The
Distribution
Management
Handbook

The
Distribution
Management
Handbook

James A. Tompkins Editor
President, Tompkins Associates, Inc.

Dale A. Harmelink Editor
Engineering Manager, Tompkins Associates, Inc.

McGraw-Hill, Inc.
New York   San Francisco   Washington, D.C.   Auckland   Bogotá
Caracas   Lisbon   London   Madrid   Mexico City   Milan
Montreal   New Delhi   San Juan   Singapore
Sydney   Tokyo   Toronto

Library of Congress Cataloging-in-Publication Data

The Distribution management handbook / edited by James A. Tompkins and
Dale A. Harmelink.
    p.   cm.
    Includes index.
    ISBN 0-07-065046-2
    1. Physical distribution of goods—Management—Handbooks, manuals,
etc. I. Tompkins, James A. II. Harmelink, Dale A.
HF5415.7.D572   1994
658.7′88—dc20   93-2309
                                                         CIP

2 3 4 5 6 7 8 9 0 DOC/DOC 9 9 8 7 6 5 4

ISBN 0-07-065046-2

*The sponsoring editor for this book was James H. Bessent, Jr., the editing supervisor
was Peter Roberts, and the production supervisor was Donald Schmidt. It was set in
Baskerville by Carol Woolverton, Lexington, Mass., in cooperation with Warren
Publishing Services, Eastport, Me.*

Printed and bound by R. R. Donnelley & Sons Company.

Contents

Part 4. Managing Distribution

Case Studies

C.   Warehouse Excellence at the Miller Brewing Company   C.1
Ric A. Schneider

**D.   Operation Desert Shield/Desert Storm: United States
Transportation Command and Strategic Deployment   D.1**
James K. Matthews and Cora J. Holt

Index follows Case Studies

Contributors

Kenneth B. Ackerman President, The Ackerman Company, Columbus, Ohio

James M. Apple, Jr. Director, Distribution Design Institute, Inc., Atlanta, Georgia

Michael R. Arledge President, Arledge & Associates, Stokesdale, North Carolina

Paul S. Bender President, Bender Management Consultants, Inc., Arlington, Virginia

Gene Bergoffen Executive Vice President, National Private Truck Council, Alexandria, Virginia

Donald J. Bowersox, Ph.D. The John H. McConnell Professor, Michigan State University, East Lansing, Michigan

Patrick M. Byrne Vice President and Managing Director of North America, A.T. Kearney, Inc., Alexandria, Virginia

Matthew Cohen Engineering Manager, Polaroid Corporation, New Bedford, Massachusetts

Frank E. Daly Regional General Manager, Tompkins Associates, Inc., Southfield, Michigan

Herbert W. Davis Chairman, Herbert W. Davis and Company, Englewood Cliffs, New Jersey

Ralph W. Fairbanks Director of Distribution, Haworth, Inc., Holland, Michigan

David J. Frayer Doctoral Student, Michigan State University, East Lansing, Michigan

Edward H. Frazelle, Ph.D Director, The Logistics Institute, Georgia Institute of Technology, Atlanta, Georgia

David E. Gibbs Director of Environmental Affairs, Webco Industries, Sand Springs, Oklahoma

Russell A. Gilmore, III President, The Focus Group, Inc., Dayton, Ohio

Craig M. Gustin, Ph.D. Principal, CGR Management Consultants, Atlanta, Georgia

James D. Hall Principal, A.T. Kearney, Inc., Cleveland, Ohio

Dale A. Harmelink Engineering Manager, Tompkins Associates, Inc., Raleigh, North Carolina

Cora J. Holt Writer, US Transportation Command, Scott Air Force Base, Illinois

Alexander Keeney, Jr. Industrial Engineering Manager, Random House, Inc., Westminster, Maryland

Bernard J. La Londe Raymond E. Mason Professor of Transportation and Logistics, The Ohio State University, Columbus, Ohio

Douglas M. Lambert, Ph.D. Prime F. Osborn III Eminent Scholar Chair in Transportation, Professor of Marketing Logistics, Director of The International Center for Competitive Excellence, University of North Florida, Jacksonville, Florida

Hank Lavery Vice President of Transportation Products, Sterling Software, Dublin, Ohio

William J. Markham Principal, A.T. Kearney, Inc., Chicago, Illinois

André J. Martin President and CEO, LogiCNet, Inc., Laval, Quebec

James M. Masters Assistant Professor of Logistics Management, The Ohio State University, Columbus, Ohio

James K. Matthews, Ph.D. Command Historian, US Transportation Command, Scott Air Force Base, Illinois

Michael F. Miller Engineering Manager, Tompkins Associates, Inc., Raleigh, North Carolina

Larry W. Moore Director of Materials Management, Fibercast Company, Sand Springs, Oklahoma

Gerhardt Muller Adjunct Professor, International Transportation and Logistics Management, City University of New York, New York

Ken L. Nixon Project Manager, Tompkins Associates, Inc., Raleigh, North Carolina

John B. Nofsinger Vice President, Material Handling Industry, Charlotte, North Carolina

David R. Olson Regional General Manager, Tompkins Associates, Inc., Dallas, Texas

Edwin P. Patton, Ph.D. Professor of Transportation, The University of Tennessee, Knoxville, Tennessee

J. Eric Peters Regional General Manager, Tompkins Associates, Inc., Soquel, California

Ric A. Schneider Operations Improvement Manager, Miller Brewing Company, Milwaukee, Wisconsin

E. Ralph Sims, Jr Associate Professor, Industrial and Systems Engineering, Ohio University, Athens, Ohio, and Chairman, The Sims Consulting Group, Inc., Lancaster, Ohio

Jerry D. Smith Executive Vice President, Tompkins Associates, Inc., Raleigh, North Carolina

Jay U. Sterling, Ph.D. Associate Professor of Marketing, College of Business Administration, University of Alabama, Tuscaloosa, Alabama

Donald E. Tepper Director of Communications, National Private Truck Council, Alexandria, Virginia

James A. Tompkins, Ph.D. President, Tompkins Associates, Inc., Raleigh, North Carolina

Gene R. Tyndall Partner, Ernst & Young, Baltimore, Maryland

Philip G. Williams President, Phil Williams & Associates, Inc., Kansas City, Missouri

Preface

The Distribution Management Handbook was developed to be a practical information reference book that will be used by managers to obtain results, reduce costs, improve customer service, enhance performance, and achieve distribution excellence. Distribution management is growing in importance, technology, and sophistication, and professionals in the field have needed a source of information upon which they could rely to gain insights and information on the full range of distribution-related topics and on understanding today's distribution state-of-the-art. This handbook is that information source. Its contents are applicable to all channels of distribution—producer, wholesaler, and retailer—and therefore readers armed with it will further elevate their knowledge of the profession of distribution.

  The Distribution Management Handbook is organized into five parts. Part 1 (Chapters 1 to 9) presents a management overview of distribution. This part explains the role of distribution in business and the important top-level distribution considerations. Part 2 (Chapters 10 to 15) and Part 3 (Chapters 16 to 22) address the two main components of distribution: transportation and warehousing. Part 4 (Chapters 23 to 30) presents the "how to" of managing distribution in today's environment. The last part (Case Studies A–D) presents four case studies that describe how others have pursued distribution excellence.

  The authors of this book are the top professionals in the field of distribution today. The editors are indebted to them for the knowledge, time, and energy they have put into their chapters in order to make this handbook an extremely valuable reference guide.

  The editors are also appreciative of the quality effort put forth by the people of McGraw-Hill, particularly Peter Roberts, Dave Fogarty, and Jim Bessent. A special thanks goes to the staff of Tompkins Associates, Inc., especially to Rhonda Smith, Jeff Lammert, Mike Halsey, and David Lane for their efforts in proofreading, communicating, and indexing. Finally, the editors would like to thank their families for their support, understanding, and love during this project.

James A. Tompkins, Ph.D.
Dale A. Harmelink

PART 1
Management Overview

1

Distribution: Past, Present, and Future

James A. Tompkins
President, Tompkins Associates, Inc.

We live in a global economy, where the pace of change is unbelievable and the demands of customers are more and more difficult to meet. Today's customer is not satisfied with quality products. Today's customer demands quality products, quality service, and increasing value. Distribution is the management of inventory to achieve customer satisfaction. It is not surprising, therefore, to find distribution in the limelight. Today many companies are discovering that distribution is not a necessary evil, but rather a major frontier for both customer service enhancement and cost reduction.

Unfortunately, in many companies, the distribution professionals are not prepared to meet the demanding needs of the customer, the pace of change, or the true integration of the distribution function. Today's distribution manager often has a strong practical background in only one area of distribution. Typically, he or she does not have a formal education in distribution, and does not have the breadth of experience to handle the breadth of the profession of distribution.

The challenge confronting many companies, therefore, is this: they desire to enhance customer satisfaction by improving distribution, but lack a knowledgeable work force to make this happen. The purpose of this book is to deal with this challenge, to deal with the increased sophistication of distribution, to present the state of the art of distribution, and to define the profession of distribution. It is the editors' goal that the improvement in distribution performance that will result from applying the material in this handbook will further elevate and promote the awareness of the profession of distribution.

The organization of this handbook mirrors the editors' goal and their definition of distribution. The goal is to elevate the level of experience in distribution management; their definition of distribution (as already stated) is *the management of in-*

ventory to achieve customer satisfaction. The overall management of inventory requires the management of inventory both when in motion and while at rest. The management of inventory in motion is the profession of transportation, the management of inventory at rest is the profession of warehousing. *The Distribution Management Handbook* is divided into five parts. Part 1 presents a management overview of distribution. It explains the role of distribution in business and the important top-level distribution considerations. Parts 2 and 3 address the two main components of distribution: transportation and warehousing. Part 4 presents the "how to" of managing distribution in today's challenging times. Part 5 presents four diverse case studies that describe how others have pursued distribution excellence.

The History of Distribution

Distribution is as old as recorded history. As set down in the earliest writings, man traveled by boats made from logs and stored food after the harvest for long winters. Over 5000 years ago the Egyptians made large boats from reeds, and over 4000 years ago the wheel was invented. As civilization developed, local warehouses were introduced. Merchandise was stored to support transportation, trading, and manufacturing. When transportation branched out from local to cross-country, warehouses became more than local storehouses. When major trade points developed during the Middle Ages, warehousing was established to handle the storage of shipped items. The first major transportation hub and the first major commercial warehouse was built in Venice, a center of major trade routes. As trading activity expanded beyond the Mediterranean, each port city developed its own terminal warehouse. Warehousing at the port city reduced the amount of time a ship was detained in port and improved transportation productivity. Truly, the profession of distribution had been born.

In the late 1700s steam-powered boats began to appear, and in the 1800s steam-powered trains, bicycles, glide planes, and cars were invented. In the late 1800s in the United States, the railroad industry provided the most responsive transportation by connecting port cities to inland cities. Freight cars began to be used as warehouses on wheels, especially during the grain harvest season, but freight-car shortages induced the railroad companies to separate the transportation and warehousing functions. With the railroad companies having a monopoly on both warehousing and freight, they were able to favor larger corporations, giving them free warehousing services with the use of the railroads.

In 1891, warehouses organized the American Warehouseman's Association (AWA). One of its first activities was to urge carriers, primarily the rail carriers, to discontinue free warehousing. The AWA succeeded in pushing through the Hepburn Act of 1906, which ended freight depot warehousing by the railroads. This legislation made "storage and handling of property transported" part of the railroading function, and required the application of published tariff rates for all such services furnished by railroads. The Hepburn Act brought railroads under government control and helped steer the development and rapid growth of the common carrier in the proper direction.

The industrial revolution brought about the combining of craft shops into factories. This resulted in mass production and manufacturing facilities that were complete from receiving to shipping. Mass production, in turn, created new aspects of warehousing. When mass production first began, goods were typically produced according to a sales forecast. The finished goods and raw materials that were necessary to meet the forecast were usually placed in the factory warehouse. However, when distribution patterns began to develop, companies moved warehouses closer to their target market areas. With the use of private and public warehousing services, both close to the factory and in the marketplace, customer service levels increased.

In the early days warehousing was offered as a supplemental service to transportation, and the facility was a part of the clearance terminal. The word *terminal* implies that the warehouses were located in the center of the city, usually close to the railroad depot and the wholesale market district. As the demand for storage space increased and the land value rose, multistory buildings were erected to provide more storage space on a minimum amount of land.

Before the end of World War I, the most common materials handling method in warehouses involved the use of hand trucks. Stacking was performed by hand and, in most buildings, stacking heights were designed in the 8- to 12-ft range. During World War II, the forklift truck and wooden pallet were introduced. Mass production of the forklift truck allowed the practical stacking height of merchandise to be increased to 30 ft, a 300 percent increase. In addition, it allowed a faster movement of merchandise within the warehouse. With the advantage of increased stacking height and the disadvantage of forklifts in multistory facilities, the use of single-story buildings replaced multistory facilities. Since the amount of land necessary for single-story warehouses was not available in the city, relocation to the outskirts of cities took place. Often, at this point, a decision had to be made with regard to continuing to ship by rail or to shift to more expensive, responsive, and reliable shipment by truck. These tradeoffs between multistory warehouses versus single-story warehouses, rail versus truck, and customer responsiveness versus the cost of transportation were the drives behind the increased sophistication of distribution. In fact, these tradeoffs continue to evolve. Today, with the focus on increasing inventory turns while improving customer satisfaction, a trend toward the substitution of transportation for inventory is prevalent.

Today's Distribution Challenges

The challenge of enhancing customer satisfaction by improving distribution requires a fully integrated approach to distribution. In many companies today, the function of distribution is done in a segregated manner. The order entry manager, warehouse manager, traffic manager, data processing manager, claims manager, etc., all operate independently. This does not work. All of distribution must work as one, with each person involved with distribution having a much greater awareness of how the totality of distribution functions. *The only way to enhance customer satisfaction is to pursue the integration of distribution.*

Given today's operational requirements, this is not an easy task. The operational requirements having the greatest impact on integrated distribution's ability to enhance customer satisfaction are business requirements, customer requirements, and distribution requirements. The business requirements reflect the changing cli-

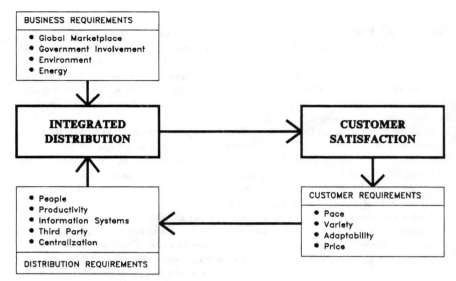

Figure 1-1. An overview of distribution challenges.

mate within which distribution must function. Business issues such as the global marketplace, the level of government involvement, the environment, and the issue of energy must be understood as the context within which distribution must function. At the same time, the customer requirements of increased pace, variety, and adaptability, while reducing costs, must be understood as a basis for customer satisfaction. Of course, these issues impact the internal pressures of distribution requirements to centralize, utilize third parties, improve information systems, increase productivity, and more fully utilize people. An overview of these distribution challenges is presented in Fig. 1.1. The remainder of this chapter is dedicated to a discussion of the requirements impacting today's distribution challenges.

The Global Marketplace

Some business leaders and managers view the global marketplace as an economic, governmental, or political issue. To the contrary, the global marketplace is a distribution issue. In fact, in today's world there is no choice but to understand the global strategy implications of all distribution decisions. As shifts occur in the world's trading patterns, this changes the distribution requirements, alters the location and number of warehouses, increases pipeline inventories, and creates new transportation opportunities and problems.

Since the early 1970s, the annual growth in free-world trade has been double the annual growth in the gross national product. Free-world trade will increase tenfold from 1970 to the early 1990s, and will double from 1980 to the early 1990s. The huge growth in free-world trade has resulted in the involvement of most companies, to some degree, in the global marketplace. This involvement may be through:

1. Export of products
2. Import of materials or components
3. Foreign partners or subsidiaries
4. Foreign competition

Whatever your involvement today, your future global involvement will be greater. This increased involvement in the global marketplace is not a result of the increased interrelatedness of the world (satellite communications and efficient global travel), nor the increased integration of political and economic systems. Of course these issues simplify a company's involvement, but they are not what motivates a company to be involved with the global marketplace. The simple fact is that companies have no choice. To compete in any market today, a company must obtain best quality and cost for its supplies. This does not mean best in their region, best in their country, but best in the world. Thus, the drive toward the global economy is very straightforward: survival.

Global distribution is not different from domestic distribution, just more complex. Global distribution complexities include:

1. Time zones
2. Languages
3. International fund transfers and currency transactions
4. Customs and customs agents
5. Government agents
6. Tariffs and trade restrictions
7. Documentation and reporting
8. Packaging
9. Freight forwarders
10. Cultural practices

However, just because the scope of the distribution network has been broadened and become more complex, this is not a justification for allowing inefficient distribution to exist. Global distribution, unfortunately, has been used to justify inefficient distribution, as exemplified in remarks such as these:

1. "We need to carry excessive inventory because global transportation times are unpredictable."
2. "There is little value in trying to provide global suppliers with advanced information, as they never understand our needs."
3. "No loads are palletized until after they arrive in our facility, as our global suppliers don't ship in unit load quantities."
4. "We never know what quantity of goods will be arriving until we unload the container, as the paperwork doesn't arrive until weeks after the shipment."

Obviously, these remarks cannot go unchallenged. The only acceptable global distribution is distribution that maximizes customer satisfaction at minimal cost.

You must first understand the complexities of global distribution, then put in place a plan for global distribution that will make the distribution network transparent to domestic or global conditions. Only then will the global marketplace become an asset to a company, as opposed to an excuse for adopting inefficient global distribution.

Government Involvement

It is not appropriate in a handbook to address specific governmental impacts on distribution. In fact, these issues change drastically from month to month and year to year. Nevertheless, it is of the utmost importance that no one overlook the tremendous impact that government involvement has on distribution.

A global trend is for governments to deregulate many activities, most notably transportation. In fact, the United States was the first country to embrace deregulation across the transportation field. Nevertheless, significant regulations still exist in the United States, and in fact in areas such as the commercial driver's license, safety inspections, and drug testing, regulations are growing. In addition, in one form or another, 42 states still regulate trucking. Issues such as the use of longer combination vehicles remain hotly contested.

Very strong transportation lobbying efforts exist in the United States, and the role of these on the government's impact on distribution should not be minimized. It is important that distribution professionals understand that just as government involvement has an impact on distribution, distribution leadership has an obligation to have an impact on government on behalf of distribution.

Environment

An issue that is closely tied to the issue of government involvement is the issue of *reverse distribution*. Reverse distribution is *the task of recovering packaging and shipping materials and backhauling them to a central collection point for recycling.* There is already a law for transportation packaging in Germany; the product manufacturer is responsible for taking back all the pallets, cardboard boxes, stretch wrap, shrink wrap, strapping, bandings, dunnage, etc. used to protect the goods during shipment. In addition, retailers must take back from consumers all product packaging. There is already a law in much of the United States for automobile batteries and soda bottles, and a law came close to adoption in 1992 in Massachusetts that would have forced package recycling on all items. As landfills continue to reach capacity, the United States Congress will continue to pursue legislation on recycling.

Handling the mechanics of reverse distribution will require significant attention by distribution professionals. Not only will they need to understand a diverse set of state and federal laws, but they will have to deal with backhauls, with handling the waste packaging in their warehouses, and with the customer satisfaction issue of recycling. So, although the environmental issue to date has not been a major distribution concern, it will become a major concern as regulations are passed to force us into reverse distribution.

Another environmental distribution issue, although nowhere near as revolutionary, has to do with the Environmental Protection Agency's push to regulate off-highway vehicles. This would include lift trucks, and would further push warehouses in the direction of electric vehicles. The internal-combustion lift trucks that will be sold in the future will need to meet much stricter emission standards, but in many applications these vehicles will be replaced by electric vehicles. Of greatest concern is the existing internal combustion lift truck fleets, and the need to replace these with vehicles that conform to the new standards.

Energy

Another issue, like the environment, that has not been a major topic of consideration by distribution professionals, is energy. Nevertheless, the cost of energy is a major concern to transportation companies. In the United States, 60 percent of all energy consumption is for transportation. Although these costs tend to be buried in the overall cost of transportation, any significant shift in the cost of energy could have a significant impact on the costs of transportation and therefore on distribution. It is therefore important that, at least as a sensitivity issue, the issue of energy costs be viewed in making all distribution decisions.

Pace

There exists an accelerating rate of change in all aspects of human endeavor—social, political, economic, technological, ecological, and psychological. It is not surprising then, that the reduction of lead times, shorter product lives, and increases in inventory turnover are resulting in significant increases in the pace of change in distribution. Distribution must be more responsive because of the demands being placed upon it by customers. Inventory turns must be increased, not only because inventories are expensive to carry due to investment, space, and handling, but increasingly due to obsolescence. As technology continues to explode, product lives get shorter and shorter. Warehouse operations and systems must be put in place to handle increased levels of crossdocking, to address supply chain management, and to support continuous flow distribution. All of distribution must focus on being responsive, on adapting to an ever-increasing rate of change, and on working smarter, not harder.

Variety

The variety of tasks to be handled by distribution will continue to increase. Special packaging, unitizing, pricing, labeling, kitting, and delivery requirements will become the norm. Distribution will be required to perform operations that traditionally have been viewed as manufacturing operations. Systems and procedures will be put in place to handle information consistent with the desires of the customers. No matter what the customer requests, distribution professionals will be able to handle, at a cost, all requirements. At the same time, customers will understand and accept the need to change for special services, and it is from this perspective that they will make their requests.

Adaptability

Due to increased pace and variety, and since customer satisfaction is an ongoing process and customers continually change their requirements, all of distribution must become more adaptable. However, what may be surprising is the confusion that results from attempting to clarify what is meant by "adaptable distribution." Adaptable distribution has different meanings to different organizations, and even to different people within the same organizations.

The most popular definition of *adaptable* is "the ability to become suitable for a new use." In distribution, *adaptable* means *the ability to respond to different distribution requirements*. Herein lies the confusion, in these two different perspectives on the word *adaptable*.

Distribution requirements may change by changing the tasks to be done or the volume of tasks to be done. *Flexible distribution* is required to address changes in the tasks to be done. *Modular distribution* is required to address changes in the volume of tasks to be done. Although flexibility and modularity are both forms of adaptability, they are totally different.

The three most important aspects of flexible distribution are:

1. Versatile equipment
2. Versatile systems
3. Multiskilled employees

The design, specification, and implementation of versatile equipment is required to achieve flexible distribution. Warehouse storage and material handling equipment, as well as transportation equipment, should be selected with sufficient versatility to handle today's distribution requirements and, when justifiable, future requirements. Similarly, versatile systems have an impact on adapting customer labeling, automatic identification, communications, and documentation requirements. We never want to find ourselves saying to a customer, "I'm sorry, our system doesn't allow us to accommodate your request."

Lastly, we must have multiskilled personnel to achieve flexible distribution. Overly restrictive work rules, excessive job classifications and labor grades, and insufficient training have often resulted in a lack of flexibility in distribution. Multiskilling eliminates barriers between tasks, and workers better understand the implications of their performance. Throughout distribution organizations there is a need to destroy the traditional barriers between tasks, and to improve distribution performance through increased visibility and understanding.

The three most important aspects of modular distribution are:

1. Modular distribution assets
2. Modular work assignments
3. Time modularity

The issue of modular distribution assets has to do with the expansion and contraction of warehouse space and the increase or decrease of transportation equipment. A consideration while planning warehouse facilities should always be how to expand or contract warehouse space to meet actual requirements. Over the short term the utilization of public warehousing may be viable, while a more long-term approach might be the expansion of a warehouse facility. Similarly, for transportation equipment, purchase and lease decisions, as well as contract terms, should be evaluated while considering both the long- and short-term fluctuations in traffic.

The challenge of modular work assignments has to do with the daily balance of work within a warehouse. Once people have been given multiple skills, it is important to be certain that they are assigned in such a way as to allow for a continuous flow of materials through distribution. As the level of case picking, layer picking, and full pallet picking shifts from day to day and season to season, it is important to make work assignments in such a way as to balance the flow of work.

Lastly, to provide modular distribution is to provide time modularity. Creativity in employee work schedules can have a significant impact on an operation's output. Issues meriting discussion include start times, 8-hour days, 10-hour days, 12-hour days, part-time employees, breaks, lunches, vacations, etc. Many distribution operations have been significantly improved by adjusting work schedules so that there is a balance between the staff on hand and the tasks to be performed. Not addressing the issue of time modularity often results in distribution operations having very low productivity.

Price

A prerequisite for the success of free enterprise is efficient, effective, and low-cost distribution. A critical element of success in the global marketplace is the existence of efficient, effective, and low-cost distribution. The issue of low-cost distribution from a customer's perspective translates directly to the price the customer must pay. The price the customer must pay consists of many factors. The customer is indifferent to the composition of these factors, but is totally focused on the reduction of the total price he or she will pay. So, although the cost of distribution is less than 10 percent of the price the customer must pay, it is of the utmost importance to the customer that even this price be reduced. Thus, it is very important that the cost of distribution be reduced.

There are a variety of measures used on a macro basis to evaluate the cost of distribution: distribution cost as a percentage of sales; distribution cost as a cost per hundredweight; distribution cost as a percentage of our gross national product; distribution cost as a percentage of our gross domestic product. Independent of which measure is used, the same conclusions may be reached:

1. Although the total distribution cost can be segmented in different ways, distribution costs basically consist of:

- Transportation—40 to 60 percent of total
- Warehousing—20 to 40 percent of total
- Inventory carrying costs—15 to 25 percent of total

2. Due to deregulation and increases in productivity, the cost of transportation has been significantly reduced in the 1980s and early 1990s. This trend will change in the mid-1990s and the cost of transportation will increase.

3. Due to stable labor rates, lower space costs, and more centralized warehouses, the costs of warehousing fell in the 1980s. Beginning in the early 1990s the cost of

labor began to increase and, with labor representing over half the cost of warehousing, this has resulted in an increase in the costs of warehousing. In the mid-1990s this trend of warehousing cost increases will continue.

4. The costs of carrying inventory fell in the 1980s, with interest rates and better inventory management. Inventory carrying costs have been flat in the early 1990s, and will increase only slightly in the mid-1990s.

5. Distribution costs have consistently been reduced in the 1980s and early 1990s. As a percentage of sales, they are down from a high in the 10 percent range to approximately 8 percent in 1992. As a cost per hundredweight, they are down from a high of over $45 per hundredweight to approximately $43 per hundredweight. As a percentage of gross national product, they are down from a high of almost 15 percent to 11 percent and as a percentage of gross domestic product, they are down from a high of almost 18 percent to below 12 percent. Distribution costs in the mid to late 1990s will increase, but hopefully an increased emphasis on integrated distribution will result in these increases being minimized.

The most important factor when addressing the customer's distribution price or the distribution cost for the future is not how the costs compare to the past but how they compare to a company's best performance. As the changes in business conditions, customer requirements, and distribution realities impact the overall price for quality distribution, the process of continuous improvement must be the focus. We need to continue to improve customer satisfaction and we must continue to reduce costs. This requires a total integrated-distribution focus and a dedication to working in a partnership relationship with our customers.

Centralization

Virtually every topic presented in this chapter will be facilitated by a trend that began in the 1980s and will continue to grow in the 1990s: centralization. There will be fewer, larger, centralized warehouses in the future, replacing the greater in number, smaller, decentralized warehouses of the past. There will be fewer managers and administrative people involved with distribution, as integrated distribution is pursued and distribution staffs are centralized. Along with the centralization of warehouses and staffs will come the centralization of order entry, customer service, and data processing. Although in the past there have been cycles of centralization/decentralization/centralization/decentralization, etc., the cycle back to decentralization will never occur. The increased responsiveness of transportation at lower costs, the focus on the total cost of distribution, the realities of customer satisfaction, pace, variety, and adaptability all point toward centralization. The trend toward centralized distribution will result in higher inventory turnover, which in turn will lead to new opportunities for automation and sophisticated information systems. As the benefits of these innovations are realized, this will further enforce the trend toward centralization.

It is very important that distribution leadership embrace the trend toward centralization and proactively plan the future of their integrated, centralized distribution operations. This is contrary to the traditional approach, in which distribution management responds to external circumstances. In today's distribution environment, distribution leadership must strategically plan for centralization, to allow distribution to become a company's tool for achieving customer satisfaction.

Third Party Distribution

Third party distribution is the utilization of an outside firm to perform some or all of the distribution functions presently performed internally. As companies better understand integrated distribution, and as distribution leadership better understands the costs of distribution, there will be an increasing trend toward the outsourcing of portions of the distribution function. Factors supporting this trend include:

1. An increasing number of professionally operated third party distribution firms offering both domestic and worldwide services in:

Freight payments	Warehousing
Customs clearance	Returns
Carrier selection	Display building
Rate negotiation	Subassembly
Vehicle leasing	Packaging
Claims processing	Kitting
Hazardous materials	Labeling
Freight tracking	Order processing
Fleet management	Customer service
Vehicle maintenance	EDI
Driver leasing	Information systems
Insurance	Data processing
Multimodal coordination	Inventory control
Financing	Documentation

2. Company leadership having the desire to reduce nonessential overhead and focus on the core elements of their business.
3. The high number of mergers and acquisitions that force an evaluation and restructuring of how business is done.
4. A desire on the part of many companies to reduce debt and lower breakeven points by restructuring operations and selling nonessential assets.
5. As companies expand into the global marketplace, there often is a lack of experience in dealing with global distribution. Rather than try to learn this new aspect of business, it is easier to use third party distribution.
6. An awareness that it is very expensive to handle peaks and remote locations while maintaining high customer satisfaction. The reality that both customer service and the costs of distribution may be better utilizing a third party.

The cumulative result of the above factors will result in a very significant growth in third party distribution. In 1990, the United States market for third party distribution services was $6 billion. By 1995 this will exceed $25 billion, and it is estimated that by the year 2000 the market for third party distribution services will exceed $50 billion. It is clear that all distribution planning must be done while considering the alternative of third party distribution.

Information Systems

Information technology is impacting everything from business to education to entertainment. It is not surprising, therefore, that information technology is having and will continue to have a major impact on distribution. Many companies are pursuing automatic identification (auto ID) and Electronic Data Interchange (EDI) as opportunities to reduce costs, improve accuracy, and improve customer service. Other companies are pursuing auto ID and EDI as their customers are mandating these technologies as a condition of continuing to do business. It has become clear that all distribution documentation must be electronic and transmitted and not mailed. All distribution paperwork needs to be scrutinized and whenever possible eliminated. It is important for distribution leadership to realize that paperwork means delays, errors, additional work, and therefore wasted time and money. Distribution information systems must be real-time and paperless and standardized throughout the distribution supply chain.

The result of the distribution information systems will be management better able to direct, control, measure, and report on the distribution system performance. More capital will be spent and more productivity will be gained in the area of distribution information systems over the next ten years than in any other portion of distribution. Distribution information system planning and implementation must include the entire scope of distribution, from order entry to satisfied customers. Warehouse and transportation management systems will be integrated into the overall distribution information system and will allow distribution to function as a focused customer satisfaction machine.

Productivity

Accountability for performance in distribution must be increased. Distribution management must establish standards, identify opportunities for improvement, measure performance, and take action to assure continuous distribution improvement. The entire distribution function must realize that productivity must be increased. The option of maintaining status quo is totally unacceptable. The improvement of distribution productivity includes labor productivity but goes well beyond labor productivity. For example, in a warehouse, it is critical to implement order picking equipment, methods, layouts, and procedures to increase labor productivity, but it is also important to look at space utilization, equipment utilization, inventory accuracy, product damage, etc., as these issues all have a major impact on the productivity of the warehouse.

Similarly, in transportation a broad definition of productivity—extending beyond labor productivity—must be utilized. Distribution must utilize a broad definition of productivity to better control distribution and to minimize uncertainty. Distribution leadership must be defining what happens in distribution and not responding to what has happened. Only when distribution has adopted this broad understanding of productivity, and proactively pursues continuous improvement, can true distribution excellence be achieved.

People

Customers drive the business of distribution, but performance depends upon distribution people. Customer satisfaction results from contact with distribution people, and so an important, ongoing distribution issue remains people. In the past, distribution people were narrowly focused, having a specialized skill or technical strength. These distribution people do not conform to today's distribution needs. The people needed in distribution today must adopt a broader view of distribution, a more integrated understanding of their field, a team-based, participative organization culture, and a total dedication to customer satisfaction. Distribution leadership must understand that the only way to achieve customer satisfaction is through empowered teams of happy and motivated distribution people. These teams must in turn work in a partnership relationship with all other organizational units, with all customers, and with all third party distribution services.

The challenge facing today's distribution leaders is how to create empowered teams of happy and motivated people. The brief answer to this question is to create an environment where people are happy and motivated and the process of continuous improvement is driven by successful teams. To create an environment where people are happy and motivated requires:

1. People development
2. Trust

The development of people requires:

1. *Visionary development.* The understanding and alignment of people with where your organization is headed, how your organization will achieve success, and the science of distribution.
2. *General development.* The general knowledge and skills needed to contribute to your firm's success. The general knowledge includes people's understanding of things such as your customers, your competition, your company's strengths, weaknesses, opportunities and challenges, etc. The general skills include problem-solving, computer literacy, planning, communications, etc.
3. *Specific development.* The understanding of the science of distribution and the company's specific methods, procedures, and systems to achieve customer satisfaction.

The issue of trust is important, because trust lays the foundation for successful, empowered teams. Distribution leadership must understand that it is only with trust that respect is achieved, and it is only with respect that people truly listen to one another. With listening comes understanding, which leads to concern for one another. True participation follows from this, and from participation comes successful teamwork, with success acting as a reinforcement of greater trust. Thus, without trust, there are no successful empowered teams.

Once people are happy and motivated, you should follow these steps to implement team-based continuous improvement:

1. Identify a team leader.
2. Identify the team.
3. Define team purpose.
4. Educate the team.
5. Assess present status.
6. Define goals.
7. Prioritize opportunities.
8. Brainstorm alternatives.
9. Identify improvement plans.
10. Evaluate improvement plans.
11. Define improvement plans.
12. Obtain improvement plan support.
13. Implement improvement plan.
14. Audit results.
15. Share and recognize success.
16. Return to step 5.

It is by following these steps with happy and motivated people that your people will create satisfied customers.

Conclusions

Distribution is the management of inventory to achieve customer satisfaction. Today many companies have realized that distribution is a major frontier for both customer service enhancement and cost reduction. This chapter has highlighted many of today's distribution challenges. The remainder of this handbook will present a more in-depth look at these challenges, and lay the foundation for you to pursue distribution excellence.

2
Marketing and Logistics

Donald J. Bowersox
The John H. McConnell Professor
Michigan State University

David J. Frayer
Michigan State University

The relationship between marketing and logistics has begun to crystallize over the past few decades. Initially, preoccupation with managing functional areas prevented firms from visualizing the benefits of marketing-logistics integration. Marketing's primary mission is to stimulate sales through coordination of product, price, and promotion activities. Logistics has traditionally been responsible for timely delivery of products and services. As enterprises face increased competitive pressure, leading-edge firms have begun to integrate marketing and logistics in an effort to achieve higher performance and positively impact customer service, satisfaction, and success.

Manufacturing companies such as Motorola, Procter & Gamble, Kimberly-Clark, and Nabisco Foods have made substantial competitive gains as a result of highly coordinated marketing and logistics. Similarly, wholesalers such as Bergen-Brunswig, McKesson, Spartan Stores, Ace Hardware, and Baxter Healthcare have built marketing programs based upon using logistical competency to achieve sustainable competitive advantages. Among retailers, Wal-Mart, Target, Kmart, and JCPenney are a few examples of those who have achieved solid market success by building strategies partially based on logistical competency.

This chapter develops the theme of growing interdependence between marketing and logistics in a technology-dominated business environment. First, the "textbook" model of marketing as a guiding philosophy of business is developed, in which logistics is positioned as a critical dimension of a firm's overall strategic initiative. Until recently, logistics was presumed to take a passive service-provider role in the managerial marketing process. A more progressive view of the contribution logistics can make toward gaining competitive superiority is introduced by viewing the challenges related to managing logistics in a life-cycle context. While a life-cycle perspective falls short of fully guiding logistical deployment, it does serve to illustrate the dynamic nature of using logistics proactively. To position logistical competency as a force for gaining differential advantage, the remaining discussion is focused on sophisticated segmentation, the supply chain process, customer-focused marketing, and customer success strategies. Finally, by way of example, a model is offered that links strategic marketing and logistical resource application, highlighting the advantages to be gained from integration.

The Marketing Concept

Firms committed to a "marketing philosophy" approach to business view customer needs as the driving force behind all business processes. Commitment to a marketing orientation serves to underscore quality initiatives designed to meet customer expectations while earning a reasonable profit.[1] This philosophy for enterprise guidance, which emerged following World War II, is referred to as the *marketing concept.*

An integral aspect of the marketing concept is the notion of a marketing mix strategy. (See Fig. 2-1.) The marketing mix is viewed as consisting of a blend of activities designed to satisfy customer requirements while simultaneously achieving business objectives. The basic activities constituting the marketing mix are the managerial aspects of product/service, promotion, logistics, and price decisions. The key to formulating a mix strategy is to blend resources devoted to these activities into a balanced effort that achieves maximum customer impact. A conventional way to position logistics within such a marketing mix strategy is to examine the managerial process that launches a marketing philosophy of business.

The Process of Managerial Marketing

The process of managerial marketing (see Fig. 2-2) involves nine interdependent steps:[2]

1. Market delineation
2. Purchase behavior motivation
3. Product-service matching
4. Channel design
5. Logistics
6. Communications
7. Pricing
8. Organization
9. Administration

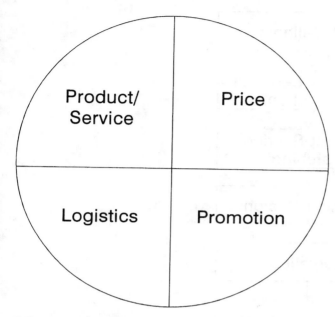

Figure 2-1. The marketing mix.

The emphasis in market delineation is on identification and measurement of potential customers and specification of their unique requirements. Purchase behavior motivation involves an assessment of factors that drive the nature and timing of customer purchasing. Product-service matching fits a firm's initiatives to market segment requirements. Channel design includes selection and coordination with associated businesses that can be deployed to position product or service assortments at the correct location in a timely manner and in a way that facilitates ownership exchange transactions. Logistics involves all information and physical activities required to transfer goods from sellers to customers. In order to establish a favorable customer purchase predisposition in the marketplace, communication is vital. Marketing communication includes advertising, promotion, and bidirectional transmission of information between buyers and sellers. Determination and administration of prices that both meet revenue objectives and facilitate ownership transfer is critical to the marketing management process. Organization is required to allocate scarce financial and human resources efficiently and effectively. Finally, administration serves to establish operating procedures and performance measurement techniques to facilitate continuous improvement.

It is important to recognize that the actual work required to complete the managerial marketing process is not, nor ever has been, performed by a single group of managers within a complex business organization. Thus, the process of managerial marketing is far larger than the job typically called "marketing." For example, while communication is partially the domain of advertising and in part a sales activity, it typically is managed on an overall basis by a marketing organization. Logistics is most often managed by a separate operating organization that also has responsibil-

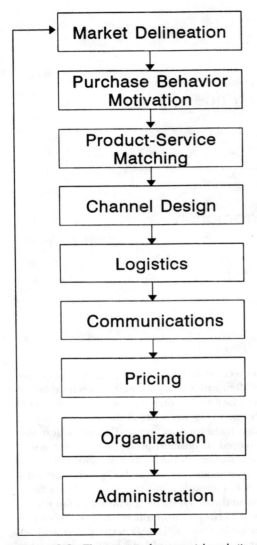

Figure 2-2. The process of managerial marketing. (*Adapted from Thomas A. Staudt, Donald A. Taylor, and Donald J. Bowersox,* A Managerial Introduction to Marketing, *3d. ed., Englewood Cliffs, NJ: Prentice-Hall, Inc., 1976.*)

ity to satisfy inbound procurement and manufacturing requirements. More often than not, product development and pricing decisions require a wide spectrum of managerial inputs, and involvement from such diverse areas as product engineering, manufacturing, accounting, finance, sales, marketing, and senior management. Recognition that the overall process of managerial marketing does not directly correspond to traditional functional work assignments is a fundamental requirement driving process integration.

Logistics in Marketing Strategy

The above discussion positions the fundamental role logistics plays in overall marketing strategy. From a logistics perspective, the marketing concept focuses managerial attention on the range of customer services available to stimulate desired purchase behavior. The impact of logistics on customers should not be passive. Alternative methods of delivery and storage are available to achieve different levels of timely inventory availability at desired locations throughout the marketing channel. In this context, viewing logistics as a cost center concerned with efficiency is important, but too narrow. Logistics should be viewed as a way to leverage overall performance and to drive competitive advantage. Customer service commitment and subsequent performance are both fundamental to creating and implementing a positive purchase environment. Performance that results in either over- or underserving customers is most often detrimental to success.

Serving Multiple Masters— Requirements for a Supply Chain Perspective

One unique aspect of logistics is a fundamental requirement to serve multiple masters. While the focus of the marketing process is to facilitate customer transactions, manufacturing, in contrast, is concerned with converting raw materials into goods and services. Each process requires logistical support to perform its mission within the overall value-added process. However, the range of inbound logistics services critical to manufacturing efficiencies are significantly different from those needed to support marketing.

Consistent and efficient inbound logistical performance is critical to manufacturing operations. The traditional practice of dealing with uncertainty by building anticipatory inventory is no longer acceptable. Likewise, low-cost bulk shipment of materials to locations that stockpile inventories to support manufacturing operations is inherently risky. The high cost of idling production, due to material shortage, necessitates that logistics managers ensure sufficient supply through inventory holdings or consistent delivery performance. Thus inbound logistics is a balancing act. The goal is to reduce idle deployment of inventories by developing just-in-time support for manufacturing requirements without introducing the risk of costly disruptions. The fact that an increasing amount of inbound logistics is accomplished across a playing field of global dimensions makes the premium placed on performance to goals all the more unforgiving.

In contrast, marketing's requirement for logistical performance typically involves unique arrangements to satisfy specific customers. Innovative logistical arrangements that involve crossdocking, sequence loading of products, stop-offs, single-invoice billing, packaging, labeling, inventory consignment, and expedited shipping are all designed to facilitate customer success. In a marketing context, logistics facilitates competitive advantage by providing tailored services to targeted customer segments. In summary, whereas inbound logistics best services manufacturing by failsafe consistency and efficiency, outbound logistics to support marketing requires the flexibility to satisfy unique customer requirements.

Supply chain management encompasses the planning and execution of internal and external logistics activities as a single process that transcends procurement, manufacturing, and finished-product distribution. The focus of supply chain management is customer success. It is a comprehensive concept of logistics which captures the objectives of functional integration and strategic deployment as a single managerial process.[3] The supply chain links suppliers and customers by managing value-added flows throughout the channel. Likewise, information requirements are exchanged between all supply chain participants. In essence, the supply chain seeks total integration of the exchange process in an effort to achieve maximum operational efficiency and effectiveness. This is accomplished through development of process management and focused responsibilities within the marketing-logistics channel.

The case for developing supply chain integration is basic. Manufacturing and marketing in isolation cannot complete transactions. A supply chain perspective (Fig. 2-3) provides an overall view of all linkages required to support successful marketing. Logistics activities provide spatial and temporal closure through movement and storage of goods and services. Unless the material or finished product is available at the right place, at the right time, in the right condition, ownership transfer transactions will not occur. The fundamental fact that transactions depend upon spatial-temporal closure highlights the critical role logistics performs in the profitable operation of an enterprise. The next section discusses the strategic imperative for marketing-logistics integration and highlights the potential benefits of acknowledging this dependency.

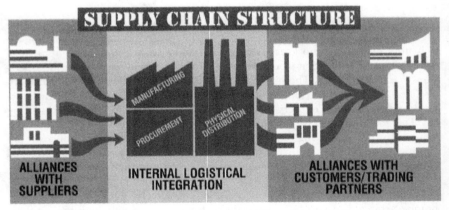

Figure 2-3. The supply chain management process. (*From Donald J. Bowersox, "Clearing Roadblocks to Supply-Chain Management,"* United Parcel Service International Update, *Spring 1992, p. 4.*)

The Imperative for Integration

The ability to successfully manage specialized functions within today's leading-edge firm requires a deep appreciation of what drives integrated performance. A perspective on integration of marketing and logistics must start by looking at the requirement to integrate within logistics as a prerequisite to integration beyond logistics. Integration of internal logistics functions was initially attempted by grouping managers responsible for specific activities, such as transportation and inventory, in the same command-and-control organization structure. The idea of functional excellence was based on the perceived need to manage expense and committed assets. The command-and-control organization offered an appropriate system of checks and balances to facilitate such control. A more recent initiative is for managers to seek logistics process integration across functions, using shared information.[4] This focus on improved information networking offers significant potential for increased leverage . With the focus on overall process integration, the importance of functional excellence is secondary to leveraging overall performance. In other words, functional excellence has relevancy only within a context of success at achieving overall goals.

Logic similar to that used to integrate internal logistics is required to arrive at a perspective on coordinating marketing and logistics. Whereas internal logistics integration is efficiency-driven, integration with marketing is more concerned with competitive advantage. Firms need to coordinate and focus all performance on achieving customer success. True integration of marketing and logistics has the potential to achieve a variety of benefits. The most significant are ease of implementing time-based competitive strategies, quality enhancement, strategic deployment of logistical competencies, multinational sourcing arrangements, and measurement efficiencies.[5]

Time-based strategies, such as just-in-time, quick response, and continuous replenishment, foster logistical efficiency by reducing assets deployed throughout the distribution channel. In the case of manufacturing, the objective of such strategies is to reduce risk. In marketing, the key is increased asset (inventory) velocity, flexibility, and overall responsiveness to customer requirements. Clearly, these drivers can be in conflict. In the past, little if any consideration was given to integrating advanced service capabilities with customer needs. Recent developments in service response logistics suggest that time-based strategies offer the potential for significant future breakthroughs.[6]

The commitment to achieving total quality, particularly in the area of manufacturing management, has driven logistics to emphasize inbound efficiencies. While efficiency is good, it must be related to doing those things better that actually make a difference to customers. Thus, inbound logistics may involve new services such as inspection, sequencing, or modification. These expanded services add value to customers. Doing the wrong things efficiently offers little value to the overall supply chain.

Strategic deployment of logistics activities poses an interesting challenge to integration of marketing and manufacturing. The desire to improve efficiency through centralization of logistical responsibility has a potential to reduce front-line marketing leverage. However, efforts to increase flexibility by decentralizing logistics decision making and to focus on unique field requirements have often resulted in loss of efficiency. What is needed is the best of both worlds: centralized logistical vision and strategy, supported by decentralized or empowered front-line decision making.[7]

As firms increase reliance on multinational sourcing, it is essential to position logistics to facilitate procurement and manufacturing. This commitment, and the need to build accommodating infrastructure, can cause obstacles or barriers to downstream integration of logistical performance and marketing requirements. The fact that some firms manage logistics, purchasing, and manufacturing through an integrated global arrangement, while marketing is done on a country-by-country basis, further complicates integration.

Measuring the interrelation of logistics performance and marketing results has been the subject of considerable attention.[5] Neither marketing nor logistics can boast superiority in assessing performance. Establishing better linkages between marketing and logistics and measuring their interrelationship is essential to deploying logistics as a strategic weapon.

Current developments in the business environment suggest that integration has begun to occur. Firms such as Dillard, Kroger, Kmart, and Target have established alliances with manufacturers to jointly reduce cost and leverage performance. These arrangements utilize joint measurement techniques and information-sharing commitment from involved parties to link logistical efficiency with marketing effectiveness. For example, Wal-Mart is reported to have invested over $600 million in information technology to facilitate sharing point-of-sale details to a group of 2000 selected vendors.[8]

Developing a Strategic Vision

The key to getting the most mileage out of logistics in terms of overall marketing is found in the development of a strategic vision. Managing logistics to minimize cost will fail to generate logistical leverage. An operational perspective driven solely by cost limits logistics activities to tactical deployment. While costs need to be held to a minimum, such deployment fails to capture synergies possible from strategic deployment of logistical competency.

The strategic potential of logistics lies in the ability to offer selected customers enhanced and unique services beyond the basic services provided all customers of the enterprise. As firms develop unique capabilities through information-sharing and technology application, these enhanced and unique services are difficult to duplicate and can generate strategic advantage. For example, L. L. Bean has built its mail order business around rapid delivery of products, utilizing premium transportation from a centralized stocking location. The Limited relies on an efficient logistics operation, which combines internal strengths with a range of partnerships designed to leverage core competencies. Other examples include:

1. Schneider National, which utilizes advanced vehicle-tracking technology in combination with highly efficient operations to offer customers reliable value-added transportation services

2. United Parcel Service, which has turned transportation reliability into strategic advantage by offering customers guaranteed delivery

3. J.B. Hunt, which utilizes its low cost position to offer customers an alternative to other carriers on "no-frills" shipments

While a growing number of examples of the strategic application of logistics to achieve competitive advantage exist, each is unique.[9] The internal characteristics of the associated firms and the strategic needs of their customers combine to form distinctive competencies which can be used to secure market advantage. The following section explores a spectrum of strategic initiatives by discussing logistics in a life-cycle context.

Deploying Logistics Service in a Life-Cycle Context

From the previous discussion, it is clear that logistics can be positioned to achieve far more than reactive or passive marketing support. Beyond achieving operational efficiency, which is essential, logistics has the potential to leverage or increase customer responsiveness. The dynamic nature of markets and competition combine to create unique opportunities for logistics value-added services. A limited but somewhat useful way to illustrate dynamic deployment of logistics competency is to use the product life-cycle framework often discussed in marketing literature.

Adjustments Across Cycle Stages

The product life-cycle model (Fig. 2-4) was developed by marketing planners to help predict competitive conditions expected during the market longevity of a product.[10] While a variety of cycle models exist, most incorporate four stages:

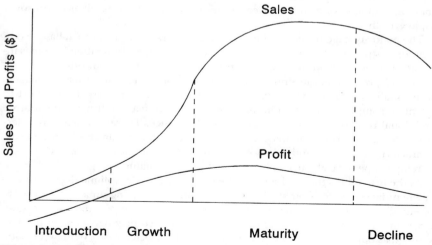

Figure 2-4. Product life-cycle.

1. Introduction
2. Growth
3. Maturity
4. Decline

Each stage may require different logistical performance to accommodate competitive conditions.

During the introductory stage, a high level of basic logistical performance is desirable. Since the primary objective is to establish market position, a premium is placed on stock availability and consistent resupply of channel inventories. Product shortages during introduction could seriously dilute the impact of the marketing launch strategy and jeopardize success, or even result in failure to gain product acceptance. For example, Gillette designed a simultaneous time-based global launch strategy for the Sensor razor. Such a strategy appeared justified because of Gillette's proven ability to provide basic logistics support. However, sales in excess of the most optimistic projections created severe product shortages and unexpected delays that placed certain aspects of the launch in jeopardy. While Gillette recovered, their experience offered timely lessons concerning the key role of logistics during new product launch.[11] Simply stated, you can't penetrate new markets from an empty wagon. Shipment sizes tend to be small, and frequency of orders erratic, during new-product introduction. As a result, the cost of logistics service failure can be great.

During the growth stage of the product life-cycle, logistical performance emphasis ideally shifts from high customer service commitment to a more balanced or segmented performance. The decision concerning what customers should be offered what service is ideally based on revenue potential and cost. Expanded market coverage and high profitability are characteristic of the growth stage. Therefore, this is the time for firms to invest in their logistical infrastructure. The key is to use logistical competency to gain market share and customer loyalty. Wal-Mart is an outstanding example of a firm that continues to use logistical excellence to propel rapid growth.

The maturity stage of the product life-cycle is characterized by broad-based competition. As product/service substitutes proliferate, price competition becomes intense. Firms who are losing market share try to hold customers by offering special price and promotional incentives. Those firms that are long-term market leaders turn to alliances as one way to be responsive to major customers. In an effort to maintain competitive position in the enterprise's core market, firms often allocate additional resources to bolster logistical performance. These resources are selectively focused on key customers. The current state of affairs in the food industry, characterized by the scramble between manufacturers and leading edge retailers to develop cooperative alliances, is common during the maturity stage.

As the firm enters the final stage of the product life-cycle, volume declines. Management faces the decision of whether to continue marketing on a restricted basis or end distribution altogether. The logistical system must support the selected strategy without overcommitting resources. Risk avoidance may become the primary strategy, as opposed to lowest cost performance. In selected cases, outdated or otherwise defective or damaged merchandise must be cleansed from the market. A prime example of cleanup logistics was stage three of the Persian Gulf War—Desert

Farewell—in which millions of dollars of unused military supplies were reclassified and logistically positioned to support future requirements.[12]

The product life-cycle, while subject to several shortfalls and being considerably short of a comprehensive theory to guide decision making, serves to illustrate how logistical deployment must be adjusted to accommodate a firm's marketing strategy. As logistics is adjusted to fit the marketing situation, the maintenance of flexibility becomes a prime concern. For a multiproduct firm, individual products are scattered across various life-cycle stages, introducing extreme complexity. Likewise, the time intervals that specific products remain in a specific life-cycle stage can vary greatly. Finally, major customers typically purchase products that are in all different "theoretical" life-cycle stages. In such complex situations, flexibility becomes the key to logistical excellence.[7] The following section examines how logistical segmentation, customer-focused marketing, and selective deployment of logistical service all facilitate logistical flexibility.

Competitive Differentiation Based on Logistical Competency

The struggle to achieve profits in an environment characterized by shrinking markets and intense global competition necessitates that firms identify and capitalize on unique offerings. Firms must seek differential advantage by distinguishing their product or service offerings from those of the competition. Traditional bases for differentiation include product, performance, price, image, channel, and service level.[1] While all of these alternatives are viable options, increasingly firms are differentiating based on logistical competency. Those who logistically perform head and shoulders above competition are positioned to launch extraordinary initiatives and take a "catch us if you can" attitude concerning competition. Such extraordinary performance requires that firms reengineer their service to match customer expectations.

Firms have traditionally assessed logistical operations on average performance, and gauged the level of overall performance as a measure of how well things were going. Such overall methods of assessment fail to recognize that individual customers have different logistical service requirements. For example, the standard trade-off in transportation has been between speed and consistency of delivery. Some customers desire or place a premium on consistency, within a longer overall order cycle. Other customers desire overnight or same-day shipments and are willing to pay a premium for such services. A practice of management based on measuring average service performance in an environment characterized by specific and diverse customer needs will lead to the failure of a marketing orientation. In many ways such an attitude of average overall performance is reminiscent of Henry Ford, who boasted that "consumers can have any color car, so long as it is black."

Service Context for Requirements Planning

When viewing logistics, two basic types of service requirements must be considered:

1. Basic service requirements
2. Special service requirements

Basic service requirements evolve to satisfy customer needs, and depend upon the product and the customer. Special service requirements are the result of enterprise plans, visions, and policy. They represent resource deployments aimed at gaining specific customer loyalty.

Examples of basic service include product availability, consistency of delivery, flexibility to expedite orders or accommodate unique delivery requests, ease of product substitutability, error-free administration, and overall support following ownership transfer. There are many business situations wherein the actual specifications of basic service will differ. In general, consumer markets are less concerned with basic service performance than industrial customers. Once a customer's basic service dimensions have been identified, a firm can develop ways and means to satisfy their requirements. As a general rule, if a customer's business is accepted or encouraged, they deserve a high-quality basic service.

In addition to identifying and servicing basic requirements, an opportunity often exists to deploy or exploit special services. Special service requirements are driven by unique customer strategies and incorporate efforts to achieve competitive advantage. A program or plan to offer enhanced value-added services to selected customers, to leverage basic service, is what leads to competitive advantage. Alliances based on developing interorganizational logistical competencies expand the potential for gaining such advantage.[13]

As firms recognize that customer loyalty can result from catering to unique requirements of customers, it becomes possible to differentiate on the basis of logistical competency. Firms can offer basic levels of reliability and response, augmented by special logistical services such as shipment tracking, crossdocking, intermodal transportation, product reconfiguration, or innovative warehousing services, when and where these fit. Positioning these and other logistics services forms the basis for differentiation. However, in order to effectively differentiate using logistical competency, managers must have a clear understanding of individual customer needs.

Operationalizing Logistical Segmentation

Segmentation builds on the fundamental premise that customers have unique needs and desire different services. By dividing the total market, which is often too large and diverse to serve effectively, into segments that share common perspectives, firms can tailor service offerings to satisfy specific needs. This segmental concept of viewing and grouping markets is fundamental to the managerial marketing process. Each firm's perspective on segmentation is unique. Segmentation allows firms to focus efforts on the requirements of customers. The driving force behind segmentation is enhanced customer satisfaction and improved profitability through the elimination of wasteful or misdirected marketing efforts.

For logistics managers, segmentation goes even further than is typical in other areas of marketing. Based on customer size and profitability, the relevant logistics segment may be an individual customer or very small groups of customers. Thus logistical segmentation means that combinations of basic and special services need to be designed to satisfy the requirements of all relevant customers or groups of customers. The overall architecture of a firm that is proactively using logistics may consist of numerous substrategies for specific target markets. The fundamental point, as noted above, is that all customers with whom a firm agrees to do business deserve high levels of basic service. The unique strategies that are driven by segmentation are those features previously identified as special services.

Segmentation is also a viable concept for services marketing. For example, the basic supply chain contains a number of target segments for transportation services. Transportation firms can target inbound transportation, interfacility transportation, outbound transportation, or final customer delivery, based upon organizational goals and customer characteristics. Specializing in a particular type of transportation service can offer competitive advantages based on increased competency, availability of specialized equipment, or tailored information technology solutions.

Similar opportunities exist for logistics service-providers to offer distinct service offerings to individual customers. Innovative arrangements designed to reduce risk, such as Exel's graduated plan for dedicated warehouse space, or to improve operational efficiency, such as single-invoice billing across multiple firms, can become the basis for segmentation plans. It is clear that logistical competency is increasingly becoming a viable means for segmenting markets to achieve improved profit performance and higher customer satisfaction.

Customer Satisfaction and Beyond

Customer-focused logistics is driven by the same basic logic as the marketing concept of the 1950s. The key is customer requirements. Customer-focused logistics does not concentrate on operational efficiency. Provision of unique service offerings tends to overshadow the importance of cost and service tradeoffs. It is through this mutual deficiency that logistical differentiation is able to reconcile these divergent concepts. Firms are able to achieve competitive advantage by combining operational efficiency and careful identification of target customer segments. This reconciliation is manifest in the shift from customer service to customer satisfaction and success.

Logistical performance was initially assessed on the basis of customer service levels. The assumption was that customers desired consistent service performance, regardless of individual market characteristics. Logistics managers became preoccupied with increasing internal performance such as fill rate, in-stock position, and delivery performance. However, such internal performance focus ignored the interface between operational considerations and customer requirements. Increasingly, firms have shifted toward customer satisfaction as the guiding principle for performance. Customer satisfaction goes beyond basic service and ensures that customers receive desired benefits from logistical performance. While satisfaction is a much better performance focus, it tends to ignore the greater goals of the overall channel environment.

Logistical service is currently evolving to a point where customer success is becoming a primary goal. In order to achieve customer success, basic service and satisfaction continue to be of concern. However, by offering services that make customers successful, the firm can help ensure long-term survival and profitability for the entire supply chain. It should be noted that customer success is not a general strategy, which can or should be made available to all customers. It should be targeted toward selected customers with whom the enterprise can establish strategic and operational synergies through an extended relationship. Customer success strategies are one part of a complete logistics service package.

Marketing-Logistics Integration: A Success Example

The previous discussion has highlighted the critical role logistics can play in the creation and implementation of a firm's strategic marketing program. The integration of marketing and logistics from a strategic perspective is anticipated to be a competitive requirement in the twenty-first century. The following discussion highlights the success of one firm in managing the process of moving from a service to a success orientation.

Bergen Brunswig, one of the nation's leading drug wholesalers, developed a long-term process that linked strategic marketing implementation and logistical resource application. The following model, illustrated in Fig. 2-5, is an adaptation of the customer success program implemented with their retail drug store customers. Each of the four stages establishes necessary prerequisites for integration of marketing and logistics activities.

Cost Effectiveness

The initial stage, referred to as "gaining cost effectiveness," consists of developing the process and related controls necessary to ensure that basic logistics services are performed in a cost-effective manner.[14] This stage establishes efficient logistics operations as the base from which to concentrate on market opportunities. Unless a firm is able to deliver on promises of quality service at reasonable cost, there is no reason for increased attention to marketing opportunities.

Market Access

The market access stage consists of across-the-board commitments to all customers regarding the firm's basic service platform.[14] Antitrust considerations prevent customer selectivity at this stage in the process. All customers to whom a commitment is made can expect a proportionate share of total logistical performance. This es-

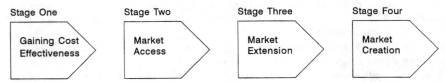

Figure 2-5. Marketing-logistics integration model. (*From Donald J. Bowersox, Patricia J. Daugherty, and Maurice P. Lundrigan, "Competitive Advantage through Electronic Information Linkage," an unpublished manuscript.*)

tablishes a broad logistical base of customer commitments from which to establish deeper marketing-based arrangements.

Market Extension

Having established a basic level of commitment to all customers, market extension seeks to intensify the business relationship with specified customers. Value-added services can be introduced to solidify and expand relationships through increased customer satisfaction. Such innovations as sophisticated bar coding, computer terminals for customers, point-of-sale encoding, retail store shelf plan-o-gramming, immediate price-change administration, profitability reports, and inventory turn reports are examples of services Bergen Brunswig used to improve customer efficiency and extend overall competitiveness. At this stage, logistics became proactive and customer-focused. Through attention to individual customer needs, logistics became a critical part of marketing strategy. Market extension links strategic marketing with logistical resource application.

Market Creation

The final stage, market creation, represents a full commitment to customer success.[14] While the impact of the stages is cumulative with regard to customer success, market creation represents initiatives beyond the typical scope of customer-focused marketing. Relational alliances, which extend beyond the basic buyer-seller transaction, serve to institutionalize business relationships. Market creation involves mutual understanding of business goals and needs, and relies on joint research and development of innovative methods for capitalizing on relationships. Electronic linkage, one of the primary facilitators of process integration, permits two-way interaction and the potential for increased control of the relationship. While market extension established the link between marketing strategy and logistical resource application, market creation utilizes this linkage for the competitive advantage of the firm.

The overall process of implementing and managing the changes required to realize a program of advanced market extension and creation requires substantial time and effort. Many firms are not able to make such commitments due to the realities of the existing business environment. However, to focus on short-term problems at the expense of long-term competitive strategy can be a fatal decision.

While the model presented is not the only method for achieving further integration of marketing and logistics, it provides a clear discussion of the basic issues involved. Marketing and logistics activities require coordination, not only within the firm, but across the entire channel. This will become even more evident as firms enter the competitive environment of the twenty-first century.

Conclusion

The interface between marketing and logistics undeniably deserves the same level of attention traditionally devoted to the separate disciplines by individual managers. This chapter has highlighted the role logistics can play in marketing strategy. In particular, attention has been focused on the type of competitive advantages attainable through superior logistical performance.

A number of experts have speculated as to the direction of logistics management in the future.[15] Their ideas can be summarized in three basic notions:

1. The basic demand for logistical services will continue to expand as logistical competency is viewed as a primary source of strategic advantage.

2. Understanding and empowering employees to meet customer needs through customer-focused activities will lead to greater process accountability.

3. Technology will continue to reshape conventional logistics processes and channels, for the betterment of the individual firm and society.

These three propositions underline the need to integrate marketing and logistics performance to achieve improved operational efficiency and enhanced customer satisfaction. By reducing or eliminating old paradigms concerning how logistics and marketing integrate, a firm can achieve superior performance. Such integration is clearly not an organizational imperative. The deployment of advanced information technology opens the door to joint planning and networked implementation that focuses responsibility. The key to deploying integrated marketing and logistics is sophisticated segmentation. Integration can secure performance levels necessary to gain and maintain customers in the highly competitive environments of the future.

References

1. E. Jerome McCarthy and William D. Perreault, *Basic Marketing: A Managerial Approach,* 10th ed., Richard D. Irwin, Inc., Homewood, IL, 1990.

2. Thomas A. Staudt, Donald A. Taylor, and Donald J. Bowersox, *A Managerial Introduction to Marketing,* 3d ed., Prentice-Hall, Inc., Englewood Cliffs, NJ, 1976.

3. Donald J. Bowersox, "Clearing Roadblocks to Supply Chain Management," *United Parcel Service International Update,* Spring, p. 4, 1992.

4. Charles M. Savage, *Fifth Generation Management: Integrating Enterprises Through Human Networking,* Digital Press, Bedford, MA, 1990.

5. Donald J. Bowersox, John T. Mentzer, and Thomas W. Speh, "The Marketing–Logistics Strategic Imperative," an unpublished manuscript, 1992.

6. Frank W. Davis, Jr., and Karl B. Manrodt, "Principles of Service Response Logistics," *Proceedings of the Council of Logistics Management,* 1991, pp. 339–55.

7. Donald J. Bowersox, Patricia J. Daugherty, Cornelia L. Dröge, Richard N. Germain, and Dale S. Rogers, *Logistical Excellence: It's Not Business As Usual,* Digital Press, Bedford, MA, 1992.

8. "O.K., So He's Not Sam Walton," *Business Week,* p. 56, March 16, 1992.

9. George Stalk, Philip Evans, and Lawrence E. Shulman, "Competing on Capabilities: The New Rules of Corporate Strategy," *Harvard Business Review,* 1992, **70:**2, 57–69.

10. Theodore Levitt, "Exploit the Product Life Cycle," *Harvard Business Review,* 1965, **43:**6, 81–94.

11. "How a $4.00 Razor Ends Up Costing $300 Million," *Business Week,* January 29, 1990, pp. 62–63.
12. Lt. William G. (Gus) Pagonis, with Jeffrey L. Cruikshank, *Moving Mountains: Lessons in Leadership and Logistics from the Gulf War,* Harvard Business School Press, Boston, MA, 1992.
13. Donald J. Bowersox, "The Strategic Benefits of Logistics Alliances," *Harvard Business Review,* 1990, **68:**4, 58–64.
14. Donald J. Bowersox, Patricia J. Daugherty, and Maurice P. Lundrigan, "Competitive Advantage Through Electronic Information Linkage," an unpublished manuscript, 1992.
15. Bowersox et al. (see reference 1) and Bernard J. LaLonde, "Three Challenges to Customer Driven Marketing," an unpublished manuscript, 1992.

3

Customer Service*

Douglas M. Lambert
Prime F. Osborn III Eminent Scholar Chair in Transportation, University of North Florida

Jay U. Sterling
Associate Professor of Marketing, University of Alabama

Customer service represents the output of the logistics system and the place component of the firm's marketing mix. It is a measure of the effectiveness of the logistics system in creating time and place utilities for a product. The level of customer service not only determines whether existing customers will remain customers, but how many potential customers will become customers. Thus the customer service level a firm provides has a direct impact on the overall satisfaction of its customers and its market share,[1] its total logistics cost, and ultimately its profitability. For this reason, it is imperative that customer service serve as the foundation and driving force in the design and operation of any logistics system.

What Is Customer Service?

The meanings of the term *customer service* varies from one company to the next. Furthermore, vendors and their customers often view the concept quite differently. In broad terms, customer service can be considered the measure of how well the

---

*This chapter is also Chapter 2 in Douglas M. Lambert, James R. Stock, and Jay U. Sterling, *Logistics Management,* to be published in 1994 by Richard D. Irwin, Inc., Homewood, Ill. It is adapted from materials contained in Chapters 4, 6, and 18 of Douglas M. Lambert and James R. Stock, *Strategic Logistics Management,* 3d ed., Richard D. Irwin, Inc., 1993. Used with permission, all rights reserved.

logistics system is performing in creating time and place utilities, such as delivering the correct product to the right place in a timely manner.

Customer service is generally presumed to be a means by which companies attempt to differentiate their product, keep customers loyal, increase sales, and improve profits. The key to customer service is understanding the customer and his or her perceptions. It does not matter what a supplier does, but rather what customers *think* the supplier does in the area of customer service. Customer service activities can be measured in quantifiable or qualitative terms. Qualitative ways involve asking customers their opinions about services they receive.[2]

Customer service should, therefore, be viewed as an integral part of marketing strategy, because it can be used to increase market share and profitability. Unfortunately, marketers have educated consumers to expect low prices that undermine brand loyalty. For companies that figure out the equation, value marketing can be a way to make a brand mean something again. Paradoxically, this means that value marketing could be a way out of the discounting trap. If a brand has value, it may be worth its premium price.[3] For instance, product availability and order cycle time can differentiate a product and increase its market penetration or influence its price, if customers are willing to pay more for better service.

A recent definition views customer service

> . . . as a process which takes place between buyers, sellers, and third parties. The process results in a value added to the product or service exchanged. This value added in the exchange process might be short-term, as in a single transaction, or longer-term, as in a contractual relationship. The value added is also shared, in that each of the parties to the transaction or contract is better off at the completion of the transaction than he/she was before the transaction took place. Thus, in a process view: customer service is a process for providing significant value-added benefits to the supply chain in a cost effective way.[4]

Successful implementation of the marketing concept requires both obtaining customers and keeping them, while satisfying the firm's long-range profit and return on investment objectives. Creating demand, obtaining customers, is often thought of solely in terms of advertising, selling, promotion, product and price, but customer service can have a significant impact on demand.[5] In addition, customer service determines whether customers will remain customers.

Management guru Tom Peters reinforces this shift to a service orientation by proposing that we say, "Bye-bye to manufacturing as we've understood it. All companies are service companies. More than 90 percent of IBM's employees, for example, perform service activities. The competitive battle rages over services added, not lumpy objects."[6] Figure 3-1 provides examples of "nonprice" services that companies such as IBM and other manufacturers can use to gain competitive advantage in the market place. This list represents services that customers most often cite as reasons why manufacturers, wholesalers, and retailers select or drop vendors. A majority of this list represents the logistics/customer service component of this marketing mix.

The concept of customer service can be applied to more than just manufacturers, wholesalers, and retailers of tangible goods. Service industries, such as hospitals, insurance companies, lawyers, dry cleaners, and transportation companies all sell intangible services. For example an Opinion Research survey of 400 executive travelers concludes that airlines, hotels, and car rental companies are concentrating on improving services that are not important to business travelers, including: in-flight

- Technical support services
- On-time delivery/high fill-rate percent
- Failure-free product (high quality)
- Breadth/depth of product line
- Knowledge/assistance of sales person
- Short lead time (stock and made-to-order product)
- Installation/training services
- Order/reorder assistance
- Return and exchange privileges
- Advance notice of shipping delays
- Ability to expedite/produce rush orders
- Ability to push/pull (change) delivery dates
- Timely and accurate order status/inventory information
- Updated/current price/specs/promo materials
- Continuity/nonobsolescence of products
- Immediate response to requests for information
- Minimize backorders and split shipments
- Commitment to TQM philosophy
- Sales force honesty (provides accurate information)

Figure 3-1. Examples of nonprice competition.

food service, late-evening room service, and wide choices of automotive makes and models. Travelers want to see improvements in: on-time arrivals, replacement of old jets, delivery of checked baggage, reasonable charges for in-room phone service, efficient hotel check-in, and rental cars in good mechanical condition. "The travel companies appear to be focusing on low-cost improvements rather than what the customer says are services which are of the greatest importance," says Joanne Brewda, Vice President, Opinion Research. "It's easier and less costly for an airline to provide upgraded food than it is to improve its baggage-handling system."[7]

Elements of Customer Service

A number of elements are commonly associated with customer service, although the degree of importance attached to any one of them varies from company to company depending on customer needs. Bernard J. LaLonde and Paul Zinszer categorized these elements into three groups—pretransaction, transaction, and posttransaction.[8] Figure 3-2 summarizes the customer service elements identified by LaLonde and Zinszer.

Pretransaction Elements.   The pretransaction elements of customer service tend to be nonroutine and policy-related, and they require management input. These activities have a significant impact on product sales and include the following:

1. *A written statement of customer service policy.* The customer service policy statement should be based on customer needs, define service standards, determine who reports the performance measurements to whom and with what frequency, and be operational.

2. *Providing customers with a written statement of service policy.* It makes little sense to provide a level of service designed to improve market penetration and then fail

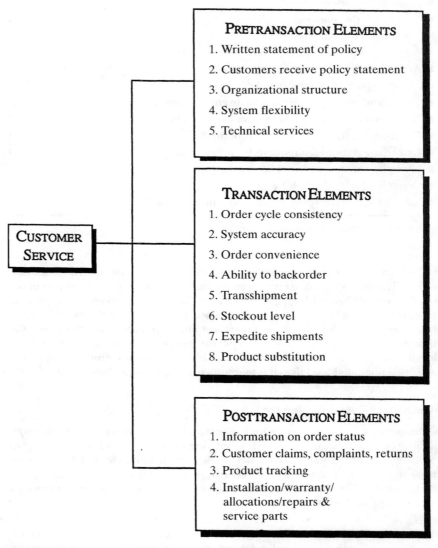

Figure 3-2. Elements of customer service. (*Adapted from p. 281 of Bernard J. LaLonde and Paul H. Zinszer,* Customer Service: Meaning and Measurement[8])

to inform the customer of what is being provided. A written statement reduces the likelihood that the customer will have unrealistic expectations of performance, and provides customers with information on how to communicate with the firm if specified performance levels are not attained.

3. *Organizational structure.* The structure selected should facilitate communication and cooperation between and among those functions involved in implementing the customer service policy. In addition, the firm should provide customers with the name and phone number of a specific individual who can satisfy their need for information. The individuals who manage the customer service components must have the appropriate responsibility and authority, and must be rewarded in a manner that encourages them to interface with other corporate functions.

4. *System flexibility.* Flexibility is required for the system to effectively respond to unplanned events such as snowstorms, shortages of raw materials or energy, strikes, and emergency needs of customers.

5. *Technical services.* Training manuals and seminars designed to help customers improve their order-processing techniques, reduce inventories, minimize transportation costs, or control concealed damage are elements of customer service.

Transaction Elements. Transaction elements are the activities most frequently associated with customer service, including the following:

1. *Order cycle consistency.* The order cycle is the total elapsed time from initiation of the order by the customer until delivery to the customer. Individual components of the order cycle include communication, order entry and processing, holding orders until backordered product becomes available, picking and packing, and delivery. Because customers are mainly concerned with consistent and reliable order cycle time, it is important to monitor and manage each of the components of the order cycle to determine the cause of variations from published standards.

2. *System accuracy.* Mistakes in system accuracy—the accuracy of quantities ordered, products ordered, and billing—are costly to both the manufacturer and customers. Errors should be recorded and reported as a percentage of the number of orders handled by the system.

3. *Order convenience.* Order convenience refers to the degree of difficulty that a customer experiences when placing an order. Problems may result from complex order forms, inefficient data-processing systems that prevent the entry of an order while the customer is on the phone, or using nonstandard terminology. All three deficiencies can lead to errors and poor customer relations. An appropriate performance measurement is the number of errors as a percentage of the number of orders. These problems can be identified and reduced or eliminated by conducting field interviews with customers.

4. *Ability to backorder.* Because no one can afford to always have every item in stock (that is, provide a 100 percent fill rate) customers must be permitted to order product that is not currently in stock and have it shipped to them when it becomes available. If this feature is not built into a company's order-processing system, then lost sales may occur and/or customers may be forced to order a product or prod-

ucts they don't want in order to comply with minimum order or truckload quantity requirements.

5. *Transshipments.* Transshipments consist of transferring product between field locations to avoid stockouts. They are often made to avoid stockouts on orders from key customers.

6. *Stockout level.* The stockout level is a measure of product availability. Stockouts should be recorded by product and by customer in order to determine where problems exist. When stockouts occur, customer goodwill can be maintained by arranging for suitable product substitution and/or expediting the shipment when the product does become available.

7. *Ability to expedite shipments.* Expedited shipments are those that require special handling in order to reduce the normal order cycle time. Although expediting costs considerably more than standard handling, the cost of a lost customer may be even higher. It is important for management to determine which customers qualify for expedited shipments and which do not.

8. *Product substitution.* Substitution occurs when the product ordered is replaced by the same item in a different size or with another product that will perform as well or better. For example, a customer may order a case of Ivory shampoo for normal hair in 15-oz bottles. If the customer is willing to accept 8- or 20-oz bottles during a stockout, the manufacturer can increase the customer service level as measured by product availability within some specified time period. Figure 3-3 demonstrates that two product substitutions will allow the manufacturer to increase its fill rate percentage from 70 to 97 percent with no change in inventory. (There is a 70 percent probability that each item to be substituted will be in stock. Thus 70 percent times the stockout percent of 30 percent will result in an increase of 21 to 91 percent with one substitution, and 97 percent with two substitutions.) If the firm

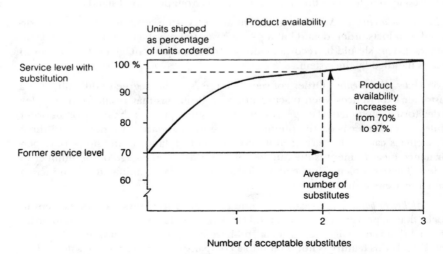

Figure 3-3. Impact of substitution on service level.

is currently achieving a 90 percent service level, then obtaining two product substitutions on an order will result in virtually a 100 percent fill rate.

In order to develop an appropriate product substitution policy, the manufacturer should work closely with customers to gain their consent. Therefore, a successful product substitution program requires frequent and clear communication between the manufacturer and customers.

Posttransaction Elements. The posttransaction elements of customer service support the product after it has been sold. The specific posttransaction elements include:

1. *Order information.* Order information is the ability to provide customers with fast and accurate information concerning inventory availability, order status, expected shipping and delivery dates, and backorder status. The number of backorders should be recorded by customer and by product categories to identify and correct poor system performance.

2. *Customer claims, complaints, and returns.* Usually, logistics systems are designed to move products in one direction—toward the customer. Almost every manufacturer has some goods returned, however, and the nonroutine handling of these items is expensive. A corporate policy should specify how to handle claims, complaints, and returns. The company should maintain data on these activities in order to provide valuable consumer information to research and development, manufacturing, engineering, marketing, and logistics.

3. *Product tracking.* Product tracking is another necessary component of customer service. In order to avoid litigation, firms may be required by the federal government to recall potentially dangerous products from the marketplace as soon as problems are identified.

4. *Installation, warranty, alterations, repairs, and service parts.* These elements of customer service can be a significant factor in the decision to purchase a product requiring after-sale service, such as machinery sold to manufacturers and big ticket items sold to consumers. To perform these functions, the following are necessary:

   a. Assistance in seeing that the product is functioning as expected when the end user or consumer begins to use it
   b. Availability of parts and/or repairmen
   c. Documentation support for the field force to assist in performing their jobs
   d. An administrative function that validates warranties.[9]

Methods of Establishing a Customer Service Strategy

A firm's entire marketing effort can be rendered ineffective by poorly conceived customer service policies. Yet customer service is often a forgotten component of the marketing mix, and the level of customer service is often based on industry norms, management judgment, or past practices—not on what customers want, or what would maximize corporate profitability.[10] What is the advantage of having a well-researched and needed product, priced to sell and promoted well, if customers cannot find it on the shelf at the retail level? However, *too much* customer service will needlessly reduce corporate profits. It is essential that a firm adopt a customer service policy that is based on customer needs, is consistent with overall marketing strategy, and advances the corporation's long-range profit objectives.

A number of methods are available for establishing a profitable customer service strategy. But the following four methods have the most merit:

1. Determining channel service levels based on knowledge of consumer reactions to stockouts
2. Cost/revenue tradeoffs
3. ABC analysis of customer service
4. The customer service audit

Consumer Reactions to Stockouts

In consumer goods companies, customer service levels normally are measured between the manufacturer and its intermediaries such as wholesalers and retailers. These measures exclude the consumer, the person who purchases the product at the retail level. However, a stockout at the manufacturer–wholesaler interface does not always result in the wholesaler's stocking out the retail accounts it services.

One way to establish the level of customer service that should be provided to wholesalers and retailers is to determine what the consumer is likely to do in the event of a stockout. Figure 3-4 illustrates consumers' possible reactions when they

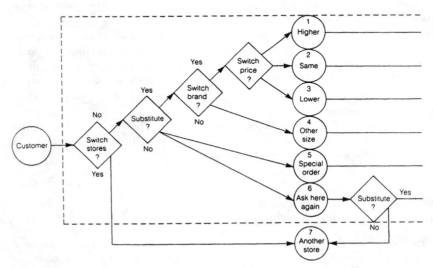

Figure 3-4. Model of consumer reaction to a repeated stockout. (*From Clyde K. Walter, "An Empirical Analysis of Two Stockout Models," unpublished Ph.D. dissertation, The Ohio State University, 1971*)

are faced with a stockout at the retail level. For example, a consumer enters a retail store to purchase Ivory shampoo for normal hair in a 15-oz bottle. If the item is unavailable, the customer can go to another store to purchase the product. Such inconvenience may not be worth it for a bottle of shampoo, but there are a number of products for which customers are willing to switch stores.[11]

Most manufacturers of infant formula do not advertise their products to consumers in national media. They spend the bulk of their advertising dollars giving the product to hospitals and doctors who, in turn, provide free samples to new mothers. Because of the high perceived risk associated with the purchase of a nutritional product for a baby, the mother will request the brand given to her by the doctor or used while she and the baby were at the hospital.[12] Although the two leading brands of products may have identical ingredients, the consumer would rather switch stores than switch brands. This information is critical when formulating a customer service strategy. While the penalty for stocking out the retailer may be very low, the manufacturer will incur a high cost if it stocks out a doctor or a hospital. For example, a service failure may cause a doctor or a hospital to switch from Ross Laboratories' product, Similac, to Mead Johnson's product, Enfamil. Ross Laboratories will lose the business of all future mothers that doctor or hospital treats. While it may be difficult to determine the exact cost of losing the business of a doctor or hospital, the customer service implications are clear. Hospitals and doctors require a high level of customer service, such as lead times of 48 hours and 99 percent in-stock availability.

Retailers, on the other hand, will most likely lose the sale if they experience a stockout on Similac. Therefore, they must be concerned about the frequency of stockouts on items for which consumers are willing to switch stores. Frequent stockouts on such items could cause consumers to permanently switch their shopping loyalties to another store.[13] With this information, the manufacturer could set a longer order cycle for retailers, but use the additional time to reduce variability in lead times and provide higher levels of in-stock availability. This would enable them to satisfy their customers' needs without maintaining excessive inventories.

In most stockout situations, consumers are not willing to accept the inconvenience of switching retail outlets. This brings us to the second decision point in Fig. 3-4. At this point, the consumer must decide if substitution is acceptable. The consumer who wants to purchase Ivory shampoo may be willing to postpone the purchase until the next shopping trip if he or she still has some shampoo left at home. If not, the consumer may substitute another brand. It is unlikely that consumers would place special orders for products like shampoo.

For some items, however, a majority of consumers are willing and may even expect to place a special order. In the early 1970s, Whirlpool and Sears, in a study of consumer purchase behavior, found that the majority of consumers would be willing to wait from three to five days for delivery of their appliances. This study had significant implications for the companies' logistics systems. First, only floor models of appliances were necessary at the retail level. Second, Sears' 60-plus retail distribution centers (RDCs) could eliminate most of their inventories.

Under the new system, all products were shipped to Sears only when the manufacturer received orders from retail stores. The product was shipped from the manufacturer's factory warehouse to Sears distribution centers (which served as wholesale warehouses in the Sears network), and from there to the consumer. All of this took place within the required three to five days. The key to implementing this program was the ability to separate the flow of information from the physical flow of product—or *channel separation*—as depicted in Fig. 3-5. In traditional channel networks, each different level (echelon) stores and distributes product as well as processes orders from its immediate contact downstream in the channel. These orders are typically transmitted upstream until eventually the manufacturing plant reacts by replenishing its immediate stocking point (factory distribution centers). It is obvious that this type of system is laden with inventories and expensive to operate. By converting the wholesale warehouse (RDC) into a flow-through crossdock operation, customer service was significantly improved and costs were dramatically reduced.

Implementation of this system substantially reduced systemwide inventories, while actually improving customer service. For example, inventory turns at Sears' distribution centers increased from 8 to 65 times, and in-stock availability improved 10 percentage points to the high nineties as a result of consolidating inventories into one location from the former 60 warehouses. The typical Sears distribution center (RDC) saved approximately $3.50 per appliance in warehousing and inventory carrying costs. Sears no longer had to predict the color, size, and features desired by consumers at each retail outlet. By 1984 the system had undergone a number of refinements, and in major U.S. markets Sears customers received 36- to 72-hour delivery on Kenmore appliances. Customers orders at retail were linked via touchtone telephone to the manufacturer's order entry system, which in turn was fed back to its manufacturing plants as input to production schedules. In addition, Sears established similar programs with vendors of other products. While this type of system may not be possible for all consumer products, it illustrates how consumer research can be used to establish a differentiated customer service strategy.

Usually, consumers will switch stores when they experience a stockout on an item with a high level of brand preference. But for other products, consumers will substitute size or brand. Figure 3-3 showed how customer service levels could be increased from 70 to 97 percent, with no corresponding increase in inventories, if

Order Flow

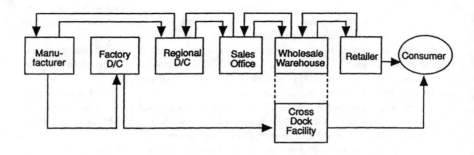

Product Flow

Figure 3-5. Channel separation.

customers were willing to accept two product substitutions. When this is the case, customer service levels should not be measured based on each stockkeeping unit (such as the 15-oz bottle of Ivory shampoo for normal hair) but on all units of that product (all sizes of Ivory shampoo for normal hair).[14]

The final option for consumers who face a retail stockout is to switch brands. Depending on the substitution strategy the consumer employs, the retailer may not experience any negative impacts on either sales or profits; for instance, the consumer may substitute an item that sells for a higher price or may buy one national brand instead of another. If the manufacturer knows the consumers are willing to substitute size, it should use this information to convince retailers and wholesalers that they too should accept these substitutes.[15]

If brand switching takes place, however, the manufacturer definitely loses at least the contribution to profit from this one purchase. By stocking out and putting the consumer in the position of switching brands, the manufacturer is allowing customers to sample competitive products and, what's worse, the competitor receives compensation for it! In addition, the substituted brand may become the consumers' first choice in the future. If this happens, the manufacturer loses the present value of all future contributions to profit that it would have realized had the consumer not changed his or her purchase behavior. These amounts are difficult, or impossible, to determine.[16]

Cost/Revenue Tradeoffs

The sum of the expenditures for all of a firm's logistics activities can be viewed as the company's expenditure for customer service. Figure 3-6 illustrates the cost tradeoffs required to implement an integrated logistics management concept. In order to achieve least-cost logistics, management must minimize total logistics costs, given a specified level of customer service. Too often companies take a reverse approach, driving down costs without considering the implications of their efforts on customer service levels. Consequently, the costs associated with improving service levels can be compared to the increase in sales required to recover the additional costs. For example, a company is currently offering a 95 percent customer service level—by its own measures—at least total cost. If sales management insists that service levels be increased to 98 percent to achieve the company's market penetration objectives, the cost of the most efficient logistics method can be estimated for the new service objective and compared to the current cost.

Assume that the cost of the most efficient logistics system for a 98 percent service goal is $2 million higher than the existing system's cost. If each dollar of additional sales yields a 25 percent contribution to fixed costs and profit—that is, if for each $1 in revenue the company incurs 75 cents in out-of-pocket manufacturing, marketing, and logistics costs—what additional sales volume will the company need to recover the increase in logistics costs? We can calculate the point at which the company breaks even on the service improvement by dividing the $2 million increase in costs by the 25 percent contribution margin. The company needs a sales increase of $8 million per year to break even. We can estimate the likelihood that this will occur by determining what $8 million represents as a percentage increase in sales. A 2 percent increase in sales volume might be viewed as likely, whereas a 20 percent sales increase might be considered unlikely, given the competitive situation.

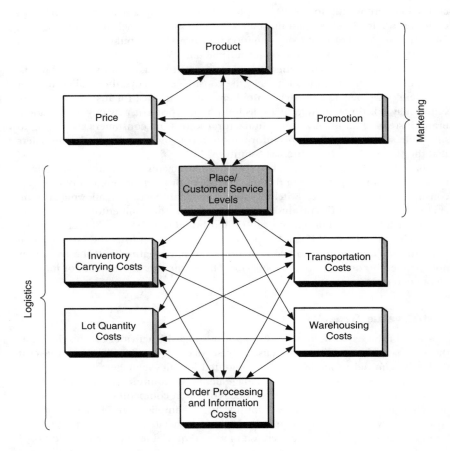

Marketing objective: Allocate resources to the marketing mix to maximize the long-run profitability of the firm. Logistics objective: Minimize total costs given the customer service objective where: Total costs = Transportation costs + Warehousing costs + Order processing and information costs + Lot quantity costs + Inventory carrying costs.

Figure 3-6. Cost tradeoffs required in a logistics system. (*From Douglas M. Lambert,* The Development of an Inventory Costing Methodology: A Study of the Costs Associated with Holding Inventory, *National Council of Physical Distribution Management, 1976, p. 7.*)

ABC Analysis

The ABC analysis used to improve customer service efficiency is similar to the ABC analysis used for inventory planning.[17] The logic behind this approach is that some customers and products are more profitable than others. Thus, a company should maintain higher levels of customer service for the most profitable customer–product combinations. Profitability should be measured on a contribution basis, excluding joint costs and fixed overhead allocations.[18] Trends in profitability also should be measured/estimated so that potential growth is considered.

Table 3-1 illustrates a customer–product contribution matrix that can be used to classify customers and products according to their impact on the manufacturer's profit performance. It is interpreted as follows:

1. Products in category A are the firm's most profitable products, followed by categories B and C. The products in category A represent a small percentage of the total product line (usually 5 to 10 percent).

2. Products in category C represent the firm's least profitable products. Typically, 80 percent of the product line falls into this category.

3. Customers in classification I are the most profitable for the manufacturer and may number no more than 5 or 10 percent.

4. Customers in classification V are the least profitable customers, because they purchase in small quantities or generate small annual sales volume. The price and service concessions they receive could easily result in a negative contribution. Classification V usually contains the majority of customers.

5. The most profitable customer–product combination occurs when products in category A are sold to customers in classification I (priority number 1). The next most profitable combination occurs when products in category B are sold to customers in classification I. The next most profitable are products in category A sold to customers in classification II, and so on until the least profitable customer–product relationship—when products in category C are sold to customers in classification V (priority number 15).

The customer–production contribution matrix can be put into operation in a manner similar to that shown in Table 3-2. In this example, customers have been grouped into three categories: high-volume, high-profit customers; low-volume, profitable customers; and low-profit spot business.

The first category of customers is assigned a fill rate standard of 99 percent on A products and a delivery standard for truckload orders of five working days, three working days for fill-in (less-than-truckload) orders. The fill rate percentages on B and C or lower product categories are reduced to 97 and 95 percent, respectively, for the most important customers.

The lowest-priority customer category (low-profit spot business) has been as-

Table 3-1. A Customer–Product Contribution Matrix

Customer classification	Product A	Product B	Product C	
I	1	2	6	Stronger franchise with best customers.
II	3	4	7	
III	5	8	11	Lower logistics costs. Higher inventory turns. Reduced expediting.
IV	9	12	13	
V	10	14	15	

SOURCE: Adapted from Bernard J. LaLonde and Paul H. Zinszer, *Customer Service: Meaning and Measurement,* (National Council of Physical Distribution Management, 1976, Chicago, p. 181.)

Table 3-2. An Example of Service Differentiation

Service action	High-volume, high-profit customers	Low-volume profitable customers	Low-profit spot business
Order cycle time			
▪ Truckload	1 week	2 weeks	3 weeks
▪ LTL (less-than-truckload)	1–2 times per week*	1–2 times per week*	–
▪ Emergency	ASAP	ASAP	–
Fill Rates			
▪ A items	99 percent	99 percent	90 percent
▪ B items	95 percent	90 percent	85 percent
▪ C items	90 percent	85 percent	If Available
Pricing/promotions	▪ Full Market Development Funds (100%)	▪ Co-op Market Development Funds (50%)	None
Claims processing	7 days	15 days	30 days

*Via consolidated, scheduled deliveries to selected market areas on prescribed day(s) each week.

signed a lead time of 15 days for truckload orders only. That is, this category is not able to order fill-in or emergency orders, in order to ensure achievement of the very high fill rates guaranteed to more important customers. Fill rate percentages are also less than other customers categories for the same reason. In fact, orders for category C products are accepted only if the product is available. This differentiated service recognizes the need to build the strongest franchise with your best customers, so as to guarantee repeat business. A firm does not want to stock out its most profitable customers on its most profitable products. Less profitable accounts can be made more valuable by reducing the costs of servicing them. For example, one method of making unprofitable accounts profitable is to limit the time when orders can be placed and then consolidate them for shipment to customers at preset intervals. By requiring that small customers in a specific geographic area place their orders on a biweekly basis, such as Mondays for delivery the following Friday, a firm can increase its profitability by reducing order processing and transportation costs. Benefits to the customer include reduced order cycle variability and higher levels of in-stock availability.

The Customer Service Audit[19]

An audit program should be conducted on a routine basis, although the length of time between audits may vary among firms. The objectives of a logistics audit are to:

▪ Identify the costs of logistics
▪ Determine current performance levels and/or deficiencies of the logistics operating system
▪ Provide data required to design or restructure the logistics strategy of the firm

- Determine operating systems or procedures that will best contribute to the company's profit goals
- Identify customer supply and market profiles, plus the factors that influence key manufacturing, marketing, and logistics decisions
- Determine the capital costs associated with logistics
- Identify tradeoffs and incremental benefits of proposed changes to the system

Because of these objectives it is necessary to identify, collect, and analyze the data that will best describe current costs and customer service levels. When conducting a logistics audit, management should follow the steps outlined in Fig. 3-7.

Figure 3-8 summarizes these steps. The process is described in the following sections.

The Logistics Task Force

Firms should use a task force approach because members of the task force are directly involved in the decision-making process and recognize that they are responsi-

---

1. A "logistics task force" should be established to assist in the review process.
2. Current corporate strategies and objectives that could impact or be affected by logistics must be determined.
3. Key questions should be constructed by the task force to serve as a basis for use in both internal and external audit interviews, identifying weaknesses in the current system, and recommending improvements.
4. An *external audit* consisting of in-depth interviews with customers should be undertaken, to determine the firm's performance, competitive practices, and performance, as well as customer desires and expectations concerning customer service.
5. An *internal audit* of current logistics performance should be conducted. This audit involves two distinct processes:
   a. Personal interviews with representatives from various functions throughout the firm.
   b. Sampling of firm records and transaction data so that the existing operating system can be statistically analyzed and performance accurately described.
6. Cost and service tradeoff alternatives should be identified and analyzed.
7. The questions identified in Step 3 must be addressed, and improvements/changes to the current system identified and recommended to management.
8. The system that will exist after the recommended changes should be described, and expected performance predicted.

Figure 3-7. Logistics review/audit sequential process. (*From Jay U. Sterling and Douglas M. Lambert, "A Methodology for Assessing Logistics Operating Systems,"* International Journal of Physical Distribution and Materials Management, *vol. 15, no. 6, 1985.*)

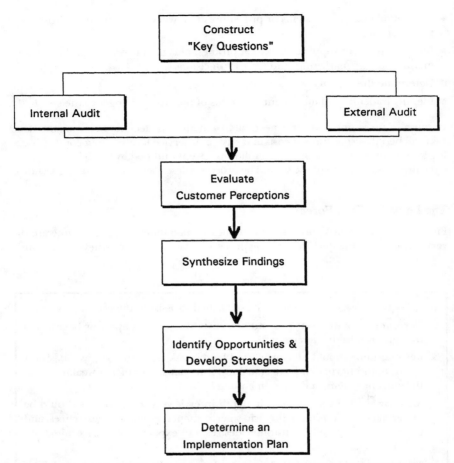

Figure 3-8. Logistics audit methodology. (*Adapted from Jay U. Sterling and Douglas M. Lambert, "Establishing Customer Service Strategies within the Marketing Mix,"* Journal of Business Logistics, *vol. 8, no. 1, p. 10, 1987.*)

ble for implementing the recommendations. The task force approach leads to a level of commitment that is not possible when recommended strategies and system changes are proposed by an outside agency, or by an individual within the firm who is not involved in the actual day-to-day operations of the function.

Two types of individuals need to be included in the task force: those involved in managing logistics activities such as traffic, warehousing, private fleet operations, customer service, and inventory management; and those representing other corporate functions that regularly interact with logistics, such as the controller's office, marketing/sales, manufacturing, and management information systems (MIS). The participation of these functions offers several advantages: corporate-wide data and information will be more accessible; cooperation across organizational areas will be facilitated; broader perspectives will evolve; and final recommendations will be more practical and more easily implemented.

Review of Company Strategies

Too frequently, one function of a company may develop objectives, strategies, and operating systems without considering their impact on the company's overall mission and stated goals. For example, a firm may desire to grow 15 percent a year, achieve a 10 percent profit before taxes, target new investment returns at 25 percent after taxes, and introduce a minimum of five new products each year. These objectives will have an impact on every activity and output controlled by the logistics function. It is useless to propose an expanded warehouse network if the projected return (ROI) would be only 10 percent or the additional inventories would decrease profits below the targeted level.

Construction of Key Questions

Before attempting to interview customers and internal operating personnel, and before measuring current logistics performance, the task force should prepare a list of questions that, if properly resolved, will enable the company to achieve a distinct competitive advantage in the markets it serves. These questions should be broad in scope, so that they do not restrict the task force's charter. They must consider the corporate mission and goals, and address the individual concerns of top management. Figure 3-9 provides an example of "key questions" developed for a logistics audit of a manufacturer of electronic controls.

Internal Audit: Personal Interviews

In addition to completing an external audit, information should also be collected from in-depth interviews with the firm's top management. Specifically, formal interview guides need to be prepared for each of the following management functions: general senior management, marketing/sales, financial control/accounting, customer service/order administration, transportation (inbound and outbound), warehousing operations, production planning and scheduling, inventory management and forecasting, purchasing/procurement, and data processing.

Sample interview guides are included in Appendix A of this chapter. They include the most important questions that need to be answered during the internal audit interviews.

Internal Audit: Sampling of Firm's Records

Various types of source documents can serve as a basis for the quantitative phase of a logistics audit. They can be obtained by modifying or extracting data from existing operating system files, or they can be compiled by using sampling techniques. Figure 3-10 summarizes the source documents which, combined with a computer-

1. What changes are likely to occur in the structure of each market segment, and how will these changes affect the relative importance of each segment?
2. What logistics systems are currently being used by competitors, and where might the firm gain a differential advantage?
3. How should the firm respond in a proactive way to the desire of customers to implement "just-in-time" inventory programs or other cost-cutting measures?
4. Will the company's current order cycle time and fill rate *standards* make it a leader in its industry?
5. What overall customer service *strategies* should be developed, and how will these differ by customer market segment?
6. What order-processing system requirements must be met in order for the company to lead the industry in terms of customer service policies?
7. Should the company utilize a centralized or decentralized/regional warehousing network?
8. How can productivity be improved in the company's distribution centers, and what measurements are required?
9. How can transportation costs be reduced, without adversely influencing customer service?
10. Should the company expand, contract, or retain its current investment in private carriage?
11. How can the company's logistics organization best interface with manufacturing, marketing, and finance/accounting organizations?
12. How should the firm respond proactively to the desire of customers to reduce inventories or other costs?
13. Are small orders a problem? How are they likely to change in the future, and what strategies should management employ to minimize the associated costs?
14. What are the best cost-reduction opportunities for the firm's logistics operations?

Figure 3-9. Logistics review/audit example of "key questions."

based statistical package, make it possible to efficiently perform a wide range of analyses.

Synthesis Process

Once the internal audit phase has been completed, in order to accurately report the effectiveness of the logistics system it is necessary to identify cost and service tradeoff opportunities; address the questions originally constructed in the "key question" phase of the methodology; and describe the recommended strategy, including required changes to the existing measurements.

1. Modify/extract existing system files.

   - Order history and/or open files
   - Bills of lading and/or shipped manifest data files
   - Paid transportation freight bills (for both inbound and outbound shipments)
   - Private fleet "trip reports"
   - Warehouse labor time cards/payroll records

2. Prepare original documents.

   - Trailer contents of all incoming and outgoing shipments for a selected time frame, such as origin and destination zip codes, contents, weight, trailer cube percentages, and damage condition upon arrival
   - Warehouse labor hours compiled by function, such as receiving, putaway
   - Private fleet movements, such as routes, miles driven, empty miles, trailer cube percentages, shipment weight, fixed and variable costs incurred

Figure 3-10. Logistics review/audit sources for sampling process.

External Audit

The external audit may be comprised of a comprehensive mail survey, or selected in-depth interviews with customers who represent the different market segments as depicted in Fig. 3-11. This technique allows a company to systematically cover all relevant segments and subsegments, such as the subgroup retailers included at the bottom of the figure. A primary purpose is to replicate the firm's overall business/product mix. This is accomplished by collecting specific information regarding the interaction between vendor and customer logistics systems, as well as determining the logistics/customer service effectiveness of major competitors. Inquiries should be made concerning both the *current* and *future* competitive environment and customer service requirements. The logistics audit will include a number of basic questions as well as unique industry/situation-specific questions. Appendix B of this chapter provides a sample of the basic inquiries that need to be included in a competitive analysis.

Many of the questions in Appendix B can be further segregated by customer segment, made-to-order versus made-to-stock products, channel segments, or product line/product group. Ideally, the identity of the firm should not be disclosed during the interview process, so that objective, industrywide data can be collected. For this reason, the assistance of university researchers or consultants is frequently preferable when conducting a logistics audit. The in-depth interviews may provide enough data to proceed with the development of a logistics strategy, or management may use them as the basis of a comprehensive mail survey of the type described in the following section.

Interviews with a firm's management often disclose the following types of problems:

1. Breakdowns/deficiencies in inventory control concerning: forecasting, production planning and scheduling, production operating systems (e.g., MRP), last-

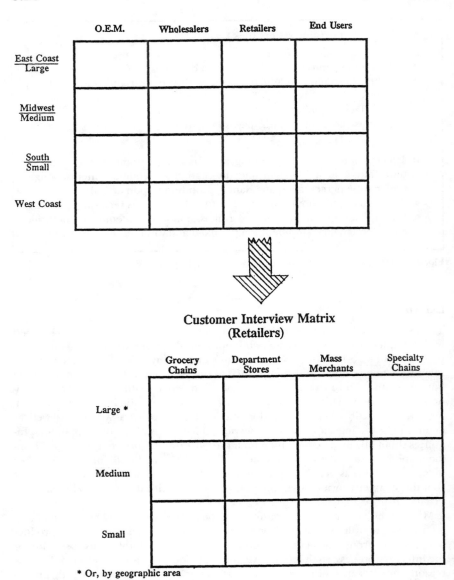

Figure 3-11. Sampling procedure for in-depth customer interviews.

minute changes in product plans, inefficient capacity planning, excessive set-ups/downtimes, inefficient sequencing of production lines, and failure to compare forecasts to actual results.

2. Order entry/processing flaws, such as: overly complex terminal input screens; failure to properly allocate inventories to orders; inability to combine multiple

orders from same customer; complex order adjustment processes; failure to differentiate service levels by product/market segments; delays due to the credit check process; and excessive manual interventions.

3. Warehousing/shipping problems, such as: excessive emergency "ASAP" orders; "will call" bottlenecks; inefficient picking processes; inefficient warehouse layouts; missed consolidation opportunities; excessive/inaccurate paperwork; inefficient stock location systems; and excessive overtime.

By analyzing internal data files, it's possible to measure order cycle times; variances; on-time or late deliveries; fill rate percentages and order completeness percentages by customer; origin shipping location; products or product group; current versus advance (future) orders; and in-stock versus made-to-order shipments. These measurements can be used to identify: causes of late deliveries (versus customers' date wanted); customers receiving superior and inferior service; weak linkages in the internal order/shipment process; excessive split shipments/backorders; orders/lines canceled; small order problems; and range in order cycle times (versus average).

The analysis of internal systems files can also reveal the following types of opportunities: the impact of slow movers and obsolete inventories on inventory turns; inventory investment and profitability; transportation malfunctions caused by a decentralized warehousing network; geographic markets that will support shipment consolidation, scheduled delivery programs, and make-build consolidation of vendor orders; opportunities for less expensive transportation modes and carriers; the advantages and opportunities for ABC analysis of products and customers; and the profitability/contribution of products (SKUs), product lines, customers, customer groups, and business units.

Customer Service Survey

Suppliers/vendors should consider the service needs of customers, as well as the costs of providing these services. Managers should group customers with similar needs, and design a specific service mix for each segment. Management must allocate scarce resources in a manner that maximizes overall marketing efficiency (low costs and high-quality products) and effectiveness (market share and value-added products). Also, it is necessary to determine if superior performance with respect to marketing services results in either a larger share of the market or a premium price, and which components of the marketing mix contribute the most to overall customer satisfaction.

For example, customer service attributes such as these can create competitive advantage for the firm:

- Delivery time
- Delivery consistency
- Product availability
- Ability to expedite orders
- Ability to substitute

- Order information and convenience
- Post sale support for the product
- Ability to resolve customer complaints/returns

The first step of an external audit is the identification of the customer service variables that are most important to the firm's customers. The relevant customer service variables might include some or all of the services contained in Fig. 3-1 discussed elsewhere in this chapter. When developing interview guides it is important to develop the list of variables based on discussions with the firm's customers. A list such as those in Fig. 3-1 or one created by management might serve as a useful starting point in discussions with customers. Marketing executives should be involved, so that the list contains other marketing mix components such as product quality, price, terms of sale, quantity discount structure, number of sales calls, cooperative advertising, and national advertising support for the product.

There are three advantages to including the marketing function:

1. Marketing involvement facilitates the implementation of tradeoffs within the marketing mix.
2. Marketing often has considerable expertise in questionnaire design, which is the next step in the process.
3. Marketing's involvement adds credibility to the research findings, which increases acceptance and facilitates successful implementation.

Several alternative sources can be used to survey customers: outside market research firms; a local university where the research might be conducted by students and/or a professor; or, a consulting firm with specific expertise. The advantages of using one of these alternatives are that the company sponsoring the research does not have to be identified, and expert assistance is available for developing questionnaires. Identifying the sponsoring firm may bias responses. That is, customers may tell vendors that they are better than they really are in the expectation that such "strokes" will result in special considerations in the event of shortages. Some customers may tell their suppliers that their performance is worse than it actually is in an effort to shock them into corrective action. It is also difficult to obtain competitive data when the sponsoring firm is directly involved.

It should be emphasized that the variables used in mail surveys must be specifically tailored to the industry under study. The quantity and type of variables used to select and evaluate vendors is complex, and not subject to simple replication of previous research endeavors. One approach is to measure the service quality of the firm.

What Is Service Quality?

Service quality involves a comparison of expectations with performance by measuring how well the service level delivered matches customer expectations. Customers accomplish this task by comparing the service they expect with perceptions of the service they receive in evaluating service quality. Thus, service quality involves a comparison of expectations to performance. Overall satisfaction with a product or service is based on the *disconfirmation theory*. That is, it is related to confirmation or disconfirmation of expectations, where the disconfirmation experience is related to the size and direction of a customer's experience with his/her initial expectations.[20] Perceived service quality is a global judgment, or attitude, relating to the superiority of the service, whereas satisfaction is related to a specific transaction. The two constructs, however, are related, in that incidents of satisfaction over time result in perceptions of service quality; that is, satisfaction soon decays into one's overall attitude toward purchasing products.[21]

Parasuraman, Zeithaml, and Berry[22] noted that significant barriers frequently prevent the successful implementation of the marketing concept, namely discrepancies (or gaps) between buyer and seller perceptions of both service quality levels and expectations. The main thesis of their "SERVQUAL" model is that consumers' quality perceptions are influenced by a series of distinct gaps occurring on the part of marketers (vendors). They operationalized SERVQUAL by measuring the degree and direction of discrepancies between consumers' perceptions of performance and expectations, using seven-point scales for each construct. Parasuraman et al. successfully tested the proposition that positive gaps indicate a higher perception of overall quality concerning the services provided by competing firms.[23] Lambert, Stock, and Sterling[24] expanded the concept and application of gap analysis by applying the model to manufacturing companies, by expanding the concept of service quality to include all components of the marketing mix, and by identifying several additional gaps.

Once gaps have been identified, definitive action plans must ultimately be developed to emphasize positive advantages and eliminate or minimize negative gaps in key marketing mix activities. Gaps can be viewed in the context of strengths and opportunities (positive gaps) or weaknesses and threats (negative gaps). Thus, gap analysis may be used in strategic logistics planning to develop a competitive advantage in the marketplace. Customers' expectations and their evaluations of how major suppliers are performing on the various marketing services provided to them are matched with the supplier's evaluations of customer expectations and of its own performance levels. Also, actual performance levels as determined from an audit of company (provider) records must be compared to customer requirements. By matching the output from these various measurements it is possible to identify the following six gaps:

1. Which vendors are meeting or exceeding customers' expectations?
2. How does our (provider) performance compare to our competitors'?
3. Are customers accurate in their assessment of our (provider) performance?
4. Do we (provider) know what's important to our customers?
5. Are we (provider) performing better or worse than customers think?
6. Do our (provider) evaluations of importance (expectations) match our perceived performance?

These six gaps are included in Fig. 3-12, as part of a framework for gaining differential advantage. Later in this chapter we will explain how these gaps can be used to

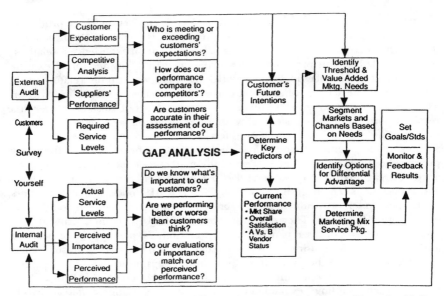

Figure 3-12. Framework for gaining differential competitive advantage. (*From Jay U. Sterling, Robert A. Robicheaux, and Carl E. Ferguson, "Identifying Differential Competitive Advantages Using an Extended GAP Analysis Model, in* 1992 American Marketing Association Summer Educators' Conference, *AMA, Chicago.*)

compare a firm's performance on key services to both customer expectations and customer evaluations of competitors' performance levels.

We will use "importance" for each marketing service attribute to measure customer "expectations."[25] Importance and expectation scores are so interrelated that the distinction between the two is insignificant. Intuitively, customers expect satisfaction on attributes they consider important. Therefore, attributes of low importance will likely engender low or ambivalent expectations, rather than high scores associated with significant prior consideration. Consequently, importance and expectation scores should be highly correlated. So, mean "importance" scores can be interpreted as barometric indicators of expectations, and can be used to weight the dimensions of the gaps. In operationalizing the model outlined in Fig. 3-12, expected service levels in addition to importance ratings should be obtained for those variables (services) that can be readily quantified by respondents, such as the number of annual sales calls required from a primary vendor/provider or length of desired lead time.

Once the six gaps have been identified for each marketing service provided by a vendor to its customers, they can be used to identify and/or predict key measurements of overall firm performance, such as:

1. Current market share of each vendor

2. Future intentions of customers (preferred, ideal market share)

3. Overall satisfaction evaluations by customers

4. Differences between "A" (primary) versus "B" (secondary) vendors.

The resulting gaps that emerge as predictors or determinants of these global measurements can also be used as the basis for:

1. Segmenting markets
2. Developing channel-specific marketing programs
3. Identifying options to gain differential advantage over competitors
4. Developing specific action programs across each of the components of the marketing mix.

Appendix C at the end of this chapter contains an example of an actual questionnaire that was used to survey customers (shippers) who used LTL motor carriers. Questionnaires should contain items that will allow the measurement of the gaps outlined in Fig. 3-11. Respondents should be asked to evaluate the importance of all of the marketing mix elements that they consider when *selecting* a new vendor or *evaluating* the performance of current suppliers. Seven point scales of importance are *anchored* on each extreme, as follows.

Respondents should be asked to assign a rating of 1 (not important) to factors not used, or that possess very little weight in the evaluation process. A rating of 7 (very important) should be assigned to factors that would cause the customer to reevaluate the amount of business given to a supplier, or cause him/her to drop the supplier in the event of inadequate performance. In addition, participants should be requested to provide evaluations of their two or three primary vendors using a 7-point scale with 1 equaling very poor to 7 equaling excellent/outstanding. It is not necessary to seek evaluations for more than two or three vendors, because in most situations this will cover the vast majority of their purchases of a given product category. Obtaining both importance and performance evaluations is critical when attempting to determine key marketing services. Variables rated most important by customers may *not* determine the share of business given to vendors because:

1. All major suppliers may be providing equal and/or "threshold" service levels
2. Variables with large variances in performance may be better "predictors"
3. No single supplier may be providing satisfactory service on important variables
4. Customers may not recognize the advantage of superior service on relatively "unimportant" variables if no supplier provides adequate service.

The questionnaire should include questions that require respondents to rate their overall satisfaction with each vendor and indicate the percentage of business they allocate to each vendor (see Part B of the questionnaire). Also, Part C of the questionnaire seeks to obtain specific levels of expected performance for key variables, such as the number of sales calls. Finally, the questionnaire also should include demographic information that will enable the firm to determine if there are significant differences in respondents across these data.

Before mailing the questionnaire, it should be pretested with a small group of customers to ensure that the questions are understandable and that important variables have not been ignored. The mailing list can be developed from an accounts receivable list; a sales/marketing department list of prospects; or lists of contracts, projects, bids lost, or inactive accounts. The accounts receivable list enables stratification of the sample to achieve an adequate number of large, medium, and small customers. If management wants an analysis of inactive accounts or projects lost, it can send color-coded questionnaires to identify these accounts.

The results of the service quality survey enable management to identify problems and opportunities. Table 3-3 illustrates the type of information that can be provided. This survey evaluated both customer service and other marketing mix variables. The two columns on the left side of Table 3-3 show that the ranking of the variables was not influenced by the order in which the questions appeared on the questionnaire. In this example, 7 of the 13 variables with the highest mean customer importance scores were customer service variables. This result highlights the importance of customer service within the firm's marketing mix. A small standard deviation in customer importance ratings means that there was little variation in the respondents' individual evaluations of a variable's importance. For variables with a large standard deviation, however, it is important to use the demographic information (see Part D of the questionnaire in Appendix C) to determine which customers want which services. The same argument holds for the last variable, "Store layout planning assistance from manufacturer." For example do large-volume, high-growth customers rate this higher in importance and small customers rate it lower in importance?

In order to determine what variables represent the best opportunity for increasing share of business and/or profitability, both importance and performance measures are necessary. For this reason, Table 3-3 also contains customer evaluations of perceived performance for the firm being researched and its four major competitors. This gives management some insight into the relative competitive position of each vendor, as viewed by the firm's customers. It is important that management determine what it is that the top-rated vendor is doing to create this perception. Management also must consider what actions it can take to improve customer perceptions of its service.

The company must also compare customer perceptions of service to internal measures of performance, as described in the preceding section of this chapter. This may show that the customer is not aware of the service being provided, or that management is measuring service performance incorrectly.

For example, Table 3-4 contains a comparison of customer evaluations and the results of the internal audit for Manufacturer No. 1 included in Table 3-3. Generally, customer perceptions of the vendor's performance match the vendor's actual performance level. When the manufacturer is equaling or exceeding customer standards/expectations, evaluations of respondents were relatively high, as in question 4a (lead time on special contract orders), where customers desired a lead time of 8.7 wk but were actually receiving their orders in 6.1 wk. Thus the vendor's performance was rated very high on this attribute. Where Manufacturer 1 was not meeting customer expectations, as in question 4b (lead time for in-stock products), customers assigned the vendor low evaluations. There were, however, a few instances where customers perceived the vendor's performance to be significantly lower than the results of the internal audit indicated: for instance, question 49a (order completeness on contract orders). Although the company was matching customer expectations (97 percent), it received a relatively low evaluation of 4.5 on a 7-point scale. In this instance a misperception exists, rather than actual subpar per-

Table 3-3. Overall Importance Compared to Selected Performance of Major Manufacturers as Evaluated by Dealers

Rank	Survey question number	Variable description	Overall importance—all dealers		Dealer evaluations of manufacturers								
					Mfr. 1		Mfr. 2		Mfr. 3		Mfr. 4		Mfr. 5	
			Mean	Std. dev.	Mean	Std. dev.	Mean	Std. dev.	Mean	Std. dev.	Mean	Std. dev.	Mean	Std. dev.
1	9	Ability of manufacturer to meet promised delivery date (on-time shipments)	6.4	.8	5.9	1.0	4.1	1.6	4.7	1.6	6.6	.6	3.3	1.6
2	39	Accuracy in filling orders (correct product is shipped)	6.4	.8	5.6	1.1	4.7	1.4	5.0	1.3	5.8	1.1	4.4	1.5
3	90	*Competitiveness* of price	6.3	1.0	5.1	1.2	4.9	1.4	4.5	1.5	5.4	1.3	3.6	1.8
4	40	Advance notice on shipping delays	6.1	.9	4.6	1.9	3.0	1.6	3.7	1.7	5.1	1.7	3.1	1.7
5	94	Special pricing discounts available on contract/project quotes	6.1	1.1	5.4	1.3	4.0	1.7	4.1	1.6	6.0	1.2	4.5	1.8
6	3	Overall manufacturing and design *quality* of product relative to the price range involved	6.0	.9	6.0	1.0	5.3	1.3	5.1	1.2	6.5	.8	4.8	1.5
7	16	Updated and current price data, specifications, and promotion materials provided by manufacturer	6.0	.9	5.7	1.3	4.1	1.5	4.8	1.4	6.3	.9	4.3	1.9
8	47	*Timely* response to requests for assistance from manufacturer's sales representative	6.0	.9	5.2	1.7	4.6	1.6	4.4	1.6	5.4	1.6	4.3	1.7

Table 3-3. Overall Importance Compared to Selected Performance of Major Manufacturers as Evaluated by Dealers (*Continued*)

Rank	Survey question number	Variable description	Overall importance—all dealers		Dealer evaluations of manufacturers								
					Mfr. 1		Mfr. 2		Mfr. 3		Mfr. 4		Mfr. 5	
			Mean	Std. dev.	Mean	Std. dev.	Mean	Std. dev.	Mean	Std. dev.	Mean	Std. dev.	Mean	Std. dev.
9	14	Order cycle consistency (small variability in promised versus actual delivery, i.e., vendor consistently meets expected date)	6.0	.9	5.8	1.0	4.1	1.5	4.8	1.4	6.3	.9	4.4	1.7
10	4b	Length of promised order cycle (lead) times (from order submission to delivery) for baseline/in-stock (quick ship) product	6.0	1.0	6.1	1.1	4.5	1.4	4.9	1.5	6.2	1.1	3.7	2.0
11	54	Accuracy of manufacturer in forecasting and committing to estimated shipping dates on contract/project orders	6.0	1.0	5.5	1.2	4.0	1.6	4.3	1.4	6.3	1.1	3.5	1.6
12	49a	Completeness of order (percent of line items eventually shipped complete)—made to order product (contract orders)	6.0	1.0	5.5	1.2	4.3	1.2	4.7	1.3	6.0	1.1	4.0	1.6
43	45	Free inward WATS telephone line provided for entering orders with manufacturer	5.3	1.5	3.6	2.5	3.8	2.0	3.4	2.6	3.5	2.6	3.6	1.8
101	77	Store layout planning assistance from manufacturer	2.9	1.6	4.2	1.7	3.0	1.5	3.4	1.6	4.7	1.6	3.4	1.2

SOURCE: Jay U. Sterling and Douglas M. Lambert, "Customer Service Research: Past, Present and Future," *International Journal of Physical Distribution and Materials Management*, vol. 19, no. 1, 1989, p. 19.

Table 3-4. Actual and Perceived Performance of Manufacturer 1 versus Required Service Levels of Respondents

Part A: Questionnaire				Expected
Question number	Description of product variable	Dealers' evaluation*	Internal audit results	performance (standard)†
9	Percent on-time delivery (contract orders)	5.9	92.6	86.9
39	Accuracy in filling orders (percent)	6.6	95.8	95.0
40	Advance notice preferred prior to arrival of order			
	a. Contract orders	6.1	delays only	8.6 days
	b. Standard, in-stock orders	3.4	not provided	2.8 days
16	Advance notice required on price changes	4.5	3 weeks	6.0 weeks
14	Order cycle consistency (range)			
	a. Contract orders (weeks)	6.1	2.7 weeks	4.6 weeks
	b. Standard, in-stock orders (days)	4.7	10.5 days	8.5 days
4a	Lead time—made to order (contract) product	6.4	6.1 weeks	8.7 weeks
4b	Lead time—in-stock (standard) product	4.9	14 days	11.1 days
49a	Order completeness percentage— contract orders	4.5	97	96.9
49b	Order completeness percentage— standard orders from in-stock product	4.5	80.8	90.0

*Based on a 7-point scale where 1 equals poor performance and 7 equals outstanding performance.
†Desired service level as expressed by survey respondents (average response).

formance. Rather than attempt to improve performance, Manufacturer 1 should try to change customer perceptions by periodically communicating their actual performance to customers and educating them regarding how their system operates or telling them how and what information can be obtained on an as-needed basis.

Identifying Potential Solutions

The external audit enables management to identify problems with the firm's customer service and marketing strategies. Used in combination with the internal audit, it may help management to adjust these strategies and vary them by segment in order to increase profitability. But if management wants to use such information to develop customer service and marketing strategies for optimal profitability, it must use these data to benchmark against its competitors.

The most meaningful competitive benchmarking occurs when customer evaluations of competitors' performance are compared to each other and to customers' evaluations of the importance of vendor attributes.[26] Once management has used this type of analysis to determine opportunities for gaining a competitive advantage, every effort should be made to identify best practice, that is, the most cost-ef-fective use of technology and systems, regardless of the industry in which it has been successfully implemented. Noncompetitors are much more likely to share their knowledge, and it is possible to uncover opportunities for significant competi-tive advantage over industry rivals.

A methodology for competitive benchmarking can be demonstrated from the data contained in Table 3-3. The analysis involves a comparison of the performance of the major vendors in the industry surveyed by this study. The first step is to gen-erate a table with importance evaluations for each of the variables as well as the performance evaluations of the sponsoring firm and its major competitors. The next step is to compare the importance score of each service attribute to customer evaluations of each vendor's (manufacturer's) performance. Table 3-3 discloses that the most important variable (ability to meet promised delivery date) received a score of 6.4 in overall importance. Manufacturer 1's perceived performance of 5.9 is significantly less than the importance score of 6.4 as well as the perceived performance of Manufacturer number 4 (6.6). Therefore, Manufacturer 1 must im-prove its performance both to meet customer expectations and to achieve competi-tive parity.

Variable number 40 (advance notice on shipping delays), which was ranked number 4 in overall importance, presents a different situation. None of the major suppliers was perceived to be meeting customer expectations (6.1). Therefore, if Manufacturer 1 were to improve its performance in this area, it could gain a differ-ential advantage over its competitors. On the other hand, variable number 45 (free inward WATS telephone lines for placing orders with manufacturers) was rated as only 43rd in overall performance. None of the suppliers received a high evaluation for their performance on this service. This indicates that customers did not per-ceive the advantages of this attribute, because such a service was not presently avail-able from any manufacturer.

If a competitor were to change its order entry procedures to allow customers the ability to phone in their orders without cost, then two things might happen: 1) cus-tomers would likely change their opinion of the advantages of this capability and consequently increase their perceptions of the importance of free WATS service, and 2) the vendor that first introduced this service could achieve a definite long-term competitive advantage. In fact, this is precisely what happened. Subsequent to this survey, one of the major suppliers implemented an on-line, interactive order entry system utilizing free inward WATS telephone service. Within three years, this capability had become the norm for all of the major vendors in the industry. There-fore, when looking for ways to improve customer service, it is equally critical to look at both important and relatively unimportant services.

Developing and Controlling
Customer Service Performance

Once management has determined which elements of customer service are most important, and which ones it must either maintain or improve the current perform-ance levels of, it must develop standards of performance. Designated employees should regularly report results to the appropriate levels of management. William

Hutchinson and John Stolle offer the following four steps for measuring and controlling customer service performance:

1. Establish quantitative standards of performance for each service element.
2. Measure actual performance for each service element.
3. Analyze variance between actual services provided and the standard.
4. Take corrective action as needed to bring actual performance into line.[27]

These recommendations are graphically illustrated in Figure 3-13.

Customer cooperation is essential if the company is to obtain information about speed, dependability, and condition of the delivered product. To be effective, customers must be convinced that service measurement/monitoring will help improve future service. Figure 3-14 contains a number of possible measures of service performance. The emphasis any manufacturer places on individual elements must be based on what that manufacturer's customers believe to be important. Such service elements as inventory availability, the ability to meet promised delivery dates, order status information, order tracing, and providing backorder status require good communications between the manufacturer and its customers. Because many companies have not kept pace with technology in order processing, this area offers significant potential for improving customer service. Consider the possibilities for improved communications if customers can either phone their orders to customer service representatives who have CRTs, or input orders on their own terminals. Immediate information on inventory availability can be provided, and product substi-

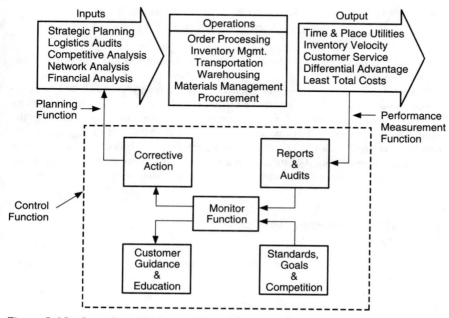

Figure 3-13. Controlling the logistics mission feedback process.

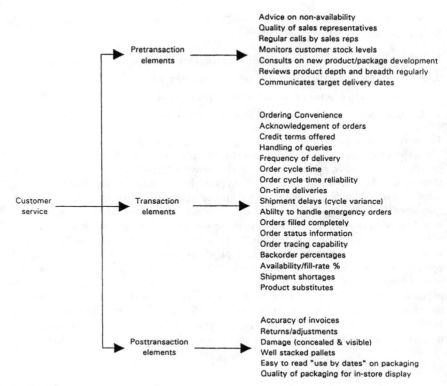

Figure 3-14. Possible measures of customer service performance.

tution can be arranged in the event of a stockout. Customers also can be given target delivery dates.

   Standards for each of the measurements contained in Figure 3-14 should be determined, based on what customers need rather than what management thinks customers need. Designated employees should measure and compare performance to the standard, and report this information to the appropriate levels of management on a regular and timely basis. The firm's order-processing and accounting information systems can provide much of the information needed to develop a customer–product contribution matrix and meaningful customer service management reports.

Improving Customer Service Performance

The levels of customer service a firm achieves can be improved by taking the following actions:

1. Thoroughly researching customers' needs
2. Setting service levels that make realistic tradeoffs between revenues and expenses

3. Making use of the latest technology in order-processing systems
4. Measuring and evaluating the performance of individual logistics activities

An effective customer service strategy *must* be based on an understanding of how customers define *service*. Therefore, customer service audits and surveys of customers are imperative:

> Many customer service surveys show that customers define service differently than suppliers and prefer a lower but more reliable service level than that currently offered. Under these circumstances, there is no reason why a firm can't improve service as the customers perceive it and at the same time cut costs. To improve service as measured by this objective standard is often less costly than to improve service as measured by arbitrary in-house standards.[28]

Once it has determined its customers' view of service, management must select a customer service strategy that advances the firm's objectives for long-range profit and return on investment. As Sabath has said:

> It should be clear that the optimum service level is not always the lowest cost level. The optimum level is one that retains customers at the lowest possible costs and meets the company's growth needs. Defined this way, an optimum service level may be achieved by trading off some [logistics] cost savings for more valuable marketing advantages or manufacturing efficiencies. The point is that with objective, customer-defined service levels and a good handle on costs, everyone knows exactly what is being traded and what is received in return.[29]

The optimum level of customer service is the one that retains the "right" or "desired" customers. Therefore, the development of an effective customer service program requires the establishment of customer service standards that do the following:

1. Reflect the customer's point of view
2. Provide an operational and objective measure of service performance
3. Provide management with cues for corrective action[30]

Summary

This chapter opened with a discussion of how to define customer service. Although the importance of the individual elements of customer service varies from company to company, we discussed the common elements that are of concern to most companies. We also saw the necessity for a customer service strategy that supports and complements marketing and corporate strategies. We saw how management can obtain better knowledge of the costs and revenues associated with different levels of customer service, and how it can implement cost/service tradeoffs.

The customer service audit is a method of determining the existing service levels, determining how performance is measured and reported, and appraising the impact of changes in customer service policy. Both in-depth interviews and mail questionnaires are a means of finding out what management and customers view as important aspects of customer service.

Although customer service may represent the best opportunity for a firm to achieve a sustainable competitive advantage, many firms implement customer service strategies that are simply duplicates of those implemented by their major competitors. The internal and external audit frameworks represented in this chapter can be used by management to collect and analyze customer and competitor information. We also learned some ways to improve customer service performance.

Appendix A. Internal Management Audit: Interview Guides

General/Senior Management

1. Describe the overall competitive environment for each industry served.
2. What is your overall marketing strategy?
3. Who are your major competitors? Describe products/markets for each.
4. How do your major competitors distribute their products?
5. Why would customers buy from your competitors?
6. What's your market share for each market served?
7. Describe the marketing channels in the industries you serve.
8. How are your logistics functions organized? Describe for each function.
9. Are standards established for each logistics function? Describe.
10. Which logistics transactions have automated computer files?
11. What logistics-related performance reports do you current compile?
12. What type of reports would you like to receive?
13. What problems do you perceive regarding marketing/production/logistics?
14. What steps (if any) are being taken to solve these problems?

Marketing/Sales

1. Describe marketing/sales organization (corporate and field).
2. Describe activities of field sales people.
3. Describe corporation's long-range strategic marketing plan.
4. Indicate perceived changes in industry over next three to five years.
5. What is the current and projected five-year marketing environment for each market segment?
6. What are the customer service requirements for each market segment?
7. Major strengths/weaknesses of company in each market segment.
8. Marketing's role in forecasting/production planning and scheduling.
9. Major strengths/weaknesses of competitors in each market segment.
10. Are there any marketing programs you'd like to try or test?

Logistics Financial Control

1. Average turnovers by product category (frequency computed).
2. Basis for computing turns (units or dollars).
3. Average dollar inventory (raw, WIP, FG).
4. What is company's hurdle rate/average RONW/ROI for new investments?
5. How are inbound transportation costs accounted for?
6. How are outbound transportation costs accounted for?
7. How are raw/WIP warehousing costs accounted for?
8. How are finished goods costs accounted for?
9. How are inventory carrying costs accounted for?
10. Does company measure profitability (contribution) of customers/products? If yes, how, and what costs are included?

Customer Service/Order Administration

1. Do you have a written customer service (C/S) policy?
2. Are different levels of C/S provided to different products or customers?
3. Describe C/S organization (corporate and field).
4. Describe what (if any) components of cycle time are measured.
5. What is the order volume processed daily/weekly?
6. Profile typical order (dollars, lines, how transmitted to company).
7. Number of order entry locations, and volume/type of orders for each.
8. Describe in detail order entry and data-processing process.
9. Describe which files (if any) are automated.
10. How are orders transmitted to ship points?
11. Type/extent of automated communications with customers.
12. Describe quantity order fill rate percentages.

Transportation (In and Outbound)

1. Total annual transportation and budget (inbound and outbound).
2. Describe freight terms on inbound receipts.
3. How are outbound freight dollars accounted for?
4. Describe channels (and the percentage of sales) used for each customer segment.
5. Describe carrier, mode, and route selection process.
6. How is carrier performance monitored, and by whom?
7. What's the basis for determining preferred carriers?
8. How do expedited/rush orders impact the transportation process?

9. Who controls selection of carriers/terms of sale for inbound freight?
10. Are inbound LTL purchases consolidated?
11. How are outbound freight rates negotiated?
12. What number of carriers used inbound/outbound?
13. What records (bills, bills of lading) are automated?
14. Do customers specify carriers/mode?

Warehouse Operations

1. Describe warehouse network (factories and field).
2. Describe ownership of each (co-owned/public).
3. Criteria used to select warehouses and sites.
4. Describe warehouse administration policies/procedures (formalized?).
5. How/what costs are included in warehousing expense?
6. How is warehouse performance measured?
7. What system is used to manage warehouse operations (is it manual/auto)?
8. What are yearly warehouse costs (in-plant/field)?
9. How are public warehouses administered and paid?
10. Percentage of receipts/shipments that are LTL.
11. Is damage a problem? Describe.
12. How is inventory controlled, and what documentation is used for picking orders?

Production/Inventory Management

1. Number of vendors who used repurchased raw/WIP materials.
2. Frequency and lead times for major purchase commodities.
3. Is an MRP system used? If yes, describe.
4. What type of specs are included in POs regarding transportation?
5. Describe production scheduling process.
6. Describe responsibilities of corporation functions in the planning process.
7. Any bottlenecks in forecasting/planning/scheduling process?
8. Any downtime problems? What percentage, by type?
9. What is length/volume of typical production runs?
10. Are target level inventories/fill rates computed? How?
11. What are normal manufacturing lead times, by product category?
12. What's the last date a schedule can be changed before production?
13. What's the frequency of schedule changes inside stated lead times?
14. Who's responsible for forecasting—at what product level?

15. How are inventory levels at DCs set? How frequently?
16. How are inventories at DCs replenished? How frequently?
17. What's the average replenishment cycle for DCs?
18. What type/kind of formal reports are generated for inventory management?

Purchasing

1. How many vendors are used?
2. What criteria are used to select and evaluate vendors?
3. What type of lead times are required/received?
4. How have vendors improved their service over the past 12 to 18 months?
5. What service would you like vendors to provide in future?
6. Are you contemplating changes in ordering procedures?
7. In techniques used to transmit POs to vendors?
8. What percentage are delivered on time?
9. What do you do if vendor can't meet your date wanted?
10. What percentage of POs are delivered on time?
11. What percentage of POs are emergency/rush orders?
12. What percentage of POs are LTL quantities?
13. Do you receive periodic reports from major vendors?
14. What modes are used to receive purchased material?
15. Do you use scheduled delivery programs or vendors?
16. How do you determine safety stocks to cover raw materials/WIP?
17. What are your inventory turns by commodity?
18. Do you quantify the cost of forward buys?

Appendix B. External Audit: Sample Questions

1. How often do you order products from your major vendors?
2. What are the typical sizes of these orders?
3. What are the typical lead times encountered when replenishing inventories from your major vendors?
4. What percentage of the product ordered is normally delivered by your requested delivery date?
5. What lead time would you prefer?
6. What percentage of your orders eventually are delivered, and how long does it typically take to receive all of your order?
7. What is the current performance by each of your major vendors with respect to order cycle (lead) time and fill rate?

8. If a supplier is unable to commit to an order by your requested "date wanted," what percentage of the time do you
   a. Cancel your order?
   b. Backorder with supplier?
   c. Request substitution?
   d. Backorder and also submit to a second source?
9. What percentage of the time do you use the following techniques to transmit orders to your major suppliers?
   a. On-line terminal
   b. Inward WATS telephone service
   c. Telephone paid by you
   d. Mail
   e. Fax
   f. Hand-deliver to salesperson
10. Do any of your suppliers use a "scheduled delivery" program? Which one(s)?
11. What percentage of your orders would you classify as "emergency" (ship as soon as possible)?
12. Do any of your major suppliers furnish you with any of the following written information/reports on a regular basis?
    a. Confirmation notices on orders submitted
    b. Open order status reports
    c. Product availability/inventory status data
    d. Advance notice of shipping information
13. Do any of your major suppliers offer incentives, such as prepaid freight, quantity discounts, claims handling for damage, or extended payment terms for ordering in large quantities?
14. What type of terms do your major suppliers offer? What terms do you prefer?
15. How many supplier sources do you normally use when purchasing your major components/products?
16. What criteria do you use to select suppliers?
17. How has the number of vendors with whom you regularly do business changed in the past three years?
18. How do you anticipate this will change in the future?
19. What are the distinguishing features or services of those suppliers who consistently provide you with desired/satisfactory customer service as compared to those who do not?
20. How have your major suppliers improved their customer service, deliveries, and information, with respect to your orders, in the past 12 to 18 months?
21. What services would you like suppliers to provide with respect to logistics/customer service that are not presently available to you?
22. What are the normal/published lead times that you provide to your customers?
23. What methods do your customers use to submit their orders to you?
24. Have you experienced, or are you experiencing, any changes in the ordering characteristics of your customers?
25. Do you have a computerized inventory record keeping/customer order status system that identifies by individual items balance on hand, on order, and on backorder?
26. What are your annual inventory turnovers by SKU, product, and product line?

27. Do you use, or are you contemplating using, a "just-in-time/zero inventory" concept in managing your inventories, or when ordering from your major vendors?
28. Do you perform tradeoff analysis to weigh the economics of quantity discounts or forward buys against the added inventory carrying costs?
29. Do you attempt to carry different levels of safety stock for fast movers as compared to low-volume items?
30. What has been your average annual growth rate during the past five years? What do you anticipate this percentage will be in the next five years?
31. Have you made any significant changes in the way you order materials from your major vendors during the past 12 to 18 months?

Appendix C. Sample Transportation Service Quality Questionnaire

See questionnaire on pp. 3.40–3.45.

APPENDIX C
Sample Transportation Service Quality Questionnnaire

SURVEY OF HOW SHIPPERS SELECT AND EVALUATE
GENERAL COMMODITIES LTL MOTOR CARRIERS

DEPARTMENT OF MANAGEMENT, MARKETING AND LOGISTICS, UNIVERSITY OF NORTH FLORIDA, JACKSONVILLE

PART A: FACTORS CONSIDERED WHEN SELECTING AND EVALUATING LTL MOTOR CARRIERS

INSTRUCTIONS: Listed on the following pages are various factors often provided by LTL motor carriers to their customers. This section involves two tasks. Each task will be explained separately. Do not evaluate small package services such as UPS or RPS.

The first task involves your evaluation of the various factors that your firm might consider when selecting a new LTL motor carrier, or when you evaluate the performance of one of your current carriers. Please circle, on a scale of 1 to 7, the number which best expresses the importance to your firm of each of these factors. If a factor is not used by your firm or has no importance in your evaluation of carriers, please circle number 1 (Not Important). If a factor is not currently provided by any of your carriers, please evaluate its importance to you if it was available. A rating of 7 (Very Important) should be reserved for those factors that would cause you to reevaluate the amount of business done with a carrier or cause you to drop a carrier in the event of inadequate performance.

The second task is to evaluate the current performance of three LTL motor carriers that you use. Please list below in the spaces labeled "Carrier A", "Carrier B" and "Carrier C" three LTL motor carriers used most frequently by your firm (if you use fewer than three LTL carriers, please evaluate those that you use). Next, using the scale labeled PERCEIVED PERFORMANCE, please insert the number between 1 and 7 which best expresses your perception of a carrier's current performance. If you perceive that a carrier's performance is poor, insert a 1. Reserve a rating of 7 for excellent performance. If a service is not available from a carrier, please write NA, "NOT AVAILABLE," in the appropriate space

YOUR LTL CARRIERS:

CARRIER A (the largest amount of your freight is handled by this carrier)   = _____

CARRIER B (the second largest amount of your freight is handled by this carrier) = _____

CARRIER C (the third largest amount of your freight is handled by this carrier) = _____

Example:

FACTORS CONSIDERED	Not Important 1	2	3	4	5	Very Important 6 7	PERCEIVED PERFORMANCE OF CARRIERS (Scale of 1 to 7) A B C
• Bar coding of shipments	1	2	③	4	5	6 7	NA 2 NA
• Reliability of transit times	1	2	3	4	5	⑥ 7	5 7 6

FACTORS CONSIDERED	Not Important 1	2	3	4	5	Very Important 6 7	PERCEIVED PERFORMANCE OF CARRIERS (Scale of 1 to 7) A B C
1. Carrier's loss/damage history	1	2	3	4	5	6 7	__ __ __
2. Adequate advance notice of rate changes	1	2	3	4	5	6 7	__ __ __
3. Provides same day delivery	1	2	3	4	5	6 7	__ __ __
4. On-time deliveries	1	2	3	4	5	6 7	__ __ __
5. Prompt action on complaints related to carrier's service	1	2	3	4	5	6 7	__ __ __
6. Quality of dispatch personnel							
- knowledge of carrier's capabilities	1	2	3	4	5	6 7	__ __ __
- prompt notification of scheduling changes	1	2	3	4	5	6 7	__ __ __
- honesty	1	2	3	4	5	6 7	__ __ __
- knowledge of my business	1	2	3	4	5	6 7	__ __ __
- concern/empathy	1	2	3	4	5	6 7	__ __ __
- friendliness	1	2	3	4	5	6 7	__ __ __
7. Carrier sales rep provides assistance/counseling on:							
- transportation solutions	1	2	3	4	5	6 7	__ __ __
- inventory management	1	2	3	4	5	6 7	__ __ __
- customer reports (i.e. transit time analysis)	1	2	3	4	5	6 7	__ __ __
- inbound just-in-time systems	1	2	3	4	5	6 7	__ __ __
- rates and tariffs	1	2	3	4	5	6 7	__ __ __
- logistics training programs	1	2	3	4	5	6 7	__ __ __
- customer service problems	1	2	3	4	5	6 7	__ __ __
- EDI information systems and usage	1	2	3	4	5	6 7	__ __ __
- packaging to reduce damage	1	2	3	4	5	6 7	__ __ __
8. Competitive rates	1	2	3	4	5	6 7	__ __ __
9. Availability of rates on a diskette	1	2	3	4	5	6 7	__ __ __

FACTORS CONSIDERED	Not Important 1	2	3	4	5	6	Very Important 7	A	B	C
10. Single point of contact with carrier to resolve operations problems	1	2	3	4	5	6	7	__	__	__
11. Rate structure simple and easy to understand	1	2	3	4	5	6	7	__	__	__
12. Electronic (on-line terminal) interface for:										
- billing	1	2	3	4	5	6	7	__	__	__
- pickup	1	2	3	4	5	6	7	__	__	__
- tracing	1	2	3	4	5	6	7	__	__	__
13. Frequency of sales calls you personally receive from carrier's sales representative	1	2	3	4	5	6	7	__	__	__
14. Lowest rates	1	2	3	4	5	6	7	__	__	__
15. Cash discounts for early payment or prepayment	1	2	3	4	5	6	7	__	__	__
16. Carrier has adequate interline arrangements	1	2	3	4	5	6	7	__	__	__
17. Literature/information available from carrier:										
- routing guide	1	2	3	4	5	6	7	__	__	__
- pricing	1	2	3	4	5	6	7	__	__	__
18. Availability of "released value" rates	1	2	3	4	5	6	7	__	__	__
19. Assistance from carrier in handling loss and damage claims	1	2	3	4	5	6	7	__	__	__
20. Pro number given at time of pickup	1	2	3	4	5	6	7	__	__	__
21. Quality of billing staff:										
- knowledge of carrier's billing procedures	1	2	3	4	5	6	7	__	__	__
- prompt follow-up	1	2	3	4	5	6	7	__	__	__
- honesty	1	2	3	4	5	6	7	__	__	__
- knowledge of my business	1	2	3	4	5	6	7	__	__	__
- concern/empathy	1	2	3	4	5	6	7	__	__	__
22. Ability to provide direct delivery without interlining	1	2	3	4	5	6	7	__	__	__
23. Information provided when pickup call placed:										
- projected pickup time	1	2	3	4	5	6	7	__	__	__
- projected delivery time	1	2	3	4	5	6	7	__	__	__
- rate information	1	2	3	4	5	6	7	__	__	__
24. On-time pickups	1	2	3	4	5	6	7	__	__	__
25. Bar coding to facilitate tracing	1	2	3	4	5	6	7	__	__	__
26. Carrier sponsored entertainment	1	2	3	4	5	6	7	__	__	__
27. Carrier's general attitude toward problems/complaints	1	2	3	4	5	6	7	__	__	__
28. Carrier's programs for claim prevention (i.e. truck alarms, surveillance equipment, statistical process control (SPC))	1	2	3	4	5	6	7	__	__	__
29. Prompt response to claims	1	2	3	4	5	6	7	__	__	__
30. Prompt and accurate response to billing inquiries	1	2	3	4	5	6	7	__	__	__
31. Promotional gifts (coffee mugs, golf balls, calendars, etc)	1	2	3	4	5	6	7	__	__	__
32. Sales rep available if customer service response is inadequate	1	2	3	4	5	6	7	__	__	__
33. Willingness to renegotiate rates	1	2	3	4	5	6	7	__	__	__
34. Length of promised transit times (from pickup to delivery)	1	2	3	4	5	6	7	__	__	__
35. If possible, advance notice of transit delays (e.g. weather, equipment breakdown, etc.)	1	2	3	4	5	6	7	__	__	__
36. Freight bill references your bill-of-lading or control number	1	2	3	4	5	6	7	__	__	__
37. Regular/scheduled check-in by driver for pickup	1	2	3	4	5	6	7	__	__	__
38. Single point of contact with carrier to resolve billing problems	1	2	3	4	5	6	7	__	__	__

Column group headers: **IMPORTANCE** (columns 1–7), **PERCEIVED PERFORMANCE OF CARRIERS (Scale of 1 to 7)** (columns A, B, C).

FACTORS CONSIDERED	CARRIER A = ___ CARRIER B = ___ CARRIER C = ___							PERCEIVED PERFORMANCE OF CARRIERS (Scale of 1 to 7)		
	Not Important 1	2	3	4	5	6	Very Important 7	A	B	C
39. Shipment security	1	2	3	4	5	6	7	__	__	__
40. Frequency of service to key points	1	2	3	4	5	6	7	__	__	__
41. Complete/understandable/legible freight bill	1	2	3	4	5	6	7	__	__	__
42. Quality of drivers:										
- knowledge of carrier's capabilities	1	2	3	4	5	6	7	__	__	__
- ability to handle problems	1	2	3	4	5	6	7	__	__	__
- honesty	1	2	3	4	5	6	7	__	__	__
- responsiveness to inquiries	1	2	3	4	5	6	7	__	__	__
- helpfulness	1	2	3	4	5	6	7	__	__	__
- friendliness/courtesy	1	2	3	4	5	6	7	__	__	__
- willingness to make inside deliveries	1	2	3	4	5	6	7	__	__	__
- appearance	1	2	3	4	5	6	7	__	__	__
- uniforms	1	2	3	4	5	6	7	__	__	__
43. Prompt availability of status information on:										
- shipment tracing	1	2	3	4	5	6	7	__	__	__
- delivery	1	2	3	4	5	6	7	__	__	__
- COD shipments	1	2	3	4	5	6	7	__	__	__
44. Liftgate availability for you and your customer	1	2	3	4	5	6	7	__	__	__
45. Provides new rate and discount sheets in a timely fashion	1	2	3	4	5	6	7	__	__	__
46. Carrier's ability to make pickups: before noon	1	2	3	4	5	6	7	__	__	__
: after 5:00 p.m.	1	2	3	4	5	6	7	__	__	__
47. Quantity discount structure based on:										
- size of shipment	1	2	3	4	5	6	7	__	__	__
- annual volume of shipments	1	2	3	4	5	6	7	__	__	__
48. Quality of sales force:										
- knowledge of carrier's capabilities	1	2	3	4	5	6	7	__	__	__
- prompt follow-up	1	2	3	4	5	6	7	__	__	__
- honesty	1	2	3	4	5	6	7	__	__	__
- concern/empathy	1	2	3	4	5	6	7	__	__	__
- friendliness	1	2	3	4	5	6	7	__	__	__
- knowledge of my business	1	2	3	4	5	6	7	__	__	__
- understanding of my customer's business	1	2	3	4	5	6	7	__	__	__
49. Timely response to requests for assistance from carrier's sales representative	1	2	3	4	5	6	7	__	__	__
50. Adequate geographical coverage:										
- major origins/destinations of your traffic	1	2	3	4	5	6	7	__	__	__
- remote regions	1	2	3	4	5	6	7	__	__	__
51. Prompt and comprehensive response to competitive bid quotations (i.e., contract discounts)	1	2	3	4	5	6	7	__	__	__
52. Accuracy of response to tracing inquiry (ETA)	1	2	3	4	5	6	7	__	__	__
53. Cleanliness of carrier's equipment	1	2	3	4	5	6	7	__	__	__
54. Carrier's reputation	1	2	3	4	5	6	7	__	__	__
55. Carrier's financial condition	1	2	3	4	5	6	7	__	__	__
56. Carriers ability to make deliveries: before noon	1	2	3	4	5	6	7	__	__	__
: after 5:00 pm	1	2	3	4	5	6	7	__	__	__
57. Ability of carrier to customize its services to meet specific and/or unique needs										
- handle emergency shipments	1	2	3	4	5	6	7	__	__	__
- handle hazardous materials	1	2	3	4	5	6	7	__	__	__
- adhere to special shipping instructions	1	2	3	4	5	6	7	__	__	__
- handle COD shipments	1	2	3	4	5	6	7	__	__	__
- rerouting/rescheduling	1	2	3	4	5	6	7	__	__	__
- inside deliveries	1	2	3	4	5	6	7	__	__	__
58. Carrier has satisfactory insurance coverage	1	2	3	4	5	6	7	__	__	__
59. Friendships with carrier personnel	1	2	3	4	5	6	7	__	__	__

IMPORTANCE

FACTORS CONSIDERED	IMPORTANCE							PERCEIVED PERFORMANCE OF CARRIERS (Scale of 1 to 7)		
	Not Important 1	2	3	4	5	6	Very Important 7	A	B	C
60. Ability of carrier to deliver damage-free goods	1	2	3	4	5	6	7	__	__	__
61. Accurate billing	1	2	3	4	5	6	7	__	__	__
62. Low frequency of split shipments	1	2	3	4	5	6	7	__	__	__
63. Proof-of-delivery available with freight bill	1	2	3	4	5	6	7	__	__	__
64. Prompt advance notice of pickup delays	1	2	3	4	5	6	7	__	__	__
65. Carrier's policy on COD/refused/returned/unclaimed freight	1	2	3	4	5	6	7	__	__	__
66. Consistent (reliable) transit times	1	2	3	4	5	6	7	__	__	__
67. Ability of carrier to respond to all customer inquiries with:										
- a single point of contact	1	2	3	4	5	6	7	__	__	__
- immediate response	1	2	3	4	5	6	7	__	__	__
68. Ability to make and meet appointments for delivery	1	2	3	4	5	6	7	__	__	__
69. Accurate rating	1	2	3	4	5	6	7	__	__	__
70. Ability to handle call before deliveries	1	2	3	4	5	6	7	__	__	__
71. Safety rating	1	2	3	4	5	6	7	__	__	__
72. Sales rep has authority to negotiate rates	1	2	3	4	5	6	7	__	__	__
73. Carrier's ability to provide formal reports on:										
- billing accuracy	1	2	3	4	5	6	7	__	__	__
- claims experience	1	2	3	4	5	6	7	__	__	__
- on-time deliveries	1	2	3	4	5	6	7	__	__	__
- on-time pickups	1	2	3	4	5	6	7	__	__	__
- transit times	1	2	3	4	5	6	7	__	__	__

PART B: MEASUREMENT OF OVERALL PERFORMANCE

1. Please indicate the percent that each carrier currently represents of your annual requirements as well as the percent that you would prefer to give each carrier under ideal conditions in the future. (Your totals should add to 100%)

	Current %	Ideal (preferred) %
CARRIER A (the largest amount of your freight is handled by this carrier)	___ %	___ %
CARRIER B (the second largest amount of your freight is handled by this carrier)	___ %	___ %
CARRIER C (the third largest amount of your freight is handled by this carrier)	___ %	___ %
Other Carriers	___ %	___ %
	100 %	100 %

2. Please mark a point anywhere on the lines below that best expresses your level of satisfaction with the above carriers. If you are extremely dissatisfied with a carrier's performance, a mark should be placed very near the left end of the line (labeled Poor). If you are exceptionally pleased with the carrier's performance, a mark should be placed very near the right end of the line (labeled Excellent). A midpoint has been placed on the line to correspond with a "Satisfactory" performance level.

OVERALL CARRIER PERFORMANCE

	Poor	Satisfactory	Excellent
CARRIER A			
CARRIER B			
CARRIER C			

3. Would you recommend these carriers to another shipper?

CARRIER A   CARRIER B   CARRIER C
___ Yes   ___ Yes   ___ Yes
___ No   ___ No   ___ No

4. Have you ever reported to these carriers a problem with the service you received?

CARRIER A   CARRIER B   CARRIER C
___ Yes   ___ Yes   ___ Yes
___ No   ___ No   ___ No

5. What percentage of on-time performance do you currently receive from your major LTL carriers during a typical month?

CARRIER A: pickups ___% deliveries ___%
CARRIER B: pickups ___% deliveries ___%
CARRIER C: pickups ___% deliveries ___%

6. For the three carriers that you have evaluated, please give the lowest price carrier a score of 0%. For the others, indicate the percentage premium that you pay for their service. If two or more carriers have the same rates, please give them the same score.

CARRIER A: ___ %
CARRIER B: ___ %
CARRIER C: ___ %

PART C: EXPECTED PERFORMANCE LEVELS OF LTL MOTOR CARRIERS

Please provide the following information with respect to the levels of customer service that you need from your LTL carriers.

1. How many contacts does your department receive from your major LTL carrier's sales rep during a typical month?
   _____ face to face calls per month   _____ telephone calls per month

2. How many contacts would your department prefer to receive from your major LTL carrier's sales rep during a typical month?
   _____ face to face calls per month   _____ telephone calls per month

3. What is the minimum number of contacts that your department would accept from your major LTL carrier's sales rep during a typical month?
   _____ face to face calls per month   _____ telephone calls per month

4. What response time do you respect from a carrier's sales representative in:
   a. Emergency situations _____ minutes   b. Non-emergency situations _____ hours

5. How much advance notice do you need from your carriers on price changes? _____ days

6. On the average, how soon do you expect a carrier to pick up your shipment after they have been notified? _____ hours

7. What is the maximum number of hours beyond the promised delivery date that you consider to be an acceptable delay? _____ hours

8. What terms of payment are offered by your major LTL carriers?
   _____ % cash discount for early payment
   _____ % discount

9. What percentage of shipments is delivered by the carrier's promised delivery date? _____ %

10. What percentage of your products arrive damage free? _____ %

11. What percentage of damage free service can be reasonably expected? _____ %

12. Do you evaluate carriers using a: (Please check one)
    a. Formal process/system _____   b. Informal process/system _____

13. How frequently do you evaluate carrier performance (please check one):
    constantly _____ weekly _____ monthly _____ quarterly _____ annually _____ never _____

14. On-time delivery to your firm means plus-or-minus (please indicate the specific number of minutes, hours or days):
    _____ minutes   _____ hours   _____ days

15. What is the percentage of on-time performance that you want from your major LTL carrier during a typical month?
    pickups _____%   deliveries _____%

16. What is the minimum percentage of on-time performance that you would accept from your major LTL carrier during a typical month?
    pickups _____%   deliveries _____%

17. What percentage increase in rates would you be willing to pay if a carrier was able to meet your service expectations? _____ %

	Strongly Disagree						Strongly Agree
	1	2	3	4	5	6	7
18. In the next five years, bar coding is going to become much more important in my selection of a LTL carrier	1	2	3	4	5	6	7
19. I require written service standards from my carrier(s)	1	2	3	4	5	6	7
20. Within the next 3 years I will not give business to a carrier that does not use Statistical Process Control (SPC) and provide me with performance reports	1	2	3	4	5	6	7

PART D: DEMOGRAPHIC DATA

This information is required in order to identify major market segments and to provide more meaningful analyses of the previous sections. Please use approximate figures in the event that exact data are not readily available.

1. What is your firm's approximate annual gross sales volume? $_____

2. How long has your firm (division) been in business? (If your answer is 4 years or less, please omit answering question 3) _____ years

3. What was the average rate of growth in gross sales for the company over the last five years? _____ %

4. What are your approximate annual freight bills: Corporate? $_____   At this location? $_____

5. How many manufacturing locations does your firm operate? _____

6. For what percentage of inbound shipments is the carrier specified by suppliers? _____ %

7. For what percentage of outbound shipments is the carrier specified by customers? _____ %

8. Please indicate the percentage of your organization's product or raw material moved via:

	Inbound % of Tonnage		Outbound % of Tonnage	
	Today	1995	Today	1995
LTL Motor Carrier	___	___	___	___

9. How many total LTL shipments do you have in a typical month?
   _____ inbound shipments   _____ outbound shipments

10. What percentage of your LTL shipments are "emergency" orders that require expedited service?
    inbound _____% outbound _____%

11. What is the weight of your typical LTL shipment? _____ lbs.

12. What is the average value of your typical LTL shipment? $_____

13. Please indicate your overall evaluation of each of the following carriers.

CARRIERS:	Insufficient Information To Evaluate	Very Unfavorable 1	2	3	4	5	6	Very Favorable 7
AAA Cooper	___	1	2	3	4	5	6	7
Alterman	___	1	2	3	4	5	6	7
Benton Bros.	___	1	2	3	4	5	6	7
Carolina	___	1	2	3	4	5	6	7
Consolidated	___	1	2	3	4	5	6	7
Estes	___	1	2	3	4	5	6	7
Gator	___	1	2	3	4	5	6	7
Old Dominion	___	1	2	3	4	5	6	7
Overnite	___	1	2	3	4	5	6	7
Roadway	___	1	2	3	4	5	6	7
Smalley	___	1	2	3	4	5	6	7
Southeastern	___	1	2	3	4	5	6	7
Southern Freight	___	1	2	3	4	5	6	7
Super Transport	___	1	2	3	4	5	6	7
Transus	___	1	2	3	4	5	6	7
Watkins	___	1	2	3	4	5	6	7
Yellow	___	1	2	3	4	5	6	7
Other (please specify) _____	___	1	2	3	4	5	6	7

14. What industries do you serve? (Please indicate the percentage of your business represented by each of the following)

Automotive	_____%	Medical equipment	_____%	
Chemicals/Plastics	_____%	Military	_____%	
Computer	_____%	Paper Products	_____%	
Construction	_____%	Petroleum	_____%	
Consumer products	_____%	Pharmaceutical	_____%	
Educational/Universities	_____%	Retail	_____%	
Food products	_____%	Telecommunications	_____%	
Industrial equipment	_____%		_____%	
Instrumentation	_____%		100 %	

15. What is your position or title? _____

16. Please indicate your responsibilities (check all those that apply).
   _____ Accounts receivable   _____ International traffic   _____ Purchasing
   _____ Customer service   _____ Inventory control   _____ Shipping—Receiving
   _____ Distribution   _____ Materials management   _____ Traffic
   _____ Inbound carrier selection _____ Outbound carrier selection   _____ Warehousing

17. What are the first three numbers of your zip code? _____

Thank you for your participation and cooperation in completing this survey. Your time and effort are sincerely appreciated. Please return the questionnaire in the envelope provided or mail to:

DOUGLAS M. LAMBERT, Ph.D. and JAMES R. STOCK, Ph.D.
Department of Management, Marketing and Logistics • College of Business Administration,
University of North Florida • 4567 St. Johns Bluff Road, South, Jacksonville, Florida 32216-6699

References

1. The relationship between customer service and market share has been documented in Jay U. Sterling, "Integrating Customer Service and Marketing Strategies in a Channel of Distribution: An Empirical Study," unpublished Ph.D. dissertation, Michigan State University, 1985.

2. Francis G. Tucker, "Customer Service in a Channel of Distribution: The Case of the Manufacturer–Wholesaler–Chain Drug Retailer Channel in the Prescription Drug Industry," unpublished Ph.D. dissertation, The Ohio State University, 1980.

3. Edward T. Fogarty, "Colgate, U.S.," *Business Week*, November 11, 1991.

4. Bernard J. LaLonde, Martha C. Cooper, and Thomas G. Noordewier, *Customer Service: A Management Perspective*, Council of Logistics Management, Chicago, 1988, p. 5.

5. Jay U. Sterling and Douglas M. Lambert, "Establishing Customer Service Strategies Within the Marketing Mix," *Journal of Business Logistics*, vol. 8, no. 1, 1987, pp. 1–30.

6. Tom Peters, "Are You Ready for Business in the 1990s?", *Marriott's Portfolio*, July/August 1989, p. 12.

7. *USA Today*, June 21, 1990.

8. Bernard J. LaLonde and Paul H. Zinszer, *Customer Service: Meaning and Measurement*, National Council of Physical Distribution Management, 1976, pp. 272–82.

9. Ibid., p. 278.

10. Harvey M. Shycon and Christopher R. Sprague, "Put a Price Tag on Your Customer Service Levels," *Harvard Business Review*, vol. 53, no. 4 (July–August 1975), pp. 71–78.

11. "Consumers may be quite willing to switch stores for a shampoo with special properties. For example, it may be the only shampoo that will solve a person's dandruff problem or prevent excess hair loss."

12. "In fact, many doctors further reduce the likelihood of brand switching by telling the mother not to switch the brand of formula."

13. A study of 7189 shoppers found that those experiencing stockouts left the store with a lower image of the store and less satisfaction and purchase intentions. See Paul H. Zinszer and Jack A. Lesser, "An Empirical Evaluation of the Role of Stockout on Shopper Patronage Process," *1980 Educators' Conference Proceedings*, American Marketing Association, Chicago, 1980, pp. 221–24.

14. Stock keeping units are individual units of product that differ from others in shape, size, color, or some other characteristic.

15. For a review of the literature on consumer response to stockouts as well as a proposed research methodology, see W. E. Miklas, "Measuring Customer Response to Stockouts," *International Journal of Physical Distribution and Materials Management*, vol. 9, no. 5, 1979, pp. 213–42.

16. For an example of how 1182 consumers responded when faced with stockouts of products they had intended to buy, see Larry W. Emmelhainz, James R. Stock, and Margaret A. Emmelhainz, "Retail Stockouts: Now What?" *Annual Conference Proceedings*, Council of Logistics Management, Oak Brook, IL, 1989, pp. 71–79.

17. ABC analysis for inventory planning is discussed in Chapter 5 of Douglas M. Lambert and James R. Stock, *Strategic Logistics Management*, 3d ed., Richard D. Irwin, Inc., Homewood, IL, 1993.

18. A method for obtaining profitability on a segmental basis is discussed in Chapter 3 of Douglas M. Lambert and James R. Stock, *Strategic Logistics Management*, 3d ed., Richard D. Irwin, Inc., Homewood, IL, 1993.

19. This section is adapted from Jay U. Sterling and Douglas M. Lambert, "A Methodology for Assessing Logistics Operating Systems," *International Journal of Physical Distribution and Materials Management*, vol. 15, no. 6, 1985, pp. 1–44.

20. Gilbert A. Churchill, Jr., and Carol Suprenaut, "An Investigation into the Determinants of Customer Satisfaction," *Journal of Marketing Research*, vol. 19 (November 1982), pp. 491–504.

21. Richard Oliver, "Measurement and Evaluation of Satisfaction Process in Retail Settings," *Journal of Retailing*, vol. 57, no. 3, 1981, pp. 25–48.

22. A. Parasuraman, Valarie A. Zeithaml, and Leonard L. Berry, "A Conceptual Model of Service Quality and Its Implications for Future Research," *Journal of Marketing*, vol. 49 (Fall 1985), pp. 41–50.

23. A. Parasuraman, Valarie A. Ziethaml, and Leonard L. Berry, "SERVQUAL: A Multiple-Item Scale for Measuring Consumer Perceptions of Service Quality," *Journal of Retailing*, vol. 64, no. 1, 1988, pp. 12–40.

24. Douglas M. Lambert, James R. Stock, and Jay U. Sterling, "A Gap Analysis of Buyer and Seller Perceptions of the Importance of Marketing Mix Attributes," in *1990 AMA Educators' Proceedings*, American Marketing Association, Chicago, p. 208.

25. Although a considerable body of research in service quality in service industries uses expectations scales with "strongly agree" and "strongly disagree" as the anchor points, research has shown that results obtained are the same as those obtained using importance scales. See Douglas M. Lambert and M. Christine Lewis, "A Comparison of Attribute Importance and Expectation Scales for Measuring Service Quality," in *Enhancing Knowledge Development in Marketing*, William Bearden et al., eds., American Marketing Association, Chicago, 1990, p. 291.

26. The material in this section is taken from Douglas M. Lambert and Arun Sharma, "A Customer-Based Competitive Analysis for Logistics Decisions," *International Journal of Physical Distribution and Logistics Management*, vol. 20, no. 1, 1990, pp. 17–24.

27. William H. Hutchinson, Jr., and John F. Stolle, "How to Manage Customer Service," *Harvard Business Review*, vol. 46, no. 6 (November–December 1968), pp. 85–96.

28. Robert E. Sabath, "How Much Service Do Customers Really Want?" *Business Horizons*, April 1978, p. 26.

29. Ibid.

30. LaLonde and Zinszer, op. cit., p. 180.

Further Reading

Christopher Martin, "Creating Effective Policies for Customer Service," *International Journal of Physical Distribution and Materials Management*, vol. 13, no. 2 (1983), pp. 3–24.

Ellram, Lisa M. and Martha C. Cooper, "Supply Chain Management, Partnerships, and the Shipper–Third Party Relationship," *The International Journal of Logistics Management*, vol. 1 no. 2(1990), pp. 1–10.

Gilmour, Peter, "Customer Service: Differentiating by Market Segment," *International Journal of Physical Distribution and Materials Management*, vol. 12, no. 3 (1982), pp. 37–44.

Kyj, Myroslaw J., "Customer Service as a Competitive Tool," *Industrial Marketing Management*, no. 16 (1987), pp. 225–30.

LaLonde, Bernard J., Martha C. Cooper, and Thomas G. Noordewier, *Customer Service: A Management Perspective*, Council of Logistics Management, Chicago, 1988.

LaLonde, Bernard J. and Paul H. Zinszer, *Customer Service: Meaning and Measurement,* National Council of Logistics Management, Chicago, 1976.

Levy, Michael, "Toward an Optimal Customer Service Package," *Journal of Business Logistics,* vol. 2, no. 2(1981), pp. 87–109.

———, "Customer Service: A Managerial Approach to Controlling Marketing Channel Conflict," *International Journal of Physical Distribution and Materials Management,* vol. 11, no. 1(1990), pp. 44–50.

Mathe, Herve and Roy D. Shapiro, "Managing the Service Mix: After Sale Service for Competitive Advantage," *The International Journal of Logistics Management,* vol. 1, no. 1 (1990), pp. 44–50.

Ozment, John and Douglas N. Chard, "Effects of Customer Service on Sales: An Analysis of Historical Data," *International Journal of Physical Distribution and Materials Management,* vol. 16, no. 3(1986), pp. 14–28.

Perreault, William D. and Frederick A. Russ, "Physical Distribution Service: A Neglected Aspect of Marketing Management," *MSU Business Topics,* vol. 22, no. 3, (Summer 1974), pp. 37–45.

———, "Physical Distribution Service in Industrial Purchase Decisions," *Journal of Marketing,* vol. 40, no. 2 (April 1976), pp. 3–10.

Sterling, Jay U. and Douglas M. Lambert, "Customer Service Research: Past, Present and Future," *International Journal of Physical Distribution and Materials Management,* vol. 19, no. 2(1989), pp. 3–23.

———, "Establishing Customer Service Strategies Within the Marketing Mix," *Journal of Business Logistics,* vol. 8, no. 1 (1987), pp. 1–30.

Tucker, Frances Gaither, "Creative Customer Service Management," *International Journal of Physical Distribution and Materials Management,* vol. 13, no. 3(1983), pp. 34–50.

Uhr, Ernest B., Ernest C. Houck, and John C. Rogers, "Physical Distribution Service," *Journal of Business Logistics,* vol. 2, no. 2(1981), pp. 158–69.

Voorhees, Roy Dale and John I. Coppett, "Marketing-Logistics Opportunities for the 1990s," *Journal of Business Strategy,* vol. 7, no. 2(Fall 1986), pp. 33–38.

4
Distribution Network Systems: Planning, Design, and Site Selection

Dale A. Harmelink

Engineering Manager,
Tompkins Associates, Inc.

Many terms describe various stages of the process of transferring product from the place of raw material to the customer. Terms such as *business logistics, logistics, materials management, distribution,* and *physical distribution* are so frequently used interchangeably that it can be confusing. The terminology can be summed up as follows.

Business logistics and *logistics* mean the same thing. In recent years the word *business* has been dropped. The term *logistics* describes the entire process of procuring goods from the supply markets, converting them by production, and distributing them to demand markets. *Materials management* describes the movement of materials and components into the firm, basically from supply markets through production. *Physical distribution* and *distribution* mean the same thing. The aim of physical distribution is to transfer goods from manufacture to the place of consumption.

Figure 4-1 illustrates the area each of the terms covers in the business process. The logistics system is the physical interface between the supply points and demand points. It is designed to react to a series of reorders. Basically, when the demand points need replenishment, this triggers an order from distribution facilities, production plants, or supply points. This material is then transported to the demand points. The depleted inventory at the distribution center may in turn generate a reorder from a supplier, or a shipment from the production plant. The production

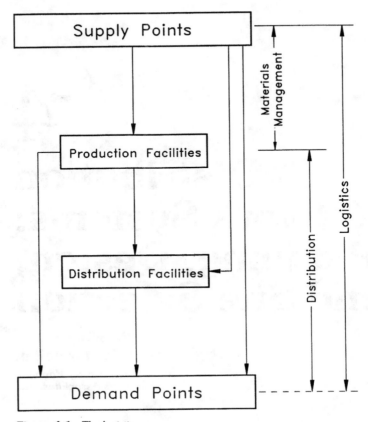

Figure 4-1. The logistics process.

plants typically replenish stock based on a sales forecast translated into a production forecast. The production plant will require goods from its supplier based on this production plan. Thus, a company's logistics system can be viewed as the link between its supply points and its demand points.

The first portion of the logistics system, materials from supply points to production facilities, is materials management. Materials management ensures that the raw materials and subassemblies needed by the production facilities to meet the production schedule are on hand.

The purpose of a distribution system is to be the link between the production of the product and the demand points, while satisfying the following objectives:

- Delivering the right goods at the right time, in the right quantity and to the right place
- Matching output to demand by holding inventory where necessary to:

  Create the capability to handle surge capacity in sales
  Support production and hold surge capacity and reserve capacity

This chapter will concentrate on the distribution aspects of logistics. Specifically the makeup of a distribution network, the various types of planning used in the field of distribution, and how to apply strategic planning to designing a distribution network and selecting a site.

Components of a Distribution System

The physical distribution system is made up of several elements. In its simplest form, the system can be described as a linked system of nodes (typically, stocking points). To move material between these nodes, all distribution networks have the following key elements: Stocking Points, Transportation, Inventory Management, Customer Service, and Management Information Systems.

Stocking points can be distribution centers, consolidation points, terminals, ports, return centers, or other points that receive goods from either production plants or suppliers and/or ship to demand points. Their job is to receive, store, pick, and ship product. Basically, any point through which produced material flows to reach the customer is a stocking point.

Transportation not only includes movement from the plant to the warehouse and from warehouse to warehouse, but also delivery from warehouse to the customer.

Inventory management is the purchasing and control of products based on a market forecast. Inventories are typically a buffer or surge between production/vendors and the customer, to permit the system to accommodate unexpected variations in demand or production. Basically, inventory management consists of: forecasting requirements, procuring orders, and managing what's on hand.

Customer service is responsible for handling the key interfaces between the company and its customers. It involves handling customer inquiries, order changes, and dealing with other situations that occur in the typical customer/supplier relationship. Customer service may also include the process of ordering. In addition it is responsible for monitoring the goals established by management for each product or market segment, i.e., order fill rate, delivery time. Customer service goals are the performance criteria to which the entire demand satisfaction process must respond.

Management information systems are any communication and/or control systems that support distribution. These systems range from taking inbound orders to managing fleet operations. The types of systems most distribution operations make use of are as follows:

1. *Forecasting*—converting sales forecast into shipping requirements; includes quantities that must be shipped on a daily or weekly basis from each location; typically a Distribution Requirements Planning (DRP) computer system.

2. *Budgeting*—takes place for the next year, and transforms the tactical and operational plans into cashflows and spending targets.

3. *Inventory management*—inventory records, safety stock calculations, inventory replenishment, historical use, and reorder points.

4. *Order processing and invoicing*—provides for customer order procedures: receipts, entry, status inquiry, and invoicing.

5. *Customer service*—provides informational support for customer service operations including: inside sales, claims handling, price quotations, order terms, and product information.

6. *Warehouse management*—supports the warehouse by generating putaway and picking list or radio frequency task, identifying inventory by storage location, cycle counting task, lot control, warehouse performance, and audit trails.

7. *Transportation management*—supports the traffic operations by providing bills of lading and other documentation required for shipment, private fleet accounting, fleet routing and scheduling, dispatching, fleet maintenance information, and freight bill auditing

In short, management information systems provide data-processing systems that support the stocking points, transportation, inventory management, and customer service functions of the business.

Organizational Structures

An organizational structure ties the stocking points, transportation, inventory management, customer service, and information systems together, and provides the building blocks to accomplish the objectives of the corporation. Just as there are many different ways to structure the components of a network, there are many ways to structure an organization. Described next are some key considerations and principles in setting up an organization.

1. *Unity of command.* This has to do with the chain of command. It is recommended that no one have more than one superior with direct authority.

2. *Span of control.* To effectively manage an organization, there must be limits applied to the number of people a manager can supervise. These limits are set based on the task being performed, the type of people being supervised, and the manner in which supervision is applied, but the general rule of thumb is no more than five to seven per manager.

3. *Responsibility and authority.* Responsibility means a manager being held accountable for the actions of his/her staff. Authority is the right of the manager to command action from a staff, or discharge responsibility to them. An often debated subject is whether managers should have equal authority and responsibility. The level of authority should be clear to the manager, so that he/she is aware of the limits of the position.

4. *Line or staff.* Line functions typically refer to those activities performed by the personnel working in a distribution center that support the everyday function of the operation. Staff responsibilities consist of those activities performed in order to assist and/or support the functions of the overall company or a division of the company.

5. *Centralized versus decentralized.* A centralized organization would have, for example, all customer service concentrated in one location, reporting to one man-

ager. A decentralized organization would have customer service representatives at each distribution center reporting to the distribution manager of that area.

Setting up an organizational structure that is efficient will help the company, but it does not guarantee a successful, motivated staff. To accomplish this an organization must have a winning culture, with such a culture being the most important part of an organization. To create a winning culture many companies are adopting team-based continuous improvement. Only by creating a unified team will a company move forward toward success. The concept of team-based continuous improvement is discussed in Chapter 26 of this handbook.

Types of Planning

There are various methods of planning or devising a scheme for helping to guide and position the organization. This planning can be for a predictable or unpredictable set of circumstances. Without plans, a firm runs the risk of insufficiently anticipating problems and failing to implement a solution within the required lead time. By planning, a company becomes active rather than passive. The framework for planning is based upon the types shown in Table 4-1.

A company must first devise a *strategic* plan that will determine the objectives of the company. The question "What is our business?" should be asked. The answers to this question will determine the overall objectives and approach, prior to the determination of any other plans. Next, *tactical* planning sets aside the resources to carry out the objectives, and *operational* planning assures that the specific tasks are carried out. Strategic, tactical, and operational are all offensive planning methods. *Contingency* planning is a defense tool that is used to guard against unanticipated events. These four planning methods are complementary.

Strategic Planning

Strategic planning is the process of deciding on: objectives of the firm, changes in the objectives, resources to attain these objectives, and policies to govern the acquisition, use, and disposition of resources. The objective of strategic planning is to define the overall approach to stocking points, transportation, inventory manage-

Table 4-1 Types of Planning

Type of planning	Reason	Need
Strategic	Determine the overall objectives and resource requirements	Policy making
Tactical	Translate the strategic objective of the distribution system into an action plan	Long-term
Operational	Process of assuring that specific tasks are implemented into the day-to-day operations	Short-term
Contingency	Exceptions or responses to emergencies	Just-in-case

ment, customer service, and information systems, and the way they relate, in order to provide the maximum return on investment.

Strategic planning is an offensive tool designed to guard against a predictable change in requirements, the timing of which can be anticipated. Strategic planning is directed at forecasting future needs far enough in advance of the actual requirements to allow sufficient lead time to efficiently meet those needs. Granted, forecasting with a long planning horizon is a risky business, and distribution plans based on such forecasts often prove unworkable. Nevertheless the forecast is a company's best available information concerning the future, and it would be foolish not to use that information to advantage. In fact, the only way to survive the rapidly changing distribution environment today is to have good strategic plans that address the future needs of distribution. Strategic planning addresses such issues as organizational structures, realignment of capacities, network planning, and impact on environmental factors.

Tactical Planning

The tactical planning time frame is one to two years. Its primary purpose is to pre-plan policies and programs and set targets, both in terms of actions to be taken and the timing that will bring the firm to the accomplishment of its long-term strategic objectives. Tactical planning must anticipate the distribution center work load to prevent overloading of the primary resource, the work force, during peak work loads. The action defined in the tactical plan is the deployment of these resources toward the achievement of the goals of the strategic plan. For example, if a firm decides in its strategic plan that it requires a new warehouse location to enhance customer service, the tactical plan will allocate resources and determine the timing of the specific resources or decisions required for successful completion of the plan. Here are some of the steps you will have to follow in relocating a warehouse:

1. Locate new facility.
2. Sign lease.
3. Design new facility.
4. Modify facility according to design.
5. Hire new employees.
6. Train employees.
7. Start transferring material from vendors and existing plants.
8. Start shipping from new facility.

The tactical plan first attempts to provide timing for each step. Second, consideration is given to major issues, such as identifying specific skills required to accomplish the plan and the quantity and duration of time needed for each step of the plan. Third, specific capital requirements are identified at each step of the plan. A fourth component is often outside services. In warehousing, this could mean anything from hiring a consultant to hiring a construction company to make modifications. Some other types of tactical planning include inventory policies, freight rate negotiation, cost reduction, productivity improvements, and information system enhancements and additions.

Operational Planning

Operational planning can vary from daily to weekly to monthly. Its purpose is to implement selected tactical policies, plans, and programs within the framework of the distribution system, and to meet the strategic objectives of the company. The major components of operational planning involve managing resources such as labor and capital assets and measuring performance with regard to both aiding operating efficiency and anticipating future operating issues. An operational plan is different from day-to-day operations. It incorporates the philosophies of the strategic plan, with general timing of events as outlined in the tactical plan, into the daily routine. An operational plan is, so to speak, where the rubber meets the road. Typically it is where the planning process fails, because the majority of the daily activities are routine; therefore no priority is put on the implementation effort of the planned activities and it becomes easy to lose sight of the planned goals. Operational planning can involve tasks such as distribution center workload scheduling, vehicle scheduling, freight consolidation planning, implementing productivity improvement/cost reduction, and operations expense budgeting.

Contingency Planning

One of the most overlooked managerial tools that has a particularly meaningful application to sound distribution management is the area of contingency planning. Contingency planning is a defensive tool used to guard against an unpredictable future change in distribution requirements. Typically contingency planning involves asking "What if?" questions. For example, "What if a major supplier is on strike?" or "What if we had a recall?" The prepared manager will look to use contingency planning to assist in countering the potentially devastating impact of the many emergency situations that may directly involve distribution. He/she will determine in advance what course of action is required if a given unanticipated change in requirements or circumstance occurs. Contingency planning is different from the common nonplanning or crisis-management (putting out fire) approach, which entails developing a plan *after* a change in requirements or circumstances has occurred. The idea behind contingency planning is to significantly reduce the lead time required to implement a plan of action. You do not wait for a fire to start to install sprinklers in the warehouse. Sprinklers are installed long before that fire may or may not take place. Some events that can affect a distribution system are now described.

Energy shortages can affect both the warehouse and the transportation system. Transportation is the most talked about segment of distribution that is affected but it can also affect the warehouse. On the transportation end, how do you maintain service? Do you offer less product line? Repackage to maximize loads? And so on. Warehouse energy shortages will affect not only lighting and heating but potential material handling equipment.

Strikes can occur within your own firm or at a key supplier of either material or services. The objectives of the strike plan will need to be determined. Items to consider are personnel and property protection, maintaining goodwill with customers, public, and employees, and resuming operation within the shortest time period. Decisions will need to be made on whether to build inventory, divert work to another plant, contract out work, lay off nonstriking employees or operate with them, hire temporary workers, etc.

Natural disasters such as forest fires, tornadoes, floods, or hurricanes can result in problems such as cleaning up, resuming operations, restoring order, dealing with employees in a disaster (wages and time), and computer backups.

Product recalls can be time-consuming and expensive. Therefore it is important to be organized properly, to minimize cost and minimize damage to the company's image. Items such as lot shipment identification, lot segregation and return procedures, legal obligations, production contingencies, and public relations should be addressed.

Strategic Distribution Network Planning

Distribution network planning is one of the main areas to which strategic planning is applied. A strategic distribution network plan is developed to meet a specific set of requirements over a given planning horizon. A good plan will determine the optimal network to provide the customer with the right goods in the right quantity at the right place at the right time, and to minimize the total distribution cost. As the number of warehouses increases, delivery cost decreases and warehouse cost increases. This is shown in a simplified manner in Fig. 4-2. The opposite is also true: As the number of warehouses decreases, the delivery cost increases. Therefore, to minimize total distribution cost it is important to find the best balance of warehouses and transportation cost.

The objective of strategic distribution network planning is to come up with a plan that indicates the most economical way to ship and receive product while maintaining or increasing customer service requirements; simply put, a plan to maximize profits and optimize service. Strategic distribution network planning typically answers the following questions:

1. How many distribution centers should exist?
2. Where should the distribution center(s) be located?
3. How much inventory should be stocked at each distribution center?
4. What customers should be serviced by each distribution center?
5. How should the customers order from the distribution center?
6. How should the distribution centers order from vendors?
7. How frequently should shipments be made to each customer?
8. What should the service levels be?
9. What transportation methods should be utilized?

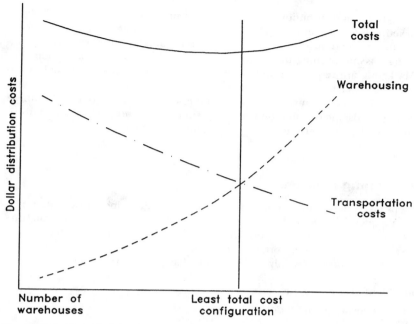

Figure 4-2. Simplified distribution cost model.

The Need for Strategic Distribution Network Planning

Basically a distribution network is a series of nodes and transportation links. Distribution networks can range from direct shipments from the source, to demand points for job-shop items, to complex multisite networks. The design of a distribution network is dependent on factors such as type of products, range and volume of products, geographic spread of service area, level of service required, and number and type of customers. However, since distribution is a dynamic environment, it is affected by such factors as:

1. Geographic shifts in production and consumption; population shifts
2. Market segmentation, new markets, and new customer service requirements
3. Cost increases in energy, plant and equipment maintenance, labor cost
4. Government regulation or deregulation
5. Product proliferation and product life-cycle
6. Competition
7. Economy

Internal organizational areas such as Marketing, Production, and Finance also affect the makeup of a distribution network. In order to understand the effects of these functions on distribution, it is important to understand their goals. The goal of marketing is to maximize sales by being next to the customer and having plenty of inventory to minimize backorders. Production wants to minimize cost by running long lots and pushing the product out the door. Therefore both Production and Marketing are requesting more inventory and more locations to hold inventory. On the other hand, Finance wants to minimize cost and conserve cash and credit, thereby lowering inventory and the number of stocking points. With these conflicting needs, the distribution network planner must find the lowest-cost distribution network that meets the service requirements.

The Planning Process

The steps taken in distribution design are listed next. Planning a distribution network is a sequential process that continually needs updating. The pitfall some companies run into is that they perform steps 3 through 6 before taking (and understanding) the most important steps, which are 1 and 2. The answer to distribution network planning is only as good as the data put into the analysis.

1. Document distribution network.
2. Identify delivery requirements.
3. Establish database.
4. Develop alternative networks.
5. Model annual operating costs.
6. Evaluate alternatives.
7. Specify the plan.

Documenting the Distribution Network

Steps 1, 2, and 3 (documenting the distribution network, identifying delivery requirements, and establishing the database) can be done simultaneously. The main goal of these steps is to gain understanding of the current system and to define the requirements of the future system. In order to document the existing systems, information must be collected on the distribution centers and the transportation system. When gathering information on the distribution centers, it is critical to collect from *all* existing sites considered, since the study could result in recommendations for the closing, moving, or expanding of these facilities. The following information needs to be collected for each site.

1. *Space utilizations.*   Determine the utilization of the distribution center. This will allow you to determine the amount of physical inventory space that will be required if this facility is to be closed when the analysis is complete. It also identifies how much more inventory can be consolidated to this location.
2. *Layout and equipment.*   List the equipment and layout of each facility. If you have a list of equipment available, it will be easier to determine the investment requirements of a new or expanded facility.

3. *Warehouse operating procedures.* Understand the order picking and shipping procedures. If there are two product lines in one location, are they picked and shipped together? Understand the differences in operating methods between facilities. This may tell you why one facility achieves a higher throughput efficiency per person. Understand how replenishment orders are pulled or pushed to the distribution center.

4. *Staffing levels.* Document levels by position. Understand which jobs could be consolidated. Collect labor rates by level, including fringe benefits.

5. *Receiving and shipping volumes.* Understand the number of incoming and outgoing trucks and the number of docks. This will be important if the facility is required to increase throughput.

6. *Building characteristics.* Collect square footage, clear height, column spacing, lighting level, etc. for the same reason as layout information, but remember to review expansion capabilities.

7. *Access to location.* Review the access to main highways. Determine if this will have an effect on freight cost.

8. *Annual operating cost.* Collect lease cost, taxes, insurance, maintenance, energy cost, and other facility costs.

9. *Inventory.* Collect information on inventory turns and levels, fill rates, safety stock levels, and ABC analysis. With this information in hand, you will be able to determine the savings to be gained by consolidating facilities. Also collect information on which and how much stock is slow-moving or seasonal, to help determine if it should be centralized in one location or if public warehouse space should be used. Get future inventory goals.

10. *Performance reporting.* Understand the performance measures for service requirements, order completeness, shipping accuracy, etc.

The following information should be collected for the transportation system.

1. *Freight classes and discounts.* Collect the freight classes and rates used. In addition to freight classes, get the discounts by carrier or location. It is also important to understand where the discounts apply (under which parameters; i.e., routes, minimum weights).

2. *Transportation operating procedures.* Understand how a certain mode of transport is selected and how a carrier is selected.

3. *Delivery requirements.* What are the delivery requirements (days of delivery) to the customer, and how is carrier performance measured? Is order completeness measured?

4. *Replenishment weight/cube.* At what weight is a trailer cubed out? Get this information from each replenishment point and for a typical load of general merchandise.

At the end of the site visits, a project team meeting should be held that summarizes the data collected and the assessment of each site. This assessment will give the team insight into their operation, and more than likely they will discover information unknown to management that will be useful in developing alternatives.

To document the future distribution network requirements, an understanding of marketing strategies and sales forecasts is required. Here are some questions that should be answered by Marketing and Sales:

- Are there any new products coming out? From where are they sourced? What is the target market area (geographically)?
- What are the ordering parameters right now? For example, what is the minimum order size? Are they changing any terms of order (i.e., charging for expedited service)?
- What is the direction of the market? (Packaging changes, wholesalers, mass merchants having more volume.)
- What is the sales increase by year?
- Are there noticeable customer shifts? Are fewer customers handling more volume?
- Are geographic shifts emerging? Have sales increased by geographic region?

Identifying Delivery Requirements

One of the key data requirements for analyzing a distribution network is that of delivery requirements, or the time from order placement to receipt of the shipment. If these requirements are not identifiable, a customer service gap analysis must be undertaken. The gap analysis is a series of questions directed at internal staff and customers. The purpose is to identify discrepancies between customer perception of service and service requirements. The gap analysis, as shown in Fig. 4-3, is an attempt to narrow down the value of service to the customer in relation to cost. In general, is it more important to have the goods faster, or at a lower price? Figure 4-4 shows distribution cost as it relates to days of delivery, and how that affects profits. The figure indicates that as delivery requirements are reduced there is a point where the cost of the product and the distribution of the product will outweigh the income achieved from sales. The figure also indicates that the longer the delivery time obtained, the higher the profits. At some point the sales sharply decline, because competition exceeds both your delivery and your cost (assuming equal product quality). The key is to find the best service that also maximizes profits.

Establishing the Database

The database of orders that are to be modeled can be established while the existing network is being documented. This information should include ship-to locations, weight of the shipments, products ordered, and the quantity ordered. Once the data has been established, the next step is to validate it. In order to ensure that the information was transferred properly, print out a few records of invoices and compare these to hard copies. Also it is a good idea to prepare a summary report (sales, cases sold, weight shipped) for a sanity check, to ensure that all the data in the files was transferred. Once the data has been proved valid, various analyses such as ABC analysis by location (geographical region), volume, and product volume by regions of the country should be run. These reports should be used to help develop alternatives.

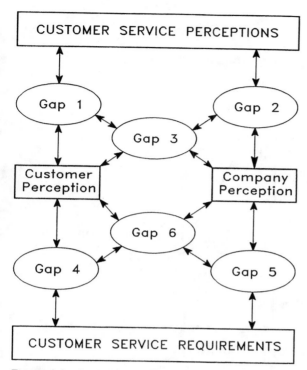

Figure 4-3. Gap analysis procedure.

Developing Alternatives

Once the data has been collected, the next step consists of developing alternative site locations and operating methods. The input used to determine alternatives are site visits, future requirements, database analysis, and customer service surveys. The methods used for the selection of each site will vary. The main factors influencing site location are listed in Table 4-2.

Typically site selection is based on the factors shown in Table 4-2, and there are methods available for determining alternative sites chosen based on customer volumes and distance. These methods range from experience, to determining the total road miles, to running a centroid (center of gravity) analysis. A centroid analysis calculates the weighted center of a customer demand by using coordinates and customer volume. It was one of the first methods used to determine site location, but it is inadequate when compared to today's modeling techniques. It assumes that transportation costs are proportional to distance, that the straight-line distance between two points is representative of actual distance, and that there is a given uniform shipment size from/to each location. It also ignores capacity constraints, service requirements, and differences in facility processing cost. However, it can be a useful tool for developing alternatives that can later be modeled. Here are the steps for using centroid analysis:

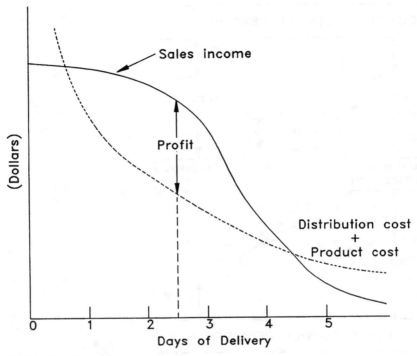

Figure 4-4. Gap analysis results.

1. Get a large scale map of the area to be examined. Superimpose this over standard graph paper.
2. Mark a uniform scale on both the horizontal (x) axis and the vertical (y) axis.
3. Pinpoint customer locations on the map, and enter these into an analysis sheet that has columns for the x (column one) and y (column two) coordinates.
4. In column three of the analysis sheet (weight), enter the weight of annual shipments anticipated from the new facility to each of the customer locations.

Table 4-2 Basis for Site Location Decisions

Basis	Reasons
Supplier and market	How quickly suppliers reach you and you reach markets (delivery days)
Transportation	Highway access, water and rail access, weather restrictions, congestion, and road limitations
Government utilities	Taxes, incentive programs, planning and zoning, energy cost
Labor	Holiday observance, unions, right-to-work laws, wages, skills available

5. Multiply the weight times the coordinates, and enter these numbers in columns four (x/weight) and five (y/weight) for each customer.
6. Total up the x/weight, y/weight, and the weight columns. To get your centroid coordinates, divide the x/weight and y/weight by the weight total. Now translate this position to the map in order to get the centroid location.

Sites are not the only option to consider as alternatives. Operating methods also must be considered, as well as criteria such as consolidating vendor shipments, centralizing slow-moving items in one place, keeping company divisions separate, and direct shipment by vendors. Once alternative sites have been determined, data must be collected on freight rates, warehouse cost, and labor cost for the alternative sites.

Modeling the Annual Operating Cost

Modeling software doesn't guarantee the right answer here. Modeling should be used only as a tool to aid in the decision process. Sometimes interpretation should be pursued. The real value in distribution planning is the knowledge gained from understanding the working of a company's distribution system, knowledge of distribution planning, and the imagination to use the model in ways that will really benefit the distribution network. Alternatives in a number of facilities can be close in cost but have a wide range; therefore it is important to have some other criteria to judge the modeling runs on. For instance:

1. Central administrative costs, and order processing costs. Typically these costs increase with the number of warehouses. It takes more effort to coordinate and manage a larger network of facilities.
2. Cycle and safety stock carrying costs. More warehouses means more total system inventory. Inventory theory supports the notion that safety stocks will increase with the number of facilities.
3. Customer order size effects. Customers who live close to a warehouse generally tend to order more frequently and in smaller quantity than customers who are farther away. This implies that delivery costs tend to increase on a $/cwt basis as the number of facilities increases.
4. Interwarehouse transfer cost. The more distribution centers there are, the greater the coordination problems and the more likely the tendency to transfer inventory between facilities due to imbalanced inventory availability.
5. Negotiated reduction in warehousing and delivery costs. The less facilities the greater their individual volume, and hence the more opportunity there is to negotiate more favorable arrangements for warehousing and delivery service.

The intent of this chapter is to document the overall approach to distribution planning, and therefore the various techniques available to model annual operating will not be discussed. However, no matter the modeling method used, the overall approach should closely resemble the following steps:

1. *Validate the existing network.* Run computer model to simulate the existing cost. Compare this cost to actual cost.

2. *Run alternative networks.* Once the model is valid, alternative networks should be run for present volumes and forecasted volumes.

3. *Summarize runs and rank.* Create a table to summarize cost by alternative. The table should list distribution center cost individually.

4. *Summarize all annual cost and service factors.* Create a table that indicates by alternative all the cost and service factors.

5. *Perform a sensitivity analysis.* Sensitivity analysis is based on the idea of setting up runs that fluctuate some components of the data. This could be a cost that is uncertain or has potential to change. By modifying this one parameter, the effect on the run can be determined.

6. *Determine all investment costs associated with each alternative.* For instance, costs of new warehouse equipment required to save space, expansion and construction costs, or any building modifications such as adding dock doors.

Evaluating Alternatives

The economic analysis compares the recommended network plan to the implementation cost. To do this analysis you must determine all the investment and savings associated with each alternative. Cost such as new warehouse equipment, construction cost, or any building modification should be included. Additionally the following information must be identified: personnel relocation, severance, stock relocation, computer relocation, taxes, equipment relocation, and the sale of existing land and buildings.

The result of this evaluation should be a return on investment of each alternative compared to the baseline. Once this step has been taken, a sensitivity analysis that fluctuates various cost and savings to see which alternatives are the most stable should be performed. To round out the analysis a qualitative analysis should be performed, looking at such factors as customer service and ease of implementation. Once a conclusion has been reached, a time-phased implementation schedule should be drawn up that lists the major steps involved in transferring the distribution network from the existing system to the future system.

Specifying the Plan

The final step in the distribution network planning process is selling the results to top management. This must be expressed in such a way that management can understand the impact of the strategy on the total business. Not only should this communication express the finances relating to transportation and warehouse costs, but also to overall sales and customer service.

To convey these thoughts to top management, project documents and presentations should be prepared. They should contain the following information:

1. *Objectives.* Typically this is in the introduction section of the report.

2. *Recommendations.* This identifies a time-implementation-phased plan. It also contains total savings and investment requirements. The recommendations should also include a map showing geographic service areas.

3. *Procedure.* This describes the methodology used and the assumptions and data that went into the study.

4. *Current network.* This describes the current network and the way it works, problems that exist, constraints on the system.

5. *Alternatives considered.* This should cover the selection criteria (cities or operating methods) for alternatives, and identify and explain the viable alternatives. Explain why some alternatives were eliminated quickly and will not be considered.

6. *Results of modeling effort.* The first thing this section should address is the method of analysis used to determine the best network. It should then list and discuss the best two or three networks.

7. *Conclusion of the evaluation of alternatives.* Once the best networks have been determined, evaluate whether it is economically and qualitatively sound to invest time and money into relocating to a new area. This section presents a summary of the investments, annual cashflows, and present value relative to the baseline for each alternative. Describe the qualitative consideration for each alternative. Tell the client which strategy is the winner, and why.

8. *Supporting data.* These include backup data, and calculations. Place them in the appendix of a report.

Site Selection

Once the prime geographical area for the new facility has been settled upon and management has approved the strategic distribution network plan, the job of selecting the best community and site begins. This is the most difficult and time-consuming part of the site selection process. Initially there may appear to be many prospective locations. One mistake frequently made at this point is starting to look at sites before the overall approach has been determined. The site selection team needs to make inquiries or get outside assistance to narrow down the potential communities, primarily because each detailed site search could take hours or even days. Support for narrowing down the communities can come from many sources, including the following.

■ *Real estate brokers* are typically tied into the multiple-listing service that lists all available property in an area. Remember that brokers are compensated upon a successful transaction. This may or may not create pressure that could affect the execution of the search.

■ *Utility companies* are a good source of information, as they typically have large service areas. However, utilities divide territories into regions and have regional salespeople who are geared toward increasing revenues in their region. So if you have decided on a particular region, a utility should provide an unbiased source for identifying industrial sites in the area.

■ *Government agencies.* State and local government development agencies, as well as local chambers of commerce, are also reliable information sources once the decision as to community has been made. Since these people are motivated to attract new industry into their area, make sure the area is where you really want to be before relying on this source of advice.

■ *Consultants* provide an unbiased source of advice and save you many hours of time. In selecting a consultant, one important consideration is whether the individual is truly independent and objective.

The best way to narrow your selection to a few communities is to create a checklist of key requirements. If a community doesn't meet these requirements then it should be eliminated from further consideration. Some of the various factors that should be put on the checklist are listed in Table 4-3.

Once the community list has been narrowed down, then site visits to view alternative lease facilities and land or buildings for sale should be made. Before you visit each site, create another checklist. This checklist should cover considerations such as zoning, topography, landscaping requirements, access to site, storm drainage, floor loadings, lighting levels, clear height, and utilities. These considerations should be prioritized, and then each site should be graded based on how well it meets the criteria. Many of the items on the list, such as utility cost, may require extensive investigation before a final evaluation can be made.

Foreign Trade Zones

One of the considerations in selecting a site is whether or not a free trade zone is applicable to your company's needs. Foreign trade zones (FTZ) or "free" trade zones are secured areas within the United States, but are considered legally outside the customer's territory. Foreign and domestic goods may generally be stopped, processed, or manufactured duty-free in the FTZ. The purpose is to attract and promote international trade and commerce. Typically zones are operated as public utilities by states or private companies performing under contract with public institutions that are the formal sponsors. Typically a FTZ is a fenced-in area with general warehouse facilities and industrial park space, with access to all modes of transportation. Located in or near U.S. customs ports-of-entry, they are the U.S. version of what are known internationally as *free trade zones*. Subzones are adjuncts to zones granted to companies that cannot be accommodated in the public zone serving area. They exist only for a single user, and strict criteria must be satisfied for subzone status. Usually a subzone must generate public benefit such as employment. Most manufacturers that assemble imported products typically fall into the subzone classification. The advantages of using a FTZ are as follows.

■ Customs duty and internal revenue tax, if applicable, are paid only when merchandise is transferred from a foreign trade zone to the custom territory for consumption.

■ Goods may be exported from a zone free of duty and tax.

■ Merchandise may remain in a zone indefinitely, whether or not subject to duty.

Table 4-3 Community Considerations

Labor	Unions (yes/no), availability of qualified personnel, wage levels, accident rate in area, community education or training programs, employment laws, right to work laws, local safety and health costs, availability of management personnel
Utilities	History of outages, rates, off-peak rates, discounts or penalties, residential rates, water conditions and chemical analysis, water source, refuse and trash collection cost, frequency and disposal methods
Community	Availability of shopping, housing availability and cost, travel and meeting facilities, news media availability, traffic levels, organizations, communications, mail service, health facilities, protective services (fire and police), education, recreation, religious activities, cultural facilities
Existing industry	Major operations in area, possible suppliers and customers, civic participation, union affiliations, environmental conditions, support to the community, number of plants gained and lost in the last five years
Local and state government	Voting record of incumbents, annual budget, sources of revenue, annexation policies, attitude during strikes, property taxes, sales tax, financial health of state and community, amount of tax-free property, any community taxes
Miscellaneous	Weather conditions (temperature, rainfall, snowfall, humidity, days of sunshine), planning and zoning history and makeup. Commercial services in area (banks, industrial distributors, office supplies, industrial repair shops)
Rail transportation	Railroad stop-off privileges for partial loading/unloading en route, demurrage charges, reciprocal switching arrangements, pickup and delivery services, freight schedules
Highway and truck transportation	State laws as to truck size and weight, toll roads and bridges, condition of roads
Miscellaneous transportation	Air: site near airport, schedule of airlines, personnel transport schedules Water: channels width and depth, terminal facilities, seasonal limitations Other: bus service, taxi service, rapid transit, auto rental agencies

Any foreign goods or materials brought into a zone for any permissible activity and ultimately shipped to a third country, either in their original or a completely altered condition, are not subject to customs duties or federal excise taxes, and usually are not chargeable against quotas. Local and state authorities should be contacted about any state or local taxes. What is not always understood and is often overlooked is the use of zone status in exporting. Companies who intend to market their manufactured goods in other countries should research the viability of FTZ.

Any foreign or domestic merchandise not prohibited by law, whether dutiable or not, may be taken into a FTZ. There are material operations that the FTZ board may exclude or deny permission to zone, if this is detrimental to the public interest, health, or safety. Certain agencies that license importers or issue importation permits may block zone entries. However many products subject to internal revenue tax may not be manufactured in a zone. These products include alcoholic beverages, tobacco, firearms, white phosphorus material, and sugar. In addition the manufacture of clocks and watch movements is not permitted in a zone. There is no retail trade permitted in a zone.

Conclusion

It is important to remember from your reading of this chapter that a good strategic distribution network plan relies upon a defined set of requirements. It should not be composed simply of ideas, thoughts, or possibilities that have not been researched as to their validity. Possible requirements should be defined, analyzed, and evaluated, and they should result in the development of a specific set of strategic requirements. Normally the planning horizon is stated in terms of years. A five-year plan is typical. A good distribution network plan is also action-oriented and time-phased. Where possible the plan should set forth very specific actions to be taken to meet requirements, rather than simply state the alternative actions available to meet those requirements. The distribution network plan is based upon a set of premises concerning future sales volumes, inventory levels, transportation costs, and warehouse costs. Most importantly, in order to sell the plan, a formally written document and maps should accompany the recommended action, to describe and illustrate how the network will be implemented and operate.

Further Reading

Attwood, P. R., *Planning a Distribution System,* Gower Publishing, Hants, England, 1971, pp. 1–39.

Geoffrion, A. M., "Making better use of Optimization Capability in Distribution System Planning," *AIIE Transactions,* vol. 11, no. 2, pp. 98–100.

Harmelink, D. A., "Strategic Logistics Planning," *Traffic Management,* August 1988.

———, "Should your company use foreign trade zones," *Network for International Material Handling,* October 1989.

Robeson, J. F. and R. G. House, *The Distribution Handbook,* Free Press, New York, 1985, pp. 110–116.

Tompkins, J. A. and J. D. Smith, *The Warehouse Management Handbook,* McGraw-Hill, New York, 1988, pp. 81–90.

5

Distribution Information Systems

Craig M. Gustin
Principal, CGR Management Consultants

"I'm convinced that using information more effectively is perhaps the single most important source of competitive advantage for firms today."
—JOHN A. YOUNG, PRESIDENT AND CHIEF EXECUTIVE OFFICER OF HEWLETT-PACKARD
Address to the Grocery Manufacturers of America (April 7, 1988), "Using Information for a Competitive Advantage."

The contribution of distribution, or logistics, to the economies of industrial nations is substantial. In 1992, logistics-related activities will represent more than $600 billion, or about 11 percent of the United States' gross national product.[1] As a percent of annual company revenues, total logistics expenditures average approximately 8 percent, although costs for a specific firm can range from 2 to 20 percent or more depending upon the type of business, geographic operations, and other factors.[2] Another measure of the impact of distribution on American companies is the fact that total (distribution) cost expenditures range from 10 to 35 percent, depending on the business, the geographic area of operations, and the weight/value ratio of finished products and raw materials involved.[3]

It has been suggested that a cost-reduction goal of 10 percent for distribution in the United States is attainable. Based on the level of logistics expenditures cited above, achieving this goal would generate savings in excess of $60 billion annually.

Challenges to Successful Distribution Systems

The foregoing suggests that there are significant benefits achievable through improved distribution operations. For example: "A physical distribution management information system is necessary in order to provide management with the knowledge to exploit new markets, to take advantage of innovative transportation systems, to make changes in packaging design, choose between common carriage or private trucking, to increase or decrease inventories, to determine profitability of customers, to establish profitable customer-service levels, to choose between public and private warehousing, and to determine the number of field warehouses and to what extent the order processing system should be automated."[4]

While significant corporate-wide benefits should be realized through improved logistics operations, a frequent reason cited for not capitalizing on this opportunity is the inability of most U.S. companies to satisfactorily measure and control their logistics activities and attendant costs. The difficulty in measuring and controlling logistics typically results from the geographically dispersed nature of logistics activities and the absence of a high-level, integrated approach to managing these activities. Another fundamental cause cited for inadequate measurement and control is the lack of suitable information systems.[5]

What are the underlying barriers precluding business from implementing needed improvements and achieving the indicated savings? For most firms, distribution activities require coordination and integration with other activities throughout the organization. Companies generally cannot deal with distribution as effectively as they should for two interrelated reasons:

1. Segmentation of distribution activities among other areas of business (i.e., marketing, production, finance, etc.)
2. Lack of distribution-oriented databases for decision making.

The first issue is largely organizational, and beyond the exclusive control of the distribution executive. Even though recent studies and publications have indicated that the distribution function is gaining recognition and status in American industry, the reality in most companies is that the heads of other major functions—finance, marketing, and manufacturing—hold more senior and influential positions than do their counterparts charged with managing the distribution function. Thus, while the distribution function may be experiencing an increased level of recognition, progress in bottom-line terms can still be difficult to quantify.

It is in the second area that more immediate and measurable success may seem more possible, since it is to a greater extent under the control of the distribution executive. To establish a distribution-oriented database, however, requires that the distribution function compete with other corporate functions in gaining approval for the necessary computer applications to be developed. Since distribution applications are frequently more difficult and require more data processing resources (both people and equipment) to implement than other applications (e.g., financial), the distribution applications are often deferred. This effect, when coupled with the subordinated and segmented role of distribution mentioned previously, can result in the lack of integrated systems to support decision making. A "distribution dilemma" thus exists, which suggests that because of the function's subordinated organizational position, only limited systems capability can be obtained, thereby precluding the identification and substantiation of improvement opportunities. With limited savings/cost reduction potential apparently available, no justification exists for strengthening distribution management or its systems capability. This "distribution dilemma" is presented in Fig. 5-1. This "Catch 22" situation has been described as "They can't have the system until they have the figures which justify it, but they can't get the figures to justify the system without a computer."[6]

Information Systems Expenditures

The investment in distribution information systems, while substantial, is difficult to quantify. One forecast estimated worldwide expenditures at more than $50 billion in 1990, with the level increasing to more than $75 billion by the year 2000. Another estimate for global expenditures by the year 2000 is $215 billion, i.e., nearly three times the first projection. With the U.S. gross domestic product being approximately a third of the global total, and assuming that the level of spending on information systems remains constant, U.S. expenditures for distribution information systems would be in the order of $25 billion by the end of the decade.[7]

In the United States, "... the cost of building and maintaining the complex infrastructure of systems, applications, and networks has risen to 15 percent of operating expenses in certain industries and soaked up as much as 70 percent of profits in others."[8] Despite these substantial expenditures, most companies have traditionally under-invested in systems development to support distribution. For example, "... apart from order entry, less than 15 percent of systems investment in the last ten years has been in logistics."[9]

Based on research conducted in 1982, 1987, and 1992, U.S. logistics executives report that expenditures for information systems range from a few percent to 15 percent or more of their logistics budget; the "average" company allocated 6.0 percent in 1982, 6.1 percent in 1987, and 5.9 percent in 1992.[10] These expenditure levels suggest that the need for information systems continues to be a critical ingredient of effective logistics management. The key role of distribution information

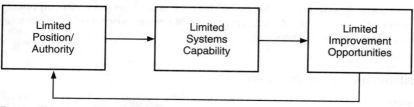

Figure 5-1. The logistics dilemma.

systems is clear when it is realized that " . . . logistics consumes 35 to 60 percent of systems development and operating budgets. In many companies, over 75 percent of all payback from applications development comes from logistics-based systems."[9]

Distribution Information System: A Definition

Distribution, or logistics, has been defined in many ways, but perhaps the most appropriate is the definition adopted in 1985 by the Council of Logistics Management:

> The process of planning, implementing, and controlling the efficient, cost-effective flow and storage of raw materials, in-process inventory, finished goods, and related information from point of origin to point of consumption for the purpose of conforming to customer requirements.

Numerous definitions exist for *information* and *system*; for example:

> *Information:* The communication or reception of knowledge or intelligence; intelligence; news; facts; data.   (*Webster's New Collegiate Dictionary, 1989, p. 620.*)

> *System:* A group of devices or objects or an organization forming a network, especially for distributing something, or serving a common purpose.   (*Webster's New Collegiate Dictionary, 1989, p. 1199.*)

Combining the three terms would give a comprehensive but probably impractical definition. Perhaps the most meaningful and operative definition was developed twenty years ago:

> The logistics information system: This system controls the flow of goods from the purchase of raw materials to the physical distribution of the finished products.[11]

Physical and Information Flows

Having established a working definition, a more complete description of a distribution information system is needed. Such a system should capture the essence of the physical distribution process, i.e., the flows of material and its associated information. As suggested by Fig. 5-2, material and information tend to flow in reverse directions, and occur both within and between each of the functions in the distribution process; in addition, flows occur to and from other functions (manufacturing, marketing, etc.).

With the evolution of global logistics and supply chain partnerships, a comprehensive system description would also include external interfaces with suppliers, customers, and intermediaries, i.e., carriers, public warehouses, brokers, forwarders, and other third party service providers.

Decision-Support Requirements

A distinction to be recognized in the information-flow segment of Fig. 5-2 relates to the level of decision making required within each component of the total system.

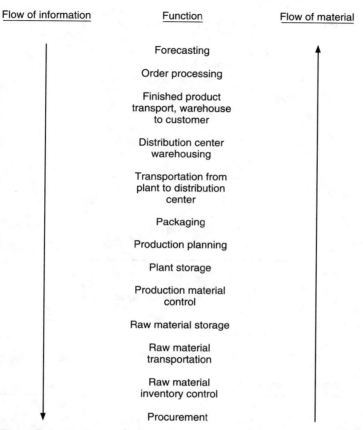

Flow of information   Function   Flow of material

Forecasting

Order processing

Finished product
transport, warehouse
to customer

Distribution center
warehousing

Transportation from
plant to distribution
center

Packaging

Production planning

Plant storage

Production material
control

Raw material storage

Raw material
transportation

Raw material
inventory control

Procurement

Figure 5-2. The logistics process. (*From James L. Heskett, "Logistics—Essential to Strategy,"* Harvard Business Review, *November–December 1977, p. 87.*)

One decision-making hierarchy, with a transaction-oriented foundation, is depicted in Fig. 5-3. A taxonomy highlighting the different perspectives required in strategic, tactical, and operational planning is shown in Table 5-1. The information characteristics associated with each decision level also can be defined as in Fig. 5-4. An alternative comparison of information characteristics considering planning, implementation, and control activities is presented in Table 5-2.

It also has been suggested that a complete system should include 10 subsystems, grouped into 3 categories according to their focus in time, i.e., past, present, or future. The 10 subsystems are:

1. Forecasting

2. Planning

3. Budgeting

4. Inventory management

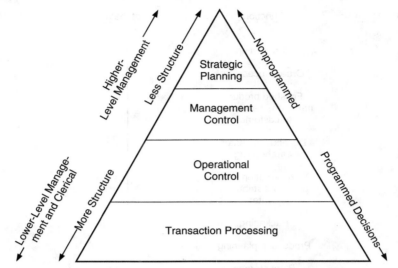

Figure 5-3. The decision-making hierarchy: strategic planning—management control—operational control. (*From Gordon B. Davis,* Management Information Systems: Conceptual Foundations, Structure and Development. *New York: McGraw-Hill, 1974, p. 222.*)

Table 5-1. Taxonomy of Decision Making

	Strategic planning	Tactical planning	Operational planning
Objective	Resource acquisition	Resource utilization	Execution
Time horizon	Long	Middle	Short
Level of management involvement	Top	Medium	Low
Sources of information	External and internal	External and internal	Internal
Level of detail of information	Highly aggregated	Moderately aggregated	Detailed
Degree of uncertainty about data	High	Medium	Low
Degree of risk	High	Moderate	Low

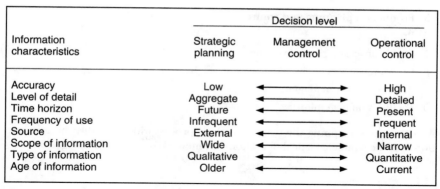

Figure 5-4. Information characteristics by area of decision. (*From Peter G. W. Keen and Michael S. Scott-Morton,* Decision Support Systems: An Organizational Perspective. *Reading, Mass.: Addison-Wesley Publishing Co., 1978, p. 83.*)

Table 5-2. Comparison of Information Characteristics for Planning, Implementation, and Control

Characteristic	Planning	Implementation and control
Focus:		
Resources	Capital amount, type	Effectiveness of application
Organization	Overall structure, interface relationship	Detailed responsibilities, objectives
Decision making:		
Structure, approach	Ad hoc	Prescribed, routinized
Judgment required	Much	Little
Information required:		
Time:		
Horizon	Over one year	Day, week, month, quarter, year
Timeliness	As needed, on demand	Immediate, real-time
Form:		
Format	Flexible, tailormade	Fixed
Accuracy	Order-of-magnitude	High-precision
Place:		
Location	Centralized	Decentralized
Source	External and internal	Internal only
Preparation	Largely manual	Largely automated

5. Production planning and control
6. Procurement
7. Order processing and invoicing
8. Customer service
9. Transportation management
10. Facilities management[12]

An example of mapping the decision-making process within the distribution function into the strategic-tactical-operational framework is presented in Fig. 5-5.

System Design and Implementation

To develop successful distribution information systems, several issues should be considered. Central points to be incorporated in the design and implementation process are addressed in this section.

Modular Architecture

To design an information system for supporting the distribution function and its related activities, as described in the preceding section, necessitates the formula-

SUBJECTS OF DECISIONS	NATURE OF DECISIONS		
	STRATEGIC	TACTICAL	OPERATIONAL
FORECASTING	• Long range • New products • Demographic shifts	• 6-12 months • Seasonality • Marketing impacts	• 12-16 weeks • Promotions • Trends
NETWORK DESIGN/ANALYSIS	• Plant and DC locations • Sourcing alternatives • Make vs. buy	• Public warehouses - usage and assignments	• Customer reassignments • Contingency planning
PRODUCTION PLANNING	• Production mix • Equipment required • Equipment location	• Production mix • Inventory vs. overtime • Crew planning	• Contingency planning
MATERIALS PLANNING	• Materials and technology alternatives	• Stockpiling and contracts • Shortage analyzer • Distribution plans	• Purchasing • Staging • Material releases

PRODUCTION SCHEDULING	• Economic analyses-dedicated
	  lines vs. multi-product
		• 6-12 month production
		  schedules
			• Daily/weekly production
			  schedules

DISPATCHING	• Fleet sizing and configuration	• Carrier contracts • Equipment location	• Daily/weekly loading and delivery plans • Billing

Figure 5-5. The distribution decision-making framework. (*Reproduced with permission of Richard F. Powers, President, Insight, Inc.*)

tion of a systems structure that can address the range of distribution activities as well as the spectrum of decision making. One such structure is shown in Fig. 5-6. This pyramid-type system recognizes the levels of decision making indicated in Figs. 5-3 and 5-4 and Table 5-1, as well as most of the planning, implementation, and control characteristics as depicted in Table 5-2. All or a portion of the 10 logistics subsystems listed above are also included, as are most of the strategic, tactical, and operational decisions shown in Fig. 5-5. It should also be noted that this system is modular in nature, meaning that one or more components may be developed independently, thereby providing the opportunity to avoid the difficulties frequently experienced in implementing corporate-wide systems intended to incorporate all essential functions at all decision levels.

Top-Down/Bottom-Up Methodology

Necessarily, systems should be tailored to fit the specific needs of each company. A design approach that combines top-down and bottom-up processes is offered in Table 5-3. This 10-step approach starts with a definition of distribution's overall mission, identifies the key distribution information requirements, and concludes with a system architecture for a distribution information system.

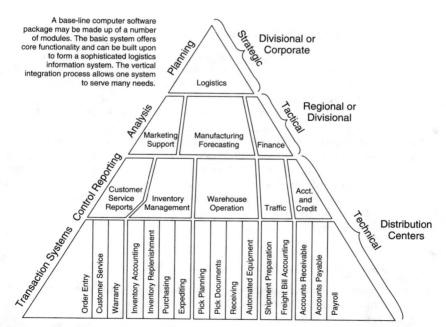

Figure 5-6. Modular logistics information system. (*From Perry A. Turnick, "Computerization: The Road Ahead for Distribution,"* Handling & Shipping Management, *April 1981, p. 54.*)

Table 5-3. Approach for Defining Logistics Information System Requirements

Step	Phase	Description
1	Top-down	Define logistics mission and objectives within the company.
2	Top-down	*Within* logistics, define the key activities and points of responsibility for performing these activities.
3	Top-down	Determine information needs from organizational functions *outside* logistics; identify key activities and points of responsibility associated with these data sources.
4	Top-down	Identify key questions and issues to be addressed in successfully managing these activities.
5	Top-down	Define the information needed to answer the key questions.
6	Top-down	Establish current data-processing applications that provide logistics information.
7	Top-down	Identify sources of this information (e.g., data files).
8	Transition	Establish data classes to support logistics activities.
9	Bottom-up	Determine the database structure necessary to integrate logistics information needs.
10	Bottom-up	Develop the information system architecture to access, analyze, and report on information in the database, i.e., a decision-support system for managing logistics activities.

Information Requirements Definition

Since distribution can assume different missions and objectives depending upon the industry, company, and top management orientation, it is worthwhile to establish a terminology for further classifying distribution activities, as presented in Table 5-4. This structure recognizes that each corporate function is made up of a number of functional areas, which, in turn, are comprised of one or more activities and related tasks.

To address the needs of each functional area within distribution, it is necessary to define the key activities that occur within these functional areas. After this step has been completed, key questions handled by each activity must be identified, as well as the information requirements that will answer these questions. The appendix at the end of this chapter contains example formats for defining the activities, questions, and information requirements for three logistics functional areas, i.e., customer service, transportation, and warehousing.

Database Structure

Having completed the information requirements definition, it is then necessary to determine the type of applications and attendant data files needed to satisfy the information requirements.

A database structure can then be established and a systems architecture developed for accessing, analyzing, and reporting on information contained in the databases. Priorities for application development should also be established, as well as

Table 5-4. Logistics Terminology

Term	Description	Examples
Function	Major operating unit within a company	Finance Logistics Marketing
Functional area	Component within a function	Accounting within finance Transportation within logistics Product management within marketing
Activity	Component within a functional area	Accounts receivable within accounting Outbound shipping within transportation Promotion within product management
Task	Specific elements within an activity	Collections within accounts receivable Manifesting within outbound shipping Competitive analysis within promotion

determining whether the applications will be developed internally, purchased from an outside vendor, or a combination of the two.

Transaction and Decision-Support Systems

It is also important to distinguish between transaction-oriented systems used in monitoring distribution operations (e.g., order processing and inventory control) and decision-support systems (DSSs) which are decision-oriented and utilized in diagnostic analyses to assist in determining future actions. These two types of systems vary significantly with respect to purpose, frequency of use, computational overhead, and data requirements (quantity and level of detail). Generally, these systems operate separately and on different equipment; for example, the transaction-oriented system will run on mainframe or minicomputers, while DSSs are resident on micro- or hand-held computers. Despite these differences, however, it is essential to allow for interaction between the two systems and to develop database structures that both systems can utilize.

A modular distribution information system with four sources of data, i.e., order processing, company records, industry and management information, has been reproduced in Fig. 5-7. Examples of database contents and report-generating capabilities are presented in Figs. 5-8 and 5-9.

Implementation

The final step to ensure successful systems implementation is to establish an installation team and schedule that will be endorsed and supported by all levels of management.

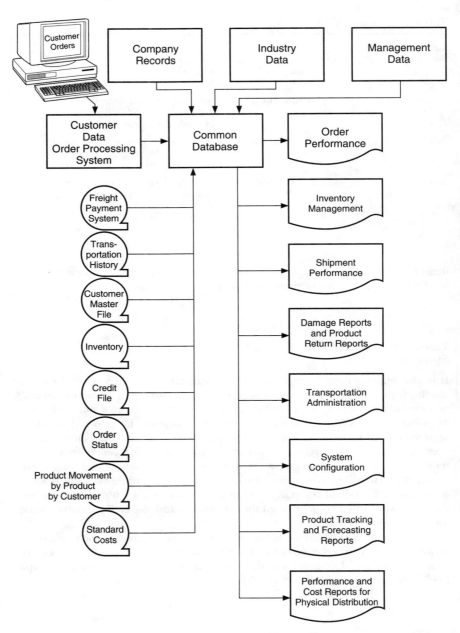

Figure 5-7. A physical distribution information system. (*From American Telephone & Telegraph Company, Business Marketing, Market Management Division, 1981, as shown in James R. Stock and Douglas M. Lambert,* Strategic Logistics Management, *2d ed., Homewood, IL: Richard D. Irwin, 1987, p. 521.*)

Customer Order Data
Customer number
Customer name
Order number
Previous order number
Customer order number
Customer billing address
Customer shipping address
Customer order date
Requested shipping date
Date product reserved
Date released to distribution center
Date picked/packed
Ship date
Date, time, and operator
Priority code
Salesperson number
Territory
Region
Partial ship back order number
Credit limit
Credit outstanding
Prepaid/collect freight
Terms
Instructions regarding shipping and product substitutions
Quantity, product number, price
Packing and shipping instructions
Transportation commodity classification
Carrier
Bill of lading number

Figure 5-8. Information that may be recorded in the modular database by customer order. (*From James R. Stock and Douglas M. Lambert,* Strategic Logistics Management, *2d ed., Homewood, IL: Richard D. Irwin, 1987, p. 525.*)

Distribution Software Solutions

One approach to automating distribution activities is to utilize one or more commercially available software packages. While most packaged solutions will require some degree of customization to address the unique characteristics of each company, the use of vendor software may be preferable to developing the system in-house.

The availability of commercial software to support the distribution function has increased dramatically during the last decade. This section presents a profile of the distribution software market.

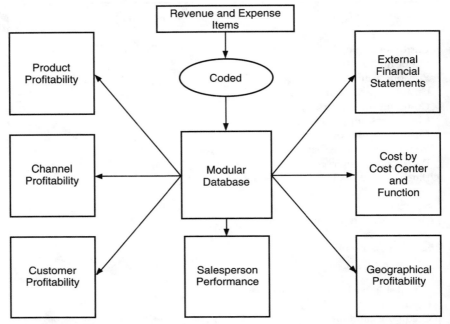

Figure 5-9. Report-generating capabilities of the modular database. (*From James R. Stock and Douglas M. Lambert,* Strategic Logistics Management, *2d ed., Homewood, IL: Richard D. Irwin, 1987, p. 528.*)

Vendor/Package Trends

As reflected in Fig. 5-10, the number of logistics software vendors grew almost exponentially from 1981 through 1989, but decreased nearly 10 percent per year during 1990 and 1991. The recent reductions are believed to be a result of a combination of merger/acquisition activity that occurred during the last two years, as well as vendors electing to redirect their business focus or cease operations in view of recessionary economic conditions.

The data in Fig. 5-10 indicate that the number of software packages—in total and for each type of platform (mainframe, minicomputer, microcomputer)—also grew significantly until 1990, with more than a thousand offerings available. As with the software vendors, however, the number of packages declined from 1990 to 1991—in fact, nearly 15 percent fewer packages were reported.

Functionality Trends

Logistics software addresses one or more individual functions—for example, order processing, inventory management, transportation, warehousing—plus related management functions. Trends in software functionality considering individual logistics functions are depicted in Table 5-5.

It should be pointed out that while the packages heavily support the traditional

VENDORS

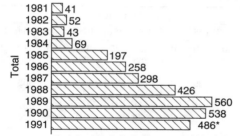

*Includes 149 offering packages on multiple platforms. Total of 337 different vendors.

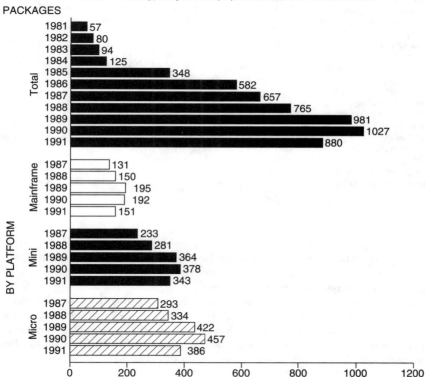

Figure 5-10. U.S. logistics software and suppliers—mainframe, mini, and micro systems. (*From the Council of Logistics Management, Chicago, "Survey of Software for Physical Distribution"; Proceedings of the 18th through 28th Annual Conferences.*)

logistics functions (order processing, inventory management, transportation, and warehousing), related functionality is becoming increasingly important, i.e., purchasing, promotion and deal accounting, and electronic data interchange (EDI).

Many systems support multiple logistics functions, as indicated in Table 5-6. It should be noted from the weighted average values that, considering all platforms, 4.5 of the 18 logistics functions (25 percent) are supported by the "average" soft-

Table 5-5. Logistics Software Functionality

Functions supported	Number of packages										
	1981	1982	1983	1984	1985	1986	1987	1988	1989	1990	1991
Order processing	18	24	30	50	125	234	257	325	423	440	378
Inventory control	26	31	38	58	153	288	322	378	496	526	452
Inventory planning and forecasting	7	11	29	29	95	184	213	246	349	363	318
Traffic routing and scheduling	24	28	33	29	96	91	112	159	200	237	200
Transportation analysis	10	10	25	33	78	172	211	194	244	236	217
Freight rate maintenance and audit	10	15	19	23	52	89	106	116	152	134	137
Vehicle maintenance	—*	—	—	—	—	42	98	82	128	136	106
Warehouse management	—	—	—	—	—	—	—	—	—	80	132
DC operations	9	13	26	21	104	—	—	—	—	—	—
Labor performance	—	—	—	—	—	60	118	148	196	227	208
Material handling	—	—	—	—	—	49	45	89	111	135	123
Stock/pallet location	—	—	—	—	—	104	142	184	246	293	249
System modeling	11	9	23	25	59	76	49	91	115	121	103
Distribution requirements planning	—	—	—	—	—	42	36	78	162	186	159
Materials requirements planning	—	—	—	—	—	—	42	93	156	178	155
Purchasing	—	—	—	—	—	—	156	231	340	381	329
Electronic data interchange	—	—	—	—	—	—	—	—	67	126	179
Promotions and deals	—	—	—	—	—	—	—	—	—	54	71
Special services/other	—	—	—	—	—	30	53	69	291	335	411

*— = not applicable.

ware package. Mainframes support about the same number of functions as the combined platform average; minicomputers support one additional function on average, while microcomputers support one less.

The most common combinations are order processing plus the inventory management functions, followed by multiple transportation functions. Most combinations involve functions at similar decision levels—that is, strategic, tactical or operational (such as order processing and inventory control); few systems offer functions at different levels (such as order processing and systems modeling).

Platform Trends

Table 5-7 indicates the functionality by platform for the logistics packages reported in 1991. The greater use of minicomputers compared to mainframes can be noted for all functions supported, particularly for order processing and inventory management. Microcomputers are increasingly being used in transportation/traffic management activities and for modeling applications.

A final observation concerns the type of computer systems supporting logistics software. IBM is predominant in both the mainframe, minicomputer, and microcomputer markets. Other major systems vendors include (alphabetically) Data

Table 5-6. Logistics Software Multiple Functionality—1991

Number of functions	Computer systems			
	Mainframe	Mini	Micro	Total
1	34	60	124	218
2	28	27	66	121
3	20	36	52	108
4	11	27	45	83
5	12	31	18	61
6	7	39	16	62
7	7	32	18	57
8	6	24	14	44
9	7	24	13	44
10	6	15	6	27
11	4	7	5	16
12	1	9	2	12
13	2	7	2	11
14	4	1	1	6
15	1	3	1	5
16	1	1	2	4
17	0	0	0	0
18	0	1	1	2
Weighted average	4.4	5.4	3.5	4.5

General, Digital Equipment, Hewlett-Packard, Honeywell, and Unisys, plus Apple for microcomputers. A lesser number of packages also run on other vendor hardware; a few can be accessed only on a time-sharing basis.

Additional Catalogs

Another reference source for identifying trends in logistics information systems development is the Distribution/Computer Expo, held annually during May in Chicago. The vendors and systems exhibited annually since 1985 are profiled in Table 5-8. It is noteworthy that while there were fewer vendors in 1991 compared to 1990, the number of system applications exhibited increased by more than 10 percent.

Several trade publications also offer catalogs of logistics-related software, as summarized in Table 5-9. It should be noted that *Traffic Management* offers the most "independent" catalog; the others typically summarize other sources (for example, the Distribution/Computer Expo). The first catalog published in 1984 contained nearly 200 software and services listings; in 1991, the total increased to more than 450 listings.

Summary

The following five points summarize the distribution software market:

1. Logistics software availability has increased substantially. From the Council of Logistics Management's *Annual Software Surveys:*

Table 5-7. Logistics Software Functionality by Platform—1991

Functions supported	Mainframe	Mini	Micro
Order processing	55	209	114
Inventory control	68	238	146
Inventory planning and forecasting	63	165	90
Traffic routing and scheduling	43	70*	87
Transportation analysis	41	55*	121
Freight rate maintenance and audit	28	50	59*
Vehicle maintenance	13	43	50
Warehouse management	24*	68*	40*
DC labor performance	37	102	69
DC material handling	26	57	40
DC stock/pallet location	42	135	72
Distribution system modeling	24	23	56
Distribution requirements planning	37	73	49
Materials requirements planning	27	68	60*
Purchasing	48	182	99
Electronic data interchange	30*	95*	54*
Promotions and deals	16*	41*	14*
Special services/other	65	189*	157*

*Increase compared to 1990

- The number of packages has increased more than 15 times since 1981, with approximately 1000 offerings currently available.
- The number of vendors has increased nearly 12 times since 1981, with a current total of more than 500 different companies.

From the Distribution/Computer Expo profiles:

- The number of vendors has increased by more than 75 percent since 1985.
- The number of packages has almost doubled since 1985.

2. The functional area most often supported is inventory management, followed by order processing, transportation, and warehousing.

3. Microcomputer software historically has been utilized for single, stand-alone applications; increasingly, however, microprocessor systems are used to handle multiple applications, thereby rivaling the capabilities of mini- and mainframe computers.

4. Microcomputer-based systems have experienced the greatest growth, and now represent 44 percent of the total number of logistics information systems; minicomputer software represents 39 percent of the total, while mainframe systems account for 17 percent.

5. Considering all logistics applications and computer platforms, over a thousand packages have been identified that address one or more application areas.

Integrated Logistics Systems

To determine the status of integrated logistics systems, a survey of U.S. manufacturers and merchandisers was first made in 1985, the results of which were reported in

Table 5-8. Distribution Computer/Expo Vendors and Systems: 1985 to 1991

	1985	1986	1987	1988	1989	1990	1991
Total vendors	79	97	113	133	152	148	139
System Applications							
Air freight	1	5	1	5	1	2	7
Bar coding	—	3	5	17	9	13	12
Computer systems/voice response	—	—	—	—	—	12	12
Consulting	—	—	—	—	—	10	17
Costing, barge	2	—	2	1	1	1	1
Costing, motor carrier	4	9	6	7	5	8	9
Costing, rail	5	4	5	4	2	2	4
Courier services	1	1	8	6	4	6	—
Distribution finance	39	28	22	32	24	22	29
Distribution management	25	26	39	54	59	56	67
Distribution requirements planning	—	8	5	8	9	9	13
Electronic data interchange	14	13	29	55	52	51	42
Freight consolidation	7	8	9	10	11	11	11
Freight payment	18	22	27	33	33	35	43
Import/export	8	9	6	9	16	14	13
Inbound transportation	—	—	—	—	—	3	9
Inventory management	11	13	7	10	8	8	11
Modeling	14	—	—	—	—	—	—
Motor carrier services	3	7	5	13	20	27	28
Order handling	9	8	9	11	10	9	8
Parcel shipping	3	3	1	3	3	2	5
Purchasing	4	5	9	12	10	7	10
Rail fleet management	16	15	18	22	17	24	13
Rating/storage/retrieval	40	42	47	58	49	50	48
Routing	9	4	5	13	14	13	18
Satellite tracking	—	—	—	—	—	4	4
Transportation management	9	18	21	34	48	56	64
Truck fleet management	39	38	50	58	40	35	28
Vehicle scheduling	7	8	10	13	13	14	13
Warehousing	10	22	8	11	13	21	43
Miscellaneous	4	6	6	1	—	—	—
Totals	302	325	360	500	471	525	582

NOTES:

1. The numbers reflect the vendors and systems contained in the published catalog; additions and deletions are not included.

2. Because many vendors offer multiple packages for a range of computers, packages may appear in several applications.

the *23rd Annual Conference Proceedings* of the Council of Logistics Management. A survey identical to one made in 1985 was conducted in 1990 to assess progress during the previous five years in implementing integrated systems; the results of the second survey were reported in the *28th Annual Conference Proceedings* of the Council of Logistics Management. Table 5-10 compares the 1985 and 1990 survey profiles.

Response rates for both surveys were substantial—i.e., 32 percent in 1985 and 39 percent in 1990. The number of usable responses for both surveys (82 and 121, respectively) also allowed meaningful statistical comparisons to be made.

To compare the 1985 and 1990 survey findings, it was first necessary to ensure

...

Table 5-9. Logistics Software Catalogs

Publication	Description	Dates
Traffic Management	11 application categories: Order processing Inventory management DC/warehouse management Logistics management Fleet management Freight rate maintenance/audit Distribution system modeling DRP Services EDI (added in 1988) International logistics (added in 1989)	May 1989–1991 Jan 1984–87
Transportation and Distribution (formerly *Handling & Shipping Management*)	Highlights and summarizes Distribution/Computer Expo held annually in May	May 1984–90 April 1991
Distribution	First catalogs in 1980 to 1985; minimal coverage since 1985, other than brief summaries of annual Distribution/Computer Expo	Jan–Dec 1987 Feb 1984–85
Inbound Logistics	Focus on applications for inbound traffic management	March–Aug 1987 March 1986

that the respondent bases were similar. Accordingly eight respondent characteristics were considered:

1. Industry classification
2. Primary business
3. Annual sales
4. Logistics organization
5. DP/MIS organization
6. Percent of sales spent on logistics
7. Percent of logistics costs spent on systems
8. Respondent position

For each characteristic, Chi-square statistical tests were conducted at the 95-percent level of confidence to compare the responses for the two years. Since no sig-

Table 5-10. Survey Profiles—1985 and 1990

	1985	1990
Targeted population	285	345
Survey respondents:		
Total	91	133
Usable	82	121
Identified	65	103

nificant differences were indicated for any of the eight characteristics, comparisons between the two respondent bases could be made.

Four areas of interest were examined to establish five-year trends in integrated logistics:

1. "Integrated Logistics Concept" interpretation
2. Success in implementing integrated logistics systems
3. Elements of integrated logistics information systems
4. Ingredients for successful implementation

The first four questions requested numerical responses using a 7-point Likert scale (high = 7, low = 1, average = 4). Mean values were calculated for each question, and comparisons made considering all respondents, e.g., 82 and 121, such that large sample sizes would exist. Two-tailed statistical tests at the 95-percent level of confidence, using the normal distribution, were then made to determine if significant differences existed between the mean values reported in 1985 and 1990.

"Integrated Logistics Concept" Interpretation

Figure 5-11 depicts the differences in interpretation of the "Integrated Logistics Concept." Organizational implications have become increasingly important, and have become virtually the same as the association with information systems.

Success in Implementing Integrated Logistics Systems

Figures 5-12, 5-13, and 5-14 indicate the degree of success in implementing integrated logistics systems. The three central findings are:

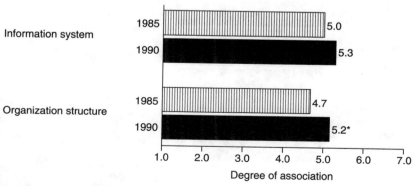

*Significant increase at 95% confidence level

Figure 5-11. "Integrated logistics concept" interpretation.

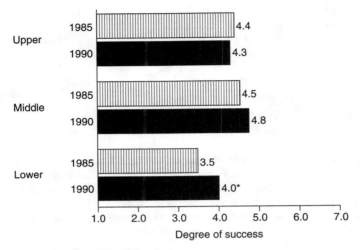

*Significant increase at 95% confidence level

Figure 5-12. Level of management.

1. As shown in Fig. 5-12, lower management has seen increasing levels of success (although the current perception is only "average"), such that their viewpoint approaches the perceptions of middle and upper management.

2. Figure 5-13 indicates that no significant difference in degree of success was reported by respondents at any of the three locations, although branch/local perceptions were somewhat less positive than at headquarters or group/division level.

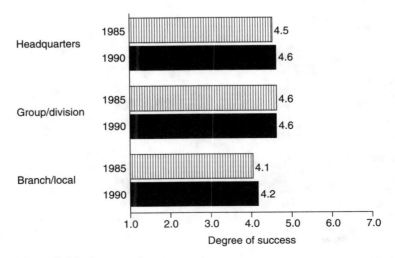

Figure 5-13. Location of management.

3. Figure 5-14 suggests that, for all logistics functions, the degree of success was unchanged during the five-year period; however, transportation/traffic did exhibit a trend toward greater success as compared to the other three logistics functions.

Elements of Integrated Logistics Information Systems

Seven perspectives were examined regarding the scope of integrated logistics information systems.

1. Figure 5-15 suggests that both customer service and warehousing data increased in importance over the five-year period; the importance of data from the other logistics activities was unchanged.

2. Figure 5-16 indicates that, while the importance of data decreased as decision making moved from the operational to the strategic level, the importance of strategic information itself increased significantly.

3. Manufacturing/production data were the most important of all related functional area information, as depicted in Fig. 5-17; purchasing data increased significantly in importance over the last five years, and was viewed as being as important as marketing/sales data.

4. Figure 5-18 reflects the growing role of micro/personal computers, rivaling or even exceeding the importance of minicomputers; however, the mainframe was still the most important database location.

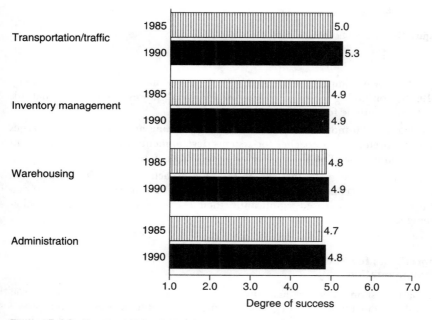

Figure 5-14. Functions within logistics.

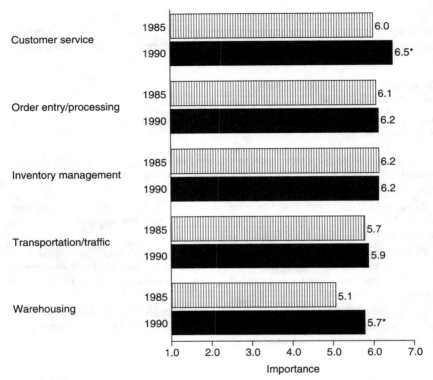

*Significant increase at 95% confidence level

Figure 5-15. Logistics activity data.

5. The greater importance of on-line/interactive data access is portrayed in Fig. 5-19; the continuing use of batch was also indicated, however, suggesting that this mode will continue for specific applications.

6. Figure 5-20 indicates that in-house programming and customized packages were the preferred approaches for systems development; however, the significant increase in the use of off-the-shelf software should be noted.

7. Figure 5-21 suggests that the preferred approach to system implementation entailed use of a combination of logistics and MIS/DP staffs; while the use of outside consultants increased significantly, their overall importance was still below average.

Ingredients for Successful Implementation

The last question requested qualitative responses regarding the ingredients for successful implementation of integrated logistics. The profile of respondent replies is shown in Table 5-11. The top four categories—which represented more than three-

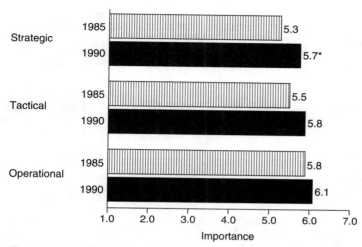

*Significant increase at 95% confidence level

Figure 5-16. Decision level data.

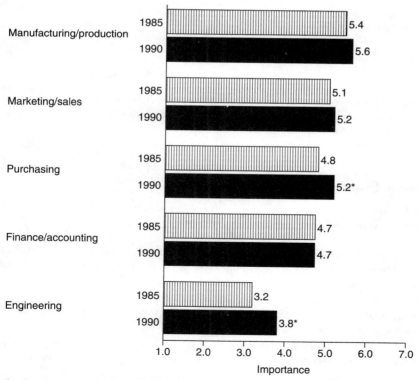

*Significant increase at 95% confidence level

Figure 5-17. Related functional area data.

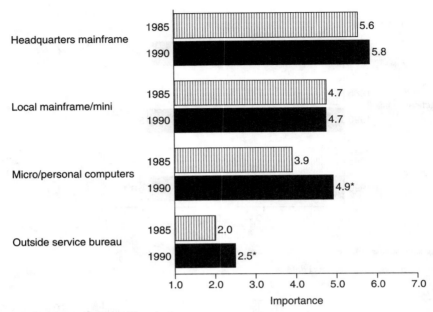

*Significant increase at 95% confidence level

Figure 5-18. Location of databases.

fourths of all responses—were similar to the results reported in 1985. As can be seen, the continuing importance of management commitment was emphasized by nearly half of all survey participants.

Survey Summary

The following points summarize the results of the survey research and subsequent interviews with a selected sample of respondents:

- Integrated systems should allow for interaction between a company's information and human resources; the information system must reflect and be responsive to the organizational structure.
- Success is most likely when integrated systems are designed and implemented on a modular basis; integration priorities will reflect the unique requirements of each specific company.
- While individual logistics activities have high and comparable levels of importance, customer service and warehousing have become increasingly important.
- Operational data is still most critical, although strategic-level data is increasing in importance; a similar comment applies to the importance of data for use by lower management personnel.

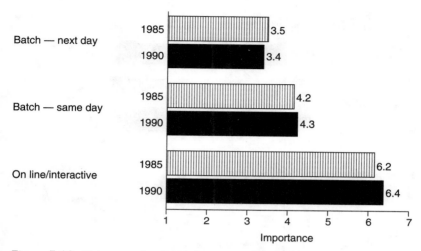

Figure 5-19. Data access/inquiry mode.

- Of the related corporate functions to be integrated with logistics, manufacturing/production is the first priority, followed by marketing/sales; purchasing is becoming increasingly important, while the finance/accounting area does not require additional attention.

- While centralized databases are still essential, the use of local, personal computing is gaining rapidly in importance.

- The use of internal resources continues to be preferred for system development; however, packaged software is increasingly a viable alternative.

- Successful systems implementation requires a coordinated effort between logistics and data processing; of comparable importance are the continued support of top management, corporate-wide communication/coordination, user involvement and training, plus sufficient time and resources (financial and human).

The summary observation to be drawn from this research is that only gradual progress has been made in implementing truly integrated distribution systems. These findings are consistent with the results of a separate survey conducted in 1988, and based on the responses from 421 U.S. distribution practitioners responsible for logistics planning; the conclusion reached from the 1988 survey was that " . . . fully integrated logistics systems are evolving in industry. . . . The degree of attainment of the modern system is rather low in current practice. . . . "[13]

Conclusion

Perhaps James H. Perry has said it best:

> Logistics managers must fully exploit the capabilities of information processing and communications technologies. This will require greater involvement in the design of management information systems.[14]

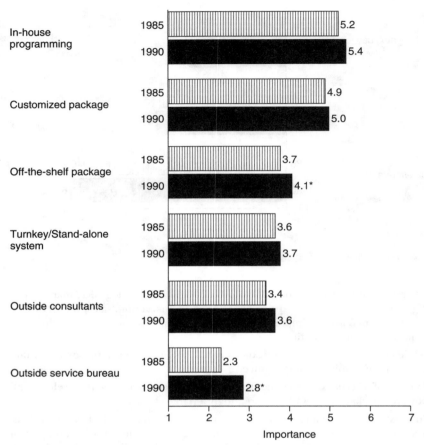

*Significant change at 95% confidence level

Figure 5-20. System development approach.

The distribution function represents a significant improvement opportunity for American business. In this chapter the challenges to implementing distribution systems were documented, as were the levels of expenditures for information systems that support the distribution function. In addition, a definition and descriptions for a distribution information system were presented. By adopting a design approach similar to the one described, a distribution information system can be developed that supports the specific needs of each company. And by proceeding in a modular fashion and implementing those applications that have been designated by management as having the greatest potential benefit for the firm, successful distribution systems should be the final result. While a plethora of distribution software is commercially available to assist in logistics decision making, a thorough analysis of internal development versus outside purchase should be completed for all planned

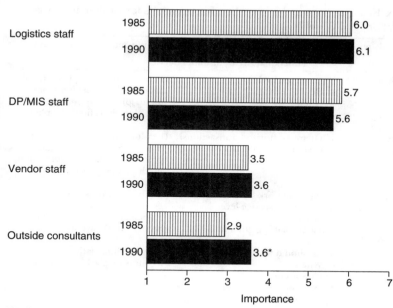

*Significant change at 95% confidence level

Figure 5-21. System implementation approach.

applications to ensure that the optimal alternative is selected. Although progress to date in implementing integrated systems has been somewhat disappointing, a sound framework has been established for developing improved distribution systems in the future.

Table 5-11. Ingredients for Successful Implementation of Integrated Logistics

Ingredient category	Responses	
	Number	Percent
Management commitment/support	54	45
Communications/teamwork/cooperation/coordination	21	17
Understanding/acceptance of concept	11	9
User participation in design/implementation	7	6
Education/training	4	3
Maintaining customer focus	3	2
Use of steering committee/task force	2	2
Recognition of logistics function	2	2
Miscellaneous (one each)	10	8
No response	7	6
Total	121	100

Appendix Key Questions and Information Requirements for Customer Service, Transportation, and Warehousing

Key activity	Key questions	Information requirements
	Functional Area: Customer Service	
Role definition	What are we to do? How? When? At what cost?	Corporate business plan, organizational chart, mission statement, job descriptions, goals and objectives, financial plan.
Order entry	What are authorized transactions? How should they occur?	Decision rules, customer information, product information, price/promotional information, methods and procedures.
Order processing	What is the work load? What are the service level objectives? What are staffing guidelines?	Number of orders to be processed, capacity compared to volume, through-put requirements—peak/average/low.
Invoicing	What should we bill? When? How accurately? How do we document and process corrections?	Shipping information. Accounts-receivable feedback.
Post-sale support	What support is required? How is it furnished?	Claims procedure. Return goods/replacement policy.
	Functional Area: Transportation	
Role definition	What are we to do? How? When? At what cost?	Corporate business plan, organizational chart, mission statement, job descriptions, goals and objectives, financial plan.
Freight classification	What are product shipping characteristics? Appropriate freight classifications? Are bills of lading correct? Do we comply with regulations?	Product weight, cube, dimensions, fragility, toxicity, combustibility. Tariffs. DOT/ICC/PUC rules.
Negotiation rates and services	Which carriers are qualified? What are their cost and service histories? What should we/can we negotiate? How do we track rates and services?	Tariffs, contracts. Traffic flow and cost data. Carrier cost structures. Alternative modes/carriers. Service histories.
Shipment routing	Which is the best carrier for each shipment?	Routing guide. Carrier performance.
Tracing/expediting	How do we locate shipments in-transit?	Routing guide. In-transit shipments status. Carrier contact points.

Key activity	Key questions	Information requirements
	Functional Area: Transportation (*Continued*)	
Auditing freight bills	Are we paying correct freight charges?	Bills of lading. Freight bills. Governing tariffs/contracts.
Claims handling	Are we recovering Freight charge overpayments? Carrier-liable loss and damage?	Signed bills of lading. Originating freight bills. Noted delivery receipt. Inspection report. Invoice value. Disposition of material.
Private fleet operation	What number and kind of transportation equipment should we operate? Should we own or lease? How do we schedule their use? What measures of utilization and performance should we employ?	Cost data for alternatives. Private and for-hire alternatives. Standards of operation for over-the-road and pick-up-and-delivery. Fleet performance measurement system.
	Functional Area: Warehousing	
Role definition	What are we to do? How? When? At what cost?	Corporate business plan, organizational chart, mission statement, job descriptions, goals and objectives, financial plan.
Receiving	How do we schedule, unload, inspect, and verify the quantity and condition of material?	Purchase orders. Product characteristics. Methods and procedures. Work load forecasts.
Storage	How is material assigned a storage location and physically relocated there?	Stock location system. Physical and demand characteristics of product. Engineered material-handling system.
Order-picking	What is the best method for scheduling and picking an order?	Size, quantity, and sequence of orders/lines to be picked. Time, manpower, and equipment available. Comparison of customer order. Picking document and available inventory.
Packing	How much space, labor, and material is required to effectively unitize multiple lines of orders, and multiple customer orders at an acceptable throughput rate?	Work load forecasts. Standard packing rates. Picking sequence schedule. Shipping schedule. Packing material usage rates.
Shipping	How do we schedule, load, and document order shipments?	Shipping orders. Bills of lading. Availability and capacity of dock. Carrier information, signatures.

5.32   Management Overview

Notes

1. 1992 data extrapolated from data developed by Robert V. Delaney of Cass Logistics, Inc., and reported in *Inbound Logistics,* July 1991, p. 3.

2. Extracted from the Herbert W. Davis distribution cost database, plus the author's 1982, 1987, and 1992 research databases on Logistics Information Systems.

3. Donald J. Bowersox, David J.Closs and Omar K. Helferich, *Logistical Management,* 2d ed., Macmillan Publishing Co., New York, 1986, pp. 4–5.

4. James R. Stock and Douglas M. Lambert, *Strategic Physical Distribution Management,* Richard D. Irwin, Homewood, Illinois, 1982, p. 323.

5. Craig M. Gustin, "Logistics Information Systems: An Appraisal of Historical Trends, Present Status, and Future Directions," Ph.D. dissertation, Golden Gate University, 1983, p. 4.

6. Tom Dulaney, "Distribution's Movers Clamor for Computerized Help," *Distribution,* August 1987, p. 38.

7. The first set of estimates was developed by Coopers & Lybrand and the author using the following assumptions:

   - 1989 Global Domestic Product (GDP) = $20 trillion
   - Of GDP, Agriculture = 6 percent, Industry = 34 percent, Services = 60 percent
   - Relevant segments for analysis are Agriculture = 6 percent, Industry = 34 percent, and Services = 20 percent; total = 60 percent
   - Logistics costs as a percent of GDP = 7.2 percent (average percent of sales for U.S. companies)
   - Logistics information systems costs as a percent of logistics costs = 6.2 percent (extracted from the author's 1982, 1987, and 1992 research databases on Logistics Information Systems)
   - 1990 expenditures = $20,000 billion × .60 × .072 × .06 = $51.8 billion
   - 2000 expenditures based on compound annual growth rate of 3.1 percent.
   - The estimate of $215 billion by the year 2000 appeared in a 1990 publication by David L. Anderson and Robert G. House entitled *Logistics and Material Handling Systems in the United States: Trends and Future Outlook.*

8. Tom Tinsley and Andrew C. Power, "Why IS Should Matter to CEOs," *Datamation,* September 1, 1990, p. 4.

9. David G. DeRoulet, "Logistics managers should be information architects," *Handling and Shipping Management,* August 1987, p. 53.

10. Extracted from the author's 1982, 1987, 1992 research databases on Logistics Information Systems.

11. John Dearden, "MIS Is a Mirage," in *Information Systems Administration,* eds. F. Warren McFarlan, Richard L. Nolan, and David P. Norton, Holt, Rinehart and Winston, New York, 1973, p. 75.

12. Paul S. Bender, "Logistics Systems Design," *Distribution Handbook,* The Free Press, New York, 1985, pp. 213–215.

13. Kenneth C. Williamson, Donald M. Spitzer, Jr., and David J. Bloomberg, "Modern Logistics Systems: Theory and Practice," *Journal of Business Logistics,* vol. 11, no. 2 (1990), p. 79.

14. James H. Perry, "Emerging Economic and Technological Futures: Implications for Design and Management of Logistics System in the 1990s," *Journal of Business Logistics,* vol. 12, no. 2 (1991), p. 14.

6

Distribution Requirements Planning

André J. Martin
President and CEO, LogiCNet

This chapter* explains the DRP (distribution resource planning) process and how it is used to solve problems in logistics, manufacturing, and purchasing. The nuts-and-bolts details will not be covered here, as there is not sufficient space. Here we focus on the ABCs of DRP logic and how it compares to the traditional reorder-point concept.

The Logic of DRP: The Big Picture

DRP is a management process that determines the needs of inventory stocking locations (ISLs)† and ensures that supply sources will be able to meet the demand. This is accomplished in three distinct phases. First, DRP receives input from the following:

---

*Reprinted From Chapter 3 of *DRP: Distribution Resource Planning*, with permission of Oliver Wright Limited Publications, Inc.

†For the purpose of this explanation, an inventory stocking location (ISL) can be any store, distribution center (DC), regional distribution center (RDC), central DC, manufacturing DC, or warehouse that maintains product for sale. The supply source can be a third party supplier, a regional distribution point, or a factory. In this chapter, the term *supply source* is used generically.

- Sales forecasts by stock keeping unit (SKU) by ISL
- Customer orders for current and future delivery
- Available inventory for sale by SKU by ISL
- Outstanding purchase orders and/or manufacturing orders by product purchased and/or manufactured
- Logistics, manufacturing, and purchasing lead times
- Modes of transport used, as well as deployment frequencies
- Safety stock policies by SKU by ISL
- Normal minimum quantity of product to be purchased, manufactured, and distributed.

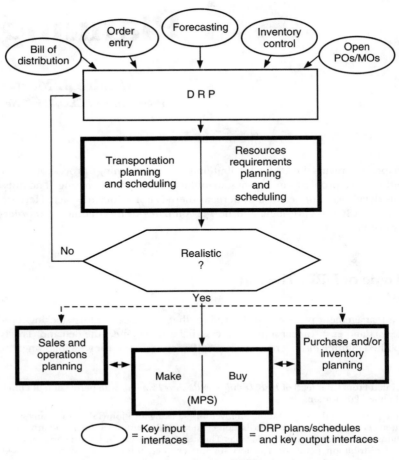

Figure 6-1. The distribution resource planning (DRP) management process.

Second, once all inputs have been received, DRP generates a time-phased model of resource requirements to support the logistics strategy. These include:

- Which product is needed, how much, and where and when it is needed
- Transportation capacity needed by mode of transport by ISL
- Needed space, manpower, and equipment capacity by ISL
- Required inventory investment by ISL and in total
- Required level of production and/or purchases, by product and by supply source

Third, DRP compares the required resources to what is currently available at supply sources, and what will be available in the future. It then recommends what actions must be taken to expedite or delay purchases and/or production, thereby synchronizing supply and demand. This third phase forces integration and feedback into the system, thus closing the loop among manufacturing, purchasing, logistics, and the customers.

DRP Logic: The Math

At the core of this management process is a very simple, yet very powerful, logic. Its power is not found in math calculations, but in the overall system's ability to time-phase future activities, predict possible outcomes, critique ongoing activities, and recommend action.

Here's how the logic works. Let's assume you're a retail store manager, and you have been asked to predict when you will run out of product. The data given to you states that you will sell a given item at the rate of 200 per week. You have 500 on hand and 600 in transit, due to arrive at your store next week. If asked how long your inventory will last, your response probably will be, "Roughly five and a half weeks." In a nutshell, that's how the math of DRP works. *It attempts to predict future shortages, then recommends action to avoid them.* Figure 6-1 shows the entire DRP management process. All of the components are described in this chapter.

DRP in Action

The math behind DRP is very simple. Let's look at an actual example of how DRP is used to plan and replan shipments to an ISL. The sample company manufactures, distributes, and sells pharmaceuticals and supports a network of six retail stores. Specifically, we'll track the planning for vitamin C tablets packaged in bottles of 100. The Los Angeles store has 500 of this product on hand, 200 as a safety stock, and a forecast that varies between 80 and 120 per week (Fig. 6-2).

In Fig. 6-2, the projected on-hand balance is determined by means of the simple computations described earlier. The logic reduces the on-hand balance by the quantities forecast for each week. In the beginning of the first week, for example, 500 are on hand. Forecast sales for the week are 100; they are subtracted from the 500 on hand, leaving a projected balance of 400 at the beginning of the next week. The same mechanism ripples through the schedule. The projected on-hand bal-

On-Hand Balance   — 500
Safety Stock   — 200

		Week							
	Past Due	1	2	3	4	5	6	7	8
Forecast		100	120	90	110	120	100	80	120
In Transit									
Projected On-Hand	500	400	280	190	80	-40			

Figure 6-2. Los Angeles store–no product in transit.

ance dips below the safety stock of 200 in week 3 (projected on-hand balance of 190), at which point the store will probably run out of stock and go on backorder in week 5.

In the sample in Fig. 6-2, no product is in transit. If that were the case, the product in transit would be added to the projected on-hand balance in the week that it is due to arrive. (Some of the later examples will include a quantity in transit.)

The situation shown in Fig. 6-2 will occur if nothing is shipped from the supply source. The store manager needs more of the product delivered in week 3 to keep the balance from dropping below safety stock, which means that more product must arrive by week 5 to keep the product from going on backorder.

The replenishment lead time for vitamin C at the Los Angeles store is two weeks, and normally 300 bottles, or four full cases, are shipped at a time. Therefore, a shipment of 300 units must arrive in week 3 to prevent the inventory from dropping below the desired safety-stock level. Since the replenishment lead time is two weeks, the shipment should be ordered from the supply source in week 1. Figure 6-3 includes this planned shipment (i.e., future order) from the supply source in the two lines labeled Plnd. Shpmts. One shows the planned shipments on the date they are

On-Hand Balance   —   500
Safety Stock   —   200
Lead Time   —   2 wks
Order Quantity   —   300

		Week							
	Past Due	1	2	3	4	5	6	7	8
Forecast		100	120	90	110	120	100	80	120
In Transit									
Project On-Hand	500	400	280	490	380	260	160	80	-40
Plnd. Shpmts.-Rcpt. Date				300					
Plnd. Shpmts.-Ship Date		300							

Figure 6-3. Los Angeles store (includes planned shipments).

On-Hand Balance — 500
Safety Stock — 200
Lead Time — 2 wks
Order Quantity — 300

	Past Due	\multicolumn{8}{c}{Week}							
	Past Due	1	2	3	4	5	6	7	8
Forecast		100	120	90	110	120	100	80	120
In Transit									
Project On-Hand	500	400	280	490	380	260	460	380	260
Plnd. Shpmts.-Rcpt. Date				300			300		
Plnd. Shpmts.-Ship Date		300			300				

Figure 6-4. Los Angeles store—the complete picture.

due to arrive at the store (Plnd. Shpmts.—Rcpt. date). The other shows the planned shipments on the date they are due to be shipped from the supply source (Plnd. Shpmts.—Ship Date).

The planned shipments provide enough stock to last until week 8, although the store will drop below safety stock in week 6. Therefore, another order must arrive in week 6. This order should be sent from the supply source in week 4. Figure 6-4 shows the complete picture for the vitamin C product at the Los Angeles store.

Now that we have seen how DRP functions in one store, let's expand it to all the stores for the vitamin C product.* The following examples (Figs. 6-5 through 6-10)

*The example includes six stores. There could be only 1 ISL, or as many as 82 if it were R. J. Reynolds, which uses DRP to manage and control cigarette inventories across the United States.

On-Hand Balance — 160
Safety Stock — 75
Lead Time — 2 wks
Order Quantity — 150

	Past Due	\multicolumn{8}{c}{Week}							
	Past Due	1	2	3	4	5	6	7	8
Forecast		40	50	45	50	40	45	40	50
In Transit			150						
Projected On-Hand	160	120	220	175	125	85	190	150	100
Plnd. Shpmts.-Rcpt. Date							150		
Plnd. Shpmts.-Ship Date					150				

Figure 6-5. Montreal store—order in transit.

On-Hand Balance — 300
Safety Stock   — 100
Lead Time   — 2 wks
Order Quantity — 300

	Past Due	| Week							
	Past Due	1	2	3	4	5	6	7	8
Forecast		120	130	115	125	140	110	125	105
In Transit									
Projected On-Hand	300	180	350	235	110	270	160	335	230
Plnd. Shpmts.-Rcpt. Date			300			300		300	
Plnd. Shpmts.-Ship Date	300			300		300			

Figure 6-6. New York store—order overdue for shipment.

show DRP displays for the other stores and are similar to the DRP display shown for the Los Angeles store.

In the case of the Montreal store in Fig. 6-5, an order of 150 is in transit. The order was shipped because the lead time is two weeks, and it is due to arrive in week 2. The in-transit quantity is added to the projected on-hand balance in the week the order is due to arrive. The store manager can now see what material is en route and when it should be expected.

In the case of the New York store (Fig. 6-6), a planned order is overdue for shipment. This is the planned shipment of 300, which appears in the past-due time period.

There could be several reasons for the past-due order. Perhaps sales were greater than forecasted, so the product was needed in New York earlier than anticipated.

On-Hand Balance — 140
Safety Stock   — 50
Lead Time   — 3 wks
Order Quantity — 150

	Past Due	| Week							
	Past Due	1	2	3	4	5	6	7	8
Forecast		20	25	15	20	30	25	15	30
In Transit									
Projected On-Hand	140	120	95	80	60	180	155	140	110
Plnd. Shpmts.-Rcpt. Date						150			
Plnd. Shpmts.-Ship Date			150						

Figure 6-7. Vancouver store.

On-Hand Balance — 120
Safety Stock — 50
Lead Time — 1 wk
Order Quantity — 150

		Week							
	Past Due	1	2	3	4	5	6	7	8
Forecast		25	15	20	25	25	20	25	15
In Transit									
Projected On-Hand	120	95	80	60	185	165	145	120	105
Plnd. Shpmts.-Rcpt. Date					150				
Plnd. Shpmts.-Ship Date				150					

Figure 6-8. Toronto store.

Or the shipment might not have been sent from the supply source on time. In that case, because of the visibility that DRP affords, the manager of the store could determine whether the supply source is shipping on time. Moreover, the manager could determine the problem well before a stockout occurs.

The situations at the Vancouver, Toronto, and Chicago stores, as shown in Figs. 6-7, 6-8, and 6-9, are similar to that at the Los Angeles store. Nothing is in transit, but there are several planned shipments from the supply source to the stores. The Chicago store is in the same city as the supply source, so its lead time for product is only one day.

The lead times, order quantities, and safety stocks are different for each store, so each store can be scheduled independently if desired. In addition the lead times, order quantities, and safety stocks can be different for different products at the

On-Hand Balance — 400
Safety Stock — 150
Lead Time — 1 day
Order Quantity — 300

		Week							
	Past Due	1	2	3	4	5	6	7	8
Forecast		105	115	95	90	100	110	95	120
In Transit									
Projected On-Hand	400	295	180	385	295	195	385	290	170
Plnd. Shpmts.-Rcpt. Date				300			300		
Plnd. Shpmts.-Ship Date				300			300		

Figure 6-9. Chicago store.

	Past Due	Week							
		1	2	3	4	5	6	7	8
Los Angeles		300			300				
Montreal					150				
New York	300			300		300			
Vancouver			150						
Toronto				150					
Chicago				300			300		
Totals	300	300	150	750	450	300	300	0	0

Figure 6-10. Summary of planned shipments to the stores.

same store. (This is not apparent in the figures, because only one of the many products is shown. Each product at each store, however, is scheduled independently.) As you can see, DRP gives the people operating the system complete flexibility in scheduling any item at any ISL.

In Figs. 6-8 and 6-9, forecasts for each store are nearly the same from week to week. Based on this, you might expect that the demand on the supply source would be smooth as well, with demand in any one week nearly the same as demands in other weeks. Yet the opposite is true. The demand on the supply source is lumpy. Figure 6-10 illustrates this point very well. For example, in week 2 the demand is only 150, but in week 3 it jumps to 750.

Lumpy demand is one of the reasons why it is so important to have visibility in the logistics system. Because the demand on the supply source can vary so much from one week to another, a planner or buyer needs to be able to see what product is needed and when it must be shipped to meet the needs of the stores in the system. Without DRP, buyers must use averages—hence the inevitability of lumpy demand. With DRP, however, buyers see the true needs of the logistics system. This gives tremendous visibility to the distribution network, and enables buyers to realistically plan for the needs of the store. The better buyers can see what the stores need in the future, the better they are able to meet those needs and resolve problems before they occur.

Flexibility through DRP

DRP can accommodate itself to the unique constraints of any business environment. The ultimate goal of DRP is to simulate the real world in a way that truly mirrors what the company does and what it wants to do in the future.

The ability to represent your own environment is a function of feeding DRP information from a bill-of-distribution module, similar to the one seen in Fig. 6-11. Users of this module define their future distribution network by indicating how many inventory stocking locations they want to manage, who the supply sources are, which products will be stocked in the various locations, what modes of transport will be used, the shipping frequency, the size of shipment, etc.

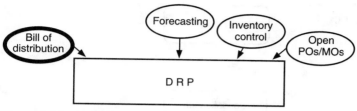

Figure 6-11. A typical bill-of-distribution module.

In some companies, the distribution network consists of only one location (in which case it really isn't a network). In others it contains three levels, as shown in Fig. 6-12. Regardless of the size or complexity of the network, DRP must have accurate and current information from the bill of distribution.

By including a bill of distribution in your DRP system, you actually induce a customer/supplier linkage. In other words, any change in any store will be passed on to its source of supply and become visible.

Managing Change

A key benefit of the visibility that DRP affords is the ability to react to change. As previously stated, the nature of the industrial pipeline is constant change. The most apparent change in the pipeline occurs when sales differ from the forecast. Such events do not cause problems for DRP, because the system not only plans each of the items in each of the stores and DCs, it also replans them continuously. In a DRP system, each item in each store or DC is replanned at least once a week. In some companies replanning takes place on a daily basis, so that people can respond quickly to change and handle large volumes of product to specific distribution points. (Companies such as Coca-Cola and R.J. Reynolds, which both use DRP, have no choice but to replan daily, given the enormous volume of product shipped from their factories to multiple distribution points every day. These are exceptions, though, and weekly replanning generally is sufficient in most situations.)

To illustrate the role of DRP in managing change, let's revisit the Los Angeles store, originally shown in Fig. 6-2. The first display in Fig. 6-13 shows a forecast of 100 in week 1. Let's assume that instead of selling the 100 that were forecast in week 1, 170 are actually sold. The following week the DRP display for this product at Los Angeles would change, as shown in the figure.

Because the sales are greater than the forecast, the planned shipments move up to earlier dates. The planned shipment of 300 due to arrive in week 6 is now needed in week 5, which is normal. In addition, a new planned shipment of 300 that did not exist in the previous week has been created for use in week 8.

In this case, the sales are so much greater than the forecast that the planned shipment dates are changed. This does not happen all the time—there must be a significant difference between what was sold and what was forecast, or the projected on-hand balance must be only slightly greater than the safety-stock level.

In Fig. 6-13, the Los Angeles store now has 300 units in transit (refer to Fig. 6-4 for original data). This 300 represents a planned shipment from the previous week.

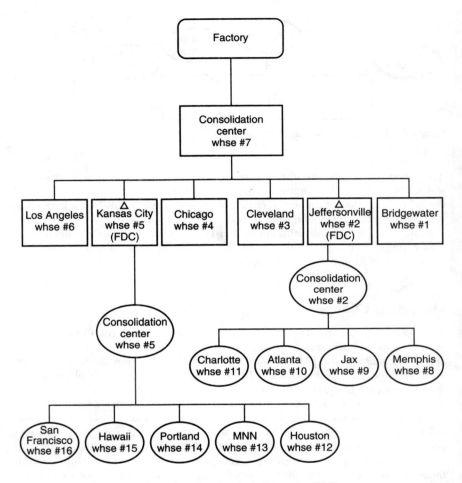

Δ = Factories planning dual roles—also FDCs.

Figure 6-12. A multitiered distribution network.

The order was shipped to Los Angeles, and now appears in transit under the week it is due to arrive.

As a result of the changes at the Los Angeles store, the total demands on the supply source have changed. Figure 6-14 shows the total demands from the previous week and the total demands for the current week.

The change in the total demands on the supply source went from 750 in week 3 to 1050; from 450 in week 4 to 150; and from 300 in week 6 up to 600. With this information, the inventory planner can determine the exact effect of the above-forecast sales in Los Angeles and other stores. The planner is also able to see the new demands on the supply source and can begin preparations to supply these needs. Conventional inventory management systems do not have this ability to look

BEFORE CHANGE IN DEMAND
On-Hand Balance — 500
Safety Stock — 200
Lead Time — 2 wks
Order Quantity — 300

		Week							
	Past Due	1	2	3	4	5	6	7	8
Forecast		100	120	90	110	120	100	80	120
In Transit									
Projected On-Hand	500	400	280	490	380	260	460	380	260
Plnd. Shpmts.-Rcpt. Date				300			300		
Plnd. Shpmts.-Ship Date		300			300				

AFTER CHANGE IN DEMAND
On-Hand Balance — 330
Safety Stock — 200
Lead Time — 2 wks
Order Quantity — 300

		Week							
	Past Due	1	2	3	4	5	6	7	8
Forecast		120	90	110	120	120	100	80	120
In Transit									
Projected On-Hand	330	210	420	310	310	490	390	310	490
Plnd. Shpmts.-Rcpt. Date						300			300
Plnd. Shpmts.-Ship Date			300				300		

Figure 6-13. Los Angeles store—DRP before and after changes in demand.

ahead accurately and revise the plan based on the changes that have occurred. The forward visibility offered by DRP allows buyers, master schedulers, and planners *to anticipate* what may change in the future rather than *react* to something that has already happened.

In the example just discussed from Fig. 6-14, the change to a planned shipment date occurred at one store (Los Angeles). In actual practice, it is likely that changes to planned shipments occurred during the week at several stores. It is even possible that a change to the planned shipments occurred at all the stores, although such a simultaneous set of changes is unlikely.

Sales that are greater or less than the forecast are not the only reasons that planned shipments change. Changes to the forecast quantities, safety stocks, lead times, and order quantities can cause the planned shipments to change. In other

BEFORE ABOVE-FORECAST SALES

	Past Due	Week							
		1	2	3	4	5	6	7	8
Los Angeles		300			300				
Montreal					150				
New York	300			300		300			
Vancouver			150						
Toronto				150					
Chicago				300			300		
TOTALS	300	300	150	750	450	300	300	0	0

AFTER ABOVE-FORECAST SALES

	Past Due	Week							
		2	3	4	5	6	7	8
Los Angeles			300			300		
Montreal				150				
New York			300		300			
Vancouver		150						
Toronto			150					
Chicago			300			300		
TOTALS	0	150	1050	150	300	300	0	0

Figure 6-14. Summary of planned shipments to the stores.

words, DRP picks up and reports any changes in the entire system. DRP can do this because it is a true simulation of a distribution network; it shows what is happening in the logistics system and what is predicted to occur.

DPR versus the Reorder Point

In this section, we'll demonstrate the difference between DRP and a reorder-point system. To make the comparison, we'll use the same data for the reorder point and DRP systems. Figure 6-15 shows a generic situation. Three locations, Chicago, Montreal, and New York, are ordering product from a supply source. This is a generic situation because it can represent virtually any company, whether it is a retailer owning three stores supported by a distribution center, a wholesaler operating three distribution centers supported by a regional or central distribution center, or a manufacturer operating three distribution centers supported by a factory.

Let's assume the company in the example is a wholesaler that operates three dis-

	Chicago	Montreal	New York
Inventory on hand	225	164	350
Forecast	115/wk	47/wk	125/wk
Reorder point	345	141	375
POQ	500	200	500
Supplier lead time	2 wks	2 wks	2 wks
		Supply Source (DC)	
Inventory on hand		1170	
Reorder point		1150	
Order quantity		2200	
Supplier lead time (factory)		3 wks	

Figure 6-15. Generic reorder-point model.

tribution centers and orders product from a manufacturer (the supply source). This manufacturer operates a number of distribution centers. In our example, Chicago, Montreal, and New York are all supplied from the same distribution center, owned and operated by the manufacturer. Both the wholesaler and manufacturer use the classic reorder-point formula—demand over lead time, plus safety stock—to manage and control inventory and order material.

The wholesaler uses a computerized inventory-control system that incorporates state-of-the-art techniques to dynamically compute and update reorder points and safety stocks, based on the most recent changes in actual sales versus forecasts. These reorder points and safety stocks are changed every week as necessary. In addition, reorder quantities are calculated for each distribution center on a period-order-quantity (POQ) rule of four-week supply. The POQ is then rounded to account for the minimum buy quantity of 100. For example, the four-week POQ for Chicago is 460, rounded to 500.

The wholesaler updates his data and makes buying decisions every Monday, taking into account sales for the previous week and inventory on hand as of the close of business Friday night. Before going further, it is important to mention that in this example, the wholesaler buys a product that is custom-packaged exclusively for him. Therefore, the only demand for this product at the supply source comes from Chicago, Montreal, and New York.

Consider what happens if you are responsible at the supply source for managing and controlling your inventory, as well as ordering from the factory. Are you okay? Are you in trouble? Do you need to do anything? You're all right, because you have 1170 on hand and your reorder point is 1150* (refer to Fig. 6-15). When your in-

---

*The reorder points in the three DCs and the supply source have all been calculated the same way:

$$(\text{demand} \times \text{lead time}) + \text{one week of safety stock}$$

For example, the supply-source reorder point in this example would be:

$$(287 \times 3) + 287 = 1148 \text{ (rounded to 1150)}$$

ventory reaches 1149 or less you will order from the factory, and when you do you will order 2200—that's your minimum, and the factory lead time is three weeks.

Now let's take a look at the wholesaler. Remember it's Monday morning, and the computer just printed out the data. The system is recommending two orders for approval, the first for Chicago and the second for New York. Both locations have gone below their respective reorder points. Montreal is okay at this time, so no action is recommended.

The wholesaler reviews the recommendations and releases two orders for Chicago and New York for 500 units each. Monday afternoon both orders are transmitted electronically, using EDI capabilities, to your distribution center. Both orders are received, verified, picked, packed, and shipped within three working days. Now

On-Hand Balance	—	225
Safety Stock	—	115
Lead Time	—	2 wks
Order Quantity	—	500

		Week								
	Past Due	1	2	3	4	5	6	7	8
Forecast		115	115	115	115	115	115	115	115
In Transit									
Projected On-Hand	225	110	495	380	265	150	535	420	305
Plnd. Shpmts.-Rcpt. Date			500				500		
Plnd. Shpmts.-Ship Date	500				500				

On-Hand Balance	—	350
Safety Stock	—	125
Lead Time	—	2 wks
Order Quantity	—	500

		Week								
	Past Due	1	2	3	4	5	6	7	8
Forecast		125	125	125	125	125	125	125	125
In Transit									
Projected On-Hand	350	225	600	475	350	225	600	475	350
Plnd. Shpmts.-Rcpt. Date			500				500		
Plnd. Shpmts.-Ship Date	500				500				

Figure 6-16. DRP display, Chicago (a), and New York (b) distribution centers.

On-Hand Balance — 164
Safety Stock — 47
Lead Time — 2 wks
Order Quantity — 200

	Past Due	1	2	3	4	5	6	7	8
					Week				
Forecast		47	47	47	47	47	47	47	47
In Transit									
Projected On-Hand	164	117	70	223	176	129	82	235	188
Plnd. Shpmts.-Rcpt. Date				200		200		200	
Plnd. Shpmts.-Ship Date		200							

Figure 6-17. DRP display for the Montreal distribution center.

it's Friday morning, and your inventory has been updated and shows an on-hand balance of 170. The computer recommends that an order for 2200 be placed at the factory. You review, approve, and release it.

That same afternoon you receive another order from the wholesaler for 200, to be shipped to the Montreal distribution center. Recall that on Monday, Montreal was okay. But now sales have materialized close to forecast, and the wholesaler has reached his reorder point.

Do you have a problem? Obviously, you can't ship the whole order—you're short 30 units. And even though you have 2200 on order, product won't be available for three weeks. So you must do two things. First, advise your customer you can only ship 170. Second, contact your factory to expedite the order you just placed the

On-Hand Balance — 1170
Safety Stock — 287
Lead Time — 3 wks
Order Quantity — 2200

	Past Due	1	2	3	4	5	6	7	8
					Week				
Forecast	1000	200	0	0	1000	200	0	0	0
In Transit									
Projected On-Hand	170	-30	-30	2170	1170	970	970	970	970
Plnd. Shpmts.-Rcpt. Date				2200					
Plnd. Shpmts.-Ship Date	2200								

Figure 6-18. DRP display at the supply source.

Sales History								
Weekly Forecast	Dist. Center	Week				Total	Current On-Hand	New On-Hand
		4	3	2	1			
115	Chicago	60	155	100	45	360	225	585
47	New York	50	33	40	45	168	164	332
125	Montreal	100	120	110	90	420	350	770

Figure 6-19. Sales history by DC, past four weeks.

same morning. You are now out of stock, and will be so for three weeks unless the factory can expedite the order.

So one day things look great, and the next day you're out of stock. One day the factory receives an order with normal lead time; a few hours later the factory is told to expedite the order. Is this typical? Indeed—it happens all the time. What's the problem? The reorder point.

With DRP (see Fig. 6-16), we have planned shipments to these Chicago and New York DCs that are overdue. In other words, the reorder point never showed the problem. Also, the safety stock in the DRP display is the forecast quantity for one week. This is the same as the quantity used in the reorder-point example.

Now let's look at a DRP display for the Montreal DC, which shows that a planned order is due for release during the current week (see Fig. 6-17). We'll also look at the DRP display at the supply source (see Fig. 6-18). The inventory planner at the supply source is getting urgent messages from the DRP display to expedite an order from the factory to cover a shortage of 30 in week 1.

The reorder-point system does not indicate any trouble until the end of week 1, when the supply source received an order for 200 from the Montreal DC and only 170 were on hand. In contrast, DRP would have given us warnings many weeks before. DRP would have predicted the shortage at the supply source and warned the inventory planner and the factory of the problem. To illustrate this, let's go back in time by four weeks. Figure 6-19 shows the sales history by DC for the past four weeks. The actual sales were added back to the inventory to give a new on-hand balance, shown in Fig. 6-20. The sales forecasts are not changed, although we know better. This gives DRP a true test.

As you can see in Fig. 6-20, even four weeks earlier DRP was planning for the distribution demands. In the example, DRP planned an order due for release to the factory in the current week, so that there will be enough to cover the distribution demands four weeks later. This order is visible at the factory as demand from the DC, and is being ordered within the normal three-week factory lead time. Here, DRP is monitoring and planning four weeks into the future. The reorder point did not anticipate the problem, and when it did note it, there was no time to fix it.

Figure 6-21 summarizes and compares the information from the reorder-point system with the information from DRP for the previous example.

Though this example depicts the situation four weeks ago, the effects would also have been similar three weeks ago, two weeks ago, and one week ago. Figure 6-22

Chicago Distribution Center

On-hand balance — 585
Safety stock — 115
Lead time — 2 weeks
Order quantity — 500

	Past due	Week 1	2	3	4	5	6	7	8
Forecast		115	115	115	115	115	115	115	115
In transit									
Projected on-hand	585	470	355	240	125	510	395	280	165
Plnd. shipments—recpt. date						500			
Plnd. shipments—ship date				500					

New York Distribution Center

On-hand balance — 770
Safety stock — 125
Lead time — 2 weeks
Order quantity — 500

	Past due	Week 1	2	3	4	5	6	7	8
Forecast		125	125	125	125	125	125	125	125
In transit									
Projected on-hand	770	645	520	395	270	145	520	395	270
Plnd. shipments—recpt. date							500		
Plnd. shipments—ship date					500				

Montreal Distribution Center

On-hand balance — 332
Safety stock — 47
Lead time — 2 weeks
Order quantity — 200

	Past due	Week 1	2	3	4	5	6	7	8
Forecast		47	47	47	47	47	47	47	47
In transit									
Projected on-hand	332	285	238	191	144	97	50	203	156
Plnd. shipments—recpt. date								200	
Plnd. shipments—ship date						200			

Supply Source

On-hand balance — 1170
Safety stock — 287
Lead time — 3 weeks
Order quantity — 2200

	Past due	Week 1	2	3	4	5	6	7	8
Forecast		0	0	500	500	200	0	0	0
In transit									
Projected on-hand	1170	1170	1170	670	2370	2170	2170	2170	2170
Plnd. shipments—recpt. date					2200				
Plnd. shipments—ship date		2200							

Figure 6-20. New DRP summary for three DCs and supply source.

Locations	Reorder Point	DRP
Chicago	Below reorder point, order from supply source.	Planned order overdue for release from supply source.
New York	Below reorder point, order from central.	Planned order overdue for release from supply source.
Montreal	Beginning of week: above reorder point, no action needed. End of week: below reorder point, order from supply source.	Planned order overdue for release from supply source this week.
Supply source	Monday a.m.: above reorder point, no problem apparent. Monday p.m.: New York and Chicago order. Friday a.m.: New York and Chicago orders shipped. Supply source orders from factory. Friday p.m.: Montreal orders, not enough stock to cover at source. Expedite the factory. Montreal will be short for 3 weeks.	Four weeks earlier: predicts a shortage of 30 five weeks into the future and below safety stock four weeks out. Source places an order on the factory to cover need. Factory order due for release in normal lead time. Planned shipments are made, no back orders.

Figure 6-21. Comparison of reorder-point and DRP systems.

shows the math for each of the four weeks. It demonstrates that except for Chicago in week 1, the reorder-point approach decremented by the actual sales, as shown in Fig. 6-19, did not generate an order for any location at any time during the past four weeks.

If the factory is able to economically produce in quantities less than 2200, the supply source might have requested a smaller quantity, since DRP shows that only 30 units are required in week 5 to cover all orders. In other words, DRP is predicting a shortage of 30, five weeks out. The reorder point reacted to this same shortage by instructing the user to secure more product.

Now, let's look at another reorder-point example, using reorder points (Fig. 6-23). In this situation, the reorder point at the supply source tripped because of an order from Chicago (1600 minus 500 equals 1100). The other two DCs had sufficient inventory, but the reorder-point system predicted that more product would be needed at the supply source immediately and an order for 2200 was placed on the factory. This order was incorrect because it was placed much too soon.

Using DRP, the situation at the supply source would appear as shown in Fig. 6-24.

Look at the difference between the two systems. DRP shows that for at least the next four weeks no additional product is needed. The current on-hand balance can satisfy the demand through the end of week 4 and most of week 5. In fact, many

4 Weeks Ago		
Chicago	OP $\longrightarrow$ 345	
	OH $\longrightarrow$ 585	
	(OH + OO)>OP	No order
Montreal	OP $\longrightarrow$ 141	
	OH $\longrightarrow$ 332	
	(OH + OO)>OP	No order
New York	OP $\longrightarrow$ 375	
	OH $\longrightarrow$ 770	
	(OH + OO)>OP	No order
3 Weeks Ago		
Chicago	OP $\longrightarrow$ 345	
	OH $\longrightarrow$ 525	
		No order
Montreal	OP $\longrightarrow$ 141	
	OH $\longrightarrow$ 282	
		No order
New York	OP $\longrightarrow$ 375	
	OH $\longrightarrow$ 670	
		No order
2 Weeks Ago		
Chicago	OP $\longrightarrow$ 345	
	OH $\longrightarrow$ 370	
		No order
Montreal	OP $\longrightarrow$ 141	
	OH $\longrightarrow$ 249	
		No order
New York	OP $\longrightarrow$ 375	
	OH $\longrightarrow$ 550	
		No order
1 Week Ago		
Chicago	OP $\longrightarrow$ 345	
	OH $\longrightarrow$ 270	
		Order something, but still too late.
Montreal	OP $\longrightarrow$ 141	
	OH $\longrightarrow$ 209	
		No order
New York	OP $\longrightarrow$ 375	
	OH $\longrightarrow$ 440	
		No order

Figure 6-22. Mathematical explanation of reorder-point example (week by week).

inventory planners and master schedulers, looking at the display shown in Fig. 6-24, realize that the supply-source order for 2200, due in week 5, is just to satisfy a true need of 100, plus safety stock of 287. But with the visibility offered by DRP, does the inventory planner really need to release this order on the factory?

Since the master scheduler can see the real demands from the supply source, he does not typically schedule a lot of 2200—most of it would be warehoused for several weeks. In such a case, the master scheduler evaluates the distribution demand in week 5 and, working with the inventory planner, decides to ship New York 400,

	Chicago	Montreal	New York
Inventory on hand	225	330	880
Forecast	115/wk	47/wk	125/wk
Reorder point	345	141	375
POQ	500	200	500
Supplier lead time	2 wks	2 wks	2 wks
Supply Source (DC)			
Inventory on hand		1600	
Reorder point		1150	
Order quantity		2200	
Supplier lead time (factory)		3 wks	

Figure 6-23. Generic reorder-point model with revised on-hand.

rather than 500. The supply source display for this item, therefore, looks like the one shown in Fig. 6-25, so no order is placed on the factory at this time. To accomplish this, a firm planned order is created for release to the factory at a future week where demand would exist. For example, if demands from any of the three DCs (Chicago, Montreal, or New York) exist in week 11, the inventory planner creates a firm planned order for release in week 8.

The forced linkage between logistics and manufacturing caused by DRP establishes the supply/demand integration between a customer and supplier. This, in turn, creates a win-win situation. DRP predicts future problems and gives people the information to solve them immediately. This often results in eliminating the problem before it occurs.

The reorder point, on the other hand, always orders material whenever the on-hand balance is below the reorder point, regardless of whether more is actually needed. In this case, there is enough on hand to satisfy the demands. But the reorder-point system doesn't look at what is needed. Instead, it blindly attempts to keep a certain amount of inventory on hand at all times.

Let's compare the reorder point and DRP for the examples in Figs. 6-21 through 6-25. Figure 6-26 gives the results.

These examples serve to show that reorder points are an obsolete technique—an invalid inventory model—and should not be used in any situation where inventories are maintained. They simply do not provide the visibility to see when product is actually needed and when problems are likely to occur.

Operating in the Real World

Thus far, comparisons between the classic reorder-point approaches and DRP have assumed that supply sources are also using reorder-point systems. In reality, that is not always the case. During the past 10 years, companies have used a variety of significantly different approaches when they plan at supply sources. The most frequently encountered approaches are represented in the following four scenarios.

Some companies plan monthly; others plan weekly. Some sources purchase prod-

Chicago Distribution Center

On-hand balance — 225
Safety stock — 115
Lead time — 2 weeks
Order quantity — 500

	Past due	1	2	3	4	5	6	7	8
Forecast		115	115	115	115	115	115	115	115
In transit									
Projected on-hand	225	110	495	380	265	150	535	420	305
Plnd. shipments—recpt. date			500				500		
Plnd. shipments—ship date	500				500				

New York Distribution Center

On-hand balance — 880
Safety stock — 125
Lead time — 2 weeks
Order quantity — 500

	Past due	1	2	3	4	5	6	7	8
Forecast		125	125	125	125	125	125	125	125
In transit									
Projected on-hand	880	755	630	505	380	255	130	505	380
Plnd. shipments—recpt. date								500	
Plnd. shipments—ship date						500			

Montreal Distribution Center

On-hand balance — 330
Safety stock — 47
Lead time — 2 weeks
Order quantity — 200

	Past due	1	2	3	4	5	6	7	8
Forecast		47	47	47	47	47	47	47	47
In transit									
Projected on-hand	330	283	236	189	142	95	48	201	154
Plnd. shipments—recpt. date								200	
Plnd. shipments—ship date						200			

Supply Source

On-hand balance — 1600
Safety stock — 287
Lead time — 3 weeks
Order quantity — 2200

	Past due	1	2	3	4	5	6	7	8
Forecast	500	0	0	0	500	700	0	0	0
In transit									
Projected on-hand	1100	1100	1100	1100	600	2100	2100	2100	2100
Plnd. shipments—recpt. date						2200			
Plnd. shipments—ship date			2200						

Figure 6-24. Revised DRP summary for three DCs and supply source.

6.21

On-Hand Balance — 1600
Safety Stock   — 287
Lead Time   — 3 wks
Order Quantity — 2200

	Past Due	Week								
		1	2	3	4	5	6	7	8
Forecast	500	0	0	0	500	600	0	0	0
In Transit									
Projected On-Hand	1100	1100	1100	1100	600	0	0	0	0
Plnd.Shpmts.—Rcpt.Date									
Plnd.Shpmts.—Ship Date									

Figure 6-25. Item supply source display.

uct; others manufacture it. Some companies plan nationally and total all inventories at all locations; others do not. The impact of these different approaches will be evident as you read these scenarios. The first two involve nonmanufacturers; the last two examine companies with a manufacturing base. Although the data are the same across all scenarios, the companies use very different approaches to interpret them.

Scenario 1

The first scenario describes a company that purchases its products. In this example, the sum of all inventories in all locations, the supply source and all distribution

Location	Order Point	DRP
Chicago	Below reorder point, order from supply source.	Planned order overdue for release from supply source.
New York	Above reorder point, no action needed.	Planned order due for release in week 5.
Montreal	Above reorder point, no action needed.	Planned order due for release in week 5.
Supply source	Beginning of week: above reorder point, no problem apparent. End of week: below reorder point, order 2200 from the factory, due in week 3.	Enough inventory to last until week 5. Master scheduler may decide to release an order next week or may ship 400 to New York and not release an order to the factory.

Figure 6-26. Comparison of reorder-point system and DRP.

Purchase Schedule Display

O/H: 1909 O/Q: 2200 L/T: 3 wks S/S: 287 (1 week)	Month								
	Past Due	1	2	3	4	5	6	7	8
Sales Forecast		1244	1244	1244					
Planned Purchases			2200						
Proj. Avail. Bal.	1909	665	1621	377					

NOTE:
1. Source and DC's inventory are totaled.
2. Planning is monthly.
3. National sales forecast is used.

Figure 6-27. Supply source that purchases product—Scenario 1.

centers, has been totaled to give a starting inventory of 1909. (See Fig. 6-27.)* The sales forecast of 1244 per month was calculated by taking the individual sales forecasts by week by DC, multiplying them by 52, and then totaling all the forecasts to arrive at a national forecast. This sum was then divided by 12 to arrive at a monthly forecast. The objective is to have as a minimum at all times two weeks of inventory available nationally for the DCs.

A company using this approach has 2200 as planned purchases during the second month. We can conclude from this example that companies using this approach are confronted with a major problem. Recall that the reorder-point example used in Fig. 6-15 indicated that when Chicago and New York ordered against supply sources, 170 units were left to satisfy the next order of 200 coming from Montreal, thus creating a shortage of 30 by the end of the week. That created a severe problem. In this case, the supply source is planning to purchase product only during the second month, so the problem is amplified.

Scenario 2

Figure 6-28 displays another approach that several companies use. In this example, only inventory available at the source is used. Companies using this approach recommend the purchase of a quantity of 2200 during their first month, and again during the third month. This still does not solve the problem. This approach is frequently encountered when inventories in the DCs are the responsibility of people other than those at supply sources. For example, the store managers may be responsible for inventory in their stores, while logistics or purchasing people are responsible for inventories in the DCs.

*The displays in Figs. 6-27 and 6-28 are a simplified version showing the sales forecast, future purchases (planned), and projected on hand (Proj. Avail. Bal).

Purchase Schedule Display

O/H: 170 O/Q: 2200 L/T: 3 wks S/S: 287 (1 week)		Month								
	Past Due	1	2	3	4	5	6	7	8	
Sales Forecast		1244	1244	1244						
Planned Purchases		2200		2200						
Proj. Avail. Bal.	1170	2126	882	1838						

NOTE:
1. Source inventory only is used.
2. Planning is monthly.
3. National sales forecast is used.

Figure 6-28. Supply source that purchases product—Scenario 2.

Scenario 3

This case involves companies that use MRP II in manufacturing. The sales forecast is shown in weeks, and the starting inventory is the total inventory available in the system, as in the first scenario. The Master Production Schedule (MPS) logic recommends that a manufacturing order be released in the third week to be available for shipping to the DCs in the sixth week, at which point the projected on-hand balance is to be below safety stock (see Fig. 6-29).*

Because these companies aren't using DRP, they still would not be in the position to accurately predict the timing of the release of the order in manufacturing to avoid a stockout.

Scenario 4

In this situation companies are using MRP in manufacturing, but only the plan inventory is being netted at the MPS level. Figure 6-30 indicates that the timing is improving. The material planning logic recommends that an order be released during the first week. Although this is closer to reality and the company is using MRP II in manufacturing, it is planning in weeks and is using only the plant inventory. The logic still recommends that a manufacturing order be released during the first week, which means that inventory will not be available to ship for three weeks.

The preceding scenarios yield four different answers to the problem. In this first instance, the approach recommends that the company purchase products sometime during the second month. In the second instance, the approach recommends that purchases be made sometime during the first and third months. In the third example, manufacture is scheduled sometime during the third week. And in the

---

*The displays in Figs. 6-27 and 6-28 are a simplified version showing sales forecasts, open manufacturing orders (Sched. Receipts), projected on-hand (Proj. Avail. Bal.), MPS receipt, and start.

MPS Display

O/H: 1909 O/Q: 2200 L/T: 3 wks S/S: 287 (1 week)	Past Due	Week							
		1	2	3	4	5	6	7	8
Sales Forecast		287	287	287	287	287	287	287	287
Sched. Receipts									
Proj. Avail. Bal.	1909	1662	1335	1048	761	474	2387	2100	1813
MPS-Receipt							2200		
MPS-Start				2200					

NOTE:
1. Manufacturing and logistics inventory is totaled.
2. Planning is weekly.
3. National sales forecast is used.
4. MRP II is used.

Figure 6-29. Supply source that purchases product—Scenario 3.

last scenario, the system indicates that the company should manufacture sometime during the first week.

In none of the cases is the company in a position in which the planning approach can predict accurately when it should begin to purchase or manufacture in order to provide sufficient inventory to handle the needs of the DCs.

You might ask why, even though companies are using MRP II in manufacturing, are planning by week, and are using the plan inventories, they are unable to predict

MPS Display

O/H: 1170 O/Q: 2200 L/T: 3wks S/S: 287 (1 week)	Past Due	Week							
		1	2	3	4	5	6	7	8
Sales Forecast		287	287	287	287	287	287	287	287
Sched. Receipts									
Proj. Avail. Bal.	1170	883	596	309	2222	1935	1648	1361	1074
MPS-Receipt					2200				
MPS-Start		2200							

NOTE:
1. Manufacturing inventory only is used.
2. Planning is weekly.
3. National sales forecast is used.
4. MRP II is used.

Figure 6-30. Supply source that manufactures product—Scenario 4.

when they truly need to create product. The point is very simple. If you refer back to the results of the DRP example, you will note that the basic difference is the forecast. DRP provides a simulation of requirements over the planning horizon that truly depicts the distribution demands as they will happen, as opposed to using a national sales forecast that may be in months or in weeks. That is the subtle difference between the two. In fact, the sum of the planned orders coming from the DCs and generated by DRP becomes the forecast that should be used in purchase planning and master scheduling. That is the key to the solution for this problem. Supply sources suddenly have visibility into distribution centers, because the forecast is an accurate picture of what the DCs really need. If you are a retailer, wholesaler, or distributor, the DCs, the stores, etc. are integrated with the external sources of supply. If you are a manufacturer, logistics and manufacturing are totally integrated via the MPS.

It is important to recognize that even though companies may have an MRP II system operating in manufacturing, unless they integrate their MRP II system with DRP to plan and schedule inventories in the distribution network, they will not achieve the results anticipated with MRP II. They will have great difficulty in developing a proper MPS that truly represents what needs to be manufactured to support logistics operations, and will constantly be confronted with timing problems of this nature.

Companies that only have MRP II in manufacturing must invest in significant amounts of safety stock at the supply source to cut down on surprises of this nature and achieve some stability in master production scheduling. With DRP, there is no need to invest in more inventory. If you are a nonmanufacturer, the same situation regarding safety stock will prevail. You will be more able to synchronize demand from the field with supply at the source, using far less inventory.

DRP Display

For the remainder of this chapter, the format of the DRP display changes from the examples presented earlier. The display is standardized—it is exactly the same for items in a store or a distribution center, for manufactured items or for purchased items. This is also the format used for purchased items.

There are a number of reasons for adopting a standardized format for retail/wholesale manufacturing and logistics. One is that the logic of the system works in exactly the same way. Therefore, there is no need to use different displays. Another reason is that it makes the system easier to understand; people in retail/wholesale manufacturing and logistics using the same display can communicate more effectively and reach a higher level of understanding.

Figure 6-31 shows an example of the DRP display using the previous format; Fig. 6-32 shows the same items using the standardized display.

Four aspects of the standardized display in Figure 6-32 differ from the DRP display in Figure 6-31:

1. The term "Gross Requirements" is used rather than "Forecast." Gross requirements are the demands for an item. If the item is a product in a store or a distribution center, the gross requirements are the forecast. If the item is manufactured or

On-Hand Balance — 140
Safety Stock — 50
Lead Time — 3 wks
Order Quantity — 150

	Past Due	Week							
		1	2	3	4	5	6	7	8
Forecast		20	25	15	20	30	25	15	30
In Transit									
Projected on-Hand	140	120	95	80	60	180	155	140	110
Plnd. Shpmts.-Rcpt. Date						150			
Plnd. Shpmts.-Ship Date			150						

Figure 6-31. DRP display, Vancouver distribution center.

purchased, the gross requirements are what is needed to be satisfied by manufacturing or outside suppliers.

2. The term "Scheduled Receipts" replaces "In Transit." Scheduled receipts are quantities scheduled to come into stock. If these items are products in a store or a distribution center, the scheduled receipts are in transit from the supply source. Although they may not actually be on the road, the scheduled orders could be in the process of being picked or packed and still be a scheduled receipt. If these are manufactured or purchased items, the scheduled receipts are either manufacturing orders that have been released to the factory or purchase orders that have been released to suppliers.

3. The term "Planned Orders" is used rather than "Plnd. Shpmts.—Ship Date." As the name suggests, planned orders are still in the planning stage and are unreleased, unlike scheduled receipts, which have either been shipped or are in-proc-

On-Hand Balance — 140
Safety Stock — 50
Lead Time — 3 wks
Order Quantity — 150

	Past Due	Week							
		1	2	3	4	5	6	7	8
Gross Requirements		20	25	15	20	30	25	15	30
Scheduled Receipts									
Projected On-Hand	140	120	95	80	60	180	155	140	110
Planned Orders			150						

Figure 6-32. Standardized display, Vancouver distribution center.

ess. If the item is a product in a store or a distribution center, the planned orders are the schedule for future shipments from the supply sources. If the item is a manufactured or purchased item, the planned orders are the schedule of what will be manufactured or purchased in the future. Planned orders are typically displayed by order start date. In the case of a distribution item, this is the date of shipment from the supply source. For manufactured and purchased items, this is the date the order is released to the shop floor or the date the order is placed with the supplier.

4. The Plnd. Shpmts.—Rcpt. Date item is eliminated from the report. It is only necessary to see the planned orders at the start date. They are still added to the projected on-hand balance, just as they would be if the planned order receipt line were on the display.

Conclusion

In this chapter, we introduced and explained the ABCs of DRP in significant detail, and showed that whether you have one inventory stocking location or a very complex multitier network, DRP will plan and schedule equally well. We also showed you how DRP deals with changes in demand and how it helps you to manage change.

We compared DRP to the reorder-point system and demonstrated the significant difference between the two and the advantages of DRP. Then we looked at four frequently used approaches to planning at supply sources in manufacturing as well as nonmanufacturing environments.

7

Organizational Trends and Career Paths in Distribution

Bernard J. La Londe

*Mason Professor of Transportation and
Logistics, Ohio State University*

James M. Masters

*Assistant Professor of Logistics Management,
Ohio State University*

Over the last 20 years, dramatic changes have occurred in logistics organizations throughout the American economy. These changes have created both challenges and opportunities for the logistics executives who have been developing their careers within these organizations. And these changes have not stopped—in fact, it seems only logical to conclude that the pace of change in business logistics will be even more rapid over the next 10 years. It is our purpose in this chapter to develop a picture of how the logistics organization of the firm has evolved and developed over time, and to point out the probable direction of future changes and developments. In doing so, we will also highlight the changing roles and functions of the logistics executive. The chapter will show how contemporary logistics executives are preparing themselves to guide their organizations into the twenty-first century.

A Brief Overview of the Economic History of the Period

Any discussion of the development of logistics organizations over the period from 1970 to the present must recognize the historical context in which these changes occurred. In many cases, changes in logistics processes and structures were strongly influenced by current events in the national economy and the world at large. The history of logistics throughout this period is largely the story of how logistics executives coped with the long series of dramatic changes that were reshaping the business environment around them. For that reason, it will be useful to briefly recount some of the most important of these historical influences.

The National Economy. In recent times, the American economy has gone through two general phases. In the 1970s the economy experienced slow or negative growth, with very high rates of inflation and interest. Among other things, these high capital costs led to increasing pressure on logistics managers to control inventory levels and costs. In the 1980s the economy experienced a long period of aggregate expansion and prosperity, although not all sectors and industries shared evenly in the boom, and the end of the decade brought a recession.

Petroleum Prices. The OPEC oil cartel was able to engineer a series of rapid price rises in the 1970s, which greatly destabilized the global economy. Since fuel costs are a large proportion of the motor carrier cost structure, this situation greatly complicated the logistics manager's task. In addition to uncertainty over price, uncertainty over availability developed. The federal government responded by building a national strategic stockpile, initiating a synthetic fuel program, and rationing fuel. Many private firms also built large fuel storage facilities and took steps to increase the fuel efficiency of their vehicles. Over the long term the cartel was unable to maintain the price increase, and by 1990 the price of motor fuel at the pump was lower in real terms than it had been in 1970. While the apparent urgency of this situation has faded into the background today, it is important to remember how much true havoc it created in logistics systems in the 1970s.

Transportation Deregulation. In 1977, the federal government began the economic deregulation of the transportation industry. These actions led to increased competition in the rail and motor carrier industries, since carriers were now able to set rates and routes virtually at will, offer new services, and enter and leave service areas. A period of great turbulence ensued. In the arena of vigorous price competition that developed, many well-established carriers perished as freight rates generally declined. Although shippers benefited from falling rates, instability in the industry created new planning problems for logistics executives to contend with.

Environmental Issues. Throughout this deregulation period, firms developed growing awareness of the importance of environmental and ecological issues. This was reflected in increased attention to the safe storage and transportation of hazardous materials, recycling of products and packaging, and industrial pollution of air, earth, and water—even noise pollution. Logistics functions in most firms were particularly visible in this regard, and this created new challenges for management. Firms that had once proudly emblazoned their motor carrier fleet with the corporate logo now sought to make their trucks as anonymous as possible.

Mergers and Acquisitions.   The 1980s were witness to a wave of corporate mergers, acquisitions, and leveraged buyouts. In a ten-year period, some corporations were bought and sold three, four, or five times. In some cases these ownership changes left the logistics organization relatively undisturbed. More frequently, however, the joining of two firms led to some form of integration of what had been two logistics organizations. This usually led to the termination of a number of logistics executives and workers, who were redundant in the newly restructured organization. While many (but not all) of these newly formed corporations made good economic sense, this process caused great turbulence in logistics organizations—and logistics careers—throughout the 1980s.

Globalization.   American firms faced growing competition from foreign firms in the battle for the American market. American firms also increased their efforts to sell in foreign markets. Companies developed offshore sources for raw materials and products and moved production facilities into low-wage-rate countries. As these practices grew, these strategies evolved from innovative ways to seize competitive advantage into necessary tactics to survive in the new business environment. Logistics executives were forced to deal with this explosion in the scope of the logistics domain. Managers who were operating national logistics networks in 1970 were operating global logistics networks in 1990, and had developed the ability to deal with international shipping, currency exchange, international law, and all the other complexities such networks entail.

Information Technology.   Perhaps the most pervasive change in the business environment during this period was the flowering of information technology. In 1970, logistics organizations used information systems on mainframe computers that were large, slow, fragile, and expensive. Processing was batch-oriented, data storage was accomplished on magnetic tape, data input was via keystroke, and outputs were often voluminous paper reports that inundated the manager with a great deal of data but very little useful information. Changes to the system software were expensive and slow, and required the efforts of a legion of programmers and systems analysts. It was very difficult to integrate the operation of data systems within a firm, and integration between firms was very rare.

By 1990, the world had really changed. Information processing was based on desktop machines, networked to one another and perhaps to a mainframe. Machines were small, sturdy, reliable, faster, more powerful, and vastly cheaper. Systems processing took place in real time, mass data storage was via disk with near instantaneous retrieval, raw data input was accomplished by automated scanning devices, and output reports were presented on video screen. User-friendly software and relational databases were widely available that allowed a manager to selectively retrieve relevant information and design tailored reports. Electronic Data Interchange telecommunications protocols allowed direct interaction and machine-controlled business transactions between corporations around the world. In the traditionally information-intensive activities of the logistics process, these new capabilities paved the way toward totally new ways of doing business.

There are other factors that have influenced the evolution of the logistics function over the last 20 years. One might cite, for example, the trends toward corporate downsizing and a reduction of the number of middle managers. Our purpose here is not to develop an exhaustive list nor to completely retell the history of this complicated period, but rather to highlight those phenomena that we believe had the most profound and direct influence on the shape of logistics practice in this era. Any useful understanding of the development of the logistics organization must be based on this historical framework. Some of these factors, such as oil prices and environmental issues, greatly complicated the logistics executive's task. Other factors, such as transportation deregulation and new information technology, presented new opportunities to improve logistics system performance. The general influence of this set of factors in most firms was to increase the visibility and relative importance of the logistics function within the corporate structure and to change the logistics organization.

Sources of Historical Data

A great deal has been written over the last twenty years in logistics textbooks, professional journals, and the trade press that deals with organizational issues. These sources provide a great deal of useful information on the subject, and where pertinent we will allude to them here. As our primary source, however, we will draw from the results of a survey entitled "Career Patterns in Logistics," which is conducted by the Logistics Faculty of Ohio State University. This is a mail questionnaire survey of logistics executives that has been conducted annually since 1971. Each year 500 to 1000 questionnaires are distributed to a set of logistics executives drawn from the membership roster of the Council of Logistics Management. This professional organization, founded in 1967 as the National Council of Physical Distribution Management, is the largest and most well-known association of logistics professionals, with a membership in 1993 of over 7500 executives. Members of the Council are employed by a broad range of manufacturing and merchandising firms. Industries that are particularly well represented within the membership include food and consumer packaged goods, chemicals, wholesaling, and retailing. Firms of all sizes are also represented. For example, in the 1992 survey, respondents reported annual firm revenues ranging from $16 million to $40 billion.

In each year the Career Patterns survey contains some new questions, while other questions are repeated annually so that comparisons across time can be made. In this way we have assembled a database that reflects organizational shifts and career pattern changes over time. On the other hand, due caution must be used in interpreting these data. From year to year the composition of the survey sample changes, due to changes in Council membership. The survey process is anonymous, so that the exact composition of any set of respondents is unknown. There is certainly random variation in the year-to-year results because of this changing sample base; perhaps only a handful of executives have participated in each and every survey. Response rates have been good, typically in the range of 25 to 40 percent. Claims of great statistical precision in these data would be difficult to support. Nevertheless, each annual survey provides a useful snapshot of the status of logistics organizations at that point in time, and comparisons across survey years frequently provide insight into general changes that are taking place in the discipline. Results of each year's Career Patterns survey have been presented at the annual conference of the Council of Logistics Management, and a written report on each survey is included in the annual conference proceedings. Most of the statistical data in this chapter is derived from these annual survey reports, and the observations and conclusions we draw are largely based on the experience and insight gained through conducting this survey over the last 20 years.

Organization of the Chapter

The remainder of this chapter will be organized into four sections. In the first section, discussion will focus on how the logistics function is organized within the firm and on how this organization has changed since 1970. The next section will develop a demographic profile of the typical logistics executive and show how that profile has changed over time. The third section focuses on educational and training issues in logistics organizations. The final section deals with estimates of the direction and extent of future changes in the logistics organization.

Organizational Trends

Functional Responsibilities

Logistics organizations are normally formed by bringing together the traditional logistics operations—freight, warehousing, and so forth—into one department with overall authority for planning and controlling logistics activities, and integrating these activities into the rest of the firm's operations. Logistics theory suggests that the logistics management task entails directing the flow of all material both into and out of the firm, and this concept seems to imply that integrated logistics management would be well supported by an organizational structure that brings "unity of command" to these activities. In fact, most firms have developed their logistics organizations by first integrating the physical distribution of their finished goods. Complete integration of the logistics organization, to include control over purchasing, material management, and inbound traffic management, is observed less frequently.

To illustrate this point, survey respondents were presented with a list of activities and responsibilities and were asked to identify those that were considered to be within the logistics organization's domain and scope of authority. Results from surveys conducted in 1972 and 1992 are compared in Fig. 7-1. These results are really quite similar, considering that 20 years had elapsed between the two surveys. While most firms included traffic and warehousing within the domain of logistics, only about half of these firms included the purchasing activity or the packaging activity, and this situation has not changed a great deal in twenty years.

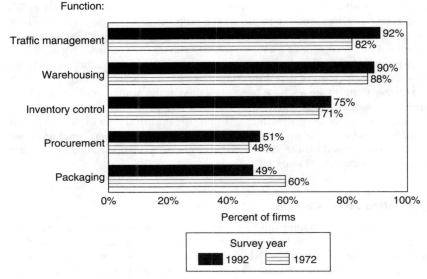

Figure 7-1. The scope of logistics responsibilities.

Reporting Relationships

As logistics emerged as an operating concept in the firm, companies began to develop organizational structures that grouped traditional functional activities such as traffic management, warehousing, inventory control, and purchasing under a single executive, to promote and institutionalize the cross-functional cost and service tradeoffs that are the essence of integrated logistics management. These early physical distribution departments were usually led by an executive with a title of manager or director, and these departments often reported to the CEO through an intermediate level; for example, the Director of Distribution might report to the Vice President of Marketing or the Vice President of Manufacturing. Over time, many firms have expanded the size and scope of their logistics organizations, and have added a Vice President of Logistics at the same organizational level as the more traditional Vice Presidents of Marketing, Finance, and so forth.

A comparison of 1972 and 1992 survey results (see Fig. 7-2) shows the extent of these changes. In 1972, 54 percent of the logistics or distribution organizations reported directly to the CEO; by 1992, 72 percent of the firms had such a structure. In 1972, 12 percent of the logistics departments were attached to Marketing, but by 1992 only one in a hundred were so organized. Similarly, the percentage reporting through the Production or Manufacturing organization has fallen from 22 percent to 11 percent over this same interval. These data point out the clear trend toward establishing a free-standing organizational entity on an equal footing with the other major organizations within the firm.

Department name

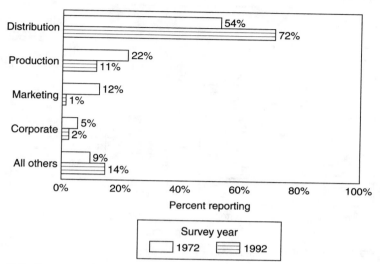

Figure 7-2. Reporting relationships.

The Emergence of the Senior Logistics Executive

Another way to measure the evolution and growth of the logistics organization is to determine when the firm created a senior executive position with a logistics title and with full authority over logistics functions and operations. A good working definition of the term "senior executive" would be a Vice President, and typical examples of position titles would be Vice President of Logistics, Vice President of Distribution, and Vice President of Materials Management and Physical Distribution.

In 1992, survey respondents were asked in what year their firm first established such a senior logistics executive position, and their responses are summarized in Fig. 7-3. Only 8 percent of these firms had established such a position by the end of the 1970s, while 49 percent created such a title during the 1980s and 1990s. On the other hand, fully 43 percent of these firms had not yet established such a position. Thus having a logistics vice president has become the dominant organizational form, but there remains a large minority of firms that have not (or at least not yet) concluded that a high-level logistics position is essential to the effective management and control of the logistics function.

Types of Logistics Organizations

Although many different organizational structures have been developed over the years, four basic types have emerged in general usage.

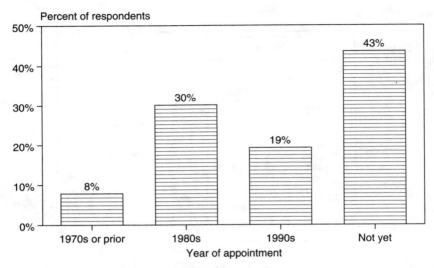

Figure 7-3. Year of first appointment of a senior logistics executive.

1. In the *centralized structure*, all logistics functions and processes are performed centrally for the firm, with control at the level of the corporate staff. This structure is typically found in a relatively small firm.

2. Larger firms typically establish a *divisional logistics structure*, where each separate operating division of the firm develops its own logistics organization, and these logistics departments operate largely independently of one another.

3. A third organizational form gathers all logistics operations of the firm into a *logistics division*, which operates as though it were a product division of the firm, often with profit and loss responsibility. The function of the logistics division is to provide logistics support for the product divisions.

4. A fourth organizational type is a *combination structure*, a blending of the first and second types. In this form some logistics functions, such as purchasing, are organized centrally, while other functions, for example warehousing and inventory control, are operated with a divisional organization.

Finally, a handful of firms have evolved unique operating structures unlike any of these four basic types.

Estimates of the relative prevalence of these organizational types can be assembled from the Career Patterns database, since each survey respondent was asked to categorize his or her firm's logistics organization. Results of the survey data from 1975 through 1991 are summarized in Fig. 7-4. These data show variability from year to year, as might be expected. If the data points corresponding to each organizational type are plotted as a trend line using linear regression, results as shown in Fig. 7-5 are obtained.

The dominant organizational type over this period was the combined or blended form, with about 40 percent of all respondents choosing this category to describe their organization. The autonomous logistics division, which had accounted for 20

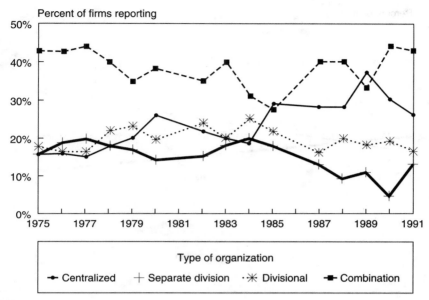

Figure 7-4. Changes in organizational types, 1975–1991.

percent of the total in 1975, was chosen by only about 10 percent by 1991. Firms with logistics functions organized along divisional lines held fairly steady, at about 20 percent of the total. The largest change took place in the growth of the centralized organizational structure. This type of organization was employed by about 15 percent of all firms in 1975, but by 1991 centralized structures were reported by about 30 percent of the respondents.

Centralization and Decentralization

As the statistics reported on the combined or blended organizational structure suggest, many firms show flexibility in their organizational structure, with some logistics functions centralized and others decentralized. Over the last few years, many analysts have noted a trend toward increased centralization of the logistics functions. Several factors have been noted that might encourage a firm to centralize. For example, efforts to downsize and reduce corporate manpower often lead to centralization schemes intended to reduce head count. The availability of modern telecommunications greatly enhances management's ability to control activities at a distance and therefore facilitates centralized control. The deregulation of the transportation industry opened an era of negotiated freight rates. In this environment, shippers could obtain maximum negotiating leverage by offering large amounts of freight. Thus a centralized traffic operation that could negotiate with national carriers began to make a great deal of sense. On the other hand, decentralized structures have their own inherent advantages, especially with regard to customer service and their ability to deal with localized requirements.

While the general trend over the last few years has been in the direction of in-

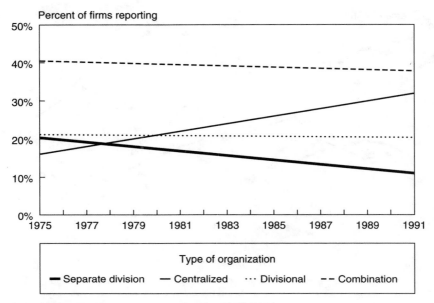

Figure 7-5. Trends in organizational types, 1975–1991.

creasing the degree of centralization of logistics functions, not all firms are doing so. Survey results from 1991 illustrate this point. Executives were presented with a list of logistics functions and were asked whether their firms had increased or de- *i* creased the degree of centralization of each function over the period from 1985 to

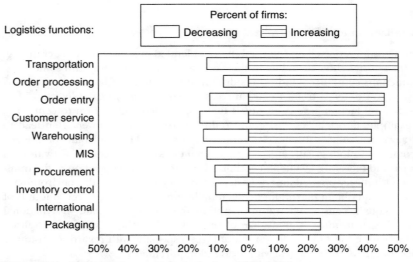

Figure 7-6. Estimated changes in centralization, 1985–1991.

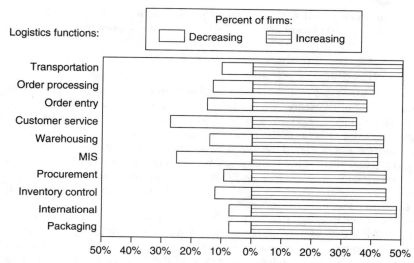

Figure 7-7. Projected changes in centralization, 1992–1995.

1991 (see Fig. 7-6), and also what they anticipated that their firm would do vis-à-vis the degree of centralization of each function from 1992 to 1995 (see Fig. 7-7).

From Fig. 7-6, it is clear that the predominant movement in the period from 1985 to 1991 was toward increased centralization, with the transportation function the activity most likely to have become more centralized. The data in Fig. 7-7 indicate that these executives expect the movement toward increased centralization to generally continue through 1995. However, it should be noted that in two areas, Customer Service and MIS, a large segment of these firms are expecting to increase the decentralization of these operations. These changes can be attributed, on the one hand, to the growing importance of customer service in the competitive environment and the belief that decentralized operations lead to more response and effective performance, and in the case of MIS, to the proliferation of powerful personal computers and user-friendly software, which has allowed many firms to dismantle the centralized data automation bureaucracies that had been developed to cope with MIS operations in the mainframe environment of the 1970s.

Thus the centralization versus decentralization issue remains unresolved, with some firms moving in one direction while others take the opposite tack. Many successful logistics organizations can be found at each end of the centralized-decentralized continuum, and at all points in between.

Executive Career Paths

A sense of the general status of the logistics discipline can be obtained by reviewing the demographic data on logistics executives contained in the Career Patterns data. Survey respondents are typically among the most senior logistics executives in their respective firms, and thus they comprise a broad sample of seasoned logistics professionals. Each year's group of survey respondents is a mix of logistics managers, directors, and vice presidents. The normal proportion for each year is about 25 percent managers, 50 percent directors, and 25 percent vice presidents.

Age and Experience

Logistics executives vary in age from the middle twenties to the middle sixties. The average age is about 43 years, and this figure has remained fairly stable over a long period. The average age reported in 1972, for example, was 42.5 years, while the average age of respondents in the 1992 survey was 44.1 years. As can be seen in Fig. 7-8, the distribution of ages in the sample is roughly bell-shaped, and has not really changed a great deal over the last 20 years. While there is some variation in average age between managers, directors, and vice presidents, with managers on average somewhat younger and vice presidents somewhat older, these variations are slight, on the order of a year or two.

The executives in these positions are generally career logisticians, who have worked in the logistics field longer than they have worked with their current employer, and who have been promoted since joining their current firm. As is shown in Fig. 7-9, the typical respondent has worked in the logistics arena for 14 to 19 years, has been with his or her current firm for 9 to 11 years, and has held the current position for 4 years. This clearly demonstrates well-established career ladders within the logistics discipline, where executives gain experience and promotion within the discipline by moving between firms as well as by being promoted within the logistics organization of the current employer. While it is possible to move laterally from another area such as marketing or production into a senior logistics position, such movement is rare. It is far more likely that the senior logistics

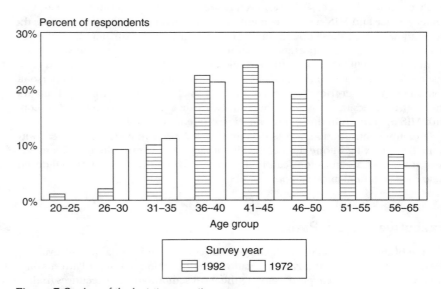

Figure 7-8. Age of the logistics executive.

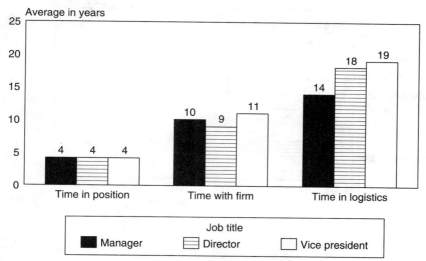

Figure 7-9. Logistics executive experience (survey year 1992).

executives in the firm are seasoned, experienced logistics professionals, who have worked their way up through the ranks and who have developed a thorough, experiential knowledge of the various aspects of the logistics discipline.

Education

In most firms, the logistics executives are college graduates. This was a well-established fact in 1972, and it remains so today. In fact, a large proportion of these executives hold graduate degrees, and this proportion is rising. As can be seen in Fig. 7-10, in 1972 about 63 percent of the survey respondents held a bachelor's degree, and another 29 percent also had a graduate degree. In the 1992 survey, 42 percent held a bachelor's, while fully 52 percent reported that they had also completed a graduate degree.

In most firms today, the bachelor's degree is a mandatory, minimum credential for consideration for an entry-level managerial position, and for many firms this policy has been in effect for decades. Over the last 20 years, the type of undergraduate study that formed the college training for the typical logistics executive has changed considerably. As is displayed in Fig. 7-11, in the 1972 survey the predominant undergraduate major field was engineering or the physical sciences; these disciplines accounted for 49 percent of all the executives' baccalaureates. Ten percent of these executives had majored in transportation or logistics, and another 31 percent had other majors within business administration. The remaining 10 percent were predominantly liberal arts degrees.

By 1992 the statistics were considerably different. Only 6 percent of these executives had training in engineering or science, while 72 percent had business degrees, with 15 percent in transportation or logistics and 57 percent in other business ad-

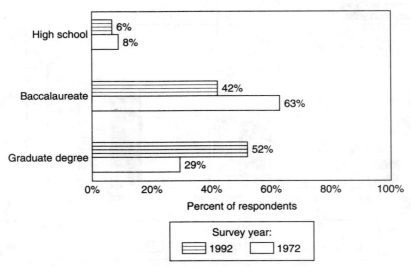

Figure 7-10. Logistics executive formal education (highest level attained).

ministration specialties. This growing focus on the collegiate study of business is particularly pronounced at the graduate level, where virtually all of the advanced degrees reported are the Masters of Business Administration. The growing popularity of the MBA among logistics executives has not yet reached the point where it, too, is about to become a mandatory ticket of admission to the managerial ranks, but it has long since passed the point of being a distinctive or even an unusual line on a job-seeker's resume. With each passing year, the community of logistics execu-

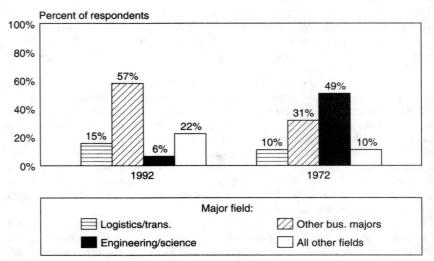

Figure 7-11. Major field of study (baccalaureate degree).

tives is continuing, one step at a time, to raise the ante as to what constitutes the baseline of professional preparation and training in the discipline. This is a natural and healthy state of affairs, and this rising level of expectation is the hallmark of a progressive discipline.

Executive Compensation Levels

Compensation levels for logistics executives are generally on a par with other comparable executives within the firm, and this has been the case for over a decade. For example, a summary of self-reported salary and bonus data from the 1992 survey is contained in Fig. 7-12. Figure 7-13 is a comparison of median reported compensation by job level, across four recent years in current dollars. As is implied by the summary data presented in Fig. 7-12, there is considerable variation in compensation level between individual executives, even at the same job level. A statistical analysis performed on the 1992 survey compensation data shows that, although there is considerable "scatter" in these numbers, compensation does tend to vary in a somewhat systematic or predictable way. As might be expected, compensation levels are related to job level (manager versus director versus vice president), the age of the executive, the size of the firm, and the executive's education level. Based on this analysis, a rough formula to estimate a logistics executive's compensation in 1992 would be as follows.

Annual compensation baseline:

$26,000 for a manager

$41,000 for a director

$83,000 for a vice president

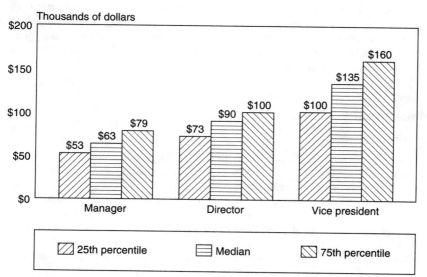

Figure 7-12. Logistics executive compensation (annual salary plus bonus; survey year 1992).

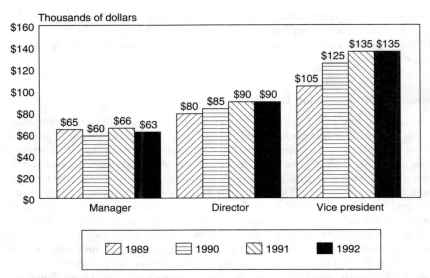

Figure 7-13. Logistics executive compensation (median values, 1989–1992).

Additive components:

$875 for each year of the executive's age

$2 for each million dollars of the firm's total revenue

$9000 if the executive holds the MBA

This formula is only a rough "explanation" of the observed variation in the compensation data; this in no way means, for example, that earning an MBA will guarantee the executive a $9000 raise. On the other hand, these relationships were statistically significant, and this formula accounts for about 53 percent of the total variation in the sample compensation data.

Educational Issues

Executive Education

Many avenues exist through which the practicing logistics executive can upgrade and update his or her skills and capabilities. A number of colleges and universities, as well as numerous private companies, offer an array of specialized short courses and seminars that are focused on logistics technology and management issues. Such courses are available on site as well as at the institution's facilities. Many progressive executives join professional logistics associations such as the Council of Logistics Management, the Warehousing Education and Research Council, and the American Society of Transportation and Logistics, to name a few. The mission of these organizations is to provide a forum for the exchange of new knowledge in the discipline and to promote the educational advancement of the membership. These organizations publish journals, newsletters, and research reports for their members, and they conduct well-attended annual meetings where corporate and academic speakers give presentations and workshops on current logistics issues.

Logistics executives are keenly aware of the need to upgrade their skills and to participate in lifelong learning. In the Career Patterns survey, respondents are asked to identify the topics they would choose to study if they were to take 90 days off and return to school. Although many different topics have been nominated, some general themes emerge that indicate important educational requirements, and perhaps perceived deficiencies, in the body of logistics executives. Figure 7-14 summarizes the results from surveys conducted in 1972 and 1992. In the earlier survey, the most popular topics included "Logistics" and "Finance," followed by "General Management" and "Information Technology." The general sentiment of these respondents was that they needed to increase their understanding of corporate finance so that they could continue to advance within the firm, since finance is often the language of the corporate boardroom. In 1972, "Information Technology" topics primarily involved learning how manual logistics processes and paper-based data systems could be effectively transferred to the mainframe computer hardware that was available.

In the 1992 survey, both "Logistics" and "Finance" still remained as popular topics, for largely the same reasons. "Information Technology" was even more frequently mentioned, and the list of potential study topics here is a long one, including personal computers, spreadsheet applications, communications technologies such as EDI and bar-coding, and inventory control tools such as MRP and DRP. As a reflection of the growing importance of global business, "International" logistics topics are common in the 1992 responses, while they were scarcely mentioned in 1972.

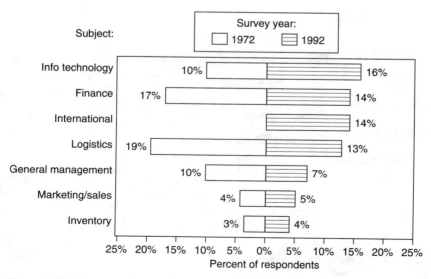

Figure 7-14. Executive education (self-selected curriculum).

Entry-Level Management Education

Logistics executives also have clearly formed ideas about what they are looking for in newly-hired, entry-level, college-educated employees. To sample these opinions, survey respondents in 1989 were asked to identify the degree of proficiency they expected, across a number of skill areas, in new graduates with bachelor's degrees and in new MBAs. Desired proficiency was to be rated on a number scale from 0 to 10, with a rating of 0 meaning that "no familiarity" was expected, a 3 indicating "basic familiarity" with the skill or knowledge of the technology, a 7 indicating "good working knowledge" of the area, and a rating of 10 meaning a "well-developed expertise" was expected. Skill requirements were assessed in three general areas: personal computer skills, information technology skills, and general management skills.

1. *Personal Computer Skills.* Many firms report that "computer fluency" is an important employment prerequisite throughout the firm, and logistics positions are certainly no exception. The relative importance of specific computer skills and abilities is indicated in Fig. 7-15, which reflects the survey respondents' average proficiency ratings across five different areas. High levels of proficiency are expected with spreadsheet analysis programs such as Lotus 1-2-3, Excel, or Quattro. Moderate levels of familiarity with database programs, such as dBase, and presentation graphics packages, such as Harvard Graphics, were also expected. Traditional third-generation computer programming languages, such as COBOL, BASIC, and FORTRAN, were not seen to be very important, nor were such relatively new and exotic technologies as expert systems. Survey respondents have also noted that personal computer usage is widespread throughout the logistics workplace, and that DOS or Windows operating systems account for approximately 90 percent of all installa-

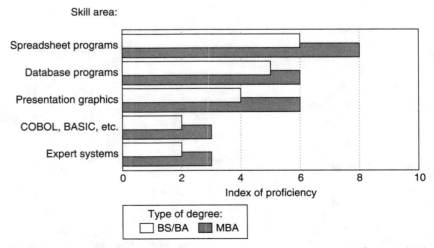

Figure 7-15. Logistics educational requirements (personal computer skills for entry-level managerial positions).

tions in logistics organizations. Macintosh, OS/2, and Unix systems account for the remainder.

2. *Information Technology Skills.* Executives are particularly sensitive to the growing importance of the new tools that are available in this area, and they have come to expect reasonably high levels of familiarity across a range of topics including MRP, DRP, EDI, and bar-coding (see Fig. 7-16). Executives also expect a thorough grounding in the basic principles and techniques of inventory control, from the traditional notions of economic lot-sizing and statistical safety stock-up through contemporary thinking as reflected in just-in-time and quick response inventory methodology.

3. *General Management Skills.* While skill level requirements are high in the areas of computer skills and information technology, the highest levels of expectation were reported in the general management skills category. Specifically, executives expect high levels of ability in writing and speaking, and well-developed analytic ability. As shown in Fig. 7-17, the degree of proficiency expected in each of these three areas is higher than in any of the more technical areas. These ratings underscore the importance of interpersonal communications skills to the successful practice of logistics management.

Work Force Preparation and Training

While logistics executives seem generally satisfied with the education and career preparation of the new college graduates being hired, the same cannot be said for the general logistics work force—the clerks, order pickers, material handling equipment operators, and all the other hourly employees who form the backbone of the typically labor-intensive logistics operation. Much has been written about the de-

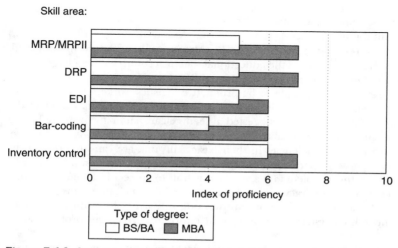

Figure 7-16. Logistics educational requirements (information technology skills for entry-level managerial positions).

Skill area:

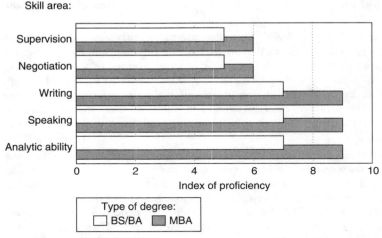

Figure 7-17. Logistics educational requirements (general management skills for entry-level managerial positions).

cline in "workplace literacy" among new high school graduates, and as might be expected, these problems are affecting the logistics workplace as well. We surveyed logistics executives in 1990 to get a sense of the size of the problem, and the results are disturbing. We asked each executive to reflect on the basic educational skills needed on the job—reading, writing, and arithmetic—and asked each executive to consider how well trained their current work force was, and how well prepared their new job applicants were to enter their logistics operations. We presented the executives with a series of statements and asked the executives to indicate their agreement or disagreement with each.

An initial statement suggested: "I am generally satisfied with the skill of the typical applicant for an entry-level job in this firm." As shown in Fig. 7-18, a total of 43 percent of the respondents agreed with this statement, but 39 percent disagreed. Most executives seem to hold the educational system accountable for a large part of the problem. Only 21 percent believe the public education system is doing a good job of preparing young people to be productive logistics workers (see Fig. 7-19), while 62 percent of the executives disagree. Regardless of the root causes of the problem, and many have been suggested, it seems clear that many firms are having trouble finding minimally qualified logistics workers, and that many current employees have serious deficiencies in their basic skills that are causing productivity problems in logistics operations throughout the American economy. Many firms have addressed this problem and are taking action to correct it. Some companies send workers to adult literacy programs; others establish such programs within the firm. Some far-sighted corporations are working in partnership with local public schools and school systems in a long-term effort to correct the problem at its source.

While some firms are working hard on this problem, many others apparently are not. Forty-three percent of these executives believe that their firms have taken appropriate steps to obtain remedial education and training for workers where

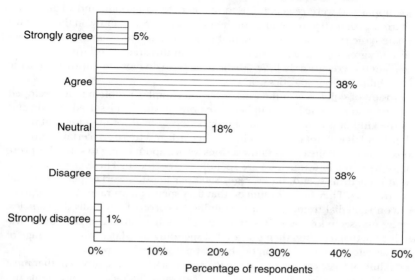

Figure 7-18. Response to survey question.

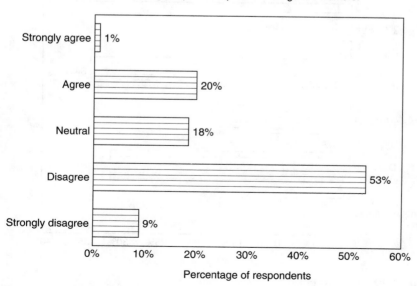

Figure 7-19. Response to survey question.

needed (see Fig. 7-20), but a disheartening 40 percent cannot agree. And the problem is far from trivial or remote. These executives estimated that 20 percent of all of their job applicants were rejected due to inadequate basic skills, and what is even more alarming, that 10 percent of all of their own workers currently on the job have inadequate basic skills and need remedial training. There does seem to be a general sense of agreement that more must be done in this area. As shown in Fig. 7-21, 70 percent of the executives believe "My firm needs to do more to improve the basic skills and abilities of our logistics workers."

The erosion of skill levels in the work force is a complex problem that developed over a long period of time for a number of reasons. It will not be solved quickly, and it is not the kind of problem that can simply be solved by throwing money at it. On the other hand, it will not go away of its own accord, and there are certainly no free solutions. One rough measure of how serious we are about trying to solve this problem might be to see how much we are spending to correct it. These executives estimate that their firms spend, on average, $500 per logistics worker per year on all forms of training. They further estimate that they spend on average $25 per worker per year on remedial training, that is, training to correct basic skills deficiencies. This figure may seem low—and it is. If we recognize that "only" 1 in 10 of our workers needs remedial training, then this level of spending translates into an average of $250 per targeted worker per year, or about $1 per worker per workday.

The decline of basic capabilities in the logistics work force is a problem that must be solved. New technology in the workplace is driving "literacy" requirements up. Workers must be ready to benefit from the training required for the new technol-

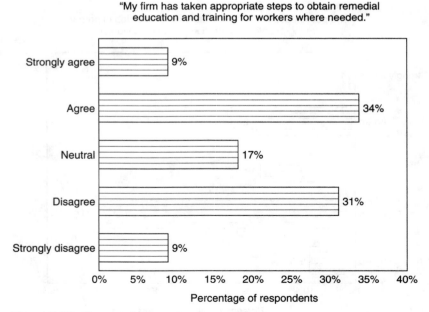

Figure 7-20. Response to survey question.

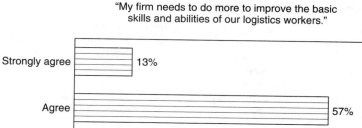

"My firm needs to do more to improve the basic skills and abilities of our logistics workers."

Figure 7-21. Response to survey question.

ogy that will define their jobs. Increasing levels of global competition are forcing us to "work smarter" every day, and globalization of the firm's activity is increasing the complexity of its logistics tasks. Healthy competition pressures us to increase the productivity and quality of our logistics operations to survive. It will do us no good to hang our quality program banners on the walls if our workers cannot read them.

A Glimpse of the Future

In the 1980s, most companies worked to build effective and efficient internal logistics organizations that would integrate the operations of the firm and provide high levels of customer service. In this context, "logistics integration" often meant serving as an interface between manufacturing and marketing. In the 1990s, firms are expanding their logistics horizons. Today's challenge is to build a seamless logistics system that will support operations throughout the whole length of the supply chain. Firms are working with vendors and customers, as well as with carriers and other third party logistics providers, to put together logistics partnerships and strategic alliances that work to the benefit of all channel members. "Logistics integration" in this context entails integrating and synchronizing logistics plans and operations between the many corporate entities with which the firm does business. Success or failure in the 1990s will largely be determined by the firm's ability to practice integrated supply chain management.

The Changing Face of Logistics

Ample evidence exists to suggest how sweeping these changes will be. As an example, consider the spread of just-in-time inventory practices. While JIT can be a fairly elusive concept to pin down to a precise, generally agreed-upon definition, most executives generally support the idea of reducing inventory levels and costs by working with large numbers of small, timely shipments. Experience shows that this kind of control requires a real commitment between buyer and seller, as well as close coordination, sharing of data, and a high level of cooperation and trust. JIT was originally conceived of as a technique to perform material management on inbound raw materials and components in a manufacturing system, but these general principles are being adapted and applied in a number of other settings as well. Many retailers, for example, are developing quick response inventory deployment schemes that apply the lessons of JIT in the distribution setting. JIT activity is growing steadily. The 1992 survey respondents were asked to estimate how much of their total shipping volume from vendors and to customers had moved under JIT control procedures in 1990 and 1992, and how much they anticipated would move in 1995 and 2000. As is shown in Fig. 7-22, JIT accounted for about 20 percent of all shipments in 1990, but by 2000, executives expect that 60 percent of all their shipping activity will be JIT.

Integration of supply chain activity will require capturing and sharing sales data, inventory data, production data, and traffic data quickly and accurately. Firms are turning to automatic identification technology such as bar codes, and telecommunications technology such as EDI, to provide these capabilities. As can be seen in Fig. 7-23, these firms received about 18 percent of their shipping volume from vendors with bar codes in 1990, and they shipped about 20 percent of their outbound volume to customers with bar codes at that time. In addition, about 10 percent of total volume was bar-coded for internal purposes within the firm's distribution system. By 2000, these executives expect to ship and receive about 50 percent of their

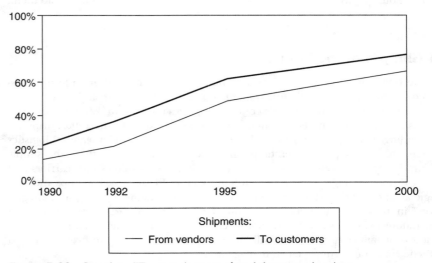

Figure 7-22. Growth in JIT activity (percent of total shipping volume).

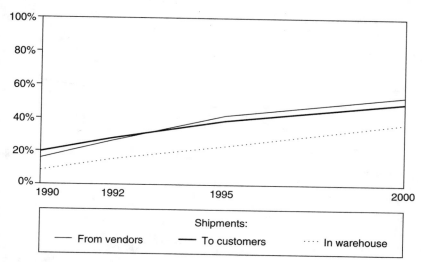

Figure 7-23. Growth in bar code activity (percent of total volume).

volume bar-coded, and to bar-code about 30 percent of volume for internal process-ing. EDI usage is also expected to climb. As is shown in Fig. 7-24, these firms con-ducted about 20 percent of their transactions with customers and warehouses via EDI in 1990, and only about 10 percent of their transactions with vendors and car-riers via this electronic means. By 2000, the executives are planning to use EDI for about 50 percent of their total transactions.

Organizational Implications

Successful supply chain management will require more than JIT and EDI. Most firms will need to rethink and reorganize their logistics organizations to support the close coordination and cooperation between firms that must be achieved. It is by no means obvious what these new logistics structures must or will look like. Some firms are trying to establish strong, top-down, centralized direction and control of logistics operations, to bring all of the firm's resources to bear on the problem in a coordinated way. Data automation and telecommunications technology, including satellite up-links and down-links, provide the capability to control worldwide opera-tions in near real time. Other firms are developing more decentralized structures to support channel integration. Such firms, for example, are building cross-functional teams with managers from marketing, manufacturing, and logistics who operate in support of a key customer or other channel member, providing close cooperation and focused attention on all aspects of the firm's relationship with the strategic partner. These firms believe that this concept of "organizing around the customer" will be the real key to future success.

Career Implications

The movement toward supply chain management will place increased demands on logistics executives. Executives will need to be multifaceted, with expertise in many

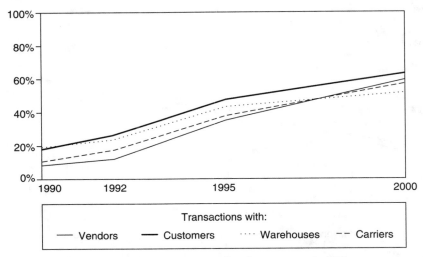

Figure 7-24. Growth in EDI usage (percent of total transactions via EDI).

areas of the business, rather than relying on their depth of knowledge within the logistics discipline. They will need to understand marketing and manufacturing, and they will need to understand their vendors' and their customers' operations just as well as they understand their own.

Since the supply chain will be a global supply chain, understanding your vendors and your customers—and your customers' markets, and perhaps your own manufacturing operations—will require a multicultural perspective. Multicultural experience and expertise will be difficult and expensive and time-consuming to achieve, but it will be necessary.

Summary and Conclusion

Many challenges and opportunities present themselves to the contemporary logistics executive. On the bright side, corporate America is now awake to the importance and significance of logistics operations to the success of the firm. Logistics really has moved "from the loading dock to the boardroom." New information technologies have emerged that may allow us to deliver on the promises of integrated logistics management. Opening global markets and rising standards of living in the developing economies provide the opportunity for real corporate growth.

On the not so bright side, many real problems face us as well. Global markets also bring fierce global competition. The educational preparation of the logistics worker is an open question, and our new technology will require well-trained workers. Operating the seamless logistics system of the future will not be simple or easy, and we will not have an unlimited amount of time to solve this puzzle. When the logistics history of the 1990s is written, the success stories will be about the leaders who found new and creative ways to build and run these new logistics systems.

8

International
Logistics

Paul S. Bender
*President, Bender Management
Consultants, Inc.*

This chapter outlines basic concepts and information, to help practitioners in their analysis of international logistic situations. In the context of a brief chapter, we do not strive for completeness. Our aim is to concentrate on important issues that may not be covered fully in the existing literature, rather than to present a complete overview of the subject or to include data and information readily available from other sources.

A basic idea underlying international logistics is that as the world economy converges toward a unified system, the distinctions between domestic and international issues become increasingly irrelevant. That is the case with logistics, where most of the concepts, techniques and practices used are becoming standardized across the world. However, there are still many differences among nations and regions that translate into different business practices. Here we focus mainly on those specific aspects that present important differences.

The chapter is divided into six sections. The first section serves as an introduction. In the second section, we start from the premise that international logistics is the physical framework of international trade and business; thus, to understand international logistics, we need to understand the basic reasons for the current globalization of business. In the third section, we provide a comparison between domestic and international logistics. In the fourth section, we discuss some of the major trends that affect international logistics. In the fifth section, we outline some of the basic characteristics of logistic systems in the regions of major economic importance in the world. In the sixth section, we examine the basic concepts and techniques used to develop competitive planetary logistics systems.

Reasons for Business Globalization

The world economy is converging toward a single, planetary market. To survive in this environment, businesses must adapt and become global in scope. The main reasons for these developments are of a strategic, tactical, and operational nature.

Strategic Reasons

The main strategic reasons leading companies to adopt a global approach to business are the following.

1. *To confront shrinking product and process lives.* There is a technological explosion under way, whose main manifestation is an informational revolution. As the technological explosion increases in amplitude, it brings about new production processes and new products. And it does so at an increasingly accelerating pace. For this reason, manufacturing companies need to recover their investments in research and development of new processes and products at an accelerating pace. To that end, they must attempt to sell new products to the largest market possible, as soon as possible. The largest possible market is the world market. For this reason alone, in the next few years we can expect an acceleration in the pace of globalization of the economy.

2. *To deny sanctuaries to competitors.* Companies competing in more markets than their competitors derive substantial strategic advantages from that fact. The typical strategy in those cases is to sell at a high profit margin in those markets with lesser competition, to compensate for sales at a lower profit margin in the other markets. In this manner, using their unique markets as sanctuaries, these companies put enormous pressure on their less sophisticated competitors. In the long term, a company that allows sanctuaries to any of its competitors is confronted by increasingly difficult competitive conditions.

3. *To bypass protectionism and mercantilism.* Many countries, mostly developing countries, practice state-directed protectionism. In this manner, they try to allow their nascent industries to gain the technical sophistication and financial strength to compete with foreign competitors that have already acquired those strengths. To minimize the impact of protectionism, companies must consider manufacturing and distributing within important protected markets.

4. *To obtain cyclic diversification.* In spite of the clear trend toward the planetarization of the world economy, different regions still experience different rates of economic growth, and different economic cycles. For this reason, companies that operate on a planetary basis can balance their business results geographically. Thus they can invest and expand in growing areas, reaping the consequent benefits while curtailing investment and expansion in other areas until the situation changes there. In this manner, their overall performance is stabilized to an extent that regional companies cannot match.

5. *To profit from global financial systems.* As manufacturing and distribution operations globalize, they are supported by an already globalized financial network.

Financial flows have become mainly a matter of data transmission. Thus they already take place instantaneously, on a planetary basis.

6. *To profit from global communications and media.* As the media expand to cover the entire world, people in a growing part of the planet are presented the same information at the same time. Thus businesses can reach simultaneously an increasing number of customers by using global media.

7. *To profit from global-demand homogenization.* The main consequence of global communications and media is that they expose an increasing fraction of world population to the same messages. The effect is an increasing homogenization of demand on a global scale. This enables businesses to offer increasingly similar products in increasingly similar manners to a growing market.

8. *To profit from location economies and efficiencies.* Since different regions and countries are at different stages of economic development, they offer different business conditions. Thus all resources, including labor, land, information, and capital, have different costs and are subject to different treatments from different authorities. Thus a planetary strategy enables businesses to maximize their long-term benefits by profiting from location economies and efficiencies, including lower resource costs and taxes and financial incentives.

9. *To maximize opportunities for symbiotic relations.* Relations between a company's suppliers and customers are changing drastically, adapting to the new conditions created by the emerging economic realities of the world environment. One of the most important changes taking place in business is that between suppliers and their clients, from arm's-length relationships based on short-term commitments and continuous reviews of the relationship, to symbiotic relationships, based on long-term commitments and close relationships. To maximize benefits from symbiotic relationships, companies must look globally for potential suppliers and customers.

10. *To establish early presence in future markets.* As economic development takes place, more regions increase their demands for products, including goods and services, and channel them into higher-quality products. Anticipating competitors in entering new markets normally results in skimming the cream off those markets when they mature and develop. Thus long-term strategy increasingly tends toward the establishment of a presence in markets that are expected to mature in the years ahead, wherever they may be located.

11. *To profit from the global trend to market economies.* The collapse of the Soviet Union and its political and economic satellites has resulted in a clear trend toward market economies of many kinds. This circumstance is bringing about the opening of many major markets hitherto closed, or severely restricted, to private companies. Those markets are principally located in Eastern Europe, the Commonwealth of Independent States, China, and India.

Tactical Reasons

1. *To profit from international trade growth.* In the 40 years between 1950 and 1990, world trade, measured in terms of exports, grew by a factor of 4. In the same period, the world economy grew by a factor of 2. Thus, the fastest-growing part of the world

economy has been and is international trade. Companies participating in international trade are therefore likely to grow faster and more profitably than their competitors that focus on national or regional markets.

2. *To participate in countertrade.* About one-third of international trade is financed by countertrade agreements. These include barter, offsets, and other practices that do not involve money as a means of payment. Countertrade is mainly used by countries lacking in hard currencies. They have the fastest-growing demand in the international market. Thus, participating in countertrade enables companies to profit from fast-growing opportunities.

3. *To obtain cyclical diversification.* In spite of economic globalization, different countries and regions still operate within different economic cycles. Thus when certain countries are in recession, others are in expansion. Working globally enables companies to stabilize their overall business, thus obtaining benefits unavailable to regional competitors.

4. *To obtain economies-of-scope.* When a company develops special functional skills in marketing, production, or logistics, they can obtain maximum advantage of such skills by applying them in the largest market possible: the world market.

5. *To maximize the benefits from transfer prices.* Global companies have the flexibility to cost their output. That flexibility enables them to transfer products across national boundaries in a manner that, within legal limits, minimizes their local taxes.

Operational Reasons

1. *To arbitrage manufacturing/logistic capacities.* Global companies acquire manufacturing and logistic facilities in many regions. At any one time, some of those facilities may have capacity in excess of their assigned demand, while others are short of capacity. Global companies can gain advantages over regional companies by arbitrating their capacities, i.e., by dynamically reallocating demands to capacities available.

2. *To arbitrage exchange and inflation rates.* Global companies operate in many markets, with different rates of exchange and inflation. By dynamically reassigning their purchasing, production, processing, sales, and financing, they can obtain additional financial benefits.

3. *To accelerate the learning effect.* As a company's processing volume increases, its costs decrease as a consequence of the learning effect. By catering to the global market, a company can maximize its processing volume in a given period. This maximizes its cost reduction through the learning effect.

4. *To exploit automation's declining breakeven point.* The use of automation makes it possible to reduce a process's breakeven point, i.e., the volume that, if sold, recovers all costs incurred. Increasing automation enables companies to disperse their production economically. Thus they can cover increasing territories economically. Global companies are in a position to maximize these benefits.

Comparison between Domestic and International Logistics

The distinction between domestic and international operations is becoming increasingly blurred. Thus, most methods and techniques that apply in the design and operation of domestic systems can be extended and used in international systems. However, there are several aspects of international logistics that make it different from the domestic practice of any particular country. International logistics must

1. *Work in three dimensions.* When working in any particular country or continent, we can assume that the earth is flat as a map. This assumption does not introduce any significant errors in the analysis. However, when intercontinental logistics are considered, the earth's curvature becomes important. Distances are not what they seem on a flat map. Even more important, facility locations must be considered in three dimensions: locations such as Alaska, that may seem to be at the periphery of the world in a two-dimensional map, may prove to be at the center of things when viewed on a globe.

2. *Work with governments.* Domestic systems, by definition, deal with one country and therefore one government: all laws and regulations are the same or similar throughout the territory considered. When dealing with international operations, it becomes essential to consider foreign governments: their different laws, regulations, duties, taxes, currencies, and the degree and form of their effect on their country's economy. In many cases, governments develop multiyear economic development plans. They may be an important input to plan operations in their countries. Many actions that may be simple in certain countries, such as setting up a facility, may require substantial work to obtain authorizations in other countries. Furthermore, in some countries the main competitor may be a government-owned company or a government-favored company, and that circumstance may complicate matters significantly.

3. *Efficiently manage inventories.* In domestic systems, in-transit inventories and their carrying costs normally represent a small fraction of total logistic costs. In international systems, they normally represent an important fraction of total costs. For this reason, managing in-transit inventories efficiently is much more important in international than in domestic systems.

4. *Consider currency exchange rates.* Planning and operating in a multicurrency environment is significantly more complex than doing so in a domestic environment, with a single currency. Continuous variations in exchange rates add significant uncertainty to management. These must be taken into account using appropriate hedging methods that are unnecessary in a domestic setting.

5. *Consider inflation rate differentials.* Different countries have different inflation rates that vary continuously. This makes planning in an international environment significantly more complex than in a single country, where only one inflation rate must be projected. To take into account the additional risk and uncertainty, it is necessary to use more powerful analysis tools than those used in domestic situations.

6. *Consider complex multimodal alternatives.* Almost any intercontinental transport move requires the use of multiple transportation modes. Coordinating and

pricing them requires significantly more information and effort than most domestic moves.

7. *Review plans and operations more often.* The added size and complexity of international logistic problems compared with domestic ones make it imperative to review strategies and operational efficiency more often than is required for domestic systems. Thus the number and location of facilities, their missions, the transportation modes used, and their resulting performances and costs should be reviewed at least twice as often as in domestic systems.

8. *Integrate marketing channels with logistics.* In global systems, the type and characteristics of logistics systems are closely linked to market channel decisions, much more so than in a domestic market. The main reason is that in a domestic market, the marketing channels are usually established and stable. In international markets, a company typically finds itself manufacturing in some countries, warehousing in other countries, and exporting to other countries. In different countries, it may need to support different channels with different requirements. As a consequence, the logistic system for the integrated international systems is more complex than that for any country. Furthermore, the logistic strategy is influenced directly by the requirements established by the different channels.

9. *Work in many languages.* From packaging and labeling to order entry, an international operation must function in many languages. This circumstance requires multilingual staffs, and multilanguage systems.

10. *Use multiple measurement systems.* Most of the world operates under the metric or International System of measurements. Only the Republic of Myanmar, the Sultanate of Brunei, and the United States of America have not yet adopted the metric system as the only one in their respective countries. To do business with these countries it is, therefore, necessary to provide packages and sizes that conform to their unique systems in addition to the metric ones. Furthermore, documentation must contain all basic measurements in their system. This circumstance increases the cost of exporting to those countries and makes their goods more expensive than necessary when exported.

11. *Provide a wider variety of stock keeping units.* Customers in different countries require or prefer different sizes of the same product or different color schemes. Thus, international businesses must typically deal with a greater variety of stock keeping units than a domestic system.

Major Trends in International Logistics

Several major trends support the growth of international logistics and determine its characteristics. They concern informational, logistic services, procurement, manufacturing, logistic operations, and organizational trends. We examine these trends below.

Informational Trends

The main informational trend affecting planetary logistics management is a consequence of the convergence and fusion of several different technologies, through the digitalization of all forms of information handling devices and their integration into multipurpose machines. This phenomenon is giving birth to a new type of device: Data-Audio-Video Integrated Digital Systems (DAVIDS). The digitalization of data processing and communications is being followed by the digitalization of radio and television signals. All of them will shortly be processed by computers linked by communications channels. Such networks will receive, process, store, retrieve, and transmit all types of digital signals. In this manner, homes and workplaces will trade their telephones; computers; faxes; radios; record, tape, and disc players; televisions; scanners; and copying machines for DAVIDS: single devices capable of performing all their tasks. Linked throughout the planet by telephone lines and satellites, they will provide instant, economical linkups to any other DAVIDS anywhere in the world.

The massive use of DAVIDS linked electronically by planetary communications links in the form of Integrated Services Digital Networks (ISDNs) will change the structures of all organizations and especially the international logistics organizations of the future. Middle managers, mainly facilitators, will disappear. Organizations will have strategists and executors working hand-in-hand, worldwide, through computer networks. The borders of the typical company will be diffused, as suppliers and customers are also linked directly electronically. Most of their strategic discussions will take place face-to-face. Most of their operational interactions will take place electronically, through Electronic Data Interchange (EDI), teleconferencing, and other applications.

Logistic Services Trends

The current trend toward subcontracting transportation and warehousing services will be extended substantially through Planetary Integrated Logistic Systems (PILS). These will offer, worldwide, all logistic services required to move anything, from any origin to any destination, anytime, quickly and economically.

PILS will encompass multimodal transportation, worldwide warehousing, customs clearance, insurance, inventory management, order servicing, financing, documentation, and any other functions required to provide single-source services to shippers.

Under these conditions, a growing number of companies operating globally will find that it is most efficient in terms of service and cost to subcontract their logistic support to PILS suppliers.

Subcontracting of PILS will likely be accompanied by subcontracting of DAVIDS, because with the right providers, shipper companies can gain several major advantages:

- Free up scarce capital and management talent that can be focused on the main business of the company.
- Improve customer service while reducing logistic and informational costs through multiuser resource-sharing.
- Reduce shippers' risks by offering them a complete array of facilities, equipment, and services that shippers can use when and where they need.

Procurement Trends

To compete in any market, companies must source their needs throughout the world to obtain the best-quality, lowest-cost ingredients available anywhere. As a consequence, plant and warehouse locations are increasingly determined on a planetary rather than a regional or national basis.

Manufacturing Trends

Increasing automation of most production processes is lowering breakeven points; i.e., in most industries it is becoming increasingly economical to manufacture in plants of decreasing size. Increasing manufacturing automation results in lower fixed costs as a fraction of total costs and in lower setup times and costs.

Increasing automation enables companies economically to confront the increasing variety of products with decreasing useful lives that characterize an increasing number of industries. As a consequence, there is a trend toward just-in-time, planetary logistic networks broadly characterized by more, smaller plants and fewer, smaller warehouses. Major exceptions to this trend are found in industries with very high fixed and setup costs, with great stability of products and processes, with low-unit-cost products and with low obsolescence risk. These include mainly the process, agricultural, and extractive industries.

Logistic Operations Trends

To operate an international business successfully, five elements must be mastered. Each one of them must approach zero frequency to ensure competitiveness and survival. These elements that we designate collectively as "the Five Zeros" are:

1. Defects
2. Breakdowns
3. Delays
4. Stocks
5. Paperwork

These five affect all types of products, goods, and services. Their performance measurements cannot be expressed in percentages but in parts, or occurrences, per billion. Let us examine them.

1. *Zero defects.* Defects on goods and services are unacceptable. Quality must approach perfection; customers expect products to perform always according to their specifications, and their deliveries must take place with the exact quantities ordered, delivered on time.

2. *Zero breakdowns.* Breakdowns of any processes are unacceptable. Availability of processes must approach perfection: customers expect to receive goods and services with absolute punctuality. Thus, suppliers must ensure uninterrupted process performance through rigorous, preventive, and predictive maintenance. Otherwise

they risk the need to provide process redundancy or stocks to live up to customers' expectations.

3. *Zero delays.* Delays must be as brief as possible. Speed is becoming the basic competitive weapon in business strategy; customers expect to receive their orders not only with the exact quantity and quality they ordered, but immediately. Suppliers must ensure that their processes are as fast as possible or they risk having to carry stocks to compensate for their slowness.

4. *Zero stocks.* Inventories are increasingly expensive to carry. Not only because of financial, handling, and storage costs, but increasingly because of obsolescence: as technology continues to explode, in most industries new products and process become available faster and faster. Thus, yesterday's offerings are not good enough today. If carried in inventory, they must be eliminated at considerable loss. Furthermore, pipeline inventories are substantial in most international logistic systems.

5. *Zero paperwork.* Documentation must be electronic and be transmitted, not mailed. Paperwork means delays, errors, additional work, and therefore wasted time and money. Suppliers must provide electronically all customer informational interfaces, using EDI technology.

Organizational Trends

We focus here on the structural changes taking place today in all types of organizations. These changes affect not only business enterprises but also all other organizations, including government, military, religious, and nonprofit. They are giving rise to a new type of organization, the network organization.

Organizational Characteristics. Two factors are determining the type and characteristics of organizations today. First, the accelerating rate of change in all aspects of human endeavor, social, political, economic, technological, ecological, and psychological. Second, the massive and increasing application of information technology to all areas of human activity, from education, business, and entertainment, to creative thinking and artistic expression.

When change was slow and the world was a stable, rather predictable place, the most appropriate organizations were stable, hierarchical structures of the type introduced by military and religious organizations several millennia ago. These were organizations headed by one person in full command, with a certain number of subordinates reporting directly to him (rarely her), who in turn had a limited number of subordinates reporting to each one of them, and so forth. Subordinates were grouped around functions, to facilitate their work and interactions. Reporting relationships were clearly established by lines of authority and communication, and the specific functions of each person could be detailed in position descriptions. Communications were mostly verbal, in face-to-face encounters, complemented by written documents such as plans, reports, and memos. This type of reporting relationship established narrow limits on the practical number of subordinates a person could have, as illustrated in Fayol's principle of Span of Control.

In a turbulent, unifying world, where change is accelerating with consequent increases in uncertainty and complexity, rigidly hierarchical, functional organizations have proven to be ineffective. Their main problem is lack of adaptability. As the environment around them changes fast, they change slowly or essentially stay the same. The first and foremost reason is that rigid hierarchies structured along strict functional lines simply cannot cope successfully with change and its resulting uncertainty and complexity. Such organizations encourage their members to clearly delimit their areas of responsibility, and that cannot be done in an efficient manner. Any functional allocation of responsibilities, being arbitrary, results in rigid, inefficient, and conflictive performance.

Rigidity is necessary for the survival of the organization in place. Typically this leads to "turf wars": every function tries to protect itself by asserting its own importance at the expense of the others. A direct consequence of rigidity is the suboptimization of the organization's performance. As different functions compete instead of cooperating with others, they in effect try to optimize their own performance at the expense of the organization's overall performance. Furthermore, rigidity results in inadaptability. As external changes take place, the hierarchical organization cannot adapt itself to them because it risks internal changes that are likely to be politically detrimental to most functions.

Thus, hierarchical organizations progressively drift away from effective contact with reality and retreat into a culture of isolation and decay. As long as their accumulated assets or access to funds enables them to do so, they can continue in their path toward alienation from reality. However, with resources always being limited, there comes a time when such organizations must confront an unpleasant reality and either remake themselves into dynamic, responsive organizations, or perish. This is becoming a commonplace story today, as evidenced by the political, economic, social, and cultural developments taking place in the world today.

Future Implications.   What are the future implications of the trends discussed above for international organization development? We provide here a brief answer focused mainly on international business requirements. However, the principles apply to any type of organization, anywhere.

To succeed in a turbulent, planetary environment, it is necessary to replace rigid, hierarchical organizations by adaptable, dynamic organizations. These must be capable of successfully confronting accelerating change and its consequent increasing uncertainty and complexity.

An effective way to structure adaptable organizations is to replace the functional orientation by a resource orientation, with individual jobs following inflexible descriptions replaced or complemented by teams with varying skills and missions making maximum use of informational technology.

In a resource-oriented, network organization, people are the critical resource, not capital or machines. Their main tool is information, not capital or machines. The organization succeeds by maximizing the opportunities of each individual to contribute to the success of the entire organization or team. In this type of organization no functional barriers exist, because it is structured around the need to manage the organization's resources rather than to perform functions. Since resources are not defined arbitrarily as functions, no arbitrary boundaries are created that result in suboptimization of the organization's performance. A resource-oriented organization functions as illustrated in Fig. 8-1.

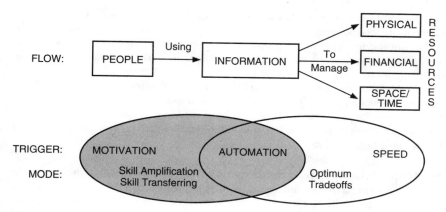

Figure 8-1. The functioning of a resource-oriented organization.

People using information manage physical and financial resources in space and time. By supporting people's performance and relationships through the use of information technology, their span of control is greatly expanded: an individual can promptly communicate with any other individual anywhere in the world instantaneously. Thus exchanges of data and information, in a variety of forms provided by DAVIDS, can take place quickly and effectively with an almost unlimited number of partners. This results in enormous flexibility and adaptability, unhampered by span-of-control problems. Furthermore, this approach frees up time for people to meet face-to-face to take care of unstructured problems such as strategy development. The result is substantially enhanced performance for the organization as a whole and heightened job satisfaction for the members of the organization.

The management of physical and financial resources in space/time (a continuum that is itself a resource), must be based on speed. High speed, coupled with product quality and service reliability, is the main competitive weapon in a turbulent business environment. Speed is attained by teams of people using automated online data processing and communications systems to process transactions and support decision making. The key to the optimum functioning of such organizations is people's motivation. Creating an environment conducive to high motivation becomes the key factor in ensuring a planetary organization's success.

Motivated people exploit information using DAVIDS computing and communication hardware to amplify and transfer skills. Computers amplify human skills by performing repetitive tasks faster, better, and cheaper than people can. They can be used to transfer skills to people by providing users access to powerful but complex decision-support technology through very-easy-to-use interfaces; in this manner, people with limited technical background can command and exploit very powerful techniques that improve their decision-making capabilities to a level unattainable by excellent managers working with manual tools.

A network organization also provides the flexibility to enhance its relations with the environment; above all, with its customers and suppliers.

In an increasingly uncertain and complex environment, success demands focused efforts. In this context, a planetary organization must bend every effort to concentrate its resources on the activities that provide it competitive advantages by adding substantial value with high productivity. Activities that cannot do so are usually better subcontracted externally to specialists that in turn can perform them more efficiently.

This flexibility of network organizations changes completely the nature of the relations between a company and its customers and suppliers. A network organization increases its performance by establishing symbiotic relationships with customers and suppliers, thus replacing the arm's-length relationships characteristic of hierarchical organizations.

Symbiotic Relationships.   Symbiotic relationships are more than mere partnerships. They bring together independent organizations into a relationship in which their success can only be ensured by the success of both parties: a "win-win" relationship instead of a "buyer beware" relationship. Symbiotic relationships are very close relationships, almost amounting to a soft form of integration. Without losing their separate identities, the parties enter into very long-term, exclusive, or almost exclusive relationships. This enables the supplier party to invest substantial resources to satisfy the needs of the customer, to contribute its knowledge without fear of being stripped of it by an unfair partner, and to react with the utmost speed by being a part of an integrated planning process. The resulting network organization is illustrated in Fig. 8-2.

The full-time members of the organization relate directly with each other, as re-

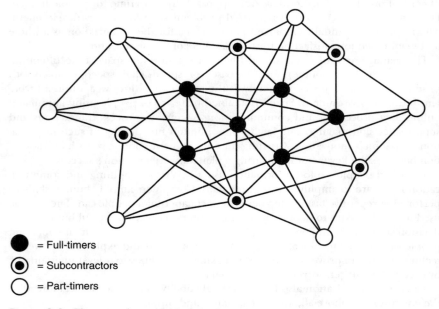

● = Full-timers

◉ = Subcontractors

○ = Part-timers

Figure 8-2. The network organization structure.

quired. They interact directly with subcontractors, who are an integral part of the network. Both are complemented by part-time individuals or companies that provide additional support as required. Toward the center of the network are the persons responsible for the formulation and implementation of strategy. Around them are the people and teams responsible for tactical management and operations. Individuals may have specific responsibilities to discharge or may work on and off as members of teams, or do a little of both, as requirements change. In this manner, the network organization embraces all the people that must function together to ensure its success and continuously adapts to the changing environment.

Managerial Consequences

The developments we have just sketched out have profound implications for managers in general and for logistic service suppliers in particular.

Implications for Managers.   The most important managerial implications deriving from the trends discussed above can be summarized as follows.

- *Planetary, long-term vision.* Even the management of domestic operations demands a planetary, long-term vision. Ignorance of competitive developments in other continents can spell disaster for managers who are not attuned to them and cannot anticipate and prepare for their impact in their domestic market.

- *Premium on leadership.* Managers cannot manage in the business environment of today and tomorrow by concentrating on resource allocation and administration problems. They must possess leadership qualities, and be able to inspire and motivate the people working with them.

- *Cross-cultural management.* Planetary management implies cross-cultural management, with teams of people of many diverse cultures working together. Providing the leadership and environment to do so effectively is a major responsibility of international managers.

- *Holistic decentralization.* The key to adaptability in a planetary environment is holistic decentralization, in which decision-making responsibilities are placed at the lowest level compatible with effectiveness, as close to the field as possible, but in an integrated, coordinated, holistic context. In this way, strategic direction can be implemented by a large number of people working in an ostensibly independent manner.

- *High quality and extensive variety.* High-quality goods and services, together with an increasingly large variety of them, are becoming the keystone of success in most industries. These requirements can be met most economically in a global environment.

- *Very high technical content.* The massive and increasing application of technology, especially information technology, to all aspects of business, makes it imperative for managers to understand its importance, and to develop the capability to harness its power to remain competitive.

- *Very high productivity.* Even in a highly differentiated strategy, high productivity provides an extra competitive edge. Thus the continuous, relentless search for improvement in quality and productivity is indispensable to ensure world-class competitiveness.

- *Very high speed.* An increasing number of companies have developed strategies around high-quality, high-variety, high-productivity product lines. Thus, competition is now moving toward high-speed service as the main weapon for competitive differentiation.

- *Customer orientation.* The very high technical content of products and processes propels companies toward research-and-development-based strategies. That is a sound base; however, only companies that start and end their strategic analysis with customer requirements can compete successfully in the long run, in a planetary environment.

Implications for Logistic Services Suppliers.   The planetary environment discussed previously presents many implications in the form of opportunities to suppliers of logistic services. The opportunities to suppliers are to

- *Offer PILS.* From an operational viewpoint, the greatest opportunities will be for companies offering Planetary Integrated Logistic Services (PILS). Such companies will be able to compete on very favorable terms with highly specialized local trucking or warehousing companies, simply by exploiting economies of scale and scope.

- *Act as risk-spreading agents.* By acting as risk-spreading agents, PILS companies will offer their customers a major incentive to subcontract all or most of their logistic needs, economically.

- *Handle small, frequent shipments efficiently.* By developing efficient means to process shipments with decreasing size and increasing frequency, PILS suppliers will offer a quality of service hard for highly specialized, local services companies to match.

- *Establish symbiotic relationships.* From a marketing viewpoint, PILS companies will be in the best position to enter into symbiotic relationships with their customers. These will provide them with long-term stability, resulting in increased profitability.

- *Exploit the power of DAVIDS.* From a managerial viewpoint, PILS companies will be in the position to exploit the power of computers and communications embodied in DAVIDS. Thus they will provide services of high and increasing quality, variety, productivity, and speed: the basic elements for success in the planetary economy.

Major Geographic Regions and Their Logistic Characteristics

Three major geographic regions account for the bulk of world economic activity and international trade: North America, Western Europe, and Southeast Asia, including Japan. These three areas produce 80 percent of the world's economic output, and account for 75 percent of world exports. For this reason, in an international logistic system it is necessary to understand the foundations of business and logistics systems in those regions.

North America

The North American Free Trade Association (NAFTA) is in the process of being created. It will join the economies of Canada, the United States, and Mexico. This area will have a larger population and domestic economic product than the European Community (EC) and the European Free Trade Association (EFTA) together. South of NAFTA is the rest of Latin America, a potential addition to NAFTA with a population of some 350 million people.

The United States and Canada have the most advanced logistics infrastructure and systems in operation in the world. North America offers a wide choice of suppliers in all transportation modes and very good, competitively priced warehousing facilities and ancillary services throughout the continent. Thus the development of logistic strategies, and logistic operations, are seldom conditioned by the physical means available.

In North America it is possible to find common, contract, and private carriers offering transportation services by air, highway, railroad, pipeline, and water. Since practically all means of transportation in the United States and most of them in Canada are privately owned, in most cases prices are negotiable, depending on freight type (e.g., hazardous materials, refrigerated goods, etc.) and characteristics (e.g., annual volumes, seasonality, shipment size, commodities, etc.).

Unitization, in the form of pallets and slip sheets, and freight containerization have been commonplace for decades. Pallets have been standardized mostly along industry lines (e.g., grocery manufacturers). Containers, mostly 40 ft and larger in length, with some 20-ft containers, have served as the basis for the International Standards Organization's standards.

The use of Electronic Data Interchange (EDI) to support logistic operations was pioneered in North America several decades ago, and the continent is the largest user of such technology in the world today.

Europe

The European continent is undergoing a major political and economic transformation that must be clearly understood to operate successfully in it.

There are four major European regions, each one with clearly differentiated subregions. These are the European Community (EC), the European Free Trade Association (EFTA), the Commonwealth of Independent States (CIS), and Middle Europe (ME).

The EC groups 12 nations: Germany, France, United Kingdom, Italy, Spain, Netherlands, Belgium, Luxembourg, Denmark, Portugal, Ireland, and Greece. This region has a population of approximately 320 million persons, with a gross regional product similar to that of the United States and a well-educated population.

The EFTA groups Switzerland, Austria, Sweden, Finland, Norway, and Iceland. This region has a population of approximately 55 million persons, the highest income per capita in the world, and a highly educated population.

The CIS and ME are trying to effect a transition from centrally planned economies to free market economies. They are expected to be in political and economic turmoil at least until the end of the current decade. Their economic problems are compounded by political volatility that is disintegrating the region into a conglomerate of smaller, tribal nations.

The CIS groups 15 republics, of which 9 are in the greater European region: Russia, Ukraine, Georgia, Belarus, Turkmenistan, Uzbekistan, Tadjikistan, Kyrgyzstan, Kazakhstan. The CIS has a population of approximately 290 million people, with a per capita income less than half that of the United States but with enormous reserves of natural resources and a well-educated population. Russia and Ukraine are the economic backbone of the CIS and encompass most of its population.

Middle Europe groups Poland, Czechoslovakia, Hungary, Romania, Bulgaria, Serbia, Croatia, Slovenia, Bosnia, Albania, and the Baltic states of Lithuania, Latvia, and Estonia. This region has a population of approximately 150 million persons with a low per capita income, adequate natural resources, and a well-educated population. In this region there are two economically different subregions: a relatively advanced one formed by Poland, Czechoslovakia, Hungary, and the Baltic states, and another, less advanced one grouping the rest.

Also economically important on the periphery of Europe is Africa, especially North Africa. This region has substantial trade with Western Europe, and is the source of massive immigration there.

In 1993 the EC and EFTA are scheduled to join, thus creating the largest trading area in the world, with a population of some 375 million persons and a gross regional product some 20 percent higher than that of the United States. We refer here to the combined EC/EFTA area as Western Europe.

In the 1990s, Western Europe will be the locomotive of the European economy. During this decade, increasing links will be developed with ME, which is likely to eventually join the EC/EFTA space, and to a lesser extent with the CIS, which is trying to develop strong links with North America.

Of major importance to companies operating in Western Europe are the following business-related issues now implemented or under consideration for implementation during this decade.

1. *Common currency.* The conversion to a common currency, the European Currency Unit (ECU). This will eliminate the costs and work of converting among currencies.

2. *Tax equalization.* The equalization of personal and corporate taxes throughout the region. This will bring logistic costs to the forefront, as the critical ones to establish facility locations.

3. *Political homogenization.* The homogenization of political institutions among all members. This will compound the benefits of tax equalization.

4. *Standards homogenization.* In January 1993, the EC implemented some 1500 safety, health, environmental, and quality standards across the EC and EFTA. The ultimate goal is to establish some 10,000 standards in Europe. The new rules are being drafted by the European Committee for Standardization, better known by its French acronym, CEN, and the International Standards Organization (ISO).

The developments affecting these issues will have major consequences on business in Western Europe, especially on logistic decisions concerning the location of plants and warehouses and the determination of their missions and areas of coverage.

However, one fact is clear from the development of optimum logistic strategies on a West European scale: the optimum number and location of plants and warehouses is substantially lower than that required to optimize the logistic networks of each individual country. Typical cost reductions obtained by optimum continental systems over optimum national systems are on the order of 15 to 20 percent. Thus, companies that streamline their logistic networks optimally on a continental basis, before their competitors, will gain major competitive advantages. If those advantages are retained for a few years, they may become insurmountable to their competitors.

The economic heart of Western Europe is a rectangle with vertices in London, Hamburg, Trieste, and Marseilles. Most production and consumption takes place in that area and is, therefore, of major logistic importance. This is the area that normally contains major distribution centers to supply West European customers or secondary warehouses.

Other major considerations governing West European logistics are as follows.

1. *Customs and transit procedures.* The EC has eliminated customs and transit procedures among its members; thus, there is a free flow of goods among its members and the EFTA nations.

2. *Transportation deregulation.* The deregulation of the transportation industry, with a common transportation policy in place possibly in 1993, will reduce transportation costs by 25 to 50 percent and will drastically reduce the optimum number of facilities required to meet customer service requirements economically.

3. *Transportation modes.* Trucks and pipelines account for the majority of tonnage transported in Europe today. They will continue to gain tonnage at the expense of rail, and coastal and inland water transportation, although the national railroads are waging a campaign to force more traffic to use rail, for environmental reasons. The result is likely to be an increase in intermodal transportation.

4. *Subcontracting of services.* Logistic services are increasingly being subcontracted to logistic services companies, rather than performed in house. This trend is likely to accelerate as the average shipment size continues to decrease, and the average shipping frequency to increase: consolidation provides substantial economies.

5. *Eurotunnel.* The opening of the Eurotunnel across the English Channel in the mid-1990s will improve service and reduce transportation cost between the United Kingdom and Europe. This will significantly affect facility location decisions.

6. *Palletization.* Palletized freight is increasingly using the International Standards Organization's (ISO) standard pallet sizes:

- 1200 × 1000 mm
- 800 × 1200 mm
- 1135 × 1135 mm

- 1220 × 1015 mm
- 1100 × 1100 mm

7. *Containerization.* Containerized freight uses mostly the ISO standard containers that have the following dimensions:

- Length: 12.20 or 6.10 m
- Width: 2.44 m
- Height: 2.59 m

Japan and Southeast Asia

The Japanese distribution system is by far the most complex and inefficient of the industrialized countries. This is a consequence of historical preferences given by the government to small business enterprises. Most aspects of goods distribution in Japan are tightly controlled by the government. The recent affluence of Japan, coupled with complaints from foreign governments and companies that consider the system a major impediment to entering the Japanese market, have provoked political actions. These have resulted in the beginning of major liberalization of the distribution system in Japan. However, distribution costs are such that retail prices are typically 5 to 10 times their respective wholesale prices.

Although Japan is an archipelago comprising more than 5000 islands, the bulk of its population lives on the four major islands of Hokkaido, Honshu, Kyushu, and Shikoku. Of these, the island of Honshu contains all the major cities and therefore, most of the population of Japan.

Some of the major characteristics of Japanese logistics are as follows.

1. *Transportation modes.* Ninety percent of domestically transported tonnage goes by truck, and this is likely to continue. Truck transportation requires licensing from the Ministry of Transport. Licenses distinguish among:

- Long-distance trucks, which carry loads between major regions; e.g., from plants to distribution centers.
- Short-distance trucks, which carry loads within a region; e.g., between a wholesaler and a retailer.
- District trucks, which can carry loads anywhere, but whose routes must originate and terminate within a designated district and can carry goods only for a single shipper.
- Route trucks, which can carry loads along their licensed route for multiple shippers.

2. *Logistic heartland.* The main area for production in Japan is the triangle Tokyo-Nagoya-Osaka, in the island of Honshu, it being about 500 km from Tokyo and Osaka. The triangle includes the metropolitan area around Tokyo known as Kanto (including Yokohama and Kawasaki), and that around Osaka, known as Kansai (including Kobe and Kyoto).

3. *Traffic congestion.* Traffic congestion on roads and highways is a critical problem in the triangle, especially in and around the major cities, where traffic speed averages less than 15 km/hr. For this reason, just-in-time systems require many small facilities, and/or substantial fleets of small vehicles, to meet customer requirements quickly, reliably, and economically.

4. *Distribution systems.* Distribution systems for different products are usually very different because of traditional differences in trade practices and channels of distribution.

5. *Distribution channels.* Nontraditional distribution channels, especially non-store channels, are booming, and often represent the best way to introduce new products into the Japanese market. These channels include mail order, catalogue sales, door-to-door sales, teleshopping, and vending machines.

6. *Shared distribution.* Shared distribution is common, with competitors delivering to the same stores sharing delivery facilities and trucks.

7. *Palletization.* Large companies tend to use ISO standard pallet sizes; however, these are not mandatory, and a proliferation of different pallet sizes significantly complicates logistic operations.

8. *Warehousing.* Business warehouses are supervised by the Ministry of Transport and regional Transport Bureaus. These distinguish among private, agricultural, co-operative, and public warehouses. Public warehouses are further classified into general-purpose, cold storage, open-air, storage tanks, floating storage (e.g., for logs), and dangerous goods warehouses. These are treated differently by the Ministry of Transport, which issues them permits.

Logistics practices in the rest of Southeast Asia present significant national differences, although most countries in the region look to Japanese practices as a model.

Ocean/Air Lanes: Intercontinental Freight

Intercontinental freight is transported by air or ocean. These are the extremes in speed and cost, with air freight moving at the highest speed and cost and ocean freight moving at the slowest speed and lowest cost of all modes.

Air freight is growing substantially faster than all other modes. Currently, most products move internationally by air. Characteristically, these are products with very high value per kilogram and with high obsolescence risk, such as semiconductors, mainframes, pharmaceuticals, fashion items, high-value spare parts and components, and instruments. In many countries air freight has taken market share away from railroads and trucks, simply because customs clearances are easier at modern airports than at old and inefficient border crossing points.

Ocean freight is used for those items with characteristics opposite to the previous ones, especially products with medium or low value per kilogram and medium or low obsolescence risk. These include grains, minerals, automobiles, microcomputers, and home electronic products.

Developing Planetary Logistic Systems

The planetarization of the economy enables companies to extend profitably the scope of their operations across the world. This requires them to establish integrated logistic networks on a planetary scale to maximize the efficiency of their logistic strategy.

The design of integrated logistic networks on a planetary scale is the fundamental technical problem that logisticians must solve. It constitutes the base upon which to build the necessary logistic management systems and organization.

The basic principles of logistic network design are similar, regardless of the scope of the network. However, the size and complexity of a planetary network, compared with a national or continental network, is much greater. For this reason the methodology to be followed to define and describe the alternatives to be considered, and the technology to evaluate them correctly, are of the utmost importance. Mediocre methods or techniques inevitably result in inferior, uncompetitive strategies.

Modeling Approaches

The size and complexity of international or planetary logistic systems design problems is such that they constitute an excellent example of the dictum "What cannot be modeled cannot be managed." Thus, when attempting to develop an optimum international or planetary logistic strategy, the main question is not whether to model or not, but how to model in the most effective manner.

The logistic modeling literature contains many descriptions of different types of modeling techniques. For this reason, we provide here only a brief summary of the approach to be taken from the international logistics viewpoint.

The most powerful technique to ensure optimal logistic strategies in use today is Mixed Integer Programming (MIP). This technique enables users to model explicitly fixed, semivariable and nonlinear variable costs, as well as nonnumerical restrictions (legal or technical condition). For these reasons, MIP is the preferred optimization tool to design large-scale, optimum logistic strategies.

One potential drawback of MIP is that it considers only deterministic conditions; i.e., it assumes that the values of every input are entirely correct. That assumption is rarely if ever true in practice. In cases where uncertainty concerning the value of inputs is high, a different type of optimization can be used advantageously: Robust Optimization (RO).

Robust Optimization is a mathematical optimization technique that enables the construction of large-scale models that recognize and reflect the probabilistic nature of the inputs. Thus, RO provides optimum strategies that maximize benefits while simultaneously minimizing risk.

The correct use of large-scale optimization techniques for the design of international logistic strategies typically saves 10 to 25 percent of the total logistic cost arrived at by inferior techniques, such as heuristics. Thus, its impact on competitiveness is of major consequence.

Management Systems

Logistic management systems for international or planetary systems are based on the same techniques used in domestic logistics. All the techniques described for forecasting, purchasing, production planning, inventory management, transportation management, etc., are applicable in the international context. However, two special considerations are worthy of consideration in this regard.

1. *In-transit inventories can be substantial.* Domestic and continental systems normally operate with relatively low in-transit inventories. That is not the typical case in intercontinental or planetary systems, where the inventory "pipeline" can represent a significant cost. For this reason, in international logistic systems, it is recommended that in-transit inventories be included in all pertinent calculations, reflected as additional inventory carrying costs.

The in-transit inventory carrying cost for a given origin-destination combination and commodity can be calculated as follows:

$$C = \frac{t}{365} \times c \times V$$

where C = total annual inventory carrying cost ($/yr); t = transit time for a given mode (days); c = unit inventory carrying cost ($/ton/yr); V = annual volume shipped between the origin and the destination (tons/yr).

2. *The problems associated with MRP and DRP are magnified.* Materials Requirements Planning (MRP) and Distribution Requirements Planning (DRP) create many operational problems for domestic users. These techniques are being replaced by more powerful ones, especially the use of optimum scheduling of production, transportation, and warehousing operations.

The problems associated with MRP and DRP center around their lack of responsiveness to market changes and the simplistic nature of the calculations used to determine logistic flow quantities. Those problems can be severely magnified in international systems, where elapsed flow times are longer than in a domestic context. For this reason, MRP and DRP techniques are to be avoided in international logistic systems, or must be complemented with better planning techniques, such as optimization, to ensure competitive results.

9

Planning and Budgeting

Gene R. Tyndall
Partner and Director, Logistics/Distribution,
Ernst & Young

Few problems threaten American business today more insidiously than uncontrolled costs. Even companies known for both excellent products and services can lose money because they fail to act on significant opportunities to improve their costs—particularly, overhead costs. Companies often adopt strategic imperatives such as total quality management, close-to-the-customer, and time-based management, yet fail to develop the proper information structure to support meaningful planning and budgeting that could help them achieve these strategic goals.

Few corporate executives are unaware of how quickly competitive pressures have intensified in recent years. The strategies for attaining market share (among them product and service innovations, emphasis on quality and speed to the market, and cost considerations) are more numerous and more complex than ever. Yet many companies continue to launch new strategic initiatives without analyzing or understanding the likely profitability of these moves. Other companies are satisfied with the status quo and fail to recognize competitive opportunities. Small wonder that many of these companies end up disappointed with the results.

In this complex world, those operational activities that comprise the functions of logistics, physical distribution, or materials management are being rediscovered. More and more companies are realizing the *value* of functions that support production and product sales. This value takes the form of logistics services, which are provided to internal "customers" as well as to external customers who purchase the company's products.

At the same time, there is the corresponding management obligation to better understand what the costs of logistics are and how they vary by activity levels (e.g., order sizes, specialized storage and handling requirements, and shipment or delivery frequencies). Studies have proven that the overall costs of logistics—sourcing, transporting, warehousing, ordering, distributing, servicing, and carrying materials and products—range anywhere from 15 to 50 percent of sales, depending on the industry, products, and company. Today's emphasis on operational effectiveness to meet customer needs can mean bottom-line improvements if companies plan, budget, and manage logistics costs (and services) properly.

The positive news is that more sophisticated, adaptable, and powerful planning and budgeting methods not only exist, but are readily available to any firm willing to try them. Collectively these new methods are called *total cost management* (TCM).

This chapter develops the elements of total cost management as applied to the planning and budgeting of logistics. It focuses on activity-based costing (ABC) as the preferred method at leading companies to plan, measure, and control expenses associated with managing and monitoring logistics.

Planning and Budgeting— The Framework

The logistics budget should be the primary tool in monitoring and controlling logistics costs. Since budgeting integrates logistics into the complete range of corporate activities, through the link between the logistics budget and the companywide budget or profit plan, it is a highly effective means of planning for integrated operations.

In the past few years, formal planning has received increased emphasis by companies and managers striving to influence and control their destiny, rather than being content to react to market and business conditions. Planning, the most basic and pervasive management function, is a formal, systematic process to ensure the direction and control of the organization's future. It includes evaluating where the company is and deciding where it should go. Planning the course of action involves deciding in advance what is to be done, who is to do it, when it has to be done, and how it is to be done.

Strategic and Operational Planning

Two major types of planning are of concern to logistics management:

1. *Strategic planning* sets long-range (3–5 year) goals and objectives that focus on the company's scope, i.e., markets, products, and customers; on its competitive position, including particular strengths or weaknesses; on specific targets for company size, market share, and profitability; and on necessary resources and how they should be applied.

2. *Operational planning* sets short-term objectives, primarily in financial terms, for marketing, sales, production, and the other corporate activities for the coming year. Its primary element is the overall corporate budgeting process.

It is important to recognize the relationship of budgeting to strategic planning. Ideally, the budgeting process commits resources to execute the strategic plan. However, if the strategic plan is absent, the budgeting process becomes more complex, because it must identify and deal with both long- and short-term issues.

This integration of planning and budgeting is indeed important for logistics. A logistic budget is most effective when it represents a commitment of resources to execute a logistics strategic plan.

The logistics strategic plan provides the framework and rationale for the logistics managers' daily decisions; thus, the budget should be responsive to the rationalization for the resources employed in logistics activities. The budget should also provide the means for measuring performance and targets for logistics management.

The first year of the logistic strategic plan, therefore, should provide the framework for the current operating budget for the logistics function. This interrelationship, performed effectively, provides the essential link between planning and budgeting.

Functions and Benefits of Budgeting

The budgeting process serves three primary functions—planning, control, and communication—the interrelationship among these three making the process a powerful and effective management tool. Let us now look at the nature of each.

1. *Planning.* The budget is the culmination of an annual planning process, and it documents the resulting plan in financial terms. The plan describes the structured approach necessary for the corporation to meet its goals and objectives, and it helps to ensure that all corporate resources and activities are directed toward a common target.

2. *Control.* The budget provides an objective means to monitor the organization's progress in meeting its goals. Inefficiencies and other causes for deviations from the annual plan can be identified by analyzing budget variances. Thus, corrective actions can be taken promptly and can be focused properly when actual results differ from expectations.

3. *Communications.* The budget provides a communication link between management and those implementing the plan. When the planning process has been completed, the budget imparts management's objectives, goals, strategies, and programs for the next year, throughout the organization. During plan implementation, monthly budget reports compare actual with planned results to communicate performance measure in a clear, concise format.

The benefits of an effective, organizationwide budgeting process go far beyond the additional focus of cost control and include:

- *Commonality of goals and objectives.* Common goals and objectives are established throughout the organization. The purpose of the organization and its specific goals can be communicated, and progress in achieving them can be monitored.

- *Periodic planning.* The preparation of the budget requires key managers to set aside time each year for planning. The budgeting process is a formal planning framework that encompasses all company activities.

- *Quantification of the plan.* The budget quantifies the activities and programs to be engaged in during the next 12 months. In addition, the benefits of each project under consideration are quantified. This enables management to review proposals, to determine which are more advantageous.

- *Effective cost control.* Periodic (e.g., monthly) variance reports provide a means to better manage and control costs. Unacceptable situations are quickly and clearly identified, and corrective action can be taken immediately.
- *Performance evaluation.* Managerial performance in each budgeting entity may be appraised objectively. Managers at each level know what is expected, so they can monitor their own progress.

The Companywide Budget

A company's overall budget, commonly referred to as the *master budget,* is comprised of two major elements:

1. The *operating budget,* or *profit plan,* which includes subsidiary budgets detailing revenues, expenses, and the resulting net income for the budget period.
2. The *financial budget,* which consists of supplemental budgets for cash, the balance sheet, capital expenditures, and a statement of changes in financial position.

The logistics budget is an element of the operating budget. It is associated with other elements of the operating budget such as the sales budget, production budget, and budgeted cost of goods sold. The assumptions used to develop these budgets provide the underlying information necessary for an effective logistics budget. They provide information on the inbound, interfacility, and outbound flow of goods that is essential to the logistics budgeting process.

Fixed Budgets

Fixed budgets, the common form for master budgets, consist of revenue and cost projections for only one level of activity. Fixed-budget performance reports compare actual performance with the single level of activity reflected in the budget. If the actual level of activity turns out to be different from that underlying the fixed budget, the performance reports, of course, become less effective.

Fixed budgets do not take into consideration cost behavior patterns. The static nature of the budget makes it difficult to isolate the impact of volume variations when analyzing budget variances. This tendency to obscure critical performance deviations, when the actual volume varies from plan, is a major deficiency.

Flexible Budgets

Flexible budgets are based on formulas that reflect fixed and variable cost components. Thus they can be adjusted easily for activity level changes. This capability allows managers to answer the question, "What should our costs be, given the actual volume level?"

The more innovative companies use flexible budgeting techniques for logistics activities, as an improved means of controlling expenses. Figure 9-1 illustrates the overall context of planning and budgeting for logistics.

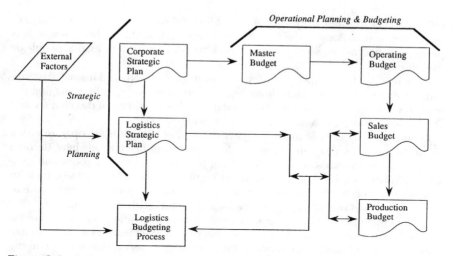

Figure 9-1. A planning and budgeting framework—the logistics perspective.

Planning Logistics Costs

Ultimately, the goal of every company must be to provide value to customers at a profit. For customers, value is a function of three interrelated factors: cost, quality, and time. Since profitability can be achieved only if a company knows the "true" cost of its products and services, the emphasis for planning logistics is on cost.

Cost Management Issues

Although management accounting was always intended to provide information for the internal use of managers, traditional accounting systems fail to provide relevant and timely information for managerial decision making. Too often, traditional cost systems provide inaccurate and misleading product and service costs. Consequently, these inaccurate product costs lead to poor decisions about product lines or logistical service. Traditional cost systems also cause (at least indirectly) dysfunctional behavior by both individual employees and functional departments. (Examples of such dysfunctional behavior include producing excess inventory to "absorb" overhead, or buying substandard raw material that causes poor-quality products to be manufactured.) By contrast, cost management (through activity-based costing, or ABC) provides reliable product costs. Cost management helps a company improve its products and services by reducing waste and eliminating dysfunctional behavior.

Much of the frustration with traditional cost systems stems from the fact that variances between actual costs and standard costs represent information that is too late and too aggregated to be of any use. Activities, by contrast, can be monitored directly and continuously. Cost management emphasized the management of activities rather than the management of costs for the simple reason that activities—unlike costs—*can* be managed. At best, costs are only *indirect* measures of efficiency or effectiveness—in other words, a cost is a historical fact that cannot be changed. Something can be done in the here and now, however, to change how an activity is performed, because an activity is simply work, or a collection of tasks, that people or machines do.

Costs remain vitally important in making strategic decisions and in analyzing customer value chains. Ultimately, however, costs are best managed by managing the activities that consume resources (i.e., costs), which is the thrust of this chapter and the key to such success in modern cost management.

Economic realities have made it necessary for most companies to operate with a "lean and mean" philosophy. In one industry after another markets have become global, with worldwide competitors offering high-quality, low-cost goods and services. Industries previously operating under regulatory rules, which allowed them to pass all costs on to the customer, now face a changed regulatory environment. Streamlining and restructuring have become common goals in all industries.

At the same time that pressures to streamline have intensified, businesses are experiencing demands to offer new services and new product features as well. Companies have worked hard to understand their customers' needs; that understanding has in turn sparked the marketers' and product designers' imaginations and enthusiasms. Those companies that are effective at rapidly bringing innovative new products and services to the market have gained a huge competitive edge in today's business world. Similarly, companies that are ineffective at quick responses are extremely vulnerable if a variety war breaks out in their industry. In fact, improving the process of introducing new products and services has become a strategic objective in company after company.

Yet the proliferation of products and services can add to the complexity of getting work done throughout an organization: in engineering, in operations, in logistics, in customer services, in human resources. This complexity is one of the chief causes of rising costs everywhere.

Finally, one other factor continues to change the business environment: automation. Much of the work previously performed by a direct labor force is now done by machines. More and more employees are now engaged in indirect or support functions. Similarly, more and more of the administrative functions are transacted with assistance from computerized information systems. All these instances help to explain why the ratio of indirect costs to direct costs keeps rising steadily.

Facing all these new challenges, executives have begun to question how well their old cost techniques provide them with the information needed to make management decisions. These techniques were developed at a time when the business environment differed dramatically from what companies face today.

The Role Cost Information Plays Today

In almost all companies, accounting departments periodically (weekly, monthly quarterly) produce a set of management reports. These reports usually appear as income statements individualized for department heads and summarized for high-level management. Typically, such reports show budgeted amounts, actual amounts, and the difference between the two for the current period and the year-to-date.

Companies using a standard cost system generate reports that show the standard cost of goods produced or services performed, along with any variances incurred.

In each of these cases the reporting basis is the predefined cost; the budget in the first case, the standards in the second.

The major purpose of periodic management reports should be to provide managers with a means of monitoring progress toward their goals and of directing their energies to situations needing attention. Yet these reports achieve their purpose only if they organize and calculate costs in such a way as to reflect the true dynamics of the business. This is achieved only if the timing of the report is synchronized with underlying activity.

The traditional transition from basic logistics starts with a function that is simply measured as a percentage of gross sales, moves toward a function that minimizes costs, and eventually creates an integrated logistics function that contributes to profitability. Proper achievement of this transaction requires a concerted management effort to incorporate logistics within the overall business strategy. In addition, more and more companies are provided "specialized logistics services" and view logistics as a competitive advantage. This trend places more emphasis on the complete understanding of logistics components, and on the need for improved methods to measure and control logistics costs across all organizational functions.

The identification, measurement, and control of total logistics costs are fundamental to the effective management of logistics and the operations of the business. Since total costs are a decisive factor in making strategic and operating decisions, it is important to understand the tradeoffs in logistics (such as transportation versus inventory), as well as the implications of functional focus across the entire product supply chain (such as cutting purchasing costs, which results in a delay of product supply). When logistics are linked to corporate strategic objectives, the proper interrelationships between such functions as manufacturing capacity and inventory management can be determined, to arrive at improved overall efficiency.

These values associated with logistics—improvements in time and cost—are increasingly important to companies in today's environment. As logistics innovations are created, how they are implemented determines their contribution; how they are planned and costed determines their value.

Activity-Based Logistics

A key component of TCM is *activity-based costing*. While business process analysis is the cornerstone concept for improving management accounting, activity-based costing (more commonly known as ABC) has become the catch phrase to describe the new techniques in management accounting. In this chapter, the term "activity-based costing" describes the specific techniques for costing business processes and for costing "objects." The objects may be products, services, product lines, service lines, customers, customer segments, or channels of distribution.

Activity-based costing is a technique for accumulating cost for a given cost object that represents the total and true economic resources required or consumed by the object.

Organizations that sell goods or services already cost their products for inventory valuation or regulatory purposes. But many people who must rely on these costs for internal decision making consider them both incomplete and distorted. They are incomplete because they include only the costs to acquire or produce the end products. They may not include any of the costs of warehousing, distribution, sales, or service. They are distorted because each product typically includes an assignment of overhead that was allocated on some arbitrary basis such as direct labor, sales dollars, machine hours, material cost, units of production, or some other volume measure.

The logic of activity-based costing is simple. Companies expend resources to fund activities. They perform activities to benefit products, services, or other cost objects. The goal in activity-based costing is to mirror this casualty among resources, activities, and cost objects in assigning overhead costs. For example, salaries, facility costs, and computer costs may be spent to support logistics planning activities, which in turn support individual products or services. In this example, the cost of each product or service should reflect the cost of the logistics planning activity required to support it.

At first glance, this ABC process may appear to require extremely elaborate data collection systems. This is not necessarily the case. Companies may want to assign overhead costs to objects more accurately, but they are also looking for ways to simplify rather than complicate the work their people do. To continue this same example, ABC would not require that staff members in logistics planning begin keeping track of how much time they spend supporting each individual product or service. Rather, ABC would make use of data that already exist as a natural consequence of the work.

Logistics planning decisions are analyzed and then communicated throughout the organization by using a computerized planning-and-control system (quite possibly, a DRP-II system). ABC data could be generated by scanning the DRP-II files and determining how many logistics or service-planning transactions were processed for each product. In fact, the very existence of rich databases is precisely what makes the actual implementation of ABC systems feasible.

The cost data contained in a company's general ledger are reorganized into *activity cost pools,* and the amounts in the activity cost pools are then assigned to products/services or other cost objects based on some causal factor. Once the object costing has been completed, the costs are compared to selling prices or revenues to analyze profitability by product, service customer, and so on.

Activity-based costing occurs in two major phases. First, we determine the costs of significant activities. Then we assign the costs of the activities to products or to other "objects" of interest, such as customers or services. This first phase is *activity-based process costing;* the second is *activity-based product costing* (or more accurately, *activity-based object costing*).

Activity-based process costing serves two separate purposes. First, it develops the costs of the activities identified in the business process itself. Second, it is a necessary intermediate step in calculating activity-based object costs. Activity-based process costing is a major link between improving the accuracy of costing and improving the performance of logistics.

The prime objective is to assign costs that reflect or "mirror" the physical dynamics of the business. A phase often used to describe the underlying concept of ABC is that "the business's resources are consumed in the conduct of activities, and activities are performed in the service of products." Activity-based costing tries to manifest this two-stage dynamic environment.

Thus, activity-based process costing applies costs through a series of activity/driver bases. The process is made up of a series of activities directed at producing an output. Activity-based process costing is the precursor to activity-based product costing and helps to facilitate performance measurements for responsibility accounting.

Activity-based product costing applies costs to products by developing cost pools within processes that represent costs that vary with a common activity/driver. An important distinction to note is that activities consume resources at the process level, while products consume activities. This allows us to integrate activity-based process and product costing by first costing the activity where incurred (process), and second, rolling up costed activities into products.

Activity-based product costing improves the tracing of costs to products, where these costs were typically and arbitrarily allocated in the past. Any costs that can be charged directly to products should be removed from the cost pools.

ABC in Logistics

Figure 9-2 provides an overview of logistics cost management.

With logistics costs of activities "outside the factory" representing as much as 40 percent of gross revenues in some industries, product cost information without the full supply chain activities is quite limited.

Most functions (or activities) of logistics lend themselves to ABC; indeed, logistics activities have typically been costed using techniques much like those used by ABC. Transportation and warehousing activities—which together comprise 40 to 60 percent of typical logistics costs—are treated as activity costs, since they primarily involve transactions that are product-related.

Once the logistics activities are understood, a company must determine cycle times and costs for the activities, which can be determined through observation and by examining historical data. The factors include:

- The time (in hours and days) required to cycle from start to finish one work product

- The cost (in labor and other expenses) associated with the cycle

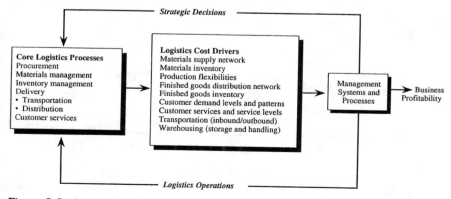

Figure 9-2. An overview of the logistics cost management process.

Figure 9-3 illustrates a sample cost and cycle time profile for labor associated with the flow of materials through the company, to delivery of one order through a particular distribution channel and finally to a customer. Note that this figure transcends the inbound-to-outbound logistics supply chain for the company itself; it does not include comparable supply chain activities for vendors, carriers, and customers.

The time line depicted in Fig. 9-3 also involves a cost associated with the dollars spent to move a product from raw material to customer delivery. This time includes "dwell activities" (such as storage, inventory, or other time-consuming activities not directly associated with flow), packaging, or labeling.

Similar cost and cycle time profiles can be developed for detailed activities undertaken within functions such as purchasing, order processing, warehousing, transportation, and information support. The sum of all such cost and cycle time profiles represents ABC for product groups, lines of business, distribution channels, customers, or other cost management interests.

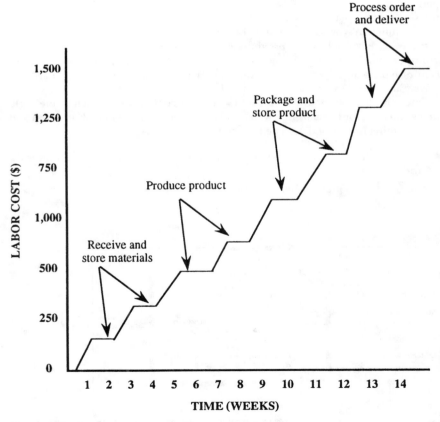

Figure 9-3. Cost and cycle time profile—an example.

Cost drivers should be identified for the logistics activities that determine the causes of cost incurred by the activity. For example, the following are typical cost drivers for logistics activities:

- Materials (number of stock keeping units (SKUs) and items)
- Materials supply network (number of vendors and locations)
- Materials inventory levels
- Production flexibilities
- Finished goods distribution network (number of locations)
- Finished goods inventory (products) levels
- Customer demand levels and patterns
- Customer services and service levels
- Transportation (inbound and outbound)
- Warehousing (storage and handling)

In other words, the logistics strategies and operating policies of the company for these key cost drivers cause costs to be incurred at the activity level. It is important to understand *why* costs are incurred for the business, as well as *how* and *when*.

A useful approach to developing logistics ABC is to develop a "cost model," typically for one business unit, one product group, one period, and one type of distribution channel. Figure 9-4 illustrates the eight steps to follow in developing the cost flow model. These are further defined as follows:

1. *Collect financial data.* Collect financial data for the current period budget (or past actual).

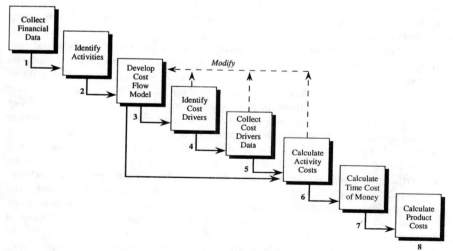

Figure 9-4. Developing the cost model.

2. *Identify activities.* Identify activities for the selected product group.

3. *Develop cost flow model.* Identify, as a preliminary step, all costs that can be assigned to the product group.

4. *Identify cost drivers.* Identify the events that initiate the activity and cause the cost.

5. *Collect cost drivers data.* Collect historical, budget, observed, or estimated cost driver data.

6. *Calculate activity costs.* Calculate activity costs per cost driver and per activity, and reconcile their scope to the sum of costs.

7. *Calculate time cost of money.* Calculate time cost of money for each product group and distribution channel; the variables are the company's cost of capital, multiplied by the total dwell time, multiplied by total activity costs.

8. *Calculate product costs.* Calculate product costs for their product group based on the appropriate drivers and activities, calculate the margins, and compare the resulting costs with traditional product costs.

The outcome of the cost flow model can thus be evaluated in light of its comparability with the firm's traditional cost methodology, its ability to accurately calculate total product flow costs across the supply chain, and its ability to calculate other measures such as gross margin, value-added costs, and profitability. Once the cost flow model approach has been deemed appropriate, the complete logistics ABC method can be developed for all product groups and all activities.

Customer Service

Customer service is *the process of providing desired goods, quality, and total support to benefit every aspect of product use at a competitive price and in a timely manner.* The management of customer service seeks to exceed customer expectations of service, while minimizing total overall cost and maintaining response flexibility to changing market conditions.

Few companies can satisfy every customer's need or perceived need without running out of resources. Customer service management involves a series of tradeoffs and negotiations that provide service at *strategically profitable* levels. The bulk of these tradeoffs involve inventory availability and packaging convenience. They may also involve undertaking those processes traditionally belonging in the customer realm but now deemed non-value-added. For instance, many customers are moving toward outsourcing functions such as purchasing for noncritical items; managing inventory between dock, stock, and production floor; and invoicing. Suppliers must be prepared to take over and manage these functions for customers if this is required to gain a competitive advantage and to establish a long-term strategic partnership. Strategically profitable customer service involves looking at the long term. Just as the experience curve dictates that pricing below current cost can increase volume and make a profit over the long term (while driving competitors out of business), as companies competing on a business battlefield they must be prepared to ignore the current costing system and provide services that will prove profitable over the longer term.

To be a viable competitor in customer service, a company will be required to commit some capital. If a strategy for customer service and a performance measurement system has been adopted, the customer service tradeoff parameters and requirements will be known. When combined with a cost management system that provides a true cost picture of product lines (by attributable cost based on cost drivers, not allocations based on labor or equipment utilization), management will be able to respond quickly and favorably to changing conditions.

Leading companies are employing strategies and ABC systems that can capture the true costs of selling and servicing the product. Several factors become important in being able to measure, determine, and control an optimum balance between cost, potential sales, and customer service. Some of the cost factors involved in these tradeoff decisions include:

- *Material cost.* The cost of the materials used in the product build.
- *Packaging cost.* The cost of packaging throughout the supply chain.
- *Marketing/sales cost.* The cost of initiating sales and leads, developing customer requirements, and processing orders.
- *Product development cost.* The cost of developing and designing the product, in terms of expended cost and time to market cost.
- *Overhead costs.* The costs associated with the manufacture of the product—tooling, capital equipment, facilities, utilities, etc.
- *Transportation cost.* The cost of the means to move the product from the last production process to the customer.
- *Storage/inventory costs.* The costs of storing and handling in-process and finished goods.
- *Service cost.* The cost of providing customer satisfaction through after-sales service and support.
- *Indirect costs.* The costs of indirect and support functions that assist in the nondirect tasks of transforming, storing, packaging, and moving the product.

It is the explicit responsibility of for-profit businesses to be profitable: there is really little other rationale for their existence. Today, with increasing customer expectations, it is obvious that customer service is not free. For instance, if inventory is maintained at a high level to service the customer through all possible demand fluctuations and operating uncertainties, the results are significant downside cost ramifications. However, if inventory is maintained at a low level, the penalty may be lost sales or customer dissatisfaction.

As sales and market penetration increase, the cost to maintain optimum service levels also increases. The important task is to maintain the balance between sales and optimum service. There is an optimum level of customer service to be achieved between the sales dollar and the cost of servicing the sale.

Providing optimum service levels may require increased levels of capital and working capital, but the benefits in terms of improved customer service and sales can be significant. Figure 9-5 illustrates certain logistics issues for major tradeoffs, while Fig. 9-6 cites methods for analyzing and deciding among choices.

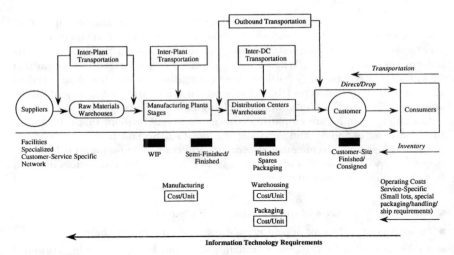

Figure 9-5. Making major tradeoffs—areas for analysis.

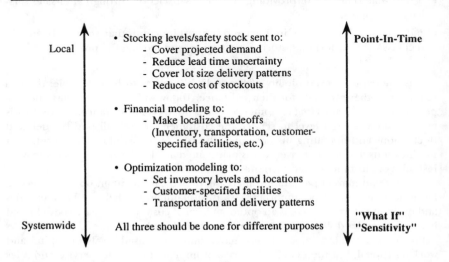

Figure 9-6. Making cost tradeoffs—methods for analysis.

Transportation

Transportation costs are driven by the overall logistics strategy and operations of the company. Since logistics encompasses all material flow functions across a company's product supply chain, from vendors to customers—transportation, warehousing and distribution, customer services, inventory management, procurement, and materials handling—transportation costs are determined by the role of the transportation function in this overall logistics environment.

Many factors contribute to the determination of transportation costs. These include but are not limited to the following:

- Shipment origin and destination
- Product shipped (i.e., its value and its specific shipped characteristics, such as special handling, weight, or packaging)
- Mode of shipment (truck, rail, air, ocean, barge, or pipeline)
- Outside carrier used
- Shipment size (e.g., full truckload, full carload, or less-than-truckload)
- Shipment weight
- Frequency of shipments
- Packaging type and unit (e.g., pallet load or air container)
- Shipment routing and total distance traveled
- Shipment tracking
- Rehandling of product (e.g., consolidation or breakbulk operations)
- Origin and destination handling
- Payment terms
- Desired speed or transit time (e.g., one-day service or cheapest route)
- Special services
- Claims (loss and damage)
- Transportation of hazardous materials (e.g., routing implications, special handling charges, or insurance costs)

In determining for-hire carrier costs, several types of special charges should be identified and measured. These include line-haul charges, occasional charges for extra services (e.g., diversions, reconsignment, demurrage, and transit privileges), claims administration (including loss and damage reimbursement), and terminal overhead.

Companies using for-hire carriers normally audit freight bills to ensure that all charges are correct and that correct amounts are paid to carriers. Freight bill audits and payments can be done internally or through third party service organizations. In either case, the systems used for auditing and paying freight bills should not only ensure correct charges and accurate payments but also provide the data required for comprehensive transportation cost management.

If a company-owned service is being used (e.g., a private fleet), all associated costs should be identified and measured. These include maintenance, terminal, and operating costs (including driver wages and fringes), fuel and oil, interest, equipment depreciation and base, and insurance. The dynamics of the deregulated transportation industry today continually change the relative economics of private versus for-hire transportation. Companies with private fleets should periodically study the possible cost and return-on-investment relationships of the for-hire option.

For costing *inbound* transportation movements, the following circumstances or factors should be considered:

- Inbound transportation costs are often incorporated into the materials purchase cost. The freight expenses need to be separated to better manage and control their incurrence.

- Inbound transportation movements typically consist of low-value, commodity-type materials. Companies often "forward-buy" to take advantage of lower prices; thus, shipments are typically made in large volumes that require minimal packaging and minimal special handling. These factors affect decisions concerning carrier selection, receiving practices (e.g., quality control and storage), and other factors affecting transportation costs.

- With the current emphasis on JIT deliveries, many companies may be paying premium transportation rates for more frequent and smaller inbound shipments.

For outbound movements, products are typically of higher value and represent lower volumes. In addition, more emphasis is placed on customer service requirements, such as loss and damage, on-time deliveries, and packaging. These factors affect decisions about mode selection (type of transport), shipment sizes, carrier selection, and use of private fleet, which contribute to total transportation costs.

Since a company's policies for customer services are a significant factor in the incurrence of transportation costs, transportation decisions and resulting costs must be consistent with—and must support—the overall customer service strategy.

Direct assignment or allocation of costs should occur at the transaction level of detail, or otherwise at the lowest level of detail practical (such as activity). For example, freight costs associated with individual shipments should be assigned to the products and destinations on those shipments and then aggregated, or rolled up, as required for management cost-reporting purposes. Good judgment must be exercised about which costs to specifically assign versus which costs to allocate as miscellaneous, or "overhead," based on their materiality.

Transportation costs that are incurred often benefit more than one cost object (e.g., the cost of a shipment containing two different products). The allocation base normally applied is weight or volume, although number of loads or number of shipments may be used. The choice of an allocation base should reflect, to the degree practical, the resources actually consumed by the elements to which costs are charged.

The objective in transportation costing is to have data available on all transportation-related costs, preferably organized by functional cost categories. Functional costs may be directly assigned to cost-behavior classifications (e.g., short-run variable, long-run variable, or fixed costs). This method permits effective marginal cost pricing, cost-volume-profit analysis, flexible budgeting, and variance analysis.

Time-related costs, such as depreciation, are frequently allocated based on hours of use. The total-hours computation for these time-related costs includes the total hours the equipment is normally in use (including the empty and loaded portion of the trip), including hours when the vehicle is in service but not being operated on the highway (e.g., loading and unloading time). Average hours generally are used for costing purposes. This procedure requires the development of average driving speed by zone, or geographic region, based on mileage brackets. The average can be determined based on continuous analysis of actual performance of each load. Alternatively, the average can be determined by using statistical sampling techniques.

For costs that are a function of miles operated, both loaded and empty miles should be included. The per-mile charge is determined using system averages or averages for each major traffic lane. This approach may be used to allocate other function costs (e.g., fuel and oil, tractor maintenance, tire and tubes, and accidents and insurance), depending on how they are incurred. The total cost of the load is calculated by accumulating the functional cost allocations using the hours, loads, and mile bases.

The accuracy of transportation costing can be enhanced through the use of cube or density factors, which are used jointly with the hundredweight (cost) miles-allocation base. This process enables the costing system to account for the weight, distance, and cube or density factors of the products shipped, when a combination of light and dense products are being shipped together.

Effective transportation information must be comprehensive enough to include all relevant costs and assets associated with transportation activities. The information should include all costs of inbound, interfacility, and outbound shipments. Both for-hire and private fleet costs should be included.

Information should be consistent across divisions and subsidiaries, to facilitate companywide decision making. The database should include all capital assets employed (e.g., trucks and rail cars) and their related depreciation costs. This categorization should reflect key cost behavior patterns. Cost variability must be identified (e.g., fixed and variable costs must be isolated). The traditional type of expense categories (e.g., labor, materials, and fuel), and organizational classifications of cost for responsibility accounting, should be provided.

With these information requirements in mind, and with today's information technology capabilities, more companies are designing and implementing information systems for transportation management. These systems increasingly take advantage of electronic data interchange (EDI) with outside suppliers and customers.

Properly designed, a transportation information system provides simultaneous capture (single-point data entry) of important operational and financial data. These data include origin and destination of shipments, cube (volume) and weight, indicators, service indicators (e.g., times and miles), and equipment capacity utilization. Ideally, a transportation system should be designed with interfaces to other logistics, distribution, purchasing, manufacturing, and accounting systems.

Warehousing

Storage and handling of products or materials have sometimes been characterized as non-value-adding activities, thus making them cost-adding steps in the product supply chain. The true value of warehousing, however, lies in having the right product in the right place at the right time. If the value of warehousing is evaluated continuously and the locations, types, and levels of inventories are determined scientifically, the costs of product flow (versus storage) can be identified as value-added for the business.

The identification and management of these costs is fundamental to the effective management of the warehouse function, because such costs often are a decision factor in making logistics and distribution decisions. Moreover, warehousing costs also can have a significant impact on product or segment profitability, product cost and pricing, and ultimately on corporate profitability.

Warehousing costs may exist for goods or products at various stages of the company's supply chain, including (1) inbound materials, (2) semifinished products at different stages of assembly, and (3) finished goods to be shipped to customers. In addition warehousing support costs, such as those associated with people and information, are included in warehousing cost management.

Information for warehousing cost management may be classified according to two distinct but related categories: (1) information on levels of inventories needed and available, and (2) information on warehousing activities. The completeness and accuracy of inventory information can affect the volume of warehousing activities required (i.e., the better the information, the lower the amount of excess storage and handling activities). This principle supports JIT programs, for example, by enabling warehousing managers to know what inventory is on hand, what product has been selling, what support is needed, and when. Most important, this information can be updated and made available for on-line inquiry.

Warehousing costs are sensitive to the different components that make up the distribution or product supply chain. For example, the raw material used in manufacturing products, along with the sources of those materials, helps to determine the capacity and size requirements of each warehouse. Also, the physical characteristics and seasonality of finished goods can affect the volume and timing of storage requirements.

Transportation costs, a major factor in considering warehouse needs and locations, influence and interact closely with warehouse costs, depending on the need for, type, and mode of movements. In general, transportation movements (i.e., shipments from plants to warehouse) increase with additional warehouses, thus increasing transportation costs. On the other hand, additional warehouses usually reduce the cost of transporting products from warehouses to customers. Therefore, the proper balance between overall costs and needs should be determined.

The costs of warehousing, however, also increase with the number of warehouses. This increase includes inventory carrying costs as well as costs for labor, activities, facilities, equipment, order processing, support, and communications.

Since a company's customer service policies play a significant role in the incurrence of warehousing costs, a key challenge to warehousing cost management is to ensure that warehousing strategies and decisions support the overall customer service strategy. This coordination may require programs such as just-in-time (JIT), high order fill rates, and customer pickups.

To the extent that it is practical and costs are material, activity-based cost information should be identified and assigned to products or groups. Products incur overhead costs by requiring resource-consuming activities, including warehousing. The costs of products, then, differ according to their different actual requirements for support activities, such as warehousing, as opposed to volume-based allocations.

Categorizing costs by specific activities is essential to determining the cost of certain warehouse practices (such as crossdock shipments) in which shipments are received and reshipped without being put in storage. It also permits the application of control methods (i.e., the managing of warehousing activities).

When there is more than one cost object involved (e.g., the cost activities to receive or ship two different products), the allocation activity costs may be directly assigned to cost behavior classifications (e.g., short-run variable costs, long-run variable costs, and fixed costs). This method permits effective marginal cost pricing, cost volume-profit analysis, flexible budgeting, and variance analysis.

These activity costs may be aggregated into the three major categories of warehousing services—handling, storage, and administration—and then allocated to products or groups. The categorization of products into a group, where necessary, is based on a detailed warehouse profile that defines each group. The specific factors often include the following:

- Mode of shipment
- Loading method (i.e., palletized, slipsheeted, or floor-loaded)
- Order size
- Line items per order
- Allowable stacking height
- Temperature or order control required
- Weight and dimensions per case or unit
- Cases per pallet
- Pallet size

Product grouping enables us to identify by product the "cost drivers" that contribute to non-value-adding activities (waste).

The warehousing function varies substantially among companies in its organization, objectives, and cost structure. Thus, different ABC methodologies may be applied. An effective costing system uses detailed cost information as well as numerous operational statistics regarding warehouse activities. The system is then able to trace direct product costs by activities and, therefore, to identify delay, excess, and unevenness in the product supply chain.

To a large extent, the appropriate volume of warehousing space and services needed depends on the timeliness and accuracy of information. The better the information on demand and activity costs, the fewer storage and handling services are needed—all other factors being equal. Thus, the quality and timeliness of information is invaluable in terms of effective warehousing cost management.

Effective warehousing information must be comprehensive enough to include all relevant costs and assets associated with warehousing activities. The information should include all costs of labor, work activities, equipment, inventory carrying, and facilities. Both public and private warehousing activities and costs should be included.

Warehousing information should provide for measures of performance and its evaluation, and for productivity improvement. It should also support capital planning (e.g., building, leasing, or disposing of storage facilities) by providing for warehouse space requirements.

Computer-Based Information Systems

With these information requirements in mind, and with today's computer hardware and software capabilities, more companies are designing and implementing computer-based information systems for warehousing management.

Properly designed and applied, these systems provide simultaneous capture (single-point data entry) of important operational and financial data. These data include activities associated with receipts, storage, handling, shipping, labor, and equipment utilization. The warehousing information system should have interfaces with related logistics activities (e.g., distribution, purchasing, manufacturing, and accounting systems). Figure 9-7 illustrates certain of these interfaces.

Activity-based warehousing cost information contributes to management decision making about product mix, product profitability, and customer profitability. The costs of warehousing activities—whether the activities are deemed value-added or not—represent resources that can make the difference to the competitiveness of a company's products and margins.

Other Logistics Activities

For logistics functions other than freight transportation and warehousing, the approach to ABC costing should be similar. Activities should be identified for each logistics function or process. For example, in procuring packaging materials, the typical activity steps would be those shown here.

Daily:

- Issue purchase order
- Receive deliveries

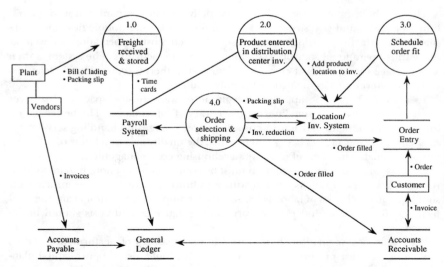

Figure 9-7. A sample data flow diagram—distribution center, and related accounting activity.

Periodically:

- Determine packaging material needs
- Determine qualified vendors
- Develop purchase specifications
- Update and evaluate sourcing strategy
- Release bids to vendors
- Select vendors
- Evaluate vendor performance

Once all the company's logistics activities have been identified and the steps delineated, basic costs can be determined for the activities. Total cost management can then be developed for the entire logistics process.

Planning Logistics Performance

Measurement Framework

Logistics performance measurement is a process whereby a company defines and measures logistics operations to support its mission, strategy, and operation. It is an extension of total cost management (TCM) that enables managers to monitor, evaluate, and improve logistics for a variety of purposes relating to both activities and products. TCM is a business philosophy of managing all company resources and the activities that consume those resources.

The design of the logistics performance measurement system should take into account responsibility and accountability, beginning at the lowest possible level (i.e., logistics activity) and flowing up to top management. It also should incorporate both enterprise-level measures (e.g., total company costs) and unit-level measures (e.g., activity costs).

A key step in the design of a logistics performance measurement system is the identification of critical success factors for all levels of the business. For enterprise-level success, factors such as the following are employed:

- Costs
- Profits
- Cycle time
- Innovation
- Quality
- Productivity
- Customer satisfaction
- Market share
- Level of investment
- Return on assets

For unit-level success, typical success factors include:

- Activity costs
- Activity cycle times
- Days of inventory
- On-time deliveries
- Order fill rates

Figure 9-8 illustrates certain key cost drivers/performance indicators in logistics. These are categorized in terms of the value chain.

Numerous other financial and nonfinancial indicators of performance are also employed. The challenge is to determine the relative importance of these factors for each customer (or group) and for each product (or group).

Once critical success factors have been identified and their relative weights determined by appropriate categories, estimates of the current state of performance and performance goals can be established for each logistics activity.

Logistics performance measures must be linked with the company's overall business strategy and with performance goals. A goal of logistics return on assets (LROA), for example, would be linked to activity performance measures such as transportation equipment productivity, warehouse facility utilization, and the like.

Logistics performance measures should not remain fixed once they are established for the activity. Rather, data-gathering problems, reporting problems, and interpretations should be monitored, and the measures, weights, or goals adjusted accordingly. The principle of continuous improvement (*kaizen*, in Japanese) should apply—that is, the relentless pursuit of improvement in the delivery of value to customer. Logistics excellence should be the ongoing goal.

Performance Information

Since logistics activities occur across the company's supply chain and thus cross traditional functions of the business, the need to develop an integrated information management approach based on a common database is increasingly important.

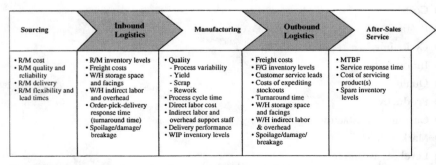

Figure 9-8. Key cost drivers/performance indicators in logistics.

This approach has been adopted by leading companies, because integrated information contributes to the providing of service to customers.

Logistics total cost management requires information that is timely, accurate, comprehensive, and shared by all operating and financial managers of the business. A single, consistent set of data—for example, information on stock status (or inventory availability)—should be accessible to parties across the supply chain, whether it is for order processing, inventory management, warehousing, shipping, production planning, or customer service.

The application of information technology (IT) to managing the logistics of the business are expanding rapidly to almost every industry. Many of these applications are deemed "mission-critical"—that is, the company has a high dependence on the system to support its business operations.

The primary function of mission-critical IT applications to logistics is the support of inventory management—especially as competition intensifies, product lines multiply, and markets increase to national, international, and global scales. These type of systems are typically referred to as "closed-loop JIT" (or quick response) management control systems that accomplish the following:

- Cover the company's (or division's) entire supply chains
- Track sales, costs, and profits by product or SKU
- Track orders, purchase orders, and stock movements
- Maximize productivity while minimizing time
- Provide for linkage with other parties through EDI
- Integrate across the supply chain functions
- Are on-line and common-database-oriented in a distributed processing environment, across the company's facilities

Expanded use of telecommunications technology has also fostered improved logistics across the product supply chain. For the inbound logistics activities, expediting materials to the point of manufacture (JIT ordering) has been aided between suppliers and producers. For outbound logistics, order cycle time is being reduced by the use of telecommunications and shared databases. These applications are generally referred to under the EDI category of "technology and systems." The most advanced EDI systems are used as integration network devices to track materials, supplies, and products from point of supply to point of sale or other customer delivery. Other applications (e.g., bar-coding) increase the accuracy of data capture and facilitate the physical handling of products (e.g., receiving and order picking). These applications reduce overall cycle time in the supply chain and have corresponding reduction effects on inventory levels and safety stock.

For logistics cost management, it is critical that advanced information systems also be able to measure, monitor, and report the true cost of products (or groups of products). Thus, as companies challenge their traditional cost-accounting systems and move toward the adoption of TCM principles, the automation of ABC methods should be an integral component of modern information technology applications.

Conclusion

The "quiet revolution" in logistics occurring in today's business world is creating significant new opportunities for profit improvements in time, cost, and service value. Supply chain management as the strategic approach to operations effectiveness is evolving into the primary means for achieving tangible improvements, and logistics is the key to its effective implementation.

Improvements in logistics operations, however, cannot be gained without effective cost management of the functions and activities that comprise the business logistics process. Although logistics costing has already been approached in the recent past by focusing on logistics activities (e.g., transportation, warehousing, order processing, and customer service), newer ABC methods should be adopted with the same rigor with which they are applied to production and other value-added activities.

Logistics (especially transportation and warehousing) has been defined here in enough depth to apply activity costing to functions that have largely been ignored. As supply chain strategies continue to be adopted, and as logistics is increasingly used to integrate cross-function activities, the value of logistics cost management should grow.

Total cost management is a sophisticated set of approaches and techniques capable of producing significant changes and cost savings in all business processes, including logistics. Its use should be guided by the following six principles.

1. *The cost information must support the strategy.* Whether the company's strategic focus is quality, close-to-the-customer, time-based competition, or something else, good information is needed to back decisions. Lacking good information, you can't reach your strategic goals. Acquiring good cost information is the fundamental power that total cost management provides.

2. *Try to see the organization as a collection of processes, not as a set of organization charts.* In fact, the view of processes needs to capture all of the interactions among the organizational units. This means that the analytical framework should be more open to concepts of how the work really gets done, and less focused on the reporting relationships used to manage the work.

3. *Once you've made the fundamental shift in how you perceive your company, manage cost by managing activities.* Only when you focus on activities can you make sustainable changes in cost structure. Total cost management makes it possible to organize information in ways that point out opportunities for reducing cost—a process that depends most significantly on identifying activities and their root causes. This focus on activities is the power behind all the TCM principles: business process analysis, activity-based costing, and continuous improvement.

4. *Organize information by identifying the value of activities to your customers.* Here too, identify improvement opportunities by determining which activities are value-added or non-value-added to your customers, and which are disproportionately costly to you.

5. *The findings of your TCM analyses must make their way into action plans.* Don't fall into the trap of simply reorganizing the numbers.

6. *Monitor the business by aligning performance measures with the critical success factors identified.* Again, the process view allows you to establish metrics for measuring and monitoring the important elements of performance.

Total cost management is not an objective in and of itself; rather, it's a way to support business objectives, whatever they may be. Reaching a new understanding of the company's numbers isn't the goal you should seek. Instead, focus on understanding the numbers so as to develop an information support structure that allows you to accomplish your strategic goals.

TCM, in short, is a means to an end. Cost management is the means. The end is greater competitiveness, and a world-class logistics process in the global marketplace.

Further Reading

B. Brinker, ed., *Handbook of Cost Management,* Warren, Gorham & Lamont, Boston and New York, 1992.

Ernst & Young, *The Ernst & Young Guide to Total Cost Management,* John Wiley & Sons, New York, 1992.

Ernst & Whinney, *Corporate Profitability and Logistics: Innovative Guidelines for Executives,* Council of Logistics Management and Institute of Management Accountants, 1987.

Christopher Gopal and Gerry Cahill, *Logistics in Manufacturing,* Business One Irwin, Homewood, Illinois, 1992.

Institute of Management Accountants, *Cost Management for Freight Transportation,* Montvale, NJ, 1990.

Institute of Management Accountants, *Cost Management for Warehousing,* Montvale, NJ, 1990.

Michigan State University, *Leading Edge Logistics: Competitive Positioning for the 1990s,* CLM, Oak Brook, IL, 1989.

Michael E. Porter, *Competitive Advantage: Crediting and Sustaining Superior Performance,* The Free Press, New York, 1985.

PART 2
Transportation

10

Transportation Modes

Gerhardt Muller

Adjunct Professor,
International Transportation and Logistics
Management, City University of New York

Until the past few decades, transportation focused on how cargo was transported and warehoused. Today, and for the foreseeable future, transportation is influenced by emerging technologies, changing world trading patterns, and deregulation nationally and worldwide. It has become a major component of the systems approach to business.

Transportation can involve either a single mode or two or more modes. Examples of modes include water, air, rail, and highway. Although not the focus of this chapter, pipelines are also an important mode for large volumes of liquid and gas products such as oil, water, and natural gas. The transfer of commodities or goods between two modes is called an *intermodal transfer.*

Before any discussion can begin about transportation, there are several issues, terms and ideas that apply to all of the modes that must be recognized.

General, Bulk, and Neobulk Cargo. Originally there were two major categories of cargo: general and bulk. Advanced transportation concepts and vehicle designs, occurring over recent years, have fostered use of a third category commonly called neobulk.

General cargo consists of finished products like machinery, packaged goods, vehicles, and equipment. Bulk cargo is coal, petroleum, various gases, grains, iron and other nonferrous ores. Bulk cargo transfer from one mode to another is normally easier and less eventful than transferring general cargo, making it easier and less costly to maintain a continuous flow.

Neobulk, a term used more widely in the last decade, involves shipment of bulk and other forms of homogeneous types of cargos in one vehicle. Oil companies use neobulk equipment to transport different grades of petroleum cargos on a single vessel, called *parcel tankers*. Other forms of neobulk include car carriers, lumber, and refrigerated products. Cargo separation is maintained during loading, transportation, and unloading processes.

Interchange Points.   Interchange points—seaports, airports, railroad sidings, and pipeline terminals, to name a few—are a part of intermodality. Competition exists not only between carriers but also between ports/airports and inland terminals for primacy as points where intermodal exchange will take place. Given the capital-intensive nature of transportation today, interchange points that once dotted the map are now becoming fewer because of the way transportation has changed. The same scenario will most likely continue for decades to come, except in certain niche cargo situations.

Government Regulations.   Railroad monopolies in the late 1800s spurred strong government regulatory controls that set a precedent for regulating other modes in later years. The history of transportation is inextricably involved with federal and state regulation and international agreements.

As the need for and practice of transportation, intermodality, and logistics management matured, government regulation was increasingly regarded as a hindrance to realizing effective transportation. Recent government deregulation in the United States, the European Common Market, and other economic blocks around the globe was initiated in large part to attain a more competitive stance in world markets. There is convincing evidence that deregulation is having a liberating effect on transportation.

Economic Impact and Rates.   A direct beneficiary of transportation deregulation is the opening of new markets. By freeing formerly restrictive trade barriers and allowing the supply and demand of the transportation industry to adjust, rates and services changed accordingly. To a large extent this freedom for shippers to select and use modal and intermodal carriers, based on a combination of rates and service, influenced the rise and sometimes the decline of carriers and interchange points beyond most expectations.

Changing trade patterns and advanced technologies, like double-stack trains and greater involvement of modal carriers in the intermodal/logistics management process, will cause similar changes in other parts of the globe as that process continues.

Growing Importance of Communications.   On the heels of transportation deregulation came what might be termed the communications revolution. Deregulation of the communications industry is giving suppliers and users of communications technologies more accurate and faster information than they had before. Communications, especially with the recent trend in national and international agreements on electronic data interchange, allow corresponding partners to move toward a paperless form of planning, implementing, and tracking cargo shipments worldwide. It is almost certain that this trend will continue at an even greater pace.

Logistics Middlemen.   At the early stages of deregulation, it was often feared that the role of the logistics middleman would be diminished, if not eliminated. In some sectors of the transportation and logistics management industry that might be the case, especially in those that were not fast enough to accept and adapt as changes in the field were taking place.

Today, however, with the growing trend toward globalization of world markets, niche markets have opened. Niche markets require specialists who have the skills and technology to serve the customer more efficiently and cost-effectively. Just-in-time (JIT) and other manufacturing and customer delivery concepts will require these specialists to continue and broaden their services to meet the ever-divergent demands of their customers.

Relationship with Distribution Management. The evolving nature of transportation and its relationship with faster and better communications has heightened the need for developing and maintaining closer attention and involvement with distribution management, which is itself undergoing constant change. The basics of transportation are and will continue to be a major component of distribution management.

Comparison between United States and Foreign Countries. For purposes of this chapter, most of the information focuses on transportation systems in the United States. This was done with two purposes in mind.

First, there is already too much that can be described about the transportation systems in the United States, given its size and impact on transportation. This would be compounded often if worldwide examples were included in every instance. This is especially true because of deregulation.

Second, changes in transportation that have taken and will take place in the United States are most likely to be similar to the changes that are now or will shortly be taking place in other parts of the globe. This does not assume that everything that has taken place in the United States should or will have the same impact in foreign countries. Most likely, however, the results will be about the same. Emerging transportation technologies, whether developed here or abroad, together with the forces unleashed because of global marketization, will force changes in transportation systems to be similar in scope, if not scale.

It is also recognized that statistics change from year to year, some radically. As a result, articles and other sources of information that contain large amounts of statistics often have short shelf lives.

Consequently, statistical information is limited in this chapter. This was done to place the emphasis on what the trends are in terms of the big picture rather than on individual components of each mode. By doing so, it is hoped that the reader will gain a better understanding of what transportation is and can be in the relatively small amount of space of this chapter.

Rail Transportation

Railroads have been viewed as one of the cornerstones of this country's expansion in the nineteenth century. Much of that expansion was achieved through oligopolistic and monopolistic competition. Today, the railroad industry serves as an example of what can be done if, after a severe downturn in fortunes, an industry is given the chance to compete again under a different set of rules that in many ways resembles a more level playing field.

Although rail lines covered a good part of the eastern half of this country up to the time of the American Civil War, expansion west of the Mississippi River did not take place until a series of laws were passed by the Congress. These laws practically gave free land to the railroads as an incentive to expand to the west coast. By 1869, the establishment of the first transcontinental railroad tied this nation together from coast to coast by a transportation system that offered both cheaper and faster transportation. For the next half-century, the railroad industry became one of the most significant players in the economic, social, and political development of this nation.

With that expansion came also the growth and sometimes the excesses of large railroads, through widespread development of monopolies. Entire communities often came under the control of these monopolies.

Because of that abuse came one of the most effective pieces of legislation that, until the last decade, had a major influence on the transportation industry. This was the Act to Regulate Commerce of 1887. Among other provisions, the Act established the Interstate Commerce Commission, which for the first time regulated the railroad industry and the other modes, both domestic and international, that evolved later.

Despite economic expansion and some of the benefits and disbenefits of regulation by the turn of the century, the railroad industry started to decline. That decline continued until the industry had reached the point of almost complete collapse by the middle of this century. Much of that decline can be attributed to the rise of alternate transport modes, primarily motor carriers and pipelines, and to a resurgence of water transportation. By the mid-1980s, with the incentives of the Staggers Rail Act of 1980 and the adoption of new depreciation methods and accounting systems, the railroads had begun to find a new incentive to become real transportation competitors. This was especially true in containerization and other forms of logistics management. Today, the American railroad industry is often viewed as a model of how the modes could be reshaped and operated in an age of deregulation and emerging technologies.

Industry Overview

In the United States, railroads that transport cargo are privately owned common carriers. As common carriers they must serve the general public. In most other places in the world, with a few exceptions such as Switzerland, railroads are owned by national governments.

The railroad industry is usually grouped by size. The largest of these are Class I railroads, sometimes known as *line-haul railroads,* which have at least $50 million in operating revenues. Supporting them in areas where the line-haul carrier does not have local access, short-line railroads perform local distribution of rail freight. Although line-haul carriers also provide switching and terminal services for large customers and other line-haul carriers, local or short-line railroad companies often furnish these services in areas where the larger line-haul carrier does not operate.

Since the Staggers Rail Act of 1980, the line-haul railroads—of which there are today 10—abandoned many local lines that did not have sufficient revenues to support operating costs, let alone make a profit. As a result, short-line railroads sprang up in larger numbers, many of which emerged from sale or abandonment by the line-haul carriers. Usually these short-line carriers have been successful, because of lower overhead and operating costs. Short-line carriers also perform terminal operations, maintain and operate bridges and other facilities such as passenger or freight stations. In some parts of the nation, they also operate ferry services.

Cost and Service Characteristics

Despite the economic operating advantages that railroads have over long and some-times shorter distances, railroads do have other competitive advantages. One of these is *right-of-way*. These right-of-ways give railroads almost monopolistic operating advantages that restrict other railroads from using the same line, especially on lines that stretch over large distances. In cases where products carried by competitors need to travel on these lines, the railroad that owns those lines enters interline agreements that at times make a good profit. Simultaneously, the owner of that fixed-right-of-way is and continues to be burdened with heavy costs that include maintenance and taxes. At this time, however, no railroad has a complete nation-wide network of lines that span the country from east to west or north to south, although interline agreements do exist to perform such services.

Carrying Capacity: Bulk and Intermodal. A large carrying capacity allows the railroads to handle large-volume movements of low-value commodities over long distances at competitive rates and services. This type of carload capacity, along with a variety of car types, permits the railroads to handle almost any type of commodity, especially bulk commodities like ores, coal, grains, and now unit trains of containers and trailers-on-flatcars (TOFC).

Fixed versus Variable. As previously noted, railroads have a high level of fixed costs, as contrasted with variable costs. Fixed costs are incurred regardless of traffic volume. Variable costs, on the other hand, vary or change with the volume of traffic moved. For example, more cargo would require more cars, locomotives, and fuel. Less demand requires more flexible or variable operations.

Terminal Facilities. Terminal facilities include both the facilities to load and unload rail cars, and rail yard facilities where trains are made up or broken depending on the destination of the cargo. Other terminal facilities include those for repair and maintenance, refueling, and crew changes.

Labor. Until the last decade, labor was often more than half the operating expense of the railroad industry. This was especially true in cases where the number of crew members on each train exceeded the capability and efficiency of the technology being used. This affected rolling stock, locomotives, and communications systems. With deregulation, more than half the labor force of the railroad industry was eliminated, despite the strong objections of unions. It has been argued by railroad management that flexible work rules have enabled carriers to be more competitive with other modes serving the same markets.

Fuel. The second largest operating expense of the railroads is fuel costs. However, with the introduction and continued development of more efficient propulsion systems, mainly diesel and electromotive locomotives, these costs have come down considerably, depending on the carrier. On average, these costs are now around 12 percent of total operating costs, and improving all the time.

Equipment

Car Types.   Most of the railroads have a standard fleet of rail cars that include plain boxcars, equipped boxcars (specially modified boxcars used for specialized merchandise, such as automobile parts), automobile carriers, open and covered hopper cars that discharge bulk commodities from the bottom of the car, flatcars that carry TOFCs and single stacks of containers, refrigerator cars for commodities that need controlled temperatures, gondola cars that have no top and have a flat bottom and fixed sides, and tank cars for liquid cargoes such as petroleum and petroleum products, chemicals and occasionally even wines and other food stocks. With the growth of intermodalism, special rail cars are designed to carry containers one on top of each other, known as *double stack*.

Locomotives.   As described above, locomotives today are more efficient in terms of fuel costs and the number of cars they can pull. The diesel and electro-locomotives of today have replaced almost entirely steam locomotives, which were the workhorses until the mid-1950s. Today, steam locomotives are mainly found in museums and on short lines that offer special tour excursions.

Unit Trains.   The unit train, which evolved from the rent-a-train concept for the movement of goods, specializes in the transport of only one commodity, usually coal or grain, from origin to destination. Often the shipper owns the cars and the train is, in effect, rented to the particular shipper for a certain time or line. With intermodalism, double-stack unit trains could have as many as 150 cars, carrying 300 containers of different sizes. These trains often stretch a mile or more in length, an awesome sight as they pass road crossings.

Staggers Rail Act of 1980, and Deregulation

As was stated earlier, the railroad industry once enjoyed a virtual monopoly over the efficient and dependable transportation of passengers and freight. Because of this the U.S. government promoted the growth of the industry, until a distinct change in public attitude toward railroads was felt. The creation of the Interstate Commerce Commission (ICC), which was a provision of the Act to Regulate Commerce, regulated minimum and maximization rates to protect the rail shipper. The ICC's objective was to promote competition from other modes of transportation while assuring the financial health of the railroads.

Over the decades, competition from other modes increased dramatically. As a result, the railroad industry's share of the intercity freight market declined to less than 50 percent during this period. In addition, railroads were also subject to operating constraints that limited them to where they could go, lines that they could not abandon because of high operating costs, and inability to own or operate other modes of transportation, such as highway, that could have enhanced their competitive position. The bottom line was that the railroad industry simply could not compete in its present market situation. Many railroads went bankrupt, especially in the Northeast.

In the spirit of deregulation that affected all of the modes one way or another, the

Staggers Rail Act of 1980 was passed. That act sought to allow market forces to operate in the railroad industry, as with other modes during this era of deregulation.

The Staggers Act deregulated the railroads only partially; the ICC was still left with enough authority to protect shippers from abuses by the railroads. Railroads were given enough freedom to enter contracts and set prices that were reasonable. Prices were determined reasonable if they fell below a threshold based on a revenue-to-variable cost ratio. The act also established faster timetables for abandonment and merger proceedings.

The result, it could be argued, is that the railroads were granted the opportunity to earn profits that allowed them to compete for survival. Railroads have shown a distinct increase in customer service levels. This is especially true with intermodalism, where performance of on-time schedules helped establish the concept of the so-called "bridge networks." These bridge networks improved service to the customer, especially for containerized cargoes subject to just-in-time (JIT). Simultaneously, on certain trade routes like the Pacific Rim–East Coast trade route, ports on the west coast grew in traffic at the expense of east coast ports. Based on the mini- and micro-land bridge systems, west coast ports like Seattle, Tacoma, Oakland, Los Angeles, and Long Beach serve the port platform function that the ports on the east coast used to serve.

Alternatively, it could be argued that cargo on the Pacific Rim–Europe route now passes through both the west and east coast ports, thus bypassing the traditional routes via the Panama and Suez Canals.

Service. The railroad cost structure makes it necessary to attract higher and regular volumes of traffic to take advantage of their scale of economies. In recent years rail management has developed several service innovations to increase traffic volume, such as the bridge systems and increased linehaul of automobiles and trucks.

The idea of piggyback service, as designed by the railroads, was to increase the service levels to intermodal customers. Piggyback, which includes both TOFC (trailer-on-flatcar) and COFC (container-on-flatcar) has grown substantially in the past few decades to the point where, especially since deregulation, it ranks second behind coal in total car-loadings.

TOFC. TOFC service transports highway trailers on railroad flatcars. It combines the line-haul efficiencies of railroads with the flexibility of local highway pickup and delivery service. On-time deliveries, regularly scheduled departures, and fuel efficiency are the major reasons for the continued growth of TOFC service.

There are many standard TOFC plans, each providing coordinated intermodal transportation services. The trailers or tractors could be either rail, highway, shipper, or consignee-owned. For example, with Plan 1, a railroad hauls the trailers of a highway common carrier while the highway carrier handles the ramp-to-door service at both ends. With Plan 2, the railroad transports and provides door-to-door service for its own trailers. Under Plan 2½, the railroad provides trailers, flatcars, and rail transportation, while the shipper and consignee arrange highway pickup and delivery from the ramps. Plan 2½ is the most widely used. By one account there are about 14 such plans in operation, the number of which could rise and fall based on market service alternatives of the railroad.

COFC.   Container-on-flatcar, better known as COFC, is the international form of transportation of containers. It is the equivalent to domestic TOFC movements. A container, minus its chassis, is placed on a flatbed rail car after it arrives at a container yard from either the shipper or container vessel. A variation of this occurs when two containers are placed on top of each other, a method known as *double stack*.

Domestic Containerization.   Building on the concept of COFC and double-stack operations is the use of ocean containers for the transportation of domestic cargos. This is often the case when containers returning to their point of origin, for example the Far East, could be used to carry cargo if there was no cargo going to the Far East. At some destination on the west coast, the container is stripped or unloaded. The empty container, if not loaded with export cargo, is then hauled by a highway carrier to the container terminal of the steamship carrier to continue its journey to the Far East.

Alternatively, ocean containers are becoming an important factor in the domestic transportation of cargo, by keeping the container in domestic service only. The advantages of on-line railroad container handling equipment for international container operations provide another cost-efficient service for domestic shippers.

Technology

EDI.   Other forms of emerging technological advances applicable to the railroad industry include electronic data interchange (EDI). The need for faster, more efficient, and cost-effective transportation, to serve the customer better, requires up-to-date information for booking, issuing of bills of lading, coordination and tracking of the cargo. EDI was originally developed to improve the location of rail cars along the line and to improve coordination of both cargo and equipment. Rapid advances in EDI extended that service, by allowing both the customer and the railroad to coordinate more efficiently each shipment and all other services that belong with the shipment.

Advanced Train Control Systems.   To improve overall railroad performance, railroads, especially the line-haul carriers, are developing advanced train control systems. These systems help the coordination of rolling stock and locomotives, improve safety standards, and in the long run, plan more efficient operations to accommodate seasonal cargo flows.

Rail Yards.   Another area of tremendous improvement has been the design and operation of rail yards. This applies to both the loading/unloading of cargo and intermodal shipments, and the making up and breaking down of line-haul and unit trains. Some of the more recent yards constructed are considered to be the latest examples of state-of-the-art rail yard operations anywhere.

Rolling Equipment.   Equal attention has been given to the advances in rolling stock, especially in the area of improved maintenance and the reduction of accidents. Some of the more high-tech equipment, such as container cars and variations thereof, are very expensive. Time out for frequent repairs is costly, and a drain on the bottom line.

Current Issues

Megacarriers.   The railroad industry is not immune to the tremendous changes in the number of players involved. As a direct result of the wave of bankruptcies and mergers that took place because of deregulation, line-haul carriers have decreased to the point where less than 10 such operators are still in business. Although the pace of bankruptcies and mergers has slowed in the past few years, it is reasonable to assume that head-to-head competition in the railroad industry will see the formation of megacarriers that could eventually span the nation from coast to coast. That could include rail lines that follow the north and south route as well. Furthermore, with the reorganization taking place of the railroads in Canada, Canadian lines such as the CN and the CP could play an increasing role in the United States' railroad industry.

Vertical Integration.   Recognition must also be given to the formation of railroad operations that embrace other modes and their ancillary services. For example, CSX is a railroad that also owns the containership line SeaLand Services, and other services including barging and intermodal/third party services. Many railroads have found that to compete, especially in high-value-added services, control or entering service partnerships with other modes and ancillary services is a requirement for survival.

Highway

Industry Overview

The transportation of intercity freight by highway carriers did not start until about 1900. Not until after World War I, however, did the industry become important as a major carrier of cargo between cities. Until then the industry was mostly small firms and operators restricted to local and regional delivery.

The growth of intercity truck transportation was supported by technological improvements such as the pneumatic tire, and better roads because of increased use of passenger automobiles. Economically, the trucking industry grew because of: the decline in competitive railroad service, especially after World War II; the completion of the National System of Interstate and Defense Highways in the past decade; ease of access to remote areas; and deregulation of transportation in the early 1980s. That influence, however, is being challenged again today by the growth in domestic containers and trailer-on-flatcar (TOFC) service by the railroads for long-haul (more than 500 to 700 mi) traffic.

The highway trucking industry makes use of an extensive road and street system that is approximately 3.9 million miles of roads and streets in the United States. Of that amount, 42,000 mi are part of the interstate and defense highway system, which was designed to connect major cities with four-lane limited-access roads.

Types of Carriers

Private versus For-Hire.   The for-hire carrier charges a fee for providing service to the public. The private carrier provides a service to the shipper that owns or leases the vehicles, and thus does not charge a fee. Private carriers may transport exempt commodities for-hire, but when operating in such a capacity the private carrier is really an exempt for-hire carrier.

Local versus Intercity.   For-hire carriers are either local or intercity operators. As local carriers they pick up and deliver interstate freight within what is commonly called a "commercial zone" of a city or region as defined by the Interstate Commerce Commission.

Common versus Contract.   Common carriers are required to serve the general public when the need to do so is there, at reasonable rates, and without discrimination. Contract carriers, on the other hand, serve specific shippers with whom the carriers have a contract, and are therefore not available to carry freight for the general public.

Exempt.   These for-hire carriers are specifically exempt from economic regulation by the ICC. These gains freed the economic regulatory control of the many types of commodity hauled (agricultural, lumber, etc.). Rates charged and services provided, and the number of vehicles used, are determined strictly by market supply and demand.

Service Characteristics

Accessibility.   Because almost every economic activity is accessible to highways, even in some of the most remote parts of the country, the highway carrier enjoys the best accessibility of all the modes. This is especially true in cases where transportation is limited to pickup and delivery with other modes.

Speed.   For shipments under 500 mi, the truck can usually deliver the freight in less time then other modes. Other modes, although faster, are restricted by fewer frequent schedules and limited access.

Small Carrying Capacity.   Trucks are often greatly disadvantaged by the weight (25,000 to 30,000 lb) and dimensions ($9\frac{1}{2}$ ft high and 96 to 106 in wide) established by state and local highway departments. On the other hand, the smaller shipping size of the motor carrier provides the buyer and seller with the benefits of lower inventory levels and inventory carrying costs.

Safety.   Although highway accidents do occur—some of which make media headlines—the general result in the past decade is that through stricter law enforcement of weight limitations, speed control, vehicle safety inspections, and national licensing of drivers, the safety of highway transportation is improving. This means less damage to the cargo, which in turn reduces the need for excessive packaging requirements and costs.

Flexibility.   Trucks have the advantage that they can be loaded and be on their way faster than most of the other modes. With rail and barge, for example, larger volumes of cargo or numbers of vehicles must be loaded before the actual transportation of the cargo can begin. Simultaneously, the number of highways or lanes trucks have available provides for faster and more efficient alternative routes when the competitive pressures of shippers require this form of service.

Cost Structure

Approximately 90 percent of the costs of the motor carrier industry are variable, and 10 percent are fixed. Motor carriers are able to increase or decrease the number of vehicles used in short periods of time and in small increments of capacity. Most terminals, because of the short stay of the cargo, are relatively inexpensive to construct and maintain. Fixed costs are largely associated with purchasing and operating fleets and, on the public side, the investment in the highway system.

Generally speaking, 94 cents of every operating dollar is consumed by operating expenses, the other 6 cents going to cover interest costs and return to investors.

Economies of Scale.   Certain economies of scale exist in the use of terminals, management specialists, and more recently information systems. This is especially true for carriers that operate over larger geographic areas. Lower operating costs are usually a part of truckload or over-the-road operations, especially if there is a return load. For shorter distances and less-than-truckload operations, frequent stops add to the overall cost of operation, especially in high cost areas such as some larger metropolitan regions.

Equipment and Operations

There are several types of vehicles, including:

Dry van:	Standard trailer or straight truck, with all sides closed.
Open top:	Top of trailer is open, to allow cargo to be lifted in and out of the vehicle vertically.
Flatbed:	Trailer with flat bed or floor, and no sides or top.
Tank trailer:	Hauls liquids such as petroleum, liquid chemicals, and waste material in liquid form.
Refrigerated:	Cargo units that provide controlled temperatures and environments.
High cube:	Trailers that have a larger than normal internal and external size, restricted only by highway safety and statutory limitations.
Special:	Special design to accommodate unique cargos such as automobiles, heavy lifts such as machinery, and certain types of gases under heavy pressure.

Line Haul.   Line-haul trucks are used to haul freight long distances between shippers and consignees. The vehicle involved is typically a tractor-trailer combination of three or more axles. State regulations determine the carrying capacity and size limitations of the vehicles, a factor that often frustrates carriers when hauling cargo between states that differ in the regulations. Standard 40-ft units are gradually being replaced by longer trailers that are 45, 48, and now 53 ft in length.

City.   Normally smaller and lighter than the line-haul vehicle, city trucks are usually one self-contained unit, meaning that the truck and driver move only when the cargo is ready. These trucks are generally 20 to 25 ft in length, although small trailers 20 to 28 ft long are often used to pick up and deliver freight in inner-city areas where larger truck restrictions are in force.

Terminals

Pickup and Delivery.   Pickup and delivery terminals are used mainly by less-than-truckload carriers where cargo is often consolidated into larger line-haul vehicles. These facilities are often located in an array of spokes that expand out from a central terminal or hub. Line-haul vehicles then travel between the hubs.

Relay/Team Driving.   Under DOT and ICC regulations and enforcement, drivers are permitted to drive a maximum of 10 hours after 8 consecutive hours off duty. At the relay terminal, one driver substitutes for another who has accumulated the maximum hours of service. (The term *slip-seat* is often used to describe this relay procedure.)

An alternative to the relay terminal is the use of sleeper team-two drivers. While one driver drives, the other sleeps in a specially furnished bunk behind the cab. These teams have been most effective where trips are long and have many destinations.

Deregulation

The highway industry was subject to regulation that severely restricted in certain parts of the country its ability to compete with other modes, if not with other motor carriers serving the same interstate markets or regions.

In response to the growing cry for deregulation of the transportation industry in the late 1970s, the motor carrier industry was deregulated in 1980. Although opposed originally by an industry that feared lower profits and greater competition, especially from nontruckers, the act eventually served to lower rates while improving service. The act eased entry for new carriers and allowed existing carriers to expand service. This included elimination by some carriers of money-losing routes that, until the act was passed, they had been required to serve. Wasteful circuitous routes were eliminated by allowing more efficient and direct routes to be used, often at substantial savings in fuel.

The act also allowed carriers and freight forwarders to set rates in response to market demand. This was made through what is known as a *zone of flexibility*, where rates rise or lower by 10 percent without ICC interference. This zone can be widened if the ICC finds that there is enough competition to let the rates float on a wider range for the benefit of both carriers and shippers. This pricing flexibility also extends to allowing a carrier and a shipper to negotiate reduced transportation rates. This, however, applies mainly to large shippers who have the volume and frequency to make such a negotiable rate attractive to carriers.

One of the direct results of deregulation is the continuing expansion and then retraction of the number of players in the motor carrier industry. Some of the larger national and regional carriers have disappeared, their place taken in part by smaller, more flexible carriers. At the same time deregulation has allowed new partnerships to develop between the motor carrier industry and other modes, especially rail.

Competition

Types of Commodities Carried. The motor carrier industry concentrates mostly on semifinished and finished products that move distances less than several hundred miles. Beyond that, rail transportation, especially as part of intermodal movements of trailers and containers, becomes more economical. Commodities such as livestock, food, and at an increasing rate of growth the waste industry, move by highway because of the lack of alternative competitive modes and rates.

Market Orientation. One of the industry's greatest advantages is that it is flexible enough to respond relatively quickly to rapid changes in the market. The smaller size of most of the carriers, especially for-hire, allows customers to receive personalized attention when and where needed. Although cost and price differences between carrier and shipper often cause sharp differences of opinion, especially when the issue of the quality of service expected and received is included in the discussion, shippers today are beginning to get the upper hand, especially in areas where the competition between carriers is severe.

Capital. The capital requirements of the LTL segment of the industry are higher, because it must invest in terminals and freight-handling equipment that is, in most cases, not needed by the TL carrier. At the same time special equipment carriers, such as refrigerated and heavy lift carriers, often have larger investments than conventional freight carriers.

Rate Structures. Since deregulation, the rate structure of the motor carrier industry has been influenced mainly by several major forces of the market, namely, supply, demand, and cost of service. Before deregulation, interstate and intrastate rates were set by government regulations and/or agencies. In times when economic conditions are tight and the supply of carriers is greater than the demand, rates in many cases are barely able to cover basic operating costs. Conversely, in a tight demand economy, rates often allow for a very comfortable rate of return, mostly at the expense of the shipper and the ultimate consumer.

Less-than-Truckload. LTL rates are usually much higher than TL rates, because of the additional cost of handling different shipments for different customers on the same truck. Part of that rate also is allocated for the additional cost of the LTL freight terminals, where individual shipments are consolidated and later broken down for further transportation to the customer.

Truckload.   TL rates reflect the economies of scale associated with almost door-to-door service for the customer. That service does not have to provide additional handling of cargo once the cargo has been loaded on the truck.

Contract.   Contract rates are negotiated between one or more carriers with one or more shippers for specified shipments. These specifications consider guaranteed volumes, frequency, schedules, and other factors that meet the competitive cost factors of both shippers and carriers over a relatively long period of time, including several years. The guaranteed nature of the contract allows all parties involved to better project expenses and other business variables.

Technology

Existing and emerging technologies in the trucking industry are reaching a new stage, where major advances in hardware are not necessarily as revolutionary as they have been for the past decade. This is not to discount the advances being made in truck operational safety, or increasing fuel efficiency caused by improved body and engine design. Alternatively, the greatest leaps forward, at least in the next decade, will most likely take place in some of the "software" used by the industry to increase competitive positions.

Electronic Data Interchange.   EDI helps carriers and shippers track shipments throughout the movement process. EDI provides shipment status information to customers by mainframe computers, personal computers, or even cellular telephones. Although EDI is still in its infancy, some larger national carriers have installed satellite-based tracking systems on most if not all of their trucks. Not only can the company trace the exact location and perhaps route of each truck, but information placed into the satellite communications systems on the truck, such as cargo manifests, traffic congestion, etc., can be transmitted rapidly to one or more central offices.

   Similar data will, in the future, be transmitted concerning the operating characteristics of the vehicle itself, including speed, engine performance, tire pressure, etc. Although all of this technology is expensive, the savings in the cost of actual operations, and in time, and improvement of service to the customer, will make it cost-efficient.

Intermodal Compatibility.   Intermodalism, especially that part of the transportation and logistics management industry that involves the increased use of containers for exclusively domestic use, will see renewed interest in the coming decade. This is especially true as double-stack service increases nationwide as the 0-railroads make clearance improvements along their rights of way to accommodate the higher double-stack trains. At the same time, piggyback or trailer-on-flatcar (TOFC) movements could either be replaced by the double-stack operation or, where the railroads cannot economically make improvements for double-stack operations, will encourage greater use of trailer carrying capacity because of the cost efficiencies associated with rail versus all truck operations.

Labor: Union versus Nonunion

The local and over-the-road trucking industry was, until deregulation, heavily influenced by the rules established by strong unions. Usually the industry was saddled with heavy expenses that were a detriment to its competitive position with the other modes, especially rail. Since deregulation, however, the bargaining power of the unions has weakened, and in some cases been eliminated completely. For the foreseeable future, whether representation is union or nonunion will depend on the degree of flexibility that labor and management needs for the carrier to remain in business in an increasingly competitive business.

Water Transportation

Water transportation takes advantage of the water highways built both by nature and man. Ever since the carrying capacity of water was discovered by man, transportation by water has served as one of the more important means of transporting cargo and passengers.

Water transportation played an important role in the development of the U.S. Ocean transportation provided the vital link to markets with Europe. Major cities developed along the coast, where their port facilities served as gateways to inland areas including an expanding frontier. In many cases, water transportation on rivers and lakes was the only means of transportation connecting inland areas with coastal cities.

Despite the emergence of other modes such as rail and highway, water transportation continues to be the main form of transportation in the United States especially for bulk commodities. Internationally, water transportation also continues to be the main form of transportation, more so for cargo than passengers. The exception, of course, is the growing popularity of cruise ships that sail from both domestic and foreign ports. Domestic water transportation consists of all water movements where the origin and destination of the shipment is in one country. Shipments that have a foreign country as either the origin or destination are classified as international shipping.

Domestic

Domestic water transportation usually consists of three different types of service.

1. *Inland water transportation* operates over the internal network of navigable waterways such as the Mississippi, Ohio, Missouri, Tennessee, Columbia, and Hudson Rivers and other smaller arteries. The vessels used include barges and towboats, mainly because of shallow-draft restrictions. Inland water carriers dominate the north-south traffic through the central portion of the United States via the Mississippi, Missouri, and Ohio Rivers. On the west coast most of the navigable rivers flow in an east-to-west direction, while on the east coast both directions are seen.

2. *Coastal carriers* serve ports on the Atlantic or Pacific Oceans or the Gulf of Mexico. *Intercoastal freight* transported between east coast and west coast ports is in most cases via the Panama Canal. Although both use oceangoing vessels, there are some operations that use oceangoing barges, some of which have a capacity of 18,000 tons or more. The majority of the freight transported is petroleum, both crude and refined. The main routes are between ports along the Atlantic coast and the Gulf of Mexico. Oil from Alaska moves via coastal carriers to refineries along the Pacific coast.

Coastal and intercoastal operations are restricted to American-flag vessels only. This regulation goes back to the earliest days of this nation's history, when it was felt that, to protect American fleet operations, foreign vessels could not carry cargo and passengers between American ports. Although under constant review and discussion, the provisions of the Jones Act, the legislation that established this regulation, are still in force today. (In most foreign countries, especially in Europe, coastal trades are open to all flags.)

Intercoastal water transportation used to be, before the advent of faster rail transportation, one of the primary forms of shipping cargo and passengers between the east and west coasts. The route used was via the southern tip of South America, then later through the Panama Canal after it was opened in the early part of the century. Today, very little intercoastal transportation is available, except in special incidences where there are disruptions in service.

3. The *Great Lakes* carriers operate along the northeastern portion of the United States and provide service between ports on the five Great Lakes that border the states of New York, Pennsylvania, Ohio, Michigan, Indiana, Illinois, Wisconsin, and Minnesota. The lake ships normally remain on the lakes, but access to Atlantic and Gulf ports is possible via the St. Lawrence Seaway. The Great Lakes-to-United States Atlantic traffic is classified as a coastal operation.

International

Despite the inroads air transportation has made in moving high-value, low-volume cargoes (see the discussion of air transportation), the overwhelming portion of international cargo still moves by water. Cargos shipped include general, bulk, and neobulk.

In the past three decades tremendous changes have taken place, primarily in the form of streamlining the flow of cargo through terminals and on ships. Whereas not too long ago bulk and breakbulk cargoes were loaded and discharged at a relatively slower pace, modern cargo-handling systems and the use of larger ships have altered international water transportation to the point where the ship is considered by many as only part of the total systems approach to transportation. Before, water transportation was often considered the main and most important component of the transportation process, around which everything else revolved.

Industry Overview

Bulk and Neobulk.   The major attraction of water transportation is that it is a low-cost service, especially for nonliquid products. Pipelines, when available, are still the lowest cost of transportation for liquid petroleum products.

Bulk/Unit Loads.   Cargo is shipped either as bulk or in unit loads. Bulk commodities such as liquids (petroleum and petroleum products) account for the largest percentage of total tonnage of domestic water commerce. Dry bulk commodities transported by water carriers are basic raw materials such as coal and coke, sand, gravel, stone, iron ore, grains and logs and lumber, waste and scrap, pulp and paper products, and if as a single vessel, automobiles. On an average-ton basis, the cost to ship bulk commodities is less than for other types of cargoes.

Unit loads are usually products that are finished or semifinished. They usually come in smaller packages, which in turn are either loaded on pallets and shipped as breakbulk cargo or in containers as containerized cargo. The cost to transport unit types of cargoes is usually more expensive per ton than bulk cargoes, although the actual cost is based on either a weight, volume, or value basis.

Private versus For-Hire.   As with the other modes, the water transportation industry is broken down into different categories depending on who the main customer is. Private carriers transport cargo only for the owner of the ship and cargo. For-hire carriers make themselves available to customers on a common carrier basis.

Common Carriers.   Common carriers are mostly involved with transporting general and sometime neobulk cargoes. The services offered are usually on liner operations, meaning that they serve a fixed route on a published fixed schedule.

Charter or Contract Carriers.   These carriers offer services to one or more parties for a particular voyage and/or time period. Although most charters are associated with bulk and neobulk cargoes, liner operators charter vessels to compensate for gaps in fleet vessel availability. This often happens when there are surges in cargo demand or when vessels are out of service for repairs or still being constructed. Oil companies are usually the largest charters, followed by dry bulk shippers of grains and ores.

Flags of Convenience.   In some cases a shipowner registers a ship in a foreign country that offers conveniences in the areas of taxes, manning, and safety requirements. Liberia and Panama are two of the largest nations known for registering these ships, which are referred to as flying "flags of convenience."

Decline of American Flag Ships.   Today, the carrying capacity of some of the larger containerships can replace up to five smaller breakbulk ships of only two decades ago. Tankers today replace smaller tankers at the equivalent of almost a 1 to 10 ratio, and sometimes even more. This has also affected the number and configuration of ports today, as ports still in business compete for fewer ships.

As far as the United States is concerned, the impact on the number of carriers has been dramatic. It can be said that three decades ago at least 25 general cargo ocean common carriers sailed under the American flag. Many company fleets had as many as 30 or more ships. Today, the number of general cargo carriers under the American flag has dwindled to less than 10. As Federal Maritime Administration subsidies, which formerly contributed to the construction and operation of these vessels, are eliminated (construction subsidies for international operations have already been eliminated), American-flag operators are finding it increasingly difficult to maintain operations under that flag. In the interim, carriers have either gone out of business or shifted over to foreign flags or flags of convenience to save costs because of more restrictive American safety and regulatory requirements. Operational subsidies are due to expire by 1997.

National Defense.   The decline of the American-flag merchant marine has often been argued to have implications for the national defense. In times of peace, American carriers compete with sometimes less costly foreign-flag carriers. One of the exceptions here is where certain government or humanitarian aid cargoes are restricted to the American flag. That competition, however, has been a major contributor to the decline in the number of American flag ships.

In times of national crisis or other emergencies, it has been argued that the lack of enough American flag ships could have a drastic effect on the moving of supplies overseas in sufficient quantities and frequency. On the other hand, as was discussed and argued in the case of Operations Desert Shield and Storm, foreign flag ships were chartered by the U.S. Navy to complement available American flag ships. The risk, it has been suggested, is that these foreign flag ships might not want to carry emergency cargoes to war zones, thus depriving them of a dependable supply of cargo. The debate has not ended.

Carriers

Vessel Sharing, Operational and Marketing Agreements.   Although the number of American-flag carriers has declined sharply in the past few decades, most of those still in operation continue to operate under the concept of rationalization. Carriers such as SeaLand and American President Lines have entered into vessel-sharing agreements with a number of foreign-flag carriers, many of which are direct competitors on the same trade routes. Oversupply of vessel space and stiff rate competition usually result in unprofitable operations. Vessel sharing and other forms of space and marketing agreements are shared between the carriers. In some cases these agreements have had some obvious benefits.

Alternatively, it sometimes happens that other operational factors such as terminal operations and priorities, and land transportation systems such as railroads involved with the bridge systems, cause scheduling conflicts between the carriers. This is especially true when delays in vessel arrivals, because of weather conditions and other mechanical breakdowns onboard the ship or onshore, have an impact on the respective lines' operations. This is especially critical when JIT operations call for very close tolerances in scheduling and service demands.

NVOCCs.   With the changes taking place in container steamship operations, many ocean carriers no longer wanted to become involved with more costly handling of less-than-container-load cargoes. This gave rise to the growth of freight forwarders called non-vessel-owned common carriers, or NVOCCs. NVOCCs consolidate less-than-containerload cargoes and load or stuff them in single containers. These containers are then transported to containership carriers. In return, the carriers offer the NVOCCs lower or volume rates. The NVOCC makes a profit between the rate it charges the shipper and the rate the carrier charges the NVOCC.

Types of Vessels

Barges. Perhaps the simplest form of water transportation is the barge, which is either towed or pushed by powerful tugboats. Inland river towing operations can sometimes consist of as much as 20 barges (1000- to 1500-ton capacity, or the equivalent of 15 rail cars or 60 trucks for each barge) on certain rivers such as the Mississippi and the Ohio. Oceangoing barge systems are usually limited to one or two barges capable of carrying several thousand tons of cargo each. This cargo can either be bulk or in general cargo form, such as container or roll on/roll off. Usually these operations are limited to coastal and inter-island routes, using tugs that travel at about 10 kn.

Tankers. Tankers carry liquid cargoes such as crude oil and petroleum products. In some cases, specially designed tankers transport acids in corrosion-resistant tanks and liquefied natural gases, the latter of which are usually stored on-board in very-low-temperature cryogenic tanks.

Some tankers, especially those that travel on large-volume trade routes like that from the Middle East to Europe, are as big as one of the towers of New York City's World Trade Center. These vessels, often classified as VLCCs (very large crude carriers) and ULCCs (ultralarge crude carriers), are limited to a relatively small number of ports because of their deep drafts (the distance from the keel to the waterline), some of which exceed 100 ft. Where deep-draft ports are not available, these super-sized vessels must offload into smaller tankers or permanent or floating offshore terminals.

Bulk and Neobulk Carriers. Bulk and neobulk carriers are like tankers except that they carry dry bulk cargoes only. Typical cargoes include ores, grains, and construction aggregates. Some bulk cargoes, like iron ore, require specially designed cargo holding areas below deck to compensate for the extra heavy weights of these cargoes. Bulk and neobulk carriers are smaller than VLCCs and ULCCs, mainly because the volumes carried are usually in smaller lots and require direct access to shoreside terminals because of the more complex cargo handling equipment involved and typically shallower channels where these shoreside facilities are located.

Breakbulk Carriers. Breakbulk carriers transport general cargo in smaller units that must be loaded and discharged on an individual basis, usually on pallets. (Pallets are small wooden platforms about 4 × 4 ft and capable of receiving the fork of a forklift vehicle to move them around on the pier and on the ship.) Up until the advent of the containership, breakbulk ships were the dominant form of water transportation for general cargo, stowing the cargo below in cargo holds and sometimes on deck. Breakbulk ships are especially useful for oversized cargoes such as railroad rolling stock and locomotives.

These vessels are also labor-intensive, often using 100 or more laborers on the vessel, pier, and terminal area. Most breakbulk operations today are found in parts of the world where more efficient container handling facilities have not yet been constructed.

Containerships.   Containerships carry containers either belowdecks in so-called "cells," or on deck where they are strapped down with lashing gear or other forms of securing mechanisms. The concept of containerization has been around for more than 200 years, but not until the mid-1950s did it start to develop into a major water transportation system. On average, containerships carry about 2000 TEUs (20-ft equivalent units) which, if placed end to end, would stretch more than 6 mi. The carrying capacity of these 2000 TEUs could be as much as 20,000 tons of cargo, three to four times the carrying capacity of a typical breakbulk cargo. Because of these larger carrying capacities and the economies of scale associated with containership operations, containerships are gradually replacing breakbulk vessels on most trade routes.

Containerships carry containers in various sizes (20, 40, 45, 48, etc.). Some container vessels are also built to carry roll on/roll off vehicles below deck.

Ro/Ro Vessels.   These vessels resemble large ferries and are capable of handling vehicles that move on and off the vessel on wheels. They are especially useful on trade routes where heavy machinery and large vehicles cannot be handled by conventional ships or, in some cases, regular containerships.

Special Carriers.   In addition, there are special-purpose vessels that accommodate activities that are unique to certain trade routes. This would include passenger vessels, auto carriers that can carry as many as 5000 smaller-sized cars, offshore oil rig supply vessels, and cable-laying vessels that are becoming increasingly important as international communications rely more on underwater cables versus satellite systems. Combination vessels usually combine different types of cargoes, such as both breakbulk and container.

Service Characteristics

Low-Cost Service.   Low-cost service is the major advantage of water transportation, especially for nonliquid products. (For liquid petroleum products, the pipeline is the lowest-cost form of transportation, but the two forms of transportation often are not in competition with each other.)

Slow Speed.   Transit time of water transportation is the longest (slowest speed) of all the modes that move most commodities. Time is generally measured in days, as compared to hours for highway and air. At the same time, however, slow speed is more than compensated for by the generally lower overall transportation cost of water transportation versus the other modes, with of course the exception of pipeline for liquid cargoes.

Service Disruption.   Winter months, periods of drought when rivers are low, siltation of navigable channels and berths, and blocking of channels because of marine accidents are some of the major disruptions that slow down, if not totally disrupt vessel-related transportation. This is especially true on waterways that have limited access.

Vessel Size and Accessibility. Vessels must have deep enough navigable channels to reach marine terminals safely. This is not a problem for some ports because of natural geological development (Seattle or Tacoma, for example). Other ports like Boston, New York, and Oakland, although channel entrances from the ocean may be relatively deep, still need channels to be deepened to allow vessels to reach the terminals further upstream and along piers.

Accessibility is also a factor in having a marine terminal close or even adjacent to rail and highway transportation. If other surface transportation modes are not that accessible, additional costs must be accounted for in the full development and operation of the terminal.

Cost Structure

High Variable Costs. Like motor and air carriers, water carriers do not provide their own rights of way, unless the navigable channel they use is for their own exclusive use. In these cases, carriers must pay for the construction and maintenance of that channel.

On the other hand, carriers pay user charges such as lock fees, wharfage (a charge assessed against the cargo for each ton or other measurement of cargo moved across the wharf), and dockage (a charge assessed against the vessel, based on length of vessel and other criteria), for use of either government or private development-provided facilities. These variable costs fluctuate based on the type and volume of the vessel.

Low Fixed Costs. Fixed costs include depreciation and amortization and general expenses. General expenses usually exceed depreciation and amortization by a 2 to 1 margin.

Capital Intensiveness. Because vessel-related operations, either on the vessel itself or onshore, are tied increasingly to the factors of faster time with increased efficiency, investment in the water transportation industry is becoming capital-intensive. That trend will continue as the demand for increased automation becomes the rule rather than the exception. Some of the larger containerships today cost as much as $100 million each, compared to the $20 million and less for earlier mid- and larger-sized breakbulk vessels.

Ports and Terminals

General versus Niche. Before deregulation, and supported in part by fairly standard vessel types such as tankers, bulk, and breakbulk ships, most ports could claim that they served almost all types of cargoes on a routine basis. Indeed most of these ports had, and in some cases still have, good inland access, especially via railroads. This gave these ports, with easily accessible inland transportation systems, a distinct advantage over ports that are somewhat limited.

Today, especially as a direct result of deregulation, emerging technologies such as containerization, and larger and more free-flowing international trading patterns, many ports are forced to reconsider their strengths and weaknesses in terms of inland access and focus their business strategies on becoming a niche port for a limited number of commodities. Some ports like Seattle and Oakland have favored containerization over bulk commodities. As a result smaller ports and terminals in the San Francisco Bay area, because of existing and easily developed facilities, took over the bulk operations. Miami became a niche port for both container and passenger operations, the latter due mainly to the port's favorable geographic position for the Caribbean-based cruise trade.

Alternatively, some ports like Los Angeles and Long Beach successfully continued on with and in some cases expanded bulk, breakbulk, and container cargo facilities and operations. These operations, especially those facilities still in the planning stages, are placing tremendous stress on financial and environmental resources.

At the other end of the spectrum are ports that determined they could no longer compete successfully with ports regionally or along the coastline. After considerable analysis and debate, these ports decided to abandon most if not all of their water transportation activities. Instead they converted valuable waterfront space for recreational, residential, and small commercial mixed-use activities. San Diego is a good example. At the dawn of the container age, it realized that it could not compete with its neighbors to the north (Los Angeles and Long Beach) for the same types of cargoes. Consequently the decision was made to switch rather than to fight, the results of which, it could be said, were profitable to each of the ports involved.

Environmental Concerns.   Many ports in the United States agree that the number one issue they face is the environment. Local communities, along with regulations promulgated by federal, state, and local environmental protection agencies, place severe restrictions on the location, development, expansion, and operation of marine activities and services. This includes the construction and maintenance of navigable channels and vessel berths. There are many examples where permits to dig or dredge channels and berths were not issued either temporarily or permanently because of these restrictions. As a result, some carriers were forced to transfer to other ports that did not face the same restrictions. Ultimately, the costs of complying with environmental issues are paid for by the carriers and the consumer.

Competition from Other Waterfront Activities.   Marine waterfront property, including in this case other marine-related activities such as vessel repair and construction, refueling and provisioning, and services such as pilotage and tow boat operations, are under considerable pressure to relocate their operations elsewhere. Much of that pressure is coming from potential non-water-transportation activities—recreational, residential, and light commercial activities—that would like those waterfront properties for themselves. This is especially true along waterfronts where traditional marine activities have declined or gone out of business completely.

Some ports like San Francisco and Seattle have had moderate success in dealing with this form of tug-of-war. Other ports like Boston and Baltimore have made the transition, and the results are in many respects quite successful. Meanwhile, other ports like Philadelphia are still weighing their options.

Distribution Management. Ports, especially niche ports, have recognized, especially in the past few years, that the port and its services are important to the concept of the so-called "systems approach" to transportation and logistics management. Consequently, some ports have actively embraced sophisticated electronic communications systems that tie shippers together with other port- and transportation-related services. This includes forwarders, carriers, and government agencies such as customs, etc. The goal is to streamline working relationships without having to depend on what seems to be an ever-increasing amount of paper.

One of the potential solutions to this information transmission problem is electronic data interchange systems (EDI). Together with third party services such as warehouses, which also prepare and ship products to the final customer based on the instructions of the owner of the cargo, these services are becoming increasingly important to the total systems approach to transportation and logistics management. Port authorities play advocacy or direct roles in making sure that these types of services are available to participants in the transportation and logistics process within the Port Authority's area of jurisdiction.

Government. Before regulation of the modes, there was a growing sense that if left to themselves, the competition within each of the modes or even between the modes could eventually harm, if not destroy, carriers. The reasoning followed that, if left unrestrained, monopolistic tendencies would begin to disrupt the flow of commerce, including passengers and cargo.

To bring some order to a rapidly deteriorating situation, the Congress enacted different pieces of legislation that, in the interim, have seen the pendulum of government interference swing both ways. In the past 80 years, two of the more important water-transportation-related acts were the Shipping Act of 1916 and the Shipping Act of 1984.

The 1916 act established a series of regulations that closely watched over international water transportation carriers, including foreign flag companies calling at American ports. It also included terminal operators and other ancillary services. It provided antitrust immunity for the water transportation industry (including terminals), permitted carriers to form open conferences, and created a U.S. Shipping Board to regulate and promote ocean commerce. The Shipping Board later was renamed the Federal Maritime Commission, which in 1961 was established as an independent regulatory agency.

The 1984 act, which focused on the last of the modes to be deregulated, at least at the international level, loosened some of the restrictions placed on both carriers and shippers. It did away with the need to file intermodal rates and divisions of those rates with the Interstate Commerce Commission. It also permitted ocean rate conferences to file joint rates covering both the inland portion and the water movement of an intermodal movement. This applied to many carriers on several routes. Freedom was allowed for carriers to establish through routes on an ad hoc basis, adjusting them daily if desired.

Even more important from the standpoint of promoting intermodalism was the ability of all participants to contract for rates and services, particularly rail and steamship operators. This had the effect of increasing the amount of competition between ports, as well as making it more difficult for competitors to obtain data (all terminal rates had to be filed with the Maritime Administration).

Overall, however, the Shipping Act of 1984 increased shipper choices, and it has made intermodal transportation a more viable option.

Cabotage.   Cabotage occurs when a nation or other sovereign entity restricts the right of foreign-flag carriers to carry cargo between that country's ports. For example, under the cabotage laws of the United States, no foreign carrier is allowed to carry passengers or cargo between Boston and New York or San Francisco and Seattle. Foreign-flag carriers can, however, carry passengers and cargo between the same port cities if that vessel makes a stop first at a foreign port such as Bermuda or the Bahamas on the east coast, and Vancouver on the west coast, before moving on to the second United States port.

Cabotage remains a sensitive issue with vested interests such as maritime unions, which have ships that call along United States coastal ports. Due to economic and other political pressures, the possibility of loosening if not abandoning cabotage completely is constantly being explored.

Competition

Since the mid-1960s, competition in the water transportation industry has been fierce. As stated earlier, much of that competition came as a direct result of emerging advanced transportation and communication technologies, changing trading patterns, and the spreading influence of deregulation. The prognosis is that over the next decade competition will move from being very niche-oriented (containership, bulk, etc.) to a field of competition where the players are fewer in number and the lineup will be head-to-head. One of the other influences on this is the bridge system.

Bridges.   The bridge system referred to in different parts of this chapter includes the use of land transportation as a key part of the total transportation route. Bridge systems replace routes and ports of the traditional all-water system.

The principal mode of transportation across the land is the railroad, especially for containerized and dry bulk cargoes. For liquid cargoes like petroleum, pipelines usually are the most efficient mode. As a result, traditional ports that might have been the main gateways along certain coastlines are replaced instead by other ports and coastlines that formerly were not part of the trade route. Furthermore, the time and cost of taking these bridge systems is usually faster and cheaper than the more traditional all-water routes. There are three principle bridge systems.

Land-bridge.   This is where containerized cargo, moving for example from Tokyo to Rotterdam, is transported by ship to a west coast port like Seattle, then carried by rail to an east coast port like Baltimore, and then reloaded aboard another vessel for the voyage to Rotterdam. This land-bridge system replaces the traditional all-ocean route via either the Panama or Suez canals.

Minibridge. Cargo moving, for example, between Tokyo and Baltimore, is transported by ship to a west coast port like Seattle, then moved by rail to Baltimore. In the process, ports on the east coast—in this case it would be Baltimore—are deprived of that cargo moving across their own piers. That marine terminal activity, and all of the economic issues associated with it, would instead be gained by one of the west coast ports.

Microbridge. Starting again, for example, from Tokyo, cargo destined for inland cities like Denver would move by container vessel to Seattle, then by rail to Denver. Formerly, the Tokyo–Denver trade route would have passed through, for example, the Panama Canal and then on to New Orleans. At New Orleans the cargo is transferred to a barge, rail, or truck or a combination of modes to Denver. Again, as was the case with Baltimore and minibridge, the traditional port gateway—in this case it is a Gulf port of New Orleans—is bypassed with the resultant loss of marine terminal activity.

Alternative Modes and Trade Routes. There are also signs that once dominant routes and systems that have lost favor to the bridge systems are the subject of renewed interest. Some of them include the following.

Air-Sea. Alternative modes and trade routes appear, disappear, and then reappear again, because of fast changes in globalization of products and the growing flexibility of transportation systems. Examples include the replacement of all-ocean or all-air routes for certain commodities by using a combination of the two modes known as air-sea. Cargoes moving by air-sea are usually those that take advantage of the cost savings of the all-sea route that is slower, but pay a sightly higher price based on the faster service of the all-air service. Examples of such cargoes are apparel starting somewhere along the Pacific Rim to a destination along the east coast of the United States. Cargo moves by ship to Seattle, where it is transferred to an airplane for the flight to New York. Such cargoes might not need to be on store shelves for several weeks, but at the same time could not afford to wait for the longer sea route and time because of market demand pressures.

Ro/Ro and Container Barges. With better cost efficiencies associated with oceangoing barge operations on certain trade routes like the Caribbean, larger and more expensive general cargo ships like container, breakbulk, and ro/ro are finding new markets for their services.

Reemergence of the Major Canals. There is also a growing interest in reestablishing the all-water route of using the Suez Canal as an alternative to land and minibridge operations between the Far East and Europe and the United States.

Megacarriers. Deregulation, among other factors, has caused the largely tradition-bound water transportation industry to change faster than might have been the case otherwise. The result is that after mergers, buyouts, and perhaps too frequently bankruptcies, the number of carriers still in the game has dwindled to the point where there are only a few players on each of the major trade routes. Except for the occasional niche carrier (automobiles, lumber and paper products, etc.), players in this new competitive environment have to be considered mega or giant companies that have the financial and operational resources to compete with each other on a direct head-to-head basis. Those that cannot match the strengths of the megacarriers most often than not fall to the wayside, or must seek niche markets in which they have a competitive edge.

Vertically Integrated Services.   Vertically integrated carriers like CSX and American President Lines have either absorbed or been absorbed by other modal carriers and services in the other modes. This was found necessary to provide their customers with what is commonly called a "seamless" transportation and logistics management system. Most often, these carriers are in the so-called megacarrier category because the resources to become fully vertically integrated require deep pockets and a worldwide network of services.

Intermodalism.   Intermodalism is usually defined as the capability to interchange freight, especially in containers, among the various transportation modes. The fact that the containers are of the same size, and have common handling characteristics, permits them to be transferred from truck to railroad to air carrier to ocean carrier, in a complete origin-to-destination movement without once disturbing the cargo.

Transportation Only versus Full Service.   Traditional transportation of cargo, regardless of the commodity, destination, and the modes and carriers involved, concentrated mostly on the actual movement (transportation) of the cargo, and how and where it was warehoused between movements. Contracts for each of the services usually were negotiated separately.

Full-service transportation, however, moves closer to what is better known as "logistics management." In this case, the transportation and warehousing (warehousing if needed; containerization is often referred to as "warehousing on wheels") are joined with a higher service level of inventory control and partial value-enhancement of the product before it moves on to the customer. Certain carriers and ports like APL and Seattle have expanded their services to include this full-service concept, especially as production methods such as JIT become increasingly important in meeting the customers' needs in a more economical and efficient manner.

Handling of Goods

Cargo, whether it is general or in bulk, requires different handling equipment. Loose, noncontainerized cargo is mostly labor-intensive, relying on the use of forklifts and conveyor belts to move it from one place to the next. This process can often be made easier if the cargo is placed on pallets.

Containerized cargo, because it is unitized in a single container, moves as a single unit weighing as much as 35 tons, depending on the size of the container and the allowable weights of the modes involved. Containers are loaded on and off different modes by a variety of lifting technologies. This includes container cranes, which are usually located on marine container terminals; straddle carriers, which straddle and then move the container before moving it to another location; and large forklift trucks, which are usually the larger cousin of the warehouse forklift.

Dry bulk commodities like coal, grains, and ores depend on large scoops, gravity feed chutes, and loading mechanisms. Liquid cargoes such as petroleum, liquefied natural gas, and even wine and beer are loaded and unloaded by pipeline.

Types of Containers.   Air or ocean containers come in all kinds of sizes, shapes, and carrying capacities. Under the International Standards Organization (ISO) classification system, ocean containers are measured in 20-ft lengths (TEUs) and are either 20 or 40 ft in length. Other container sizes used include 10-, 24-, 30-, 35- and more recently 45-, 48-, and 54-ft sizes. Most containers are 8 ft 6 in in height. High cube containers are usually 9 ft 6 in in height. Except for special cases, almost all containers are 8 ft wide. Nearly 9 out of 10 containers are made of steel, with the remaining containers of either aluminum or special materials.

The standard 20-ft/40-ft closed-top dry freight container is the most popular in use, and accounts for more than two-thirds of all the containers. The remaining group of container types are mostly open-top, integral reefer, and flatrack and platform types. Other containers handle strictly liquid cargoes such as concentrated fruit juices, acids, and chemical products. Today, as improvements are made in minimizing damage due to condensation, some containers are built to handle bulk commodities such as coffee, raw rubber, and grains.

Labor.   Automation of cargo transportation, especially containerization, is capital-intensive. In most cases, capitalization reduces the amount of labor used at considerable cost savings.

With traditional breakbulk operations, several hundred laborers were used to off-load and load a ship (this is especially true in parts of the world where local labor laws restrict the use of automated equipment). The time required could be as long as one week. Today, with the automation of containerization, the number of laborers needed to handle the equivalent of three to four times the amount of cargo of the more traditional cargo ship is often less than 10 to 20 percent. The time required is often as little as 24 hours.

Whereas breakbulk operations relied heavily on human muscle, container operations, except for some terminal processing operations on the pier, utilize specialized skills that take time and effort to develop. This is especially true for specialists such as container crane operators, who load and unload as much as 35 tons in one lift, at speeds that could average 25 containers/hr.

Technology

Refinement.   The technology of ocean transportation has reached the point where major breakthroughs in size and speed will be incremental at best for at least the next decade. It is true that some countries such as Japan are developing hull designs and propulsion systems that are said to move between Tokyo and Seattle in about three days, at least half the time it takes today. These specialized vessels will carry as many as 50 containers. But these vessels will most likely be the exception.

Instead, we will most likely see vessels that will have improved propulsion systems that use more efficient fuel mixtures and other refinements of the power plant. At the terminal, cargo will move faster on and off the vessel, including container, bulk, and liquid. Advanced navigation systems will increase the safety of navigation at sea and in port.

Improved Flow of Activity.   The biggest breakthroughs, however, will most likely come in moving the cargo through the terminal faster and more efficiently. This will involve closer coordination between each phase of operation on the terminal and what takes place before and after the cargo arrives at the terminal. The goal will be to reduce as much as possible the time cargo remains on the terminal. This will require closer cooperation between shipper, carrier, third party services such as freight forwarders, custom house brokers, etc., and government agencies such as Customs Service, Immigration, etc.

Communications.   The key, or perhaps it could be said the glue that will bind all of these activities together, is communications. With the use of faster and more powerful computers and electronic data interchange (EDI), information will flow through the transportation system faster, more accurately, and with less cost. By comparison with the evolutionary state of containerization and where it is today, it could be said that the communications revolution is still in its infancy, with most of the players involved still learning to crawl before they can walk.

Labor.   Similar to other economic activities, labor will be one of those most affected by the coming changes in transportation and logistics management. One obvious result is that machines and automation will continue to replace most of the manual tasks involved in moving passengers and goods to, through, and out of the terminal.

At the same time, there is the continued strain between union and nonunionized work forces on and off the ship and terminal. In the United States, the larger carriers and ports still have unions. However, because of the acceptance of technological advances combined with the recession of 1990–1992, there have been fewer strikes or other labor disruptions. Other parts of the globe are witnessing a similar pattern, except in countries where economic activities are still in the process of shifting from central management to market forces.

Smaller Crews.   All of this automation has reached the point where the size of crews aboard ship and on the terminal will be a fraction of what they were less than a decade ago. This raises an issue that is receiving growing recognition: the social factor of reduced human contact as a result of less persons on the job, especially on ships.

As an example, a German containership operator recently built a class of containerships that have the capability of sailing with a crew of four. But, as the company found out later, it had a difficult time finding qualified and skilled persons willing to live under such conditions. Consequently, the size of the crews was increased to more than 12, a number that is still less than half that of the average ship.

Skilled versus Low or Semiskilled.   At the same time, and as has often been said in the media and on the shop floor, skilled jobs are replacing unskilled and in some cases semiskilled jobs. On some of the more modern vessels today, licensed officers and certified crew members are required to handle more technology, which often means they must master several disciplines.

Although this shift from muscle to brains is having a profound impact on the number of jobs lost, perhaps permanently, many carriers, terminal operators, and unions have joined forces to develop training or retraining programs that meet the technological needs of the industry as it exists today and conform to the shape it will take in the future. Some carriers and terminal operators, especially in Europe and Japan, have taken the extra step of involving ship and terminal staff to be part of the technological development process right from the start. Although a full evaluation of that process is still under way, it can be argued that in most cases this form of cooperation between management and labor has lessened the fear of technology by both management and labor. Furthermore, this dialogue has gained certain inputs that could have been missed had that input not been available.

Safety. Vessel collisions, groundings, and sinkings, as well as accidents on the terminal, have always taken place. Today, however, because of faster and larger amounts of information that can be gathered, analyzed, and disseminated, the frequency, scale, and magnitude of these accidents seem to have a larger impact than when less was known about them several decades ago. As a result the risk to life, property, and the environment now receives closer attention, and may prevent such accidents from happening in the first place.

This is especially true with greater use of more accurate vessel-positioning technology based on advanced terrestrial and satellite navigation systems. Some of these systems have the capability of locating the position of a vessel to within 100 ft or less of its actual position.

Other improved safety measures benefit from more efficient design of vessels and shoreside equipment, and better training.

Current Issues

Drug and Alcohol Abuse. Investigation of water transportation related accidents has brought to light more and more incidents where the abuse of drug and alcohol were major contributors. To deal with this problem, federal agencies like the U.S. Coast Guard and other substance-abuse agencies have instituted and followed up closely on very strict rules affecting these substances. It is more often than not the case that loss of job and potential banishment from the transportation industry is the penalty if found guilty. At the same time, companies and government agencies have started extensive substance-abuse counseling programs designed to prevent, rather than punish, potential abusers from starting.

Conferences. Conferences for rate agreements and services were originally formed and protected by various American laws to stabilize rates and service competition on designated trade routes. This may change. In the last few years there has been increased pressure to become more competitive, both ashore and at sea, to respond faster to changes in transportation and communication technology. Under these conditions, the conference system is under pressure to reform itself. This could mean that the conference system as we know it today will in the next few years have a new set of purposes, or disappear completely.

Air Transportation

On December 17, 1903, Orville Wright left the ground from the sand dunes off Kitty Hawk, North Carolina. As he drifted into the air, he was the pilot of what was to become the world's first controllable powered flight. That first flight covered 120 ft.

The progress in air transportation since then can be measured by saying that the wing span of a Boeing 747 is greater than the length of that first flight. Putting that in further perspective, the first airplane was nothing more than an oversized glider on which a 16-hp engine had been placed. The first sustained flight lasted only 12 sec. By contrast, the modern jet engine on today's airliners develop many thousands of pounds of thrust horsepower and are capable of covering distances of 6000 mi and more nonstop.

Air transportation in the United States, and indeed in many other countries at the time, really got its most important support from government mail service. Up until then, aviation was more of a curiosity that allowed experimenters to test their ideas on what and how aviation could do for both fun and profit. Many of this country's largest airlines that are still in business today started out in the mail business in one way or another, including American and United. Others, like Delta, started out as local service carriers, including crop dusting, etc.

By the early 1930s, airlines began to establish themselves across the country and in foreign countries. Many still had airplanes that flew little more than 100 mi/h. At the same time, competition and services for the general public continued to lag. To provide some help, including incentives to branch out into other potential revenue-producing fields, the Civil Aeronautics Act of 1938 was passed. One of its more important provisions was the improvement of coordination of the industry by the government and its sometimes overlapping agencies by creating the Civil Aeronautics Authority, which later became the Civil Aeronautics Board (CAB) in 1940.

Additional provisions provided incentives for the carriage of air mail. Carriers that were in business prior to the act were issued a Certificate of Convenience and Necessity for the routes that they were serving. This meant that carriers that had the certificate could operate in a market where on certain routes the number of players was limited.

The growth and development of international and foreign air transportation did not parallel the progress of domestic air transportation in the United States. Air carriers in the United States were privately owned corporations, while foreign air carriers for the most part were either wholly or partially owned by their governments. This often led to differences in financial and political support the American carriers had to face when dealing with heavily subsidized foreign carriers.

Although there were several important pieces of legislation passed by the United States designed to give some support to the industry, the Bermuda Agreement of 1946 was perhaps one of the most far-reaching and influential up until the present. The Bermuda Agreement was the first bilateral agreement involving civil aviation entered into by two countries, namely the United States and Great Britain. It served as a model for other bilateral agreements because of its flexibility. Each country granted to the other the "Five Freedoms" in accordance with certain general provisions: government approval of rates, inadequate traffic capacity, and a review of the carriers' operation in compliance with these principles. The two also agreed that international rates and fares would be subject to agreements to be made through the International Air Transport Association.

Air carriers like Pan American Airlines and Trans World Airlines, in cooperation with the United States government, used these agreements to its maximum advantage to gain and retain access to foreign countries. Up until deregulation in the late 1970s, these two carriers were the primary international air carriers for the United States. Other carriers like Northwest Orient were restricted to limited international routes to the Far East, for example.

Perhaps one of the most dramatic breakthroughs in air transportation was the introduction of the jet plane from the late 1950s to the late 1960s. Not only did it fly faster and further than conventional propeller-driven aircraft, but its payload also increased several-fold per flight. Right behind the jet came the realization that airport authorities must prepare for and construct larger airports to handle the increased volume and sometimes frequency of passengers and cargo that these planes could handle.

With the advent of jet airplanes, the air transportation industry changed dramatically almost overnight. And, for the first time, air cargo became an important player in generating revenue for carriers. Although the air transportation industry is very dependent on passenger revenues to maintain its financial viability, on average about 14 percent of operating revenues that combination passenger and cargo carriers receive comes from cargo.

The aviation industry, as part of the larger aerospace industry, includes all the activities involved with building and flying aircraft.

Despite national and international interruptions such as downturns in the economy and the impact of Operations Desert Shield and Desert Storm on transportation in general, the expectation is that aviation worldwide should grow between 4 to 9 percent annually. In the United States the greatest increase will most likely come from air cargo, as businesses become more informed and take advantage of advanced logistics management concepts to better serve their customers. In Europe, in contrast with the phenomenal double-digit growth in the Far East and to a certain extent South America, aviation increases are expected to be less. Alternative competing transportation systems, and closer distances between major centers of economic activity, have slowed down the growth potential of the industry there.

Carriers

Major.   Major carriers in the United States are usually those that generate more than $1 billion or more in annual revenues. Such carriers also provide services between major population areas within the United States and with other countries. Most of the larger routes served are usually highly sensitive to price competition—especially since deregulation went into effect in the early 1980s—and use mostly large-capacity planes for longer routes that often stretch across the continent. Because of the need to increase if not control market share, many of these airlines also serve medium-sized population centers such as Cleveland and New Orleans.

National.   National carriers usually operate scheduled services on relatively shorter distances (Cleveland and Chicago) and in other cases large, regional areas (Cleveland and Washington). Many of these carriers are also stiff competition for the major carriers on many routes between less-populated areas and major population centers, using smaller planes. Generally speaking, these carriers have annual revenues between $75 million and $1 billion.

Regional and Local.   These carriers operate within a particular region of the country, such as the southwest corner of the United States or New England, and connect less populated areas with larger population centers. These carriers are usually grouped into two categories: large ($10 to $75 million) and medium (less than $10 million.) For competitive purposes, many of the major carriers like American own or have agreements with these smaller carriers to act as feeders.

International.   Because of deregulation at both the domestic and international level, many U.S. carriers are also international carriers. They operate between the continental United States and foreign countries and between the United States and its territories. The president of the United States is usually involved in determining which carriers, both American and foreign, will be given new or expanded routes. Selection of carriers is often based on both economic and political issues, especially on routes that have the potential to generate large numbers of passengers and cargo over the years.

Charter.   Although charter carriers use the same type and size planes as national and international carriers to carry passengers and freight, they operate without fixed schedules or designated routes. Rather, they charter the entire plane to a group or companies between specified origins and destinations at agreed-to prices, schedules, and other terms of limitation. In return, the customer gets a lower price for the service.

   Many of the large domestic and international air carriers are restricted by international agreements that limit them to specific routes. To take advantage of occasional charter arrangements, many of these same carriers created charter subsidiaries. In this way, and perhaps softened somewhat by bilateral restrictions between the two countries involved, carriers can offer a larger range of services that are competitive with the charter market.

Small Package and Overnight Express.   Since deregulation, one of the fastest growth areas in aviation has been in the small package and overnight express business. Companies such as Federal Express and United Parcel Service specialize in a service that is in most cases in direct competition with the postal services of this and other countries. They can do this because of logistical operations that start at the point where the package is picked up (usually at the shipper's own premises or central collecting points) and end at the final destination of the recipient. The fee for this service is usually several more times than what postal services might charge. In return, however, it is usually faster (overnight, or two or three days for international shipments) and more reliable.

Types of Aircraft and Service Equipment

Widebody versus Short-Haul.   Aircraft are usually classified by size (regular or widebody) and short-haul versus long-haul. Economics and the concept of hub-and-spoke operations have sharply changed the role of plane sizes in the transportation of passengers and cargo. For shorter distances, or where takeoffs and landings are more frequent, air carriers use smaller planes like the Boeing 737 and DC-9. For longer distances, especially transcontinental and across the ocean, the economics favor larger widebody planes. Although the cost of the widebody plane is higher initially (as much as $125 million each), the cost of operation per seat mile or cargo mile is considerably less.

Airframe Manufacturers. The high cost in development (often $2 to $4 billion), and the time from the drawing board to the customer (five to nine years) has reduced the number of major airframe manufacturers in the past few decades. In addition, projected cuts in defense budgets, which often include provisions for commercial airframe manufacturers to use the same or modified technologies, have placed additional strains on the profitability of building newer models. This is especially true for radically new design and performance planes, like hypersonic planes capable of reducing flight time over very long distances.

Nevertheless, two of the three largest commercial airframe manufacturers are American (Boeing and McDonnel-Douglas). The third is AirBus, which is a consortium of major airframe and parts manufacturers from Germany, England, France, and Spain. The competition for new orders is becoming more fierce all the time, often spilling over into squabbles about political and international agreements. Other advanced industrial countries like Japan are looking for opportunities to become a player in this high-tech business, followed in turn by other Far East countries like South Korea and Taiwan.

Ground Handling Equipment. The high cost of air transportation for both passengers and cargo is placing pressure on other sectors of the industry to develop and operate more efficiently. One of these sectors is ground handling equipment for passengers, cargo, and planes. Such equipment, if it breaks down or is very expensive to operate, could have severe impact on time and other service activities. Not only does this include actual handling of passengers, baggage, and cargo, but also the servicing of the aircraft, such as fueling, provisioning of supplies, and routine maintenance between flights.

Service Characteristics

Air Transportation. Air transportation in general is usually considered to be scheduled and on fixed routes, and therefore categorized as common carriers of passengers and cargo. This includes most of the airline companies regardless of size and the markets they serve.

General Aviation. General aviation usually serves private owners (generally corporations), using smaller aircraft and flying on a demand basis. General aviation also includes smaller pleasure aircraft.

Speed. The single most important characteristic of aviation is speed in covering larger distances in a shorter period of time when compared to alternative modes.

This is especially important given today's need to move passengers and cargo almost overnight to practically any part of the world. For shorter distances, modes such as high-speed rail are strong competitors of the aviation industry. This is especially true in high-population-density parts of the world like Europe and Japan, where large population centers are relatively close.

Flight Frequency.   In addition to speed, many carriers compete on frequency of service between locations. The larger carriers, especially some of the megacarriers like American, United Airlines, and Delta, have competed effectively against smaller and in some cases emerging airlines. Larger carriers have larger fleets and services that the smaller carriers cannot match on the same terms of competition.

Congestion.   At the same time, all airlines face the rising tide of too many planes in the air and on the ground. This is especially true in and around airports in larger population centers.

Airlines, in cooperation with and sometimes at the insistence of airport operators, have established landing and takeoff schedules that assign slots designed to avoid potential congestion periods, especially during peak hours of operation. At the same time some airlines, especially those that compete with some of the megacarriers, provide service to alternate airports in the same regions where available, to offer passengers and cargo alternatives to this congestion problem. It is interesting to note here that one of the largest areas for future advances in aviation might be on the ground rather than in technological advances of the aircraft. Unless the congestion problem can be solved in an amicable way, the advantages of speed that the aviation industry has to offer the air transportation customer could be negated.

Accessibility.   The aviation industry also faces the growing realization that carriers, whether flying to large population centers like Los Angeles or Houston, or less dense areas like Salt Lake City, are limited by the number of airports that each of these population centers has available. On the ground, intermodal accessibly to and from the airport is another growing challenge that local communities which support their airport industries are striving to improve. Airports that offer their passengers and customers reliable transportation to and from the airport find that such services are sometimes just as important as the airplane service itself.

High Value/Low Volume.   Due to the high cost of aviation service to both passengers and cargo, service is usually limited to high-value/low-volume clients. This results in transporting passengers who find that the cost of transportation is expensive, but in the total scheme of logistics management for both passengers and cargo, time is sometimes more valuable. This is especially true when the need to arrive at a certain destination is one of the keys to conducting important meetings or to meeting manufacturing and assembly schedules that are based on tight schedules and have very little room for error.

Cost Structure

Air carriers, like motor carriers, have a cost structure that is based on high variables and low fixed costs. Approximately 80 percent of the total operating costs are variable and 20 percent are fixed. This is attributable to government investments and operation of airports and airways. The carriers pay for the use of these facilities through landing fees, which are also variable in terms of the size and weight of the aircraft and, in some cases, the number of passengers and cargo on board.

Maintenance. Maintenance of both aircraft and ground facilities also includes administrative activities. The cost of this can reach as much as 22 percent of total operating expenses, and as a result is subject to some of the more stringent cost-reduction efforts by both carriers and airports. However, with increased pressure on reliability of service, many carriers and airports find that too many restrictions and cutbacks in maintenance result in a loss of customers. With increased use of better materials, more efficient operations, and closer attention to what the customer demands, the aviation industry has made tremendous strides in this area.

Commissions. Commissions are fees paid to travel agents and air cargo forwarders by carriers who book flights. Travel agents receive a percentage of the air fare for tickets issued on behalf of the carrier. This commission, usually less than 10 percent of the cost of the ticket or tariff, is deducted from the air fare that the carrier charges. Many air cargo carriers continue to rely on air freight forwarders, especially in cases where niche cargoes and other special circumstances require the time and effort that air cargo forwarders offer and that the air carrier cannot match because of usually higher overhead expenses.

Fuel and Labor Costs. Perhaps one of the largest cost categories that air carriers must support is in fuel and labor. In the United States it is generally stated that for every increase of 1 cent in the cost of fuel, the overall cost to the industry is about $1 billion. This is especially important in making the decision as to what kind of aircraft to use. On average, a 747 uses about 3300 gal of fuel per hour while in the air, whereas a smaller 727 uses 1300 gal/hr. On the other hand, the cost per unit (passenger or cargo weight) is smaller for the larger plane than the smaller aircraft if the load factor is high enough to at least break even. Labor costs, especially since deregulation, have also received closer attention by the carriers, many of which have turned to nonunion labor where possible because of generally lower wages and benefits needed to support that labor.

Plane Size. Plane size depends on many factors, including the route being served, the number and volume of the payload (passengers and cargo), and the market being served. The largest commercial aircraft are typically the MD-11s and the Boeing 747, the latter of which can carry as much as 100 tons of cargo for distances greater than 3000 mi. Smaller aircraft, although still large, carry only half as much as the larger aircraft and usually specialize in routes that are much shorter and perhaps more frequent.

Routes. Air carriers specialize in routes that they are best equipped to handle. National and international carriers usually have the equipment (planes, airport facilities, etc.) to serve routes that are longer and perhaps greater in volume. They also use hub-and-spoke systems (see below) which allow them to take advantage of the benefits that these systems offer. Smaller local and regional carriers usually serve shorter and perhaps specialized markets such as overnight courier and small package services. Because of the competitive issues that developed from domestic and now international air transportation, many carriers are finding that they need to rationalize their route systems in cooperation with other carriers, thereby offering easier schedules and other services at a lower cost to the passenger and cargo.

Load Factor.   Air carriers strive to maximize the load factor for each type of aircraft used on each route served by the carrier. Typically the breakeven load factor is about 60 to 70 percent, depending on the type of plane being used and the route. However, many carriers find that even higher load factors do not sufficiently cover all costs on particular routes, such as the North Atlantic and cross-continental, because not serving that particular market could mean the loss of customers on other routes that connect with the main route and that are usually more profitable.

Equipment Substitution.   Cost of operations, and competition, often require carriers to switch equipment, and in some cases schedules, when the demand of the service fluctuates, often seasonally. Thus some of the megacarriers, because of the larger range of types of planes in their fleets, have the ability to switch planes to accommodate the market. Other carriers, especially regional and specialized carriers (for limited niche markets such as automobile parts), may find that their operational costs do not allow them to be flexible enough to allow for easy substitution, thus placing increased pressure on operational budgets.

Communications

Perhaps one area that has seen the greatest advancement in aviation in the last decade is in communications. Customers today demand faster and more accurate schedule and cost-of-service information to meet their own intense competitive pressures. Computers and more efficient transfer of electronic data has allowed carriers and their customers, including travel agents and freight forwarders, to assess the range of services and costs available to determine the best carrier to use. American Airlines SABRE and similar systems of other carriers, some of which have joined forces to provide this type of service, find that such technology is the key to profitable operations. At the same time, carriers that use these advanced communication systems are able to apply the concept of yield management to change almost at a moment's notice the price and schedule of a particular service as market conditions change. Communications is now also being used not only to book passengers and cargo faster and more accurately, but also, in the case of international transportation, to clear cargo through customs even before the plane lands at the foreign destination.

Airports

Most airports are developed and operated by public agencies as part of the public transportation infrastructure. Airports usually are designed and operated to accompany both passenger and cargo operations, although a few are almost exclusively cargo. Operational procedures dealing with the safe operation of the planes on the ground follow the directions and sometimes the control of government agencies such as the Federal Aviation Administration. Other functions such as immigration, handling of food (especially imported), and clearance of passengers and cargo are the responsibilities of other agencies.

User Fees.   To help pay for their development, operation, and maintenance, airports usually charge user fees. These user fees can include a charge for landing and takeoff of aircraft, usually on a set charge per weight classification (e.g., per 1000 lb), rental of plane gates and other ramp areas where passengers and cargo are handled on and off the aircraft, passenger waiting areas, surcharges on fuel and other services, etc. Other user fees are charged to services that passengers require such as car rentals, food and other convenience stores, restaurants, etc. Cargo areas, usually located away from the main passenger terminal area, are leased to air cargo carriers and/or air freight forwarders.

Hub and Spoke.   Before deregulation, most airlines provided nonstop or limited one- or two-stop flights between origin and destination airports. Although this form of direct service provided the passenger and/or cargo the most efficient form of service, many flights did so at less than compensatory conditions. Besides, the number of routes covered across the continent and other places in the world placed increased pressure on safety of operations, both on the ground and in the air, because of congestion.

One of the direct benefits of deregulation was the establishment and now almost universal use of what are commonly called "hub-and-spoke operations." Instead of a large number of flights crisscrossing the continent from east to west or from north to south, for example, carriers will use smaller passenger planes as feeders to fly in passengers from several smaller original airports and meet at one central airport, where all the passengers will be placed on one or more larger planes for the transcontinental portion of the trip. At the hub airport located at the other end of the continent, passengers will transfer to smaller planes for their final destination. Hence, the hub-and-spoke system looks like the wheel of a bicycle, where all of the spokes fan out from the center or hub.

For example, passengers arriving on a smaller plane like a DC-9 or B-737 from Boston, Albany, Buffalo, Philadelphia, Washington, Pittsburgh, and Norfolk would transfer to a larger plane such as a 747, DC-10, or L1011 and fly to a hub airport like San Francisco. At San Francisco, passengers would transfer to smaller planes and then continue their flight on to Sacramento, Las Vegas, Portland, and Seattle.

Airport Services.   As described above, airport services range from direct servicing and maintenance of the aircraft to the servicing of the passengers and cargo on the ground. These services might be performed by the carriers themselves or by other carriers or service companies on a contract basis. Major aircraft maintenance is performed at specified airports, especially those where some of the carriers have their hub operations. Aircraft servicing includes refueling, loading of passengers and their baggage, cargo, supplies (food), etc. Other services include surface transportation companies, including car rentals and limousine service, convenience stores, and at some airports, hotels, and conference centers where meetings and overnight stays can all be handled at the airport.

Congestion. As deregulation began to encourage more flights, particularly between major cities, services on those routes began to become more congested, not only in the air but at the airport as well. As a result, the time it takes on the ground getting to, through, and then out of the airport may be as long as the flight itself.

Expansion and the Environment. Airports, especially those that have seen tremendous growth in passengers, cargo, and air and surface transportation, especially in a relatively short period of years, place heavy burdens on the environment, and also cause the frustration that comes from congestion, especially at peak periods of travel. One way of relieving this situation is to expand or perhaps even construct new airports in the same region. This strategy, however, has met increasing opposition, especially from those who feel that the extra burden will add to the deterioration of the environment, especially air and noise pollution. As a result, many airport authorities who had visions of expanding their operations have either had to cancel their plans or modify them enough that in many cases they no longer represent the original plans.

Deregulation

Deregulation of the transportation industry started with the Air Cargo Act of 1977 and was followed the following year with the Air Passenger Deregulation Act. Both acts went into effect the year each was passed by the Congress. The results were phenomenal in terms of what the air transportation industry looked like before, during, and after the deregulation process started.

Before deregulation the air transportation industry, like the other modes, was heavily regulated to protect both carriers and the passenger/cargo from cutthroat competition and other competitive abuses. Those restrictions, however, restrained the air transportation industry in the wake of emerging newer technologies and changes in worldwide trading patterns. After much debate and strong opposition from some of the larger established domestic carriers, deregulation finally was enacted. The industry since then has never been the same.

Air Cargo Deregulation Act of 1977. Deregulation of transportation in the United States started with the air cargo industry because it was one, if not the smallest, of the transportation markets. The Air Cargo Act of 1977, which actually went into effect one year later, allowed new carriers to openly compete on routes which had up until then been protected for carriers that had been considered as having "grandfather" rights to operate without the fear of competition. It also called for open competition for rates and other services that are determined by the demands of the market.

One of the big results of this form of deregulation was the emergence and later spectacular growth of overnight package carriers and couriers like Federal Express, DHL, and Emery among others. These carriers were able to compete directly with the Postal Service for overnight delivery at rates that were perhaps slightly more than what the Postal Service was charging, but with guaranteed service.

The lessons learned from this act of breaking away from a regulatory past cleared the way for the other part of the aviation to be deregulated shortly thereafter, followed by deregulation of the rest of the transportation industry over the next few years.

Airline Deregulation Act of 1978. The Airline Deregulation Act amended previous acts that dealt with the regulation of the domestic airline industry. The act placed more reliance on free market forces to establish competition by extending operation authority to carriers that offered low-fare proposals. Furthermore, the CAB was itself designated to go out of business on January 1, 1985. At that time the regulation of certification and rates ceased and other responsibilities of the CAB were transferred to other federal agencies, including the Department of Transportation. Legal issues such as mergers and agreements went to the Justice Department. The expiration of the CAB removed all industry protection from the antitrust laws (protection that the industry had enjoyed during a period of regulation).

The act established "zones of reasonableness" which indicated that, within a specifically defined zone, airlines would be free to set fares without having to worry about them being suspended, unless the rate was deemed too predatory. The act also indicated that an individual carrier would not have to charge equal fares for markets of equal distance. As a result, carriers could actually charge more for a shorter distance than a longer one, if the competition and other factors called for such a fare structure. Routes also could be added or abandoned without going through a long and cumbersome application process, which had formerly been the case under previous regulations.

International Deregulation. Deregulation of international air transportation started much later, and is still emerging at different rates of change around the globe. It started basically in the middle and late 1980s on the North Atlantic route between Europe and the United States. Although route and rate structures are still subject to bilateral agreements between the countries involved, the pace and perhaps need to deregulate has been enhanced by the growing influence of EC '92 and the unification of 12 western European countries into one market that removed trade and other international barriers between member nations. Today, air deregulation at the international level has influenced bilateral agreement around the Pacific Rim, Central and Eastern Europe, and Latin and South America. The so-called "North American block" of Canada, United States, and Mexico calls for similar deregulation in order to compete against other trading blocks and for reshaping of international trade and transportation agreements.

Competition

Service versus Price. Up until perhaps the past few years, the most important issue in deciding the carrier to be selected for the transportation of passengers and cargo was price. Price, after all, was what mattered in establishing the final cost to the customer for the shipment of passengers and goods over a particular trade route.

However, as competition grew, largely as the impact of deregulation made itself felt, the issue that was beginning to receive more attention was service: service that the customer demanded. This is especially true when applied to the systems approach to transportation, including logistics management. Air transportation is one of the more costly forms of transportation, but when matched against other factors such as inventory, JIT, security, and the cost of capital, among others, air transportation offers an alternative.

Low Profit Margins.   Open competition, primarily through deregulation and expanding markets for the services that air transportation can best provide, has placed additional strains on already stretched operations and cost structures. Low return on investment, especially investment needed to replace technologically obsolescent equipment and systems, separated the carriers that were successful in making the change from those that eventually dropped out. Deregulation made entry into the air transportation market easy, but deregulation also made the road to failure faster and in most cases assured that profitability was not maintained.

Megacarrier versus Niche.   One of the direct results of deregulation, especially after the so-called "fare wars" were fought, was the rise of the megacarriers. These carriers represented the winners in the almost winner-take-all sweepstakes on most of the more heavily traveled transcontinental and international routes. All other carriers, on the other hand, had to either merge, sell out, or leave the route and/or business of air transportation completely.

At the same time, a number of smaller carriers were still able to offer services, sometimes on the same route, at a much smaller scale. These carriers identified and satisfied a niche in the market that the larger carriers could not fill, because their overhead and other operational requirements precluded them from competing head-to-head with the smaller niche carriers. These smaller carriers are niche carriers.

Advanced Technologies.   Advanced aerotechnologies and similar technological advances on the ground (passenger and baggage handling, faster and more efficient cargo handling, refueling, etc.) contributed greatly to lowering the unit cost of air transportation operations. Larger planes using more efficient engines resulted in a lowering of the unit cost of moving passengers on longer trips and in a faster time. Smaller planes, especially those that have more efficient payload space and overall lower operating costs due to engine and plane design, reduced the cost of flying shorter distances. Advanced technologies increased the reliability of operations for longer periods of time, including actual flight time, thus removing the need for costly downtime of the aircraft. In some cases, the need for backup equipment and planes was also reduced if not eliminated entirely.

Where technological advances did not compromise minimum safety regulations, either by regulation or the carrier itself, crews in the cockpit were reduced from three (captain or pilot, copilot, and flight engineer) to two (the flight engineer gave way to the computer). Several decades earlier, with the gradual acceptance of the reliability of both on-board and on-the-ground navigation guidance systems, the navigator also lost his position.

Today, modern computers have made it possible for the plane to almost fly itself from the moment of takeoff to final landing. It might be said that the cockpit crew is only along for the ride. This is said in jest, for the experience of qualified crews will in all likelihood still be needed in cases of emergency, where the need for human decision making will be as urgent as it is today.

Likewise, communications both on the aircraft and on the ground have reached new levels of sophistication that ensure that the information being transmitted is reliable, faster, and more useful when a quick decision is necessary.

Air-Sea. The transfer of cargo between air and ocean carriers, air-sea cargo, is part of the intermodal chain that takes advantage of the speed and cost efficiencies of each of the modes. Such transfers usually take place without benefit of the same intermodal container, because of the incompatibility of modal container characteristics (sea containers are heavier than air containers).

The types of cargo that usually travel by air-sea are mostly higher-value, smaller-volume consumer electronics, automated office equipment, and high-technology parts that are less time-sensitive than other air freight. An estimated 133,000 tons of cargo traveled by this combined system in 1988. This number is expected to grow in the double digits in the next decade, depending on origin and destination points. For the moment, most of these shipments travel between the Far East and Europe, although the South American/North American/European block of nations is growing on an annual basis.

Labor. Stiff competition within the air transportation industry has taken a major toll on labor. Since deregulation, the American air transportation industry has actually gained jobs, most of which were on the ground. Managements were forced to seek cost economies with labor (much of which was usually union), because labor still represented sometimes more than half of the operational and administrative costs. In some cases where bankruptcies and other redistribution of air transportation related functions were massive, the consequence of lost jobs and careers, and the impact on lives, was devastating. Alternatively, some of the megacarriers added employees to provide the kinds of services that expanded operations required. Many of these new jobs were often filled by nonunion labor, or by establishing what is commonly called "tiered labor," in which newer employees are paid at substantially lower wages and benefits than those who might be working alongside them and have longer seniority with the carrier.

These issues of disparity of labor are still evolving.

Skills. The high-technology nature of today's operations calls for higher levels of skills. At the root of those skills is the need for training and retraining, especially as more sophisticated communication and operational equipment is brought on-line.

Current Issues

Safety. The one area where carriers and their customers cannot compromise cost is safety. The added pressure of moving larger amounts of passengers and cargo more efficiently often leads to compromise on the issue of how long a piece of equipment can go before the need of replacement or maintenance becomes acute. Nevertheless, both labor and management realize that if a carrier develops a reputation for unsafe operations, some of which might include plane crashes or other forms of accidents on the ground, the paying customers will turn elsewhere, even if it means that the cost to do so is higher.

Congestion.   Congestion in the air can be solved by establishing more stringent air traffic control procedures, including landing slots when planes can take off and land. Not only does this save fuel when planes do not have to circle above congested airports, but these traffic-control measures also relieve congestion at the terminal, where passengers and cargo are processed in more reasonable volumes.

At the same time, the congestion in getting to and from the airport has grown, especially at airports that have limited transportation facilities and systems. Airports in heavily populated areas like Los Angeles and New York are constructing better and faster road and rail systems to whisk both passenger and cargo in and around the terminal area. In some cases like Schipol Airport (Amsterdam), authorities are looking to add rail service for cargo during those periods of high peak air transportation, as an alternative to conventional highway transportation.

Low Profits.   All of these improvements are placing added pressure on carriers and airports to pay for them. These improvements are often costly, and efforts are made by all parties to have the other players pay for them. If these costs are passed on to paying customers, they will be constantly on the lookout for lower-cost transportation alternatives.

Megacarriers.   One of the few players to successfully deal with all of these new constraints on cost, and with the need to increase efficiency, are the megacarriers. Not only are the megacarriers looking to cut costs at the airport, they are also developing innovative ways of sharing costs with other megacarriers and in some cases with niche carriers, by coordinating schedules, sharing marketing costs, and in some cases sharing equipment through the concept of "rationalization."

Emerging Trends

Progress in transportation and logistics management is being fueled by changing trading patterns, technological advances, deregulation, and the spreading adoption of computerization and electronic communications. The history of transportation has shown that changes in these influences sometimes require a fairly long period before there is commercial, financial, legal, and social acceptance. Advances in transportation, and more recently in logistics management, have shown that what progress is made is often part of a dynamic, lurching process.

Strategic Issues

Central to that process are several important issues. Some of the more notable include the following.

Global Economy.   Rapid changes in the world's trading patterns, often referred to as *globalization,* will create new opportunities for carriers and terminal operators of all the modes to develop new business opportunities that might not have existed a few years earlier.

Ports that once served manufacturing hinterlands like the midwest now find that most of the cargo traffic has shifted from bulk and semibulk to one of finished and semifinished products that are more efficiently handled in containers. For these ports, massive investments in capital container handling facilities are required, to at least maintain a credible market share of that traffic.

Meanwhile, other transportation centers that find it difficult if not impossible to play the central role in transportation they once did must look for alternative uses for once-active modal and intermodal facilities. San Diego did. At the dawn of containerization, the Port of San Diego realized that shifting economic trading patterns and expanded use of containers to move cargoes could no longer support the traditional water and rail transportation services of that port city. A tough decision was made, which in retrospect can be considered a success. Where large terminal facilities once dotted the city's waterfront, mixed-use recreational, residential, and small commercial activities today contribute to the social and economic well-being of that city. Other transportation centers and ports are now making the same decisions, sometimes reluctantly.

Social and Demographic.   Shifts in economic centers of activity that take place within nations, and now more often among nations themselves affect the social and demographic growth and sometimes decline of regions. These shifts place considerable strain on the existing infrastructure. Major transportation centers like Los Angeles and Long Beach are stretching economic, environmental and limited land resources to accommodate the expanded growth of cargo, which continues to pass across their marine, rail, and highway terminals and access routes. On the other hand a once-prosperous port like Philadelphia, which once served the social and industrial heartland of this country, now finds that many of its transportation facilities are underutilized.

Energy.   The cost of energy is still a major concern of carriers of all modes, when it comes to determining the most efficient equipment to use and the routes to be served. Now, however, the growing concern as to energy's impact on the environment has forced both the carriers and the communities in which they operate to reevaluate the need to remain competitive versus the need to preserve the environment. Perhaps the answer lies somewhere in between.

Governments and Deregulation

Governments in most parts of the globe have started deregulating many of their economic activities, most notably transportation. The United States was the first of the larger countries to fully embrace deregulation across the transportation field. The process has been painful in many cases, but basically it has made the utilization of emerging technologies more important. Other nations, and now trading blocks like the European Economic Community, have paid close attention to the lessons learned from the American experience with deregulation. These lessons will also serve as the basis for other experiments in deregulation now taking place in Latin America and parts of the Far East.

It should be cautioned here, however, that regardless of how far deregulation has gone, there are still elements of regulation that remain. This is particularly true of safety. It can be argued that safety regulations in the transportation industry have become perhaps more restrictive than was the case a decade ago.

Megacarriers and Niche Players.   Deregulation of the transportation industry nationally and internationally has spawned the growth of megacarriers, which face each other in head-to-head competition. Each of the modes will be affected by this form of battle. Meanwhile, there will be many parts of the field of competition that are better served by niche players. Niche players will fill needs of the transportation customer that the megacarriers are not willing to serve, or even capable of serving.

Human Resources

Any discussion about changes expected to take place in transportation would be incomplete without at least some mention of the "doers" and managers who operate and control the various activities involved. Until recently, each operation of any transportation system had its usual cadre of skilled and semiskilled operators. In some cases this still remains the primary method of operation, especially in large multilayered companies that stretch across several modes and functions.

Now, however, there is a slow but dawning realization that the systems approach to providing a service no longer allows for specialists to remain isolated from the rest of the corporation. Intermodalism, as opposed to intramodal transportation, is more dependent on personnel who are informed about many different operations. This is critical to most sectors of the industry, where being flexible is crucial if they are to accommodate rapid changes in business activity and patterns.

To some extent, the challenge of improving the caliber of personnel in transportation and logistics management is being met through formal university-level education programs and professional seminars. But this will be only part of the solution. What is also needed is a period in the early stages of training when the individual gains actual field experience in all functions contributing to overall operations. The Europeans and the Japanese have known this for a long time.

Further Reading

Coyle, John J., Edward J. Bardi, and Joseph L. Cavinato, *Transportation*, 3d ed., West Publishing Company, St. Paul, MN, 1990.

Coyle, John J., Edward J. Bardi, and C. John Langly, Jr., *The Management of Business Logistics*, 4th ed., West Publishing Company, St. Paul, MN, 1988.

Eno Foundation for Transportation, *Transportation in America*, 9th ed., Waldorf, MD, 1991.

Journal of Commerce, recent editions, Knight-Ridder, Inc.

Muller, Gerhardt, *Intermodal Freight Transportation*, 2d ed., Eno Foundation for Transportation, Westport, CN, 1990.

Stock, James R., and Douglas M. Lambert, *Strategic Logistics Management*, 2d ed., Richard D. Irwin, Homeward, IL, 1987.

Wells, Alexander, *Air Transportation: A Management Perspective*, 2d ed., Wadsworth Publishing Company, Belmont, CA, 1989.

11
Private Fleet

Gene Bergoffen
Executive Vice President,
National Private Truck Council

Donald E. Tepper
Director of Communications,
National Private Truck Council

More than 30 years ago, a study conducted for the Commerce Committee of the United States Senate identified three reasons why a company would begin a private carriage operation: (1) cost savings, (2) customer service, and (3) convenience.

The congressional study found: "Usually the decision will rest upon some combination of these factors."[1]

Today, those same three factors continue to affect the establishment and growth of a private fleet. But on the other hand, these same factors can cause a company to reduce or eliminate its private fleet operation.

In a recent survey, *Private Fleet Benchmarks of Quality and Productivity,*[2] private fleet managers identified five factors that influence fleet size. Managers who reported that their private fleets had grown cited Customer Demands (57 percent), Fleet Service Performance versus Alternatives (42 percent), Fleet Cost versus Alternatives (32 percent), Availability of Alternative Service (20 percent), and Carrier Rates (19 percent) as factors influencing fleet size.

On the other hand, fleet managers who reported that their fleets were shrinking cited the same five factors, in nearly the same order and roughly the same percentages, to explain the decline in their fleet sizes.

Assuming that private carriage will continue to have an important role in distribution and transportation, the challenge then is to make the above-listed factors work in favor of private carriage, rather than against.

Defining Private Carriage

First, however, what exactly is private carriage? The Interstate Commerce Commission exercises economic regulatory authority over interstate for-hire motor carriers. Specifically, its jurisdiction extends only to motor common and contract carriers, defined as carriers that "provide motor vehicle transportation [of passengers and property] for compensation."

"Motor private carriers" are specifically exempted from ICC regulation, and private carriers therefore do not need ICC operating authority to conduct private carriage operations. The precise test for private carriage is the "primary business test," set forth in § 10524. The ICC does not have jurisdiction over property by motor vehicle when

> the property is transported by a person engaged in a business other than transportation;
>
> the transportation is within the scope of, and furthers a primary business (other than transportation) of the person.

Under the "primary business test," if the truck operation is "within the scope of, and furthers a primary business (other than transportation) of the person," it is considered to be private carriage, not subject to ICC regulation.

Colin Barrett, in *Practical Handbook of Private Trucking*, states: "The law envisions that private carriage will be a secondary, logistical-support activity of an individual, partnership, corporation, etc., who or which is primarily involved in other business activities—generally producing and/or distributing goods."[3]

The regulatory reforms that began in the late 1970s and continued through the 1980s greatly blurred the legal distinctions between private and for-hire carriage. As a practical matter, however, private fleets continue to exist fundamentally to support the transportation and distribution needs of a parent company.

The definition of private fleets is also blurred by the range of services performed by the fleet and the driver. A fleet and driver for an oil refiner may have one set of goals and responsibilities; a fleet and driver for a paint manufacturer, where the driver helps stock hardware stores, fits another profile; and a fleet and driver for a lawn-care service, where the driver primarily tends lawns and only drives to get from one job to another, fits yet another profile.

And finally, accurately describing private carriage is made difficult by the sheer scope of private fleet operations. For example, private fleets:

- Transport an estimated 56 percent of all truck tonnage.
- Operate 80 percent of all commercial trucks.
- Annually run 48 billion miles.[4]

What all this means is that, while private carriage may often resemble "trucking" (for-hire motor carriage), it is more accurately described as a transportation and distribution function of a parent company. Thus, to operate a successful private fleet, a fleet manager needs to look far beyond conventional trucking issues.

The Private Carriage Decision[5]

Should a company operate a private fleet? Barrett points out that a company must recognize that operation of a private fleet involves a substantial commitment of corporate resources. And if a company devotes resources to a private fleet operation, it may not have those resources available for other uses perhaps more related to its principal business activities.

On the other hand, those resources can be minimized through, for example, equipment leasing and driver leasing. Further, resources are already being expended for for-hire carriage, so what may be involved is simply a reallocation of resources.

Second, a private fleet has effects beyond the transportation function itself. Decision making in such areas as marketing, production, procurement, accounting, legal, industrial relations, and administration will be affected by whether the company does or does not provide its own transportation services.

Third, the success of the private fleet itself will depend in part on the cooperation of other departments. Barrett points out that if those other departments fail to participate actively in the private carriage operation, reaping all possible benefits for them, part of its advantage to the company as a whole will have been negated.

Barrett also lists seven steps of decision making, with tips on applying them to the private carriage decision.

1. *Defining the problem.* Why is the company thinking about a private carriage operation? Is it dissatisfied with the cost and/or service of its present means of transportation? Does it want additional transportation support to expand its markets? In brief, what is wrong with the way the transportation function is being performed today?

In this context, a "problem" simply means any deviation of the actual (what's going on today) from the ideal (what the company would like to see occurring). This means the company must have a fairly good idea of how it would *like* to see the transportation function performed.

2. *Defining the objective.* This, the "transportation audit," begins with the simple question: "If our company could have anything we wanted in terms of transportation service, what would we wish for?" The resulting "wish list" is the initial phase of the transportation audit.

The audit should extend beyond transportation. Would the company benefit from having its name and/or advertising on vehicles hauling its products? What about sales efforts, as goods are delivered to customers? Could inventory costs be reduced through the transportation process?

After having compiled a wish list, the company should identify the mandatory items (what it absolutely needs), and the remaining items (what is wanted but not needed) should be ranked. The product of this exercise will be a clear picture of the company's ideal transportation process.

3. *Identifying the alternatives.* Begin examining the options by looking at whatever service the company presently is using. Since problems with that service have been identified using the steps above, is it possible to negotiate improvements with existing for-hire carriers? What about other for-hire carriers? Contract carriage? Other modes of transportation? Private carriage is another option, but it should be

compared with all the choices; the question must be broader than "status quo vs. private carriage."

4. *Evaluating the alternatives.* The comparisons must be realistic. When comparing rates, for example, the manager must use actual or realistic for-hire rates, not published rate bureau class rates. Similarly, when comparing service levels, consider the service levels that for-hire carriers might be willing or persuaded to provide. On the private carrier side, be realistic about the regulatory and financial difficulties of establishing and running a private fleet.

5. *Assessing the overall impact.* Any decision of corporate importance will have side effects that impact many areas of the company. The objective is to: (1) review for a second time the differences between private and for-hire carriage alternatives in the nontransportation areas already identified, and (2) examine those impacts in other areas that have not yet received consideration.

How would they affect marketing? Production? Accounting? Legal? Human resources?

6. *Comparing the alternatives.* Having established the basic parameters of each alternative, the manager should continue the process by carefully comparing them. This step is important not only in terms of examining the options, but also in "selling" the decision to others in the company.

7. *Making the decision.* At this point, it's likely that one of the options under consideration will have emerged as superior to the others. But that doesn't mean that the other choices should be discarded entirely. Barrett points out that there will seldom be a single "right" transportation choice for any company that fits all the traffic it needs to ship. Thus, it may well develop that the best choice for the company is a blend of two or more of the options that have been considered.

Four Core Areas

The National Private Truck Council, the national association representing private fleets, has developed a Certified Private Fleet Manager (CPFM) program. The CPFM program is designed to foster and promote continuing professional education and development in private fleet management. While there are undoubtedly dozens of ways in which to analyze and categorize the information and knowledge that private fleet managers need, the CPFM program offers one clear and time-tested approach.

The CPFM program defines four "core areas" in which private fleet managers should be proficient:

1. *The role of the private fleet—value versus cost considerations.* This deals with the knowledge and understanding of logistics issues concerning costs, service, profit justification, and the dynamics of private fleet operations.

2. *The legal and regulatory environment of today's private fleet.* This deals with the principal laws and regulations affecting private fleet operations.

3. *Managing a safe and effective private fleet work force.* This deals with the practical do's and don't's for managing a safe and productive fleet and work force.

4. *Making better use of private fleet resources.* This deals with the variety of approaches, tools, techniques, and technologies available to improve fleet productivity.

The subjects covered in this chapter touch on some of the critically important private fleet management issues. However, there are many other subjects of importance to fleet managers that could not be included because of space limitations.

Legal and Regulatory

It is beyond the scope of this chapter to set forth the legal and regulatory requirements imposed on private fleets. Further, the law and regulations are constantly changing. Although general discussion of some of the broader areas of legal and regulatory responsibility are outlined below, companies considering establishing private fleets, or private fleets with questions pertaining to the law or to regulations, should consult with a lawyer or practitioner experienced in transportation issues.

Operating Options

The Motor Carrier Act of 1980, and changes in regulations and policy of the Interstate Commerce Commission (ICC), have provided private carriers with a number of new operating options. These options allow for more efficient use of fleet equipment and fewer empty miles. Several of these expand the definition of private carriage, which is exempt from ICC regulation, while others allow private fleets to engage in for-hire operations within the Commission's jurisdiction.

Supplemental For-Hire Authority ("Toto" Authority)

In *Toto Purchasing and Supply Co., Inc.*, 122 M.C.C. 873 (1978), the ICC held that it was permissible for motor carriers to engage in both private and for-hire operations through a single entity. A private carrier that obtains common carrier authority pursuant to 49 U.S.C. § 10922, or contract carrier authority pursuant to 49 U.S.C. § 10923, however, is subject to ICC regulation with respect to its operations conducted under such authority.

Common versus Contract Carriage Authority.   Most private fleets that have obtained supplemental for-hire operating authority have become contract carriers, rather than common carriers. There are a number of advantages—for example, contract carriers are not required to file tariffs with the ICC, and they are not subject to the "common carrier obligation" to provide service to any shipper who tenders freight for transportation within the bounds of the carrier's authority.

Applications for Operating Authority.   The application process for a common carrier certificate or a contract carrier permit, set out in 49 C.F.R. Part 1160, has been simplified by the ICC.

An applicant for authority must establish that it is "fit, willing, and able" to provide the service, and must present evidence that the proposed operation will serve a useful public purpose, responsive to a public need or demand.

The ICC requires that all motor carriers of property request commodity and territorial authorizations sufficiently broad to provide a complete service to the shippers desiring the service. Additionally, carrier applicants seeking contract authority may seek to serve an entire industry or industries or class of persons, rather than named shippers.

Licensing Requirements.   Before beginning operation, a successful motor carrier applicant must comply with certain ICC licensing requirements. Basically, these requirements include: (1) filing proof of adequate insurance ($750,000 liability coverage, unless the authority encompasses hazardous materials, in which case either $1 million or $5 million of coverage is required; common carriers must also have $10,000 cargo insurance); (2) designating agents in each state through which operations will be conducted, and who will accept legal filings on a carrier's behalf; and (3) if the application is for common carrier authority, filing a copy of the rates and rules tariffs.

Compensated Intercorporate Hauling

A corporation that provides truck transportation for compensation to another corporation (CIH) is exempt from ICC regulation if the corporations involved in the movement are part of the same "corporate family" (i.e., 100-percent-owned by the same parent, directly or indirectly).

A corporation engaging in exempt intercorporate hauling must comply with minor administrative requirements set forth in 49 U.S.C. § 10524(b) and with the ICC's regulations implementing that subsection.

Private carriers with interstate CIH operations may also have to register with state regulatory agencies, and show proof of insurance, in those states in which they operate. A number of states require registration of interstate-CIH operations conducted into or through their states.

Vehicle Leasing

Leasing of Vehicles to or from For-Hire Carriers.   Leasing of vehicles by private truck operators to for-hire (common or contract) carriers, or vice versa, is subject to the regulations of the ICC on "Lease and Interchange of Vehicles," 49 C.F.R., Part 1057.

The ICC permits private carriers to trip-lease their equipment and drivers to authorized drivers. The ICC requirements for private carriers engaged in trip-leasing to for-hire carriers are these:

- The lease must be for at least 30 days.
- There must be a written agreement that the lessee shall have control and responsibility for the operation of the equipment while in its possession.
- There must be a receipt for the equipment.

- The trip-lease agreement must be carried in the equipment.

- The equipment must be placarded with the ICC certificate or permit number of the for-hire lessee while in the lessee's possession.

The ICC also allows private carriers and shippers to lease equipment and drivers from regulated carriers, with no minimum lease term.

Leasing of Vehicles to or from Persons Other than For-Hire Carriers.
Under the ICC's policy, for a lease of equipment and driver from a nonregulated entity to a private carrier to result in legitimate private carriage by the lessee, the shipper must exercise control and responsibility over the transportation service and must perform the critical organization and management functions. These include dispatch, scheduling movements, and general coordination, all of which characterize a transportation company.

Exempt Commodity Hauling

The Interstate Commerce Act (49 U.S.C. § 10526[a][6]) also exempts from ICC regulation the transportation of certain livestock, fish, agricultural and horticultural commodities, livestock and poultry feed, seeds and plants, and other specified commodities. This exemption for transportation of agricultural commodities provides another opportunity for private fleets to fill empty backhaul miles with revenue-generating freight.

Safety Regulations

The Federal Motor Carrier Safety Regulations (FMCSRs) are administered and enforced by the U.S. Department of Transportation, Federal Highway Administration, Office of Motor Carriers.
   The OMC was established by the Bureau of Motor Carrier Safety within the Federal Highway Administration, when the Department of Transportation was created in 1967. It became the OMC in 1985. Its mission is to:

- Reduce commercial vehicle accidents

- Decrease fatalities, injuries, and property losses involving commercial motor vehicles

- Help reduce casualties and economic loss due to all types of commercial motor vehicle interpretations

   The complete FMCSRs are contained in Title 49, Chapter III, Subchapter B, of the Code of Federal Regulations.
   In carrying out its responsibilities, FHWA issues the FMCSRs, which, among other things, prescribe the records that carriers subject to the FMCSRs are required to maintain. In many instances, such records will be the basis of proof that carriers are complying with the FMCSRs, in general. To ensure carrier compliance, FHWA conducts periodic on-site inspections and audits of carrier records.

The FMCSRs specify records in two types, or forms: (1) the *prescribed form,* which the carrier must use, and (2) the *required content,* which must be contained in the record.

As a general rule, the records that carriers are required to maintain must be centralized and kept at a carrier's "principal place of business." FHWA will consider requests from individual carriers for permission to maintain certain records at terminal locations.

A company with a large fleet operation and multiple terminals should establish companywide standard procedures and record forms for all of its locations. Carefully designed forms can help assure that the FMCSRs requirements will be met. Standard procedures also enhance internal monitoring, which, in turn, will help to ensure consistency in compliance with the FMCSRs.

Generally, all private carriers of property and for-hire motor carriers operating in interstate or foreign commerce must comply with the FMCSRs. In addition, state and local laws must be obeyed.

There is seldom any question as to the applicability of the Federal Highway Administration rules to a commercial vehicle that is actually interstate in nature. The problem arises when a commercial vehicle operation operates wholly within one state (intrastate).

Nevertheless, there are two reasons why a carrier should comply with the federal rules, even when operating within one state.

First, the federal regulations state that if a commercial vehicle is engaged in any interstate commerce, then all truck operations involving hazardous materials in quantities that require placarding of the vehicle are subject to the federal regulations, regardless of whether commercial vehicles operate intra- or interstate.

In this case it is the commodity, not the vehicle, that determines whether the movement is intra- or interstate. For example, a customer orders a product that the private carrier does not have in stock. The carrier orders it from an out-of-state supplier. When it has been received at his dock, he reloads it on his own truck for delivery to the customer, who is in the same state. That "continuing movement" of the product on its own truck is considered to be interstate commerce.

This gray area of "continuing movement," however, is subject to continuing change. If in doubt, consult a transportation attorney.

The second reason for compliance with federal regulations, even for intrastate carriers, is that most states have adopted the federal safety regulations in whole or in part for truck operations within their states. Even in those cases in which a private fleet never operates a truck beyond the borders of the state, there is a strong likelihood that the state regulations impose at least some of the federal rules on its operations.

Part 392—Driving of Commercial Motor Vehicles. There are seven subparts (not listed here) describing the requirements while driving commercial motor vehicles.

Part 383—Commercial Driver's License Standards. The standards in Part 383 require that no driver have more than one driver's license. It disqualifies drivers who do not safely operate commercial motor vehicles.

Part 391—Qualifications of Drivers. Part 391 says drivers of commercial motor vehicles must be qualified. This part also explains what a motor carrier must do to qualify drivers.

This part also contains regulations dealing with driver physical qualifications and examinations. Recent legislation—particularly the Americans With Disabilities Act—and regulatory interpretations require fleets to stay current on the latest regulations.

And this part sets forth mandatory requirements for drug testing of truck drivers.

Part 393—Parts and Accessories Necessary for Safe Operation. Every motor carrier, its officers, agents, drivers, representatives, and employees involved with the maintenance of equipment must understand and obey the rules of this part. A motor carrier cannot operate any commercial motor vehicle unless it is properly equipped.

Part 394—Accident Reporting. This part was the subject of a rule-making proceeding, and fleets should check with appropriate authorities to determine what their obligations are.

Part 395—Hours of Service. This part also was the subject of a rule-making proceeding, and fleets should check with appropriate authorities to determine the restrictions on the number of hours a driver may drive.

Part 396—Inspection, Repair, and Maintenance. Every motor carrier must make sure that all its vehicles are regularly inspected, repaired, and maintained. All vehicle parts and accessories must be in a safe and proper working order at all times. This part also specifies where maintenance records must be kept, and for what period of time.

Part 397—Transportation of Hazardous Materials: Driving and Parking Rules. The rules in Part 397 apply to each carrier transporting hazardous materials by a commercial motor vehicle that must be marked or placarded in accordance with 49 CFR 177.823. The rules also apply to each officer or employee of the carrier who performs supervisory duties related to the transportation of hazardous materials, and to each person who operates or is in charge of a commercial motor vehicle containing hazardous materials.

Value versus Cost

Benchmarking[6]

Most companies today are trying to improve customer service, increase productivity, reduce costs, and implement other steps that will sharpen their competitive edge in the global marketplace.

As part of this effort, they are carefully examining their business operations (including the private fleet) and looking for ways to handle each function better. Being under the microscope is, of course, not new to the private fleet. But the level of today's scrutiny is, perhaps, more intense than ever, the potential outcome more radical.

While the private fleet provides an essential function (transportation of goods and services) this function is not the company's basic business activity. Nevertheless, transportation costs often range from 2 to 10 percent of a company's total operating expenditures and may tip the profit-loss scale in the wrong direction.

These factors make the private fleet, on the one hand, an excellent candidate for improvement, and on the other a potential nominee for being outsourced in full or in part.

Senior management's decision (whether to improve or to outsource) could very well depend on the fleet manager's ability to answer a number of important questions about the private fleet operation. More than ever, senior management points to superior customer service as the best way to differentiate the company in the marketplace and to achieve and maintain a competitive advantage. Therefore, the question most often asked is: "How good is the customer service offered by our private fleet?"

In asking this question, senior management does not want to know merely how quickly the product is delivered. It wants to know an array of quantitative and qualitative aspects of customer service. Is the product delivered without damage? Is it exactly what was ordered? How complete is the private fleet's paperwork and billing process?

Beyond these questions, senior management wants to know if the private fleet is serving customers efficiently, cost-effectively, and productively. It is asking: How does the fleet's cost and productivity compare with those of other private fleets? How do they compare with those of common carriers aggressively marketing their services to senior management? How does the fleet fit into the company's overall strategy?

The manager of the private fleet must provide answers. Moreover, the answers must be focused. They must take into account senior management's limited knowledge of transportation and its perspective on the private fleet's role within the company. They must clearly demonstrate how effectively, productively, and competitively the operation is being run today, and what improvements are being made to keep the function ahead of the competition. In short, they must be meaningful to senior management.

To provide such answers, the fleet manager must understand what needs to be looked at, measured, tracked, and documented.

Benchmarking, defined as *a search for those best practices that will lead to superior performance,* can provide input for these answers. This tool, benchmarking, highlights both the "Best of the Best" practices by activity across industries and the "Best of the Best" performance levels within those activities.

The private fleet manager can use benchmarking to measure the practices and performance of his/her private fleet operation and then to compare these findings with those of other private fleets and of common carriers.

With this information, the manager can thoroughly answer any questions senior management may ask about fleet performance. Moreover, the fleet manager can set goals and establish a framework for developing an implementation plan and actions based on the "Best of the Best" practices.

Benchmarking offers specific, useful, comparative information. It identifies the types of measures companies use to track current performance levels, and the types of practices they use to improve specific areas such as customer service, driver efficiency, and equipment. (See Table 11-1.)

This information tells the private fleet manager what should be measured, how it should be measured, and what kind of performance results should be achieved. It also shows the fleet manager which areas have given other companies the biggest return, so he/she can first implement the most important measures used by the

Table 11-1. Benchmarking Measures

Measure	Percent using
Labor	
Miles per driver per year	71
DOT accidents per million miles	70
Driver turnover	48
DOT violations per month	46
Labor utilization	37
Trip performance (actual time vs. standard)	26
Actual vs. dispatched miles	22
Total cost per labor hour	22
Equipment	
Miles/tractor per year	83
Trailer/tractor ratio	71
Average vehicle replacement cycle	59
Equipment utilization	32
Total cost per equipment hour	13
Maintenance	
Cost per gallon diesel fuel	57
Maintenance cost per mile (excl. tires)	48
Tire cost per mile	43
Percent PMs completed on time	38
Tractor/mechanic ratio	25
Road failure per million miles	15
Revenue	
Operating ratio	49
Outbound revenue per mile	32
Inbound revenue per mile	29
Customer service	
On-time delivery performance	71
Damage-free delivery performance	44
On-time pickup performance	31
Percent shipments with claims	31
Percent shipments with 100 percent paperwork accuracy	29
Inquiry response time	17
Claims-handling cycle time	17

SOURCE: Reported in *Private Fleet Benchmarks of Quality and Productivity: 1991.*

"Best of the Best" companies and then move on to others as time and resources allow.

The benchmark process consists of a number of critical steps. These have been well illustrated by Robert C. Camp in his book, *Benchmarking: The Search for Industry Best Practices That Lead to Superior Performance.*

These have been summarized into five steps. By following these steps, the private fleet manager can achieve superior performance and, along the way, can profit from a number of benefits offered by the benchmarking process.

The five steps, greatly condensed, are:

1. Plan benchmarking.
   a. Select areas to be benchmarked.

   b. Identify other companies as benchmark candidates.
   c. Identify additional data sources.
2. Conduct benchmarking.
   a. Measure own operation.
   b. Gather benchmark data from other sources and on-site visits to other companies.
   c. Determine the gap between own operation and "Best of the Best."
   d. Project future performance levels.
3. Gain acceptance of benchmarking results.
   a. Management can gain acceptance of private fleet line operations people by openness, validation of results, and communication.
   b. Management may ask operations people to participate on the benchmarking team.
4. Carry out improvement.
   a. Set clearly identified and defined goals.
   b. Plan improvements; identify specific actions necessary to accomplish the goals.
   c. Implement.
5. Recalibrate.
   a. Take another look at the "Best of the Best" to learn what new practices they now have in place.
   b. Incorporate the latest "Best of the Best" practices into the private fleet operations.

Backhaul Programs[7]

In today's complex and highly competitive transportation environment, it is extremely difficult to justify the operation of a private fleet based only on the higher cost of using for-hire, commercial carriers. Especially in the truckload market, there are times when the selective use of for-hire carriers may be the lower-cost alternative to private carriage.

With this in mind, some private carriers have made the transition from a "profit center" operation to a "cost center" operation. In making this change, the emphasis becomes operating the fleet at the lowest possible cost. That cost is then compared to the cost of using commercial carriers to perform the same services. Thus, the operating cost of the fleet must be kept as low as possible.

To accomplish this, a backhaul program is almost mandatory. According to one recent survey of private fleets (*Private Fleet Profile*), approximately half of all private fleets are engaging in activities suggestive of a backhaul program. For example, 33 percent have contract carriage authority, 31 percent engage in compensated intercorporate hauling, and 14 percent have common carrier authority.

Private Fleet Benchmarks produced a similar pattern, with 56 percent of the fleets engaging in compensated intercorporate hauling, 41 percent holding contract carrier authority, and 15 percent holding common carrier authority.

The implementation of a backhaul program can generate revenues, which can be credited against the gross operating cost of the fleet, thus lowering the total delivery cost of the operation.

For example, assume a fully distributed fleet has an operating cost of $1.00/mi. The fleet operator is delivering a load to a customer located 500 mi from its manufacturing facility. Therefore, this delivery will result in a round-trip run of 1000 mi at a cost of $1.00/mi for a total delivery cost of $1000.

The actual delivery cost is $2.00/mi ($1000/500 mi). However, if this operator had the ability to generate a backhaul load, rather than to return empty, and the backhaul load generated revenue of $400, this revenue could be applied as a credit against the total round trip expense of $1000. The net delivery cost would then be $600, or $1.20/mi.

The question then is: Could a for-hire carrier have been used to deliver the original outbound load for less than $600, or $1.20/mi?

This example demonstrates how a backhaul program can reduce delivery costs by improving the utilization of manpower and equipment. Backhaul revenue can also be below fully-distributed operating cost and still be effective. However, before making the decision to embark on such a program, several issues must be addressed.

Scheduling, Equipment, and Manpower Considerations

Before making the decision to establish and maintain an ongoing backhaul program, two preliminary questions must be reviewed and resolved:

1. *Can drivers and equipment be delayed long enough to accommodate the pickup and delivery of backhaul loads?* Unfortunately, many loads are not always ready for pickup when drivers and equipment are available to load. This could result in driver and equipment downtime, or possibly an extended layover. The operation must have the scheduling flexibility to handle such situations, if and when they occur.

2. *Is the equipment suitable for the implementation of a backhaul program?* Some fleet equipment is highly specialized to meet the specific needs of the company. If this is the case, it may be extremely difficult to haul general commodities in a backhaul program. Examples of such equipment include: single-axle tractors, single-axle trailers, drop-deck trailers, cage-type trailers, flatbeds, and tankers.

Considering For-Hire Carriage Operations.
If a private carrier can load most of its returning equipment with its company's raw materials or parts, perhaps a pure private carriage operation is all that needs to be considered.

However, this is not always the case. As a result, some consideration should be given to establishing a for-hire operation, giving the carrier an opportunity to fill empty backhaul miles with outside revenues.

However, there are costs and legal requirements associated with being a for-hire carrier. These include the following:

- Application for operating authority must be made to the Interstate Commerce Commission. The cost is minimal.
- Resident agents must be established in each state in which operations will be conducted. These agents will act as the carrier's representatives in those states, in the

event legal notices or documents must be served. This service is available at fees typically ranging from a one-time charge of $75 to annual fees of $150–$200.

- The operating authority received from the ICC must be filed with each state in which operations will be conducted on a for-hire basis. Those states will impose charges for evidence that the carrier's operating authority has been registered with the state.

- Depending on the type of operating authority requested, specific minimum insurance limits are required.

Depending on the scope of the operation, a private fleet may have several thousand dollars invested in federal and state fees before the first for-hire load is ever moved.

It must be remembered that private carriers are exempt from all ICC economic regulations; however, for-hire carriers are not. If the decision is made to conduct a for-hire carriage operation, these regulations and requirements must be thoroughly reviewed and completely understood.

Additional Managerial Requirements

Planning.   The operation of an effective, full-service backhaul program requires a number of additional managerial tasks, over and above those required in a typical private carriage operation.

If an operation is pure private carriage, with no for-hire carriage involved, the only sources for backhauls are company vendors, distributors, customers, and others who make shipments to the company. These shipments consist of materials or products to which the company holds title.

If the operation is a combination of private and for-hire carriage, additional sources for backhaul loads will be available from licensed property brokers and/or other outside shippers.

In either case, a great deal of communication and coordination is required between the fleet operations people, the purchasing department, and others involved in the program.

To be efficient and cost-effective, backhaul movements must be preplanned and coordinated, in order to maximize the use of drivers and equipment and to minimize empty miles. Without preplanning and proper communications and coordination, a backhaul movement can cost more than it is worth.

Responsibilities.   To properly preplan and coordinate an effective backhaul program, several areas of responsibility must be assigned; for instance:

- Potential freight sources must be identified.
- Rates must be established or negotiated.
- Pickup and delivery of backhaul loads must be coordinated.
- All required documentation should be prepared and processed.
- A billing and collection procedure must be established and maintained.
- Pickup and delivery records must be maintained for future reference.
- Any loss/damage claims that may be filed must be processed and resolved.

The cost to staff a department to handle these responsibilities must be included in the construction of the fully-distributed costs to operate the fleet. If not, costs will be understated. If effective, the backhaul program should generate the revenue and savings to more than offset the cost of administering the program.

Private Fleet Resources

Life-Cycle Costing[8]

Life-cycle costing is a technique to help you determine which items can be cost-justified, what it really costs to operate equipment, and when it's time to replace equipment.

Most often, fleet managers want to use life-cycle costing as a discipline for determining, "When should I trade or buy new equipment?" They seek a reasonably uncomplicated formula or software package that will allow them to input a minimum of data and produce an ironclad answer.

The search for a simple solution sometimes results in a graph with a descending line representing depreciation and an ascending line representing running costs. Where the lines cross is supposed to trigger a buy decision.

There are at least four major problems with this approach to life-cycle cost analysis:

1. With this scenario, the cost of ownership is always constant, with rising running cost being offset by descending depreciation and interest costs.

2. As maintenance people know, running costs do not follow a straight, or even curved, line.

3. Generally, part of the costs associated with operating a group of vehicles does not appear in running data. For example, older vehicles need more mechanics, better shop, overhaul room, and tools.

4. This approach would suggest that all cost considerations for this model are internal to the vehicle (book value and running cost). They are not.

Let's consider some issues in detail.

Fixed cost is easy to calculate. Fuel cost/saving is also relatively straightforward.

Service or maintenance capability of the shop is an easily forgotten life-cycle cost issue, since these costs do not normally appear on a repair order. They are, however, very real.

Let's assume that your calculations indicate you can cost-justify replacing old equipment with new state-of-the-art power units. But do these calculations include such items as:

- The $5000 cost of engine diagnostics tools?
- The $1500 cost of antilock brake diagnostics?
- Electronic air-conditioning controls? ($1000)
- Electronic tools? ($500)
- Mechanic training? ($10,000)
- Building modification (12-ft doors)? ($20,000)

Technology issues should be very carefully reviewed, because they could have a major impact on future life-cycle costs. Timing purchases to take advantage of or avoid technology changes can rearrange the cost/saving equation considerably.

Also to be factored into the equation are economic outlook, the need for that capital in manufacturing equipment, the benefits of leasing versus purchasing, and so forth.

In view of all this, a fleet manager might think he/she will never get agreement that the time is right for new equipment. He/she might be right.

The time to make the decision as to when to sell should be made *before* you *buy*. For example, a 27,000-GVW diesel straight truck that is going to run 40,000 mi/year for 5 years, if speced wisely, is a much different animal than one that must run 60,000 mi/year for 8 years.

Further, these two trucks should be set up on different maintenance schedules. If your shop size, tools, and mechanic skills are such that you should not plan on over-hauling engines and transmissions, then plan on selling the vehicles before those needs arise.

In short, establish a plan based on needs and resources, then work the plan, adjusting for special circumstances, as you go. Then, the vehicle running cost records (which you should keep) primarily provide you with feedback that lets you know that part of the plan is either working or needs modification. If the plan is not followed, it won't work.

It doesn't much matter whether you buy new tractors and sell at 400,000 mi or 4 years, or buy new tractors and sell at 1.5 million miles. The keys are:

- Decide first what your plan is to be.
- Buy equipment that meets your needs and fits that plan.
- Do preventive maintenance to protect your investment against surprises and uncontrolled cost through the life of the plan.
- Get out of the equipment when the plan (not current cost) calls for it.
- Review, review, review.

Some LTL common carriers are very successful running four years and 400,000 mi. Others take the same general kind of equipment to 1.5 million miles. Which is right? Both. They are successful because they have a plan and follow it.

According to several studies of private fleets, private fleet managers who own equipment tend to base vehicle-replacement criteria on age of vehicle, followed by mileage of vehicle.

In *Private Fleet Profile* the average replacement cycle for tractors was 5.8 years, although some replaced as often as every 3 years, while others reported 17-year cycles. Those who used mileage as a guide averaged 627,000 mi before replacing, although some replaced as often as 150,000 mi, while others had adopted 1.5-million-mile replacement cycles.

In *Private Fleet Benchmarks*, the average vehicle replacement cycle was 673,000 mi or 5.6 years.

The average replacement cycle for trucks, as reported in *Private Fleet Profile*, was 7.1 years or 377,000 mi.

A few final points on life-cycle costing:

- Numbers and calculations made a year ago are no longer valid.
- Formula and repair cycles established with an earlier group of tractors are no longer valid.
- Even a change in oil suppliers, or kind of oil from the same supplier, can affect time to overhaul.
- Keep/trade decisions should never be made on vehicle life-cycle cost alone.
- Establish a sell time before you buy.

There is no single perfect formula for life-cycle costing. There are many cost considerations in total life-cycle costing other than initial cost and running cost. If you narrow your focus too much, you will make costly mistakes in establishing your plan. And finally, you must constantly document results and review that plan.

Outsourcing

Outsourcing, simply put, means turning over to an outside firm some or all of the functions that your company performs internally. In its various permutations, it may be called *contract logistics, strategic alliances, third party logistics,* or something else. But, regardless of what it's called, outsourcing is growing dramatically—at an estimated annual rate of 20 percent.

In fact, a recent study by Arthur D. Little, Inc., shows that 43 percent of firms are currently outsourcing two or more functions. The same study found that 31 percent of the respondents expect outsourcing to grow over the next three years; only 12 percent expect outsourcing to be used less frequently. (See Table 11-2.)

Trends In Transportation. To understand the growth in outsourcing, it's necessary to examine the trends in transportation. Charles Lounsbury of Leasway

Table 11-2. Factors Accounting for the Increase in Logistics Outsourcing

Success factor	Changes
Integrated logistics management	Foreign competition Major success stories Information resources
Window of opportunity	Mergers & acquisitions Operations restructuring Inventory velocity
Decision-making environment	Focus on core business Deregulation dividends Productivity measures
Receptive decision makers	Reorganizations, retirements Post-deregulation managers Interdisciplinary teams

SOURCE: Cass Logistics.

Transportation has pointed out that the transportation function is being integrated more closely with other corporate functions, i.e., marketing, purchasing, and manufacturing. Information systems are becoming more sophisticated, and there's a trend toward centralized transportation operations.

More emphasis is being placed on benchmarking various factors. Meanwhile, globalization is placing new pressures on the logistics responsibility.

These trends, coupled with competitive forces and economic trends, can be translated into a current reality that consists of:

- Economic effects of leveraged buyouts, management buyouts, mergers, and acquisitions
- Regulatory trends such as the Commercial Driver's License, safety inspections, and drug testing
- Labor shortages and a changing labor force
- The relationship between a firm's capital budget and its operating budget
- The substitution of transportation for inventory, and the focus on inventory turns

According to Robert Delaney, Vice President of Cass Logistics:

> In terms of windows of opportunity, every time a merger or acquisition takes place it is necessary to reoptimize logistics operations. In our current decision-making environment, managers are focusing on making their core business more efficient and deciding which operations can be outsourced.
>
> Thinking managers are interested in controlling their bottom line, not investing in assets and managing large staffs of personnel. This is especially true among companies who must lower breakeven cost and pay down an overload of debt. They are prime candidates to leverage off balance-sheet assets.

Outsourcing isn't a new concept to industry. It has already been applied in such areas as manufacturing, data processing, accounting, engineering, and marketing. What may be new is the economic and business climate. Lawrence Collett, President of Cass Logistics:

> A new wave is about to sweep across the business logistics system. It involves operations restructuring. Manufacturers and distributors are selling assets to pay down debt and lower their breakeven costs. The impacts on business logistics systems are major. The availability of timely and reliable information is key. We believe that this climate favors outsourcing.

The benefits can be many. If properly applied and executed, outsourcing can provide a company with known and predictable costs, and sometimes reduce a company's overall costs. It can allow the company to redeploy its assets and improve service levels. It can open new doors. For example, allow access to new technology and ensure the availability of insurance.

Outsourcing, if properly implemented, may reduce labor costs and provide insulation between a company and labor. And it can minimize compliance hassles. However, if improperly implemented, it can be counterproductive.

Transportation Outsourcing.   Outsourcing in transportation is provided by a variety of firms: mega-carriers, niche players, and logistics intermediaries (brokers, forwarders, agents, freight payment services, and information services). Nevertheless, outsourcing isn't for everyone.

What transportation functions are typically outsourced? They include:

- Freight payment
- Customs clearance
- Warehousing
- Carrier selection
- Rate negotiation
- Freight tracking
- Information systems
- EDI
- Fleet management
- Order processing
- Inventory control
- Labor recruitment

Private Fleet Outsourcing.   The main transportation functions that are outsourced, and the percentage of private fleets using this function, are shown in Table 11-3.

International Outsourcing.   Dr. Theodore Levitt of Harvard University recently observed that 80 percent of U.S. commerce is international. Global and competitively intense, business practices are the engines driving the interest in outsourcing.

The benefits of integrated logistics management are steadily becoming more accepted. According to Cass Logistics, "Major success stories are emerging. H.J. Heinz sells 40 percent of its products outside the United States. Heinz has assigned their product lines to five group vice presidents who are responsible for sourcing, manufacturing, quality, marketing, and distribution throughout the world."

Other big-name companies that have gone to partial or total outsourcing, according to Lounsbury, include General Motors, Wang, Toyota, Safeway, A&P, Pepsi,

Table 11-3. Selected Functions Outsourced by Private Fleets

Function	Percent
Vehicle leasing: full service	49
Routine maintenance: leasing facility	44
Routine maintenance: outside shop	9
Major maintenance: leasing facility	44
Major maintenance: outside shop	19
Driver leasing	9

SOURCE: *Private Fleet Profile.*

Sears, Xerox, Rank Xerox, Unilever, N.V. Philips, Land Rover, Marks & Spencer, Whirlpool, Stone Container, McDonalds, and many more.

Success Factors.   As noted above, outsourcing can offer a company numerous benefits. But Lounsbury says that for outsourcing to work (to work well) there must be commitment across the organization ranks. Outsourcing must satisfy the mutual needs of the company and the outsourcing provider. There must be organizational and cultural compatibility, as well as strong communication between the parties and within the organization.

The commitment and communication must be reflected in the sharing of both goals and information. And while there must be specific goals and methods for measuring effectiveness, there must also be flexibility and the freedom to reposition if and when necessary.

Failure Factors.   When outsourcing fails to live up to its potential, one or more factors may be responsible. It may be an internal problem such as the lack of top management support, or an external one such as the wrong choice of partner. Or somewhere in between: lack of mutual trust, poor communication. Or the failure may be in the implementation, such as insufficient lead time for start-up, short-versus long-term planning horizon, or a struggle between quality and profits.

Added to these are the understandable concerns of the distribution manager as to loss of control, loss of status, unmet service expectations, and the risk of relying on a sole source.

Outsourcing may be one of the major trends of the 1990s, but it isn't an all-or-nothing proposition. Companies will pick and choose the functions they want outsourced; they will be influenced by factors as diverse as economics and corporate culture. And just as a wide range of functions may be outsourced, a wide range of suppliers will be willing to provide those services. The keys to success will be choosing the right functions to outsource, choosing those functions for the right reasons, and choosing the right suppliers to perform those functions.

Safety And Labor

Employment[9]

A high driver turnover rate results in additional training costs, safety problems, lost business, increased insurance rates, idle equipment, and a host of other business problems. Certain segments of the motor carrier industry, such as truckload, report turnover rates of 100 percent or more.

The Upper Great Plains Transportation Institute has conducted studies looking at the job satisfaction of commercial drivers. In one study, 13 truckload firms located through the United States were surveyed. The results are based on the responses to a 20-page questionnaire by 3910 drivers who worked for the truckload carriers. The sample was not random, but it was intended to be representative.

The study identified several key findings as displayed in Table 11-4. Most importantly, no single factor causes turnover. Conversely, there is no simple solution to the problem. Thus, any plan developed by a private fleet must be comprehensive and long-range.

Table 11-4. Job Satisfaction of Commercial Drivers

Why drivers are leaving	
Reason	Percent
Low pay	19
Away from home too much	17
Unpredictable schedules	13
Working conditions	11
No advancement	10
Poor treatment	9
Other	8
Poor supervision	6
Retirement	5
Poor health	3
Requirements	1
What drivers like	
Reason	Percent
Driving the truck	91.0
Independent lifestyle	83.3
Meeting safety requirements	75.2
Present company	67.9
Drug testing	67.2
Traveling out-of-town	66.7
Maintenance	66.0
Other drivers	65.6
What drivers dislike	
Reason	Percent
Hand (un)loading	72.9
Slip-sheeting	71.9
Company speed limits	44.5
Commercial driver's license	43.8
Palletized (un)loading	34.5
Vehicle inspections	33.4
Paperwork	29.4
Highway patrol	28.2

SOURCE: Upper Great Plains Transportation Institute.

Specific findings ranged over several aspects of the driver's job and its relationship to the company. These suggest that the industry is underutilizing its largest and most important resource: drivers.

Specifically, drivers:

- Derive a great deal of job satisfaction from certain aspects of their job

- Are very dissatisfied with several elements of the working environment

- Strongly desire to be more fully integrated into the firm as contributing employees

- Are very interested in receiving additional training that would allow them to conduct their job better

- Desire personal contact with supervisors and other company employees when giving and receiving information

- Had expectations that differed from the reality, when first starting the job
- Have a strong desire for some form of career advancement based on performance

As brought to life by these findings, drivers are independent, responsible, resourceful individuals seeking additional responsibility and involvement with the firm.

Drivers like several inherent aspects of their job: driving the truck, the independent lifestyle, meeting safety requirements, the responsibility associated with being a driver, relations with customers and maintenance.

These aspects describe the work itself, for which they indicate a strong liking. They derive personal satisfaction from this type of work. This provides a strong base from which to develop additional, meaningful, motivational aspects of the job and improve the work environment itself.

On the other hand several elements of the job, those that describe the work *environment,* provide driver job dissatisfaction. These include: pay and benefits, hand-loading and unloading of freight, company speed limits, road pavement conditions, variations in state laws, irregular schedules, and the amount of time away from home.

Although these aspects of the job need to be improved, easing work environment problems will not provide a great deal of job satisfaction leading to motivation and growth in the workplace. However, they must be addressed if fleets hope to focus on the motivational opportunities of the job.

Drivers express a strong desire to influence management in several areas, including: maintenance, dispatch procedures, safety improvements, improving customer service, and ways to cut costs. Additionally, drivers want to get more involved in customer relations, cost reductions, safety, equipment purchases, maintenance and repair, training, sales, and recruiting.

These driver interests indicate a need to be more fully involved and integrated into the company as an equal with other employees.

Training. A strong appetite for additional training is expressed by drivers over a wide variety of survey topics. The areas of training selected would allow them to conduct their jobs better. Seventy-five percent or more of the drivers expressed interest in defensive driving, safety regulations, injury prevention, accident procedures, first aid, company strategy, equipment inspection, customer service, problem-solving skills, hazardous materials, and maintenance procedures.

This would indicate that fleets have an excellent opportunity to develop achievement-oriented training programs that could result in a more motivated and satisfied employee.

Personal Contact. Drivers seek personal contact when giving information to and receiving information from management. However, they also show a practical side: notices in paychecks and newsletters were both ranked in the top 4 out of 11 categories of methods of receiving information. Talking with a supervisor was ranked number one in receiving and giving input.

One of the key causes of dissatisfaction is unmet expectations, i.e., those occasions when reality conflicts with perception. Sixty percent of the drivers said they had expected less waiting time; 48 percent had expected more pay; 42 percent had expected better benefits and less job-related stress; and 40 percent had expected a better lifestyle than they actually experienced.

This indicates that many drivers do not have an accurate picture of the job when they start. Therefore, fleets need to do a better job of informing new entrants of the work environment. Further, the data suggest that new drivers should receive a great deal of attention in the first 6 to 12 months to assist them in adjusting their expectations to reality.

Career Advancement. Drivers expressed a strong desire for a system of career advancement based on personal performance. Eighty-one percent of drivers said that an opportunity for career advancement was important or very important to them. Seventy-five percent of the drivers favored or strongly favored a classification system of career advancement based on personal performance. Yet 56 percent of them felt that opportunities for career advancement in the trucking industry were either poor or very poor.

The four defining characteristics of career advancement most frequently cited by drivers were (in order of frequency): (1) more money, (2) regular schedule, (3) home more often, and (4) advancement in a classification system based on performance.

The desire to be challenged and have a career path available to them was overwhelming. This indicates that fleets need to redefine the job of driving to accommodate this desire for achievement, responsibility, and recognition and reward it with better pay, a more regular schedule, and so forth.

Conclusion. What provides motivation, satisfaction, and fulfillment in any job has to do with a complex array of factors. This seems to be the case with driving. There is no simple solution to retaining drivers, but a variety of things must be accomplished to improve the working environment and redefine the job of driving in a way that will emphasize those elements that motivate people.

Driver Management[10]

A fleet manager, like a mechanic, needs a "toolbox" full of good tools for those seemingly stubborn and difficult problems that surface all too often. This toolbox is composed of three main tools: trust and openness, a human value ethic, and a common goal/purpose. These three work together.

Trust. Rensis Likert, in *New Futures of Management* (McGraw-Hill), finds that supervisors with the best records of performance focus their attention on the human aspects of their subordinates' problems and on trying to build effective work groups with high performance goals. These managers are *employee*-centered, as opposed to *job*-centered. Likert calls this type of manager a "System 4," and describes him/her as having complete confidence, openness, and trust in all matters.

These managers motivate by using a compensation system developed through group participation and involvement in setting goals, improving methods, appraising progress toward goals, and so forth. There is communication up and down the hierarchy and among peers.

Because of the socio-psychological isolation each driver faces, it is important for fleet managers to be open and trusting. Drivers come in after days (and perhaps weeks) on the road, cut off from the daily interchange of ideas and information other employees share. It is paramount that they be made to feel part of the company community and its decisions.

As managers learn to trust and to be more open, they begin to share responsibility with the drivers. As this happens, an unusual thing takes place. The manager actually begins to *gain* control. This additional control is the result not of a vertical authoritarianism, but of an intensified commitment on the part of the drivers to share goals.

Human Value Ethic.   The second tool in the fleet manager's toolbox is his/her conviction that all employees, regardless of position or job assignment, are of equal and infinite worth.

According to psychiatrist Dr. William Schutz, each person (driver) has at least two basic, interpersonal needs: to be included, and to have some degree of control.

Inclusion.   It is the isolation of the driving job that makes inclusion difficult, but the failure of a manager to be aware of this aspect of the driver's job forces the driver into even greater isolation. According to Dr. Schutz, most drivers want others to pay attention to them. And their biggest fear is being ignored. This may help to explain why drivers have a strong tendency toward self-sufficiency.

One of their deepest anxieties is that of low self-esteem. While most of today's truck drivers have finished high school and many have completed two or more years of college, it is easy for fleet managers to judge them according to inaccurate, outdated stereotypes.

Companies often go to extreme measures, spending inordinate amounts of money to fix a piece of equipment so that a delivery can be made as promised. Meanwhile they spend little time or resources on making a good driver out of a troublesome one.

Control.   The desire for control is central for drivers. They feel they must be in control of the roads they take, the hours they drive, the type of equipment they drive, the truck stop at which they eat. The control aspect of their nature can and should be put to positive use by giving them more control, more voice in decisions.

For example, one fleet manager was having trouble getting his drivers to accept the weekly dispatch schedule as fair and equitable. Various drivers each week thought they were being given the less desirable or lower-paying loads. One option was to dispatch according to seniority. This, however, favored the highly tenured drivers, and the drivers with two or three years suffered financially—a factor contributing to high turnover in many fleets.

A better idea was to involve the drivers themselves in the writing of the weekly fleet schedule. Now each week the schedule is drawn up at a specific hour on a specific day, with the help of one or more volunteer drivers. They do not get paid extra for this service, but they derive enjoyment and a sense of usefulness from helping the fleet resolve an irritating problem. The other drivers feel they are being fairly represented by one or two of their own; consequently there is an aura of increased trust and openness, as well as a sense of equal value to the company and each other.

Common Goals. The third tool in the manager's toolbox is the sharing of common goals and purpose. L. Coch and J. R. P. French, in *Group Dynamics: Research and Theory,* find that when manager and employees discuss proposed changes, productivity increases and resistance to change decreases. This study, and others, suggest that involving drivers in decision making tends to be very effective.

Peter Drucker's *Management by Objective* is a valuable tool in working with employees. This is especially true with truck drivers, because their personality type, as mentioned above, craves control. The idea is that goals should be jointly established. The review of the drivers' performance in achieving these goals is also mutually accomplished.

Management by objective is not simply a lofty idea, available only to those with advanced business degrees. It also can be used by fleet managers with everyday applications.

Begin by discussing some goals one-on-one with a driver. Be open and honest, and mutually set a simple, easily obtainable, short-term goal such as reduced idling. Do not offer the driver anything in return, other than the satisfaction of learning to be a better driver, helping the company lower costs or improve productivity, and most of all giving him/her a feeling of personal satisfaction and involvement.

Significantly, when there is mutual goal-setting and a mutual review of the results, there can appear a goal synergism. In other words, the results of the combined actions of the drivers and manager will produce a greater effect than the sum of the various individual actions.

Lastly, be aware of restraining forces. These are forces acting to restrain or decrease your efforts. In the fleet manager's work environment, they could be apathy, hostility, or poor equipment or maintenance. These negative goals need not stop the goal-setting, but managers must compensate by adjusting the goals.

Safety Fitness Ratings

Section 215 of the Motor Carrier Safety Act of 1984 directs the Secretary of Transportation, in cooperation with the Interstate Commerce Commission (ICC), to establish a procedure to determine the safety fitness of owners and operators of commercial motor vehicles operating in interstate or foreign commerce, including private carriers. The Secretary, in turn, delegated this responsibility to the Federal Highway Administration.

To meet the safety fitness standard, a motor carrier must demonstrate to the FHWA that it has adequate safety management controls in place that function effectively to ensure acceptable compliance with the applicable safety requirements.

Under DOT's procedures, carriers are assigned one of three possible ratings: "satisfactory," "conditional," or "unsatisfactory." According to recent FHWA figures, approximately 53 percent of the carriers that have been rated to date have received satisfactory ratings, 41 percent have received conditional ratings, and 6 percent have received unsatisfactory ratings.

Satisfactory, conditional, and unsatisfactory ratings are now used as a standard sorting criteria for the FHWA's comprehensive education, compliance, and enforcement activities. Carriers that receive an unsatisfactory rating are prohibited from operating vehicles that require a hazardous materials placard or that transport more than 15 passengers, including the driver. Carriers with an unsatisfactory rating are also prohibited from obtaining ICC operating authority as a for-hire carrier. In addition, shippers and insurance companies have recently begun using safety ratings to minimize potential liabilities involved in highway transportation.

The Safety Review Process. FHWA's program for evaluating the compliance status and safety management practices of motor carriers not previously reviewed or audited is called the Educational and Technical Assistance (ETA) program. The evaluation process is conducted through the Safety Review (SR).

The DOT or state safety auditor uses a Safety Compliance Form to check a fleet's compliance with the safety regulations.

Safety Review. A safety review is an on-site assessment to determine if a motor carrier has adequate safety management controls in place and functioning to comply with the FMCSRs and, if applicable, HMRs. The SR includes a review of selected carrier records and operations. It is used to gather information for assigning ratings to unrated carriers.

Carriers receiving an unsatisfactory or conditional safety rating can expect to be reevaluated at a later date through a more comprehensive compliance review.

Compliance Review. A compliance review is an on-site investigation of motor carrier operations, such as drivers' hours of service, vehicle maintenance and inspection, driver qualifications, commercial driver's license requirements, financial responsibility, accidents, and other safety and business records to determine a motor carrier's degree of compliance with the FMCSRs or, if applicable, HMRs.

A CR may be conducted to: (1) review a motor carrier's operation in response to a request to change a safety rating; (2) investigate a complaint; (3) investigate the operations of an unsatisfactory or conditionally rated motor carrier identified by an SR; or (4) as part of a routine periodic inspection of a carrier that has been rated satisfactory. The CR may result in the initiation of an enforcement action.

Safety Ratings. A satisfactory safety rating means that a motor carrier has in place and functioning adequate safety management controls to meet the safety fitness standard prescribed in Section 385.5.

A conditional safety rating means that a motor carrier does not have adequate safety management controls in place to ensure compliance with the safety fitness standard, which could result in the occurrences listed in Section 385.5 (a) through (h).

An unsatisfactory safety rating means that a motor carrier does not have adequate safety management controls in place to ensure compliance with the safety fitness standard, which has resulted in occurrences listed in Section 385.5 (a) through (h).

The Safety Fitness Rating Process. FHWA's Office of Motor Carriers is in the process of evaluating and assigning a Safety Rating to every company operating commercial vehicles in interstate commerce in the United States. Companies that haul hazardous materials are at the top of the list for evaluation and rating. The rating process is based on the Safety Review (SR) and the Compliance Review (CR).

Safety Review.   The Safety Review is an assessment survey conducted by federal and state safety specialists for unrated motor carriers. The SR generally takes four to six hours, during which time the safety specialist interviews management officials and inspects samples of the records and files to be maintained under the federal safety regulations and hazardous materials rules.

The SR contains 75 questions designed to assess carrier compliance with the regulations in the following eight areas:

1. General knowledge
2. Minimum levels of financial responsibility
3. Accident notification and reporting requirements
4. Driver qualification requirements
5. Requirements applicable to driving of motor vehicles
6. Vehicle inspection, repair, and maintenance
7. Hours of service and records of duty status
8. Requirements for the transportation of hazardous materials

The SR questions are answered by the safety specialist either yes or no, depending on the specialist's observation of the carrier's operations, records, management controls, the information provided by the company's representative, and the carrier's reportable/preventable accident history for the prior year.

As a result of the information determined in the SR, the carrier will receive a safety rating of satisfactory, unsatisfactory, or conditional.

Compliance Review.   The Compliance Review is a more in-depth examination of a motor carrier's operations and is used as a follow-up investigation of carriers rated conditional or unsatisfactory, or in response to complaints about a carrier, or in response to the carrier's request for a reevaluation of its rating. In the CR, driver qualification files, driver logs (records of duty status), and vehicle maintenance records are thoroughly examined for compliance with the regulations, and accident information is also collected.

Notification.   The FHWA will provide the motor carrier with a written notification of the safety rating assigned. If the motor carrier is assigned a safety rating of unsatisfactory, the written notification will advise of the statutory limitations on the carrier's further operations.

Any carrier that receives an unsatisfactory safety rating will receive an administrative order from FHWA directing the motor carrier to cease the transportation of HazMat in quantities requiring placarding or the carrying of 15 passengers or more, including the driver, by all commercial vehicle operations.

Petition for a Review/Change of Safety Rating.   There are two ways to request a change in the unsatisfactory rating and thereby prevent the hazardous materials transportation ban from becoming effective.

First, if the carrier believes that the unsatisfactory rating was the result of inaccuracies, factual errors, or other disputed factual or procedural issues, the carrier may petition for a review of the assigned rating. Under the regulations, the carrier must file the petition in writing, listing all the disputed issues and any information or documents to support its claim, within 90 days of receipt of the rating.

Additionally, a carrier receiving an unsatisfactory rating will be given the opportunity to take the action necessary to upgrade the rating during the 45-day period. The basis for the request should be evidence of corrective actions and overall compliance with the regulations.

Although at present the sanctions for an unsatisfactory safety rating apply only to carriers of hazardous materials and passengers, there is a consensus building that Congress will extend the sanctions to transportation of general freight as well in the next few years. In addition, FHWA is becoming more aggressive in issuing fines for noncompliance with the regulations, and is less likely than before to reduce the fine significantly after negotiation with the carrier. The bottom line for carriers is that a safety compliance program is now a necessity for any well-run fleet.

ICC Operating Authority.   If your fleet seeks common or contract operating authority from the Interstate Commerce Commission, you must include your safety fitness rating for your private fleet on the ICC application. Carriers with an unsatisfactory rating (or applicants for new operating authority that are owned or controlled by carriers with an unsatisfactory rating) are not eligible to obtain ICC authority.

Selective Compliance and Enforcement Program.   If, as a result of the safety review, a carrier is issued either a conditional or unsatisfactory rating, the carrier will be assigned to the Selective Compliance and Enforcement Program (SCE).

Carriers assigned to the SCE program are sorted by types of operations posing the greatest risks to highway safety and then scheduled for an extensive "compliance review."

The compliance review entails an in-depth examination of the carrier's operations. If a serious degree of noncompliance is uncovered during a compliance review, FHWA may initiate an enforcement action against the carrier. The enforcement action may include: disqualifying all or some of the carrier's drivers; issuing a written cease and desist order against the carrier; initiating successive civil or criminal actions with increasingly higher fines for noncompliance; and/or intervening in an application proceeding for authority from the ICC.

A carrier will remain in the SCE program until it obtains a satisfactory rating. Upon obtaining a satisfactory rating, the carrier will be transferred to the ETA program. Once in the ETA program the carrier can expect to be monitored approximately once every five years, unless, as previously noted, its name begins to appear repeatedly on roadside inspection reports, indicating serious deficiencies in the carrier's safety program.

Selling Safety to Senior Management

Senior management often professes total support for safety, yet asks why significant dollars need to be committed to the safety effort.

How should a private fleet manager answer? It is unlikely that management will be convinced by vague generalities or "What if" scenarios. A fleet manager needs to provide hard figures on accident costs and present a quantitative analysis of them.

Experts and studies indicate that 90 percent of all accidents are caused by driver error, with as many as 20 percent being the result of aggressive driving habits. It is essential to examine the total costs of these accidents.

Vehicle accidents are the number-one cause of job death. Vehicle accidents result in over one-third of the job deaths—approximately 3900 people. The total cost of traffic accidents in the United States is over $74 billion annually.

In order to more easily identify costs, they can be broken down into three categories: hard costs, soft costs, and incalculable costs. Hard costs include:

- Collision repair
- Replacement transportation
- Medical costs
- Worker's compensation
- Temporary labor charges
- Towing charges

Soft costs include:

- Civil/criminal lawsuits
- Physical and vocation rehabilitation
- Employee downtime
- Investigative and reporting costs

The incalculable costs are:

- Lower productivity
- Loss of goodwill
- Loss of customer relationships
- Loss of sales to competition

We'll now examine each of these in more detail.

Hard Costs. The costs of repairing collision damages are obvious and relatively easy to calculate. One must note, however, that these costs are continually escalating, and at a nearly exponential rate.

Medical costs are also rising at a phenomenal rate. Like the collision repair expense, these direct costs are relatively simple to calculate.

Worker's compensation costs are also related to the accident. Even a minor mishap may result in significant worker's compensation expenses.

The cost of temporarily replacing an injured worker must also be a part of the total cost calculation. In the case of a driver, this may mean either the cost for a less-skilled replacement or the cost associated with lost fleet revenue from turning loads over to carriers.

As the pool of qualified, full-time drivers shrinks, so will the availability of qualified temporary replacements.

The cost of towing and renting replacement vehicles is also easily identified and easily calculated.

Soft Costs. What are termed "soft" costs are much more difficult to assess. It is these costs, however, that if overlooked will severely distort the accident cost calculation.

The cost of defending or initiating lawsuits and/or court action is very high. Whether one purchases legal assistance or absorbs it as part of a corporate overhead expense, the cost remains high.

The private fleet manager may find himself the recipient of "nuisance" actions simply because the vehicles are very identifiable from corporate logos. They often represent familiar products or companies to the public.

The costs of physical and vocational rehabilitation also must enter the calculation. These costs must also be coupled with nonproductive employee downtime.

One must also consider the cost of a formal accident investigation or, at the very least, the expense of administrative time to complete reports and documentation.

Incalculable Costs. Finally, there is a group of expenses that are impossible to quantify but are no less real.

Lower productivity will result from all those involved, even peripherally, with the accident. The manager or fleet supervisor must adjust his or her organization to compensate for the loss of the individual and equipment. Fleet revenue may be lost. Budget considerations may have to be made. Reports must be completed.

The dispatchers may have to revise delivery schedules. Drivers may be forced into unfamiliar territory.

Regular delivery schedules may be interrupted, resulting in decreased customer satisfaction, deteriorating goodwill, and ultimate loss of sales to the competition.

One must also consider the negative effects of a highly identifiable fleet vehicle conspicuously involved in a highway accident. Remember, thousands of people see your equipment daily.

One of the significant difficulties for many fleet managers is that they themselves will see relatively few of these costs.

The fleet manager should be aware of the collision repair charges, replacement costs, towing costs, and temporary labor expenses. In many cases, however, they will be unaware of the actual medical costs, worker's compensation charges, legal costs, rehabilitation costs, investigative and administrative costs. This is to say nothing of those costs designated as incalculable.

While it varies with each organization, a good rule of thumb is to assign a 1 to 5 ratio of direct, identifiable costs to indirect, less often identified charges. What this means is that an accident with identifiable costs of $2000 will probably result in charges of nearly $10,000 when all costs are considered.

A related idea involves self-insured companies with fleets of company cars, particularly those of salespeople. A poor driving record, or a high accident frequency for an individual, is often excused with: "That's my best salesperson!"

Consider this: If a self-insured company is operating on a 10-percent margin and one salesperson totals a $15,000 automobile, $150,000 in sales must be generated merely to cover the cost of the car. And this takes no account of the additional costs just discussed.

When selling to senior management the need for safety programs, be sure to consider *all* the costs of having accidents. The numbers are compelling.

References

1. *Report of the Committee on Commerce, United States Senate, by its Special Study Group on Transportation Policies in the United States,* p. 507, U.S. Government Printing Office, Washington, D.C., 1961.

2. National Private Truck Council and A.T. Kearney, Inc., *Private Fleet Benchmarks of Quality and Productivity,* p. 39, National Private Truck Council, Alexandria, VA, 1992.

3. Colin Barrett, *Practical Handbook of Private Trucking,* p. 3, The Traffic Service Corporation, Washington, D.C., 1983.

4. Ronald D. Roth, *America's Private Carriers: Who Are These Guys?* Transportation Technical Services, Fredericksburg, VA, 1991.

5. Adapted from Barrett, *Practical Handbook of Private Trucking.*

6. Adapted from *Private Fleet Benchmarks of Quality and Productivity.*

7. Adapted from a paper by Joseph BenVenuto of Tompkins Industries.

8. Adapted from Blaine Johnson, "Life Cycle Costing: How To Compute Equipment's True Costs," *The Private Carrier,* pp. 4–14, August 1992.

9. Adapted from Julia Rodriguez and Gene Griffin, "Driver Satisfaction: What Do Drivers Like and Dislike?" *The Private Carrier,* pp. 4–8, November 1991.

10. Excerpted from Elden Steilstra, "A Manager's Toolbox: Three Techniques For Better Driver Management," *The Private Carrier,* pp. 4–9, December 1991.

12

Carrier Rates and Tariffs*

Edwin P. Patton

*Professor of Transportation,
University of Tennessee at Knoxville*

Pricing/Costing Concepts and the Carrier–Shipper Interdependency

The price that the carrier offers the shipper, together with the service provided for that price, has short- and long-run implications for both parties involved. If the price is accepted, the carrier moves a freight shipment from one point to another in exchange for revenues sufficient to earn a profit, or at least to minimize a loss. Depending on similar shipments' returns over a period of time, the carrier will make long-run decisions as to the future suitability of the market of which the shipment is a part, such as whether to remain as present in that market, to expand in it, or to exit it altogether.

Shipper rejection of the carrier's price-service package forces the carrier to recalculate its cost and/or reconsider the price charged for the service involved. Whether its prices are accepted or rejected, the carrier continually must analyze its prices for services offered to its current and potential customers.

The shipper, on the other hand, by accepting the carrier's offer, incurs a cost that must be added to the manufacturing cost of the product moved that equals a delivered cost to the buyer. Regardless of whether the seller or buyer pays the cost of moving the product to the buyer, the carrier must be paid.

*Reprinted with permission of the author. See Chapter 1 of Edwin P. Patton, *Transportation Costing and Profit Analysis,* Graphic Creations, Knoxville, TN, 1992.

The lower the transportation cost, presumably the better the shipper's situation will be, vis-à-vis its competitors. Thus, the buyer of a freight transportation service continually pressures freight carriers for lower rates, while at the same time demanding improved services. The transportation industry in the 1990s is exciting because carrier management often is meeting those demands.

However, transportation management walks a tightrope as it fights to survive in this most competitive of industries. A wrong marketing decision here, inadequate attention to a cost problem there, and a company can face loss of market share or even bankruptcy. Particularly in trucking, many once-prominent haulers now are buried in the motor carrier graveyard. Mason and Dixon, Spector Red Ball, Smith's of Staunton, McLean—all leaders in the early years of motor transportation—now are only memories.

Railroads too have had to revise their traditional approach to freight procurement by offering reliable services and placing emphasis on customer needs rather than on carrier requirements. The rails' shrinking share of the monies received for moving the nation's freight is testimony to the mode's inability to retain or recapture high-value freight. No mode can avoid the demands and consequences of the current competitive pace in the transportation marketplace.

Definition of a Transportation Market

Before analyzing the role of carrier price in the shipper-carrier relationship, and the interdependency of the two parties, it is necessary to define a transportation market and to understand the carrier's short- and long-run costs of doing business in each market.

Five factors work together to define a transportation market:

1. One or more related commodities, moving
2. From an origin to a destination
3. In a particular quantity
4. Within an established timeframe at a designated standard of performance, and
5. Of a certain value to the shipper or the buyer of the shipment.

Using the above factors in an example, a transportation market might exist for the movement of:

1. Heavy, industrial wrapping paper, on rolls,
2. From Savannah, Georgia, to Philadelphia, Pennsylvania,
3. In volume quantities (10,000 lb and upward),
4. With an origin-to-destination transit time of three days and a 98 percent on-time reliability standard,
5. For which the transportation buyer (seller or buyer of the wrapping paper) is willing to pay a cost based on a combination of factors, primarily
   a. The actual or anticipated market value of the wrapping paper in Philadelphia, compared to the paper's production cost and market value in Savannah;

b. The seller's own competition in the marketplace, namely the wrapping paper market in Philadelphia; and

c. The transportation buyer's perception of a reasonable price for moving wrapping paper from Savannah to Philadelphia, given other transportation options for moving the paper.

Continuing with this example, additional markets for the movement of wrapping paper from Savannah to Philadelphia might include shipments in smaller-quantity lots (less-than-truckload, or LTL) and shipments allowing storage-in-transit. The carriers wanting to move the LTL quantities may or may not be those wanting to move wrapping paper in volume lots or to offer storage. Which carriers offer what services will depend on individual carrier managements and what each determines to be its strengths. This includes its competitors, both for-hire intramodal and intermodal, private carriers (companies moving their goods in their vehicles), and operators of intermodal services.

Analyzing a market includes entering, deciding to remain in, or expanding present services in that market. In this analysis, the carrier evaluates: (1) the performance standard offered and price charged by the competition and (2) whether it can meet this competition given its own cost structure. Serious appraisals reduce market possibilities from seemingly endless (particularly when considered on a national scale) to a realistic, manageable number.

Control of Profit Determinants and Market Decisions

In this country, freight carriers are profit-seeking organizations. The survival of each is a function of its cumulative profit or loss generated in the different markets it serves. In evaluating a market, the carrier looks at profit potential. Profit in a transportation market is defined as in any market: *Profit* (or loss) on a shipment moved equals *Revenue* generated by the shipment minus *Costs* incurred to move the shipment

$$P = R - C$$

In breaking down the equation, revenues received for moving the shipment equal price (or rate) charged per weight unit (e.g., per ton) multiplied by the number of weight units moved in the shipment, usually abbreviated: $TR = P \times Q$, where TR is shipment total revenue, P is price or rate per weight unit, x is multiplied by, and Q the number of units moved.

The factors that affect the price a carrier charges for a transportation service usually are beyond the individual carrier's control. The market value of wrapping paper in Philadelphia, or what the average buyer will pay for wrapping paper there, may affect the rate to move the paper to Philadelphia; however, one carrier's ability to influence this amount should be negligible. Also, the number and location of the shipper's wrapping paper-producing competitors is beyond the carrier's control, as is the number of competitors in the carrier's own Savannah-to-Philadelphia marketplace.

Carrier management, therefore, must look to the area of costs if it is to influence its profit situation effectively. Even here management may have trouble, especially in the very short run. For example, the price of fuel for a small motor carrier most likely is fixed for the next 24 hours.

However, as the time period lengthens, opportunities increase for management to control its costs. To operate profitably, management not only must know the costs themselves but also their degree of flexibility, and how to take advantage of this flexibility.

Cost Variability and Management Flexibility

Cost variability plays a crucial role in shipment cost determination and in carrier management's resulting market decisions. In particular, management must distinguish between variable and fixed costs and establish a time frame for when the short run ends and the long run begins. This chapter uses the following definitions for the two costs.

Variable costs are *costs incurred by the carrier when it chooses to move a particular shipment.* If these costs cannot be covered by shipment revenue, the carrier should not move the shipment nor participate in that particular market.[1]

Fixed costs, on the other hand, are *costs assigned to the shipment that carrier management must pay whether it chooses to move the shipment or not.* In other words, these costs must be paid by other shipments actually moved if the shipment in question is not moved. While all fixed costs assigned to a shipment do not have to be covered, at least a portion must be paid.

The following two questions often are asked about fixed costs:

1. While it is easy to say that in the long run all costs are variable, how does such cost behavior affect management's decision to accept or reject a certain shipment today, right now?

2. Does "the long run" mean that different costs change from fixed to variable at a single point in time? In other words, at a single stroke of the clock, do all costs treated as fixed suddenly become variable, and suddenly have to be covered by revenues if management is to remain in the market?

To answer these questions, consider the following motor carrier example. Management of a multistate truck line purchases an annual license for a vehicle to operate in one of the states it serves. The license cost of $500 is a fixed cost, in that it must be covered by shipment revenues either carried by the licensed vehicle itself or by other vehicles in the carrier's fleet in the year the license is effective. Otherwise, management is not covering all its costs in that particular year.

When the license expires, management must decide whether to renew it for another year. Management now controls the license expense; the cost is fixed, but only for one year. At the end of one year it becomes variable, because management can renew the license or sell or retire the vehicle.

Management renews the license. The moment the fee is paid, management enters a new fixed cost, short-run period of one year.

Meanwhile, how is the cost of the license assigned to freight shipments the vehicle carries during the year's service to the carrier? A general rule is to allocate the costs logically and fairly while not discouraging movement of the freight by the transportation buyer. With fixed costs, the absolute amount assigned per shipment does not have to be covered by each shipment; however, when all fixed costs are not covered by an individual shipment's revenues, the deficit must be made up by revenues from other shipments.

If the $500 license fee has not been covered by the end of the short run, management should consider using the vehicle to carry other commodities or to operate over different routes where its fixed costs can be met.

Individual Vehicle versus Company Fixed Costs

In addition to each vehicle's cost, some assignment of a carrier's headquarters' and top management costs must be made on a per-shipment basis. One procedure is to estimate for an appropriate time frame (usually one year) the fixed costs of operating and maintaining the carrier's headquarters unit, including the costs of top management, the company's sales and marketing programs, information systems, and a sum required for profit or return on investment (e.g., $1 million). Next, estimate the quantity of transportation to be performed in the same time frame (e.g., 20 million revenue miles). In this example, fixed cost for the headquarters unit per revenue vehicle mile will be 5 cents ($0.05).

Although this example involves a motor carrier, the short-run/long-run principles discussed apply equally to rail, barge, air, and pipeline carriers. In the railroad and pipeline modes, railways and pipeways incur fixed maintenance costs that are not applicable to those carriers using public highways, waterways, and airways. Public way costs, which usually take the form of use taxes, are totally variable; if no traffic moves, use taxes are zero.

It is important to remember, however, that fixed railroad and pipeline maintenance costs are *only* those that occur at zero traffic levels. The difference between total maintenance of way cost and zero-traffic-level maintenance costs will be variable costs.

The Long Run as a Planning Tool

Carrier management must make short-run/long-run decisions, as in the motor carrier license renewal example, every year, if not every minute. Licenses, permits, and insurance policies expire. Leases terminate. Mortgages mature. Units need overhauls. Facilities need maintenance. Short runs end all the time. What does management do in each case? Does it renew, sell, overhaul?

Because of the decisions required to juggle short- and long-run costs, the long run actually is a planning device. By making long-run decisions, the carrier is forced into long-run planning.

Therefore, the long run for each carrier asset or liability actually is a series of short runs. At the end of each short run, management must decide the disposition of each asset and how to handle each liability. These judgments, cumulatively, determine the future direction of the carrier and its ultimate success or failure.

Variable Costs

Variable costs are incurred when the carrier chooses to move a freight shipment. Major variable costs are labor, fuel, and operating maintenance. In the motor carrier industry, the highest variable cost is labor, which may account for over 50 percent of total shipment cost. This includes driver cost plus support personnel such as dock (un)loaders, rating, billing, claims, and communications employees.

Fuel usually is the second highest variable cost. Its importance can change, however, because fuel supplies vary with the political situation in the Middle East. Another factor in fuel costs is the efficiency of the power unit. Fuel economy has improved in all transportation modes since truck tractor, locomotive, aircraft, and towboat builders have made fuel conservation a top priority.

Operating maintenance is the third largest motor carrier variable cost. Sometimes called "running maintenance," this factor includes tire and power unit costs. Management usually employs a combination of new and recapped tires on its vehicles. Recapped tires represent a lower-cost alternative to new tires, but their operating life is shorter and they are perceived as less reliable.

Power-unit-engine operating maintenance cost generally increases per mile as power units get older; however, of greater concern to management is an older vehicle's decreased reliability. The same is true of power units in all modes. A basic decision confronting virtually every carrier is when to trade a high-maintenance-cost and fuel-inefficient but paid-for unit for a new low-maintenance-cost, fuel-efficient unit that carries a high price tag.

Assignment of Common Costs

In addition to shipment costs being either fixed or variable, they also must be classified as identifiable or common. Consider the following: A shipment weighing 5000 lb moves in a trailer of less-than-truckload (LTL) shipments. How is the depreciation of the tractor-trailer rig allocated to the shipment? How is the driver's salary allocated to it? The shipment incurs variable costs, and some fixed costs must be assigned, but the shipment incurs those costs together with one or more shipments. No clearcut method exists to assign these costs to the individual 5000-lb shipment. What to do?

Costs that cannot be identified with an individual shipment are called *common costs,* and the answer to the question is to assign them arbitrarily, but logically, just as fixed costs such as vehicle depreciation, maintenance, license, and insurance are assigned.

Costs not classified as common costs are identifiable costs. The driver's salary is easier to allocate if the truck he or she is driving contains a single shipment of one commodity moving from a single shipper to a single receiver; however, the allocation of top management, marketing and sales, and information systems expenses remains.

The problem of common cost assignment affects all transportation modes. A unit train (a trainload of one commodity with a single origin and single destination) is the railroad's equivalent of a truckload. A single- or multiple-car shipment within a train, moving several commodities with a variety of origins and destinations, is comparable to a highway trailer full of less-than-truckload shipments. A tow of barges could be moving a single commodity from one origin to one destination, like a truckload, but more likely is composed of barges carrying different goods to different places. Commercial aircraft carry people, cargo, mail, and baggage. The common cost assignment task is universal in transportation.

Shipment costing in a competitive environment such as that found in U.S. transportation in the early 1990s, where a few cents per unit of transportation provided can mean profit or loss, survival or death, for a carrier, demands accuracy and a willingness to include *all* costs associated with the handling of a shipment. Just because the cost-assignment methodology is arbitrary is no reason to exclude one or more costs, particularly when bidding for desirable freight against one or more rivals. Whether a carrier does so by oversight or purposely, quoting prices below costs virtually assures financial failure in transportation as in any business endeavor.

Total Compared to Per-Unit Costs

Once total shipment cost has been determined, management converts it into a form comparable to the price or rate charged to move the shipment. The most popular rate forms include:

1. Per (revenue) hundredweight (cwt)
2. Per (revenue) ton (2000 lb)
3. Per (revenue) vehicle mile
4. Per (revenue) ton mile

The word *revenue* is shown in parentheses because it is necessary to differentiate between the weight of the shipment being moved and the weight of the vehicle doing the moving. Also, *deadhead miles* (miles a vehicle moves empty) must be considered, as opposed to *revenue miles* (miles the vehicle moves with the freight).

Total or gross weight includes both vehicle weight and shipment weight. Total miles includes both empty and revenue miles. The word *revenue* is not always included when calculating per-unit costs, especially when using per-hundredweight rates. However, it is understood to be revenue hundredweight, and revenue should be included in the per-unit figure, as in the following example.

A 30,000-lb volume shipment is moved by a motor carrier a distance of 375 mi. The move is broken down into three sub-moves as follows: (1) PICKUP: 15 mi deadhead from the carrier's origin terminal to the shipper's loading dock, and return to the terminal with the shipment; (2) LINE HAUL: 350 mi, origin terminal to destination terminal with the shipment; (3) DELIVERY: 10 mi from the carrier's destination terminal to the receiver's dock with the shipment, and return to the terminal deadhead. Total cost: $480, of which $320 is variable cost and $160 is fixed.

The four per-unit costs discussed above are determined by breaking down total cost as follows:

1. *Per revenue hundredweight (cwt).* Divide 30,000 by 100 to compute the number of hundredweight units in the shipment.

$$30,000 \text{ divided by } 100 = 300$$

Next divide $480 by 300. Answer: $1.60, or the rate per revenue cwt is $1.60.

2. *Per revenue ton.* Assume a ton is 2000 lb. How many tons in 30,000 lb?

   30,000 divided by 2000 = 15.

   $480 divided by 15 = $32 per revenue ton.

3. *Per revenue vehicle mile.* Review the volume move and divide into deadhead versus revenue miles, or miles the tractor-trailer rig actually moved with the shipment. Deadhead miles total 25: 15 from the carrier's origin terminal to the shipper's dock, and 10 from the receiver's dock to the carrier's destination terminal. The remainder of the miles were with the shipment and totaled 375; that is, 15 from the shipper's dock to the origin terminal, *plus* 350 terminal to terminal, *plus* 10 from the destination terminal to the receiver's dock. Therefore, total miles are 400, but revenue vehicle miles are 375. Per revenue vehicle mile? $480 divided by 375 equals $1.28, or 8 cents more per mile than per total vehicle mile cost (deadhead plus revenue miles). To cover total costs, the carrier charges either $1.20 per *total* vehicle mile or $1.28 per revenue vehicle mile. Carriers usually employ the latter.

4. *Per revenue ton mile.* Use the figures in (2) and (3) to determine revenue ton miles. In (2), shipment weight is 15 revenue tons. In (3), shipment distance totals 375 revenue miles. Multiply the two to determine revenue ton miles: 15 revenue tons times 375 miles equals 5625 revenue ton miles. Dividing $480 by 5625 revenue ton miles equals $.0853, or 8.53 cents per revenue ton mile.

Per-unit costs are used to compare carrier costs to the rates or prices charged shippers, and also are important in comparing individual carrier costs to costs of both intramodal and intermodal competitors.

Two Kinds of Profit

Two kinds of profit should be considered when analyzing the financial repercussions of carrier price. One profit is that required by the company's investors to keep them in the business. If a carrier does not realize a certain return on the monies devoted to the business of providing transportation, those monies are moved into another market or area of opportunity where they will earn what their owners feel is a reasonable return. The amount or percentage of return required will vary among carriers according to the expectations of the investors vis-à-vis the risk levels of the markets in which each company participates.

This return is termed *normal* or *required profit* or *target yield* and is included as a *shipment fixed cost* in the basic formula: Shipment profit *equals* total revenues from moving a freight shipment *minus* shipment total cost (STC), which, in turn, is the total of shipment variable cost (SVC) plus shipment fixed cost (SFC).

When a surplus exists after total costs have been deducted from total revenues, this surplus is termed *pure* profit (some prefer *economic* or *exploitive* profit). This surplus is not required by the carrier's investors to keep them providing transportation; nevertheless, it can play an important role in a carrier's short-term survival. Specifically, when a carrier charges a shipper *less* than total cost to move a shipment in the short run (price covers variable but not total cost on a certain move) the difference between costs covered and total cost must be made up on shipments where revenues earn *more* than total costs.

Goals of Carrier Pricing

The goal in setting a price or rate for a transportation service depends on the carrier being interviewed. Three responses currently are being heard:

1. To maximize profit or net income
2. To maximize contribution to overhead or fixed costs
3. To maximize total (gross) revenues.

Although all three goals appear similar, if not identical, important differences do exist among them, as shown in Table 12-1.

The table shows a railroad's demand schedule for a relatively low-value, packaged commodity that moves in boxcars with a maximum capacity of 50 revenue tons. The schedule was drawn up by a pricing manager based on knowledge and/or assumptions on the value of the transportation service to the shipper of moving the commodity to an actual or potential buyer in a particular market. It is, in effect, a *derived demand* schedule, as is the price schedule constructed for any for-hire freight service.

The table indicates the quantity demanded in revenue tons (column 2) at a series of prices per ton (column 1) and the resulting total revenues at each price (column 3). Columns 4 and 5 list shipment variable and total costs, respectively, for each quantity moved. The last two columns (6 and 7) indicate contribution to fixed costs (column 6) and profit or loss (column 7) at each possible price.

The three responses mentioned above are illustrated in the table. To maximize profit, the carrier equates marginal revenue, which is the change in total revenue for moving one additional revenue ton of freight, with marginal cost, which is the change in cost of moving the additional ton. In reality this may be difficult to accomplish, due to inadequate cost data or methodology. In the table, a rate of $10 a ton produces total revenues of $300, a pure profit (above required profit) of $79.34, highest of the predicted profit possibilities. Marginal revenue is $4.20 and marginal cost is $4.01 at this level of traffic.

To maximize contribution to overhead, a rate of $9.20 is charged, which contributes $160.58 (column 3 minus column 4) but does not maximize profit. Maximizing contribution to overhead is how one noted transportation economist defines "charging what the traffic will bear."[2]

Charging a rate that maximizes gross revenues is called *yield management* by an increasing number of carriers. It involves charging a price such that *any further* change in price, either up or down, will result in a decrease in total revenue. This price, or point of service output, is termed *the point of unitary elasticity* in economics. In the table, total revenues are maximized at $8 a revenue ton. At this rate, pure profit is $20.12 *less* than at a price of $10 a ton, and contribution to overhead is $8.28 *less* than at $9.20 per ton.

A rate of $4 per revenue ton is the lowest the railroad should charge under any circumstances. This is the lowest rate at which shipment variable costs are covered and a contribution ($3.66) is made to fixed costs. In the short run, when certain costs are fixed, the question arises: If total revenues do not cover total costs of handling certain traffic, should the carrier continue to handle the freight or should the traffic be refused?

The answer: Continue to operate if revenues cover variable costs *and* contribute

Table 12-1 Demand Schedule for 400-Mile Freight Shipment in Boxcars

(1)	(2)	(3)	(4)	(5)	(6)	(7)
Price per Revenue Ton ($)	Quantity Demanded: Revenue Tons	Total Revenue (1) × (2) ($)	Shipment Variable Costs ($)	Shipment Total Costs* ($)	Contribution to Fixed Costs ($)	Profit or (Loss) (3) − (5) ($)
12.00	20	240.00	116.10	180.54	123.90	59.46
11.80	21	247.80	118.68	184.55	129.12	63.25
11.60	22	255.20	121.26	188.56	133.94	66.64
11.40	23	262.20	123.84	192.58	138.36	69.62
11.20	24	268.80	126.42	196.59	142.38	72.21
11.00	25	275.00	129.00	200.60	146.00	74.40
10.80	26	280.80	131.58	204.61	149.22	76.19
10.60	27	286.20	134.16	208.62	152.04	77.58
10.40	28	291.20	136.74	212.64	154.46	78.56
10.20	29	295.80	139.32	216.65	156.48	79.15
10.00(1)	30	300.00	141.90	220.66	158.10	**79.34**
9.80	31	303.80	144.48	224.67	159.32	79.13
9.60	32	307.20	147.06	228.68	160.14	78.52
9.40	33	310.20	149.64	232.70	160.56	77.50
9.20(2)	34	312.80	152.22	236.71	**160.58**	76.09
9.00	35	315.00	154.80	240.72	160.20	74.28
8.80	36	316.80	157.38	244.73	159.42	72.07
8.60	37	318.20	159.96	248.74	148.24	69.46
8.40	38	319.20	162.54	252.76	156.66	66.44
8.20	39	319.80	165.12	256.74	154.68	63.03
8.00(3)	40	**320.00**	167.70	260.78	152.30	59.22
7.60	41	311.60	170.28	264.79	141.32	46.81
7.20	42	302.40	172.86	268.80	129.54	33.60
6.80	43	292.40	175.44	272.82	116.96	19.58
6.40	44	281.60	178.02	276.83	103.58	4.77
6.00	45	270.00	180.60	280.84	89.40	(10.84)
5.40	46	248.40	183.18	284.85	65.22	(36.45)
4.80	47	225.60	185.76	288.86	39.84	(63.26)
4.00(4)	48	192.00	188.34	292.88	**3.66**	(100.88)
3.00	49	147.00	190.92	296.89	(43.92)	(149.89)
2.00	50	100.00	193.50	300.90	(93.50)	(200.90)

(1) Price at which profit is maximized (marginal revenue equals marginal cost, as close as possible on a whole ton basis).

(2) Price that maximizes contribution to overhead or fixed costs.

(3) Price where change in price will decrease total revenues.

(4) Price beyond which carrier should not offer service, since shipment variable costs are not covered.

*Total costs are railroad operating costs, which define fixed costs as *those costs that remain if a particular shipment is not accepted for transportation.* This fixed cost factor is $.00358 per gross ton mile. (See E. P. Patton, *Handbook for Railroad Costing,* Graphic Creations, Knoxville, TN, 1992, pp. i, 36, and 74.)

to fixed costs. If revenues do not cover the costs incurred because the carrier chooses to move the freight (variable costs), the freight should be refused. This rule minimizes losses until the carrier enters the long run, when all costs are variable. Then the company can decide whether to continue in or abandon a particular market.

The Zone of Negotiation

The *zone of negotiation* defines a reasonable rate to be charged by the carrier. Before 1980, this zone was called the *zone of reasonableness,* and a rate that fell within this zone was said to be reasonable. Zone of negotiation is a more popular term currently because of the passage of the Staggers and Motor Carrier Acts of 1980. These acts largely replaced regulated price-setting with prices set by market forces, as reflected in carrier-shipper negotiations. The limits of the zone of negotiation are exactly the same as the limits of the zone of reasonableness.

A rate is deemed reasonable if it falls between an upper and a lower limit. These limits are defined as follows.

1. *Upper Limit.* The value of the transportation service to the shipper, which is the *difference* between the product's value at its origin point *and* its market value at destination. *Origin point* means point of receipt by the carrier, and usually equals the production cost of the product.

2. *Lower Limit.* The cost to provide the service to the shipper by the carrier. Whether variable or fixed cost is employed depends on the carrier's capacity situation in the direction the shipment is moving. If the carrier has excess capacity (the usual case), variable cost is the lower limit. If the carrier is fully utilized and has no excess capacity in the shipment direction, total cost is used as the lower limit.

Note that where the value of the service to the shipper is less than either the variable or total cost to the carrier, depending on which cost applies, no zone of negotiation exists.

The zone of negotiation is shown schematically in Fig. 12-1.

Factors Affecting the Zone of Negotiation

The following factors can affect the *upper* limit of the zone of negotiation. They represent the concerns of the shipper and the carrier during price negotiations:

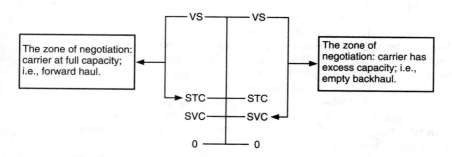

VS is the value of the transportation service to the shipper.
STC is the total cost to the carrier to move the shipment.
SVC is the variable cost to the carrier to move the shipment.

Figure 12-1. The zone of negotiation.

1. *Shipper* concerns
   a. Location of competitors
   b. Price and service provided competitors by other carriers
   c. Public acceptance of the product; e.g., is it new or established? Acceptance is measured by market value, which in turn is a function of (1) consumer tastes, (2) consumer incomes, and (3) substitutability of other products.
2. *Carrier* concerns
   a. Carrier's own competition for the shipper's business
   b. Shipper's competition from other shippers in other locations
   c. Future potential of shipper's business; for the transportation of the product being negotiated as well as other moves.
   d. Desirability of the shipper's freight; cost of service characteristics such as size, frequency, and direction of moves, claims potential, single-line or interline requirements.

The Shipper-Carrier Interface

The important relationship between the shipper and the carrier is demonstrated in the following example, which shows how transportation cost directly influences shipper profit and, in turn, how the shipper's ability to compete in his or her marketplace affects the carrier's own financial success or failure.

The Shipper's Situation. The shipper currently ships 500 lb of Piddies to a market 400 mi from the shipper's Piddie production plant. Piddies are packed in 25-lb packages that measure $1 \times 2 \times 3$ ft equaling 6 cu ft per package. Piddies cost a total of $1.25 to manufacture, including normal profit, of which 75 cents represents variable cost, before transportation cost to market. Piddie market price is $1.50 each, with the producer having no control whatsoever over that price. A Piddie weighs 1 lb.

The Carrier's Situation. The carrier's costs to move Piddies to market are developed using actual cost data for average less-than-truckload (LTL) shipments.[3] Carrier price closely approximates that of a major LTL carrier that wishes to remain anonymous. Both costs and rates are updated to January 1992. Carrier rates are given with no discount and with discounts of 20, 40, and 50 percent off the applicable class rates. Four shipment sizes are used: 500, 1000, 1500, and 2000 lb. In the market being analyzed, 500 Piddies are sold by the producer each week. Therefore, movements of 1000 (two weeks' sales), 1500 (three weeks' sales), and 2000 Piddies (four weeks' sales) will require storage costs at the point of sale to the public. One week's sales (500 Piddies or lb) will not involve storage. However, one week's storage is required with 1000 Piddie shipments, two weeks with 1500, and three weeks with 2000 Piddie (lb) shipments. Storage costs are $2.50 per square foot if the producer provides the service in house, and $3.75 per square foot if a for-hire storage facility is used. Piddie cartons are stacked five-deep, with the 2×3-ft side of the cartons resting on the floor.

Under these conditions, the shipper and carrier's profit-loss situations, as indicated by the upper (shipper) and lower (carrier) limits of the carrier's zone of negotiation, are shown in Table 12-2. The carrier has excess capacity in the shipment move direction.

The table indicates that Piddies will not move, in any shipment size, without a discount. Carrier cost exceeds the value of the transportation service to the Piddie producer, at least on a total cost basis, for all sizes at no discount pricing.

With a 20 percent discount, 500 Piddie shipments net the producer $1 of pure profit (25-cent Piddie × 500 = $125 profit − $124 transportation costs) while the carrier earns $19. Twenty percent discounts also are profitable on 1500 Piddie shipments ($15), if in-house storage is utilized. Total costs (including normal but not

Table 12-2 Shipper-Carrier Situations and the Zones of Negotiation (Piddie market price is $1.50 per unit)

Shipments and Discounts	Trans-portation Cost ($)	Value at Destination (1) ($)	Upper Limits		Lower Limits	
			(1): Less In-House Storage ($)	(1)Less For-Hire Storage ($)	Carrier Total Cost ($)	Carrier Variable Cost (2) ($)
500 Piddies		125	125	125	105	83
No discount	155	−30	Storage is not required.	Storage is not required.	50	72
20% discount	124	1			19	41
40% discount	93	32			−12	10*
50% discount	78	47			−27	−5
1000 Piddies		240	190	160	122	94
No discount	240		−50	−80	118	146
20% discount	192	Storage is required.	−2	−32	70	98
40% discount	144		46	16	22	50
50% discount	120		70	40	−2	26*
1500 Piddies		375	255	195	166	129
No discount	300		−45	−105	134	171
20% discount	240	Storage is required.	15	−45	74	111
40% discount	180		75	15	14	51
50% discount	150		105	45	−16	21*
2000 Piddies		500	320	230	184	140
No discount	400		−80	−170	216	260
20% discount	320	Storage is required.	0	−90	136	180
40% discount	240		80	−10	56	100
50% discount	200		120	30	16	60

(1) Piddie value at destination, *before* transportation cost deduction, derived as follows, for 500 Piddies:

$$\text{Revenue Per Piddie: } \$1.50 \times 500 \text{ Piddies} = \$\ 750$$
$$\text{Variable cost per Piddie: } .75 \times 500 \text{ Piddies} = \$(-)375$$
$$\text{Fixed costs per Piddie: } .50 \times 500 \text{ Piddies} = \$(-)250$$
$$\text{Pure profit per Piddie: } .25 \times 500 \text{ Piddies} = \$\ \ 125$$

For 1000, 1500, and 2000 Piddies, multiply the above revenue and cost figures by 1000, 1500, and 2000, respectively.

(2) Carrier fixed costs are as follows: 500—$22, 1000—$28, 1500—$37, and 2000—$44.

*Covers variable costs and contributes to fixed costs only.

pure profit) are covered on 2000 Piddie shipments, again using in-house storage. The carrier earns pure profits on all size shipments with a 20 percent discount.

Forty and 50 percent discounts mean manufacturer pure profits in all cases except one (2000 Piddies with for-hire storage—$10) and, while the carrier earns profits at the 40 percent discount level on all traffics above 500 lb, it profits giving a 50 percent discount only on 2000-lb shipments.

The most profitable situation for the shipper is 2000 Piddies with a 50 percent discount, using in-house storage; the most profitable for the carrier is 2000 lb with a 20 percent discount.

Piddie Market Price Falls.   Consider what might happen if a new foreign or domestic competitor were to introduce a new product that is a close substitute for a Piddie. For whatever reason, the market price for Piddies drops to $1.45 and the manufacturer considers the change permanent. Table 12-3 reflects the immediate consequences of the price change before either party can make any short- or long-run adjustments.

With the new product price, the shipper needs at least 40 to 50 percent discounts, on all sized shipments, to cover all costs. Specifically, on 500 Piddie shipments, 40 percent nets $7 and 50 percent nets $22, but the carrier covers variable costs only with a 40 percent discount and loses money at 50 percent. On 1000-lb shipments, the shipper nets a pure profit only with a 50 percent discount, while the carrier covers only variable costs in this situation.

On 1500-lb shipments, with in-house storage, the shipper earns normal profit and carrier-pure profits with a 40 percent discount. Fifty percent discount shipments generate pure shipper profits while the carrier contributes to fixed costs only.

A 50 percent discount on 2000 Piddie shipments nets the shipper $20 pure profit, if in-house storage is utilized, while the carrier nets $16 above all costs.

Thus Piddies still should move at the new market price, but only shipments of 1500 and 2000 lbs (and the shipper must use in-house storage), at 40 and 50 percent discounts, respectively, will interest the carrier.

Short-Run Carrier Adjustments.   In response to shipper pleas to help neutralize the effects of the price decline, the carrier does two things: first, reviews the value of its service to the shipper if higher discounts are granted to the movement of Piddies; second, recalculates its costs if the Piddie shipper is willing to make certain adjustments in his or her shipping policies.

Specifically, first the carrier reviews shipper profit-loss possibilities under price discounts of 55, 60, 65, and 70 percent. Second, it recomputes fixed and variable costs of pickup operations, assuming the shipper guarantees three shipments every time the company's driver stops at the Piddie production facility. When three shipments can be picked up by a driver in the same amount of time that a single shipment is handled, lower-rated moves become attractive to the carrier. The results of the carrier's review are shown in Table 12-4.

The higher discounts offer several pure profit opportunities to the shipper, but the carrier, to cover total costs, cannot price below a 55 percent discount. On 500 Piddie shipments, the carrier at best contributes to overhead. Heavier shipments produce pure profits for the carrier with a 55 percent discount, contribute to overhead with 60 percent off (at all three weights) and 65 percent off (on 1000- and

Table 12-3 Shipper-Carrier Situations and the Zones of Negotiation (Piddie market price decreases to $1.45 per unit)

Shipments and Discounts	Transportation Cost ($)	Upper Limits			Lower Limits	
		Value at Destination (1) ($)	(1): Less In-House Storage ($)	(1) Less For-Hire Storage ($)	Carrier Total Cost ($)	Carrier Variable Cost (2) ($)
500 Piddies		100	100	100	105	83
No discount	155	−55	Storage is not required.	Storage is not required.	50	72
20% discount	124	−24			19	41
40% discount	93	7			−12	10*
50% discount	78	22			−27	−5
1000 Piddies		200	140	110	122	94
No discount	240	Storage is required.	−100	−130	118	146
20% discount	192		−52	−82	70	98
40% discount	144		−4	−34	22	50
50% discount	120		20	−10	−2	26*
1500 Piddies		300	180	120	166	129
No discount	300	Storage is required.	−120	−180	134	171
20% discount	240		−60	−120	74	111
40% discount	180		0	−60	14	51
50% discount	150		30	−30	−16	21*
2000 Piddies		400	220	−130	184	140
No discount	400	Storage is required.	−180	−270	216	260
20% discount	320		−100	−190	136	180
40% discount	240		−20	−110	56	100
50% discount	200		20	−70	16	60

(1) Piddie value at destination, *before* transportation cost deduction, derived as follows, for 500 Piddies:

$$\text{Revenue per Piddie: } \$1.45 \times 500 \text{ Piddies} = \$ \quad 725$$
$$\text{Variable cost per Piddie: } .75 \times 500 \text{ Piddies} = \$(-)375$$
$$\text{Fixed cost per Piddie: } .50 \times 500 \text{ Piddies} = \$(-)250$$
$$\text{Pure Profit per Piddie: } .20 \times 500 \text{ Piddies} = \$ \quad 100$$

For 1000, 1500, and 2000 Piddies, multiply the above revenue and cost figures by 1000, 1500, and 200, respectively.

(2) Carrier fixed costs are as follows: 500—$22, 1000—$28, 1500—$37, and 2000—$44.

*Covers variable costs and contributes to fixed costs only.

2000-lb shipments only). Seventy percent discounts do not cover variable costs at any weight.

Therefore, if the shipper is willing to revise shipping policies, he or she can continue to sell Piddies at a pure profit in the market in question, while the carrier can move them profitably. In the long run, however, both shipper and carrier will want to develop lower-cost methods to produce and move Piddies. The shipper, particularly, may benefit from a long-run reevaluation of the situation. Should Piddies be manufactured elsewhere? Have different product components? Be sold in different-sized lots? Transportation-wise, should less-than-truckload shipments be re-

Table 12-4 Shipper-Carrier Situations and the Zones of Negotiation
(Carrier considers new discounts and lower operations costs)

Shipments and Discounts	Transportation Cost ($)	Upper Limits			Lower Limits	
		Value at Destination (1) ($)	(1) Less In-House Storage ($)	(1) Less For-Hire Storage ($)	Carrier Total Cost ($)	Carrier Variable Cost (2) ($)
500 Piddies		100	100	100	89	69
55% discount	85	15	Storage is not required.	Storage is not required.	−4	16
60% discount	62	38			−27	−7
65% discount	54	46			−35	−15
70% discount	46	54			−43	−23
1000 Piddies		200	140	110	107	80
55% discount	132		8	−22	25	52
60% discount	96	Storage is required.	44	14	−11	16
65% discount	84		56	26	−23	4
70% discount	72		68	38	−35	−8
1500 Piddies		300	180	120	145	110
55% discount	165		15	−45	20	55
60% discount	120	Storage is required.	60	0	−25	10
65% discount	105		75	15	−40	−5
70% discount	90		90	30	−55	−20
2000 Piddies		400	220	130	163	121
55% discount	220		0	−90	57	99
60% discount	160	Storage is required.	60	−30	−3	39
65% discount	140		80	−10	−23	19
70% discount	120		100	10	−43	−1

(1) Piddie value at destination, *before* transportation cost deduction, derived as follows, for 500 Piddies:

$$\text{Revenue per Piddie: } \$1.45 \times 500 \text{ Piddies} = \$\ 725$$
$$\text{Variable cost per Piddie: } .75 \times 500 \text{ Piddies} = \$(-)375$$
$$\text{Fixed cost per Piddie: } .50 \times 500 \text{ Piddies} = \$(-)250$$
$$\text{Pure Profit per Piddie: } .20 \times 500 \text{ Piddies} = \$\ 100$$

For 1000, 1500, and 2000 Piddies, multiply the above revenue and cost figures by 1000, 1500, and 2000, respectively.

(2) Carrier fixed costs are as follows: 500—$20, 1000—$27, 1500—$35, and 2000—$42.

*Covers variable costs and contributes to fixed costs only.

placed, at least in certain markets, by less-volume intermodal services, by a consolidator-forwarder operation, or by an in-house system? A single best way to move freight is a rarity in the 1990s' highly competitive transportation freight market.

Costing and Pricing in Excess-Capacity Situations

Transportation is a service, not a product. A service cannot be stored or inventoried as a product can. For example, a commercial airliner has empty seats as the departure hour of 10 a.m. approaches. If the empty seats are not filled, the opportunity to sell capacity is lost forever once the loading gates have been closed. An identical service may be offered at 10 a.m. tomorrow or at one or more times today, but those flights are new-capacity situations.

The empty seats on today's 10 a.m. service represent excess capacity, and most carriers, passenger and freight, have excess capacity at least part of the time on certain routes or runs. To fill this capacity, carriers resort to pricing strategies that often appear totally unrelated to the cost of providing the service. The time frame in which such pricing and costing is used is termed the *immediate run,* and the following example shows how it works.[4]

If the plane mentioned above, with ticketed passengers in place and ready to leave, is treated as a fixed cost, the expense to fly one or a few additional passengers to fill the empty seats should be relatively low, amounting to whatever refreshment is provided plus ticketing preparation, baggage handling, and fuel. These costs, incurred because the airline chooses to fly the fill-in capacity passengers, are the variable costs, and should be covered by a relatively low price. Meanwhile, standby ticket passengers risk not getting to their destinations at personally convenient hours.

If all of the plane's passengers paid the fare that standby passengers paid, in all likelihood total revenues would not cover the run's variable costs, much less fixed costs. However, when used selectively, excess-capacity costing and pricing can fill empty space while contributing to overhead costs. The trick lies in recognizing which costs are fixed and which are variable in excess-capacity situations.

Now using a freight example, consider a train that is ready to leave a terminal. Locomotives are fueled, the train is inspected, the crew is receiving its orders.

Assume that the train is not filled to capacity. Its locomotives could pull several additional cars without significant wear and tear or fuel consumption. Crew size remains unchanged. If a last-minute shipment of cars turns up for a move in the same direction, how should the railroad cost it?

Answer? Exactly as the airline costs its empty seats. The train's cost is fixed. All costs incurred to move the last-minute shipment to and from the train, plus extra fuel used during its move with the original train, are the variable costs. Thus, immediate-run pricing is no different than short-run/long-run pricing: cover variable costs and contribute to overhead, or do not enter the market.

While excess capacity can be found on any route, in any direction the carrier operates, it usually is thought of in connection with backhauls. With the exception of pipelines, which represent one-way transportation, virtually every carrier confronts the problem of empty backhauls. Equipment moving in revenue service in one direction, called the *forward* or *head* haul, automatically generates the need for a return-to-origin move, called the *backhaul,* so that equipment again may be used in the forward haul.

Consider an empty tractor-trailer rig returning from a destination to an origin terminal so that it again may offer service in the forward direction. To return to origin a driver must be paid, fuel consumed, tires worn thinner, some maintenance incurred, etc. The carrier must pay these costs whether or not freight moves in the vehicle during the backhaul move. In effect, these costs are fixed costs.

Meanwhile, if the carrier accepts freight to fill the empty space, all costs associated with moving it become variable, including what normally are treated as fixed costs.

Thus, costing and pricing to fill excess capacity are the same in both the forward hauls and the backhauls. Two challenges face carrier management when it engages in immediate run activity: first, being realistic in classifying costs into fixed and variable categories and pricing accordingly; second, resisting the temptation to offer relatively low immediate-run rates to shippers who do not need them.

Summary

Never before have rate and service negotiations between carriers and shippers been as challenging as they are in the early 1990s. Carrier management must meet increasingly higher service demands while holding the line on price. The savvy shipper knows the transportation options available and, in the best carrot-and-stick tradition, plays the movement vendors off against each other. However, the more cost and market information the two parties have about each other, the better the chances that each will be satisfied with the negotiated service-price package and the greater the probability that each will survive in the long run.

Legalities of Rate Publication

The Deregulation Movement

April 5, 1992, marked the thirtieth anniversary of President John F. Kennedy's transportation message to the Congress, which is regarded by many as the beginning of the deregulation era in U.S. transportation history.[5] The president called for "greater reliance on the forces of competition and less reliance on the restraints of regulation."[6] Just as this message stirred up controversy three decades ago, the issue of transportation regulation and competition remains equally controversial today. After three-quarters of a century of government control, President Kennedy asked Congress to loosen the regulatory shackles affecting carrier initiative. Today, Congress again may be asked to loosen the shackles of a long-standing regulatory fixture, that being the necessity of the carrier to charge, and the shipper to pay, only those rates on file with the Interstate Commerce Commission (ICC). This time, however, it is the entire shipping community doing the asking, and the money involved is estimated at $32 billion.[7]

Whether the responsibility of a guild, a monarchy, or a regulatory agency, the regulation of rates charged by privately owned carriers has been in place for centuries.[8] In this country, rate control dates back to individual states' attempts (the Granger Laws) to neutralize the abuses inherent in monopoly rate-setting by the railroads.[9] On April 5, 1887, Congress reflected the country's dissatisfaction with railroad pricing policies when it passed the Act to Regulate Commerce and, in the very first sections of the legislation, declared unreasonable and discriminatory rates to be unlawful.[10]

As a corollary to Sections 1–4 of the new legislation, rates were required to be published and adhered to strictly. Primarily because only the railroads, and not the shippers, were liable for penalties for Section 6 violations of the act, Congress passed the Elkins Act in 1903, which provided penalties for all parties associated with charging anything other than the published rate.[11]

Although the 1887 legislation demanded reasonable, nondiscriminatory rates, subsequent litigation determined that the Commission had no authority to set rates.[12] This deficiency was corrected partially in 1906, and completed in 1920 when the ICC was given control of maximum, minimum, and exact rates.[13] Virtually identical rate control was extended to regulated motor carriers in 1935 and to airlines in 1938.

President Kennedy made his plea for more competition in 1962, but the idea was not new. Economists had acknowledged the new competition and issued similar pleas previously.[14] Although Kennedy's message did not produce an official new national transportation policy for regulation, it did, in the words of a popular text, "set a new tone, establishing a new goal and a new approach to regulation."[15]

Several reasons can be given for deregulatory rumblings in the early 1970s that resulted in: limited rail deregulation in 1976 (4-R Act); complete airline deregulation in 1977 to 1978 (cargo in 1977 and passengers in 1978); and the Motor Carrier and Staggers Acts of 1980. In terms of the country overall, this era saw the rise of consumerism and the conclusion of the Vietnam conflict, both of which cast a shadow over the effectiveness of government as a protector of the individual and the national interest.

Within the transportation industry, the virtual completion of the National Interstate and Defense Highway System provided new incentives for shippers to move their own goods and to become even less dependent on regulated carriers that offered restricted services at perceived inflated prices. The fuel crisis in 1972 to 1973 spawned congressional hearings that brought to light the inefficient uses of energy due to ICC regulation such as limited carrier operating authorities that resulted in empty backhauls.[16]

Finally, in 1970, history's largest bankruptcy of a privately owned company—the Penn Central Transportation Company—was a particularly sensitive development in view of the Commission's close supervision of the company's founding and operations in the previous decade.

Writers refer to the legislative upheaval of 1976–1982 alternately as "deregulation" or "reregulation."[17] Whichever term is chosen, the result of the various acts was a "new philosophy of more reliance on market competition" that changed "markedly . . . the regulatory environment of all transportation."[18]

Motor carrier deregulation unleashed a frenzy of competitive activities. With virtual freedom of entry, the ability to engage in common and contract carrier services simultaneously and to revise rates on a day's notice, Congress's intent "to promote competitive and efficient transportation services," was realized.[19] With unfettered competition, however, came the not-surprising consequences of such activity, which included unsound pricing policies (rates-setting below variable costs) and the charging of rates not filed with the ICC.

In the former case, carriers quoted noncompensatory rates to expand their market share or minimize losses while in their death throes. A lack of appropriate cost data and price-setting expertise also contributed to unreasonably low rates being charged.[20] The charging of nonfiled rates, on the other hand, merely reflected the vicissitudes of the free market, stated the Commission, and did not represent carrier-shipper efforts "to establish secret, discriminatory rates" in violation of the Interstate Commerce Act.[21]

An example of the latter practice involved Quinn Freight Lines, a common motor carrier and subsidiary of Maislin Industries, U.S., Inc. Quinn negotiated with Primary Steel, Inc. from 1981 into 1983, then charged rates to Primary that were lower than its ICC-filed rates.[22] In fact, Quinn never filed the rates charged to Primary Steel with the ICC during this period.

In 1983, Maislin Industries filed for bankruptcy. The bankrupt estate then billed Primary Steel for the *difference* between the negotiated, nonfiled rates charged for the 1981–83 period *and* Quinn's higher, filed rates for the same period. Primary Steel refused to pay the claim, whereupon the Maislin estate brought suit in Federal District Court.

Both the District Court and the Court of Appeals, supported by the ICC's interpretation of the 1980-amended Interstate Commerce Act, supported Primary Steel. Then on June 21, 1990, in a decision that shocked the world of commerce, the Supreme Court reversed the decisions of the two lower courts and, in effect, the ICC's liberalized approach to the carriers' charging nonfiled rates. The Court stated: "Although the Commission has both the authority and expertise generally to adopt new policies when faced with new developments in the industry . . . it does not have the power to adopt a policy that directly conflicts with its governing statute."[23] Further, "Generalized congressional exhortations to 'increase competition' [stated in the National Transportation Policy—see note 19] cannot provide the ICC [with the] authority to alter well-established statutory filed rate requirements."[24] Finally, on page 2771 of the decision: "If strict adherence to Sections 10761 and 10762 [original Section 6 of the Act] as embodied in the filed rate doctrine has become an anachronism in the wake of the MCA [Motor Carrier Act of 1980], it is the responsibility of Congress to modify or eliminate these sections."

In a rousing dissent, Justice John P. Stevens, with Justice William H. Rhenquist concurring, argued that "even wearing his famous blinders, old Dobbin would see through the tired arguments" used by the majority in supporting the "filed rate doctrine."[25] Stevens concluded: "The Court's analysis is plausible only if read as a historical excursus about a statute that no longer exists. Nothing more than blind adherence to language in cases that have nothing to do with the present situation supports today's results."[26]

Justice Stevens' interpretational fireworks notwithstanding, shippers continued to be liable for the difference between filed and nonfiled rates charged by carriers, as they had been since 1935 and as they remain today.

The high court's decision united shippers in an effort to have Congress repeal the filed rate doctrine retroactively.[27] In mid-1992, however, chances appeared slim of such legislation being enacted, a major reason being opposition by the Teamsters Union, whose members often were the largest creditors of the bankrupt carriers.[28]

While shipper groups worked to find a legislative solution to resolve the claims against them—the results of carrier trustee–shipper litigation, in particular—two circuit court of appeals decisions in June, 1992, produced decisions that some observers have argued will eliminate the need for such a solution.

The first, released June 17 by the Ninth Circuit Court of Appeals, prohibited the trustee of Transcon Lines, once the twelfth largest motor carrier in the U.S., from collecting as much as $1 billion in undercharges; and, it was predicted for carriers as a whole, from collecting $25 billion or more from shippers.[29]

In this case, Transcon's discounted rates were filed with the ICC, but over 98 percent were published in code numbers that identified the shipper receiving the discount. The codes were known only by Transcon and were not filed with the Commission, nor were they available for public inspection. The district court declared the coded rates invalid, thereby opening the way for Transcon's trustee to collect the higher rates used by the carrier.[30]

In its reversal of the district court's decision, the circuit court admitted "to being troubled by the ICC's policy of allowing codes to identify shippers" and the policy's encouragement of secrecy and the potential for discrimination in rate-setting.[31] Nonetheless, the court found the discounted rates legal, meaning the shippers using them had paid in full. The attorney for Transcon's trustee stated that an appeal was "likely."[32]

The second case was decided June 26 by the Fifth Circuit Court of Appeals. In a familiar scenario, the estate of a bankrupt carrier, Advance United Expressways, Inc. (United), billed the Eastman Kodak Company (Kodak) for the difference between rates charged Kodak *and* rates filed with the ICC. Kodak challenged the reasonableness of United's filed rates. In August 1989, United sued Kodak in federal district court for over $450,000 in undercharges. The ICC, meanwhile, found United's applications of discounts to be unreasonable.[33]

The district court delayed United's suit against Kodak until the Supreme Court's decision in the *Maislin* case, since the two undercharge suits were similar. The Maislin decision upheld the filed rate doctrine, as discussed earlier, but did state that the doctrine could be overturned if ICC-filed rates were found to be unreasonable, which Kodak was arguing in its dispute with United. On the basis of Maislin, however, the district court ruled in favor of United, completely rejecting Kodak's challenge as to the unreasonableness of United's rates.

The circuit court reversed the district court, stating, first, that the issue of reasonableness of ICC-filed rates must be considered *and* that the ICC was the agency of primary jurisdiction in ruling on rate reasonableness.

Second, and perhaps of equal importance, shippers did not have to pay overcharge claims to carrier estates *before* filing suits challenging reasonableness of rates, which constituted a break with traditional practice. Previously, shippers had paid the disputed rate, and then if the ICC ruled in the shipper's favor, the amount paid in excess of what the ICC determined to be reasonable, i.e., a *reparation,* was refunded to the shipper by the carrier by court order.[34]

In bankruptcy cases, however, the court recognized that once monies had been paid to a carrier's estate, there was virtually no chance of a refund, no matter how valid the shipper's case. This represented a reversal of an earlier ruling by the same circuit court, and generally followed the thinking of other circuit courts. In the one exception, the Fourth Circuit Court of Appeals had ruled that the shippers must "pay first," but this decision had been accepted for review by the Supreme Court.[35]

Thus, recent court decisions have given shippers hope in rate discount litigation with bankrupt carrier trustees. However, these decisions probably will be reviewed by the Supreme Court. Meanwhile, legislation to modify or repeal the filed rate doctrine faces an uncertain future in Congress. One thing is certain: motor carriers must charge and shippers must pay only rates on file with the ICC. There are various methods by which shippers can be assured they are being charged filed rates. To understand these methods, a brief review of rate-filing (publication) requirements, by the different modes, is warranted.

Filing (Publication) Requirements—Motor

Motor common carrier rates must be filed with the ICC and charged to the shipper on shipments moving under those rates. Documents containing filed rates are called *tariffs.* Tariffs are published by rate bureaus on behalf of member carriers or by individual carriers themselves.

Bureaus publish a range of tariffs, including those of general applicability affecting the movement of all commodities, by all carriers for their customers within the areas covered by the bureau. Also published are tariffs that apply to one or a few specifically named commodities, moving between a restricted number of origins and destinations, by one carrier for a single shipper. Rates may be nondiscounted, discounted, or published as a basis for discounts. An advantage of using rate bureaus is knowing that all bureau tariffs are filed automatically with the ICC.[36]

Carrier tariffs are published for individual and multiple shipper accounts and include rates that may have initial discounts built in.[37] Shippers concerned about proper tariff filings with the ICC can utilize one of several so-called "watch services" located in the ICC building in Washington, D.C. For a fee, these services will assure clients that rate-filing requirements have been met.[38] With over 40,000 common motor carriers, each obligated to file their rates, shippers are justified in checking to be sure they are paying legal rates.

Before May 5, 1992, motor contract carrier rates were spelled out in individual, written instruments, called contracts, that detailed the obligations of both shippers and carriers in specific reference to "a series of shipments over a stated period of time."

In a decision released May 5, the Commission deregulated motor contract carriage, stating that its regulations no longer were required by the Interstate Commerce Act. This decision followed a sequence of events whereby motor contract carriage became subject only to the requirements of federal and state laws of contracts. The decision reflected a complete turnaround in this country's approach to the use of contracts in highway transportation, as indicated by congressional statute and its interpretation by the ICC.[39]

From the initial federal motor carrier regulation of 1935 to the Motor Carrier Act of 1980, transportation policy had been designed to protect motor common carriers from contract carriers. This has been accomplished by limiting the number of shippers a contract carrier can serve and by requiring that contracts detailing the services to be provided and rates to be charged be filed with the Commission.[40]

Under the 1980 legislation, however, and in keeping with the congressional change from a policy of protectionism and restraint to one of competitiveness and flexibility, the Commission removed its restrictions on the number of contract shippers per carrier, the number of commodities carried per contract, and the extent of geographical areas served.[41] Further, carriers now could offer both common and contract services, called *dual operations,* to their customers. Warming to its task of promoting competition, the Commission later decided that neither the written contracts for service nor the rates charged by the carriers for those services had to be filed.[42]

On May 5, the ICC dropped the written requirement for contracts and the specific information that had to be contained in carrier–shipper contracts. This left the agency's limited role in the regulation of motor contract carriage, in its words, to distinguishing "between statutory common and contract carriage when called upon to do so in a particular situation."[43] Referring to this difference, the ICC wrote in its decision: " . . . it is the ongoing relationship, service commitment, and legally enforceable commercial link between a carrier and its shippers . . . that render contract carriage inherently different from common carriage service alternatives. . . . It is the totality of the circumstances surrounding any particular movement, not the presence or absence of a written contract, that determines whether the transportation is contract carriage."[44]

How soon the Commission will assume this limited role was blurry in mid-1992, because substantial opposition to further contract carriage deregulation was registered during the agency's hearings on the matter by regulated common carriers, rate bureaus, the Teamsters Union, and others. Commissioner J. J. Simmons noted in his dissent: "At each stage of this proceeding, a majority of commentors has favored retention or limited modification of our contract carrier regulations. These parties have advanced sound, practical reasons and policy considerations which demonstrate the need for Commission guidelines on valid motor contract carriage."[45] Vice Chairman Gail C. McDonald perhaps best summarized the majority's policy when she wrote in her dissent: "In opting for repeal (of contract carrier regulation) rather than modification, the majority has ignored the call from the parties for guidance and direction in favor of a philosophy that the only good regulation is no regulation."[46]

On June 12, 1992, 10 motor carrier rate bureaus, joined by the Regular Common Motor Conference of the American Trucking Associations, Inc., and the Teamsters Union, filed suit against the ICC's decision and asked that existing contract carrier regulations remain in effect until the court's review had been completed.[47] This move had been predicted by industry observers.[48]

To summarize: In mid-1992, motor carrier shippers, to keep their transactions with regulated carriers from becoming embroiled in expensive litigation, were warned to be sure that the common carrier rates being charged them were filed with the ICC and, if contract services were used, that the contracts were in writing and the services distinctly different from those of common carriers.

Filing Requirements—Rail

Compared to motor carriers, the legalities surrounding railroad rates are relatively free from litigation. Rail carriers provide three types of freight service in a legal sense: regulated common, contract, and exempt.

Before the Staggers Act of 1980 was passed, virtually all rail traffic moved under close ICC regulation, with all rates published and subject to the filed rate doctrine. Under the Staggers legislation, contract rate-making was not only allowed but encouraged; several freight categories, namely unprocessed agricultural commodities (except grain) and intermodal traffic, were declared exempt from economic controls; and rates on most remaining freight were allowed to be set according to market forces.[49]

By mid-1992, the Association of American Railroads estimated that close to 60 percent of all rail freight traffic moved under contracts, as opposed to tariff rates.[50] Contracts were used in pricing 86 percent of coal tonnage moved by the carriers (the industry's leading commodity), 54 percent of chemicals, and 40 percent of grain traffic.[51] Each rail carrier–shipper contract had to be filed with the Commission. Each contract consisted of a confidential and a nonconfidential section. The latter was open for public inspection, the former was not. In that year, the Commission recommended doing away with the requirement that the confidential section of the contract be filed with the agency.[52] The Commission stated that some 70,000 contracts were filed annually, and its storage space was shrinking. Under its proposal, the Commission would continue to require filing of the nonconfidential section of contracts and would retain authority to subpoena confidential sections if required in carrier–shipper disputes.[53]

Intermodal freight traffic, primarily the coordination of the rail and motor modes (called *trailer* or *container-on-flat car*, TOFC/COFC), was the rail industry's fastest-growing traffic segment. The service was offered under a series of plans, with price a function of several service variables, including trailer or container ownership, provision of pickup and/or delivery, and transit time.[54] Each railroad published its own intermodal rates. On joint services involving two or more railroads, shippers were advised to contact the origin carrier for price and service offerings.[55]

While disputes regarding railroad pricing strategies arose in the early years following passage of the Staggers Act, most had been resolved by the early 1990s and the trend toward deregulated rail rate-making seemed assured. Other rail issues such as abandonment, labor relations, and safety seemed more important than pricing strategies of the carriers.

Filing Requirements—Air, Pipe, Barge

Air.   Since air cargo service was deregulated in 1977, there are no rate filing requirements with any government agency for any air freight carrier. The Airline Tariff Publishing Company (ATPCO), which publishes tariffs for joint passenger–cargo carriers such as Northwest, American, United, and Delta, warns users at the beginning of its tariffs:

> This tariff is not published pursuant to state or federal regulation requirements. It is published on behalf of the participating airlines to provide information to the public. ATPCO cannot guarantee that specific rates or rules will be in effect on the date shown or continue in effect until the next issue of this publication.[56]

ATPCO's set of cargo tariffs, collectively, covers rates and rules governing the application of those rates on both cargo (including individual package, bulk, and container-sized shipments) and small packages, by one or more major trunk and/or commuter airlines, including pickup and delivery charges as appropriate.[57]

All-freight carriers, including Federal, United Parcel, Airborne, Burlington, and Emery, issue their own individual tariffs.[58]

Some discount programs exist that apply to all shippers; for example, Delta's Density Discount—"special discounts for shipments with a density of 25 pounds per cubic foot or more."[59] Depending on the carriers' capacity situation, discounting for select shippers similar to motor carrier practices also may occur.[60] Contracts sometimes are used, but this is the exception not the rule in air freight pricing.[61]

Pipe.   In the oil pipeline business, the carrier and the shipper usually are the same; that is, most of the major pipeline companies are owned by the oil companies that patronize them.[62] Pipelines that move products belonging to shippers other than their owners are regulated as common carriers, and each company individually must file its rates with the Federal Energy Regulatory Commission. No departures may be made from these rates under any circumstances.

Some carriers offer incentive rates for large tenders of product, but this pricing practice is not universal. No discounting exists in pipeline transportation as in trucking, for there is rarely excess capacity.[63] Pipeline is one-way transportation.

The reason for strict regulation of the mode is the perceived need to provide reasonably priced pipeline service to independent refiners so that they may compete with their megasized competitors who otherwise would shut them out. In reality, regulation is limited to trucklines and certain large gathering lines. Small-diameter feeder or gathering lines from individual wells to larger gathering or trunkline pumping stations are treated as proprietary and are not available for the public's use.[64]

Barge. Although barge transportation service operated over this country's inland waterway system has been regulated by the ICC since 1940, over 90 percent of it is exempt from economic regulation.[65] In 1992 only 4 to 6 percent of barge traffic, referred to as "mark and count" freight, must be moved according to rates filed with the ICC.[66] Since the last domestic water carrier rate bureau, the Waterways Freight Bureau of Fairfax, Virginia, closed "eight to ten years ago," rates are filed by the individual carriers charging them.[67] Barge carrier-shipper contracts, also subject to ICC scrutiny at one time, now presumably are left strictly to the negotiating skills of the parties involved and the requirements of contract law.[68]

Filing Requirements—International

Water. Two types of rates exist in international transportation: contract rates that are exempt from economic controls, and a close equivalent to domestic filed common carrier rates. Contract rates, called *charters,* apply to shiploads of freight and are negotiated on a per-voyage (voyage charter) or longer (time charter) basis, with price and service terms being strictly a function of the demand for and supply of ships in the worldwide marketplace.[69]

Liner service is international water's equivalent to common carrier transportation. Liner rates are set by rate bureaus, called *steamship conferences,* whose rates must be filed with the U.S. Federal Maritime Commission (FMC). Discounts are available through the conferences, depending on capacity available in the shipping area covered by each conference. These reductions also must be filed with the FMC.[70]

Air. International air cargo rates are set primarily by a cartel called the International Air Transport Association (IATA), located in Montreal, Canada, whose rates then must be approved by the governments of the countries to and from which the rates apply.

Airlines serving international routes do so only with the consent of the government of each nation served, through what are called bilateral agreements. Consequently, rates charged can be called *bilaterally approved rates.*

U.S. air carriers in the past have been frustrated by IATA rates, feeling they were too high to promote growth and development of air cargo in global markets. Many foreign carriers, on the other hand, are nationalized companies whose goals are national prestige and world recognition of the owning country. These carriers do not seek profits or compete for market share. IATA rates somehow must compromise between these differing objectives.[71]

Mexico and Canada. As to the United States' portion of rates between this country and our trading partners north and south, the same rules and regulations apply as to domestic rates discussed previously. Individual carriers should be consulted to determine what special services are offered by each one to these countries.[72]

Interchange of freight equipment, long a problem in United States–Mexico motor carrier transportation, is being resolved as an increasing number of U.S. carriers are forming partnerships with Mexican-owned companies. New United States–Mexico intermodal services also are removing some of the traditional obstacles to a freer-flowing commerce between the two countries.[73]

Summary

In 1980, deregulation of transportation rates replaced pricing by bureaucrats with pricing by marketplace, and the repercussions still are being felt 12 years later. One thing is certain: More opportunities exist for shippers and carriers to negotiate innovative rate and service schemes than ever before. However, a word of warning to both parties may be in order. The ongoing undercharge controversy in motor carriage, and the continuing shakeout of firms in both the motor and air modes, indicate that some degree of appreciation of shippers' and carriers' long-term goals is advisable if their relationship is to be enduring and financially satisfactory.

Rate Determination and Publication

Class Rates—The Simplification Devices

The task of publishing a rate to cover every possible commodity that moves in commerce, from every conceivable origin to every conceivable destination, at an amount of money such that the carrier covers its costs while the shipper profits in the marketplace, boggles the mind. Yet rate-making is centuries old, and its principles are relatively simple and quite logical.

Rate-making is made manageable through the use of three simplification devices. The first, the *classification,* organizes the vast array of products that shippers tender to carriers into a limited number of categories, called *classes,* according to the ease or difficulty of movement.

The second device, the *rate group guide,* reduces the number of possible origins-and-destinations to a reasonable quantity by having rates to and from all points in an area apply to and from a single point within that area, called a *rate base point.*

The third device, the *rate scale,* relates the results of the classification procedure to the distance a product moves, and assigns a shipment transportation charge that, ideally, is reasonable and satisfactory to both shipper and carrier. The rate scale incorporates the cost and value factors analyzed in the first section of this chapter and, together with the Classification and Group Guide, reflects a systematic approach to establishing transportation rates.

Classification. The earliest classification activities can be traced to the 1700s, when wagoners, operating over this country's primitive roads, assigned rates to "light" goods as compared to "heavy" goods and assigned higher rates to the former. Steamship companies on the Mississippi and Ohio rivers used the same commodity differentiation in the early 1880s.[74] Since those times, the carriers and their representatives, called *classification committees,* aided by shippers and since 1887 overseen by the Interstate Commerce Commission (ICC), have crafted a relatively simple, if thorough, uniform document that provides a basis for setting rates on every commodity that moves in commerce.

The classification reflects the process of categorizing commodities according to each one's shipping characteristics. These characteristics include the bulkiness of the product (its density), the ease with which it can be damaged, and its degree of appeal to thieves, since the carrier is liable for safe delivery to the receiver. Any special handling requirements may entail above-ordinary costs, and so enters the classification process. The need to assign a rate to over a million possible products is thus reduced to assigning rates to a dozen or so product categories called *classes.*

Each class can be considered a *rating,* with *class* and *rating* having the same meaning and being used interchangeably. To each class or rating, a rate is assigned. The rate comes from a different publication than the classification. The rate comes from a *tariff.*

Therefore, in rate-making, two important distinctions must be made: ratings of commodities are found in a *classification,* and the rates assigned to the ratings are published in *tariffs.* A rating is a classification number only; a rate is a dollar amount that, multiplied by the weight of a shipment, will give a total charge for that shipment.

Class 100 is the base to which all other classes are anchored. When a commodity is classified as "class 200," this means it will move at twice the rate of a commodity rated at class 100. Herein lies the beauty of the rate-simplification procedure. Once a rate has been assigned to class 100, rates are immediately established for all classes of freight. These rates are a percentage of the class 100 rate, as reflected in the class number or rating.

For example the railroad classification, called the Uniform Freight Classification (UFC), uses 31 classes for all commodities moved by rail. On the other hand, the National Motor Freight Classification (NMFC) employs 23 classes. The classes used by both classifications are: 400, 300, 250, 200, 175, 150, 125, 110, *100,* 92.5, 85, 77.5, 70, 65, 60, 55, 50; and for volume shipments only, classes 45, 40, 37.5, and 35.[75]

The NMFC has a class 500 category for particularly valuable goods. The UFC has classes 32.5, 30, 27.5, 25, 22.5, 20, 17.5, 16, 14.5, and 13 for low-value commodities that tend to move only by rail.[76] The NMFC equivalent for the low-rated, rail-oriented commodities is class 35.

What is the secret to the classification procedure? In the words of Thurman Van Metre, Professor Emeritus of Columbia University:

> The consideration upon which a classification committee leans most heavily in reaching a decision as to what rating an article should receive is comparison. The

whole process of classification is largely one of comparison, and the object of the committee is to put into the same class articles which from a transportation point of view are alike.

It is impossible to make any hard and fast rules which a committee can follow in reaching a decision. The members must use their best collective judgment and endeavor to the best of their ability to give each article a rating which is fair and reasonable and which does not involve any unjust discrimination against some other article.[77.]

Thus, no exact definition or formula exists for classifying freight. Consider the following group of 10 commodities, keeping in mind the amount of space consumed compared to the weight of each product, the ease with which it can be damaged, and/or its attractiveness to thieves. All are rated class 100 in the NMFC and are packaged in boxes.

Toasters	Bathtubs, china or earthenware
Guns or rifles, air	Razors, safety, not gold-plated
Flasks, glass, leather-covered	Rooms (sauna), knocked-down (KD)
Life preservers, pneumatic	Spark Plugs, NOI, card-mounted
Adding machines, NOI*	Umbrellas, NOI, folded

Some of the 10 commodities have additional listings according to the way they are shipped. For example, umbrellas shipped set-up (not folded), are class 400; sauna rooms, set up or assembled, are class 200; and spark plugs, not card-mounted, are class 85.[79]

The type of container is important, because the carrier is liable for damages while the product is in its care, and physical damage can be caused by the container used. All 10 items are packed in boxes, but one's concept of a box may differ from that of the NMFC, which needs 11 pages to define the qualifications of a box.[80] Over 200 pages of the NMFC, approximately one-quarter of the document, are devoted to defining the requirements of various shipping containers.[81]

To further understand the classification process, consider the following 10 commodities, again packed in boxes, all of which are rated class 200.[82] By way of comparison, note that these commodities will move at twice the rate of those on the first product list. Their shipping characteristics, particularly their density and susceptibility to damage, warrant such rates. Do you agree?

Cookies, fortune	Afterburners, jet aircraft
Life rafts, NOI	Skeletons (anatomical specimens)
Bones, human, NOI, prepaid	Lanterns, paper, other than flat
Tripods, camera, set up (SU)	Sunglasses, on cards
Curios, NOI	Sponges, natural, NOI

Finally, 10 commodities rated class 50 are listed, to further illustrate the results of the freight-classification process. These commodities will move at one-half the rate of the class 100 group, again based on their shipping characteristics:

---

*NOI means "not more specifically described herein."[78]

Boxes, water meter, iron

Clay, ball or china (Kaolin)

Coal or coal briquettes, NOI

Cullet (broken glass)

Creosote, pitch or tar

Gravel, NOI

Grits, NOI, groats or hominy

Tracks, including shoe nails, NOI

Material, incendiary bomb extinguishing, dry

Tanks, septic, reinforced concrete, KD

Undoubtedly, the class 50 items reflect their ability to withstand damage and the fact that thieves should not be interested in such relatively low-value products.[83] Because they do not damage easily, many class 50 commodities do not require containers. Examples include iron or steel (I/S) boiler plates, reinforced concrete beams, I/S circus grandstand parts, highway guardrails, wood logs, and railway car couplers.[84]

The Future. The classification of new products, and reclassification of existing ones as the result of carrier-shipper discussions, is an ongoing process. Since commodity ratings lead directly to rates being established, rating negotiations can be just as important as rate negotiations. A lower rating often can be obtained for a product merely by changing its packaging. On the other hand, shippers have been shocked by rate increases when, in efforts to merchandise a product differently, a new packaging method has placed the product in a higher class. It is advisable to check the classification before making any changes in packaging procedures.

Several large shippers argue that the classification is outdated and no longer has a purpose in distribution. These companies usually have entered into long-term partnerships with a select number of carriers, where the shipping characteristics of the commodities moved are well known by each of the parties and rates are negotiated without going through the usual classification procedure.[85]

Another way to circumvent the classification is to use Freight, All Kinds (FAK) rates, where a single rate is negotiated that applies to a group of products moving in single shipments.[86] Although long-term partnerships and the use of FAK rates are growing in number, they represent the exception and not the rule in carrier rate-making in the early 1990s.

Rate Groups. The second simplification device is the assignment of a single point to represent all points in an area for the purposes of rate application. That is, an area, such as a state, is divided into sub-areas. Then a single point within the sub-area (usually the largest shipping point) is selected. This point is called a *rate base point* (RBP). Rates to and from the RBP apply not only to and from the RBP but to and from all locations within the sub-area.

Motor RBPs. The Southern Motor Carriers Rate Conference (SMC), a leading rate bureau and tariff-publishing agency located in Atlanta, publishes RBPs for all localities in its Rate Group Tariff, SMC 115. However, particularly in motor carrier tariffs, the RBP method of origin-destination reduction is being replaced by the use of three-digit zip codes found in the U.S. Postal Service zip code directory. The distance between zip codes is determined using the Household Goods Movers Mileage Tariff ICC HGB 100 series, which represents "the shortest regularly traveled available highway route" between code areas.[87] Distances between RBPs and zip code areas are published in rate tariffs and are termed *rate basis numbers* (RBNs).

Rail RBPs. A railroad rate group area covers "a square of about 40 miles," or

1600 sq mi.[88] However, exceptions to this rule do exist. Tennessee, with 41,797 sq mi of land surface, has approximately 90 rail RBPs, or one for every 40-plus sq mi.[89] The distances between railroad RBPs "generally speaking, are the shortest workable mileages over which carload traffic can be handled without transfer of lading."[90] Rail distances also are published in rate tariffs and termed rate basis numbers.

Rate versus Governing (Support) Tariffs. So far in this chapter, tariffs have been mentioned only in connection with the publication of rates. This overlooks the other important function of these documents, which is the publication of rules, regulations, and other pertinent information surrounding the application of rates given in the rate tariffs. Rate group guides or tariffs are considered *governing tariffs.*

Rate Scale. The third simplification device relates the classification of a commodity to the distance it moves, to determine a rate per weight unit (usually per 100 lb or hundredweight) for its movement. Because this rate applies to a class of goods, it is called a *class rate.* A class rate exists for every product, at any weight, between any two points in the country.

The most famous rate scale prescribed by the ICC was the result of a thorough investigation, initiated in 1939, of railroad pricing practices. The study was not concluded until 1952, when the Uniform Freight Classification (UFC) was published along with the Docket 28300 rate scale.[91] The rationale and characteristics of this rate scale underlie all rate scales in effect today and, therefore, are worth reviewing briefly.

1. *Use of distance blocks.* "In the typical distance-rate system (scale) the rates do not change with each additional mile of distance. Instead a distance-block system is used, with blocks varying in length." In Docket 28300, "5-mile blocks were used for the first 100 miles, then 10-mile blocks up to a distance of 240 miles, then 25-mile blocks up to 2200 miles, and 50-mile blocks" up to 3000 miles.[92]

2. *Use of the tapering principle.* "Most distance rates are constructed on the tapering principle; that is, the rates increase with distance, but not as rapidly as distance increases."[93] The original Docket 28300 scale (it has been increased many times since 1952) increased, or tapered, is shown in Table 12-5.

Locklin discusses the tapering rate scale: "There are several reasons for not making freight rates increase in exact proportion to distance. In the first place, terminal costs are the same regardless of the length of the haul. The longer the haul, the

Table 12-5 Docket 28300 Rate Scale: Major and Individual Mileage Blocks, with Per-100-Pound and Per-Mile Rates at Block Mileage Points

Major Blocks (Mi)	Major Block Size (Mi)	Individual Block Size (Mi)	Number of Individual Blocks	Rate		
				At Mileage Point	Per 100 lb ($)	Per mile ($)
0–100	100	5	20	100	1.14	0.01140
100–240	140	10	14	240	1.62	0.00675
240–800	560	20	28	800	3.05	0.00381
800–2200	1400	25	56	2200	5.85	0.00266
2200–3000	800	50	16	3000	7.45	0.00248

Table 12-6 Item 15000 Rate Scale: Major and Individual Mileage Blocks, with Per-100-Pound and Per-Mile Rates at Block Mileage Points

Major Blocks (Mi)	Major Block Size (Mi)	Individual Block Size (Mi)	Number of Individual Blocks	Rate		
				At Mileage Point	Per 100 lb ($)	Per mile ($)
0–40	40	40	1	40	12.19	0.305
40–100	60	20	3	100	15.40	0.154
100–800	700	25	28	800	32.18	0.040
800–1500	700	50	14	1500	44.99	0.030

greater the distance over which the constant terminal cost can be spread." Another "reason for the use of the tapering principle is to prevent the rates from restricting the movement of long-distance traffic."[94]

Motor carrier rate bureaus adopted the 28300 scale in many areas, except where "competitive situations" did not permit it.[95] Motor carrier rate scales later were separated into less-than-truckload (LTL) and truckload (TL) versions, then into weight groups within those two basic segments.[96]

Table 12-6 shows a recent motor carrier rate scale for class 100 rates, published by the Southern Motor Carriers Rate Conference (SMC) for LTL shipments weighing less than 500 lb. The rates are significantly higher than the 28300 scale rates (as expected), the mileage blocks differ, and the maximum distance is 1500 mi due to limited coverage by the rate bureau. However, the tapering principle is obvious when comparing Tables 12-5 and 12-6. Figure 12-2 is a graph of the rate scale and shows how the rates taper as distance increases. The straight line is included for comparison, and plots a scale based on a uniform rate increase of 3 cents per mile for the same distance.[97]

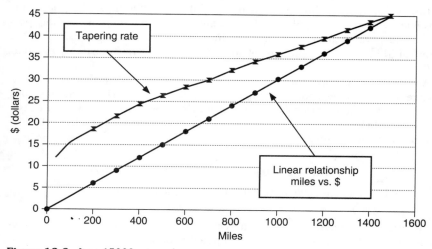

Figure 12-2. Item 15000 rate scale.

Table 12-7 Determination of Rate Breaks: Item 15000 Rate Scale, Class 100 Rates, 81- to 100-Mile Block

(1)	(2)	(3)*	(4)	(5)*	(6)*
Rate (LR) per 100 lb ($)	Minimum Weight at which rate applies (MW) (lb)	Minimum Total Charge using (LR) Rate ($)	Higher Rate (HR) ($)	Weight Break (RBW) (lb)	Percent off Highest Rate
15.40	290.9†	44.80†	—	—	—
14.26	500	71.30	15.40	463.1	—
10.52	1000	105.20	14.26	737.7	7.4
7.78	2000	155.60	10.52	1,479.1	31.7
6.10	5000	305.00	7.78	3,920.3	49.5
6.06	10,000	606.00‡	6.10‡	9,213.1	60.4
2.81	20,000	562.00	6.10	9,213.1	60.4
2.25	30,000	675.00	2.81	24,021.35	85.4
2.02	40,000	808.00	2.25	35,911.1	86.9

*(3) = (1) × (2); (5) = (3) ÷ (4); (6) = [(4) − (1)] ÷ (4).

†Shipments weighing less than 290.9 lb move at a minimum charge of $44.80. The $15.40/100 lb rate applies to shipments whose total charge is between $44.80 and $71.30 (first RBW).

‡The rate of $6.06/100 lb, 10,000 minimum weight, is a "paper rate," that is it is published but not used, because the 20,000-lb rate (at $2.80/100 lb) is cheaper ($562 versus $606). The $6.06 rate is used only where the carrier indicates specifically that it does not participate in the 20,000-lb rate, in which case the rate giving the higher total charge (the $6.60 rate) would apply.

3. *Use of weight groups.* For reasons of cost and competition, motor carriers list a series of rates for each commodity class and distance block, according to different possible shipment weights. Rates are shown in Table 12-7 for shipments weighing more than 500 lb. An origin-to-destination distance of from 81 to 100 mi is used in the table.[98]

Rate Breaks. With different rates being applied to different weight groups, it is possible for two rates to apply to a single shipment. When this occurs, the rate producing the lower total charge (rate × weight) will apply. For example, in Table 12-7, a rate of $14.26/100 lb applies to 500-lb shipments, and a rate of $10.52/100 lb to 1000-lb shipments.

Assume a 950-lb shipment is tendered for movement. In determining the total charge, the 500-lb rate should be applied, at least for starters. Here, since 950 lb is close to 1000 lb, rating the shipment as if it actually weighed 1000 lb and consequently would move at the lower rate should be computed. The results of the two computations are as follows:

At actual weight: 950 lb at $14.26/100 lb = $135.47.

905 lb rated as 1000 lb: 1000 lb at $10.52/100 lb = $105.20.

Here the lower rate applies. Whenever multiple rates apply to a traffic movement, the rate break point should be computed to be sure the correct rate is used. To determine the rate break point use:

$$\text{Higher} \atop \text{rate (HR)}} \times {\text{rate break} \atop \text{weight (RBW)}} = {\text{lower} \atop \text{rate (LR)}} \times {\text{minimum weight at which the} \atop \text{lower rate applies (MW)}}$$

In this example:

$$\$14.26 \times RBW = \$10.52 \times 1000 \text{ lb}$$

$$RBW = 737.7 \text{ lb}$$

Therefore, shipments weighing less than 737.7 lb will use the $14.26/100 lb rate; all shipments weighing more, at least up to the next rate break point (1479.1 lb), will use the $10.52 rate. Rate break points between all rates are shown in the next-to-last column of Table 12-7.

The table also demonstrates the cost advantages of shipping in large quantities, as was shown when shipping Piddies. The table lists the percentages off the less-than-500-lb rate for each rate group. The savings range from 7.4 to 86.9 percent, up to 60.4 percent on LTL shipments (shipments weighing less than 10,000 lb) and 86.9 percent on TL quantities. Of course, not every shipper is in a position to move truckload quantities and, as previously discussed in the Piddies example, storage cost at destination point can neutralize the savings in movement costs.

Looking up a Class Rate. The three simplication devices, the classification, the rate group, and the rate scale, now will be used to determine a class rate. Assume that the commodity to be rated is one of the class 100 products listed earlier, toasters. The shipment consists of 500 lb of toasters, to move from Greensboro, NC, to Mobile, AL. Documents needed are the NMFC and SMC Tariff 500-D (Southern Class Tariff).

If the rating for toasters is not known, find it in two steps using the NMFC. First, find the item number for toasters in the Index to Articles (item 63360). Then find its rating and any special instructions concerning its movement (page 436, class 100 LTL; there are none, if packing conforms to NMFC rules).

Next find the three-digit zip codes for Greensboro (274) and Mobile (366) in a zip code directory. With these codes find the distance (the *rate basis number,* or RBN) between 274 and 366 in SMC Tariff 500-D. Page 53 shows it to be 703 mi.

Finally, using the rate scale in the same tariff, with an RBN of 703, a class 100 product and shipment size of 500 lb, page 81 indicates a rate of $28.31/100 lb. Total charge to ship the toasters: $28.31/100 lb × 5 (100-lb units) = $141.55.

Locating the toaster rate and determining the shipment total charge seemed simple enough. In reality, a rate analyst's job can be tedious and frustrating. Rates are, in effect, laws of the land, and like other laws they must be written in such a way that misinterpretations are minimized. Thus both the publishing and use of rates, and the specifying of conditions under which they apply, are exacting, complicated tasks.

Expertise in analyzing rates can be expensive to learn, and consequently to hire. In the toaster example, the person seeking the rate must be familiar with the National Motor Freight Classification, its ratings and its rules. Knowledge of class rates, and the fact that a rate bureau, the Southern Motor Carriers Rate Conference, publishes class rates from Greensboro to Mobile, is necessary. In Tariff 500-D, due to the competitive nature of motor carriage and the fact that competing carriers cannot act collectively to set rates (as they once did), ten class 100 rates apply between the city-pairs in that document alone. The rate expert knows which one to apply. Shippers must know this rate also or the law may be violated, and if they are caught, fines may be assessed and/or litigation initiated, with its attendant cost.

This is a reason many shippers farm out their carrier-rated bills to professional rate auditors to be sure they have not been over- or undercharged.[99] It also is a reason many companies are interested in creating partnerships with a few reliable carriers, so that rates charged can be reduced in number and complexity.

So far, only class rates have been addressed. In terms of complexity, these rates pale when compared to special rates established for specific shippers or commodity groups. Such rates are known collectively as *commodity rates*.

Commodity Rates

Commodity rates traditionally have been established to attract freight, usually in truckload or volume lots, that the carrier felt could be moved, but only at rates lower than class rates. This situation continues today when a number of competitors are willing to lower rates to obtain the traffic, or when it is felt the commodity cannot bear existing rates and still be sold profitably in the marketplace. Commodity rates continue to be published, but their importance has declined since deregulation in 1980, being replaced by discounting and contract rate-making.

Although commodity rates usually apply to volume movements, the following examples using 500-lb shipments of class-100-rated commodities reveal significant differences between commodity and class LTL rates.

■ From Atlanta, GA, to Chattanooga, TN, 133 mi, on corrugated paper boxes, KD flat, the class rate is $15.86/100 lb versus a commodity rate of $8.14. Thus, a savings of 48.7 percent is realized—or could it be termed a *discount* of 48.7 percent?

■ From Louisville to Memphis, 376 mi, the class 100 rate is $22.18 on "500 pounds" of liquor, alcoholic, NOI, while the commodity rate is $8.26, a savings of 62.8 percent.[100]

Commodity rates take as many forms as there are methods of publishing rates. Charles Taff describes the three most popular types of commodity rates as follows:

1. Those tied to class rates, usually expressed as a certain percentage of Class 100, and termed "column rates."

2. Those rates not tied to class rates but constructed on a systematic basis, such as a distance scale.

3. Those special point-to-point rates not built upon any systematic basis but adjusted to meet the needs of particular shippers, localities, or competitive conditions.[101]

Commodity rates are published in commodity tariffs, with "commodity" being a part of the tariff's title, just as "class" is included in the title of a tariff that consists of class rates.

There are two kinds of commodity tariffs. A specific tariff applies to a certain category or group of goods such as textile products, iron or steel articles, or foodstuffs, and identifies the commodity group in its title. A general tariff consists of rates on a variety of commodities, with no reference to any particular commodity type in its name. All three types of commodity rates described by Taff may be found in a specific or general commodity tariff. In fact rates on the same commodity, from the same origin to destination, may be found in two commodity tariffs. Which rate will apply to the actual shipment being moved will depend upon precedence.

Precedence. Because a commodity rate is established for a particular commodity moving under a special set of operational circumstances, the carrier usually publishes a rule in the tariff that no other rate shall be applied to the movement in question. Where more than one rate is published for a particular move, the rule of precedence applies, which states that the more specific tariff and/or rate will be used before the less specific tariff and/or rate. For example, the rate in a specific commodity tariff takes precedence over a rate published in a general commodity tariff. The rule is necessary whenever a commodity rate is published for a freight movement, because at least one other rate, a class rate, is always available, and would apply to the shipment in the absence of the commodity rate.

Alternation. The alternation provision can negate the precedence rule by stating that whichever tariff rate produces the lowest (if three or more rates apply) or lower (if two rates apply) total charge on a shipment, that tariff rate must be charged.

Participation. A final step in rate determination is participation. Each tariff bureau issues a Participation Tariff that indicates which member carriers participate in or charge the rates shown in the tariffs published by the bureau. Despite how appealing a rate in a particular tariff may be to a shipper, a carrier is not obligated to charge rates published in a tariff if it does not officially participate in that tariff; in fact, it would be illegal to do so.

A General Procedure. In checking the rate applied or figuring what rate to apply to a shipment, a general procedure should be followed. Assume that commodity and weight, origin and destination, and any special requirements such as refrigeration or placarding (hazardous materials) are known. First specific commodity tariffs are checked, then general commodity tariffs. Each commodity tariff has an index to articles, origins, and destinations. Obviously, a rate on towels or automobile tires would not be found in an iron or steel articles tariff. If shipment origin is Spartanburg, SC, and a tariff shows no rates to or from the SC city, the rate analyst goes to the next tariff in line, using the rule of precedence. The last tariff used is expected to be the class tariff. Familiarity with the commodities moved and traffic lanes utilized will accelerate the process.[102]

Railroad Tariffs

Except for the development of the 28300 rate scale, the discussion of tariff construction in this chapter has centered on motor carrier tariffs. This is not to underrate the scope and importance of rate publication in the railroad industry. Rail tariffs are as demanding as motor, if not more so. Indeed, the motor industry reaped the benefits of decades of rail experience when it became regulated in 1935.

Railroads still must observe filed rates published in class and commodity tariffs, but class rates are about equal in importance to filed rates charged by barge carriers. Only 5 percent or so of rail freight moves by class rates. Tariff-controlled rates used in the rail industry are commodity rates, but the application of these charges is predicted to decline in the decade's remaining years.

In mid-1992, the railroads asked the ICC to declare 31 commodities exempt from rate regulation that accounted for roughly 15 percent of the industry's business, including motor vehicles, coke, primary forest and wood raw materials, blast furnace products, and primary iron or steel products.[103]

In rail, long-term contracts and exempt spot (one-time) rates are where the action is in the early 1990s. Over a century of experience with regulated construction of rates may assist in the publication of today's exempt rates, but only if the requirements of the railroads and their customers are met.

Additional Rate Definitions

Several types of rates have been analyzed in this chapter, including bureau and individual carrier, filed and exempt, class and commodity, and contract rates. Eight additional kinds of rates should be mentioned because of their direct impact on transportation monies exchanged between shippers and carriers.

Local or Single-Line Rate.   A rate applicable over the line of a single carrier. The term "local" seems misleading if the carrier operates coast-to-coast, as several motor carriers and airlines do. New York to San Francisco is a local rate when moved by a single carrier. A local rate means terminal expenses are included only once, as opposed to a combination rate, explained below.

Joint Rate.   A rate applied over the lines of two or more carriers that is the same amount as a local rate, where terminal expenses are counted only once. A routing guide or the equivalent is required to determine which carriers offer joint rates in conjunction with each other. In the next definition, the savings of joint rates are compared to combination rates.

Combination Rate.   A rate applied over the lines of two or more carriers where, unlike a joint rate, each carrier applies its own local rate to its portion of the origin-to-destination move. This means that terminal expenses are included by each carrier participating in the move. As an example of the difference in joint and combination rates, the Greensboro-to-Mobile class rate of $28.32/100 lb, determined earlier, was equivalent to a local or joint rate. If a combination of rates, such as Greensboro-to-Atlanta plus Atlanta-to-Mobile, had applied, the rate would have been $42.95, an increase of 51.7 percent.

Through Rate.   Merely the total rate from shipment origin to its destination, whether it be a local, joint, or combination rate. The term *through rate* usually is used synonymously with *joint rate*. However, a *combination rate* also counts as a through rate, which can be confusing. It is better to use the terms local, joint, or combination rate, whichever applies, rather than through rate.

Exception Rating or Rate. An exception to the rating in an appropriate classification (motor or rail), and the rate applicable to the rating found in the appropriate tariff. Exception ratings/rates usually are lower than class ratings/rates on the same commodities. An exception rate is another form of commodity rate. Discounting accomplishes the same goals as using the exceptions publication mechanism.

Released Rating or Rate. Published on commodities of unusually high value, where the carrier agrees to a lower rating/rate in exchange for reduced (being "released" from full) liability if the goods are lost or damaged in transit. Such ratings are particularly popular in the movement of "drugs, chemicals, medicines, toilet preparations" and like products, as named in Item 60000 of the NMFC, 100-O.

Density Rating or Rate. Rating based strictly on the space occupied by a product relative to its weight (its density). This type of rate is the basis for the motor carrier classification employed in "six New England states and in parts of New York and New Jersey."[104] This classification is called the Coordinated Freight Classification (CFC), and all commodities are grouped into 9 classes instead of 23 as used by the NMFC. The object of the Coordinated Classification's method is "to develop rate tables so that, regardless of the product's density, a vehicle load will produce about the same total revenue."[105]

Any Quantity (AQ) Rating or Rate. Usually a lower rating or rate is granted (through use of an exception or commodity rate, contract or discount) to a shipment in volume (be it truckload, carload, or multiple-carload) that is not available to a less-volume (LTL) shipment. These lower-volume rates represent actual or perceived lower costs of moving freight that does not require multiple handlings.

For some products, however, no savings are felt to exist, regardless of quantity shipped. These commodities are given AQ ratings. Four examples from the NMFC include shuttlecocks, NOI (class 300), balsa wood (class 100), cotton candy (less than 4 lb per cu ft, class 300), and clothing, NOI (in wheeled containers, class 150).[106]

Summary

In most cases, the setting, determining, and charging of rates is not as exciting or rewarding as influencing the establishment or management of a firm's total distribution system. Rates are but a part of the total picture and are couched in complicated legalese, which is perhaps not the place for a future shining star or fast-tracker.

However, rates are important, and even if tariffs are avoided in favor of long-term contracts, the law still must be observed in these shipper-carrier relationships. Rate negotiations are challenging and their results are of vital concern to both parties, even though one side may not realize the consequences of one or more settlements until the rates have been in place for some while. Without proper rate and tariff orientation when entering rate negotiations, a negotiator is, to use a familiar expression, a sitting duck.

Notes

1. The word *choose* is used in the definition of *variable cost* to reflect the more liberal attitude toward carrier obligations to accept freight, as reflected in the Staggers and Motor Carrier Acts of 1980 and similar legislation affecting other modes passed in the late 1970s and early 1980s.

2. D. Philip Locklin, *Economics of Transportation,* 7th ed., Richard D. Irwin, Inc., Homewood, IL, 1972, p. 160.

3. Edwin P. Patton, *Handbook for Motor Carrier Costing,* Graphic Creations, Knoxville, 1991, pp. 31–35.

4. Immediate-run pricing and costing concepts are credited to Dr. Frank W. Davis, Jr., Professor of Marketing and Service Logistics, The University of Tennessee, Knoxville.

5. Roy J. Sampson, Martin T. Farris, and David L. Schrock, *Domestic Transportation: Practice, Theory, and Policy, Sixth Edition,* Houghton Mifflin Company, Boston, 1990, p. 289.

6. Sampson et al., loc. cit.

7. Wade Lambert, "Truckers' Bid On Discounts Is Set Back," *Wall Street Journal,* June 18, 1992, p. A3.

8. Marvin L. Fair and John Guandolo, *Regulation of Transportation,* Wm. C. Brown Company, Dubuque, IA, 1970, p. 7.

9. Locklin, op. cit, pp. 212–221.

10. Ibid., pp. 224–226.

11. Ibid., pp. 228–229.

12. Ibid., pp. 230–231.

13. Ibid., pp. 240–250.

14. For a discussion of the advantages of early truck transportation, see: D. Philip Locklin, *Economics of Transportation,* revised ed., Richard D. Irwin, Inc., Chicago, 1946, pp. 767–780. This is the only reference to Locklin's Revised Edition. All other Locklin references refer to the Seventh Edition.

15. Sampson et al., op. cit., p. 289.

16. Ibid., pp. 289–291.

17. Ibid., p. 305.

18. Loc. cit.

19. Title 49, US Code #10101, National Transportation Policy. For a review of the 1980 legislative changes and their effects on motor carrier competition, see Ex Parte No. MC-177, *Petition to Institute Rulemaking on Negotiated Motor Carrier Rates,* 5 ICC 623 (2d) at pp. 632–634.

20. Two conclusions of the Shipper LTL Pricing Practices Roundtable, held at the University of Tennessee, Department of Marketing, Logistics, and Transportation, June 18, 1992.

21. Ex Parte No. MC-177, op. cit., pp. 631–632.

22. 110 S.Ct. 2759 (1990), 2760.

23. 110 S.Ct. 2759 (1990), 2770.

24. Loc. cit.

25. 110 S.Ct. 2759 (1990), 2772.

26. 110 S.Ct. 2759 (1990), 2780.

27. John Schulz, "Shippers beset by undercharges urge repeal of 'filed-rate' doctrine," *Traffic World*, 229:11, pp. 20–21.

28. John Schulz, "Teamsters 'strongly support' trustee, blast ICC in Transcon bankruptcy," *Traffic World*, 229:10, pp. 7–8.

29. John Schulz, "Shippers, attorneys divided on post-Transcon undercharges," *Traffic World*, 230:13, pp. 30–31.

30. Loc. cit.

31. Loc. cit.

32. Loc. cit.

33. John Schulz, "5th Circuit overturns 'pay first' rule as shippers, ICC rack up another win," *Traffic World*, 23:1, pp. 9–10. Also see: 1992 WL 142813 (5th Cir. [Tex.]).

34. For an explanation of reparations and overcharge claims, see: Charles A. Taff, *Management on Physical Distribution and Transportation, Sixth Edition*, Richard D. Irwin, Inc., Homewood, IL, 1978, pp. 539–542.

35. "5th Circuit Overturns . . . ," op. cit., p. 10. Also see: David Cawthorne, "Shippers seek Justice probe of P-I-E undercharge practices," *Traffic World*, 230:8, p. 18.

36. Personal interview with Mr. Jerry Patterson, Graduate Assistant and Candidate for the Ph.D. degree in Logistics and Transportation, University of Tennessee, Knoxville, June 18, 1992.

37. Loc. cit.

38. Loc. cit.

39. 8 ICC 2d 520 (1992), Contracts for Transportation of Property, p. 5.

40. Ibid., p. 4.

41. Loc. cit.

42. Loc. cit.

43. Ibid., p. 6.

44. Loc. cit.

45. Ibid., p. 8.

46. Loc. cit.

47. David Cawthorne, "Truckers sue ICC over contract rules," *Traffic World*, 230:12, p. 34.

48. David Cawthorne, "Shippers welcome ICC contract ruling as they prepare for judicial battles," *Traffic World*, 230:9, pp. 10–11.

49. For a discussion of rail maximum rates and "market dominance," see: John E. Tyworth, Joseph L. Cavinato, C. John Langley, Jr., *Traffic Management: Planning, Operations, and Control,* Addison-Wesley Publishing Company, Reading, MA, 1987, pp. 66–68.

50. "AAR endorses ICC proposal to end rate contract filings," *Traffic World*, 230:8, p. 21.

51. Loc. cit.

52. Loc. cit.

53. Loc. cit.

54. For definitions of railroad intermodal pricing plans, see: Tyworth et al., op. cit., p. 42.

55. Telephone interview with Mr. James A. Giblin, Intermodal Market Manager—Mexico, Santa Fe Railway, Schaumburg, IL, July 21, 1992.

56. Airline Tariff Publishing Company (ATPC), The Official Local Cargo Rates Tariff (No. 87) (Washington: ATPC, 1988), p. A-1.

57. Ibid., p. A-2.

58. Telephone interview with Ms. Ginger Hughes, Customer Service Supervisor, Burlington Air Express, Knoxville, TN, July 20, 1992.

59. "Density Discount, Delta Cargo Services," advertisement issued by Delta Air Cargo, Delta Airlines, May 1990.

60. Paul Page, "Cargo fare wars? Shippers find rates sharply discounted on spot markets," *Traffic World*, 230:13, pp. 26–27.

61. Telephone interview with Mr. Travis Childress, Supervisor, Delta Airlines Air Cargo, Knoxville, TN, July 20, 1992.

62. Frederick J. Stephenson, Jr., *Transportation USA,* Addison-Wesley Publishing Company, Reading, MA, 1987, pp. 262–263.

63. Telephone interview with Mr. Noel Griese, Colonial Pipeline Co., Atlanta, GA, July 20, 1992.

64. Telephone interview with Ms. Michele Joy, Association of Oil Pipelines, Washington, DC, July 20, 1992.

65. Sampson et al., op. cit., pp. 249–251.

66. Telephone interview with Ms. Jennifer Kelly, Manager of Regulatory Issues, American Waterway Operators, Alexandria, VA, July 21, 1992.

67. Telephone interview with Mr. Jack Simpson, Editor, *Waterways Journal,* St. Louis, MO, July 23, 1992.

68. Telephone interview with Ms. Jennifer Kelly, op. cit., July 23, 1992.

69. Telephone interview with Dr. David Menachof, Assistant Professor of Marketing Logistics, Intermodal Transportation Program, School of Business, University of Charleston, Charleston, SC, July 23, 1992.

70. Loc. cit.

71. Loc. cit., and F. J. Stephenson, op. cit., pp. 435–449.

72. Telephone interview with Mr. James A. Giblin, op. cit.

73. Loc. cit., and telephone interview with Mr. Robert Gaither, Sales Representative, Consolidated Freightways, Knoxville, TN, July 23, 1992.

74. William Way, Jr., *Elements of Freight Traffic,* Regular Common Carrier Conference, Washington, ATA, 1956, pp. 76–77.

75. The greatest number of changes in classification procedures occurred in the railroad industry where, at one time, each carrier published its own classification. By the time motor carriers were regulated in 1935, many principles by which commodities were assigned into classes had been set. The earliest motor classification heavily reflected the rail classification, the result of using a rail classification and "scissors and scotch tape." Lecture in Transportation 311 by Dr. James W. Bennett, Jr., Professor of Transportation, University of Tennessee, Knoxville, August 7, 1957.

76. Charles A. Taff, op. cit., pp. 361–363.

77. Thurman Van Metre, *Industrial Traffic Management,* McGraw-Hill, New York, 1953, p. 57.

78. *National Motor Freight Classification (NMFC) 100-O,* American trucking Associations, Inc., Alexandria, VA, 1988, p. 856. Classification item numbers of the 10 articles shown, in order: 63360, 84340, 88020, 111210, 115760, 158040, 168820, 170650, 177080, 188100.

79. Ibid., items 188100, 170650, 177080.

80. Ibid., pp. 234–244.

81. Ibid., pp. 227–259, 678–848.

82. Ibid., items 21212, 25000, 27780, 39785, 55120, 114030, 176580, 153520, 58320, 177360.

83. Ibid., items 28820, 48140, 49977, 86600, 49992, 90160, 89550, 97050, 134210, 50660.

84. Ibid., items 25690, 32020, 47895, 105460, 112800, 166090.

85. Shipper LTL Pricing Practices Roundtable, op. cit.

86. Tyworth et al., op. cit., p. 135.

87. Southern Motor Carriers Rate Conference (SMC), *South Commodity Tariff, Tariff 200-L,* SMC, Atlanta, 1987, p. 88.

88. Charles A. Taff, op. cit., p. 383.

89. Americana Corporation, *The Encyclopedia Americana,* 1957 ed., vol. XXVI, Americana Corporation, New York, 1957, p. 413. Western Trunk Line Committee, Agent et al. (WTL), *National Rate Basis Tariff, Tariff NRB 6000-A,* WTL, Chicago, 1981, pp. 236–241.

90. Charles A. Taff, op. cit., p. 383.

91. Ibid., pp. 357–362, 380–385.

92. D. Philip Locklin, op. cit., pp. 187–188; Charles A. Taff, op. cit., p. 382.

93. D. Philip Locklin, op. cit., p. 188.

94. Ibid., p. 189.

95. Charles A. Taff, *Commercial Motor Transportation, Fifth Edition,* Cornell Maritime Press, Cambridge, MD, 1975, p. 355. This is the only reference to Taff's *Commercial Motor Transportation.* All other references to Taff are to his *Physical Distribution and Transportation* text; see reference 34.

96. Tyworth et al., op. cit., pp. 92–93.

97. SMC, Southern Class Tariff, Tariff 500-D, SMC, Atlanta, 1987, items 150, 597, 15000, pp. 6, 19, 71–86.

98. Ibid., p. 73.

99. "Freight Bills Audited," *Traffic World,* 231:3, p. 49.

100. Commodity rate references: SMC, *South Commodity Tariff, Tariff 200-L,* SMC, Atlanta, 1987, items 22180 and 73180.

101. Charles A. Taff, op. cit., p. 385.

102. The Southern Motor Carriers Rate Conference (SMC), of Atlanta, GA, publishes an excellent short course in the Construction and Application of Motor Carrier Tariffs in which all of the material discussed in the third section of this chapter is analyzed in detail with questions and rate problems from eight governing tariffs, including the NMFC, and nine rate tariffs. Contact: C.E. Medlin, SMC, 1307 Peachtree Street N.E., P.O. Box 7219, Atlanta, GA 30357.

103. "Railroads seek rate exemptions," *Traffic World,* 231:2, p. 36.

104. Tyworth, et al., op. cit., p. 85.

105. Loc. cit.

106. NMFC, op. cit., items 17260, 21400, 39925, 49880.

13
Transportation Operations

Michael R. Arledge
President, Arledge and Associates

The two foundations of quality traffic operations are:

1. A knowledge of the characteristics and requirements of the product to be shipped, thus ensuring that the product arrives without degradation.
2. A knowledge of alternative transportation options, and the ability to match transportation method with shipping requirements to maximize service at a minimal cost.

The management of today's traffic operations requires not only an understanding of the four modes of transportation (rail, motor carrier, air, and water) but also:

1. The integration of any two modes: intermodal
2. Private fleets
3. Outsourcing

Today, intermodal travel is the fastest-growing mode, private fleets are the largest source of transportation, and outsourcing is a hot topic of consideration as companies continue to cut overhead and downsize their internal staffs.

The key factor in traffic operations today is customer service. The cost of transportation is a secondary factor. It is of the utmost importance that you communicate your requirements to your carriers, that you share with them your decision process and the issues that are important to you to provide quality transportation. Without these clear and open communications with your carriers, you will not be able to create the win-win relationship you must have to maintain quality traffic operations.

Mode Selection

In selecting a transportation mode, the first step is to define as accurately as possible the requirements of the transportation to be provided. The following seven factors must be taken into consideration:

1. Nature of freight
2. Packaging and handling
3. Volume
4. Traffic lanes
5. Transit times
6. Access to the product
7. Tracing

Nature of Freight.   The obvious starting point is the identification of the major products requiring transport. Typically, these are best identified by using the Standard Industrial Classification (SIC) codes. Generally speaking, SIC codes consist of four digits, with the first two showing the industrial group, into which there are 10 divisions ranging from 01-09 (e.g., agriculture, forestry, and fishing) to 60-70 (e.g., finance, insurance, and real estate).

Some transportation modes require more detailed product identification. For example, when shipping hazardous materials, rail requires the specification of a six-digit SIC code. It is very important not just to deal with SIC codes but to truly understand the nature of the freight to be transported. For example, if your business is the transportation of food, it will be important not to allow your product to have any contact with a carrier that handles medical waste or trash from a landfill.

Packaging and Handling.   The single most important factor leading to a product's being received in the same condition it was in when it was loaded, is the packaging and handling of the load. If an item is packaged properly, the product will arrive at its destination properly. There are an unlimited number of packaging alternatives, and therefore it is important to talk with several carriers to understand how best to package the material. Similarly, it is important to understand any special handling requirements of your product. Just as there are many packaging alternatives, so too there are many different handling alternatives. Are you shipping industrial generators that require cranes to load on flatbeds, or are you shipping apple pies on a special-exchange pallet, or are you shipping product from Florida to Washington, where you need twice-daily updates on the conditions of the product?

Whatever the special handling requirements, it is your duty as the manager of the traffic operations to communicate these requirements to the carrier. Although not always enforced, it is illegal to force a driver to load or unload your freight through the use of loading and unloading personnel that you select and have the carrier pay the personnel involved. The responsibility of the carrier starts and ends with picking up a load, transporting and tendering it in the same condition as it was originally to the destination. The carrier has no obligation to load or unload your freight unless specially stated and agreed to in advance by your organization and the carrier.

Volume. The factor of volume refers to the business level or the frequency of move. When shipping LTL, the more you ship, the better the discount you should obtain from your carrier. If you ship more than one pallet that weighs 500 lb or more to a given destination, then you must investigate the consolidation of your freight with others through a freight consolidation service or a freight broker.

Traffic Lanes. To many managers of traffic operations, traffic lanes, or geographical coverage, is the sole factor in selecting transportation mode. Today, many traffic managers are seeking a single carrier for door-to-door service on one through bill of lading and one freight bill. As a result, if your traffic lanes are of the regional variety, then you may be best satisfied dealing only with regional carriers. On the other hand, if you ship to and from several different regions of the country or world, you may decide to work with several large multiregional carriers. The advantage of utilizing one carrier is the ease of operation, making one phone call and dealing with a select number of people. The disadvantage is that no carrier can economically cover all traffic lanes.

Transit Times. Transit times are most often indirectly related to cost: the shorter the transit time, the more expensive the cost of transportation. For domestic transport of trips greater than 300 mi, air is typically fastest, then motor carrier, then rail, and lastly water. Interestingly, for trips less than 300 mi, sometimes water can be faster than air or truck. The manager of traffic operations must clearly understand for all trips which transit times are needed and which can be provided by the different modes of transport.

Access to the Product. This refers to how important it is, when the product is in transit, that you gain access or direct your cargo to another destination. Although this is an unusual requirement, when it does come into consideration it may be the most important factor in mode selection.

Tracing. *Trackability* is the ability to track a shipment while in transit. *Traceability* is the ability to go back and trace a shipment from the point of origin to the destination. Although all modes are traceable, the speed and cost of tracing a shipment varies considerably by mode.

The Four Modes

The following discussion presents an overview of the four basic modes of transportation. When this discussion is combined with the requirements of the product to be transported, then a mode selection may be made:

1. Rail
2. Motor carrier
3. Air
4. Water

Rail. Historically, railroads have been confined to carloads and the transportation of heavy common items such as coal, grain, chemicals, food, agricultural products, lumber, paper goods and automobiles. Today, carload shipments clearly dominate both volume and revenue. Interestingly, however, volume and revenue are not always related. For example, automobile shipments account for only 2 percent of the volume but 11 percent of the revenue, as opposed to coal, which accounts for 40 percent of the volume but only 25 percent of the revenue, and agricultural products, which account for 20 percent of the volume but only 10 percent of the revenue.

As railroads have been trying to both expand their carload business and attract business other than carload business, they are becoming more sensitive to the topic of customer service. In some cases, partnership agreements between rail and motor carriers are being created.

The advantages of rail remain the low cost of transport and the ability to move large volumes of freight. The disadvantages are the limited traffic lanes and slow transit times. However, as rail continues to forge intermodal agreements and become more responsive, many, many loads will be shipped by rail.

Motor Carrier. Of all modes of transportation, motor carriers are the most independent. Motor carriers are able to carry a large assortment of items to any domestic destination, while allowing you the flexibility to direct the shipment while in transit. Motor carriers link rail to your loading dock, your container to the steamship, and air freight to the aircraft. The disadvantages of motor carriers are the lack of real-time contact and the fact that motor carriers have reached a saturation point and rates will begin to increase, making other modes more competitive.

Air. Air freight within the United States became a viable mode of transport with the enactment of the Motor Carriers Act of 1980. The advantage of air freight is the ability to respond to overnight cross-country shipments. Certainly for small-parcel shipments, the transit time of air cannot be matched by any other mode. Other air freight advantages include guaranteed delivery, dependable services, and almost real-time tracking. Of course, the disadvantage is the premium cost.

Water. Water is very similar to rail. The price is very good, but the traffic lanes are limited and most often transit times are slow. Tracking capabilities with water also are often limited.

The reality of traffic operations is that mode selection evolves over time. The never-ending process of mode selection follows a four-step process. You must

1. *Define alternatives.* If you are establishing a new traffic operation, you need to begin by defining the potential transportation candidates. A call to local traffic managers will almost always result in a preliminary understanding of the available transportation alternatives. Your local telephone directory yellow pages will most often list the available local transportation companies under the appropriate headings, such as Air Freight, Trucking–Motor Freight, Transportation Brokers, Steamship Lines, etc.

   If you are located in a small rural area, the nearest metropolitan area yellow pages should be consulted. In addition, other local information may be obtained from Delta Nu Alpha, the Council of Logistics Management, *Chilton Distribution Magazine, Transportation Topics, Transportation and Distribution,* etc. The most single comprehensive list of motor carriers is the *National Directory of Motor Carriers.* Another good source of candidates is the organization to whom you are shipping. Give your customer the option of selecting a carrier. If they wish for you to make the choice, ask them for options.

2. *Establish evaluation factors.* Now that you have many alternatives, what you need to do is to establish the factors that are important to your organization in selecting a carrier. Factors that may be of importance, and questions you will want to ask, include:

   a. *Current business.* What other items does the carrier transport? Does it mix with our freight? Does the carrier participate in a pallet exchange program?

   b. *Financial strength.* How long has the company been in business? How stable is the company? How are the alternatives ranked in various carrier journals by revenue, by operating ratios, etc?

   c. *Company size.* How many employees? Quantity and type of equipment? Backup equipment for peak periods?

   d. *Tracking capabilities.* Is tracking done automatically, or just on troubled shipments? How will the carrier notify us if there is a problem? How will communications take place?

   e. *Bill processing.* How will freight rates be calculated? Will we have a fixed rate? Can we identify individual freight bills for specific shipments?

   f. *Rates.* What would be the rates for the orders in question? How do we establish a long-term relationship? How will rate changes be handled?

   g. *Reliability.* How has the carrier performed for others? What similar experience has the carrier had? How customer-oriented is the carrier?

3. *Establish operating guidelines.* Now that you have defined what is important to you, you will want to establish written operating guidelines to communicate your expectations with the carriers. These guidelines should state in simple language what level of transportation service you desire, and they should be specific. For example, don't just state that "appointments should be made"; explain that "appointments should be made within four hours of a load being picked up by calling XXX-YYYY."

4. *Select carrier.* After you have established your guidelines, present each alternative carrier with your transportation requirements. Give each one several loads,

evaluate its performance, and discuss that performance with the carrier. Select the carrier that consistently meets your requirements.

Private Fleets

To gain an insight into current private fleet challenges, listen in to the following interview with William Foust, Operations Manager for Dillard Transportation Company.

What problems are private carriers facing?

I personally feel that working within the regulations of the government is the biggest problem facing the private carrier.

What regulations specifically?

The hours-of-service rules, which limit the distance your drivers can legally drive. Limits of 60 hours per week. For instance, a driver who can drive 10 hours per day in a 55-MPH zone legally can only average 50 MPH. We have 500 total miles per 24-hour period that we can cover.

It costs an average of $1.43 per mile to operate a private truck. Do you feel that is accurate?

For 1992, yes, that is a good number.

Don't you think you could do it cheaper with outside carriers?

In my particular instance it is not the cost that is important, but the service we provide. A private carrier can provide specific services that contract carriers cannot provide. For example we have very tight schedules—we deliver to 25 different warehouses before 7 a.m. every working day, with only 12 trucks. It's the LTL delivery service that we provide that no contract carrier could ever handle.

So actually, even though you are paying $1.43 per mile, considering the multiple stops that you provide that's still cheaper than running LTL service?

Yes. Well, I don't know if it's cheaper, it's a better service. LTL carriers could not give the service that we do.

What are the advantages of private carriers as opposed to contract carriers?

The biggest advantage is the service, because there is the element of control within the private fleet that does not exist with the common carrier.

What are the disadvantages?

The cost involved. You have the constant cost of maintaining the fleet, regardless of the volume, so you don't have much flexibility. If the volume drops off in your business, you can't sell all your trucks and lay off all the drivers. If you're going to have a private fleet, you must ensure that you have the volume to produce revenues necessary to maintain that fleet.

So you need a well-balanced traffic department?

You have to be sure you have the people on staff to operate the fleet efficiently. If you are not moving that equipment a certain percentage of time, then you're not going to be able to pay for that fleet. In our case, as an LTL carrier, we have no authority, so we can't just go out and pick up additional freight to fill our trucks, so we have to tie our system together and keep the equipment running the percentage of time we require. Once you start running your equipment empty, that's when you take the profit out of the private fleet.

What regulating compliances that carriers are faced with present the biggest problem?

Government compliance.

What do you see as the future of private carriers?

I see a bright future. They will continue to grow. As companies grow larger due to buyouts and takeovers, I think you will see an increased need for private carriers. When you look at the cost versus service, larger companies see the value of the private fleet and will invest capital in the fleet.

Today's Private Fleet Motor Carrier

Private fleets carry approximately 50 percent of the trucking industry expenditure, comprising approximately $85 billion in 1991. The reasons most often given for having a private fleet are service reliability and responsiveness to customers. As seen in the above interview, private fleets are not pursued as a way of reducing the cost of transportation.

Often, what starts out as a private carrier ends up as a common or contract carrier, one example being Monfort Transportation, an excellent refrigerated carrier based in Greeley, Colorado. Monfort Transportation got its start to ensure timely, dependable service of their parent company, Monfort of Colorado, one of the largest beef-packing houses in the United States. The sole purpose of Monfort Transportation was to carry beef to destination and return as quickly as possible for the next trip. As a result, the inside lane of Interstate 81 became known as "the Monfort Lane." Then, with the passage of the Motor Carriers Act of 1980, Monfort Transportation became a contract carrier. Today they are the premier refrigerated carrier from all points to the beef patch of the United States. Although Monfort is no longer a private fleet, their corporate management, like most management, requires their fleet to be cost-effective. However, the primary reason private fleets exist is to give service. Not only is service important, it is expected. Customers demand responsive quality service from their transportation providers, with the same fervor as they demand product quality. On-time performance isn't a service differentiator, it's a basic requirement.

Outsourcing

In today's global economy, many organizations are downsizing. In many cases, what was once a very large, complex bureaucratic corporation is today a lean corporate business, with business management concentrating only on their core business. The corporation is headed by managers who demand a profit from each department, including transportation. If the transportation department is showing a profit, it is left alone. If it is not showing a profit, management is looking for other alternatives. One alternative is to outsource one or more of the logistical functions.

In the late '80s and '90s, the third party contract logistics market has been undergoing a very rapid growth period. The biggest motivator in outsourcing logistical services is cost retainment or cost reduction. There are two distinct types of outsourcing, asset- or space-based and consultant- or non-asset-based. Asset-based companies are those that are owned or own logistical assets such as transportation equipment and/or warehouses. Non-asset or consultant-based companies have no financial interest in transportation or warehouses. There are advantages and disadvantages to each, although they both offer virtually the same services. Asset-based companies can show real assets and signs of financial weakness or strength. Their disadvantage is their inability to prove that they are nonbiased. The advantage of non-asset-based companies is that they are nonbiased, because they have no financial interest in transportation equipment or warehouses.

Factors to consider when selecting outsource logistical third parties are the type of industry serviced by the company, and if that interest matches yours. To list only a few of the different types of services you might consider: information systems, order processing, warehousing, inventory control, transportation arrangements by their own or other's equipment, credit and collections, technical support, assembly of components, direct store delivery, order picking, crossdocking, bar coding, billing, etc.

Another form of third party service is freight forwarders and brokers. The biggest difference between a freight forwarder and a broker is warehousing. Generally speaking, a freight forwarder does four things that a broker does not do:

1. Assembly
2. Consolidation
3. Breakbulk
4. Distribution

A freight forwarder uses its own bill of lading, as opposed to the broker, who uses the shipper's bill of lading. In the eyes of the Interstate Commerce Commission, the broker acts as an agent for the shipper, as opposed to the freight forwarder, who *is* the shipper. Both have advantages and disadvantages. The following four points must be considered in determining if you should use freight forwarders or brokers:

1. Consolidation of smaller shipments, as opposed to using the more traditional LTL carrier.
2. Dealing directly with a carrier, and increasing the linkage between the traffic manager and the driver.
3. Time delay in billing, when an original bill of lading or proof of delivery is a requirement for paying a freight bill.
4. Processing of claims, with the exception of the freight forwarder. It is not the obligation of the third party to file the claim; the claim is between the carrier and the traffic manager. Sometimes, as a courtesy to the traffic manager, third parties will process freight claims.

Personnel

Traffic operations is not an easy job. Few people other than the traffic people themselves understand it. Typically, traffic operations personnel were not educated to handle traffic operations but rather just grew into the function. Good traffic operators require accounting skills to work with all the numbers (billing, auditing, and reporting), dispatcher skills to deal with the minute-by-minute assignment of tasks, management skills to deal with the service requirements, and even legal skills to deal with the complex topic of transportation law. In many small companies, all these skills reside in one person. In larger companies, these tasks may be divided. Sometimes they are divided by type of task, sometimes by geographical region, by type of product, and many other ways. The dispatcher is key to determining how to divide the traffic operations task. A good dispatcher can handle 40 to 50 loads per week, an excellent one 50 to 60. Although the management of traffic operations is not necessarily different than the management of other functions within an organization, due to the complexity of traffic operations and the critical impact on customer service it is important that only people who have an intimate understanding of a company's specific traffic operations be assigned the task of managing the traffic operations.

Effect of Transportation on Profits

Most businesses have one paramount objective: to return a profit to the owners of the company for their investment into the business. I can think of no product that does not have a logistical cost associated with it. Logistical costs include the cost of transportation, warehousing, order processing, administration, and inventory carrying. Of these, the largest single cost is transportation. On average, transportation consumes 41 percent of the total logistical dollar. Warehousing is the second highest cost with 25 percent. Inventory cost is third with 22 percent. In 1990, total domestic transportation expenditures were $353 billion, with 79.3 percent or $279.9 billion going to trucking, 8.6 percent or $30.4 billion going to rail, and the remainder being divided between water, air, and pipeline.

It is through effective utilization and becoming more efficient at doing our jobs as traffic managers that we can contain the cost of transportation. On the average, logistical costs in the consumer nondurable market are 8 percent of sales, so if you cut transportation costs 1 percent, the result will be the same as increasing sales approximately 12.5 percent. It is critical in traffic operations that we focus on the costs of transportation so that our companies may maximize profits.

The Transportation Business

Since the passage of the Motor Carriers Act of 1980, rates have become negotiable. The traffic manager, wanting to reduce costs, will play carrier A against carrier B. Carrier B, wanting to haul the freight, will take the freight away from carrier A by proposing lower rates. Carrier A will lose the freight—enter carrier C. The traffic manager, under pressure to further reduce costs, will use carrier C. Carrier B will have the choice of reducing the rate or losing the freight. Carrier A may come back again to get the freight and be faced with a repeat of the situation. The typical plan would be to use carrier A against carrier B, carrier B against carrier C, and so on. As a result transportation companies, truckers in particular, go bankrupt. In reality, there hasn't been much negotiation. Just the dog-eat-dog transportation game.

Today, with a saturated market, the tide is turning. Carriers have to make a living, and traffic managers have to prove their worth. Drivers are now demanding more money, and carriers can no longer increase their profit by buying other carriers. Insurance companies control the issue of who drives and who doesn't. This, coupled with the new commercial driver's license, has created a shortage of drivers. Therefore, as we move into the 1990s we will start to see carriers increase their rates, and it is going to take a very studious traffic manager to keep rates in line. The game of traffic operations has never been easy, and it is not getting easier. It is not just rates.

For example, in moving a certain product from Greensboro, North Carolina, to Rochester, New York, carrier A tells you that its rate is 95 cents/mi while carrier B's rate is $1/mi. Looking at the unit cost of 95 cents, carrier A would seem to be cheaper, but you must look at all the variables. Carrier A has 1100 mi and carrier B has 1000 mi; now that you've made the comparison of both variables, carrier B looks cheaper. LTL works the same way; when making comparisons, you must compare all the variables to include weight, class, base rate, then discount. When considering LTL, you may want to take into account the number of times the product is broken down and reassembled and how many breakbulk points your product has to go through.

Conclusion

As stated earlier, the game of traffic operations is not getting easier to play. The only way to reduce costs is to look at all the variables and all the costs and only then chart a course for traffic operations. An example:

1. Volume, truckload, Los Angeles, CA, to Greensboro, NC.
2. Customer requires pallet exchange.
3. Cost of pallets delivered to the point of origin is $5 each.
4. You need 20 pallets.
5. Truckload motor carrier costs $2400, and does participate in pallet exchange.
6. Intermodal carrier costs $2100, and doesn't participate in pallet exchange.
7. Assume all equal transit times.

Question:
What would be the most cost-efficient way to move your product?

Answer:
Intermodal. You would save $200, and that would include disposing of the pallets at the destination. If you wanted to do more homework, you could weigh the cost of cheap pallets and look into the cost of selling them at the destination, which would further reduce the cost.

The astute traffic manager will do his homework and weigh out all his options before selecting the proper method that will reduce costs, thereby increasing company profits.

14

Transportation Documentation

Hank Lavery

*Vice President, Transportation Products,
Sterling Software*

The history of transportation documentation is as old as civilization itself. Ancient civilizations in Egypt, Crete, and Babylon maintained meticulous records of goods. Early sea carriers such as the Phoenicians kept careful track of cargo with detailed manifests. Roman carriers used legalistic, precise lists of goods to limit liability and stipulate payments.

Transportation today requires the use of a variety of documents. Documentation is a record of the what, who, how, where, and when of a given shipment, specifying such things as cargo contents, carriers, routings, departure and arrival dates, and points of origin and destination. Because domestic and global transportation is governed by national and international law, the most important documents are those that are required by and that must conform with legislative statutes. These documents range from the basic bill of lading to the extensive documentation typically required for import/export activities. Moreover, special situations such as the filing of loss and damage claims or the transport of hazardous cargo necessitate still more documentation, again regulated by law.

As a result of the profusion of paperwork associated with transportation during the past three decades, there has been, in recent years, a great need to simplify the administrative burden and cost of processing transportation documentation. For this reason, the transportation industry has seen the rapid growth of computerization.

The computer application that is perhaps most important to transportation documentation is Electronic Data Interchange. Electronic Data Interchange (EDI) is the computer-to-computer exchange of business documents in a standardized, machine-readable format. EDI is revolutionizing the transportation industry. When used in conjunction with just-in-time and quick response applications, EDI makes possible the complete automation of the manufacturing, warehousing, transportation, and distribution cycles. An electronic and paperless form of business communication, EDI plays an important role in controlling the "paper explosion."

This chapter will discuss the basic transportation documents involved in shipping and billing. In addition, it will examine various documents and procedures associated with claims for losses, damages, and overcharges. The specific uses of EDI for transportation documentation will also be addressed.

Key Shipping Documents

Bill of Lading

A bill of lading is a negotiable or nonnegotiable document acknowledging receipt of goods and serving as a contract for the transport of cargo. Also sometimes called the *shipping order*, the bill of lading is the most important and most basic document used between shippers and carriers. It contains all the information the carrier needs to properly transport the shipment.

Regulation.   Early in this century, American carriers attempted to limit their legal liability through the use of a bill of lading contract, and this led to a variety of forms and provisions for this document. As a result Congress, after considerable legislative activity, legally standardized the document's form and provisions in 1917 with the Pomerene Bill of Lading Act. This Act provided penalties for altering, forging, counterfeiting, or falsely making a bill of lading for criminal purposes. Currently, the form and the use of the bill of lading are regulated by the Interstate Commerce Commission (ICC). An example of a bill of lading format widely agreed to by shippers and carriers may be seen in Fig. 14-1.

Functions.   The ICC has explained the functions of the bill of lading as follows:

> As a receipt for goods, it recites the place and date of shipment; describes the goods, their quantity, weight, dimensions, identification marks, conditions, etc., and sometimes their quality and value.
> As a contract, the bill names the contracting parties, specifies the rate or charge for transportation, and sets forth the agreement and stipulations with respect to the limitations of the carrier's common law liability in the case of loss or injury to the goods and other obligations assumed by the parties or to matters agreed upon between them.
> That part of the bill which constitutes a receipt may be treated as distinct from the part incorporating the contractual terms.

The first function of a bill of lading is to serve as a receipt issued by a carrier to a shipper for goods received for transport. The carrier (or the carrier's agent), upon receipt of the freight, issues and signs the bill of lading and gives the original of this document to the shipper. The signed original of the bill of lading is the shipper's legal proof that the carrier received the freight.

A bill of lading must show, in detail, several pieces of information. These include:

STRAIGHT BILL OF LADING
ORIGINAL - NOT NEGOTIABLE

PAGE   OF

CARRIER NAME

SHIPMENT IDENTIFICATION NO.

CARRIER ADDRESS
& ZIP

FREIGHT BILL PRO NO.
CARRIER USE

SCAC   DUNS

TO:
Consignee

On Collect on Delivery shipments, the letters "COD" must appear before consignee's name or as otherwise provided in Item 430, Sec. 1

TRAILER / CAR NUMBER

Street

Destination   ZIP

ROUTE

(Code)

FROM:

Shipper

SPECIAL INSTRUCTIONS

Street

Origin   ZIP

(Code)

FOR PAYMENT, SEND BILL TO:

SHIPPER'S INTERNAL DATA

Name

Street

City / State   ZIP

SID NO.

NO. SHIPPING UNITS	H/M	KIND OF PACKAGING, DESCRIPTION OF ARTICLES, SPECIAL MARKS & EXCEPTIONS (CODE)	WEIGHT (SUBJECT TO CORR.)	RATE	CHARGES

REMIT C.O.D.
TO

COD AMT: $

C.O.D. FEE
PREPAID
COLLECT $

ADDRESS

NOTE - Where the rate is dependent on value, shippers are required to state specifically in writing the agreed or declared value of the property.
The agreed or declared value of the property is hereby specifically stated by the shipper to be not exceeding

Subject to Section 7 of conditions, if this shipment is to be delivered to the consignee without recourse on the consignor, the consignor shall sign the following statement:
The carrier shall not make delivery of this shipment without payment of freight and all other lawful charges

TOTAL
CHARGES $

FREIGHT CHARGES ARE PREPAID
UNLESS MARKED COLLECT

$ per

(Signature of Consignor)

CHECK BOX IF COLLECT

RECEIVED, subject to the classifications and tariffs in effect on the date of the issue of this Bill of Lading, the property described above in apparent good order, except as noted (contents and condition of contents of packages unknown), marked, consigned, and destined as indicated above which said carrier (the word carrier being understood throughout this contract as meaning any person or corporation in possession of the property under the contract) agrees to carry to its usual place of delivery at said destination, if on its route, otherwise to deliver to another carrier on the route to said destination. It is mutually agreed as to each carrier of all or any of said property, over all or any portion of said route to destination and as to each party at any time interested in all or any said property, that every service to be performed hereunder shall be subject to all the bill of lading terms and conditions in the governing classification on the date of shipment.
Shipper hereby certifies that he is familiar with all the bill of lading terms and conditions in the governing classification and the said terms and conditions are hereby agreed to by the shipper and accepted for himself and his assigns.
This is to certify that the above named materials are properly classified, described, packaged, marked and labeled and are in proper condition for transportation, according to the applicable regulations of the Department of Transportation.

SHIPPER   CARRIER

PER   PER   DATE

* Mark with "X" or "RQ" if appropriate to designate Hazardous Materials or Hazardous Substances as defined in the department of Transportation Regulations governing the transportation of hazardous materials. The use of this column is an optional method for identifying hazardous materials on bills of lading per Section 172.201 (a) (1) (iii) of Title 49, Code of Federal Regulations. Also, when shipping hazardous materials, the shipper's certification statement prescribed in Section 172.204 (a) of the Federal Regulations must be indicated on the bill of lading, unless a specific exception from this requirement is provided in the Regulations for a particular material.

Figure 14-1. Bill of lading.

the name and place of business of both the shipper and receiver; a full description of the goods and the manner in which the articles are packed; the gross weight, agreed weight, or estimated weight; the car or container initials and number on carload freight; and, at the option of the shipper, the route. In addition, the bill of lading must specify any special service or handling, as well as whether the goods are considered hazardous cargo. As a receipt, the bill of lading confirms that the cargo received is in apparent good order except as noted, and is marked, consigned, and destined as specified by the shipper.

Second, the bill of lading serves as a contract of carriage in a legally standardized form. When properly executed and signed by carrier and shipper, the bill of lading is a binding contract specifying the duties and obligations of both carrier and shipper. It describes the cargo that the carrier agrees to transport, and may name the rates to be applied and charges to be collected.

Like all contracts, a bill of lading must specify any special conditions and/or limitations of the agreement; on a *long form bill of lading,* these are shown in detail on the back of the bill and are, in many cases, the most important part of the contract. Typically, these fine-print items relate to the carrier's liability (or lack of it) under various circumstances, although the ICC limits the extent to which a carrier may disclaim liability in a bill of lading. Unfortunately these items, because they are usually printed in extremely small type, are seldom read, understood, or analyzed by the parties involved. By signing the bill of lading, however, the parties do imply that they are familiar with all terms and conditions of the contract, including every word on the front and reverse sides of the document.

Unlike the long form, a *short form bill of lading*—more widely in use today—does not note the special conditions and limitations on the reverse of the document. Instead, the terms and conditions are incorporated by reference, and on the front of the form the shipper acknowledges understanding of these terms and accepts them. One value of the short form is that its use can save approximately one-third of the bill's printing costs.

Whether in its short or long form, the bill of lading contains the following statement on its front side, which constitutes the contract of carriage:

> It is mutually agreed, as to each carrier of all or any of said property over all or any portion of said route to destination, and as to each party at any time interested in all or any of said property, that every service to be performed hereunder shall be subject to all the conditions not prohibited by law, whether printed or written, herein contained, including the conditions on back hereof, which are hereby agreed to by the shipper and accepted for himself and his assigns.

It is worth noting that even if either party fails through error or oversight to sign the document, the bill of lading is still a binding document. As the ICC has specified, "It is sufficient if the shipper accepts the carrier's bill of lading without himself signing it. It becomes binding upon him by his acceptance, he being presumed to know and accept the conditions of the written bill of lading." The same reasoning holds when it is the carrier who neglects to sign. Moreover, a carrier cannot escape liability by failing to issue a bill of lading.

Third, the bill of lading is legal, documented evidence of title to the goods, in case of a dispute or controversy. A bill of lading has long been held to serve as documentary evidence of title to the goods. A transfer of the bill of lading is a legal transfer of the goods specified, and possession symbolized by the bill of lading is the same as actual legal possession. This issue is especially important in the case of an order bill of lading (described below). In every bill of lading, a person or organization must be named as consignee, the entity to whom the goods are to be delivered.

It is the carrier's legal duty to issue the bill of lading, but often the shipper will choose to prepare the forms. In such cases, the documents must conform to the format prescribed by the ICC. Shipper's bill of lading forms typically have the shipper's name preprinted on them, are prenumbered according the shipper's numbering system, and contain a classification description of the products generally shipped. A bill of lading issued by the shipper typically is in the long format, while a carrier usually utilizes the short form. The use of shipper-provided short form bills of lading is encouraged by transport organizations such as the National Industrial Transportation League (NITL) and the International Trade Facilitation Council (formerly the National Committee on International Trade Documentation, or NCITD).

Problems. As with any kind of document, a bill of lading is subject to clerical and other errors. There is, then, a question of whether a corrected bill of lading can replace the original, especially where freight charges, weights, load, and count notations are concerned. This is an important question, because it is often the shipper—and not the carrier—that weighs, loads, and counts the goods being shipped.

When a bill of lading specifies a certain weight, load, and count, the carrier must deliver the weight, load, and count noted or be held liable for the shortage. However, when the shipper does the weighing, loading, and counting, the carrier has no way (outside of the time-consuming process of reweighing, reloading, and recounting) of knowing whether the information furnished by the shipper is correct. Is it fair, therefore, to hold the carrier liable for the shipper's errors?

The Pomerene Bill of Lading Act specifies that when the goods are loaded by the shipper and the notation specifies "*shipper's* weight, load, and count," the carrier cannot be held liable for damages caused by improper loading or by incorrect description of the goods. Further, the ICC has held that when freight is not actually checked or weighed by the carrier, it is reasonable for the carrier to specify "*shipper's* weight, load, and count." Such a notation does not fully release the carrier from liability for losses and damages, but in instances where a smaller shipment arrives than the one specified in the bill of lading, the burden of proof is on the shipper and not the carrier.

Straight and Order Bills of Lading

A *straight bill of lading* is a nonnegotiable document that cannot be bought, sold, or traded, and one that shows a consignee. Most shipments are sent under the straight bill of lading. Under a straight bill of lading, the carrier is legally obligated to deliver the goods to the named consignee and to no one else. Typically, the carrier will deliver the freight without presenting the bill of lading. If the carrier is in doubt as to who is the correct consignee, it may request that the party claiming the shipment produce proof of identity, such as a copy of the shipping order, or a purchase order.

An *order bill of lading*, however, is negotiable, and can be bought or sold or conveyed by endorsement, with the shipper retaining title or control of the property until the invoice charges are paid. The name of the actual consignee is not specified, although the freight is consigned to the order of the shipper. The order bill will, however, contain a name and address of the person or organization that is to be notified when the cargo reaches or nears its destination. This designation of the party to be notified does not, however, give that party title to the shipment.

An order bill of lading may be used when the goods leave the shipper before a buyer has been found. Once a buyer is found, the shipper endorses the original copy of the order bill and takes it, along with a sight draft in the amount of the invoice, to a bank. The two documents are sent by that bank to a bank near the buyer. Upon receipt, this second bank will notify the party on whom the sight draft is drawn. The buyer pays for the goods through the second bank, which forwards the funds to the shipper's bank, and the buyer receives title to the goods when the order bill of lading is received from the bank in return for payment. The buyer then takes the bill of lading to the carrier and exchanges it for the cargo.

When an order bill of lading is negotiated, the person or organization to whom ownership of the cargo has been transferred acquires an obligation by the carrier to hold possession of the cargo, according to the terms of the bill, just as if the carrier had contracted directly with this new owner.

The Pomerene Bill of Lading Act requires that the original bill of lading, properly endorsed to the new owner of the cargo, be surrendered to the carrier before delivery of the cargo. If the original has been lost, destroyed, or delayed, however, the cargo may be delivered in advance of the bill of lading. This may be done without the carrier being held liable for mishandling the goods, as long as certain conditions are met.

An order bill of lading can be used for rail, motor, and water shipments, but it cannot be used for cargo shipped via domestic air freight or parcel post. Further, the use of an order bill of lading may be inconvenient for both buyer and carrier, because the goods typically will arrive at the destination prior to the arrival of the bank draft and order bill of lading at the buyer's bank. For these reasons, besides the order bill of lading, two other methods may be used to secure payment before delivery. These are the straight bill of lading with a release order letter, and COD service on a straight bill of lading.

The *straight bill of lading with a release order letter* is used only for rail shipments, and it eliminates the concern over possible loss of an order bill of lading. On the straight bill of lading, the shipper lists itself as the rail car's consignee and specifies the buyer to be notified upon arrival. The shipper further instructs that the rail car be delivered only after the buyer has surrendered a written release order letter or delivery order. This release order letter is an official document authorizing the railroad agent at the destination to release the rail car to the specified buyer. The railroad is obligated to follow the instructions on this bill of lading.

Another option that eliminates the need for an order bill of lading is the use of *COD service on a straight bill of lading*. COD service is offered for domestic air freight and parcel post, and, more often, by motor carriers. When delivery is made without COD charges being collected, the initial motor carrier on interline traffic is held liable. Consequently, most motor carriers do not offer COD service on shipments beyond their own lines. Others limit COD service to certain carriers whom they trust to deliver the goods after collecting COD charges.

Other Types of Bills of Lading

In addition to the straight and order bills of lading, several other variations exist and are used in particular shipping circumstances.

The *domestic bill of lading* is simply the commonly used straight or order bill of lading used for shipments in the U.S. or to Canada or Mexico.

The *livestock bill of lading* is a special form that is used for livestock shipments and that serves as the receipt given to the livestock shipper when the animals are delivered to the carrier. Because special conditions and circumstances accompany the shipping of live animals, the terms and conditions of the livestock bill of lading differ from those of the uniform straight bill of lading document. For example, the shipper must specify whether the animals are "ordinary," that is, being shipped for grazing, fattening, or slaughtering; or "other than ordinary," that is, shipped for breeding, show, or racing.

Although the livestock document differs from the uniform straight bill of lading, the purpose of the two documents is essentially the same. It is worth noting, however, that only a straight bill of lading may be used for the transport of livestock. In other words the name of the consignee must be specified, and the consignee claims title to the goods regardless of payment. The livestock bill of lading is used primarily for rail transport.

The *ocean bill of lading* may be used for domestic or export shipments. Traditionally an ocean carrier is, like a land carrier, liable for the goods being transported. Because of perils associated with water transport (storms, piracy, war, fires, etc.), a carrier's liability has historically been more limited for water transport than for surface carriage; hence, a distinct bill of lading that delineates these limitations is required for ocean cargo. Unlike inland bills, an ocean bill of lading for coastal and intercoastal shipments is prepared by the carrier only, and its use is regulated by the Carriage of Goods by Sea Act of 1936. In keeping with an ancient tradition that sailors are not expected to be skilled animal-keepers, this Act does not apply to livestock as cargo. An ocean carrier may append additional terms and conditions to the standard ones, provided they are in accordance with the law.

Issued in either long or short form, and as straight or order bill, the ocean bill of lading typically is prepared by the shipper or export agent at the port of departure, using forms provided by the ocean carrier. Any number of copies may be included to satisfy the needs of the carrier, shipper, bank, insurer, consignee, etc., but six is the most common number. Customarily three copies—called a "full set," with each containing a signature of the carrier's agent—are given to the shipper. All three are marked "original," and each contains a notation signifying the number of originals.

The full set is used to guard against documentation loss or delay, and the set is often split up and mailed at intervals. When a single original is negotiated, the others are automatically voided. Additional copies of the ocean bill of lading may be used for filing information with U.S. Customs, with a consular office overseas, and with banks.

An ocean bill of lading usually will be endorsed as referring to goods "on board" or goods "received for shipment." The on-board bill is neither signed nor surrendered until all cargo has been loaded on board. The more commonly used received-for-shipment bill signifies that cargo is being held on the dock by the carrier company, without guaranteeing transport by any particular vessel. For shippers whose cargo is still on the docks and who wish assurance that a particular vessel will be used, a carrier may issue an on-board certificate in advance of loading. But if no date certification is given, there is no guarantee as to when the goods will be shipped.

Cargo that is being held on a dock is protected by a *dock receipt* or other receipt signed by the carrier. The dock or other receipt is subject to the contract terms and conditions of the carrier's regular long-form bill of lading.

Many large-volume shippers prepare their own ocean bills, but usually freight forwarders, acting as agents for shippers or carriers, prepare the bills.

An ocean bill of lading will normally contain the following information: carrier name and address; shipper; consignee; party to be notified; booking number; bill of lading number and date; point and country of origin; loading pier and terminal; type of service being provided by carrier; mode of transport prior to ocean carriage; place of receipt by prior carrier; exporting vessel, voyage number, and voyage flag; port of loading; port of discharge; final place of delivery by subsequent carrier; marks, container numbers, and seal numbers; number of packages; description of packages and goods; gross weight; measurements; shipper's declared value; and place where freight and other charges are to be paid. The following additional information may also be included, when applicable: second party to be notified; routing; special instructions; export references; forwarding agent; and full name and address of payer of freight charges. Finally, the following information is optional: details of freight and charges; place where original bill of lading is to be released; and on-board certification that goods have been loaded.

The carrier will not surrender the ocean bill to the shipper or agent until all freight charges have been paid or special arrangements been made. Once the carrier's requirements have been satisfied, the consignee, agent, or subsequent carrier takes delivery of the shipment at the pier.

A "frustrated" ocean bill of lading refers to a bill for cargo that cannot be shipped to its destination. This usually occurs because of severe conditions such as war, political upheaval, or natural disaster. When this happens, the cargo is sent to another port, and the carrier is released from further obligation.

A *through ocean bill of lading* is used when a single bill of lading is issued by the ocean carrier to cover inland, ocean, and subsequent transport. The cargo is loaded into a container at the inland point of origin, and the same container is transferred intermodally until reaching the final destination.

This procedure has several advantages. First of all, transport rates tend to be lower than for combined ocean and surface charges, since the container makes loading and unloading easier and the consolidation reduces costs. Second, the container minimizes losses and damages due to theft. Third, because of the lower risk of loss and damage, insurance rates are lower using the container method of transport.

The *air bill of lading* (also called the *airbill* or *air waybill*) is used for air freight. Because of the relative newness of air transport compared to land and water transport, shipping by air lacks the body of traditions and customary liabilities and procedures that exist for surface and ocean travel. As a result, air carriers' responsibilities are not as well defined as are those of other carriers. The fundamental law regulating commercial air transport in the U.S. is the Federal Aviation Act of 1958. This act outlines some of the duties of air carriers; for example, they must provide reasonable through-service in conjunction with other air carriers, and they must provide safe and adequate service, equipment, and facilities. The act does not, however, discuss the transportation contract or the air carrier's liability, nor does it prohibit air carriers from limiting their liability.

Without legal precedents, air carriers have relied upon legal cases in related fields to establish liability guidelines. The guidelines are as follows: air carriers are liable only for losses and damages that result from their own negligence on their own lines; this liability is limited to a specified valuation by the shipper per shipment or per pound; and the contract of carriage is held to be the air bill of lading, which serves the same essential function as the uniform straight bill of lading.

An air bill of lading is similar to a uniform straight bill of lading in many ways, but as with the ocean bill of lading, the terms, conditions, and liabilities of transport by air differ substantially from those for transport over land. An airbill requires a valuation of the cargo. The airbill carries a customary valuation of $50 per shipment or 50 cents per pound for shipments exceeding 100 lb, unless a higher value is declared and additional charges paid. As in the case of ocean transport, air carriers are not liable for livestock as cargo.

An airbill is always issued as a straight bill only, and always uses the short form. The air carrier supplies the shipper with blank forms, and the shipper must prepare and present an airbill with each shipment. If the shipper fails to do so, the carrier will accept the shipment only when a nonnegotiable shipping document or memorandum is substituted.

An *international air bill of lading* is used in export by air. The form used is customarily that specified by the International Air Transport Association (IATA). It is issued as a through waybill by the carrier or forwarder, and it is typically prepared with at least 10 copies.

For international air transport, different liability terms apply from those for domestic air shipping. International air shipping liabilities, along with international ocean shipping liabilities, are governed by the rules of the 1929 Warsaw Convention and by the Hague Protocol of 1955. In general, unlike domestic carriers, international air carriers are not held to strict standards of liability for losses or damages; however, international air carriers are subject to a higher degree of liability than are ocean carriers.

The *government bill of lading* is a special form used for U.S. government and U.S. military shipments when goods are transported to or from government agencies. The American federal government is the world's largest shipper, using every form of transportation and shipping nearly every commodity. Because of the volume of government shipping, the U.S. prints its own documents to control transport of goods and payment of freight charges. In essence, the government bill of lading is a draft on the U.S. Treasury Department, since it is an order for payment by the federal government of freight charges.

Government regulations prohibit prepayment of freight charges; thus, a government bill of lading must be used if commercial carriers are to be paid. Shippers of goods sold to a government agency may substitute their own commercial bill of lading, but they will be billed by the carrier for freight charges. A government office may, however, authorize a carrier to use a commercial bill of lading and later substitute a government bill of lading, as long as all copies of the commercial bill contain the words "to be converted to a government bill of lading at destination." In the case of a commercial consignee for a government bill of lading shipment, the consignee is relieved of the responsibility of paying freight charges by completing the "Consignee's Certificate of Delivery" section on the bottom of the government bill of lading and giving it to the carrier.

The federal government's General Accounting Office prescribes the form and issues regulations concerning government bills of lading. Instructions to carriers and commercial shippers are found on the reverse side of the original copy. On the face of the original, the information is essentially the same as that on commercial bills, but some additional internal accounting and control information may also appear. A short-form government bill of lading has been authorized and is sometimes used.

Electronic Data Interchange and the Bill of Lading

Electronic Data Interchange (EDI) is *the computer-to-computer transmission of business information in a standardized, computer-readable form.* Using EDI, transportation documents can be transmitted electronically between shipper and carrier in seconds, eliminating data reentry errors and costly delays.

Not only is EDI faster than the traditional paper-based system, it is also more accurate because it eliminates errors associated with hard-to-read or illegible copies. EDI is more cost-effective than paper-based documentation. It is common for international shipments to require as many as 40 separate documents, many having multiple copies. While domestic shipments require less documentation, the transportation industry has long been known for being paper- and people-intensive. Using EDI, the costs of paper products, paper shuffling, and paper storage—as well as related staffing expenses—are reduced.

For both shippers and carriers, paper transportation documentation is normally generated from internal business computer applications. Using EDI, the basic information already contained in both parties' computer systems can be communicated electronically. EDI also allows additional data to be added to a transaction without rekeying the original source document.

A shipper's internal computer system can send an EDI bill of lading to a carrier. The carrier can electronically acknowledge receipt of the document, provide electronic tracking information as the shipment moves to its destination, and issue an electronic freight bill to the shipper. Using financial EDI applications, this freight bill can then be paid automatically using Electronic Funds Transfer (EFT), and the carrier can be notified with an electronic remittance advice. All of this can be accomplished economically, quickly, and accurately, with little or no human intervention.

EDI Bill of Lading

The *EDI bill of lading* is revolutionizing the transportation industry. Getting a shipment started in a timely and accurate fashion depends on the accurate and timely shipment information being sent to the carrier; an EDI bill of lading accomplishes this. The uses of the EDI bill of lading vary depending on whether the mode of transportation is rail, motor, ocean, or air carrier.

Rail.   The railroad industry was the first to use EDI bills of lading between themselves and their shippers. Prior to the advent of EDI, special couriers in automobiles picked up paper bills of lading from shippers, since a rail carrier always requires a bill of lading before a rail car can move. The courier would bring the paper document to the rail yard, where information would be key-entered and the rail car containing the cargo would be okayed for movement.

The time-consuming, error-prone nature of this process makes it easy to see why the rail industry was the first carrier mode to take advantage of EDI. The electronic bill of lading not only eliminated the need for these couriers, it also served to minimize the errors and labor costs associated with the initial key-entry of information from paper documents into the carrier's data system.

A unique aspect of rail transportation is that several rail companies are frequently involved in moving cargo from one part of the country to the other. Prior to EDI, paper waybills (routing documents) generated from the original bills of lading would be passed manually from one rail system to another, with the shipment information being key-entered again each time. The use of waybills transmitted via EDI eliminates the need for repeated key entry and the accompanying errors. This rail-carrier-to-rail-carrier use of EDI paved the way for EDI bills of lading between shippers and rail carriers.

To accommodate their shippers and to broaden the use of EDI, many major railroads have developed PC-based software that is provided to shippers. These packages allow shippers to use a PC at the shipping dock to key in information about the shipment. The PC program converts this information to standard EDI format and, in some cases, the PC will then dial the railroad's computer and transmit the information via modem.

The function of the bill of lading in the rail industry is somewhat unique, since the bill of lading does not really serve as a shipment tender. This is the case because the rail carrier either already has the rail car on the shipper's siding, or has already sent its rail car to the shipper to be loaded by the time the bill of lading is received. Thus, the rail company already knows that it will handle the specified cargo, and the document's function as a tender by the shipper is not required.

Motor.   In the motor industry, the EDI bill of lading was the last of three shipment-related EDI documents to be adopted by motor carriers. The motor carrier industry has some different constraints than the railroad industry. One way in which the motor industry differs is the existence of less-than-truckload or LTL carriers. These LTL carriers specialize in moving many shipments in a single trailer from multiple shippers to multiple destinations. Such shipments are consolidated at carrier origin terminals into "road trailers," and moved either to destination terminals or to intermediate transfer terminals.

Under this system, paper bills of lading received from all shippers are usually entered on-line into the LTL carrier's central computer system and are subject to the error-prone nature of key entry. Freight handling and information-processing systems of such LTL carriers are designed for efficient, cost-effective cargo movement. As EDI volumes grow, labor-intensive, error-prone, key-entry processes are reduced. For example, LTL carriers serving major customers with large volumes of shipments can receive EDI bills of lading at their central computer site, process the data, and send instructions back to their origin terminal as to the proper movement of the cargo.

For the second type of motor carrier, the truckload or TL carrier, scheduling of shipments usually takes place farther in advance than scheduling of LTL shipments. The shipper sending the bill of lading in such cases will truly be tendering an offer to the carrier, saying in effect, "Can you handle this shipment? If so, please let me know in a predetermined number of hours, or I'll try another carrier." EDI in this case has replaced phone calls between the shipper's scheduling staff and the carrier's dispatchers. Indeed, some of the newer information systems may be so highly automated that cargo movement can be arranged almost without human intervention.

Ocean.   The EDI bill of lading is relatively new in the ocean industry, and once again the document has some unique applications. Three important EDI documents—the booking, the booking confirmation, and the bill of lading—are used by ocean carriers to reduce errors, reduce labor costs, and speed the goods through the export process.

Typically ocean carriers ask their exporters or forwarders to transmit booking requests. The electronic booking document in the ocean industry fulfills the shipment tender function of the bill of lading. The booking document says in effect, "I've got cargo to ship to this country on this date. Can you handle it?" The ocean carrier responds with an EDI booking confirmation if it can in fact transport the cargo. After the exporter or forwarder has received this confirmation, an EDI ocean bill of lading is sent, containing specific details relevant to the shipment.

Air.   Of all transportation modes, the air industry is the one for which timeliness and accuracy are the most important. For this reason, in the late 1960s air carriers developed electronic formats for the interchange of shipment information. Today the industry uses a variety of electronic formats, but it is making a serious effort to implement a single, standardized EDI format.

Uses of the EDI Bill of Lading

Whatever the mode of transport, an EDI bill of lading ordinarily may be used in several ways. First, it may (except in the rail industry) be used as an initial shipment tender between the shipper and the carrier; in other words, the shipper sending an EDI bill of lading is offering the carrier the opportunity to transport the cargo.

Second, the EDI bill of lading may be used as a pickup notification. In addition to offering the carrier the opportunity to transport the cargo, a shipper may also specify the shipping location, commodities, quantities, and dates.

Third and most importantly, like a paper bill of lading an EDI bill of lading is a legally binding contract, once receipt has been acknowledged by the carrier via an EDI acknowledgement. The ICC has ruled that an EDI bill of lading is a permissible legal agreement, as long as a paper version of the bill of lading can be produced when and if required. Further, the ICC encourages the use of the EDI bill of lading and declared in 1983, "The electronic transmission of a B/L [bill of lading] would appear to be in the public interest . . . [and] would advance the national transportation policy goals." For legal purposes, when a paper bill is available to serve as a written receipt and as prima facie evidence of title to goods, an acknowledged EDI bill of lading is the exact equivalent of the paper document as a legally binding contract.

Future of the EDI Bill of Lading

As carrier cargo movement information systems become more sophisticated, and as shippers integrate the distribution function into their EDI-based manufacturing and logistics systems, the EDI bill of lading will expand in use and value. Because of the complexities and volumes of paper bills of lading—not to mention the rising costs of doing business, and the error-prone nature of manual rekeying—automation of the manufacturing, warehousing, transportation, and distribution cycles is inevitable. An electronic and paperless form of business communication, EDI will play an important role in extinguishing or at least controlling the "paper explosion." As a natural part of this process, transportation documentation requirements will be modified accordingly.

Other Shipping Documents

The *waybill* is the carrier's routing document; it identifies the shipper and the consignee, specifies routing, describes the goods, indicates the shipment weight, and presents other important information related to the shipment. A waybill moves with the freight; after transport is concluded, it serves as a historical record of the shipment. A freight waybill will sometimes be issued as a quadruplicate copy of a bill of lading; copies of this document may be sent to interested agents of the carrier. A waybill may also be a separate document created from information contained on the shipping order, which is a duplicate of the bill of lading.

The *delivery receipt*, frequently a copy of the freight bill (to be discussed in a moment), specifies that the shipment has arrived at its destination. It is signed by the consignee to acknowledge receipt. The consignee may note exceptions on the delivery receipt, but if none is noted, it is assumed that the contract of carriage has been fulfilled and the shipment has arrived in good order. All modes and all carriers use some form of delivery receipt, as a record of delivery and as a record to be used in the event that future claims are filed.

Special Documents

Hazardous Materials and Hazardous Wastes. Hazardous materials documentation is an area of growing importance. The shipping of dangerous goods can potentially endanger the lives of agents of the shipper, carrier, and consignee, not to mention countless uninvolved "innocent bystanders" along the transport route. The transport of dangerous cargo has been federally regulated since 1838, and as the volume of hazardous goods being transported has ballooned during the past 20 years, regulation has increased accordingly. The Hazardous Materials Transportation Act of 1974 consolidated the regulation of hazardous materials and substances under the Materials Transportation Bureau of the Department of Transportation. It also established training requirements for shippers and carriers, allowed the DOT to regulate routing and loading/unloading, and increased previous penalties for violations of regulations. The DOT subsequently established numerous classifications, definitions, and tables, related to hazardous materials and substances, to be used as guidelines by shippers and carriers.

As a result of such federal legislation, hazardous cargo is subject to special marking, handling, packing, and stowage. For example, a red warning label typically is prominently displayed on containers of highly flammable materials. It is the responsibility of the shipper to label and mark the packages. Special placards for the carrier vehicle may also be required, and the shipper is usually the one required to provide these. If a carrier knowingly accepts a shipment that is not marked in accordance with federal regulations, the carrier also becomes liable for fines and penalties. Moreover, regulations forbid the loading of hazardous materials in the same vehicle with certain other products; for example, a package bearing a poison label may not be loaded in the same car with edibles. In addition, special routings may be required for dangerous cargo; for example, many municipalities forbid the through transport of hazardous goods and mandate the use of circuitous routings and outerbelts.

A shipper is required to notify the carrier regarding the existence of hazardous cargo, and Section 6 of the bill of lading long form protects the carrier from liability in the event that dangerous goods are being shipped without written disclosure to the carrier. The disclosure must appear on the bill of lading and all related documents, and the proper shipping name (not an abbreviation) for the materials, as specified by the DOT, must be used. Opposite the shipping name, certain related information must be provided, including: special symbols; the hazard classification; identifying numbers; labels; packaging requirements or exceptions; and aircraft and water carrier restrictions. For all domestic and international shipments, all of the above information must be written legibly and in English. The bill of lading must further contain the following statement:

> This is to certify that the above-named materials are properly classified, described, packaged, marked, and labelled, and are in proper condition for transportation according to the applicable regulations of the Department of Transportation.

Shipments by water are regulated both by the DOT and the International Maritime Organization (IMO). Shipment by air requires that two copies of the airbill be provided, with the following statement

> I hereby certify that the contents of this consignment are fully and accurately described above by proper shipping name and are classified, packed, marked, and labelled, and in proper condition for carriage by air according to applicable national governmental regulations.

Each certification must be legibly signed by a representative of the shipper.

Special EDI hazardous materials messages are currently being developed. The English port of Felixstowe is working on *EDI hazardous materials messages* that would communicate information regarding hazardous materials. These documents would alert the destination port to be ready to receive, handle, and store dangerous cargo. The information received in such documents could greatly facilitate cleanup operations, security procedures, and evacuation programs in the event of leakage or spillage. It would minimize the impact of accidents involving dangerous cargo, and prevent major disasters from occurring.

Deregulation and Freight Billing

For many years, freight charges were regulated by the government. Today, deregulation has substantially changed the transportation industry. In 1978, the Airline Deregulation Act was passed and the Intercoastal Shipping Act of 1933 was amended; in 1980, the Motor Carrier Act, the Staggers Rail Act, and the Household Goods Transportation Act were passed; in 1982, the Bus Regulatory Reform Act was passed; and in 1984, the Shipping Act was passed. The result of all of this legislative activity is that carriers now aggressively vie in a free marketplace for cargo through competitive freight charges and services, while logistics managers can negotiate for better rates.

Freight Bill

The freight bill (see Fig. 14-2 for a widely used format), prepared from information found on the bill of lading, is the carrier's invoice for the transport of goods. It shows the total freight charges to be collected.

An original and multiple copies of the freight bill are typically created by the carrier. Some copies are used at the point of origin; one copy usually goes to the carrier's general office for accounting purposes; several copies are sent to the shipper or consignee, or their agent, for payment. Additional copies travel with the

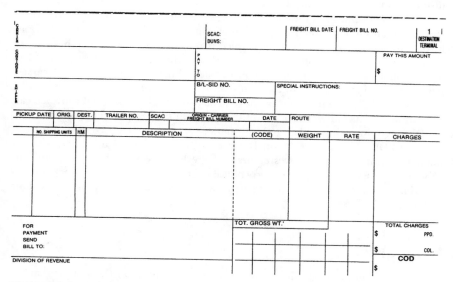

Figure 14-2. Freight bill.

freight and are used for freight handling as the cargo moves. At the destination, two copies are given to the consignee, one being retained and the other being signed and used as a delivery receipt.

Federal regulations mandate that carriers collect on freight bills within specified credit periods. Moreover, regulations provide for fines for carriers who fail to remind customers of past due bills and who neglect to cut off credit to delinquent customers. Shippers, too, may be subject to similar penalties under federal law.

The *EDI freight bill* is growing in popularity (see previous section, "EDI Bill of Lading"), especially among larger carriers, shippers, and consignees. The task of handling paper invoices can be complicated and tedious; when volumes of paper invoices—as many as several thousand a day—are involved, the invoicing procedure can be extremely error-prone and time-consuming at both ends. The EDI freight bill has the typical advantages of electronic documentation: speed, accuracy, and economy. Its use can minimize errors and result in financial savings for carriers, shippers, and consignees.

Few other industries generate the large volumes of invoices seen in the transportation industry. One shipment usually equals one invoice, and the very large LTL motor carriers, for example, are likely to handle more than 70,000 shipments per day. In the retail industry, shippers and consignees process enormous volumes of shipments, and invoices in excess of one million per year from a single carrier are not uncommon. Given this immense volume, it should come as no surprise that the freight invoice was the first EDI document to be implemented by motor carriers who looked to EDI as a means of improving their billing procedures.

Another factor other than volume spurred the adoption of EDI freight invoicing. In the years prior to deregulation, motor carriers were required by the ICC to collect freight charges within seven days, and rail carriers were required to collect within five days. Companies thus had an incentive to process and pay their freight invoices correctly and promptly.

A primary advantage of the EDI freight invoice is its accuracy. Invoicing on paper typically entails several potential errors, including the following: carrier mails paper invoice to wrong company; carrier invoice is not in same format as other carrier invoices, causing confusion by payer's processing clerks; carrier invoice is not legible; shipper processes paper invoice incorrectly; shipper incorrectly enters carrier payment reference number or amount due. In many cases, correcting errors such as these may involve a full hour or more of staff time. The EDI freight invoice can substantially reduce these errors and the amount of time required to correct them.

EDI freight invoicing is likely to be even more accurate when used in conjunction with the EDI bill of lading. Manual data entry at any stage of the transportation documentation process involves errors that are likely to be carried through into subsequent stages. But when the procedure gets off to a good start by being automated in its earliest stages, invoicing errors are likely to be minimal or nonexistent later on.

Filing Claims

The freight claim is a significant area of potential conflict in the shipper/carrier relationship. With the enormous volume of shipments that carriers transport daily, it is inevitable that some loss and damages will occur. In addition to damage due to improper handling, claims may arise from thefts, unnecessary transfers, spoilage of perishable commodities, and accidents. Traditionally, the carrier is legally liable to some degree for transporting the goods without loss or damage, and for billing according to prearranged rates. As we have seen, the bill of lading was originally an attempt by carriers to limit liability, and legal liability for cargo has historically varied with carrier mode. In addition to loss and damage claims, shippers have recourse to file for alleged freight overcharges.

Loss or Damage Claims

Shipper Responsibilities. Freight is naturally subject to a certain amount of rough handling by the carrier, and it is expected that shippers will anticipate this and package goods accordingly. A carrier will not be held liable for loss or damage occurring en route when it can be proven that the shipper has failed to: prepare and pack goods properly; use suitable containers for the goods; properly load, stow, and brace the goods; give proper, definite, and legible shipping instructions, both in the bill of lading and in marking the packages; and make reasonable and definite requests for temperature control, when desired.

The shipper is further expected to give the carrier notice of special conditions that would result in loss or damage when unforeseeable delays occur. Such notice must be prompt, complete, and in writing; the written notice should communicate the eventual purpose or use of the goods and should specify the need for promptness. Limited and vague notations such as "Please Rush" on a bill of lading ordinarily are not sufficient to make the carrier fully liable for damages resulting from delays. In addition, the shipper has special responsibilities when the cargo being shipped constitutes hazardous materials, substances, or waste.

Carrier Responsibilities. A carrier is expected, when receiving a shipment, to verify that goods are: adequately packed; properly marked; labeled accordingly when fragile or perishable; and labeled accordingly when other special handling is required. After shipment has been accepted for transport, the carrier is responsible for handling the cargo safely and for delivering the cargo to the consignee in the same condition in which it was received from the shipper.

In the event of a claim, the carrier is expected to make the claimant "whole," that is, to satisfy the claim as if no loss or damage had occurred. If the articles cannot be repaired or reconditioned, the carrier is considered liable for the full actual cost of the losses or damages. If the goods can be repaired, the carrier is liable for repair costs, plus incidental expenses that occur while repair work is being done.

Consignee Responsibilities. In general, the consignee is expected to accept damaged property and to use reasonable means to minimize the loss, where possible. Acceptance by the consignee of a damaged or delayed shipment does not jeopardize any just claim by the shipment's owner.

Procedures for Filing Loss and Damage Claims

Perhaps surprisingly, for all its control over transportation, the ICC has no authority over disputed claims. The ICC has, however, set up a series of principles and procedures for the filing and administration of claims documents; this is in keeping with its duty to lay down rules for the handling of claims. The ICC specifies the following: a claim must be filed within the time limit specified in the bill of lading terms (these vary according to mode and type of claim—nine months is usual); a claim must be specific and in writing; the carrier must acknowledge, within 30 days, receipt of each claim and indicate in writing the need for additional information; the carrier must pay, refuse, or compromise a claim within 120 days, or the carrier must advise the claimant of the claim status and reason for delay within 60 days; and, when retained by the carrier, damaged freight may, after notice to and with permission from the claimant, be sold as salvage.

On the claimant's side, the cost of preparing the claim should be taken into account when deciding whether to file. For this reason, some companies have minimum values for claims filing, below which the claim is not filed. It is illegal for the claimant to deduct money for loss and damage claims from freight charges for subsequent shipments by the same carrier. Claims should be filed promptly, since a delay may cause a greater delay in satisfaction of the claim.

Sometimes losses or damages are simply noted on the *delivery receipt*. This method of identifying losses and damages is commonly used when the loss or damage is evident at the time of delivery. In such cases, the consignee should carefully inspect the damaged items, making precise notation of the damage, in some cases even photographing the goods. When the loss or damage is significant, the situation is reported immediately to the shipper, and the shipper's logistics department requests that an *inspection and claim report* be prepared by the carrier and signed by the consignee. This report is not an admission of carrier liability, but it may represent an agreement by the carrier as to the condition of the shipment. Whenever possible, damaged items should be separated from the rest of the shipment until the claim has been resolved.

Another type of damage is concealed damage, which does not become apparent until after delivery. This situation represents a particularly problematical area, since the damage may have occurred before or after the carrier handled the goods. As a result, concealed damage claims are often difficult to collect, and the courts often side with the carrier in such disputes, unless it is clearly proven that the cargo was in good condition when accepted for transport and in damaged condition when delivered.

A special *consignee concealed loss or damage form* is ordinarily used, and is filed with the shipper. Concealed damage ought to be reported as soon as it is discovered, ideally within 15 days after delivery, if possible. As with evident damage, the concealed-damage goods should be carefully inspected, recorded, and perhaps even photographed. Legal regulations regarding the maximum reporting time for concealed damages vary depending on carrier mode.

Whether for concealed or evident loss or damage, the claim is commonly filed against the initial or delivering carrier. For filing the claim, the *standard form for presentation of loss and damage claims* is used. This form gives the particulars of the claim situations and requests reparation in a specific dollar amount.

After the claim has been filed, the carrier will return a *claim acknowledgment* form within 30 days, as required by the ICC. This response verifies the claim number and amount, assigns a carrier claim number, and makes note if additional documentation is needed to process the claim.

EDI Loss and Damage Claims

Electronic loss and damage claims filing is currently being used between rail carriers and automobile manufacturers. The use of EDI loss and damage claims is not yet widely extended, but testing is also being done by several motor carriers.

Some carriers receive electronic loss and damage claims and respond automatically from internal databases with faxed copies of the delivery receipt and bill of lading for the shipment in question. The claim can thus be filed and handled promptly, and there is little or no waiting for additional documentation. This results in a faster and more accurate claims settlement, providing better customer service on the part of the carrier and greater customer satisfaction on the part of the claimant.

By the mid-1990s, paperless loss and damage claims filing is expected to become more widespread, especially among the larger carriers.

Overcharge Claims

The number of freight bills received by some of the larger shippers is staggering. As with loss and damage claims, the sheer volume of business in America makes overcharges inevitable. Careful auditing of freight bills is critical, and recovered overcharges for a single high-volume shipper may run as high as $1 million per year.

It is of course illegal for a carrier to intentionally overcharge a shipper or consignee, but such overcharges occur through mistakes and oversights. Since deregulation has made freight charges negotiable, shippers and carriers must keep careful records of agreed-upon rates.

Sloppy, illegible, or inaccurate bill of lading information is almost sure to result in billing problems. Since the freight bill is prepared from information found on the bill of lading, proper preparation and handling of the bill of lading can help both parties avoid overcharges. Overcharges typically result from any one or more of the following: errors in calculating charges; errors in copying information onto the freight bill from the bill of lading; errors in recording shipment weight; errors made in commodity descriptions; errors in applying rates; and differences in rate interpretations.

As mentioned above, overcharges due to clerical errors can be greatly minimized by the use of electronic documentation, especially the EDI bill of lading and the EDI freight bill. When the electronic loop is completed by using EDI for the bill of lading, freight bill, funds transfer, and remittance advice, overcharge claims can be reduced almost to the point of nonexistence.

Unlike loss and damage claims, overcharge claims ordinarily fall within the jurisdiction of the ICC. The ICC has approved a *standard form for the presentation of overcharge claims*. All sections of this form are to be completed. It should be filed by the party paying the freight charges, although it may be filed on the party's behalf by the external auditor. In the event that the movement of goods involves more than a single carrier, the claim is filed against the carrier that presents the freight bill containing the overcharge. The error should be identified on the overcharge claim form. The only required accompanying document is the original of the paid freight bill, but typically the original of the bill of lading and the freight bill should both be attached. If these originals are not available, photocopies may be substituted, along with an indemnity agreement explaining why the originals cannot be produced. As with claims for loss and damage, it is illegal for the claimant to deduct money for overcharge claims from freight charges for subsequent shipments by the same carrier.

Summary

Accurate documentation for every shipment, and prompt handling of transportation claims, is not only good business practice, it is the law. The bill of lading is the most important of all transportation documents and serves as a cargo receipt, certificate of title, and legal contract of carriage. As such it should be completed carefully and accurately, since it protects both the shipper and the carrier.

Since deregulation of the transportation industry in the late 1970s and early 1980s, carriers now vie for freight in a free marketplace. Shippers are looking for carriers that provide high levels of customer service, consistent on-time pickup and delivery, competitive pricing, and state-of-the-art technology.

Electronic communications—such as EDI bills of lading, EDI freight invoices, and EDI claims—bring speed, accuracy, and economy to the transportation documentation process. EDI is changing the way companies conduct their transportation business. The use of EDI in transportation is encouraged by the ICC and is growing rapidly, especially among the larger shippers and carriers. EDI is expected to be widespread throughout the transportation industry by the year 2000, even becoming a condition for doing business with most shippers.

Further Reading

Bowersox, Donald J., David J. Closs, and Omar K. Helferich, *Logistical Management,* 3d ed., Macmillan, New York, 1986.

Buys, Clifford R., *Motor Carrier/Shipper Electronic Data Interchange,* American Trucking Associations, Alexandria, VA, 1985.

Cavinato, Joseph L., ed., *Transportation-Logistics Dictionary,* 3d ed., International Thomson Transport Press, Washington, DC, 1989.

Colton, Richard C., and Edmund S. Ward, *Practical Handbook of Industrial Traffic Management,* 5th ed., rev. by Charles H. Wager, The Traffic Service Corp., Washington, 1973.

Flood, Kenneth U., Oliver G. Callson, and Sylvester J. Jablonski, *Transportation Management,* 4th ed., Wm. C. Brown Co., Dubuque, IA, 1984.

Interstate Commerce Commission, *Electronic Transmission of Loss and Damage Claims and Freight Bills,* ICC, Washington, 1982, 1983.

Johnson, James C., and Donald F. Wood, *Contemporary Physical Distribution,* 2d ed., Petroleum Pub. Co., Tulsa, Oklahoma, 1982.

Knorst, William J., *Transportation and Traffic Management,* 12th ed., vol. 1, College of Advanced Traffic, Chicago, 1970.

McElhiney, Paul T., and Charles L. Hilton, *Introduction to Logistics and Traffic Management,* Wm. C. Brown Co., Dubuque, IA, 1968.

National Committee on International Trade Documentation (NCITD), *Ocean Bill of Lading: Identification and Location of Transportation Data Elements,* NCITD, New York, n.d.

————, *The Paper Work Explosion,* NCITD, New York, 1968.

Rose, Warren, *Logistics Management: Systems and Components,* Wm. C. Brown Co., Dubuque, IA, 1979.

Sampson, Roy J., and Martin T. Farris, *Domestic Transportation: Practice, Theory, and Policy,* 4th ed., Houghton Mifflin Company, Boston, 1979.

Sigmon, Richard R., *Miller's Law of Freight Loss and Damage Claims,* 4th ed., Wm. C. Brown Co., Dubuque, IA, 1974.

Taff, Charles A., *Management of Physical Distribution and Transportation,* 6th ed., Richard C. Irwin, Homewood, IL, 1978.

Toffler, Alvin, *Powershift,* Bantam Books, New York, 1990.

Wood, Donald F., and James C. Johnson, *Readings in Contemporary Distribution,* 2d ed., PennWell Books, Tulsa, 1983.

Wortman, Leon A., *A Deskbook of Business Management Terms,* AMACOM, New York, 1979.

15

Hazardous Materials Management

David E. Gibbs
Director, Environmental Affairs,
Webco Industries

Larry W. Moore
Director, Materials Management,
Fibercast Co.

The recent proliferation of regulations regarding the management of hazardous materials and hazardous waste is unprecedented. The media has been quick to point out evidence of damage to human health and the environment from past and current hazardous materials management practices. As the public becomes more aware of issues affecting the environment, elected officials are becoming more responsive in terms of environmental legislation. Love Canal, Times Beach, and Bhopal, India, are a few of the places where ecological damage, illness, and even death has been attributed to improper and sometimes irresponsible management of hazardous materials. Events such as these have helped to hasten enactment of the Resource Conservation and Recovery Act (RCRA) of 1976; the Comprehensive Environmental Response, Compensation and Liability Act (CERCLA) of 1980, better known as Superfund; and the Superfund Amendments and Reauthorization Act (SARA) of 1984.

Transportation is a vital element of hazardous materials management. When hazardous materials are offered for transportation, the shipper passes all control of the materials to the transporter. However, the shipper retains the ultimate responsibility and liability for any damages that may result during transportation.

In the case of hazardous waste, federal law dictates that the generator of the waste is perpetually responsible for the waste, regardless of any contractual indemnity offered by either the transporter or the treatment, storage, and disposal facility (TSDF). Many manufacturing companies have found themselves involved in expensive Superfund enforcement actions and subsequent litigation due to the inappropriate management practices of their transporter or their TSDF. However, Superfund's axiom of "strict liability" excludes any requirement of negligence to establish liability. Liability is incurred when environmental damage has been caused, regardless of the events leading to the damage.

The *Environmental Manager's Compliance Advisor,* published by Business and Legal Reports (BLR), summarized 1990 transportation incidents involving hazardous materials. Approximately 8500 accidents in 1990 resulted in nearly $33 million of damages. BLR reports that truckers make an average of 500,000 hazardous materials shipments each day. With this volume of hazardous materials on the public highway system, it is imperative that Department of Transportation (DOT) regulations be interpreted accurately and implemented unequivocally.

Selection of the hazardous materials transporter must be made with the utmost caution. A physical audit of the facility is essential. Most reputable transporters will welcome an audit or inspection by a potential customer. References, compliance history, up-to-date permits, driver training, emergency preparedness, insurance coverage, and transportation equipment should be carefully examined during the audit.

Regulatory Review

History of Transportation Regulations

The first federal regulation of hazardous materials occurred a few years after the end of the Civil War. Many accidents occurred, causing loss of lives and damage to property, during the transport of sensitive explosives over land and sea. The Nitroglycerine Law was enacted in 1866 to restrict transportation routes and reduce accidents.

Many more regulations followed the 1866 law. The majority of the regulations were intended to help protect the public's safety and property while maintaining a healthy commerce. However, the laws were enacted by many different governing entities who had little or no knowledge of what type of regulations the other regulating authorities were promulgating. The result was a quagmire of confusing, conflicting, and overlapping regulations, making it nearly impossible for a shipper to be certain of full compliance.

Different regulations on labeling, placarding, shipping papers, etc. existed for air, water, and land. The Hazardous Materials Transportation Act (HMTA) of 1975 reorganized nearly a century of piecemeal regulations under a single authority designated as the Department of Transportation. The only exceptions to Department of Transportation authority are those hazardous substances and materials shipped in bulk by water. These types of shipments are regulated by the United States Coast Guard.

Rule-Making Procedures

Transportation regulations are found in Title 49 of the *Code of Federal Regulations,* more commonly referred to as 49 CFR. A proposed regulation begins with a piece of legislation drafted by Congress. In some cases this will go through many changes and revisions. After the final form of the bill has been passed by Congress, the statute is sent to the regulating agency for codification.

FR (Federal Register).   After the Department of Transportation's RSPA (Research and Special Projects Administration) codifies the legislative language into a regulation, the proposed regulation is printed in the *Federal Register* (FR). The *Federal Register* is published each business day. The daily FR includes proposed regulations, final regulations, and announcements concerning administrative decisions on many different subjects.

A public commenting period allows industry, trade groups, and citizens to challenge, question, and comment on the proposed regulations as published in the FR. Significant comments and their responses will be published in the FR. Depending on the level of complexity and controversy, several rounds of public commenting periods may be necessary before the proposed regulation is finalized and published in the *Code of Federal Regulations* (*CFR*).

Code of Federal Regulations (CFR).   After careful consideration of all comments submitted during the public commenting period, the final form of the regulation is printed in the CFR. Updated CFRs are issued each year. However, in many cases the regulated community is subject to the requirements of the new regulation many months before the CFR is available. Therefore it may be risky to depend on the CFR alone to ensure regulatory compliance. In addition to the daily FR, many updating services are available to the shipper to aid in maintaining compliance.

Updating Services, and Other Helpful Publications

Unless one has the luxury of perusing reams of *Federal Register*'s on a regular basis, it is difficult to keep current with recent regulatory developments. Due to the time lag between the time a final regulation is published in the FR and the time the next CFR is printed, a hazardous materials transporter may not be aware of the new regulation. This could lead to a situation that finds the transporter not in compliance and subject to enforcement actions, including penalties.

Several methods of obtaining current regulatory information are available other than daily reading of the FR. Some trade groups have excellent resources available that monitor regulatory developments pertaining to their industry. Also, publications such as the BLR's *Environmental Manager's Compliance Advisor* (mentioned earlier), J. J. Keller and Associates, and the Bureau of National Affairs publish periodicals on proposed regulations and other regulatory information. In addition to providing timely notice of pending regulations, many of these publications offer regulatory interpretation and advisory services that may aid the shipper in selecting the best compliance method for a particular situation. Although these are excellent services, it is the shipper who must make the final decision as to how compliance will be met.

Definitions of Hazardous Materials

Depending on what set of regulations is being used, several definitions of regulated materials exist. Figure 15-1 illustrates the overlapping between the various agencies' classifications of regulated materials.

In addition to DOT's hazardous *materials,* there are hazardous *wastes* and hazardous *substances.* Each term has a unique meaning, and refers to specific lists found in the federal regulations.

49 CFR and HM (House Measure) 181

The Department of Transportation lists over 3000 materials that may potentially pose a hazard while being transported. The list of DOT hazardous materials, sometimes referred to as "the Commodities Table," may be found in 49 CFR 172.101 for domestic shipments and 49 CFR 172.102 for international shipments.

HM (House Measure) 181 has consolidated these lists into a single list, found in 172.102. RSPA has developed the table in HM 181 to conform with international shipper requirements. Other important changes in HM 181 include incorporation of International Hazard Classes, replacement of DOT packaging design specifications with performance-oriented packaging specifications (POPS), packing group designations, elimination of the ORM (other regulated material) designation (with the exception of ORM D), and adoption of new hazard labels and placards.

OSHA

OSHA (Occupational Safety and Health Administration) is concerned with employee exposure to chemicals in the work environment. Worker safety, container labeling, material safety data sheets (MSDS), and hazard communication are gov-

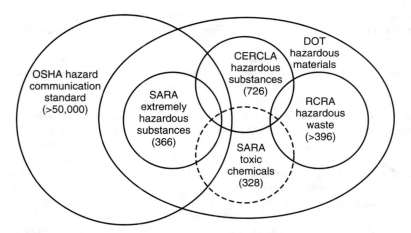

Figure 15-1. Approximate overlapping between different lists of regulated materials.

erned by OSHA regulations. OSHA's Hazard Communication Program is known as "Employee Right to Know." OSHA container markings and labeling are required at all times, not only while the material is in transit. OSHA's regulations supplement DOT's requirements.

CERCLA

CERCLA (Comprehensive Environmental Response, Compensation, and Liabilities Act) is commonly referred to as Superfund. CERCLA-regulated materials are called *hazardous substances.* Hazardous substances are chemicals that could pose a threat to human health and the environment if not properly controlled. CERCLA also has strict reporting requirements concerning hazardous material spills. These spill reporting requirements are stringent, and heavy penalties can be levied if there is a failure to report. Spill reporting requirements will be discussed in more detail in a later section of this chapter.

SARA

SARA (Superfund Amendments and Reauthorization Act) is an amendment to the Superfund Law. SARA Title III requires reporting of chemicals in storage and chemical use. The inventory reporting is known as Tier 1 or Tier 2 reporting. The report used to document chemical use is known as Form R. Only facilities meeting certain SIC (standard industrial classification) codes and other criteria are required to report.

The Form R is concerned with documenting certain chemicals entering the environment, either as a product, a component of a product, or a waste. This information is reported before each July 1 for the previous year's activity. The reporting rules under Form R have had major changes each year since reporting was first required in 1987. Many consider Form R reporting to be one of the most onerous of all EPA reports. Generally, most shippers are in the fortunate position of being excluded from these reporting requirements.

Tier 1 and Tier 2 are usually somewhat simpler to complete than Form R. In most cases, either the Tier 1 or the Tier 2 form may be used. Both forms require essentially the same type of information. The Tier 2 is slightly more detailed and is usually recommended, or sometimes may be required, by the agency receiving the reporting information.

Basically, Tier 2 or Tier 1 reports are necessary for all chemicals on the OSHA List. Any chemical for which OSHA has established exposure limits is considered to be on the OSHA List, and a material safety data sheet (MSDS) is required. If the chemical is located at a covered facility, in excess of the 10,000-lb TPQ (threshold planning quantity), at any time during the calendar year, a report is required. A covered facility is designated by certain SIC Codes. If, however, a facility stores a chemical on the SARA EHS (extremely hazardous substance; 40 CFR, part 355, appendixes A and B) List, the TPQ may be less than 10,000 lb. Tier 2 or Tier 1 reports are due by each March 1 following the reporting year.

An additional requirement for facilities that store an EHS chemical is to participate with local emergency response agencies in emergency planning. The local emergency response agency is often a local fire department. SARA has designated the agency with this responsibility as the LEPC (Local Emergency Planning Committee). Each LEPC then coordinates with their respective State Emergency Response Commission (SERC) to develop a statewide emergency response plan.

RCRA

RCRA (Resource Conservation and Recovery Act) governs hazardous waste generators and hazardous waste transporters. Treatment, storage, and disposal facilities (TSDF) are also subject to regulation under RCRA. Later in this chapter, specific RCRA regulations regarding hazardous waste transportation requirements will be discussed in detail.

Hazardous Materials Tables

In 49 CFR there are two tables of hazardous materials. Part 172.101 is to be used for domestic shipments and 172.102 is for international shipments. Quantity limitations are shown for either highway, water, or air transportation. An appendix to 172.101 lists the hazardous substances, their common synonyms and reportable quantities. This list is also known as the CERCLA list. A copy of the first page of the table is shown in Fig. 15-2.

The two tables found in 49 CFR, domestic and international, have been combined in HM 181 to form one table consistent with international regulations. The CERCLA List is discussed in more detail in a later section of this chapter.

Table in 49 CFR 172.101

The table in 49 CFR 172.101 lists DOT hazardous materials. A copy of the first page of the table is shown in Fig. 15-3. Proper shipping names, hazard class, label(s) required, placarding, and packaging information are shown for each hazardous material listed. Additionally, quantity limitations are shown for either highway, water, or air transportation. The Hazardous Materials Table in 49 CFR 172.101 contains seven columns of information. The information listed in each column is now described.

Column 1. Column 1 contains three symbols as appropriate:

+ fixes the proper shipping name and the hazard class for that entry, without regard to whether the material meets the definition of that class.

A (abbreviation for Air) indicates that the DOT regulations apply when this material is transported by aircraft.

W (abbreviation for Water) indicates that the DOT regulations apply when this material is transported by vessel.

Column 2. Column 2 is entitled "Hazardous Materials Descriptions and Proper Shipping Names." The proper shipping names are shown in Roman type, but the words in italic may be used in addition to the proper shipping name. Shipping names may be used in the singular or plural and in either upper- or lowercase let-

LIST OF HAZARDOUS SUBSTANCES AND REPORTABLE QUANTITIES

Hazardous Substance	Synonyms	Reportable Quantity(RQ) Pounds(Kilograms)
Acenaphthene		100 (45.4)
Acenaphthylene		5000 (2270)
Acetaldehyde *	Ethanal	1000 (454)
Acetaldehyde, chloro-	Chloroacetaldehyde	1000 (454)
Acetaldehyde, trichloro-	Chloral	1 (0.454)
Acetamide, N-(aminothioxomethyl)-	1-Acetyl-2-thiourea	1000 (454)
Acetamide, N-(4-ethoxyphenyl)-	Phenacetin	1 (0.454)
Acetamide, N-fluoren-2-yl-	2-Acetylaminofluorene	1 (0.454)
Acetamide, 2-fluoro-	Fluoroacetamide	100 (45.4)
Acetic acid *		5000 (2270)
Acetic acid, ethyl ester	Ethyl acetate	5000 (2270)
Acetic acid, fluoro-, sodium salt	Fluoroacetic acid, sodium salt	10 (4.54)
Acetic acid, lead salt	Lead acetate	5000 (2270)
Acetic acid, thallium(I) salt	Thallium(I) acetate	100 (45.4)
Acetic anhydride *		5000 (2270)
Acetimidic acid, N-[(methylcarbamoyl)oxy]thio-methyl ester	Methomyl	100 (45.4)
Acetone *	2-Propanone	5000 (2270)
Acetone cyanohydrin *	Propanenitrile, 2-hydroxy-2-methyl-	10 (4.54)
Acetonitrile *	2-Methyllactonitrile	5000 (2270)
3-(alpha-Acetonylbenzyl)-4-hydroxycoumarin and salts	Ethanenitrile	100 (45.4)
Acetophenone	Warfarin	5000 (2270)
2-Acetylaminofluorene	Ethanone, 1-phenyl-	1 (0.454)
Acetyl bromide *	Acetamide, N-fluoren-2-yl-	5000 (2270)
Acetyl chloride *		5000 (2270)
1-Acetyl-2-thiourea	Ethanoyl chloride	1000 (454)
Acrolein *	Acetamide, N-(aminothioxomethyl)-	1 (0.454)
Acrylamide	2-Propenal	5000 (2270)
Acrylic acid *	2-Propenamide	5000 (2270)
Acrylonitrile *	2-Propenoic acid	100 (45.4)
Adipic acid	2-Propenenitrile	5000 (2270)
Alanine, 3-[p-bis(2-chloroethyl)amino]phenyl-, L-	Melphalan	1 (0.454)
Aldicarb	Propanal, 2-methyl-2-(methylthio)-, O-[(methylamino)carbonyl]oxime	1 (0.454)
Aldrin *	1,2,3,4,10,10-Hexachloro-1,4,4a,5,8,8a-hexahydro-1,4:5,8-endo,exo-dimethanonaphthalene	1 (0.454)
Allyl alcohol *	2-Propen-1-ol	100 (45.4)
Allyl chloride *		1000 (454)
Aluminum phosphide *		100 (45.4)
Aluminum sulfate *		5000 (2270)
2-Amino-1-methyl benzene	o-Toluidine	1 (0.454)
4-Amino-1-methyl benzene	p-Toluidine	1 (0.454)

Figure 15-2. Appendix to part 172.01, aka the CERCLA list.

8172.101 Hazardous Materials Table

(1) +/A/W	(2) Hazardous materials descriptions and proper shipping names	(3) Hazard class	(3A) Identification number	(4) Label(s) required (if not excepted)	(5) Packaging (a) Exceptions	(5) Packaging (b) Specific requirements	(6) Maximum net quantity in one package (a) Passenger carrying aircraft or railcar	(6) (b) Cargo only aircraft	(7) Water shipments (a) Cargo vessel	(7) (b) Passenger vessel	(7) (c) Other requirements
	Accumulator, pressurized (pneumatic or hydraulic), containing nonflammable gas	Nonflammable gas	NA1956	Nonflammable gas	173.306		No limit	No limit	1,2	1,2	
	Acetal	Flammable liquid	UN1088	Flammable liquid	173.118	173.119	1 quart	10 gallons	1,3	4	
	Acetaldehyde (ethyl aldehyde)	Flammable liquid	UN1089	Flammable liquid	None	173.119	Forbidden	10 gallons	1,3	5	
A	Acetaldehyde ammonia	ORM-A	UN1841	None	173.505	173.510	No limit	No limit	1,2	1,2	Stow separate from nitric acid or oxidizing materials
	Acetic acid (aqueous solution)	Corrosive material	UN2790	Corrosive	173.244	173.245	1 quart	10 gallons	1,2	1,2	Stow separate from nitric acid or oxidizing materials
	Acetic acid, glacial	Corrosive material	UN2789	Corrosive	173.244	173.245	1 quart	10 gallons	1,2	1,2	
	Acetic anhydride	Corrosive material	UN1715	Corrosive	173.244	173.245	1 quart	1 gallon	1,2	1,2	
	Acetone	Flammable liquid	UN1090	Flammable liquid	173.118	173.119	1 quart	10 gallons	1,3	4	
	Acetone cyanohydrin	Poison B	UN1541	Poison	None	173.346 173.3a	Forbidden	55 gallons	1	5	Shade from radiant heat. Stow away from corrosive materials
	Acetone oil	Flammable liquid	UN1091	Flammable liquid	173.118	173.119	1 quart	10 gallons	1,2	1	
	Acetonitrile	Flammable liquid	NA1648	Flammable liquid	173.118	173.119	1 quart	10 gallons	1	4	Shade from radiant heat
	Acetyl acetone peroxide, in solution with not more than 9% by weight active oxygen. See Organic peroxide, liquid or solution, n.o.s.		UN2080								
	Acetyl acetone peroxide with more than 9% by weight active oxygen	Forbidden									
	Acetyl benzoyl peroxide, not more than 40% in solution. See Acetyl benzoyl peroxide solution, not over 40% peroxide		UN2081								
	Acetyl benzoyl peroxide, solid, or more than 40% in solution	Forbidden									
	Acetyl benzoyl peroxide solution, not over 40% peroxide	Organic peroxide	UN2081	Organic peroxide	None	173.222	Forbidden	1 quart	1,2	1	Keep dry. Glass carboys not permitted on passenger vessels
	Acetyl bromide	Corrosive material	UN1716	Corrosive	173.244	173.247	1 quart	1 gallon	1	1	Stow away from alcohols. Keep cool and dry.
	Acetyl chloride	Flammable liquid	UN1717	Flammable liquid	173.244	173.247	1 quart	1 gallon	1	1	Separate longitudinally by an intervening complete compartment or hold from explosives

Figure 15-3. First page of table in 49 CFR 172.101.

15.8

ters. The word *or* in italics indicates that any terms in the sequence may be used (e.g., Isobutane *or* Liquefied petroleum gas). When one shipping name references another by the use of the word *see,* and if both names are in Roman type, either name may be used as the proper shipping name (except for organic peroxides). For an organic peroxide, the technical name must be used as the proper shipping name.

The abbreviations used in Column 2 have the following meanings:

"n.o.s." means "not otherwise specified."

"n.o.i." means "not otherwise indexed."

"n.o.i.b.n." means "not otherwise indexed by name."

If the hazardous material to be transported is a hazardous waste, the word "Waste" must precede the shipping name (e.g., Waste acetone).

Column 3. Column 3 lists the hazard class corresponding to each proper shipping name or the word "Forbidden." A material shown as "Forbidden" in Column 3 is prohibited from transportation unless the materials are diluted, stabilized, or incorporated in devices, and it is classed in accordance with the definitions of hazardous materials contained in 49 CFR 173.

Column 3(a) lists the identification numbers assigned to hazardous materials. Numbers preceded by "UN" (abbreviation for United Nations) are appropriate for international shipments as well as domestic shipments. Numbers preceded by "NA" (abbreviation for North America) are associated with shipments within the United States and Canada.

Column 4. Column 4 specifies the labels required to be applied to each package.

Column 5. Column 5 references applicable packaging regulations in 49 CFR 173. Column 5(b) indicates specific packaging requirements. Column 5(a) references exceptions to some of the packaging requirements.

Column 6. Column 6(a) specifies the maximum net quantity allowed in one package for transportation by aircraft or passenger railcar. The term "Forbidden" in this column means the material may not be transported by aircraft or passenger railcar. Column 6(b) lists the maximum net quantity permitted in one package for transportation by cargo-only aircraft. These materials must bear the CARGO AIRCRAFT ONLY label.

Column 7. Column 7(a), (b), and (c) specifies each of the authorized locations on board cargo vessels and passenger vessels, and certain additional requirements. The numeric symbols represent the following vessel locations where the materials must be stowed during transportation:

1—on deck

2—under deck

3—under deck, away from heat

4—limited quantities, cargo vessel stowage

5—forbidden from vessel transportation

6—explosives carried in a magazine

The Optional Hazardous Materials Table, 49 CFR 172.102, describes requirements for hazardous materials being transported by international shipments. This Optional Hazardous Materials Table is being replaced by HM 181. HM 181 is discussed in detail in a subsequent section of this chapter.

DOT Proper Shipping Name. The shipping description of a hazardous material on the shipping paper must include the proper shipping name for the material in 49 CFR 172.101, the hazard class prescribed for the material in the same CFR section, and the UN or NA identification number prescribed for the material in the same CFR section. If appropriate, RQ (reportable quantity) may also be required either at the beginning or at the end of the DOT proper shipping name. RQs are discussed in a later section of this chapter. The basic description must be shown in the sequence just described. For example: "Gasoline, Flammable Liquid, UN1203."

Placarding. Each person who offers for transportation or transports any hazardous material must place placards on each end and each side of the transport vehicle, with some exceptions. These placards generally describe the primary hazard of the material with a symbol and a word or words. Most placards are approximately 10 in square and are diamond-shaped (square on point). Placarding requirements are described in detail in 49 CFR 172.500.

The specific placard required for a particular material is determined by identifying the Hazard Class of the material in the Hazardous Materials Table (49 CFR 172.101), then cross-referencing Table 1 or Table 2 in 49 CFR 172.504. Table 1 identifies placards for the listed classes of materials shipped in any quantity, while Table 2 generally identifies placards for the listed classes of materials shipped in quantities of 1000 lb or more. Copies of Tables 1 and 2 are shown in Figs. 15-4 and 15-5, respectively.

Numerous placarding exceptions and special cases are described in 49 CFR 172.500. For instance, vehicles containing two or more classes of materials requiring different placards specified in Table 2 may be placarded DANGEROUS, in place of

TABLE 1

If the transport vehicle, or freight container contains a material classed (described) as—	The transport vehicle or freight container must be placarded on each side and each end—
Class A explosives	EXPLOSIVES A.[1]
Class B explosives	EXPLOSIVES B.[2]
Poison A	POISON GAS.[1]
Flammable solid (DANGEROUS WHEN WET label only)	FLAMMABLE SOLID W.[3]
Radioactive material	RADIOACTIVE.[4, 5]
Radioactive material:	
Uranium hexafluoride, fissile (containing more than 1.0 pct U 235)	RADIOACTIVE [4] AND CORROSIVE.[6]
Uranium hexafluoride, low specific activity (containing 1.0 pct or less U 235)	RADIOACTIVE [4, 5] AND CORROSIVE.[6]

[1]See § 172.510(a).
[2]EXPLOSIVES B placard not required if the transport vehicle or freight container contains class A explosives and is placarded EXPLOSIVES A as required.
[3]FLAMMABLE SOLID "W" placard is required only when the DANGEROUS WHEN WET label is specified in § 172.101 for a material classed as a Flammable solid.
[4]Applies only to any quantity of packages bearing the RADIOACTIVE YELLOW III label. (See § 172.403.)
[5]For exclusive use shipments (see § 173.403) of low specific activity radioactive materials transported in accordance with § 173.425 (b) or (c).
[6]CORROSIVE placard not required for shipments of less than 1000 pounds gross weight.

Figure 15-4. Table 1 in 49 CFR 172.504.

TABLE 2

If the transport vehicle, or freight container contains a material classed (described) as—	The transport vehicle or freight container must be placarded on each side and each end—
Class C explosives	DANGEROUS.[1, 9]
Blasting agents	BLASTING AGENTS.[9, 10]
Nonflammable gas	NONFLAMMABLE GAS.[8]
Nonflammable gas (chlorine)	CHLORINE.[7]
Nonflammable gas (fluorine)	POISON.
Nonflammable gas (oxygen, cryogenic liquid)	OXYGEN.
Flammable gas	FLAMMABLE GAS.[8]
Combustible liquid	COMBUSTIBLE.[3, 4]
Flammable liquid	FLAMMABLE.
Flammable solid	FLAMMABLE SOLID.[5]
Oxidizer	OXIDIZER.[9, 10]
Organic peroxide	ORGANIC PEROXIDE.
Poison B	POISON.
Corrosive material	CORROSIVE.[6]
Irritating material	DANGEROUS.

[1] Applies only to a class C explosive required to be labeled with an EXPLOSIVE C label.
[2] [Reserved]
[3] COMBUSTIBLE placard required only when a material classed as a combustible liquid is transported in a packaging having a rated capacity of more than 110 gallons, a cargo tank, or a tank car.
[4] A FLAMMABLE placard may be used on a cargo tank or portable tank during transportation by highway, rail or water, and on a compartmented tank car containing materials classed as flammable liquid and combustible liquid.
[5] Except when offered for transportation by water, a FLAMMABLE placard may be displayed in place of a FLAMMABLE SOLID placard except when a DANGEROUS WHEN WET label is specified for the material in sec. 172.101. (See table 1, this section.)
[6] See § 173.245(b) of this subchapter for authorized exceptions.
[7] CHLORINE placard required only for a packaging having a rated capacity of more than 110 gallons; the NON-FLAMMABLE GAS placard for packagings having a rated capacity of 110 gallons or less.
[8] A NON-FLAMMABLE GAS placard is not required on a motor vehicle displaying a FLAMMABLE GAS placard or an OXYGEN placard.
[9] BLASTING AGENTS, OXIDIZER and DANGEROUS placards need not be displayed if a transport vehicle or freight container also contains Class A or Class B explosives and is placarded EXPLOSIVES A or EXPLOSIVES B as required.
[10] Except for shipments by water, OXIDIZER placards need not be displayed if a freight container, motor vehicle or rail car also contains blasting agents and is placarded BLASTING AGENT as required.

Figure 15-5. Table 2 in 49 CFR 172.504.

the separate placarding specified for each of those classes of materials specified in Table 2. However, when 5000 lb or more of one class of material is loaded therein at one loading facility, the placard specified for that class in Table 2 must be applied. This does not apply to a portable tank, cargo tank, or tank car. Other situations, exceptions, and special cases are detailed in 49 CFR 172.500 but are too numerous to be included in the scope of this writing.

Packaging.   DOT specifies packaging requirements for hazardous materials in 49 CFR 173. The information contained in this section is primarily very specific, because it deals with individual hazardous materials or groups of hazardous materials. Packaging exceptions and specific requirements are referenced in the Hazardous Materials Table (49 CFR 172.101), Column 5, or the Optional Hazardous Materials Table (49 CFR 172.102), Column 6. The types of packaging information contained in this 49 CFR 173 section are: Class A, B, C Explosives; Flammable and Combustible Liquids; Flammable Solids; Oxidizers; Organic Peroxides; Corrosive Materials; Gases; Poisonous Materials; Radioactive Materials; Other Regulated Materials (ORM-A, ORM-B, ORM-C, ORM-D, ORM-E).

More general packaging and preparation-for-shipment information is contained in 49 CFR 173.1 through 173.34. Examples of the types of information contained in these sections are: exceptions for small quantities; agricultural operations; oil field service vehicles; air shipments; tank car shipments; standard requirements for all packages, authorized packages, and overpacks; use of cylinders; and classification of material having more than one hazard. Because of the specific nature of these sections, the CFR should be consulted for the individual material of concern.

Labels.   Each person who offers a package, overpack, or freight container containing a hazardous material for transportation shall label it, when required. Labels prescribed for the material are specified in the Hazardous Materials Table (49 CFR 172.101), Column 4, or the Optional Hazardous Materials Table (49 CFR 172.102), Column 5. Specific labels are described and illustrated in 49 CFR 172.411 through 172.450. Each label required must be printed or affixed to the package near the marked proper shipping name, and must not be obscured by markings or attachments. The label must be durable and weather-resistant. Each diamond (square on point) label must be at least 4 in on each side, with a black solid-line border ¼ in from the edge. When two or more labels are required they must be displayed next to each other. The 49 CFR 172.400 should be consulted for details of other labeling exceptions and special cases. Most available labels now meet the HM 181 configuration. (HM 181 is discussed in the following section). HM 181 labels may be used interchangeably with labels described in 49 CFR until the transition to HM 181 regulations is complete. After HM 181 has been fully implemented, previous labels will be obsolete.

Hazardous Materials Table in HM 181 (172.102)

House Measure 181 is the nomenclature given to the final rule that comprehensively revises the Hazardous Materials Regulations (49 CFR 171–180) with respect to hazard communication, classification, and packaging requirements. The changes are based on the United Nations' *Recommendations on the Transport of Dangerous Goods*; i.e., it is consistent with international transportation standards. The final rule was published in the *Federal Register*, vol. 55, no. 246, Friday, December 21, 1990, and became effective October 1, 1991. Even though the regulation went into effect on October 1, 1991, the required dates of compliance with certain sections of HM 181 are being phased in until October 1, 1996. Because of this extended implementation period, users of 49 CFR, Parts 100–180, are urged to retain the October 1990 editions of the CFR containing the superseded rules. HM 181 is expected to be codified into 49 CFR. The Hazardous Materials Table in HM 181 replaces both the Hazardous Materials Table in 49 CFR 172.101 and the Optional Hazardous Materials Table in 49 CFR 172.102. A copy of the first page of the HM 181 table is included in this chapter and is identified as Fig. 15-6. The information listed in each column is now described.

   Column 1.   Column 1 of the Hazardous Materials Table contains five symbols: "+," "A," "D," "I," and "W."

+ fixes the proper shipping name, hazard class, and packing group for that entry, without regard to whether the material meets the definition of that class or packing group.

A (abbreviation for Air) indicates that the regulations apply when this material is transported by aircraft.

Sym-bols	Hazardous materials descriptions and proper shipping names	Hazard class or Division	Identifica-tion Numbers	Pack-ing group	Label(s) required (if not excepted)
(1)	(2)	(3)	(4)	(5)	(6)
	Accellerene, see p-Nitrosodimethylaniline				....
	Accumulators, electric, see Batteries, wet etc.				
D	Accumulators, pressurized, pneumatic or hydraulic (containing non-flammable gas).	2.2	NA1956		NONFLAM-MABLE GAS.
	Acetal..	3	UN1088	II	FLAMMABLE LIQUID.
	Acetaldehyde..	3	UN1089	I	FLAMMABLE LIQUID.
A	Acetaldehyde ammonia..	9	UN1841	III	CLASS 9...........
	Acetaldehyde oxime	3	UN2332	II	FLAMMABLE LIQUID.
	Acetic acid, glacial or Acetic acid solution, more than 80 per cent acid, by mass.	8	UN2789	II	CORROSIVE....
	Acetic acid solution, more than 10 per cent but not more than 80 per cent acid, by mass.	8	UN2790	II	CORROSIVE....
	Acetic anhydride...	8	UN1715	II	CORROSIVE....
	Acetone..	3	UN1090	II	FLAMMABLE LIQUID.
	Acetone cyanohydrin, stabilized...	6.1	UN1541	I	POISON...........
	Acetone oils	3	UN1091	II	FLAMMABLE LIQUID.
	Acetonitrile, see Methyl cyanide				
	Acetyl acetone peroxide with more than 9% by mass active oxygen.	Forbid-den			....
	Acetyl benzoyl peroxide, solid, or more than 40% in solution......	Forbid-den			
	Acetyl bromide...	8	UN1716	II	CORROSIVE....
	Acetyl chloride...	3	UN1717	II	FLAMMABLE LIQUID, CORROSIVE.
	Acetyl cyclohexanesulfonyl peroxide, more than 82 per cent wetted with less than 12 per cent water.	Forbid-den			
	Acetylene, dissolved	2.1	UN1001		FLAMMABLE GAS.
	Acetylene (liquefied)	Forbid-den			....
	Acetylene silver nitrate...	Forbid-den			
	Acetylene tetrabromide, see Tetrabromoethane				
	Acetyl iodide	8	UN1898	II	CORROSIVE...
	Acetyl methyl carbinol	3	UN2621	III	FLAMMABLE LIQUID.
	Acetyl peroxide, see Diacetyl peroxide, etc.				
	Acetyl peroxide, solid, or more than 25 percent in solution..........	Forbid-den			
	Acid butyl phosphate, see Butyl acid phosphate........................				
	Acid, sludge, see Sludge acid..				
	Acridine...	6.1	UN2713	III	KEEP AWAY FROM FOOD.
	Acrolein dimer, stabilized	3	UN2607	III	FLAMMABLE LIQUID.

Figure 15-6. First page of the HM 181 table.

Special provisions	(8) Packaging authorizations (§173.***)			(9) Quantity limitations		(10) Vessel stowage requirements	
	Exceptions	Non-bulk packaging	Bulk packaging	Passenger aircraft or railcar	Cargo aircraft only	Vessel stowage	Other stowage provisions
(7)	(8A)	(8B)	(8C)	(9A)	(9B)	(10A)	(10B)
	306	306	None	No limit	No limit	A	
T7	150	202	242	5 L	60 L	E	
A3, B16, T20, T26, T29.	None	201	243	Forbidden	30 L	E	
	155	204	241	200 kg	200 kg	A	34
T8	150	202	242	5 L	60 L	A	
A3, A6, A7, A10 B2, T8.	154	202	242	1 L	30 L	A	12, 21, 48
A3, A6, A7, A10 B2, T8.	154	202	242	1 L	30 L	A	112
A3, A6, A7, A10, B2, T8.	154	202	242	1 L	30 L	A	40
T8	150	202	242	5 L	60 L	B	
2, A3, B9, B14, B74, B76, B77, N34, T38, T43, T45.	None	227	244	Forbidden	30 L	D	25, 40, 49, M2
T7, T30	150	202	242	5 L	60 L	B	
B2, T12, T26	154	202	242	1 L	30 L	C	8, 40
A3, A6, A7, N34, T18, T26.	None	202	243	1 L	5 L	B	40
	None	303	None	Forbidden	15 kg	D	25, 40, 57
B2, T9	154	202	242	1 L	30 L	C	8, 40
B1, T1	150	203	242	60 L	220 L	A	
	153	213	240	100 kg	200 kg	A	
T1	150	203	242	60 L	220 L	A	40

Figure 15-6 (*Continued*)

D identifies the proper shipping names that are appropriate for describing materials for domestic transportation, but may be inappropriate for international transportation.

I identifies the proper shipping names that are appropriate for describing materials in international transportation. An alternate proper shipping name may be selected when only domestic transportation is involved.

W (abbreviation for Water) indicates that the regulations apply when this material is transported by vessel.

Column 2. Column 2 lists hazardous materials descriptions and proper shipping names. Note the following:

1. Proper shipping names are limited to those shown in Roman type (not italics).
2. Proper shipping names may be used in the singular or plural, and in either capital or lowercase letters.
3. Punctuation marks and words in italics are not part of the proper shipping name.
4. The abbreviation "n.o.i." or "n.o.i.b.n." may be used interchangeably with "n.o.s."
5. Except for hazardous wastes, when qualifying words are used as part of the proper shipping name, their sequence in the package markings and shipping paper description is optional. However, the entry in the Table reflects the preferred sequence.
6. When one entry references another entry by use of the word "see," if both names are in Roman type, either name may be used as the proper shipping name (e.g., Ethyl alcohol, *see* Ethanol).
7. Use of the prefix "mono" is optional in any shipping name, when appropriate.
8. Hazardous substances. The appendix to this section lists materials that are listed or designated as hazardous substances under section 101(14) of the Comprehensive Environmental Response, Compensation, and Liability Act (CERCLA). Proper shipping names for hazardous substances shall be determined as follows:
   a.. If the hazardous substance appears in the Table by technical name, then the technical name is the proper shipping name.
   b.. If the hazardous substance does not appear in the Table and is not a forbidden material, then an appropriate generic or "n.o.s." shipping name shall be selected corresponding to the hazard class (and packing group, if any) of the material.
9. If the word "Waste" is not included in the hazardous material description in column 2 of the Table, the proper shipping name for a hazardous waste shall include the word "Waste" preceding the proper shipping name of the material. For example: "Waste acetone."
10. A mixture or solution comprised of a hazardous material identified in the Table by technical name and a nonhazardous material shall be described using the proper shipping name of the hazardous material. The qualifying word "mixture" or "solution" should be used as appropriate. See 172.101(c)(10) for listed exceptions.

Column 3. Column 3 contains a designation of the hazard class or division corresponding to each proper shipping name, or the word "Forbidden." A material for which the entry in this column is "Forbidden" may not be offered for transportation or be transported. This prohibition does not apply if the material is diluted, stabilized or incorporated in a device, and it is classed in accordance with the definitions of hazardous materials contained in part 173.

Column 4. Column 4 lists the identification number assigned to each proper shipping name. Those preceded by the letters "UN" are associated with proper shipping names considered appropriate for international transportation as well as domestic transportation. Those preceded by the letters "NA" are associated with proper shipping names not recognized for international transportation except to and from Canada.

Column 5. Column 5 specifies one or more packing groups assigned to a material corresponding to the proper shipping name and hazard class for that material. Classes 1, 2, and 7 materials, combustible liquids, and ORM-D materials do not have packing groups. Packing Groups I, II and III indicate that the degree of danger presented by the material is either great, moderate, or minor, respectively.

Column 6. Column 6 specifies the hazard warning label(s) required for a package filled with a material conforming to the associated hazard class and proper shipping name.

Column 7. Column 7 specifies codes for special provisions applicable to hazardous materials. When column 7 refers to a special provision for a hazardous material, the meaning and requirements of that special provision are as described in 172.102.

Column 8. Columns 8A, 8B, and 8C specify the applicable sections for exceptions, nonbulk packaging requirements, and bulk packaging requirements, respectively, in part 173. Columns 8A, 8B, and 8C are completed in a manner which indicates that "part 173" precedes the designated numerical entry. For example, the entry "202" in Column 8B associated with the proper shipping name "Gasoline" indicates that for this material conformance to nonbulk packaging requirements prescribed in 173.202 is required.

Column 8A contains exceptions to some of the requirements. Column 8B references the section in part 173 that prescribes packaging requirements for nonbulk packagings. Column 8C specifies the section in part 173 that prescribes packaging requirements for bulk packaging other than IM (intermodal) portable tanks. A "None" in either column 8A, 8B, or 8C means that no packaging exceptions are authorized. Authorizations for use of IM portable tanks are set forth in column 7.

Column 9. Columns 9A and 9B specify the maximum quantities that may be offered for transportation in one package by passenger-carrying aircraft or passenger-carrying railcar or by cargo aircraft only.

"Forbidden" means that the material may not be offered for transportation or transported in the applicable mode of transport. For example, methyl ethyl ketone peroxide (MEKP) containing in excess of 9 percent oxygen is forbidden. The MEKP would have to be diluted to below a 9 percent oxygen concentration to be acceptable for transportation.

Column 10. Column 10A (Vessel Stowage) specifies the authorized stowage locations on board cargo and passenger vessels. Column 10B (Other Provisions) specifies codes for stowage requirements for specific hazardous materials. The meaning of each code in column 10B is set forth in 176.84. The authorized stowage locations specified in column 10A are defined as follows:

Stowage category A means the material may be stowed "on deck" or "under deck" on a cargo vessel and a passenger vessel.

Stowage category B means the material may be stowed "on deck" or "under deck" on a cargo vessel, but must be stowed "on deck" on a passenger vessel.

Stowage category C means the material must be stowed "on deck" on a cargo vessel and on a passenger vessel.

Stowage category D means the material must be stowed "on deck" on a cargo vessel, but is prohibited on a passenger vessel.

Stowage category E means the material may be stowed "on deck" or "under deck" on a cargo vessel, but is prohibited on a passenger vessel.

Proper DOT Shipping Name. The shipping description of a hazardous material on the shipping paper must include the proper shipping name prescribed for the material in column 2 of the 172.102 Table, the hazard class or division as shown in column 3, the identification number prescribed in column 4, the packing group, if any, prescribed in column 5 preceded by the letters "PG," and the total quantity of the hazardous material covered by the description. "Dangerous when wet" shall be entered on the shipping paper for those types of materials.

The basic description must be shown in sequence, with no additional information interspersed. For example: "Gasoline, 3, UN 1203, PG II." The letters "RQ" shall be entered either before or after the basic description to indicate that a "Reportable Quantity" is being shipped. For example: "Allyl alcohol, 3, UN 1098, PG I, RQ." RQs will be discussed in greater detail later in this chapter.

The technical name of the hazardous material must be entered in parentheses in association with the basic description. For example: "Corrosive liquid, n.o.s., (Caprylyl Chloride), 8, UN 1760, PG II"; or "Corrosive liquid, n.o.s., 8, UN 1760, PG II (contains caprylyl chloride)."

If a hazardous material is a mixture or solution of two or more hazardous materials, the technical names of at least two components most predominantly contributing to the hazards of the mixture or solution must be entered in parentheses.

Numerous other special cases and exceptions to these proper shipping name guidelines are applicable. Proper shipping descriptions are covered by sections 172.202 through 172.203.

Placarding. Each person who offers for transportation or transports any hazardous material must place placards on each end and each side of the transport vehicle, with some exceptions. These placards generally describe the primary hazard of the material with a symbol and a word or words. Most placards are approximately 10 in square (as described by 172.519[c][1]) and are diamond-shaped (square on point). Placarding requirements are described in detail in 172.500 through 172.560.

The specific placard required for a particular material is determined by identifying the category of material (hazard class or division number, and additional description as appropriate) from the Hazardous Materials Table (172.102), then cross-referencing Table 1 or Table 2 in 172.504 to find the corresponding placard name and placard design section reference. A copy of Table 1 and Table 2 is shown in Fig. 15-7.

Table 1 identifies placards for the listed categories of materials shipped in any quantity, while Table 2 generally identifies placards for the listed categories of materials shipped in quantities of 1000 lb or more.

Numerous placarding exceptions and special cases are described in 172.500. For instance, vehicles containing two or more classes of materials requiring different placards specified in Table 2 may be placarded DANGEROUS, in place of the separate placarding specified for each of those classes of materials specified in Table 2. However, when 5000 lb or more of one class of material is loaded at one loading facility, the placard specified for that class in Table 2 must be applied. Other situations, exceptions, and special cases are detailed in 172.500 and the sections following, but are too numerous to be included in the scope of this writing.

Packaging.   HM 181, section 178, details the requirements for nonbulk packaging. This regulation is a major departure from 49 CFR packaging specifications, because HM 181 uses performance-oriented standards rather than design-oriented standards. A performance standard states the criteria that must be met in order for a package to be acceptable. Performance standards are stated in terms of leak testing, drop testing, etc. This is in contrast to a design standard, which states specifically how each package must be constructed. A design standard will specify the type of lumber, the dimensions of the lumber, the type of nails, the number of nails, etc.

HM 181 uses 20 performance standards to replace approximately 100 design standards for packages. These performance standards are consistent with international transportation requirements. Section 173 contains general and specific information on shipments and packagings, while section 178 contains standards for manufacturing and testing packagings.

Labels.   Each person who offers a package, overpack, or freight container containing a hazardous material for transportation shall label it, when required, with labels prescribed for the material as specified in the Hazardous Materials Table (172.102), column 6. Specific labels are described and illustrated in 172.411 through 172.450.

Each label required must be printed or affixed to the package near the marked proper shipping name, and must not be obscured by other markings or attachments. The label must be durable and weather-resistant. Each diamond (square on point) label must be at least 4 in, with each side having a black solid-line border $\frac{1}{4}$ in from the edge. When two or more labels are required, they must be displayed next to each other. Section 172.400 should be consulted for details of other labeling exceptions and special cases. Some examples of labels are shown in Fig. 15-8.

Hazardous Materials Table Appendix

Following the list(s) of hazardous materials in HM 181 and 49 CFR is an appendix. The appendix is also known as the CERCLA List. Chemicals on the CERCLA list are

Table (a)

Category of material (Hazard class or division number and additional description, as appropriate)	Placard name	Placard design section reference (§)
1.1	EXPLOSIVES 1.1	177.522
1.2	EXPLOSIVES 1.2	172.522
1.3	EXPLOSIVES 1.3	172.522
2.3	POISON GAS	172.540
4.3	DANGEROUS WHEN WET	172.548
6.1 (PG I, inhalation hazard only)	POISON	172.554
7 (Radioactive Yellow III label only)	RADIOACTIVE	172.556

(a)

Table (b)

Category of material (Hazard class or division number and additional description, as appropriate)	Placard name	Placard design section reference (§)
1.4	EXPLOSIVES 1.4	172.523
1.5	EXPLOSIVES 1.5	172.524
1.6	EXPLOSIVES 1.6	172.525
2.1	FLAMMABLE GAS	172.532
2.2	NON-FLAMMABLE GAS	172.528
3	FLAMMABLE	172.542
Combustible liquid	COMBUSTIBLE	172.544
4.1	FLAMMABLE SOLID	172.546
4.2	SPONTANEOUSLY COMBUSTIBLE	172.547
5.1	OXIDIZER	172.550
5.2	ORGANIC PEROXIDE	172.552
6.1 (PG I or II, other than PG I inhalation hazard)	POISON	172.554
6.1 (PG III)	KEEP AWAY FROM FOOD	172.553
6.2	(None)	
8	CORROSIVE	172.558
9	CLASS 9	172.560
ORM-D	(None)	

(b)

Figure 15-7. (a) Table 1 and (b) Table 2 in 172.504.

Figure 15-8. Hazardous materials labels.

referred to as hazardous substances. However, when DOT refers to a hazardous substance, a slightly modified definition is used. This will be discussed in more detail in the following section on reportable quantities. In addition to listing reportable quantities, common chemical synonyms are also found in the appendix.

When selecting a proper shipping name, the synonyms listed in the appendix can be very useful. When determining a proper shipping name, one may not be found to match exactly the name of the chemical on the container label or the Material Safety Data Sheet. When this happens, it is helpful to check the CERCLA List in the appendix for possible synonyms. Where the name of the hazardous material is marked with an asterisk, the material will be listed by that name in the commodities table.

DOT Hazardous Substances and Reportable Quantities

Enactment of SARA Title III included provisions and procedures for reporting releases of hazardous substances. A reporting threshold was established for each hazardous substance. These reporting thresholds are referred to as *reportable quantities,* or *RQs.* All RQs may be found in the appendix to the hazardous materials table. As previously mentioned, this appendix is also known as the CERCLA or Superfund list. RQs are calculated based on the amount of the listed chemical in a single shipping container. If the chemical is a mixture, then only the CERCLA hazardous substance component is used to calculate the RQ.

Reportable quantities are frequently the source of much confusion to the shipper. To determine if RQ is required on the shipping papers, container markings, or the hazardous waste manifest, first determine if the material in question is listed in the appendix.

If the material is listed in the appendix and if the listed RQ is in a single container, then DOT's definition of a hazardous substance applies. In this case RQ should be noted on all the shipping paperwork, container markings, and hazardous waste manifest as an integral component of the proper DOT shipping name.

If the RQ quantity is not in a single container, DOT's definition of a hazardous substance does not apply. In this case, do not list RQ along with the proper DOT shipping name on shipping papers, container markings, or the hazardous waste manifest. See 49 CFR 172.8, "Definitions and Abbreviations," for DOT's definition of a hazardous substance.

General Operating Requirements

Shipping Papers

Most shipments of hazardous materials require some form of shipping papers or other documentation to accompany the material while in transit. Shipping papers are often referred to as a *bill of lading* or *waybill.* Exceptions to shipping paper requirements and other shipping information may be found in 49 CFR 172.200.

When a hazardous material is required to be listed on shipping papers, the following procedure must be followed:

1. When nonregulated materials are to be shipped with regulated materials, the regulated material must be listed first, or . . .
2. The regulated material description must be highlighted in some way such as written in contrasting ink, or . . .
3. Must be identified by placing an X in the column marked "HM." RQ may be entered instead of an X if appropriate.

The shipping papers must be printed in English and be legible. Use of unauthorized abbreviations is prohibited. An emergency-response telephone number must be included. The shipper must also certify that the material meets the DOT requirements, using the specific language found in 49 CFR 172.204.

Shipping papers must be within reach of the driver at all times while the vehicle is in operation. When the driver is not in the vehicle, the shipping papers must be either in the driver's seat or in a pocket on the inside of the driver's door.

Commercial Driver's License (CDL)

DOT regulations require that all transportation workers operating vehicles on public roads obtain a CDL. The CDL requirement is intended to reduce the number of bus and truck accidents and fatalities by standardizing licensing criteria. All commercial vehicle drivers are required to obtain a CDL, and may not possess any additional type of driver's license. A driver is allowed to carry a CDL upon successful completion of knowledge and skills testing.

Driver Training

There are many driver training programs to help prepare transportation workers to successfully operate the sophisticated transportation equipment in use today. In addition to understanding how to safely operate the large tractor-trailer units on the public highway system, the driver must also be familiar with emergency response procedures to protect himself/herself and the public. Knowledge of hazardous materials and proper loading procedures is essential. The driver also must be familiar with chemical spill or release reporting requirements, and with the personal protective equipment that may be required in an emergency. Training should also include recognition of the limitations of the emergency equipment. If not properly trained in use of emergency equipment, the driver may develop a false sense of security that may lead to catastrophic consequences.

Since it is the transporter that has information supplied by various shippers regarding the nature of hazardous materials on the vehicle, the transporter must be familiar with materials that are not compatible. For example, a vehicle must not carry acids and cyanides at the same time.

Emergency Equipment

The emergency equipment required depends on the type of materials transported. For example, if a load contains a corrosive material, a neutralizing agent should be available in the event of a small spill or leak. Certain equipment, however, should be standard on all vehicles. Fire extinguishers, emergency flares, first-aid kit, flashlight and spare batteries, and other equipment depending on road conditions and the environment are essential.

Emergency Response

Any person who offers for transportation or accepts for transportation or storage any hazardous materials must provide and maintain emergency-response information. According to 49 CFR 172.600, this emergency-response information must be immediately available and include:

- A 24-hour emergency-response telephone number, monitored at all times by a knowledgeable person or someone who has immediate access to a knowledgeable person. The telephone number must be on the shipping paper.
- The basic description and technical name of the material

- The immediate hazards to health
- The risks of fire and explosion
- Immediate precautions to be taken
- The initial methods of handling spills
- Preliminary first-aid measures

The information must be printed legibly in English, available for use away from the package, and presented on a shipping paper. Emergency information may also be found on the MSDS or other emergency-response guidance document. Carriers must maintain this information in the same manner as a shipping paper. Facility operators must maintain the information in a location that is immediately accessible.

Spills and Leaking Containers. It is nearly impossible to provide an exhaustive compilation of the many different scenarios involving hazardous materials spills. Attempting to cover all possible situations is beyond the scope of this chapter. A driver should be trained in the proper spill-response techniques for whatever materials are in transport.

The driver must be aware of the reportable quantity for each hazardous substance on the vehicle. As explained in an earlier section of this chapter, DOT only uses the term hazardous substance when the material is listed on the CERCLA list (appendix following the hazardous materials tables in 49 CFR) *and* the RQ quantity is contained in a single shipping container.

For example, a driver may be transporting a chemical with an RQ of 1000 lb. If the chemical is contained in several 55-gal drums weighing 500 lb each when ready for shipment, then the RQ notation is *not* to be entered as part of the proper DOT shipping name. In this case, the chemical does not meet DOT's definition of a hazardous substance, even though the chemical is on the CERCLA List and has an RQ.

On the other hand, if the chemical is being transported in containers that contain 1000 lb or more of the chemical (e.g., a tank truck), the RQ notation is required as part of the DOT proper shipping description. In this case, the DOT definition of a hazardous substance applies.

In the event of a spill or other unpermitted release of the chemical to the environment, the driver must immediately notify either the shipper (via the 24-hour emergency number on the shipping papers), the transportation company supervisor, or someone who is familiar with the various agency reporting requirements. If a volume of material meeting or exceeding the RQ is released into the environment, certain reporting requirements may be required. Severe penalties may be assessed for not reporting a reportable spill. If a reported spill is later found not to be reportable, the reporting individual is not likely to be penalized. In other words: *If in doubt, report!!!*

An additional requirement that transporters and facility managers must be aware of is the potential liabilities they share whenever a transportation vehicle with a leaking container comes onto a facility's property. The owner or operator of the facility shares the responsibility of the leaking container, regardless of whether or not a business relationship exists between the facility and the transporter. If the vehicle were to leave the property with the container still leaking, the facility owner or operator could share the liability with the transporter for any subsequent damage caused.

DOT Emergency Response Guidebook.   Each driver transporting hazardous materials should be familiar with the *DOT Emergency Response Guidebook*. This book gives brief instructions on the proper responses to hazardous materials releases. The hazardous materials are listed by common name and also are listed by UN or NA number.

Reporting Hazardous Materials Incidents.   Certain incidents involving hazardous materials may require reporting to the DOT or other regulating agency. According to 49 CFR 171.15, at the "earliest practical moment" each carrier who transports hazardous materials (including hazardous wastes) shall give notice that, during transportation, loading, unloading, or temporary storage, an incident has occurred. The reportable incident must involve one of the following situations:

1. As a direct result of hazardous materials
   - A person is killed
   - A person receives injuries requiring hospitalization
   - Estimated carrier or other property damage exceeds $50,000
   - An evacuation of the general public occurs lasting one or more hours
   - One or more major transportation arteries or facilities is closed or shut down for one hour or more
   - The operational flight pattern or routine of an aircraft is altered

2. Fire, breakage, spillage, or suspected radioactive contamination occurs, involving shipment of radioactive material.

3. Fire, breakage, spillage, or suspected contamination occurs involving shipment of etiologic agents.

4. A situation exists of such a nature that, in the judgment of the carrier, it should be reported even though it does not meet the criteria above.

Each notice shall be given to the DOT by telephone by dialing 800-424-8802. If the notice involves etiologic agents, the Center for Disease Control in Atlanta, Georgia, should be contacted at 404-633-5313 rather than the DOT. Each notice must be followed by a written report in duplicate on DOT Form F5800.1, within 30 days.

Each notice given by phone must include the following information: name and phone number of the reporter; name and address of the carrier represented by the reporter; date, time, and location of incident; extent of injuries; classification, name, and quantity of hazardous material involved; and whether a continuing danger to life exists at the scene.

In addition to the notices and reporting mentioned above, DOT requires each carrier who transports hazardous materials to report any unintentional release of hazardous materials from a package (including a tank), or any quantity of hazardous waste that has discharged during transportation, loading, unloading, or temporary storage. If the report pertains to a hazardous waste discharge, a copy of the hazardous waste manifest must be attached to the report. The report must also contain an estimate of the quantity of the waste removed from the scene, the name and address of the facility to which the waste was taken, and the manner of disposition of any removed waste. A copy of the report shall be retained for a period of two years at the carrier's principal place of business.

Reporting is not required for unintentional releases of hazardous materials being transported under the following proper shipping names:

- Consumer commodity
- Battery, electric storage, wet, filled with acid or alkali
- Paint and paint-related material, when shipped in quantities of 5 gal or less

These exceptions do not apply to incidents involving transportation aboard aircraft, incidents involving transportation of hazardous waste, or incidents requiring immediate notification by telephone, as described earlier in this section. Note: EPA requires reporting of releases of hazardous substances in any quantity equal to or greater than the reportable quantities as stipulated in 40 CFR 302.6. These requirements are in addition to the DOT notices and have been previously discussed in this chapter.

Hazardous Waste Transportation

In addition to DOT regulations, EPA also regulates shipments of hazardous wastes. The EPA's transportation requirements may be found in 40 CFR 262. EPA's definition of a hazardous waste may be found in 40 CFR 261. It is the responsibility of the waste generator to determine at what point in a process a material is a waste. If the material is a waste, the generator of the waste must determine if it meets any of EPA's definitions of hazardous waste. It is the generator's responsibility to properly identify the waste. A careful review of 40 CFR 261 is necessary in order to make this determination. A specific sequence must be followed when determining if a waste is hazardous.

A hazardous waste may be generated from a production process. Examples include spent solvents from degreasing of parts in an assembly operation, or emission-control dust generated from secondary lead smelting. Unused chemicals that have become contaminated from cleanup of spills or leaks may also be hazardous. A chemical may have exceeded its recommended shelf-life and no longer be a useful material. The chemical may have become contaminated with some other substance that renders the product useless for its intended purpose. Additionally, a chemical substance may simply no longer be used in the process, due to production changes or elimination of a product.

To determine the appropriate EPA Hazardous Waste Code, first consider wastes generated from specific sources. The generating process must be compared to the list of processes and their associated wastes in 40 CFR 261.32. This list is broken down into various industries. Wastes fitting any of these processes are considered listed hazardous wastes by the EPA. All EPA Hazardous Waste Codes in this category begin with the letter K. These wastes are referred to as "specific source" listed wastes by the EPA.

If a generated waste does not fit any of the industrial categories on the K list, the next list to consider is the F list. The F list is known as the "non-specific source" list and is found in 40 CFR 261.31. These wastes are generated from processes generally not associated with a particular industry. For example, waste solvents generated from degreasing or cleaning operations, waste-water-treatment sludges, and incineration residues are all F-listed wastes. All wastes having EPA Hazardous Waste Codes beginning with F or K are referred to as "listed" hazardous wastes.

If a waste is not accurately described by any of the descriptions on the F list or the K list, then the next section of 40 CFR to consider is 261.24. These wastes are referred to as "characteristic wastes." All of these EPA Hazardous Waste Codes begin with the letter D. These wastes may exhibit either toxicity, ignitability, corrosivity, or reactivity characteristics. Some wastes may exhibit a combination of hazardous characteristics, e.g. a corrosive material that is also flammable. Generally, these types of wastes require a laboratory analysis to establish the concentration of specific hazardous constituents or physical properties that warrant special handling to protect human health and the environment. If the concentration of the listed contaminant exceeds values listed in 261.24, or if any of the physical properties of ignitability, corrosivity, or reactivity are identified by the laboratory, then the waste is considered characteristically hazardous and an appropriate D hazardous waste code is assigned by the generator. For example, if a waste is determined to have a pH of 2.0 or less, the proper EPA hazardous waste code is D002. The same waste may also be flammable and contain 5.0 ppm or more chromium. This waste would be classified as D002, D001, and D007, due to corrosivity, ignitability, and toxicity, respectively.

To determine EPA hazardous waste codes for wastes such as off-specification chemicals resulting from inadvertent contamination, container residues, or spill remediation, locate the name of the chemical on one of two lists in 40 CFR 261.33. One list in this section is referred to as the U list. The other list is called the P list. The P-list chemicals are considered acutely hazardous and are regulated in smaller quantities than the chemicals listed on the U list.

Uniform Hazardous Waste Manifest

In addition to the shipping documentation required by DOT, EPA requires use of the Uniform Hazardous Waste Manifest. The manifest is described in 40 CFR 262.20 and detailed instructions for completing the manifest may be found in the appendix to 40 CFR 262.

If the state receiving the waste has its own manifest, use of that state's manifest is required. If the receiving state does not have its own state manifest, then the manifest from the originating state should be used. If neither state has its own version of a hazardous waste manifest, use the EPA form 8700-22, as discussed in 40 CFR 262.20.

The generator of the hazardous waste is responsible for completing the hazardous waste manifest. After completing the information on the manifest, the generator must sign the manifest. By signing the manifest, the generator is certifying that all the information on the manifest is correct and accurate. The transporter must also sign the manifest, indicating acceptance of the load for transportation. After the manifest has been properly completed, and the transporter and shipper have signed the form, the shipper retains one copy and the transporter takes the other copies.

When the waste reaches its destination, the receiving site acknowledges acceptance and receipt of the material by signing the manifest. The copy of the manifest with the original signatures is then returned to the shipper by the receiving site. Copies are retained by the transporter and the receiving site. Individual state requirements vary regarding the reporting of manifest information. Some states require submission of manifest copies along with other reporting on hazardous waste activities.

The manifest system serves as a paper trail for tracking hazardous waste. Hazardous waste generators are required to receive the original signature manifest from the receiving site within 35 days from the date of shipment. If the generator does not receive the manifest, a thorough investigation must be initiated by the generator to locate the manifest. After 45 days have elapsed since the waste was shipped, and if the generator is still unable to locate the manifest, an Exception Report must be submitted to the EPA, describing the situation and the generator's efforts to locate the missing manifest. Exception reporting requirements are described in 40 CFR 262.42.

Further Reading

Code of Federal Regulations, Title 40, Parts 260, 261, 262, 265, and 300–372, July 1, 1989.

Code of Federal Regulations, Title 49, Parts 172–177, July 1, 1989.

Code of Federal Regulations, Title 29, Part 1910.1200, July 1, 1990.

Federal Motor Carrier Safety Regulations, sections 383 and 390, J. J. Keller and Associates, April 10, 1992.

Federal Register, vol. 55, no. 246, pp. 52,402–52,729, December 21, 1990.

Federal Register, vol. 56, no. 181, pp. 47,158–47,163, September 18, 1991.

1990 Emergency Response Guidebook, U. S. Department of Transportation Research and Special Programs Administration, American Label Mark Company.

Wray, Tom, *Business and Legal Report Environmental Manager's Compliance Advisor,* no. 332, March 2, 1992.

PART 3
Warehousing

16

Warehouse Space and Layout Planning

Jerry D. Smith

Executive Vice President,
Tompkins Associates, Inc.

Kenneth L. Nixon

Project Manager,
Tompkins Associates, Inc.

What is the thing one always runs out of in a warehouse? One might answer this question with the response, "Capital." In reality, one can get more of that and other resources if one's salesmanship skills are honed. The true response is "Space." Of all the common denominators in warehousing, space is the primary finite resource. All too often, there is a deficiency in the planning of this key physical factor which then hinders the operating efficiency of the warehouse. Examples of these deficiencies are products being stored in public warehousing immediately after the facility opens, or extended travel distances due to a poor layout, or even something as simple as a column in the middle of the aisle. Therefore, in order to meet the objectives of the warehouse, proper planning of the warehouse space and layout requirements is imperative. This chapter addresses the methodologies and philosophies for correct space and layout planning for the receiving/shipping area and the storage areas.

Space Planning for Receiving and Shipping

The most important functions of a warehouse occur on the receiving and shipping docks. This is where the transfer of control of merchandise occurs, whether product is brought into the warehouse or taken from it. If these transfers of control are not accomplished efficiently, safely, and accurately, it is impossible for the warehouse to meet its objective of satisfying the customer, regardless of the quality of the other aspects of the warehouse. Unfortunately, these are the most neglected areas of a warehouse. Therefore, most warehouses are behind the proverbial eight ball from the beginning, and find it difficult to perform their functions in an efficient manner.

An important prerequisite of efficient, safe, and accurate receiving and shipping activities is enough space in which to perform them. The following sections detail the steps to be taken to provide adequate space for the dock area, by first defining what materials are to be received and shipped, determining the dock requirements and the maneuvering allowances inside the warehouse, and then calculating the staging requirements and other dock-related requirements. This methodology should be followed to determine the space requirements of receiving and shipping activities.

Defining the Materials Received and Shipped

The first step in space planning for receiving and shipping operations is to define what is to be accomplished; that is, to define the materials to be received or shipped and the related frequencies. Therefore, data defining the physical characteristics of the product are required. The following information is critical:

Unit length, width, height

Unit cubic feet

Unit weight

Units per load

Load length, width, height

Load weight

Received on pallets or slipsheets

Stackability

Classification (flammable, corrosive, radioactive, etc.)

It is seldom practical to collect this data for each individual SKU, and in fact it typically is impractical, because most warehouses store thousands of different SKUs and determining the dimensional information for each would be an extremely time-consuming task. If the facility being planned is a new one and forecasted data are used, these forecasts are inevitably wrong. Consequently, planning a warehouse based on specific item requirements will result in a time-consuming and inaccurate waste of time.

A much better strategy is to establish generic categories of items and then determine the physical characteristics for representative items in each generic category. The items in a given generic category should have similar characteristics with respect to type of item and unit load received, stored, or shipped. Developing generic categories reduces the number of entries to a manageable level. Another advantage is that fluctuations in requirements for individual SKUs will have less impact because they will affect a whole generic category, not just one unit.

Determining Frequency of Activity

The frequency with which items are received and shipped should be determined. To do this, you will need the following information:

1. Receiving activity
   a. Units (or loads) per truck
   b. Frequency of receipt
   c. Unload time per truck
   d. Total trucks per day
2. Shipping activity
   a. Units (or loads) per truck
   b. Frequency of receipt
   c. Unload time per truck
   d. Total trucks per day

Determining Dock Bay Requirements

After materials to be received or shipped have been defined, the next step is to determine the requirements for the receiving and shipping dock bays. Three questions must be addressed:

1. What kind of vehicles are at the docks?
2. How many dock bays are required?
3. How should the dock bays be configured?

Types of Vehicles at the Dock Bays.   To determine this, you will need to collect the following information:

- Type
- Exterior/interior length
- Exterior/interior width
- Clearance height to the top of the carrier
- Height of the carrier bed off the road

Number of Dock Bays.   Typically the answer is obtained by means of one of three techniques:

Guessing

Waiting-line analysis

Simulation

Of these techniques, only *simulation* will consistently result in an accurate assessment of the number of dock bays required for a typical warehouse. Unfortunately, *guessing* is most commonly used. The guess is usually based on some historical experience of the guesser, such as the number of dock bays in the old warehouse or in other warehouses in the area. Although guessing may very well result in the correct answer, success can be usually attributed to luck, not knowledge. Furthermore, a warehouse plan based on guessing will rarely withstand the scrutiny of upper management.

Waiting-line analysis, or *queuing theory,* is often suggested as the correct technique for determining the number of dock bays required if the time between carrier arrivals and the time to service the carriers at the warehouse vary randomly. However, this rarely is the case in most warehouse operations. Instead of being random, carrier arrivals usually follow a pattern. For instance, more trucks may be received in the first two weeks of the month than in the last two weeks, and more shipments may occur during certain parts of the week or day. Because dock activity generally does not occur in a random manner, waiting-line analysis will rarely result in an accurate determination of the number of dock bays required.

Simulation, then, is the recommended technique for warehouses in which carrier arrivals and service times are not random. Contrary to what complicated statistical models and computer programs imply, simulation is a straightforward, simple tool.

Dock Simulation: An Example.   XYZ Company is building a warehouse. The company has completed a receiving and shipping analysis chart. Truck activity tends to surge at 10 a.m. and 2 p.m., and the same pattern is expected at XYZ Company's new facility.

How many receiving dock bays should XYZ Company construct, and what is the anticipated performance of this number of bays? Based on the experience of local warehouses and the anticipated volume of flow into XYZ Company, the expected time between truck arrivals from 8 to 10 a.m., from 11 to 2 p.m., and from 3 to 5 p.m. is given in Table 16-1.

Table 16-1 Truck Arrivals

Time between arrivals (hr)	Relative frequency	Cumulative frequency	Random-number range
0.25	0.02	2	0–1
0.50	0.07	9	2–8
0.75	0.22	31	9–30
1.00	0.30	61	31–60
1.25	0.27	88	61–87
1.50	0.07	95	88–95
1.75	0.04	99	95–98
2.00	0.01	100	99

The expected time between truck arrivals from 10 to 11 a.m., and from 2 to 3 p.m., is given in Table 16-2.

Table 16-2 Truck Arrivals

Time between arrivals (hr)	Relative frequency	Cumulative frequency	Random-number range
0.25	0.32	32	0–31
0.50	0.41	73	32–72
0.75	0.27	100	73–99

Experience has also shown that the time to unload a truck follows the distribution given in Table 16-3.

Table 16-3 Unloading Times

Unloading times (hr)	Relative frequency	Cumulative frequency	Random-number range
0.50	0.01	1	0
1.00	0.11	12	1–11
1.50	0.20	32	12–31
2.00	0.21	53	32–52
2.50	0.20	73	53–72
3.00	0.16	89	73–88
3.50	0.08	97	89–96
4.0	0.02	99	97–98
4.50	0.01	100	99

The relative frequency columns of Tables 16-1, 16-2, and 16-3 represent the percentage of time that the interval between truck arrivals (Tables 16-1 and 16-2) and the unloading time (Table 16-3) is equal to the values indicated in column one. For example in Table 16-1, between 8 and 10 a.m., the interval between truck arrivals will equal 0.25 hr, 2 percent of the time. These relative frequencies can be represented by an assignment of an appropriate range of numbers between 0 and 99. Thus, a relative frequency of 0.02 would be assigned two numbers between 0 and 99. This assignment has been made in the random-number range columns of these three tables.

Some other information required to complete the XYZ Company receiving dock simulation:

1. The dock opens at 8 a.m. for incoming trucks.
2. Dock personnel take breaks and eat lunch according to this schedule: break, 9:30–9:45 a.m.; lunch, 12–12:30 p.m.; break, 2:15–2:30 p.m.
3. The receiving dock closes to incoming trucks at 3 p.m. Trucks arriving after 3 p.m. must return the next day.
4. Dock personnel receive overtime pay for work performed after 5 p.m.

The simulation model to help determine the feasibility of various numbers of docks should be constructed by following these steps:

1. Generate a series of random numbers from 1 to 100. (Choose any numbers from that group.)
2. Transform the random numbers into a series of truck arrival times using Tables 16-1 and 16-2, which indicate the times at which trucks arrive.
3. Generate a series of random numbers from 1 to 100.
4. Transform the random numbers into a series of truck unloading times using Table 16-3.
5. Assume there are to be three bays.
6. Assign trucks to dock bays and, if a bay is unavailable, to a queue. Unload the trucks. Perform the truck operations for the entire day and maintain statistics.
7. Determine if steady state is reached.* If so, and if more than five docks have been considered, terminate the model.
8. If steady state is reached and fewer than five dock bays have been considered, add a bay and return to step 1.
9. If steady state is not reached, return to step 6 and simulate another day's operation.

Figure 16-1 presents the simulation of one day's operation of XYZ Company's receiving dock. It assumes that three dock bays are available. After the day's operation has been simulated, statistics describing the performance of the dock for that day should be summarized. They are presented in Table 16-4.

The simulation of the receiving dock with three dock bays is repeated for several days of operation until steady state is achieved. Then the process is repeated for receiving docks having four and five dock bays. The cumulative summary statistics for each alternative are summarized in Table 16-5.

Analysis of the statistics presented in Table 16-5 indicates that, as the number of dock bays increases, the carrier costs decrease, while the dock costs (the costs of dock space and unloading labor) increase because dock bay usage declines. XYZ Company owned the carriers; therefore, the cost of having over-the-road trucks sitting idle was extremely high. A four-dock-bay receiving dock was judged to be more economical than a three-dock-bay receiving dock. A comparison between four dock bays and five dock bays, however, revealed that the reduction in carrier cost gained by using five bays was not significant enough to justify the additional dock space and unloading crew. Consequently, the decision was made to construct a four-dock-bay receiving dock at the XYZ Company.

The simulation worksheet presented in Fig. 16-1 is an excellent method of keeping track of carrier arrival times, load/unload times, and assignment of carriers to

---

*Steady state is reached when incorporating the summary statistics for another day's simulated operation into the cumulative summary statistics has no significant impact on the cumulative summary statistics. A baseball player's batting average has achieved steady state toward the end of the season, when hitting a home run or striking out has little impact on his or her season's batting average.

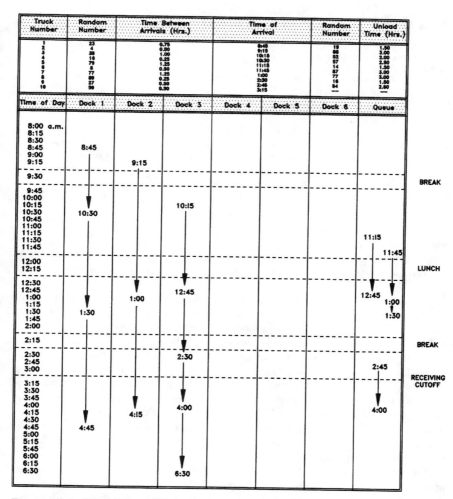

Figure 16-1. Simulation worksheet.

bays or the queue in a dock simulation. The top portion of the simulation worksheet records the random numbers, carrier arrival times, and carrier service (load/unload) times. The bottom portion of the worksheet simulates the assignment of carriers to dock bays to study the impact of having various numbers of dock bays.

Unfortunately, simulation will not give an unequivocal answer to the dock bay question. It will, however, reveal how dock performance will vary with different numbers of dock bays, and provide valuable data upon which one can base sound management decisions. Simulation is significantly more valuable than the other methods of determining the number of dock bays required.

Dock operations, particularly receiving functions, generate a tremendous

Table 16-4 Summary Statistics for the Three Dock Bays—Day One

Average truck-waiting (queue) time (hr)	0.50
Longest truck-waiting (queue) time (hr)	1.50
Average time truck spent at warehouse (hr)	3.10
Longest time truck spent at warehouse (hr)	4.50
Average dock bay usage (percent)	82

amount of trash, including corrugated boxes, binding materials, broken and disposable pallets, bracing, and other packing materials. Therefore, a refuse container is a requirement. Most companies find the ideal location for this to be at a dock door. Therefore, it is a good idea to add an additional door to the planned number of doors.

Dock Bay Configuration. The third step in determining the dock requirements is to ascertain the dock configuration. There are several basic dock types. The basic configurations are 90° (flush) docks and finger (staggered) docks, with the variations being whether or not they are enclosed. Another configuration that exists is the open dock.

With the 90° dock, the truck is positioned perpendicular to the building. The ideal configuration for a 90° dock is one with a relatively level driveway approach pitched slightly toward the building, as seen in Fig. 16-2. The slight decline assists in holding the truck against the dock bumpers while being loaded or unloaded, and also aids in drainage. In another configuration of the 90° dock, the driveway is depressed. This occurs when buildings are placed on grade and the driveway must be depressed to create the proper dock height. If the depressed configuration is necessary, care must be taken to ensure that the truck does not hit the building wall. In either configuration, the 90° dock is the most popular of the dock options, because it provides the advantage of taking up a minimum amount of inside warehouse space. This popularity is directly attributable to the relatively high cost of inside warehouse space compared to outside space.

However, when there is limited maneuvering area between the dock and the nearest obstruction or street, then finger docks are much more attractive. Finger docks require a minimum amount of outside warehousing space, but do reduce the total available dock space and interior warehousing space. As seen in Fig. 16-3, a 45° finger dock occupies twice as much interior space per position as a 90° dock. Tables

Table 16-5 Cumulative Summary Statistics for Dock Simulation

	Number of Dock Bays		
Factor	3	4	4
Average truck-waiting (queue) time (hr)	0.80	0.30	0.10
Longest truck-waiting (queue) time (hr)	1.00	0.40	0.10
Average time truck spend at warehouse (hr)	2.80	2.30	2.10
Longest time truck spent at warehouse (hr)	3.50	2.50	2.10
Average dock bay usage (percent)	85	65	49

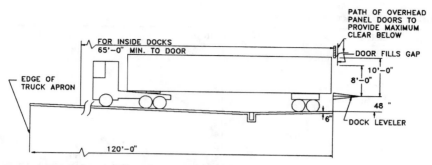

Figure 16-2. Ideal configuration for a 90° dock.

16-6 and 16-7 provide general guidelines for required dock bay widths and apron depths for 90° and finger docks, respectively.

Note as well that the apron depths given in Tables 16-6 and 16-7 assume clockwise backing by trucks into the dock area. Trucks should enter the dock area in a counterclockwise direction of travel, to allow the truck to back into the dock berth in an clockwise direction. Clockwise backing enables the driver to clearly see the rear of the truck as it turns into the dock berth. By contrast, when backing counterclockwise, drivers must rely on rearview mirrors to guide their approach to the dock. At first glance this issue may appear trivial; however, experience has shown that counterclockwise backing requires the apron bay to be 20 ft deeper than the bay required for clockwise backing.

An option for either of the aforementioned dock configurations is to enclose them. The enclosure has inherent advantages. It provides excellent weather protection, accessibility to trucks, and offers a very good security environment. However, enclosing docks is expensive because of the additional construction cost and the cost associated with the extra space and the installation of an exhaust system to remove fumes from truck engines. Also, energy usage will be higher to provide lighting and heating.

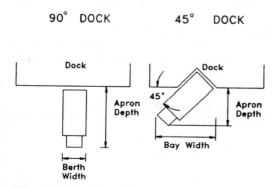

Figure 16-3. 90° and 45° docks.

Table 16-6 Space Requirements for 90° Docks

Truck length (ft)	Dock width (ft)	Apron depth (ft)
40	12	43
	14	39
45	12	49
	14	46
50	12	57
	14	54
55	12	63
	14	58
60	12	63
	14	60

NOTE: Dimensions are for unobstructed docks. Where trucks must back into the dock alongside other trucks, the apron depths are equal to the apron depth plus the length of the truck.

The least desirable dock alternative is an open dock. However, where conditions dictate, the open dock should have a canopy that extends to cover the work area and a minimum of 4 ft beyond. The outer edge of the canopy should have a minimum clearance of 15 ft from the road. The dock should be wide enough to accommodate two-way traffic. To determine the proper width, take the width of the material being handled, multiply it by four, and add the length of the dock levelers. If any staging is required on the dock, the dock width needs to be increased to accommodate it.

Maneuvering Allowances Inside the Warehouse

Directly inside the warehouse, behind the dock doors, is the maneuvering space required for a receiving or shipping dock. This space consists of two components, the first being the area occupied by the dock-leveling device, the second the aisle located between the dock-leveling device and the back edge of the staging area.

The amount of space a dock-leveling device occupies will vary according to the type used. Generally, temporary inside dock-leveling devices will occupy 3 to 7 ft, measured from the dock face. Permanent inside dock-leveling devices will require 4 to 10 ft of inside warehouse space.

The aisle behind the dock levelers allows unloading/loading personnel and equipment to enter and exit the carrier and travel to the appropriate staging area. This aisle should be restricted to these operations only. The existence of other traf-

Table 16-7 Space Requirements for Finger Docks for a 65-Ft Truck

Dock width (ft)	Finger angle (deg)	Apron depth (ft)	Bay width (ft)
12	10	49	66
14	10	47	67
12	30	74	62
14	30	70	64
12	45	92	54
14	45	87	56

fic within the dock maneuvering aisle will inevitably result in injuries to both dock personnel and other traffic. The required width of the aisle is dependent on the type of material handling equipment. Six to eight feet are generally recommended for manual handling and nonpowered material handling equipment. For powered material handling equipment, 10 to 12 ft is sufficient.

Staging Area Requirements

The majority of warehouses require a staging area directly behind the dock maneuvering aisle. The functions and size of this area are the topics discussed in this section.

The staging area for receiving serves as an immediate depository for materials unloaded from the carrier. Thus dock personnel are able to concentrate on unloading the carrier and releasing the carrier quickly. This is particularly important to companies with large investments in their private fleets. For companies that utilize common carriers, demurrage or detention charges can be avoided. Once the carrier has been released, a more thorough check-in can be performed.

The shipping staging area serves as an accumulation point for the merchandise that comprises a shipment. Various levels of accumulation may be established within the shipping staging area. Different types of accumulation include individual line items that make up a customer order, the customer orders making up a shipment, or shipments that go to a particular region. Activities performed within the staging area might be packing, unitizing, or verifying that the shipment is ready for loading on the carrier.

The functions performed in the staging area are easy to delineate. Determining the size of this area is entirely another matter, and if not calculated correctly it can be a source of inefficiency for the entire warehouse. The impact will be particularly severe if too little staging space is provided, because congestion will occur, as will lost product, damaged material, and erroneous shipments. Determining the amount of staging space required is contingent on the degree of control that exists over the workload of the dock area. The more uncertain the receiving or shipping workload is throughout the day, the more flexible the staging areas have to be. Thus, if a carrier arrival schedule is in existence and strictly adhered to, there is a good possibility that the staging area can be limited to one truckload of material per dock bay. Otherwise, surges in carrier activity will require that the staging area be increased.

To determine the amount of staging area needed, the same options are available as when determining the number of docks. Guessing is the most commonly adopted option and, as mentioned before, may provide the correct answer. However, one cannot expect that method to withstand any scrutiny, and it would be foolish to "take a stab" at calculating such an important area. Historical activity can be reviewed, and patterns identified, as another way of determining the amount of space required. This allows for surges in activity, and for larger volumes to be accommodated. The danger is that an excess of space may be allocated, which increases construction and operating costs. Simulation, then, is the recommended technique for warehouses in which carrier arrivals and service times are not random.

The previous example for dock doors also can be used to determine the number of lanes. By assuming that the time between arrivals is the time that a lane is filled with a truckload, and that unload time is the time it takes to empty the staging lane, one can use the same methodology to determine the number of staging lanes. One determines the size of the lane to accommodate the typical load, either a full truckload, less-than-truckload, or a UPS shipment. Then one determines the amount of time required to fill that space with the expected deliveries or picking activities and assigns that time to be the time that the lane is filled. The unload time is the time required to empty the staging lane. With this data, one can simulate the staging lane requirements. The same drawback is evident as before: Simulation will not give you an unequivocal answer to the staging lane question. Simulation will, however, reveal how lane utilization varies with different numbers of lanes, and give valuable data upon which one can base a sound decision.

Dock-Related Space Requirements

There are several other support activities that require space in this area that are imperative for a successful warehouse. These support activities are:

Office area for supervision/clerical

Quarantine area

Empty pallet storage

Truckers' lounge

The receiving and shipping offices must be included in the dock area. Approximately 125 sq ft per person regularly occupying this area is a good rule of thumb to use. Clerical functions may or may not be included in this same office area, since data processing responsibilities are often combined with other activities in the warehouse.

A quarantine area is essential for accumulating material that has been rejected for any reason. This area should be separate from the main staging area, and may be used to temporarily store material that has failed a quality-control inspection, been damaged in transit, or requires a quality-control sample. The amount of space required is dependent on the type of material likely to be rejected, the specific inspection process followed, and the timeliness of the disposition of the rejected material.

A large percentage of warehouses use pallets for transporting and storing unit loads. Incoming product may or may not be palletized, and shipments the same. Thus a pool of pallets is required. Space must be allocated, whether on the floor or on cantilevered racks above the dock doors, to accommodate this requirement.

A truckers' lounge is an area to which truck drivers are confined when not servicing their trucks. The truckers' lounge should include seating, private toilet facilities, and a telephone. General space requirements for a basic truckers' lounge are approximately 125 sq ft for the first trucker and an additional 25 sq ft for each additional trucker. The purpose of the lounge is to effectively control the movements of the trucker while on-site. Doing so eliminates many potential problems related to trucker safety, theft and pilferage, labor union campaigning, and warehouse employee productivity.

Space Planning for Storage Activities

Storage space planning is particularly critical, because the storage activity accounts for the bulk of the space requirements of a warehouse. Inadequate storage space planning can easily result in a warehouse that is significantly larger or smaller than required. Too little storage space will result in a world of operational problems, including lost stock, blocked aisles, inaccessible material, poor housekeeping, safety problems, and low productivity. On the other hand, too much space will breed poor use of space. The familiar situation of a homeowner filling all the available closets with "essential" junk comes to mind. The result of too much space will be high space costs in the form of land, construction, energy, and equipment. To avoid these problems, storage space planning must be thought out carefully, using quantitative analysis. Understanding and pursuing the following methodology will generate a defensible assessment of storage space requirements.

Defining Materials to be Stored

Generally, the same SKU information required for receiving and shipping can be used here. Once again, the generic categories that were identified for receiving and shipping should be used. The following additional information is needed:

Usage (units) over time

Popularity (times sold)

Average inventory (units)

Maximum inventory (units)

Planned inventory (units)

Choosing a Storage Philosophy

There are two major storage philosophies: fixed location storage, and random location storage. In fixed location storage, each SKU is always stored in a specific location, and no other SKU may occupy that location even though the location may be empty. Random location storage allows any SKU to be assigned to any available location. Thus, in a random location storage system, one could find SKU number 1 stored in location A this week and in location B the next week.

Fixed Location Storage.   The simplest of the two philosophies is the fixed location system, where all that is required is a fixed place for each SKU. Thus when a new SKU is introduced by marketing, another location must be defined, and conversely when an SKU is discontinued, the location is reassigned to another SKU. To initiate a stock locator system with a fixed location system, a detailed drawing showing the locations and their associated SKU's is all that is required. After a short period of time, the operators have memorized the layout and are able to go directly to the location without referring to the drawing. In large warehouses with thousands of SKUs, the operator's memory is ineffective and must be enhanced by having the location entered into the computer containing a file with each SKU and its related location. Therefore, during picks or putaways, the operator can be told where the SKU is either by printed pick list or an RF terminal.

The advantage of simplicity must be weighed against a very serious disadvantage, poor space utilization. This is due to the requirement that enough space must be provided to store the maximum amount of inventory of each SKU. This, in turn, is due to the two components of inventory, reserve stock and order quantity. Reserve stock is the component required for "just in case"; just in case the incoming shipment is delayed, just in case the part is backordered, and a host of other possibilities. Therefore, the reserve stock component of inventory is a constant until an emergency.

The sum of reserve stock and order quantity is the inventory level. Inventory level peaks when a shipment is received and is depleted as orders are filled against it until another shipment arrives. Therefore, even though the expected inventory level in total will be all of the reserve stock and half of the order quantity, one must plan for the peak periods of inventory. Thus one can easily see how the average space utilization of a fixed location storage warehouse is 50 percent before taking into account aisle losses and staging areas.

Random Location Storage. When one thinks of something done at random, the usual image is of something close to anarchy, a state where confusion reigns. In warehousing, this should not be the case. Effective random storage has a locator system identifying every SKU and its relative information; i.e., date produced, date received, lot number, etc. With the locator system, the SKU can be placed anywhere within a designated storage area. An example might be a fast-moving SKU designated for bulk storage in close proximity to the shipping doors. Once a shipment of this SKU has been received, it may be placed in any of the available storage lanes as directed by the locator system. The locator system then tracks each SKU once it has been stored.

The locator system maintains the orderliness of the random storage warehouse. Thus, zones may be assigned to different-velocity products, where the fastest are closest to the docks and the slowest are placed in remote areas of the warehouse. The obvious benefit here is a lowering of the travel distance required to pick and place inventory. Without the locator system defining these zones, a reverse ABC storage configuration occurs, which actually increases travel distance. When an SKU is received and placed in the first available location, no matter what its velocity, slower-moving items eventually will tend to occupy all the storage locations closest to the dock. Fast-moving items will migrate away from the dock, and an increase in travel distance will occur.

Why use random storage? The primary reason is that random storage permits a superior utilization of space. Since inventory may be stored anywhere (within specific guidelines), the storage system can accommodate the peaks and valleys of inventory. When one SKU has high inventory, another SKU likely will have low inventory. The cost is an ability to plan space for random location systems on the *average* inventory expected.

With these tradeoffs, which alternative is best? A clearcut decision cannot be made. The only general conclusion that can be made is that the poor use of space associated with fixed location storage is a very large factor to consider. Fixed location storage will generally require 65 to 85 percent more space than random location storage. The expense of developing and maintaining a material locator system for a random location storage scenario is easily justified when compared with the high cost of construction and land. However, the accessibility to material may be such a driving factor that it will be enough to offset the high cost of space. An example would be an operation with extremely small and extremely valuable items, where accountability and accessibility is imperative, such as microchip or jewelry storage. Thus, one should closely evaluate using random location storage before deciding to use fixed location storage.

Space Requirements for Alternative Storage Methods

In Chapter 20, alternative material handling and storage equipment are reviewed. When evaluating alternative storage equipment, the relevant costs for each must be available. Among the costs relevant to a storage alternative is space cost. To determine the space costs for a storage alternative, the space requirements must be calculated. This section presents the basic methodology for the determining of storage space requirements.

The space requirements of a storage alternative are directly related to the volume of material to be stored and to the use-of-space characteristics of the alternative. Use-of-space characteristics include honeycombing allowances and aisle allowances. Honeycombing allowances are the percentage of storage space lost because of ineffective use of the capability of a storage area. In other words, honeycombing occurs whenever a storage location is only partially filled with material. It may occur both horizontally and vertically. An example of horizontal honeycombing can be seen in Fig. 16-4, where 3 lanes of bulk storage are occupied by 3 different SKUs (A, B, and C) and each SKU has 4 pallets of inventory. Thus, the capacity of the storage area is 12 pallets, assuming the pallets cannot be stacked. In the second part of Fig. 16-4,

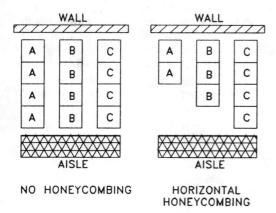

Figure 16-4. Horizontal honeycombing.

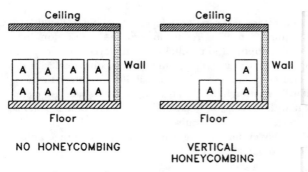

Figure 16-5. Vertical honeycombing.

an order requiring 2 pallets of A and 1 pallet of B has been picked. No other items may be placed in these 3 open slots, or the back pallets will be blocked. Until the remainder of the items in the lanes are picked, these open slots are considered honeycombing losses.

Similarly, vertical honeycombing can occur. Fig. 16-5 shows a side view of the lane that SKU A occupies. However, in this example the assumption will be that pallets can be stacked 2 high and the lanes are still 4 deep. Therefore, SKU A has 8 pallets occupying a lane. Suppose an order requiring 5 pallets is picked. Therefore, as can be seen in the second part of Fig. 16-5, no product may be placed in those open slots without blocking pallets. Those open slots are also considered honeycombing losses. Honeycombing, while it should be minimized, must be considered a natural and allowed-for aspect of the storage process. For each storage alternative, the expected honeycombing allowances should be estimated and applied to the inventory. Examples of honeycombing allowances for storage equipment are included in Table 16-8.

It is obvious that warehousing is the business of storing product. However, much effort has been expended in establishing handling performance measures, such as labor performance and equipment utilization. The reason for this emphasis on labor is that it has traditionally been treated as a variable cost, with space cost being considered a fixed cost. Thus, management has tended to focus on controlling the labor cost, while accepting the monthly charge for the building as inevitable. However, space is as important to the total cost picture as labor, and one needs some method to determine current and future space utilization. A *space standard* is the benchmark that defines the amount of space required per unit of product stored. For new facilities, once a space standard has been calculated for a given class of

Table 16-8 Honeycombing Allowances

Alternative	Honeycombing allowance
Bulk Storage	75
Drive-In Rack	75
Flow Rack	70
Single-Deep Selective Rack	100

items being stored, using a given type of storage equipment, the total storage space can be determined for that class of items. Then, for alternative methods of storage, similar calculations can be made, and total storage space for each alternative determined.

To determine a space standard, one needs to determine the total square feet of the storage alternative "footprint" and then determine the number of unit loads that can be stored in that area. For single-deep selective rack, the formula for determining the square footage of the footprint is:

$$\text{Square feet/footprint} = \frac{A \times D}{144}$$

A footprint in this case equals a bay of single-deep selective rack. Thus, A is the length of one rack opening, measured from center of upright to the center of the other upright, and D is one half the aisle width, in inches, plus the depth of a single bay of rack plus one-half the flue space. Figure 16-6 graphically depicts these dimensions. To calculate the square footage per unit load stored, determine the number of unit loads stored within the footprint and then divide into the square footage of the footprint. Thus the formula is:

$$\text{Square feet/unit load} = \frac{\text{square feet per footprint}}{\text{quantity of unit loads stored in the footprint}}$$

Let's say we're calculating a space standard for a counterbalanced lift truck using single-deep selective rack. The following are the required parameters:

Unit load dimensions: Length, $U_L = 48''$

Height, $U_H = 50''$

Width, $U_W = 40''$

Beam width, $R_W = 42''$

TOP VIEW

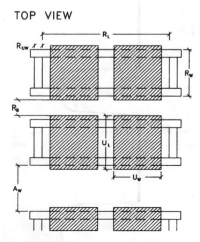

SIDEVIEW

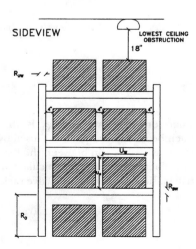

Figure 16-6.

Rack dimensions: Beam length, $R_L = 92''$

Back-to-back spacing, $R_B = 4''$

Upright width, $R_{UW} = 3''$

Beam height, $R_{BH} = 3''$

Rack opening height, $R_O = 54''$

Building dimension: Clear height, $C_H = 21'$

Load weight: 2500 lb

Stacking aisle width: $A_W = 144''$

The calculations are:

$$\text{Square feet/footprint} = \frac{[R_L + 2(\tfrac{1}{2}R_{UW})] \times (\tfrac{1}{2}A_W + U_L + \tfrac{1}{2}R_B)}{144}$$

$$= \frac{(92 + 3) \times [(\tfrac{1}{2} \times 144) + 48 + (\tfrac{1}{2} \times 4)]}{144}$$

$$= \frac{95 \times 122}{144}$$

$$= 80.5$$

To determine the number of pallets that occupy this 80.5-sq-ft footprint, one must calculate the number of levels of rack that can fit in the clear height of the building. The first load beam of the single-deep selective rack is 54 in from the top of the floor. This allows 4 in between the unit load and the bottom of the beam in order to lift the unit load. For each level above, one must add the width of the beam, thus 54 in + 3 in will provide 57 in total per level. To calculate the number of levels, it is a simple division of available clear height by the distance per level. The available clear height must have 18 in subtracted from it for fire protection, thus the true clear height is 234 in. The calculation is:

$$\text{Levels per bay} = \frac{(C_H \times 12) - R_O - 18}{R_O + R_{BW}}$$

$$= \frac{(21 \times 12) - 54 - 18}{54 + 3}$$

$$= 3.16$$

Therefore there are four levels: three, in addition to the first level on the floor. Each beam has two pallets. This allows 4 in between each of the loads and the upright, as well as 4 in between the loads. (The calculation is: 4 + 40 + 4 + 40 + 4 = 92 in.) Therefore, one can calculate the space standard for a counterbalanced lift truck using single-deep selective rack:

$$\text{Square feet/unit load} = \frac{80.5 \text{ ft}^2/\text{footprint}}{2 \text{ pallets/level} \times 4 \text{ levels/footprint}}$$

$$= 10.0$$

One can then determine the effects on space when using an alternative material handling method. A reach truck can operate in an 8-ft aisle as opposed to the 12-ft aisle for the counterbalanced truck. Thus, using the same calculations, the square feet per unit load would be 8.1. The tradeoff in space savings for utilizing this type of equipment is offset by potential higher initial cost and limited flexibility, as it cannot load trailers. This and other types of material handling equipment will be covered in detail in other chapters.

The space standard calculated must have main and cross aisles added before it can be an accurate projection of the required footage. Main aisles allow two-way travel and, as the name implies, are heavily accessed. The cross aisle allows the material handling equipment to access another aisle without having to travel to either end. Both main and cross aisle widths are dependent on the material handling equipment utilized.

Warehousing Layout Planning

Determining the Objectives of a Warehouse Layout

Before layout planning can begin, the specific objectives of a warehouse layout must be determined. In general, the objectives of a warehouse layout are to

1. Use space efficiently
2. Allow the most efficient material handling
3. Provide the most economical storage in relation to costs of equipment, use of space, damage to material, and handling labor
4. Provide maximum flexibility in order to meet changing storage and handling requirements
5. Make the warehouse a model of good housekeeping

The objectives of both a warehouse itself and of the warehouse layout are virtually identical. Without a good warehouse layout, it is impossible to have a good warehouse. The objective of layout planning is to arrange and coordinate the space, equipment, and labor resources of the warehouse. Poor layout planning can undermine superior space, equipment, and personnel planning. Put another way, accomplishing the objectives of warehousing depends on having a good layout. If the warehouse layout is bad, the warehouse as a whole will be bad; and if the warehouse as a whole is bad, chances are the warehouse layout is bad.

The fourth objective of a warehouse layout, as just listed, recognizes the fact that warehousing exists not within a static, unchanging environment, but within a dynamic, everchanging one. If the mission of a warehouse changes, the warehouse layout should very likely change as well, in order to adapt to the new mission. However, a good warehouse layout possesses the flexibility to absorb minor variances in expected storage volumes and product mixes with few or no alterations required. This flexibility allows the warehouse to function even if the forecasts on which it was planned prove to be wrong, as they so often and inevitably do.

The last objective of warehousing springs from the principle that there is efficiency in order. Good housekeeping is essential to good warehousing: a good ware-house cannot exist without good housekeeping. Yet good housekeeping by itself will not ensure a good warehouse. If the space, equipment, personnel, and layout are not properly planned, all the housekeepers in the world could not get a ware-house to function. But poor housekeeping will surely undermine good space, equipment, personnel, and layout planning.

Following a Layout Planning Methodology

Warehouse layout planning methodology consists of two steps:

1. Generating a series of warehouse layout alternatives
2. Evaluating each alternative according to specific criteria, to identify the best warehouse layout

Generating Alternative Layouts.   Generating alternative warehouse layouts is as much art as it is science. The quality of the layout alternatives will largely depend on the skill and ingenuity of the layout planner. This fact is crucial to the most common approach to generating layout alternatives: template juggling. The word *juggle* means to skillfully manipulate a group of objects to obtain a desired effect. Consequently, template juggling is *the skillful manipulation of a group of templates, models, or other representations of warehouse space, equipment, and personnel in order to obtain a warehouse layout that meets its objectives.* In other words, template juggling is a trial-and-error approach to finding the proper arrangement and coordination of the physical resources of the warehouse.

The quality of the alternatives created from template juggling will depend on the creativity of the layout planner. Unfortunately, layout planners often either lack creativity or do not attempt to express their creativity. Many of them approach the problem with a preconceived idea of what the solution should be. They tend to judge the layout planning process toward that preconceived solution. As a result, creativity is stifled. Oftentimes, the layout chosen for a new warehouse looks exactly like the layout used in the old warehouse. Layout alternatives are generated by the creativity of the layout planner, yet many layout planners fail to harness this force.

To generate warehouse layout alternatives, follow the five steps described here.

1. *Define the location of fixed obstacles.*   Some objects in a warehouse can be located only in certain places, and they can have only certain configurations. These objects should be identified and placed in the layout alternative first, before objects with more flexibility are located. Some fixed obstacles are building support columns, stairwells, elevator shafts, lavatories, sprinkler system control, heating and air-conditioning equipment, and, in some cases, offices. Failure to consider the location of these types of items first will prove disastrous. The warehousing corollary to Murphy's law states, "If a column can be in the wrong position, it will be." Don't be the layout planner who designs a warehouse and buys the storage and material handling equipment only to find that, when the equipment is installed, the location of the building columns makes an aisle too narrow for the handling equipment.

2. *Define the location of the receiving and shipping function.* Oftentimes, the configuration of the warehouse site will dictate the location of the receiving and shipping functions. When this is not true, however, the receiving and shipping location decision becomes an important one. Receiving and shipping are high-activity areas and should be located so as to maximize productivity, improve material flow, and properly utilize the warehouse site. The location of access roads and railroad tracks, if rail service is required, are important considerations in locating receiving and shipping.

The question of whether receiving and shipping should be located together or in different areas of the warehouse must be addressed. Common receiving and shipping docks can often result in economies of scale related to sharing space, equipment, and personnel. Separate receiving and shipping areas may, on the other hand, be best, to ensure better material control and reduce congestion.

Energy considerations are important. Where a choice exists, receiving and shipping docks should not be located on the side of the building that faces north. Avoiding this location reduces the amount of heat loss in the winter form northerly winds entering the warehouse through open dock doors. The preferred location of the receiving and shipping dock is the south side of the warehouse, with east and west as second and third choices. The particular weather patterns around each warehouse site should be examined, however, to identify the prevailing wind direction at that particular site, and the docks should be located away from the prevailing wind.

3. *Locate the storage areas and equipment, including required aisles.* The types of storage areas and equipment to be used will indicate to some extent the configuration of the storage layout and the aisle requirements. Be sure to make allowances for the fixed obstacles in the facility. Main warehouse aisles should connect the various parts of the warehouse. The cross aisle at the end of the storage area may need to be wider than the aisles within the storage area, depending on the type of material handling equipment used. For example, a side-loading fork truck that can operate with a 7-ft-wide storage aisle may require 12-ft-wide cross aisles at the ends of the storage aisles to allow maneuvering into and out of the storage aisle.

4. *Assign the material to be stored to the storage location.* This step in the generation of layout alternatives ensures that storage allowances have been made for all the items to be stored. In addition, it allows the performance of a mental simulation of the activities expected within the warehouse.

5. *Repeat the process, to generate other alternatives.* Once a warehouse layout alternative has been established following the four steps just outlined, the process must be repeated many times to generate additional layout alternatives. Different layout configurations, building shapes, and equipment alternatives should be used. The creativity of the layout planner should be taxed to ensure that each succeeding layout alternative is not essentially identical to the first.

Evaluating the Alternative Layouts. A number of warehouse layout philosophies exist to serve as guidelines for the development of an effective warehouse layout. Each warehouse layout alternative should be evaluated against the specific criteria established for each of these warehouse layout philosophies.

1. *Popularity philosophy.* An Italian economist named Pareto once stated that 85 percent of the wealth of the world is held by 15 percent of the people. On closer examination, Pareto's law actually pertains to many areas other than wealth; one of these areas is warehousing. In a typical warehouse, it is not unusual to find that 85 percent of the product throughput is attributable to 15 percent of the items, that another 10 percent of the product throughput is attributable to 30 percent of the items, and that the remaining 5 percent of the product throughput is attributable to 55 percent of the items. Consequently, the warehouse contains a very small number of highly active items (often called *A items*), a slightly larger number of moderately active items (often called *B items*), and a very large number of infrequently active items (often called *C items*).

Popularity philosophy suggests that the warehouse should be planned around the small number of items that are at the center of most of the activity in the warehouse.

It maintains that the materials having the greatest throughput should be located in an area that allows the most efficient material handling. Consequently, high-turnover items should be located as close as possible to the point of use.

The popularity philosophy also suggests that the popularity of the items helps to determine the storage methods used. For example, if bulk storage is used, high-turnover items should move into and out of storage at a relatively high rate; the danger of excessive honeycombing losses will be reduced, and excellent use of space will result from the high-density storage. Low-throughput items in deep bulk storage blocks will cause severe honeycombing losses, because no other items can be stored in that location until the low-throughput item has been removed.

2. *Similarity philosophy.* Items that are commonly received and/or shipped together should be stored together. For example, consider a retail auto parts distributor. Chances are that a customer who requires a spark plug wrench will not buy, at the same time, an exhaust system tailpipe. Chances are good, however, that a customer who buys the spark plug wrench will also require spark plugs. Because these items are typically sold (shipped) together, they should be stored in the same area. The exhaust system tailpipe should be stored in the same area as the mufflers, brackets, and gaskets. Certain items are commonly received together, possibly from the same vendor; they should be stored together. Similar types of items should be stored together. They will usually require similar storage and handling methods, so their consolidation in the same area will result in more efficient use of space and more efficient material handling.

An exception to the similarity philosophy arises whenever items are *so* similar that storing them close together might result in order picking and shipping errors. Examples of items that are too similar are two-way, three-way, and four-way electrical switches; they look identical, but function quite differently.

3. *Size philosophy.* The size philosophy suggests that heavy, bulky, hard-to-handle goods should be stored close to their point-of-use. The cost of handling these items is usually much greater than that of handling other items. That is an incentive to minimize the distance over which they are handled. In addition, if the ceiling height in the warehouse varies from one area to another, the heavy items should be stored in the areas with a low ceiling, and the lightweight, easy-to-handle items should be stored in the areas with a high ceiling. Available cubic space in the ware-

house should be used in the most effective way, while meeting restrictions on floor-loading capacity. Lightweight material can be stored at greater heights within typical floor-loading capacities than heavy materials can.

The size philosophy also asserts that the size of the storage location should fit the size of the material to be stored. Do not store a unit load of 10 cu ft in a storage location capable of accommodating a unit load of 30 cu ft. A variety of storage location sizes must be provided so that different items can be stored differently. In addition to looking at the physical size of an individual item, one must consider the total quantity of the item to be stored. Different storage methods and layouts will be used for storing 2 pallet loads of an item than will be used for storing 200 pallet loads of the same material.

4. *Product characteristics philosophy.* Some materials have certain attributes or traits that restrict or dictate the storage methods and layout used. Perishable material is quite different from nonperishable material, from a warehousing point of view. The warehouse layout must encourage good stock rotation so that limitations on shelf life are met. Oddly shaped and crushable items, subject to stacking limitations, will dictate special storage methods and layout configurations to effectively use available cubic space. Hazardous material such as explosives, corrosives, and highly flammable chemicals must be stored in accordance with government regulations. Items of high value or items commonly subject to pilferage may require increased security measures, such as isolated storage with restricted access. The warehouse layout must be adapted to provide the needed protection. The compatibility of items stored close together must also be examined. Contact between certain individually harmless materials can result in extremely hazardous reactions and/or significant product damage. Specific steps must be taken to separate incompatible materials. Oftentimes, the easiest way to accomplish this objective is through the warehouse layout.

5. *Space utilization philosophy.* This philosophy can be broken down into four components:

   a. Conservation of space
   b. Limitations on use of space
   c. Accessibility of material
   d. Orderliness

a. The conservation of space principle asserts that the maximum amount of material should be concentrated within a storage area, the total cubic space available should be effectively used, and the potential honeycombing within the storage area should be minimized. Unfortunately, these objectives often conflict. Increased concentration of material will usually cause increased honeycombing allowances. Therefore, determining the proper level of space conservation is a matter of making tradeoffs among the objectives that maximize use of space.

b. Limitations on use of space must be identified early in the layout planning process. Space requirements for building support columns, trusses, sprinkler-system components, heating-system components, fire extinguishers and hoses, and emergency exits will affect the suitability of certain storage and handling methods and layout configurations. Floor loading capacities will restrict storage heights and densities.

c. The warehouse layout should meet specified objectives for *material accessibility.* Main travel aisles should be straight and should lead to doors in order to improve maneuverability and reduce travel times. Aisles should be wide enough to permit efficient operation, but they should not waste space. Aisle widths should be tailored to the type of handling equipment using the aisle and the amount of traffic expected.

d. The *orderliness* principle emphasizes the fact that good warehouse layout planning begins with housekeeping in mind. Aisles should be well marked with aisle tape or paint; otherwise, materials will begin to infringe on the aisle space and accessibility to material will be reduced. Void spaces within a storage area must be avoided, and they must be corrected when they do occur. If a storage area is designed to accommodate five pallets, and in the process of placing material into that area one pallet infringes on the space allocated for the adjacent pallet, a void space will result. Because of this, only four pallets can actually be stored in the area designed for five pallets. The lost pallet space will not be regained until the entire storage area is emptied.

To evaluate the alternative warehouse layouts, each should be looked at in the light of specified expectations relative to the layout philosophies discussed above. The layout planner must determine which layout philosophies are most important under the specific circumstances and attempt to maximize the extent to which the recommended layout adheres to these philosophies.

Remember, however, that warehousing exists within a dynamic environment; therefore, the layout chosen as best today may not be so as conditions change. The extent and timing of changing requirements in the future should be forecast, and a warehouse master plan established that will effectively compensate for the changing mission of the warehouse. Your challenge is to utilize the tools for space and layout planning to formulate an effective warehouse strategic master plan and to become one of those elite warehouse facilities that have balanced the resources of space, equipment, and labor.

17

Receiving and Shipping Systems

Kenneth B. Ackerman
President, The K. B. Ackerman Company

As we look at receiving and shipping, it will be helpful to understand the factors that make receiving and shipping so critical to physical distribution. Therefore, we will look at the purposes of receiving and shipping systems. If the activity in your business is growing in velocity, how does your receiving and shipping system change to cope with this increased velocity? Both receiving and shipping can create a disaster unless they are done accurately. Furthermore, they must be done with reasonable security, which includes protection from theft or mysterious disappearance. Everybody favors safety, and we never appreciate the value of a safe warehouse until there is an accident.

The physical layout of the warehouse will substantially influence the effectiveness of receiving and shipping.

Before anything can be shipped, the order must be selected. Before anything is fully received, it must be put away. Therefore the intermediate steps of order selection and putaway should be explored.

No warehouse operation is perfect, and unfortunately materials handling damage is a consequence of the distribution process. Not all of this damage occurs in the warehouse, and the alert manager must identify warehouse damage and accurately assess the probable cause as well as the means of preventing such damage in the future.

The velocity of inventory turns in business in the 1990s is generally faster than it was in the 1980s, and that velocity seems to increase every year. If we can assume that velocity will continue to increase, then a primary purpose of a receiving and shipping system is to adapt to these increases in velocity.

Another primary purpose of such systems is the improvement of both accuracy and security. Electronic identification systems have done a great deal to facilitate an increase in accuracy in both receiving and shipping. Unfortunately, growing crime rates have created new challenges in maintaining security. Both accuracy and security are ultimately essential to the successful operation of any logistics system.

Federal statistics show that the most dangerous work in a warehouse is the loading and unloading of freight vehicles. Therefore, any receiving and shipping system must put a high priority on improvement of safety.

Since any dynamic logistics system is in a state of constant change, part of the purpose of a receiving and shipping system is to adapt to those changes that can reasonably be anticipated. These might include growth or consolidation of warehouse operations, adaptation of older buildings, and automation.

Adapting to Growing Velocity

A hallmark of logistics development in the past 20 years has been the increase in velocity of inventory turns. Two things have happened in the past two decades. First, the cost of money rose and the presumption of constant inflation disappeared. Second, improved communications and computing capabilities allowed a degree of inventory control that was not cost-effective before. Logistic managers have both the incentive and the ability to turn inventories faster than ever before.

The ultimate in high velocity is to have merchandise move in through one door and almost immediately move out through another. The term for this movement is *crossdock operations,* and in a moment we will look at it in detail. Bar coding is one technological change that has allowed velocity to increase at no compromise in accuracy. Locator systems allow the operator to move rapidly without losing control.

Crossdock Operations

The ultimate in fast inventory turnover is crossdocking, a distribution system in which freight moves in and out of a distribution center without ever being stored there. Crossdocking involves the receipt, sorting, routing, and shipment of products in a minimum amount of time. On occasion, some value-added services may be included in a crossdock situation. Usually these are limited to repackaging or kitting.

The movement of freight from one vehicle to another is nothing new. For many years, shippers assembled pool cars and sent them to distributors. Pool car distribution involved the unloading and reshipment of segregated loads consigned to smaller customers. The difference in freight costs between full boxcars, truckloads, and small shipments exceeded the cost of handling pool distribution. Crossdocking is different, because the warehouse operator receives bulk shipments and then assembles the smaller orders on the warehouse floor. When comparing costs of crossdocking to conventional warehousing operations involving receipt, stowage, order picking, and shipment, the results are dramatic. For example, one grocery products distributor achieved significant savings by changing from conventional warehousing to a crossdock operation.

Crossdocking works best when it is limited to the relatively small number of SKUs that are the most popular. These items typically sell on the basis of fast and precise delivery.

Information is a key to crossdocking. To function effectively, the crossdock operator should receive information on both the incoming shipment schedule and the outgoing customer orders. Until accurate information has been received, the sorting operation of a crossdock system cannot be completed.

New technology provides breakthroughs in information and in controls. One operator who uses crossdocking extensively has controlled the flow of merchandise through the facility by using bar coding and real-time information systems. In this operation, forklift operators are equipped with radio frequency terminals that are either hand-held or mounted on the truck itself. Through the use of bar coding scanners and RF terminals, each lift operator is instructed as to the movement requirements for each unit load. Using this system, the crossdock warehouse runs with virtually no paper.

Simpler methods can also be used to control a crossdock operation. By recording all of the numbers for both inbound shipments and outbound bills of lading and keeping those numbers in the same place, a manual tracking system can be used to trace movement of product through the crossdock facility.

Other operations achieve similar results with a minimum of technology. Each outbound bill of lading also makes reference to the inbound shipment numbers. This provides an audit trail to track the physical inventory.

A crossdock operation may utilize specialized equipment, though it certainly could also use the typical counterbalanced forklift truck. Because stacking is seldom needed in a crossdock operation, use of a high lift truck is wasteful, since the stacking capabilities of the vehicle are seldom if ever needed.

Crossdocking by its nature is primarily horizontal rather than vertical product movement. The ideal vehicles are low-lift pallet movers or standup lift trucks that allow the operator to mount and dismount from the machine with great ease. Conveyors and automatic guided vehicle systems (AGVS) are sometimes used very effectively in a crossdock operation.

Integration of information handling and materials handling equipment is critical. When RF terminals are used, they may be mounted on the lift trucks.

While most crossdock operations are part of a careful planning process, others are unplanned and motivated only by a certain series of events. When urgently needed goods are received under normal process, the best warehouse procedures call for immediate crossdocking of the "hot" items so that their handling is expedited and the goods are never moved into a storage or pick line area. This kind of crossdocking is typically truck to truck, with the hot items moving out of one truck and directly into another.

One manufacturer has identified that five SKUs represent 25 percent of dollar value shipped, and these hot items are in a "warehouse on wheels" program. To reduce warehousing costs, these items are moved from either factories or a few central distribution centers direct to breakbulk points, where they are merged with the slower-moving SKUs for immediate shipment to customers. These five popular items are never stored in the regional distribution centers.

Another consumer goods company eliminated a whole group of warehouses by the crossdocking of its several most popular items. In this situation, the popular items were shipped directly from factory to crossdock facility on a precise delivery schedule. They arrived at approximately the same time as another truck carrying the slower-moving items in the order. The fast movers are merged with the remainder of the order, and the stock moves directly to the customer in a shipment that previously originated at a regional distribution center in that same city. In this situation, the manufacturer is giving virtually identical service and yet has eliminated a local warehouse.

One grocery distributor uses crossdocking primarily for promotional buys. The crossdock merchandise sits a maximum of three days in the distribution center, and it is never placed in storage racks.

One wholesale distributor uses crossdock procedures as a support for private trucking, moving sufficient additional tonnage in a crossdock situation to create an economical truckload for the private fleet.

Crossdocking also can be used to facilitate the consolidation of inbound materials. Rather than suffer the confusion and expense of many small shipments arriving at a receiving dock, some buyers arrange for inbound consolidation at a remote consolidation terminal. Under such as program, all vendors in the Chicago area would ship their products to a consolidation terminal on a timed delivery basis so that goods arrive shortly before they are needed. The consolidator converts the small shipments into a single truckload shipment. If a company truck is used, the purchases provide a needed backhaul, which reduces the cost of private trucking. Otherwise a common carrier may be used. In either case, the cost of inbound transportation is reduced through the use of a consolidation terminal.

Will crossdocking work for you? Consider the three primary advantages. First, crossdocking should allow you to eliminate some field warehouse operations that exist today. By substituting a crossdock for a regional warehouse, you will eliminate all of the expenses connected with keeping that warehouse operation. Second, you should also eliminate some field inventories that were formerly stored in those regional warehouses. Third, the elimination of regional warehouses results in some simplification of operations, and the elimination of administration and paperwork associated with a warehouse that no longer exists.

While crossdocking has its benefits, it also has some drawbacks. Handling activity must be timed to coincide with the arrival of inbound loads and the availability of outbound trucks, so there may be substantial peaks and valleys in volume. This can pose a significant challenge to labor utilization, because having enough people to handle the peaks means that labor is wasted when no merchandise is flowing through the terminal. Facilities and equipment also are used unevenly. The number of pallets needed must meet peak requirements, and not all of them will be fully utilized. Dock doors and floor space also may be idle for part of the time.

Some regional warehouses have already been replaced by crossdock operations. Yet the function of storage of goods will always exist, because it is seldom possible to achieve a perfect balance between production and consumption. There will always be manufacturing processes that are governed by seasonality, such as the processing and packing of fresh vegetables as the crop becomes ripe. While improved production planning techniques have leveled off the peaks of seasonal production and consumption, it is unlikely that they will ever be completely flattened. Therefore, storage will always be required to balance seasonal variations in consumption and production.

Storage will also be needed to provide the buffer of inventory necessary to make crossdocking work. A crossdocking operation will clearly break down unless all of the merchandise necessary to support the operation is flowing across the dock at the right time. This means that stockouts at the master warehouses cannot occur.

Though crossdocking will never eliminate warehousing, it will cause relocation of some warehouses and elimination of others. The consumer products distributor who once used 30 regional warehouses to support a national market may do the same thing today with 3. However, the function of those three will be more critical than ever before.

Reverse Order Picking

One food distribution warehouse installed an order picking system that is both simple and effective. The system combines the function of receiving with the makeup of outbound customer orders. The reverse order picking system will work only if completed outbound orders are available when the inbound shipment arrives. The system is designed to allow the unloading crew to make up all available outbound orders as the product is received. This saves a second order picking operation and restaging. The warehouse saves time and money.

In nearly every large warehouse, receiving and shipping are segregated, frequently on opposite sides of the building. The receiving function is designed to be handled with a minimum time commitment, and the goal is to unload each vehicle as quickly as possible and release it promptly.

In reverse order picking, a computerized recap sheet (Fig. 17-1) contains a vertical column representing each item on the inbound load. The horizontal lines list each outbound order by order number and name of customer. Using the sheet shown in Fig. 17-1, an office worker creates warehouse pick tickets that identify customers, load number, and number of cases ordered.

A ticket is made for each stock item. For example in Fig. 17-2, product code 17315 has shipments destined for five different consignees. Using the pick ticket, the receiver segregates the merchandise for each of the five outbound orders as he unloads and checks the freight from the truck. Once these five orders have been segregated on separate pallets, each pallet is labeled to show the name of the customer and load number.

Before the product is put in the staging area, the pick tickets are compared to a tally sheet to ensure that the total of cases on the pick ticket matches the total on the tally sheet. Then each pallet is put in a staging area and when it is time to ship, the order is available for immediate loading. To provide a doublecheck, a bill of lading is reviewed by the loader to be sure that the entire load has been segregated properly.

Some claim that reverse order picking will severely slow down the receiving process. Admittedly it complicates receiving, but the total amount of effort in receiving and shipping is greatly reduced. The system works best if strict time schedules for inbound and outbound truckers are followed. You can receive as much product as the staging area allows. Therefore, the best way to implement this system is to spread the appointment schedule for inbound merchandise, thus allowing a maximum number of hours per day to be devoted to receiving. Note that the dock area must be designed with an ample amount of staging space, possibly including drive-in pallet racks to hold staged orders.

How much time is saved? With a conventional receiving and shipping system,

	15045	15116	17315	17354	18518
434718 Grocer 1		10	200		25
434732 Grocer 2	30			50	10
434744 Grocer 3		25			
434740 Grocer 4	40	30	400		
434745 Grocer 5		15	200	25	
434729 Grocer 6	40			20	10
434741 Grocer 7	15	20	10		
434728 Grocer 8	200	50		25	15
434728 Grocer 9	10	10		100	200
434731 Grocer 10		15	30	15	50

Figure 17-1. A computerized recap sheet.

four people are needed: receiver, putaway, selector, shipper/loader. Under the new system, the same work is done with just two people, a receiver/selector and a loader.

The greatest virtue of the system is its simplicity. The more complicated computer-printed master sheet is not used in the warehouse. Warehouse workers deal with easy-to-read pick tickets. By assembling outbound orders at the time of receipt, the picking, staging, and shipping process is greatly simplified. Like the proverbial better mousetrap, warehousing operations can be improved through the use of this approach to receiving and order picking. Once the employees have learned the system, picking errors are greatly reduced.

Bar Coding

Bar coding, more than any other technology used in warehousing, has often been discussed and rarely implemented.[1] However, bar coding will reduce the amount of time required to process information in your warehouse. Consider the receiving process as an example.

Without bar coding, the warehouseman writes up a receiving report while unloading each inbound shipment, then carries the receiving report and the accompanying packing list to the office for entry into the inventory system. A clerk compares both documents for discrepancies and then enters the information on

Product Code	*17315*	
Order	**Load**	**Case Quantity**
GROCER # 1	5	200
GROCER #4	9	400
GROCER #5	1	200
GROCER #7	3	10
GROCER # 10	13	30
		840

Figure 17-2. Warehouse pick ticket.

the receiving report. After entry the clerk might obtain the appropriate storage lo-cations for the merchandise and write those locations on the receiving report. The report is then returned to the warehouseman for stock putaway. The warehouse-man puts the stock away in the assigned locations.

One large manufacturer crossdocks materials coming to the distribution center from many different origins each day. Each origin ships the total quantity of materi-als to be used on that day. The same material is used at more than one manufactur-ing location, and the distribution center ships to all manufacturing locations. The arrival of a consolidated shipment to each manufacturing location is scheduled to meet a predetermined appointment; however, materials have continuously been ar-riving at the distribution center over the previous 24-hour period. These materials must be received, repacked, staged, and shipped—all within a very short period of time. Accountability is critical, and there is no margin for error. Old methods of paper-pushing would retard product flow and require more inventory as a buffer or safety valve. In this case, bar coding is not only affordable but also provides measur-able economies.

Using a bar code system, you begin the receipts process by obtaining a pallet label from a bar code printer on the receiving dock. The warehouseman attaches the label to the pallet, scans the bar code, then key-enters the quantity of cartons on the pallet. In less than two seconds, the system tells you if there is a discrepancy and gives you the location to which the pallet should be taken.

Locator Systems

An increasing number of warehouses today have formal stock locator systems re-corded on paper or computer records. Our first consideration should be whether or not such a system is needed at all.

The need for locator systems is governed both by layout and complexity of the inventory. A warehouse that contains only one stock keeping unit, such as a bulk silo full of grain, obviously needs no system to tell where the grain is located. A warehouse with only two or three stock keeping units may not need the locator system either.

A fixed location system might function without a stock locator, but few would argue that a random storage system can function effectively without a stock locator. Therefore, the argument over stock locator systems is frequently an argument about random versus fixed storage layouts. Some warehouses have a combination of the two, with a pick line that has fixed stock locations and an overflow stock area that has random locations. In this situation, some would argue that the locator system is needed only for the overflow section of the warehouse.

When stock locators are used, there are at least seven advantages that occur from their use.

1. *A locator system will save space.* When an item is stored in more than one location, look for ways to consolidate locations and open up a new slot that can hold an additional item.

2. *A locator system saves time.* On inbound, the operator does not have to search for a spot to put the new merchandise—an empty location has already been assigned before the stock is put away. Search time on outbound is saved, because the order picker does not have to search the warehouse to find the needed item.

3. *The locator system provides an extra control.* Some order pick lists require the operator to first go to a specific location, then to find a given item there. If location and item do not match as called for in the order, there must be an error in either the location or the item. If every item and location discrepancy is doublechecked, there will be fewer shipping errors.

4. *Order picking is expedited with a locator system.* Careful selection of picking locations can provide a shorter path for picking outbound orders, so the speed of picking is increased.

5. *A locator system can provide control of individual lots for product recall.* In production of some chemicals, each batch from the production line is considered to be a separate lot. Therefore a single stock keeping unit may consist of several lots. When each lot is in a separate location and is specifically identified, the control of these lots is greatly improved.

6. *A locator system improves "first-in, first-out" (FIFO) control.* By seeking the location that holds the oldest stock, control of FIFO is centralized and improved.

7. *Locator systems can be used for product quarantine.* Some products are held in quarantine for a brief period until a quality-control check has been completed. A locator system can provide the means of controlling the quarantine.

When a locator system is working well, the procedure starts with space planning for inbound merchandise. Empty locations available for storage are easily discovered in the system. Empty locations are increased by consolidating partial pallets or partial rows of merchandise that is already in the warehouse. When new merchandise is scheduled to be received, a space planner assigns an empty location to the inbound item. The person who unloads the truck already knows the designated storage slot for the inbound item. Then the merchandise is moved directly from the receiving dock to the empty storage location.

When goods are shipped, the order pick list contains the location first, then the item that will be found there. If the order picker does not find the item in that location, the discrepancy is immediately reported so that the source of the error can be discovered and corrected. That individual who is responsible for space planning makes a frequent location check of the entire warehouse. The purpose of this check is to discover empty locations and record them, to discover opportunities to save space through rewarehousing, and to improve space utilization by changing locations as necessary. An effective locator system requires good communications, discipline, and immediate correction of errors. Intercoms are frequently used to report and resolve location problems. When a physical inventory is taken, the locator system provides a time-saving control over the counting process.

Many warehouse managers can operate without a formal locator. However, nearly every busy distribution center will function far more effectively with a stock locator system.

Unitized Handling

Pallet History

Some attempts to unitize marine freight go back to very ancient history. But unitized handling as we know it today really had its inception with the technologies developed to supply the military during World War II. At that time the industrial truck was still in its earliest development stages. A wood platform or pallet was recognized as the best way to allow the industrial forklift truck to transport a number of small pieces of freight. The first such platforms were skids, consisting of a deck of wide boards nailed across two or more runner boards that raised the platform enough to allow the forks to move underneath and pick it up. Because of the need for stability in high stacking, the skid evolved into today's warehouse pallet, in which additional boards are nailed across the bottom of the runner boards to provide stability. Pallets were and are primarily made of wood, simply because wood is the lowest-cost construction commodity available in most countries.

Skids and pallets come in a wide variety of sizes, with the most common ones measuring as little as 3 × 3 ft up to 4 × 8 ft. Early in the 1960s, one warehouse operator made a survey of grocery chains in his community to explore the possibility of exchanging pallets. At that time, each food chain had a storage rack system based upon a different size pallet, and standardization seemed impossible.

The Standard Pallet

The decade of the 1960s saw the acceptance of a standard pallet specification in the United States. Overseas, such standardization had come much earlier. The U.S. military had generally used a standard pallet, and huge quantities of these pallets were war surplus in 1945. The Australian government had a particularly large supply of materials handling equipment left over after the war. It formed a Common-

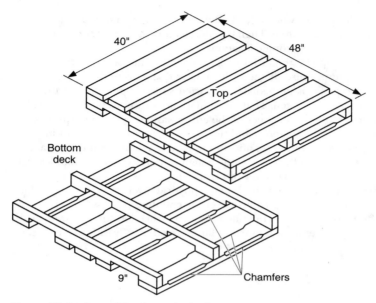

Figure 17-3. General Foods standard pallet.

wealth Handling and Equipment Pool, later abbreviated as CHEP. CHEP adopted a standard-size pallet, so that Australia was probably the first place in the world to achieve a practical standardization of pallet sizes as a legacy of its military surplus.

Within the U.S., General Foods deserves prime credit for the pressure it created in the early 1960s for a standard pallet. This standard (see Fig. 17-3) specified the size and spacing of the boards on the top and bottom deck as well as the size of the runner boards or stringers. The General Foods pallet was to be made of hard wood, with a specified weight per unit of approximately 80 lb. Notches on the stringer boards allowed the pallet to be entered from all four sides, though it is handled most easily from the 40-in face with its larger openings.

Because of its influence on both suppliers and its customers, General Foods had achieved growing acceptance of a standard pallet when the program was transferred to the Grocery Manufacturers of America (GMA). Through the cooperation of its members, GMA finished the job of establishing the General Foods specification as an industry standard. Wholesalers and chains adapted their materials handling and storage rack systems to the new standard pallet. Subsequently the program was transferred to a Grocery Pallet Council, and then efforts to maintain standards disintegrated. The hardwoods specified in the original General Foods design became scarce and expensive. Up to half of America's hardwood lumber was being consumed by the pallet industry, and prices became prohibitive. To cut costs, many pallet users found cheaper and softer types of wood. Others made changes in thickness and the spacing of deckboards that made for a cheaper but less durable pallet. Eventually the Grocery Pallet Council disbanded, and today the only pallet standard that has been preserved is that for the length and width dimensions. The

48 × 40-in pallet remains the most common size used, and the predominant size used in the grocery products industry. Most storage rack systems are designed to accommodate the 48 × 40-in unitized load.

Alternatives to Pallets

While use of the wood pallet is the oldest and easiest method of handling unitized loads, it is not the only method available. The first developments of substitutes for pallets arose as early as the 1940s, when materials handling manufacturers cooperated with paper companies in developing a thin and disposable shipping platform that became known as a *slipsheet*. Constructed of high-tensile laminated paper, the sheet is much thinner than a wood pallet. However, it cannot be lifted with conventional forks without damage. Handling equipment manufacturers developed a special device known as a *push/pull attachment*. The device is designed to grip a protruding tab of the slipsheet and pull the entire sheet with its load onto the flat metal plates that support the load while it is being transported. At destination, a plate pushes the loaded slipsheet onto the floor of a trailer or onto the floor of the warehouse. Figure 17-4 shows the slipsheet and push/pull attachment in use.

A simpler alternative to the slipsheet is a *skee sheet,* so named because one end curves up like the front of a ski. It is made of wood veneer and was developed by the

Figure 17-4. Slipsheet and push/pull attachment in use. (*Courtesy of Cascade Corporation*)

Elberta Crate and Box Company, which changed the spelling to *skee* in order to register the word as their trademark. The skee sheet does not require a push/pull attachment, but it does require a lift truck equipped with polished and thinly tapered fork tines. Badly trained or improperly equipped lift truck operators can damage loads if they try to handle skee sheets with blunt forks. Therefore, both the slipsheet and the skee sheet require special truck attachments and a high degree of training.

Another special device that has been in use for over three decades is the *carton clamp* or *grab truck*. Figure 17-5 shows a clamp truck with a load. This truck has paddles that squeeze the sides of the load enough to allow it to be lifted. This device was originally designed for cotton bales and rolls of paper, and some clamps are designed to rotate the load so that it can be inverted or placed on its side. The clamp truck works best with relatively large and sturdy packages. Because it requires side pressure to lift the unit, improper pressure adjustment, or packaging that is not designed for clamp use, can cause the clamp to damage the product. In the early days of clamp truck use, extensive damage to home laundry appliances occurred when a warehouse operator used improperly adjusted clamps that dented each unit as it was lifted. The device must be carefully maintained, since it too can be damaged by operator abuse. Some warehousemen have used clamp attachments to pick up everything from bicycles to bailing wire, causing damage to both the clamp attachment and the merchandise handled. Because of the way it functions, the clamp truck does not require any loading platform. It can pick up a load and transfer it from one loading platform to another. There is some space loss in both storage and freight vehicles, because a few inches of side void are left to allow access by the arms of the clamp attachment.

Figure 17-5. Clamp truck with a load. (*Courtesy of Cascade Corporation*)

Challenges of Unitized Load Handling

As you consider the various options in unitized handling, it is well to consider the advantages and disadvantages of each.

The wood pallet is the fastest and simplest way to store and transfer unitized loads. It is easier to operate an industrial truck equipped with forks than with any other kind of loading attachment. The generous-sized openings in standard pallets allow them to be safely stowed and retrieved, even when they are in a high stack and the lift driver is maneuvering a load that is 20 ft off the ground. However, if the pallet is to achieve full savings in materials handling, it should be transported with the load from origin to destination.

If the material is hand-stacked from a warehouse pallet to the floor of the truck, or if the process is reversed, the loading or unloading process will take more than six times as long as unitized loading. One time study of the process showed that manual loading of 22-lb cases is done at a rate of 8 pallets or 480 cases/man-hr. The loading of full pallets can be accomplished at the rate of 50 pallets/man-hr, or 3000 cases/hr.

If full pallets are loaded, the shipper has the option of donating them or taking other pallets in exchange. Pallets are costly, and most users of them are reluctant to donate a platform that costs between $6 and $10. On the other hand if they exchange pallets with the trucker, vendor, or supplier, they run the risk of exchanging a high-quality pallet for a cheap one. Very few warehouse people would recognize the difference between the durable and expensive species of wood and the cheap ones, or well-cured versus green wood. Few warehouse operators have the time or the inclination to measure and check to be sure that the thickness and spacing of deck boards and bottom boards is in compliance with a standard specification. As a result, there is no practical way to enforce the design standard on warehouse shipping and receiving docks. Industry frustration with the high costs of "junk" pallets increased after efforts to police a standard system had collapsed.

Fire protection is another significant problem. Underwriters consider high stacks of wood pallets to be one of the worst hazards in a warehouse, since the spaces between boards allow combustion to create a "flue effect" that can result in a very dangerous fire. Therefore, risk underwriters typically restrict the height of stacks of pallets in a warehouse. To avoid wasting valuable storage space, warehouse operators typically move empty pallets outdoors.

When they are outdoors, pallets are subject to contamination and deterioration by birds and rodents. They are exposed to the elements and are further deteriorated by rain, snow, or ice. Finally, wood does not lend itself to steam-cleaning or other effective cleaning methods.

Slipsheets or skee sheets are more compact and less costly than wood pallets. Their compactness allows them to be stored in a much smaller space, and because of their construction they do not present the fire hazard of a wood pallet. However, there are no standard specifications for these devices either. Slipsheets can be made of anything from paper to plastic. One major brewing company uses plastic slipsheets and recycles and remanufactures the sheets at its own facility. Both skee sheets and slipsheets require special equipment and special handling. They cannot be handled by the conventional lowlift pallet truck, which was designed specifically for wood pallets. Therefore, when loads that are unitized in this way are received at a company that uses conventional forklift and lowlift equipment, they must be transferred to a wooden pallet.

The clamp truck offers the ability to effect this transfer, since it can lift a load and place it onto a platform. Procter & Gamble developed its "trucker-owned pallet system," abbreviated as TOPS. Each transportation company wishing to enjoy the labor savings of a unitized load brings pallets to the company's dock, and clamp trucks are used to place unitized loads onto the trucker's pallets. However, clamps don't work well on every kind of load. Unitized loads of very small boxes are not practical for clamp loading, since the smaller cartons are more likely to drop out of the center of the unitized load.

The Future for Unitized Loads

In 1989 and 1990, frustration with the damage caused by "junk" pallets caused an intensive search for alternatives. Cleveland Consulting Associates developed two studies for the Joint Industry Shipping Container Committee, a new group sponsored by Food Marketing Institute, Grocery Manufacturers of America (GMA), and National American Wholesale Grocers Association (NAWGA). They concluded that the cost of the current system in the grocery industry alone is $1.9 billion per year, which translates to 16 cents per case of groceries or $10 for each full pallet load. These costs represent product damage caused by poor pallets, replacement and repair of damaged pallets, extra cost to motor carriers in transporting pallets, productivity loss as pallets are sorted and selected, workers' compensation costs from pallet caused injuries, and administration of pallets. One grocery wholesaler states that 7 out of 10 injuries in his warehouse are caused by pallets.

There were two reactions to the data developed by Cleveland Consulting Associates. One was a competition announced by the joint industry committee to develop a one-way disposable shipping platform that would allow unitized loads to be moved in transit on something other than the conventional wood pallet. Whether or not an acceptable shipping platform will be widely adopted remains to be seen. At this time, there is no platform that meets the specifications of the committee.

At least four alternative expendable pallets have been designed. Pressed wood fiber pallets have about the same durability as wood, and they save space since they are designed to be nested. They are nail-free, which avoids product damage. Corrugated fiberboard pallets are less durable than wood and not repairable, but they could be suitable for single-use shipping applications. Plastic pallets are more durable than wood. While they are not repairable, they can be made of a recyclable material. They are typically used in a closed-loop system, where the pallet is always recovered for reuse. Metal pallets have similar characteristics and have the same uses. Both plastic and metal can be sanitized to meet FDA requirements for food processing. The U.S. Postal Service has experimented with both a nestable wood-fiber pallet and a nestable plastic pallet.

The other reaction to the Cleveland data is a concept that is widely used in Australia, New Zealand, and Europe. In 1958, the Commonwealth Handling and Equipment Pool (CHEP) was purchased from the Australian government by Brambles Industries Limited. This newly privatized pallet pool offered pallets on a lease basis to users in a variety of industries. After proving the concept in Australia, Brambles expanded into New Zealand. To launch the European campaign, Brambles merged with a British firm, GKN. A pallet-leasing pool started up in the United Kingdom in 1974 and spread throughout Europe. GKN Brambles launched its leasing program in the United States in September of 1990. Procter & Gamble announced its commitment to the program, though it will still offer other options such as "TOPS," mentioned earlier. The CHEP pallet seems to closely follow the original General Foods specification, with one exception. The wood specified is southern pine or Douglas fir, which would not be classified as the "hardwood" of the original standard pallet. The CHEP pallet has an average weight of 65 lb, as compared to 80 lb in the General Foods specification, probably because the wood is lighter. The loading deck covers 81 percent of the 40 × 48-in surface, and the bottom deck covers 57 percent of the surface. CHEP pallets have a bright blue paint on the side surfaces that allow the pallets to be easily identified and separated.

The truly distinctive feature of the CHEP system, however, is that the pallets are never sold, only leased. Therefore the pallet owner, not the user, is responsible for maintenance of the pallets. CHEP management says that the average cost of its pallet is $10 per unit, substantially higher than the $6.92 cost found in the Cleveland Consulting Associates study. The pallet rental pool is based on a fee of $1 per pallet as the pallets are issued. A rental charge of $.035 per day is charged for each pallet in use, and an 88-cent transfer charge is made when the product is shipped to another party on the same pallet. Procter & Gamble will offer CHEP pallets to its customers at no charge while the pallet is under first load. As soon as that pallet has been emptied, it must either be returned to the lessor or released from CHEP. A fee is paid if the pallet is lost, but presumably there is no way to levy a fee for damage unless it can be proven that the pallet has been abused. GKN Brambles plans to establish depots all over the country to store, maintain, and control pallet inventories. Initial plans call for an inventory of about one million CHEP pallets in the United States, as compared to their inventory of eight million pallets in Australia, a country with less than one-tenth the population of the United States.

Predictably, there is already a competitive alternate in pallet leasing. Libla Industries, Inc. published an announcement of its new subsidiary, First National Pallet Rental, Inc. Based in Missouri, Libla cooperates with other pallet manufacturers in other regions. Like CHEP, the First National Pallet will have a distinctive color code. However, it is made of hardwood (oak) with 71 percent deck coverage. The pricing system differs as well. A grocery manufacturer rents the pallet for a flat fee of $4 plus a returnable deposit of $3.50. When the loaded pallet is delivered to a customer, the new user is billed $3.50 for the deposit, which is then returned to the original manufacturer.

As the two options of pallet leasing or disposable shipping platforms are considered, the user must also remember the advantages and disadvantages. Empty wood pallets, whether leased or owned, are still a fire risk when stored in quantity indoors. If outdoor storage is used, the contamination and deterioration problems remain. CHEP will assume much of this burden by keeping idle pallets at its own depots, but a two-day supply of pallets will be kept by each grocery manufacturer using the system.

The one-way shipping platform is presumably designed only for material handling, not for storage. It is unlikely that a low-cost shipping platform would also be strong enough to use for high-piled, free-standing storage stacks. Therefore the load will have to be transferred from the shipping platform to a more durable warehouse pallet. Such transfer is clearly feasible, but it represents an additional expense.

A leased pallet made of some material other than wood could be an attractive alternative, particularly if this would allow indoor storage and steam cleaning. However, this alternative has not yet surfaced.

The challenge of unitized loads will be resolved in the next few years, simply because there is so much attention being given to it. The eventual result is likely to significantly change many warehousing operations in the United States.

Maintaining Accuracy and Security

In many operations, errors are the worst problem that management faces. In some industries, errors mean lost customers; in a few situations, a shipping error can mean the loss of a life. As long as you have human beings in the warehouse, there will be some errors. Still, it is management's job to reduce them to the smallest number possible.

Reducing Errors in Receiving and Shipping

Cost of errors varies widely in different operations, and you should try to get an estimate of the cost of mistakes in your operation. If the wrong item is shipped, you will have an undetected stockout when inventory is exhausted, with a corresponding overage in some other item. If physical counts are not taken frequently, the undetected stockout can cause customer relations problems with the delivery you could not make because you did not have the item that you thought you had.

If the shipping error is to be corrected, you have the cost of taking back a customer return and replacing it with the right freight. Typically this triples the delivery cost that would have been incurred if the correct item had been shipped in the first place. In some industries, the shipper will allow the receiver to keep the wrong item in order to avoid some of the excess transportation costs. Obviously this cannot be done with expensive merchandise. The cost of taking back the wrong item and putting it into stock is many times the cost of a normal warehouse receipt. Part of this cost is the administrative burden of correcting a shipping error and handling a receipt of just one or a few packages.

Finally, the most serious cost of an error is the creation of an unhappy customer.

There are many steps that can be taken in your operation to minimize the possibility that an error will be made. One cause of errors is a misunderstanding as to what was ordered, when the order was taken by telephone in the office. Such misunderstandings are minimized if the order is repeated on the telephone. Additionally, some companies will call back their customers to confirm their orders. Consider the procedure used by a fast-food company that makes home deliveries. This firm asks for the telephone number whenever a phone order for its product is taken. Then the operator phones back the customer to repeat the order. This second phone call prevents a high percentage of errors.

Reducing Errors in Order Picking

Warehouse locator systems originally were designed to cut search time with a complex inventory. However, they have a second advantage—that of preventing shipping errors. The order picker is instructed to go to a given location to pick a given item. If the picker finds that the item is not in that location, there is either an error in the locator system or an error as to the item specified. If the order picker always questions it when the locator system and the item do not match, this provides an additional chance to find errors in the selection system.

A surprising number of warehouse errors are made because the labels or markings on packages are confusing or sometimes even misleading. Nonessential markings should be eliminated, and care should be taken to be consistent in the marking or labeling system. Any marking system should have the trade name first, then size, color, and item number. Some markings are too small to be adequately read in normal warehouse light. Others are done in a color that does not show up under some warehouse lighting systems. If you have a high error rate, consider whether the marking on the packaging could be changed in a way that would make it easier to read.

Another source of error in marking systems is the use of shelf packages or packages within a package. You may have a shipping case that contains inner packs, each of which contains three bottles. With unclear terminology, the warehouse order picker may not know whether the customer wants one case, shelf pack, or bottle. Confusion of this sort can result in overshipments that create a substantial loss, or an undershipment that leaves you with an unhappy customer. Be sure that your system makes it absolutely clear how many pieces the customer really wants.

In these days of computer-generated paper, picking documents are frequently carbon copies that are garbled and difficult to read. To prevent errors, the picking document should be designed primarily for the order filler. The list should be as legible as you can make it, and it should use as few letters and numbers as are needed to identify the product. Every effort should be made to eliminate unnecessary information that might distract the order picker. If there is unrelated information on other copies of the order, blackout techniques can mask this information from the order filler. Improving legibility on a pick list will reduce errors. This includes leaving enough space to ensure that the information is easily readable, and using horizontal ruling to ensure that the order picker does not misread the quantity of one item for the one on the succeeding line.

A picking document often has four columns. The first shows the warehouse location of the product, the second the identification numbers for the product. The third column is left blank, for the order filler to place a check mark when the item has been picked. The fourth column will show the quantity to be selected. Any changes in the order go only in the third column.

A surprising number of warehouse picking documents do not list the product in the same sequence in which it appears on a pick line. As a result the operator must either change the paper to match the freight, or else move through the warehouse in a zigzag pattern as the operator retrieves the material in the sequence in which it appears on paper. Sometimes warehouse travel time can be cut by more than half simply by putting the order pick list in the same order as products appear in the pick line.

Sometimes the environment of your warehouse invites order picking errors. The most common failure is lack of sufficient lighting. While minimum lighting may be adequate for bulk storage situations, an order-pick area should have illumination of at least 50 foot candles to keep you relatively free of errors. Those items that are most popular and most frequently picked should be at levels that eliminate reaching or stooping by the order picker. The fastest-moving items should be no less than 16 in above the floor and no more than 6 ft high, in order to reduce the effort involved in selecting the most popular items. Some products invite errors because of similar markings or similar appearance. Try to keep from storing these confusing items next to each other.

One of the more controversial personnel practices is the elimination of full-time checkers. Many warehouse operations have eliminated full-time checking personnel with great success. Other operators feel that this is impossible. The decision is influenced by the quality of your work force and the nature of the merchandise being selected. In many cases, elimination of the checker results in proven economies—error-correction costs are less than the salary of the checker, and workers feel more responsible because they know that the only checker is the customer. In other cases, a checker is absolutely necessary to maintain desired quality.

Preventing Theft and Pilferage

Almost any product that is received and shipped could be stolen. Those products that are most likely to be stolen are either very valuable, easily marketable, or both. Some merchandise may be expensive but not readily sold, and other products may be of lower value but easily sold. Thieves generally will consider marketability of product more closely than value. Some basic grocery products that do not have a high value have been the object of mass thefts because there was a market for the item. Some commodities have changed in their attractiveness to thieves. There was a time when computers were valuable but difficult to sell. Today the cost per cubic foot of computer product has gone down, but the marketability has gone up. Law enforcement officials can give you a good idea of which products are frequently stolen for resale.

Many warehouse operators apply selective security standards, using the highest security measures for those products that are considered most attractive to thieves.

Thefts of merchandise in and around warehouses can be divided into two types of occurrences. The first, a *mass theft*, is the hijacking of a freight vehicle or breaking into a warehouse building and removing substantial quantities of goods. The second is *pilferage*, or "mysterious disappearance."

Mysterious disappearance may involve collusion between truck drivers and shipping employees to deliberately overload an outbound vehicle. Similar collusion with receivers may cause a failure to receive all of the merchandise on an inbound vehicle. The excess merchandise remains on the truck, to be sold at a later date. Other pilferage involves the clandestine removal of small amounts of merchandise from the warehouse. Small products may be taken out in lunch boxes or pockets, or put into a trash barrel for removal at a later time.

There are two defenses against theft and pilferage. The first is the development of physical deterrents in the facility that make it difficult for thieves to remove products. The second is defense through personnel, by making sure that warehouse employees are all honest people who would not condone theft or pilferage.

The most elaborate protective devices can be defeated by a dishonest worker. The only way to control this kind of theft is to try to hire only honest workers. This has become increasingly difficult, particularly now that the use of polygraph or lie detector tests in the U.S. is legally banned. Use of detailed credit checks is also illegal in certain states.

A newer method of testing a job applicant's honesty is preemployment screening through voice-stress analysis. Some claim that the results are superior to the polygraph. When the person being questioned intends to deceive in his or her answer, the voice contains stress that may not be audible to the human ear but that can be measured by a trained analyst using a special recorder. While most interviews are conducted in the presence of the speaker, it is also possible to analyze a tape recording or a telephone conversation.

The 1988 ban on use of the polygraph caused renewed interest in handwriting analysis, a personnel technique that is more widely used in Europe than in the United States. The effectiveness of this technique has been debated, yet many claim that handwriting analysis reveals a great deal about the personality of the writer.

A good way to defeat collusion is to have a "second-count" check. Ideally, the person who makes it should be a foreman or supervisor who is a member of management.

There are at least three ways you can use a foreman as a first line of defense against collusion theft:

1. Make the placement and breaking of all seals the responsibility of a foreman, accompanied by the truck driver whose vehicle was sealed.

2. See to it that, upon receipt of any load, the foreman as well as the receiver verifies merchandise in the staging area. In a busy or crowded warehouse, this verification may take place in a storage bay, since the load is taken directly from the vehicle to storage.

3. Because only a random check of certain loads can be made, be sure the check is done by a member of management.

This does not mean that a collusion ring could not extend to management, or could not include more than two persons. However, experience has shown that few collusion thefts involve more than two individuals.

Personnel policies in receiving and shipping can be structured to encourage honesty. A strict policy on the acceptance of gifts is one example. At some busy grocery warehouses, a convenient unloading appointment depends on a "gift" to the receiving clerk. When this kind of corruption exists, the moral atmosphere that encourages pilferage of merchandise is also likely to be present.

Adherence to security procedures must be strictly enforced. For example, if only foremen are to break and apply seals, you must create—and use—paperwork that certifies that only a certain foreman has performed the task.

Every empty container is a potential repository for stolen merchandise. An empty trailer left at a dock could be the staging area for a theft. The same is true of empty boxcars and even trash hoppers. One approach is to restrict access to such containers. Empty freight vehicles should either be kept under seal, or inspected as they leave the warehouse. Furthermore, this inspection should be covered by a written record that it took place.

Customer pickups create an additional risk of theft. One way to control this risk is to have merchandise for pickup pulled from stock by one individual, with delivery to the customer made by a different worker. Again, this procedure is based on the fact that usually there are only two people involved in collusion thefts.

Customer returns present an unusual security problem—particularly if the merchandise is returned in high volume or in nonstandard cartons. If this is the case in your warehouse, be sure all customer returns are checked thoroughly as soon as the merchandise arrives at the dock. If you don't keep your returned-goods processing current, you're inviting pilferage.

Control of documents can be as important as control of freight. Since fraudulent parcel labels can be used to divert small shipments, the best way to prevent this is to supervise the issuing of labels.

Many shipping crews break for lunch or coffee at the same time, with no one available to inspect exposed docks or entrance doors. It's a good idea to stagger rest breaks, with a few individuals always on duty to protect against unauthorized entry.

A first line of defense in theft security is electronic alarm systems, which generally are more reliable than a watchman. But it is important to remember that an electronic system can always be defeated. Any system designed by one human can be overcome by another, especially since a sophisticated ring of thieves may include a former employee of an alarm company. Furthermore, some alarm companies use outside electricians as subcontractors to install equipment. One dishonest electrician can defeat almost any system.

Yet it is harder to defeat the electronic systems being installed today, thanks to the increasing sophistication of the new equipment. An example is the use of closed-circuit television cameras. These are most effective when combined with videotape to give a reviewable record of an occurrence seen by the camera. Some closed-circuit TV systems are activated by the opening of a dock door, so that the camera operates only when a loading door is open. The tape systems can be set to operate through an evening or weekend when the warehouse is closed, with high-speed review of the tape by supervisory personnel after the warehouse has reopened.

In many warehouses, closed-circuit TV is used primarily as a psychological deterrent. However, when properly installed, it also can be a material aid both in detecting theft and in convicting those involved.

The possibility of false alarms is one drawback of any electronic system. A too-sensitive system tied directly to police stations can set off so many false alarms that it quickly becomes a nuisance. While most law enforcement officials encourage the use of electronic systems, they naturally want the devices to be reasonably reliable.

In a warehouse, the most sensitive electronic systems are sometimes those most likely to send the most false alarms. Heading the list would be ultrasonic systems, which are designed to detect noise or movement. The problem, however, is that most warehouses are located in or near railroad yards, and the normal switching of freight cars may be sufficient to trip the alarm. Some warehouses have an interior rail dock that must be accessible to railroad crews for switching cars at night. Under these conditions, use of ultrasonic alarms is most difficult, if not impossible.

The cheapest electronic alarms for a warehouse provide protection for the doors only. However, this type of system is not going to stop a determined thief who is willing to take the time to cut through a warehouse wall. The walls of most modern warehouses are relatively thin, and whether they are constructed of masonry or metal, a thief will take little time in cutting a large enough hole in the wall to allow a mass theft.

In one such case, thieves backed a truck against a wall of the warehouse. Working from inside the van, they removed concrete blocks from the exterior wall to gain entry, then loaded the van with the highest-value product in the building.

Because of the vulnerability of nearly all warehouse walls, the best electronic alarms include a "wall of light" surrounding most of the storage areas. With this, the thief who manages to penetrate an exterior wall will still sound an alarm when entering the storage areas.

Skylights and roofs also are easily entered, primarily because of the lightweight materials used in modern construction. Protecting an entire roof area with electronic beams is not practical. Fortunately, however, it is equally impractical to take out any significant volume of freight over a roof.

One answer to the compromises necessary with alarm systems is to install sectional alarms, providing one standard of security for most inventory of normal value and a high-security storage area for high-value items. Even the ultrasonic system can be practical in an isolated room designed for a small portion of the inventory.

The typical alarm system used in warehouses usually must be switched on or off as an entire system, so if there is a breach it's difficult to pin down where it occurred. Warehouse supervisors may have difficulty "setting up" the system at night when one of many doors is partially ajar, or one electronic beam is blocked. However, more sophisticated systems have an "annunciator panel" to show exactly which doors or beams have been breached.

Such a system may also permit you to keep certain doors on alarm but take others off. This enables you to activate the system for portions of the building not in daily use. In a very large or lightly staffed building, this system may be worth its additional cost.

Fire codes in most communities require many safety pedestrian doors along the walls of the warehouse to allow workers to escape from the building in case of fire. Since such doors can also make it easier to pilfer merchandise, you should put a stop to any casual use by having alarms on each personnel door that ring whenever it is opened.

Perhaps the best way to keep thieves from breaking into your warehouse building is to restrict or deny access to the land surrounding the warehouse. Both the physical arrangement of the grounds, and the access to your warehouse, can either invite or discourage theft. No busy warehouse can totally cut off access to the property, since any high-volume movement of freight will involve the placement and removal of trucks and boxcars at docks. Access to the docks by trucking and rail employees must be allowed, and such access is often required at night or after working hours.

High fences and gates help to control access to the property. After-hours patrol of the grounds by a guard dog and trained handler is an excellent psychological deterrent. Some guard dog services operate on a roving basis, with protection provided for a number of facilities by the same guard team.

Where you locate employee and visitor parking can also deter or encourage theft. Persons entering or leaving a warehouse should all use a single entrance, with other personnel doors available only for an emergency. Parking should never be permitted adjacent to warehouse walls or doors.

A seal is a thin metal strip (with a serial number) that is fastened so that it can't be broken without the break being evident. Properly used, the seal is a good physical deterrent to cargo theft. Because theft in interstate commerce may be investigated by the FBI, for years the mere presence of a seal on a boxcar was enough to discourage unauthorized entry. More recently, however, bolder thieves have attacked the boxcars themselves.

If a boxcar is broken into while spotted at the shipper's or receiver's plant, the railroad has a legal right to disclaim responsibility, as the car was not under its control. For this reason, the use of an inside rail dock may be the only means of protecting yourself against theft from a railroad car. A parked truck-trailer presents similar problems. You can buy electronic alarm systems that extend coverage to trailers parked on your property.

To use seals effectively, you must have procedures that are carefully followed, as well as good communication between shipper and receiver. You can't allow seals to be either applied or removed by unauthorized personnel if you expect them to serve their purpose.

One way to reduce losses of highly vulnerable products is to place them on the upper levels of storage racks, where they can be readily removed only by a trained lift truck driver. By limiting access in this way, you see to it that storage racks improve security as well as storage productivity.

Only warehouse employees should have access to storage areas. Bank customers aren't offended by barriers that prohibit them from walking behind the counters where the money is stored, and so too no user of a warehouse should be offended if his or her movements are restricted in the same manner. Even warehouse employees should understand that they are authorized to enter only those areas involved in their own work.

Yet many warehouses have no physical restrictions that prevent visitors from wandering at will. Furthermore, many warehouses don't prevent visiting truck drivers from walking or loitering in storage areas. Posting signs or painting stripes may not be good enough. Look into how fencing, cages, or counters can be used to prevent unauthorized persons from entering storage areas.

Good management must actively combat theft, focusing on the three aspects of defense: physical, personnel, and procedural. No one of the three will be effective without the other two, and a "Maginot line" mindset can be as fatal in warehouse security as it was in military history. The greatest enemy of security is complacency. An outside security audit is a good way to guard against management complacency.

A periodic spot check of outbound truck shipments may be the best way to impress both warehouse employees and truck drivers of your vigilance. Under this audit procedure, perhaps one truckload per month leaving the warehouse is stopped, returned to the dock, and thoroughly recounted to check loading accuracy. Common carrier management will cooperate with such a procedure when its purpose is understood, and in this way you demonstrate to employees that you are serious about discovering any "errors" that could lead to "mysterious disappearance."

Hiring Honest People

At the end of 1988, a Federal law banned most businesses from using polygraphs as a preemployment screening tool. A polygraph, popularly known as the lie detector, is a device that measures changes in blood pressure, heart rate, and other bodily functions to help determine if a person is lying. In response to this law, some warehouses have begun to use other examinations as part of their employee screening systems. To replace the polygraph, many companies have begun to use honesty tests for employee screening purposes.

The best honesty tests have two categories of questions. The first looks primarily at the applicant's *attitudes* towards honesty, by asking direct questions about possible illegal activities. The second is a broader test of *personality*. These two look at a wide range of work behaviors. The evaluation of the multiple-choice responses is designed to detect whether a respondent has answered questions truthfully. The tests try to detect potential thieves and other dishonest people with a combination of subtle and not so subtle questions. The most direct questions simply ask the respondent if he or she has stolen from an employer in the past. Surprisingly, many people will mention past incidents of stealing, and look on this not as a confession but as a description of behavior that in their minds is perfectly acceptable. Other questions are designed to discover attitudes commonly found in those likely to steal. For example, a dishonest person often believes the whole world is dishonest. While the tests vary in length, they normally take no longer than one hour to complete.

The critical features of any employment test are validity, legality, implementation, and cost. Will the test be valid as a predictor of dishonest employees? On a high-quality test, each question is thoroughly studied for its predictive ability by both in-house and third party groups. The in-house studies, those performed by the test companies themselves, report excellent validity figures. Some academics have expressed concern that the tests may give false indications on any given individual. Others have pointed out that the polygraph was not perfect either. Honesty tests may reject a few employees who are honest, and they may fail to screen out a few dishonest employees. However, the number of times that this will happen is quite small. The testing companies' literature suggests that the tests cannot with certainty predict the behavior of every applicant, but that over a range of applicants the validity is extremely high. Studies have also been conducted to determine whether or not applicants could fake their way through the test. The results show that even when test groups deliberately give fake responses, the high validity of the tests is still maintained.

One advantage of honesty tests is their relatively low cost. At around $7 to $12 per applicant, honesty tests cost less than polygraph tests, which may run as high as $40. One employer told us that if the test screens out only one or two dishonest people per year, that will have paid for the whole testing program.

Implementation of honesty tests into the preemployment process is relatively easy. Another user presents the test to each applicant as an attitude survey, and warns that no one is hired unless the survey is completed. Many applicants are not even aware that the test is being used as a screening tool. Completed tests can be sent to the test company via the telephone, computer, or mail for evaluation. Immediate feedback is available if needed. All results are evaluated by the test company to ensure the accuracy and integrity of the process. This process can be completed in relatively little time, and therefore will not significantly impact the time frame of your preemployment process. The analysis returned to an employer shows how an applicant compares as to honesty, drug use, and other work-related areas with others who have taken the test. Sometimes the feedback will suggest areas for further review. For example, if an applicant admits he took $20 worth of goods from a previous employer, the feedback might recommend a follow-up interview to find out exactly what was stolen.

Ensuring Safety and Preventing Damage

Because so much lifting, pushing, pulling, and human interaction with power equipment and large mechanical devices is involved, the potential for accidents and damage in warehouses is extremely high. Any of the hundreds of different tasks performed daily can create a condition where serious accidents or damage may happen.

Accidents in Receiving and Shipping

Most injured warehouse workers are not newcomers. A federal study shows that workers with five or more years' experience in warehousing are more likely to be injured than others. Those with one to five years are second, and those with less than one month have the least likelihood of injury. Apparently experience causes carelessness, which leads to injuries. The same study shows that extreme fatigue may not be a factor in most accidents. Twenty-nine percent of accidents occur after only two to four hours on the job, and another 23 percent occur after less than two hours on the job. Only 8 percent occur after eight or more hours in the workplace.

The most dangerous work in a warehouse is the loading and unloading of freight vehicles. The warehouses having the most accidents are those of wholesalers and retailers. Sixty-eight percent of all warehouse injuries are in these warehouses, as contrasted with only 8 percent in warehouses devoted to transportation and public utilities. Presumably, public warehousing is in this smaller category. More of the study's findings:

- Injuries are more frequent in larger warehouses. Those with 11 or more employees had 82 percent of the injuries.
- Older workers are safer. Seventy-four percent of injured workers were 34 or younger.
- Though personal protective equipment will prevent injuries, the majority of warehouse workers do not wear such equipment. The most commonly used protectors are gloves and steel-toed safety shoes. Hardhats and goggles also are frequently used.
- While safety training is common, many workers never receive it. Training in proper manual lifting is the most popular, but only 28 percent of injured workers have been exposed to it. Only 23 percent have received a forklift operator training course.

Two types of accidents account for nearly two-thirds of all injuries:

1. Overexertion, accounting for 38 percent of injuries
2. Being struck by a falling or flying object, accounting for 26 percent of injuries

Three types of injuries account for nearly all those that occur in warehouses:

1. Muscle sprain or strain (the most common)
2. Bruise or contusion
3. Cut, laceration, or puncture

Although injuries requiring hospitalization accounted for only 9 percent of the total, more than three out of four injuries resulted in some time lost.

When workers were asked why accidents happen, 54 percent felt that it was not conditions at the work site that had caused the accident. However, 22 percent felt that lack of space in the workplace was a factor. Some felt that working too fast or working in an awkward position was a contributing cause.

Figure 17-6 shows what activity workers are engaged in when accidents take place.

Metal or plastic banding used to seal many types of containers is also a common source of injuries. When this banding is cut away to open the containers it can fly back, causing serious lacerations or eye injuries. Eye protection and gloves could prevent this. In addition, employees should be trained to stand to the side of the container, away from the banding, so they will not be hit if the banding flies. After the banding is cut, it should be disposed of so it doesn't trip someone or wrap around the wheel of a forklift.

Redesigning Lifting Tasks

Overextension of muscles, particularly those of the lower back, is an injury that accounts for 30 to 40 percent of health claims, totaling up to $9 billion a year. With

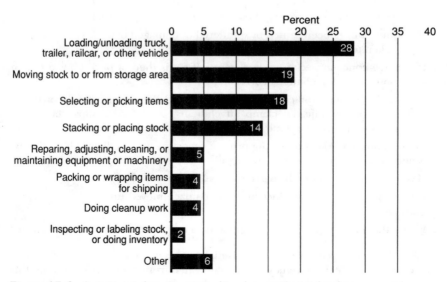

Figure 17-6. Activities workers are engaged in when accidents take place.

these figures in hand, many employers have begun to seriously address this problem and have devised methods to reduce the risk.

The substantial amount of research and training applied to the manual lifting problem has not been very effective. Employers train workers in the traditional "squat lift," yet injuries still occur. Many workers find this method very unnatural, since it requires more effort than a natural lift. The more effective approach to reducing injuries for these tasks is to apply mechanical aids such as lift trucks, conveyors, and dolly wheels.

The most effective way to eliminate back injuries is to redesign the workplace using ergonomics. Ergonomics is a big word to describe a simple process—arranging work for human comfort. In this situation, the goal is to eliminate the need for employees to lift. Although all lifting can never be eliminated, many tasks can be made less strenuous. Each task where employees are experiencing back injuries should be analyzed to determine how it can be redesigned to eliminate the cause of injury. Some solutions are simple. For instance, the height of offloading can be changed so that the worker doesn't have to bend over as far or reach up as high. Other solutions are more complex and may require mechanical devices such as conveyors or power hoists to make the job easier. These solutions are best implemented during the design phase of the facility, so that costly redesign is not needed further down the road. Studies indicate that the ergonomic approach will reduce about one-third of back-related injuries.

Preventing Damage

As you work to reduce damage in receiving and shipping, the following checklist may provide some loss-prevention ideas.

1. Is some of the "warehouse damage" actually unreported carrier damage? If so, what steps can be taken to stop the acceptance of damaged freight?
2. Has some damage been caused by splintered or damaged pallets? What steps are being taken to control pallet quality?
3. Is damage concentrated in certain items? If so, is there a packaging problem with those items that could be corrected?
4. Have maintenance problems in lift trucks caused damage, such as protruding forks, improperly adjusted clamp attachments, or defective slipsheet attachments? If so, what can be done to improve lift truck maintenance?
5. Are warehouse workers providing prompt reporting and feedback about the existence and cause of warehouse damage?
6. Has damage been caused by narrow aisles and overcrowding?
7. Has the percentage of product suffering damage moved up or down since last year?
8. What other changes in warehousing practices might reduce warehouse damage?

When damage of sensitive materials is discovered, it is important that the damaged cases immediately be removed and segregated from good stock. At times this removal is not easy because it could involve depalletizing, for which there is no labor available. One answer is the development of a *drip pan,* a piece of sheet metal a little larger than a pallet with corners turned up and sealed to hold leaking fluid. In this way, leakage from the damaged pallet is captured in the drip pan and not allowed to seep through the warehouse.

Another answer is the use of fiber or metal drums as a temporary repository for damaged cases or bags. Like the pan, the drum keeps the spillage from causing further damage.

One showcase warehouse handles nothing but carbon black, one of the most sensitive products from the standpoint of secondary damage. Carbon black is the same material used as toner in photocopy machines, and bags of this material, when broken, can cause substantial discoloration of goods stored nearby. In this warehouse, every lift truck is equipped with a portable vacuum as well as broom and dust pan. When a leak is discovered, cleaning and controlling the leakage has higher priority than completing the shipment. By placing the emphasis on damage control, the carbon black warehouse maintains superior housekeeping even with a dirty product.

Planning New Construction for Future Receiving and Shipping

Whenever construction of a new building is planned, you must face the probability that the receiving and shipping areas will become inadequate long before the structure is actually worn out. The building could become obsolescent for reasons of changes in volume, outdated design, or reduced location value. If the volume and storage pattern for which the building was designed changes, the building will lose its value. New warehousing technology could create needs that cannot be met in the existing building. Even when the function and design are still good, changing markets may make the location less effective than it was previously. Substantial expansion or contraction of volume may cause the structure to be either much too large for current purposes or too small, with no practical means of expansion.

All of these eventualities can be avoided if the real estate planner anticipates the problems of the future.

How does future obsolescence affect building design? Consider the fact that a building designed specifically for your use may have very limited appeal if it must be put on the market for a quick sale. In general, there is a somewhat smaller market for very large warehouses than for those of a more common size. If your use is quite large, running from 500,000 to several million square feet, consider whether that need could be met by a cluster of separate buildings rather than one huge structure. Separate buildings can be leased or sold to different users when no longer needed. Furthermore, the use of a cluster of separate buildings creates a substantial improvement in fire risk, since it is relatively easy to control the spread of fire from one building to another. While some warehousing operations require a single building for effective shipping and receiving, many others can be managed in a way that does not require all merchandise to be under the same roof. Don't assume that one building is essential just because one manager thinks so. Carefully simulate an operation that separates different product lines or inactive reserve stock into adjacent and separate buildings.

In essence, nearly every warehouse building is designed to accommodate storage, order picking, and a combination of receiving and shipping. Receiving and shipping can be considered together, since they can be performed over the same docks. Storage and order picking may require specific building design features. As you plan a new building today, you are likely to have in mind certain specifications for these three basic functions. Consider what will happen to the building design if these specifications should change. In some industries, storage has been practically eliminated as materials flow quickly through the building from receiving docks to shipping docks. In others, there have been radical changes in methods of order picking or methods of receiving and shipping. The six most common functions of warehousing are stockpiling, product mixing, production logistics, consolidation, distribution, and customer service. The building you are designing presumably fills one or more of these functions and is designed to do so. How effective will that building be if the emphasis is on a different function 10 years from now? It is possible to design sufficient versatility into your building so that its function could change. At least, if the function does not change, the building has been designed for ready resale to another user.

Transportation considerations must also be measured. You may choose a rail-served site for your warehouse even though no rail transportation is planned. This is done in recognition of the fact that a rail-served site has a wider resale market than one not so served. Legislation that allowed wider highway trailers made some warehouse buildings obsolescent, because shipping and receiving doors were too close together to accommodate the wider trailers. While this defect is usually correctable, there could be situations where such changes greatly impaired the utility of the building.

Using Idle Rail Pits

Many rail-served distribution centers, particularly those constructed between 1960 and 1980, have extensive indoor rail sidings that are either unused or seldom used today. Changing business conditions, including deregulation, have caused many companies to use less rail service today than when these buildings were designed. Unfortunately, an inside rail dock represents space that is wasted when it is not used for the intended purpose of holding boxcars.

Several creative alternatives have been used to correct this situation.

The first and most permanent answer is to fill the rail pit with sand and pour a concrete floor. Some users have created concrete slabs that include hooks or cables that would allow the slab to be lifted back out at a later date.

Another solution is to create a bridge over the railroad siding, designed to be moved at a later date. Others have created an asphalt floor around the railroad tracks that would allow storage over the rail track. Access to the rail pit is gained by using an outdoor ramp and moving a lift into the rail pit from its open end.

One creative approach is the use of leased railroad flatcars to create a platform for storage of materials in the rail pit. This method provides maximum flexibility, since the railroad cars can easily be removed if increased rail activity should cause the dock to be used a future date.

If your warehouse is full and you want to avoid finding more space, you should look at ways to use the space that is standing idle in an empty railroad pit. As you pursue this course, remember that we have no way of knowing whether our abandonment of railroad boxcars is a long-term trend or a short-term fad. Is there a possibility that your rail pit, which is empty today, might be very busy in the future? None of us can be sure of the answer, and therefore a flexible approach is probably the safest.

Receiving

Receiving starts with acceptance at your dock of a vehicle with material consigned to you.[2] You unload the material, count and confirm the quantity with shipping documents, and inspect for quality assurance. Inspection ends with a decision to accept or reject the load. If accepted, the load is moved to storage.

There are three ways to receive material, and they are listed here in order of efficiency:

1. Unload from a carrier, and move across the dock for outbound. This is the simplest warehousing method because it requires no storage.
2. Unload from the carrier and move material directly to storage. This is the second-best receiving method, because it does not require rehandling.
3. Unload the material from the carrier to temporary storage near the dock. This step is taken if
   a. The material requires additional checking, inspection, or price marking
   b. Storage space is not available or assigned
   c. Material handlers are not available to store the material.

Number three is the least preferred receiving method, because it requires rehandling the material from the dock. Storage space is required on the dock to hold unloaded material until it is moved to storage. If space is scarce, use pallet racks in or near the receiving dock.

If the physical activities of receiving are not closely supervised, you may be charged with damage for which you are not responsible. Furthermore, whether through accident or deliberate dishonesty, you could sign for material that was never actually received. Training of the receivers and material handlers is an often neglected function. As you look at your receiving, ask yourself how you could change your system to go directly from truck to truck, or truck to storage.

Receiving is a process of sequential steps. You may not require every step, but omit steps only for good reasons. Here are the steps in the truck receiving process:

1. Following a call from a carrier, an appointment time is given for the unloading of the truck.
2. Before the truck arrives, the receiver verifies that a manifest is available and that it applies to this load. If not, the shipper is contacted by phone to provide the manifest or packing list.
3. A receiving dock door is assigned to the trucker when he arrives.
4. The vehicle is safely secured before unloading, with confirmation by a supervisor that all security steps have been taken.

5. The truck driver is present when the seal is broken and initial inspection completed.
6. If accepted, the load is removed from the truck with three variations:
   a. Unitized or palletized material is unloaded by lift truck.
   b. Loose or floor-loaded material is properly stacked on pallets for movement to storage.
   c. Material is removed by conveyor to a shipping dock or staging area.
7. Material is counted and inspected constantly, to be sure that quality and quantity conform to specification.

As you review the process in your warehouse, ask yourself if it would be possible to convert all receipts to unitized loads to eliminate palletizing by hand.

Check-in requires absolute accuracy. The methods used to achieve accuracy may be any one or combination of the following. Listed in order of their likelihood to give you error-free receiving, they are:

1. Bar code wanding. Scan each package with a hand-held unit. The scanner feeds the information into a computer to register receipt.
2. Blind receiving. The checker writes down the received quantity and items, without reference to the manifest or packing list that shows the expected quantity.
3. Where the receiver knows the quantity and item, there are two variations:
   a. The receiver has a listing of the items but records the quantity received.
   b. The receiver has a listing of quantity and item. The receipt is simply checked.

The design of the receiving tally, the first document prepared at the warehouse, should contain only necessary receiving information. Figure 17-7 offers a format to use in designing your own form.

The receiving tally is the start of the audit trail. Therefore, this document must contain the required information plus any exceptions including overages, shortages, and damage recorded in detail. The rule is "Always count twice before signing once."

Checking is the most critical step in the receiving operation, and receiving is not complete until:

- Documents match the manifest or packing list.
- You note any discrepancies and document them fully.

The final step in receiving is to assign a storage location to the material, or move it to the next area for processing. Move damaged material to a recooperage area, or immediately refuse it and return it to the truck driver. In the recooperage area, you dispose of damaged material by:

- Shipping it to the vendor
- Salvaging what is repairable by the repacking of good items and the removal of damaged ones
- Scrapping

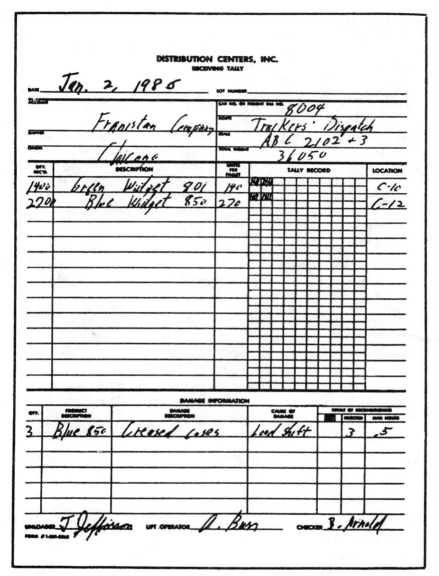

Figure 17-7. A receiving tally, the first document prepared at the warehouse.

Equipment for Receiving

Equipment used on truck docks receives the hardest use of any in the warehouse. For lift trucks used on the dock, the work requires short runs and frequent starting, stopping, and maneuvering. This activity accelerates wear and requires more maintenance.

Stationary equipment is subject to impact from trucks and lift trucks. Equipment needs to be rugged and well maintained to stand up to receiving dock use. Choose the heavy-duty options when it comes to equipment for receiving. Increased uptime will more than cover the increased cost.

In choosing lift trucks for dock work, you should be sure to

- Install the biggest, widest tires possible. Wider tires reduce damage to both warehouse and trailer floors.
- See to it that lowered height for lift truck masts does not exceed 83 in. This height allows entry into even the oldest of trailers. Specify a free-lift upright for both unloading and loading of trailers. The freelift upright elevates the load without increasing the overall lowered height of the forklift mast, which allows you to remove double-stack loads inside a trailer.
- Specify a sideshift attachment, to allow you to hydraulically move loads away from the wall of the trailer. This allows removal and storage of the load with less damage. It also allows more precise stacking.

Stationary dock equipment is as important as the mobile equipment at your receiving dock. Specifications for dock equipment should include:

- Automatic dock-levelers, to provide full height adjustment for variances in truck heights. Be sure the leveler includes bumpers, to protect the dock from the impact of the truck.
- Dock seals or shelters, to shield inside dock area from outside weather, reduce heat loss, and prevent unauthorized entry into the warehouse.
- A vehicle restraint system, to prevent trailers from being pulled away from the dock prematurely or pushed away by the lift truck repeatedly entering and exiting the trailer.
- Lighting that will illuminate the inside of the trailer and help to avoid accidents.

Receiving refers to the time at which you take possession of the material. You must know you have

- The material ordered
- The quantity ordered
- Material that meets your quality standard
- An accurate record of the transaction

Receiving is both a material handling and an auditing function. It is most efficient when the flow of material from carrier to storage is continuous.

Summary

As distribution systems have grown in size and scope, the role of the receiving and shipping system has become increasingly critical. Fortunately, new technology such as reverse order picking and bar coding, along with faster and more economical information systems, has allowed receiving and shipping to be accomplished faster and more accurately than ever before. While speed is important, there can be no compromising of accuracy and security.

Both federal regulation and growing insurance costs make management more sensitive to safety issues than ever before, and fortunately we have learned a few new things about the prevention of accidents in receiving and shipping.

We have also learned how to adapt our distribution buildings to meet the physical changes required by acceleration of receiving and shipping. The heart of the process is the actual function of receiving and its reverse, order picking. Finally, we must accomplish all of this with a minimum of damage, and when there is damage it must be handled quickly and safely.

References

1. Adapted from Russell A. Gilmore III, "A User's View of Bar Coding," *Warehousing Forum,* vol. 6, no. 11, Ackerman Co., Columbus, OH.

2. From an article by William J. Ransom, *Warehousing Forum,* vol. 7, no. 7, Ackerman Co., Columbus, OH.

18

Storage Equipment

John B. Nofsinger
Vice President, Marketing and Administration, Material Handling Industry

Storage equipment is to the distribution process what roads are to transportation. It is essential infrastructure, and will to a very large degree determine the scope and success of the distribution operation. Storage equipment, when applied in support of and consistent with overall business plans, will be one of your greatest assets and, indeed, a competitive advantage.

This chapter will profile both basic and advanced storage equipment/systems for use in the warehousing element of the distribution process. It will speak to features/characteristics of the various equipments, while reminding the reader of the benefits that might be achieved through proper application.

Since it will be impossible to fully address all of the design/technical considerations, this chapter ends with a bibliography that provides useful additional information important to the success of your installation.

Loads. Before proceeding with equipment-specific issues, it is important to briefly discuss the load and functional characteristics of the process of handling, storing, controlling, and protecting materials. This is necessary, as the equipment discussions following will outline characteristics that make each better suited to particular conditions. Within the distribution process you are likely to deal with some or all of the following load/storage conditions:

1. Unitized loads

2. Contained loads

3. Long and random lengths

4. High-value/security/bonded materials

5. Returns

6. Broken packages

7. Damaged/off-spec/obsolete materials

8. Loose materials

The storage function will be asked to support both end users directly and resale distribution organizations, and as such the process(es) being serviced may call for full pallets, full cases, or various individual or combination packages.

The process is served by both basic and advanced storage equipment/systems solutions. The equipment/systems are many, and the solution will often require application/integration of several different equipments from the many that are discussed in this chapter.

As a practical matter, there is a great deal of overlap in how different types and styles of storage equipment/systems perform in the distribution environment. As a result, I will avoid the temptation to generalize the ideal application of the technologies we will discuss.

Justification and Benefits

Virtually any item being manufactured or processed in a conventional facility may be "idle" as much as 95 percent of the time—in receiving, storage, or in transit from one operation to the next (see Fig. 18-1). But managing these idle assets is often overlooked in the effort to create value in products or services, or for stockholders.

The profit potential of a smooth, continuous flow of materials has been widely discussed and documented. With continuous flow you need less material on hand, so the reduction in inventory contributes directly to profitability. But the cost of moving, storing, protecting, and controlling what remains on hand is not always easy to quantify, since costs may be spread across several product lines or functions. As a result, material handling and storage costs are often lumped with company overhead. Determining the amount of value created by each business activity is essential to the realistic allocation of costs and is a prerequisite for an effective cost management program.

Most profitable companies recognize that increased value comes from operating

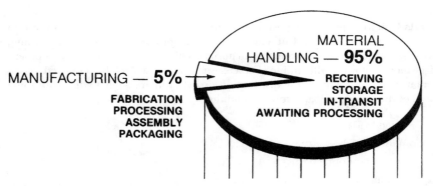

Figure 18-1. Material handling versus manufacture.

efficiencies, not solely from financial manipulations. They recognize that improving material handling efficiency is a way of significantly reducing costs and lowering invested capital, thus increasing profitability while providing better service to customers. Some of the primary areas in which storage equipment/systems can add value to the distribution operation include:

- *Space Savings.* This is the most obvious and visible result of well-organized/-designed storage. Floor space utilized is often compressed by one-half to two-thirds, allowing expansion within an existing building.
- *Productivity.* Consolidation and reorganization of the operations affected offers tangible benefits in reduced handling, movement, and idle time. Direct labor and order picking operations can be significantly enhanced. Properly selected storage equipment will enhance productivity objectives.
- *Cost Avoidance.* Another of the more obvious results of proper equipment application, and often the most compelling. The effective use of inner space and cube can avoid or minimize very costly facility expansion/construction programs.
- *Labor Reduction.* By reconfiguring operations into a more efficient arrangement under improved control, you can expect to reduce indirect handling and movement and even improve the efficiency of direct labor operations.
- *Cost Savings/Waste Elimination.* In addition to labor- and space-saving opportunities, other direct savings are available since you are already heating, conditioning, lighting, paying taxes, etc. on the overhead space. You can expand up without a proportional increase in these traditionally high-cost areas.
- *Inventory Reduction.* Consolidation and reorganization offers a distinct opportunity to improve the control over inventories and affect a corresponding reduction. This area alone can free substantial amounts of working capital for productive uses.
- *Security.* Properly applied storage equipment/systems lend themselves to limiting access to authorized personnel, resulting in improved security and reduced shrinkage.
- *Safety/Housekeeping.* The installation should result in a reduction of clutter, tripping hazards, and, in a great number of cases, fatigue and strain, by organization of operations more efficiently.
- *Damage Avoidance.* Reduction in the number of handling cycles can have a dramatic effect on internal product damage/rework costs.

Of course a careful matching of your equipment/systems to the business plan will provide additional opportunities to add real value and productivity throughout the distribution process.

Industrial Steel Storage Racks

Industrial steel storage racks are structures designed to store palletized, containerized, or long-length loads. The storage and retrieval function is typically accomplished by operator-assisted mechanical handling equipment. Industrial storage racks generally are of three basic types:

1. Stationary, or fixed
2. Portable
3. Movable-aisle

Stationary or *fixed racks* can be free-standing or can be designed to provide the dual purpose of supporting roof and wall systems (commonly referred to as *rack-supported buildings*). Stationary racks can be further broken down into a series of types or styles, each providing features suited to particular loads or functions. These types or styles include:

- Selective pallet racks
- Double-deep racks
- Push-back racks
- Drive-in/drive-through racks
- Cantilever racks
- Pallet or case flow racks

Selective pallet racks (see Fig. 18-2) are constructed by attaching horizontal shelf beams to upright frames assembled from pairs of columns with horizontal and diagonal bracing. Attachment of the shelf beam to the upright frame is typically by means of mechanical bolting or by use of a specially designed adjustable boltless

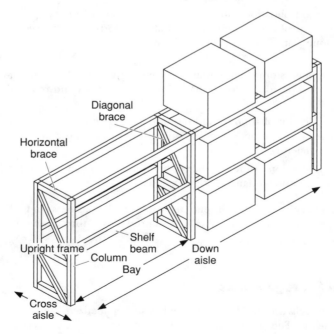

Figure 18-2. Selective pallet racks.

connector. In some cases, connections can be welded. Selective racks are commonly produced from hot rolled shapes or from cold roll-formed sections. There is a very high degree of application overlap, where designs of either style will perform acceptably. Selective pallet racks are generally arranged in either single or back-to-back (double) rows. Each row will consist of a number of *bays* in the down-aisle direction. A bay is defined as *the horizontal space between two uprights containing pairs of shelf beams (vertically)*. Pallets are stored side-by-side in the down-aisle direction at each level of the bay. All pallets are accessible from the facing aisle, giving flexibility to location or inventory technique.

An aisle between rows of racks allows access by mechanical equipment. Aisles can be conventional, narrow, or very narrow, and will range from as little as approximately 4 ft to as much as approximately 14 ft in selective applications. The aisle width becomes a function of the load itself and the design of the truck. The proper selection criteria consider throughput, space utilization, and style of truck.

Heights of freestanding selective rack systems will range from as little as approximately 6 ft (2 pallets high) through heights in excess of 80 ft (requiring, of course, specialized mechanical equipment). *Rack-supported buildings* (see Fig. 18-3) tend to be more common in taller applications and can offer some tax (depreciation) incentives.

One-way density of selective racking is enhanced is by arranging back-to-back rows with shelf beams at the same elevation. This is called *double-deep rack* (see Fig. 18-4). A special double-reach truck allows two pallets deep to be accessed from one aisle. The tradeoff here is space savings versus selectivity and equipment considerations.

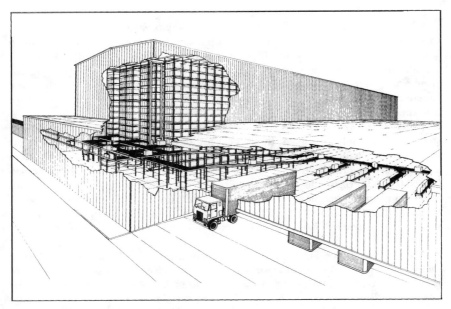

Figure 18-3. Rack-supported buildings.

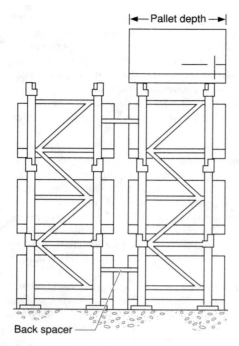

|←— Pallet depth —→|

Back spacer

Figure 18-4. Double-deep rack.

Another way density is enhanced is with *push-back rack systems* (see Fig. 18-5). In this case the rack structure is equipped with a carriage allowing two-or-three-deep storage with conventional mechanical equipment. Pallet/container loads are pushed into the opening until all positions are full. When a load is picked, the carriage gravity delivers the next pallet. This system demonstrates some of the same functional characteristics of drive-in systems, except that the truck does not drive into the rack.

Drive-in/drive-through racks (see Fig. 18-6) are structures designed for high-density storage. Unlike selective styles, these racks are designed for storing several pallets deep, thus reducing the number of aisles and increasing the cube utilization (density). The truck actually enters the drive-in/drive-through bay and deposits the palletized/containerized load onto load rails. Drive-in racks require a last-in, first-out (LIFO) inventory technique, while drive-through (accessible from both ends) allows for either first-in, first-out (FIFO) or LIFO techniques. Drive-in/Drive-through racks are constructed from columns, load rails, and various structural framing members.

Pallet flow racks (see Fig. 18-7) are for practical purposes back-to-back selective racks into which inclined conveyor wheel sections have been installed. Loads are input to the rear, and flow by gravity to the front pick face. This system is useful for fast-moving like items where FIFO techniques are desirable. The primary advantages are density and throughput.

High-density dynamic storage (see Fig. 18-8) is another way in which density is en-

Figure 18-5. Push-back rack systems.

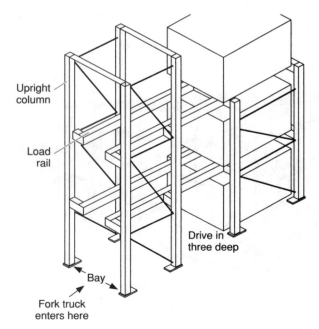

Figure 18-6. Drive-in/drive-through racks.

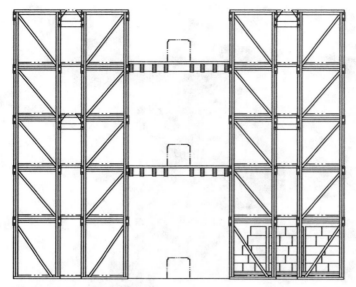

Figure 18-7. Pallet flow racks.

hanced. While similar to pallet flow racks in function, the load remains horizontal and is indexed intermittently by a series of mechanical or pneumatic motions.

Cantilever racks (see Fig. 18-9) are designed for long or irregular-length materials. They are constructed from load-bearing arms cantilevered from vertical columns. Either loads can span the arms, or decks can be installed between arms to store loads that might not span a pair of arms. Decking also provides a continuous stor-

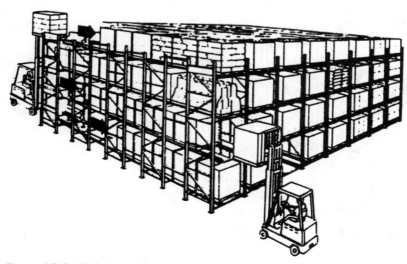

Figure 18-8. High-density dynamic storage.

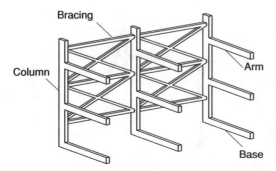

Figure 18-9. Cantilever rack.

age surface without any intrusive structure. Picking is generally accomplished by a side-loader mechanical truck.

Case (package) flow racks (see Fig. 18-10) are similar in concept to pallet flow, except that depositing/picking is with individual cases/cartons with manual operator assistance. Bar coding, electronic systems known as *pick-to-light*, and intelligent picking carts have enhanced the order picking utility of this traditional solution.

Portable racks (see Fig. 18-11) are self-contained units comprised of decks and posts. The units are designed to stack on top of one another and, when empty, to be nested or knocked down to conserve space.

Pallet stacking frames (see Fig. 18-12) typically attach to a standard pallet, thereby enabling loads to be multiple-stacked. When empty, the frames can be disassembled to conserve space. Both portable racks and pallet stacking frames are particularly useful for mobility, protection of crushable loads, and movement through processing.

Movable-aisle storage systems (see Fig. 18-13) are created by installing rows of storage racks onto a carriage or platform. The carriage operates on tracks, allowing fewer aisles and higher-density storage. This technology is well suited to high-quantity/low-activity applications, where conservation of floor space is desirable or necessary.

A variety of special-purpose racks and accessories for more standard racks are available for storing drums, coils, reels, etc., and for interfacing with other handling equipment like overhead cranes. Additional accessories like *column protectors* and *aisle guide angles* are also available to minimize the chance of undesirable impact by mechanical equipment.

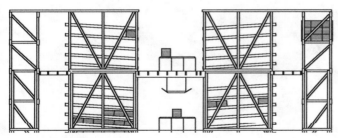

Figure 18-10. Case flow racks.

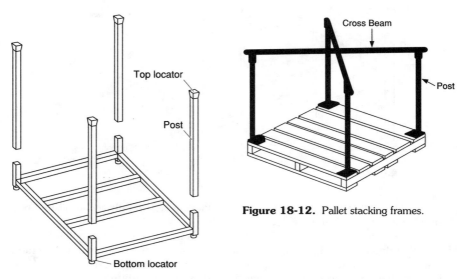

Figure 18-12. Pallet stacking frames.

Figure 18-11. Portable rack.

Figure 18-13. Movable-aisle storage systems.

Industrial Shelving Systems

Industrial shelving systems are structures designed to handle nonpalletized loads, generally placed in the systems by hand. Shelving (see Fig. 18-14) is offered in either open, closed, ledge, or countertop styles and can be installed in multilevel configurations. Open-style shelving in its simplest form consists of columns, braces, shelves, and connecting hardware. A wide variety of column designs is offered as a function of capacity and application. Braces are mechanically fastened to the columns, and the shelves are attached by a combination of mechanical fasteners and/or specially designed connection clips to create units. Closed-style units consist of solid panel uprights in lieu of braces. The panels function both structurally and to enclose the unit for function and organization. Units are generally installed in single or double rows and single or double faces.

Units/shelves are offered in a range of capacities from light loads (generally 200 lb or less/shelf) through heavy loads in excess of 1000 lb/shelf. Shelf rating is based on evenly distributed loads (EDL). Manufacturers' load-tables allow for some deflection at the rated load (length of shelf ÷ 140). While this deflection is normal, you will want to ensure that it does not interfere with the opening below. This is particularly important where the available cube is fully utilized (viz., records or archival storage). Increased capacity is typically accomplished by a combination of

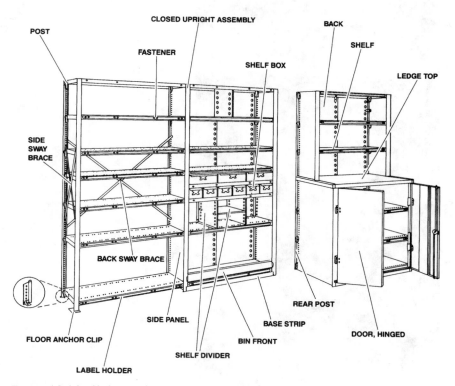

Figure 18-14. Shelving styles.

design geometry, material, and in some cases, reinforcement. Most standard shelving comes in a 36-in width. Sizes over 48 in tend to be referred to as *wide-span shelving* and demonstrate many of the characteristics of steel storage racks except for the lighter hand-loading application. Units can be installed in two-level or multilevel applications (see Fig. 18-15) by tiering the units and providing intermediate service aisles. This approach offers particular advantage in utilizing vertical space. However, you need 15 ft or more of clear building height to accommodate a second functional level. Shelving systems can also be constructed in high-rise configurations (generally over 10 and less than 30 ft). In these configurations, picking is usually done by rolling ladders and/or mechanical stock picking vehicles. Savings in space is traded off against cost of equipment and throughput when justifying this popular application.

Figure 18-15. Multilevel shelving.

One of the advantages of industrial shelving systems is the ability to accessorize with a wide variety of options to create specific functionality. These accessories include:

- *Dividers.* Allow shelves to be subdivided in either fixed or variable compartments.
- *Label holders.* Steel or plastic strips attached to the shelf face to insert identifying labels, bar codes, etc.
- *Shelf boxes.* Steel, molded or corrugated open-top boxes with label holders, handles, and subdividers to organize small parts.
- *Bin fronts.* Steel or molded strip affixed to the front of the shelf to contain the load on shelves.
- *Doors.* Hinged and sliding doors to add security and cleanliness to the units.
- *Modular drawers.* Full-extension, full-width modular drawers, designed to organize small parts in a high-cube, utilization, higher-security situation.
- *Movable bases.* Allow fewer aisles and improved density. Can be moved either mechanically or under power.
- *Counter or ledge surfaces.* Allow for a work surface in front of shelving.

In applying industrial shelving, as with any storage equipment, a number of issues need to be addressed to arrive at the most efficient and cost-effective application. Those issues are:

- Volume
- Dimension
- Quantity (activity will dictate)
- Configuration
- Accessories

Since shelving is designed for hand loading, you will want to position high-activity items to minimize lifting/reaching. Units containing the most active items should be located near the output end of the system. Aisle widths and traffic patterns should allow for peak activities and avoid building columns and other obstructions. In the case of multilevel applications, a number of additional variables must be addressed. These include ingress/egress (primary and secondary where appropriate), lighting and fire safety considerations, allowances for pallet drop areas, penetrations for conveyors, lifts, etc.

Maintenance of the shelving is important to assure the continued fitness of the system. Some things to look for are loose, missing, or mispositioned hardware, damage from impact and overloads. Post damage is particularly important to watch for, and if noticed the unit(s) should be immediately unloaded and repaired before being returned to service. Overturning is a consideration to be aware of (see Fig. 18-16). This can arise from a number of factors, including nonuniform loading, out-of-plumb installation, and impact. Common ways to prevent this from occurring include anchoring and tying units together across the service aisle.

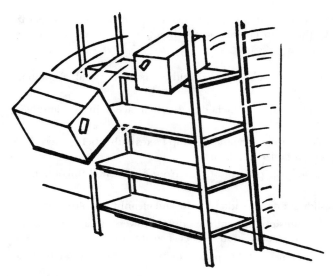

Figure 18-16. Overturning.

Mezzanines

Mezzanines are available in many formats, depending on intended use. Careful attention should be given during the conceptual stage of a project to what type of system will best suit current needs. Design flexibility must encompass all aspects of the intended use of the structure. Will it be used for storage, offices, manufacturing, conveyor or equipment support, etc., or a combination of uses? Is the loading requirement uniform or concentrated? Are there obstructions or fixed building characteristics that must be considered in the design? In short, are there any conditions that the designer should be aware of in order to make an accurate assessment for correct design? Most applications can be accomplished utilizing manufacturer's standard designs, with few or no alterations. There will, however, be situations in which it will be advantageous for the mezzanine to be custom-designed. Potential future requirements may immediately point toward a freestanding system or one supported by another product such as rack or shelving. Rack- and shelving-supported mezzanines depend on rack uprights or shelving posts for deck support.

Freestanding mezzanines (see Fig. 18-17) are available in two formats: *modular* and *custom.* Modular mezzanines are usually standardized, prefabricated modules of various sizes, which can be assembled into many mezzanine configurations by utilizing different combinations of modules. Modular formats are often used when there are no unusual loading or configuration requirements.

Custom mezzanines are designed to the user's specifications for load and configuration. This format allows for complete freedom in design, from column spacing to unusual loading characteristics. The manufacturer will assist with final design specifications after determining how the mezzanine will be used along with user requirements.

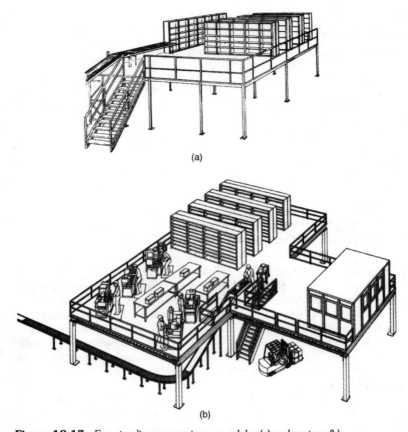

Figure 18-17. Freestanding mezzanines—modular (a) and custom (b).

There are many potential benefits associated with mezzanines. If you have a mezzanine you may be able to

- Virtually double available floor space, through efficient use of existing cube in the facility.
- Increase productivity.
- Avoid or minimize moving expenses.
- Have minimal disruption of production during installation.
- Avoid need to rent, build, or purchase additional space.
- Avoid or minimize additional property taxes.
- Make optimum use of existing heating, ventilating, and cooling.
- Demount and relocate (in most cases).

- Expand.
- Get a tax advantage through accelerated depreciation.
- Save on outside engineering cost with preengineered mezzanines.
- Save time.

There are six basic technical considerations, regardless of the type of mezzanine. These are:

1. Loading requirements
2. Column spacing
3. Flexibility of design
4. Deflection
5. Seismic considerations at the project location
6. Supporting substructure (floor slab or footings)

Determining the size and shape of the mezzanine is a primary concern. If walled in on all four sides by partitions or other equipment, the available area is plain to see. Usually, however, the available space permits options in size. It may be economically prudent to maximize the mezzanine area, as there are efficiencies of scale in the design engineering, manufacturing, and installation processes. Height is determined by the importance of underclearance and code restrictions. Is the distance from ground floor to the mezzanine deck surface, or to the mezzanine underclearance, more important? Headroom above the mezzanine deck should also be considered. Codes dictate minimums.

What type of loads will be applied to the deck surface? Will they be relatively uniform, or will there be concentrated loads or perhaps some specific heavily loaded areas? Estimate the anticipated values and locations of additional and/or concentrated loads for design purposes. Deck surfaces can be of many types, ranging from plywood to specialized overlays. Decking is a very important part of any mezzanine and should be selected carefully, considering strength required and intended use. The manufacturer will usually offer several decking options, or you may wish to incorporate some other type of specialty flooring system.

Consider whether the mezzanine columns are potential hazards for traffic and material flow. If this is of no concern, specify the most cost-effective design. If column interference is of concern, the manufacturer may be able to offer advice and assistance in determining the most effective column spacing. If the mezzanine is to interface with other equipment, such as conveyors, rack, shelving, offices, vertical lifts, etc., the mezzanine manufacturer will require a detailed layout of the existing or proposed plan to assure compatibility. If the possibility of future vertical or horizontal expansion of the mezzanine is foreseen, it is important to inform the manufacturer at the time of his initial proposal. The system can then be designed to accept expansion that will eliminate the potential for costly restructuring later. Also, stair and railing locations should be established with the first concern being the safety of the user. Code requirements and efficiency of material and traffic flow are other important considerations.

Industrial Containers/Pallets

Industrial containers are effectively used in every type of manufacturing plant and distribution center. This is because items of any size, weight, or shape become unitized loads when placed inside industrial containers. Industry has long recognized the value of industrial containers and the contribution they make to increased productivity and space utilization.

Industrial containers contribute significantly to efficient space utilization in today's distribution centers. A few of the multiple benefits of efficient space utilization obtained with industrial containers include reduced labor and handling requirements, reduced lighting requirements, better organization of storage materials, and the opportunity to expand production and distribution into areas previously occupied by unorganized storage of materials. Inventory becomes visible, accessible, and readily transferable.

Containers are ideally suited for use in all modern material handling systems. In fact, many of today's storage systems are specifically designed to accommodate industrial containers. Common formats include pallets, skids, containers, and tote boxes. The format of the contained or unitized loads warrants particular attention, as it can dictate storage and handling equipment and throughput of the Distribution Center. Materials are as variable as formats including steel, plastic, and corrugated board. Steel containers for large unitized loads break down further into welded wire and corrugated metal. *Welded wire containers* (see Fig. 18-18) are used universally because of their light weight in relation to their load capacity, and because the strong welded wire construction accepts great punishment. The advantages of welded wire containers include the following.

- They are light in weight in relation to load capacity.
- They make possible visual inventory and ventilation.
- Their self-cleaning features promote product cleanliness and good housekeeping.
- They are stackable—usually four units high, utilizing warehouse cube.
- They provide uniform tare weights.
- They are interstackable with all ANSI spec. containers of the same dimensions.

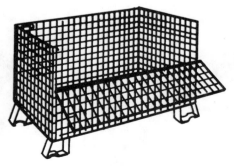

Figure 18-18. Welded wire containers.

Welded wire containers are available in a variety of configurations, including folding and rigid.

Corrugated metal containers (see Fig. 18-19) have tremendous strength and damage resistance, and can be furnished in a wide variety of configurations. Standard design consists of corrugated sides and ends welded to a corrugated bottom, available with a variety of stacking features. Corrugated metal containers are rigid and resist abuse. Many options and designs are offered, such as:

- Dump bottoms
- Rollover units
- Crane-handling accessories
- Skid bases
- Wire mesh panels
- Hinged gates
- Sliding doors
- Heavy-duty forging boxes

Plastic (*structural foam*) *container formats* (see Fig. 18-20) for large unitized loads are also common, and demonstrate many of the same characteristics and features as steel format containers. Some points to be made about plastic containers include the following.

- All containers are designed primarily to be loaded by hand or automatic feed and to be moved by machine, and they are easily cleaned with liquid or steam.
- These containers are ideal for handling within and between manufacturing and distribution operations, and are suited to shipping, storage, and handling.
- Containers for smaller items accessed by hand are generally of molded polymer or corrugated-board construction.

Figure 18-19. Corrugated metal containers.

Figure 18-20. Plastic (structural foam) container formats.

- Materials range from molded polymers to conductive and antistatic materials for electronics applications. Flame-retardant polymers are also available.
- Principal features of plastic containers include stackability, nestability, dividability, modularity, and durability.

Containers designed to interface with storage structures and handling equipment provide an efficient, cost-effective, integrated infrastructure for the distribution operation, and may eliminate a great deal of manual handling and transfer of materials.

Pallets used in the distribution environment will generally be wooden or of structural foam, reinforced molded polymer, or steel. Before choosing a pallet, one should ask oneself: Will the pallet be captive to the distribution center? One-way? Returnable/reusable? Each operating scenario will suggest different styles and corresponding costs. Some questions that will help you select the best container/pallet for your needs include:

1. How will the container/pallet be stored/conveyed? This will influence both foot and base design along with structure, if the conveyance is other than a base support.
2. What is to be stored? Size? Weight? Quantity? This will suggest material, structural design, and configuration.
3. Will the container/pallet be used in an automated system? Very early in the planning stage, this consideration should bring the suppliers of your Automated System, modes of conveyance, and container/pallet manufacturer into joint-planning communications to avoid the need for costly design changes that can occur in the absence of these communications.
4. Is this a captive container/pallet? Will it remain in the plant? Should there be plans to use this container/pallet in over-the-road transport, impact loading should be considered in the design. Cube versus gross weight ratios in your truck or other transport should also be considered, as shipping air and dunnage is expensive. Empty backhauls may dictate consideration of a folding container.
5. How will the container/pallet be used? Abused? Are there unusual demands such as temperature extremes, chemical exposure, or impact-loading abuse that should be considered?
6. Do the people buying the container/pallet have knowledge of special conditions in satellite plants or customer facilities? Here again, accommodating special conveyance, storage systems, and other applications need to be considered. It is very important in selection of pallets or containers to consider the total distribution system internally and externally. The pallet or container has to work correctly with the internal conveyor and storage system, provide for economical transport in standard conveyances, and be receivable at its destination, which may be a user's plant or warehouse or your own facility. Total interface is the key.
7. What does the future hold? Is there a possibility of some of the following?
   a. Modification of a rack system?
   b. A dramatic change in product mix?
   c. The addition of satellite operations, which would dictate using the containers/pallets for shipping and receiving?
   d. The revision of work-station automation, which might dictate using the containers/pallets in work stands?

One additional consideration is provision of storage space for stacked storage of idle containers or pallets. Selection of this location can be critical to fire safety, in the instance of wood or plastic material. Easy access is also important.

Automated Storage and Retrieval

Automated storage and retrieval has long been successfully applied within the distribution environment. AS/R systems incorporate many of the storage equipments discussed in this chapter and add additional elements of integration and control. Automated storage/ retrieval systems offer particular benefits in the areas of space savings, labor savings, control and security, inventory reduction, and productivity improvement. Real-time control is being achieved through automated material handling technology: minicomputers talk to microprocessors on-board material handling machines, directing them to move, store, or manipulate materials while simultaneously reporting their status back to a computer. Or a computer may direct equipment operators and require verification of tasks completed.

In this section we will briefly discuss the styles and principal characteristics of automated storage-and-retrieval systems in three broad areas that parallel industry descriptions of the technologies:

1. Automated storage-and-retrieval systems (AS/RS)

2. Vertical automated storage-and-retrieval systems (VAS/RS)

3. Carousel storage-and-retrieval systems

In all cases, these technologies are supporting an active order picking fulfillment strategy. Automated storage/retrieval systems (AS/RS) integrate the storage structure, storage/ retrieval machinery, and the unitized/containerized load under varying degrees of computer control.

A typical system consists of rows of rack storage structures accessed by a floor-running, top-guided storage/retrieval machine that is captive to the aisle. The S/R machine moves horizontally and vertically (simultaneously) within and between the rows. Loads are delivered to and picked from a pickup and delivery (P&D) station under computer control and are stored and retrieved automatically. Systems can generally be broken into two primary categories, those handling large palletized or containerized loads (typically called *unit load AS/R systems*) and those handling smaller containerized loads (typically called *miniload* or *microload AS/R systems*).

Unit load AS/R systems (see Fig. 18-21) generally handle palletized (or similar for-

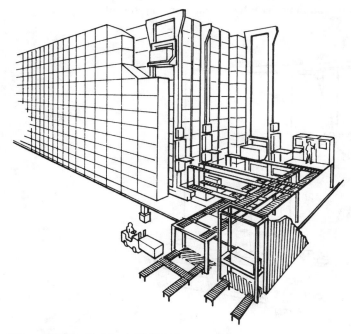

Figure 18-21. Unit load AS/R systems.

mat) loads that exceed 1000 lb. They are typically large structures that can operate effectively in heights exceeding 100 ft without direct operator involvement. Unit load AS/R systems are constructed both as freestanding (standalone) structures and as rack-supported buildings.

Miniload AS/R systems generally handle smaller and lighter loads in the category of 750 lb or less. Products/materials are placed into containers (typically of steel or molded design) that are generally 12 to 24 in wide by 24 to 48 in deep by various heights. Containers are usually captive to the Distribution Center. Containers are often subdivided to allow storage of a variety of items and to support kitting/throughput objectives. Microload systems (see Fig. 18-22) are generally applied to smaller and lighter loads under 250 lb. Products/materials are placed into small storage containers similar to, although normally smaller than, those found in miniload AS/R systems.

Vertical AS/R systems (see Fig. 18-23) are similar to miniload and microload systems, in that an S/R device automatically stores and retrieves small containerized loads to/from a storage structure. The primary structural difference is that each vertical bay (facing bay) is equipped with its own storage/retrieval device that delivers and picks to/from an operator control station.

Carousel storage and retrieval is typically found in two forms, horizontal and vertical. *Horizontal carousels* (see Fig. 18-24) consist of a motorized revolving framework that rotates vertically tiered storage shelves into which materials/loads are stored and from which products/materials are retrieved. All storage locations are rotated to an operator station under full or semiautomated control.

Vertical carousel systems (see Fig. 18-25) rotate shelves or carriers along a vertical enclosed loop. Stored on the shelves are containers (totes or pans) that are delivered to the operator station under full or semiautomatic control.

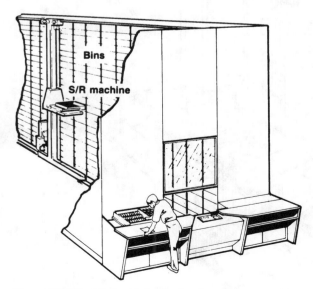

Figure 18-22. Miniload/microload systems.

Figure 18-23. Vertical AS/R systems.

Figure 18-24. Horizontal carousel.

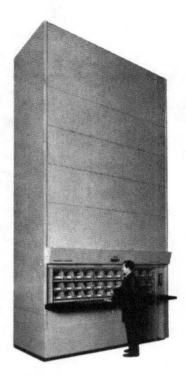

Figure 18-25. Vertical carousel.

It is typical for AS/R technologies to operate either independently or as part of an integrated environment within the distribution center.

Modular Drawer Storage

Modular drawer storage (see Fig. 18-26) consists of drawers contained in either cabinets or shelving units. Cabinets can be fixed in position or be movable by means of casters or fork trucks. Drawers are mounted to a suspension system that allows the drawer to be fully opened for access to a wide variety of internal compartments. Capacities of each drawer are generally in the 400-lb range. A variety of sizes and compartmentalization options make modular drawers an effective and productive high-density storage solution for small- and high-value parts. Modular drawer units are designed with flexibility in mind for either floor or multilevel application. Primary benefits include space savings, labor savings, security, cleanliness, and flexibility.

Figure 18-26. Modular drawer storage.

Permits, Codes, and Certifications

Storage equipment used in the distribution process will have to comply with a wide variety of permitting and codes requirements. There are several issues that are particularly worthy of note in this chapter. Additional technical references and resources will be included at the end of the chapter.

Compliance to all applicable codes should be determined prior to final design and fabrication of structural storage equipment. Federal, state, or local fire, building safety, and health codes should be obtained, when appropriate, as should any special requirement of insurance companies. Applicable codes for structures may include, but are not limited to, the following.

Model Building Codes*:

BOCA National Building Code
Building Officials and Code Administrators International, Inc.
4051 Flossmoor Road
Country Club Hills, IL 60478-5795

---

*Model building codes may not be applicable unless they have been adopted by a political entity or "governing body" such as a city, county, or state.

Standard Building Code
Southern Building Code Congress International
900 Montclair Road
Birmingham, AL 35213-1206

Uniform Building Code
International Conference of Building Officials
5630 Workman Mill Road
Whittier, CA 90601-2298

Fire Codes:

    FM (Factory Mutual)

    NFPA (National Fire Protection Association Life Safety Codes)

Life Safety Codes:

    OSHA (Occupational Safety and Health Administration)

    State or local building departments and/or equipment manufacturers should be able to offer assistance in determining which codes apply to a specific installation.

    The three model building codes listed deal with the designation of areas of varying seismicity. It is the responsibility of the user to establish which seismic zone or ground acceleration coefficient should be used, based upon the geographical location of the structure (see Fig. 18-27). The user also must state the intended occupancy or use of the building in which the structure is to be located. The manufacturer may have knowledge of the most likely zone or coefficient and, upon receipt of occupancy information allowing determination of Seismic Performance

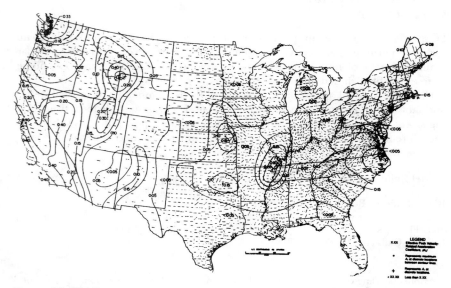

Figure 18-27. Seismic map.

Category, be able to design accordingly. Local building departments may also assist in determining appropriate seismic design criteria for the location and occupancy under consideration.

Designing for the appropriate seismic criteria is critical to the integrity of the structure, the safety of people, and design approval by building officials. In order to properly perform a seismic design it is also necessary to know the intended occupancy or use of a building in which a structure is to be constructed. For certain types of occupancies, building code requirements may result in increased design forces or other additional design requirements that could greatly affect design. Occupancies that fall into this category include but may not be limited to: schools, hospitals, any that contain sufficient quantities of hazardous or toxic materials, and other critical facilities. It is recommended that users make manufacturers and suppliers aware of the intended use or occupancy in which a structure is to be installed.

Failure to consider the correct occupancy/use and zone or acceleration coefficient in the design may result in rejection during the plan check by building authorities. In many areas of the country, plan review and the issuance of building permits for construction have become commonplace. Should the installation of a system require a building permit or certification, it is best to make the supplier or contractor (if different) aware of this. Obtaining a building permit need not be a problem as long as proper preparation is made. Visiting the building department and asking them exactly what will be required when the plans are submitted for review will prove to be very helpful.

Certification of the design and drawings by a registered professional engineer may be required. The company responsible for design can normally provide such certification. On occasion, drawings in addition to those normally provided by the manufacturer may be required as part of a plan-check procedure. The applicable local building department should be consulted and the supplier advised of these requirements, as extra engineering activity may be involved.

Permit applications and associated costs are normally the responsibility of the owner. Permits, if required, should be obtained prior to installation. Failure to do so may result in fines, withholding of an occupancy permit, or, possibly, being ordered to dismantle and remove the structure.

Fire Safety

The National Fire Protection Association (NFPA), Factory Mutual (FM), several other fire underwriters and associations, and the codes community regularly advance rules and policies that have a dramatic effect on the distribution center. Fire safety is a function of many things: commodities stored, building occupancy, geography, and lifeline safety, to name a few.

New sprinklering technologies are being developed and incorporated into distribution centers to deal with this important issue. One relatively new technology known as Early Suppression Fast Response (ESFR) promises a great savings over earlier methods in most circumstances where buildings are under 35 ft in height. In addition, additives have been developed for some molded products that dramatically improve fire retardance.

Industrial Floors

One commonly overlooked area in distribution center design is the interaction that takes place between soils, floor slabs, and storage structures. It is important that this factor be addressed to avoid slab distress and minimize maintenance. All loads are transmitted to the supporting floor through the columns and base plates of a storage structure. The concrete floor acts as the footing. The model building codes define a footing as that portion of the foundation of a structure that spreads and transmits loads directly to the soil. Consideration should be given to the quality and thickness of the existing or new concrete, along with the properties of the supporting soil.

When unusually large column loads from storage equipment are applied, the allowable capacities of the concrete floor slab or soil may be exceeded. Appropriate options in designing for these loads may include spreading the loads through larger base plates, creating new footings under the columns, or, in some cases, spreading the load over more columns.

The end user, typically, is expected to take responsibility for analyzing the adequacy of the supporting substructure under the columns of the structure to be provided. The equipment provider should, however, provide column loading and base plate dimension information, which can allow a building owner or his consultants to make an analysis and verify the adequacy of the substructure.

Conclusion

Distribution and warehouse storage and logistic functions that are managed to support the company's strategy for competitive advantage invariably make a measurable contribution to profitability. Correspondingly, the most successful storage applications are those that are designed and arranged to support operating strategies.

Companies will realize the most value from their storage equipment and systems installations by seeking out and forming alliances with experienced consultants and/or storage equipment systems providers. These people bring to the partnership a depth of real-world storage experience unavailable anywhere else.

The storage function is clearly not a static element of the distribution process. It is in fact a very dynamic infrastructure that to a very large extent will dictate the capability of the operations to carry out an ever-changing mission. As such, it deserves the highest and most senior attention and respect.

Acknowledgments/Resources

Special thanks are given to the Storage Council and its sponsoring organizations of The Material Handling Institute for providing a substantial portion of the materials used throughout this chapter.

The reader is encouraged to contact the Storage Council and other organizations listed herein for a more comprehensive treatment of equipment/application specific issues. While the list is certainly not all-inclusive, you will find answers and help for most of your storage equipment/systems application questions.

American Concrete Institute (ACI), Detroit, MI

American Institute of Steel Construction (AISC), Chicago, IL

American Iron & Steel Institute (AISI), Washington, DC

American National Standards Institute (ANSI), New York, New York

American Society for Testing & Materials (ASTM), New York, New York

American Welding Society (AWS), Miami, FL

Association of Mezzanine Manufacturers, Charlotte, NC

Association of Professional Materials Handling Consultants (APMHC), Charlotte, NC

Automated Storage/Retrieval Systems Product Section (MHI), Charlotte, NC

Building Officials and Code Administrators (National Building Code), Country Club Hills, IL

College Industrial Council for Material Handling Education (CIC-MHE), Charlotte, NC

Conveyor Product Section (MHI), Charlotte, NC

Council of Logistics Management (CLM), Oakbrook, IL

Factory Mutual (FM), Norwood, MA

Industrial Distributors Association (IDA), Atlanta, GA

Industrial Metal Containers Product Section (MHI), Charlotte, NC

Industrial Truck Association (ITA), Washington, DC

International Conference of Building Officials (Uniform Building Code), Whittier, CA

Material Handling Equipment Distributors Association (MHEDA) Vernon Hills, IL

Material Handling Institute (MHI), Charlotte, NC

Material Handling Industry of America, Charlotte, NC

Materials Handling & Management Society (MHMS), Charlotte, NC

National Earthquake Hazards Recommended Provisions, c/o Building Seismic Safety Council, Washington, DC

National Electrical Manufacturers Association (NEMA), Washington, DC

National Fire Protection Association (NFPA), Quincy, MA

National Wooden Pallet & Container Association (NWPCA), Washington, DC

Plastic Products Product Section (MHI), Charlotte, NC

Rack Manufacturers Institute, Charlotte, NC

Shelving Manufacturers Association, Charlotte, NC

Southern Building Code Congress International (Standard Building Code), Birmingham, AL

Storage Council, Charlotte, NC

Warehousing Education and Research Council (WERC), Oakbrook, IL

19
Material Handling Equipment

David R. Olson
Regional General Manager,
Tompkins Associates, Inc.

In the broadest terms, material handling equipment includes all hardware that is used to manipulate, position, weigh, elevate, transport, or control the flow of raw material, work-in-process of manufacture, purchased components, or finished goods. As defined by the Material Handling and Management Society, the broad topic is divided into the following subdivisions:

1. Conveyors
2. Cranes, elevators, and hoists
3. Positioning, weighing, and control equipment
4. Industrial vehicles
5. Motor vehicles
6. Railroad cars
7. Marine carriers
8. Aircraft
9. Containers and supports

These subdivisions are certainly comprehensive, but not entirely relevant in the context of the distribution of finished goods. The Material Handling Institute of America has defined material handling as "the movement, storage, control, and

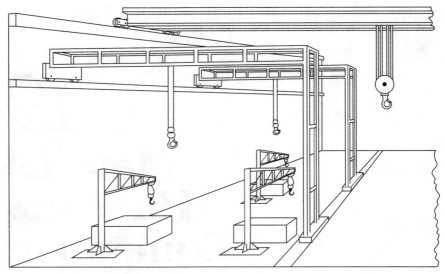

Figure 19-1. Overhead equipment.

protection of materials and products throughout their manufacture and distribution." For the purpose of this handbook the following simplified classification will be used:

- *Industrial trucks.* All nonhighway equipment utilized for intermittently moving material within a wide area.
- *Conveyors.* All equipment utilized for continuously moving material between fixed points.
- *Overhead equipment.* All equipment utilized for intermittently moving material between points within a limited area defined by the span of the equipment (see Fig. 19-1).

This chapter presents an overview of Industrial Trucks and Conveyors, as they are the dominant classifications in distribution. The focus is on the variety of alternatives that are available and their attributes that, when matched with warehouse requirements, lead to successful applications. Table 19-1 presents an overview of the three classifications.

Industrial Trucks

Industrial trucks have many classifications, taking into account the mode of locomotion (manual labor, electric-powered, internal combustion), method of load support (platform, forks, clamps), method of operation (manually driven, automated), and method of control (operator-directed, computer-directed). The major

Table 19-1 Comparative Characteristics

Characteristic	Industrial trucks	Conveyors	Overhead equipment
Material:			
Volume	Low–High	High	Low–high
Shape	Regular, uniform	All	Irregular
Size	Mixed, uniform	Uniform	Mixed, variable
Weight	Medium, heavy	Low–heavy	Heavy
Move:			
Distance	Moderate	Unlimited	Moderate (area)
Rate, Speed	Variable	Uniform, variable	Irregular, variable
Frequency	Intermittent	Continuous	Intermittent
Origin, Destination	Variable	Fixed	Variable
Area Covered	Variable	Point to point	Defined
Sequence	Variable	Fixed	Variable
Path	Defined	Fixed	None
Route	Variable	Fixed	Variable
Bypassing	Yes	No	Yes
Primary Function	Stack, carry	Transport, storage	Lift, carry, position
Methods:			
Load Support Method	Pallet, crate, container	Carton, tote, pallet	Hook, sling, chain
Load/Unload	Along path	Designated points	Any point
Operator Interaction	Unless automated	At fixed points	Normally
Building:			
Floor Space Cost	Medium–high	Low–medium	High
Clear Height	Low–high	Low–high	High
Floor Load	Medium–high	Low–medium	Low–high
Running Surface	Fair–very good	Not applicable	Not applicable
Aisles	Necessary	Not applicable	Not applicable
Operability, Congested Areas	Undesirable	Fair	Good

types of industrial trucks are hand trucks, powered industrial trucks, and automated guided vehicle systems (AGVS).

Regardless of whether the trucks are powered manually, by an electric motor, or by an internal combustion engine, or whether they are operated by an operator or automatically, there are common features that define the type of truck.

- *Platform trucks* have a wide surface for supporting the load (typically skids, cartons, and totes), whereas *fork trucks* have two narrow surfaces that support the load (typically pallets or pallet containers).

- *Low-lift trucks* lift a load 4 to 6 in, in order to clear the floor for transportation, whereas the *high-lift trucks* lift the load in order to stack loads and for transportation.

- *Walkie and walkie/rider trucks* are controlled by an operator that leads or follows the truck on foot, whereas *rider trucks* are controlled by an operator in either a *standup* or *sit-down* position.

Hand Trucks

A hand truck is a wheeled device that is capable of supporting a load while being manually propelled. A two-wheeled hand truck is the simplest, used for handling cased goods between floor storage locations. A typical application is from storage to dock areas, and on and off road vehicles. A special application is the *drum truck,* specially designed to secure the upper lip of a drum while supporting the bottom rim.

A *pallet jack* (see Fig. 19-2) is used to raise a pallet or skid off the floor and move it horizontally. It is versatile and is used over short distances, in a relatively confined space. Another common hand truck is the *platform truck* (see Fig. 19-3). This typi-

Figure 19-2. Pallet jack.

Figure 19-3. Platform truck.

cally has two fixed wheels and two swivel casters for maneuverability. A cart is a multishelf platform truck.

A *dolly* is a low platform truck with three or four wheels, all of which swivel, and a platform that may be either open or closed. The most complex type of hand truck is the *hand lift truck* (see Fig. 19-4). It is capable of raising loads above normal carrying heights by hydraulics actuated by a foot pump. Hand trucks are typically low-cost, maintenance-free, and relatively safe to operate. They are used for horizontal transportation where loads are light, distances are short, throughput is low, and maneuvering space is limited.

Powered Industrial Trucks

The Industrial Truck Association has established seven major classes of industrial trucks. They are defined in Table 19-2. These classifications represent a number of choices to the user. One is electric versus internal combustion (IC) power.

Class I, IV, and V Trucks. As the traditional choice for warehouse operators, IC-powered trucks are typically lower in initial cost, but have greater annual fuel and maintenance costs due to the nature of the internal combustion engine. Electric-powered trucks have environmental advantages in that they are quiet and do

Figure 19-4. Hand lift truck.

not emit potentially harmful exhaust gases. There has been a clear shift toward electric-powered trucks for indoor use in industry, while IC trucks are clearly the choice
in outdoor applications, for safety reasons.

The choice of tires is based on the surface conditions on which the truck will
operate. Cushion tires work well on smooth, dry surfaces, or where the risk of puncture is great. Where water, grease, or oil are a factor, or the surface is irregular,
pneumatic tires offer additional traction.

Class 1, 4, and 5 trucks are commonly referred to as *counterbalanced trucks* (see Fig.
19-5). Their design is similar to a teeter-totter: the load is suspended on the forks,

Table 19-2 Industrial Truck Association Lift Truck Classifications

Class	Description	Applications	Typical load capacities (lb)	Typical lift heights (ft)
I.	Electric motor rider trucks	Indoor, general-purpose	2500–12,000	16 to 18
II.	Electric motor narrow-aisle trucks	Indoor, narrow-aisle and very-narrow-aisle	2000–4500	Up to 40
III.	Electric motor hand trucks	Indoor, general-purpose	4000–8000	
IV.	Internal combustion, cushion tire	Indoor and outdoor, general-purpose	2000–15,000	Up to 20
V.	Internal combustion, pneumatic tire	Outdoor, general-purpose, paved surfaces	2000–15,000	Up to 20
VI.	Tow tractors	Indoor, long-distance	n/a	n/a
VII.	Rough-terrain lift trucks	Outdoor, construction sites	4000–20,000	Up to 20

the wheels behind the forks are the fulcrum, the weight of the chassis, engine (motor), fuel (battery), and ballast keep the wheels on the ground and the load in the air. Counterbalanced trucks are often described as *wide-aisle vehicles,* as they typically require a 10- to 15-ft clear aisle for right-angle stacking in rack or on the floor. The actual dimension is a function of the truck's turning radius and the length of the load. They are available in sit-down and stand-up versions. The stand-up version requires a smaller aisle, because the truck is shorter. It is a good choice when the operator must get on and off the truck frequently during the work shift. For horizontal transportation over long distances and infrequent dismounts, the sit-down version is preferred. These trucks are commonly used for loading and unloading over-the-road trailers and in bulk floor storage, since the space lost for aisles is small in relation to the depth of storage.

Class 2 Electric Motor, Narrow-Aisle Trucks.   These are typically standup riders that have a shorter chassis, which reduces the required right-angle-stacking aisle.

Straddle trucks (see Fig. 19-6) use outriggers on wheels that extend in front of the mast on either side of the forks. The load is carried between these outriggers. In order to pick up pallets from the floor, the outriggers must "straddle" the load, unless it is placed on a support that allows the outriggers clearance underneath. Typically, the bottom level of a pallet rack is placed on a pair of beams for this reason, for ease of operation.

Order picker is a special type of straddle truck (see Fig. 19-7). It has a platform between the mast and the forks that allows the operator to control the truck while elevated with the load, and store and retrieve goods by hand in shelving and rack. Because right-angle-stacking turns in a storage aisle are not made, wire or rail guid-

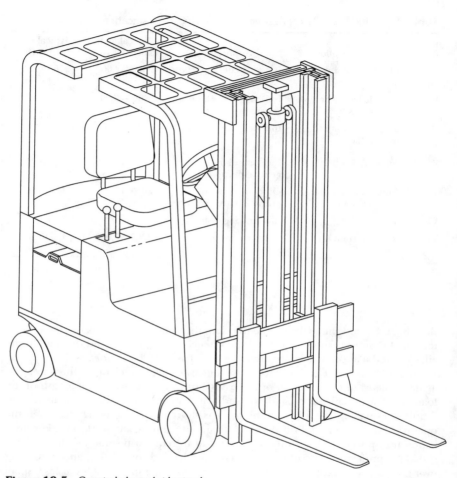

Figure 19-5. Counterbalanced rider truck.

ance may be used to reduce the side clearances to 4 to 6 in. These trucks should never be used for stacking or storing pallets.

Reach trucks (see Fig. 19-8) eliminate the need for a pair of beams for the bottom level of the pallet rack, by incorporating either a pantograph mechanism between the mast of the truck and the backrest for the load or telescoping forks. It also allows the operator to pick up a load too wide to fit between its outriggers, because it can "reach" beyond the outriggers to pick up or deposit a load.

Double-reach trucks provide a second pantograph extension, which permits the truck to be used for storing loads two pallets deep in pallet rack. Typically, the bottom level is supported on a pair of beams (as for the straddle truck). The front load is stored as with the reach truck. The rear load requires outrigger clearance under the

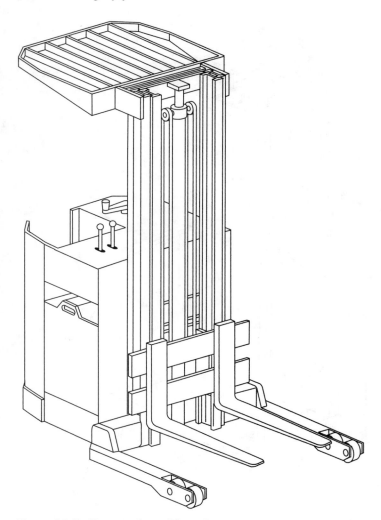

Figure 19-6. Narrow-aisle straddle truck.

beams, and if necessary a second "bite" of the pallet. The first step places the pallet as deep as possible, based on the maximum extension of the reach mechanism. The second step retracts the reach mechanism several inches, and then the load is partially lifted and pushed into position. When specifying a double-reach truck, it is important to be sure that the rack opening is large enough to provide clearance for the pantograph mechanism when the load is placed in the rear position.

Class 2 also includes trucks that may be referred to as *very-narrow-aisle trucks*. They further reduce the width of storage aisles because their design does not require them to make a right-angle turn within the storage aisle, as do the wide-aisle

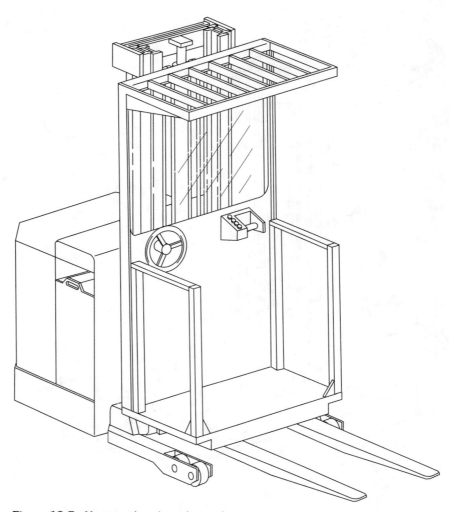

Figure 19-7. Narrow-aisle order picker truck.

and narrow-aisle trucks. An order picker truck could be described as a very-narrow-aisle truck. These trucks operate with minimal clearances when guided by wire or rail.

Wire guidance operates by sensing the electromagnetic field that emanates from a wire that is embedded in the floor, through which an electric current flows. The current is provided by a "line driver," and is sensed by a device mounted underneath the truck that transmits control signals to the steering system. Wire guidance is characterized by high onboard vehicle costs and low-aisle guidance costs, as well as a clean floor. *Rail guidance* is purely mechanical. Angle iron is lagged to the floor on both sides of the aisle. Steel casters are welded to each of four corners of the

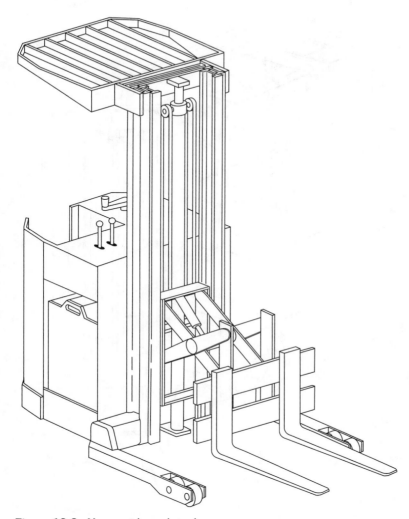

Figure 19-8. Narrow-aisle reach truck.

truck chassis. Rail guidance is characterized by low vehicle costs and higher aisle-guidance costs, as well as high reliability.

Swing mast trucks (see Fig. 19-9) are designed with a special mast that rotates 90° to the right and also side-shifts to place a load in a rack position. These trucks operate in an aisle whose width is a function of the widest dimension of the truck or load, plus operating clearances on each side. However, the additional weight of the rotating mast requires a substantially heavier truck to achieve the same load-carrying capacity as a counterbalanced truck. Also, since these trucks can rotate only 90° to the right, the operator must consider on which side of the aisle to store or retrieve the load before entering the aisle.

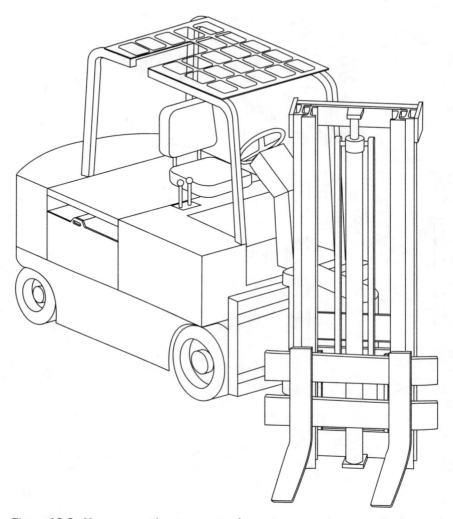

Figure 19-9. Very-narrow-aisle swing mast truck.

Turret trucks (see Fig. 19-10) are able to store loads without turning in the aisle, because the forks and backrest are designed to rotate the load perpendicular to the aisle, left or right. Once rotated, the forks and backrest traverse toward the rack to place the load. Man-up and man-down versions are available. The man-up version has the advantage of locating the operator close to the load for better control. It can also be used for order picking from pallet locations. The man-down design requires a shelf-height selector or the calibration of the truck mast for the tallest storage locations, but has the advantage of faster operating speeds. As a result, the

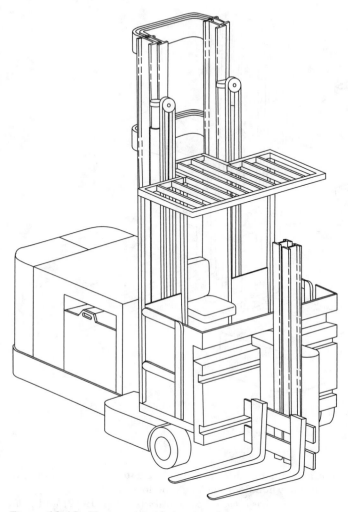

Figure 19-10. Very-narrow-aisle turret truck.

man-down turret truck is used in low-bay applications, and the man-up trucks are popular when the shelf height exceeds 20 to 25 ft.

Side-loader trucks (see Fig. 19-11) are designed to handle long, heavy materials that are difficult to palletize. They are typically used in conjunction with cantilevered rack in guided aisles. They travel in the aisle, with the long axis of the truck and load parallel with the aisle. Either a pantograph or rolling mast design eliminates the need to make 90° turns in the aisle for storage and retrieval. These trucks can either be man-up or man-down.

Four-directional trucks function similarly to the side loader. They have the addi-

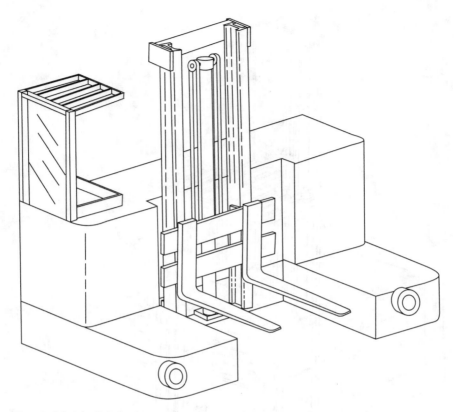

Figure 19-11. Side-loader truck.

tional advantage of moving along the aisle, and then into a storage location without turning. This feature is useful when floor-stacking long loads in deep lanes.

Class 2 also includes the very basic *low-lift pallet truck* (see Fig. 19-12) and *pallet rider truck*. These are relatively low in cost, and are commonly used for loading and unloading trailers of palletized goods that do not need to be stacked or de-stacked. Some are designed to carry as many as four loads at once (two high, two deep). They are both inexpensive and high-productivity transportation devices.

Fixed-mast storage/retrieval machines (see Fig. 19-13) combine fork truck and automated storage-and-retrieval features. When operating in an aisle, they receive electric power from a buss mounted overhead, and from batteries when outside these aisles. The mast extends to a guide rail at the top of each aisle, which facilitates stability and guidance of the vehicle in the aisle. High operating speeds and simultaneous horizontal and vertical travel reduce cycle time and increase productivity. A man-up design is typical, as is a shuttle-table to store and retrieve pallets in the rack structure, similar to a storage/retrieval machine. The aisle widths are minimal, based on the width of the load or the truck, whichever is greater, plus minimal

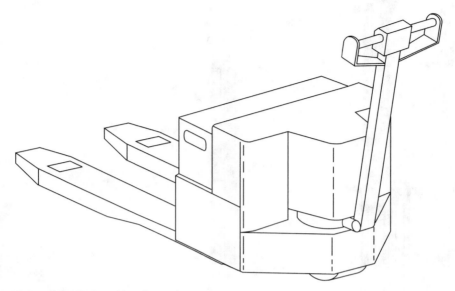

Figure 19-12. Low-lift pallet truck.

clearances on each side. Some designs can handle storage heights up to 60 ft. Yet they are more versatile than dedicated-aisle AS/R machines.

Class 3 Electric Motor Hand Trucks.   Class 3 trucks (see Fig. 19-14) are characterized by a swivel control arm that allows the operator to control the truck while walking in front or behind the vehicle in the case of a "walkie," or while walking or riding in the case of the "walkie/rider." This control arm is equipped with forward, reverse, lift, lower, and speed functions, as well as a dead-man brake that activates when the arm is released, allowing it to return to its normal vertical position. Directional control is achieved through horizontal rotation. There is typically a feature that stops the truck when the arm senses a resistance when operating in reverse.

Low-lift platform trucks are used primarily for transporting skids and bins. The minimum lowered height of the platform is usually 6 in. Two adaptations are common. The platform of these versatile trucks is often modified to accept customized unit loads, such as steel coils, wire and cable reels, bolts of yarn, paper flat stock, or other units with distinctive configurations. A *low-lift walkie pallet truck* is similar to the pallet rider truck, except that it requires the operator to lead or follow the truck on foot.

Tractors are typically used to pull one to five wagons or trailers. The number is dependent on the draw-bar pull rating of the tractor. These rider trucks are intended for transporting large-volume loads over long distances.

Electric motor hand trucks are also available in straddle, reach, and counterbalanced *high-lift* designs. They are similar in design to the Class 2 trucks, except that they are walkie trucks and the typical lift heights are up to 15 ft.

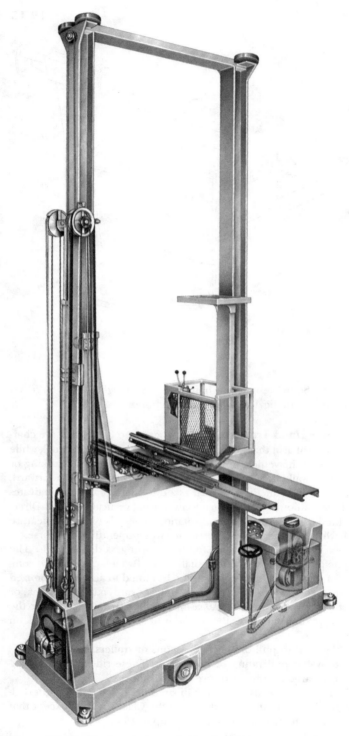

Figure 19-13. Fixed-mast storage/retrieval machine.

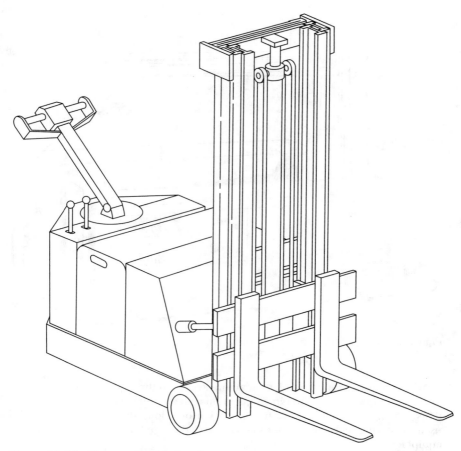

Figure 19-14. Electric motor hand truck.

Automated Guided Vehicle Systems

Automated Guided Vehicle Systems (AGVS—see Fig. 19-15) are battery-powered driverless vehicles that are controlled by computers for task assignment, path selection, and positioning. The typical AGV system has four components: one or more vehicles, pick-up/drop-off (P/D) locations, a guidance system, and the control system. Because they do not require an operator, they have low operating costs relative to powered industrial trucks, especially in a multishift, around-the-clock operation. However, at speeds that range from 150 to 250 ft/min (1.7 to 2.8 mi/hr), they are slower than the typical industrial truck that may operate at 3 to 5 mi/hr. Economic justification is typically a tradeoff between lower operating cost against higher investment. They provide a high degree of discipline in an operation. They also require a higher degree of skill and knowledge relative to industrial trucks, but the difference is narrowing as electric-powered trucks are incorporating increasingly sophisticated electronic controls.

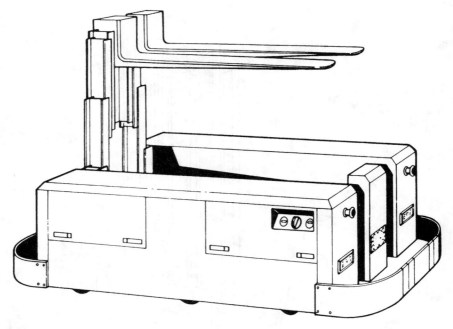

Figure 19-15. An AGV.

AGV systems are found in the most automated, high-throughput, high-utilization distribution operations, often in conjunction with automated storage/retrieval systems (AS/RS) or for repetitive transportation over long distances. They are also used for storing high-value goods that are easily damaged with operator-controlled equipment.

Vehicles and Pickup/Delivery (P/D) Stations

There are five vehicle types: tractors, pallet vehicles, unit load carriers, fork vehicles, and light-load carriers. The pickup and delivery station is dependent on the vehicle, and will be described along with the vehicle.

Tractors towing trailers were the earliest application of AGV technology. The simplest design uses flatbed trailers that are loaded by fork trucks or by hand. Trailers with nonpowered roller decks can be used to interface with fixed, nonpowered conveyors, using manual assistance for load transfer. Trailers with powered roller decks are less commonly used in systems with fixed powered-roller conveyors for automatic load transfer. They are powered from the tractor battery. Loading and unloading may be from either side, and each trailer can be designed to carry two loads.

Pallet vehicles are similar to the industrial pallet truck. They are typically loaded like a pallet truck but they travel and unload themselves automatically. After loading, the vehicle is programmed for the appropriate destination and placed on the guide path. Pallet delivery stations are located on spurs off the main guide path. As a truck enters a spur, it slows down to creep speed and stops at a predefined location. The truck lowers the load automatically, placing the pallets on the floor. The truck restarts, pulls out from the pallets, and proceeds to its next destination. Platform trucks are similar to pallet trucks but have the forks replaced with a solid deck or platform for handling skids.

Unit load carriers are designed to handle one or two loads at a time, with the vehicle below and supporting the load. They are compact and highly maneuverable in both forward and reverse, can rotate 180° in their own length, and are available as either rollertop or lift-and-carry vehicles. The rollertop AGV has powered rollers that can receive or discharge a conveyable unit load from or to a roller conveyor P/D stand at the same height as the rollers on the AGV. Power for the onboard rollers is provided by the AGV battery, and the P/D rollers are driven off the vehicle by a friction drive. Lift-and-carry vehicles require loads to be placed on load stands that allow the vehicle to drive underneath the load. When in position, the load support lifts to clear the load from the stand and transport it to its destination. Unloading is similar, but in reverse sequence.

Fork vehicles allow loads to be picked up and deposited at P/D stations that are simply floor locations. Straddle, counterbalanced, and side-loader models are available. They can also handle loads at a variety of levels: floor, conveyors, and racks. The straddle and counterbalance vehicles store and unload in conjunction with right-angle turns. This maneuver requires a significant aisle width. The sideloader operates in a very narrow aisle, since the right-angle turn is not necessary. However, the vehicle must leave and reenter an aisle to combine a drop-off on one side with a pickup on the other, unless the aisle is sized for 180° turns.

Light-load carriers are vehicles that are typically loaded and unloaded by hand. Loads may be totes, cartons, or loose items.

System Controls.   An AGVS control system includes an interface to a host computer, a local material handling system control computer, control software, onboard processors, a guidance system, and a means of communication between the local computer and the individual vehicles. The most basic AGVS control strategy uses an operator to enter a destination code at an on-board terminal, and release the vehicle. The vehicle travels to the intended destination and waits for further instructions. The early tugger AGVSs used this method. Early AGVSs used a centralized control hierarchy. The material handling control computer maintained control of vehicle functions, routing, and traffic. Guidance and safety functions were at the machine level. These vehicles were considered to be "dumb." In keeping with the philosophy of Distributed Processing, many suppliers are using vehicles that have the onboard intelligence to receive, store, and process information. Those that have routing and traffic management functionality, and therefore can operate independently, are referred to as "smart" vehicles. All AGV control systems must provide guidance, communications (including positional control and dispatching), routing, and traffic control.

Guidance.   There are five techniques that may be used to guide the vehicle.

1. *Inductive wire guidance* is the most commonly used method for large-load AGVs. Similar to the wire guidance used by narrow-aisle industrial trucks, a wire that is buried in a slot in the floor serves as the centerline of the travel path. A current in the wire provides an electromagnetic field. An onboard sensor measures

the strength of the field and adjusts the steering mechanism to keep the vehicle centered over the wire. For reliability, the floor should be smooth and the wire must be continuous. It is becoming common for turns to be configured with wires that are at right angles. The vehicle will follow the wire to a predetermined point, leave the wire, execute a specific radius turn under the control of an onboard processor, and then reacquire the wire as it completes the turn. This approach reduces installation costs.

2. *Optical guidance* uses tape or paint to identify the centerline of the path to the vehicle. Photocells sense the light that is reflected when an onboard light source illuminates the reflective path. Signals fed to the steering control indicate reflectance, which is maximized when the vehicle is centered over the path. Optical paths have the advantage of flexibility: they may be altered at little cost. However, their lack of durability makes them suitable only in clean industrial, office, and laboratory environments.

3. *Chemical guidance* uses a phosphorus-type paint that is invisible to the eye. When illuminated by an ultraviolet light, the fluorescent particles glow, thereby identifying the path to the vehicle.

4. One of the newest vehicles, known as "self-guided vehicles" (SGVs), uses a combination of advanced *dead reckoning navigation* for general control in conjunction with triangulation to make corrections. The triangulation method uses infrared lasers and reflective bar codes or retroreflective targets to identify the actual location of the vehicle, compare it to the planned location, and then make appropriate adjustments.

5. *Vision systems* are the latest innovation in AGV guidance. An onboard camera records the view ahead and compares it to an image that has been programmed and stored in memory. Typically, that image will be the marker lines on either side of an aisle.

Communications.   The local control computer and the vehicles need a means to communicate location, task assignment, task completion, routing, and traffic conditions. Four methods of communications are available:

1. Inductive wire
2. Floor devices
3. Radio frequency transmission
4. Optical infrared

The inductive wire uses the same floor path as the guidance does. Except for when operating off-wire, communication is continuous. Floor devices may include magnets, radio frequency transponders, and additional inductive loops installed adjacent to the guide path in specific patterns and locations. Because they require the vehicle to be close enough to receive its signal, the communication is intermittent. This approach is used for determining vehicle position. Radio frequency transmission between the vehicles and system control allows continuous communication, unless dead spots exist in the facility. The use of radio frequency identification tags provides intermittent communication. These can be used to identify the vehicle and receive data at P/D stations. Optical solutions typically require a line-of-sight, and are therefore intermittent.

Routing. System-level control of routing uses path-switching to direct the vehicle to its destination. Inductive wire guidance systems are divided into zones that may be turned on and off. Machine-level control of routing is based on frequency selection. The AGV knows its location and is assigned a destination. A system map in memory defines the routing and frequency signal to follow along the guidepath. Internal controls monitor the correct frequency.

Traffic Control. The purpose of traffic control is to prevent collisions between vehicles. Decisions are made to stop, slow down, or proceed according to vehicle locations and the queue of pending material moves. AGVSs using dumb or semi-intelligent vehicles will locate this intelligence at the system level. Smart vehicles are able to determine the location of other vehicles, in order to make stop and proceed decisions.

Unit Load Conveyors

A conveyor is defined by the Conveyor Equipment Manufacturers Association as:

> A horizontal, inclined, or vertical device for moving or transporting bulk materials or objects in a path, predetermined by the design of the device and having points of loading and discharge fixed, or selective . . .

The definition goes on to define examples, and presents a list of 109 specific conveyor types. The definition suggests two broad categories: bulk handling and object handling. Bulk handling conveyors include bucket, pneumatic, screw, trough, and vibratory designs. These are rarely used in distribution. Most distribution applications involve packaged finished goods. The packaging may be a bag, a carton, a pallet or a drum. Sometimes loose items are conveyed using a tote or a hanger for ease of conveyance. In this chapter, the term *unit load* will be used to describe the variety of discrete objects that may be conveyed. The most common types of conveyors that are applied in distribution warehousing to transport unit loads will fall into one of the following classifications:

1. Gravity conveyor
   a. Chute
   b. Ball transfer
   c. Wheel (skate wheel)
   d. Roller
2. Powered conveyor
   a. Belt
   b. Live roller
   c. Chain
3. Special designs
   a. Accumulation
   b. Transfer cars
   c. Sortation systems

Each of these designs and their typical applications in distribution are described in this section.

Gravity Conveyors

Chute Conveyors.   A chute conveyor (see Fig. 19-16) is used to change the elevation and position of a unit load, using gravity to overcome friction. It consists of a smooth metal trough that may be straight, curved, or spiral in shape. Chutes are an alternative for short distances and durable loads. Chute conveyors are often part of a sortation system.

Ball Transfer Conveyors.   A ball transfer (see Fig. 19-17) is a section of conveyor that consists of an array of balls that are mounted and retained by a sheet-metal section over a bed of many more smaller balls. It is used as a manual assist, for purposes of changing the orientation of the unit load within a gravity conveyor configuration. Ball transfers are commonly used for in-line weigh stations, as in a parcel manifest system. Because the bearing surface is relatively small, ball transfers may mark the surface of soft materials such as brass and wood, as well as highly polished steel. They should not be used for soft or irregular-bottom loads, such as soggy cartons, bags, pallets, drums, baskets, or crates.

Wheel Conveyors.   A wheel or skate wheel conveyor (see Fig. 19-18) is used to reduce the lifting force required to transport a load under manual force or gravity. It consists of small wheels that are mounted on axles. The axles are mounted in a metal frame, perpendicular to the flow of the load. It is available in straight sections, curved sections, spurs, and switches, as well as expandable, telescoping designs, and portable designs. A wheel conveyor is appropriate for loads with a smooth and durable bottom surface. Loads with a high weight-to-hardness ratio may not roll easily. Gravity wheel conveyors are used for supporting a "pick to" container in order picking, and for loading and unloading floor-loaded trailers.

Roller Conveyors.   A gravity roller conveyor is used for the same purposes as the gravity wheel conveyor, where the weight or bottom surface of the load would make it difficult to roll. It consists of rollers that are mounted on axles between supporting frames and span the full width of the conveyor. The gravity roller conveyor is available in straight, curved, and spiral sections. It is installed level and inclined.

Powered Conveyors

Belt Conveyors.   A belt conveyor is an endless fabric (rubber, plastic, leather, metal mesh) that is mounted on a drive-and-idler roller and supported by either a sheet-metal bed (slider bed) or rollers. As a horizontal transportation device it is used for incline, decline, controlled spacing, and accurate positioning of loads. It is also used for loads with soft and irregular surfaces. It is available in straight, curved, turntable, and spiral sections.

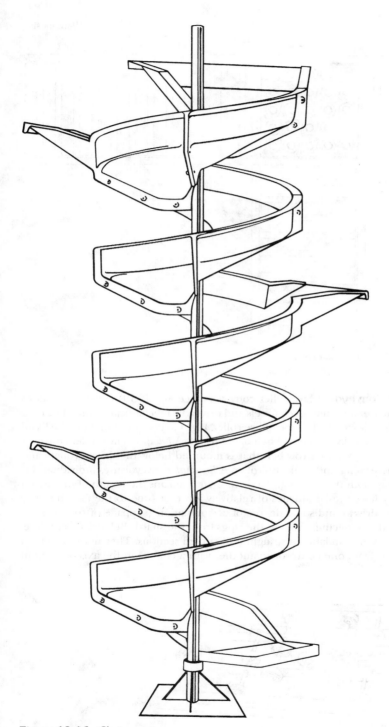

Figure 19-16. Chute conveyor.

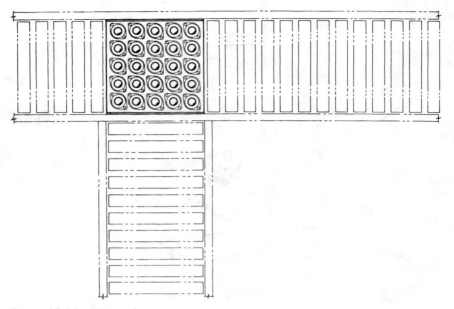

Figure 19-17. Ball transfer conveyor.

Live Roller Conveyor. Live roller conveyors (see Fig. 19-19) consist of a series of rollers that are mounted on channels and driven by mechanical means. The driving mechanism describes the type of live roller. Light loads (those that may be lifted manually) are typically driven by a belt or "O" rings. A *belt-driven* live roller conveyor uses the friction from a narrow belt that is mounted below the driven rollers and between a drive roller and a take-up roller. A *line-shaft* conveyor uses individual "O" rings that wrap both the rollers and a drive shaft that runs the length of the driven section. They have the advantages of relatively low cost (due to the fact that they require fewer drives) and some degree of accumulation (slippage of rollers is encouraged by disconnecting some of the rings from the shaft). Belt-driven and line-shaft conveyors are available in straight and curved sections. They use transfers to move the load from one conveyor to another with a change in the axis of motion.

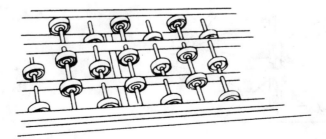

Figure 19-18. Skate wheel conveyor.

Figure 19-19. Live roller conveyor.

These may be pop-up roller, pusher, or puller designs. They use diverters to move the load from one conveyor to another, with no change in the axis of motion. These may be swing-arm, powered-belt, chain, or skewed/steerable wheel designs.

Heavy loads are conveyed on a *chain-driven* live roller conveyor. Each roller has a gear, and the chains may be roller to roller, or span several rollers. Chain-driven live roller conveyors are available in straight sections. Changes in direction and axis of motion are typically accomplished by right-angle transfers or turntables. Power-section-to-power-section transfers use a pop-up chain conveyor, mounted between the delivering rollers. Power-to-gravity transfers may use a pop-up tilt gravity section also mounted between the delivering rollers. Changes in direction without a change in the axis of motion are accomplished with a turntable. The delivering conveyor loads the turntable, and forward motion stops until the 90° rotation is complete. Chain-driven live roller conveyors are used to transport pallet loads when the throughput between fixed points is high.

Chain Conveyors

Chain conveyors (see Fig. 19-20) use two or more continuous strands of chain that are mounted between a drive sprocket and an idler sprocket, and are supported by a low-friction continuous surface. They include sliding, rolling, pusher, and vertical designs. Chain conveyors are used to transport loads that must be carried with the runners perpendicular to travel. They are also used for heavy loads such as large castings, stacks of steel sheets, or steel coils. In distribution, the most common chain conveyor is the *sliding-chain* conveyor, in which the chain is dragged on a wear surface with the load carried directly on the chain. Because of the higher friction of

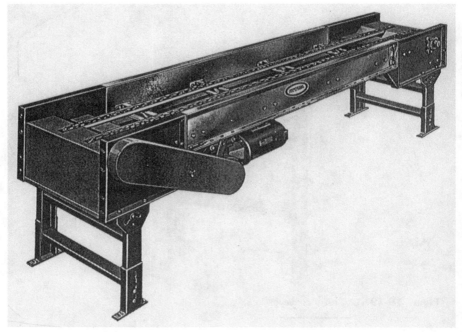

Figure 19-20. Powered chain conveyor.

this design, it is commonly used for relatively light loads and shorter distances (e.g., right-angle transfer). Rolling chains incorporate a roller at each bushing or barrel to reduce the friction against the supporting surface, and therefore can be used for heavier loads and longer conveyors. A *pusher-chain* conveyor has bars at specific intervals between two strands of chain that push the load along a slider bed. A *roller-slat* conveyor is a continuous chain that consists of rollers that span the width of the conveyor. The load can be conveyed on the slat or accumulated on the rollers. In the slat conveyor design, fixtures or other special mechanisms can be mounted to the slat for positioning or carrying a load. *Vertical-chain* conveyors are either of a reciprocating or continuous type. *Reciprocating* conveyors are used to shuttle loads between floors in a multistory facility. *Continuous-type* chain conveyors are a variation on the roller slat design, where gaps between slat sections provide spacing of the loads.

Special Designs

Accumulation Conveyors.   The purposes for accumulation capability in a conveyor system are to

- Buffer irregular input flow rates
- Provide continuous activity during interrupted flow
- Consolidate related or similar loads that were separated

In a distribution environment, accumulation is used as a part of a conveyor system that either delivers product to the warehouse or handles the loads created during the order fulfillment process, including picking, packing, and staging for shipment. Typical locations, in the context of the conveyor system, are

- Before the intersection of two lines
- In a staging zone before a sorter
- Before induction at a sorter
- After a sortation zone
- Wherever a smooth, metered flow is required

In general, accumulation should be only in straight sections, and the length and pitch of gravity lines must be engineered according to the weight of the load.

While there are many electromechanical designs for accumulation conveyors, functionally there are two: zone, or zero/minimum pressure, and continuous accumulation. Minimum pressure designs divide the conveyor into zones. Each zone has a load sensor which, when activated, will remove the power from that zone. The zone at the end of the accumulation line is controlled by the system controller. A stationary load in the last zone removes the power from the next zone, and so on to the beginning of the line. The release from a zone-type accumulation can occur individually or in a slug of loads. Case sealers, stretch-wrap equipment, and shrink wrappers require individual release, whereas palletizers require metered slugs according to the cases per layer. Variations in line pressure and slug releases are typically due to the variance in load size relative to the zone length.

Continuous-type accumulation may take place on gravity or live roller conveyor. The first load in the line is stopped, either mechanically or by removing power from a metering section. The live roller designs are continuously powered, but once the slug reaches critical length the drive force is reduced either by removing power from the line or by mechanical adjustment. The mechanical adjustment reduces friction between the power source and the roller to the point that the roller does not move under the slug.

The key design parameter in live roller continuous-type accumulation conveyor is line pressure. Crushing or buckling of the slug can occur if the line pressure is too great. There are three factors to consider in determining line pressure:

1. Integrity of the load itself
2. Length of slug
3. Coefficient of friction of the conveyor

The metering section of conveyor is designed to release a single load at a time. Release of the line may be by sensor or by mechanical stops. Often a speed-up section is used to create a constant gap at the discharge point.

Transfer Car.   A transfer car (see Fig. 19-21) consists of a short section of conveyor that is mounted on a frame with wheels. The wheels are typically designed to ride on a pair of rails. Transfer cars are used to route loads from many inbound lines to many outbound lines, when throughput is low. The car is loaded, it moves

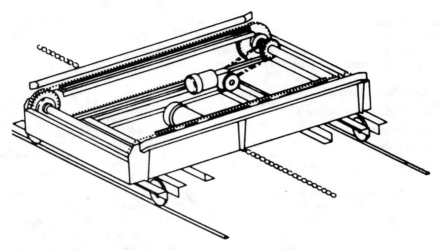

Figure 19-21. Transfer car conveyor.

perpendicular to the intended direction of travel to align with the intended takeaway line, and the load is discharged. The cycle is completed as the car moves to the next line to pick up a load. The transfer car can be either manual or powered.

Sortation Systems. Sortation systems will be discussed briefly in this chapter, and in more detail in Chapter 22. Sortation systems (see Fig. 19-22) are used in distribution centers to organize mixed products that are to be

- Dispatched to specific storage zones
- Palletized in specific unit load configurations
- Routed to specific dock doors for shipping

Where throughput is moderate, sortation can be accomplished using powered conveyors with transfers and diverters feeding spurs consisting of gravity and chute conveyors. High-speed sortation systems handle cartons and have four subsystems: (1) merge, (2) induction, (3) sort, and (4) takeaway.

The *merge* subsystem receives product from various sources in the distribution center, and provides a controlled release of cartons to the downstream sortation-induction equipment. The specific design of the merge is dependent on the number of infeed conveyors that it serves and the desired throughput rates. In general there are two types: *parallel-design* and *perpendicular-design*. The infeed flow-control device regulates the flow of cartons to the merge bed, where cartons in two or more columns feed a funneling device. The result is that a single column of cartons feeds the induction subsystem.

The *induction* subsystem provides spacing between the cartons and identifies them individually. Low rates (10 to 40 cartons/min) are accomplished by an operator visually identifying the carton and keying an identifier into the control console. Moderate rates (40 to 80 cartons/min) are accomplished by adding manual key-entry induction stations, or by laser-scanning bar code labels. Multiple induction sta-

Figure 19-22. Sortation system.

tions typically require another merge between induction and sortation. Tilt-tray sortation systems are moderate rate systems. High rates (80 to 200 cartons/min) are accomplished by a sophisticated system. One to four servo-driven indexing belts release the cartons to a merge device one at a time with a precise gap. A second series of indexing belt conveyors optimizes the gap and feeds an omnidirectional scanner for identification.

The *sortation* subsystem divides the flow of cartons into separate streams according to a downstream destination, using a diverter. Once identified, the carton is tracked until it reaches the divert point, where the system controller activates the divert device. The type of divert used depends on the speed and weight of the carton. Low-rate devices include barrier-type arms, pop-up transfers, and pushers. Moderate-rate devices include pop-up skewed wheels and steerable rollers. High rates are accomplished with sliding-shoe and tilt-tray diverters. They are both fast and bidirectional. Sliding-shoe diverters are typically slat conveyors with "shoes" that slide between the slats to push or pull the load off the line. They are gentle. Tilt trays "dump" the product to either side of the line. In general they are suitable for soft goods as well as cartons. Some designs provide a parabolic trajectory that can handle breakable goods without damage. A tilt-tray system can handle a large number of divert locations.

The takeaway conveyors must accept diverted material without affecting the sorter. The type of conveyor used depends on the operating rate, product mix, product weight, and product durability. Powered takeaways are either live roller or belt conveyor. They typically run faster than the sorter conveyor, so that they can pull the cartons away. The gravity wheel conveyor is preferable to the roller conveyor, due to its lower inertia. It is used with positive sortation, such as the sliding shoe diverter, as its speed of up to 350 ft/min provides significant momentum. It is also used on slow systems. Chute conveyors are often used with tilt-tray systems, where orientation is not important.

20

Facilities Design and Maintenance

E. Ralph Sims, Jr.

Chairman,
The Sims Consulting Group, Inc.

The role and configuration of the distribution facility, or warehouse, in a modern physical distribution operation is defined by the marketing and materials management policies of the enterprise. The distribution facility's system design is the physical manifestation of the marketing policy, and the building is the weather cover for the system. Building design must not dominate the operation.

To achieve optimal operational performance and capital-investment efficiency, the building should be designed around the system. The system must accommodate inbound materials movement, inventory storage, order picking, packing, and outbound transportation.

It is seldom desirable to "stuff" a distribution system into an existing building, but circumstances sometimes require that a system be fitted to a facility. Material handling systems usually can be designed to deal with existing building parameters.

Coordination of the material handling and storage system with functional facility design and planned maintainability will provide effective support to the physical distribution operation.

Defining the System Configuration

The first step in the design of a distribution facility is definition of the qualitative and quantitative characteristics of the operation required to perform the desired physical distribution functions. It is essential to define product mix, product handling characteristics, inventory and transaction profiles, seasonal and periodic activity variations, order characteristics, shipping and receiving volumes and patterns, in and out vehicle traffic schedules, and storage environment requirements. These data should be gathered on a statistically valid historical sampling basis for a period of at least 12 months prior to the beginning of the design process in order to capture seasonal variations and business trends. In the design of a new "green field" facility without an operating history, these factors must be projected from the management's business plan.

The aggregation of these data will provide a basis for defining the required operating parameters of the planned distribution facility. In addition, it is essential to introduce a market-and-activity forecast and management-planning criteria in order to extrapolate the data (usually from a 12-month history) into a 5-to-10-year projection. A good rule of thumb is to plan for a "design target year" that is 5 years from the projected opening date of the facility and to provide land and a site arrangement for doubling the facility in 10 years. Changing markets and inventory policies may limit or expand this projection, but "capacity insurance" is usually less costly than future relocation and/or construction of multiple facilities. This type of study will also permit analysis and validation (or rejection) of existing facilities in a modernization program.

Once the "design target year" parameters have been defined, the system designer must analyze the operation, identify alternative materials handling and storage system configurations, and screen the equipment market for the best hardware applications. As discussed in Chapters 16, 17, 18, 19, and 22, definition of the possible alternative system configurations must include the development of space requirements for each activity area, a general arrangement flow and layout study, a projection of the number, location, and type of truck and/or rail docks, the selection of storage and handling equipment alternatives, and the definition of the level of sophistication to be used in the operation. This preliminary design work must also deal with such environmental issues as controlled substance security, hazardous/flammable materials storage, coolers, refrigerated storage, overall security, fire defense, personnel service areas (personnel administration, toilets, showers, lockers, first aid, etc.), and management offices.

The product of this early analysis effort should include, but not be limited to, the following, for each alternative system configuration plan.

1. *Preliminary system flow charts* showing the steps in the operation, the quantities of materials and/or unit loads flowing through each step, and the control points or computer interfaces that the materials flow.

2. *Preliminary materials handling and storage system concept drawings* and space layouts showing the types of materials handling equipment to be used, the handling volumes and/or speeds to be expected in each segment of the handling system, the storage area requirements and the types of storage systems to be used (AS/RS, pallet racks, floor storage, etc.) and the areas required, the location and number of truck and/or rail docks, and the support area requirements.

3. *A preliminary general-arrangement building and site plan* for each of the alternative preliminary system concepts.

4. *A preliminary operating narrative* describing the operation and the functions of each element of the system, with expected "design target year" transaction volumes and inventory levels.

These documents should include sufficient detail to allow equipment vendors and/or system integrators to generate preliminary "budget" quotations or estimates of the cost of the system and its equipment. These budget estimates will then be used in conjunction with labor (Chapter 21) and operating cost estimates to compare and evaluate the economics of the alternative system configurations and to choose the most promising one(s) for further study and detail design.

The System Design

The design of a distribution facility requires an application engineering approach to both the operating equipment and the building. It is seldom practical to design material handling and storage equipment on a special-machinery basis. In most cases the system is a composite design, based on the blending of a variety of equipment components from many specialist vendors. The system designer's job is to define the overall system configuration and the relationships between the components. The system designer writes an operating specification in response to the user requirements and operational projections. The equipment vendors design the actual hardware and control systems to meet the requirements of the operating specifications developed by the system designer.

Once the overall system configuration has been defined and the preliminary cost estimate has supported its selection, the next step in the design process is a thorough search of the materials handling and storage equipment market to identify the most applicable and appropriate equipment and the most reliable and qualified vendors.

It is essential to recognize the complexity and segmentation of the materials handling and storage equipment market. The system designer, whether an in-house engineer, outside specialist consultant, or contract system integrator, cannot always be up-to-date with the ever-changing galaxy of equipment and system components that are available in the market. It is necessary to search the market and to evaluate the many component options and their compatibility with the overall system. It is essential to choose vendors who will work together in the design and implementation of the system.

Each hardware element of the system must be evaluated carefully by applying selection criteria that measure its fit to the overall system. Some of these criteria are:

1. Does the equipment unit have the right dimensions and capacity to perform the required operation(s) (i.e., conveyor width, conveyor speed, lift truck capacity and lift height, pallet dimensions, pallet rack capacity and dimensions, etc.)?

2. Is the equipment configuration the most appropriate for the function required at this point in the system (i.e., belt versus live roller conveyor, counterbalanced versus reach or turret forklift trucks, pallet racks versus AS/RS machines, roll-

through pick rack versus conventional shelving, manual versus automated operation, etc.)?

3. Is the equipment well engineered (i.e., sturdy construction and adequate design safety factors, meets or exceeds OSHA standards, failsafe design, ease of maintenance, ease of installation, etc.)?

4. Are the power requirements and controls compatible with a centralized system management arrangement (i.e., motor voltages, motor controls, AC versus DC, computer interfacing, speed variability and stability, etc.)?

5. Are purchased components standard and interchangeable, and/or compatible for ease of maintenance and minimum maintenance inventories (i.e., motors, belts, bearings, connections, controls, tires, batteries, engines, etc.)?

6. Are dealer or manufacturer service facilities and warranties acceptable and available (i.e., service engineers, repair shops, spare parts, loaner equipment, etc.)?

Once the equipment suppliers have been screened, it is usual to request more definitive quotations with technical specifications from two or three competitive vendors. These are not final quotations, but they are more refined than the above suggested preliminary estimates and they include sufficient technical data to allow a final selection of equipment sources. With these technical estimates and equipment specifications in hand, the system designer can then prepare detailed layout and elevation drawings of the system, a space layout, building envelope drawings, and final operating specifications. These documents are then combined into a "bid package" and issued to the selected vendors as part of a "request for quotation" (RFQ) to solicit final bids. The successful bidder usually prepares the final design and installation drawings and submits them to the owner or the owner's consultant for approval before manufacture and installation of the system.

In most cases, the system designer will define the building envelope or functional design (dimensions, shape, dock arrangement, office location, site plan, etc.) and prepare a general-arrangement drawing.

The actual design of the building to house the system is based on a combination of operational needs and architectural aesthetics. From a purely practical point of view, a distribution center can operate just as effectively in a preengineered building as in a stylized edifice. The designer of the building must accommodate the system configuration and consider all of its functional requirements. The building design should include planned expansion, system configuration fit, overhead clearances, structural durability, ease of maintenance, resale value, compliance with building codes, building cost control, community acceptance, and corporate image. Again, the complex building materials and construction market requires careful study before the owner commits to a final design.

The Building Design Process

From a physical distribution management point of view, the critical issues in the building design process are the definition of the building's structural envelope, the sizing of the building, establishment of the required clear height and column spacing, floor capacity, the location, arrangement, and number of truck and rail docks, the internal environmental control systems, the sizing and location of offices and employee services, the security of the facility, and the overall site arrangement. Let us examine these design issues one at a time.

Sizing of the Building

Building size is a function of both the choice of system configuration and the inventory/service policy of the owner management. It is essential to define inventory mix and turnover objectives or targets in order to safely determine the quantities and characteristics of the goods to be stored and handled in the proposed distribution warehouse. This management parameter is the basis for the definition of the configuration of the storage system to be used.

The choice of storage system determines the overhead clearance requirements, the floor capacity, the aisle dimensions, and the fire defense system criteria. These technical parameters, coupled with projections of the inventory profile and volumes, will dictate the layout of the storage system and, in turn, the area and height of the storage portion of the building. The building envelope dimensions are usually dictated by these space and height requirements. In turn, the building envelope dimensions will be the basis for selecting the proper structural system for the building.

Once the building envelope's dimensional requirements have been established, the next step is the development of its general shape and arrangement. In this effort, the system configuration and material flow patterns dominate the design and the building is "wrapped around" the system. In the development of the "wrap," the designer must consider construction economics, supporting work and service areas, offices and employee services, truck and rail access, truck aprons, parking, the direction of and expectations for expansion, and general site arrangement.

Structural Envelope

The structural envelope of the building includes the clear height, the column spacing and size, the number, location, and configuration of truck and rail docks, the roof design, the floor design, the fire defense system, and the environmental system. Each of these elements of the building envelope must be selected to conform with the design and objectives of the operating system. However, there are some practical considerations that may dictate the design characteristics of the building envelope.

In some jurisdictions the height, setback, appearance, fire defense system, structural design, and site arrangement of the building are dictated by building codes. Most communities follow the National Building Code and OSHA Regulations. However, many also have stricter rules for construction of industrial buildings, plus local appearance and environmental codes. All of these restraining influences must be accommodated in the building design. In some cases, commercial and economic factors will prompt the granting of site waivers by local governments or zoning boards. This possibility should be explored.

Another government-based factor that applies to the design of a storage facility is the possible tax advantage of a rack-supported warehouse building. It is often possible to amortize a rack-supported building under machinery depreciation rules rather than as a building structure. This has obvious tax advantages, which can be a significant consideration in the design of the building and the system. Building height codes, fire defense regulations, and land cost also enter into the decision process when comparing conventional structures to rack-supported facilities.

The choice of the "common denominator" (pallet, tote, unit load, etc.) for the system, and the choice of the handling and storage system, have a direct impact on the dimensioning of the building structure. For example, the size of the pallet dictates the dimensions of pallet racks or automated storage/retrieval machinery and the size and capacity of materials handling vehicles. These in turn have a direct impact on the spacing of columns, the sizing of aisles and doors, and the floor load capacity requirements. The choice of the storage system is the basis for establishing the required "clear height" (height under all overhead obstructions) of the building. The combination of the storage system design, the inventory profile (lot size and product mix), and the peak inventory volume lead to the definition of the space requirements and "footprint" of the warehouse facility.

Once the column spacing, clear height, floor loading, and "footprint" of the storage structure have been defined, the next element of the design is the definition of the order picking and shipping operation. These functions may or may not require a high building structure, and the system may or may not involve vehicles or automated machinery. Nonetheless for building economics, layout flexibility, and future resale value, the owner may prefer a constant roof height and therefore sacrifice the unusable "air rights" above the picking, shipping, and receiving areas. In many cases, offices and employee service facilities can be located on a mezzanine above the shipping area to utilize the cube. Under current building codes and EEOC/ADA Regulations, such a mezzanine will require an elevator for handicapped access, and most fire codes require a minimum of two fire tower stairwells.

After defining these operating features, projecting future expansion, and estimating the size of the building, the general arrangement or shape of the facility can be developed. In this design stage, it is necessary to define the material flow pattern, the location and size of the supporting employee service areas, the maintenance and building service areas, offices, shipping and receiving docks, and pedestrian entries. In most cases the locations of the truck and rail docks, pedestrian entries, and parking areas are also a function of the site configuration, site layout, rail and road access, building and setback codes, and the aesthetics of the facility.

Thus, in the most operationally effective and aesthetically acceptable structure, the "structural envelope" consists of a preliminary dimensioned building design, a preliminary site plan, an expansion plan, and the accommodation of the required system configuration and layout.

Building Design Considerations

These include such things as the choice of the basic framing or structure, the selection of wall materials, security and fire defense, floor design, and internal structural flexibility. There are several philosophically different approaches to building design. The most common in warehouse design are these:

- To design the system and cover it as cheaply as possible
- To build the cheapest possible facility, provide the minimum-sized space, and stuff the operation into it

- To minimize capital cost for both the system and building
- To design the optimum system, with flexibility and expandability, and house it in the least expensive "weather cover"
- To design the optimum system, with flexibility and expandability, and build the optimum building around it

In this chapter, let us consider only the last two options. The others are obvious designs and generally least cost-effective in the long run.

If a professionally competent design study is undertaken, the system configuration and the size and shape of the required structure will be well defined. Many managers and engineers will then take a "practical" or "cheap" approach to the building and simply design a "weather cover" to protect the system. The most common of these is a steel frame structure with a flat, built-up pan roof, insulated panel siding, and a good concrete floor. Such a building is functional, inexpensive, expandable, resellable, and capable of a reasonably maintenance-free life of 25 or more years. The cost will vary with the selection of materials for the roof and wall panels and with the thickness and flatness of the floor.

But this basic building may also require other design considerations based on functions and codes. Management may have plans for future expansion, and therefore the structure and wall-panel system should be designed for rearrangement and growth. The siting of the building must allow for expansion, and the sewers, power supplies, and other utilities must anticipate growth. If internal offices or mezzanines are included, consideration of future relocation should be a part of their design. Provision must also be made for additional truck and/or rail docks as the business grows. This will require larger apron space and rearranged or expanded parking areas.

If high-rise vehicular systems are to be used, it is essential to have super-flat floors in the storage areas, and adequate floor load capacity to handle the very heavy machines without cracking or sagging. If a combination of a freestanding and a rack-supported structure is to be used, it is essential to treat the design in a manner acceptable to the IRS in order to gain the tax advantages of the rack-supported building. In very high buildings and flat-roof structures, it is necessary to consider prevailing winds and expectations of severe storms.

In the construction of a large and high warehouse building, the National Building Code and OSHA specify fire defense systems. These systems include high-density and multilevel in-rack sprinklers, floor drains and wall scuppers leading to catch basins (which can separate fire-water-collected contaminants), a separate onsite water supply to supplement public water systems, fire curtains or fire walls, and well-marked multiple employee escape routes. In many cases, the use of a steel frame and panel wall structure is inconsistent with the conditions or requirements. For example, a precast/prestressed concrete frame structure with either precast or tilt-up concrete walls and a concrete pan-type roof may be the wisest construction because of weather conditions, fire defense, security, or in some areas, construction cost. This type of construction may also provide the best aesthetic opportunities, and it will usually retain the design flexibility required for expansion.

The use of concrete block wall panels with steel or precast framing may provide the same fire resistance with a lower construction cost. In some areas, as in the northwest of the United States, laminated and treated redwood framing is preferred. This type of construction is fire-resistant and, in those areas, often less expensive. In any case, a good phrase to remember is "the terrible permanence of poured-in-place concrete." The designer should always lean in the direction of flexible construction and expandable facilities.

Heating, Ventilating, and Air Conditioning

Internal environmental control and the internal operating environment is another consideration in the design of the warehouse building. This involves the design of the heating, ventilating, and air conditioning systems (HVAC) for employee comfort, and the need for special systems to store and handle cooler, refrigerated, or frozen products, hazardous and flammable materials, and controlled substances. In addition, the general security of the facility and the provision of security for pilferables and high-value merchandise must be included in the system design. These requirements will vary with the company's needs and the location of the plant.

It is obvious that southern locations will have less need for heat than northern facilities, and the desirability of air conditioning in hot climates is self-evident. The questions of capital and operating costs, employee relations, and product care must all be considered when dealing with the HVAC system design. If the product requires a controlled environment, this is an overriding consideration, and the work force will benefit or be inconvenienced as a by-product of the system.

In general, temperatures of 50 to 75°F are comfortable for warehouse work, and 68 to 72°F temperatures are acceptable in office operations. It is well known that high work-area temperatures reduce productivity, and that air conditioning can pay off in lower summer labor costs. The size of the payoff will depend on the climate and the size of the labor force. Conversely, except in very cold climates, the provision of warm work clothing for warehouse workers can reduce the need for heating in the storage areas. (This is generally not the case in order picking operations.) Door heaters (often overhead radiant units) are generally desirable at the shipping and receiving docks. Office areas should always be heated to the 68 to 72°F level for good performance.

There are several schools of thought as to the design of warehouse heating systems. Some designers prefer under-floor radiant heating by electricity, steam, or hot water. This method is theoretically sound, but it is expensive to install and very difficult to maintain against heavy forklift traffic. Another form of radiant heating is based upon ceiling-mounted gas, steam, or electric heaters over aisles and work areas. The advantages of this system are its localized nature, relocation flexibility, and often operating economy. The disadvantage is that it heats people's heads and often leaves their feet quite cold, with resulting discontent. Radiant systems are also confined to heating and require additional systems for cooling and/or air conditioning.

The most common approach to heating and ventilating a warehouse is based on convection. There are several types of convection systems and some are dual-purpose, with the capability to air-condition with the same equipment. The dual systems are usually either floor-mounted central units in multiple locations, with large blowers to circulate the air, or ceiling mounted units. In some cases these central units are equipped with distribution ducts to carry air to different parts of the building. This is most often the case in ceiling-mounted equipment. Many of these units are equipped with hot water or steam coils to provide heat from a central boiler. They can also be individually gas-fired or electrically heated systems. The choice of heating energy is dependent upon local utility rates, capital cost, and fire protection considerations. When the dual units are used, the air conditioner is built into the system and the same blower and ducts are used for cooling.

Another type of warehouse heating is based on the use of a multiple of individual gas-fired or steam-heated space heaters. These are usually mounted on the ceiling over aisles and work areas. They are equipped with blowers, but do not have air-cooling capability. There are two basic classes of this type of equipment. The typical space heater is a "box" with a burner or steam or electric heating coil in front of a blower. The unit is equipped with adjustable louvers to aim the hot air at the floor and is controlled by a work-level thermostat. These are usually high-velocity, intermittent heaters, and result in variable-temperature convection heating.

Another type of ceiling heater is a low-velocity, mass-flow unit that is usually round, with a slow fan blowing straight down through dispersal louvers. This type can also use a variety of heat sources and usually results in more stable temperatures.

In all of these convection systems, outside return air is used to assure positive ambient pressure, provide combustion air in gas units, and reduce drafts. The gas units are also vented to the outside. This feature also allows these systems to provide air circulation without heating or air conditioning in the summer.

Another type of air heating system is the "air gate," which can be used between buildings, for outside doors, and for truck and rail docks. These systems, which are common in department store and hotel entrances, create a downdraft curtain of air at the door to contain heat in the winter and the air-conditioned interior atmosphere in the summer. They are very effective and generally economical.

When special environments are required for the preservation of the stored merchandise, the systems are usually designed for the specific application. Refrigerated storage usually breaks down into two categories. The freezers are often at $-12°F$ and the refrigerators are at 32 or 50°F depending on the merchandise to be stored. These facilities are usually designed in the form of large insulated buildings within the main building, or as a separate facility built for the purpose. They are heavily insulated, equipped with special doors and safety devices, and are usually equipped with racks. Their refrigeration plants are independent of the HVAC systems of the rest of the distribution warehouse.

Another special-purpose segment of the distribution facility may be a "cooler" for storing produce or candy. These are usually air-conditioned to about 54°F by a separate unit. They too are usually insulated internal structures within the overall warehouse facility. In most cases they are partitioned off from the main warehouse with insulated panels and roof insulation.

Lighting

The lighting requirements of a distribution warehouse will vary with the functions to be performed and the types of handling and storage systems installed. Good and economical general lighting is essential, but each work area usually has special local requirements. In conventional warehouses it is customary to install either high-intensity roof-mounted flood type units (mercury halide or high-pressure sodium) or fluorescent fixtures in the ceiling. These deliver a general lighting level of about 20 foot candles at the working level. This is usually adequate for safe vehicle and pedestrian movements, fire defense, and security. The general lighting is then supplemented by additional fixtures as required, for high-traffic operations and work locations that involve the reading of documents. Work areas receive special treatment to suit their specific needs.

There are also those who say that no lighting is required in a fully automated warehouse. This is usually impractical from a safety and maintenance point of view, and fire lighting is usually required.

In order picking, shipping, receiving, and inspection areas, where documents and labels must be read, it is desirable to have 70 to 100 foot candles of light at the working level. When deep (24- and 36-ft) shelving is used in manual picking operations, it is often necessary to use cross-aisle lighting to allow light to penetrate the bins from the opposite side. In such cases (and often in multideck shelving systems), strip fluorescents are installed at the top of the shelving on both sides of the picking aisle.

In high-bay, narrow-aisle, turret truck storage operations, adequate and even lighting of the storage face is needed to assure safe fork penetration of pallets. At the same time, care must be taken to prevent high-intensity roof lighting from causing blinding glare in the most critical upper-level fork positioning operations. In such installations, diffusers can be installed on the high-intensity units, or aisle-centered fluorescents can be used to provide the best results.

In all cases where racks, shelves, or other storage furniture is in use, the lighting should be aligned with the aisles to be most effective. Lighting should be arranged to fit the layout and to suit the specific needs of each operation. Fixtures can be track-mounted to permit rearrangement as layout changes occur. Local lighting is also often required to supplement the general system. Examples are the special arm-mounted lamps that are used to light the interior of highway trailers during loading and unloading operations, the automobile-type headlights that are often mounted on lift truck masts to improve high-storage and deep-stack visibility, and the cab lighting on high order picking vehicles.

Lighting controls are another consideration in a warehouse. Lighting should be wired in overlapping segments to allow variable coverage and intensity without the expense or maintenance problems associated with variable-intensity switching. Most warehouses have large low-traffic areas that require high lighting only during input/output activity and when rewarehousing for space consolidation. In such cases, a low level of safety lighting can be installed, with separately wired and remotely switched supplementary zone lighting for use when activity requires more light. Switching can be controlled from the warehouse vehicles via radio frequency, infrared, or sonar tone. A garage door type of switch on each forklift truck can be coupled with a timer or a departure sensor. Motion or infrared detectors can also be used to turn on the bright lights for television security systems.

Exterior lighting is another key part of the system. If night operations are normal, truck yards and parking areas should be lighted for traffic safety and personnel security. Security lighting of the perimeter of the site and building is a good defense against burglars and vandals, particularly when used in conjunction with infrared motion detectors and television surveillance. The outdoor systems usually consist of pole- and roof-mounted floodlights. In addition decorative lighting is often used for aesthetic purposes, and it too enhances security.

Fire Defense

Fire defense is a major consideration in the design of a distribution warehouse. The OSHA Regulations, the local and national fire codes, and the insurance companies impose certain fire defense design standards on the industrial community. Compliance with the code of the National Fire Protection Association (NFPA) is required, and NFPA Bulletin 231C specifies the rules for warehouse fire defense systems.

In general sprinklers are required, and high bay storage must comply with special regulations. For example, any rack storage with combustible merchandise or packaging that exceeds 12 ft in height requires in-rack sprinklers, and floor storage of similar material over 15 ft high requires high-density ceiling sprinklers. There are other rules that must be applied in narrow-aisle, flammable, and large-area situations. There are specific codes concerning the water supplies and valving of the sprinkler systems, the escape routes and their markings, roof venting, fire curtains and fire walls, etc. These items must all be considered in the design of the facility, and it is best to consult a fire defense system specialist in order to assure compliance with the required codes.

Another factor in fire defense is the selection of the type of structural system to be used in building the facility. An all-steel structure does not have good fire survivability. In a hot fire, the steel will weaken and the building will collapse on the interior system and inventory, often knocking out the sprinkler system in the process. Prestressed, precast concrete structures are the most fire-resistant. The concrete structural members will spall in a fire but are not likely to collapse. This type of construction is also a better defense against sabotage or burglary in vulnerable locations.

As stated above, properly treated timber construction is also quite fire-resistant. Heavy or laminated timber structures are common in the northwest of the United States and in other locations. If properly sprinklered, this type of construction will char in a fire but is less likely to collapse than a steel structure. In all cases, the lack of a sprinkler system is an invitation to disaster.

In most urban jurisdictions, suitable fire water capacity can be connected from the city fire supply, and city hydrants can be installed adjacent to the site. However when this is not possible, insurance companies and fire codes require either a fire water tower, a ground tank and fire pumps, or a fire pond and pumps. The size of the water supply depends upon the size of the building and local code and insurance company requirements. In cold climates, freezing protection is also required.

Truck Docks and Truck Aprons

Truck docks, truck aprons, rail docks, and rail sidings, are the material handling interface between the distribution warehouse and the outside world. They are often the most active and difficult to manage areas of the operation. Industrywide, they are the most dangerous part of a warehouse. Most truck and rail docks experience high activity, with forklift trucks and other vehicles, random pedestrian traffic, and very-difficult-to-schedule carrier vehicle operations.

In cases where automated guided vehicle systems (AGVS) or towlines deliver goods to the shipping dock, the material flow pattern is easily organized because of the system's fixed geography and machine-paced activity. However, the primary scheduling factors in shipping operations are the customer order activity pattern and the shipper's ability (or lack of it) to schedule the arrival and loading of trucks. This situation makes flexibility a primary issue in the design of truck and rail shipping docks and their supporting truck aprons or rail sidings. The same issues are present in a reverse form in the design of receiving facilities. There, the work schedule and material flow pattern is dictated by the arrival rate of inbound vehicles.

Another factor that requires a flexible shipping and receiving dock design response is the variation in the sizes and dimensions of inbound trucks, trailers, and rail cars. Street or "straight" trucks will vary in length and width, with deck heights ranging from 24 to 60 in. Highway semitrailer bodies will vary in width from 96 to 102 in, in length from 20 to 45 ft, and in deck height from 36 to 60 in, or higher for container-carrying flatbed trailers. The truck docks must either be specialized to handle a type of vehicle or be flexible enough in their design to accommodate the majority of carrier equipment.

In the case of rail docks, freight cars vary in length from 40 to 90 ft and have a variety of door configurations. Cushion cars also exhibit instability when driving on and off with forklift trucks. For this reason it is almost impossible to space rail dock doors in a universally compatible arrangement. Fifty-foot spacing is most common on building face doors, and this forces the movement of car strings during loading and unloading. A more practical approach, particularly in new buildings and in cold climates, is the use of inside docks, for here car length and door spacing becomes a moot issue. Track-mounted and movable dock bridges or movable bridge plates are used for inside siding installations. Figure 20-1 shows a section through such a rail dock.

In the design of truck docks, the height variations can be met with a variety of designs. The rear wheels of the very low vehicles can be raised on ramps or blocks, or on a hydraulic lift. The ramps usually are not a satisfactory method and are used only in cases where a consistent vehicle mix is assured. The hydraulic lift provides more flexibility. In most cases, the deck heights of highway trailers range from a low of 48 to a high of 60 in, and permanently installed dock levelers can deal with this variation. When there is a great proportion of traffic with low "straight" trucks or over-the-road "low boys" with 36-in decks, specifically assigned docks can be equipped with raised outside ramps to bring the truck's deck level with the warehouse floor and within the range of the dock leveler.

In most cases, a dock height of 51 in will put the leveler in a median position. Most levelers range from 9 in below level to 12 in above the floor level of the warehouse. By designing the dock with a height of 48 in and a dock leveler as shown in Fig. 20-2, the full range of movable tandem trailers and trucks can be handled with a sloped apron. A well-located storm drain will minimize ice buildup and flooding. A weather seal and canopy can also be installed to protect both workers and cargo and to limit warehouse heat or air conditioning loss.

Modern truck docks are normally equipped with counterbalanced dock levelers

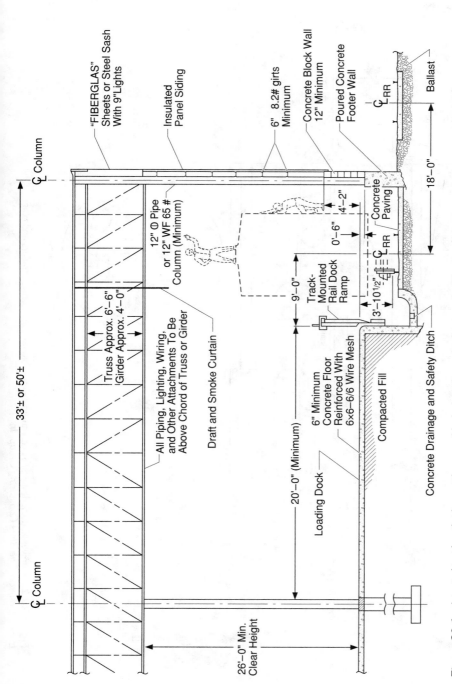

Figure 20-1. A typical inside rail siding, with a movable dock bridge and safety trench. (*Courtesy The Sims Consulting Group, Inc.*)

Ç Column

Ç Column

33'± or 50'±

"FIBERGLAS" Sheets or Steel Sash With 9"Lights

Insulated Panel Siding

6" 8.2# girts Minimum

Concrete Block Wall 12" Minimum

Poured Concrete Footer Wall

Ç RR

Ballast

Truss Approx. 6'–6" Girder Approx. 4'–0"

All Piping, Lighting, Wiring, and Other Attachments To Be Above Chord of Truss or Girder

Draft and Smoke Curtain

12" Ø Pipe or 12" WF 65 # Column (Minimum)

Concrete Paving

4'–2"

0'–6"

Ç RR

Track-Mounted Rail Dock Ramp

9'–0"

3'–10½"

18'–0"

20'–0" (Minimum)

Loading Dock

6" Minimum Concrete Floor Reinforced With 6×6–6/6 Wire Mesh

Compacted Fill

Concrete Drainage and Safety Ditch

26'–0" Min. Clear Height

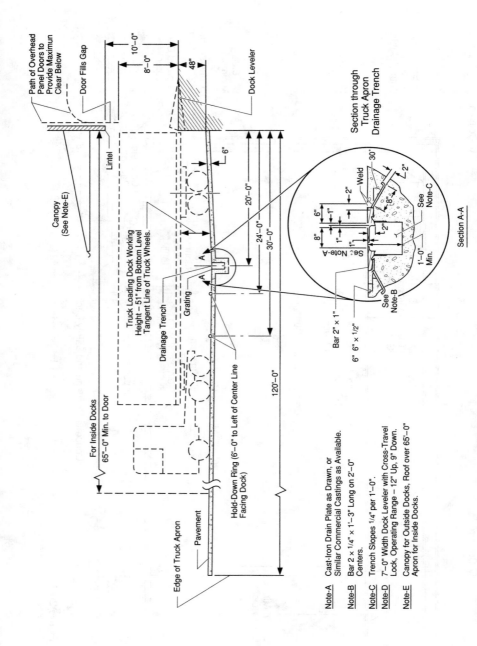

Figure 20-2. A universal dock design, to accommodate movable tandem highway trailers and other trucks. (*Courtesy The Sims Consulting Group, Inc.*)

Path of Overhead Panel Doors to Provide Maximun Clear Below

Door Fills Gap

Canopy (See Note-E)

Lintel

10'-0"

8'-0"

48"

Dock Leveler

Truck Loading Dock Working Height – 51" from Bottom Level Tangent Line of Truck Wheels.

Drainage Trench

Grating

6"

20'-0"

24'-0"

30'-0"

For Inside Docks 65'-0" Min. to Door

Hold-Down Ring (6'-0" to Left of Center Line Facing Dock)

120'-0"

Edge of Truck Apron

Pavement

Section through Truck Apron Drainage Trench

Weld

30°

2"

6"

1"

8"

8"

2"

1"

1"

See Note-C

See Note-A

See Note-B

1'-0" Min.

Section A-A

Bar 2" × 1"

6" 6" × 1/2"

Note-A Cast-Iron Drain Plate as Drawn, or Similar Commercial Castings as Available.

Note-B Bar 2 × 1/4" × 1'–3" Long on 2'–0" Centers.

Note-C Trench Slopes 1/4" per 1'–0".

Note-D 7'–0" Width Dock Leveler with Cross-Travel Lock, Operating Range – 12" Up, 9" Down.

Note-E Canopy for Outside Docks, Roof over 65'–0" Apron for Inside Docks.

20.14

and "dock locks" to provide for safe forklift loading and unloading of the trailers. The dock leveler usually has a built-in safety device to prevent it from dropping out of level if the truck moves out prematurely. The "dock lock" hooks onto the ICC bumper on the rear of the trailer to keep it in place during forklift entry and loading/unloading. Dock levelers are also installed with cross-travel locks to keep them at floor level when idle and to permit free vehicle movement on the dock when no highway trucks are present.

Another critical factor in the design of truck docks is the lateral spacing of the docks. Modern trailers are 102 in wide and 45 ft long. The whole tractor/trailer unit is often 65 ft long (and may be longer in the future if truckers have their wish). These dimensions, when coupled with the fact that the rear of a tractor/trailer unit turns at least 6 ft inside the track of the tractor, make close spacing both a hazardous and a labor- /time-costly design. In addition there is a need for space on the dock between the dock levelers for checkers, spare pallets, and often, computer terminals or bar code stations. When conveyor loading is combined with forklift loading, there is an additional need for space between docks for people and forklift truck movement. Depending on your pick requirements, center-to-center spacing of truck docks could be 15 ft or more. This will allow smooth working conditions on the dock, easier maneuvering of the trailers, and easier opening of trailer doors. If desired, it also allows space for stairs or ladders, and a man door between docks for driver entry to handle checking, driver loading, and tailgate delivery operations.

The truck apron or yard is another element of the system and building design that requires operational attention. The distance from the face of the dock to the nearest obstruction should be at least 120 ft, to allow single-swing spotting, pull-out operations, and yard-cross traffic. Aprons should also be laid out so that the driver can back into the spot in a reverse left turn to assure good maneuvering vision. Figure 20-3 shows a good dock spacing and truck apron layout.

Dock security is another design factor that must be considered. False shipments, pilferage, receiving dock theft, and many other security problems can develop on the truck docks. A cardinal rule is to be sure that shipper personnel control the outbound cargo and carefully check it before signing the bill of lading or loading the vehicle. In modern systems that use conveyor loading and forklift drive-on loading, this creates a cost-and-control problem by forcing the use of shipper loading personnel. This can sometimes be avoided, and carrier self loading can be used, if product is checked by shipper personnel or an automated bar-code-checking system is installed. The reverse is applicable to receiving. In both cases close control of outside personnel, control of freight, control of carrier vehicle traffic, and enough space to avoid congestion will aid in maintaining dock security.

Parking

Parking has become a major site planning issue in the design of warehouses, industrial facilities, commercial centers, and residential developments. Off-street parking is required in most communities and industrial parks. In some situations, limited land availability or the high cost of real estate has caused firms to build highrise parking garages for employees. In addition, industrial facilities need parking space for highway trailers and waiting trucks. In some cases the highrise garages are built

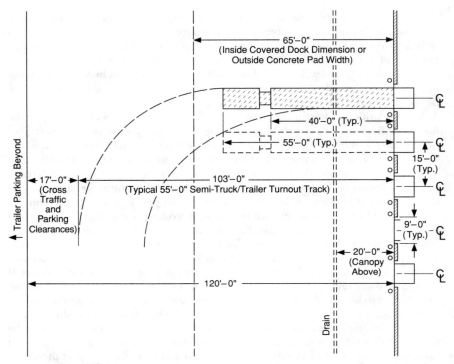

Figure 20-3. A flexible truck apron layout, with good truck dock spacing and adequate clearance for single-swing tractor-trailer spotting. (*Courtesy The Sims Consulting Group, Inc.*)

above the truck apron area, to make use of air rights and to conserve land. There are some rules of thumb that can be applied to the definition of parking requirements, but the problem is best solved by a common-sense application of traffic engineering and compliance with local building codes.

Whether the new plant (or modernized facility) is scheduled to operate on a one-, two-, or three-shift schedule, the formula for the minimum required number of employee parking spaces should be more conservative than predictive. In the case of a multishift operation with overlapping shift ending and starting times, employee parking spaces must be available for two shifts' cars. The required number of spaces must be defined on the basis of the predicted, fully staffed, work force head count. The finally defined parking lot capacity must be a function of the work force size, the shift schedules, the availability of public transportation, the demographics of the area in which the plant is located, and the rules or building codes enforced by the local government and/or industrial park management. The space per vehicle, roadway widths, highway access curb cuts, distances from buildings and adjacent highways, and traffic control methods are often spelled out in the local building codes or in the rules of the industrial park. In some cases the allowable visibility of the parking area from the street is also specified.

The configuration of the truck yard or apron was described in a previous paragraph. However, the relationship of the passenger car parking area to the entrance and exit of the truck yard is a critical traffic safety issue. If the plant is on a well-traveled road or highway, it is essential to provide a deceleration lane for both cars and trucks entering the plant site. It is also desirable to provide traffic control in the form of a stoplight at each exit for use during shift-change periods. The truck entry should be located "upstream" from the truck exit, and both the truck exit and entry curb cuts should be far enough "downstream" from the passenger car entry and exit to avoid the need to pass a truck when entering the parking lot or truck yard.

As a security and fire defense consideration, employees' cars should be parked no closer than 50 ft from the building walls or entrances. This will help to prevent pilferage and will assure adequate fire engine access. Employee parking should also be within the perimeter security fence of the plant site. Visitor parking can be in a limited area adjacent to the office entrance, but it should be on the far side of the entry road for the same security and fire access reasons.

Offices

Offices are an integral part of every warehousing and physical distribution facility. If the operation is a part of a manufacturing plant, the office requirements are usually limited to the supervision and documentation support of the warehousing operation. If it is a freestanding distribution facility or a public warehouse operation, the office requirements will expand to include general management, personnel administration, accounting, sales, and other management-support functions. For the purposes of this handbook, this commentary addresses only the offices required to conduct the operational business of the warehouse. This will include the documentation of receiving and inspection activities, the handling of stock location records, the processing of orders, the documentation of shipments, traffic management, security, labor control, and maintenance management.

The office requirements for these activities will differ sharply when comparing manual and computer-supported operations. In view of the prevalence of desktop and other small computers, it will be assumed herein that these operations are computer-supported, and space considerations are based on that assumption. Manual operations will usually require much more space.

The design of the warehouse management and administrative offices in a computer-based operation will depend upon the type of warehouse and the transaction rate of the system. Although there is a trend toward paperless transactions, and bar code data entry eliminates keystrokes on the computer, it is usually still necessary to enter bills of lading and other hard documents into the computer in receiving and shipping operations. Bar code stations at the shipping and receiving docks can also be used to wand bar codes from packages and documents to make direct data entries into the computer system. These stations usually are equipped with a computer terminal and printer to bring documents and files up on the screen and to produce working documents, bills of lading, and receipts. It is also necessary to handle paper for order picking activities even when the system is highly mechanized.

If the workload requires the capacity of a mainframe computer and multiple terminals to handle the posting of receiving documents and stock location data, the office probably will be laid out in "bull pen" fashion. If only a relatively few transactions are involved, a single high-capacity desktop computer may suffice. Office space requirements will therefore be a function of the transaction rate and the number of work stations needed to process the documents. Work station areas will vary from 36 to 100 sq ft per person, depending upon their arrangement and the type of furniture and equipment used.

In mechanized warehouses, there may also be a requirement for a central computer control facility. Such a facility may manage one or more automated storage/retrieval machines, a conveyor network, AGVS operations, order picking, and the flow of information through the system. The same control center may also house a dispatcher and include a two-way radio base station for forklift truck management and supervisory communications, plus a loudspeaker system for directing highway trucks in the yard and at the docks. The dispatcher should have direct visual window access to the truck apron, plus closed-circuit television surveillance of both the truck apron and the warehouse operations. This work area can also be the control center for the security system. In many cases these facilities are placed on a mezzanine above the shipping dock, with windows looking out on both the truck apron and the interior of the warehouse.

In addition to the documentation areas, most warehouses will have at least one private office for the warehouse manager, and often several for foremen or supervisors. There will also be a requirement for trucker access to the office personnel through a teller-type window, in order to handle transport documents. In many cases there will also be a dock-level or gate house control center, for security surveillance via television monitors. A typical dock-level warehouse office layout is shown in Figure 20-4.

In situations where there is a need for a great deal of clerical office space, or in a freestanding warehouse that has need for other management offices, it is common practice to place a mezzanine above the truck dock area. As stated above, the computer center and dispatcher may be housed on the mezzanine level. This is also a good location for the warehouse manager's office and for such employee service facilities as lunch rooms, locker rooms, showers, and conference or training facilities. Overhead clearances under the mezzanine can be reduced to approximately 15 ft without impairing the shipping and truckloading operation. Under current equal employment opportunity regulations, such an office requires an elevator for handicap access, and most fire codes require two exit stairwells to the main floor. Toilets must also be provided, in accordance with local building codes.

Maintenance

Maintenance is a major factor in the design of a warehouse. The building should be designed in a manner that minimizes maintenance requirements. However all structures will require care, and the floors are the most critical component of the building. In most warehousing operations, building maintenance is handled either by a central companywide plant engineering and maintenance department or by an outside contractor service. Floor maintenance must include periodic scrubbing, sealing, and restriping. In addition, cracks must be monitored and repaired. Janitor services can be either an in-house activity or a contracted operation.

The maintenance of lighting, heating, air conditioning, forklifts, conveyors,

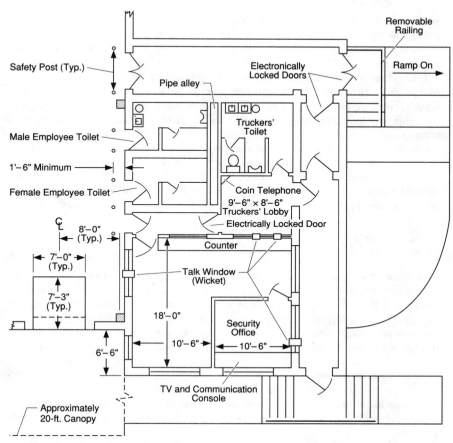

Figure 20-4. Typical warehouse office arrangement, with controlled trucker access and security surveillance. (*Courtesy The Sims Consulting Group, Inc.*)

AS/RS machines, and other materials handling machinery is usually managed by an in-house maintenance department within the warehouse organization. This arrangement requires a shop area and, if electric vehicles are used, a battery-charging facility. The battery-charging area must be properly ventilated and in compliance with OSHA regulations. There is also a need for fuel service, if internal combustion equipment is in use. This requires outside storage of propane and/or gasoline.

The extent of the maintenance operation is a matter of management policy. Total inside maintenance of mechanical and electrical equipment requires a skilled staff, extensive shop facilities, and spare parts inventories. Such an activity is not generally compatible with a freestanding warehouse or physical distribution operation. It may be a good practice in a warehouse that is a part of a manufacturing facility that already has extensive maintenance capabilities.

In a freestanding warehouse, the maintenance operation is usually confined to "first-echelon" maintenance. This would include fuel, oil changes, battery charging, preventive maintenance, troubleshooting, operating adjustments, tires, belts, and environmental control problems. Any major repairs, overhauls, breakdowns, or modifications would usually be handled under a vendor service contract. Backup machinery would be kept on hand or be available on rental from the vendor.

In any case it is desirable to establish a sound, and strongly enforced, preventive maintenance program. Vehicle and equipment operators should be trained to recognize, react to, and report, any malfunction in their equipment or any apparent building problem. This training should be a part of a strong safety training program. In addition regular inspections, prefailure parts replacement, and service records should be used to anticipate and prevent breakdowns. As a further defense against shutdowns, some firms overbuy the needed equipment and have a fully failsafe system based on the presence of onsite backup facilities. This is an expensive form of operational insurance, but it may be justified in some instances where long lead times are a problem when it comes to spare parts or service support.

Summary

The warehouse or physical distribution facility is the physical manifestation of marketing and distribution policy. It is a physical response to management's inventory policy and the marketing practices of the company or institution. Its design and system configuration must reflect management's objectives and policies. It must also comply with government regulations and community relations limitations. The design of the facility must meet the needs of the sales and shipment system in a manner that will satisfy customers and minimize operating costs. These operating costs include the amortization of the investment, maintenance of the plant, operation of the equipment, and utilization of labor. The adequacy and durability of the facility, its location and site arrangement, its equipment and maintenance, and the facility impact on employee morale and productivity are all factors in the profitable performance of the business.

Warehousing and distribution are all cost operations. Any savings are a direct improvement in profit, with no impact on product performance or production cost. However, inadequate facilities can generate nonproductive costs and unfavorably impact on customer service and marketing effectiveness. The distribution facility is a key factor in the successful performance of the enterprise!

21
Personnel Planning

Alexander Keeney, Jr.
Manager, Industrial Engineering
Random House, Inc.

Labor Standards

In order to plan for the staff of a distribution center, it is necessary to identify and establish standards for the tasks to be performed and the amount of time each task should take. This includes each and every function, from receiving to shipping. As the activities grow in size, the standards of a department or activity may multiply and become more complex, but certain standards are basic in each of the center's activities.

The distribution center can take on any of several generalized functions. It can distribute a single product to many outlet points. It can handle many different products to be moved to outlet points. It can combine products into new sales packages for final outlet sources, and it can fill direct customer orders. To carry out its purpose, there are 11 basic functions that must take place in the distribution center in order to maintain good management control. These identified functions are:

1. Receiving
2. Inspection
3. Inventory control
4. Storage
5. Replenishment
6. Servicing
7. Order picking

8. Checking

9. Packing and marking

10. Staging and consolidating

11. Shipping

While discussing the necessary record keeping in a distribution center, the text of this chapter will address the functions in terms of a manual system. The reader should keep in mind that capturing, recording, and transmitting data also can occur using an electronic keyboard as well as fixed and hand-held scanners.

If the suppliers that are shipping to the distribution center are not providing bar-coded data, then it is in the Receiving area that bar-coded labels must be created and applied to the containers or items. This action in Receiving assures us that the items traveling through and out of the distribution center can be identified and quantified at any internal function. The duties of the employees in each of the 11 basic functions are now discussed.

Functions of the Distribution Center

Receiving. The basic responsibility of the receiver is to unload incoming material, count the material, and record any overage, shortage, or damage on the receiving ticket and driver's copy of the freight bill. The receiver also records on a receiving form the name and address of the supplier, date, name of item received, part number, quantity received, purchase order shipped against, discrepancies in quantity, and/or notation of possible damage. Purchasing and Inventory Control receive documents of this receipt.

Typical of state-of-the-art receiving is the use of scannable bar code data labels (as shown in Fig. 21-1) on inbound products. If not already on the product, the label should be created in the Receiving area so that the container or pallet can be scanned as it travels though the distribution center.

Inspection. The purpose of the inspection is to determine if the product meets the specifications and drawing requirements of the purchase order. Documents are prepared by the inspector to notify Purchasing and Inventory Control as to the status of the material. Some businesses eliminate incoming warehouse inspection by having source inspection. However, a sample check of the inventory should still take place during order fulfillment to discover in-house damage. The degree of inspection is relative to the methods and frequency of handling in the distribution center. Another benchmark for determining where and how often to inspect is the input from your Customer Service department.

Inspection should be just a sampling of distribution center activity. If more frequent and in-depth inspection is found to be necessary, management must find new suppliers and/or find the activity or employee causing the defect.

Inventory Control. Materials are moved from the inspection area to one of two points: (1) the picking location (in the case of a picking outage), or (2) a storage location (i.e., a bin, shelf, or rack). To control the location and quantities of materials on hand, it is important that the responsibility for routing materials to the

Figure 21-1. A pallet-load bar code label used at a book distribution center. Label is applied by bindery supplier.

proper locations be assigned. This is a clerical function. It is executed by the manual mode of paper forms and pencil. Or, as in modern distribution centers, the product labels are scanned and the data transmitted by radio frequency (RF) to the computer.

Storage.   The physical act of moving materials from inspection and placing them in storage is generally a lift truck operator's function. In very small operations, a manual lift truck can be used for the horizontal move, the product then being hand-transferred from the pallet to the storage shelf.

If the work site is state-of-the-art, the product is scanned, the storage location's bar code is scanned, and the system confirms that the storage function has been executed.

Replenishment.   When distribution management assigns a special area for picking stock, it is necessary to move cartoned stock from general storage to the prime picking area. This is the replenishment function.

Servicing.   Some distribution centers must do something to the product received from a supplier before the product can be shipped. Those dealing in cigarettes and liquor must apply a state tax stamp to each unit of retail sale. Other scenarios call for packaging for sale two or more items from different suppliers into a sellable unit.

Order Picking.   With an invoice or customer order ticket, the order picker goes about selecting the items in the quantity requested and unitizing them in a container, on a pallet, or at a station. The most critical part of this function is the document on which the order is written. The document must be a legible copy; preferably a typed original, well spaced and of characters large enough to see under distribution center lighting.

Other means of order picking are basically electronic. An order number is keyed or scanned into a control system, and the picker is directed by an electronic voice (headset and microphone), or by an LCD display, at the desired SKU bin. The display indicates the quantity to be picked.

These paperless picking systems are easily 50 percent more efficient than the typical one-arm order picker (one hand does the picking while the other does nothing but hold the paperwork). These systems do impact the size of the order picking work force. They also provide the employer with an opportunity to utilize a disabled or handicapped person, a person who has the use of only one hand.

Checking.   Each order should be checked for accuracy of item, quantity, and condition. If experience dictates, a sampling checking plan can be put into effect. The level of sampling is determined by the incidence of damage or error found in house or reported by customers. The latter case excludes damage in transit due to abnormal handling. It is assumed that the product package has passed the National Safe Transit Test procedures.

Packing and Marking.   Less-than-full-carton quantities of products have to be packaged and packed for shipment. In some distribution operations, split-case handling is avoided by shipping the next full case if the order for a broken case lot is 50 percent or more of a carton, or by shipping short if the order for a broken case lot is less than 50 percent of a carton. This technique generally is practiced within the same firm, as when a central distributor ships stock to a regional distribution center. The marking or labeling of a container must contain the consignor, consignee, invoice number, purchase order, account number, quantity, and description. There are variations of this data, such as bar code labeling, industry marking practices, governmental marking requirements, and international symbology.

Staging and Consolidation.   This function is necessary for gathering together the various orders for a single customer. The orders may have entered the cycle at different times or, if entered into the cycle as a group, may have been held up within the cycle for several legitimate reasons. Orders also are staged by carriers that service different regions of the distribution area that the business serves.

The actual staging is executed by several methods. Some distribution centers will route cases to an accumulation line, then release the line to palletizing stations. In the case of small-size orders, the cases or cartons enter a sorting loop and are diverted to multiple palletizing stations.

Depending on the level of system sophistication, the sortation can either be very labor-intensive or a single employee can oversee the automatic sorter and automatic palletizer.

Shipping.   The actual loading of the carrier generally is accomplished by one of four methods or a combination thereof: hand-pallet truck; forklift truck; mobile containers, of the kind that are used in grocery and retail-drug distribution; and "bricklayering," i.e., hand-stacking cartons in a trailer or truck in much the same fashion as laying bricks one upon another when building a wall.

Defining Daily Routine Tasks

With the 11 basic distribution center functions well understood, the next step in establishing standards is to determine the tasks performed within a given function. Some are performed with a fair degree of frequency during any given work period or shift. Other tasks are performed only a few times per day or week. When establishing work standards for a given function, the frequently performed tasks should have a time value assigned, expressed as an amount of time per unit or cycle, or a number of units per hour. The infrequently performed duties can be summarized as a total amount of time per day or week. Such nonroutine tasks found in a warehouse could include:

- Obtaining supplies such as carton tape
- Totaling receiving reports
- Writing inspection summaries
- Replacing missing or damaged merchandise on order

As shown in Table 21-1, identifying the repetitive and nonrepetitive duties of each department enables department supervisors and distribution center management

Table 21-1 Repetitive and Nonrepetitive Tasks

Weekly Functions	
1. Receive 800 Pallets @ 0.05 hr/pallet	40.00
2. Receive operating supplies @ 1.0 hr/day	5.00
3. Move 800 pallets to Inspection Department @ 0.02 hr/pallet	16.00
4. Deliver operating supplies @ 1.0 hr/day	5.00
5. Take receiving bills to office @ 0.25 hr/day	1.25
6. Clean up work areas @ 0.25 hr/day	1.25
7. Obtain and deliver lift truck to Maintenance for service @ 0.25 hr/day	1.25
8. Obtain operating supplies @ 0.50 hr/wk	.50
Total	70.25

Normal Calculations

$$\frac{70.25 \text{ hr weekly workload}}{40 \text{ hr/wk/employee}} = 1.75 \text{ employees required}$$

Recommended Calculation

$$\frac{70.25 \text{ hr weekly workload}}{37.5 \text{ available hr/wk/employee}} = 1.88 \text{ employees required*}$$

*See "Documenting Nonproductive Activities" below.

to determine the approximate crew size or staffing requirement for each distribution function.

From such a basic summary, one can better manage people and time and evaluate the impact of any changes in procedure or work assignment. If you are in a situation in which employees can be assigned to departments as needed, it can be seen by the example that, if the function has two employees, one can work in another area for 9.75 hr (normal) during the week. Any change in procedure can be identified, and the impact noted. If freight bills are to be taken to the office more frequently, an employee's availability to another department will be reduced. If obtaining operating supplies is taking longer, it can highlight the need to investigate the cause and reschedule the trip to the supply center, if necessary.

Documenting Nonproductive Activities

In addition to having standards that define the tasks in each employee activity and the time needed to perform them, it is also important to know about and control employee activity that is not operations-oriented. It is surprising what an analysis can reveal of normal, justifiable actions that occur daily. Supervisors are responsible for a given number of employees. Management expects these employees to be productive during their 40 hr/wk, with reasonable allowances for fatigue, personal time, and uncontrollable delays in the work process. Yet there are legitimate daily occurrences that reduce the number of hours the employee is available for productive work. In establishing work standards, some managements use a 7.5-hr shift per worker. This recognizes the two-coffee-breaks system so popular in American industry, as well as a shift start-up and cleanup allowance. Expected productivity then is measured against the 7.5 hr of "productive time" per employee, and the crew size for the expected work to be produced is determined accordingly. The frequently made management error is to consider 800 hr of work to be done at the rate of 8 hr/employee/day. This calculation requires 100 employees. This is not a pragmatic approach to staffing an operation. More correctly, 800 hr of work to be done at 7.5 hr/employee indicates that 107 employees are required. This more nearly reflects the reality of the situation.

Table 21-2 illustrates a typical situation that occurs in industry. It would serve supervision and management well to analyze how employees legitimately spend time away from the job during the work shift. In the exhibit, there are 10 employees. Each is paid for 40 hr during the week being analyzed, except for Carter, who went home ill one day (36 hr). It is important to note that the supervisor does not have the employees available to work for the full 396 hr in the example.

Column 1 represents the clocked hours, which is the number of hours normally said to be available to do an assigned amount of work. It is the number of hours for which an employee is paid (excluding sick pay). Column 2 is the amount of time lost each 40-hr work week due to a 10-min start-up, two 10-min coffee breaks, and a 10-min cleanup time allowance. The allowed nonproductive time will vary with local practice.

Column 3 is the time an employee requires, from the moment work stops until it is resumed, for dispensary aid, be it a cut finger, fever, headache, dizziness, lift truck operator eye examination, or a company-required physical.

Column 4 represents time lost due to Personnel visits or programs. Column 5 concerns union business, which, depending on company practice, could be conducted on company time. Column 6 documents the amount of time employees temporarily are loaned to another department. Column 7 documents unmeasured work for a work assignment outside the normal duties of a worker. Column 8 documents no-fault lost time, during which one or several group members cease productive functions through no fault of their own, such as owing to a machine malfunction or a supervisor's instruction time. Column 9 represents the total of columns 2 through 8. Column 10 is the total amount of work theoretically assigned for this example and completed. Column 11 is the net amount of worker time available to do the work. Using the summary line for evaluating the group's activity, the gross percent effective to payroll is found by dividing column 10 by column 1. It indicates that the group was only 85.4 percent effective. The percent effective to availability is found by dividing column 10 by column 11. It indicates the group was 100.8 percent effective.

If managers and supervisors do not perform some sort of record keeping and have some standards to measure their performance against, it will be very easy to go astray in not recognizing employee efforts for what they are. Also, if nonproductive activities are not recorded, it will be difficult to spot trends in accident- or health-related incidents, excessive socializing when legitimately excused to visit other areas, or similar situations that affect the effective utilization of distribution center labor.

Establishing Labor Standards

Labor standards are important if one expects to have control of any given operation. Somewhere it has been said that one must measure to manage. Managerially speaking, one must have benchmarks to determine if progress is being made and

Table 21-2 Labor Utilization Index

Employee	Payroll hours (1)	Allowed nonproductive (2)	Aid station visits (3)	Personnel visits (4)	Union bus. (5)	Out of dept. (6)	Day work (7)	Loss time (8)	Total col. 2–8 (9)	Assign std. hr. (10)	Hr act. avail. (11)
Adams	40	2.5	.6						3.1	40.0	36.9
Brown	40	2.5				12.0			14.5	28.0	25.5
Carter	36	2.3	1.5	1.2			5.5		10.5	22.0	25.5
Davis	40	2.5			2.7				5.2	31.0	34.8
Ewell	40	2.5		.8					3.3	35.0	36.7
Fox	40	2.5	.2					.7	3.4	38.0	36.6
Grey	40	2.5	.2			4.0	2.0		8.7	31.5	31.3
Howe	40	2.5			.4				2.9	38.0	37.1
Inn	40	2.5						3.1	5.6	35.0	34.4
Joy	40	2.5	.5						3.0	40.0	37.0
Summary	396.0	24.8	3.0	2.0	3.1	16.0	7.5	3.8	60.2	338.5	335.8

Gross efficiency: Column 10 ÷ Column 1 = 85.4 percent

Net efficiency: Column 10 ÷ Column 11 = 100.8 percent

whether progress is being made at an acceptable rate. The benchmark must be consistent to be a valid reference of measurement. Labor standards are the benchmarks. They are determined or established based on a given sequence of events. First, management must establish the basic functions of distribution center activity. For each function, management must determine the duties to be performed and how they are to be performed. This includes such characteristics as:

1. Frequency of an action, such as once per stock keeping unit (SKU) or once per three SKUs or twice per SKU.

2. Degree of detail in performing a given duty. This could vary from tossing SKUs into totes to requiring the exact placement of the SKU into Cell #1 in the tote, or, in the case of paperwork, "print in block letters only."

3. Quality consciousness should be considered. Receiving functions require alertness to damaged incoming materials. A packer's standard may require a cursory examination of items being packaged for shipment.

4. Impositions of weight handling, and limitation of weight being handled by a person or machine. This can include volume limits and limits on the mass of an item. In many distribution activities there are SKUs that are within the prescribed weight limits of an individual's lifting range, but the mass of the SKU dictates that either two or more employees or powered equipment is necessary to lift it safely. For example, a 35-lb item may be packed in a carton $75 \times 75 \times 5$ in. This would indeed be difficult for one employee to manage.

Ergonomics has moved to the forefront. The National Safety Council and OSHA now are taking a closer look at the shape, weight, distance moved, and employee body positions involved in handling a given item, be it an SKU or a shipping container. To staff properly, you must become knowledgeable in the area of ergonomics.

Following the above characteristics, after the task has been described to management's satisfaction, it must be measured in terms of time to become a labor standard.

Labor Measurement

Labor measurement can be an excellent tool in controlling the costs of distribution. However the measurement must be acceptable and accurate, and the administration of the labor-measurement program must be within acceptable cost constraints. Before any further comment on distribution labor measurement, let us consider the environment of the work area relative to work measurement.

Work measurement began in the repetitive production environment. Consequently, emphasis was placed on very precise time measurements of highly repetitive tasks or actions. Tasks had to be identical to the activity units that were time-studied if one expected the same time values to apply. The industrial engineers who were the time-study observers would question an elemental time if it varied by 3 percent from the arithmetic means. It is very difficult to obtain this precision in warehousing activity and, for this reason, the industrial engineering "purist" avoided the warehouse and distribution centers as an area of practice.

Since the measured-work concept grew and flourished in the assembly area, it seems to have been tagged as a management tool for the production area only, and both labor and management avoided its use elsewhere. Education in business, economics, commerce, accounting, and industrial engineering focused the student's attention on production problem solving and control of direct costs (labor and material); indirect costs such as warehouses and distribution centers were ignored as areas in which traditional industrial engineering management techniques could be applied.

Measures of Distribution Productivity

In a survey conducted by this author, it was found that distribution center management is using several methods to measure productivity. The most common methods used are:

1. Cases per man-hour
2. Lines per man-hour
3. Pounds shipped
4. Lines per day
5. Orders per day
6. Dollar volume per day
7. Unit loads per hour
8. Hours actual versus hours standard

The first seven means of measurement are not very reliable, because too many variable factors affect an employee's performance. The weight, size, and shape of cases and the variability of these physical features (1) drastically affect the productivity of the worker. The impending move to more rigorous enforcement of the ergonomic aspects of materials handling either will increase the use of additional labor to help handle cases or result in a reduction of personnel through the use of mechanized or automated equipment. Lines per man-hour (2) does not reveal the volume per line (3), which is a significant factor. For example, a line item of 100 lb of steel is moved quickly and easily with a lift truck. However, moving 100 lb of feathers could be a time-consuming, voluminous job. Lines per day (4) and orders per day (5) similarly do not take into account the physical variables. Dollars per day (6) does not correlate with the physical energies expended. Any price changes would require a mathematical analysis to plot and compare past and current activity to establish a performance standard. Unit load per hour (7) also would be similar to (2), in which variables in the task go unrecognized.

The most constant labor measurement is obtained by setting a time standard on each stock keeping unit (SKU). The SKU is what the employee touches, moves, manipulates, inspects, packages, and ships. If it changes in physical or chemical composition, the labor standard should change. The labor standard also should change if there is a change in the method of working or in the environment in which the tasks are performed.

The hours actual versus hours standard system is the most effective means of measuring warehouse labor. Time values are developed for the various general elements of the tasks, and a sum value is assigned to each invoice or to a batch of job tickets. In establishing the time values, one cannot be an industrial engineering purist. While each act of picking a box of pencils, a box of ballpoint pens, and a box of felt-tip markers has a slightly different value, the warehouse industrial engineer should take the practical and realistic approach of establishing one value for all three items. The value could be based on average weight or on the most frequently occurring event. Hands-on experience in a particular environment should indicate the proper course of action. Time-studying the various activity functions is time-consuming and can be expensive, but the managerial control that results and the savings realized are worth the cost. With accurate measurement techniques, management can, with a high degree of accuracy:

1. Determine staffing levels for a given activity
2. Plan personnel changes well in advance of need
3. Budget payroll needs realistically and accurately, and eliminate generalizations for distribution center budgets
4. Develop long-range distribution center labor forecasts, based on long-range production and sales forecasts
5. Use work measurement in model simulation for analyzing, altering, or expanding site activity

Sources of Labor Standard Systems

The United States Department of Agriculture and the Department of Defense both have published basic standards for warehousing and the steps for establishing warehouse standard costs systems. Due to the functional environmental, equipment, and mission similarities, these government standards will be applicable to the distribution center environment. These data include elemental descriptions, basic time values, and allowances. These data along with other useful charts, formulae, and analytical forms can be obtained in a booklet entitled, *Digest of Warehouse Cost Calculations and Handling Standards.*[1]

For those interested in developing their own standards or gaining a working knowledge of applying work measurement to the distribution activity, there is a comprehensive dissertation in the *Handbook of Industrial Engineering.*[2] There are also several consulting firms that will accept a company's employees as students for two- and three-week accelerated courses or send their staff members on site to conduct an on-site program of time-study analysis and work-standards development.

Benefits of Labor Measurement

Once labor measurement is in effect, there are several benefits to be gained:

- Both the worker and supervisor should have a clear understanding of how long any task should take.
- Incidents that cause delays in meeting the standard can be noted, isolated, and corrected.

- Staffing requirements can be easily determined when man-hours are related to product activity.

- Analytical charting is easier when working in hours per unit or hours per 1000 units or units per hour.

- Management can predict, with reasonable accuracy, the consequences of changes in inventory loading, software, methods, or layouts.

A word of caution! The use of measured labor alone is not sufficient to judge changes in operational schemes. Seasonal peaks and valleys also must be reckoned with as legitimate and very influential characteristics of planning and evaluation. Management, in some cases, also must be aware of where a product is in its life-cycle to make judgments about its volume activity. A physically small SKU may not impact space requirements if it's rising or declining in product life-cycle. On the other hand, giant-screen TVs or similar-size SKUs will significantly impact space requirement and handling requirement.

Labor standards also must be prudently used by management and, especially, first-line supervisors. Labor measurement is a guide to what can be reasonably expected as a consistent daily effort of output. One must recognize that the work environment and the employee's personal psyche affect daily performance. Good employees have bad days and fall below the established standard. Employees will also accept the challenge and exceed or "beat" the standards with some frequency. Supervisors must learn to recognize a periodic versus a patterned decline in productivity. The work standard never must become a device whereby the supervisor enforces continuously higher achievement as a means of gaining management recognition. Productivity is increased and recognition is gained through improving the method, simplifying the process, or changing the layout. The cliché of "working smarter, not harder" applies. Management must lead workers to increase productivity intelligently, not threaten, bully, or deceive to obtain improved results.

Labor Standard Maintenance

To be a meaningful tool, labor measurement values must be kept current. In the dynamics of daily routine and the pressing nature of everyday business, the maintenance of time values often is forgotten. If job conditions change so that there is difficulty in meeting the standard, time value maintenance will be self-policing; there will be complaints. However, creeping changes may go unnoticed and unreported. The labor measurement system then becomes valueless and also can be costly.

An actual case involved a standard that was not reviewed in total for 25 years. The time values for various subassemblies were changed individually as methods and equipments were improved. However, the formulae for some major components were ignored. This resulted in the company's paying for more product than the shop actually produced.

Administration of Labor Measurement Systems

The administration costs of a labor measurement system are the second reason for a lack of work measurement in the distribution center environment. Sometimes it simply is not practical to undertake a program the benefits of which are exceeded by the cost of its administration. Operations are frequently so varied that a large pool of clerical help would be necessary to apply time values to each order or invoice. However, some manual systems have been developed wherein orders or invoices are identified by zones of like activity, and a time value is applied per frequency of occurrence in a particular zone. This helps to reduce administrative clerical labor. For example:

- Value A would be for picking all 24-count cartons of dry cereal. (Time value × number of cartons.)
- Value B would be for picking 24-count cartons of #303 cans of fruit, vegetables, and soups. (Time value × number of cartons.)

Computerized Administration of Standards.   The use of computers and computer-generated invoices or picking documents has opened the field of applying time values to the picking documents. It can be done in a fraction of a second by the computer. This eliminates the problem of excessive clerical help for a manual time value program. A computerized time value program requires an in-depth study of the order picking program so that the industrial engineer knows each basic function of picking. Then the elemental data have to be grouped in natural and logical order. The data must be kept as simple as possible. Variable elements of a like nature should be combined to keep the program formula simple. This is where the work measurement purist must give way to reality in order to have a workable and manageable program. A sufficient number of observations have to be made to be sure that what is observed is representative of the work being done over a long time period.

To computerize time values, a detailed breakdown of the time values is of the essence, but the most important consideration is to know how the computer identifies specific products. The computer logic must be understood thoroughly in order to organize time-study observations and develop standard data tables. If the computer has no way of recognizing a keg of nails, per se, or of differentiating between a keg of nails and a box of carpet tacks, there are significant problems ahead. The computer recognition of commodities must be categorized so that basic standards can be developed for like items. In one case, the problems may exist in weight per stock keeping unit to be handled, cubic volume to be handled, and the dexterity with which both weight and volume are handled. As weight and cube vary, the time value by category will vary. There are many ways to categorize products in computers. Be sure each category or sphere of activity is organized and identified logically, so that the programmed time values will be properly indexed and applied to the picking document.

In a particular case of computer-generated work standards, the computer customized the picking standards as each invoice was generated. There were four basic order picking concepts. As each invoice was being generated, the computer totaled the order by each picking concept and held these four totals in memory. The criteria of "picking concept by category" was determined by the total number of items per order and the total weight. Once volume and weight had been determined, the correct standard was selected from the memory and printed on the invoice. Such a technique saves many clerical hours, is relatively easy to maintain, and results in a standard tailored to each invoice.

Short Interval Scheduling

In addition to establishing work standards for traditionally indirect activities—warehouses, distribution centers, storerooms, receiving, and shipping—two additional tools are required to measure work effectively. The work must be scheduled, and all time must be accounted for during the shift.

Short interval scheduling (SIS) or a variation of this scheduling technique should be used to allow for close supervisory control. Twenty-minute batches of assigned work for each order picker keeps the supervisor current with orders picked and picking problems or time delays encountered. The problem may be people, documents, stockouts, or equipment. If these problems, as well as accomplishments, are reported on by each worker in 20-min intervals, the involved supervisor will be more aware of the work situation than most counterparts on other work sites. If work measurement is to be meaningful, management must act or react to that which affects measured work.

Computerized Control

Modern distribution centers and warehouses are being equipped with radio frequency (RF) systems, onboard computer terminals on forklifts, order-pick trucks, and even powered pallet jacks or "walkies." All receipts, inspections, storage, picking, packing, and shipping are being assisted and monitored by mobile and fixed terminals in conjunction with bar-coded products, activity charts, and bar-coded employee badges.

Employees clock on and off assignments and into and out of departments via bar-coded employee badges. A permanent chart of bar-coded activities is scanned to indicate "started picking," "completed," "shipped." Jobs are tracked through activity areas by scanning bar codes on the invoices as the job enters and exits the area.

At some distribution centers, employees function in a totally paperless environment. A computer-driven system lights up the SKU lanes or slots to be picked, and LCD numbers indicate the quantities. Voice systems also are on the market. The employee wears a headset consisting of earphone and microphone and verbalizes with the computer.

Supervision

The supervisor is the primary managerial contact with the worker. Generally, this is the level at which there is a set tone of conduct regarding hourly employees' attitudes toward both production and the company in general. The supervisor's personality, leadership capability, technical competence, attitude toward employees, comprehension of changing social conditions, awareness of currently developing situations, and constant focus on the future will determine his or her success. Distribution center supervision basically is the same as supervision in an assembly or production operation. The most important function is the proper utilization of people. This is brought about by the supervisor influencing the opinions, attitudes, and behavior of the workers to bring about optimum productivity. The only two areas in which distribution center supervision differs from supervision in the production and assembly environment are the technical knowledge peculiar to the distribution center environment and the ability to supervise employees who frequently are out of sight of the supervisor (spread throughout various storage and picking aisles).

Distribution centers vary in physical size and in the size of staff. Since this handbook is intended to cover all distribution centers, readers must keep in mind as they read the size of their own organization and its degree of development. Larger businesses generally have a human resources or personnel department that can assist in training and developing supervisors and provide help and guidance in the complex areas of labor relations, human behavioral science, and understanding and complying with various employment regulations and laws.

The state-of-the-art of distribution centers varies from a totally manual environment to sophisticated paperless systems using bar codes, laser scanners, radio frequency real-time control, and worldclass software programs. The degree of mechanization and/or automation will have a bearing on the size of the operating staff. It also will impact the degree of knowledge and control at the supervisor's fingertips.

Dynamics of Supervision. The position of supervisor has changed dramatically during the twentieth century. The age of the authoritarian supervisor has passed. Modern supervisors must execute through good leadership. Those chosen to be supervisors must continue to develop leadership skills. Occupying a position of authority does give one authority, but does not make one a leader. Leadership skills must be learned and developed, and the development is ongoing. The dynamics of the work force require changing managerial attitudes. Supervisors should take advantage of any supervisory, labor relations, human relations, industrial psychology, or like programs being offered by the company, community, and four-year colleges, industrial management clubs, or technical societies. Even degreed supervisors should take courses in the above to reinforce and remain current with concepts and trends in these areas. The relationship that develops between the supervisor and work force is most critical. This relationship frequently determines if there will be an adversarial "we-they" attitude or a harmonious "we-are-one" attitude. The worker and company are interdependent on each other. The company cannot function without employees, and employees cannot achieve economic goals without an employer. Working together in a harmonious atmosphere is what the supervisor must establish as a general goal.

Good supervision is a learned skill. The subject is very broad and has much depth. If a supervisor intends to progress through the ranks of management, the development of leadership skills is very important. The further one progresses into middle management, the more one needs to know how to accomplish company goals through the leadership of people.

Supervisory Responsibilities. A supervisor is responsible for knowing, understanding, and working with a variety of tasks, situations, and problems. The following is a list of duties, responsibilities, and concerns that a supervisor faces either daily or at some less frequent interval.

Planning. This includes setting present and future goals and establishing procedures and policies to meet them. In some organizations, a Production Control function sets the daily production goal; in other organizations, the supervisor must do this.

Organizing.   This involves assigning workers to tasks. Decisions have to be made that best utilize individual talents to achieve the goals of the group, department, and company. If you do not have a production standard in place, the supervisor must determine the crew size of each function that is performed.

Staffing.   This includes selecting and training workers. Some businesses have a human relations department to assist in recruiting, selecting, and training workers. In less structured organizations, a supervisor may be responsible for recruiting workers. This is one of the areas in which the responsible supervisor must be aware of all the laws and regulations that govern the acts of the employer. The text of a help-wanted ad could be in violation of a law or regulation regarding discrimination as to age, sex, and/or physical ability. The employment application form may be in violation of law. For example, "date of birth" is a legitimate piece of employment information after a person is hired. However, on an employment application, it is considered to be age discrimination unless there is a bona fide reason for asking; e.g., when the company doubts the majority age of the applicant in reference to child labor laws or for valid insurance consideration.

Directing.   This includes the daily supervision of employees, as well as the providing of needed training to individuals or groups.

Controlling.   This involves determining the priorities of the work tasks to accomplish the goals.

Technical Competence.   This is the ability to operate the machinery and comprehend the operations and processes of the department.

Developing Employee Loyalty.   This involves creating an atmosphere of trust between the workers and company. Create a "we-are-one" outlook. Earn the respect and approval of the employees by being firm but fair, being worthy of their trust, and helping them as well as allowing them to help you.

Praising Good Work.   Constructively criticize errors. Praise is a public acclamation; criticism is personal and private.

Providing Opportunities.   Give employees a chance to function with a minimum of supervision. However, be able to recognize and give close support to those who need it and who seek it out.

Building Morale.   Help develop your employees' attitude or frame of mind, be it toward the work task or the company.

Discipline.   Be fair, firm, and keep a record of disciplinary actions that is signed by the employee and, if represented, by the shop steward.

Drugs and Alcohol.   Be able to identify the problem and handle it in accordance with company policy.

Unionism.   If the workers are under contract, be sure you know and understand the contract. Check and be sure that you are interpreting it in the same manner as other members of management.

Motivation.   Understand what motivates employees to produce, and how motivational factors will fluctuate.

Off-the-Job Influence.   Be able to recognize, understand, and deal with nonwork factors that influence production, such as employee problems with finances, health, marriage, illness of other family members, children's welfare, behavior, well-being, and similar categories that worry people. You are not expected to counsel in these areas, but by all means recognize that these factors affect employee attitude and performance and be ready to recommend that your human resources personnel talk with the employee.

Absenteeism.   Learn its causes and the corrective actions to take.

Adjusting to a Changing Work Force.   Work forces change for many reasons, and the supervisor must be aware of these changes and respond accordingly. Laws and regulations, as well as population mobility and immigration, can affect a work force. As the makeup of the work force changes, the supervisor must come to understand the needs, desires, and social nature of the emerging majority of workers in order to maintain the necessary leadership skills. The work force may change with regard to age, sex, race, ethnic origin, and education.

Handling Grievances.   Be it a union or nonunion shop, the supervisor must learn how to handle an employee grievance. The nature of the grievance may be such that it needs to be resolved at a higher level.

Grievance decisions, like disciplinary decisions, should be made only after the supervisor has had ample time to reflect on the subject and detach himself or herself from the emotions of the situation.

Budgeting.   Be aware of operating costs and function within the established cost limits, keeping track of and reporting to higher management those that interfere with cost containment.

Quality.   Meet the standards of performance established for the task.

Accident Prevention and Safety.   Identify practices and conditions that could lead to accidents. Thoroughly investigate the circumstances of any accident, recording facts and not conjecture. Be an example; be safety-conscious.

Terminations.   A properly handled termination can be beneficial to both the employer and employee. It should be done with an explanation of the reason(s) for termination, and only after the emotions of the moment have subsided and the situation has been clearly thought out.

Preventing Theft.   The distribution center environment, with its availability of finished goods, makes it a prime area for theft. The supervisor here must be more aware of theft possibilities than supervisors in areas where the product is of little or no value to potential thieves.

Communications.   Frequently, the art of listening and reading body language is emphasized as a way of improving communications. These are beneficial techniques. However, communications frequently are carried on by telephone and/or memo. The person originating the communication already knows the problem and circumstances. The difficulty is in conveying this knowledge to another party, being able to have another person visualize and comprehend what you already know. Using proper shop terminology and being specific is an effective aid to good communications.

Laws and Regulations Important in Supervision.   Supervisors in small distribution centers generally do not have the staff support found in larger firms. Consequently, they personally must gain a working knowledge of laws and regulations affecting employment. There are at least 16 areas of concern:

1. State employer's liability and compensation act

2. Unemployment insurance

3. Social Security

4. State old-age and assistance programs

5. Fair Labor Standards Act

6. Acts governing the employment of females and minors

7. Walsh-Healy Act

8. Taft-Hartley Act

9. Veteran's Reemployment Rights Act

10. Equal Employment Opportunity Commission

11. Vocational Rehabilitation Act (governs employment of the disabled)

12. Civil Rights Act

13. Occupational Safety and Health (OSHA)

14. State-level OSHA

15. Employee Retirement Income Security Act (ERISA)

16. The Americans with Disabilities Act

Basic Knowledge Requirements.   Supervisors who function without staff services also should expand their background to include a functional knowledge of methods analysis, work simplifications, building layout, equipment evaluation techniques, space utilization analysis, and materials handling principles.

Modern-day supervisors need a very broad background to meet all the responsibilities of the position. Continuing education in the various categories of supervisory duties and responsibilities is necessary to keep skills current.

Personnel.   The personnel or human resources department is a highly developed staff function that handles many facets of a distribution center, as well as other types of businesses. This section deals only with those subjects that pertain especially to distribution centers.

Safety.   A safety program should be part of the operation, and the personnel department either should spearhead the program or actively monitor and guide the distribution center management in this area.

Lift Truck Operator Training.   By OSHA regulations, only trained and authorized operators shall be permitted to operate powered industrial vehicles. Source material can be obtained from the published OSHA regulations and ANSI B56.1.[3] A complete training and testing program, including slides, test-course layout, and reference materials, can be purchased from the Materials Handling and Management Society (MHMS).[4] Lift truck manufacturers also have been a source of these programs. Industrial truck operator training is important. Remember, possession of a motor vehicle driver's license does not qualify an employee as a powered industrial truck operator. The training section of the personnel department should coordinate this program.

Physical Examinations.   Personnel also should arrange for periodic examinations of powered industrial truck and crane operators. Good natural or corrected vision, as well as good depth perception, are important. Good hearing also is necessary, especially for crane operators who use a system that combines audible communication and visual signals.

Training.   Personnel may be responsible for employee training. For example, employees will need training when converting from a paper-and-pencil transaction system to an on-line or microcomputer system of record keeping, or from mechanical lift truck operation to those using onboard microprocessors.

Testing.   Lift truck operators must be able to read load tickets, move tickets, and shelf or pallet locations. They must be able to read and comprehend the address system used in a distribution system. The personnel department should establish a battery of tests to evaluate candidates for distribution center positions.

Unions

People are very conscious of unions and union activity but, surprisingly, only about 15 to 20 percent of the industrial work force in the United States is union-represented. Employees' attitudes concerning unions vary geographically as well as demographically (e.g., urban versus rural, skilled versus unskilled workers). Probably the greatest influence concerning unions is whether the employees see themselves in a "we-are-one" environment with the employer or in a "we-they" situation.

Actions during Union Organizing.   If the work place is nonunion and there is an indication that there is organizing activity taking place, management quickly should obtain the services of a professional specialist or labor lawyer for advice and direction. There are laws and rulings that specifically deal with the allowed and nonallowed activities of management, the employees, and the organizing union during the organizing period. Supervisors and managers should refrain from any comment or opinion on unions or organizing activity until professional advice has been obtained by the company. The National Labor Relations Board has very specific guidelines as to what and how company representatives, managers, and supervisors may comment on, or whether they may answer employee questions.

Labor law is a very complex subject, and negotiations should not be undertaken by nonprofessionals. Management that has had proper counsel should be able to properly advise its employees and answer their questions concerning an organizing campaign. It is essential to have professional advice in such a critical matter and to have it early.

If the distribution center is functioning under a union contract, it is important for management to remember that all management rights and policies stand, except as limited or prohibited in the contract. Actions and expectations are governed by a specific contract. What happens in labor relations at other businesses may be noteworthy, but each company's obligations and rights are established in its own contract. What was done under one labor contract may be entirely inapplicable to another situation.

Discipline in a Union Environment.   Management—especially first-line supervisors—should be trained. This training in dealing with disciplinary procedures also should be frequently reviewed. Such acts as fighting, drinking, drug use, gambling, stealing, and refusing a legitimate order require immediate supervisory action. It is important that this action be swift and correct, but it is just as important not to overreact. When possible, the supervisor should allow for tempers to cool before making a disciplinary decision. Cooling a temper can be as simple as going to the personnel manager or to the next echelon of management to discuss the situation and the intended disciplinary action. A rash action can be detrimental to the morale of the department if there is a "we-they" attitude and the supervisor has to back down from an impulsive decision. Such incidents contribute to the polarization of attitudes.

Probably the most frequent union situation a supervisor will deal with is a grievance. There are several steps or levels a grievance can travel through, and there is the potential for the grievance to be resolved at any of those levels. The first step is an informal one-on-one discussion in which a represented employee cites to the supervisor what is believed to be a violation of the existing labor agreement. The supervisor explains to the worker his or her understanding of the administration of the contract. If the disagreement cannot be resolved, a process as spelled out by the contract begins, whereby different levels of management and union officers attempt to resolve the issue. The contract frequently provides that, if an issue cannot be resolved between the parties of the contract, the issue is submitted to arbitration for a third party determination of a solution.

Arbitration is expensive, and both parties share the expense of the arbitrator's fee. It does bring an outsider's view into a situation that is really the business of two parties. Precedent has very little to do with an arbitrator's decision. Each case is evaluated independently based on the contract and included agreements. Even though one case may very closely parallel a previous case, the decision in the former may not be the same.

Labor law is a field unto itself and differs from other law. *Criminal law* is based on guilt beyond a reasonable doubt. *Tort law* is based on the preponderance of evidence. Labor law is based on contract and the intent of the parties.

Management and supervision should take advantage of every opportunity to improve their knowledge and understanding of unions and labor relations. As mentioned before, management needs labor to be able to engage in economic activity, and labor needs business in order to realize its monetary goals. We should strive to bring about an atmosphere in which both parties can achieve their goals to their mutual benefit.

Incentive Systems

Incentive systems can be utilized effectively in distribution centers when customized to the conditions of the distribution center environment. The incentive system is a means of rewarding increased skill and effort with increased pay. Traditionally, the incentive system has been based solely on employee skill and effort. To earn incentive pay, the employee has to expend more energy in performing the task, become more skillful, utilize time better during the shift, and develop better personal methods (workers are generally entitled to the benefits of their own methods improvements, unless they are shared through the suggestion system).

In production operations, the repetitive nature of the work contributes to the justification of personal incentive programs. The implementation and administration of individual incentive programs has been profitable. However the diversification of work, the broad base used to establish standards in a distribution center, plus the costs of administering such a program, make an individual incentive program very difficult. In such a situation, group incentive is the more practical approach.

Before any incentive system is placed into operation, there should be a firm commitment by management to back the plan and follow through with the administration of the program. The plan should be explained thoroughly to the worker, along with the benefits that are to be realized by both management and the worker. The explanation should cover the effects on the system when new methods, new equipment, and/or new products enter the picture.

This differs from management-directed work simplification, acquisition of technically advanced machinery, changes in product design, changes in shop and workplace layout, and changes in tooling that affect productivity potential. In these cases, benefits generally accrue to the employer and constitute a methods change.

Once a new level of productivity has been achieved, it is expected to be maintained and the economic benefits permanently shared between employees and employer. From the beginning of the twentieth century, there have been about 10 popular incentive plans that centered around individual skill and effort. These plans have all but passed away. The three most popular productivity plans are the Scanlon Plan, the Rucher Plan, and IMPROSHARE (IMproved PROductivity through SHARing).[5] These plans provide an incentive to improve productivity, from which both the employees and employers gain. Rather than measure the results of individual skill and effort, the work force is evaluated as one. The gains are derived more from the permanent group improvements than from fluctuating individual skill and effort improvements. Hence the improvement in productivity is more constant.

Developing an incentive system for a particular distribution center should be done by people with expertise in the field. It is necessary to analyze the work site and attitude of the employees, and develop what is best suited to the type of operation under consideration.

Hand in hand with a productivity program, managers and supervisors must be aware of *product quality*, the *timeliness* of each order delivery, and the control of *cost*, if they are to accomplish their goal of keeping the distribution center's customers satisfied. The framework of a distribution center productivity measurement system should include factors to evaluate timeliness of order filled, percentage of each order filled, handling damage versus shipping damage, and whether these goals are being achieved within the acceptable cost range. It is easy to excel in one area at the expense of the other one or two goals.

In today's distribution center, personnel must be able to respond to the emerging demand for "quick pick" or "rapid reorder," and do so within the time, quality, and cost restraints of good business.

References

1. Out of print, but copies may be obtained by contacting Leslie Harps, Silver Spring, MD, 301-585-0730.

2. Gavriel Salvendy, ed., *Handbook of Industrial Engineering*, 2d ed., John Wiley, New York, 1992.

3. American National Standards Institute, 345 East 47th Street, New York, NY 10017.

4. Materials Handling and Management Society, 8720 Red Oak Blvd., Suite 224, Charlotte, NC 28217.

5. IMPROSHARE was developed by Mitchell Fein, New Rochelle, NY. For more information contact: Industrial Engineering and Management Press, Institute of Industrial Engineers, 25 Technology Park, Norcross, GA 30092.

22

Warehouse Operations

Edward H. Frazelle
Director, The Logistics Institute,
Georgia Institute of Technology

James M. Apple, Jr.
Director, Distribution Design Institute

The recently completed 1992 Warehousing Education and Research Council's annual conference was titled, "Meeting Increased Demands." It is no wonder!

The just-in-time operating philosophy has moved from manufacturing to distribution. Where it used to be sufficient to ship 100 units of a product on a Monday to complete a week's supply, today we must ship 20 units on each day of the week. The same amount of material is shipped, but there are five times as many transactions.

Quick response programs have reduced the amount of time allowed to respond to customer demands. Very quickly the standard for order cycle time is becoming same-day or overnight shipment. The compressed time schedules limit the available strategies for productivity improvement, and place increased importance on the functionality and capacity of warehouse control and material handling systems.

The quest for quality has also moved from manufacturing into warehousing and distribution. As a result, the standards for accuracy performance have increased dramatically. Today, the average shipping accuracy in U.S. warehouses is about 99 percent. However, the Japanese standard of 1 error per 10,000 shipments is rapidly becoming the acceptable standard.

A renewed emphasis on customer service has increased the number and variety of value-added services in the warehouse. The extra services may include kitting, special packaging, label application, etc. For example, a large fine-paper distributor counts and packages individual sheets of paper for overnight shipment. A large discount retailer requires vendors to provide slipsheets between each layer of cases on a pallet to facilitate internal distribution.

Increased emphasis on customer service and evolving consumer demand patterns in the United States have also increased the number of unique items in a typical warehouse or distribution center. The result, SKU proliferation, is perhaps best illustrated in the beverage industry. Not many years ago the beverage aisle in a typical grocery store offered two or three flavors in 12-oz bottles in six-packs. Today the typical beverage aisle offers colas (regular and diet, caffeinated and non), clear drinks, and fruit-flavored drinks in 6-, 12-, and 24-pack glass and plastic bottles and cans and 1-, 2-, and 3-liter bottles.

Finally, an increased concern with the preservation of the environment, the conservation of natural resources, and human safety have brought more stringent government regulations into the design and management of warehousing operations.

The traditional response to increasing demands is to acquire additional resources. In the warehouse those resources include people, equipment, and space. Unfortunately, those resources may be difficult to obtain and maintain. Before the recent recession, economic forecasts identified a coming labor shortage. As the economy recovers, we will again begin to experience the effects of the labor shortage. In addition, we will have to adjust to a work force characterized by advancing age, minority and non-English-speaking demographics, and declining technical skills. Also, increased safety standards brought on by OSHA and the Americans with Disabilities Act will make managing large work forces increasingly difficult. New standards for work force safety and composition, through OSHA's lifting standards and the Americans with Disabilities Act, also make it difficult to rely on an increased work force as a way to address the increased demands on warehousing operations.

When labor is not the answer, we typically turn to mechanization and automation as a means to address increasing demands. Unfortunately, our history of applying high technology in warehousing operations as a substitute for labor has not been distinguished. In many cases we have over-relied on high technology as a substitute for labor problems. In addition, high levels of technology are becoming more difficult to justify as capital becomes more restrictive, as downsizing becomes more prevalent, as mergers, acquisitions, and the introduction of new competitors make it increasingly difficult to forecast the future.

In the face of rapidly increasing demands on warehouse operations, and without a reliable pool of additional resources to turn to, the planning and management of today's warehousing operations is very difficult. To cope, we must turn to simplification and process-improvement as a means of managing warehouses and distribution centers. Toward that end, this chapter is meant to serve as a guide for warehouse operations improvement through the application of best-practice procedures and available material handling systems for warehousing operations. We begin with an introduction to the missions of the warehouse. One way to reengineer warehousing operations is to justify each warehouse function and handling step relative to the mission of the warehouse. If a function is not clearly serving the warehouse mission, it should be eliminated. Likewise, one or more functions may need to be added to bring the warehouse operations more closely in line with the mission of the warehouse. For example, to improve response time within the warehouse, a crossdocking function may need to be included. We then turn our attention to individual functions and activities within the warehouse. In the introduction we introduce each function and describe its objective. Then each function is described in detail, and best-practice principles and systems for executing each function are defined. We conclude with a look at the next-generation warehouse.

Comprehensive coverage of the topic of warehousing operations should, and does, fill entire books. Necessarily, this chapter serves as an overview of warehousing operations. Other chapters in this section (Part 3) of the handbook cover specific warehouse operations in more detail.

Missions of a Warehouse

In a distribution network, a warehouse may meet any of the following requirements:

1. It may hold inventory that is used to balance and buffer the variation between production schedules and demand. For this purpose the warehouse is usually located near the point of manufacture, and may be characterized by the flow of full pallets in and full pallets out, assuming that product size and volume warrant pallet-sized loads. A warehouse serving only this function may have demands ranging from monthly to quarterly replenishment of stock to the next level of distribution.

2. A warehouse may be used to accumulate and consolidate products from various points of manufacture within a single firm, or from several firms, for combined shipment to common customers. Such a warehouse may be located central to either the production locations or the customer base. Product movement may be typified by full pallets in and full cases out. The facility is typically responding to regular weekly or monthly orders.

3. Warehouses may be distributed in the field, in order to shorten transportation distances and thereby permit rapid response to customer demand. Frequently single items are picked, and the same item may be shipped to the customer every day.

Figure 22-1 illustrates warehouses performing these functions in a total distribution network. Unfortunately, in many of today's networks, a single item will pass in and out of a warehouse serving each of these functions between the point of manufacture and the customer. When feasible, two or more missions should be combined in the same warehousing operation. Current changes in the availability and cost of transportation options make the combination possible for many products. In particular, small high-value items with unpredictable demand are frequently shipped worldwide from a single source, using overnight delivery services.

Functions within the Warehouse

Although it is easy to think of a warehouse as being dominated by product storage, there are many activities that occur as part of the process of getting material into and out of the warehouse. Most warehouses engage in these activities:

1. Receiving
2. Prepackaging (optional)
3. Putaway
4. Storage

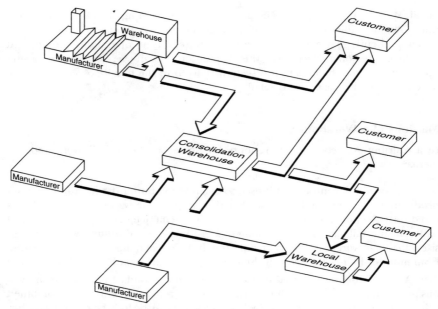

Figure 22-1. Warehouse roles within the distribution network.

5. Order picking
6. Packaging and/or pricing (optional)
7. Sortation and/or accumulation
8. Packing and shipping

These functions may be defined briefly as follows.

   1. *Receiving* is the collection of activities involved in (a) the orderly receipt of all materials coming into the warehouse, (b) providing the assurance that the quantity and quality of such materials are as ordered, and (c) disbursing materials to storage or to other organizational functions requiring them.

   2. *Prepackaging* is performed in a warehouse when products are received in bulk from a supplier and subsequently packaged singly, in merchandisable quantities, or in combinations with other parts to form kits or assortments. An entire receipt of merchandise may be processed at once, or a portion may be held in bulk form to be processed later. This may be done when packaging greatly increases the storage-cube requirements or when a part is common to several kits or assortments.

   3. *Putaway* is the act of placing merchandise in storage. It includes both a transportation and a placement component.

   4. *Storage* is the physical containment of merchandise while it is awaiting a demand. The form of storage will depend on the size and quantity of the items in inventory and the handling characteristics of the product or its container.

5. *Order picking* is the process of removing items from storage to meet a specific demand. It represents the basic service that the warehouse provides for the customer, and is the function around which most warehouse designs are based.

6. *Packaging and/or pricing* may be done as an optional step after the picking process. As in the prepackaging function, individual items or assortments are boxed for more convenient use. Waiting until after picking to perform these functions has the advantage of providing more flexibility in the use of on-hand inventory. Individual items are available for use in any of the packaging configurations right up to the time of need. Pricing is current at the time of sale. Prepricing at manufacture or receipt into the warehouse inevitably leads to some repricing activity, as price lists are changed while merchandise sits in inventory. Picking tickets and price stickers are sometimes combined into a single document.

7. *Sortation* of batch picks into individual orders, and *accumulation* of distributed picks into orders, must be done when an order has more than one item and the accumulation is not done as the picks are made.

8. *Packing and shipping* may include the following tasks:

- Checking orders for completeness
- Packaging of merchandise in an appropriate shipping container
- Preparation of shipping documents, including packing list, address label, and bill of lading
- Weighing of order to determine shipping charges
- Accumulation of orders by outbound carrier
- Loading trucks (in many instances, this is a carrier's responsibility)

For the purposes of this brief chapter we include, in receiving, those activities described above as receiving, prepackaging, and putaway; in order picking, those activities described above as order picking, packaging, and sortation/accumulation; and in shipping, those activities described as packing and shipping. Storage operations and systems are described in Chapter 18 in this handbook. Receiving and shipping systems and operations are described in detail in Chapter 17. Hence, the emphasis in this chapter is on order picking operations.

Receiving Operations

The primary objectives of a receiving system are (1) safe and efficient unloading of carriers, (2) prompt and accurate processing of receipts, (3) accurate maintenance of records and activities, and (4) rapid disbursal of receipts to appropriate locations for subsequent use, and access to material as soon as possible for order filling.

We now list the primary functions of a typical receiving system. Concentration on an efficient procedure to fulfill each of these functions will accomplish the objectives of a receiving system.

1. Analysis of documents for planning purposes, including:

- Determining approximate dates of arrival in terms of type and quantity of material
- Scheduling carrier arrivals as much as possible

- Furnishing carrier or incoming traffic controller with spotting information
- Preplanning temporary storage locations

2. Unloading carriers, and clearing the bill of lading or carrier responsibility
3. Unpacking goods as necessary
4. Identifying and sorting goods
5. Checking receipts against packing slips
6. Marking records to call attention to unusual actions to be taken
7. Recording receipts on receiving slip or equivalent
8. Noting overages, shortages, and damaged goods
9. Disbursing goods received to appropriate location for subsequent use
10. Maintaining adequate and accurate records of all receiving activities

Receiving Principles

The efficient completion of each of the tasks just enumerated depends on the successful application of the following best-practice operating principles. The principles are meant to serve as guidelines for streamlining receiving operations. They are intended to simplify the flow of material through the receiving process, and to ensure that the minimum work content is required. In order, they are as follows.

1. *Don't receive.* For some materials, the best receiving is no receiving. Often *drop shipping*—having the vendor ship to the customer directly—can save the time and labor associated with receiving and shipping. Large, bulky items lend themselves to drop shipping. An example is a large camp and sportswear mail-order distributor, drop-shipping canoes and large tents.

2. *Prereceive.* The rationale for staging at the receiving dock, the most time- and space-intensive activity in the receiving function, is often the need to hold the material for location assignment, product identification, etc. This information often can be captured ahead of time by having it communicated by the vendor at the time of shipment, via EDI link or fax notification. In some cases, the information describing an inbound load can be captured on a *smart card,* allowing immediate input of the information at the receiving dock, or can be communicated in *RF tags* readable by transponders located along the road as executed by a large textile manufacturer.

3. *Crossdock "crossdockable" material.* Since the ultimate objective of the receiving activity is to prepare material for the shipment of orders, the fastest, most productive receiving process is crossdocking—essentially, shipping directly from the receiving dock. Palletized material with a single SKU per pallet, floor-stacked loose cases, and backordered merchandise are excellent candidates for crossdocking.

4. *Putaway directly to primary or reserve locations.* When material cannot be crossdocked, material handling steps can be minimized by bypassing receiving staging and putting material away directly to primary picking locations, essentially replenishing those locations from receiving. When there are no severe constraints on product rotation, this may be feasible. Otherwise, material should be directly put away to reserve locations. In direct putaway systems, the staging and inspection ac-

tivities are eliminated. Hence the time, space, and labor associated with those operations is eliminated. In either case, vehicles that serve the dual purpose of truck unloading and product putaway facilitate direct putaway. For example, counterbalanced lift trucks can be equipped with scales, cubing devices, and on-line RF terminals to streamline the unloading and putaway function. The most advanced logistics operations are characterized by automated, direct putaway to storage, and will be described in a moment. The material handling technologies that facilitate direct putaway include roller-bed trailers and extendable conveyors. In addition to prereceiving, prequalifying vendors helps to eliminate the need for receiving staging.

5. *Stage in storage locations.* If material has to be staged, the floor space required for staging can be minimized by providing storage locations, for receiving staging. Often, storage locations may be live storage locations with locations blocked until the unit is officially received. Sometime spaces are provided over dock doors.

6. *Complete all necessary steps for efficient load decomposition and movement at receiving.* The most time we will ever have available to prepare a product for shipment is at receiving. Once the demand for the product has been received, there is precious little time available for any preparation of the material that needs to be done prior to shipment. Hence any material processing that can be accomplished ahead of time should be accomplished. Those activities include:

a. Prepackaging in issue increments. At a large office supplies distributor, quarter- and half-pallet loads are built at receiving in anticipation of orders being received in those quantities. Customers are encouraged to order in those quantities by quantity discounts. A large distributor of automotive aftermarket parts conducted an extensive analysis of likely order quantities. Based on that analysis, the company is now prepackaging in those popular issue increments.

b. Applying necessary labeling and tags

c. Cubing and weighing for storage and transport planning

7. *Sort inbound materials for efficient putaway.* Just as zone picking and location sequencing are effective strategies for improving order picking productivity, inbound materials can be sorted for putaway by warehouse zone and by location sequence. At the U.S. Defense Logistics Agency's Integrated Material Complex, receipts are staged in a rotary rack carousel and released and sorted by warehouse aisle and location within the aisle to streamline the putaway activity. Automated guided vehicles take the accumulated loads to the correct aisle for putaway.

8. *When possible, combine putaways and retrievals.* To further streamline the putaway and retrieval process, putaway and retrieval transactions can be combined in a dual command to reduce the amount of empty travel for industrial vehicles. This technique is especially geared for pallet storage and retrieval operations. Again, counterbalanced lift trucks that can unload, put away, retrieve, and load are a flexible means of executing dual commands.

9. *Balance the use of resources at receiving by scheduling carriers and shifting time-consuming receipts to off-peak hours.* Through computer-to-computer links and fax machines, companies have improved access to schedule information on inbound and outbound loads. This information can be used to proactively schedule receipts and to provide advance shipping notice information.

10. *Minimize or eliminate walking by flowing inbound material past work stations.* An effective strategy for enhancing order picking productivity, especially when a variety of tasks must be performed on the retrieved material (i.e. packaging, counting, labeling), is to bring the stock to stationary order picking stations equipped with the necessary aids and information to perform the necessary tasks. The same strategy should be employed for receipts, which by their nature require special handling. At the flagship distribution center of a large retailer, receipts flow out of inbound trailers on skatewheel conveyor, past a stationary receiving station equipped with a touch-screen terminal. At the stationary receiving stations, inbound cases are weighed, cubed, and tagged with a bar code label describing all necessary product and warehouse location information. In addition, if the material is needed for an outbound order, a receiving operator diverts the inbound case down a separate conveyor line for crossdocking.

Order Picking

A recent survey of warehousing professionals identified order picking as the highest-priority activity in the warehouse for productivity improvements.[20] There are several reasons for their concern. First and foremost, order picking is the most costly activity in a typical warehouse. A recent study in the United Kingdom[5] revealed that 63 percent of all operating costs in a typical warehouse can be attributed to order picking.

Second, the order picking activity has become increasingly difficult to manage. The difficulty arises from the introduction of new operating programs such as just-in-time (JIT), cycle time reduction, quick response, and new marketing strategies such as micromarketing and megabrand strategies. These programs require that (1) smaller orders be delivered to warehouse customers more frequently and more accurately, and that (2) more stock keeping units (SKUs) be incorporated in the order picking system. As a result, both throughput, storage, and accuracy requirements have increased dramatically.

Third, renewed emphasis on quality improvements and customer service have forced warehouse managers to reexamine the order picking activity from the standpoint of minimizing product damage, reducing transaction times, and further improving picking accuracy. Finally, the conventional responses to these increased requirements, to hire more people or to invest in more automated equipment, have been stymied by labor shortages and high hurdle rates due to uncertain business environments. Fortunately, there are a variety of ways to improve order picking productivity without increasing staffing or making significant investments in highly automated equipment. Twelve ways to improve order picking productivity in light of the increased demands now placed on order picking systems are now described.

Order Picking Principles

1. *Encourage full-pallet as opposed to loose case picking, and full case as opposed to broken case picking.* By encouraging customers to order in full-pallet quantities, or by creating quarter- and/or half-pallet loads, much of the counting and manual physical

handling of cases can be avoided both in your warehouse and also in your customer's warehouse. In similar fashion, by encouraging customers to order in full-case quantities, much of the counting and extra packaging associated with loose case picking can be avoided. A pick line profile illustrating the distribution of the portion of a full pallet or full case requested by customers should reveal an opportunity to reduce the amount of partial pallet and/or partial case picking in the warehouse.

2. *Pick from storage.* Since a majority of a typical order picker's time is spent traveling and/or searching for pick locations, one of the most effective means for improving picking productivity and accuracy is to bring the storage locations to the picker, preferably reserve storage locations. A large wholesale drug distributor and a large discount retailer have recently installed systems that bring reserve storage locations to stationary order picking stations for batch picking of partial case quantities. In so doing, order picking travel time has been virtually eliminated. In addition, the same system can transfer storage locations to/from receiving, prepackaging, and inspection operations, thus virtually eliminating travel throughout the warehouse. Though expensive, the systems may be justified by increased productivity and accuracy.

3. *Eliminate and combine order picking tasks when possible.* The human work elements involved in order picking may include:

- Traveling to, from, and between pick locations
- Extracting items from storage locations
- Reaching and bending to access pick locations
- Documenting picking transactions
- Sorting items into orders
- Packing items
- Searching for pick locations

A typical distribution of the order picker's time among these activities is provided in Figure 22-2. Means for eliminating the work elements are outlined in Table 22-1. When work elements cannot be eliminated they can often be combined to improve order picking productivity. Some effective combinations of work elements are now outlined.

a. Traveling and extracting items. Stock-to-picker (STP) systems such as carousels and the miniload automated storage/retrieval system are designed to keep order pickers extracting while a mechanical device travels to, from, and between storage locations, bringing pick locations to the order picker. As a result, a man-machine balancing problem is introduced. If the initial design of stock-to-picker systems is not accurate, a significant portion of the order picker's time may be spent waiting on the storage/retrieval machine to bring pick locations forward.

b. Traveling and documenting. Since a person-aboard storage/retrieval (S/R) machine is programmed to automatically transport the order picker between successive picking locations, the order picker is free to document picking transactions, sort material, or pack material while the S/R machine is moving.

c. Picking and sorting. If an order picker completes more than one order during a picking tour, picking carts equipped with dividers or totes may be designed to allow the picker to sort material into several orders at a time.

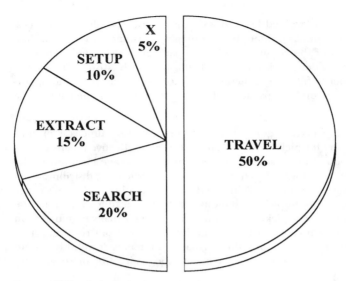

Figure 22-2. Order picker's time distribution.

d. Picking, sorting, and packing. When the cube occupied by a completed order is small, say less than a shoebox, the order picker can sort directly into a packing or shipping container. Packing or shipping containers must be set up ahead of time and placed on picking carts equipped with dividers and/or totes.

4. *Batch orders to reduce total travel time.* By increasing the number of orders (and therefore items) picked by an order picker during a picking tour, the travel time per pick can be reduced. For example, if an order picker picks one order with two items while traveling 100 ft, the distance traveled per pick is 50 ft. If the picker picked two orders with four items, the distance traveled per pick is reduced to 25 ft.

A natural group of orders to batch is single-line orders. Single-line orders can be batched by small zones in the warehouse to further reduce travel time. Other batching strategies are enumerated in Figure 22-3. Note that when an order is assigned to more than one picker, the effort expended to reestablish order integrity is significantly greater. The additional cost of sortation must be compared with savings generated with batch picking.

a. Strict order picking. In strict order picking, each order picker completes one order at a time. For picker-to-part systems, strict order picking is like going through the grocery store and accumulating the items on your grocery list into your cart. Each shopper is concerned only with his or her list.

The major advantage to the strict order picking strategy is that order integrity is well maintained. The major disadvantage is that the order picker is likely to have to travel over a large portion of the warehouse to pick the order. Consequently, the walking time per line item picked is high. However, for large orders (i.e., those greater than 10 line items), a single order can create an efficient picking tour.

b. Batch picking. A second operating strategy for order picking is batch picking. Instead of an order picker working on only one order at a time, orders are batched

Table 22-1 Order Picking Work Elements, and Means for Elimination

Work element	Method of elimination	Equipment required
Traveling	Bring pick locations to picker.	Stock-to-picker system —Miniload AS/RS —Horizontal carousel —Vertical carousel
Documenting	Automate information flow.	Computer-aided order picking Automatic identification systems
Reaching	Present items at waist level.	Vertical carousels Person-aboard AS/RS Miniload AS/RS
Sorting	Assign one picker per order and one order per tour.	
Searching	Bring pick locations to picker. Take picker to pick location. Illuminate pick locations.	Stock-to-picker systems Person-aboard AS/RS Pick-to-light systems
Extracting	Automated dispensing.	Automatic item pickers Robotic order pickers
Counting	Weigh count. Prepackage in issue increments.	Scales on picking vehicles

together, and each order picker becomes responsible for a batch of orders. In the grocery store context, batch picking can be thought of as going to the grocery store with your shopping list and those of some of your neighbors. In one traversal of the grocery store, you will have completed several orders. As a result, the travel time per line item picked will be reduced by approximately the number of orders per batch. The major advantage of batch picking is a reduction in travel time per line item.

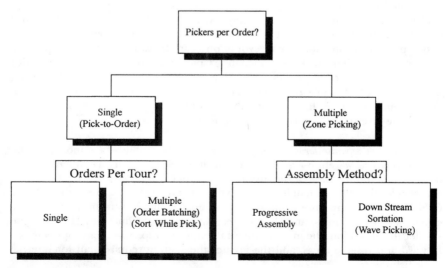

Figure 22-2. Order picker's time distribution.

The major disadvantage of batch picking is the loss of order integrity, and hence the cost to sort the line items of different customer orders and the potential for picking errors.

Orders may be sorted in one of two ways. The order picker may use separate containers to sort the line items of different orders as he or she traverses the warehouse. Special pick carts and containers are available to facilitate such an approach. Or the line items and quantities of different orders may be lumped together, to be sorted later. It is the cost of this sortation process, not required in strict order picking, that determines whether batch picking is a cost-effective strategy.

Batch picking can also be used in part-to-picker systems. In those cases, all the line items requested in the batch of orders are picked from each location as it is presented to the picker. Again, the benefits of reduced travel time must be weighed against the cost of sortation and the potential for order filling errors. Batch picking is especially effective for small orders (one to five line items).

c. Zone picking. In zone picking, an order picker is dedicated to pick the line items in his or her assigned zone—one order at a time or in batches. In the grocery store context, zone picking can be thought of as assigning one individual to each aisle in the grocery store.

That individual would be responsible for picking all the line items requested in that aisle, regardless of the customer order that generated the request.

One advantage of zone picking is travel time savings. Since each picker's coverage has been reduced from the entire warehouse to a smaller area, the travel time per line item should be reduced from that of strict order picking. Again, however, these travel time reductions must be weighed against the costs of sorting and the potential for order filling errors. Additional benefits of zone picking include the order picker's familiarity with the product in his or her zone, reduced interference with other order pickers, and increased accountability for productivity and housekeeping within the zone.

Two methods for establishing order integrity in zone picking systems are progressive assembly and wave picking. In progressive assembly (or pick-and-pass) systems, complete orders are established as their components are passed from zone-to-zone in tote pans or cartons along a conveyor or on a cart. In wave picking, order picker's truly work in an item picking mode. In a typical wave picking system, an order picker applies a bar code label to each unit picked. Unit-by-unit or in batch, labeled units are placed on a takeaway conveyor for induction into a sortation/accumulation system. As before, the productivity gains in order picking must be weighed against the investment in sortation/accumulation systems.

5. *Establish separate forward and reserve picking areas.* Since a minority of the items in a typical warehouse generate a majority of pick requests, a condensed picking area containing some of the inventory of popular items should be established. The smaller the allocation of inventory to the forward area (in terms of the number of SKUs and their inventory allocation), the smaller the forward picking area, the smaller the travel times, and the greater the picking productivity. However, the smaller the allocation, the more frequent the internal replenishment trips between forward and reserve areas, and the greater the staffing requirement for internal replenishments.

Some typical approaches for making forward reserve decisions include: (1) allocating an equal time supply of inventory for all SKUs in the forward area, or (2) allocating an equal number of units of all SKUs in the forward area. However, a near-optimal procedure for solving the forward-reserve problem was recently developed.[6] The procedure makes use of math programming techniques to decide for each SKU whether it should receive a location in the forward area or not, and if it should, its proper allocation. The annual savings in picking and replenishment costs is on the order of 40 percent.

For a simplified approach to the configuration of a forward/reserve system, follow these steps:

a. Determine which items should be in the forward picking area. Because most inventories include many slow-moving items that have relatively small storage cube requirements, a forward picking area may include the entire inventory of each of the slow movers and only a representative quantity of the fast movers. Alternately, to provide the fastest possible picking, very slow-moving items may be stored elsewhere in the warehouse in a less accessible but higher-density storage mode.

b. Determine the quantities of each item to be stored in the forward picking area. As mentioned, slow movers may have their entire on-hand inventory located in the forward picking area. Storage allocation for other parts may be determined by either (1) an arbitrary allocation of space, as much as one case or one shelf, or (2) space for a quantity sufficient to satisfy the expected weekly or monthly demand. (It is common to select large quantities from reserve storage and smaller quantities from forward storage.)

c. Size the total storage cube requirement for items in the forward picking area. Space planned for each item must be adequate for the expected receipt and/or replenishment quantity, not just for the average balance on-hand.

d. Identify alternative storage methods that are appropriate for the total forward picking cube and that meet the required throughput

e. Determine the operating methods within each storage alternative, in order to project personnel requirements. The description of the operating method must also include consideration of the storage location assignment (i.e., random, dedicated, zoned, or a combination of these), because this will have a significant impact on picking productivity. It is also necessary to evaluate the opportunity for batch picking (picking multiple orders simultaneously).

f. Estimate the costs and savings for each alternative system described.

6. *Assign the most popular items to the most easily accessed locations in the warehouse.* Once items have been assigned to storage modes, and space has been allocated for their forward and reserve storage locations, the formal assignment of items to warehouse locations can commence. In a typical warehouse, a minority of the items generate a majority of the picking activity. This phenomenon can be used to reduce order picking travel time and reaching and bending. For example, by assigning the most popular items close to the front of the warehouse, an order picker's or S/R machine's average travel time can be significantly reduced. In automated storage/retrieval systems, average dual-command travel time can be reduced by as much as 70 percent over random storage.[5] In miniload automated storage/retrieval systems and carousel picking systems, order picking productivity can be improved by as much as 50 percent depending on the number of picks per bin retrieval and

the other tasks assigned to the order picker (e.g., packaging, counting, weighing, etc.).

The phenomenon can also be used to reduce stooping and bending, consequently reducing fatigue and improving picking accuracy. Simply, the most popular items should be assigned to the picking locations at or near waist height. In an order picking operation for small vials of radio-pharmaceuticals, a stock location assignment plan was devised that concentrated over 70 percent of the picks in locations at or near waist level.

The most common mistake in applying this principle to the design of stock location systems is the oversight of the size of the product. The objective in applying the principle is to assign as much picking activity as possible to the locations that are easily accessible. Unfortunately, there are a limited number of picking locations that are easy to access—those near the front of the system, and/or at or near waist height. Consequently, the amount of space occupied by an item must be incorporated into the ranking of products for stock assignment. A simple ranking of items based on the ratio of pick frequency to shipped cube (the product of unit demand and unit cube) establishes a good baseline for item assignment.

7. *Balance picking activity across picking locations to reduce congestion.* In assigning popular items to concentrated areas in picker-to-stock systems, congestion can reduce potential productivity gains. Care must be taken to distribute picking activity over large enough areas to reduce congestion, yet not over so great an area as to significantly increase travel times. This is often achieved in horseshoe configurations of walk-and-pick systems. A typical picking tour will require the picker to traverse the entire horseshoe. However, the most popular items are assigned locations on or near the horseshoe. In stock-to-picker systems, system designers must be careful not to overload one carousel unit or one miniload aisle. Balanced systems are more productive.

8. *Assign items that are likely to be requested together to the same or nearby locations.* Just as a minority of items in a warehouse generate a majority of the picking frequency, there are items in the warehouse that are likely to be requested together. Examples include items in repair kits, items from the same supplier, items in the same subassembly, items of the same size, etc. Correlations can be identified from order profiles[5] and can be capitalized on by storing correlated items in the same or in nearby locations. Travel time is in turn reduced, since the distance between pick locations on an order is reduced. In a carousel or miniload AS/RS application, storing items that are likely to be requested together in the same location minimizes the number of locations visits to complete an order and therefore helps reduce order picker idle time and wear and tear on the system.

At a major mail-order apparel distributor, nearly 70 percent of all orders can be completed from a single size (e.g., small, medium, large, extra large) regardless of the type of item ordered (e.g., shirts, pants, belts, etc.). At a major distributor of health care products, a majority of the orders can be filled from a single vendor. Since material is also received that way, correlated storage by vendor improves productivity in picking and putaway.

A computerized procedure for jointly considering the popularity and correlation of demand for items in developing intelligent stock assignment plans was recently developed.[5] In the example, order picking productivity was improved by nearly 80 percent. The procedure suggests that items be clustered into families containing items that are likely to be requested together, the families then being assigned to warehouse locations on the basis of pick frequency and space occupied.

9. *Sequence pick location visits to reduce travel time.* In both picker-to-stock and stock-to-picker systems, sequencing pick location visits can dramatically reduce travel time. The order picking travel time for a person-aboard AS/RS picking tour can be reduced by 50 percent by simply dividing the rack into upper and lower halves and visiting pick locations in the lower half in increasing distance from the front of the rack on the outbound leg, and in decreasing distance in the upper half on the rack during the inbound leg. Location visits should also be sequenced in walk-and-pick systems. In case picking operations, where an order may occupy one or more pallets, the picking tour should be sequenced to allow the picker to build a stable load and to reduce travel distance. A major distributor of photographic supplies uses an expert system to solve this complex problem.

10. *Organize picking documents and displays to minimize search time and errors.* A majority of picking errors are the result of picking documents and displays that are confusing and/or difficult to read. Large, bold characters, color coding, eye-level displays, and floor markings can all be used to minimize confusion. In addition, every attempt should be made to remove similar colors and/or stock numbers from adjacent picking locations. One major distributor of cosmetics uses body parts as opposed to alpha-numerics to name pick locations in bin shelving units. A major distributor of office machines and supplies color-codes all putaway tags to simplify product identification.

11. *Design picking vehicles to minimize sorting time and errors and to enhance the picker's comfort.* The order picking vehicle is the order picker's work station. Just as work station design is critical to the productivity and comfort of assembly and office workers, the design of the picking vehicle is critical to the productivity and morale of the order picker. The vehicle should be tailored to the demands of the job. If sorting is required, the vehicle should be equipped with dividers or tote pans. If picking occurs above a comfortable reaching height, the vehicle should be equipped with a ladder. If the picker takes documents on the picking tour, the vehicle should help the picker organize the paperwork.

Unfortunately, the design of the picking vehicle is often of secondary concern, yet it is at this work station that order picking really takes place. A major wholesale drug distributor recently installed picking vehicles that are powered and guided by rails running in the ceiling between each picking aisle. The vehicle automatically takes the order picker to the correct location and with an on-board CRT communicates the correct pick location, quantity, and order or container to place the pick quantity into. The vehicle can accommodate multiple containers to allow batch picking, and is equipped with on-board scales for on-line weigh counting and pick accuracy verification.

12. *Eliminate paperwork from the order picking activity.* Paperwork is one of the major sources of inaccuracies and productivity losses in the order picking function. Pick-to-light systems, radio frequency data communication, and voice input/output are existing technologies that have been successfully used to eliminate paperwork from the order picking function.

Order Picking Systems

A detailed review of order picking systems follows. The review includes an operating description, plus pros and cons of each system type. The review describes both full case and broken case picking systems. Case picking systems can be categorized by whether or not the pallet travels to the pick face or not. Those systems in which the pallet travels to the pick face are typically less expensive but more labor-intensive than those in which palletization is established downstream from the pick face.

Pallet-to-Pick-Face Systems

Pallet Jack or Pallet Truck Picking.   In pallet jack or pallet truck picking, order pickers pull pallet jacks or drive pallet trucks along the floor, picking cases to pallets on the vehicles. Order pickers typically pick one order at a time, and since they do not have to pick above positions on the floor or the first or second level of pallet rack, the productivity can range from 100 to 250 cases/hr. Productivity may be enhanced by picking more than one order at a time. This batch picking practice is sometimes facilitated with a double pallet jack, capable of handling two pallets at a time. Nonpowered pallet jacks cost around $1000. Powered pallet trucks cost around $10,000.

Stock Pickers.   Stock pickers, sometimes referred to as *order picker* or *cherry picker trucks,* allow the order picker to travel to pick locations well above floor level. In so doing, picking productivity is reduced to between 50 and 100 cases/hr. Productivity can be enhanced by minimizing vertical travel through popularity-based storage and/or intelligent pick tour construction. Typical order picker trucks cost approximately $30,000.

Pick-to-Roller Conveyor.   Empty pallets are inducted onto a pallet roller conveyor at the beginning of a case picking line. Pallets pass by order pickers stationed at zones along the pick line. In so doing, the travel time for the order picker is nearly eliminated. In addition, the pickers are essentially palletizing and establishing order integrity as they pick. The productivity of these operations ranges from 175 to 350 cases/hr. The initial system cost is about $1000 per linear foot of pallet roller conveyor.

Automated Case Picking

Pick-to-Belt.   In pick-to-belt, or *wave picking* systems, order pickers are assigned to small zones along a case picking line. The case picking line is typically comprised of pallet floor positions, single-deep pallet rack, or pallet flow lanes. A powered belt or roller conveyor runs along each location on the picking face.

During a pick wave, typically ranging from 20 to 60 min, an order picker walks down the locations in his or her zone, picking cases from locations on the pick line directly to the belt or roller conveyor. Since travel distances are limited and order pickers have no knowledge of order composition, productivity can range from 250 to 400 cases/hr. Note that since order pickers have no knowledge of order composition, order integrity must be established downstream from the picking operation. This is typically accomplished with one of the many mechanized sorting systems described below.

End-of-Aisle AS/RS.   End-of-aisle case picking systems are typically comprised of a unit load AS/RS for pallet storage and retrieval and a conveyor delivery system to transport pallets to remote case picking stations. Order pickers are stationary, and located at remote picking locations serviced by a pallet roller conveyor. As pallets are presented to the order pickers, the order pickers remove the correct number of cases and return the pallet to the AS/RS for storage. The principal advantage of the end-of-aisle system is the excellent floor space utilization provided by the high-rise AS/RS and the elimination of travel for the order pickers. Picking rates range from 200 to 300 cases/hr. The system cost is comprised of the AS/RS cost ($250,000 to $400,000 per S/R machine) and the pallet conveyor cost ($1000 per foot).

Automatic Extraction.   Automated case extracting systems are comprised of case flow rack for case storage and an automated storage/retrieval machine for case putaway and retrieval. The automated storage/retrieval machines run on guide rails in the floor and ceiling and are equipped with telescoping conveyors for case handling to/from the putaway/pick face. While one machine puts cases into the back of the case flow rack, another retrieves cases from the front of the flow rack. Each machine operates at a rate of approximately 500 to 800 cases/hr and costs between $150,000 and $200,000.

Tier Picking.   When the typical number of cases ordered for an item is at least a pallet layer, case picking productivity can be enhanced by selecting layer or tier quantities from the pallet, as opposed to individual cases. One method for tier picking is to transport pallets to a device that clamps the top tier on the pallet and singulates the cases along a takeaway conveyor. This device is sometimes referred to as a "depalletizer." The depalletizer works at rates between 1000 and 1500 cases/hr and costs around $150,000. For cost comparisons, the cost of the system must also include the pallet conveyor used to feed the depalletizer and to transport pallets back to storage.

Broken Case Picking Systems

The primary distinguishing feature in broken case picking systems is whether or not the order picker travels to the picking location. The systems in which the picker travels to the pick location are classified as *picker-to-location* or *picker-to-stock* systems (PTS).

In PTS systems, the selection of the storage mode is usually separated from the retrieval mechanism. The order picker either walks or rides a vehicle to the pick location. The four major equipment groups under the heading of picker-to-part or in-the-aisle systems are bin shelving, modular storage drawers/cabinets, gravity flow rack, and man-aboard AS/RS. The key feature distinguishing the first three systems listed here from the man-aboard AS/RS is the mode of travel of the order picker. In the first three systems, the order picker typically walks to the pick location using a cart to accumulate, sort, and/or pack orders (i.e., cart picking) or picks to a tote pan transported with roller or belt conveyor. In the man-aboard AS/RS alternative, the picker rides aboard a storage/retrieval (S/R) machine to the pick location.

Bin Shelving Systems.   Bin shelving systems (see Chapter 18, Fig. 18-14) are the oldest and still the most popular (in terms of dollar sales volume and number of systems in use) equipment alternative in use for small-parts order picking. Their low initial cost ($100 to $150 per unit), easy reconfigurability, easy installation, and low maintenance requirements are at the heart of this popularity.

It is important to recall that the lowest initial cost alternative may not be the most cost-effective alternative, or the alternative that meets the prioritized needs of the warehouse. With bin shelving systems, savings in initial cost and maintenance may be offset by inflated space and labor requirements.

Space is frequently underutilized in bin shelving systems, since the full inside dimensions of each unit are rarely usable. Also, since people are extracting the items, the height of shelving units is limited by the reaching height of a human being. As a result, the available building cube may also be underutilized.

The consequences of low space utilization are twofold. First, low space utilization means that a large amount of square footage is required to store the products. The more expensive it is to own and operate the space, the more expensive low space utilization becomes. Second, the greater the square footage, the greater the area that must be traveled by the order pickers, and thus the greater the labor requirement and costs.

Two additional disadvantages of bin shelving are supervisory problems and item security/protection problems. Supervisory problems arise because it is difficult to supervise people through a maze of bin shelving units. Security and item protection problems arise because bin shelving is one of a class of open systems (i.e., the items are exposed to and accessible from the picking aisles).

As with all of the system types, in order to make an appropriate system selection these disadvantages must be evaluated and compared with the advantages of low initial cost and low maintenance requirements.

Modular Storage Drawers/Cabinets.   Modular storage drawers/cabinets (see Chapter 18, Fig. 18-26) are called "modular" because each storage cabinet houses modular storage drawers that are subdivided into modular storage compartments. Drawer heights range from 3 to 24 in, and each drawer may hold up to 400 lb worth of material. The storage cabinets can be thought of as shelving units that house storage drawers.

The primary advantage of storage drawers/cabinets over bin shelving is the large number of SKUs that can be stored and presented to the order picker in a small area. The cabinet and drawer suppliers inform us that one drawer can hold from 1 to 100 SKUs (depending on the size, shape, and inventory levels of the items), and that a typical storage cabinet can store the equivalent of two to four shelving units worth of material. This dense storage stems primarily from the ability to create item housing configurations within a drawer that very closely match the cubic storage requirements of each SKU. Also, since the drawers are pulled out into the aisle for picking, space does not have to be provided above each SKU to provide room for the order picker's hand and forearm. This reach space must be provided in bin shelving storage, otherwise items deep in the unit could not be accessed.

Several benefits accrue from the high-density storage characteristic of storage drawer systems. First, and obviously, the more material that can be packed into a smaller area, the smaller the space requirement. Hence, space costs are reduced. When the value of space is at a true premium, such as on a battleship, an airplane, or the manufacturing floor, the reduction in space requirements alone can be enough to justify the use of storage drawers and cabinets. A second benefit resulting from a reduction in square footage requirements is a subsequent reduction in the travel time and hence labor requirements for order picking.

Additional benefits achieved by the use of storage drawers include improved picking accuracy and protection for the items from the environment. Picking accuracy is improved over that in shelving units, because the order picker's sight lines to the items are improved, and the quantity of light falling on the items to be extracted is increased. With bin shelving, the physical extraction of items may occur anywhere from floor level to 7 ft off the ground, with the order picker having to reach into the shelving unit itself to achieve the pick. With storage drawers, the drawer is pulled out into the picking aisle for item extraction. The order picker looks down onto the contents of the drawer, which are illuminated by the light source for the picking aisle. (The fact that the order picker must look down on the drawer necessitates that storage cabinets be less than 5 ft in height.) Item security and protection are achieved, since the drawers can be closed and locked when items are not being extracted from them.

As one would expect, these benefits do not come for free. Storage cabinets equipped with drawers range in price from $1000 to $1500 per unit. Price is primarily a function of the number of drawers and the amount of sheet metal in the cabinet.

Gravity Flow Rack. Gravity flow rack (see Chapter 18, Fig. 18-10), or just *flow rack,* is another popular picker-to-part equipment alternative. Flow rack is typically used for active items that are stored in fairly uniform sized and shaped cartons. The cartons are placed in the back of the rack from the replenishment aisle, and advance/roll toward the pick face as cartons are depleted from the front. This back-to-front movement ensures first-in, first-out (FIFO) turnover of the material.

Essentially, a section of flow rack is a bin shelving unit turned perpendicular to the picking aisle, with rollers placed on the shelves. The deeper the sections, the greater the portion of warehouse space that will be devoted to storage as opposed to aisle space. Further gains in space efficiency can be achieved by making use of the cubic space over the flow rack for full pallet storage.

Flow rack ranges in price from $3 to $10 per carton stored, depending on the length and weight capacity of the racks. As is the case with bin shelving, flow rack has very low maintenance requirements and is available from a number of suppliers in a wide variety of standard section and lane sizes.

The fact that just one carton of each line item is located on the pick face means that a large number of SKUs are presented to the picker over a small area. Hence walking, and therefore labor, requirements can be reduced with an efficient layout.

Mezzanines. Bin shelving, modular storage cabinets, flow rack, and even carousels can be placed on a mezzanine. The obvious advantage of using a mezzanine is that nearly twice as much material can be stored in the original square footage inexpensively ($10 to $20 per square foot). The major design issues for a mezzanine are the selection of the proper grade of mezzanine for the loading that will be experienced, the design of the material handling system to service the upper levels of the mezzanine, and the utilization of the available clear height. At least 14 ft of clear height should be available for a mezzanine to be considered.

Mobile Storage Equipment. Bin shelving, modular storage cabinets, and flow rack can all be "mobilized." The most popular method of mobilization is the "train-track" method. Parallel tracks are cut into the floor, and wheels are placed on the bottom of the storage equipment to create "mobilized" equipment. The space savings accrue from the fact that only one aisle is needed between all the rows of storage equipment. The aisle is created by separating two adjacent rows of equipment. As a result, the aisle "floats" in the configuration between adjacent rows of equipment.

The storage equipment is moved by simply sliding the equipment along the tracks, by turning a crank located at the end of each storage row, or by invoking electric motors that may provide the motive power.

The disadvantage to this approach is the increased time required to access the items. Every time an item must be accessed, the corresponding storage aisle must be created.

Picker-to-Part Systems—
Retrieval Systems

Cart Picking. A variety of picking carts are available to facilitate the accumulation, sortation, and/or packing of orders as an order picker makes a picking tour. The carts are designed to allow an order picker to pick multiple orders on a picking tour, thus dramatically improving productivity as opposed to strict single order picking for small orders. The most conventional vehicles provide dividers for order sortation, a place to hold paperwork and marking instruments, and a stepladder for picking at levels slightly above reaching height. Additional levels of sophistication and cost bring powered carts, light-aided sortation, onboard computer terminals, and onboard weighing.

Tote Picking. In tote-picking systems, conveyors are used to transport tote pans to successive picking zones to allow order completion. The tote pans are used to establish order integrity and for merchandise accumulation and containment. Order pickers may walk one or more totes through a single picking zone, partially completing several orders at a time, or an order picker may walk one or more totes through all picking zones, thus completing one or more orders on each pass through the picking zones.

Man-Aboard AS/RS. The man-aboard AS/RS, as the name implies, is an automated storage-and-retrieval system in which the picker rides aboard a storage/retrieval machine to the pick locations. The storage locations may be provided by stacked bin shelving units, stacked storage cabinets, and/or pallet rack. The storage/retrieval machine may be aisle-captive or free-roaming.

Typically, the picker will leave from the front of the system at floor level and visit enough storage locations to fill one or multiple orders, depending on order size. Sortation can take place on-board if enough containers are provided on the storage/retrieval (S/R) machine.

The man-aboard AS/RS offers significant square footage and order picking time reductions over the previously described picker-to-part systems. Square footage reductions are available because storage heights are no longer limited by the reach height of the order picker. Shelves or storage cabinets can be stacked as high as floor loading, weight capacity, throughput requirements, and/or ceiling heights will permit. Order pick times are reduced because travel is automated, allowing the order picker to do productive work while traveling. Search time is also reduced, since the picker is automatically delivered to the correct pick location.

As you might expect, these reductions in square footage and pick times come with a price tag. Man-aboard automated storage-and-retrieval systems are far and away the most expensive picker-to-part equipment alternative. Aisle-captive storage/retrieval machines reaching heights of up to 40 ft cost around $100,000.

Robotic Retrieval Systems.   In rare instances, robotic retrieval systems are applied. Each robotic picking vehicle is equipped with a small carousel to permit order sortation, accumulation, and containment. The carousel travels up and down a mast on the robot as the robot traverses the picking aisle(s). A storage drawer is pulled from a storage location onto the picking vehicle.

Stock-to-Picker Systems

The major difference between *stock-to-picker* systems and *picker-to-stock* systems is the answer to the question, "Does the picker have to travel to the pick location, or does the pick location travel to the picker?" If the pick location travels to the picker, the system is termed a *part-to-picker* system.

In stock-to-picker systems, the travel time component of total order picking time is shifted from the picker to a device for bringing locations to the picker. Also, the search time component of total order picking time is significantly reduced, since the correct pick location is automatically presented to the order picker. For well-designed systems, the result is a large increase in the pick-rate capacity of the order picking system. In poorly designed systems, the potential improvements can be quickly eroded if the picker is required to wait on the device to present him or her with parts.

The two most popular classes of part-to-picker systems are carousels and the miniload automated storage-and-retrieval system (AS/RS). A third less popular class is the automatic item picker. Each class is now described.

Carousels.   Carousels, as the name implies, are mechanical devices that house and rotate items for order picking. Three classes of carousels are currently available for order picking applications: horizontal, vertical, and independently rotating racks.

Horizontal Carousels.   A horizontal carousel (see Chapter 18, Fig. 18-24) is a linked series of rotating bins of adjustable shelves, driven on the top or on the bottom by a drive motor unit. Rotation takes place about an axis perpendicular to the floor at about 80 ft/min.

Items are extracted from the carousel by order pickers who occupy fixed positions in front of the carousel(s). The order pickers may also be responsible for controlling the rotation of the carousel. Manual control is achieved via a keypad that tells the carousel which bin location to rotate forward, and a foot pedal that releases the carousel to rotate. The carousels may also be computer-controlled, in which case the sequence of pick locations is stored in the computer and brought forward automatically.

A management option with carousel systems is the assignment of order pickers to carousels. If an order picker is assigned to one carousel unit, he or she must wait for the carousel to rotate to the correct location between picks. If an order picker is assigned to two or more carousels, he or she may pick from one carousel while the other is rotating to the next pick location. Remember, the objective of part-to-picker systems is to keep the picker picking. Humans are excellent extractors of items; the flexibility of our limbs and muscles provides us with this capability. We are not efficient searchers, walkers, or waiters.

Horizontal carousels vary in length from 15 to 100 ft, and in height from 6 to 25 ft. The length and height of the units are dictated by the pick-rate requirements and building restrictions. The longer the carousel, the more time required, on average, to rotate it to the desired location. Also the taller the carousel, the more time required to access the items. Heights over 6 ft necessitate the use of ladders or robot arms on vertical masts to access the items.

In addition to providing a high pick-rate capacity, horizontal carousels make good use of the available storage space. Very little space is required between adjacent carousels, and the only lost space is that between parallel sections of bins on the same carousel unit.

One important disadvantage of horizontal carousels is that the shelves and bins are open. Consequently, item security and protection can be a problem.

The price of a carousel unit starts at $5000 and increases with the number of bins and the weight capacity.

A "twin-bin" horizontal carousel was recently introduced to the material handling market. In the twin-bin carousel, the traditional carousel carrier is split vertically in half and rotated 90°. This allows for more shallow carriers, thus improving the storage density for small parts.

Vertical Carousels.   A vertical carousel (see Chapter 18, Fig. 18-25) is a horizontal carousel turned on its end and enclosed in sheet metal. As with horizontal carousels, an order picker operates one or multiple carousels. The carousels are indexed either automatically, via computer control, or manually, by the order picker working a keypad on the carousel's work surface.

Vertical carousels range in height from 8 to 35 ft. Heights (as lengths are for horizontal carousels) are dictated by throughput requirements and building restrictions. The taller the system, the longer it will take, on average, to rotate the desired bin location to the pick station.

Order pick times for vertical carousels are theoretically less than those for horizontal carousels. The decrease results from the items always being presented at the order picker's waist level. This eliminates the stooping and reaching that goes with horizontal carousels, further reduces search time, and promotes more accurate picking. Some of the gains in item-extract time are negated by the slower rotation speed of the vertical carousel. Recall that the direction of rotation is against gravity.

Additional benefits provided by the vertical carousel include excellent item protection and security. In the vertical carousel, only one shelf of items is exposed at one time, and the entire contents of the carousel can be locked up.

The price of a vertical carousel begins at $10,000 and increases with the number of shelves and the weight capacity. The additional cost of vertical carousels over horizontal carousels is attributed to the sheet metal enclosure, and the extra power required to rotate against the force of gravity.

Independent Rotating Rack Carousels. Independent rotating rack carousels are like multiple one-level horizontal carousels stacked on top of one another. As the name implies, each level rotates independently. As a result, several pick locations are ready to be accessed by the order picker at all times. Consequently, the order picker is continuously picking.

Clearly, for each level to operate independently, each level must have its own power and communication link. These requirements force the price of independent rotating rack well above that of vertical or horizontal carousels. Specific price estimate information is scarce and unreliable, because there are relatively few system installations of this type.

Miniload Automated Storage-and-Retrieval System.   In the miniload automated storage-and-retrieval system (see Chapter 18, Fig. 18-22), a storage/retrieval (S/R) machine simultaneously travels horizontally and vertically in a storage aisle, transporting storage containers to and from an order picking station located at one end of the system. The order picking station typically has two pick positions. As the order picker is picking from the container in the left pick position, the S/R machine is taking the container from the right pick position back to its location in the rack and returning with the next container. The result is the order picker ping-ponging back and forth between the left and right pick positions.

The sequence of containers to be processed is determined manually by the order picker, keying in the desired line-item numbers or rack locations on a keypad, or the sequence is generated and processed automatically by computer control.

Miniloads vary in height from 8 to 50 ft, and in length from 40 to 200 ft. As in the case of carousels, the height and length of the system are dictated by the throughput requirements and building restrictions. The longer and taller the system, the longer the time required to access the containers. However, the longer and taller the system, the fewer the aisles and S/R machines that will have to be purchased. At between $150,000 and $300,000 per aisle, the determination of the correct system length, height, and number of aisles to meet the pick-rate, storage, and economic return requirements for the warehouse becomes critical.

The transaction rate capacity of the miniload is governed by the ability of the S/R machine (which travels approximately 500 ft/min horizontally and 120 ft/min vertically) to continuously present the order picker with unprocessed storage containers. This ability, coupled with the human factors benefits of presenting the containers to the picker at waist height in a well-lit area, can produce impressive pick rates.

Square footage requirements are reduced for the miniload, due to the ability to store material up to 50 ft high, the ability to size and shape the storage containers and the subdivisions of those containers to very closely match the storage volume requirements of each SKU, and an aisle width that is determined solely by the width of the storage containers.

The disadvantages of the miniload system are probably already apparent. As the most sophisticated of the system alternatives described thus far, it should come as no surprise that the miniload carries the highest price tag of any of the order picking system alternatives. Another result of its sophistication is the significant engineering and design effort that accompanies each system. The consequence of this effort is a delivery time ranging from 4 to 18 mo. Finally, greater sophistication leads to greater maintenance requirements. It is only through a disciplined maintenance program that miniload suppliers are able to advertise up-time percentages between 97 and 99.5 percent.

Automated Dispensing. Automatic item pickers act much like vending machines for small items of uniform size and shape. Each item is allocated a vertical dispenser ranging from 2 to 6 in wide and from 3 to 5 ft tall. (The width of each dispenser is easily adjusted to accommodate variable product sizes.) The dispensing mechanism acts to kick the unit of product at the bottom of the dispenser out onto a conveyor, running between two rows of dispensers configured as an A-frame over a belt conveyor. A tiny vacuum conveyor or small finger on a chain conveyor is used to dispense the items.

Virtual order zones begin at one end of the conveyor and pass by each dispenser. If an item is required in the order zone, it is dispensed onto the conveyor. Merchandise is accumulated at the end of the belt conveyor into a tote pan or carton. A single dispenser can dispense at a rate of up to 6 units/sec. Automatic item pickers are popular in industries with high throughput for small items of uniform size and shape. Cosmetics, wholesale drugs, compact discs, videos, publications, and polybagged garments are some examples.

Replenishment is performed manually from the back of the system. This manual replenishment operation significantly cuts into the savings in picking labor requirements associated with pick rates on the order of 1500 picks/hr/pick head.

One new design for automated dispensing machines is an inverted A-frame that streamlines the replenishment of automated dispensers and increases the storage density along the picking line. In so doing, the price per dispenser has been reduced from nearly $650 per dispenser to around $250. Another new design allows automated dispensing for polybagged garments.

Sorting Systems

Sorting systems are used to congregate material (i.e., cases, items, totes, garments, etc.) with a similar characteristic (i.e., destination, customer, store, etc.) by correctly identifying the like merchandise and transporting it to the same location. The components of a sorting system include transport systems, divert mechanisms, induction systems, identification/communication systems, and accumulation media.

Transport Systems

Conveyor systems are by far the most common mechanism for transporting merchandise through a series of diverters. Both belt, roller, and carriers on chain conveyor are used. The application of each type of conveyor will become clear in our description of alternative divert mechanisms.

Divert Mechanisms

The wide variety of divert mechanisms available for mechanized sortation is evidence of the variety of throughput, size, and weight requirements that can be satisfied with alternative sorting systems. The divert mechanisms can be classified into four major categories: surface sorters, pop-up sorters, tilting sorters, and carrier sorters.

Surface Sorters. Surface sorters are distinguished from other types of sorting mechanisms by the fact that the material to be sorted is diverted along the surface of the belt or roller conveyor. Surface sorters break down into four types: deflectors, push diverters, and rake puller or moving slat sorters.

Deflectors consist of stationary or movable arms that deflect product flow across a belt or roller conveyor to the desired location. They are necessarily in position before the item to be sorted reaches the discharge point. Stationary arms remain in a fixed position and represent a barrier to items coming in contact with them. With the stationary arm deflector, all items are deflected in the same direction. Movable arm or pivoted paddle deflectors are impacted by the item to be sorted in the same manner as the stationary arm deflector. However, the element of motion has been added. With the movable arm deflector (i.e., the paddle), items are selectively diverted. Pivoted deflectors may be equipped with a belt conveyor flush with the surface of the deflector (a *power face*) to speed or control the divert. Paddle deflecting systems are sometimes referred to as *steel belt sorters*, since at one time steel belts were used to reduce the friction encountered in diverting products across the conveyor. Deflectors can support medium (1200 to 2000 cartons/hr) throughput for up to 75-lb loads.

Push diverters are similar to deflectors, in that they do not contact the conveying surface but sweep across to push the product off the opposite side. Push diverters are mounted beside (air- or electric-powered) or above the conveying surface (*paddle pushers*) and are able to move items faster and with greater control than a deflector. Overhead push diverters are capable of moving products to either side of the conveying surface, whereas side-mounted diverters move conveyed items in one direction only to the side opposite that on which they are mounted. Push diverters have a capacity of 3600 cases/hr for loads up to 100 lb.

The *rake puller* sorter is best applied when the items to be sorted are heavy and durable. Rake puller tines fit into slots between powered or nonpowered roller conveyors. Upon command, a positioning stop device and the tines pop up from beneath the roller conveyor surface to stop the carton. The tines pull the carton across the conveyor, then drop below the roller surface for a noninterference return to the starting position. During the return stroke, the next carton can be moving into position.

The *moving slat sorter* is differentiated from the other surface sorters by the fact that the diversion takes place in-line along the roller conveyor.

Pop-Up Sorters. In *pop-up sorters,* a wheel, belt, chain, or roller pops up at the divert point to deflect products to the proper sortation lane.

Pop-up skewed wheels are capable of sorting flat-bottomed items. The skewed wheel device pops up between the rollers of a powered roller conveyor or between belt conveyor segments and directs sorted items onto a powered takeaway lane. Rates of between 5000 and 6000 cases/hr can be achieved.

Pop-up belt and chain sort devices are similar to pop-up skewed wheels, in that they rise from between the rollers of a powered roller conveyor to alter product flow. Belt-and-chain sortation devices are capable of handling heavier items than the wheeled devices.

Pop-up rollers rise up between the chains or rollers of a chain or roller conveyor to alter the flow of product. Pop-up rollers provide a relatively inexpensive means of sorting heavy loads at rates of 1000 to 1200 cases/hr.

Tilting Sorters. Tilting sorters are distinguished from other sorters by the fact that the conveyor belt or slats that support the load and individual carriers are not distinguished along the conveyor.

In a tilting slat sorter, the product occupies the number of slats required to contain its length. The sort is executed by tilting the occupied slats. Hence, tilting slat sorters are best applied when a wide variety of product lengths will be handled. The tilting slat is capable of tilting in either direction. Slats may be arranged in a continuous over-and-under configuration.

Carrier Sorters. Carrier sorters are distinguished from other sorters by the fact that each individual item is transported on and diverted by a dedicated carrier. These are typically tilt-tray or cross-belt sorters.

Continuous chains of *tilting trays* are used to sort a wide variety of lightweight merchandise. The trays may be fed manually or by one of the many types of induction devices available. Tilt tray systems can sort to either side of the sorter. Tilt tray sorters do not discriminate as to the shape of the product being sorted. Bags, boxes, envelopes, documents, software, etc. can all be accommodated. The tilt tray sorter is not appropriate for long items. The capacity of the tilt tray sorter, expressed in pieces or sorts per hour, is expressed as the ratio of the sorter speed to the pitch or length of an individual tray. Rates of 10,000 to 15,000 items/hr can be achieved.

Cross-belt sorters are so named because each item rests on a carrier equipped with a separate powered section of belt conveyor, which operates orthogonal to the direction of material transport. Hence the sorting capacity is enhanced, and the width of the accumulating chutes can be reduced.

Induction Systems

The simplest induction is a gravity roller conveyor section placed next to the sorter. An operator codes each article as it passes this section, then pushes the article onto the moving sorting conveyor. This push-off type of induction is suitable for surface, pop-up, and tilting sorters.

When distribution systems are used for lightweight articles, the coding operator simply places each article onto the sorter with one hand while entering the sort code on the keyboard with the other. A beam of light, moving synchronously with the sorter conveyor, indicates the correct spot for the article to be placed. This type of hand induction is typical to tilt tray sorting systems.

In some situations it is possible to induct articles "on the fly." A belt conveyor carries the articles past a coding operator (at a speed at which he can recognize the code), then conveys them directly onto the sorter. Throughput can be increased by adding a second coding operator, the two operators coding alternate items as they pass by.

Automated induction systems accept, orient, and deposit items on sorters without losing proper orientation. The physical induction is typically executed with a belt conveyor operating at a 45° angle to the direction of the sorter.

The fundamental control requirement in mechanical sorting is the ability to identify a product, a product's destination, and the product's place on the sorter. Product identification may be done manually, with induction operators reading labels related to product codes and types. The identification may be automated, with bar code or optical character recognition labels applied to or integrated into the product packaging. The product identification is then communicated by hand (with keyboard data entry), by mouth (with voice input), or automated (with bar code scanners or vision systems).

Accumulation Lanes and Chutes

The last major component in a sorting system is the mechanism used to accumulate merchandise at a discharge point. Depending on the weight and dimensions of the items and the number of divert points, the range of options for lanes and chutes is vast. For surface and pop-up sorters, accumulation lanes are usually comprised of some type of wheel or roller conveyor ranging from simple gravity flow rack or skate wheel conveyor to heavy-duty pallet roller conveyor. For tilting and carrier sorters an even greater array of chute designs is available. Chutes are widely variable in configuration (i.e., single-lane, double-lane, drop-door, etc.) and material (i.e., metal, wood, or cloth).

Shipping Operations

Shipping typically encompasses the sortation, accumulation, consolidation, packaging, staging, and loading of outbound orders. Shipping is another space- and labor-intensive function in a distribution center. However, through direct loading of outbound trailers, the staging activity and the associated space, labor, and time are eliminated. The labor content in the remaining shipping activity, trailer loading, can also be minimized through the use of automated forklifts and conveyors that extend into outbound trailers. When the staging activity cannot be eliminated, the space requirements can be minimized through rack systems.

Shipping Principles

Many of the best-practice receiving principles also apply in reverse in shipping, including direct loading (the reverse of direct unloading), advanced shipping notice preparation (prereceiving), and staging in racks. In addition to those principles we have chosen to introduce best-practice principles for unitizing and securing loads, automated loading, and dock management.

1. *Select cost- and space-effective handling units:*
   a. *For loose cases.* The options for unitizing loose cases include wood (disposable, returnable, and rentable) pallets, plastic, metal, and nestable pallets. The advantages of plastic pallets over wood pallets include durability, cleanliness, and colorability. The Japanese make excellent use of colored plastic pallets and totes in creating appealing work environments in factories and warehouses. Metal pallets are designed primarily for durability and weight capacity. Nestable pallets offer good space utilization during pallet storage and return, but are not very durable and have limited weight capacity. Other options for unitizing loose cases include slipsheets and roll carts. Slipsheets improve space utilization in storage systems and in trailers, but require special lift truck attachments. Roll carts facilitate the containerization of multiple items in case quantities, and facilitate material handling throughout the shipping process from order picking to packaging to checking to trailer loading. The selection factors for unitizing loose cases include initial purchase cost, maintenance costs and requirements, ease of handling, impact on the environment, durability, and product protection.
   b. *For loose items.* The options unitizing loose items include totes (nestable and collapsible) and cardboard containers. As was the case with unitizing loose cases, the selection factors include impact on the environment, initial purchase cost, life-cycle cost, cleanliness, and product protection. For an excellent review and comparison of carton and tote performance, consult the article listed as number 22 in the References section at the end of this chapter.
2. *To minimize product damage:*
   a. *Unitize and secure loose items in cartons or totes.* In addition to providing a unit load to facilitate material handling, a means must be provided to secure material within the unit load. For loose items in totes or cartons, those means include foam, peanuts, popcorn, bubblewrap, newsprint, and airpacks. The selection factors include initial and life-cycle cost, impact on the environment, product protection, and reusability. An excellent review of alternative packaging methods is provided in the article just mentioned.
   b. *Unitize and secure loose cases on pallets.* Though the most popular alternative is stretch-wrapping, velcro belts and adhesive tacking are gaining in popularity as environmentally safe means of securing loose cases on pallets.
   c. *Unitize and secure loose pallets in outbound trailers.* The most common methods are foam pads and plywood.
3. *Eliminate shipping staging, and direct-load outbound trailers.* As was the case in receiving, the most space- and labor-intensive activity in shipping is the staging activity. To facilitate the direct loading of pallets onto outbound trailers, pallet

jacks and counterbalance lift trucks can serve as picking and loading vehicles, thus bypassing staging. To go one step further, the automating of pallet loading can be accomplished with pallet conveyor interfacing with specially designed trailer beds, to allow pallets to be automatically conveyed onto outbound trailers, with automated fork trucks, and/or automated guided vehicles. Direct, automated loading of loose cases is facilitated with an extendable conveyor.

4. *Use storage racks to minimize floor-space requirements for shipping staging.* If shipping staging is required, the floor-space requirements for staging can be minimized by staging in storage racks. A large automotive aftermarkets supplier places racks along the shipping wall and above dock doors to achieve this objective.

5. *Route on-site drivers through the site with a minimum of paperwork and time.* A variety of systems are now in place to improve the management of shipping and receiving docks and trailer drivers. At one brewery, trailer drivers use a smart card to gain access throughout the distribution center site, to expedite on-site processing, and to ensure shipping accuracy. At another brewery, terminal stands are provided throughout the site to allow drivers on-line access to load-status and dock schedules.

Integrating Material and Information Flow

The principles and systems that have been described above are designed to streamline the operations of individual functional areas within the warehouse. To complete our objective of achieving streamlined, minimum-work-content warehouse operations, the flow of materials and information must be well integrated. The principles and systems described briefly in this chapter are designed to help the reader understand the integration of material and information flow in warehouse operations. A more detailed description of information flow is presented in Chapter 27, Warehouse Management Systems.

The integration of the physical flow of material in warehouse operations is achieved with a variety of material handling technologies, including conveyors (belt, roller, accumulation, sortation, towline, trolley, and car-on-track) and industrial vehicles. A detailed description of these material flow systems is provided in Chapter 19 of this handbook.

Automatic, Paperless Communication Systems

Automated status control of material requires that the real-time awareness of the location, amount, origin, destination, and schedule of material be achieved automatically. This objective is in fact the function of automatic identification technologies, technologies that permit real-time, nearly flawless data collection. Examples of automatic identification technologies at work include

- A vision system, reading bar code labels to identify the proper destination for a carton traveling on a sortation conveyor (see Chapter 27 for a full discussion)

- A laser scanner, to relay the inventory levels of a small-parts warehouse to a computer via RF
- A voice recognition system, to identify parts received at the receiving dock
- A radio frequency (RF) or surface acoustical wave (SAW) tag, used to permanently identify a tote pan
- A card with a magnetic stripe that travels with a unit load, to identify the load through the distribution channels

Radio-Frequency Data Communication. Again, although not technically a member of the automatic identification systems family, hand-held and lift-truck-mounted radio data terminals (RDTs) are rapidly emerging as reliable tools for both inventory and vehicle/driver management. RDTs incorporate a multi-character display, full keyboard, and special function keys. They communicate and receive messages on a prescribed frequency via strategically located antennae and a host computer interface unit. Beyond the basic thrust toward tighter control of inventory, improved resource utilization is most often cited in justification of these devices. Further, the increasing availability of software packages that permit RDT linkage to existing plant or warehouse control systems greatly simplifies their implementation. The majority of RDTs installed in the plant environment use hand-held wands or scanners for data entry, product identification, and location verification. This marriage of technologies provides higher levels of speed, accuracy, and productivity than could be achieved by either technique alone. In 1989, initial installations of RDTs and voice data entry devices provided equally promising results.

Light- and Computer-Aided Order Picking. The objectives of light or computer-aided order picking (CAOP) are to reduce the search time, extract time, and documentation time portions of total order picking time, and to improve picking accuracy. Search time is reduced by having a computer automatically illuminate a light at the pick location(s) from which the next pick(s) is (are) to be made. Extract time is reduced by displaying the quantity to pick on a display at the pick location. Documentation time is reduced by allowing the order picker to push a button at the pick location to inform the computer that the pick has been completed. The result is accurate order picking at a rate of up to 600 picks/man-hr.

CAOP systems of this type are available for bin shelving, flow rack, and carousel systems, and cost around $100 per storage location.

Systems of this type are also available for use with the miniload AS/RS. These systems provide a computer display over each pick station. On the display is a picture of the configuration of the storage container in that pick station. The compartment in the container that is to be extracted from is illuminated, and the quantity to select is displayed on the computer screen.

The basic solution approach of CAOP systems is to take the thinking out of order picking. Consequently, an unusual human-factors challenge is introduced. The job becomes too easy, and hence boring and even mentally degrading to many people.

Voice Input/Output. Voice recognition (VR) is a computer-based system that translates spoken words into computer data without special codes. VR systems are attractive when an operator's hands and eyes must be freed up for productive operations. Though VR systems are in their infancy, some systems recognize up to 1000 words and are 99.5 percent accurate. VR systems are still relatively expensive, and must be dedicated to one operator at a time.

Smart Cards.   Smart cards (essentially credit cards) are now used to capture information ranging from employee identification to the contents of a trailer load of material to the composition of an order picking tour. At a large cosmetics distribution center, order picking tours are downloaded onto smart cards. The smart cards are in turn inserted into a smart card reader on each order picking cart. In so doing, the picking tour is illuminated on an electronic map of the warehouse that appears on the front of the cart.

Automatic Control Systems

Warehouse efficiency and accuracy are largely a function of the control system used to direct and track activity. Control system principles and requirements are now described by functional area.

Receiving Control.   The receiving function is primarily one of information processing rather than physical handling. Consequently, it is desirable to plan and concentrate the information-related tasks into as few steps as possible. Accomplishing this requires on-line accessibility to receiving information and real-time interaction with the database.

Receiving tasks might be thought of as a series of questions to be answered regarding each item that crosses the dock. The basic questions that should be built into a control system for each receipt are listed next. Yes answers indicate straight-through flow, with little cause for delay. A no answer requires resolution, or exception processing, and usually interruption of flow. It becomes obvious that the best improvements in receiving operations are a direct result of ensuring that the answers will be yes.

- Am I expecting a shipment from this company on or before this date?
- Do the cartons/pallets match the freight bill?
- Does the merchandise appear to be undamaged?
- Are the items on the packing slip included on open purchase orders?
- Do the items and quantities in the shipment match the packing list?
- Is the merchandise in good condition, and do the parts match the purchasing specifications?
- Is the merchandise received needed by production or a customer now, and what are the destinations?
- If it is not needed immediately, where should I store it?

The information-processing requirements are used to generate a physical handling system. Each of the decision points should be reviewed, to determine which ones can be performed at a single station. The consolidation of information-processing tasks into groups should be based on the following three principles:

1. Simplify the workplace.
2. Utilize personnel.
3. Minimize materials movement.

The most effective receiving systems consist of layout and handling equipment that permits material to flow through or past a receiving station. At this point as many of the tasks as possible, including exception processing, should be done at one time.

Two major objectives must be achieved for this type of flow-through receiving to be possible:

1. Immediate availability of information
2. Capacity to handle peak demands

Solving the first problem usually speeds up the process so much that capacity is no longer a problem. Having information immediately available will eliminate the time wasted by personnel searching for the information. Most of the delays in the receiving process result from lack of correction or of adequate information. Easy access to information will reduce the need for staging space as well.

Computerized databases with on-line terminals would appear to be the logical solution. And indeed they are—when the computer is up, the response time is short and the data is all there. For years large, central, mainframe computers have forced us to grow accustomed to batch processing of data and long response times—approaching, or even exceeding, a minute for a reply to a command. Data-processing system designers felt successful when they were able to consistently respond within three seconds. However, recent studies have indicated that subsecond responses provide a dramatic increase in productivity at computer terminal operations.

With today's computer costs falling, the problems of availability and response time are frequently addressed by means of a processor dedicated to the warehousing or even the receiving function. Data completeness and accuracy result from a truly integrated system design, which requires that data relevant to receiving be in place in the files before purchase orders are released.

Working in conjunction with computers, automatic identification systems also play a vital role in speeding data entry, maintaining system integrity, and facilitating automatic operations. It is common for documents, containers, and even individual parts to be labeled with a code.

Stock Location Control.   There are a number of ways to assign the space provided in racks, shelving, bins, and drawers for the storage of material. Each assignment system provides a different combination of cube utilization, throughput, or productivity and control. In general, the following objectives apply to stock location planning:

1. Good space utilization
2. Facilitating placement into storage

3. Facilitating efficient and accurate order picking
4. Matching control system capability
5. Flexibility to accept change

In many instances where limited control system capability exists or when absolute simplicity of controls is necessary, merchandise may be stored in part-number sequence, grouped by product line or manufacturer. This system is easy to implement and to learn, but when applied strictly it compromises both cube utilization and productivity. It is usually difficult to add part numbers or to increase the inventory of selected items.

When an individual part number can be put away in any available storage slot, it is subject to random location assignment. Storage slots may be classified by size, so that there can be a closer match between the cube of the item to be stored and the available locations.

There are two types of randomized storage: (1) true randomized storage, in which all locations have an equally likely chance of having product stored in them, and (2) closest-available slot (CAS). Outgoing items may be picked automatically on a first-in, first-out (FIFO) basis, or they may be selected based on the opportunity to complete the pick from a single location. Yet another option is to select based on an opportunity to empty partially filled locations to make them available for the storage of new items. The CAS type of randomized storage is the most common in today's industrial environment. If the storage levels remain fairly constant and at a high level of utilization, there is little difference between the two types of randomized storage. However, if utilization is low and inventory levels vary, the CAS method of randomized storage will increase throughput in the system.

Dedicated storage based on activity will maximize throughput at the expense of storage space utilization. Conversely, randomized storage will optimize storage space but reduce throughput of the system. Studies have shown that dedicated storage can yield savings in increased throughput of 15 to 50 percent over pure or true randomized storage, while dedicated storage can yield savings in increased throughput of 15 to 50 percent over pure or true randomized storage. Additionally, studies have shown that dedicated storage can require from 20 to 60 percent more storage slots than are required for random storage. Thus, the selection of the appropriate storage location assignment method depends on the importance given to space versus throughput levels.

When items are often used or sold together they may be colocated to increase picking productivity. When locations are next to or close to one another, travel time is reduced. In automated-bin storage systems, several picks may be made with a single bin retrieval. With the exception of colocation, storage assignment in automated systems is more likely to be random, in order to maximize the utilization of the expensive storage cube. Rapid horizontal and vertical travel, combined with relatively slow positioning and load transfer moves, make total cycle times, and hence throughput, less dependent on optimized location assignment. The control systems typically associated with automated storage can accommodate random locations easily.

Order Picking and Shipping Control.   Most of the general issues discussed in the section on receiving control apply to picking and shipping control as well. Particularly important are the concepts related to performing as many information-related tasks as possible at a single station. This is applicable when picking is done at the end of the aisle, as in miniload or carousel systems, and for verification, packing, and shipping functions.

As random storage systems become more common in order to conserve space, it is mandatory to include the picking location along with the item and quantity to be picked. Since the same item may be stored in several locations, it is also necessary to include logic in the control system that maintains first-in, first-out product movement if required, or that facilitates picking by directing the operator to a location with sufficient quantity to satisfy the pick. Other logic may attempt to clear out partially used locations to make space available for new merchandise.

Real-time receipt of orders and allocation of stock is now commonplace, and, for many operations, orders received today are shipped today.

Printing picking instructions in the same sequence as the merchandise appears in the storage system improves efficiency for in-aisle picking. Picks for several orders may be interspersed and separated by the operator as the picks are made, so that one trip down the aisle will satisfy several orders.

Product cartons, picking lists, and tote boxes are commonly identified with bar codes to facilitate tracking, sorting, accumulation, and data entry.

Many software packages are available to manage warehouse operations. Selecting the right package requires careful matching of the specific needs of a particular physical and operation design with the features in the alternative packages. Most often, some modification of the package must be done, or some customized input/output modules must be developed, to make a package fit exactly. Obviously, the fewer changes the better. That way costs stay down and reliability remains high.

Next-Generation Warehouse Operations

Before speculating on the nature of the next generation of warehouse operations, we need to speculate on the next-generation *requirements* for warehouse operations. In doing so, we can only imagine that

1. The standards for shipping response time and accuracy will tighten—overnight shipping and near-perfect accuracy will be the norm.
2. A continued emphasis on customer service will make tailored services and packaging the norm, and will place a premium on flexibility in design and management.
3. A labor shortage (in quality if not in quantity) will make work environment a competitive advantage for those firms attempting to attract high-quality labor.
4. The resulting emphasis on ergonomics and human safety, and rapidly declining costs and risks in automated material handling systems (already achieved by some Japanese material handling suppliers), will make the application of automated material handling systems more prevalent.
5. An emphasis on the preservation of natural lands will make industrial-use land areas more scarce. The resulting premium price on working space will make storage space utilization a critical factor in the design of new warehouse and distribution centers.

6. Rapidly advancing capabilities in automatic identification, communication, and control systems will eliminate all need for paperwork and keyboarding.

With those requirements in mind, we now revisit each of the functional areas within the warehouse, to speculate on how the operation of each area may look in the next generation.

Let us first recall that the traditional receiving process includes unloading inbound trailers, staging inbound loads, inspecting and inchecking inbound material, and putting material away in reserve storage locations. In direct putaway systems, the staging and inspection operations are eliminated. Hence the time, space, and labor associated with those operations is eliminated. Consequently, the next generation of receiving operations will be characterized by automated, direct putaway to storage. The material handling technologies that facilitate direct putaway include roller-bed trailers and extendable conveyors.

With the new requirement to simultaneously minimize landspace requirements and maximize throughput capacity, storage systems must break the historical trade-off of storage density for product accessibility. A variety of systems have been applied to successfully make the breakthrough, including twin-shuttle automated storage/retrieval systems, multicrane AS/RS aisles, rotary-rack carousels, and high-velocity input/output systems for AS/RS. These systems will populate the next-generation warehouse.

Recall that order picking typically encompasses the extraction of material from storage locations to satisfy customer orders and the replenishment of depleted picking locations. It is the most labor-intensive, error-prone, and time-critical activity in a typical warehouse or distribution center. Hence it has been the focal point for the application of a wide variety of automated systems, including multiload vehicles, tier picking, light aids, intelligent picking vehicles, batch picking for direct sorter induction, and dynamic pick-line configuration. These technologies will be the norm in the next generation.

Shipping typically encompasses the sortation, accumulation, consolidation, packaging, staging, and loading of outbound orders. Shipping is another space- and labor-intensive function in a distribution center. However, through direct loading of outbound trailers, the staging activity and the associated space, labor, and time are eliminated. The labor content in the remaining shipping activity, trailer loading, can and will be minimized through automated forklifts and conveyors that extend into outbound trailers. When the staging activity cannot be eliminated, the space requirements will be minimized through rack systems.

The design of material transport and sorting systems is governed by high throughput requirements and high precision requirements to interface with automated systems throughout a distribution center. Automated guided vehicles, automated electrified monorails, car-on-track conveyor, cross-belt and surfer sorters, and sorting transfer vehicles all meet these requirements.

References

1. Warehousing Education and Research Council, "A Guide for Evaluating and Implementing a Warehouse Bar Code System,"Oak Brook, IL, 1992.

2. Apple, James M., *Material Handling System Design*, Ronald Press Co. (John Wiley), New York, 1972.

3. Frazelle, E. H., "Automated Storage, Retrieval, and Transport Systems in Japan," U.S. Department of Commerce Technical Report, December 1990.

4. ———, "Small Parts Order Picking: Equipment and Strategy," Material Handling Research Center Technical Report Number 01-88-01, Georgia Institute of Technology, Atlanta, GA, 30332-0205.

5. ———, "Stock Location Assignment and Order Picking Productivity," Ph.D. Dissertation, Georgia Institute of Technology, December 1989.

6. Frazelle, E. H., S. T. Hackman, U. Passy, and L. K. Platzman, "Solving the Forward-Reserve Problem," Material Handling Research Center Technical Report, Georgia Institute of Technology, May 1992.

7. Frazelle, E. H., S. T. Hackman, and L. K. Platzman, "Intelligent Stock Assignment Planning," Proceeding of the 1989 Council of Logistics Management's Annual Conference, St. Louis, MO, October 1989.

8. Frazelle, E. H. and L. F. McGinnis, "Automated Material Handling," in *The Encyclopedia of Microcomputers*, A. Kent and J. G. Williams, eds., Marcel Dekker, New York and Basel, 1988.

9. Hale, C. A. and M. N. Harrell, "Lift Truck Storage," SysteCon Technical Presentation, SysteCon, A Division of Coopers & Lybrand, Atlanta.

10. Hill, J. M., "Automatic Identification Perspective 1992," Proceedings of the Material Handling Short Course, Georgia Institute of Technology, Atlanta, March 1992.

11. Horrey, R. J., "Sortation Systems: From Push to High-Speed Fully Automated Applications," 1983 International Conference on Automation in Warehousing Proceedings, Institute of Industrial Engineers, Atlanta, pp. 77–83.

12. Jenkins, Creed H., *Modern Warehouse Management*, McGraw-Hill, New York, 1968.

13. Kulwiec, Raymond A., "Material Handling Equipment Guide," *Plant Engineering*, pp. 88–99, August 21, 1980.

14. Material Handling Engineering, 1984 Casebook Directory, Boston, Cahners Publishing Co., 1984.

15. Kulwiec, Raymond A., ed., *Materials Handling Handbook*, John Wiley, New York, 1985.

16. Frazelle, E. H., ed., *Material Handling Systems and Terminology*, Lionhart Publishing, Atlanta, 1992.

17. Muther, Richard, *Systematic Layout Planning*, CBI Publishing Co., Inc., Boston, 1973.

18. Suzuki, J., "Guide to the Installation of Automated Sorters," 1990 International Conference on Automation in Warehousing Proceedings, Institute of Industrial Engineers, Atlanta.

19. Tompkins, J. A. and J. A. White, *Facilities Planning*, John Wiley, New York, 1984.

20. Warehousing Education and Research Council, "Warehousing Education and Research Council's Annual Membership Survey," Oak Brook, IL, 1988.

21. *Warehouse Modernization and Layout Planning Guide*, U.S. Naval Supply Systems Command Publication 529, U.S. Naval Supply Systems Command, Richmond, VA, 1988.

22. Wilde, J., "Container Design Issues," Proceedings of the 1992 Material Handling Management Course, sponsored by the Institute of Industrial Engineers, Atlanta, June, 1992.

PART 4

Managing Distribution

23

Distribution Network Monitoring

Herbert W. Davis
President, Herbert W. Davis and Company

You cannot manage what you cannot measure. That old thought is still current—perhaps even more so, given today's complex, sophisticated distribution networks. Monitoring, therefore, has emerged as an area of vital concern.

Current management objectives require three things from the distribution network and its managers.

1. *The network has to supply product to customers exactly when, where, and how they want it.* Customer service, therefore, is a key objective of the network. Service excellence helps to assure competitive survival.

2. *Networks need to operate with far less inventory than in the recent past.* Planning, manufacturing, and distribution have to be redesigned for reduced cycle times. That means substituting information for inventory, and processing that information almost instantly.

3. *Low-cost distribution is a competitive necessity, so the network must operate with high productivity.* Accuracy and precision in operation are hallmarks of today's best distribution networks.

Thus, proper monitoring of the distribution network is crucial to logistics management. The monitoring system needs to be set up to measure performance in the three crucial areas described: customer service satisfaction, inventory availability, and cost control. Monitoring systems for each will be described separately in this chapter.

Two Concepts of Monitoring

A major problem with monitoring systems in today's corporate environment derives directly from the plethora of data that is available. Current sensing and automatic recording systems (bar code readers, cash registers, electronic data interchange, radio frequency transmissions, etc.) provide the opportunity to collect vast quantities of data. Computers permit accurate, fast processing of this data. Unfortunately, the manager can drown in oceans of information unless monitoring systems are designed to separate the important from the merely interesting.

So the first concept of network monitoring is to *concentrate on the important facts*. Don't waste time sorting through irrelevant detail data. The essence of monitoring is *focus*. Focus on those indicators that tell how well the network is functioning and where problems are developing. Later, some of the interesting background detail data will help isolate and then correct the problems uncovered by the monitoring system.

For example, in customer service, measure those service elements that have the largest impact on the customer's perception of service; things such as number of perfect orders delivered, total order cycle time as seen by the customer, percent of orders and lines filled complete, telephone line hangups, etc. In warehousing, concentrate on labor and equipment utilization and efficiency; for example, how many lines are picked per labor hour.

The second important concept to observe in monitoring is to *set the reporting interval properly*. What is meant by "properly"? Ideally, the interval or reporting frequency needs to be set based on the activity being controlled. If the system is to monitor costs at public warehouses or other third party logistics providers, the proper monitoring interval is probably 30 days, because not much can be done about costs on a real-time basis.

On the other hand, to monitor and control labor utilization in a company-owned distribution center, hourly and daily results are needed. A monthly report won't detect problems early enough to provide any chance to improve throughput efficiency.

Some suggestions on interval and frequency include the following.

Customer Service:

1. Customer satisfaction: Monthly
                                    Annual surveys

2. Order and line fill rates: Measure weekly
                                    Report monthly

3. Total order cycle time: Monthly

4. Telephone responsiveness: Daily
                                    Report monthly

Inventory:

1. Quantity by SKU, lot, and location should be controlled in real time.

2. Reports by item for comparison to budgets should be at the same frequency as the replenishment system—daily, weekly, or (occasionally) monthly.

Labor Utilization:

1. In-warehouse monitoring might be in real time as part of a computerized warehouse management system. Reports should summarize results by facility and department daily, weekly, monthly, and year-to-date.

2. In manually controlled warehouses, recording frequency should be at least daily, with management reports weekly.

Accuracy:

1. Inventory quantity and location accuracy are best controlled by cyclical counts made continuously. Frequency of control for the item is a function of the A, B, C classification; that is, count the high-value or fast-moving items more frequently than the slow movers.

2. Order accuracy should be built into the system by the use of scanning and bar codes. Thus, frequency of monitoring is real-time, while reporting is best done daily and weekly, with monthly summaries.

These are merely examples to illustrate the concept of monitoring and reporting intervals. The proper answer for each element measured depends on the element and the control system used. More detail will be presented in the sections covering each monitored element.

To repeat the major point: In setting up a distribution network monitoring system, be sure to follow the two cardinal rules:

1. Concentrate on the important facts.

2. Establish the appropriate monitoring interval.

Monitoring Customer Service

The logistics department has primary responsibility in the corporation for the elements (i.e., warehousing, transportation, etc.) that result in a successful distribution network: "delivery of the product when and where the customer wants it." The objective of this delivery service is customer satisfaction. Thus, the customer service monitoring system needs to measure two broad variables:

1. *The customer's satisfaction with the product delivery process.* This is essentially an area of soft data—inexact and somewhat subjective, but nevertheless vital.

2. *A series of internal, statistical-data measurements that show the level of performance on those variables that most influence customer satisfaction.* The list of variables changes over time and by industry. The most common customer concerns are product availability, delivery order cycle, and responsiveness of the information and communication system. Performance levels for all of these can be measured. However, it is important to remember that at times any industry may concentrate on other areas that are just as important. Currently, for example, there is great concern with the impact of packing materials on the environment.

Thus, the monitoring system that measures customer service level is fairly complex. Follow these five steps to ensure proper design and installation:

1. *Conduct a customer survey.* A survey can help determine customer needs, competitor capabilities and performance level, and the economic gain (or loss) that will result from changes in the present service level.

2. *Perform an internal audit.* An audit will help you to ascertain current levels of service, the cost to achieve these levels, service problem areas that need to be fixed, and the cost implications of better (or lower) service.

3. *Set service objectives.* Objectives for each attribute measured should be established by the company on the basis of customer needs, competitive offerings, internal capabilities, and economics.

4. *Design the monitoring system to measure each service variable.* Measurements usually are done in real time by accumulating statistics drawn from the transaction-processing system. In some cases it is necessary to draw information from third party logistics partners. Good examples of third party reports are the time of delivery by motor carriers and the order-processing time by public warehouses.

5. *Design the reporting system.* The measurements of each service element are accumulated and presented in a regular management report. Reports typically are prepared and distributed monthly, while the department responsible may review the detailed results daily or weekly. A typical report on internal service measurement is shown in Fig. 23-1. Four major service attributes are measured, and a composite score calculated.

The Customer Service Survey

There are three key issues to address in surveying customers to determine their perception of service level and satisfaction: (1) what contact method to use, (2) what specific service areas need to be examined, and (3) how many customers to contact.

Contact Method. Customer satisfaction surveying is a derivative technique that originated in market research. The research field uses a wide range of approaches in surveying customers, but in distribution, the four most commonly used methods are as follows.

Team Meetings. A four- or five-person team representing sales/marketing, order entry/customer service, distribution center operations, transportation, and computer support systems arranges to meet with a counterpart team from the most important accounts. Usually only four or five giant accounts are visited in this way; there is a lot of preparation, some presentations, and a meeting facilitator. The team leader prepares a written report on the visit, and follow-up sessions are held to assure maximum responsiveness to the account's needs.

Personal Interviews. A trained interviewer visits one or more customer buyers or representatives. A predetermined series of questions is asked, partly to get numerical data but primarily to draw from the customer their perceptions of key service issues and concerns. An important by-product sought is a measure of competitive capabilities and performance.

Telephone Interviews. Many customers resist personal interviews (too time-consuming), so the telephone serves as a backup. Results are usually more quantitative, and less background information is developed. The method, however, is much less expensive.

	Warehouse				
	East		West		Total
Order Fill Rates (50%)	No.	%	No.	%	No. %
Lines Filled Complete Target					
Performance (%)					

	Number In ( ) Days					Number Within Standard
Order Cycle Time (30%)	1-7	8-14	15-21	22-28	+28	
Northeast						
Southeast						
Midwest						
Southwest						
West Coast						
Total						
% On Time						

Error Rates (10%)	No.	%	No.	%	No.	%
Order Entry						
Warehouse						
Transportation						
Billing						
Other						
Total						
Target						

Complaints (10%)			
Number Received			
% of Accounts			

Total Orders Processed			
Total Lines Processed			
Total No. of Accounts			
Overall Performance (%)			

Figure 23-1. Customer service measurement report—internal.

Mail Questionnaires. This is the method most used by distribution departments. A questionnaire, with a stamped return envelope, is sent to key customer personnel. The information sought is principally quantitative, and only limited customer comments and perceptions can be expected. Broad competitive comparisons can be found, but details are hard to get in a mail contact.

Questionnaire Design. The survey design is usually developed by outlining the questions or issues that need to be addressed. There are two major factors: (1) how important is service, and (2) what are the elements that, taken together, contribute to the customer's ranking of the supplier in terms of satisfaction. The questionnaire design, then, usually contains one to five open-ended questions about service importance, overall satisfaction, and areas that need improvement. The bulk of the questionnaire, however, consists of a listing of the service elements (product availability, cycle time, damage, etc.). A sample questionnaire shown in Fig. 23-2 lists many of these service elements. Then, three questions are asked:

Please rate the following attributes for their importance in your evaluation of the quality of service, our current performance, and how well we compare to competitors.

Attribute	IMPORTANCE IN EVALUATING THE QUALITY OF SERVICE (Circle One)			CURRENT PERFORMANCE (Circle One)			COMPETITORS' PERFORMANCE (Check One)		
	Irrelevant	Moderately Important	Essential	Does Not Meet Our Requirements	Sometimes Meets Our Requirements	Meets All Our Requirements	Worse Than	Same As	Better Than
1. Total order cycle time (speed of delivery)	1 2	3 4 5	6 7	1 2	3 4 5	6 7	—	—	—
2. Availability of product	1 2	3 4 5	6 7	1 2	3 4 5	6 7	—	—	—
3. Meeting requested delivery dates	1 2	3 4 5	6 7	1 2	3 4 5	6 7	—	—	—
4. Availability of information on inventories, open orders, delivery times, etc.	1 2	3 4 5	6 7	1 2	3 4 5	6 7	—	—	—
5. Procedures for placing orders	1 2	3 4 5	6 7	1 2	3 4 5	6 7	—	—	—
6. Procedures for correcting errors	1 2	3 4 5	6 7	1 2	3 4 5	6 7	—	—	—
7. Procedure for processing performance claims	1 2	3 4 5	6 7	1 2	3 4 5	6 7	—	—	—
8. Field salesperson (helpfulness, visit frequency)	1 2	3 4 5	6 7	1 2	3 4 5	6 7	—	—	—
9. Customer service representative (attitude and helpfulness)	1 2	3 4 5	6 7	1 2	3 4 5	6 7	—	—	—
10. Accuracy of invoices	1 2	3 4 5	6 7	1 2	3 4 5	6 7	—	—	—
11. Accuracy of shipments	1 2	3 4 5	6 7	1 2	3 4 5	6 7	—	—	—
12. Response to emergency requests	1 2	3 4 5	6 7	1 2	3 4 5	6 7	—	—	—
13. Procedures for returns	1 2	3 4 5	6 7	1 2	3 4 5	6 7	—	—	—
14. Condition of product when received/packaging	1 2	3 4 5	6 7	1 2	3 4 5	6 7	—	—	—
15. Proper markings (labels, identification)	1 2	3 4 5	6 7	1 2	3 4 5	6 7	—	—	—
16. Proximity of inventory (nearby warehouse required to supply you)	1 2	3 4 5	6 7	1 2	3 4 5	6 7	—	—	—

Do you have any comments? _____

Figure 23-2. Sample customer service questionnaire.

1. How important is the element?
2. How satisfied are you with our performance?
3. Is the competitor's performance better than, same as, or worse than ours?

The customers' answers are the major measure of current satisfaction level.

Sample Size.   The required number of customer interviews or completed questionnaires can be determined statistically. Usually, the customer list is divided into three categories based on sales volume (giant, top 100 or 200, all others). The giants are handled by action team meetings. The top 100 accounts are sampled using both personal and telephone interviews, with a 50 percent sample or larger desired. The other accounts can be covered by phone or mail. Typically, questionnaires are sent to perhaps 1000 accounts, with returns expected from 20 to 40 percent of those contacted. Numerous techniques are used to improve the percent returned.

Statistical tests are used to determine the confidence level and accuracy of the results. As a rule, enough research is completed to assure 90 percent confidence that the customer segment sample result reflects the population's opinion, accurate to within plus or minus 10 to 20 percent.

Customer Service Monitoring Interval.   It is important to monitor customer satisfaction on a continuing basis. This can be accomplished by means of two different approaches.

1. Repeat the customer service survey every year or two, refining the sample and the questionnaires but retaining several key, long-term measures that will provide a continuous track record.

2. Follow the example of some companies and do sampling by mail and telephone each quarter, contacting 25 of the top 100 accounts. This supplies the monitoring system with quarterly data to compare to the internal statistical measures. A sample report is shown in concept in Fig. 23-3.

Monitoring Cost and Productivity

Seen from an historical perspective, distribution costs today are relatively low. Although physical distribution as a concept—giving time and place utility to a product—is very old, industry didn't develop the first organizational structures for it until the early 1960s. Publication of Peter Drucker's *The Dark Continent* and the formation of the National Council of Physical Distribution Management (by William Beckmann in 1963) were the early milestones.

Consolidated, accurate information on distribution costs has been available since those times. Figure 23-4 shows distribution cost as a percentage of sales revenue by year since 1961. Figure 23-5 shows the same information for the three major components: transportation, warehousing, and inventory.

Costs have been low historically because industry pays a lot of attention to distribution cost. It is a direct cost of doing business and, at about 8 percent of sales, it's

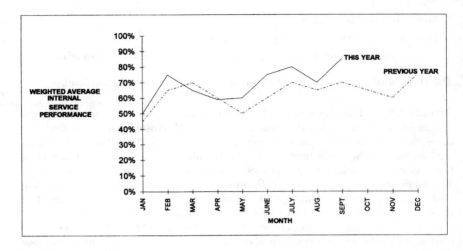

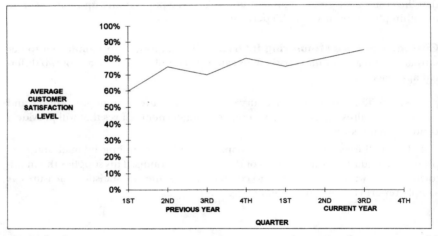

Figure 23-3. Customer service report—consolidated.

as large as total corporate profit for the average manufacturer. Table 23-1 shows cost by major distribution activity. The three major reasons why costs are relatively low are now given.

1. *Transportation deregulation.* The trend toward deregulation of many business areas started with air and motor carriers in the late 1970s. Increased competition and higher carrier efficiency sharply reduced freight rates over the entire decade of the 1980s.

2. *Management techniques.* The advent of just-in-time inventory and the sharp reduction in manufacturing cycle times have more closely coupled inventory and sales demand. Modern quick response systems result in better control of the entire supply chain.

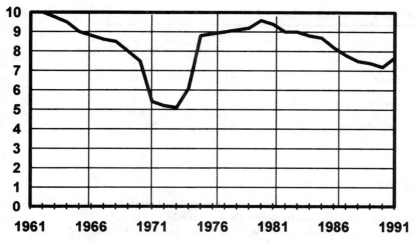

Figure 23-4. Distribution cost (percent of sales).

3. *Global competitiveness.* As exports climbed from below 10 percent of gross manufactured product to the current 30 percent, American companies had to reduce costs to retain and expand their markets. A countertrend, the enormous rise of imports, further encouraged this drive to reduce costs.

Thus, monitoring of distribution network cost is a vital activity for the distribution department. This discussion of monitoring will focus on two levels of control:

1. Overall, or total, distribution cost, segmented by facility or product and by major function (transport, warehousing, etc.).
2. Productivity, primarily a set of input/output ratios that describe the effectiveness of an operation, person, or machine.

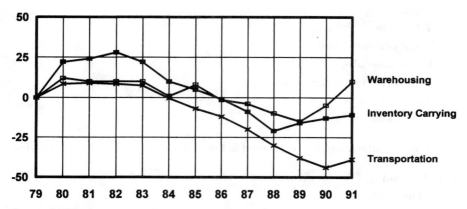

Figure 23-5. Distribution component cost (percent of sales).

Table 23-1 Distribution Costs—1991

	Distribution costs in	
	Percent of sales	$/CWT
Transportation	3.31	$11.73
Warehousing	2.03	10.96
Customer service	0.56	4.04
Administration	0.39	2.13
Inventory carrying	1.82	9.86
Total distribution costs	8.11	$38.72

Monitoring Distribution Cost

The typical corporate cost-monitoring system is based on the classifying to a specific account of each cost as it is incurred. Costs generally can be related to (1) a product or (2) a period. Typically, costs for labor or material can be assigned readily to a specific product or order. Some costs, like rent or depreciation, are time-related. These costs can be allocated to a product flow that takes place concurrently.

In the cost system, these two expense categories are tabulated by functional activity and facility, and are reported as the department's cost for an accounting period, normally a month.

The distribution network cost, then, can be developed from the elemental costs shown in the monthly statement for each facility managed. The distribution department, therefore, will know distribution cost by activity, facility, and cost center. Each cost is usually analyzed by month and year-to-date, and each is compared to the annual operating plan or budget and to the same period in previous years.

A normal breakdown of these distribution center costs will include:

Supervision

Labor

Fringe benefits

Rent (or building depreciation)

Light, heat, power

Telephone

Taxes: personnel, building

Direct materials

Equipment rent or depreciation

Miscellaneous

Facility total

Transportation costs may be charged to the facility under one of these categories:

1. Inbound
2. Outbound
3. Interfacility

Freight paid by others can be subtracted. Each company tends to have its own conventions as to where freight cost is allocated. However, totals are universally available because of freight's significance.

While all of these cost breakdowns may yield some interesting information, monitoring or controlling cost requires further analysis. Typically, the distribution manager will deal with cost ratios to facilitate control. Absolute numbers are difficult to evaluate because of daily, weekly, and seasonal volume differences. The two ratios most frequently used are now described.

1. *Cost as a percent of revenue.* Most corporate budgets are established in relation to sales. Thus, the warehouse function will be allocated some amount based on the historical relationship of freight cost to sales. The amount is significant, and may be expected to total around 2 percent of sales.

2. *Cost per hundredweight.* This ratio is mostly used where third party or public warehouses are engaged to handle storage and shipping. Similar ratios can be based on the number of order lines, customer orders, cases shipped, etc.

Very similar systems are used to monitor other distribution costs, such as order entry and customer service and the distribution network management.

Finally, transportation cost is accumulated for the accounting period and divided by the pounds (or hundredweight) handled, and by the sales revenue for the same period.

These and other useful ratios form the most basic distribution cost-monitoring systems. Frequently a lot of data is processed, usually requiring a PC computer spreadsheet program.

Monitoring Distribution Productivity

Cost monitoring using the techniques described has been used by distribution management for many years. The techniques are flexible, and the system can monitor many facilities and product flows. Cost control, however, requires much more detailed ratios, and monitoring closer to the time when the cost was incurred. This is called *productivity monitoring.*

Technically, all productivity monitoring requires development of a ratio that shows how many units of output work were accomplished for a given input unit or time. In monitoring warehouses, for example, the ratios of cost as a percent of revenue or per hundredweight shipped are useful primarily in comparing to historical performance or to competitors. More detailed information is needed to evaluate productivity and to isolate actionable problems.

In warehousing, the common output units used are:

Orders

Order lines

Cases

Pounds

Units

Pallets

The input measures are:

Labor hours or minutes

Labor dollars

These measures can be normalized to improve comparability. For example in a furniture warehouse, the unit may be one piece or chair. A sofa could be rated as equivalent to three chairs; so the shipment of two chairs and one sofa would result in an output of five equivalent units of work.

Similarly, labor input might be rated in equivalent paid hours to level the effect of different wage rates and overtime, or shift differentials.

Using these methods, then, let's illustrate with an example.

Assume a warehouse ships 2000 orders this month. The orders average 5 lines each. Therefore, the warehouse shipped 10,000 lines in total. This is the output.

The normal input measure is labor hours. Assume there are 16 warehouse employees. If they all work a normal month (168 hr), the total input is 2688 hr.

Productivity for the month, then, can be expressed in several ways:

0.74 orders/labor hr

3.72 lines/labor hr

1.34 hr/order

0.26 hr/line

Productivity Measurements

Similar data could be developed for the customer service department, and the measurement could be kept in all warehouse facilities to develop comparisons. To be a useful control tool, however, the measurement system needs to be broken down to report productivity for each individual and for various working groups such as picking, packing, loading, etc. Many companies do this; for example, tabulate productivity by individual, function, and in total, and post this information prominently in their corporate warehouses.

A simple procedure for setting up a productivity measurement system is as follows:

1. *Prepare a list of all jobs done in the warehouse.* This list can be determined at a general meeting of supervisors or by a detailed work-measurement or ratio-delay study. A suggested starter list for a facility is:

Receiving
Stocking
Pick-line replenishment
Order picking
Order assembly and packing
Shipping and loading
Returns processing

Care is needed to be sure that the list is not too long or detailed, as each category must contain enough work to provide for some statistical averaging over time and between people.

2. *Analyze each job to determine the basic work content and to establish a measure of performance.* Again, the analysis can be a detailed methods engineering study or as simple as a meeting of supervisors to discuss the job. For each job, set up a list of the key things to be done and the best measure of performance. For example, the following might be adequate for the job of order picking.

Job: Order picking
Job content:

- Select order from basket.
- Get pallet jack and pallet.
- Make rounds of picking bins, selecting the number of cartons and pieces needed for each line on the order.
- Place completed order in packing area.

Measure:

- Lines picked, or
- Number of orders picked, plus number of lines picked

3. *Total the hours, production and productivity—daily and weekly.* The productivity control clerk should complete a computer spreadsheet displaying all of the job functions for the week. The calculations to determine each person's productivity and the average for the whole work force can be done using the spreadsheet software.

4. *Determine work standards.* Finally, the question of work standards needs to be addressed. This is a step beyond productivity measurement, but it is an important element in controlling personnel costs. Standards can be established in a number of ways. This will be discussed here only briefly, as Chapter 21 discusses this subject in detail.

a. Accumulate data for a period of time, and compare current performance levels to those of the past. For example, tabulate how many hours are assigned to inbound transport unloading and also tabulate the number of received lines handled. Then calculate an individual and an average performance for the receiving group. Typically the standard is calculated by removing all individual results less than the average, then recalculating the average. These are *historical* standards.

b. Compare productivity between facilities. The number of lines unloaded per man-hour from transports might be compared to the average for all facilities, which would be used as a standard. These are *comparative* standards.

c. Conduct time studies to assign reasonable performance levels to each activity. Use a stopwatch and time the best forklift operator, and use this as a standard for unloading transports. This is an *engineered* standard.

d. Use predetermined, or standard, times. Define the steps in unloading a truck. Look up in a standards book how long it should take to do each of these tasks. Then add up the elemental times and calculate a standard for each operation. This is another form of *engineered* standard.

This last method is preferred today by most distribution departments. Essentially, the method requires that the analyst:

1. Subdivide the task for which a standard is desired into a series of elemental activities or movements that are fairly universal in content.

Table 23-2 Sample Work Standard

Element	Elemental time in minutes
Drive to pallet	0.10 min/pallet
Insert forks	0.05
Elevate forks	0.10
Drive 100 ft to staging area	0.40
Set pallet down	0.15
Drive back to starting position	0.40
Subtotal	1.20
PF&D	0.18
Total	1.38 min/pallet

2. Look up the proper time for each elemental movement in a standard time database.

3. Accumulate the times for each element or movement into a total for the entire operation.

4. Add cushion factors to allow for personal time, fatigue, and unforeseen interruption or delays (PF&D).

An example based on a simple forklift operation is seen in Table 23.2. The work standard arrived at in Table 23-2 could then be used to evaluate a forklift operator's performance in a day, as shown in Table 23-3.

A monitoring report can compare the performance level for a number of operators to determine how effective each person is and also determine the overall performance of the group.

As a practical matter, it is quite feasible to develop productivity standards for most activities in a warehouse, and to determine the overall performance or productivity of the work force. If a sound job is done in calculating these standards, they can be used to:

■ Establish the proper staffing level for the facility for every volume level.

■ Compare daily performance to targets set up especially for a facility, rather than compare performance to that of another, somewhat different facility.

■ Improve productivity by providing a full workload for every operator.

Table 23-3 Sample Performance Evaluation

Number of pallets moved	250
Time worked	510 min
Less 2 breaks @ 10 min	(20) 490 min
Earned time (1.38 min × 250)	345 min
Performance (345 ÷ 490)	0.70 percent

Monitoring Public and Contract Warehouses

Conceptually, monitoring of outside contract operations is very similar to the systems used in company-operated facilities. Most distribution departments monitor contractor costs on the basis of revenue and throughput—that is, cost as a percent of sales volume handled or hundredweight shipped.

These overall numbers can be expanded to include the base handling units specified in the contract, usually cases, pieces, orders, or lines. Thus, the monitoring system for a third party warehouse would include:

1. Cost for the period:

   Handling $ _____
   Storage   _____
   Accessorial   _____
   Special services   _____
   Total $ _____

2. Output measures such as orders, lines, cases, or pounds:

   Inbound
   Outbound
   Stored

3. Input/output ratios

Frequently, third party contracts also specify service levels and productivity targets, much as for company-operated facilities. Obviously, since daily and hourly control has been assigned to the contract operator, the distribution department is inhibited in short-term cost control. Long-term control is retained by the contractual terms and by competitive bidding.

Transportation Network Monitoring

Transportation cost from the point of manufacture to the customer is high, averaging just under 4 percent of sales revenue in the typical product distribution system. Thus it is important to minimize the expense, consistent with supplying adequate service to customers.

The monitoring system usually deals with both private truck operations and for-hire carriers. Also, there may be two or more levels in the system:

1. *Full or large loads used to transfer material between facilities and to supply large-volume customers.* These loads may be made up of packaged or palletized freight, or be in dry or liquid bulk form. The transport mode may be rail, highway, water, or air.

2. *Smaller loads shipped from distribution centers to customers.* Again, all modes and product forms are possible.

The monitoring system has to keep track of the products shipped, the customer service levels achieved, and the cost incurred. This happens in two related but separate systems.

1. *Product tracking.* Modern, service-sensitive distribution networks have to provide real-time information as to the location and status of materials and shipments. The information is needed by service and sales personnel and customers to assure efficient operation. Modern product-tracking systems are costly, but provide the shipper with a significant competitive advantage because of the service improvement.

2. *Freight bill audit and payment.* For-hire carriers bill for their services on the basis of contractually developed rates. The rate considers the origin-destination locations, freight classification, shipment weight or cube, delivery distance in miles, packaging format, and geographic area. Bills have to be audited and then paid. The processing system, either captive or contracted to another processor, usually handles the receipt, audit, and payment of invoices, and supplies detailed data for the control system.

Both of these distinct systems can be either manual or computerized. Most today rely on bar code and other scanning systems and highly developed processing software. The typical distribution department contracts for these services from one or more third party operators. In many companies, there are three separate groups of such third party operations:

1. One or more networked carriers that pick up the shipments at the distribution center and deliver product to the consignee. The primary carrier then prepares a freight bill that is sent to a freight bill payment service company.

2. A traffic service company that audits the freight bill by comparing it to the shipper's shipment advice and to the negotiated tariff. The service then may pay the corrected bill on behalf of the shipper, or forward the audited transaction to another party for payment.

3. A tracking network that reports on the movement and delivery of materials. This network features electronic data interchange (EDI) and may be operated by any of the entities in the supply chain: shipper, consignee, carrier, distribution center operator, or outside network provider.

Monitoring Inventory

The cost to store and protect finished goods inventory is a major consideration in the distribution network design. Two factors are involved.

1. *Inventory,* a major part of every company's invested capital. On average, American manufacturers achieve about four turns annually. Inventory cost, on average, is about 50 percent of sales value. Thus, a company may have $12.5 million invested in inventory for every $100 million of sales.

2. The cost of carrying this inventory, which can be very high. Interest alone, at the prime rate of 8 percent, represents in the example a cost of $1 million. Other

costs are for obsolescence, spoilage, insurance, ad valorem taxes, etc. The average company puts this total cost to carry inventory at around 18 percent of value, or $2.25 million including interest.

Most of this inventory is in the distribution network. Frequently, distribution orders product from manufacturing plants and outside sources based on sales forecasts and distribution requirements. Monitoring this investment and safeguarding the materials are major functions of the network.

The monitoring system requirements derive fairly easily from the function itself. It is necessary to know, by stock keeping unit (SKU), exactly how many units are in stock and where they are currently located.

In smaller, older warehouses, the total inventory count was maintained in a central inventory file. The stock location within a warehouse was found in another file on the warehouse floor. Modern practice, using elementary or complex warehouse management systems, combines both functions (quantity and location).

The inventory information is updated either real-time (concurrent with transaction recording) or in a batch mode hourly or daily. The latest systems improve the accuracy of inventory records by the use of bar codes and scanning of both product and location.

Nevertheless, errors do occur. To minimize problems, the best current method is by regular cycle counting. In this monitoring method, a person or team makes a blind count of a product and a location, reporting the information to a computer terminal. The terminal software compares the information to the record and reports the result. The computer system may signal the items to be counted, frequently based on zero or low stock levels or on product value. In other systems, the inventory counters simply count and report on all locations on a regular rotation.

Inventory accuracy is reported, usually monthly, as a normal part of the network's quality assurance program. Typical results in non-bar-code-controlled warehouses are in the 95 to 98 percent area. That is, each count has two possible errors (quantity and location) and total good counts shouldn't be less than 95 percent of count locations. In bar-coded systems, accuracies of over 99 percent are common. When errors are found, they tend to be system-related rather than warehouse problems, with the exception of theft and/or product spoilage.

Summary

This chapter has described the concepts and proposed specific measurements needed to monitor the distribution network. The key point made right at the start bears repeating: You cannot manage what you cannot measure.

Measurements derive from mission—they should focus on recording the performance of the distribution network as compared to the network's objective. Normally, the objective is to provide a high level of service while keeping costs down.

Many companies lose sight of this when designing their monitoring systems. Too many measurements are published that track only the departments' or functions' achievements, primarily to protect turf or to transfer responsibility.

The appropriate monitoring system measures and reports data in three areas: customer satisfaction, inventory level, and cost/productivity. It is important that reports on current performance levels contain monthly, year-to-date, and other historical information, and that all of this is compared to objectives.

The typical system used in major corporations is complex. The current data are usually entered into a PC or mainframe database. Multipage reports are produced on regular schedules and/or on demand. The most interesting monitoring systems that are coming into use now are prepared from real-time databases. Inputs are made from scanning devices in the distribution center. In such systems, monitoring reports can be prepared that are current to the instant of printing. These offer significant advantage in supporting corporate efforts to achieve higher levels of customer satisfaction at ever-lower inventory and operating cost—clearly, the overall goal of the distribution network.

24

Transportation Management

Philip Williams

President, Phil Williams and Associates, Inc.

The old rules of transportation management have given way to the free-for-all world of deregulation. Many shippers, however, remain unaware of the "new" basics of transportation management. The major goal of this chapter is to reveal the changes and to provide the opportunity to put the system to work for you.

After more than a decade, the question remains: Has the public really benefited from deregulation? Consider the fact that the telecommunications industry was deregulated at the same time as the transportation industry. With all the advertising, how confident do you feel in selecting a long-distance phone service? Do you find it any easier to understand your monthly telephone bill(s)?

This same kind of challenge exists within the transportation industry. Granted, with deregulation shippers have the opportunity to reduce their costs and to improve the level of services. But there remains on the opposite side of that coin the dreaded possibility of being sued over a tariff or a contract deficiency of one sort or another—even with the most discerning logistics choices.

Just when we think freight management has become more relaxed and easier to understand, we find that it has instead become far more complicated. Much of what we are learning is only partially the result of changes in Interstate Commerce Commission rules and regulations. Much more is the result of court decisions, including the affirmation of the filed rate doctrine by the U.S. Supreme Court.

Many who knew and understood the old regulatory scheme have retired or became casualties of the "downsizing" as American industry restructured. The ability to read and understand a tariff has virtually disappeared. Additionally, more and more shippers are relying on contracts and "third parties" to purchase transportation services for them.

Many who are responsible for purchasing transportation services remain confused and fail to ask the right questions in protecting their company and in truly understanding the price and service he/she has purchased. It is important to know that discounts may not apply to shipments in the following situations:

Single shipment charges	Joint-line shipments
Short-haul territory	Minimum charges
Fuel or insurance surcharges	Over 10,000 or 20,000 lb
Canada or Mexico shipments	Congested areas (like New York City)
Third party billing	Intrastate shipments
FAK rates	Commodity rates
Extraordinary value shipments	Government shipments

It is also important to know that virtually everything is negotiable—the rate level, the discount, the minimum charge, credit terms, liability limits, single shipment charges, everything!

The carriers have introduced a whole set of revenue-enhancing rules and charges. The following are some items to look for.

1. *Application of the discount.* The carriers will normally apply the discount only on direct point or single-line shipments. The long-haul or nationwide carriers also restrict the use of the discount to their so-called "market areas." Normally, this excludes a 500-mi radius around the shipping point.

2. *National Motor Freight Classification (class rating).* All less-than-truckload shipments are subject to the "class rating" tariff in helping to determine the proper rate. The carriers appear to be making changes in this system to increase their revenue.

3. *Single shipment charges.* Carriers may assess a single shipment charge on shipments weighing less than 500 lb. This appears as a separate line-item charge, and is normally around $16.50. Discounts do not apply to this charge.

4. *Third party shipments.* Third party shipment rules are changing. The bill of lading on such shipments must be prepared properly. The vendor is shown as "shipper." The terms are "prepaid," with a note to "send freight bill to" followed by the complete name and address of the payor. Section 7 of the bill of lading *should not* be signed.

5. *Minimum charges.* There is an absolute minimum charge, which can vary. For example, one major carrier charges $46.95 as its absolute minimum and for other carriers it is around $45.

6. *Shipped weight.* The actual weight of the shipment will have a direct impact on the calculation of the carrier's charges. New rules have been proposed to make the packing and the skid a part of the shipment weight.

7. *Freight not adjacent to vehicle.* There is a charge of from $45 (minimum) to $475 (maximum) if the material to be loaded is not readily available, *or* if the unloading space is not immediately adjacent to the carrier's position of loading/unloading.

8. *Shipments delivered at one time.* There will be an added charge if the total shipment cannot be delivered to the same location at the same time.

9. *Order-notify shipments.*   Maximum discounting will not apply if the carrier is requested to call ahead, notify a party, or make the delivery at any time other than normal working hours.

10. *Intrastate, local, or "nonmarket areas".*   Shipments that are short-haul or not within the negotiated state-to-state market areas may not be covered by the discount.

11. *COD shipments.*   All collect-on-delivery shipments normally are exempt from discounting.

12. *Joint or interline shipments.*   Occasionally, two or more carriers will be required to move the shipment from point of origin to point of destination. Because of the interline, the discount may not apply or may at least be reduced.

13. *Fuel surcharge.*   A fuel surcharge is instituted by the carriers when the price of fuel reaches about $1.10/gal. This charge appears as a separate line item on the freight bill and is not subject to the application of the discount. A shipper may be able to persuade the carrier to use a standardized scale for calculating the fuel surcharge. The method to accomplish this is indicated later in this chapter. But the rule of thumb is that if the carrier produced a revenue of $1/mi or less, use a percentage factor. If the revenue per mile is more than $1.01, apply the surcharge in cents per mile. This method is in the best interest of the shipper.

14. *Insurance surcharge.*   An insurance surcharge may also appear, should insurance rates climb dramatically.

15. *Cubic capacity and density rule.*   Carriers have instituted rules that are generally designed to ensure profitability where lightweight shipments require a great volume of space (cube) as loaded on the trailer. These rules vary by carrier. For example, Yellow Freight applies the rule to shipments over 2000 lb that occupy more than one linear foot of vehicle floor space for each 350 lb of shipment weight. Such shipments are subject to a minimum charge based on class 77.5 rates multiplied by the calculated weight. The calculated weight is determined by multiplying the linear foot of floor space occupied by (times—×) 350 lb for each linear foot or portion thereof. This charge is *not* subject to discounting.

The Mess

With the onset of deregulation, business practices became lax. Many of the ICC tariff-filing requirements were ignored, as carriers failed to publish (or properly publish) discount pricing agreements. Shippers failed to request proof of publication, or simply could not understand the provisions of the tariff items shown to them. Some shippers were handed documents that gave the impression and assurance that the discount pricing was legally in effect, when it was not.

So how does one go about obtaining competitive transportation services? What does a company need to know? The following information is intended for use as a primer of sorts on the "New Basics" in buying transportation services. It is necessary for one to have a foundational understanding in order to cut through the new rules in choosing the right carriers and in keeping it legal in the struggle for survival.

Transportation deregulation is actually a myth! What really occurred would more accurately be termed "re-regulation." Additionally, 42 states continue to impose some form of economic control over the intrastate transportation industry. While deregulation increased competition, it did so at the cost of concentration in the trucking and airline industries. Fewer carriers are now chasing the same freight. In Texas, 90 percent of the freight is handled by just 2 carriers. In California, 85 percent of the freight is handled by 8 carriers. On a national basis, only 8 of the top 50 carriers from 1965 are still in operation today.

The major changes under deregulation came in two areas: pricing and service. Pricing means more than just the amount or level of discounting. The whole approach to pricing changed as carriers moved away from the Rate Bureau Systems and instituted the use of their own private tariffs—which are now giving way to contracts. Service encompasses the area of Operating Authority, plus a whole host of customer-service-oriented delivery and information systems.

Prior to 1980, a carrier could hold only one type or kind of ICC operating authority. Today a carrier can be common or contract, a broker, or even a freight forwarder—all at the same time. The trick is to know with whom you are dealing and on what basis.

We must also recognize the importance of the carriers' Rules Tariff, which governs the applications of rates and charges. When was the last time you requested a copy of the Rules Tariff, or even looked at one? Ask the next sales representative who comes through the door if they have ever received a request for a copy of their rules. Or get *really* bold, and ask the representative if *he/she* has ever read it!

Our remarks here are largely confined to the less-than-truckload (LTL) motor carrier industry, and the changes that affect the pricing and the services offered for sale. The nationwide less-than-truckload carriers, (i.e., Yellow, Roadway, Consolidated Freightways, etc.) are referred to as *regular route common carriers*. They operate over regular routes through a network of terminals and breakbulk centers.

In contrast, the nationwide truckload carriers (i.e., J.B. Hunt, Schneider, Werner, etc.) are referred to as *irregular route carriers*.

Both regular route and irregular route carriers are usually common carriers offering rates through published tariffs or contract carriers offering rates through contracts. Tariffs must be legally on file with the Interstate Commerce Commission. There is no filing requirement with a contract carrier, but the contract must be retained on file by the carrier.

A broker is a legal transportation entity but is not a carrier. For a fee, a broker arranges for the shipment and helps to establish the agreed-upon price.

Just a few words about the use of a broker. One of the key elements here is to clearly establish the agency relationship between the broker and the carrier. Your broker agreement must state that the broker is the agent of the carrier and is, therefore, able to bill and receive payment on behalf of the carrier. Payment to the broker is the same as payment to the carrier.

The broker must also be responsible for qualifying the carrier (authority, insurance, etc.) and for maintaining a valid contract with contract carriers.

A freight forwarder is recognized as a carrier and arranges for the shipment in the same way as a broker.

Admittedly these are simplistic definitions, and much could be written about each of these services. But again, we are confining our remarks to the LTL common carrier segment of the industry.

There are six basic components of the cost of transportation:

1. The underlying tariff, or schedule of rates
2. The application of the NMFC (National Motor Freight Classification) class rating, and rules covering the material being shipped
3. The weight and/or cube of the shipment
4. The origin and destination of the shipment
5. The application of the carrier's rules tariff
6. The shipper/carrier pricing agreement

Under section 10706 of the Interstate Commerce Act (49 U.S.C. 10706), the ICC is permitted to recognize carrier rate bureaus. The members of the bureaus (the carriers) are accorded limited antitrust immunity in order to jointly set the rates.

All bureau pricing is basically the same for each member carrier. The major difference is in the level of discount and in the service offered. Today the bureau system is being used by a diminishing number of local or regional carriers.

In place of the bureau system, the carriers have instituted the use of their own private tariffs. These tariffs were built on the old bureau rates, but modified to accommodate either a three-digit or a five-digit zip code determiner.

A 1991 article written by Jace A. Baker of the University of California, entitled "Emergent Pricing Structures in LTL Transportation",[1] included tables that compared competing carrier rates on class 100 shipments between 64 key markets. The rate variance ranged from a low of .59 percent (between Seattle and San Francisco) to a high of 60.01 percent (between St. Louis and San Francisco).

In establishing carrier pricing, there is more to consider than just the level of discount. And as we move farther away from the bureau rating system, these pricing differences may become even more pronounced.

Rate Increases

When a carrier announces a rate increase (for example, of 5.5 percent) it does not mean that all rates have increased the same amount. It means that, on average, the rates have increased by the stated amount.

In fact, the carriers have selected certain lanes (city pairs), certain weight breaks, and/or certain class ratings for both increases and decreases, which then go together to affect the increase "on average." Again, one must always ask: "A discount off of *what*?"

Classification

The National Motor Freight Classification (NMFC) is a tariff used to determine the class rating, and sets forth shipping rules, bill-of-lading terms and conditions, claims and packaging specifications.

A *class rate* is a rate that applies to a grouping of commodities that share similar shipping characteristics. Factors such as risk in handling, weight, bulk, and value are used in assigning a specific rate classification to a commodity.

Class ratings are established through the National Motor Freight Classification Committee, made up of representatives from most of the major less-than-truckload carriers.

If the Committee were to propose changes in the rating on your product, would you know it? For an annual fee you can obtain a copy of the docket that details all proposed changes. You also have the right to appear before the Committee and argue against proposed charges affecting your company. Or you can petition the committee to establish a more favorable class rating on new or existing products.

What to Do

A key strategy in gaining control over the cost of transportation has been to "magnify the corporate clout" by reducing the number of authorized carriers. Using fewer carriers, each handling a larger volume of business, will reduce the cost.

A second strategy has been to gain control of the inbound freight (and its volume) by purchasing FOB origin, freight collect, and dictating the use of specific carriers.

The New Basics of Transportation Management must be mastered in order to understand exactly what you are buying and with whom you are dealing, and in keeping it legal.

Getting Started

Now the work begins. Consider, what are you really attempting to accomplish? Obviously, to reduce/control the cost while improving the level of services. But where do you start?

Figure 24-1 outlines the specific questions a carrier will ask in either a bid situation or in attempting to negotiate on a one-to-one basis.

The source documents for this information are (1) on outbound, the bills of lading and the carrier freight bills, and (2), on inbound, receiving reports and freight bills. Do not overlook the carriers themselves. Don't hesitate to call in a sales representative. Most carriers maintain shipment reports and files on their accounts. But you must ask the right questions. What is the time frame of the information? Does the information reflect the volume from/to all your facilities? Are the inbound prepaid and outbound collect shipments shown? What is the average revenue per bill and the average weight per shipment? Which origins/destinations ship/receive the most volume?

Many carrier representatives are unaware of the fact that their home office may be able to identify the average class rating. By combining this type of information, gleaned from a number of carriers, you can develop a fairly complete picture of what is actually happening.

The Bid Process

If you decide to develop a bid package, we have included a sample as Figure 24-2. As discussed earlier, you must have the ability to evaluate the effective rate (base rate, less discount). Experience has proven that with a representative sampling of specific shipment information, the carriers will bid "apples to apples" and simplify the evaluation procedure.

1. Name and title of customer contact: _____

2. Is this customer an affiliate or subsidiary? (Y/N) _____ If yes, of what Corporate/National Account? _____

3. If this is a National Account, does this request require clearance with the customer's corporate office? (Y/N) _____ If so, has it been cleared? _____

4. Does this location control routings? (Y/N) _____ At this location only? _____ At other locations? _____

5. State in precise terms exactly what is being requested _____
   _____:

6. Is this a bid situation? (Y/N) _____ If yes, attach a copy. When is the response due? _____

7. Does this request involve O/B, I/B, or both? _____

8. List all of our discounts, refunds, and allowances currently in effect:
   Tariff _____ Item _____
   Tariff _____ Item _____
   Tariff _____ Item _____

9. Points of origin and/or destination (specify if not shown in bid package):
   (A) Outbound to _____
   (B) Inbound from _____

10. Unless otherwise requested, O/B discounts apply on prepaid shipments only. Is a collect application necessary? (Y/N) _____ Why? _____

11. What is the total revenue/month potential to or from our service area?
    Total _____ Outbound _____ Inbound _____

12. Outbound freight charges: Prepaid _____ % Collect _____ %
    Inbound freight charges: Prepaid _____ % Collect _____ %

13. Will figures change? (Y/N) _____ If so, explain: _____
    _____

14. Is this request designed to meet a competitor's pricing? (Y/N) _____

15. Name the top three carriers currently handling this customer's business and their percent (%) of total revenue.
    (A) _____ _____ %
    (B) _____ _____ %
    (C) _____ _____ %

Figure 24-1. What the carrier needs to know.

16. Supply competitor tariff # and item # if available:
    Competitor _____ Tariff # _____ Item # _____
    Competitor _____ Tariff # _____ Item # _____
    Competitor _____ Tariff # _____ Item # _____

17. Will our business level increase (I) or remain constant (C) if this request is affected? (I/C) _____ If it will increase, state by how much: _____
    From _____ % to _____ % of total service area traffic.
    Estimated loss of business if request is not granted or competitive? _____ %

18. NMFC item #'s and/or description covering commodities involved:
    O/B _____
    I/B_ _____

19. Average revenue per bill? O/B _____ I/B _____

20. Average weight per shipment? O/B _____ I/B _____

21. O/B bills per day? _____ Per week? _____

22. I/B bills per day? _____ Per week? _____

23. Average number of shipments per pickup? _____

24. Average number of pieces per shipment? _____

25. What are the principal traffic lanes? _____

26. Unitized? O/B (Y/N) _____ I/B (Y/N) _____

27. Palletized? O/B (Y/N) _____ I/B (Y/N) _____

28. Density (pounds per cubic foot)? O/B _____ I/B _____

29. If a full trailer load of this traffic were tendered at one time, how much could be loaded on a 28-foot trailer? _____ 45-foot trailer? _____

30. Describe any special qualities or characteristics of the traffic: _____
    _____

31. Describe any additional cost or labor involved in the pickup, transfer or delivery (such as sorting and segregating): _____
    _____

32. Do you have a commitment from the customer? (Y/N) _____ If yes, in what form? Verbal _____ Routings _____ Other _____

33. If this request involves a loading/unloading allowance, will the customer actually perform the loading/unloading service? (Y/N) _____

Figure 24-1 (*Continued*). What the carrier needs to know.

CARRIER BID PACKAGE
(Company Name)
(Contact)
(Title)
(Address)

(Telephone/Fax No.)

SUBJECT: Carrier Bid Package
Request for Quotation No. _____

THE ABC COMPANY WILL RECEIVE BIDS UNTIL____(DATE/TIME)____.

Transportation companies are to furnish service and pricing proposals within the scope and limits of their insured operating authority.

NAME OF CARRIER: _____ DATE: _____

REPRESENTATIVE'S NAME: _____ PHONE: _____

NOTE: 1) Due to the pending appeal of *ICC v. TRANSCON* in the Ninth Circuit, we request that all current and future discount items be published by name rather than a "code number."

   2) Further, it is our intent to eventually discontinue dealing with carriers under their common carrier authority and to switch to contracts in order to avoid the filed rate doctrine altogether.

1. Describe your services: (Check all that apply.)
   _____ LTL Carrier _____ TL Carrier _____ Contract Carrier
   _____ Nationwide _____ Regional _____ Missouri Intrastate
   _____ Broker _____ Freight Forwarder

2. Attach a list of states served. Indicate any which are only partially served. Indicate the number of terminal facilities in each state.

3. What is our current level of pricing with you? (Provide proof of publication.)

4. What level of discount are you proposing? _____

5. Does the discount apply on minimum shipments/charges?_____

6. Is there a floor or absolute minimum charge? _____

7. We request that the discount apply equally on inbound and outbound shipments. Please clarify your proposal:

Figure 24-2. Carrier bid package.

TERMS	YES	NO
INBOUND PREPAID	——	——
INBOUND COLLECT	——	——
OUTBOUND PREPAID	——	——
THIRD PARTY PAYMENT (BILLED TO ABC)	——	——
CONNECTING LINE (INTERLINE SHIPMENTS)	——	——
AT ORIGIN	——	——
AT DELIVERY	——	——

8. The attached rate and delivery service matrix is designed to aid us in the evaluation of your proposal. Please provide specific information concerning the rates.

   NOTE: The rates quoted must be taken from the same tariff as that proposed for use by your company in rating our shipments.

   TARIFF NAME: _____ NO. _____
   SCHEDULE: _____
   This is a: PRIVATE TARIFF _____ BUREAU TARIFF _____
   These rates were effective on: _____
   The last increase was taken on: _____ Percent: _____
   The last increase is reflected in the rates quoted: _____
   An increase of _____ % is proposed to be taken on _____ .
   Is this increase included in the rates quoted? _____
   A fuel surcharge of _____ % was or will be implemented on _____ .

9. ABC requests that the level of rates be held or maintained for one (1) year. Would you be willing to waive any increases or to adjust the level of discount to compensate?
   (Circle one.)   YES   NO
   EXPLAIN: _____
   _____

10. Will you waive the application of single shipment charges?
    (CIRCLE ONE.)   YES   NO

11. A listing of our facilities has been attached for your review. The primary receiving locations have been marked.

    Do arbitraries apply to any of the facilities? If so, which ones? Would you agree to waive these charges?

    Please indicate any facilities not served by your company on a direct basis.

    Are these facilities served by interline? If so, provide the name of the carrier and whether or not the discount will be protected.

Figure 24-2 (*Continued*). Carrier bid package.

12. Will you agree to waive the assessment of any so-called density or linear foot rule charges? _____

13. Provide a copy of any current or proposed rules which change or affect the normal fifteen-(15) day credit terms.

    Do you have any rules which negate the discount if the freight charges are not paid within a certain amount of time?

14. Provide a copy of any rules which might limit or affect liability for loss and/or damage. This includes the use of any so-called release value rates.

    Does your tariff include an inadvertent clause? If yes, please provide a copy, and explain the application.

15. Provide details concerning your EDI capabilities. ABC is interested in zip code rating systems, electronic tracing, pre-delivery notification and transportation management reports.

16. Provide your company's operating ratios (ICC method) for the last 18 months.

17. What was your company's claim ratio for the past 18 months?

18. Provide any additional information which you feel we should know about your company or its services.

19. The rate/service matrix which follows must be completed and returned with your response to the questions. Be certain to properly rate, extend and subtract the proposed discount in calculating the charges.

    NOTE: A If the tariff calls for the application of additional charges, i.e. arbitraries, etc., they must be included in the "Calculated Charges" column.
    B. Make certain to indicate the average in-transit time (service) we can expect.
    C. If you do not have authority for handling the intrastate shipments, do not complete the intrastate rate study.
    D. If you handle the regional shipments, complete that portion of the rate study for which you are offering service *and* protecting the discount.

20. Please return to: _____ Name
    _____ Address
    _____ Address

Figure 24-2 *(Continued).* Carrier bid package.

NATIONWIDE

Note: Complete rates for city pairs only where you offer direct service and/or protect the discount by interline.

Origin	Zip	Weight	Class	Destination	Zip	Rate or M/C	Disc. %	Calc. chgs. rate × wt. less disc.	Average in-transit time	Indicate direct service or interline
Doraville, GA	30360	255	55	Whittier, CA	90601	—	—	—	—	—
Houston, TX	77043	243	77.5	Birmingham, AL	35233	—	—	—	—	—
Clifton Hts., PA	19018	180	77.5	Duluth, MN	55806	—	—	—	—	—
Pittsburg, CA	94565	500	50	Greeley, CO	80631	—	—	—	—	—
Atchison, KS	66002	164	55	San Diego, CA	92102	—	—	—	—	—
LaGrange, GA	30240	623	70	Bloomsburg, PA	17815	—	—	—	—	—
Highland, IL	62249	520	77.5	Long Beach, CA	90804	—	—	—	—	—
Rockville, CT	06066	3541	85	Warrensburg, MO	64093	—	—	—	—	—
Norcross, GA	30071	375	55	Univ. City, MO	63130	—	—	—	—	—
Pacolet Mills, SC	29373	112	70	Univ. City, MO	63130	—	—	—	—	—
LaGrange, GA	30240	769	70	Kansas City, MO	64108	—	—	—	—	—
Chicopee, MA	01020	500	70	Warrensburg, MO	64093	—	—	—	—	—
Winnsboro, SC	29180	500	100	Warrensburg, MO	64093	—	—	—	—	—
E. Rutherford, NJ	07073	1125	70	Warrensburg, MO	64093	—	—	—	—	—
Kalamazoo, MI	49009	1000	77.5	Warrensburg, MO	64093	—	—	—	—	—
Altamahaw, NC	27202	286	100	Kansas City, MO	64108	—	—	—	—	—
Warrensburg, MO	64093	6513	100	Atlanta, GA	30336	—	—	—	—	—
Warrensburg, MO	64093	2644	77.5	Atlanta, GA	30336	—	—	—	—	—
S. Plainfield, NJ	07080	1120	100	Kansas City, MO	64108	—	—	—	—	—
Warrensburg, MO	64093	2700	70	Costa Mesa, CA	92667	—	—	—	—	—
New Bedford, MA	02741	296	100	Warrensburg, MO	64093	—	—	—	—	—

Figure 24-2 (Continued). Carrier bid package.

INTRASTATE

Note: Complete rates for city pairs only where you offer direct service and/or protect the discount by interline.

Origin	Zip	Weight	Class	Destination	Zip	Rate or M/C	Disc. %	Calc. chgs. rate × wt. less disc.	Average in-transit time	Indicate direct service or interline
				Missouri						
N. Kansas City, MO	64116	186	55	University City	63130	—				—
				California						
Pico River, CA	90660	3996	55	Long Beach, CA	90804	—				—
Lamirada, CA	90638	1100	55	Union City, CA	94587	—				—
Industry, CA	91748	991	100	Milpitas, CA	95035	—				—
Montebello, CA	90640	195	77.5	Union City, CA	94587	—				—
				Illinois						
Sycamore, IL	60178	1440	70	Schaumburg, IL	60194	—				—
				Texas						
Dallas, TX	75229	338	100	Harris, TX	77506	—				—
				Georgia						
Atlanta, GA	30336	2200	100	Bremen, GA	30110	—				—

Figure 24-2 (*Continued*). Carrier bid package.

REGIONAL

Note: Complete rates for city pairs only where you offer direct service and/or protect the discount by interline.

Origin	Zip	Weight	Class	Destination	Zip	Rate of M/C	Disc. %	Calc. chgs. rate × wt. less disc.	Average in-transit time	Indicate direct service or interline
Mt. Airy, NC	27030	736	100	Atlanta, GA	30336	——	——	——	——	——
Collierville, TN	38017	1000	70	Warrensburg, MO	64093	——	——	——	——	——
Star City, AR	71667	2568	100	Kansas City, MO	64141	——	——	——	——	——
Dallas, TX	75229	383	70	Thornton, CO	80229	——	——	——	——	——
Neely, MS	39461	370	100	Atlanta, GA	30336	——	——	——	——	——
Muscatine, IA	52761	275	92.5	Ft. Smith, AR	72914	——	——	——	——	——
Philadelphia, PA	19154	1000	70	Charlotte, NC	28217	——	——	——	——	——
Galesburg, IL	61401	1338	100	Kansas City, MO	64141	——	——	——	——	——
Sycamore, IL	60178	1190	125	Glenwood, IA	51534	——	——	——	——	——
Birmingham, AL	35233	400	70	Rome, GA	31061	——	——	——	——	——

Figure 24-2 (Continued). Carrier bid package.

The point here is to review both the underlying base rates and the in-transit times in a controlled, measurable environment.

The shipper should identify the factors that are most important, and systematically evaluate the carrier's responses and capabilities. Figure 24-3 "Carrier Evaluation Worksheet," details a number of the pricing and service factors—along with the suggested point values—that objectively evaluate the carrier's responses and capabilities. The carrier may be strong in one area and weak in another. This method selects the best carrier "on balance."

The information that follows may appear to have limited the evaluation factors. It does, on purpose. Attempting to evaluate everything would soon result in discouragement. Besides, you have already evaluated and agreed on the price, now you must become familiar with the details and begin the fine tuning that will lead you to an understanding of what you have agreed to purchase.

Reviewing the Carrier Rates and Rules

After receiving notification that it has won the bid, the carrier will initiate the publication of the discount.

Once the carrier reports that the discount has been published and is effective, the shipper must request a copy of the proof of publication of the tariff item, evidenced by the ICC's perforated stamp on the tariff page.

Without this "proof of publication," the shipper will simply be relying on the carrier's word. In view of the Supreme Court's affirmation of the filed rate doctrine, you must take the proper steps to protect your company—and perhaps even your job.

It is also important to request a copy of the carrier's rules tariff. The shipper must

Factor		Value
1. Pricing		40%
a. Base rate less discount	15%	
b. Minimum charge	10%	
c. Exception class rating	10%	
d. Inbound and Outbound discount	5%	
2. Service		40%
a. Number of states served	10%	
b. Number of terminals	10%	
c. In-transit time	10%	
d. Direct service w/o interline	10%	
3. Administrative capabilities		15%
a. Zip code rating diskette	5%	
b. Computerized manifest/tracing	5%	
c. Monthly management reports	5%	
4. Profitability/Claims		5%
a. Operating ratio	2.5%	
b. Claims ratio	2.5%	
Total		100%

Figure 24-3. Carrier evaluation Worksheet.

review the "proof of publication," making certain he/she understands *all* the provisions and, in particular, any references to other tariffs, tariff items, and/or footnotes.

Here are some specific details to look for:

1. The published item must identify the full legal name of the entity benefiting from the application of the negotiated discount. If the discount is applicable to a subsidiary, it must also be identified by name. If the discount is published by account code (a code in place of the shipper's name) be aware that the legality of coded tariffs is being challenged. At the very least the tariff must contain an item that links or otherwise identifies the code number with the shipper, *by name.*

2. The tariff must also specify the location of all the shipper's facilities. If a complete listing of the facilities is uncertain or subject to periodic change, the item should state: "all facilities of ABC Mfg." or similar wording.

3. On occasion, the beneficiary of a discount item may not be shown as either the consignor or the consignee on the carrier's freight bill. The beneficiary, with "third party" responsibility for the freight charges, still wants to receive the discount. The tariff item must permit the application of the discount to third-party payors.

Be certain to check the carrier's rules tariff. As stated earlier, a common restriction is that the shipper's bill of lading must show the shipment as "prepaid, third party bill to:" with the complete name and address of the party responsible for the payment.

Recently, carriers have begun to add a new rule, stating that on third party shipments the shipper must *not* sign section 7 (the so-called "no-recourse clause") on the bill of lading.

4. Be alert to any item that attempts to name the products to which the discount applies. If the carrier insists on this method, then it should identify the products by National Motor Freight Classification item number. But this is still a poor method. It is highly recommended that the discount reference the products as "freight all kinds (FAK)." This eliminates any controversy over commodities that are somehow overlooked or otherwise not identified by specific reference.

5. Make certain that the tariff indicates the agreed level of the discount and its application to outbound prepaid, outbound collect, and inbound collect, and that the tariff permits a third party payer of the freight charges. If the discount is equally the same for outbound and inbound, it should show "between the facilities of ABC Mfg. and all points served by the carrier, from and to the facilities of ABC Mfg." or "for the account of."

6. Please note that generally discounts apply only on single-line shipments. If the agreement applies to joint-line traffic, the item must show the level of discount and any limits of application, i.e., specific states, inbound collect when _____ is the originating carrier, or outbound prepaid when _____ is the delivering carrier or any other such restrictions. NOTE: Require from the carrier issuing the discount a copy of the concurrence agreements established with the connecting carriers, who now become parties to the negotiated discount.

7. Some carriers may set forth certain qualifications in order to obtain the discount, such as a "sign-up" or other participatory request like specific bill of lading

"references" that must be initiated by the shipper. Also, some carriers might require the tender of a specified monthly or yearly gross or net dollar amount of traffic in order to activate the discount.

Such restrictions are often used to "trap" the shipper and should be avoided if possible.

8. Most discounts are shown as "on-the-bill" discounts, and the tariff item should affirm that this is the case. If all or part of the discount is to be applied as an "additional discount" or an "off-the-bill" refund allowance, the tariff item must specify whether the refund is automatic (voluntary on the part of the carrier) or only upon presentation of a weekly or monthly bill by the shipper.

Further, the "off-the-bill" discount must state how the refund is to be determined, i.e., from the "gross" or "net" freight charges.

Here is an example that clearly demonstrates the difference between net and gross calculations on a split 50 percent discount.

	Net	Gross
Total freight charges	$100.00	$100.00
On bill discount (25%)	−25.00	−25.00
Net charges	$ 75.00	$ 75.00
Rebate percentage (25%)	−18.75 (25% net)	−25.00 (25% of gross)
	$ 56.25	$ 50.00

Obviously gross is better, but net is more common, because it provides greater revenue for the carriers.

The discount tariff may also contain a provision restricting the time frame for payment or stipulating a time limitation for presentation of the refund invoice. The carrier may also decline payment until a certain minimum dollar amount has been met. In any case, proper procedures for record keeping and accounting must be established to ensure a timely and accurate settlement.

9. Most carrier Rules Tariffs contain a schedule of accessorial charges. Some of these charges will be associated with services such as notify-on-arrival, single-shipment, reconsignment, diversion, inside pickup/delivery, etc. If the carrier agrees to waive or otherwise exempt these charges, this must be clearly stated in the negotiated discount item.

10. Carriers are also required to maintain in full force and effect a minimum level of cargo, liability, and property damage insurance. The carrier's adherence to these provisions should be evidenced. The shipper may also ask to be specifically identified as insured and be provided with a copy of a certificate of insurance. The certificate must identify the coverage and state the limits, plus name the carrier, the insuring agent, the underwriter, and the effective dates.

Limits of Liability

For some time, the carriers have been attempting to shift their responsibility for loss and damage over to the shipper.

The ICC has ruled that motor carriers can establish or set limits on their liability through tariff provisions. For example, Yellow Freight limits its liability based upon the definition of "extraordinary value." Articles are judged to be of extraordinary value when the shipper's invoice value is $50/lb or greater. Yellow is neither higher in the assessment of charges nor alone in establishing them. What is true of Yellow is equally true of Roadway and Consolidated Freightways.

If the shipper fails to declare the extraordinary value on the bill of lading at the time of shipment, the liability is automatically limited to $50/lb. If the value is stated and exceeds the $50/lb/package limit, the shipper may request additional coverage, which is assessed at 25 cents per $100 of value.

If extraordinary-value articles are inadvertently accepted without the excess coverage, such shipments will be considered to have been released by the shipper at $50/lb/package. Some more specific points:

1. The negotiated tariff provisions must identify the applicable scale and effective date of the rates applicable to the shipment. If agreed, provisions must also be stated that "freeze" the applicable scale of rates for a specified period, i.e., six months, one year, etc. Said negotiated items must also identify what constitutes a minimum charge.

2. An analysis of the carrier's tariffs should be rendered to determine if they contain "bumping" provisions that will permit the application of the discount on minimum weights up to 10,000 lb or up to 20,000 lb as "less-than-truckload" (LTL) and higher weights as "truckload" (TL), whichever is cheaper. We recently encountered a couple of restrictive rules that are not common. The first states that if the carrier chooses to interline the shipment (even when they ordinarily serve the point direct), the discount will not apply.

The second compares the application of the volume or truckload rate against the LTL charges *before* the discount rather than after the normal discounted LTL charge. Hence the higher volume rate applies and increases the carrier revenue.

Do *not* assume that all carriers have the same bumping provisions. They do not, and the way such rules apply will have a great bearing on the charges.

3. Many carriers offer what is called "spot pricing" agreements or contracts. Such agreements are generally either for a specific shipment or for a specific period of time, i.e., 30 days. Shippers are offered lower rates, enabling the carriers to reposition equipment in specific lanes.

Be cautioned that some authorities feel that these agreements may be flawed, leaving the shipper open to the application of higher rates if the agreement is ever declared illegal or otherwise declared invalid.

4. Care should be exercised to examine the carrier's rules that address shipments that meet the definition of full visible capacity, cubic capacity, density, lineal foot, exclusive use, order notify, etc. Such provisions usually negate the application of a discount and actually increase the charges for the shipment. Further, the tariff may also provide for higher charges if the carrier must provide copies of the bills of lading or delivery receipts along with the freight bills.

If import/export shipments are to be excluded from the discount provisions, this must be clearly stated in the tariff.

5. The Code of Federal Regulations, 49 CFR 1320(3)(C), requires the payment of the original freight bill within 30 days of presentation. The carrier's tariffs should be examined to determine if there are any rules that impose a stated monetary pen-

Subject: Truckload Fuel Surcharge

Dear

Although unpopular, ABC Corporation recognizes that carriers cannot be expected to absorb dramatic and unforeseen diesel fuel prices without eroding margins. Therefore, we realize fuel surcharges are necessary.

In order to effectively administer a fuel surcharge, we must insist that our truckload carriers abide by one matrix, so we can know where we are in terms of costing.

After studying several carrier's proposals we have developed our fuel matrix as follows, based on the ICC national fuel price index:

Fuel price (cents/gal)	Surcharge (cents/mi)	Fuel price (cents/gal)	Surcharge (cents/mi)
112.9–115.8	1.0	157.9–160.8	8.5
115.9–118.8	1.5	160.9–163.8	9.0
118.9–121.8	2.0	163.9–166.8	9.5
121.9–124.8	2.5	166.9–169.8	10.0
124.9–127.8	3.0	169.9–172.8	10.5
127.9–130.8	3.5	172.9–175.8	11.0
130.9–133.8	4.0	175.9–178.8	11.5
133.9–136.8	4.5	178.9–181.8	12.0
136.9–142.8	4.5	181.9–184.8	12.5
142.9–145.8	5.5	184.9–187.8	13.0
145.9–148.8	6.5	187.9–190.8	13.5
148.9–151.9	7.0	190.9–193.8	14.0
151.8–154.8	7.5	193.9–196.8	14.5
154.9–157.8	8.0	196.9–199.8	15.0

Formula: (current price minus base price 106.9)÷ by 6 mi/gal = fuel surcharge (in cents/mi).

The surcharge will be applied to all shipments made on the day the fuel surcharge becomes effective and will remain in effect until the following Tuesday, at which time the ICC price may be adjusted up or down, or remain the same.

Please acknowledge acceptance of our fuel matrix by signing in the space provided below, and faxing a copy back to us.

Your cooperation is appreciated.

Yours truly,

Accepted by:_____ (carrier)_____

Title: _____

Date: _____

Figure 24-4. Shipper's letter describing fuel surcharge.

 __(Name of Institution)__ reserves the right to designate the carrier when Common Carriers are used.

1. Will deliveries be made by:
    A. Vendor-owned equipment   Yes _____ No _____
    B. Common carriers   Yes _____ No _____

2. If delivery will be made by common carriers, will you agree to use carriers designated by __(Name of Institution)__ ? Yes _____ No _____

The *shipping point* and *shipping weight* MUST be stated for *each line item* quoted to enable __(Name of Institution)__ to determine the low bid and to assign the appropriate carrier. Failure to include this information could result in disqualification.

1. FOB destination delivered price $ _____
    (cost to include freight)

2. FOB destination freight collect $ _____
    (cost to exclude freight)
    Freight allowance (#1–#2) $ _____

    Source (shipping point):
    City _____ State _____ Zip _____

    (NMFC) Commodity class (50–500) _____ Class rating

    Shipping information (by individual line item):

Item	Weight	Class Rating
_____	_____	_____
_____	_____	_____
_____	_____	_____

    Total shipping weight _____ lb

Indicate here if the material requires any special handling,   Yes ____ No ____
                             is of extraordinary value,   Yes ____ No ____
         and/or requires a cubic density rating.   Yes ____ No ____

Figure 24-5. Vendor request for freight information.

alty for late payment or even provide for the loss of the discount under certain conditions.

   6. The carriers will also implement fuel and insurance surcharges as provided in the tariffs. These provisions must clearly state the formula and/or method by which these charges are to be determined. The shipper may be able to institute its own

---

Vendor routing instructions

Ship freight collect, FOB origin, via __(carrier)__ or contact __(name)__ at __(phone number)__ if your (vendor) shipping location and our designated receiving facility are not serviced direct (origin and destination) by this carrier. Call also if your shipping location changes from __(location)__ . The vendor assumes responsibility for any/all loss of discount resulting from the use of a carrier other than that authorized above. The excess charges and a $25.00 administrative handling fee will be billed to your company.

Figure 24-6. Purchase order routing instructions.

scale of fuel surcharges. Figure 24-4 provides an example of one shipper's effort to retain control over the fuel surcharges.

7. It is reasonable and strongly suggested that the shipper require a statement of the carrier's current operating ratio, claims ratio, and safety rating, as recorded by the Interstate Commerce Commission.

Handling the Inbound

Whenever possible, inbound material should be purchased on an FOB origin, freight collect basis. The assumption is that your negotiated rates are better than those of the vendor (shipper).

But how do you really know? Figure 24-5 provides a copy of a form that solicits shipment information, allowing you to compare the vendor delivery charges against your own. This permits you to determine which method (collect or prepaid) provides for "least delivered cost." Figure 24-6 provides an example of purchase order routing instructions.

Experience has proven that only about 50 percent of the vendors actually pass on the full discount to their customers. Are you one of them? Failure to pass on the discount is behind our assumption that your discount is better. Additionally, every shipment adds to your volume and clout with the carriers.

Conclusion

The changes in rates and rules continue at a rapid pace. Admittedly, it is hard to keep up with them all. Will the ICC exist a year from now? Will the states abandon their hold on intrastate shipping? How many more carriers will file for bankruptcy? Will Congress finally pass an undercharge relief bill? Change—it is what keeps this industry interesting.

Reference

1. Jace A. Baker, "Emergent Pricing Structure in LTL Transportation," *Journal of Business Logistics,* vol. 12, no. 1, 1991, p. 195.

25

Inventory Management

Michael F. Miller
Engineering Manager,
Tompkins Associates, Inc.

The purpose of this chapter is to provide the reader with critical information on key tactical aspects of inventory management in the distribution environment. Two broad areas are discussed as the basis for tactical understanding:

1. Inventory maintenance through the use of cycle counting and physical inventory
2. Inventory planning models, and the impact of external and internal forces on their use

The information presented in each area is sufficient to gain an understanding for day-to-day operation discussions. Implementation of programs in these areas should be preceded by much more detailed information collection and topic instruction. Before discussing the primary topic areas, it is necessary to set in context inventory management's role in the distribution environment.

Customers demand service because they pay the bills. This is true for both the external and internal customers of a distribution center. How this demand for service is balanced against efficient operations determines whether payments create profits. All companies are in business to make money, not to save it. Distribution management's ability to use inventory to make money while containing costs is what determines success.

Unfortunately, the external customer is not the only one making demands. Distribution management is caught in a constant tug of war with other internal organizations. As Fig. 25-1 shows, many conflicting demands are made. As we know, each internal organization has its own idea as to the best way to run distribution operations. The most significant weapon you have to meet all your demands, and the

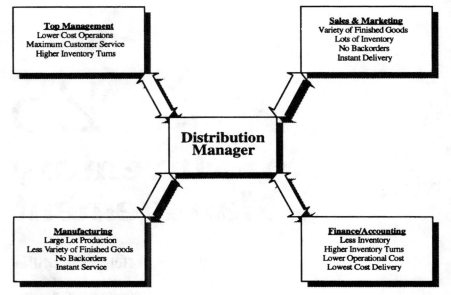

Figure 25-1. Demands on distribution management.

outside customer's, is inventory. Your ability to manage this weapon will determine success. The basic inventory process is straightforward.

Receive —> put away —> pick —> ship —> order replenishment

Given this simple process, how can inventory management be a difficult task? A few of the key reasons are forecast accuracy (or inaccuracy), product lead times, and delivery requirements. Each of these factors makes the inventory management task anything but simple. Each will be considered throughout the chapter.

The final point of this introduction is to define simply the ultimate value of your ability to manage inventory. To any given customer, inventory's ultimate value is in its *time* and *place*. Your ability to provide inventory at the *right time* and *right place* is your value.

Inventory Maintenance

Inventory management's ability to maintain accurate records is their first responsibility. Accomplishing any other goals is impossible without accurate inventory records. Significant challenges exist in keeping inventory records accurate, and this section addresses that challenge.

Inventory accuracy suffers for a number of reasons. High-volume repetitive activities induce errors. Obsolescence from both spoilage and model outdating occurs. Damage in the distribution environment claims additional saleable product. Direct theft and pilferage takes inventory. Then, even if no inventory is lost due to the above, it is misplaced or incorrectly recorded and unavailable when required. These specific challenges require focused solutions to improve inventory accuracy and maintain the level of accuracy. The two common techniques are physical inventories and cycle counting. Only cycle counting ultimately proves successful.

Improving Inventory Accuracy

In the distribution center, a high volume of material is processed in a very repetitive manner. This repetition and volume lead to incorrect counts, data entry errors, and missed items. The problems caused by these factors can be reduced through the use of automatic identification systems, vision systems, and weigh checking.

Automation identification systems support data entry through automated recognition of either bar codes or characters. These systems do not miscount materials. An incorrect read fails to be processed by the system. No manual keying of data is required, eliminating the chance of data entry errors. Recognition is the benefit of automated identification technology. Automatic identification technology also reduces the repetitive job content of distribution staff, improving quality of work life.

Vision and weighing systems perform similarly to automatic identification methods, in that they "see" the product for us. Vision and weighing systems can perform counts on materials being processed both in and out of the distribution center. These counts can then be used to reconcile with recorded activity to identify errors.

Obsolete materials tend to be the most difficult component of maintaining inventory. Just a small amount of direct effort on the part of distribution management can reduce obsolescence. Good FIFO control and emphasis on just-in-time can help reduce the amount of time material is held in inventory, thus reducing obsolescence. Indirect efforts applied from other parts of the organization helps the most. These efforts can include technical improvements in product, "vanilla" generic products, improved forecasting, and special marketing efforts. Technical improvements in the physical products or storage conditions may extend the shelf-life. The design of generic models that can be customized just prior to shipment can reduce the number of components that can become obsolete. Improved forecasting helps to reduce the amount of inventory held and the length of time stored. Recognition of outdating or soon-to-spoil by marketing or sales can initiate programs to increase current sales volumes through special offers.

Inventory lost to damage will be reduced through improved material handling, better packaging, and just-in-time. Improved material handling systems, and/or improvements in the use of these systems, directly reduces product damage. Better package designing will result in less damage in the distribution center and less in-transit damage received by the customer. Just-in-time's ability to increase turns reduces the stay of material in the distribution center and therefore the opportunity for damage.

Theft and pilferage directly affect inventory accuracy. Increased security, audits, and just-in-time will help reduce the chance of missing material. Security is straightforward and too often overlooked. Audits of inbound and outbound shipments also provide an added measure of security. Just-in-time again reduces the stay, and therefore the opportunity for theft.

Very often you have the material you need but you cannot locate it. Material is incorrectly placed, or incorrectly recorded during putaway operations. Warehouse control system technology, together with automatic identification, can dramatically improve inventory maintenance. These systems are discussed in detail in other chapters. The bottom line from an inventory maintenance standpoint is that the putaway of material is *directed* to a location, and *verified* at that point. This directed putaway ensures that the right material is in the right place. Picking of material is then *directed* back to the correct location and *verified* at that point. The closed-loop verification of modern warehouse control systems is essential to improving and then maintaining inventory accuracy.

Maintaining Inventory Accuracy

Any effort to improve inventory accuracy will prove futile if there is no planned program to maintain the established level of accuracy. For many years the formal system to maintain the level of accuracy has been physical inventories taken either periodically, such as annually, or at some fixed interval. While physical inventories still take place in some distribution centers, cycle counting has been established as the best method of maintaining inventory accuracy. To understand why cycle counting is the best, it is necessary to understand how both methods function. In a few very special cases, physical inventory may also be required.

Physical Inventories.   Short of the words "you're fired," no others exact the painful response that "physical inventory" does for distribution managers. Physical inventory is the process utilized to physically record the on-hand quantity and location for all items currently in inventory. This process almost always entails a complete shutdown of operations during the count. Typical time frame for physical inventory is once per year. In most cases the distribution operations do not have a choice in taking a physical inventory. Corporate auditors often require this process to establish the inventory value for financial reporting. Given the time and cost incurred to complete a physical inventory, it should be well planned and executed.

A well-managed effort using the proper techniques with the proper tools, equipment, and staff is necessary to maximize the efficiency and effectiveness of the physical inventory. The managed effort must exist all year to coordinate the team, complete advanced preparations, and ensure that timing is executed properly. A high level of integrity in the process requires that the correct techniques be utilized. Finally the tools, equipment, and staff sufficient for the effort must be put in place.

Managing the physical inventory process may require a full-time, year-round coordinator. This individual must work with all the external organizations to ensure that the planned process meets all requirements. The completion of any advance preparations such as tagging, precounts, etc. are also part of this management task. The ability to complete as much advance work as possible is directly proportional to the efficiency achieved during the actual physical inventory process. Management of the physical inventory process must also schedule the physical event, as well as the servicing of customers up to a cutoff date and immediately following physical inventory. Timing during physical inventory must include sufficient time for each counting team, independent auditors, and the reconciliation effort.

The basic technique for a successful physical inventory requires a minimum of two counts for each stock location. To improve integrity and speed, the distribution center is typically divided into count areas. Each count area consists of locations that require the same types of tools to complete the count. Count areas are sized so that the team members have an achievable limit of work in the scheduled time. Individuals assigned to count areas should be those typically supporting work in that area. In addition to the second group assigned to count an area, a roaming group of independent auditors also provides the highest level of integrity to the process.

The physical inventory process requires the proper tools, equipment, and staff. Tools for counters should include calculators, and bar code readers if available. Tags should be designed to support scanners that read tags automatically. If materials are of the proper type, scales should be used to weigh-count rather than hand-count bulk. Finally, an efficient counting and auditing group will not produce a timely process unless a sufficient number of data entry staff are available for tag entry.

While the physical inventory process is not the most desirable for effective maintenance of inventory accuracy, it is still commonly used. Until such time as this process is eliminated, it should be managed as efficiently as possible to minimize costs and the impact on customers.

Cycle Counting. The recommendation is always the same: Eliminate annual physical inventories and implement cycle counting. Nevertheless, there still are many distribution centers that stumble along with an annual physical inventory. This is not smart. There is no way to manage a distribution operation today and achieve customer satisfaction without implementing cycle counting. Allow me to be perfectly clear; annual physical inventory is

1. A waste of time, effort, and money
2. A cause of inventory errors
3. Not required by auditors, accountants, or tax people
4. A source of frustration to the distribution staff
5. An interruption to the operation of the distribution

If you already have cycle counting, continuously report inventory accuracy of 98 percent plus, and have management's awareness that inventory accuracy is a prerequisite of quality distribution, you don't need to read the rest of this section. Otherwise, keep reading; this section could have a significant impact on your ability to manage inventory accuracy.

Inventory accuracy is necessary for customer satisfaction, for replenishment to occur on a timely basis, and for excess inventory to be identified. No one knows the true cost of inventory inaccuracy. However, when we realize that the level of inventory in the United States is equal to approximately 10 percent of the gross national product, the effect of inventory inaccuracy of even 1 percent can be seen to be very significant. Consider what inventory inaccuracy costs your company. Include the cost of lost sales, missed schedules, premium freight charges, wasted distribution labor, unhappy customers, and surprises.

A critical portion of every distribution center manager's job is inventory accuracy.

The best way to achieve inventory accuracy is to count a small percentage of the inventory on a regular cyclical basis. This sample of the total inventory can be easily compared to the inventory records. By continually counting, when errors are identified you have an excellent opportunity to define the cause of the error and take corrective action. This process of making regular cycle counts, reconciling them with inventory records, and identifying and correcting errors is called *cycle counting*.

It is important to realize that the objective of cycle counting is not accurate inventory. The objective of cycle counting is the identification and elimination of errors. A by-product of identifying and eliminating errors will be an accurate inventory.

The first question is "What to count?" To respond to that question, we must realize that it is really two questions in one: 1) "How often should an item be counted?" and 2) "When should each specific item be counted?" The answer to the first question lies in Pareto's Law. Pareto's Law, or "the ABC concept," has many different applications. The ABC impacts for cycle counting in your distribution center are as shown in Table 25-1. The obvious cycle-counting application is that the A items should be counted much more frequently than the B items, and the B items much more frequently than the C items. A typical scenario would involve counting 6 percent of your A items each week, 4 percent of your B items, and 2 percent of your C items.

Question number two, "When should each specific item be counted?", is relatively straightforward. An item should be counted when it is easiest and cheapest to get the most accurate count. When is this?

1. When an item is reordered and replenishment is being completed
2. When an inventory balance is zero or a negative quantity (Counting to zero is something anyone can do easily.)
3. When an order is received at the dock
4. When the inventory balance is low
5. When a person is at a location with time to spare

All of these times are appropriate for executing a count of an SKU or location, with the least effort, cost, or operational interruption. Thus the answer to the question, "What to count?" is that you should count based upon an ABC analysis, and count when it is easy to count.

How do you determine who should count? The number of people who should do cycle counts depends upon the number of items in inventory, the desired count frequency, the number of storage locations for each item, and the number of count irregularities such as number of recounts, accessibility of items, and physical characteristics of the items. A realistic standard is that a cycle counter can count 40

Table 25-1 Impact of ABC (Pareto's Law) on Cycle Counting

Classification	Percent of dollars	Percent of SKUs
A	80	10
B	15	40
C	5	50

items per day. The cycle counters should be very familiar with the stock location system, the distribution layout, and the items being counted.

Cycle counters should be assigned to cycle counting on a permanent basis. This does not mean that cycle counting is necessarily a full-time job, only that each person assigned to cycle counting should be a permanent team member and should not be rotated through this function. In many modern distribution control systems, the cycle-counting activities may be interlaced between ongoing distribution operations. For example, if there are no orders for an order picker to pick, the control system automatically assigns the order picker cycle-counting tasks until orders become available. Using order picker *dwell times* in this manner results in the cycle counting being done for free.

Cycle counters must recognize the probability of crossovers. A well-established cycle-counting procedure will include checks of those items that are likely to be incorrectly shipped. Therefore, when a cycle count reveals an overage in one item, there is an immediate check of those items that would normally be confused with the one that is not in balance.

Although some auditors are concerned with "proper checks and balances" within a distribution center and, therefore, believe that only people outside of the distribution center, assigned full-time, should be involved in cycle counting, this issue has not been shown to be valid. In fact, to the contrary, it has been shown that true inventory management will begin once management realizes that the job of maintaining accurate inventory is not one for accountants and auditors, but for distribution staff and distribution center managers. Thus the whole "checks and balances" discussion is irrelevant.

Having determined what to count and who should do the counting, the remaining question is, "What are the procedures for cycle counting?" A critical cycle-counting procedural decision involves establishing valid cutoff controls. Since cycle counting should take place without affecting normal operations, a very careful coordination of counting and transaction processing must be planned.

Any transaction that takes place after the inventory balance has been reported and the actual count has been made must be isolated, so that an accurate inventory reconciliation may take place. This can be done in one of four ways:

1. By recording all inventory transactions and cycle counts in a real-time mode.
2. By recording the time when each location is counted and reporting transaction times.
3. By coordinating transactions with the count process, so that counts are taken when transactions do not occur.
4. By *not* processing any transactions for items scheduled to be counted until after the items have been counted.

Once the issue of cutoff controls has been addressed, the next issue to be addressed is that of count documentation.

The information that initially should be recorded on the cycle-count document or on the portable terminal is shown in Fig. 25-2. The cycle-counting transaction then should be forwarded to a reconciler. Counters should not reconcile their own counts. Reconcilers should compare the cycle count to the inventory record and

Cycle Count Transaction	
Location:	A43D9
Unit of Measure:	Feet
Part Number:	12345
Part Description:	Copper Wire
Quantity: Counter Name: Date/Time:	
Reconciliation: (OK) Date/Time	

Figure 25-2. Cycle count transaction ticket.

determine if a good count occurred. To determine if a good count occurred, you need to have established a cycle-count tolerance limit.

Cycle-count tolerance limits should be based upon the value of the items being counted. For example if a $1500 item is counted and a cycle count of 490 is made, and this is reconciled against an inventory record of 500, it is clear that this is a bad count. To the contrary, if a 2-cent item is counted and a cycle count of 490 is made, and this is reconciled against an inventory record of 500, it is clear that this is a good count. A typical count tolerance limit would be $50. That is, if the cycle count is within $50 of the inventory record, the count is considered to be a good count. If the cycle count indicates a discrepancy of $50 or more, the count is considered a bad count. Cycle-count tolerance for individual items should also reflect the impact of planned safety stock for each item. Incorrect counts exceeding 20 percent of the planned safety stock quantity should be reconciled.

When a bad count occurs, the item should be recounted. The recount will verify if the original count was truly a bad count or if an error was made and the item count is within the tolerance limit. Whether the recount variance is within the count tolerance limit or not, the reconciler should initiate action to adjust the inventory record to agree with the verified recount. If the variance of the recount is outside the tolerance limits, further investigation is required to determine why the inventory record is incorrect. If the counted quantity is verified as less than the inventory record, there are two relatively easily checked possibilities:

1. An outstanding allocation of this item may have been filled without any recording of the transaction, or
2. A recently completed sales or production order may have been incorrectly subtracted from inventory.

If the variance shows that the count quantity is higher than the inventory record, replenishment orders should be checked to see if any product was received and not properly recorded, and recently completed sales or production orders should be checked for erroneous subtraction from the inventory records. It is important to

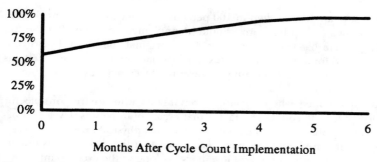

Figure 25-3a. Inventory accuracy over time.

recall that the objective of cycle counting is the identification and elimination of errors. Thus, the error investigation process is critical to the viability of cycle counting.

At the end of each month, a cycle-counting accuracy plot should be given to management. A simple equation for arriving at cycle-counting accuracy is:

$$\frac{\text{Good Counts}}{\text{Total Counts}} = \text{Cycle-Counting Accuracy}$$

Figure 25-3a presents a graph illustrating the typical progress made once cycle counting has been implemented. If a problem occurs such as that shown in Fig. 25-3b, it is critical that either the error investigation identify the problem and action be taken to resolve the problem, or that the cycle-counting quantities be increased until the errors can be identified and eliminated.

Implementation of a cycle-counting program is mandatory for successful warehouse generations. Implementation should occur in two phases, three steps. The first phase involves three steps:

1. Identify approximately 100 items. These items should be A, B, and C items.
2. Complete repeated counts on these items; count frequency should be whatever is necessary to identify errors.
3. Eliminate errors.

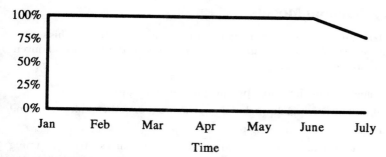

Figure 25-3b. Problem requiring corrective action.

Once the first phase has resulted in 100 percent accuracy for several weeks, the full cycle-counting system, phase two, should be implemented. Even after the full cycle-counting system has been implemented, the original 100 items should continue to be counted for at least two months. The special counts on these 100 items should be continued until 98 percent-plus inventory accuracy has been achieved overall by the full system.

Some have questioned whether public accountants who are responsible for audits will accept a cycle count. The fact is that cycle counting was developed because of frequent problems with the accuracy of annual physical inventories. As cycle counting has matured, auditors have recognized that the procedure is usually far superior to the traditional physical inventory. As long as the cycle-counting system is cleared with the audit team, a cycle count is recognized as a superior means of checking inventory.

Cycle counting results in the accurate management of inventory. It makes possible the identification of errors in a timely fashion. It may be designed in many ways that work, this section having described one method. The keys for your successful implementation are to

1. Determine what to count
2. Determine when to count
3. Decide who should count
4. Establish cutoff controls
5. Define count documentation
6. Define count tolerance limit
7. Implement phase one
8. Implement phase two, full cycle-counting system
9. Aggressively pursue improvements
10. Manage inventory accuracy

Cycle counting has become the industry standard for maintaining inventory accuracy. A program to implement cycle counting is the only way to move beyond knowing how bad things are, to making things better.

Inventory Planning Models

Inventory planning models exist as an attempt to maximize your profit. This section will offer answers to the following questions, which serve as the basis for all inventory planning problems.

1. What problems are the inventory planning models trying to solve?
2. What goals will be reached through the implementation of the models' answers?
3. What types of inventory are being planned?
4. Which models should be used, based on the circumstances of the planning problem?
5. What strategies beyond models will maximize effectiveness of the inventory plan?

6. What is the bottom line for inventory planning problems in the distribution environment?

The Problem

If inventory is the weapon you have to make profit, then you must determine how much to have and when to have it. In the distribution environment a third factor exists: where to have it. Therefore, to answer three basic questions inventory models are required. Only three answers, and you have all you need for successful inventory planning in the distribution environment. The three questions can be answered easily:

Three basic questions	Three simple answers
1. How much inventory do we need?	1. Enough to meet the highest projected demand.
2. When do we need this inventory?	2. Often enough to maintain the quantity in number one, based on the highest projected frequency of demand. Order early!
3. Where do we need this inventory?	3. In all our locations, the amount in number one, when number two requires.

No inventory models are required here, just three questions and three easy answers. Unfortunately, you will not be able to maximize profit by using the three easy answers. So the problem is how much, when, and where?

Inventory Model Goals

We started this chapter with the premise that you want to maximize profit in your distribution system. The various inventory planning models trying to answer the three questions work toward maximum profits. Each, however, approaches it with a different goal set. Distribution costs can be broadly divided into labor, material, and customer service. Different inventory models approach goals set around each area.

Cost of labor is based on stabilizing the work flow to minimize the total labor cost required to service requirements. In distribution, seasonality, production economics, and employment stability all affect labor costs. Models that evaluate each of these factors work toward a lowest total cost of labor.

Material cost for distribution operations is based on purchase price, order cost, and transportation costs. Purchase price is the direct charge per unit of inventory at the warehouse dock. Order cost reflects the amount per order expended, regardless of order size. Each order carries an associated direct cost of processing all the transactions from determination of need to receipt at the dock of each customer. Transportation costs are those required to have the material moved to a dock.

Customer service costs are not easily defined or calculated. Various models attempt to assign costs both negative and positive to the process of customer service. Positive cost is money lost indirectly through lost sales, incorrect orders, backorders, rush shipments, etc. Negative costs are best viewed as the positive results of increased customer satisfaction. More orders, more customers, and reduced cost of transactions are all examples.

As we shall see, each group of inventory models approaches these goals in one or more of the above cost areas.

Types of Inventory

Before discussing the models specifically, there is one more topic to be covered. Inventory can be classified in many different ways. It is important to establish a common understanding of the types of inventory. The five basic types are:

1. Order lead time (on-hand)
2. Safety stock
3. Purchase economics
4. Manufacturing economics
5. In-transit (pipeline)

Order lead time or *on-hand* inventory is that required to fill the projected demand through the next replenishment period. As the lead time changes, so should the order inventory to ensure availability. Order lead time inventory is best thought of as the *need*. This need of customers must be filled until such time as a new order can be received.

The second type of inventory is *safety stock*. Safety stock is the amount above project demand you require to meet customer service levels when replenishment is delayed. The greater the volatility of demand, the greater the safety stock requirement.

While the lead time inventory is just what we should need to meet demand, we often obtain some amount more. The third and fourth types, *purchase economics* and *manufacturing economics,* reflect this amount. Purchase economics represents the quantity obtained at least cost, given some incentive to obtain a certain amount above the specific need. Where a manufacturing operation supports distribution, quantities shipped reflect an effort to balance manufacturing costs with the total cost. This includes balances for setups, lot economics, and seasonality.

The last type of inventory most common to distribution operations is *pipeline* or *in-transit* inventory. Very often when we need to service demand above available inventory levels, the material is "in the mail." Material has been shipped, but has not yet arrived. The material is somewhere within the transportation cycle from the plant to the distribution center. This in-transit or pipeline inventory must be closely tracked, because it will be the first amount available to us following a stockout.

The Models

In the context of this chapter, we will discuss at the tactical level three broad model types or areas:

1. Economic Order Quantity and Reorder Point
2. Total Cost Model

3. Distribution Requirements Planning (DRP), Manufacturing Requirements Planning (MRP), and Just-In-Time (JIT)

There are many other special case models utilized in the inventory planning field that are beyond the scope of this discussion. These three are the most common used.

Economic Order Quantity and Reorder Point.   EOQ and Reorder Point are two concepts that work together to form an inventory model. Reorder point is concerned with when a replenishment transaction should take place, while EOQ tries to determine the quantity to obtain in the order. Reorder Point is based on two alternatives: variable-interval and fixed-interval.

In the first alternative, the reorder point is some amount of inventory that when reached causes an order to be generated for replenishment. Very often this alternative is described as the "two-bin" system. Some distribution operations actually store a "second" or reserved location that represents an inventory level at which a reorder is required. This inventory level must represent "available" inventory, which is represented by this equation:

Available Inventory = (On-Hand + On-Order) − (Back Orders)

At some point this may mean you have available inventory, with no inventory on hand, only on order. This would mean that customers' orders have to wait for on-order materials to arrive. When this is the case, very often customer service suffers.

The "reorder point" inventory level requires a straightforward calculation of the lead time and projected demand over lead time units, either days or weeks. Unfortunately, the demand over time or usage is rarely constant. Given modern techniques of forecasting and error approximations, you may be able to determine some reorder point level appropriate for your customer service levels.

The second alternative for reorder point is based on fixed-interval review. Common for many low-end parts, fixed intervals are established for review of inventory levels. To determine a reorder quantity, the inventory level is measured and compared to the projected demand over the next review period. Before modern inventory control technology, fixed-interval review provided a least-cost policy for inventory review. Current computerized systems with perpetual inventory tracking of both on-hand, on-order, and demand make fixed-interval less appealing.

In both of the above alternatives, some amount of inventory is ordered. This quantity has traditionally been calculated using the EOQ model.

$$EOQ = \sqrt{\frac{2AS}{iC}}$$

EOQ attempts to determine the optimum quantity of material to order in a single transaction. This attempt is made by determining the lower total costs of ordering and carrying inventory. These four variables are:

A = $ of demand (annual usage)

S = $ cost per order (setup cost)

i = $ cost per unit (individual unit costs)

C = % carrying cost (cost per unit per year)

The first variable A, $ of demand, assumes you can project with a high degree of certainty the total annual usage for a particular part. The setup cost(s) assumes a known cost, to completely process an order from determining the need to having replenishment in stock, and that this is constant for all orders. Unit cost is the standard cost of a single inventory unit. Carrying cost is all costs associated with providing physical space for a single unit of inventory for one year. This would include space, insurance, utilities, etc.

Understanding this model is the basis for understanding what each numerical model is trying to achieve. By minimizing the *total cost* of inventory we can achieve maximum profit. The costs associated with all the order models of inventory are the *order cost* and *carrying cost*. As the *order size* increases, the *order costs* decrease because there are less orders placed in the system, reducing the order cost. This is not the cost per order, but the cost of all orders placed. As the order size is increased, the average on-hand cost of inventory, carrying cost, is increased. The sum total of these two cost curves, order cost and carrying cost, create a *total cost curve,* which at its lowest point represents the least cost balance. An order size is therefore defined to meet the least cost objective.

The first variable, annual demand, is a precisely determined number based on Marketing's and Sales' expert knowledge of customer demand. Second, the Manufacturing department will be able to provide the setup cost per item, to an accuracy of three decimal places. The third variable is always precisely known: individual unit cost. Carrying cost is the percentage of cost assigned to individual units, which if taken of all units would cover all nondirect (order) costs. The carrying costs would include rent, insurance, other overhead, etc.

If the tone here seems sarcastic, that's because it is. No company can precisely determine these variables. Annual demand is at best a guess. Setup cost is usually some scientifically calculated guess. Individual cost is accounting's precise guess, and carrying cost is management's best guess. So what does EOQ formula really look like?

$$EOQ = \sqrt{\frac{2 \times \text{guess} \times \text{scientific guess}}{\text{precise guess} \times \text{management's guess}}}$$

Obviously, no precision is available from EOQ. EOQ numbers should be treated as such, and utilized only as guidelines for ordering based on your confidence in the variables.

Total Cost Model. The total cost model is based on an expanded understanding or interpretation of the total cost curve. This model tries to balance the level of customer service based on the cost to carry inventory. This is shown in Fig. 25-4.

By assigning a level of cost to "sales and service" at each level of customer service and combining the "carrying cost" required to reach that level, a "total cost" curve can be obtained. An argument can be made that the level of customer service should always be increasing, and that the extra cost is worth it. It is obvious from the calculation, though, that the total cost does go up to achieve the higher levels of customer service. This is not worth it. Your profit will decrease. This will happen unless you determine that the cost to "sales and service," which includes goodwill, direct losses, backorders, rushed shipments, etc., is increasing. Given that this is

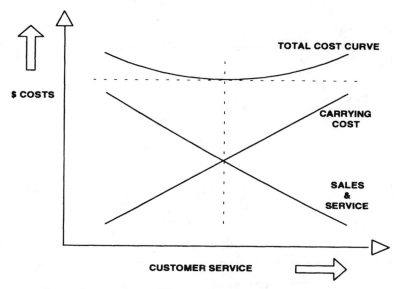

Figure 25-4. Economic order quantity based on customer service level.

true, the lowest total cost point will move to a higher level of customer service (see Fig. 25-5).

The examples shown in Figs. 25-4 and 25-5 strive to improve profit through achieving the lowest "total cost." Both are trying to determine the level of inventory based on this point. The goal is to operate at the optimum order quantity and service level that provide the level cost operation.

DRP, MRP, and JIT. This section will try to explain the basic concepts of current inventory models, and their evolution. The advent of high-powered, low-cost computing has introduced new models of inventory management, such as, Material Requirements Planning, or MRP. The evolution of MRP in the distribution environment led to Distribution Requirements Planning, or DRP. Study of Japanese management techniques has led to pursuit of Just-In-Time, or JIT. DRP is the technique for current distribution-based inventory management. But first it is necessary to understand DRP's evolution from MRP and JIT.

MRP, Materials Requirements Planning, is a concept developed in the 1970s to make use of high-speed computers to model the requirements of materials for manufacturing operations. The MRP model utilizes information about how products are put together (bills of materials) and characteristics of components (inventory master file) to calculate the projected need for orders of material over time. MRP is constantly updated based on the progress of production, customer needs, and deliveries of material to run the manufacturing business.

Just-In-Time is a concept that has been branded a system, a model, and/or a savior for manufacturing and distribution. JIT is primarily a philosophy that by itself does nothing to help plan or manage your inventory. JIT's focus is on the systematic

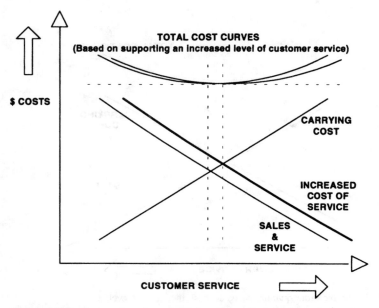

Figure 25-5. Economic order quantity based on adjusted total cost of customer service.

reduction of waste and inefficiencies in operations to improve overall performance. One end result is often the delivery of products at just the right place, in just the right quantity, and at just the right time. Where, how much, and when—the same answers inventory models seek are those JIT pursues.

Distribution Requirements Planning is the application of MRP principles to the distribution environment, integrating the special needs of distribution. DRP is a dynamic model that looks at a time-phased plan of events that impact inventory. These events may include any or all of the following:

- In-transit
- On-order
- Allocated to ship
- Backorders
- Planned orders
- Actual orders
- JIT requirements
- Consolidation

The key to "dynamic" is the rapid updating of events as they occur through the use of high-speed computers. This dynamic nature allows distribution management to ask "What if?" questions about events through simulations. By simulating events, management can select the best or most likely paths to make profit by delivering exactly how much, when and where it is needed.

The specifics of the DRP process allow management to determine the needs of inventory stocking locations and ensures that supply sources will be able to meet the demand. DRP uses selected inputs to generate outputs that create recommendations for actions. Fig. 25-6 shows a summary of the process.

Distribution Requirements Planning is your most important inventory tool to

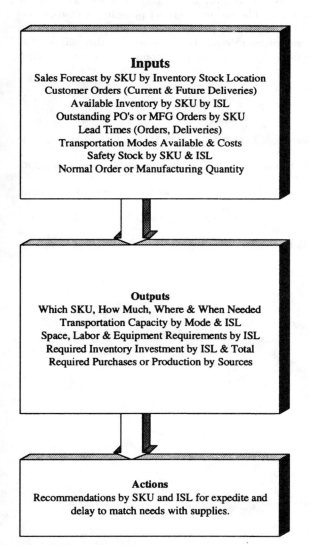

Figure 25-6. The DRP process.

meet your customers' needs from your factories and/or supplies while maximizing profits through the optimal use of your limited resources.

Conclusions

Inventory management in the distribution environment is *not* simple. As we have seen, many internal and external forces affect your ability to control and plan inventory, to make profit. The key to control is constant attention to accuracy through a cycle-counting program. The key to inventory planning is Distribution Requirements Planning; a comprehensive, dynamic model, allowing optimum use of available resources to meet customer demands. Remembering that your tool to maximize profits is effective use of inventory, use cycle counting to control it, DRP to plan it. Good luck!

Further Reading

Ackerman, Kenneth B., *Practical Handbook of Warehousing*, Van Nostrand Reinhold, New York, 1990.

Blanchard, Benjamin S., *Logistics Engineering and Management*, Prentice-Hall, Englewood Cliffs, NJ, 1974.

Coyle, John J. and Edward J. Bardi, *The Management of Business Logistics*, 3d ed., West Publishing Company, St. Paul, MN, 1984.

Martin, Andre J. *DRP: Distribution Resource Planning*, 2d ed., Oliver Wright Limited Publications, Inc., Essex Junction, VT, 1990.

Robeson, James F. and Robert G. House, *The Distribution Handbook*, The Free Press, New York, 1985.

26

Personnel Supervision

Frank E. Daly
Regional General Manager, Tompkins Associates, Inc.

When distribution is discussed, we often start talking about common carriers, bar coding, sortation systems, EDI, etc. Our goal is to maximize the use of our resources, while satisfying the demands of our customers. One of our most important resources is often taken for granted—people. People are our most important resource. People are our greatest competitive weapon. What is easier to replace—a four-million-dollar distribution center, or 100 good employees?

Distribution is not a pallet or truck business, but a people business. In fact, good distribution people have the following characteristics. They are

- Honest
- Self-starters
- Good team players
- Highly motivated

and they

- Enjoy variety
- Accept responsibility

It can be argued that a worker in distribution should be even more trained and educated than a typical manufacturing worker. In manufacturing, workers perform a predefined set of tasks, often within a narrow scope. Manufacturing supervision is highly visible and close at hand. On the other hand, a distribution center is an excellent hiding place. The work is dynamic. The worker must have personal integrity to find and complete the next task at hand.

Thus, the objective of this discussion is to examine ways in which we can better understand and deal with this most important resource. In this way we can improve our operations and make our jobs as distribution managers/supervisors more rewarding. Specifically, we will be discussing

- The organizational role of supervision
- Leadership
- Planning/organizing
- Delegation
- Motivation
- Communication
- Team Building

The Organizational Role of Supervision

The supervisor is the link between management and staff. The supervisor is the borderline, but is part of management. Unfortunately, supervisors often are not treated as a part of management. Many supervisors are promoted from the distribution staff. In fact, many are promoted without the benefit of any formal training in good management practices. Typically, the promotion goes to the best forklift driver or the fastest order picker. While these traits are admirable, they do not necessarily imply that an individual will make a good supervisor. As a result, many supervisors become overworked and are underpaid for their efforts.

The supervisor is expected to motivate and lead the worker to achieve management objectives. This is the role of the supervisor. As the translation point from intention to action, the supervisor is the most important link in the management chain.

To do this, we, as supervisors, must direct workers. Workers are people. Workers are not fork trucks. We understand how fork trucks work. There are instruction manuals and training programs available. If there is a problem with our fork trucks, we can call a mechanic to fix it. We have a preventive maintenance program to maintain this equipment. We do not put a new vehicle into operation without understanding its capabilities.

On the other hand, we often do not understand our workers or how they work. If a problem occurs, we generally use a hit-or-miss approach to addressing it. We do not try to maintain the worker until a problem does occur. We generally do a poor job of dealing with people. We will not tolerate inefficiencies in equipment, but we will with people.

What can we learn, now that we know workers are not fork trucks? First, before we can learn, we must study workers. If we knew half as much about people as we do machines, we could double our productivity.

Second, we must know how to troubleshoot human problems. We have to know our workers as individuals, so that we can understand why certain actions occur and how to detect problems.

Third, we have to exercise human preventative maintenance. We must learn what we can do as supervisors to keep people cooperative, motivated, and productive. We should not ignore problems and hope they will go away.

Finally, we have to devote considerable time to new workers. It is interesting to note that, except for the initial job interview, many distribution workers are injected directly into the work force with little formal training. We naively call this approach on-the-job training (OJT). Often, new employees have more loyalty to the few individuals in the work force who have helped them survive than to the supervisor. This is wrong. A supervisor has to spend time with new employees. It is important to develop an understanding of the new employee's goals so as to help him/her achieve them. We need to establish performance goals for the new employee. We need to gradually develop him or her and allow him/her to succeed.

On the other side of the coin is upper management. As supervisors, we learn to successfully work with this group. We all work as part of a larger organization. We become a rectangle in an organization chart, or wire diagram. This chart presents clearly defined relationships and "pecking" orders. Unfortunately, these charts do not accurately reflect reality. Relationships are fuzzy and overlap. We often, in reality, have multiple bosses.

The first thing you must do to successfully deal with upper management is to understand the boss's job, including objectives and responsibilities. How can you make the boss look better, so that you will look better?

Secondly, always keep your boss informed if you have been given directions directly from higher management. What happens when the president gives you specific directions? Put yourself in your boss's position. You need to communicate, so that everyone knows the direction in which you are headed.

Always tell your boss at the first opportunity if you have to go over his or her head in an emergency. It is bound to happen. As soon as your boss goes on vacation, the forklift breaks and a higher authority is needed to initiate a repair. The boss needs to understand what has occurred upon his or her return.

Think your problems through so that you can suggest solutions before asking for advice. This accomplishes two objectives. First, by presenting an alternative solution, it often makes it easier and quicker for the boss to make a decision. Second, this demonstrates your own job competence.

Accept new responsibilities, and become a reliable assistant who can be counted on to complete every assignment successfully. In this way you can demonstrate and develop self-confidence and your readiness for new responsibility. At the same time, you must encourage your employees to demonstrate this philosophy. You must develop your employees so that you can identify potential candidates to take your place. Many supervisors do not do this. They fear that they will lose their job unless they can portray themselves as indispensable. This is a mistake. When management considers a supervisor for a promotion, his or her replacement is always a concern. If a likely candidate already exists, then the process can continue smoothly.

Many believe that what workers really want is a supervisor who lets them loaf, gets them regular pay, and lets them take time off all the time. This simply is not true. More people complain about not having enough to do and not being asked to perform to their potential than they do about being overworked. The U.S. Department of Labor conducted a nationwide survey to determine the characteristics of a successful supervisor. (The results are listed here in order of importance.) The successful supervisor

1. Makes sure everyone understands what is expected
2. Follows rules and procedures consistently
3. Listens and tries to understand
4. Allows everyone to participate in decisions
5. Praises when praise has been earned
6. Is willing to compromise
7. Is fair
8. Is firm and decisive
9. Admits errors
10. Controls anger
11. Is creative—a source of, and open to, new and interesting ideas
12. Is friendly and sociable

You should concentrate on the first two characteristics. Making sure everyone understands what is expected and is consistent is critical to being a successful supervisor. This is what your workers want. These characteristics permit your workers to execute the correct tasks in a secure environment. The worst supervisors always violate these two principles.

Thus far, we have reviewed the organizational role of the supervisor and identified the characteristics of a successful supervisor. We will now address issues that will aid you in improving your supervision skills.

Leadership

"The most powerful weapon on earth is a human soul on fire."
MARSHAL FERDINAND FOCH

Great leaders know how to inspire others to give that extra effort. Ordinary people will accomplish extraordinary things for a good leader. Leadership, however, requires thought, practice, and constant attention if it is to be developed. It is different from management. We control resources through management. It is through leadership that we direct and motivate people. We can categorize leaders into four generic stereotypes:

1. *Autocratic/Parent.* These individuals use a high-pressure approach to achieve their goals. They tend to dominate an environment. Their basic philosophy is "I'm OK, you're not OK." They are lone decision makers who criticize people instead of problems. When these individuals are absent, no decisions are made and everything stops.

2. *Democratic/Adult.* These are self-confident individuals with a mature perspective. Their basic philosophy is "I'm OK, you're OK." These individuals listen, set goals, and measure performance.

3. *Laissez-faire/Child.* These are insecure individuals who are afraid of making decisions. They seek acceptance by others. Their basic philosophy is "I'm not OK, you're OK." They retreat from their position, and operate with a "hands-off" policy.

4. *Alienator/Brat.* These are completely negative individuals who could care less about the circumstances they find themselves in. Their basic philosophy is "I'm not OK, you're not OK." They are rarely in a leadership position.

These stereotypes illuminate different approaches, both good and bad, to leadership.

Leadership is practiced using four basic styles or behaviors:

1. *Directing.* The leader makes all decisions and directs all activities. The leader closely monitors performance.

2. *Coaching.* The leader still provides much direction, but is now explaining decisions.

3. *Supporting.* The leader begins to subordinate decisions and share responsibility.

4. *Delegating.* The leader passes some responsibility on to subordinates, and participates in problem solving.

Considering these basic styles, it is important to understand that leadership is a *dynamic* activity. The style of leadership exercised is dependent upon the person, task, or situation. Good leaders adjust their style accordingly.

This is best exemplified by considering employee development. Development is measured by employees' competence (their ability to do the job) and their commitment/motivation. Table 26-1 illustrates various levels of employee development and the appropriate leadership styles that should be used.

We can conclude that leadership is not a static activity. If it is to be practiced well,

Table 26-1 Employee Development Levels

Level	Characteristic	Competence	Commitment	Leadership
1	■ Makes mistakes ■ Wants to Succeed	Low	High	Directing (Prevent mistakes)
2	■ Discouraged ■ Lack of confidence	Growing	Falling	Coaching (Explain and praise)
3	■ Confidence grows	Good	Growing	Supporting (Increase employee responsibility)
4	■ Good performance ■ Confident	High	High	Delegation (Fully developed)

the leader must understand his or her employees. Treating everyone as equal is not effective. A leader should determine at what level of development an employee is, and on that basis decide on the best style for that employee.

What are some indicators of good leadership? A good leader

- Permits workers to operate in a democratic atmosphere that encourages efficiency
- Uses the "What do you think?" approach
- Sets attainable goals that offer a challenge and in which everyone has a stake
- Keeps workers informed about how each job contributes to the success of the entire organization
- Knows the workers
- Fosters trust and confidence
- Is positive and optimistic
- Is reasonable and tolerant
- Sets a good example
- Leads the way

Conversely, the following are indicators of poor leadership:

- Indefinite or vague instructions
- Poor job distribution
- Poor training for replacements
- Failure to dispense rewards or punishments
- Poor communication of policies
- Temper flare-ups, grouchiness, and irritability
- Trying to do all the work
- Trying to be one of the gang
- Making most of the decisions oneself

In summary, a leader commits people to action, turns followers into leaders, and converts other leaders into agents of change. A leader's job is to establish a mission and define its goals. A leader must believe in the organizational mission and display confidence in it.

Planning and Organizing

The primary responsibility of the supervisor is to plan and organize. It is interesting to note how little planning many supervisors do. The most often repeated excuse is that they have insufficient time. They point to all the fires they are constantly battling. Yet a closer examination reveals that if the supervisor had taken the time to plan, there would be fewer fires to fight. We will examine planning and organization from two perspectives: the workers' and the supervisor's. When planning and organizing the jobs of workers, a simple three-step approach should be used:

1. Define the objectives.
2. Develop procedures to reach those objectives.
3. Assign the steps of those procedures to individuals or organizational units.

Defining the objectives essentially establishes the mission for the organization. Care must be taken when defining objectives, for they should not establish goals too high or too low. If the goal is too high, it can never be achieved and becomes frustrating. On the other hand if the goal is too low, achieving the goal has little value.

It is important to be specific when establishing goals. For instance, establishing a goal of "improving inventory accuracy" is admirable, but it is too vague. Rather, we should set a goal of improving inventory accuracy by 10 percent. We now have specificity against which we can measure and provide feedback.

In this regard, it is often prudent to involve the workers in setting their own objectives. Often our workers will set higher goals for themselves than we would. Involving the workers develops a commitment to achieve the goal and promotes understanding of it. Additionally, it is better to develop group goals rather than individual goals. Group goals encourage teamwork.

Once the objectives have been established, we must develop procedures to reach those objectives. It is important to explore alternatives. We should avoid tunnel vision. There are always alternative approaches. Again, involving our workers can be both educational and productive. For each alternative, we should assess the consequences. We should evaluate cost, time, safety, quality, and ease of implementation. We must think through the entire process. We can then develop a plan of action. We should specify who, what, where, why, and when. We should constantly be aware of details. This will aid in implementation. After implementation, it is helpful to follow up on the results. In this way, we can gauge our success or learn from our failures.

Once a plan of action has been developed, we can assign the steps of those procedures to individuals or organizational units. Here is a partial checklist for good planning and organization:

1. Have you planned and organized the work assigned your unit?
2. Have you placed people well?
3. Is the work schedule completed on time?
4. Are you making sincere, continuous efforts to be fair to all workers?
5. Have you made sure the right kinds of equipment, forms, documents, etc., are available?
6. Have the workers received the necessary training and demonstrated the required proficiency to do the work assigned?
7. Do your follow-up assignments assure reasonable control without supervising too closely?
8. Do you keep workers informed of how they're doing?

9. Do you plan ahead for unexpected conditions or emergencies, so that work flows smoothly?

While many supervisors adequately plan and organize their employees' jobs, they often neglect their own. Either a supervisor runs the job or the job runs the supervisor. To determine if your job is running you, quiz yourself on the following:

1. Do I have too much to do?
2. Do I frequently work overtime to catch up?
3. Am I spending too much time at my desk?
4. Do I find myself making guesses because I don't have accurate data on hand?

If these symptoms sound familiar, then either you are truly overworked or you are poorly organized. In any event, you must take control. The following is a simple eight-step procedure to help gain control.

1. *List all the different things you do.*   During the course of a month, establish a running list of everything that you do. It helps to be specific and comprehensive.
2. *Figure the time now spent on each job.*   Monitor the time spent on each task identified in the first step. You should monitor the time spent between planned and unplanned activities. Be realistic in your time estimates.
3. *Classify all things you do according to their importance.*   The following classifications are useful:
   - Essential every day
   - Essential at stated intervals
   - Essential at unpredictable intervals
   - Advisable and important
   - Emergencies
   - Planning activities
   - Unimportant
   - Social
4. *Eliminate any duplications or unnecessary jobs.*   It is often surprising to examine our list of activities and find duplications. We do not want to do the same job twice.
5. *Delegate appropriate tasks.*   Some jobs can be easily delegated to our subordinates.
6. *Adjust your estimate of the time required to perform the streamlined list of jobs.*   After eliminating some tasks and delegating others, summarize the time required to complete the remaining tasks. If the time required still exceeds 40 hr/wk, then perhaps you really are overworked. At that point, it is helpful to see your supervisor and present your streamlined list of activities in an effort to help further reduce the task list or get you some additional help.
7. *Develop a realistic timetable.*   You can now establish a personal work schedule. You should remember not to schedule 100 percent of a day. You should leave time for unpredictable events that generally occur. You should also ensure that you schedule time on the floor each day.
8. *Set the plan in motion and update as necessary.*   It generally takes about four to six weeks to implement this methodology; however, most who have done this have

distinctly improved their personal productivity. Also, it is important to realize that your job changes over time. It is prudent to review the plan occasionally so that you can adapt to changing conditions.

To help control your job, the following hints are provided:

1. *Beware of details.*   Forgetting the details today will lead to extra work later.
2. *Set daily objectives.*   Making a "To Do" list works well. During the day we should cross off those items that we complete. By the end of the day we can measure our personal performance by examining the number of items we have completed.
3. *Avoid interruptions, or at least keep them to a minimum.*   If you have allocated time to complete a task, then you should avoid interruptions where possible. You should screen phone calls and establish an appointment calendar to schedule meetings.
4. *Whenever appropriate, verify oral communications in writing.*   This verification ensures that both parties are in agreement.
5. *Conduct standup conferences whenever possible.*   When someone enters your office, you should stand up. This naturally forces your guest to remain standing until you can determine the need to sit down and have a meeting. Frequently, your guests immediately sit down after entering your office. When this occurs, you tend to drift through a variety of issues rather than close the meeting. Standup conferences tend to keep the topic focused.
6. *Don't be a perfectionist.*   This usually results in nothing being accomplished.
7. *Avoid clutter on your desk.*   Many distribution supervisors have desks that look as though a tornado had recently landed. They struggle to find the documents and reports they need. The last thing you should do before leaving for the day is to organize your desk.
8. *Do it right the first time.*   It is always true that we will make time to redo it if we make a mistake the first time.
9. *Handle paper only once.*   Many of us fail to realize how often we handle the same piece of paper as it makes the circuit around the piles on our desk. This wastes valuable time. It is educational to put a small red dot in the corner of a piece of paper every time we handle it. Some papers will soon look as though they are bleeding to death.
10. *Do things now.*   Procrastination only increases the pressure.

Delegation

The essence of supervision is delegation. It is the process of assigning projects/tasks and accountability to subordinates to reach goals. Delegation is a powerful time-management strategy. Do not do for yourself what others can do for you. This allows you to be a manager and not just a "doer." Those who believe that in order to "get it right you have to do it yourself" have not learned how to delegate properly.

Delegation does not mean getting rid of your undesirable work. There are a number of reasons to delegate. Delegation provides training through participation.

It provides an opportunity to assess the skills and competency of each worker. Delegation is the best way to provide growth and development. Confidence is developed in both the delegator and the delegatee. Knowledge is shared, and the chain of management is strengthened. Delegation increases accountability. Delegation encourages innovation and change. It is a way to maintain a steady work flow. Delegation is cost-effective. Staff who are delegated to are usually highly motivated.

Delegation can create anxiety for both parties. The key to minimizing the potential for failure is to approach the process methodically. The first step is to determine what to delegate. Some questions to ask when you are considering which tasks to delegate are:

- Is it a job that someone else could do as well or better than I?
- Can I afford to delegate it?
- Do I have someone who could do the job competently?

Next, we should consider to whom to delegate. It is important that we spread assignments and do not create "favorites." Remember to delegate slowly in order to develop your employees.

When an individual is selected, clearly define which tasks you are delegating. Explain what you want done and why. Be sure to define specific results expected. Agree on a deadline. Remember that through delegation you must shift some authority to the employee to make decisions. An indicator that you have not communicated clearly is if the individual is continually asking, "What do I do now?" or makes decisions outside the scope of the delegated authority.

When you delegate to someone, tell others about the delegation so that the individual can do the job. Indicate any shift in authority so that there is no confusion about roles.

Delegate for results. This is your objective. Evaluate results more than methods. Remember that there are always alternative approaches to accomplishing a task. Follow up carefully by requesting feedback on progress. Conduct regular meetings, but try not to become a "nag" or the individual will lose confidence.

In conclusion, delegation is an important management tool. If done properly, it can establish a "win-win" scenario for all parties involved.

Motivation—Why People Work

Why do you work where you do today? Why do your employees work for you? These questions can be quite perplexing. The same U.S. Department of Labor survey that addressed supervisory traits also asked these questions. The responses, in order of importance, are listed below:

1. Recognition for good work
2. "Feeling in on things"
3. Sympathetic help on personal problems
4. Job security

5. Good wages
6. Interesting work
7. Opportunity for promotion
8. Supervisor "stands up" for the workers
9. Good working conditions
10. Helpful discipline

It is somewhat surprising that job security and good wages ranked in the middle of the pack; however, this perhaps best illustrates the difference between coming to work and "grinding through the day" versus true work enjoyment. Yes, people need jobs and wages to care for themselves and their families, but these will not motivate an individual to improve performance above bare minimal requirements.

On the other hand, let us consider the top two responses. Recognition for good work is indeed a powerful motivator. This does not imply that we should have a parade for an employee who reports to work on time. All of us, however, remember the verbal "attaboys," the letters of appreciation, and the awards we have received over the years. Brief words of encouragement to our employees can work wonders. Unfortunately, we tend to emphasize the negative. We always remember the things an employee has done wrong, but take for granted those things done right. We need to make that effort to look for the good things that occur.

"Feeling in on things" highlights the social nature of our species. We like to be part of a group or "family." If we can create this type of environment in our work environment, we can foster a team effort.

While this survey accents some important motivational issues, it is critical that we recognize that a person's motivation comes from within. All we can do is to create an environment that will foster motivation. In truth, there will be individuals we cannot motivate. We simply cannot find their specific motivational "button." Often this is because the key to that individual's personal goals cannot be found in the work environment. As a result they "grind it out," expending as little effort as possible. Perhaps it would be better to help these individuals find a different job. One that they might enjoy, rather than destroying the motivation of our group.

There have been numerous motivational studies. The first one was an accident. It occurred in 1927, at the Hawthorne works of Western Electric (Chicago) where relays were assembled by large groups of laborers. The original objective of the study was to increase production by improving the lighting at the assembly benches. To conduct the study, a select group of laborers was selected to be tested in a special work environment that could be modified. The engineers increased the lighting, and group production increased. To test the lighting relationship, the engineers reduced the lighting below normal levels. They were stunned to find that regardless of what was done, production went up. This became known as "the Hawthorne effect," and it illustrates the motivational power of "feeling in on things." The Hawthorne effect says that if workers feel involved, they will work better. When questioned, the workers in the test group said they felt part of a "special group" and therefore worked harder.

Perhaps the most famous motivational theory was developed by Douglas McGregor of M.I.T. in 1954. He developed theories "X" and "Y." Theory X employees dislike work and will avoid it. They prefer to be directed and wish to avoid responsibilities. They have little ambition, and only partially use their mental capacity. To the contrary, Theory Y employees like work and are happy with rewards that satisfy their need of self-respect. They like responsibility, and want to make full use of their mental capacity. In summary, McGregor tried to define motivation as an inherent trait of a person.

The Hertzberg two-factor theory, however, first attempted to define motivation environmentally. Hertzberg defined *motivational* and *maintenance* factors. Motivational factors lead workers to be motivated. They include achievement, recognition, participation, and growth. Maintenance factors are the foundation of motivation. In other words, maintenance factors must be satisfied before an individual can become motivated. Maintenance factors include physical conditions, security, economic factors, and social factors.

A. G. Maslow's approach was similar to Hertzberg's. Maslow developed a hierarchy of needs in which each worker has basic needs that can be placed on a hierarchy. Each need is filled contingent upon the fulfillment of former needs. Maslow's hierarchy of needs, in order, are:

1. Physiological
2. Safety and security
3. Social
4. Esteem
5. Self-actualization

As these studies demonstrate, there is still much confusion with regard to motivation. These studies, the survey, and practical experience have been used to develop a list, presented below, of motivational factors that can be initiated by supervision:

1. *Recognition.* As the survey demonstrated, this is the most effective motivator. Programs such as the "Order Picker of the Month" work. One warehouse gave everyone a turkey if they exceeded the inventory accuracy goal. It is vital that any program you develop be sincere and not faked. Your workers can always tell if they are being asked to make only a fake effort.

2. *Participatory management.* This again exploits the Hawthorne effect. People like to be involved. In addition, workers know much about the operation. Use that knowledge through participation.

3. *Clearly defined goals and objectives.* As discussed in regard to leadership, people perform best when they understand what is expected of them. Feedback on progress is important.

4. *Adequate training.* This is especially important when implementing a change to the operation, such as a new computer system.

5. *Trust and confidence.* We must develop a different attitude towards our people based on trust. When trust exists, employees and managers have respect for each other. From respect comes a sincere desire to listen. Listening results in understanding the other's perspective. Understanding results in a concern for the well-being of one's partner. Concern grows into a participative style that allows

management and employees to openly discuss goals and directions. This leads to success, which gives way to positive reinforcement. Positive reinforcement makes employees happy, and they are motivated to work for further positive reinforcement.

6. *Supervisory support.* Workers appreciate a supervisor who will work with them to resolve difficult issues. For instance, the work force contains many single parents who need support and understanding if a child is sick.

7. *Consistent supervision.* This again refers to the results of the survey on the traits of good supervisors. People like to know what to expect. Surprises create anxiety.

8. *Upward mobility.* The distribution center can often become a one-way road to nowhere. We need to provide a path for our employees who wish to grow. This will be discussed in greater detail.

9. *Adoption of constructive suggestions.* This demonstrates that we are listening.

One motivational area often missed by most organizations is upward mobility. Warehouse personnel do fit elsewhere in our organizations. They can contribute to production control, inventory control, quality control, purchasing, traffic, and customer service. Upward mobility will build morale if you do the following.

1. *Promote on the basis of qualifications.* This is often more difficult in a union environment. Unfortunately, the most senior individual is not necessarily the most qualified.

2. *Look for and develop workers' abilities.* Many workers have abilities that you were not aware of but that could be used constructively on the job. In any event, you should continually develop your employees.

3. *Have the courage to turn down the popular but unqualified.* Many make the mistake of not doing this, and soon regret it.

4. *Reconcile the disappointed, and retain their cooperation.* Often there are several candidates for an open position. Although we may have selected the best candidate for the promotion, we need to make the effort to reconcile the losers and assure them that they will be considered for the next opening.

5. *When you find it necessary to go outside your department for qualified people, explain why.* In warehousing, more often than not, supervisors are selected from outside the warehouse. This is baffling. Sometimes qualified candidates are truly not available, and choosing a person outside the department is necessary. This should be explained to the work force so that they do not perceive a closed door.

Another area of concern is the impact of positive discipline on motivation. The world is not perfect. Employees will test our interpretation of rules. Others will test to see how far they can push before a reaction occurs. Sooner or later, discipline will have to occur. In order to be effective, discipline should not be punishment. The objective is to change behavior, not to get revenge. When you approach it in this way, you can have positive discipline. Positive discipline is teaching, correcting, strengthening, and molding.

Positive discipline is based on rules that are: easy to understand, easy to enforce, and enforced the same way every time. The five rules of positive discipline are:

1. Be reasonable.
2. Stay out of private lives.
3. Don't make examples.
4. Keep personalities out of discipline.
5. When it's over, it's over—forget it.

The 10 steps to positive discipline are:

1. Get the facts. Do not operate on hearsay. Document the violation thoroughly.
2. Step up to the violations as they happen. Discipline cannot be effective unless it occurs soon after the undesirable behavior occurs.
3. Reprimand in private. This will ensure that you have the individual's full attention. If you reprimand in public, he or she wallows in embarrassment and fails to understand.
4. Stay calm and objective. Control your temper and use a level voice. Bellowing accomplishes nothing.
5. Talk straight. Address the issue and get to the point.
6. Avoid threats. Threats become empty promises.
7. Be fair and firm. Do not play favorites. Be consistent with discipline.
8. Discipline one infraction at a time. Again, this ensures understanding.
9. Criticize the work, not the person. You want to change behavior, not the individual.
10. Give words of encouragement. Remember, there is always something positive that can be said about everyone.

When it is time to talk to an employee regarding disciplinary action, remember the following seven points:

1. Talk privately on your own territory. In your office is the best place to have the discussion.
2. Don't take on someone else's problem. Many people try to confuse the issue and shift blame.
3. Do your homework and have documentation handy. Be prepared to back up what you say.
4. Stick to the problem. Do not allow the individual to change the subject.
5. Make employees accountable for their actions. Ensure that each employee understands this personal responsibility.
6. Get specific on charges—what was the infraction and when did it occur. This enhances the clarity of the communication.
7. Review and follow up. Monitor subsequent behavior to ensure that changes have occurred.

In summary, discipline is the hard part of supervision. Avoiding it only makes the situation worse. Consistency is critical to the impact of discipline. Remember to focus on the behavior, not the individual. When workers feel they are treated fairly and with respect, receiving constructive guidance rather than abusive criticism, then discipline will be positive.

Communication

As previously stated, the supervisor is the link between management and staff. Thus, communication is a critical process. Communication is the process through which one person's ideas and feelings are made known to another person. It is the means through which supervision gets the job done.

The most important element of communication is not speaking, or reading, or writing, but listening. To be an excellent communicator, we must learn to listen. Listening is the foundation of good communication. To this end, never interrupt or argue with an upset worker. This generally worsens the situation. Let the worker take advantage of this opportunity to vent his/her pent-up anger.

Try your best to show that you are genuinely concerned. Establish eye contact, and remove distractions. If the individual feels that you don't really care, you will worsen the situation by increasing the distance between you and the employee. Distance is a very difficult barrier to overcome.

Be patient if the employee has difficulty putting feelings into words. Don't be thinking about a response; control the urge to tell your side of the story. Give the employee your undivided attention. Do not shuffle papers. Do not answer the telephone. Be careful of passing judgment. Entering a discussion with preconceived thoughts creates a listening block.

If you wish to be a good communicator, you should

1. Communicate frequently
2. Give instructions in small portions
3. Continually reassure workers
4. Explain why actions are taken
5. Be truthful in your comments and act on what you say
6. Accentuate the positive
7. Be specific
8. Solicit comments, questions, and feedback
9. Give meaningful praise
10. Repeat instructions
11. Avoid surprises
12. Spend time on the floor
13. Be familiar with the company's rules and benefits
14. Be prepared to clear up misunderstandings
15. Avoid generalities and use simple, direct language
16. Keep your written memos and notices simple

17. Pay as much attention to the way you say things as you do to the words you use
18. Keep your meetings informal and encourage discussion

Sometimes communication becomes distorted or occurs unexpectedly. This usually results in rumors. The truth is everyone enjoys juicy gossip. Rumors occur in small organizations as well as large organizations. As a supervisor, we should act to curb rumors.

Accordingly, remember that a supervisor's word carries weight; weigh your words carefully. Be discreet in discussing one employee with another. This is often analogous to playing Russian roulette. Do not let planned criticism or discipline slip out ahead of time, and keep personal information to yourself. As a supervisor, never knowingly repeat a rumor.

Keep the grapevine under control by waiting for official word on company business. Cut down speculation by keeping workers informed. If a vicious rumor arises, it may be an indicator of discontent and anxiety in the organization. Set up a "rumor box" to allow employees the chance to contradict a widespread rumor.

Another type of communication a supervisor must deal with is complaints. Complaints are inevitable. How we address complaints is important. If we dismiss them out of hand, then we are not listening and therefore not communicating. When a complaint occurs, listen carefully to the complaint. We should not be sarcastic. We should realize that the complaint may be symptomatic of deeper concerns.

After listening to the complaint, first decide what is the objective of the employee's complaint. Next, explain to the employee what actions you will take to investigate the complaint. Then get the facts regarding the complaint. If the complaint has merit, take action to correct the situation, then follow up with the employee. If the complaint does not have merit, provide an explanation to the employee.

Also, consider the source and type of the complaint. Often our harshest critics are our best performers. They complain about not having the right tools, or about nonproductive activities. Our low producers complain about not having enough time for lunch.

Team Building

One survey reports that 23 percent of U.S. workers claim they are not working to potential. Many workers feel "pigeonholed" by their companies. While some question the American work ethic, university studies have shown that in fact the U.S. has an extremely strong work ethic, one of the strongest in the world. Perhaps then, the key to improving productivity is not necessarily resident in the worker. Perhaps the key resides in the organizational structure, and we need to develop organizations to tap these resources.

Traditional U.S. organizational principles can be summarized as follows:

- Specialization of work
- Departmental organizations based on function
- Separation of planning, control, and improvement functions from operations
- Information systems to support top management
- Top-down decision making

Unfortunately, the characteristics of organizations that are based on traditional principles are:

- Little flexibility
- Organizational inertia
- Lack of product identification
- Large inventories
- Higher operating costs
- A feeling that improvement is someone else's job

In fact, the individual worker no longer feels capable of making a difference in a traditional organization. He or she cannot comprehend where the organization is heading.

Teamwork and people are the key strategies to improving our productivity, because all improvements involve people implementing change in a system. A system is the combination of social and technical systems. Traditional organizations have attempted to maximize the technical systems. Maximizing technical systems results in poor social systems and little improvement. On the other hand many have discovered that better social systems, even at the expense of the technical systems, yield better results. The reason is simple, and can be presented by means of these statements:

- No meaningful change occurs without people.
- People are the single greatest competitive advantage that any organization has.
- People do things that make sense to them.

This implies that we need to optimize both the social and technical systems. When this occurs, productivity gains of 15, 30, and 50 percent have been reported.

The optimal social system is the Self-Managing Team (SMT) concept. Organizations that use this approach develop a series of work teams both on the warehouse floor and in administrative areas. A SMT typically has 5 to 12 members who rotate jobs and produce an entire product or service with minimal supervision. The team assumes all responsibilities and makes all decisions regarding their product or service.

SMTs have been extremely effective, because they challenge all workers to mentally participate rather than mindlessly execute policies. Workers begin to use "brain power rather than horsepower." This results in continuous productivity and quality improvements, and ultimately, success. Meaningful participation by workers always has a positive impact on productivity, never a negative or neutral one.

As a result, SMTs are spreading rapidly: to autos, aerospace, electronics, food processing, paper, steel, wood, and even financial institutions. Some examples of big companies using work teams include:

- Boeing
- Caterpillar
- Champion International
- Cummins Engine

- Digital Equipment
- Ford
- General Electric
- General Motors
- LTV Steel
- Procter & Gamble
- A.O. Smith
- Tektronix
- AT&T Credit Corporation
- Miller Brewing Company

While the benefits of SMTs are clear, implementing them is not a small undertaking. Often it entails wiping out entire levels of management and removing interdepartmental bureaucracies in order to place meaningful authority in the hands of the teams so that they can act quickly (see Fig. 26-1). Resistance to SMTs is still widespread. Many managers resist sharing power. Supervisors feel threatened. At the same time, some employees do not wish more responsibility and job rotation. The turnover rate at General Electric's Salisbury plant increased to 14 percent when it converted to a team concept.

What Is a Team?

A team is an energetic group of people, committed to achieving common goals, who work well together. Members enjoy working with other team members to produce high-quality results. The basic tasks of any team are:

- Achieving its goal
- Maintaining itself
- Continuously improving

While all teams share these common tasks, there are many types of teams. For instance, consider a tennis team as compared to a basketball team. Each wishes to achieve its goal, maintain itself, and continuously improve, but the manner in which each of the members of each team interacts to accomplish these tasks is completely different. Clearly, the members of a basketball team interact more closely than the members of a tennis team.

Some types of teams are temporary. They are formed to achieve a specific goal. Campaign workers for an individual running for an elected office are one example. Other teams are permanent and ongoing.

There are three basic types of industrial teams: problem-solving, special-purpose, and self-managing (SMTs). A comparison is provided in Table 26-2.

A GAO survey in 1987 found that 70 percent of 476 large companies had installed some form of team approach. Many of us believe that industrial teams were a Japanese development. In reality they were developed in Britain, Sweden, and the U.S. long before being adopted by Japanese auto companies on a widespread basis. Many believe that the success of Japanese industrial teams (most notably Quality

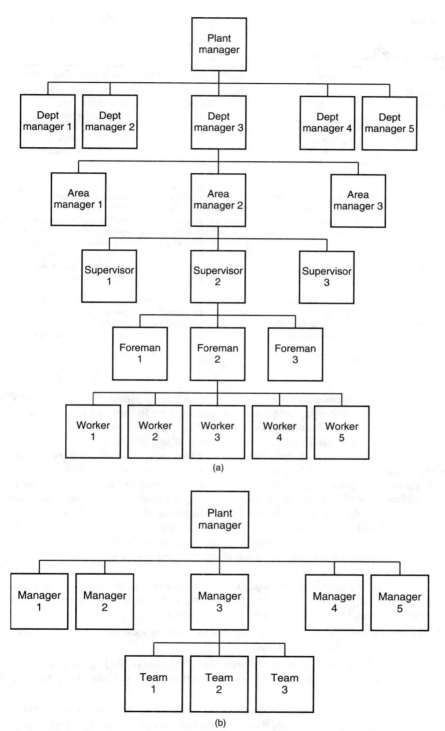

Figure 26-1. Organizational structures: traditional organization (a), team organization (b).

Table 26-2 Industrial Teams

	Problem-solving teams	Special-purpose teams	Self-managing teams
Structure and Function	5 to 12 volunteers from different areas of a department. Meet 1 to 2 hr/wk. Identify ways to improve productivity, quality, and work environment. No power to implement ideas.	May address designing work reforms, new technologies, vendor/ customer relations.	5 to 15 employees who produce an entire product/service. Members learn all tasks and rotate jobs. Teams take over managerial duties.
Results	Can reduce costs and improve quality, but do not organize work more effectively. Tend to fade away.	Involve workers in decisions at higher levels, creating an atmosphere for improvement. Creates foundation for self-managing teams.	Can increase productivity 30 percent and dramatically increase quality. Fundamentally changes work organization, giving control to workers. Creates flatter organizations.
Evolution	Small-scale efforts in 1920s and 1930s. Widespread use in late 1970s as Quality Circles.	Evolved from problem-solving approach in 1980s. Still spreading.	Used by a few companies in 1960s and 1970s. Rapid spread in late 1980s. Wave of the future.

Circles) is due to Japanese culture. This is also untrue. Japanese "transplant" auto plants in the U.S. are equal in quality and productivity to those in Japan. Honda now produces motorcycles and automobiles in U.S. plants for export to Japan.

Today, it can be argued that U.S. companies that are adopting SMTs are in fact ahead of the Japanese. If we examine the most successful example of Japanese industrial teams, Quality Circles, we find that these teams are merely "off-line" discussion groups that present recommendations for improvement but have little power to implement their recommendations. Self-managing teams diverge from the Japanese approach. Workers function as a team throughout the workday. They are empowered to take control and make decisions rather than merely recommend improvements. In some ways the SMT becomes a small, focused company.

The four main characteristics of self-managing teams are these:

1. *Task interdependence and interaction.* The team members perform a series of tasks dependent upon each other. In other words, the function performed by the team requires a team to accomplish the function.

2. *Specified purpose.* The team has a specific reason for existence that can be defined in a vision/mission statement.

3. *Open communications.* The key and inherent advantage of SMTs is their ability to communicate among themselves quickly and frequently without having to cope with a bureaucracy.

4. *Empowerment.* This is the most important characteristic that energizes the SMT. Empowerment does not imply that the team has unlimited authority. Rather, em-

powerment implies accepting responsibility for group goals and for individual contribution to those goals. The objective is to organizationally push down the ability to share, contribute, and make decisions from upper levels of management to the shop floor.

Effective teams achieve results individuals cannot accomplish working alone. They have identifiable missions, with strong personal commitment by team members. Members exhibit high energy and involvement. Members understand and manage questions of power, control, leadership, conflict, and team roles. Members trust each other, are committed to developing satisfied customers, and seek to continuously improve.

It is interesting to note that team members do not have to like each other to be an effective team. There have been many examples of professional sports teams that have competed well even though the personal relationship among team members was volatile. One might consider the stormy relationships among the New York Yankees.

The impacts and results of implementing SMTs are dramatic. First, employing SMTs increases organizational flexibility. Team members learn a number of jobs performed by the team and can react to employee sickness or operational changes. Team members help each other and increase individual utilization. This results in leaner staffing and improved productivity. The team accepts responsibility for its own operations. This accountability yields improved quality. SMTs improve the quality of work life, and there is less turnover because of the resulting high employee satisfaction. Individual responsibility is increased, and greater employee development is achieved. This results in increased self-esteem. Finally, because staffing is leaner and at the same time individual employee development is greater, there is increased job security. Organizations simply cannot afford to lose a team member.

Developing a Team-Based Culture

While the benefits of SMTs are clear, implementation is not. The entire nature of an organization must undergo change. The entire organization is literally turned upside down. This requires change, and people fear change. Change involves modifying and eliminating paradigms. Perhaps the best discussion of understanding and eliminating paradigms is a video by Joel Barker titled "Discovering The Future: The Business of Paradigms."* Many traditional paradigms must be eliminated if SMTs are to be implemented.

The entire culture of the organization must change. The culture of an organization is its personality. It is the foundation on which much decision making occurs. Traditional organizational culture is driven from the top. Team-based culture is driven from the bottom. Management provides guidance, but operational decision making is made at the lowest levels.

In order for this to happen, everyone within the organization must understand the vision of where the organization is going. Unquestionably, the most critical mis-

---

*Available from Charthouse Learning Corp., 221 River Ridge Circle, Burnsville, MN 55337; 1-800-890-1800.

take made by many companies is a lack of vision. Yet vision alone is not enough. Vision alone will not adequately describe how to be successful in any organizational pursuit. Successful companies have evolved according to a model of success (Fig. 26-2). As can be seen, this model incorporates four basic components in a layered fashion.

The first, obviously, is vision. Simply put, vision is a description of where the organization is headed. It is the bulls-eye of the target. The mission defines how to accomplish the vision. The foundations of success are the values that will guide us to accomplish our mission. These represent the code of ethics that an organization uses to make decisions. Finally, enabling concepts are the means that we use to accomplish our mission. Not shown in Fig. 26-2, but still part of the model of success, is the requirement for evidence of success. Requirements of success are essentially road markers that provide feedback to the organization with respect to its performance.

To implement SMTs, a transition plan is required. The transition plan compares the present reality of the organization to the desired state of a team-based culture. The present reality is the current state of team building in the organization. The desired state is an organization that is committed to customer satisfaction, that has a clear mission, structure, and roles, that employs teamwork, that exercises empowerment, and that is dedicated to continuous improvement. Team building is a continuous process of assessing present reality and clarifying desired state. In this way, the organization evolves.

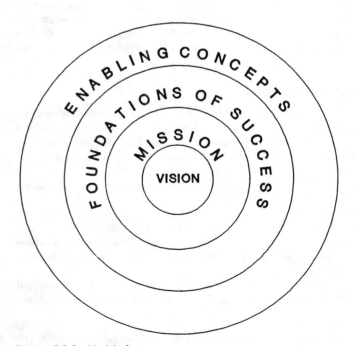

Figure 26-2. Model of success.

Implementing SMTs requires, first and foremost, total commitment by top management. Management must lead the way and present the concept to the work force. The work force, in turn, must then acknowledge and commit to the team concept. In effect, management must sell the concept. Teams cannot simply be formed and begin operating. An *extensive* amount of training must be given to all employees before teams can function effectively. Teams will be given the responsibility to make operational decisions. To make these decisions, they must develop or be provided with financial information and/or performance statistics. Team members must first be trained on how to understand and use this information. Training must be provided on how to run a meeting and how to make decisions as a group. Management must make the investment in time and money to undertake this training.

Finally, management must be willing to let go of some decision making. A basis of trust must be built. This is perhaps the hardest part.

All of this takes time. It is not done in a weekend or a month. Developing a team-based culture takes years. Some suggest that larger organizations may require up to five years to undergo this change. This implies a long-term commitment by all parties.

Conclusions

In truth, dealing effectively with people is just plain hard. It takes patience, and requires attention to detail. We need to develop a better understanding of our employees. We must be consistent in our actions and ensure that everyone understands what is expected. We need to practice leadership, rather than management, when working with our employees. We need to delegate for results. We should remember that recognition is a powerful motivator, and that the most important part of communicating is listening. Finally, we need to implement an organization that allows the worker to use both his mind and his muscles. The concepts of team building and of SMTs are finding wider acceptance. Distribution is, in the end, a people business.

Further Reading

Beaumariage, Kimberly, and Dan Shunk, *Issues in Migrating to Teamwork,* Computer and Automation Systems Association of the Society of Manufacturing Engineers.

Daly, Frank, and James A. Tompkins, "Trenton Brewery Management Development Course: Trenton Brewery Vision," Tompkins Associates, Raleigh, NC, 1991.

Daly, Frank, John C. Spain, and James A. Tompkins, "The Dynamics of Warehouse Supervision Seminar," Tompkins Associates, Raleigh, NC, 1988.

Hauck, Warren C. and Victor Dingus, *Achieving High Commitment Work Systems,* Institute of Industrial Engineers, Norcross, GA, 1990.

Tompkins, James A., *Winning Manufacturing: The How-To Book of Successful Manufacturing,* Institute of Industrial Engineers, Norcross, GA, 1989.

Tupper, Tim, "Trenton Brewery Management Development Course: Teambuilding," PDS Press, 1991.

27

Warehouse Management Systems

J. Eric Peters

Regional General Manager,
Tompkins Associates, Inc.

The objectives of warehousing are to maximize the use of warehouse resources while satisfying the customer requirements. The key to maximizing resources is control. The key to attaining the highest levels of customer service is control. The tool to creating control is a warehouse management system.

A management system is a means, mechanism, or procedure by which we manage our operations. The basic objectives of a management system, be it manual or computerized, are to

1. Identify and coordinate the work that needs to be done
2. Direct the accomplishment of the work so as to maximize performance (productivity of warehouse resources, and satisfaction of customer requirements)
3. Report the status of the work that needs to be (or was) done

A manual system uses paper and manual techniques to attempt to optimize warehousing operations. A computerized warehouse management system (WMS) is the integration of bar coding technology, RF communications equipment, hardware, and warehouse-oriented software. This software is used to optimize warehousing and warehouse-related operations. Whereas the sophistication levels of manual systems are low, the levels of sophistication for WMSs can vary from simple stock location control methodologies to systems that truly optimize space, labor, and equipment in the warehouse.

It is important to note at this time that one should not confuse WMS technology with business systems applications that impact the warehouse. A mainframe inventory management application is not a warehouse system. A mainframe inventory management package is primarily interested in the financial aspects of inventory. An MRP system is not a warehouse system. MRP is concerned with managing the manufacturing operations. As we will discuss shortly, a warehouse system is an application whose solution is based upon the needs of the warehousing operations.

Four critical areas will lead up to the discussion on WMS technology: bar coding, printing, data collection, and radio frequency (RF) technology. An understanding of these technologies will allow for a discussion of the functionality, justification, and implementation methodologies of a WMS. The sections that follow will address these issues.

Bar Coding

Bar coding and the related technologies were first discovered and patented in the 1930s. Up until the 1960s, the primary use of bar coding was in the area of direct machine focus and control. In the early 1960s, the railroad industry started to use bar coding technology for automatic rail-car identification. The purpose of this experiment was to improve fleet utilization through visibility of car locations. Shortly thereafter, grocery stores became involved in the technology. Today bar coding is becoming as necessary to a distribution operation as a pitcher is to a major league baseball team. Bar coding is here to stay.

Put in the most simplistic terms, a bar code functions much like Morse code. Whereas Morse code is the use of dots and dashes to represent alphabetic and numeric characters, the bar code uses parallel dark bars and spaces to represent these same characters. The method may vary from code to code, but the principles remain the same. Light is reflected from a light surface and absorbed by the dark surfaces. Dark bars absorb light; white spaces reflect light. The bar code is illuminated, and a photo sensor "sees" the reflective differences between the bars and spaces and generates a proportional electronic signal that is decoded by the system.

Bar Coding Considerations

An understanding of the following factors can impact the effectiveness of a bar coding project. They should be evaluated when designing a bar coding application.

1. *Source coding.* Item coding/labeling should take place as close to the beginning of the process as possible. This will allow for maximum utilization of the bar code and the appropriate automatic identification technology.

2. *Numbering scheme.* The more characters in the bar code, the more difficult it is to read. Thoroughly examine your current numbering scheme to determine if it can be reduced to cut label size, label printing time, and scanning complexity. If the numbering convention cannot be changed, consider the use of shorter-length license plates, to which related data can be linked via a computer system directory.

3. *Symbology.* Evaluate available symbologies on the basis of their ability to accommodate your current and projected item-identification requirements, their potential value outside your plant to both carriers and customers, ease of printing or producing, and vendor (printers and readers) support. Do not select a symbology that lacks a broadly endorsed standard.

4. *Code density.* Code density refers to the number of characters per inch on the bar code. Low-density bar codes have fewer characters per inch than medium- and high-density bar codes. Although some applications will require high-density encoding because of space limitations, larger bars and spaces are easier to read and less subject to contamination. Use low-density codes whenever possible.

5. *Scanner field of view/code density.* A reasonable rule of thumb states that scanner range will be equivalent to 1000 times the narrowest bar's thickness; i.e., a 10-ml (.010-in) bar can be read at a distance of 10 in. Depth of field will normally be half the range; i.e., the code using 10-ml narrow bars could be read from 5 to 10 in. Although extended ranges can be obtained by reducing the height of the field or through auto-focusing techniques, these approaches should be used only if other alternatives have been exhausted.

6. *3 to 1 wide/narrow ratio.* The wide-to-narrow ratio refers to the width ratio of the bars to spaces. Most codes permit narrow bar/space ratios of 2 or 3 to 1. To minimize the effect of printing anomalies, dirt specks, etc., use the 3 to 1 ratio or a ratio as close thereto as possible.

7. *Aspect ratio/quiet zones.* Overall bar code height should be at least 15 percent of code length for hand-held scanning and 25 to 100 percent for automatic scanning, to accommodate variations in operator performance or label presentation. The quiet zones preceding and trailing the bar code should be .5 in or 10 times the size of the narrowest bar, whichever is greater.

8. *Scanner resolution.* Match scanner resolution (i.e., the size of the spot of light exiting the scanner) through the required field of view to the density of the code. Spot size should be equal to or slightly smaller than the thickness of the narrowest bar.

9. *Substrate opacity.* Media selection for bar code labels must include consideration of shelf life, so that background discoloration or aging does not reduce bar/space contrast. The label material should be sufficiently opaque to cover dark backgrounds that, if the label is translucent, could turn spaces into bars.

Bar Code Symbologies

Numerous bar code symbologies exist in the marketplace. Accordingly, several factors play a role in the selection of a bar code that is correct for your operation. The following are several factors to consider when selecting your bar code symbology.

Most industries have defined bar code standards for their particular industry or sector. These standards were typically defined by either of the following two methods.

The usual method a company will use to define their bar coding strategy is through user groups. User groups may dictate the industry specification. The specification definition usually includes:

- How anyone in the industry can use the symbol
- Data to be encoded
- Fields of information
- Detailed quality-control specifications to ensure universality
- Location and size of code on item

Examples of this industry definition would include the Automobile Industry Action Group (AIAG), and the U.S. Grocery Industry (UPC).

A second method used to determine your bar coding requirements is to look at your customer requirements. Many industries, particularly in the retail sector, are having their bar coding symbologies and methodologies dictated by the major companies in their sector. This trend is likely to continue, as large retailers and customers force conformance with their requirements.

And finally, the issue of cost plays a role in a company's selection of a bar code. There are two approaches to bar code generation: preprinted and on-demand labels. Preprinted labels are bar codes that are usually printed off-site in bulk quantities. These bar codes are generally sequential unique bar code license plates. A bar code license plate is a bar code that contains no information aside from the actual bar code number. License plates are unique tag identifiers for each individual unit load, carton, or piece.

Typical applications for a preprinted bar code include high-volume applications, sequential applications, and preprinted boxes. The advantages of preprinted bar codes are that they are low-cost and provide a better, consistent print quality. The downside to a preprinted bar code is that it provides little flexibility. Usually, though, this flexibility is not required, as most bar code applications are for internal use only.

The second type of bar code is an on-demand label. This bar code is exactly what the name implies. The bar code is printed on demand, as needed. On-demand bar codes are useful when one has random, specific part number applications, or wishes to imbed customer information in the bar code. On-demand bar codes are extremely flexible. The two negatives, when compared to the preprinted label, are the higher cost (especially in hardware) and print quality, which must be closely monitored.

The two most popular bar codes used in warehousing and distribution today are the Code 3 of 9 bar code and the Code 2 of 5 bar code. Other bar code symbologies are gaining more widespread popularity, and these symbologies will also be discussed in detail.

The Code 3 of 9 (or Code 39) bar code is an alphanumeric bar code that allows for both uppercase alphanumeric characters and numeric digits. Code 3 of 9 is a binary-encoded bar code that uses wide and narrow bars and spaces to represent the alphanumeric characters (see Fig. 27-1). Three out of nine bits are used to indicate a character. The Code 3 of 9 bar code can be of variable length, and bidirectional as well. Code 39 is widely used in warehousing, both because of its alphanumeric capabilities and because it is the Department of Defense's primary bar code.

The second popular warehousing bar code is the Code 2 of 5 bar code. Code 2 of 5 is a bidirectional numeric-only bar code. The Code 2 of 5 bar code is usually interleaved (see Fig. 27-2). Interleaving occurs when the odd positions are encoded into

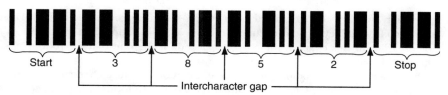

Figure 27-1. Code 3 of 9 bar code.

bars and the even positions into spaces. Interleaving allows the characters to over-lap, thus creating a higher-density code. Code 2 of 5 is more compact than Code 39. This is evident when you compare Figs. 27-1 and 27-2, which represent the same code (3852). It should be noted that Code 2 of 5 does not allow for check charac-ters with the bar code.

A special type of Code 2 of 5 bar code is the UPC code. The UPC bar code is a popular standard, used in many retail applications. In fact, the UPC code was devel-oped for grocery supermarket point-of-use sale applications. As will be borne out by the grocery industry, the UPC code is best suited for fixed-length coding for unique manufacturer and item identification only. The UPC code, being a 2 of 5 bar code in a fixed format, is a 12-digit pattern. The first digit represents the product cate-gory, the next five digits represent the vendor ID, the following five digits represent the part number, and the last digit is a check digit. There are numerous variations of the UPC code, depending on the particular industry application.

Code 128 is a recently popularized bar code symbology. Code 128 is a high-den-sity encoding of the full 128 ASCII character subset. Code 128 is also a variable-field-length bar code, like Code 3 of 9. One of the principal benefits of Code 128 is that it provides elaborate character-by-character and full-symbol integrity checking. Code 128 is commonly used today to perform shipping container identification and tracking.

Code 93 is another bar code symbology that uses all 128 ASCII characters. Code 93 can provide the highest alphanumeric data density. Two check characters are used in Code 93 to ensure data integrity.

A fifth bar code symbology worth noting is Codabar. Codabar was one of the ear-lier symbologies. Codabar is a numeric-character set, with six unique control char-acters and four unique stop/start characters. Codabar is commonly used in nongrocery point-of-use sales, blood banks, and libraries. Codabar is very rarely found in warehousing or distribution applications.

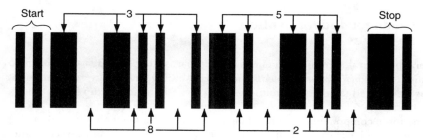

Figure 27-2. Code 2 of 5 bar code (interleaved).

A variety of other codes exist, including Code 49, binary coded decimal (BCD), bilevel code, bull's-eye code, decimal code, geometric code, among others. As noted earlier in this chapter, the correct bar code is the one that fits your application.

One other coding symbology that deserves mention is optical character recognition (OCR) technology. OCR uses human readable code to identify product and materials. OCR is the Department of Defense backup identification code to the Code 3 of 9. OCR technology typically has been confined to document reading. One challenge associated with OCR technology is that it requires a near-contact reader to read the code. Inkspots and voids can easily transpose or obscure characters. It is for these reasons that OCR technology is typically confined to document reading only.

Bar Coding Benefits

The two main benefits of bar coding are these:

1. *Labor reduction.* Labor reductions are brought about by bar coding through a reduction in the time required to identify loads and locations. This helps to support real-time RF communications transactions. Labor-intensive keystrokes are replaced by virtually instantaneous label scans.

2. *Data acquisition accuracy.* RF and non-RF communications transactions involve a series of load and location identifications. These identifications are critical to system operation; therefore, the accuracy of data acquisition is essential. Keystroke data entry, with a typical error rate of 1 in 300 keystrokes, is both time-consuming and error-prone. Bar code data entry, with a typical error rate of 1 in 1 to 2 million scans, is both fast and highly accurate. Bar code data entry for the number of transactions occurring is important to the success of real-time RF communications.

The most significant benefit to be gained from the use of bar coding is the effective support of data collection and real-time RF communications. Without the bar code, data collection and real-time communications through manual terminal keystroke inputs will be a drag on productivity and replete with errors. Bar code data acquisition offers a fast and accurate medium through which real-time communications can reach their peak.

Miscellaneous Identification Technologies

There are several identification alternatives to bar coding. The first technology to be discussed is *radio frequency identification* (RFID). RFID technology can be thought of as a protected tag that communicates back to an RF reader with respect to item identification.

The three components of an RFID tag are the transponder, antenna, and reader. The transponder tag is a small printed circuit board that contains a receive-and-transmit antenna, a small number of discrete components, and an integrated circuit (IC) chip for data storage, housed in a heavy-duty industrial package. The size of the transponder is dependent upon antenna size, which in turn is a function of required range and speed. Two basic tag types are passive and active (battery-powered) tags. Passive tags are activated by an external RF signal, and respond with a unique multicharacter signal preprogrammed at the factory. Active tags are self-activating. Because the RFID tag is a protected and enclosed tag, RFID technology is used primarily in harsh environments where bar coding is not feasible.

A second type of identification technique is the *magnetic strip*. The magnetic strip identification technology is the same identification technology you see on the back of your credit card or ATM card. Magnetic strip technology is a ferromagnetic tape with binary code "written" on it. Magnetic strips are excellent in dirt/grease environments. The downside to this technology is that it is restricted by read distance (near-contact).

The final technology to be discussed is *voice recognition*. Voice recognition systems perform discrete word recognition based on a vocabulary of 50 to 1000 words. The principal benefit of a voice recognition system is that it allows the operator total use of the hands. The downside of this technology is that tone and pronunciation can affect accuracy, and it is questionable whether voice recognition is any faster than conventional data collection methods. The use of voice recognition technology has generally been limited to nonwarehouse applications.

Printer Technology

Several different printers exist to print bar code labels. The following is a discussion of some of these printers. With any of these printers, the requirements of your bar code will drive the selection of your printer.

The first type of printer is a *dot matrix impact printer*. This printer was originally designed for printing pages of data. A dot matrix printer is composed of many needles evenly spaced across a movable horizontal shuttle. These needles create the image of the bar code. It is usually recommended that overlap printing occur, to get the best density. Generally the quality of a bar code on a dot matrix printer is average. It is for this reason that most bar coding applications are not performed on a dot matrix printer.

The second type is a *thermal printer*. A thermal printer uses a light-colored substrate, impregnated with clear coating. The clear coating changes to a dark color when heat is applied. Small thermal heaters are in the print head to effect this change. A thermal printer has a typical speed of $\frac{1}{2}$ to 5 in/sec and is generally used indoors due to temperature constraints. Thermal-printed bar codes are affected by ultraviolet light.

A *thermal transfer printer* is similar to a thermal printer except that it uses plain paper instead of special impregnated paper. A thermal transfer printer also has a special ribbon that reacts with the thermal print head to darken the bar code. Thermal printers and thermal transfer printers are two of the most popular bar code printing methods.

Data Collection Methods

Data collection devices are devices that collect information to be entered electronically into a computer system. These devices have a small screen and an alphanumeric keypad with function keys. Information is entered into the data collection device either through the keypad or through a reader. Data collection devices can either be hard-wired to the computer system or not. Nonwired data collection devices are either batch readers or real-time radio frequency (RF) readers. RF devices will be discussed later in this chapter.

Batch collection devices (batch readers) are devices that operate in a batch (or non-real-time) manner. Most batch readers are hand-held devices. Batch readers typically interface with the computer system through a docking station. A docking station is a device that interfaces with the computer system to transfer information between the batch readers and the computer system. Batch readers have information periodically downloaded into them through the docking station. The operator then performs the set of tasks that has been loaded into the batch reader. Most batch readers can hold a significant amount of information.

Data collection devices, whether RF or non-RF devices, usually have some type of data reader attached to the data collection device. The two principal methods by which to read are *contact wands* and *noncontact readers*. The following is a discussion of both types of technologies.

Contact wands are sometimes called *light pens* or *wedges*. A contact wand must physically touch the code. Light pens can either be stationary devices attached to a CRT or portable devices attached to a batch reader. In either case, the contact wand generally utilizes light-emitting diodes (LEDs) and is a low-cost data reader.

In choosing a contact reader, one must take several factors into account. The first that must be considered is character density. The type of contact wand that is chosen is dependent upon the type of bar code that is used, the relative sizes of widest bar or space versus smallest bar or space, and the smallest width of a bar or space. The second factor is the aperture size of the contact reader. The aperture size must be matched to the code density of the bar code. A high-resolution wand that is used to read a low-resolution code can sometimes inadvertently read a dirt smudge as a bar. The third factor to consider is the angle of the read. This can affect the first-pass read rate. And finally, the speed of the pass must also be considered, because this too can affect the first pass read rate.

The second type of reader is a noncontact reader. This type of reader can be either a *fixed beam reader* or a *moving beam reader*. Noncontact moving beam readers are sometimes called *scanners*. Scanners can be attached to both RF and non-RF devices. Almost all RF devices will utilize a scanner. The following is a discussion of these two types of readers.

A fixed beam noncontact reader is a stationary beam through which the bar code passes. The bar code is in one fixed location on the object. A fixed beam reader is a one-read-per-pass type of scanner. Fixed beam readers typically use LED, incandescent, or fluorescent lights to read the bar code. Fixed beam scanners are typically used in applications where the product is moving past the scanner at a constant distance from the reader.

The second type of noncontact reader is a moving beam scanner. A moving beam scanner uses a light spot to transverse an angular path, searching for a bar code on the object. Moving beam scanners can scan at rates of up to 1400 passes/sec, and thus can allow for multiple read. Multiple reads can ensure a high level of accuracy.

The selection of a moving beam scanner requires the consideration of several factors. The first consideration is whether or not the scanner will be mounted. If it is a mounted scanner, it must be determined if the scanner will be mounted overhead, on the side, or underneath. The second consideration is the symbol speed. A mounted scanner is immobile, so the object speed will affect the scan rate of the scanner. Portable hand-held scanners are not affected by symbol speed, as the product typically being scanned is stationary. The third factor that must be considered is the depth of field. A camera cannot take an accurate photograph from any distance, nor can a scanner read from any distance. The moving beam scanner requires a minimum and maximum distance at which the symbol will be read. The fourth factor to consider is the placement and orientation of the symbol. Especially for mounted scanners, the placement and orientation of the symbol is critical if one is to get a successful read on the first pass.

Real-Time Radio Frequency Communications

An RF data collection device is a second method of interfacing the data collection with the host computer. Whereas the batch reader must have information transferred to it through a docking station, an RF device will communicate with an RF base station through radio waves. The RF base station then typically communicates with the computer system. Information transfer is virtually instantaneous. The primary benefits realized from real-time RF communications can be classified as follows:

1. *Information availability.* Real-time status updates of receipts, manufacturing requests, and customer orders give warehouse management the responsiveness to manage ongoing activities as they occur. This information availability allows the warehouse to be responsive to changing needs, and gives management the capability to redeploy its labor, equipment, and space resources as required to maximize performance. Each transaction results in an update of some system record, which can be queried to determine status and to determine the next action to be taken.

2. *Labor pacing.* Real-time communications between the system and the operator allow the system to pace the operator from one assigned task to the next. The operator does not need to return after each task to a central location to get the next instruction. The system can select the next task for an operator based on what needs to be done *now,* where the operator is, and what the operator is capable of doing. The result is work load management that maximizes task accomplishment and minimizes labor idle time.

3. *Material tracking.* Real-time communications allow verification of all transactions that affect material location. This verification updates status records to be used for future transactions, eliminates most material location errors, and provides immediate instructions for resolving errors that are identified. Real-time communication allows the warehouse to operate more efficiently in a fuller state, in that the

system is immediately aware of empty storage locations as they are created and can assign these to putaway loads immediately, without manual searching of the rack.

Two basic RF devices are used in warehousing: hand-held devices and truck-mounted units. The primary differences between truck-mounted RF devices and hand-helds are that truck-mounted devices are more rugged, have a larger keyboard, and use a larger screen. Hand-held units should not be substituted for truck-mounted units on a lift truck. Lift truck operators need to pay attention to what they are doing and not have to be fumbling with a hand-held unit.

There are several issues that one must consider when selecting and installing an RF system. First, a site survey must be done. The issue of coverage is critical. An RF system that does not provide 100 percent coverage is ineffective. Issues of concern include the physical environment, radio transmission techniques, the power of the transmitted signal, and receiver sensitivity. This survey should be done by the RF vendor you have chosen to install your system.

There are two principal RF technologies utilized in warehousing: narrow band primary frequencies and spread spectrum frequencies. Narrow band frequencies are licensed by the FCC, whereas spread spectrum frequencies do not require a license. Spread spectrum systems are a recent development in WMS RF communications. Spread spectrum was developed in the 1940s as a jam-resistant, interference-free radio communications method. Initially it was a military application. Simply put, a spread spectrum frequency is distributed over a wide range of frequencies, as opposed to a primary frequency, which is confined to one narrow band.

The benefits of spread spectrum systems are that they require lower power requirements, need no FCC license, and are resistant to radio interference. Spread spectrum technology also has very high data-transmission rates. The benefits of narrow band frequencies are that they are FCC-protected and have a longer broadcast range. Spread spectrum systems may sometimes require more base stations and repeaters, due to the shorter broadcasting range.

Real-time RF communication is a very worthwhile operational enhancement. The opportunities afforded to improve inventory and stock location accuracy, labor management, and responsiveness to manufacturing, result in tangible cost savings. Warehouse installations of RF technology are plentiful; the technology is proven. Truck-mounted and hand-held RF terminals are relatively inexpensive, and most up-to-date warehouse management system packages will support RF communications.

Warehouse Management System Functionality

In general, every warehouse performs four basic functions. It (1) receives product, (2) stores product, (3) picks product, and (4) ships product. These functions can be further broken down thus:

1. Receive product
   a. Purchased items
   b. Third party finished goods
   c. Customer returns

2. Store product
   a. Quality inspection
   b. Putaway
   c. Location and lot control
3. Pick product
   a. Raw materials picking
   b. Work-in-process picking
   c. Finished goods picking
4. Ship product
   a. Internal customer shipments
   b. External shipments

Supporting these functions are order entry, order scheduling, inventory status reporting, and other miscellaneous activities.

The following is a brief discussion of the functionality requirements for each of the operational areas.

Order Entry

The function of order entry is to quickly and accurately place orders into the warehouse system. A WMS accomplishes this mission by fulfilling the following requirements.

1. The WMS must be able to *record special customer requirements.* Special packaging, palletizing, labeling and/or documentation requirements should be noted in the WMS, as should any additional miscellaneous customer information.

2. The WMS must *make inventory available for use as close to real time as possible.* Instant availability of inventory allows Customer Service to make the product available for immediate sale. Instant availability also allows the planners to make incoming product available for immediate use in Manufacturing. Ultimately, lead times will be significantly reduced by reducing the time it takes to make inventory available for productive use.

3. The WMS must *provide for inventory preallocation.* Preallocation will allow Order Entry to hold incoming goods for a certain customer or a selected manufacturing run.

4. The WMS should *record an anticipated shipping date for a customer order.* The anticipated shipping date will allow the warehouse to productively plan its picking schedule.

Order Scheduling

The function of order scheduling is to plan the day's activities. The order scheduling decision-making process is as follows.

1. The WMS must be able to *allocate the shift's labor to the day's activities.* A WMS can either automatically plan the day's labor activities or a supervisor can intervene

and alter the recommended allocation. Manpower allocation must also take into account the material handling method that each operator will use, and ensure that the equipment is properly allocated based on the tasks.

2. A WMS must be able to *schedule the work load based on the manpower and equipment allocation.* The WMS must manage the work pending, the work in the queue, the work in process, and the work completed. The WMS must also be able to handle emergency order generation and be able to alter the work load schedule to accommodate these emergency orders.

3. Labor task interleaving is *the ability to optimize labor and equipment assignments based on queued labor tasks.* Interleaving refers to the fact that the system must have the ability to select the next labor task from a queue of all pending activities, and not just from one module or labor subgroup. Interleaving expands the pool of tasks available to an operator, and thus minimizes travel distances. Minimizing travel distances results in a direct labor productivity increase. Several other capabilities of the WMS must exist if the system is to task-interleave. The system must time-stamp and manage task times in the queue, contain a travel path methodology, and operate in a real-time manner. If these and the above requirements are met, then task interleaving is possible. Without interleaving, labor productivity is still improved, though not to the optimal level.

Receiving Functionality

Proper identification and tracking of materials in receiving lays the groundwork for efficient, accurate warehousing operations. A lack of control in receiving generally equates to a poor, difficult-to-manage operation. Generally, receiving operations have the following needs.

1. The need to *have accurate receipt information,* with advanced notice of the anticipated receipts to facilitate quick and accurate receiving operations. Electronic downloading of detailed shipment information from the host system to a WMS must quickly and accurately translate this data into usable information.

2. A WMS must be able to *provide receipt validation of incoming goods.* The WMS should electronically validate incoming materials. This validation should be real-time, so as to support the immediate correction of any discrepancies.

3. The WMS should *quickly provide receipt confirmation to the mainframe system.* This confirmation is necessary so that incoming materials can quickly be made available for use.

4. The need to *reduce the time product spends in staging.* After the incoming receipt's bill of lading has been checked, the warehouse must sometimes wait until Quality Control completes inspection, Purchasing or Planning rectifies discrepancies, operators are available, or space is found to store materials. These scenarios, coupled with the fact that most warehouses suffer from a chronic lack of staging area, requires that product move quickly and accurately through staging. A WMS minimizes the time product sits in staging, because of operator-directed putaway and system-selected putaway locations. A WMS minimizes staging times by monitoring the time product sits in staging and by working to create a con-

tinuous flow of material into and out of staging. In short, a WMS monitors staging to reduce the total cumulative time products spend in staging.

5. A WMS must *have the ability to handle discrepancies*. It should be able to handle overages, underages, wrong items, and missing items. It should be able to print out a discrepancy report that notifies purchasing of the discrepancies on the inbound receipt.

Inspection and Quality Control

Many warehousing operations require an inspection process between receiving and storage. A WMS will support the inspection process as follows:

1. A WMS is able to *notify the operator of inspection requirements for incoming materials.* This notification allows for the immediate delivery of goods to inspection, or the immediate notification to an inspector to come to the receiving area.

2. A WMS can *provide inspection confirmation and release.* Product can be stored in the warehouse, and the storage location can be quarantined from picking. Upon completion of the inspection process, the storage location can be released, and the material is now available for picking. A WMS can eliminate the need for physical segregation of material.

Storage Functionality

The functional needs with respect to product storage include:

1. The need to have *positive identification and tracking of loads* that have completed receipt and are ready for putaway. This tracking includes the need to identify whether a pallet is available for use or not.

2. The need to have *automatic selection of storage locations* for pallet loads, based on parameters designed to maximize space utilization and picking efficiency and minimize putaway labor. This storage location selection process should attempt to utilize an ABC storage philosophy, rewarehouse product where possible, and ensure lot integrity.

3. The need for a *stock location system that tracks the identity and quantity of each SKU by unique storage location.* This feature is necessary to ensure product traceability to the customer.

4. The ability to *cycle count inventory by storage location,* as opposed to doing a total on-hand physical inventory. The warehouse must also be able to correct discrepancies as they occur. A WMS, through directed picking and putaway, inherently uses cycle-counting techniques.

5. The *real-time update of inventory, lot, and stock location records,* to provide timely information upon which subsequent putaway, picking, and manufacturing decisions can be made. The more real-time the update, the greater the reduction in the information lead time.

The primary deficiency in many warehousing operations today is the absence of a formal stock location system. Knowing not only *what/how much* is in the warehouse, but also *where* it is, is fundamental to the success of the operation. Many of the problems we encounter in a warehouse revolve around the lack of an effective stock location system. With such a system, loads can be stored randomly, subject to practical parameters, in any available empty location. The result is a significant increase in storage location utilization.

Knowing where product is stored will also have an inherent positive impact on product retrieval efficiency; however, it does not necessarily increase putaway efficiency. In fact, knowing where the product is *not* is often more important to putaway. By having the system automatically select the best location based on parameters such as cube size, product type, frequency of order, etc., and by having the system inform the putaway personnel of the assigned storage location, significant labor and space productivity can be gained. With the assigned location in hand, the putaway personnel will not be forced to cruise through the warehouse searching for an empty location; travel time will be reduced, particularly as the warehouse becomes fuller. Furthermore, the possibility of mismatching loads to storage openings will be minimized, and overall cubic space utilization will increase. Finally, the opportunity to combine partial pallets into larger locations will increase. This rewarehousing will also help to improve overall space utilization.

The absence of a stock location system typically requires that the warehouse inventory accuracy be confirmed by counting the entire on-hand inventory for an SKU. The first challenge is finding all of it. The second challenge is completing the count in a timely manner, such that order processing is not hindered and reconciliation of transactions completed during the count is not overly burdensome. A warehouse system provides the potential to cycle count by location. Record accuracy can be verified by location; there is no need to restrict transaction activity, or reconcile transactions and total on-hand balances. The result is a drastic decrease in the time and labor required to maintain inventory records and a dramatic increase in inventory accuracy.

A stock location system is essential. The directed putaway capabilities will result in significant labor and space savings.

Picking Functionality

The typical picking functional needs of a warehouse include:

1. The ability to *optimize picking paths, preroute and prepost customer orders in storage location sequence,* in order to minimize picker travel distance.
2. The need to select *specific storage locations for picking based on parameters such as lot number, stock rotation, primary pick location, and order quantity versus location quantity.* The system must also be flexible, to allow for variations in FIFO requirements and location selection.
3. The WMS must have *the ability to manage inventory at the warehouse level.* The WMS must record inventory on hand, inventory allocated, inventory quarantined, expected receipts, and inventory picked and/or shipped.
4. The need to *perform case picking and less than full case picking.*

As stated above, the stock location system provides the foundation for efficient order picking. The picking functionality provided by a WMS is designed to exploit the existence of the stock location system to further maximize picking efficiency. The functional abilities of a management system are designed to minimize picker travel time between picks and to maximize actual time spent picking. Zone picking allows pickers to specialize in certain types of storage or handling equipment, product types, or picking units (full pallet versus full case versus broken case). Location selection parameters are important, to avoid product obsolescence and to minimize the number of locations accessed to pick an order. Prerouting items on a pick list eliminates backtracking, particularly for pick lists with many line items. Batching, particularly for full case and broken case picking in a primary or forward pick area, allows separate orders to be combined for picking to maximize pick time by minimizing travel between pick locations.

Shipping Functionality

The shipping functions are designed to maximize control of orders moving through packing, checking, and loading. Additionally, packing list and bill of lading generation, and customer order file updating, are designed to minimize manual clerical tasks and thereby reduce labor and improve accuracy. The shipping functional needs of a warehouse typically include:

1. Routing of picked goods to specific staging lanes for order control. The WMS will match an order to a staging lane to ensure accurate setdown of the order in staging. This management of the staging area reduces the amount of time a product will sit in staging. This management also reduces the amount of staging that is required to effectively manage the shipping operation.

2. Automatic bill of lading generation upon the completed pick of the order. This ensures that the bill of lading is an accurate reflection of the goods that are being shipped.

3. Automatic updating of open customer order files throughout the day. Customers can inquire about the status of their order. Management can review the number of orders that are pending. The WMS can also provide immediate ship confirmation to the order entry system. This immediate confirmation can reduce the lead time required to invoice the customer.

4. Providing of weight and cube calculations for outbound shipments. These calculations can help in planning the day's picking activities and sequences. A WMS can also provide carrier scheduling, and detail any special packing or palletizing requirement.

Cycle Counting

Two types of cycle-counting scenarios exist. The first is the issuance of a cycle count in the event of anomalous detection during putaway or picking. The second is routine cycle counting by product, zone, or location, according to the schedule established by the warehouse or the financial department.

The first scenario occurs when an operator goes to a putaway location and that location is either full for a putaway, has the wrong product for a pick, has the wrong quantity for a pick, or is empty for a pick. In all four circumstances, the operator must perform a cycle count. The system will ask the operator to verify what is in that location and then update the inventory records. At the end of the day the warehouse manager can print a report that shows all the inventory discrepancies reported that day.

The second-cycle counting scenario exists when an operator is asked to perform a cycle-counting operation as part of his regular daily routine. This employee would perform a minimum number of cycle counts per day, as determined by the warehouse and its auditors.

In both cycle-counting scenarios, the WMS should have the ability to determine how many times an item should be counted per year. The number of times an item should be counted will be based on the popularity of that item. Most WMSs not only determine but also change the number of times an item is to be counted per year based on its item popularity.

Inventory Adjustments

The WMS must accommodate authorized adjustments to inventory. Authorized adjustments include customer returns, cycle-counting adjustments, etc. The WMS must be able to receive these items into inventory. A screen is sometimes provided to adjust the inventory by part number and reason for adjustment.

Inventory Rewarehousing and Stock Rotation

The WMS must be able to perform stock consolidation and stock rotation tasks by shade code. It will be necessary to consolidate like SKUs so as to maximize storage utilization in the warehouse. The WMS must also identify the need to replenish and stock the oldest stock in the closest pick locations to shipping for each item.

Performance Reporting

Performance reporting is perhaps the single biggest benefit a WMS can provide to a warehouse manager. Because the WMS creates an audit trail for all warehouse activities, the warehouse manager is able to develop warehouse reports that help manage the operations. The following is a brief list of typical performance reports. These reports are in addition to the numerous reports that can be created by querying the audit trail that is recorded by the WMS.

1. Customer service reports can be generated that highlight the number of orders filled, shipping errors, customer tendencies, etc.

2. Inventory accuracy reports can be printed that document not only the dollar accuracy of the inventory, but also the count accuracy. The count is the truest reflection of how well a warehouse is managing its inventory.

3. Order accuracy reports can be generated that highlight the percent of correct orders shipped.

4. Space utilization reports can be printed that document the free space in the warehouse and the percent full for each storage location. Space utilization reports can be used to signal trends in storage.

5. Labor productivity reports document the activity or performance levels for individual employees and for the warehouse staff as a whole. These reports can be activity- and performance-based.

6. Item activity reports can be provided. These will show each item's movement and usage histories. These histories can then be used to identify the causes of damage; loss; and shipping, receiving, and storage errors.

All of the above needs are value-adding functions, and would be consistent with the objectives of the physical operations of most warehouses. The above functionalities serve to highlight the true reason for installing a WMS: to control your operations.

Material Handling Interfaces

In addition to directing warehouse personnel to perform specific tasks in the warehouse, a WMS can also control and/or interface with various types of material handling and storage systems. These types of equipment include horizontal carousels, automated storage-and-retrieval systems (AS/RS), automated guided vehicle systems, and conveyor systems. WMSs can also interface with manifesting systems, postage metering systems, in-line scales, and freight rating systems.

System Justifications

An intelligent warehouse integrates computer systems, material handling equipment, storage equipment, and people into a single cohesive working unit. The quality of information is vastly improved. The improvement in information quality, in turn, results in a reduction of errors. The improvement of information quality also results in the minimization of unproductive labor hours. Minimizing errors and improving labor productivity results in better customer service. Better customer service results in higher sales. Higher sales promote growth.

After quality information has been attained, a reduction in the information lead times then occurs. A reduction in the information lead time provides a faster customer response. A faster customer response further perpetuates customer satisfaction and growth. Once errors have been eliminated and information lead times minimized, customer satisfaction is guaranteed. The warehouse has accomplished its customer goal, having become a truly efficient unit that maximizes customer satisfaction. The final step then, is to use this information to optimize the use of space, equipment, and labor. Figure 27-3 is an illustration of the benefits of an intelligent WMS system.

The first characteristic of an intelligent system is zero information errors. Two types of errors exist, errors that affect customer service and errors that affect warehouse operations. Errors that affect customers must be eliminated.

It is a well-known fact that poor information will result in inaccurate inventory. What is not always understood is the far-reaching effect inaccurate inventory can have on one's operations. The costs of inaccurate inventories include:

1. Lost sales

2. Backorders

3. Excessive inventory

4. Excessive safety stock

5. Missed schedules

6. Low labor productivity

7. Excessive expediting

8. Excessive freight costs

9. High obsolescence

One-hundred-percent-accurate inventory records will have a dramatic impact not just on warehousing operations but also on the total business.

The first method by which an intelligent warehouse achieves zero errors is through 100 percent information verification. A warehouse receives, stores, picks, and ships goods. When a product is initially received, it is verified, bar-coded, and entered into the management system. All future movements are tracked against that bar code. The product has now been uniquely identified. A significant chance for tracking errors has been eliminated.

The second method by which an intelligent warehouse achieves zero customer service errors is through system-directed operations. Every receiving, putaway, picking, and shipping operation is system-directed. Product will move only if it is system-directed, and the operator can complete the move and go on to the next operation only if the previous operation has been verified as correct. Operator errors associated with misplaced inventory and operator carelessness are eliminated.

The third method by which an intelligent warehouse achieves zero customer service errors is through continuous cycle counting. Since every operation in an intelligent warehouse is system-directed, the system knows every location's status. When the system directs a pallet to a location and that location is not empty, then the system will call for a rectifying of that location's inventory. Inventory errors will be

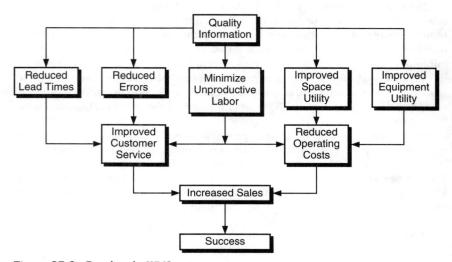

Figure 27-3. Benefits of a WMS system.

caught at the first opportunity. As a result, backorders due to inventory discrepancies will be virtually eliminated, as will the need to perform costly annual physical inventories.

In fact, all of the problems associated with inaccurate inventory will be minimized through zero information errors. These savings are in addition to savings found in other areas, including reductions in manufacturing overruns and reductions in manufacturing disruption costs due to material unavailability. Accurate information will have a significant impact on all aspects of your operations.

Zero Information Lead Times

Total information verification results in quality information. Once quality information has been attained, the information lead time must decrease. Eventually, the information lead time will approach zero. When this occurs, then the intelligent warehouse information side of the equation is complete.

There are two types of information lead time: customer-oriented, and warehouse-oriented. Customer-oriented lead times relate to the time it takes to transfer customer order information to and from the warehouse. Customer-oriented information going to the warehouse generally means information that is entered either manually or through electronic data interchange (EDI) into the corporate data-entry system. This information is then transferred by paper or electronically to the warehouse. To achieve zero customer-oriented information lead times, the information must be electronically transferred as it is received into the corporate system.

Customer-oriented information flowing from the warehouse means shipping information that is transmitted by paper or electronically to the customer. Bills of lading and packing lists are not preprinted. They are printed as the order is completed, to represent an accurate count of the material shipped. This information is then transferred electronically to the customer so that the customer can plan for an anticipated receipt.

The second type of information is warehouse operations related. This is data that is used to guide the intelligent system. This information is transaction-based and provides feedback as to what was picked or put away. By recording the transaction, and by interfacing with the customer-oriented information, a variety of calculations can be performed. Examples include: truck loading plans, freight rating, personnel requirements, and other prioritization, among others. The warehouse information lead time must be zero if these tasks are to be optimized.

At this point, the quality of information is high. The lead time of information is low. Customer service has improved. The next step is to improve operations.

Improving Warehouse Operations

The first step to take to improve warehouse operations is to increase labor productivity. The increase in computer processing speeds will allow for the development of algorithms that will maximize labor productivity by allowing more decisions to be evaluated prior to the assignment of the next work task. It has already been determined that system-directed operations are required to reduce errors. Directed operations also improve labor productivity. Operators no longer have to think about the next operation, for the system does the thinking. The more pending tasks the system can draw upon to make a decision, the more optimal the decision. Intelligent warehouse management systems will use labor task interleaving techniques to maximize labor productivity.

There are five factors that must be considered to optimize labor: operator location, equipment availability, task prioritization, queue times, and task criticality. An intelligent warehouse must address and optimize these factors. The method by which an intelligent warehouse optimizes labor is through labor task interleaving. Labor task interleaving is the ability to optimize labor and equipment assignments based on queued labor tasks. Interleaving refers to the fact that the system must have the ability to select the next labor task from a queue of all pending activities, not just from one module or labor subgroup. Interleaving expands the pool of tasks available to an operator, and thus minimizes travel distance. Minimizing travel distances results in a direct labor productivity increase. Several other capabilities of the intelligent warehouse system must exist if the system is to task-interleave. The system must time-stamp and manage task times in the queue, contain a travel-path methodology, and operate in a real-time manner. If these and the above requirements are met, then task interleaving is possible. Without interleaving, labor optimization is marginal.

The net result of a WMS is an increase in driver productivity, due to:

1. A reduction in driver time, owing to a decrease in driver time spent searching for a product

2. Optimizing the travel distances and paths

3. A reduction in rewarehousing

4. Wasted driver time, owing to lack of an ABC storage philosophy

These labor savings are in addition to reductions in data entry labor that occur because of a reduction in key entry labor and a reduction in data entry errors.

An added benefit of improved labor utilization is an increase in equipment utilizations. Improvements in equipment utilizations can result in a reduction in future capital equipment expenditures and in reduced future maintenance costs.

The fourth characteristic of an intelligent warehouse management system is improved space utilization. Because inventory is more accurate, more locations are available for putaway and storage. Improved inventory accuracy and system-directed operations allow for higher storage densities. The traditional problem of worker productivity suffering as storage utilization increases is diminished. The hunting and searching aspects of picking and putaway are eliminated.

In addition to improving space utilization, dock staging requirements are reduced. Product does not have to sit as long in staging. As soon as a pallet has been bar-coded and verified, it is available for putaway. This faster turnover results in smaller staging requirements.

Intelligent systems also use crossdocking techniques to reduce handling and storage requirements. Crossdocked material is received, staged, and shipped without ever being placed in storage. Because product is not actually put away, storage requirements are reduced. Only an intelligent system that has visibility to anticipate receipts, customer orders, and material movements can maximize crossdocking opportunities.

Finally, an intelligent warehouse reduces storage and handling requirements through rewarehousing. When the overall storage utilization falls below an acceptable level due to honeycombing, the system will implement a rewarehousing program. Partial locations are combined, and deep-lane storage materials are rewarehoused to their proper lane depths. Honeycombing is minimized. As a result, space utilization is improved.

The final justification for a WMS is improved management control. With increased management visibility to data and the operations, management can more efficiently run the operations. This improved efficiency will directly impact the bottom line.

Implementing an Intelligent Warehouse Management System

The first step to take toward implementation is to document your needs. This documentation includes operational procedures, transaction levels, and space, equipment, and labor requirements. Documenting your needs will require a complete understanding of the methods by which the warehouse operates. The needs document should attempt not only to define the present but also to strive to optimize operations regardless of existing constraints. You must not let your paradigms restrict the potential of your operations. Just because you've done it the same way forever, or just because that's how everyone else in the business operates, does not mean that you cannot change the rules. Your defining of your needs must reflect thinking that is unconstrained. If you cannot perform this type of thinking, then you should consider engaging an independent consultant to help you define your opportunities.

The second step is to translate your needs into a functional bid specification. A functional bid specification document clearly defines your needs in a format that will allow vendors to quote on your system. The specification must be concise, yet not restrictive.

The functional bid specification will prove to be the project crossroads. A poorly written specification results in ambiguity, and sometimes in disaster. Two completely different interpretations can be drawn from a single illustration. These problems can be avoided by clearly understanding and documenting your needs before making any formal commitment.

The third step is to select a vendor. If you've understood the characteristics of intelligent management systems, if you've documented your needs and written a concise functional bid specification, then this part is easy. The vendor understands your expectations, and hopefully will help make your systems a reality.

Common Pitfalls

In the 1990s, software will play a major role in our warehouse operations. Most equipment that we purchase will require some type of computer interfacing. These requirements will tax your skills. You will be asked to provide input to the system requirements. You will have to help implement the system. You will have to live with the system. Poor and hastily made decisions will have a dramatic impact on your operation. There are dozens of documented success stories. Success stories that tell how warehouse computerization works. Success stories that don't tell of the struggles involved to become a successful case study. Case studies certainly don't prepare the warehouse manger for the challenges that lie ahead—challenges that are made much more difficult when one encounters an unexpected pitfall. What we would like to share with you, then, are some of the pitfalls associated with warehouse software implementation from a warehouse manager's perspective.

Misunderstanding the Benefits of a Warehouse Management System

A warehouse management system is not an inventory locator system. A locator system locates, tracks, and manages inventory. A warehouse management system manages the warehouse operations. It is an integrated package whose components consist of RF communications devices, dedicated localized computer hardware, automatic identification equipment, and the necessary applications software. It works to minimize the costs associated with space, equipment, and labor, and, performing in real-time, it directs and manages labor, maximizes equipment utilization, and tracks and controls inventory.

Quite often an inventory locator system is confused with a warehouse management system. The significant difference between the two is that the locator system does not manage the labor. While it is true that a locator system can minimize pick-path requirements, the locator system cannot optimize all labor by directing puts, picks, and other tasks in the warehouse. Over 50 percent of a lift truck operator's time can be spent deadheading in the warehouse. A warehouse management system can help to capture some of this time by combining put tasks with pick tasks in a real-time environment. A simple locator system cannot.

Failure to Identify Your Needs

If you fail to document your needs, how will you know what is required of the system? If, when buying a new delivery truck for your business, you do not have a budget in mind and have not done some preliminary investigative work, how will you buy that truck? You will probably buy that truck on impulse, and not based on value or need. The truck salesman has determined your need. This, unfortunately, is how many of us buy warehouse management systems.

Many companies will begin to contact warehouse management system vendors before they understand their needs. This approach causes problems for both the buyer and the seller. The vendor must spend considerable time helping to identify your needs, which costs it time and money. If the vendor is presented with vague or poorly defined specifications, it is going to have to develop a quotation that is based on speculation. That speculative quotation is going to contain a "fudge factor" to reflect your uncertainty in your definition of the system. The vendor spends considerable time and money in putting a bid specification together, and someone has to pay for those. It benefits you to make the vendor's job easier in providing you with a quotation.

Problems also are created by selecting a single vendor to help you identify your needs. A sole-source approach to selecting a warehouse management system will result in a needs-requirements document that fits the parameters of that vendor's particular solution, a solution that may not be the best or most cost-effective for you. The vendor's solution is the best that fits within the vendor's parameters, not necessarily your parameters. You must determine your needs. If you are not comfortable determining your needs, then you should hire an unbiased party who can help you to do so. Don't limit your options or fail to solve your problems by shortcutting the needs-definition development.

Function versus Design

The desire to develop a design bid specification as opposed to a functional bid specification can be disastrous. Who is the expert in the functions of your operation? You are. Who is the expert in the design of the warehouse management system software? The vendor is. Why should you tell the vendor how to design software? Why should the vendor tell you how your operations should function? Tell the vendor what your functional requirements are. The vendor's experience and software package will determine how to meet your functionality. If the vendor is given some latitude, the amount of customization that will be required will be minimized. By minimizing customization, the software development costs will be kept down. This in turn may result in savings for you, the buyer, which in turn may result in a better system for you, the end user.

The second problem with a design bid specification is that the burden is now placed on the buyer to specify how the needs are to be met. You have told the vendor what you want and how you want the vendor to get it done. The vendor will then provide you with a system that meets these requirements. But will this system optimize your solutions? Probably not. Will a functional bid specification that allows the vendor some degree of design latitude provide you with a system that performs your required functions? If you have selected the correct vendor, the answer is yes. But remember who the expert in which field is.

Forgetting Who's the Boss

Understanding the role of the warehouse and the Information System (IS) department is the first key to a successful implementation. The IS department supports the value-adding functions of warehousing and manufacturing. Every product has three values: a function value, a time value, and a place value. Manufacturing adds the value of function by producing a product that satisfies the customer's needs. Warehousing provides a time and place value by getting the product to the correct location at the correct time. The IS department provides information that supports the operations that provide the value. You can run a warehouse or a manufacturing facility without an IS department and still have a product and provide a value. You can run the IS department, but without a warehouse or manufacturing operation there is no product and no product value.

The product is what makes a company profitable. We must not lose sight of this fact. Information is something that is not to be guarded by the few, but shared by the many, and this information is intended to support, not isolate, the groups who would most benefit from this information. Don't be forced to proceed along a path that you may later regret. If someone tries to convince you to use a system that doesn't meet your needs, don't do it. Remember, you have to live with the system.

Unrealistic Scheduling

Ambitious scheduling of a project may look good on paper, but it can become a painful reminder when that schedule is not met. Expectations, operational decisions, and future sales strategies all hinge on your anticipated completion date. It is important that you not mislead the people involved with these decisions and strategies. An ambitious schedule can affect many more people than just those working in the warehouse.

It is equally dangerous, however, for a schedule to have a distant, safe, and unrealistic completion date. If the project is a 9-month project, *state* that the project is a 9-month project. A 6-month project may disrupt operations when the goal is not met, but a 15-month projection may doom the project to failure before it ever gets approved. Don't be pressured one way or the other into making an unrealistic estimate of the projected cycle time.

Customizing the Common

"Gee, wouldn't it be great if the warehouse management system could schedule important shipments according to the safety record of the carrier?" Wow, that *would* be great, but would it be cost-effective? It's great to have your head in the clouds when you document the needs of your warehouse management system, but only if your feet stay on the ground as you determine the functionality of the system. The desire to use a customized software package can be ruinous. If it is possible to alter the functionality of your system to solve your problem through a proven solution, then an attempt should be made to have the functionality addressed by the proven solution. Don't micromanage or pie-in-the-sky the solution. Once a customized package has begun to fall apart, it is very time-consuming to reverse the process. The software is unique, the problem is unique, and the solution to the problem becomes unique.

Testing

"When we get near the completion of the project we will determine the testing schedule." If finger-pointing is a favorite activity of yours, then this is the approach you should take. On the other hand if you like a no-surprise ending to the project, then agree to the acceptance-testing parameters at the beginning of the project. Software is an inexact science. More likely than not there will be bugs or quirks in the software that will have to be debugged. Don't come down to the end of the project and leave your testing criteria a topic of discussion. Tie the final payments to the testing plan. This will ensure that the vendor is 95 percent complete, and will not walk away from the job until it is complete. The testing criteria are your last measure of protection. Don't be foolish and squander this safeguard.

Selling

Warehouse managers don't like to think of themselves as salespeople. But the fact is, if you want the system, you must sell the system. There will be resistance to your ideas. Other people will think that they know what is best for you. Make sure that what they *think* is best for you *is* best for you. By defining your needs, you are in a strong position to sell your needs. By putting yourself in a strong position to sell your needs, you increase your chances of getting the system that you truly require. Don't let bits and bytes bog you down. To paraphrase real estate agents, the most important thing about a warehouse management system is function, function, function. To sell your functions, you must first know your needs.

System Design Inflexibility

"The software has to be purchased from the 123EZ Software Company and the software must operate on an ACME computer platform." Many people probably will find humor, or perhaps anguish, in that statement. The solutions have been dictated before the needs have been defined. One of the single biggest challenges the warehouse must overcome in designing a warehouse management system is the force-feeding of a hardware platform and software system into the warehouse by the IS department. You, as a warehouse manager, must first determine your needs before you can find a solution to meet these needs. If two plus two is four, and two times two is four, does that mean that three times three equals six? Of course not. Each solution to each application must be determined. In identifying the needs, it is true that some solutions may be similar, but in most cases our problems will be like the addition and multiplication tables. All needs will have to be identified and understood before a hardware platform and software system can be defined.

A Final Thought

The future of warehousing is bright. Intelligent warehouse management systems will revolutionize operations. The warehouse will become a customer-driven operation with virtually instantaneous access to information. Don't stand on the sidelines while others prosper.

28

Supply Chain Management

James D. Hall
Principal, A. T. Kearney, Inc.

Supply chain management is an approach to controlling the physical flow of products from source to point of use by aligning the capabilities of suppliers, manufacturers, channel partners, and customers. Supply chain management is also a tool to achieve sustainable competitive advantage. It supports both differentiation-based and cost-based strategies. The supply chain management approach contributes to world-class performance by progressing beyond functional excellence and cross-functional integration. It focuses on the practices used by the different businesses that together produce the product and service the customer. It integrates the activities of all members of the value-added chain to produce higher levels of performance than can be achieved individually. Supply chain management practices create supply chain integration that yields superior business performance.

Supply chain integration utilizes a variety of business practices such as Just-In-Time Manufacturing, Quick Response, and Continuous Replenishment. The art of supply chain management is to blend appropriate practices in a way that increases productivity and value at all stages of the chain of activities, from source to delivery. Integration of the supply chain raises customer satisfaction. Supply chain integration provides increased value to customers by coordinating activities to reduce costs for all participants and to create value by eliminating duplicate or non-value-added functions. The supply chain approach recognizes that customers evaluate suppliers on more than simply product attributes and availability. Value extends beyond price and includes total cost and service. Innovation can create new markets, quality will permit long-term presence, but differentiation from competition can be achieved only through a capability that increases value to customers and protects margins.

The progress and success of supply chain management should be measured against objectives. Supply chain integration can be evaluated against the objectives of:

- *Service.* Do customers receive what they ordered, when they want it, in the manner they desire?
- *Cost.* Is the net landed cost to the end user optimized with service and time requirements?
- *Assets.* Does inventory exist within the supply chain merely to respect the variability of consumer demand, or to create operational efficiencies?
- *Time.* Is the cycle time from source to delivery limited only by physical constraints?

Supply chain integration is practiced in a broad range of industries. While the actual techniques and practices may be tailored to specific issues and business characteristics of supplier, manufacturer, channel partner, and customer, the benefits of supply chain integration are available to all.

Supply Chain Management in Practice

In the automotive industry, manufacturers and suppliers integrate component assembly and final assembly to create just-in-time delivery of components. The final assembly plant receives only the components needed for the specific production schedule, in a manner that eliminates buffer inventories, rehandling, and extra transportation. The final assembly location transmits the detailed production schedule to suppliers only hours before assembly. The component supplier finalizes assembly according to the models to be produced, then configures the components in sequence, according to the production schedule, so that the components can be delivered directly to the point of use. The flow of product between supplier and manufacturer is integrated to eliminate costs while maintaining service to production.

Consumer goods manufacturers and retailers practice supply chain integration to better respond to consumer demand without duplicate investments in finished goods inventory. Leading companies have established programs of continuous replenishment of retailer's distribution centers to provide high store service at lower cost. Retailers provide daily sales information as well as store order and distribution center inventory levels to manufacturers, who then determine the proper replenishment quantity to achieve both high service and high inventory turns. In this example of supply chain integration, the manufacturer takes responsibility for creating the purchase order quantity. Practitioners report dramatic increases in inventory turns and significant gains in sales.

Supply chain integration practices can be tailored to unique industry situations. A leading distributor of hospital supplies offers a program to deliver hospital products directly to the nursing station, bypassing storage and handling in a hospital storeroom. Orders are issued based on nursing station use, and replenished directly from the distributor's inventory. Timeliness and accuracy are paramount, yet an entire step in the traditional flow of products is eliminated, reducing operating costs and investment.

These examples of supply chain integration, from diverse industries, illustrate the universal applicability of the supply chain management approach to the flow of product from source to delivery to the customer. A focus on the objectives of service, cost, assets, and time, when coupled with creative thinking, bring forth new approaches to traditional business practices. In the examples cited, responsibility for some processes is transferred between channel partners: automotive suppliers configure orders in sequence of production, consumer goods manufacturers determine replenishment quantities for retailer's distribution centers, and distributors of health care products maintain inventory and a distribution capability for customers. The benefits of these changes are seen not only in elimination of structural costs and improvements in productivity, but in the creation of stronger partnerships among members of the supply chain. Relationships can shift from an adversarial buyer/seller interaction, focused on price, to a relationship of mutual dependency and mutual gain. For in the end, supply chain integration seeks to create profitable growth for all members of the chain.

Supply Chain Processes

Supply chain integration links suppliers, manufacturers, channel partners, and customers through the processes used from order creation to customer delivery. Each supply chain partner should support the others to create greater productivity, value, and customer satisfaction. Processes that are well aligned will produce higher service, lower manufacturing costs, lower costs of distribution, and higher quality. The key processes within the supply chain are depicted in Fig. 28-1. Each of these processes results in a clear output, and the potential to contribute to supply chain integration.

Order creation results in the customer's decision as to the quantity, frequency and composition of an order. The opportunity to manage pricing structures and incentives creates the potential to establish those relationships by which the customer receives products in a manner that supports its business objectives, while the supplier receives orders in a manner that supports its business objectives. Some customers may wish to pick up large quantities of single items directly at the production site. Others may require smaller quantities of multiple products on a frequent basis. Some may accept long lead times, while others require next-day service. Supply chain integration through the order creation process requires deep understanding of marketing strategy, competitor's capabilities, and cost structures. Leaders in supply chain integration establish operational capabilities that allow their customers alternatives in order creation. But these capabilities are coupled with managed service, time, and cost, to permit a mutual benefit.

The order entry process enables a customer's desires to be acted upon. The opportunity to manage the method of order entry creates the potential to solidify marketing strategies, create sales opportunities, and build relationships. Supply chain integration through the order entry process requires thorough knowledge of customer requirements, customer business practices, and technology. Leaders in supply chain integration provide a variety of order entry methods so that customers can

Figure 28-1. The supply chain process.

order in the way they desire. Computer-to-computer Electronic Data Interchange (EDI) and voice response expand traditional, but often valid, approaches such as phone or mail.

Production planning establishes the location, quantity, and schedule of product generation. The opportunity to coordinate consumption and production creates the potential to minimize investments in finished goods, storage space, and handling costs. Producing closer to the point of need minimizes the risk of obsolescence or rework. For producers of fashion items, it minimizes the costs of markdowns. For producers of products with short shelf life, it contributes to higher-quality products for the consumer. Supply chain integration requires linkages with purchasing, production, and customers, to balance the multiple objectives of each in a manner that achieves overall objectives. Leaders in supply chain integration have established the shop floor procedures and the analytical, yet swift, planning tools that leverage manufacturing flexibility to achieve customer objectives while maintaining production efficiencies.

The purchasing process results in decisions on source of supply, purchase quantity, purchase frequency, and purchase order composition. Correct decisions maximize availability and minimize cost. Making the correct decision requires a detailed knowledge of production requirements and an intimate understanding of each supplier's business drivers. Supply chain integration transforms the procurement process from an adversarial relationship based primarily on price to a partnering relationship based on total cost. Leaders in supply chain integration establish customized order quantities and frequencies based on mutual understanding of the activities required to create material on the part of the supplier and the process by which the material will be used in production. Customized transportation programs between supplier and manufacturer are often developed to manage total cost and create mutual efficiencies.

The production process generates product. Supply chain integration is strengthened by a production process that exhibits flexibility and responsiveness. The benefits of coordination between customer and manufacturer are lost if the production process cannot routinely respond with quality products.

The inventory management process establishes the available product to respond to customer demands. A business strategy of make-to-stock or make-to-order creates different issues, but the objective remains the same. The opportunity to establish single-inventory investments between supplier and manufacturer or manufacturer and customer establishes a potential benefit in capital reduction through integrating this process. An objective of maintaining inventory only to respect the variability of consumer demand, or to create an operational efficiency in production or procurement that reduces net landed cost, establishes a stretch goal. Leaders in supply chain integration routinely share demand and inventory information among partners. Transfers of responsibility for inventory to the manufacturer, with clear performance objectives established, permit each party to benefit and to share a commitment to partnership for performance.

Inventory deployment determines the location of product awaiting orders. Decisions on inventory deployment strongly influence the customer service parameters of order cycle time and order completeness. Inventory deployment presents the opportunity to create competitive advantage through responsiveness and service quality. An investment in inventory by a manufacturer may be leveraged into a value-added offering that replaces the customer's investment. Leaders in supply chain integration are deploying inventory to not only meet cycle time and availability objectives, but to enable multiple parties in the supply chain to leverage one investment.

Order fulfillment results in the configuration of products that conform to the customer's desires. The opportunity to customize an order provides the potential to create additional value by avoiding duplicate efforts and rehandling. Supply chain integration through order fulfillment requires detailed understanding of customer requirements, flexibility in order selection, and efficient processes that permit mutual benefit. Leading companies establish the capabilities to respond to a broad range of order configuration requests and the flexibility to use any method routinely. In advanced examples, the manufacturer's or distributor's order fulfillment process negates the need for one on the part of the customer, providing product ready for use at the point of use.

The delivery process produces the cycle time, delivery precision, and arrival quality of the customer's order. The opportunity to manage shipments and carriers provides the additional opportunity to minimize cycle inventory, reduce buffer inventories, and create cost efficiencies. Supply chain integration through the delivery process requires careful monitoring of transportation economics, a commitment to long-term business relationships, and a willingness to act in partnership with others. Leaders in supply chain integration employ near-exclusive relations with carriers, who in turn invest in the equipment, technology, and management knowledge that will better support both the manufacturer and its customer.

These supply chain processes are applicable to a broad range of businesses. By focusing on the process outputs, progressive organizations can develop new business practices that achieve improved results. Without a results-oriented process approach, attempts at true breakthroughs among supply chain partners may not be achieved. Attention may focus on functional performance and tradeoffs among functions, and channel partners may not be achieved. Supply chain integration must therefore be judged against performance rather than by technique. Does the end customer receive what it ordered, when it wants it, in the manner it desires? Is the net landed cost to the end user optimized with service and time requirements? Does inventory exist within the supply chain only to respect the variability of consumer demand or to create operational efficiencies? Is the cycle time from source to delivery limited only by physical constraints?

Integrating the Supply Chain

Initiating supply chain management requires top management involvement. Supply chain integration may produce fundamental changes in the relationship among channel partners. Such change must have the full support and commitment of senior executives. In addition, the supply chain management approach will call for a cultural change within an organization. Remaining barriers between functions must be eliminated. Integration with suppliers or customers requires a new mindset, which must be supported by the appropriate organization, incentives, and performance measures. Once the commitment to supply chain integration has been achieved, specific actions to identify supply chain management opportunities can be initiated.

Identifying opportunities for supply chain integration requires a deep knowledge of customer satisfaction objectives, documentation of the existing supply chain economics, and understanding of practices used in other businesses and industries. From these, thoughtful analysis will reveal gaps in practices or gaps in execution that can lead to a prioritized action plan. This approach is shown in Fig. 28-2.

Establishing customer satisfaction objectives requires quantitative analysis of customer requirements and an analysis of the customer's business issues. Customer requirements for many criteria such as order cycle time, delivery precision, item availability, and order fill rate can be established by a variety of survey approaches and methodologies. Understanding the customer's true business issues, however, is usually more challenging, but yields higher potential-to-surface opportunities to integrate along the supply chain. It is important in this analysis to understand business strategies, sources of differentiation, service strategies, infrastructure, and organizational structure. Knowledge gained in this research has the potential to reveal opportunities for mutual benefit through supply chain integration.

Understanding current business practices requires an ability to explain not only how key business processes work but what drives the process. Utilizing a framework

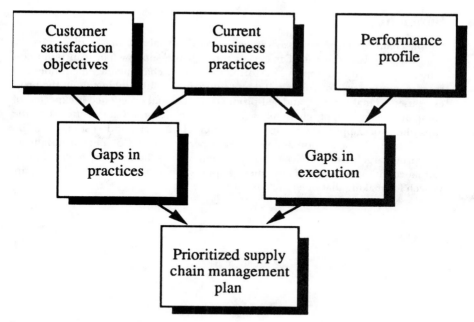

Figure 28-2. Integrating the supply chain.

based on business processes assists in moving toward supply chain integration, since processes produce results. This provides a means for a range of functional managers and supply chain members to describe their impact and contribution to a business result. Close attention must be paid to identifying the rules, beliefs, values, and principles that are incorporated within a business process. Once key business processes are understood, it is then possible to benchmark these processes against other companies in a variety of industries to best understand how the processes are being addressed. Completion of these steps ensures analysis of supply chain integration and contains an understanding of existing business practices and alternative approaches used by others.

The performance profile quantifies performance along the entire supply chain: supplier, manufacturer, channel partner, and customer. The dimensions of time, cost, and investment should be applied to understand the service, quality, and financial performance that results along the supply chain. With this knowledge, opportunities will surface and leverage points may be identified. Leverage points represent the places along the supply chain where large improvements are possible with a relatively small investment.

From these three building blocks an objective assessment of gaps in practices and gaps in execution must be made. Potential improvement opportunities may be revealed, and sufficient knowledge will exist to suggest how such opportunities could improve customer satisfaction and business performance. These can then be synthesized and prioritized, so that efforts initiated for supply chain integration yield substantial benefits.

Summary

Supply chain management assists in achieving financial and marketplace success. The integrated movement of materials through the supply chain can build customer satisfaction and improve performance. Supply chain management does not require massive scale or volume. It does require insightful thinking about the processes used to make, move, and sell products. Functional excellence is expected of companies today. Supply chain management moves beyond that to better align the capabilities of suppliers, manufacturers, channel partners, and customers, to increase customer satisfaction and yield better performance. Competitive advantage will spring largely from service-focused commitments—the result of intelligent performance with suppliers and customers. Supply chain management provides an approach for making that objective a reality.

29

Third Party Logistics

Russell A. Gilmore, III
President, The Focus Group, Inc.

In the 1980s, third party logistics was attracting more attention in the U.K. than in the United States. The use of third party warehousing was widespread, and the development of logistics partnerships had long been used to gain competitive advantage.

In the U.S., upper management typically thought of logistics as a support activity buried in a purchasing or marketing budget, and it seldom received top management attention. During that decade, however, companies were making major breakthroughs in providing excellence in customer service and developing true quality systems to enhance product value and eliminate waste. Just-in-time (JIT) and direct store delivery (DSD) programs were gaining interest, even though in their infancy these programs may not have done much more than rearrange inventory in the integrated logistics channel.

These same companies began to examine the validity of placing confidence in the idea that the corporation can perform all steps, from sourcing raw materials to delivering finished goods to the final customer, with equal skill and cost effectiveness. During the late 1980s a movement began to "reinvent" the corporation, allowing it to concentrate upon its core competency and perform internally what it does best, while looking to third parties to support other activities.

Simultaneously, the information technology revolution was well under way. The cost per transaction for computer technology was falling rapidly, and software was being developed to accurately separate the cost of logistics from other processes, to efficiently support logistics activities, and to manage the flow of goods in the logistics channel. The strong emphasis on replacing inventory with information opened opportunities for third party logistics providers to add value at an affordable cost to companies seeking to improve their competitiveness.

The purpose of this chapter is to help the reader develop an understanding of third party logistics, evaluate its effectiveness to the firm, and develop criteria for selecting a third party partner.

Understanding the New Third Party Environment

In the last decade, interest from suppliers of segments of logistics operations has expanded to provide additional logistics offerings. During the last three years, however, the number of full-service logistics providers has increased dramatically. A number of factors have contributed to this increase. Consider some answers to the following two questions:

1. What catalysts have smoothed the way for third party logistics evaluations?
   - Increased awareness of the importance of logistics to top management
   - Return to core competency—manufacturing companies are learning how *not* to make things
   - Current trend to outsource activities that divert corporate capital
   - Emphasis upon decreasing human resource levels
2. What advantages do these third party providers bring?[1]
   - Provide operational flexibilities with flexible resources to meet changing needs without obsolescence.
   - Improve balance sheet economics by eliminating capital investments in warehouses, material handling equipment, and private fleets.
   - Enhance human resources by gaining expertise in systems, logistics, and marketing, without the investment necessary to keep talent on staff.
   - Develop strategy. Outsourcing logistics forces decision making and tends to break up internal communications log jams. For a successful outsourcing experience, a company must define its expectations and requirements before entering into the third party relationship.
   - Be the catalyst for change. Through other cross-industry experiences, third parties can benchmark and maximize the third party logistics experience. Looking out of the industry for benchmarking information brings a completely different focus to the benchmarking results to be achieved, and in many cases can cause logistics performance to exceed expectations.

As the field of logistics is constantly being expanded to involve additional business processes, so is the list of services offered by third party logistics suppliers. Figure 29-1 illustrates the many different services that can be outsourced. For years, third party involvement in logistics was limited to freight payment programs of certain warehousing or transportation activities. Now the list has grown in breadth to include activities that were formerly never considered for outsourcing.

The number of companies that supply third party logistics service has expanded significantly. Major players who entered the industry early through involvement in components of integrated logistics include motor carriers, air freight forwarders, rail carriers, and national warehousing chains. Now some of these providers are major players in the industry, having grown through acquisition of many smaller

What can you outsource?

Here's a compilation of services available from numerous third parties. Consider this a starting point for exploration. Evaluate your needs, then talk with service providers about how those needs can best be met.

1. *Capital Asset Management*
- Eliminate capital investments.
- Flexible resources
- Level business cycle peaks and valleys.

2. *Marketing*
- Target or test markets.
- Penetrate markets—domestic or global.
- Serve fringe areas.
- Zoned vending
- Multiple customer service strategies

3. *Sourcing*
- Vendor scheduling
- Single-source varied services
- Manage total supply pipeline.

4. *Packaging/Labeling*
- Differentiate packaging for domestic or international markets.
- Repackaging
- Overwrapping
- Value packing
- Shrink wrapping
- Labeling
- Price stickering
- Couponing for specific regions or markets
- Build display pallet packs.
- Point-of-sale displays

5. *Transportation*
- Manage time-sensitive performance and expedited transportation.
- Guaranteed delivery dates
- Sequencing
- Route and load planning
- Blocking and bracing
- Real-time information management
- Tracking & tracing
- Freight consolidation

- Pool business of small companies to increase leverage.

6. *Distribution*
- On-site warehouse managing
- Manage inventory systems, yours or theirs.
- Manage fulfillment programs.
- Serial and date control (Categorize kill date or manage recall capability using EDI.)
- Scheduling and replenishment
- Crossdocking
- Assembly
- Subassembly
- Pick and pack lines
- Bar coding
- Inspection/testing
- Order entry—accept orders from customers and process via EDI.

7. *Installation, setup, and training*
- Inside deliveries
- Videotaped training sessions
- Ship and assemble for home delivery, even after hours.

8. *Reverse distribution*
- Repairs
- Disassembly and scrapping of product
- Returned goods management

9. *Global/import/export*
- Create seamless global operation, offer import/export support, process paperwork.
- Customs clearance
- Nonresident importer services
- Foreign trade zone assistance

10. *Personnel*
- Screen employees—yours or theirs.
- Contract labor.
- Manage productivity.

Figure 29-1. Services offered by third party logistics suppliers. (*From* Transportation and Distribution, *July 1992. Used by courtesy of the Focus Group, Inc., Dayton, OH.*)

players. Additionally, foreign investment provided resources for even further consolidation of large integrated logistics service providers. Furthermore, companies that have traditionally provided one segment of integrated logistics, for example long-distance LTL transportation, have made major investments in facilities, human resources, and systems in order to be considered a single-source provider.

Some of these providers have even pushed the definition of integrated logistics to the extreme by offering total package services through partnerships in dedicated alliances with other professionals who are experts in some part of the logistics process. This enables a well-financed major player to offer seamless logistics services without making significant financial commitment but at the same time truly offering services provided by experts.

In logistics discussions, considerable debate has arisen over the benefits or detriments of using third parties to perform logistics services.[2] Those advocating the use of third party services contend that their use enables companies to concentrate on their core business while allowing others to manage the logistics business. Others warn that use of third party partners leads to a loss of control, less direct contact with customers, and substantial costs related to terminating internal operations.

To bring the present perspective to the use of third party logistics in industry during 1992, *Fortune* magazine surveyed the chief logistics executive of each of the 500 largest manufacturers in the U.S. Twenty-six percent of those surveyed submitted a response, and 37 percent of those who responded indicated that their companies used third party logistics services. Nine out of ten executives who responded reported that when all factors were taken into account, their company's use of third party logistics has been a positive development for their corporation.[3] Table 29-1 illustrates which logistics services are most frequently used.

The results of the survey indicated that a substantial segment of the largest U.S. manufacturing companies use third party logistics as an acceptable way of doing business. Corporate interest in the process appears to be increasing as a method of improving productivity, enhancing customer service, and reducing overall logistics costs. Few logistics providers offer, and can substantiate through experience, a full range of logistics services; however, there are many providers who can adequately provide the multiple services shown in Fig. 29-1. Judging from the positive feedback *Fortune* received from the respondents, there appears to be a growing market for

Table 29-1. Logistics Services Most Frequently Used

Logistics process	Percent of respondents using third party logistics company for that service
Warehouse management	45
Shipment consolidation	45
Logistics information systems	32
Fleet management	28
Order fulfillment	26
Carrier selection	21
Rate negotiation	21
Order processing	6
Production assembly	6
Product returns	2

third party logistics services. Service offerings from third party logistics companies will most likely increase in the next few years.

Definition of Third Party Logistics

The term *third party logistics* has taken on different meanings as it has received more widespread attention during the last decade. Furthermore, I submit that its definition will continue to be refined as the process gains even more attention during the 1990s. Accordingly, as we attempt such a definition we must do so with a view toward the constant change and continuous improvement that has fostered logistics growth. I happen to like the definition of logistics offered by Lt. General William "Gus" Pagonis in the book he wrote about his team's remarkable undertaking in the Gulf War:

> The careful integration of transportation, supply, warehousing, maintenance, procurement, contracting, and automation into a coherent functional area, in a way that prevents suboptimization in any of these activities; and in a way that permits and enhances the accomplishment of a given goal, objective, or mission.[4]

To add the concept of third party to his definition, we could simply begin it with the words "By using others to provide . . . " Time spent reading Pagonis's book, *Moving Mountains,* will underscore the importance of the logistics process to government and industry. Lessons learned from this massive undertaking can greatly help private industry learn to refine logistics practices and rely upon experts to accomplish logistics objectives. Reading this book is a must for today's logisticians.

Selecting a Third Party Logistics Provider

Many companies have struggled to approve the concept of using third party logistics providers, only to realize that choosing a third party operator can be a little like looking into a long dark tunnel. Long before beginning the search for acceptable candidates for logistics partnerships, the company has several important hurdles to cross. It must do the following:

1. *Develop a concise scope of work.* Understand what you wish to accomplish in the logistics venture in detail, and never assume anything. The logistician who assumes things too quickly goes down the chute.[5] When working with others outside the corporation, it is even more important to spell out exactly what is to be accomplished and how the attainment of those stated objectives affects every functional area in the corporation. There is a misconception that an internal group can effectively make up their plans as the project progresses. While this may be possible in some circumstances, it is virtually impossible for a third party to function effectively with such a lack of planning. The scope of work details physical characteristics of all items distributed, all handling and transportation needs, movement patterns, information flow, and every detail of the logistics process.

2. *Establish objectives and selection criteria.* Determine what is to be obtained from the relationship to allow the user to realize the fullest benefit from a third party

logistics relationship.[6] By developing such goals or objectives, as well as a concise understanding of the selection criteria that will be used, companies can more successfully determine which third party logistics supplier will be the most compatible with their requirements and with the company processes that are to benefit from the relationship. The process of establishing selection criteria and objectives should be designed such that all company processes that are affected by the outsourcing decision have input. This sounds good on paper but is usually not done in practice, which contributes to underutilizing the third party partner and occasionally to failure with the third party logistics project.

3. *Identify qualified providers.* Third party logistics is realizing a tremendous increase in growth and is written about frequently in respected business reviews. This has increased the number of users of third party logistics and significantly increased the number of companies who portend to be providers of third party logistics services. Identifying qualified providers without first spending time on the selection criteria is akin to walking through a minefield without a map. Many providers who are new to the industry seem to think "deep pockets" or domination in one facet of logistics qualifies them to be experts in integrating the logistics process as a third party. This may or may not work for the company seeking to outsource its logistics process.

Many resources are available to identify potential third party logistics partners. Associations such as the Warehousing Education & Research Council (WERC) and Council of Logistics Management (CLM) are good sources of information about third party logistics. Many of their members are providers and users of this service, making available networking opportunities to select the providers that most closely fit a company's requirements. Additionally, trade publications such as *Traffic Management, Distribution,* and *Transportation & Distribution* often publish articles, success stories, and lists of their views about the top third party logistics providers.

4. *Call for proposals.* When developing a request for proposal (RFQ), the design phase is most critical. The best RFQs are detailed enough to explain the business and objectives of the company as well as the particulars of the logistics project. The RFQ should be designed with the assumption that the potential vendors know little about the company: product lines, shipping volumes, growth forecasts, and industries served are all important.[6] With this background, the bidders can put the specific information to develop a cost for the logistics project into a proper perspective. More specific information provided should include but is not limited to such items as:

- Specific scope of work
- Final customer requirements
- Information technology requirements
- Value-added services required
- Location(s) and specialized facility/equipment needs

5. *Evaluate the bids.* Evaluating the bids and bidders is more complicated than picking lowest price or expanding services provided by a current vendor. Since these relationships usually are designed for multiple years, care must be taken to select the third party provider who most closely fits the needs and complements the culture of the selecting company. Remember to

1. Look at customer service—meet the person who will service your account.
2. Understand the geographic location—inspect the facility/equipment, understand current carrier service, look for best opportunity.
3. Look at the big picture on cost—include the costs of transportation, consolidation, storage, value-added services, length of term on rates, union contract and history. Also examine rate cost models and understand how they measure profitability.
4. Check customer references—understand the customer's background and experience, relate their experience to your goals, litigation exposure, top management commitment, and accessibility.
5. Evaluate capability in information technology (IT)—EDI, RF, and bar coding skills and experience, programming skills and depth, ease with which they use IT in their own business operations.
6. Evaluate strengths and weaknesses—learn about their strongest point and about where they are trying to get better.
7. Evaluate long-term plans—look into their long-term planning process to see how their plans fit with the plans of the company selecting the third party partner.
8. Evaluate financial stability—obtain financial statements and have credit manager run a credit check. Evaluate financial strength over the long run. Examine new product offerings, and compare their effects upon the logistics partnership.
9. Evaluate flexibility—determine the third party provider's ability to respond to changes in business cycles. If the scope of work changes significantly, determine the effect upon the logistics partnership.[8]

Developing a Contract for Third Party Logistics

The reasons for deciding to enter into a relationship with a third party logistics supplier usually have to do with assets, scarce capital, growth over a long term, global markets, and other interests that divert risk from the user to the provider. Sometimes, when companies outsource their logistics process, the third party is asked to purchase assets, hire long-term employees, and assume facility leases. These commitments on the part of the third party logistics supplier are often expensive, and may have a substantial effect on the supplier's balance sheet. The supplier will insist upon a long-term contract to shelter it from this risk. Conversely, the company seeking to outsource its logistics process needs the assurance that if the third party logistics provider fails to perform as expected, the contract can be terminated in favor of another alternative.

Two principles must be a part of every contract for logistics:

1. Investment amortization for the provider
2. Without-cause cancellation options for the customer

While the principles of immediate cancellation and complete investment amortization may seem to fit like oil and water, a review of the following agreement will demonstrate how these concepts can be brought together. This sample agreement is one that actually has been used in practice and that focuses primarily upon warehouse-related services. Of course, sections may be added and subtracted to fit the particular situation; nevertheless, many hours of legal and practical expertise are spent in drafting a service agreement between two parties, so use of the following as an outline may greatly reduce the time and expense required to arrive at a suitable agreement:

> *THIS AGREEMENT, effective the _____ day of _____, _____ is entered into in City, State, by and between Third Party, Inc., an _____ corporation, hereinafter referred to as "Third Party", and _____ hereinafter referred to as "Customer";*
>
> *WHEREAS, Customer desires that Third Party perform certain logistics and inventory management services; and*
>
> *WHEREAS, Customer desires that Third Party perform such services for Customer on the terms and conditions contained herein;*
>
> *NOW THEREFORE, the parties hereto agree as follows:*
>
> 1. SERVICES, PAYMENT AND TERM. *Third Party shall perform the services described in Scope of Work in consideration of the payments to be made for such services as described in Schedule A. In the event that the dollar volume of logistics services performed under this agreement in any one month shall be less than the monthly minimums as set forth in Schedule A, Customer shall pay the minimum fee and no less. In addition to logistics service fees, Customer shall pay Third Party a monthly fee for storage services performed under this Agreement of _____ ($_____). The term of this Agreement shall be for a period of three (3) years commencing _____ ("Original Term") and shall automatically renew itself for successive periods of one (1) year ("Renewal Terms") unless either party gives written notice of termination in accordance with Section 8 (a) herein. Sixty (60) days before the end of the Original Term or any Renewal Term, the parties hereto shall renegotiate new logistics and storage service fees to be effective for the next successive term.*

The key element of this section is the reference to the Scope of Work (Scope). As mentioned earlier in this chapter, many third party relationships overlook the importance of this document. The Scope is particularly important in first-time ventures between a user and a supplier of logistics services. Without it the supplier may not have a clear definition of what he has quoted to do, and the user may not know just exactly what he is paying for. Nevertheless, the Scope is the most frequently overlooked part of the relationship. The Scope of work details physical characteristics of all items distributed, all handling and transportation needs, movement patterns, information flow, and every detail of the logistics process. This Scope should be jointly developed by the user and provider of logistics services and involve representatives from functional areas on both sides of the relationship. For example, in the section of the Scope about packaging, both the user and supplier should have their packaging experts develop that portion of the Scope. Specific performance objectives are another example of that which should be covered in the Scope:

> 2. SHIPPING.
>
> (a) Goods Shipped with Third Party as Named Consignee. *Customer agrees not to ship goods to Third Party as the named consignee. Third Party shall have the right, in its sole discretion, to refuse or accept goods with Third Party named as consignee. If Third*

Party accepts goods with Third Party named as consignee, Customer shall immediately, upon notice of such fact from Third Party, notify the carrier with copy of such notice to Third Party that Third Party has no beneficial title or interest in such property.

(b) <u>Nonconforming Goods</u>. *Customer agrees not to ship goods to Third Party that do not conform to: (i) the description of goods set forth in the Manifest as defined in Section 3 herein and (ii) the description of the goods on the packing slip for each such shipment. Third Party shall have the right, in its sole discretion, to refuse or to accept any nonconforming goods. If Third Party accepts such nonconforming goods, Customer shall pay Third Party the rate set forth therefore in Schedule A or a reasonable rate if no such rate is set forth in Schedule A. Third Party will attempt to promptly notify Customer upon the delivery of any such nonconforming goods to Third Party in order to obtain instructions; provided, however, that Third Party shall not be responsible for miscommunications as a result of oral communications.*

Frequently, during a successful relationship between the user and supplier, others from the user's company may begin to use the third party relationship in a manner not contemplated during the design phase. The Scope of Work should make reference to this eventuality and should suggest a means to handle unanticipated materials. The third party provider usually should have the ability to accept or reject materials received that were not referred to in the Scope of Work but that might have an overall effect on the logistics service. For example the receipt of hazardous materials that were not planned would wreak havoc in any distribution center or transportation channel:

3. <u>TENDER FOR STORAGE</u>. *All goods for distribution by Third Party shall be delivered at the warehouse properly marked and packaged for distribution. It is acknowledged that Customer has prepared the list of goods to be delivered to Third Party as set forth in Scope of Work. The parties may agree that Third Party will store and handle other goods at a mutually agreed price provided that such agreement must be in writing. The list of goods set forth in Scope of Work and any further items which may be added to such list in the future are herein referred to as the "Manifest". All goods delivered to Third Party shall be goods described in the Manifest.*

4. <u>DELIVERY REQUIREMENTS</u>.

(a) No goods shall be delivered or transferred except upon receipt by Third Party of complete instructions properly signed by Customer. However, goods may be delivered upon instructions by telephone, but Third Party shall not be responsible for miscommunications as a result of oral communication.

A troublesome concept to smooth between two parties trying to work out a new agreement is the absence of third party responsibility. Typically, companies who are moving to third party logistics have grown accustomed to communicating shipment and delivery instructions orally. It is preferable to handle such communication by EDI or in writing. When oral communications are the accepted practice, responsibility for the accurate receipt and performance of those instructions must be negotiated in advance:

(b) When goods are ordered out of the warehouse by Customer, a reasonable time will be given Third Party to carry out instructions, and if it is unable because of acts of God, war, public enemies, seizure under legal process, strikes, lock outs, riots and/or civil commotions or for any reason beyond Third Party's control, or because of loss or destruction of goods for which Third Party is not liable, or because of any other excuse provided by law, Third Party shall not be liable for failure to carry out such instructions. If any of the proceeding

events or difficulties occur, Customer and Third Party shall agree upon a reasonable extension of time for performance.

   5. EXTRA SERVICES (SPECIAL SERVICES)

      (*a*) *Third Party labor required for services other than ordinary logistics (i.e. the logistics services described in Scope of Work) will be subject to an additional reasonable charge at Third Party's regular rates.*

      (*b*) *Special services requested by Customer including but not limited to compiling of special stock statements, reporting marked weights, serial numbers or other data from packages, physical check of goods, and logistics transit billing will be subject to an additional reasonable charge at Third Party's regular rates.*

      (*c*) *Dunnage, bracing, packing materials or other special supplies may be provided for Customer at a reasonable charge at Third Party's regular rates.*

      (*d*) *By prior arrangement, goods may be received or delivered during other than usual business hours, subject to an additional reasonable charge at Third Party's regular rates.*

      (*e*) *Communication costs including postage, teletype, telegram or telephone, will be charged to Customer if such concern more than normal inventory reporting or if, at the request of Customer, communications are made by other than regular United States Mail.*

      (*f*) *It is also acknowledged that at times it may be desirable or necessary for Third Party to incur "unusual" expenses without prior written approval of Customer and Customer hereby agrees to reimburse Third Party for any reasonable and appropriate expense arising therefrom; however, whenever it is reasonably possible to do so, Third Party will obtain authorization from Customer prior to incurring any such expense and any such authorization may be verbal provided that Third Party shall not be responsible for miscommunications as a result of oral communications.*

The important issue to recognize in the above section is that there will be a need for the supplier to perform extra duties or, at the minimum, to act in the user's behalf to carry out the mission of the third party agreement even through adverse operating conditions. In many cases that translates into a reason for an extra charge. Some agreements set forth limits or notification periods for the performance of extra work:

   6. LIABILITY AND LIMITATION OF DAMAGES.

      (*a*) Liability for Loss. *Customer as bailor shall deliver to Third Party as bailee the personal property referred to herein, and Third Party as bailee agrees to receive such personal property as follows: Third Party shall not be liable for any loss or injury to goods stored however caused unless such loss or injury resulted from the failure by Third Party to exercise reasonable care. The property covered by any receipt will not be insured by Third Party for the benefit of Customer against fire or any other casualty, and Customer agrees to insure such property against loss or damage by fire or any other casualty with waiver of subrogation against Third Party.*

      (*b*) Insurance. *Goods are not insured by Third Party against loss or injury however caused. However, Third Party does agree to continue in effect its present insurance policy which states that the insurance company will pay on behalf of Third Party all sums (subject to the policy limits) which Third Party shall become legally obligated to pay by reason of liability imposed upon the insured as a bailee for loss or destruction of or damage to personal property of others situated at Third Party's warehouse at which this Agreement is to be performed during the term of this Agreement or any extension thereof. This policy shall remain in full force and effect, subject to the exclusions contained in said policy, during the term of this Agreement including extensions thereof. A copy of such policy shall be provided to Customer upon request.*

Discussing who will provide insurance is always a difficult hurdle to cross when negotiating a third party logistics agreement. The user generally has obtained insurance for the materials to be handled through the logistics channel through some type of corporate umbrella or contents policy that may be subject to a deductible. For the supplier to purchase contents coverage in a warehousing environment, or transit coverage in a transportation environment, may cause duplicate coverage and duplicate expense. Since only one insurance company is likely to pay off in the event of a loss, the extra coverage may be superfluous. Additionally, if the third party supplier is required to include insurance in the rate for services performed, the user is probably overpaying for services purchased. A more cost-effective manner of handling the situation in a warehousing environment is to insist that the supplier provide warehouseman's legal liability coverage. This coverage allows the user's insurance company to subrogate against the supplier in cases where the supplier was negligent. That way, paying twice for contents insurance is avoided, when inventory is in the care and custody of the third party supplier:

> (*c*) <u>Calculation of Damages</u>. *In the event Third Party shall be deemed liable for any loss or damage to Customer's goods, then for the purpose of calculating such damages such goods shall be valued at their inventory cost of sale value.*
> (*d*) <u>Loading and Unloading</u>. *Third Party shall be liable for demurrage charges caused by delays in unloading inbound shipments or delays in loading outbound shipments. Third Party shall use its best efforts to perform its services to be provided hereunder in a timely manner.*
> (*e*) <u>Consequential Damages</u>. *Third Party shall not be liable to Customer for any consequential damages arising out of any act or omission of Third Party.*

Consequential damages sometimes becomes either an uninsurable risk or a potential deal-breaker. From the perspective of the user, an incident that results in a lost sale, or a missed delivery that forces a production line to shut down and workers to be sent home for the day, can be very expensive. The user would like to collect damages from the supplier. Conversely, the supplier may not be able to insure against such an eventuality or the cost of such insurance may be prohibitive. To add this additional cost to a third party transaction rate may result in a cost-prohibitive relationship to insure, an occurrence for which the user would be primarily responsible if the incident occurred when there was no third party relationship:

> 7. <u>RESPONSIBILITIES</u>. *Third Party shall be responsible for supervision, clerical staff, hourly employees, janitor service, material logistics equipment, office furniture, normal security (including locking doors at end of work shifts and activating electronic security systems), pallets and packing materials and banding (to be ordered by Third Party and rebilled to Customer), and maintenance of the premises at which this Agreement is to be performed.*
> 8. <u>RISK SHARING</u>. *The parties hereto acknowledge that Third Party will be making certain commitments and capital expenditures in order to perform hereunder. Accordingly, the parties hereto agree as follows:*
> (*a*) <u>Termination</u>. *Notwithstanding anything in this Agreement to the contrary, this Agreement may be terminated by either party without cause upon ninety (90) days written notice of such termination being given by the terminating party to the non-terminating party which notice shall specify a date of termination. In the event of such termination for any reason, whether such termination is by Customer or by Third Party, or by operation of law or otherwise, Customer agrees to reimburse Third Party in full for the unamortized portion of all loans or leases, without markup but including any prepayment penalties, interest and principal that Third Party has incurred in regard to any and all assets purchased or leased by Third Party in connection with this Agreement, including but not limited to the Premises described in Section 12(a) herein and any lease hold improvements in connection*

therewith. All assets purchased or leased by Third Party in connection with this Agreement, including the Premises and leasehold improvements in connection therewith, are hereinafter referred to as the "Assets". Customer specifically agrees that upon termination for any reason whatsoever Customer shall assume that certain lease by and between _____ as lessor and Third Party as lessee, dated _____, 199__, commencing _____, 199__, for the lease of those premises described in Schedule C attached hereto (the "Lease") and Customer shall thereafter be solely responsible for all obligations of the Lessee under the Lease, including but not limited to the obligations to pay rent or any other sum.

It is the intention of this Section 8(a) that in the event of any termination of this Agreement by either party, by operation of law or for any other reason, that Third Party shall be fully reimbursed with the result being that Third Party suffers no financial loss as a result of such termination and that Third Party is relieved from any liabilities it might have to any banks, to other lenders, to lessors of any personal or real property, to the lessor under the Lease, or to any other party.

Termination is perhaps the most important section of the agreement. When two parties enter into a third party arrangement, one will most likely be making a significant investment (the supplier) and one will be concerned about how to deal with its perceived loss of control and conformance to performance standards (the user). One method of dealing with this situation is to allow the user to terminate on relatively short notice for any cause. If the user elects to trigger this termination option, the user must agree to pay for unamortized loans and owned (not loaned) assets, and assume leases that involve the third party project. This provides the user with the comforting knowledge that he/she may terminate with or without cause should circumstances arise later in the relationship that warrant such action. Given the "safety valve," the supplier can make investments for the project knowing that, should termination occur, payment for the assets has been prearranged according to a preset schedule. The supplier must itemize all assets at the beginning of the relationship and keep the user informed about any assets purchased during the relationship:

In addition to the reimbursement provisions set forth herein, title and possession of the Assets, excluding leasehold improvements, shall be determined, upon termination of this Agreement, in the following manner:

(i)   If Third Party terminates this Agreement at any time during the three (3) year Original Term of this Agreement, Customer shall be vested with title and possession of the Assets, after Customer has met all of its financial obligations as set forth under Article 8 herein.

(ii)   If Customer terminates this Agreement at any time during the first eighteen (18) months of the Original Terms [or if terminated by operation of law or by reasons other than Third Party terminating during the first eighteen (18) months], Customer shall be vested with title and possession of the Assets, after Customer has met all of its financial obligations as set forth under Article 8 herein.

(iii)   If Customer terminates the Agreement at any time during the remaining portion of the Original Term or thereafter [or if terminated by operation of law or by reasons other than Third Party terminating after the first eighteen (18) months], and, after customer has met all of its financial obligations as set forth under Article 8 herein, then Customer shall have the following choice:

(1)   Customer shall be vested with title and possession of the Assets upon payment to Third Party by Customer of $_____; or

(2)   Third Party shall be vested with title and possession of the Assets and Customer shall not be obligated to make the payment of $_____ to Third Party.

Customer shall notify Third Party of its choice, if applicable, of either (1) or (2) above no later than the termination date.

Any reimbursement payments provided for in this Section from Customer to Third Party shall be made no later than the termination date specified in the notice of termination.

In the event that such reimbursement payments are not made by the termination date, Customer agrees that it will, until final reimbursement payments have been made, pay to all lending institutions and lessors of personal property all payments due by Third Party to such lending institutions and lessors of personal property, on a timely basis, so as to prevent any defaults in Third Party's loans or leases of personal property. It is further agreed that said lending institutions and lessors shall have the right to enforce payment against Customer of all sums due to them under said loans and leases, and for this purpose, said lending institution or lessor shall be considered a third-party beneficiary of this Agreement.

The payments or obligations to be made or performed by Customer as set forth herein and in Section 12(a) herein, shall be Third Party's exclusive remedies in the event of termination; provided however, that Third Party shall also be entitled to recover from Customer any amount earned by Third Party prior to such termination.

In the presence of an accelerated depreciation schedule or a contract of relatively short-term duration, one question is often asked: "If we terminate, who gets the assets?" One way to solve that dilemma might be to allow the user to automatically take title to the assets during the first half of the agreement. If the supplier figured the residual value of owned assets as a factor in pricing the service, he might be entitled to an additional payment in the event of cancellation during the last half of the agreement:

(b) <u>Labor Rates.</u> *It is acknowledged by the parties hereto the prices quoted for services in Schedule A and the minimum charges for logistics and storage services contained in Section 1 and Schedule A herein are based upon certain labor rates which Third Party reasonably believes will be applicable to the services to be performed under this Agreement. In the event that actual labor rates are in excess of Third Party's present assumptions contained in Schedule A, the parties hereto shall adjust the compensation and minimum monthly compensation to be paid to Third Party with the result being that Customer shall pay Third Party an additional amount to cover Third Party's excess labor costs.*

During start-up situations, a supplier is frequently asked to price his/her services based upon the labor rate that research has shown would apply in the subject area. However, often six months to a year may pass between the RFQ submission and start-up dates. Should local conditions change during that period, the supplier may need the opportunity to document a one-time labor rate adjustment:

9. STATUS OF PARTIES.

(a) It is the mutual understanding of the parties that Third Party is not engaged in the business of storing goods for hire and shall not be deemed to be a "warehouseman" under the laws of the State of _____, the State of _____ or under the laws of any other state, and Third Party expressly agrees for all time not to assert any claim, lien, privilege, right of offset, or the like against any of the goods handled by Third Party under this Agreement and that full, sole and unquestioned title to the goods shall remain in Customer.

(b) Notwithstanding anything in this Agreement to the contrary, it is hereby agreed that with respect to the goods which are to be subject to this Agreement that Third Party is a bailee and that the relationship between Third Party and Customer is a bailee-bailor relationship. It is further mutually agreed that Third Party shall have sole and complete control or discretion concerning the manner and means of performing its obligations hereunder and is not an agent or employee of Customer. For the purpose of enabling Third Party to perform its

duties imposed upon it under this Agreement as a bailee, Customer grants to Third Party exclusive control, subject to the right of Customer to inspect the goods and premises at any reasonable time.

Typically, under the Uniform Commercial Code of most states, the term *warehouseman* has a legal definition that may allow the supplier to place a lien upon the user's goods in the event of nonpayment of an invoice or for other reasons. Accordingly, a bailee-bailor relationship restricts the supplier from the ability to automatically exercise any lien. A more complete legal opinion from counsel should be obtained, to learn which term best fits the third party logistics situation:

10. NOTICE OF CLAIM AND FILING OF SUIT.
    (*a*) *All claims hereunder must be presented in writing prior to bringing any court action thereon.*
    (*b*) *No action may be maintained by either Customer or Third Party unless such claim has been made in writing and unless such action is commenced within one (1) year after the event, action or inaction to which such claim relates.*
    (*c*) *This provision shall survive any termination or expiration of this Agreement, however arising.*
11. ORAL COMMUNICATIONS. *Sections 2(b), 4(a) and 5(f) place responsibility for miscommunications as a result of oral communications upon Customer. Notwithstanding anything in said Sections to the contrary, however, Customer hereby agrees to confirm all oral communications in writing within twenty-four (24) hours after the occurrence of such oral communication. Upon receipt of such written confirmation, Third Party shall no longer have the right to rely upon its understanding of the oral communication but shall instead rely upon the written confirmation; provided, however, that in no event shall Third Party be responsible for any action it takes in reliance of oral communications prior to the time of receipt by Third Party of the written confirmation.*
12. WAREHOUSE.
    (*a*) Premises and Effect of Termination. *The warehouse to be utilized for the performance of services hereunder shall be certain premises located at _____, ("Premises") leased by Third Party from _____ for a term of _____ ( ) years commencing _____, 199__, which premises are more particularly described in the attached Schedule C ("Lease"). In the event of the termination of this Agreement for any reason whatsoever, Customer shall assume the Lease upon such termination, and, thereafter, Customer shall be solely responsible for all obligations of the Lessee under the Lease and Third Party shall thereupon be relieved of all such obligations, including but not limited to the obligations to pay rent or any other sum. Upon termination, Third Party will transfer its interest in all leasehold improvements to Customer.*
13. ASSIGNMENT. *Third Party shall not assign, transfer, pledge or otherwise alienate this Agreement, or any part hereof, or any rights inuring to it hereunder without the express written consent of Customer, and said consent shall not be unreasonably withheld.*
    Nothing contained in this assignment clause, however, shall prevent Third Party from assigning its interest under this Agreement to any corporation for which the stock is either owned or controlled by the principal shareholder of Third Party, and such assignment or transfer shall not require the consent of Customer.
14. AUTHORITY. *The undersigned officer, agent or employee represents and warrants that all necessary actions have been taken and that they have the authority to bind their respective organizations.*
15. DEFAULT. *The following shall be deemed to be events of default by Third Party:*
    (*a*) *If Third Party shall materially default in the performance of or compliance with any of the terms and provisions of this Agreement; or*
    (*b*) *If Third Party shall file a voluntary petition in bankruptcy or shall be adjudicated bankrupt or insolvent or shall make a general assignment for the benefit of its creditors or shall seek or consent to the appointment of any receiver or liquidator of Third Party, of all or substantially all of its assets.*

If such default shall continue for a period of thirty (30) days after written notice of such default is received by Third Party, then and in such event Customer shall have the right to terminate this Agreement, subject to the provisions for payment of the termination fee set forth in Section 8(a). Notwithstanding the foregoing, Third Party shall have thirty (30) days after the date of such notice of default to cure such default.

"How much time should the supplier be allowed to take to cure his/her default condition?" This is a common item of debate among parties negotiating an agreement. The user wants to be able to step in and ensure a smooth flow of goods to his/her customers, while the supplier needs time to cure his/her default condition. The key is timing and severity. In a default situation, the user should have representatives on site to monitor the situation, yet should not prevent the supplier from curing the conditions that led to the default. The 30-day period suggested in the sample contract may work in certain situations but be unworkable in others. Nevertheless should a default occur, and should that default not be corrected in a timely fashion, termination and payment for termination will then occur, subject to the terms and conditions of the termination section of the agreement:

16. <u>SUCCESSORS AND ASSIGNS</u>. *This Agreement shall be binding upon the successors and assigns of the parties hereto.*
17. <u>CAPTIONS</u>. *Captions are for reference purpose only and are not limited to expand or restrict the actual wording of the provisions herein.*
18. <u>GOVERNING LAW</u>. *This Agreement shall be governed by and construed according to the laws of the State of_____.*

The "smaller" of the two parties to the agreement might choose to have the agreement interpreted in his/her home state, to minimize the impact of probable legal expenses. The reason for this is that generally attorneys are most familiar with law practice in a single state. Adjudicating a contract in a different state may result in either increased legal fees or the need to deal with an out-of-state attorney unfamiliar with the company. On the other hand, "larger" parties generally have legal representation in many states, so for this company, out-of-state legal representation may not be an issue:

19. <u>MODIFICATIONS—FINAL AND COMPLETE AGREEMENT</u>. *This Agreement may not be changed, modified, waived, discharged or terminated orally or in any other manner, except as provided herein or except by a writing signed by the parties hereto. This writing contains the entire agreement between the parties hereto, and no other representations, oral or written, have been made. All prior negotiations, whether oral or written, of either party have been merged herein and are superseded hereby.*
IN WITNESS WHEREOF, the parties have hereunto set their hands on the day and year set under their names but effective on the day and year first above written.

Lessons Learned

The courtship that takes place between two companies often does result in a long-term satisfying relationship. The Scope of Work and Agreement often took weeks or in some cases months to develop, and involved many participants from several functional areas of both companies. Frequently others were heavily involved in the process, including attorneys, equipment suppliers, creditors, and financial experts. During this development process there was a strong temptation to cut corners so as to race into early production, in the belief that the agreement file, which has by now grown fat and expensive, will merely sit in a filing cabinet, never to be opened. It would be gratifying if that were always the case.

Experiences related by successful users and suppliers of third party logistics services suggest that some relationships and agreements do end; that stipulation of an orderly manner for terminating a contract is an absolute necessity; and that a strong, well-written agreement often encourages a healthy relationship between a buyer and a seller.

We have often heard it said that the most important ingredient in a third party relationship is the presence of a "champion" of high authority on each side of the relationship. Unfortunately, these champions often are promoted or change jobs during the term of the agreement, which puts their replacements in the position of administrating their own interpretation of how the relationship between buyer and seller should look. In the absence of a strong agreement, this situation, which happens all too often, almost always spells disaster.

Summary

Never before in the history of the logistics industry has the future looked so bright. Universities are graduating more students who have received training in logistics and who are eager to develop their careers in the field. Experienced logisticians are sought after by major corporations who use or supply logistics. Investment in companies who provide the third party logistics service has increased dramatically. *Harvard Business Review* and other highly respected publications have given logistics and parts of the logistics process unprecedented coverage and in-depth research. And finally, operations Desert Shield, Desert Storm, and Desert Farewell have provided a universally observed practical application of logistics, combining the skills of the military and third party logistics providers in a tremendously successful undertaking that will be analyzed in case studies for years.

The field of logistics has become a new frontier that provides substantial investment advantages and cost-reduction opportunities for users and providers of the third party logistics process.

References

1. Helen Richardson, "Outsourcing: The Power Worksource," *Transportation & Distribution,* July 1992.
2. Robert Lieb, "The Use of Third-Party Logistics Services By Large American Manufacturers," *Journal of Business Logistics,* CLM, vol. 13, no. 2, 1992.
3. Ibid.
4. Lt. General William G. Pagonis, *Moving Mountains,* Harvard Business School Press, Cambridge, 1992.
5. Ibid.
6. James Potochick and Mark Richards, "How to choose a third-party company," *Traffic Management,* July 1992.
7. Ibid.
8. Richardson, op. cit.

30

Customer Satisfaction*

Patrick M. Byrne
*Vice President and Managing Director of
North America, A. T. Kearney, Inc.*

William J. Markham
Principal, A. T. Kearney, Inc.

In today's dynamic business environment, innovative companies are searching for a means to differentiate themselves from the competition and become the supplier of choice. The rules of the marketplace are changing, and suppliers are only just beginning to focus on one of the most critical components of success: customer satisfaction. Leading-edge suppliers recognize that satisfying customers is a key to achieving competitive advantage in the 1990s and beyond. As customers become more sophisticated and demanding, customer satisfaction is being incorporated into the strategies and goals of successful companies.

As a strategy for achieving competitive advantage, the ability to satisfy the customer is determined by the value created and added to the customer operation. While all business processes must work in concert to maximize satisfaction, logistics process excellence drives distribution service quality—perhaps the most highly val-

---

*This chapter is based on the results of A. T. Kearney's 1991 study and survey on logistics quality and productivity for the Council of Logistics Management. Many of the concepts and ideas discussed in this chapter are more fully explored in the book prepared for the Council of Logistics Management and entitled *Improving Quality and Productivity in the Logistics Process—Achieving Customer Satisfaction Breakthroughs.*

ued customer service. The logistics process directly touches the customer and affects customer satisfaction in three ways:

1. Through distribution, the logistics process provides the essential value-added services required by the customer—time and place utility.
2. Logistics directly impacts the ability of other business processes to satisfy customers.
3. Distribution and other logistics staff frequently come in direct contact with customers, influencing their perceptions of the product and the associated services.

As a result, planning, operating, and managing logistics for performance excellence differentiates suppliers, creates value, drives customer satisfaction, and is an important source of competitive advantage.

This chapter examines the link between value and customer satisfaction, presents a framework for a customer-focused distribution strategy, and describes the benefits and suggests techniques for achieving and measuring logistics and distribution excellence.

The Customer Value-Satisfaction Link

Evolution of Competitive Advantage

During the 1980s, the product quality and customer service revolution was the new strategic focus of many U.S. and foreign companies. Total quality management (TQM) and continuous improvement presented the path to competitive advantage. Many CEOs adopted the teachings of Deming, Crosby, Juran, Taguchi, and others to meet the demand of the day: a top-quality product. Today, product quality and customer service are the battleground on which companies pursue a higher competitive goal: customer satisfaction. Leading companies are beginning to recognize that a top-quality product is only one step toward satisfying customers and ultimately achieving increased market share and profits. A total customer focus in all business processes, including distribution, is today's strategy for competitive advantage.

What Is Customer Satisfaction?

Satisfying customers is an ongoing process—a cycle of continuous change. Customer satisfaction includes the sum of every relationship a firm has with its customers, both external and internal, touching all business processes. It is based on the product as well as support-service performance. In the end, customers select one supplier over another based on the product and service value they receive relative to the cost they incur. Companies create value in two ways: by meeting customer requirements, and by exceeding customer expectations.

Customer Requirements and Expectations

Companies meet requirements and exceed expectations through business-process excellence. Total quality continues to be the framework through which most companies pursue excellence. However, as service performance and product quality are continuously improved, customer expectations spiral upward to new standards of excellence. To maintain a competitive advantage through total customer satisfaction (TCS), all business processes must be managed to meet and even exceed customers' ever-changing expectations, thereby creating value and driving customer satisfaction.

Customer service is generally defined as *an activity, performance measure, or effort that increases a product's value or utility to the customers.* Customer service as a business process adds value by fulfilling minimum requirements and exceeding expectations, as do all other customer-focused business processes. Therefore, customer service is more accurately described as *a process resulting in customer satisfaction.*

Quality, also a significant component of customer satisfaction, is defined by Juran as "Those product features which meet the needs of customers and thereby provide product satisfaction."[1] Quality, like customer satisfaction, must be defined by the customers. The ability to integrate a level of product and service quality that is consistent with customer expectations into the company's business processes is imperative for creating value. For example, a major pharmaceutical company scheduled production runs for cost efficiency, disregarding actual customer demand. As a result, its customers were dissatisfied when the distribution department was unable to deliver products on time because they were not available to ship. This problem underscores why every participant business process must apply a customer-focused strategy to its operations in order to meet customer service requirements.

Logistics: A Key Business Process

Customer–Shareholder Value Relationship

Companies must add value not only to their customers but to shareholders as well. Still, creating value for customers is key to meeting shareholder requirements and adding shareholder value. Every business process adds varying levels of value to each; it is a company's *key business processes* that add high value to both customers and shareholders. Logistics is a key business process, and within it, distribution takes a lead role in providing value to the customer.

Distribution is critical, because it provides a variety of value-added services and directly affects many other business processes. Distribution spans a wide range of business functions, all of which must be customer-focused to optimize performance and maximize satisfaction. Functions involved in distribution usually include warehousing and storage, transportation, finished goods inventory management, order entry, material handling, distribution planning, and return goods handling. All of these responsibilities can contribute to value-added services that ultimately affect the customers.

Distribution performance also affects other components of the business. Order management, inventory planning and control, information availability, credit/accounts payable, manufacturing, sales, and marketing are all affected by distribution. In order to satisfy customers, all these departments must coordinate their efforts.

Distribution contributes directly to a product's value by providing time and place utility. As quick response inventory replenishment, one-stop shopping, electronic data interchange (EDI), and special packaging and labeling become the norm, today's customers expect and demand time and place utility. To satisfy its customers, distribution must provide the service levels they require and exceed their expectations.

The distribution process is unique because employees have frequent, direct contact with customers, as when they receive orders, make delivery arrangements, or actually deliver products. This frequent customer contact gives distribution a key role to play in achieving customer satisfaction.

Distribution service quality adds high value to customers and contributes to logistics performance excellence. This in turn drives productivity and impacts profitability, a critical shareholder requirement. In addition, efficient distribution operations can positively impact the balance sheet. For example, reduction in order cycle time and inventory levels may improve cashflow and free up capital for alternative uses. Therefore, value is maximized when service quality and productivity are properly balanced—and this results when a company has achieved logistics excellence.

Characteristics of Logistics Excellence

Logistics excellence speeds the journey toward superior customer satisfaction by

- Enhancing capability to tailor service and offer higher service levels
- Improving service quality (consistency and reliability)
- Accelerating cycle times
- Increasing supply chain efficiencies and productivity
- Strengthening customer-company relations

These benefits ultimately will result in increased market share, revenue, and profit—making logistics excellence a management imperative. The best way to assess logistics excellence is through an evaluation of the approaches companies use to plan and manage the logistics process. These approaches group into eight key dimensions used to determine a company's Stage of Logistics Excellence (see Table 30-1, and the following descriptions of the three stages).

Stage I. A company whose logistics process exhibits Stage I characteristics has yet to pursue quality and productivity improvement in a meaningful way. Generally, the Stage I logistics process lacks fundamental control over the supply chain, creating a substantial barrier to improvement.

Table 30-1. Characteristics of the Stages of Logistics Excellence

Dimension	Stage I	Stage II	Stage III
(1) Service goal setting	■ Handle each transaction as a separate situation ■ "Keep noise level down"	■ All customers treated the same ■ Attain internally-set goals	■ Provide differentiated service ■ Meet/exceed customer requirements
(2) Long-range planning	■ Not formally carried out ■ Fragmented planning	■ Narrow scope (e.g., distribution) ■ 1- to 3-year horizon	■ Full logistics scope ■ 3- to 5-year horizon
(3) Operations planning	■ Today ■ Each transaction	■ Period (e.g., monthly) ■ Budget-period based	■ Period/annual ■ Rolling periods
(4) Ongoing improvement process	■ Quick-fix, "stop the bleeding"	■ Cost reduction	■ Continuous improvement toward goals ■ Quality and productivity
(5) Relationships between employees and management	■ Employees versus management	■ Limited employee involvement	■ Training ■ Empowerment ■ Shared goals/rewards
(6) Information management capabilities	■ Process transaction ■ Little or no data ■ No analysis capabilities	■ Report period's financial results ■ Fragmented data ■ Limited analysis capabilities	■ Support planning with operational data ■ Easy-to-use shared data ■ Flexible analysis capabilities
(7) Measurement approach	■ Cost versus last year ■ Cost as percent of sales ■ Service "noise level"	■ Cost versus budget ■ Productivity versus past levels ■ Service versus competition	■ Service versus customer requirement ■ Productivity versus goal ■ Cost versus standard
(8) Relationships with suppliers and service providers	■ Unmanaged ■ Crisis-driven ■ Adversarial	■ Cost-driven ■ Multiple sources ■ Competitive bid-oriented	■ Partnership ■ Results-driven ■ Joint improvement
Constraints to further improvement	■ Lack of control	■ Bureaucracy	■ Parochialism

© Copyright A. T. Kearney, Inc., 1990

Stage II. These operations are control-oriented by nature, and typically are internally focused. Budget performance is critical. While some degree of control is necessary, excessive Stage II controls usually create bureaucracy, which stifles improvement efforts.

Stage III. In Stage III, the various functions participating in the logistics process are *functionally* excellent. Each performs its part of the process to the best of its ability. Unfortunately parochialism can set in, suboptimizing overall supply chain performance and inhibiting excellence.

A profile of logistics excellence along the eight key dimensions includes:

1. Service goal setting—involves customers, requirements-driven, updated regularly
2. Long-range planning—formal, long-term horizon, full logistics scope
3. Operations planning—formal, cross-functional, results-oriented
4. Ongoing improvement process—formal (tied to overall process), includes continuous and breakthrough improvements, integrates quality and productivity
5. Relationships between employees and management—includes training and empowerment, ties rewards to success
6. Information management capabilities—supports planning, operations, transaction processing; tied to customers and suppliers; cross-functional
7. Measurement approach—goal-based, covers quality and productivity
8. Relationships with suppliers and service providers—performance-driven, involves joint improvement and information-sharing

A final factor shown in the table, "Constraints to Further Improvement," identifies the hindrances that must be overcome for a company to move from one stage to the next.

A logistics process with these characteristics can create customer value and in turn drive customer satisfaction. Given the potential contribution of logistics toward achieving superior customer satisfaction, logistics excellence provides the best foundation upon which to build an entire customer-focused business strategy.

Achieving Superior Customer Satisfaction

The long-term success of a commitment to increased customer value depends on several critical factors. First, the company must adopt a strategy of total customer satisfaction. This means understanding and meeting all customer requirements the first time, every time. It also means exceeding customer expectations of high-value, high-priority services. Service quality has established itself as the preeminent point of differentiation among competitors, as product quality becomes a minimum basic requirement.

Second, if a company depends on service to successfully differentiate itself, then the logistics process, and consequently distribution performance, must be the key driver in executing that strategy. It is at the heart of the day-to-day, order-by-order delivery of customer satisfaction. No other process cuts so deeply across a corporate organization; no other process links so closely with the customer (see Fig. 30-1).

All operating functions must work in concert to achieve logistics excellence and execute a customer satisfaction strategy effectively. As a result, responsibility for orchestrating the logistics process across these functions rises to the chief operating officer, the first level in the organization with accountability for the full logistics process. These success factors serve as the prerequisites to a successful customer-focused distribution strategy.

Common Obstacles

Before a company can set out to build competitive advantage based on superior service quality and customer satisfaction, it must first close four gaps that act as obstacles to improvement:

1. Understanding customer requirements
2. Identifying/prioritizing value-added factors
3. Setting meaningful customer service goals
4. Measuring and communicating service performance

The first gap exists because many suppliers don't fully understand customer service requirements. Instead of asking the customer directly, they rely too heavily on

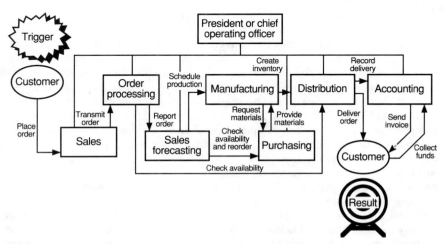

Figure 30-1. The logistics process. (*From Patrick M. Byrne and William J. Markham*, Improving Quality and Productivity in the Logistics Process: Achieving Customer Satisfaction Breakthroughs, *Council of Logistics Management, Oak Brook, IL, 1991*)

sales force input, competitors' service levels, or customer complaints. Research shows that fewer than two-thirds of suppliers bother to conduct in-person interviews with their customers to understand service requirements. And when suppliers directly contact customers, typically only about one-third find a match between customer expectations and their own perceptions.

The second obstacle is a direct result of not communicating with the customer up front; customers and suppliers frequently disagree on what constitutes "value-added." Without an in-depth understanding of customers' operations, suppliers lack the knowledge needed to identify, develop, market, and deliver value-added services to customers. One complication is that value varies according to customer, industry, and product line. For example, for an infrequent purchase such as a mainframe computer, customers might emphasize service attributes such as technical support, postsales support, and customer service as the most important criteria. With repetitive buying, however, other service attributes may be viewed as critically important. On-time delivery, first-time order accuracy, and consistency are significant when supplying a manufacturing process with critical components.

The third gap is the setting of meaningful, accurate, service goals. Most companies set their customer service goals based primarily on internally focused factors or competitor-focused factors. As many as one-third of companies set performance targets simply as a percentage improvement over the previous year, at the same level as the previous year, or at a level of parity with the competition. None of these common approaches establishes the most effective goal for maximizing value: to meet or exceed customers' expectations.

The final obstacle exists because of a gap between customer and supplier perceptions of actual performance. Research shows that across important dimensions of service (e.g., order cycle time, unit fill rate, invoice accuracy, order completeness, etc.), almost four times as many suppliers believe their service consistently meets their customers' needs as do the customers. One reason for this is that suppliers and customers are not always measuring the same thing. For example, a computer manufacturer had historically been proud of its order completeness rate. Each division boasted rates above 90 percent. However, when the company asked its customers to rate its order completeness performance, customers generally rated the supplier around 50 percent. The gap occurred because most customers bought complete systems that required components from as many as seven or eight divisions. With a 5 to 10 percent likelihood of incomplete shipment from any one division, the customers' chance of getting a complete order was only 50-50. With a computer system, one missing component can render the entire system inoperable.

Given the pervasiveness of these obstacles, it is not surprising that most companies have just begun the journey toward meaningful improvements in customer satisfaction. Research has revealed that prior to 1987, only 17 percent of companies had implemented corporate-wide quality and productivity improvement programs. Another third began between 1987 and 1989, and another 17 percent between 1990 and 1991. The final 33 percent of research respondents have not yet begun as of this writing (1991). And in the logistics process—the driver of service quality and customer satisfaction—only about 55 percent of companies reported formal improvement processes in place.

Customer Focus Success Stories: Common Characteristics

Overcoming the four obstacles mentioned above is critical. Customers continue to be more demanding of suppliers, because their own downstream customers are placing new demands on them. Unless a company constantly updates its understanding of customer requirements and its knowledge of how well it is performing against those requirements, it will be left behind by the competition. For companies with established quality improvement programs, these obstacles have diminished as customer focus continues to sharpen.

Over the past decade, the growth rate in the stock price for a portfolio of 21 recognized quality and customer satisfaction leaders, including Xerox, Milliken, and Federal Express, averaged 16.9 percent annually, compared to 10.9 percent for the Standard and Poor's 500 over the same time period. This superior performance is largely the result of several common characteristics shared by these 21 TQM and TCS leaders:

- *Customer-driven service strategy.* These firms focus on customer needs and requirements using the *customers'* definition of quality. Customers are contacted regularly to determine and reconfirm requirements. The companies' explicit goals are to meet requirements and exceed expectations, thereby expanding customer value.

- *Senior management commitment.* Positioning the company to meet and even anticipate customer needs often requires a fundamental shift in culture and management style, as well as radical changes in operating methods. Such shifts in culture and style can occur only with absolute commitment at the top. Only senior management can oversee the cross-functional coordination necessary for meaningful process improvement. It is processes, which unlike functions produce tangible outputs for specific customer requirements, that create value.

- *Formal process for continuous improvement.* This process includes an improvement framework that encompasses performance measures, analysis tools, and benchmarking programs. Most companies initiate continuous improvement processes, with pilot programs that achieve early successes. These "wins" are then publicized, setting the tone for future success.

- *Aggressive goal-setting.* The most successful companies all agreed that aggressive goal-setting was key to their programs. These are often referred to as "stretch" goals. Customers tend to notice when stretch goals have been reached, but may fail to notice incremental improvement. Stretch goals act as magnets, pulling an organization forward. But successful companies are careful not to abuse stretch goals, thus ensuring that employees view the target as attainable.

- *Employee ownership and empowerment.* In successful companies, employee ownership of improvement is the fuel that drives the engine of change. Employees are involved in the process at all levels and are held accountable for performing up to customer-focused goals. Training emphasizes teamwork, and empowers employees to initiate improvements and take risks. Reward and recognition programs reinforce ongoing improvement efforts.

These characteristics are the key to success for customer-focused programs designed to build competitive advantage, and they suggest the steps necessary for building an effective customer-focused logistics strategy.

Implementing a Customer-Focused Logistics Strategy

Step 1: Understand Customer Requirements and Expectations

Increased competition, changing consumer demands, and pressures for continuous quality improvement mean that the customers' requirements constantly change. The supplier must anticipate and react to these changes, continually redefining its business goals. As requirements change, business processes must adapt in order to maintain customer satisfaction.

As an example of the benefits of understanding customer-defined value-added, consider a perishable foods distributor that aimed to deliver all orders within 24 hours. The distributor had a large number of warehouses in order to meet the promise of 24-hour delivery. The products were delivered within the promised time frame, but because there were so many warehouses the produce was not always fresh when it arrived at the stores. Upon asking customers what they value, the distributor realized that 24-hour delivery is not crucial, but fresh products are. The distributor was then able to satisfy customers by providing fresh products and to save money by reducing inventory and eliminating excess warehouse capacity.

When creating a customer-focused logistics strategy (see Fig. 30-2), distribution personnel must understand exactly what customers require and expect from the distribution process. Different customers have different requirements and expectations. For example, customers' requirements for the delivery component of distribution might include:

- Timely, reliable delivery, with good communication
- On-time delivery

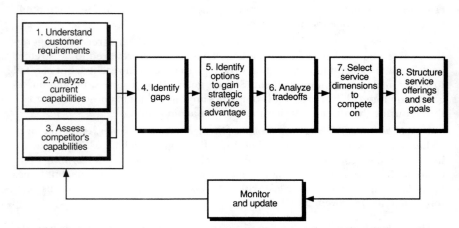

Figure 30-2. Implementing a Customer-Focused Logistics Strategy. (*From Patrick M. Byrne and William J. Markham,* Improving Quality and Productivity in the Logistics Process: Achieving Customer Satisfaction Breakthroughs, *Council of Logistics Management, Oak Brook, IL, 1991*)

- Frequent deliveries
- Availability of order status information
- Product receiving standards
- Availability of customer pickup
- Shipment routing preferences/restrictions
- Efficient returns processing
- Immediate handling of emergencies
- High damage-free rate
- Courteous claims processing
- Accurate and timely billing
- Responsiveness to inquiries

The process of defining customer requirements can be complex, and is unfamiliar to most companies. Management must learn to understand and focus on external customer requirements if it is to deliver value. Follow these three steps to determine what customers value:

1. Understand the customer's business, the buyer, and the user.
2. Identify customer requirements and expectations.
3. Explore the importance of requirements and expectations with customers; determine the customer's willingness to pay for services.

Now let's look more closely at each of these three steps.

1. *Understand the customer's business, the buyer, and the user.* If it is to offer a product and service package that provides value, the supplier must understand the customer's business. This understanding will make it easier for the supplier to translate customer satisfaction requirements into operational standards. A good example is understanding how orders differ by order type. Emergency, stock replenishment, custom, promotion, and test/trial orders may each have different distribution requirements. Requirements may also differ by product type. Core items, line extensions, custom items, critical and noncritical items may be treated differently by the customer. Identifying these requirements, and tailoring service accordingly, increases customer satisfaction and is likely to reduce costs.

In addition, it is important to distinguish the buyer's needs from those of the user, which are often quiet different. F.A.O. Schwarz, a luxury toy store company, understands this difference. It tailors services to parents (the buyers), who can sip coffee in quiet living room-like lounges where sales representatives demonstrate the latest toys, while their children (the users) play with toys in the store. The adults can purchase prewrapped gifts or leave lists with sales representatives who select, wrap, and ship the gifts later.

In most large companies the buyer is not the user, and thus may have different satisfaction criteria. The buyer of parts for an electronics manufacturing firm—the purchasing department—may be influenced by other departments such as production, quality control, logistics, product development, and finance. The buyer may be most concerned with price and delivery terms, while the influencers may be most interested in quality. The user—the production line—may regard product availability and product characteristics as most important. Understanding the role the buyer and the user play in the purchasing decision helps the supplier to discern requirements and meet expectations.

2. *Identify customer requirements and expectations.* Suppliers must explore with customers which service attributes are most critical. It is important to ask qualitative, open-ended questions that give customers the flexibility to express their true requirements and desires. Giving customers a list of "requirements" from the suppliers' perspectives can be a starting point, but usually is insufficient. It promotes an internal focus, fails to reveal all important issues, and does not probe into the rationale for requirements. An oft-quoted anecdote talks of a home tool and appliance maker that once thought it was in the business of selling $1\frac{1}{2}$-in drill bits; eventually it realized that its customers didn't really want $1\frac{1}{2}$-in drill bits. All they wanted were $1\frac{1}{2}$-in holes.[2]

In Norway, Toyota used to think of cars simply as products, until it began to look at the total car experience and to ask customers what they expected. It discovered that car buyers were concerned with reliability and performance, as well as with the ease of buying a car, insurance, and repair. Toyota responded to this new knowledge by offering competitive financing, insurance services, and a free diagnostic service. Between 1985 and 1986 sales increased 30 percent, and profits almost doubled. Toyota moved up to be the best-selling foreign car manufacturer in Norway, surpassing Ford, which had been the best seller for the previous 15 years.

It is also important to assess what role current business practices play in the creation of value and satisfaction. For example, are sales representatives specifying delivery dates based on when the customers want the delivery, or on when they know the company can make the delivery? This was the case with a parts distributor who reported 99.9 percent on-time delivery. The measure was based on the delivery date agreed to by its customers, but the date was not necessarily when the customers really wanted the parts. Often a customer requested delivery on Tuesday, but the distributor could not make the delivery until Thursday. Negotiations would lead to the customer agreeing on a Thursday delivery date, although he was not satisfied. Upon discussing distribution requirements with its customers, the distributor realized that its sales force and distribution system were not customer-focused and therefore did not contribute to the customer satisfaction process.

One of the most popular ways of determining what is important to customers is to ask the buyer and user open-ended questions in personal interviews or focus groups. Questions, of course, will vary by industry, but might include:

- *What's important to you?* Which service dimensions make a difference in your buying decision? How do you prioritize those service dimensions?

- *What constitutes discernibly superior and inferior performance?* What levels of performance prompt you to increase your purchases? On what criteria? What levels of service problems reduce your purchases, or cause you to disqualify a supplier?

- *What is current performance, and how do you measure it?* How well does our company meet your requirements? How well do competitors meet your requirements?

- *How can we be easier to do business with?* What things are we doing that we should not be doing? What things aren't we doing that we should be doing?

■ *How can we create value?* What are we doing today that you like or value? What are competitors doing that you like or value? How can we do a better job of meeting your needs?

Assignment of responsibility for gathering information from customers is an important consideration. In some companies management has enough contact with customers, and is willing to listen to customer feedback with an open mind. For example, Square D requires its middle managers to make at least three customer calls per week. In this way, management gains significant insight from talking to customers. In other circumstances, however, managers' preconceived notions regarding customer requirements might be too strong, and taint what customers tell them. Using an outside firm specializing in customer satisfaction is one objective method of identifying customer requirements and expectations. The downside to a third party approach is that management and other employees do not have the opportunity to hear customer responses firsthand. A mix of management contact and a third party approach often provides the most comprehensive information. Most customers and suppliers (90 and 74 percent, respectively) agree that suppliers should update their understanding of customer requirements at least annually.

There are four common approaches to determining what product attributes and services customers value:

1. Direct customer input

2. Customers' statements

3. "Noise levels"

4. Benchmarking

Each approach has its merits, but a comprehensive understanding comes from implementing a combination of the four, with an emphasis on direct communication.

a. Direct customer input. Asking customers directly what they value is an accurate method of determining what customers want and need. Effective techniques for gathering direct customer input include personal interviews, focus groups, and surveys. Personal interviews are the most comprehensive because they involve direct customer contact. Although the time commitment is considerable, interviews allow the supplier to better understand the customer's business and probe the reasons behind why specific services add value. Some companies require that managers visit their top 5 or 10 accounts a few times a year to discuss performance and satisfaction. A visit to the customer's facility can be crucial in obtaining a true understanding of what is important to the customer and why.

Focus groups are generally used to uncover the reasons behind buying patterns. They are usually comprised of 8 to 12 customers from different companies. Although some customers may be reluctant to discuss certain issues with competitors present, focus groups are particularly useful if the customer base comes from a broad cross-section of industries.

Mail and telephone surveys are effective and efficient methods of gathering statistical data. Surveys are most accurate when they are designed around feedback from direct customer contact and are not based on management's idea of which issues are critical. Offering 800 phone numbers to solicit direct customer feedback is also effective and increasingly popular.

b. *Customers' statements.* Many customers issue unsolicited statements of their minimum requirements to suppliers. These statements are often very explicit, listing specific requirements and expectations. Although this information is crucial to doing business, it may only cover the basics—the minimum a customer expects. For example, a major office supply company's statement specifies requirements regarding order completeness, cycle time, carton labeling, palletization methods, paperwork consistency, and freight bill documentation. Baxter's Hospital Supply Division has a 10-point supplier requirements program that sets out its expectations of suppliers. The requirements for suppliers include assuming responsibility for product and service quality; delivering 100 percent of orders, filled complete, within established lead times; providing 100 percent accurate invoices 100 percent of the time; adhering to minimum notification requirements for any changes to products, service, or terms of doing business; and becoming "EDI-ready" in support of Baxter's efforts to operate in an EDI environment.

Once minimum requirements have been understood, further discussions with customers should build on this framework and help suppliers to understand customer expectations for other value-added services.

In addition to existing customers' statements, lost business reports are an excellent source of feedback from potential customers.

c. *Noise levels.* Noise levels can be used as supplements to direct customer contact. Although a reactive approach, they offer specific feedback on a customer's "hot buttons." Many companies encourage the identification of complaints through 800 numbers, employee investigation of complaints, and exit interviews with lost customers. Some companies even have a formal exit interview with lost customers. Preston Trucking views these exit interviews as a valuable source of information. The chances are great that if one customer has a problem, others who will not complain have the same problem.

A disadvantage of relying on noise levels to handle customer satisfaction issues is that only about 5 percent of customers actually complain. While this does provide some information for future improvement, it does not offer a broad foundation upon which to base satisfaction efforts. Sandoz Chemicals has developed a method of entering customer complaints or inquiries into a system and automatically routing the complaint to the appropriate functional manager for a response. The Sandoz System also allows sales representatives to record recent customer-complaint data on their laptop computers so that they don't make "blindsided" sales calls. This system not only improves service but promotes increased sales effectiveness.

d. *Benchmarking.* Benchmarking against the competition is another approach that can be used to supplement direct customer contact. It provides feedback on current performance relative to the competition, but it does not help to define requirements or expectations. The disadvantage of benchmarking is that there is no indication that the competition is satisfying customers. Basing service goals on the competition, therefore, may be to move in the wrong direction.

3. *Explore the importance of requirements and expectations with customers.* Once customer minimum requirements and expectations have been identified, suppliers should explore the relative importance of each. They must discuss with customers which performance standards the customers consider crucial, important, not im-

portant, and why. This information will help to distinguish between requirements and value-added services. If value-added services are provided but basic requirements are not met, satisfaction will not result.

Another area for discussion is customer perception of current service levels. This provides a rating of current performance and a gauge of which services contribute to competitive advantage. For example, is responsiveness to inquiries, availability of order status information, on-time delivery, or damage-free delivery critical or insignificant in the customers' eyes? How critical is each, relative to the others? What type of an advantage would result from improving these service levels?

Because it may be impractical to satisfy all customer desires at a price the customers are willing to pay, it is important to understand which services are minimum requirements and which would exceed expectations. Providing value-added services costs money, and customers are willing to pay only for services they consider valuable. Suppliers should discuss with customers their willingness to pay for the services they define as important. Upon realizing the cost involved in providing a service, some customers may reevaluate the importance of that service. For example, a major appliance manufacturer discussed product features with its customers and determined that customers, if given the option, would prefer a lower price rather than an expensive ice-maker on the refrigerator door. The manufacturer eliminated the ice-maker from some of its models and was able to lower the price as the customers had requested.

Step 2: Assess Current Service and Capabilities

Once suppliers understand what customers want, suppliers must identify gaps between their current service capabilities and actual service offerings. This involves specifying what it would take to meet specific service goals and identifying current services offered by the competition. This helps to determine which services provide a competitive advantage and which are simply expected from every player in the industry. If the competition offers EDI, the supplier that does not may be at a competitive disadvantage. Similarly, if EDI is a service valued by customers and only one supplier offers it, that company possesses a competitive advantage.

Step 3: Interpret the Gaps between Current Operations and Customer Requirements

Once suppliers understand what customers want as opposed to what suppliers offer, the gaps between the two can be analyzed. Before talking to customers, many companies think the gaps between requirements and current services are small. After talking to customers, they often discover they have misinterpreted customer requirements. Peter Drucker understood the concept of customer satisfaction over 30 years ago when he wrote *Managing for Results*. He said, "What people in the business think they know about the customer and the market is more likely to be wrong than right. There is only one person who really knows: the customer."[3] Once gaps have been identified, they must be examined to determine the benefit (i.e., increased customer value) to be gained from closing them.

When asked about their requirements and expectations, a consumer products company's customers reported that on-time delivery and damage-free delivery are their two most important criteria when evaluating distribution service. When the company examined its service offering compared to what the customers desired, it found a large gap in on-time service but no gap for damage-free delivery. The company also looked at how the competition was rated in these areas. It realized that its customers had reported that the competition offered superior on-time and damage-free delivery services. Given this information, the consumer products company determined that closing the gap for on-time delivery was crucial to its success, and that improving damage-free rates to exceed customer expectations would provide a competitive advantage. The next step for the company is to identify options for eliminating the gaps to gain strategic advantage. To improve on-time delivery, the company could work with existing carriers to improve performance or it could hire new carriers, manage delivery-date promises, and improve shipment-tracking capabilities. Steps to improving damage-free delivery might include better packaging, better loading and unloading techniques, and enhanced employee training in product handling.

Once improvement alternatives have been identified, the company must analyze the tradeoffs, benefits, costs, and risks associated with closing the gaps. Some benefits of closing the gaps include increased customer satisfaction as a result of improved service levels. Although it is difficult to directly measure the benefits of improved service, one way is by means of an improved customer satisfaction rating on a survey or questionnaire administered periodically throughout the improvement process. Other benefits may include increased revenues, customer loyalty, competitive advantage, and referrals. Avoidance of lost sales due to poor service is also a benefit of closing these gaps. Based on this analysis, the company must decide if the benefits outweigh the costs. Of course these dimensions vary by customer or market segment, and require detailed analysis in each specific situation.

Step 4: Tailor Service to Meet Customer-Specific Needs

When suppliers ask customers what is important to them and then analyze the results, it becomes obvious that different groups of customers require different services and service levels. In order to satisfy as many customers as possible, companies should establish customer segments with similar requirements and expectations. Many suppliers segment customers by industry, product type, volume, or profitability. The underlying criterion, however, should always be similar requirements. For example, segmenting by "overnight" or "second-day" delivery makes more sense than segmenting by business type—supermarket versus wholesale club. Some customers like to receive products on pallets, others prefer slipsheets. By examining these natural segments, suppliers will be better able to tailor services.

A major airline company failed to recognize its customer segments and therefore provided unsatisfactory service to a segment of travelers, who in turn switched to a different airline. The airline in question used Europe to New York flights to feed its

New York-to-west coast flights. Because European flights are frequently delayed due to congestion and weather, the airline held the New York-to-west coast flights for the European travelers to make their connections. As a result the airline often departed late, offering travelers from Europe exceptional service while alienating bicoastal travelers. Finally, lost business forced the airline to review its strategy and identify the needs of its various customer segments.

Identical products may have different service requirements, depending on how customers use them. In the paper industry, newspapers order newsprint based on relatively long lead times. Their delivery requirements are fairly flexible—generally "week of," or "month of." Exact quantities are not required; newspapers allow a variance of as much as 10 percent on total tons ordered. Although commercial publishers use essentially the same newsprint, their requirements are much more stringent. Lead times seldom extend beyond 72 hours, with 24 hours commonplace. At the very least, the delivery requirement is "day of," and specific delivery times are often required. Because commercial publishers order to specific press runs, they require exact quantities. It is critical to a supplier's success that these segments are recognized and that service is tailored to their individual needs.

No matter what the industry, differentiating service must be weighed against the cost of providing that service. If a service is valuable enough to customers, they may be willing to pay a premium for it if the competition does not offer the same product package at a lower price. It is important to segment those customers who are willing to pay for services from those who are not. Raising prices and increasing services may drive some customers to the competition while satisfying others. General Electric experimented over a two-year period with varied levels of repair service for out-of-warranty appliances. GE found that the law of diminishing returns is applicable: There is a point at which each incremental investment yields lower returns than the previous investment. To find that point, customers must be segmented so that suppliers can provide the appropriate level of service for each customer. Optimally, segmentation provides a method to operate profitably while satisfying as many customers as possible.

Step 5: Create Service Offerings Based on Customer Requirements

The next step in implementing a customer-focused distribution strategy is to create service offerings based on customer requirements and expectations. Based on its analysis, the consumer products company mentioned earlier must next determine what service levels it will strive for. Exact levels of on-time delivery and damage-free delivery must be established as goals, and the methods to achieve these goals must be put in place. For example, "on-time" must be defined for each customer segment and a corresponding goal must be set. This segmentation will help to avoid underserving some customers and overserving others. A multitiered service package offers higher service levels to customers who want them and are willing to pay for them.

When AT&T's computer group placed a 99.8 percent incoming acceptance rate requirement on Intel's materials, the original equipment manufacturer had to increase its quality standards from the current 97 percent incoming acceptance rate.

This meant an improvement of 1500 percent! Intel, in turn, demanded better quality from its suppliers, and got it by working with them in a quality improvement process. Thus, Intel was able to achieve the level of service its customers required.

In order to satisfy customers and exceed their expectations, suppliers must not only meet requirements but provide value-added services. As competitors begin to leverage customer satisfaction as a competitive advantage, suppliers are focusing on customer perceptions of value. Suppliers are working to meet customers' minimum requirements in order to cross the threshold of customer satisfaction. If these requirements are not met, the supplier is generally evaluated negatively by the customers. If the requirements are met, the supplier is often given no credit, because the customers expect them. It is when the supplier *exceeds* minimum customer requirements that it begins to achieve customer satisfaction and add value. These value-added characteristics are the differentiating factor that creates competitive advantage. As one author put it, "Meeting minimum requirements keeps a company in the race, but it seldom helps it win one."[4]

Step 6: Measure and Track Performance and Improvement

Measurement of the satisfaction process is crucial both to determining performance and to motivating employees. Quantitative performance measurement plays a key role in the ongoing improvement process by facilitating statistical analysis. However, customer feedback is the only accurate indicator of actual satisfaction, because a company's success at meeting customer requirements is based on customer perceptions of the product and service package. A customer satisfaction index (CSI) is one way to quantitatively measure overall satisfaction levels. It is important to measure all of the product package attributes, because satisfaction is interpreted based on the customers' entire experience. A CSI is designed to evaluate where the supplier stands in the customers' eyes by rating relevant criteria on a scale from 1 to 10.

When developing a CSI, suppliers must comprehensively understand customer requirements and expectations. These requirements and expectations are then expanded into criteria that must be met in order to achieve requirements and exceed expectations. For example, postsales support is a common value-added service across many businesses. Criteria for providing postsales support differ by industry but may include timeliness of response, convenience of service, timeliness of problem resolution, and employee courtesy.[5]

CSIs should be administered to rate suppliers on pertinent satisfaction criteria and to measure performance and improvement over time. The CSI, along with direct contact, helps to identify problem areas, recognize changing requirements, and monitor improvement. American Express conducts frequent focus groups and follow-up interviews to determine what customers value. The company then uses this information to develop customer satisfaction surveys. These surveys are distributed to 12,000 customers a year. How often CSIs are administered varies, based on the industry and the frequency of other types of contact. Some companies offer the opportunity to fill out a CSI upon each contact with the company; others use CSIs on a quarterly basis as a tool to gather quantitative, concrete feedback. Marriott's Guest Service Index is an example of one kind of CSI. Questionnaires are left in every guest's room to continuously monitor feedback. The CSI is also a beneficial tool in communicating improvement progress to employees. Marriott bases rewards and incentives on CSI improvement, to motivate employees to be more customer-focused. Dell Computers includes a questionnaire disk when it delivers its computers. Panasonic attaches reply cards to each product sold.

Step 7: Maintain Continuous Improvement Process

Customer satisfaction must be an ongoing process, because customer requirements change as a customer's manufacturing process, product line, and customer base change. In order to maintain the desired level of customer satisfaction, suppliers must be in touch with these shifting requirements. There is no successfully proven level of customer contact, but customers agree that frequent contact is necessary. The types of customer contact vary, but they can be categorized in three ways: initial information gathering, periodic updates, and continuous contact.

1. The initial information gathering is the first time customers are formally contacted regarding their needs and their level of satisfaction. As mentioned earlier, this contact can take the form of a personal interview, focus group, mail or telephone survey, sales call, etc. The purpose of this interaction is to gauge customer perception of supplier performance on a variety of factors, segment customers, and determine improvement initiatives.

2. Once suppliers understand what customers initially require and expect, suppliers must periodically check the status of both their ability to meet the requirements as well as changes in customer requirements since the previous contact. Because customer perception of service is the most important factor in achieving customer satisfaction, only the customers can ascertain whether service has improved or not. Periodic contact gives the supplier an idea of how well it is meeting customer requirements and how well it is responding to customer needs. Often a downturn in survey results indicates that customer needs are changing and the new requirements are not being met. As mentioned earlier, customer requirements can change for a variety of reasons including new products, new distribution channels, new competitors, new customers, or new customer demands. Periodic contact by mail or telephone surveys, personal interviews, and even focus groups help suppliers meet customer needs and avoid future lapses in satisfaction. Xerox contacts each customer at least twice a year to measure satisfaction levels. Federal Express conducts quarterly surveys across various segments of its business.

3. Continuous customer-specific communication is significant for key accounts and for the most profitable customers. Ongoing discussion of satisfaction levels, customer facility visits, and other communication methods provide immediate feedback and allow suppliers to anticipate changes and problems before they occur. Both customers and suppliers can benefit from such an interchange by designing and executing process improvements that benefit both parties. For example, key suppliers of Bose Corporation place representatives at Bose facilities to ensure that requirements are constantly being met, reviewed, and updated. Nalco Chemical assigns teams of engineers to work full-time at customer facilities to ensure that to-

day's requirements are being met and tomorrow's requirements are proactively identified.

Harley-Davidson motorcycle company sends a letter from the president of the motorcycle division to every customer one month after it receives the warranty card to inquire about the customer's level of satisfaction. Twelve months later, a follow-up letter is sent to update the customer's satisfaction. In addition, Harley executives must attend Harley-Davidson rallies wearing T-shirts that identify them as the "guys from the factory," and customers are encouraged to discuss their product and service experiences with these executives. Other continuous customer contact includes unannounced random dealer visits and discussions with the competition's customers to find out why Harley-Davidson does not have their business.

Achieving Logistics Excellence: Tools and Techniques

Once the strategic framework has been established for an effective customer-focused logistics process, there are several critical tools and high-leverage techniques that can be employed at the tactical level to achieve excellence and breakthrough improvements. Most companies have not yet established a foundation of logistics excellence to support a customer satisfaction strategy. This foundation should be built on a few critical logistics management tools including goal setting, performance measures, and nontraditional methodologies. In addition, high-leverage breakthrough techniques include failsafing the logistics process, reducing cycle times, integrating operations management, implementing shipper–carrier partnerships, and implementing customer–supplier partnerships.

Logistics Management Tools: Goal Setting

Goals give meaning to measures; they help determine performance effectiveness. They also drive improvement toward increased customer value and satisfaction. Without goals, value measurement is impossible.

There are two basic philosophies for setting goals: incremental and quantum improvement. Incremental goals target gradual improvement, and while frequently attainable, they rarely challenge employees to think differently about a problem. There is a real danger that competitors in pursuit of quantum improvements will pass by the incremental goal setter. On the other hand, "stretch" goals are typically set according to best or leadership practices (often identified through external benchmarks). The only way to realize a stretch goal is to think differently about a task or process, often resulting in fundamental change, quantum improvements, and a noticeable increase in value-added activities.

In their book, *Maximum Performance Management,* Joseph Boyett and Henry Conn describe three kinds of goals managers should use in their goal-setting processes.[6] The first is a long-term goal, i.e., a desired level of performance one to two years in the future that usually represents significant improvement over the current performance level. The second type is a short-term goal, normally attainable over a 3-to-12-month horizon. A short-term goal should be set at a level that exceeds the average but not the current best and should be negotiated between management and employees. Finally, a minimum goal is less than or equal to the current average, but not below the current worst. Minimum and short-term goals act as specification limits for the activity or process being measured. Boyett and Conn believe that this three-tiered goal-setting process combines the best aspects of incremental and stretch goals.

Logistics Management Tools: Performance Measures

Performance measurement plays a broad role in the pursuit of logistics excellence and creation of customer value. Companies use measurement programs to:

- *Facilitate communication.* Clearly defining measures in a way that is meaningful to each party involved simplifies the task of communicating potential problems and identifying improvement opportunities.

- *Identify areas that need improvement.* If the answers to "how much? how many? how far?" etc. aren't what the manager expects, the measures have helped to identify potential improvement areas.

- *Gather data to understand problems.* Understanding problems often requires looking beyond *what* is going on to *why* it is occurring.

- *Evaluate alternatives.* Measures provide an objective means of comparison.

- *Monitor progress.* Once goals have been set, measures enable managers to track progress and make any necessary corrections.

- *Quantify and report results.* By having measures to quantify results, management can identify the benefit of its investments and report results to customers and shareholders.

There are three major categories of measures used to track quality and productivity in logistics. These are service quality (to customers and from vendors), productivity, and process effectiveness.

1. *Service quality.* These measures are typically more sensitive than productivity measurement, because service quality lies in the eyes of the beholder. Suppliers view service quality measures as a surrogate for customer perceptions of service. In most companies, service quality focuses on the essentials (often internally determined) of customer service. However, some quality leaders have begun to measure quality against value-added service requirements. And recently, more customers are implementing their own measurement systems for tracking and feeding back service quality.

2. *Productivity.* Measuring logistics productivity means measuring the efficiency with which the logistics process meets requirements. Generally, productivity is calculated as the ratio of real output produced to real input consumed. Effective logistics measures include inputs (direct hourly labor, inventory levels, fuel, cycle times, etc.) and outputs (orders, costs, shipments, line items, etc.).

3. *Process effectiveness.* This measurement includes both internal customer service quality (an order entry clerk processing an order from a sales representative, a

warehouse operator receiving a pick list from the order entry department, etc.) and key external benchmarks of process effectiveness. This dual measurement is based on the assumption that a process cannot consistently satisfy the customer if internal activities break down.

These measures form the logistics measurement system. There are two major steps in designing a measurement system: (1) selecting the key measures and (2) developing a reporting capability. There are four key questions that help to identify the best measures:

a. What are we trying to accomplish?
b. What is a good measure of this?
c. What is the formula for calculating this?
d. What are the best data sources?

By following this logic flow, companies can avoid data overload and ensure that their measures are on target. The effectiveness of the measures ultimately selected can be tested against seven characteristics: validity, coverage, comparability, completeness, usefulness, compatibility, and cost effectiveness. There is no perfect set of measures; only a blend of potential measures can create an overall logistics quality and productivity measurement system that supports the customer-focused strategy.

Designing an effective measurement-reporting capability requires access to information technology. Leading quality companies make information support and technology available to aid measurement and analysis throughout the organization. They use these systems to measure, track, and report the quality of suppliers, logistics service providers, internal processes, and most importantly, the ultimate service value delivered to customers.

Logistics Management Tools: Nontraditional Methodologies

To establish competitive advantage based on customer value, future improvements in logistics must come from nontraditional areas. Traditionally, improvements to logistics performance have been measured in terms of cost reduction and productivity gains. The primary sources of these improvements were within the distribution function: transportation and warehousing. In the future, leading quality companies will rely less heavily on these incremental improvement areas and drive toward quantum improvement in nontraditional areas, with nontraditional methods. One such method, quality function deployment (QFD), also referred to as the "House of Quality," is discussed in detail in the appendix at the end of this chapter.

Breakthrough Techniques

Leading-edge companies that have achieved high levels of logistics excellence employ five techniques on which they build a logistics competitive advantage.

1. *Failsafing the logistics process.* Failing to get the basics right undermines the value-adding services, no matter how good they are. Therefore, preventative systems, procedures, and techniques that reduce the likelihood of failure of essential

services allow companies to proactively protect their advantage and their customers' value.

2. *Reducing cycle times.* This technique yields substantial quality and productivity benefit, squeezing out low-value activities to streamline operations and enhance value-added activities.

3. *Integrating operations management.* Many firms use this approach to draw together all major operational functions at the strategic, tactical, and transaction processing levels. Current applications rely less on formal organizational restructuring and more on common goals, shared accountability, and integrated systems.

4. *Implementing shipper–carrier partnerships.* Once a company has begun the internal logistics integration process, it may be ready to establish shipper–carrier partnerships, typically characteristic of Stage III companies. These partnerships rely heavily on concentrated business through supplier reduction, joint improvement efforts, formal measurement systems, information sharing, and shared savings for mutual benefit. Ultimately, the end customer will benefit from improved service quality.

5. *Implementing customer–supplier partnerships.* Throughout all industries, customers are concentrating their business with a limited number of suppliers to simplify their business processes, increase leverage, improve quality, and reduce cots. Shipper–carrier partnerships are only one example. While some resistance still exists, partnership momentum is increasing, and true partnering provides the greatest potential for increased value and satisfaction.

These tools and techniques are management's best resources in the pursuit of logistics excellence, the foundation for a successful customer-focused satisfaction strategy.

Keys to Successful Implementation

Customer satisfaction improvement efforts involve all business processes and, therefore, require commitment from all aspects of an organization. Four key principles govern successful implementation of a customer-focused distribution strategy and the realization of distribution excellence:

1. Commitment from the CEO
2. Companywide customer satisfaction strategy
3. Customer satisfaction focus in all business processes
4. Employee empowerment

Commitment from the CEO

Because achieving customer satisfaction requires the integration of all business processes, support must come from the CEO. Concentrating on the customer requires a new way of thinking and doing business that often elicits a skeptical response from employees. Support from the top is crucial in motivating employees to change their current practices and focus on the customer. The commitment of the CEO and senior management reinforces the importance of customer satisfaction and motivates employees by example. Additionally, a customer-focused company does not evaluate employees on internal standards alone, but management incorporates customer satisfaction into employee and department evaluation criteria.

An excellent example of CEO support is Brunswick's CEO, Jack Reichert. Reichert found out from one of his customers that a bowling ball his company produced was defective. The bowling ball performed extremely well and was used to win many professional tours, until it was put into mass production and a chemical compound mistake was made. When left in extreme heat, the bowling ball turned to the consistency of a marshmallow. The CEO, concerned with customer satisfaction, ordered every ball replaced free of charge and the customers' money refunded. Reichert confronted the responsible department heads, who were aware of the mistake and thought the problem could be handled through warranty adjustments. The managers who did not think that the problem was severe are no longer with Brunswick. Overall, the catastrophe cost the company $2.5 million but earned the loyalty of many customers.

Companywide Customer Satisfaction Strategy

The overall company must have a customer-focused strategy as its foundation. Then every business process must interpret and implement the strategy to make a positive contribution to customer value. Senior management must make customer satisfaction a part of its mission statement and vision, moving the entire company in the direction of customer satisfaction. Once all aspects of a company are focused on customers, shareholders begin to reap the benefits of the efforts.

Customer Satisfaction Focus in All Business Processes

As mentioned above, customer satisfaction requires the commitment of all parts of an organization. In order to reach the goal of satisfied customers, all business processes must be customer-focused. If just one business process is internally focused, the entire value chain is endangered. Each process builds off of or is indirectly affected by the others, making the commitment toward customer satisfaction throughout the entire organization crucial.

Employee Empowerment

Customers drive business, but performance (e.g., logistics) excellence depends on the employees. Without employee commitment, customer satisfaction is bound to fail. Often customer contact occurs with front-line employees, giving them great influence over the customer satisfaction cycle. It is these employees who must be empowered to do whatever it takes to satisfy customers. These individuals must be motivated and rewarded for satisfying customers.

Implementation Pitfalls

In addition to these keys to success, there are several common pitfalls that should be considered prior to implementation. First, don't focus so intently on improving performance against a certain set of requirements that a change in requirements goes unnoticed. To prevent such a mistake, the logistics quality and productivity improvement process should tie in to regular updates of service strategy, offerings, and goals. Other common obstacles to watch out for include inadequate systems support, internal functional organizational boundaries, and inadequate employee training.

Summary of Benefits

Satisfying customers yields many tangible and intangible benefits. Satisfied customers will bring repeat business and promote new business through referrals. Because competitors are able to produce the same product at the same price, companies are turning to customer satisfaction to gain market share and increase profits. The Strategic Planning Institute published a study that reports that companies perceived to be providers of high service experience an annual increase in market share of 6 percent, while low service providers lose market share at a rate of 2 percent/yr. Attention to customer needs is driving the success of innovative businesses.

Satisfied customers are repeat customers. Business is a two-way street. If a company works to satisfy its customers, it will be rewarded by increased revenues and repeat business. Of 100 satisfied Chrysler owners, 58 purchased their next car from the same dealer. Of the dissatisfied customers of a U.S. capital goods manufacturer, 82 percent switched to the competition. Even when a product failure occurs, if it is handled in a manner that meets or exceeds the customer's expectations and he is satisfied with the results, his loyalty will increase despite the product failure. Chances are high that satisfied, repeat customers will eventually become multiple-product, high-volume customers. As long as services meet their ever-changing needs, these customers will remain loyal and demonstrate a willingness to pay for a company's ability to meet their requirements.

This loyalty directly impacts the bottom line. It costs five to eight times as much to attract a new customer as it does to maintain a current customer. Satisfied customers also refer friends and colleagues, increasing revenues without additional marketing costs. A market analysis conducted by a major German frozen foods delivery company determined that 1000 satisfied customers generate a 3 percent increase in the customer base. That equates to 30 new customers for every 1000 satisfied ones. On the other hand, customers that are not satisfied voice their dissatisfaction more than satisfied customers talk about their positive experiences. Negative publicity can significantly damage a supplier's reputation, making satisfaction a necessity.

Satisfaction Is an Ongoing Process

Customer satisfaction is not measured solely at the time of purchase or at the time of use but spans from prepurchase to past the life of the product. The level of satisfaction associated with a product or service can increase or decrease over time. It is affected by pre- and postpurchase contact with employees, long-term product performance, maintenance and warranty service, and any other incident during which the customers come in contact with or are affected by the company, its employees, products, or services. Therefore, a customer-focused logistics strategy that incorporates a formal program for ongoing improvement supports value creation and ensures customer satisfaction and long-term benefit.

Conclusion

Companies around the world are recognizing that satisfying customers is key to achieving competitive advantage in the 1990s and beyond. As customers become more sophisticated and demanding, close attention to their needs is driving the success of innovative businesses. Leading companies understand that product quality is no longer sufficient for competitive positioning. Only superior customer value can ensure complete customer satisfaction and ultimately lead to increased market share and profits. And only customers can determine when the products and services they receive meet or exceed their expectations.

Successful companies also know that logistics and distribution service quality is a critical component in achieving customer satisfaction. Companies with customer-focused logistics strategies will be able to identify and meet the high service levels customers are coming to expect. And because satisfying customers is an ongoing process, companies will have to continually monitor and adapt their customer satisfaction strategies just to stay ahead of the competition. Across all business processes and on all organizational levels, companies must follow a strategy that focuses every effort on the customers. Though these efforts are not without cost, the loyalty of satisfied customers who know they are valued will reap rewards far into the future.

Appendix:
The "House of Quality"

In Japan, a widely used approach to arrive at a customer satisfaction strategy is called *quality function deployment* (*QFD*). It adds discipline and rigor to the strategy development process. Specifically, QFD is a structured approach that relates customer requirements to design characteristics of a product or a process. It has been used widely in product development, but only recently adapted for analyzing service requirements and structuring offerings. Many U.S. companies that are implementing QFD consider the technique a major tool for gaining competitive advantage.

The QFD approach is a framework for analysis that will be widely used in customer service strategy development in the future. The framework is often called "the House of Quality" because of its shape. Although visually complex, the House of Quality follows a sound, logical approach for understanding and analyzing customer requirements and preparing a response (see Fig. 30-3).

Part 1 of the diagram lists customer requirements—what customers say they want. Typically, these are stated in the customers' own words: on-time delivery, easy order

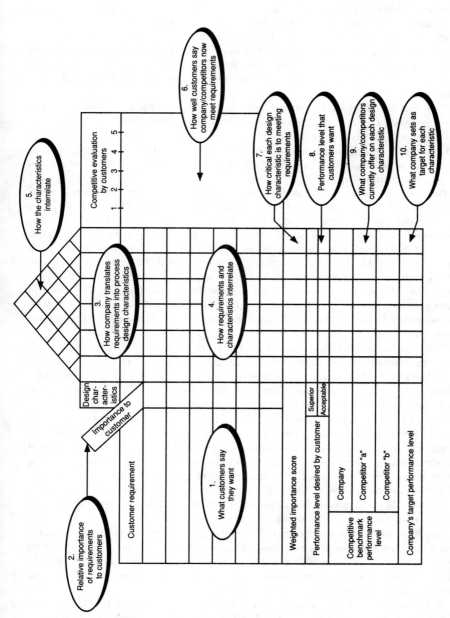

Figure 30-3. The House of Quality. (*From Patrick M. Byrne and William J. Markham, Improving Quality and Productivity in the Logistics Process: Achieving Customer Satisfaction Breakthroughs, Council of Logistics Management, Oak Brook, IL, 1991*)

placement, undamaged product, etc. Part 2 of the diagram ranks the relative importance of the requirements to the customers, usually on a 10-point scale. The information for parts 1 and 2 comes directly from the customers.

Part 3 of the diagram lists how the company translates customer requirements into product or process design characteristics. For example, if on-time delivery is a customer requirement, then the process characteristics that drive "on-time" might include the level of inventory on hand, carrier equipment availability, and order lead time.

Part 4 of the diagram is a simple relationship matrix that examines how each process design characteristic relates to each customer requirement. Here, the typical approach involves using three levels of relationship—strong, moderate, and nonexistent—and placing symbols in the cells of the matrix to indicate the nature of each relationship. Using these symbols helps people visually understand and interpret the relationships.

Part 5 of the diagram (the peak of the house) tracks the interrelationships between the various process design characteristics. Here, too, a symbolic scale helps show a strong positive correlation, a medium positive correlation, a medium negative correlation, or a strong negative correlation. Characteristics that have a positive correlation support one another, while those with negative correlations work against one another (and indicate the existence of a tradeoff decision). An example of logistics process characteristics that are negatively correlated is local inventory stocks in branch locations (to support same-day delivery) and high product fill rates across a broad product line. Dispersing a broad product line of inventory to 50 or more local branches makes it difficult and expensive to achieve high fill rates on all items.

The first five parts of the House of Quality focus on customer requirements and how the company can respond to meet those requirements. Part 6 is an evaluation from the customers' perspective of how well the company and its competitors are doing in meeting customer requirements. Typically, this is done on a five-point scale, and the input comes from surveys such as CSIs.

Part 7 of the diagram estimates how critical each design characteristic is to meeting the requirements listed above. The score is calculated by weighting each requirement a characteristic meets against the importance to the customer of that requirement and the degree to which that characteristic relates to the requirement. Thus, if a requirement had an importance score of 8 and the characteristic strongly addressed the requirement (i.e., had a weight of 9), the characteristic would get a score of 8 × 9, or 72 against that requirement. Adding the scores across all requirements yields the total weighted importance score.

Part 8 of the diagram represents the company's interpretation of performance levels that customers want. For example, if the customer survey process identifies 92 to 95 percent as the acceptable range for line-item fill rate, and pinpoints 98 percent as clearly superior, then these would be the values used here for the process design characteristics related to order fill rates.

Part 9 benchmarks the company and its competitors on each of the design characteristics. This helps the firm to decide if it is at a competitive advantage, at parity, or at a disadvantage. Using these data along with the performance levels the customers want (Part 8) and the weighted importance of each characteristic (Part 7), a company can decide what the target performance level should be for each of the design characteristics (Part 10).

QFD is an emerging tool for understanding customer requirements and establishing service responses. It is a structured way of planning, communicating, and documenting customer requirements as well as the company's planned responses. Based on widespread successes in manufacturing and a few service-oriented examples in North America, it promises to be a major step forward in formalizing the service strategy development process.

References

1. J. M. Juran, *Juran's Quality Control Handbook*, McGraw-Hill, New York, 1988.
2. "CE Roundtable—Can't Get No (Customer) Satisfaction," *Chief Executive*, Sept./Oct. 1989, pp. 72–92.
3. Peter Drucker, *Managing for Results*, Harper and Row, New York, 1964.
4. Craig Cina, "Creating an Effective Customer Satisfaction Program," *Journal of Business and Industrial Marketing*, Summer/Fall 1989, vol. 4, pp. 33–42.
5. William Band, "Create a Customer Satisfaction Index to Improve Your Performance," *Sales and Marketing Management in Canada*, July 1990, pp. 58–59.
6. Joseph Boyett and Henry Conn, *Maximum Performance Management*, Glenbridge Publishing Ltd., Macomb, IL, 1988.

References

PART 5
Case Studies

Case Study **A**

Distribution in the Office Furniture Environment

Ralph W. Fairbanks

Director of Distribution, Haworth, Inc.

Company Data

Haworth, Inc., of Holland, Michigan, is one of the largest manufacturers of office furniture in the world. Haworth's motto, "Excellence in Office Furnishings," is a commitment that is taken seriously.

Founded in 1948 as Modern Products by G. W. Haworth, the company became a major factor in the floor-to-ceiling movable partitions market during the 1950s and 1960s. In the 1970s the company began development of an open-plan office furnishings system, and redirected the company's efforts exclusively to that market in response to the changing needs of the office environment.

HAWORTH®

The company name was changed to Haworth, Inc. in 1975, and in 1976 the company's founder, G. W. Haworth, was elevated to chairman of the board. His son, Richard, became the new president.

In 1976, Haworth sold its floor-to-ceiling movable partitions interest and concentrated its efforts on its UniGroup® open-plan office furniture system. That year began a period of rapid expansion and growth. After 1976, sales increased annually by 20 to 60 percent for many years—and continue to increase at a rate twice the industry growth average. Sales of Haworth furnishings exceeded $600 million in 1991.

Today, Haworth is a full-line manufacturer of office furniture, employing more than 4500 worldwide. Products include UniGroup®, PLACES®, and RACE® open-plan systems, freestanding and panel-hung electronic office furniture, wood and metal desks and credenzas, modular furniture, files, and numerous seating lines.

Haworth has acquired several companies in recent years, to broaden its product lines and position the company to meet customer needs. Acquisitions include, in 1988, the German-based Comforto, which manufactures office, auditorium, reception, lounge, and institutional seating and conference tables; in 1990, Mueller Furniture Company, which manufactures executive seating and wood furniture, Lunstead, Inc., which produces wood casegoods lines, and Kinetics, Inc., which

added institutional furniture and office seating to the Haworth line; in 1991, Myrtle Desk Company, which offered wood desks and seating lines. The acquisition of a significant interest in Cortal and Seldex, the two largest office furniture manufacturers in Portugal, and in Mobilier International, a leading French manufacturer of office furniture, has created new European manufacturing and distribution opportunities for Haworth.

Haworth is recognized as an accomplished company that has gained recognition for industry firsts in electrified panel-based systems office furniture and electronic support furniture. Today, Haworth continues on with the dynamic growth and innovative, award-winning product development program that have made it a world leader in the office furniture industry.

The following distribution study explains how these challenges have been met. Providing product at the right time, in the right sequence, in the right quantity and condition are the standards of excellence at Haworth that ensure total customer satisfaction.

Distribution at Haworth

Over the years, the distribution function has been transformed from a shipping department to a key player in the corporate strategy. The departments that make up Distribution include Receiving, Raw Material Storage, Finished Goods Warehousing, Truck Load and LTL Shipping, and Transportation. Also included are Distribution Engineering, Packaging Engineering, International Distribution, and Sales Aid Fulfillment Operations. Each of these departments is responsible for the efficient flow of material to and from the plants. And they must also ensure that finished goods arrive at the customer's location on time and damage-free.

The raw material storage function has systematically been transferred to individual plants, where appropriate. Point-of-use receiving has allowed raw material to be stored as closely as possible to the manufacturing area where it will be used. For example, panel fabric is received through the panel plant receiving doors and is stored near the panel assembly area. Steel is brought into the file and pedestal drawer plant on flatbed trucks, and likewise is stored as closely as possible to the fabrication area. The remaining raw materials in the Distribution warehouse remain there due to space constraints in the plants.

The critical factor in point-of-use receiving was a close working relationship with the various suppliers. The delivery of their products had to be made to a specific dock door according to a daily schedule. This meant that the supplier had to adjust his production scheduling and warehousing plan to support a JIT (just-in-time) environment. Additionally, the quality of their products had to be high, because any delay due to defective parts would stop production lines. Haworth worked with suppliers at their locations to certify them for consistent levels of error-free parts. This then eliminated the need for incoming inspection, and the parts moved directly into manufacturing. The net result was a better utilization of space, improved quality of product, and faster throughput, with the ability to be flexible to the changing demands of the customer.

Today's customer has more choices than ever before. A typical concern about a company's distribution system is the number of stock keeping units (SKUs) it handles. In the office furniture business, this is almost irrelevant. At one time, office furniture was fairly standard. One could order a wood desk or a steel desk, and there were few color choices to be made. The color of the office might be determined by the paint on the wall or the color of the carpeting. With the advent of systems furniture, all that changed. Panels and components can now be specified from hundreds of choices of colors and fabrics. The size and style of the panel depends on the configuration of the office. Panel options offer further choices—power, nonpower, ported, glass, gabled, etc. The combination of panels alone creates the possibility of over 100 million SKUs! By adding work surfaces, overhead storage units, chairs, files, pedestal drawers, lights, and special products, the choices are almost limitless.

Because the choice of colors, sizes, styles, and options is nearly unlimited, virtually all product is made to order. Customer orders are received, raw material is ordered, and product is manufactured to the specific order. Distribution becomes a final assembly point for product arriving from various plants and suppliers. Just as a plant takes pieces and produces parts, Distribution takes parts and produces customer orders. In this way, Distribution operates similarly to manufacturing.

Over the years, lead time for shipment of product diminished from nearly 24 weeks between order placement and shipment to 5 weeks or fewer. In order to produce the specific items requested on an order, the suppliers must be given a general forecast of shipment levels so that capacity planning can be determined. Fabric, for example, can be spun but not dyed or woven. When the final color and style is known, the finished fabric can be delivered within two to three weeks. This allows Haworth to build panels within the published lead times. A similar process occurs for steel, wood, and other materials.

In addition Haworth offers a Quick-Ship program, where certain colors, fabrics, and options can be delivered in five days. These products are produced and shipped through the same distribution system as regular product, but are expedited to ensure prompt shipment.

After production, the furniture arrives at the Distribution Center from the various plants and suppliers, according to a schedule that was determined just after order entry. Products are either stored briefly to await completion of the order or sent directly to the loading dock. They are then shipped on the most appropriate mode of transportation. Since most large orders are going to an office site, the trailers frequently are loaded in sequence to arrive in a specific order. This allows the installation crew to unload, unpack, and install with efficiency.

Product movement requires continuous control. Communication with the manufacturing plants, planning, and customer service is critical to the successful completion of each order.

Restrictions at the job site must also be taken into consideration during delivery. Areas under construction, or the unavailability of elevators, may interfere with the arrival of the delivery vehicle or with unloading of the product. Move-in schedules also play an important part in the installation. Office buildings may be available for furniture installation only in the evening or on weekends. Elevators must be scheduled to avoid jams at the unloading dock. These are all issues that Distribution must take into consideration when servicing the customer.

In order to make this complicated process work, two things are critical to the support of manufacturing and distribution operations: well-trained people, and computer support systems.

Employees at Haworth are referred to as "members," because everyone is critical to creating the teamwork required to meet customer expectations. Participative management has been ingrained as a way of life at Haworth. Members expect that everyone is part of a process and should contribute to the success of the process. Likewise, in Distribution, members have formed numerous QIP (quality improvement process) teams, which address opportunities for improvement in every area. All members receive training in problem solving, just-in-time, and quality improvement processes, in addition to technical job training.

Computer support systems allow members to track the progress of the customer order from Order Entry, through Manufacturing, to Distribution. These systems have become more sophisticated as lead times have decreased and product offerings have increased. For example, the locator system in Distribution is available 23 hours a day, and Manufacturing operates on a daily MRP (material requirements planning) run. Members can access the data through fourth-generation languages like NOMAD to measure past performance and assist decision making.

Distribution monitors the completion of product from the plants and provides them with feedback as to the successful completion of their orders. In this way, Distribution serves as Haworth's internal customer. In an environment where products are made to order, problems that arise at the end of the manufacturing process must be corrected immediately in order to meet expected customer delivery dates.

Quality

The business world is undergoing a quality revolution. Nowhere is this more apparent than in logistics. Customer expectations must be met for companies to stay in business, and logistics significantly impacts customer expectations. It has been described as an operation that provides time and place utility. Basically, this means that goods are delivered where and when they were intended to be. This coincides with a basic definition of quality: *to meet or exceed the customer's expectation.* When customers expect to receive a shipment at a promised time, they are gravely disappointed when it doesn't happen. Or, when it is damaged or shorted, they may consider this the next time they order. A successful logistics organization is sometimes referred to as "invisible," because every operation happens as planned. Therefore no corrections need to be made, no last-minute helter-skelter takes place, and the customer is not put in an embarrassing situation if they were relying on accurate and timely delivery.

Haworth is particularly sensitive to this, since the final product, an office furniture system, is actually constructed at the job site. Because the product is assembled in the customer's building, each part is subject to scrutiny by the customer. Everything must be there and be in the proper size and color.

Imagine buying an automobile that was to be delivered in pieces to your garage, where a special team would come in and completely assemble it. What if the steering wheel were missing from the shipment! It's not enough that 99 percent of the car was delivered; it still remains unusable. This also applies to office furniture. It would be difficult to work in an office if there were no chair to sit in or desk to write on, and almost impossible to function if the lights didn't work.

To prevent incomplete orders, Haworth Distribution monitors the shipping process at several points, ensuring that the right product is delivered at the right time to the right customer. These checkpoints are described in the Haworth Distribution Quality Plan, a document that describes the authority and responsibility of each member to maintain quality standards. Distribution has established the plan in order to monitor critical areas where processes must be followed correctly. All Distribution members have authority to establish and support the Quality Assurance process. They have been charged with the responsibility of complying with the procedures defined in the Distribution Quality Plan, departmental procedures, and training programs. Members may halt any process or stop any shipment that violates applicable quality standards. They may also determine when the condition has been corrected so that shipments may continue.

Quality improvement is a never-ending process. As such, zero defects is the ultimate goal. And a defect, whether it is in a product or service, is defined by the customer. Haworth has established intermediate goals that progressively lead to zero defects.

Quality and service goals are based on feedback from customers. Product or service complaints are documented on Field Problem Reports (FPRs). This information is analyzed, and preventive measures are taken to avoid recurrence. The Top 10 field complaints are identified, and action plans are established to address each issue. The resulting objectives become part of both management and hourly individual performance objectives. At least 35 percent of a member's individual performance objectives, the highest category on an individual's performance evaluation, are quality-related.

The highest recognition for a company's quality efforts is the Malcolm Baldrige National Quality Award. Just applying for the award is a worthwhile process, as it provides a means of objectively measuring the organization's total quality commitment to meeting customer requirements. Strengths and weaknesses in the organization's various processes are identified. Improvement in products and services to Haworth customers is the greatest reward for the extensive application process.

Customer Service

Haworth Distribution works closely with Haworth's Customer Satisfaction department in providing on-time delivery of shipments. The primary communication link between departments is an electronic mailing system called OSR, or Order Service Request. As many as 80 requests to change orders come each day from customers. This may be a request for a change in the "ship to address," delivery times, sequence of delivery, or product changes. The OSRs are processed as quickly as possible, sometimes while the product is being loaded. The OSR system provides documentation of the request so it doesn't get lost in the verbal communication between members.

To assist the customer in a proactive manner, Distribution has established a Project Liaison Coordinator position. The Coordinator contacts the installation crew two weeks ahead of the planned delivery date to determine if any special requirements are needed. It is not uncommon to have 20 or more trailers delivered at two-hour intervals with products in each trailer loaded in a particular sequence. This requirement arises from the need to install product in a particular sequence within a limited amount of time and space.

Another installation consideration is the job site itself. In many metropolitan areas, some older buildings are not equipped to handle larger trailers, and accommodations must be made early in the schedule so that proper equipment can be ordered for loading. If this information is known far enough in advance, delays at the job site can be prevented.

The greatest benefit of the Project Liaison Coordinator's activities has been the improved communication between Haworth and the installer. On the first call the coordinator establishes a communication link, and subsequent calls keep the installer informed of any changes to the schedule. A call after installation checks with the installer to learn how the project went. Installers often are surprised to be called after completion, and appreciate the opportunity to give their suggestions for improving future service.

On occasion, interruptions in the shipping process occur. They may be due to material shortages or defective products. Early notification allows the installer to take alternate action in the time before the end user must move in to the new office. When shipping is interrupted, the liaison function ensures early notification.

The following example demonstrates what can go wrong if upfront information is not properly communicated. In New York City, electrical unions are responsible for performing any work that requires electrical power distribution. For this reason, electrical raceways are preinstalled not in panels at the factory, but at the customer's site. If this information were not communicated to manufacturing, all work on the job could be halted while the raceways are removed and then reinstalled once the panels are taken into the building.

Haworth has established a program called LTL Personalized Delivery Service, which adds an extra level of service to normal LTL deliveries. Normally a common carrier will have several stops to make during a typical day of deliveries. Being delayed in the beginning of the delivery sequence causes subsequent deliveries to be delayed. This situation is unacceptable to most Haworth customers. Job site restrictions that apply to truckload orders (freight elevator availability, for example) also apply to less-than-truckload orders. With the Haworth LTL Personalized Delivery Service, product is received at regional breakbulk terminals, and if it is destined to the adjacent major metropolitan area, it is placed on a box truck for delivery. The same driver always makes the deliveries. The driver helps unload, and has developed a close working relationship with the customer. The product is checked in and inspected for damage, and any discrepancies are noted and resolved with Haworth and the customer. This program has prevented mix-up of orders, and customers appreciate the extra service.

Warehousing

Haworth has studied various methods of warehousing and has applied many of these, depending on the product and the location of storage. Conventional racks are utilized throughout the finished goods warehouse. Square footage of the main Haworth warehouse in Holland, Michigan, is 334,000 sq ft, with 28 ft of clear height. The building is racked with Paltier and Republic racks. Rack locations vary widely in size, depending upon the product being stored. Office furniture comes in many sizes, from bulky desks and files to small hardware parts, and all must be accommodated in the warehouse without wasting space. As product lines, sizes, and colors have expanded, the size of rack locations has become more varied, with the addition of more "mini" locations. Whenever possible, only one part number is stored in a location. This prevents inadvertent picking of the wrong part.

The warehouse is divided into types and categories, and each product is assigned to the proper area for storage. In this manner, product can be stored in a specific zone so that the most efficient pick paths can be set. The lower levels are set up for higher-turn products, to minimize picking machine up-and-down travel.

The key to efficient warehousing is accuracy. When product is turning rapidly, accuracy is even more critical. Inaccurate inventories would cause tremendous backup of the flow of material coming from manufacturing. Inventory accuracy is measured not by piece part but by location; typical measurements of inventory accuracy are 98 percent plus. The main reason for high accuracy levels is the self-discipline of all members who work in the warehouse. The practice of measuring accuracy by location emphasizes the need for precise inventory control.

"Locator" is the computer system that helps maintain these high levels of accuracy. A mainframe, in-house-designed inventory control system, Locator monitors each inventory transaction and maintains an on-line, real-time record of all product movement in or out of the warehouse. The key to proper inventory control is that no parts are moved without Locator input.

Product is received from manufacturing either on automatic guided vehicle (AGV), lift truck, or shuttle truck. Upon entering the warehouse, the product is assigned to a location. As it is put away, the part number and the pieces are doublechecked and are put in the assigned location. When an order is complete, Locator indicates to the pickers where the product is stored, so that it can be picked, brought to packers for final packing of the order, and labeled.

Automatic data capture (bar coding) has been utilized in Haworth's warehouse for several years. It has added to the accuracy of the inventory and has improved inventory turns. LXE terminals and Symbol Technology laser guns have been successfully used in nearly all inventory transactions. This equipment is utilized in an RF (radio frequency) environment, and location updates can be done instantly. For example when product is picked, the member drives to the location as indicated on the terminal, picks the parts required, scans the location, and hits the transmit button on the terminal. This transaction is passed directly to the mainframe for updating. If the location has been depleted, Locator instantly notes its availability for storage.

Some products that Haworth sells are purchased from outside suppliers. These products come directly into the Distribution warehouse and are planned and managed by Distribution management members. This has made Distribution into an organization similar to Manufacturing. The decentralization of the planning function to Distribution has improved communication with suppliers, minimized inventory, and maximized product throughput.

A case in point concerns the corrugated material Haworth uses for packaging. Prior to decentralization, nearly one-fourth of the raw material warehouse was dedicated to corrugated packaging supplies. After the planning function was transferred to Distribution, negotiations with the local corrugated supplier and transportation companies resulted in just-in-time deliveries. Now, only the corrugated that is needed is brought in on a daily basis, and the free space is used for finished goods.

The proliferation of product lines significantly increased the requirements for small hardware parts storage. Vertical carousels are now used to store hardware items and sales aid materials, such as promotional items and literature. The carou-

sel storage system freed valuable space in the conventional racks, and made picking of these parts more efficient.

Despite these space-saving efforts, an entirely new storage problem arose when freestanding furniture, such as files and pedestal drawers, was added to the product line. A large, heavy, five-drawer file could not be handled by one person, and it took up considerable space in the warehouse. Automatic storage-and-retrieval systems were investigated as solutions, but were thought to be too restrictive because Haworth products are offered in a wide assortment of colors and sizes. Furthermore, such a system would be inflexible as volumes increased. Consequently, a new storage system that addressed this problem was devised in house.

Roller conveyors were placed in conventional racking systems for easy handling into and out of location. The rollers were slightly tilted down at the rear of the rack location, and cables were strung at the back so product could not fall from the rear. Files and pedestal drawers were then mechanically handled from production to shipping by automatic guided vehicles, which offloaded them onto a conveyor in Distribution. Lift truck equipment was fitted with manual rollers so the files could be simply rolled onto them and locked in place. The operator-controlled lift truck traveled to the narrow-aisle conventional rack system. Here it was guided onto a buried cable in the floor, where an onboard system guided the lift truck between the racks. At the proper location the driver stopped, raised the file to the proper location, and rolled it into place. This system was relatively inexpensive, and provided flexibility at the same time.

As shipments have increased over the years, throughput in the warehouse has increased tenfold since the Distribution Center's origin in 1982. Automatic data capture, decentralization of the planning function, "mini" locations, reduction in unallocated resources, and improved material handling methods have significantly reduced the need for warehouse expansion.

Wherever possible, product is shipped directly from the plants or is sent to the Distribution Center loading docks, bypassing the warehouse. This minimizes handling, storage space, and possible damage. The Transportation department must be prepared to handle product when it is ready. Haworth's solutions to this are discussed in the next section.

Transportation

Haworth Transportation supports the main function of the company, which is manufacturing office systems furniture. Traditionally, office furniture companies have employed private fleets for large customer deliveries, but Haworth chose to focus on that which they do best: building office furniture. Consequently, product is shipped to customers by common or contract carriage. To ensure that service levels are met, Haworth works closely with the freight companies and provides them with continual feedback on their performances.

For example, the Haworth Transportation Quality Plan establishes guidelines for the carriers to follow so they know exactly what is expected of them. As an extension of Haworth, these companies must provide the same level of quality and service that Haworth would expect if it was delivering the freight. To provide the carriers with feedback on their performances, routine surveys are conducted and the data is shared with them.

On each truckload shipment, surveys are included that can be filled out by the customer and the driver. These surveys are returned to the Haworth traffic department (self-addressed with prepaid postage) and are analyzed. The information is shared with the carrier company and is tracked on a monthly basis to watch for negative trends in service levels. The carriers appreciate this system, since it provides them with hard data to share with their drivers. Some companies provide a monetary incentive for deliveries that arrive error-free.

As a follow-up, telephone surveys also are conducted to determine the level of service. These surveys have proven to be an exceptional method of receiving feedback directly from the field sales force, dealers, installers, and end users on deliveries. Frequently information is received that does not pertain to Distribution issues, and this is forwarded to the appropriate department for resolution and follow-up.

Because product is made for a specific order and is not stored longer than necessary, carriers are required to keep a pool of trailers available at a Haworth location. Then, as product becomes available, the trailers are pulled to the loading docks. Frequently product must be custom-loaded for the job site according to the office floor, or by product line. Products can be blanket-wrapped, stretch-wrapped, containerized, or cartoned, depending on the situation. Air ride equipment is preferred, because damages from rough transit are reduced.

Less-than-truckload deliveries are handled through a breakbulk network. Small shipments destined to regional areas of the country are consolidated and shipped to a regional breakbulk carrier. Here the orders are unloaded, inspected for damage and completeness, then reloaded on local trucks for final delivery.

Orders for a local metropolitan area are shipped via the Haworth Personalized Delivery Service. In this program, the truck of the regional carrier is painted with the Haworth logo. The driver calls for delivery appointment and assists with the unloading at the customer's site. Most of these deliveries are made to dealer warehouses, so the driver often develops a rapport with dealer personnel and they work together to ensure that all deliveries are complete and damage-free. If there are discrepancies, the driver can call Haworth for immediate resolution.

Orders going outside metropolitan areas are handled through the regional carrier's normal system. These are delivered with the same care and attention given to the Personalized Delivery Service program.

Haworth has established a Carrier Quality Plan that spells out the expectations of the company. The plan includes:

- A Quality Statement from the carrier
- Quality reports and measurements

- Quality-improvement projects
- Benchmarking world-class performance
- Haworth Quality Carrier award

The Quality Statement is a statement of the quality objectives and responsibilities of the carrier, indicating their plans for customer satisfaction.

Each carrier also submits a quality performance report to Haworth, which includes the following:

- Survey performance
- Safety performance or records of accidents, DOT inspections, and tickets
- Claims records for their entire company and Haworth shipments
- Fuel mileage
- Driver training and hiring programs
- Mechanical performance (breakdowns), preventative maintenance, and replacement strategy
- Quality incentive programs
- New programs to stimulate continuous improvement
- Images of equipment and drivers

On a monthly basis, carriers are requested to submit recent projects they have completed relating to quality improvement, such as the purchase of new equipment, company newsletters, safety programs, etc.

Benchmarking world-class performance allows the carrier to compare itself to other leading companies, either within or outside of the industry. Topics for benchmarking can include better equipment, service, operating efficiency, and communication. For example, a company might investigate onboard communications devices that allow en route changes or report trip progress.

At the end of the year, Haworth awards all carriers who met the expectations of the Quality Plan. The award recipients are invited to Haworth, where they select a chair produced by one of the Haworth companies. This functional award serves as a reminder of the excellent service they provided during the previous year. Frequently this chair is given to the dispatcher who works daily with Haworth, setting up loads, sharing information, and expediting shipments.

Carrier quality performance and awards are determined annually, just before carriers are selected for the upcoming year. This creates a direct link between continued business relationship with Haworth and the carrier's quality performance. Carriers that exceed the Quality Plan requirements are given special considerations in the truckload bidding process described next.

Each year, bids are sent out to interested truckload carriers who desire to do business with Haworth. Included with the bid letter are the operational guidelines that specify Haworth requirements, as follows:

- Product description
- Origin and destination points
- Work hours

- Weight and cube information, and packaging
- Sales and freight terms
- Trailer inspections and trailer pool requirements
- Bill of lading information
- Loading procedures
- Dispatching and delivery instructions
- Instructions for the survey forms
- Delivery constraints and commitments
- Claims instructions
- Recommended equipment
- Freight bill auditing
- Detention time

The carrier responds with the following:

- A list of states it is interesting in serving
- The number of trailer loads it can handle each week
- Per-mile freight rates
- Insurance coverage
- Mileage guide used
- Effective and expiration dates of proposed rates
- Copies of operating authority
- Scheduled holidays
- Evidence of fiscal responsibility
- Normal working hours for dispatch
- Calculations for fuel surcharges, if applicable
- Ratio of owner-operators to company-employed drivers
- Terminal locations
- Separate bids for blanket-wrapped versus cartoned freight
- Age of their tractor and trailer equipment
- Availability of load bars
- Time allowances for unloading

After the information from the carriers has been received, it is formatted in a matrix for review. The traffic department makes the first cut of those carriers that do not meet the Haworth requirements, then a crossfunctional team composed of Distribution, Accounting, and Purchasing managers reviews the remaining carriers. The selected carriers are notified of Haworth's decision before year's end. This procedure is intended to be as fair and objective as possible.

The selection process has brought up the level of service from our contract carriers and, in many cases, exceeds the levels that can be provided by a private fleet.

Until 1987 Haworth utilized a private fleet, but discontinued it due to the service improvements of the contract carrier. Three keys to this decision to switch were (1) the realization that customers are more impressed by the product quality and service of Haworth than by the appearance of a truck, (2) creating alliances with contract carriers who understand the importance of quality and customer satisfaction, and (3) measuring these services on a routine basis and linking the performance of the carrier to continued business.

The result is a win-win relationship. Haworth receives outstanding service from trucking companies who are operating as efficiently as possible, and the carrier receives a long-term business relationship, supplemented by objective feedback to improve their operations.

Packaging

Packaging is a critical element in the distribution process. In traditional organizations, packaging is often treated as an afterthought. The product is designed to meet marketing and production objectives, but the package is not considered until late in the new product introduction cycle.

At Haworth, packaging engineering is part of the distribution organization. Most damage occurs to product when it is handled, and most handling takes place during warehousing and delivery to the customer. Therefore it is appropriate that damage prevention be a paramount consideration in the distribution process.

The primary purpose of industrial-type packaging is to prevent damage to the contents of the package. Packaging must identify the product and provide pertinent information required for delivery.

The packaging engineers design and test various packaging methods, both in the laboratory and under actual warehousing and shipping conditions. Their objective is to maximize product protection while minimizing packaging cost, which can be a delicate balance to strike.

Another factor that the packaging engineers take into consideration is the environment. Packaging materials make up an estimated 30 percent of the 160 million tons of solid waste materials discarded in the United States every year. While Haworth's contribution to this waste is extremely small, on large orders it can become very visible.

The packaging engineers at Haworth have initiated several programs to address these environmental issues, including those centered around Source Reduction (eliminating as many package materials as possible) and Recycling (working with our suppliers to develop returnable and recyclable packages).

Source Reduction programs:

- *Blanket Wrap.* Most of the exterior packaging is eliminated, and furniture pads are placed around the product as it is loaded onto the trailers and for the duration of the shipment.

- *Bulk Packs.* Outer packaging is reduced, and product is placed on pallets and secured by banding or stretch wrap.

- *Stretch Wrap and Honeycomb.* A combination of these two materials eliminates many large, corrugated boxes.
- *Packaging Material Content Reduction.* Reducing the actual amount of material in a package. This includes making poly bags thinner, and using ECO BRITE, cartons that are made, in part, from recycled newspaper.

Recycling programs:

- Wire pinracks and special bulk bins are employed, which eliminate the need for corrugated boxes.
- Haworth has built an on-site recycling center to capture scrap packaging and material that was previously transported to a landfill. Various metals, wood, plastic, cardboard, computer reports, and office paper are sorted and sold to local recycling centers.
- Members are also encouraged to bring their old newspapers, cans, and bottles to an on-site drop-off container for recycling.

To come up with strategies for the 1990s, the Packaging group is working with the School of Packaging at Michigan State University to develop corporate environmental strategies for packaging materials. Goals for source reduction and recycling will be determined, as well as identification of opportunities to expand our current bulk pack and blanket-wrapping programs.

In 1990 the recycling effort saw significant payback, both to Haworth and the environment. Haworth recycled:

- 4600 gal of oil
- 600,000 lb of fabric
- 800,000 lb of aluminum
- 5 million lb of steel
- 800,000 lb of computer paper
- 1 million lb of wood materials
- 13,000 gal of cleaning solvents
- 1.4 million lb of cardboard

Summary

This case study has been an overview of Haworth's distribution operation, provided in order to share with other distribution practitioners the corporation's methods of product storage and delivery.

One of the best methods of improving a distribution operation is to benchmark companies. Understanding the systems of successful companies enables a company to identify improvement areas in its own operations. The key to improvement is to know that there is always room to improve. Haworth has of course set goals for the upcoming year that are "stretch" goals but are also realistic, forcing us to continually look at how we can improve our processes.

Case Study **B**

An Integrated System at Polaroid

Strategic Planning, Design, and Implementation

Matthew Cohen
*Engineering Manager,
Polaroid Corporation*

Polaroid Corporation has undertaken a major upgrade at its largest photographic film manufacturing facility. A strategic master plan for an integrated system of automated process machinery and continuous-flow material handling has significantly reduced manufacturing costs while increasing product quality and employee safety. The project scope included conceptual design, economic justification, simulation, detailed specifications, vendor analysis, installation, startup, and postaudit functions. The process equipment includes coating and converting machinery. The material handling equipment includes a roll-turning and transport system, an automated guided vehicle system, a flexible packaging line, a robotic sortation palletizer, and an automatic storage-retrieval system. Portable radio frequency bar code data terminals are used to link and verify materials identification to the plant-wide information network. The technical aspects of the system integration were synchronized with a transition from a traditional organizational design to a team-based management concept. This article presents a case study of the planning, design, implementation, and assessment phases of this integrated production system.

Plant and Operations

Polaroid Corporation manufactures and markets instant photographic camera and film systems for worldwide distribution. The Spectra and Sun 600 product lines are for family imaging and amateur photography. The PolaColor and Black & White product lines are primarily for business imaging and professional photography. All Polaroid instant film products contain a light-sensitive component called "the negative." This material is manufactured in a world-class facility located in New Bedford, Massachusetts. The site includes a chemical building, a coating building, a power plant, a waste treatment plant, and an electrical substation. Additional expansion facilities are under construction.

The New Bedford complex was constructed in the early 1970s and originally included an array of traditional material handling and process equipment. A high-rise, narrow-aisle warehouse was added in 1978. Wire-guided turret trucks and a bar code labeling system have been in place since 1979. The material movement, packaging, and palletizing operations were essentially manual, labor-intensive functions for almost 20 years.

Conventional Material Handling System

With the exception of a few short moves, all Polaroid material handling was done by conventional forklift trucks. Counterbalanced, turret, and deep-reach forklift trucks were utilized. There are three groups of material flow throughout the plant: photographic film, chemicals, and packaging material.

Rolls of raw photographic film stock are delivered and staged at the main receiving dock by counterbalanced lift trucks. The lift trucks deliver the vertically oriented rolls to a narrow-aisle warehouse, where a turret truck stores the rolls in high-rise racking. When rolls are to be coated with photographic emulsions, the turret truck retrieves them and they are delivered via lift truck to a manually operated downender. The roll is downended into a rack, delivered by lift truck, and pushed manually into the coating operation on a transfer car. After coating, the roll is returned to a horizontal rack and stored by lift truck at a work-in-process area. The slitting, packaging, and palletizing operations occur in a similar manner, utilizing manual transfer cars, lift trucks, and walkie pallet jacks.

Pallets of chemicals in 55-gal drums are delivered and staged at the main receiving dock by counterbalanced lift trucks. The lift trucks take incoming chemicals, weigh them on floor scales, stage some chemicals for double-deep reach trucks, and store other chemicals in a bulk floor storage area. Chemicals to be stored in racks are handled by double-deep reach trucks. When needed for production, the pallet loads of chemicals are delivered to the scales by either the double-deep reach trucks or by counterbalanced lift trucks. After weighing, chemical pallets are placed on a tractor trailer by lift truck to be delivered to the chemical receiving dock, or they are taken by pallet walkie through the plant to the chemical production area. It is interesting to note that due to poor layout planning when the plant was originally designed, chemicals had to be transported around the building via tractor trailer to get from the storage warehouse to the chemical receiving dock. Chemicals or intermediates (work-in-process) returning to the chemical warehouses from production are also moved by either tractor trailer or pallet walkie.

Packaging materials are delivered and staged at the main receiving dock by counterbalanced lift trucks. The packaging materials are stored on the floor in a block-stacked storage area. The materials are delivered by manual pallet jack or lift truck from the staging area to the packaging operation. Finished goods move from the packaging area via lift truck and turret truck to the finished goods storage warehouse, where they await shipment to the customer. Domestic shipments are made via tractor-trailer trucks. International shipments are made via ships using temperature-controlled ocean containers.

Project History and Strategic Planning

Almost every case study related to improvements in a manufacturing process requires some initial funding to get started. This project was no exception. Several thousand dollars were required immediately just to even consider a feasibility study and an economic analysis. The payback from this initial study was not apparent at the outset. When compared to the several million dollars, however, that might eventually be invested in process changes or high-technology equipment, it became a straightforward matter to obtain authorization to proceed with an investigation of alternatives to the status quo. The feasibility study led to the formation of a strategic plan for an integrated production system.

There were six individual departments in the plant that were directly concerned with the operations described above. These departments were Coating, Slitting, Packaging, Warehousing, Quality Control, and Maintenance. Supporting these departments were Engineering, Planning, Finance, and Purchasing. These departments were organized in a conventional manner along functional responsibilities. Each department operated independently on a nonintegrated basis. They had a history of false starts in attempting to upgrade or automate their own portion of the total operation. A number of separate equipment proposals were turned down by plant management, because in each case the plant either fell short of the corporate investment criteria or had an adverse affect on the neighboring department.

The plant management decided that an integrated solution would not only help to solve the existing problems but would also lead to further opportunities to improve their basic manner of doing business. They realized that a piecemeal approach to equipment replacement could not be justified, but that a strategic master plan that encompassed each segment of the entire system could lead to substantial savings in materials, labor, and inventory. Furthermore, the potential improvements in product quality that could be achieved via totally integrated automation would represent an order-of-magnitude change in customer satisfaction. The plant was already moving toward a computer-integrated manufacturing (CIM) system to handle the flow of information. A CIM approach to materials handling and process equipment integration would benefit the flow of current products and streamline the introduction of new products to the marketplace.

A strategic plan called the "Finishing Automation Project" was conceived as a way of combining and integrating the six individual departments into one common operation. The project began with the establishment of a clear set of goals and objectives. These goals were in the areas of quality, capacity, and organization. The strategic plan called for a long-range timetable; in fact, this project was one of the first formal attempts in the plant to establish a program that spanned a four-year period in detail. It became apparent at the start that the expertise of an outside consultant could be extremely beneficial in terms of the design and integration of the material handling system. The process of hiring a consultant, however, was quite traumatic, because the internal engineering departments had always done everything themselves. The approach that was taken was not to attempt to justify making use of the services of a consultant only, but to justify the total project, then agree that the most effective way of completing the project on schedule would be to employ some consulting services.

The overall strategic plan was divided into four phases. These were:

Phase I   Project Initiation and Feasibility Study
Phase II   Conceptual Design
Phase III   Detailed Design Specifications
Phase IV   Implementation

Phases I, II, & III required 18 months to complete. Phase IV, Implementation, required an additional 18 months to complete, with some portions of the process equipment requiring an additional 12 months. An interim post audit was conducted at the 24-month point and a continuing audit is conducted on an annual basis to ensure that the project is realizing its objectives.

Conceptual Design

The most important decisions regarding the design of an integrated system take place at the very beginning of the project. The concepts that are envisioned form a framework for further development in order to achieve the expected goals and objectives. As can be seen from the description of the existing operation, there was significant potential for improvement in both the process equipment and the material handling methods. The following savings objectives were identified and documented.

Quality

The existing process equipment, specifically the coating-line winder, utilized a manual transfer method when changing from the end of one completed roll to the beginning of the next. This method required the use of a double-sided tape to attach the product to the surface of the winding core. The sticky residue from the tape created quality problems at the subsequent slitting operation. Furthermore, at relatively slow line speeds, the winder was incapable of completing a full-length roll without some degree of winding off-center (telescoping) and damaging the product. This, in combination with extensive product damage due to forklift handling, manual packaging, manual sorting, and rework all contributed to quality problems that could not be culled from the process and eventually found their way to the customers.

A major focus on improving product quality by reducing damage from known and unknown sources became the prime objective of the integrated system. The concept that was adopted was to conceive a manufacturing system in which no one would touch, handle, or rework the product. This would eliminate all quality variances at their source.

Capacity and Continuous Flow

The throughput capacity of the process-coating line exceeded the ability of the downstream slitting and packaging operations that finish the product. This restricted flexibility, increased manning costs, and promoted a high inventory level of coated work-in-process rolls. It typically required two and a half weeks to slit and package rolls that were coated in one week, and thus the support operations were dictating the production schedule of the primary process. This throughput disparity was a direct result of the coating operational design as a continuous process, whereas the slitting design was a batch or intermittent process. Two-thirds of the slitting cycle time was spent in loading or unloading material from the machines, while only one-third of the cycle time was spent actually slitting the product. The product schedule mix, and various format requirements, added additional setup time that accentuated this mismatch to create a severe bottleneck in the operation.

On-line, in-line, and off-line slitting were considered as a means of improving the slitting operation. The selected concept was a change to a continuous-flow, real-time, off-line slitting process with automated material handling. This conceptual design would change that part of the operation from an operator-paced batch mode to a machine-paced continuous mode. The resulting throughput increase would allow a just-in-time inventory policy, reduced labor requirements, and provide a more responsive overall system.

Safety

Due to the forklift orientation, the length of the moves, and the double and triple handling of material, there was a significant safety concern in this part of the manufacturing operation. The finishing process included a high level of manual tasks. These tasks required operators to push, pull, or lift sensitive and valuable materials. The roll-handling operation involved push/pull forces in excess of 125 lb. The finished product palletizing and sorting operation involved lifting loads of 45 lb at a rate of 1/min. The roll-turning and storage operation included fork truck movement of rolls weighing over 2000 lb in darkroom conditions. Also, the line speed of the coating equipment was somewhat limited, due to the inability of winding rolls large enough to be unloaded safely. Faster line speeds translate into shorter cycle times between rolls, unless the length of each roll is also increased.

The coating, slitting, and warehousing departments had consistently poor safety performance, due in part to the design of the equipment in use. Over 50 percent of the job-related accidents in those departments were back injuries. Any time an operator was injured he or she had to be replaced or covered with overtime to keep the process running. This is one obvious example where safety directly figured in the economic analysis and capital equipment justification procedure. Safety improvements were the third major consideration in the conceptual design for an integrated system.

Definition of Responsibilities

Specific responsibilities were identified at the inception of the Finishing Automation Strategic Plan. The Technical Production Manager in the plant had overall responsibility for project implementation. The engineering and organizational responsibilities were assigned to teams.

The process equipment, including the coating-line winder and slitter, were the responsibility of the local plant production engineering group. The packaging equipment was the responsibility of the corporate engineering group. The material handling equipment was the responsibility of the local plant industrial engineering group, with the outside consultant as a primary resource. The computer hardware and software was the responsibility of the local plant systems group. Members from each of these groups worked directly on teams with the production organization.

Prior to the Finishing Automation Project at the New Bedford plant, it was standard procedure to design, build, install, and debug most major pieces of manufacturing equipment with internal resources. A large portion of corporate overhead was being absorbed by an internal engineering organization. This internal engineering organization had been appropriate during periods of large-scale production expansion and plant construction, but this was no longer a cost-effective means of operating in a competitive, mature manufacturing environment. In fact, contracting external engineering services as required was a much more economical way of doing business.

The primary mission of the local plant engineering group was to directly support the manufacturing operation on a daily basis. The expertise and value of this group was to solve manufacturing problems as they occurred, so that high-quality photographic products could be produced. Designing and building machinery was not the reason for having an engineering department in the plant. The internal group developed the concepts, specifications, and performance requirements for the equipment. Then, using procedures recommended by the consultants, they chose the best machinery builders from around the world to design and construct the equipment. This ensured that the internal experts were free to concentrate on the total system integration and make certain that it fulfilled the established goals and objectives.

In parallel with the upgrade to the manufacturing production equipment, the production departments were assigned the task of redesigning their organizations to fully realize the benefits of factory automation. A key part of Polaroid's modernization effort is the change from a functional organization structure to a matrix structure, through the application of STS concepts.

STS stands for "socio-technical systems," a framework for designing and managing effective organizations. STS utilizes the knowledge and skills of the people who actually do the work in redefining the methods and procedures needed to perform the future jobs more efficiently. STS is one of many organizational development programs developed by behavioral scientists in the 1950s. What distinguishes STS from other programs is its focus on self-managing teams responsible for overall performance.

The assumption here is that a work environment based on STS will be more rewarding and satisfying to the individual worker. As a result, the organization gains a higher level of performance and commitment from its employees. This provides a high-energy workplace in which the dedication to quality and creativity support the application of new technology.

In a traditional work setting, a worker performs simple or repetitive tasks under the direct control of a supervisor. Assigned to a station or machine, this worker performs his or her work autonomously, with little or no interaction with other workers. This is, by definition, a nonintegrated system.

In contrast, STS creates a self-managing team that organizes, plans, and controls its work. Tasks are interchangeable, and workers can acquire many new skills. Every employee understands and performs the quality function. At Polaroid these self-managing teams are headed by team coordinators, who report to three business managers in a matrix structure. Each team coordinator functions as a consultant to the team. The work is accomplished in an integrated system, in which each team is responsible for continuous improvements to the system.

Specifications and Vendor Selection

Detailed specifications are one of the most important components of any integrated project. After the conceptual design has been completed and a design direction chosen, the detailed specifications are necessary to convey to the potential designers the functionality of the system. The detailed specifications are not intended, however, to be the actual documents or drawings used to construct the system. They are, rather, the documents prepared by the customer to describe the exact system requirements, expectations, and contractual obligations. They describe in detail such items as system configuration, throughput, layout, product and process parameters, operating constraints, construction and safety standards, documentation, and schedule.

The detailed specifications, after preparation by the customer, are used by the supplier in preparing a bid or quotation package. The detailed specifications require the successful bidder to prepare a functional system specification as part of the initial design review after a contract is awarded. The reason for this apparently duplicate documentation is to assure the customer that the supplier has a complete understanding of the system requirements before the equipment is constructed. The functional system specification is the designer's interpretation of how the equipment will meet the customer's specific needs.

In the case of the Finishing Automation Project, the specifications for the major pieces of process equipment, the winder and the slitter, were prepared by Polaroid individually. The material handling and support equipment specifications were prepared on a system basis. This was chosen because the integration of all the parts was critical to the eventual success of the project. A project schedule, developed early in the detailed design phase, had to be strictly adhered to, because of installation windows that were available only twice per year. In order to facilitate the tight schedule, potential vendors were brought in during the early stages of the project. Polaroid utilized an extensive list of vendors that had either worked with us before or had been recommended by the consultants.

The bid specification packages were comprised of the following 10 sections:

1. Introduction—a general description of the overall project.
2. Functional Specifications—a specific description of the operating requirements.
3. Instructions to Bidders—schedule, pricing, and commercial terms.
4. General Conditions—insurance, indemnity, warranty, patents, etc.
5. Special Conditions—confidentiality, inspection, change in orders, etc.
6. Equipment Specifications—safety standards, drawings, documentation, environmental considerations, utilities, etc.
7. Installation—delivery, storage, handling, assembly, and schedule.
8. Acceptance—performance trial, acceptance tests, and acceptance procedures.
9. Maintenance—spare parts recommendations, lubrication, preventative and predictive measures, and reliability data.
10. Training—operational procedures, troubleshooting techniques, manuals, and ongoing vendor-support capabilities.

Vendor Analysis

A quantitative evaluation of all vendor quotations was conducted by both Tompkins Associates, Inc. (consultant) and Polaroid Corporation. A joint recommendation was made to the project team and the plant management prior to establishing firm contracts with all successful bidders.

We established eight quantitative factors for vendor evaluation and assigned a relative weight to each factor as follows:

	Factor
1. System cost	15
2. System Design	
a. Hardware	15
b. Software	15
3. Quotation completeness	10
4. Implementation schedule	10
5. Training and documentation	10
6. Related experience	10
7. Support capability	10
8. Financial strength	5
Total	100

All of the vendors for each specific quotation were rated (0 points for the worst, 10 points for the best) on each of these factors. By multiplying the rating times the weight, the score for each factor is established. The sum of all the scores for each vendor results in the vendor's total score.

Cost evaluation involves examining the quoted price and determining which bid provides the best value for the equipment, whether or not the quotation meets the originally requested specifications. Flexibility, maintainability, safety, reliability, and other design criteria are considered when rating the system hardware and software design. Quotation completeness examines whether or not the vendor properly addressed all of the issues in the original bid specifications. This is important, as it allows us to compare bids equitably. Implementation scheduling capabilities are important due to the strict time frames a vendor maintains to allow the customer to adhere to his own project timeline.

Due to the complexity of most integrated systems, training and documentation must also be clear and concise. Factors related to experience include prior systems of similar design, prior projects with the customer, and individual experience of the vendor's personnel. Support capability of the vendor is evaluated to assure the customer that the system will work for a long period of time, and to determine if the vendor has support people available on a 24-hour basis. Finally, financial strength is examined to assure the customer that the supplier will be in business for future years' requirements.

Systems Implementation

Winder

The winder is considered to be the single most important piece of equipment associated with this project. It is directly responsible for the physical quality of the photographic products produced in the plant. As described earlier, the existing winder was determined to be a main source of quality problems and was a prime candidate for replacement. It is interesting to note that all of the equipment upgraded during this project, with the exception of the winder, was installed in parallel with the existing equipment. This enabled us to use the old equipment as a backup during the installation and startup periods. The winder, however, was a complete replacement, and had to be fully operational upon installation in order for the rest of the system to function effectively.

The winder consists of a two-station turret mechanism that allows the process-coating line to operate continuously while a roll of photographic film is being unloaded or a new core for the next roll is being loaded. The cutting of the film and the attachment of the product to the core is done automatically, without stopping the line. Before a finished roll is removed from the machine, a quality-control sample is taken from the outer wraps of the roll.

A pair of hydraulically operated roll-handling arms lifts the finished roll from the winder mechanism and deposits it on a waiting precision roll carrier. The roll carrier is taken out of the area via the roll transport system, which then interfaces with an automatic guided vehicle. The guided vehicle arrives with a roll carrier holding an empty core. An exchange of roll carriers takes place, and the guided vehicle takes away the finished roll. The roll transport system brings the carrier with the empty core back to the roll handling arms, and the winder is then ready for the next roll change cycle. This entire sequence takes place in total darkness. The operator monitors the sequence via an infrared television system with remote control.

Slitter

The slitter is the machine that converts the wide-width film products from the coating line to narrower-width products that are assembled into consumer film packs. This operation also takes place in total darkness with minimal operator involvement. The process is monitored and controlled remotely from a computer terminal. Like the winder, the slitter receives its product rolls from an automatic guided vehicle and transport system.

The unwind station of the slitter consists of a two-station turret mechanism that can be loaded or unloaded while the machine is operating. The turret has an adjustable centering device that allows off-center or variable-width rolls to be handled automatically. The operator attaches the leading wrap of the product to an automatic threading bar, which runs on a chain along both sides of the machine. The product is automatically threaded into the machine and placed on a vacuum splice table. An automatic traversing device cuts the product and applies a splice tape that attaches to the expiring end of the previous roll.

After the product has been run through a set of precision slitting knives, it is separated into individual webs and rewound onto individual cores on a triple-station turret winder. The unloading of finished product and reloading of new cores is accomplished automatically with a pair of synchronized robots. The robots deposit the finished product on two belt conveyors, which deliver the product through a wall into the packaging area. This allows the slitting operation to run continuously, without having to stop for material handling functions. The productivity improvement of this new operation represents a fourfold increase over the previous method and a dramatic improvement in product quality.

Roll-Turning System

The roll-turning system consists of an automatic roller conveyor, a hydraulic roll-turner, and an overhead bridge-mounted C-Hook. The system has operated satisfactorily since installation, and has virtually eliminated all edge damage in handling mill rolls.

The roller conveyor is made up of seven independently driven zones for roll accumulation. Load capacity for each zone is 4000 lb. Zone 1 is a delivery station for rolls brought in from the warehouse via automatic guided vehicle. Zone 7 is also a delivery station for rolls that may need to be inserted at the beginning of the queue. Queue size is maintained at six rolls. This allows a production operator to bypass the queue for a particular roll without having to unload the entire conveyor.

The downender is a heavy-duty hydraulic table with 90° of rotation. A pair of centering clamps is used to position the load on the center of the table. This positions the core of the roll in line with the overhead C-Hook. The hook is driven in vertical and horizontal travel by a pair of programmable servomotors. The program is written to prevent the operator from placing the load in the wrong position or trying to pick up the load before the downender has finished its cycle. The entire sequence is controlled via a four-way "joystick" for crane positioning and a single-sequence button for roll movement.

Roll Transport System

The Roll Transport System is used to load and unload product rolls from the process machinery, and for temporary storage for work-in-process rolls. The system consists of air flotation transporters, stationary "slideveyors," and precision roll carriers. The transporters interface with the roll-turning system and the process machines. The slideveyors and precision roll carriers interface with the automatic guided vehicle system.

The system operation is based on handling product rolls on extended cores. The face of the product roll ("the web") is never allowed to touch or contact another surface. The precision roll carriers support the product in a horizontal position. The automatic guided vehicle delivers or picks up the loaded carrier from a slideveyor. The slideveyor has a ball-screw pusher mechanism that slides the carrier onto low-friction rails that match up with rails on the transporter. The roll transporter rests on conical landing pads on the concrete floor for loading or unloading. For travel in or out of the process machines, the transporter floats on four air casters and is driven by a variable-speed motor. Positioning is determined by an encoder that feeds location pulses to the system's programmable controller.

Installation of the transport system required extensive trench work in the concrete floor. The air supply, electrical cables, and guide rails are all located below floor level. The system layout requires the automatic guided vehicle to travel across the guide rail in three locations. This necessitated making the AGV capable of leaving its wire guidance system for approximately 5 ft while dead-reckoning across the transporter guide rail.

The roll transport system operates automatically from a series of push-button panels located near each transporter station. The system is interlocked with the AGV traffic controller to prevent AGV and transporter collisions. The precision roll carriers are used for work-in-process storage of rolls in a darkroom area. They are stored and retrieved by the automatic guided vehicles. The identity and location of each carrier is tracked by the AGV system computer. The carriers are classified as unloaded, loaded with good product, or loaded with scrap product. Approximately 20 percent excess storage space was allocated in the work-in-process area to allow the AGVs to shuffle carriers for random access of specific rolls. When a carrier shuffle takes place, the AGV computer automatically updates the carrier location map before allowing a roll to leave the darkroom.

Automatic Guided Vehicle System

Prior to the detailed design and construction of the Automatic Guided Vehicle System, a simulation model of the proposed system was developed. The purpose of the model was to evaluate the system design in a statistically valid manner and to provide a base model to be used for alternate configurations. An independent simulation consulting firm was used to develop the model, in conjunction with the AGV vendor and Polaroid.

It took approximately two months of effort to construct the simulation model, conduct the experiments, and interpret the results. The finished model provided all of the information needed to meet the above objectives. We designed the final system to incorporate a number of guidepath changes, parking areas, priority sequences, and retrieval functions that would otherwise have been overlooked without the simulation model.

The AGVS consists of three automatic fork-type wire-guided vehicles, a PC-based traffic control computer, a DEC MicroVax-based multiuser system computer, and approximately 12,000 linear feet of guide path. There are seven operator terminals stationed throughout the plant. The system can handle six different types of unit loads, and it operates in both light and dark areas. The vehicles can pick up or deliver to two different types of conveyors, or to floor locations within the warehouse aisles.

The system has been brought on-line in phases, beginning with the shortest delivery paths and expanding outward to the longer delivery routes. This method has enabled the engineers and operators to keep the vehicles within eyesight and shouting distance during the debug and start-up period.

Each AGV contains an onboard programmable logic controller, a microprocessor and modem for communication, and a forklift mast with an electric ball-screw drive. The vehicle uses a center-mounted guidance system for forward travel, and outrigger-mounted guidance for reverse travel. Safety features include four-way flashing lights, a strobe light, a beeper, infrared collision-avoidance detectors, and a continuous outboard bumper system. Load presence and positioning are determined by inward- and outward-looking photosensors, and by limit switches on the fork carriage. Load height is controlled via an encoder on the ball-screw mast drive. Load capacity is 4000 lb, with a maximum lift height of 30 in. Wobble sticks are automatically extended as an additional safety measure whenever the loads carried are wider than the vehicle.

The system traffic controller dispatches vehicles throughout the plan on a priority basis, monitors vehicle locations, opens and closes automatic doors, and uploads system transactions to the MicroVax database. Additionally, temperature sensors were installed at the fire door locations to prevent an AGV from attempting to pass through a doorway in the event of a fire.

In the narrow-aisle warehouse areas of the plant, the AGVS is used to pick up and deliver raw rolls of negative base, or to deliver and move pallet loads of finished film. A turret truck is used to store or retrieve loads from the warehouse racks. The turret truck operator places the loads in the aisle, between guidelines that have been painted on the floor. The operator then goes to an AGVS terminal to request a load pickup. The AGV travels down the requested warehouse aisle, picks up the load, and delivers it to the proper destination. The operator can preprogram a series of moves to keep the AGV busy for an entire shift in certain aisles while the turret trucks are operating in other aisles.

Packaging Line

The packaging line consists of a series of darkroom belt conveyors, an automatic bag-loading machine, an automatic carton-erecting and -loading machine, two bar code printer/applicators, and two bar code scanners.

The darkroom belt conveyors transport the finished "cuts" of product from the automated slitter to the packaging operation. The bag-loading operation takes place in total darkness. Once the product has been loaded and sealed in the light-tight bag, it can then be conveyed into a lighted area for labeling and final cartoning. The conveyor system operates with an elaborate control logic, to assure that the individual identity of each product is maintained in the event of a system failure. A number of light locks have been installed to allow sections of the conveyor to be run independently, for product removal in case the lights need to be turned on.

The bag-loading machine is built around a rotary index table with four individual product stations. At station #1, the product is positioned on its centerline and measured with ultrasonic sensors. The measurement data is used to select the proper bag size for sealing the product. Stations #2 and #3 are bag-loading stations for two different sizes of light-tight bags. Station #4 is a folding and sealing device for loaded bags. The machine is designed so that in the event of a failure or a jam the operator can remove the product without turning on the room lights. An infrared television system is used to monitor the machine performance from a remote location.

Bar code labels are automatically applied to each sealed product bag immediately after exiting the darkroom conveyor. The label includes a product code, date of manufacture, length of the roll, and a unique identifying number. The labels are scanned and verified by two omnidirectional bar code scanners as they enter the infeed station of the cartoning machine.

The cartoning machine is capable of receiving bagged product of different sizes in random order and loading them into the appropriate-sized carton. Information from the bar code scanners is used to activate one of three hoppers containing different-sized carton blanks. While the product is being positioned for insertion into the carton, the blank is transported via a chain conveyor to the erecting station. The different-sized cartons are always erected with a common reference edge. Once the product has been loaded, the carton flaps are folded, sealed with hot melt glue, and labeled with a duplicate label to match the bag. Only one product is allowed in the machine per cycle, so that if the next product requires a different carton size, servomotors adjust the guide bars in the machine before the product is loaded.

Palletizer

The palletizer system consists of the final delivery conveyors for finished product, two fixed-head bar code scanners, two pallet dispensers, a robotic sorting and palletizing cell, and an automatic stretch wrapper with accumulating pallet conveyor. Four vendors were required for the design and installation of the system, making project management and coordination an important step in the implementation phase.

The system is capable of handling four different product types with two different palletization patterns. Product cartons are picked up at two input stations and can be sorted and stacked on up to 12 different pallets. When a pallet load is completed, the product is transported to the stretch wrapper and prepared for AGV pickup. Reject conveyors are included in the system, to allow the robot to continue operation in the event of a misread label or insufficient product data for proper sortation.

The control system includes a PLC for cell control, a microprocessor for robot control, and a MicroVax link for transmitting sortation data between the mainframe VAX inventory system and the robotic cell. A personal computer and customized spreadsheet software are also included to allow sortation data to be entered directly into the PLC without the use of the MicroVax.

The robot itself is a four-axis Cartesian coordinate machine with a payload capacity of 110 lb. It is programmed for specific palletization patterns by leading it through a series of moves with a hand-held teach pendant. The robot arm is equipped with a four-cup vacuum gripper for picking up the corrugated cartons of finished product. The vacuum pump is self-contained and travels with the robot.

The robot is mounted on a precision transporter that can travel up to 60 ft on a pair of floor-level tracks. There are 12 nonpowered pallet stations located along both sides of the tracks. The transporter is positioned via an onboard encoder and variable speed drive. A driven section of roller conveyor, large enough for one palletized load, is also attached to the transporter. For pallet transfer, the transporter is positioned opposite the appropriate pallet station, a slave-drive roller unit is energized, and the pallet is transferred from the transporter to the station. Clamps are then activated to hold the pallet in a precise location while the product is being stacked by the robot. When the unit load is completed, the above procedure is reversed and the finished pallet is ready to be stretch-wrapped and delivered to the finished goods warehouse by AGV.

AS/RS and RF Bar Code System

Concurrent with the Finishing Automation Project, Polaroid was challenged with designing an integrated material handling delivery system for pallet loads of chemical drums that would be used in a newly constructed, adjacent multifloor production building. The initial plan for material delivery in the new facility was to duplicate the material handling system found in the existing production facility. The new building was to use a second freight elevator to deliver pallets of chemical drums from the dock area to and between the different floors in the building. Production materials and work-in-process would continue to be staged on the various production floors.

It soon became apparent to the project team that existing material handling approaches probably would not work in the new facility. Significant throughput problems were occurring, with pallet loads of chemicals congesting narrow access aisles and valuable floor space. We sought an integrated approach using the AGV, bar code, and computer technology already in place in other parts of the plant.

After conducting another extensive analysis of systems and alternatives, we selected a computer-controlled automatic storage and retrieval system (AS/RS) to stage and deliver palletized drums of chemicals used in the manufacturing process. The AS/RS interfaces with an extension of the AGVS, which is used to deliver chemicals to the primary material input station located in the receiving area adjacent to the high-rise storage system.

The AS/RS resides in a freestanding structure located between the two chemical process buildings. It is enclosed in a fireproof shaft measuring 40 ft long × 15 ft wide × 80 ft high. A single-aisle racking network provides 168 single-deep storage locations. An automated storage/retrieval machine operates in this aisle to transport loads between the rack locations and the infeed/outfeed stations located on each level of the five-story building.

Due to the nature of the construction and the timing of the implementation, all of the rack components and the S/R machine were installed by lowering them through an 8×8-ft opening in the roof of the building. It was a very complicated installation and rigging job. The roof installation was a significant factor in the vendor analysis and selection of the prime contractor.

The ground floor infeed/outfeed station uses a powered conveyor with an AGV pickup and delivery spur, an incoming load sizing and weighing station, a laser bar code scanner, and a conveyor crossover section for reject loads. Each of the infeed/outfeed stations located on the upper floors of the building utilizes a single-position static pickup and delivery stand. The static stand is equipped with an array of photosensors, which perform a size check on all loads entering the system. The S/R machine accesses the static stands directly, by reaching through an automatic door with a double-deep shuttle fork arrangement. The fork capacity is 3000 lb at a 120-in extension.

Control of the material flow is performed on a DEC MicroVax computer system with operator terminals at each floor. The computer is used to direct the storage and retrieval activities, provide inventory and equipment control functions, interface with the mainframe VAX inventory system, and transmit orders to the AGV control system.

Load tracking and control is accomplished using a combination of fixed and portable bar code scanners. Each drum of chemicals is labeled with a unique bar code identification tag upon receipt into the plant. The portable hand-held scanners communicate with the MicroVax computer via a radio frequency link. This RF system allows us to have real-time control over the movement of chemical loads. Each time a load is moved by an operator, it must first be identified with a hand-held scanner. The operator will then receive a confirmation from the computer of the correct move or location for that chemical. If a chemical load is moved via AGV or conveyor, it must first pass by a fixed-head scanner that performs the same type of load verification. In either situation, the operator also has the option of identifying the load via the computer terminal to access further information in the database. The combination of AS/RS for load staging and RF scanners for real-time tracking has enabled us to provide the right material, at the right place, at the right time.

The RF bar code system consists of a base station transmitter/receiver, a multiplexer, portable hand-held scanners, spare batteries and chargers. The system is capable of communicating with up to 100 portable scanners. We are currently using 12 scanners. The multiplexer is connected to a communications port on the MicroVax computer. The computer treats the data from the portable scanners just the same as it handles data from conventional stationary terminals.

The bid specifications for the RF bar code system required the successful bidder to perform an electronic site survey prior to the installation of any radio frequency devices. This site survey was used to determine the most efficient location for the antenna and transmitter/receiver equipment. The survey was our guarantee that the equipment would provide complete site coverage and that we could utilize the portable scanners for any application within the plant. This real-time, mobile information system will serve as the basis for future integration of the remaining manufacturing operations throughout the facility.

Project Assessment

The equipment described in the systems implementation section was installed in phases during the semiannual plant shutdowns, which occur during the months of July and December. These two periods are used for major equipment upgrades or replacements, and for most large-scale preventative maintenance programs. We used the six-month period between phases to perform an ongoing assessment of the equipment installed to date, and to determine what improvements could be made for each succeeding phase.

We initiated an audit procedure for each major piece of operating equipment and for the portions of the system that were operating in an integrated manner. The audit began with data collected by the operating production departments. The data was summarized and reviewed by the project team and production management. The summary was then evaluated by an outside organization for a nonbiased assessment of our performance against the original strategic plan.

A number of quantitative categories were used in performing the project assessment. These categories included measurements in the areas of quality improvements, safety improvements, productivity improvements and the actual implementation schedule. In addition to these measures a series of interviews and surveys were conducted to ascertain the qualitative results of implementing the project. This information was used to provide recommendations on how to improve the planning process and how to continue to improve the performance of the integrated system. Included in this qualitative analysis were subjects such as customer feedback, vendor follow-up, and training programs. The combined assessment with both quantitative and qualitative factors provides an objective analysis of the project performance and gives direction for further improvements on future systems.

Conclusion and Lessons Learned

Polaroid Corporation has installed a number of sophisticated, integrated systems with a high degree of automation. This experience has taught us to proceed with full awareness of the potential for problems. There are many, many pitfalls along the way to achieving successful integrated systems. The system and concepts presented in this case study have not only served to improve the operation, they have also served as the foundation for learning the way to success in future endeavors.

The case study described in this chapter has enabled us to document the following lessons learned:

1. Formulate a strategic master plan with clear goals and objectives.
2. Pursue integrated solutions that correct existing problems and lead to further opportunities.
3. Involve plant personnel at all levels right from the beginning.

4. Establish a dedicated project team with the authority to make decisions.
5. Prepare detailed, in-depth, performance specifications.
6. Require prospective vendors to visit the site before submitting bids, visit the selected vendor's facility before awarding a contract, and make regular visits to the vendor's facility during the project.
7. Don't try to automate everything.
8. Perform a simulation of automated systems before finalizing the design.
9. Once a design is released for construction, freeze it to minimize changes.
10. Purchase equipment with installation costs included by the supplier.
11. Require a performance trial at the equipment vendor's site before giving authorization for shipment, and an acceptance test at your facility to replicate the vendor's performance trial.
12. Establish a fixed payment schedule based on significant milestones.
13. Don't accept equipment without full operating instructions, maintenance procedures, spare parts lists, drawings, and other documentation.
14. Require software to be warranted as well as hardware, and make backup copies of all software the instant you receive it.
15. Plan extensive training sessions for operation and maintenance of high-tech equipment.
16. Retrofitting new technology into an existing operation is always more difficult than you think.
17. Include start-up costs, spare parts, and training expenses in the economic justification analysis.
18. Perform a post audit of the project to confirm that it met the original goals and objectives.
19. Anticipate continuing improvements to projects after their completion.
20. Take lots of pictures. Take pictures before, during, and after the project.

The foundation of a successful manufacturing operation must be a long-term commitment to a broad-based, common-sense, structured process of continuous improvement. The theme of this case study is *dynamic consistency*. Dynamic, in that the key to success is the process of continuous improvement, and consistency, in that all of manufacturing must share a common vision of where manufacturing is headed. Polaroid's commitment to supplying its customers with high-quality, innovative products, processes, and services has helped to maintain a competitive edge in a worldwide marketplace.

Further Reading

Auguston, K. A., "Polaroid's Journey to Materials Handling Excellence," *Modern Materials Handling*, July 1989.
Avishai, B., "A CEO's Common Sense of CIM—An Interview With J. Tracey O'Rourke," *Harvard Business Review*, January–February 1989.

Bower, J. L. and T. M. Hout, "Fast Cycles Capability For Competitive Power," *Harvard Business Review,* November–December 1988.

Cohen, M. and J. E. Peters, "Economic Justification and the Management of Risk," *AGVS Forum '88,* The Material Handling Institute, Charlotte, NC, 1988.

Cohen, M. and J. A. Tompkins, "Material Handling: The Manufacturing Integrator," *Proceedings of the World Productivity Forum,* 2d ed., Norcross, GA, 1987.

Cohen, M. and J. A. Tompkins, "Handling System Design—A Case Study," *The 36th Annual Material Handling Management Course,* Norcross, GA, 1989.

DeGevs, A. P., "Planning as Learning," *Harvard Business Review,* March–April 1988.

Dumaine, B., "How Managers Can Succeed Through Speed," *Fortune,* February 13, 1989.

Hitchcock, N., "Polaroid Launches a Major Quality Initiative," *Modern Materials Handling,* April 1992.

Tompkins, J. A., *Winning Manufacturing: The How-To Book of Successful Manufacturing,* 2d ed., Norcross, GA, 1989.

——, "Successful Facilities Planner Must Fulfill Role of Integrator in the Automated Environment," *Industrial Engineering,* May 1984.

——, "Giving CIM a Chance," *Modern Materials Handling,* May 1987.

Tompkins, J. A. and J. A. White, *Facilities Planning,* John Wiley, New York, 1984.

Tompkins, J. A. and J. D. Smith, *The Warehouse Management Handbook,* McGraw-Hill, New York, 1988.

Wallach, S. L., "For Users of CIM, The Plan's The Thing," *Managing Automation,* July 1988.

Warehouse Excellence at the Miller Brewing Company

Ric A. Schneider

Operations Improvement Manager,
Miller Brewing Company

Warehouse excellence at the Miller Brewing Company started with the development of a Master Plan Strategy. This strategy began with a change in operating philosophy, from the old school of placing production into storage to the ideal of every pallet coming off a production line and going directly into a trailer or rail car. This may be idealistic, but the focus was on a flow-through concept. One of, "We don't store it, we ship it."

This effort began at Miller in late 1989, when the Industrial Engineering Department suggested that a planning strategy be developed to standardize and simplify distribution operations prior to the implementation of automation. As a result, executive management formulated, directed, and guided the development and implementation of a strategic vision to reduce operating costs while increasing customer service. Today, performance of each brewery is measured against the strategy to ensure continuous improvement.

The implementation of the strategy is split into the following three phases:

1. Standardization and simplification of operations
2. Becoming more responsive to customer needs, while establishing a culture and attitude of continuous improvement
3. Utilizing improved responsiveness to aggressively meet market demands

The basic model for the continuous improvement process utilized at Miller was developed by Tompkins Associates, Inc. The following steps outline the process:

1. Develop an understanding of the vision.
2. Assess present status.
3. Identify and prioritize opportunities.
4. Identify and evaluate alternatives.
5. Develop and implement plans.
6. Measure and report results.
7. Return to Step 2.

Company Background

The Miller Brewing Company is a wholly owned subsidiary of Philip Morris Companies, Inc. With approximately 10,000 employees, the company operates eight breweries, five can manufacturing plants, and a glass bottle plant. In addition to these facilities, Miller operates a hops-processing plant, a malt plant, and a packaging printing plant.

Miller is the second largest U.S. brewing company, with a sales volume of 43 million barrels. Miller currently produces 4 of the top 10 domestic brands: Miller Lite, Miller Genuine Draft, Miller High Life, and Milwaukee's Best. Other major brands include: Meister Brau, Miller Reserve, Lowenbrau, Leinenkugel, Magnum, and Colder's 29. Miller also produces Sharps, a nonalcoholic brew.

The brewing industry in the United States operates under a three-tiered system: brewery to distributor (wholesaler) to retail account. Miller has 690 distributors located throughout the country, and owns 5 of them. To service sales accounts, Miller operates 24 regional offices.

The balance of this chapter describes the approach utilized by Miller to develop its strategic plan for distribution, and shows how the process of continuous improvement is supporting implementation.

Project History

As stated earlier, this effort was initiated in late 1989 owing to concerns over increasing distribution costs and a lack of coordination between breweries. Executive management assembled a crossfunctional task team to develop and implement a five-year plan to reduce warehouse costs by one-third while improving customer service. This task team began work in February 1991.

The development of the strategic plan document took six months. The plan is titled "The Warehouse Operations Master Plan" (WOMP). By the end of 1991, Miller's Operations Division and its Executive Management had approved the strategic plan for implementation and hired an outside consultant (Tompkins Associates, Inc.) to support implementation. The original task team that developed the plan took on an advisory role to oversee and guide implementation.

To date, the process of continuous improvement has been established at all breweries to support implementation of the strategic plan. The effort has been extremely successful and has resulted in millions of dollars in savings and improved customer responsiveness in just a couple of years.

Implementation of those recommendations from the strategic plan related to interface points with independent distributors (wholesalers) has just begun. From there, changes will be made to aggressively meet market demands.

Strategic Plan

The strategic direction to make Miller's Brewery Operations more responsive to market demands includes the following major operating changes:

- Direct loading of production
- Reduction of process and order variability
- Producing to schedule
- Lower inventories
- Improved product availability
- Employee involvement/flexibility
- Total cost optimizing

Approach

The approach utilized by the task team to develop the strategic plan was to look at warehousing from an entirely new perspective. "What are the requirements to become world-class?" was the question asked. The team utilized the 17-point "action agenda" outlined by Richard Schonberger in his book, *World Class Manufacturing: The Lessons of Simplicity Applied,* as a point of reference. The team also visited with a number of companies with similar distribution requirements to benchmark Miller's operations.

From the information gained, the team decided to focus on the following:

- Improving customer service
- Reducing process variability
- Reducing inventories
- Increasing production frequency
- Increasing flexibility
- Incremental automation
- Total cost optimization

To be competitive, product distribution must be responsive and reliable. Miller's distributors (customers) require accurate, timely, and dependable performance.

With significant production and order variability, it is impossible to provide good customer service.

The team took a look at "What is customer service?" from both a Sales (customer) and an Operations perspective. Most of the time the customer is the one who should define good service. However, there is that small percentage of time when customers have not yet realized their needs have changed. For Miller, the Sales perspective is providing the freshest product available to support market demands, while meeting distributor preferences for order placement. The Operations perspective is to ship all orders on confirmed date and time, while providing production flexibility to react to changing market demands. Slightly different understandings of the same goal.

In looking at various automation alternatives, the team first established a baseline from which to measure potential benefits. In other words, what were the best practices, procedures, and methods that could be employed prior to investing in automation? In a "world-class operation," automation is done incrementally once process variability can no longer be reduced. As a result of the benefits to be gained without automation, it became apparent that it would be extremely difficult to cost-justify automation on a marginal basis.

Organization

The development of the strategic plan along with the implementation process has been coordinated through a team-based organization structure. The establishment of this multidisciplined team was the catalyst for developing a standardized and simplified operating plan. The varying backgrounds and expertise of the individual members provided the crosspollination required. A large portion of what this group accomplished was the education of one another to develop a higher-level understanding of distribution operations, customer service, and their impact on the overall company mission.

From the start, this project has been supported and guided by executive management. The initial crossfunctional task team that developed the strategic plan now functions in an advisory role to each of the continuous improvement team at the breweries. An outside consultant has been utilized during implementation to ensure that the process of continuous improvement is understood and working. The following are brief descriptions of the roles individuals have within the organization structure.

Executive Steering Committee. Provide support and direction, and assure accountability.

Corporate Advisory Committee (crossfunctional). Act as integrator, clearinghouse, communicator, motivator, facilitator, and refiner of plant improvement. Resolve identified corporate issues.

Project Manager. Work to assure the success of all plant and corporate projects and to maintain a high comfort level of plant and executive management.

Outside Consultant. Work to assure the success of all plant projects and to implement the process of continuous improvement. Provide cultural and technical training. Assess operations and identify barriers to change.

Plant Team Leader. Assure progress, oversee implementation, document savings, and report progress. Manage the plant's adoption of the culture of continuous improvement.

Plant Action Teams (salaried and hourly members). Identify and implement projects. Lead and motivate others in the continuous improvement process.

Strategic Plan Detail

The strategic plan document is a manual that provides a path into the future. It also includes information and analysis of existing operations. The following are some of the key recommendations from the plan:

- Maintain finished goods inventory below 1.5 days.
- Reduce production variability at daily SKU level within ±5 percent of schedule.
- Increase SKU run frequency to match removals.
- Direct-load 40 percent of total production.
- Computer-generate work assignments/control.
- Implement order writing in even-pallet quantities when feasible.
- Reduce weight cuts to 3 percent or less of orders.
- Schedule dunnage returns.
- Increase spot service/capacity.
- Limit placement of orders outside of published availability windows, specifically single-product orders.

The first three recommendations support an optimum finished goods inventory. These recommendations provide increased product availability and improved order matching, which in turn reduces overall inventory requirements. The purpose of having an inventory of finished goods is to maintain effective order servicing when orders do not match production. To operate efficiently between a 1.0- and 1.5-day inventory level requires close maintenance of the following to avoid hindering customer service.

1. Daily variability of production to schedule at the SKU level is a major cause of inventory. Production overruns create product availability prior to order availability. Underruns cause poor customer service or cause product to be loaded from stock that otherwise could have been directly loaded/staged.

2. When matching product to orders, variability in the shipping schedule has the same negative impact as production variability. Later arrival of trucks, no-shows, equipment shortages, and orders loaded out of sequence cause product to be placed into storage.

3. Lags and expansions are scheduling tools used to allow for unpredictable line performance and to create windows of availability. This allows orders to be matched

properly. The time to change over a line and the subsequent accumulation of inventory to service orders is the lag. If production is better than planned, excess product is placed in storage. If production is worse than planned, product shortages result in order swaps/substitutions. The expansion is the availability window through which a given SKU is offered to the distributors. Without an expansion, mixed orders could never be matched to production. Excess expansion creates inventory, which is held until a future order is processed.

4. Ordered within availability windows and produced with minimal variance to schedule, product should be shipped within five days of production. The exception is interplant transfers (IPTs) due to built-in double-handling requirements. IPTs are always the minor package on an order. Companion packages are produced and inventoried until all products are available. A few hundred pallets of IPT product can become a thousand pallets awaiting shipment.

5. Orders that are placed outside of published product availability windows result in inventory built to cover future orders. The primary cause of such misplacement is orders with multiple packages that cannot be matched until the last product is available.

6. Control of finished goods inventories is often hindered by over-/under-ordered simulations. Plants attempting to smooth production and level manpower find themselves "out of sync" with orders.

Direct loading, along with computer-generated work assignments and control, are two recommendations that provide the largest opportunity for improved productivity. Computer-generated work assignments and control are obtained with a real-time communication link between forklift drivers, system needs, and warehouse management. This link is dynamic, and utilizes forklift drivers to satisfy least-cost product flows; i.e., direct loading/staging opportunities are maximized by connecting current production to current order requirements and directing operations through the transaction.

It is estimated that, on average, each pallet is handled five times. To reduce one pallet move equates to an annual reduction of 7.5 million pallet moves. The greatest opportunity we have for reducing pallet handling is to direct-load product. The basic premise of direct loading is that the beer and the trailer have to arrive at the dock at the same time. In order to obtain this, process variability has to be minimized. Some flexibility exists by utilizing the two-hour window for loading live trailers and by managing spot loads (24-hour window) to preship overruns and delay underruns.

As a number of SKUs increase, fewer single-pallet orders will be written. Even though the percentage of direct loading today is close to zero, the current opportunity is 40 percent. However, without properly matched orders and predictable production, increased SKU requirements will minimize direct-loading opportunities and increase pallet handling.

The remaining recommendations support the standardization of operating procedures. In the development of these recommendations, we created process flow charts of the operation, generic to all our plants. These charts identify the least-cost path to the loading vehicle, and highlight the cost-added routines caused by current operating inefficiencies.

The number-one item identified by the process flow charts was the opportunity for reducing pallet handling with direct loading. Other items identified include: single-pallet handling, inventory accuracy, product/load stabilization, and system communication.

Single pallets create double handling and significantly reduce productivity. The main causes for single pallets are orders written in odd-pallet quantities and weight cuts. When a single pallet is created due to a weight cut, excess inventory is also created without being matched to an order.

Increasing the emphasis on producing to schedule assumes an accurate schedule, which in turn assumes an accurate inventory. Inaccurate inventories reduce customer service, involve allocation of manpower resources to reconciliation, cause stock rotation, and decrease the predictability of the shipping schedule. Even minor inaccuracies cause work delays and reduced productivity until the problem is resolved. Product must be found, orders must be modified, and schedules must be revised to reconcile the problems.

The 10 key recommendations outlined in the strategic plan provide a target that establishes the baseline of operations. From this base line, various levels of automation were reviewed. This comparison showed that a conventional forklift operation provided the greatest benefit, required the lowest capital investment, and would impact operations the least.

Finished Goods Control System

To support this approach, Miller is installing a new Finished Goods Control System at each brewery. The Finished Goods Control System incorporates both radio frequency technology and bar-coded pallet labels. This provides the mechanism to enable direction of warehouse activities utilizing vehicle-mounted RF terminals and hand-held scanners. By providing instantaneous product and location confirmations, the system optimizes both product movement and warehouse activities. In many instances, excessive handling or stacking of product is eliminated, as product is delivered directly from the production line to the loading dock.

The Finished Goods Control System provides "active" management of product flow and eliminates "reactive" measures by warehouse management. Automatic storage allocation eliminates the need to search for empty locations or to find matching product. Picking algorithms ensure proper stock rotation and minimize product movement. Automatic location and part consolidation improves both space utilization and product flow.

The Finished Goods Control System is a "tool" that helps provide:

1. *Less operating variance.* When random or periodic events skew normal activities, the Finished Goods Control System automatically adjusts activity priorities and assigns additional resources to process those events. This allows the warehouse to function smoothly not only during normal periods but also during periods when certain activities peak.

2. *Improved inventory accuracy.* Activities are verified as they occur rather than after the fact. Bar-coded labels provide accurate and fast identification of operations, products, and locations.

3. *Reduced product spoilage.* Product spoilage due to inaccurate or untimely inventory information is eliminated.

4. *Reduced inventory levels.* Improved product flow and labor productivity increase warehouse throughput. Increased warehouse throughput ensures that the warehouse can deliver products in a timely and consistent manner. This provides the capability for warehouse management to reduce stock levels that protect against untimely deliveries or stockouts.

5. *Improved product traceability/recall.* By maintaining product shipment history, the ability to trace all product shipments (by pallet label, plant, production line, SKU number, and code date) is available in the event of any recall.

6. *Improved space utilization.* By providing *real-time* functions for location consolidation, purge picking, and direct truck and rail loading, warehouse throughput can be increased. By increased throughput, warehouse space utilization is optimized, and warehousing space needs for the facility can be reduced.

7. *Virtual elimination of paperwork.* Paperwork within a warehouse tends to be very labor-intensive and error-prone, and significantly contributes to the lack of timely inventory information. Since most warehouse operations are directed by radio frequency terminals, the paperwork normally associated with those operations is eliminated. Reports have been designed to print by exception rather than as a part of normal everyday procedures.

8. *Maximized operational efficiency.* Through radio frequency terminals, the Finished Goods Control System, interacts with personnel on the warehouse floor to provide real-time operations within the warehouse and distribution facility. This real-time interaction eliminates the necessity for paperwork, reduces errors, and provides immediate System confirmations and updates. It also eliminates waiting for work and deadheading conditions.

Implementation Steps

The first critical step in the implementation of the strategic plan is the establishment of a culture and attitude of continuous improvement. To take this step, a series of training programs was developed. The training classes, along with team-building sessions, were set up in various degrees from plant to plant. The following three programs are given at each plant:

1. *Adaptability to Change.* The natural resistance to change, and the barriers that must be overcome to implement changes.

2. *Team Dynamics.* A foundation for teamwork, interpersonal skills, problem solving, and continuous improvement.

3. *World-Class Manufacturing.* The concepts of continuous flow, low or no inventory, flexible, modular, responsive, high-quality manufacturing.

At the same time that the individual plant teams are being formed and trained, an assessment is made of existing operations. The next step is to establish criteria to measure progress toward the vision. This criteria relates back to the baseline developed from the assessment. Once this is complete, the team begins identifying and prioritizing improvement projects.

At times, continuous improvement of an operation is difficult to measure. This is specifically true when the game rules of the business change quickly. Some of the factors that make continuous improvement a moving target include:

- Additional brands and packages
- Market demand
- Competitive pressures
- Environmental issues
- Government regulations
- Social pressures
- New technology/automation

To demonstrate the implementation process utilized, the following describes the activities that have occurred at the Fort Worth, Texas, brewery.

In the fall of 1990, the warehouse master plan strategy was presented to the senior plant management and warehouse management staffs. This three-hour presentation covered how the plan was developed, the recommended operating changes, and the dollar impact of each change. The four categories used to develop the plan were: inventory/scheduling, operating procedures, new technologies, and staffing requirements.

In January 1991, an implementation schedule was developed by the corporate task team (including a member from Fort Worth) to roll the plan out to the plants. It was decided to phase plants into the implementation schedule and to hire a consultant to support the effort. Based on a number of factors, Fort Worth was identified as the fourth plant on the schedule, and would begin the fourth quarter of 1991. The main objective established for each plant was to develop an action plan to individually address the recommendations.

With the nine months available to them, Fort Worth management decided to utilize the extra time by preparing and educating their people in the operating philosophies and proposed changes detailed in the master plan. In the first quarter of 1991, this information was presented to the Fort Worth personnel on all shifts. Then in April 1991, Dr. James A. Tompkins, the president of the consulting firm hired to support implementation of the plan, visited the plant so the people could become familiar with him and his theories on world-class manufacturing/warehousing, and to review the continuous improvement process that would be utilized for implementing the plan.

The continuous improvement process, as covered at the beginning of this case study, is the means utilized to make changes happen. Over the next few months, the plant began to address some of the recommendations outlined in the plan (e.g., adherence to schedules, weight cuts, etc.). They also started to assess who was interested in being part of a continuous improvement team.

At the end of September 1991, the plant officially started the implementation process, utilizing the support of the corporate task team and the consultant. The first step was the selection of a full-time plant coordinator and the creation of a plant advisory committee for the project. The role of the plant coordinator is to ensure that the master plan is successfully implemented. The advisory committee (senior plant management) provides direction and overall support of the continuous improvement process.

At the start, the project team consisted of 22 salaried and hourly members. This group, along with the senior plant management staff, was provided the training discussed earlier (adaptability to change, team dynamics, world-class manufacturing/warehouse principles). During this training process, an assessment was made of the existing operation to establish a baseline and to identify opportunity areas.

From the assessment and a questionnaire given to all warehouse personnel, the team identified over 100 potential projects. These project proposals were reviewed, approved, and prioritized by the advisory committee. Individual teams were then created to address the priority projects. In the beginning, these teams were formed only on first shift.

In April 1992, additional teams were formed on second and third shift. All new members were provided with the training given to the initial members. On an ongoing basis there are eight active teams. Each team addresses one opportunity at a time. A number of these teams are headed up by hourly employees.

As a result of the early efforts to inform people of what the master plan was and how it would be implemented, Fort Worth has experienced a smooth and successful transition. Within the first six months, over $500,000 in cost reductions were obtained.

Results

In the two and one half years since this effort began, Miller has been very successful in obtaining positive results. These results include:

1. An improved understanding of operations and customer requirements
2. Cost reduction savings
3. Benefits to customer "distributor"
   a. Reduction in order movements
   b. More predictive product availability
   c. Less product handling/damage
   d. Improved shipment accuracy
4. Benefits from improved responsiveness
   a. Reduced operating cost at customer level
   b. Increased product throughput
   c. Lower inventory requirements

Reasons for success include:

- Team organization/structure
- Multiplant/division involvement
- Plant action teams being made up of salaried and hourly members
- Executive management involvement
- Utilization of outside consultant

The support gained from the use of a consultant has been instrumental in maintaining momentum. During the course of this effort, a consultant has been utilized for two reasons on two separate occasions. The first reason was to audit the strategic plan content and applicability to a goal of World Class Status. The second and ongoing reason has been to support implementation of the plan. The consultant's role has included:

- Assessing operations and identifying barriers to change
- Providing cultural and technical training
- Creating and structuring continuous improvement teams
- Providing technical expertise
- Being a troubleshooter

Summary

The Miller Brewing Company effort is a results-driven improvement program that is focused on achieving specific, measurable improvements within a short time frame, even though the change process is a long-term commitment. The greatest risks of failure are losing focus and not understanding how cultures vary from one facility to another.

The annual savings potential from this effort has been estimated at over $20 million. A large portion of this savings is due to a productivity increase attributed to loading directly off the production line into a trailer. This reduces the number of pallet handlings by two to three times. As stated earlier, the RF/inventory control system provides the required real-time coordination between production and shipments to enable direct loading to be maintained at a level greater than 20 to 30 percent.

As discussed, the key factors that have allowed Miller Brewing Company to achieve warehouse excellence are:

- Standardization and simplification of operating practices and procedures. This first creates a target for improvement and, once obtained, becomes the baseline for future changes.
- Becoming more responsive to customer needs, while establishing a culture and attitude of continuous improvement.
- Utilizing improved responsiveness to aggressively meet market demands. (Knowing and understanding your business better enables you to establish a leadership position.)

Case Study **D**

Operation Desert Shield/ Desert Storm

United States Transportation Command and Strategic Deployment

James K. Matthews
Command Historian,
U.S. Transportation Command

Cora J. Holt
Writer,
U.S. Transportation Command

Strategic Deployment Overview

Strategic Lift Accomplishments

The strategic deployment for Desert Shield/Storm ranks among the largest in history. From 7 August 1990 (C-Day, beginning of deployment) to 10 March 1991 (R-Day, beginning of redeployment), United States Transportation Command (USTRANSCOM), in concert with its Transportation Component Commands—Military Airlift Command, Military Sealift Command, and Military Traffic Management Command—moved to the United States Central Command (USCENTCOM) area of responsibility (AOR) nearly 504,000 passengers, 3.7 million tons of dry cargo, and 6.1 million tons of petroleum products, as seen in Table D-1. This equates roughly to the deployment and sustainment of two Army corps, two Marine Corps expeditionary forces, and 28 Air Force tactical fighter squadrons. To paraphrase Churchill, no nation ever moved so many and so much, so far, so quickly.

Table D-1 Desert Shield/Storm Strategic Lift Summary, Passenger and Cargo (As of 10 March 1991—Cargo in Short Tons)

	Airlift					Sealift			
	Unit cargo	Sustainment	Desert Express*	European Express*	Pax	Unit cargo†	Sustainment	Pol‡	Pax
Aug. 90	46,946§	—	—	—	67,263§	253,263	—	333,640	315
Sep. 90	49,738	19,142	—	—	60,476	252,013	—	508,534	681
Oct. 90	33,781	20,512	2	—	51,154	326,930	78,059	517,038	436
Nov. 90	9663	34,028	235	—	20,553	206,416	58,073	1,011,243	186
Dec. 90	52,045	38,064	399	375	105,413	356,025	113,651	894,061	465
Jan. 91	80,903	36,372	580	488	132,095	712,373	198,006	1,088,825	516
Feb. 91	52,009	42,611	637	442	45,562	297,888	183,779	1,336,807	147
Mar. 91 (1–10)	9831	14,396	213	136	18,204	27,210	69,941	412,858	12
Total	334,916	205,125	2,066	1,441	500,720	2,431,878	701,509	6,103,006	2,758

Total air cargo: 543,548 (14.78%)
Percentage on all cargo, including pol‡: (5.56%)
Total air pax: 500,720 (99.45%)

Total sea dry cargo: 3,133,387 (85.22%)
Total including pol‡: 9,236,393 (94.44%)
Total sea pax: 2758 (.55%)

Air and Sea total dry cargo: 3,676,935
Total air and sea including pol‡: 9,779,941
Air and Sea total pax: 503,478

*Includes both war-stopper requirements (9AU) and Desert Shield/Storm airlift cargo (9BU) cargo.

†Includes ammunition.

‡Petroleum, oil, and lubricants.

§As of 4 September 1990.

SOURCE: Military Sealift Command (MSC) Lift Summary Reports and USTRANSCOM Situation Reports (SITREPs).
Prepared by: U.S. Transportation Command, Office of History (TCHO).

The deployment's immensity invites historical comparison. During the first three weeks of Desert Shield, USTRANSCOM moved more passengers and equipment to the Persian Gulf than the United States transported to Korea during the first three months of the Korean War. By the sixth week the total ton-miles flown surpassed that of the 65-week-long Berlin airlift. Desert Shield/Storm sealift was equally historic. For instance, the number of cargo ships arriving in the Persian Gulf in the first five months of Desert Shield matched that of the 18-month-long allied convoy operations to Northern Russian during World War II. In contemporary terms, the command moved to the Persian Gulf area, via air and sea, the rough equivalent of Atlanta, Georgia—all its people and their clothing, food, cars, and other belongings—halfway around the world in just under seven months. The supported Commander in Chief, United States Central Command Army Gen. H. Norman Schwarzkopf, called the task "daunting" and the result "spectacular." Secretary of Defense Dick Cheney termed the deployment "a logistical marvel," while the Chairman of the Joint Chiefs of Staff, Army Gen. Colin L. Powell, told Congress it had proven USTRANSCOM's worth. He called Desert Shield/Storm the command's "graduation exercise," and as far as he, Secretary Cheney, and President George Bush were concerned, USTRANSCOM had "graduated magna cum laude."

The New World Order and Strategic Deployment

Desert Shield/Storm marked the end of an era. In the post-Cold War world, the perceived threat had changed and so had U.S. strategy. Shifting focus from a superpower conflict in Europe to regional contingencies worldwide prompted a reduction of overall U.S. forces and, more importantly, resulted in fewer forces forward-deployed. These circumstances put increased emphasis on strategic lift. The first major military confrontation in the post-Cold War era, Desert Shield/Storm showed that the United States Transportation Command must be prepared to deploy U.S. forces great distances with little warning. USTRANSCOM's Status of Forces as of August 1990 are outlined in Tables D-2 through D-5.

Fortuitous Circumstances

At first glance, the deployment to the Persian Gulf seemed a "worst-case" scenario. USTRANSCOM had to move troops and equipment a tremendous distance. By air, it was 7000 miles from the east coast. Some troops had to travel from as far away as

Table D-2 United States Transportation Command (As of August 1990)

Commander:	General Hansford T. Johnson, USAF
Headquarters:	Scott AFB, Illinois
Personnel:	406 Active-duty military and civilians 36 reserve recall/mobilization (50 percent manned)
Mission:	To provide global air, sea, and land transportation to meet national security needs

Table D-3 Military Airlift command (As of August 1990)

Commander:	General Hansford T. Johnson, USAF
Headquarters:	Scott AFB, Illinois
Personnel:	89,048 active-duty military and civilians (2,742 headquarters, 86,306 field) 73,937 reserve recall/mobilization
Mission:	Strategic and tactical airlift Aeromedical evacuation
Strategic Airlift Forces under U.S. Transportation Commmand:	234 C-141B 110 C-5A/B

the west coast, and that was 10,000 miles by air. The distance by sea through the Mediterranean and the Suez Canal was 9000 miles from the east coast and 11,000 from the west coast. However, the situation could have been much worse. Fortunately, the Suez Canal was open, and traveling around Africa, a distance of 12,500 miles, was not necessary. Air and sea lines of communication were unchallenged by enemy action. As it turned out, transporters did not have to deal with combat attrition. Furthermore there was not a second, concurrent crisis.

Other favorable circumstances facilitated deployment. In-theater air and seaports of debarkation were among the most modern and capable in the world. (USCENTCOM's preferred seaport of debarkation was Ad Damman, Saudi Arabia. It was the principal logistics support base in the AOR, it allowed cargo to be delivered directly into U.S. military control, and it met USCENTCOM's "goal of delivering cargo as far forward as practical with the most efficient mode." The command's number two preference was Al Jubayl, Saudi Arabia.) Saudi Arabia supplied extremely generous host nation support, particularly food, water, and petroleum products. The strategic lift provided by friendly governments and allies made a significant contribution to the deployment. Most importantly, Saddam Hussein's decision not to continue his drive south into Saudi Arabia in early August 1990, and

Table D-4 Military Sealift Command (As of August 1990)

Commander:	Vice Admiral Francis R. Donovan, USN
Headquarters:	Washington, D.C.
Personnel:	6784 Active-duty military and civilians (479 headquarters, 6305 field) 2337 reserve recall/mobilization
Mission:	Provide sealift necessary to deploy military forces. Sustain operational forces. Provide fleet support. Special mission support.
Forces under U.S. Transportation Command: MSC Force Ready Reserve Force	40 dry cargo, 23 tanker 83 dry cargo, 11 tanker, 2 passenger

Table D-5 Military Traffic Management Command (As of August 1990)

Commander:	Major General John R. Piatak, USA
Headquarters:	Falls Church, Virginia
Personnel:	3675 active-duty military and civilians (302 headquarters, 3373 field) 4149 reserve recall/mobilization
Mission:	Provide responsive traffic management support to the nation's armed forces. Operate common-user ocean terminals. Administer programs for national defense and serve as the Department of Defense land-transportability agent.
Forces under U.S. Transportation Command:	Defense Freight Railway Interchange Fleet 1421 flatcars 32 boxcars 1173 tank cars 22 other train cars 2648 total cars

Iraqi inaction from the time of President Bush's decision to send troops on 7 August 1990 until 15 January 1991, provided USTRANSCOM and USCENTCOM a deployment time of 161 days prior to offensive actions.

Joint Operations and Deployment Synergism

The Desert Shield/Storm deployment followed the fundamental tenets of joint operations. Supporting Commander in Chief General Schwarzkopf established requirements and set priorities. Supporting Commander in Chief, United States Transportation Command, Air Force Gen. Hansford T. Johnson directed his component commands to provide strategic lift and to execute the deployment so that troops and materiel arrived in the USCENTCOM AOR as required: major combat units first, followed by their support forces and sustainment cargo.

USTRANSCOM's success was based on a synergism of military and commercial landlift, port operations, prepositioning, airlift, and sealift. Trucks, trains, and buses moved troops, equipment, and materiel to airports and seaports for loading and deployment to the Persian Gulf. Airlift carried the first deterrent, show-of-force Army, Marine Corps, and Air Force combat units. Supplemented by afloat prepositioning, airlift also carried their supplies and equipment. Throughout Desert Shield/Storm, airlift delivered high-priority, war-stopper cargo. As planned, airlift carried nearly all (99 percent) of the troops to the AOR, as shown in Table D-1. (In December, USTRANSCOM investigated the possibility of moving troops from Europe to the AOR via sea, but rejected the idea due to bad weather and the time and money it would take to make a transport seaworthy. The few troops who deployed by sea, called supercargoes, for the most part did so to guard and maintain their equipment.) Airlift's speed and flexibility allowed USTRANSCOM to deploy troops to the Persian Gulf as their equipment arrived in the region by sea. Such close coordination expedited the movement of forces forward, thus improving readiness and decreasing the burden on Saudi port areas to store cargo and support large numbers of troops. Limiting the time troops were concentrated in the cities and at the air and seaports decreased their vulnerability to enemy attack by ballistic missiles and aircraft.

Sealift carried most of the supplies and equipment too large to fit on aircraft, although not as much as originally anticipated. During Desert Shield/Storm, ships carried 85 percent of the dry cargo, compared to the planning factor of 95 percent developed from the United States' experiences in the Vietnam War and in Europe during World War II. The differences between Desert Shield/Storm and the other two wars helps explain this discrepancy. The great distance to the Persian Gulf, rapidly changing requirements and priorities, lack of in-theater storage and reception facilities, the relatively small amount of prepositioned materiel in the region, the relatively short period of time to deploy, and shortages of critical items such as atropine, uniforms, boots, and chemical weapons gear, resulted in a heavier reliance on airlift than planned. Combining petroleum, oils, and lubricants with total dry cargo sealifted, and comparing it to total cargo airlifted, gives a 94.4/5.6 ratio. As expected, nearly all POL (99 percent) traveled by sea (see Table D-1). The transport of fuel for reconnaissance aircraft via C-141s accounted for the remainder. Perhaps most importantly, USTRANSCOM was heavily dependent on the civil sector. The command estimated that commercial industry provided, as expected, 85 percent of the transport during Desert Shield/Storm.

Airlift Operations

Overview

As directed by USTRANSCOM, Military Airlift Command (MAC) managed the Desert Shield/Storm strategic airlift. MAC's active-duty force jointed with MAC-gained aircraft and crews from the Air Force Reserve and Air National Guard to make up a total strategic airlift force of 110 C-5s and 234 C-141s. During the operation, this organic airlift force was supplemented by Air Force KC-10s (Strategic Air Command tanker assets available to MAC for cargo missions as required) and Navy C-9s (nine aircraft loaned to MAC in January for transport from Europe to the Persian Gulf). U.S. military aircraft flew 13,103 strategic airlift missions in support of Desert Shield/Storm. Missions flown in the common-user role follow, by aircraft type: C-141 (8536); C-5 (3770), KC-10 (379); and C-9 (209). Commercial airline augmentation was crucial. On 3309 missions, commercial aircraft delivered 321,005 passengers and 145,225 tons of cargo. That equaled 64 and 27 percent respectively of the total passengers (500,720) and cargo (543,548) carried via strategic airlift during Desert Shield/Storm.

Military Fleet

The Desert Shield/Storm airlift effort was enormous. By mid-August, 95 percent of operable C-5s and 90 percent of operable C-141s, along with aircraft volunteered by the airlines, were flying what became known as the "aluminum bridge." The rate of

C-141 missions slowed in September and October as the airlift shifted from unit deployment to sustainment, which allowed resumption of scheduled maintenance and gave crews a chance to rest. The greatly increased number of C-141 missions in December and January reflected wartime tempo deployment. During this period, up to 127 planes landed daily in Southwest Asia, averaging one arrival every 11 min.

To meet the massive requirement, MAC took extraordinary measures. The command stopped unit air crew training and waived the requirements for the crew duty day and crew maximum flying time. It also waived aircraft home station maintenance requirements, stopped depot maintenance, and even put aircraft stripped for painting into the airflow.

Civil Reserve Air Fleet

Early in the deployment it became apparent that USTRANSCOM needed additional aircraft to meet requirements, and the U.S. airline industry was quick to respond. The first volunteer commercial aircraft flew on 8 August in support of Desert Shield, and within days the volunteer civilian force numbered 30 aircraft, 15 passenger and 15 cargo. Then, on 17 August, General Johnson activated Stage I of the Civil Reserve Air Fleet (CRAF) program, which guaranteed USTRANSCOM the use of an additional 17 Long Range International (LRI) passenger and 21 LRI cargo aircraft. An arrangement dating from 1951 in which commercial airlines agreed to make aircraft available for Department of Defense deployments in exchange for peacetime military business, CRAF had never before been activated. These 38 (which MAC intentionally took from 16 different airlines to help spread out the economic hardship they might face by removing their aircraft from the commercial market) gave USTRANSCOM an additional daily airlift capacity of 1920 passengers and 490 tons of cargo. With 412 strategic airlift aircraft (68 civilian and 344 military), USTRANSCOM directed an air fleet that surpassed any air deployment in history.

Supporting the President's call for additional forces just prior to hostilities, and to help ensure a steady stream of resupply, Secretary of Defense Cheney, acting on General Johnson's request of the previous day, activated Stage II of CRAF on 17 January 1991. Stage II provided USTRANSCOM access to a total of 76 LRI passenger and 40 LRI cargo aircraft. Of these, the command was primarily interested in the cargo aircraft. The U.S. commercial airlines industry continued to provide 30 additional cargo aircraft above those required by activation of CRAF Stage II. (Under CRAF Stage II, USTRANSCOM could also call on the following aircraft: 23 Short Range International (SRI) passenger; 38 domestic cargo; and four Alaskan cargo.)

The military seriously considered activating CRAF Stage III to tap its cargo and aeromedical assets. On 21 January 1991, with the air war well under way and the C-141 and C-5 forces stretched to their maximum, General Johnson told the Chairman, Joint Chiefs of Staff, that USTRANSCOM had "an airlift shortfall for already validated, rapidly emerging requirements." CRAF Stage III included the following additional aircraft: 110 LRI cargo, 176 LRI passenger, 38 aeromedical, 25 SRI passenger, and 51 cargo (SRI, domestic, and Alaskan). However, USCINCTRANS wanted only 31 of the LRI widebody cargo aircraft as follows: Federal Express (6); Northwest (2); Pan American World Airways (6); United Parcel Service (2); Evergreen International Airlines (6); Emery/Rosenbalm (6); and World Airways (3). Facing the possibility of a bloody ground war, and believing that USTRANSCOM would be unable to spare C-141 aircraft for aeromedical airlift operations, the Air Staff also wanted MAC to have access to Stage III's 35 aeromedical aircraft should the DOD need them. As it turned out, the short duration of the war and a rapidly diminishing backlog of air eligible cargo, due to several USTRANSCOM initiatives, made activation of CRAF Stage III unnecessary.

Four tables detail the contributions of commercial airlines to Desert Shield/Storm. Showing by month the total passengers and cargo transported by commercial carriers, Table D-6 highlights the commercial sector's tremendous contribution under CRAF Stage II. For instance, with Stage I assets, MAC moved in September and October 77,053 passengers. That compares to 155,000 passengers in December and January under Stage II. In January and February, under Stage II, commercial airlines carried 67,105 tons, compared to 24,728 tons in September and October Stage I operations.

Tables D-7 and D-8 show by airline and Stage the number of LRI passenger and LRI cargo aircraft obligated to MAC under CRAF. Upon activation of Stage II, 14 airlines had 76 LRI passenger aircraft committed to the program. Four of those—

Table D-6 Desert Shield/Storm Strategic Airlift Summary Completed by Aircraft Type as of 10 March 1991 (Cargo in Short Tons)

		C-141*	C-5	KC-10	Commercial	Total
Aug. 90	Passengers	19,353	20,956	102	32,559	72,970
	Cargo	19,663	23,437	407	8,948	52,455
Sep. 90	Passengers	7,860	13,259	112	27,274	58,505
	Cargo	18,772	31,698	3,491	14,001	67,962
Oct. 90	Passengers	2,138	7753	102	39,779	49,772
	Cargo	12,447	25,895	1,816	10,727	50,885
Nov. 90	Passengers	4,041	3,138	141	13,111	20,431
	Cargo	12,754	1,586	9,362	9,362	45,647
Dec. 90	Passengers	18,988	13,541	519	85,126	118,174
	Cargo	26,921	34,355	3,520	27,425	92,201
Jan. 91	Passengers	28,664	16,443	135	69,874	115,116
	Cargo	33,466	43,108	1,309	33,502	111,385
Feb. 91	Passengers	6,661	8,133	0	29,699	44,493
	Cargo	30,513	34,035	0	33,603	98,151
Mar. 91	Passengers	5,421	1,162	0	13,583	20,166
(1–10 Mar)	Cargo	4,926	7,571	0	7,657	20,154
Total	Passengers	93,126	84,385	1,111	321,005	499,627
Total	Cargo	159,462	222,024	12,129	145,225	538,840

*Represents Desert Shield/Storm, Desert Express, and European Desert Express.

SOURCE: Military Air Integrated Reporting System (MAIRS) Database, Military Airlift Command, Operations and Transportation, Command Center (MAX/XOCR). Prepared by: U.S. Transportation Command, Office of History (TCHO).

Table D-7 CRAF Long-Range International (LRI) Passenger Aircraft by Carrier

Carrier	Total LRI aircraft	Committed Stage I	% fleet	Committed Stages I & II	% fleet	Committed Stages I, II, III	% fleet
American	131	2	2	8	6	12	9
American Trans Air	10	1	10	3	30	10	100
American West	4	0	0	0	0	4	100
Continental	23	2	9	6	26	23	100
Delta	69	0	0	0	0	4	6
Federal Express	2	0	0	0	0	1	50
Hawaiian	11	0	0	0	0	11	100
Northwest	58	3	5	14	24	52	90
Pan American	38	3	8	10	26	37	97
Sun Country	1	0	0	0	0	1	100
Tower	4	1	25	1	25	4	100
Trans World	60	2	3	12	20	29	48
United	131	4	3	21	16	61	47
World	4	0	0	1	25	3	75
Total	546	18*	3	76	14	252	46

*There were only 17 passenger aircraft in State I when activated 17 August 1990. One Continental was later added.

SOURCE: Military Airlift Command, Plans and Programs, Readiness, Civil Air and Operability Plans (MAC/XPXO). Prepared by: U.S. Transportation Command, Office of History (TCHO).

United (21), Northwest (14), Trans World (12), and Pan American World Airways (10)—had 57 aircraft committed, equaling 75 percent of the total. Upon activation of Stage II, 13 airlines had 40 LRI cargo aircraft committed to the program. At that point, by far the largest participant for cargo hauling was Federal Express, with 14 aircraft equaling 35 percent of the total. Emery/Rosenbalm's commitment of seven aircraft was the next largest in the Stage II LRI cargo category.

As seen in Table D-9, by war's end 34 airlines had made significant contributions to the lift, while several others had also participated. Five companies carried more than 10,000 tons: Federal Express (33,845), Northwest Airlines (19,078), Pan American World Airways (12,419), Evergreen International Airlines (12,185), and American Trans Air (11,818). This accounted for 52 percent of the total tonnage airlifted. Six companies carried more than 30,000 passengers: Northwest Airlines (63,155), American Trans Air (61,740), Pan American World Airways (51,900), Trans World Airlines (46,046), Tower Airlines (41,906), and United Airlines (35,150). This accounted for 65 percent of the total passengers airlifted. Thus three airlines—Northwest Airlines, Pan American World Airways, and American Trans Air—stand out among all the others for their contributions to both cargo and passenger transport. World Airways, carrying 9002 tons and 24,448 passengers, was also a major participant in the deployment.

Federal Express's role was also exceptional. That company carried 19.8 percent of all the cargo delivered by the U.S. commercial sector in support of Desert Shield/Storm. Northwest, the second largest commercial carrier of cargo during the operation, moved 11.2 percent of the total commercial sector tonnage.

MAC listed nine commercial aircraft types as making significant contributions to

Table D-8 CRAF Long-Range International (LRI) Cargo Aircraft by Carrier

Carrier	Total LRI aircraft	Committed Stage I	% fleet	Committed Stages I & II	% fleet	Committed Stages I, II, III	% fleet
Air Transport International	5	1	20	2	40	4	80
Arrow Air	10	1	10	1	10	6	60
Buffalo Airways	4	0	0	0	0	4	100
Connie Kalitta	12	1	8.5	2	17	8	67
Emery/Rosenbalm	26	4	15	7	27	22	85
Evergreen	11	2	18	3	27	9	82
Federal Express	41	8	19	14	34	41	100
Florida West	7	0	0	0	0	4	57
Northwest	8	2	25	3	38	8	100
Pan American	18	0	0	0	0	18	100
Southern Air	6	1	17	1	17	4	67
United Parcel	50	2	4	4	8	13	26
World	9	1	11	3	33	9	100
Total	207	23*	11	40	19	150	72

*There were 21 cargo aircraft in Stage I when activated 17 August 1990.

SOURCE: Military Airlift Command, Plans and Programs, Readiness, Civil Air and Operability Plans (MAC/XPXO). Prepared by: U.S. Transportation Command, Office of History (TCHO).

Desert Shield/Storm. The obvious workhorse of the operation was the widebody Boeing 747. It carried 108,535 tons and 262,195 passengers, representing 63.4 percent and 64.7 percent, respectively, of the total tonnage and people moved by U.S. commercial aircraft during Desert Shield/Storm. Ranking numbers two, three, and four, in tons transported were, in descending order, the Douglas DC-8 (29,296), Lockheed L-1011 (14,939), and Douglas DC-10 (12,287). Ranking numbers two, three, and four, in passengers airlifted, were, in descending order, the L-1011 (79,732), DC-10 (43,131), and DC-8 (8643).

The airlines also contributed crews. MAC required each CRAF carrier to maintain at least a four-to-one crew ratio for each airplane committed to the program. However Captain John Saux, Executive Vice President, Airline Pilots Association, admitted that airlines "had not kept track of the people current, qualified, and available to fly CRAF, keeping in mind that the reserve and guard people would already be called back to active duty before CRAF was activated. This made it difficult to assess the airlines' true capability to support CRAF." (He estimated that nearly half of his organization's 3000 crew members were reservists called back to duty.) To assure they could meet all their requirements, the airlines stepped up recruiting and qualification training.

Under CRAF agreement, airlines maintained overall responsibility for their crews and aircraft. Airlines set up round-the-clock control centers at their headquarters (Evergreen Airlines management called theirs the "War Room") to monitor commercial aircraft operating under military call signs. They communicated with Headquarters MAC and MAC's Numbered Air Forces over secure telephones, which they were authorized under the CRAF program. Carriers operated through intermediate bases in Europe where they positioned relief crews and management and maintenance personnel. Commercial airlines' en route maintenance operations were

Table D-9 Commercial Airlift Summary

Carrier	Code	Missions	Tons	Passengers
American Airlines	AAL	64	2516	15,514
American Trans Air Inc	AMT	307	11,818	61,740
Arrow Air	ARW	77	2161	13
Air Transport International	ATN	115	2879	65
American West	AWE	17	980	5662
Buffalo Airlines	BVA	15	329	0
Connie Kalitta Services	CKS	354	8706	471
Continental Airlines	COA (CRA)	41	2266	12,023
Delta Airlines	DAL	16	600	2996
Eastern Airlines	EAL	22	775	4602
Evergreen International Airlines	EIA	219	12,185	1471
Federal Express	FDX	382	33,845	4565
Florida West Air	FLW (FTL) (FWL)	28	951	352
Hawaiian Airlines Inc	HAL	160	3596	19,783
International Loaned Lift	ILL	45	2929	0
Key Airlines	KEY	6	69	284
Northwest Airlines Inc	NWA	290	19,078	63,155
Pan Am World Airways	PAA	190	12,419	51,900
RAF	RAF	7	253	360
Rosenbalm Aviation	RAX	300	8753	591
Reeve Aleutian	RVV	126	984	7096
Sun Country Air Transport	SCX	17	608	3533
Southern Air Transport	SJM	186	4541	0
Transcontinental Airlines	TCW	6	95	452
Tower Air	TOW	106	6763	41,906
Trans World Airlines	TWA	116	7560	46,046
United Airlines	UAL	100	5778	35,150
United Parcel Services	UPS	92	8508	358
World Airways	WOA	193	9002	24,448
Other	999	7	270	914
Total		3604	171,167	405,450

SOURCE: Military Air Integrated Reporting System (MAIRS) Database, Military Airlift Command, Operations and Transportation, Command Center Reports (MAC/XOCR). Prepared by: U.S. Transportation Command, Office of History (TCHO).

manned continuously throughout the operation. Some airlines also stationed management and maintenance personnel at airfields in the Middle East.

A usual routine was for crews to operate from Europe to the Middle East for two to three weeks, then return to the States for domestic flying for the same period before returning to Europe for additional Desert Shield/Storm duty. Because of the long distances flown, each chartered aircraft came with four crews. CRAF used the double crew method, where one crew rested while the other crew flew. Back-to-back missions with double crews became routine. Average monthly flight time for crews during the operation was about 100 hr. However, the Federal Aviation Administration extended the monthly limit during the emergency to 150 hr of flight time.

All volunteers, CRAF crews, like their military counterparts, carried hazardous cargo and faced possible Iraqi conventional, chemical, and biological weapons attacks. Consequently, MAC operations and intelligence specialists in Europe briefed the civilian crews on safety precautions, security issues, diversion plans, flight routes, and air traffic control procedures prior to each mission (although several airline executives complained that their crews did not receive such preparation until well into the deployment). MAC frequently changed civil aircraft routings to make it more difficult for the enemy to find and track them. Upon arrival in Saudi Arabia, the crews were again briefed on the latest security precautions and what to do if the base came under attack. Ordinarily, commercial crews did not remain overnight in Saudi Arabia. Turnaround time there was about 2 to 3 hr for commercial cargo aircraft. During Desert Shield/Storm there were no commercial aircrews or aircraft casualties. Neither were any crew members hurt nor any aircraft damaged, according to William W. Hoover, Executive Vice President, Air Transport Association of America.

The U.S. air carriers' service went beyond that required by the CRAF arrangement. They waived restrictions on nonrefundable tickets for troops volunteering and activated for service in Desert Shield/Storm. Also, airlines offered discount fares to family members of troops traveling to visit them in hospitals. On return trips, commercial passenger aircraft transported civilian evacuees, mostly women and children, back to the United States following their release from Baghdad, Iraq, and Kuwait City, Kuwait. Evergreen evacuated Asian refugees from Amman, Jordan, to Sri Lanka and Bombay, India, and Tower Airlines evacuated Americans from Israel on its scheduled operations between Tel Aviv and New York. Because military cargo loads for the most part went one-way, commercial cargo aircraft often brought mail out of the United States Central Command Area of Responsibility (AOR) on return flights. Southern Air Transport, Evergreen, and other commercial carriers moved ammunition and other supplies into the Persian Gulf for coalition countries. Furthermore, several CRAF carriers took over MAC Pacific and Atlantic channel missions to free C-5s and C-141s for Desert Shield/Storm operations. When aircraft backed up at Dover AFB, Delaware, Federal Express used its trucks, some of which it had to modify, to move cargo from Dover to John F. Kennedy International Airport, New York, for airlift to the AOR, which eased the pressure on Dover and expedited the lift.

Allied Commercial Aircraft

Allied commercial aircraft also played a role in the deployment. Initially, USTRANSCOM and MAC were concerned that few foreign-flag airlines would be willing to fly at the compensatory rates established by MAC. Under the Fly America Act, MAC could not pay higher rates as long as American airline aircraft remained available on the market. As it turned out, their fears were not realized. Airlines offered their services at the MAC established rates. (USTRANSCOM gained, but did not exercise, authority to charter foreign airlift.) Additionally, the United States could legally accept lift donations from foreign countries subject to the carriers undergoing a technical safety evaluation (pursuant to 10 U.S. Code 2640). By the end of March, four countries had flown 200 Desert Shield/Storm cargo missions free of charge, as follows: Japan (124), South Korea (54), Italy (21), and Kuwait (1).

Tactical Airlift

While U.S.-flag and allied commercial aircraft augmented strategic or "intertheater" airlift, C-130s provided the tactical or "intratheater" airlift for Desert

Shield/Storm. Although USTRANSCOM assets, C-130s operated under the direct control of the theater commander, Army Gen. H. Norman Schwarzkopf. Eventually numbering 149 aircraft (including five from South Korea), C-130s completed nearly 13,900 missions, carrying about 242,000 passengers and 174,000 tons of cargo in support of the theater commander.

The tactical airlift force performed a wide variety of missions. There were two types of scheduled missions. "Star" missions transported people and "Camel" missions, for the most part, hauled cargo. At their peak, Star and Camel missions numbered 25 each per day. Some of the first C-130s on the scene moved ammunition, tents, fuel, and other supplies from prepositioned stocks at Thumwait, Masirah, and Seeb, Oman, to establish logistical bases for arriving air and ground forces. In mid-January, C-130s on 1175 missions carried nearly 14,000 passengers and 10,000 tons of cargo for the XVIII Airborne Corps from King Fahd to Rafha, Saudi Arabia. Between 18 and 28 February, C-130s on 3100 sorties moved about 8600 troops and 12,700 tons of cargo to forward positions near the Iraqi border in support of the "Hail Mary" flanking maneuver. Soon thereafter, the aircraft on 500 sorties shifted part of the Marine Corps forces to the northwest so they could penetrate Kuwait at the bend in the elbow. They also dropped 15,000-lb BLU-82 bombs (nicknamed "Big Blue 82s" and "daisy cutters") on Iraqi fortifications and airdropped food and water to Iraqi prisoners of war.

Aeromedical Airlift and Medical Planning

USTRANSCOM and MAC planned and carried out aeromedical airlift. They developed the "Aeromedical Evacuation (AE) Concept of Operations for Desert Shield." In support of the operation, the entire airlift force—commercial, active-duty, reserve, strategic, and tactical—transported nearly 16,400 patients in the AOR, from the AOR to Europe, and from Europe to the United States. Also they moved via air human remains from the AOR to the mortuary at Dover AFB, Delaware, and wrote the "Integrated CONUS [Continental United States] Medical Mobilization Plan (ICMMP) Aeromedical Evacuation Concept of Operations for Operation Desert Storm." Fortunately, it was not put to the test.

Channel Airlift

Strategic airlift aircraft accomplishments during Desert Shield/Storm were many. In the United States, regularly scheduled channel missions moved cargo and passengers from Tinker AFB, Oklahoma, and Dover AFB, Delaware, to Cairo, Egypt; and to Dharain, Riyadh, Al Jubayl, and King Khalid Military City, Saudi Arabia. From Norfolk, Virginia, strategic airlift channel missions flew to Sigonella, Italy; King Faisal, Saudi Arabia; and Bahrain. Also from the east coast, MAC channels ran from McGuire AFB, New Jersey, to Dhahran and Riyadh. On the west coast, MAC operated a channel from Travis AFB, California, to Clark AFB, Philippines; Diego Garcia in the Indian Ocean; Cubi Point, Philippines; Masirah, Oman; and Al Fujayrah, United Arab Emirates (UAE). A channel connected Clark to Diego Garcia and Dhahran, and in Europe a channel tied Sigonella to King Faisal. As requirements changed during the operations, so did channel mission frequency and airports of embarkation and debarkation.

Navy C-9 Aircraft

During Desert Shield/Storm, for the first time, Navy C-9 aircraft served in the common-user role. In late December 1990, four Naval Air Reserve squadrons, each with three aircraft and about 245 personnel, deployed from their home stations to Europe. Transport Squadron VR-55, Naval Air Station (NAS) Alameda, California, and VR-57 from NAS North Island, California, operated from Semback, Germany. VR-59, NAS Dallas, Texas, deployed to Bitburg, Germany, and VR-58, NAS Jacksonville, Florida, deployed to Naples, Italy. The German-based units received mission tasking from the Navy Air Logistics Office Detachment Alpha, which worked with MAC's 322d Airlift Division, Ramstein AB, Germany. Those nine aircraft flew some of their missions in the common-user role. VR-58 took its orders from the Air Service Coordination Office, Mediterranean. Through the month of January, Navy C-9s primarily moved passengers to Saudi Arabia and Turkey. Later in the month, a rotating two-aircraft detachment from the German-based units began to operate from Al Fujayrah, UAE, while the remaining aircraft continued their operations from Germany and Italy.

By February, the Navy C-9s had shifted to a primarily resupply mission. The aircraft were reconfigured to handle eight pallets of cargo and they began shuttling bombs and fuses to Moron, Spain, for B-52 bomber operations. As the war intensified, the Navy airlifters flew Eastern European routes in support of coalition forces in Turkey. During their Desert Shield/Storm operations, from 1 January to 24 March 1991, the 12 Navy C-9s moved about 18,000 passengers and 3750 tons on approximately 700 missions, of which MAC estimated 209 were in the common-user role.

Special Assignment Airlift Missions

Special Assignment Airlift Missions in support of Desert Shield/Storm were many and varied. They included 16 Puma helicopters from the United Kingdom to Saudi Arabia on four C-5s in October and November 1990; a chemical defense battalion (183 passengers and 63 vehicles) from Czechoslovakia to Saudi Arabia on 13 C-5s in December; a Patriot missile battalion from the Netherlands to Turkey on one C-5 in January 1991; and in February a Roland surface-to-air missile system from Germany to Turkey on 10 C-5s, and 100 passengers, two tanks, and two trucks from Paris to Saudi Arabia on two C-5s. Also of note, MAC established an "air-bridge" to move nearly 50,000 tons of M-117 munitions from the United States to the AOR in January 1991 for the air offensive against Iraq.

Patriot Missile Deployment to Israel

For political as well as military reasons, the deployment of Patriot missiles to Israel stood out among all other Desert Storm airlift operations. At 0030Z on 18 January 1991, Iraq fired SCUD missiles into Israel, prompting President Bush to assure Israeli Prime Minister Shamir that the United States would help defend Israel against further attacks. The United States feared that an Israeli military response would fracture the fragile Arab coalition against Iraq. As a result the Chairman, Joint Chiefs of Staff, at 0130Z the following day, ordered United States Commander in Chief, Europe (USCINCEUR), as the supported commander, and Commander in Chief, United States Transportation Command (USCINCTRANS), as the supporting commander, to deploy two Patriot fire units—personnel; launchers; missiles; and command, control, and communications gear—to Israel within 24 hours. The first Patriot unit had to be operational within 48 hr of the deployment order. Twenty-two missiles had to be delivered within 18 hr of the deployment order. Another 42 missiles had to be delivered within the next 30 hr. At 0245Z on the 19th, USCINCTRANS directed MAC to deploy two Patriot batteries from Europe to Ben Gurion IAP, Israel. Shortly thereafter, MAC diverted two Saudi Arabia-bound C-141s, one over Germany and the other over Egypt, and each carrying eight Patriot missiles, to Ben Gurion. Between 1230Z and 1245Z those two aircraft and eight C-5s from Rhein Main AB, Germany, carrying eight Patriot launchers, arrived at Ben Gurion. About four hours later, two C-141s with 14 more missiles arrived at Ben Gurion from Ramstein. Therefore, 30 missiles, 8 more than were required, were in place within $15\frac{1}{2}$ hr, $2\frac{1}{2}$ hr ahead of schedule. At 2300Z on the 19th, USCINCEUR reported 2 Patriot missile batteries operational, $26\frac{1}{2}$ hr ahead of schedule.

Meanwhile, loading of the remaining 42 missiles had already begun at Little Rock AFB, Arkansas, and Cape Canaveral, Florida. They arrived in Israel at 1855Z on the 20th, $6\frac{1}{2}$ hr ahead of schedule. The Iraqis launched their second SCUD on Israel on the evening of 22 January, and the newly arrived Patriots intercepted and destroyed the missile.

The deployment was extraordinary. Just $21\frac{1}{2}$ hr after receiving their orders, United States European Command and United States Transportation Command had delivered Patriot missiles to Israel and put them on alert outside Tel Aviv. In all, 9 C-141s and 30 C-5s had airlifted 544 passengers, 70 missiles, 8 launchers, and unit equipment totaling 2776 tons from the United States and Germany to Israel in less than 42 hr. Most importantly, the airlift, the largest to Israel since the Yom Kippur War of 1973, kept Israel out of the war with Iraq. To help assure the safety of innocent Israeli citizens and the continued military neutrality of their country, MAC, over the next several weeks, deployed another 122 Patriot missiles and support equipment from Germany and the United States to Israel on 19 C-141 and 17 C-5 missions.

Desert Express and European Desert Express

To help cope with "priority creep," the tendency for transportation users to continually increase the amount of their high-priority air cargo, USTRANSCOM established Special Priority Code 9AU and an airlift system to support it. Named Desert Express, the operation was one of the command's most successful Desert Shield/Storm initiatives. USTRANSCOM designed Desert Express to meet United States Central Command's war-stopper requirements—such as spare parts for aircraft, tanks, and other high-tech equipment—and patterned it after commercial airlines' overnight delivery service. Rarely did it carry passengers.

Initiated by MAC on 30 October at USTRANSCOM's direction, Desert Express carried Army, Air Force, and eventually Navy and Marine Corps cargo daily via a C-141 from Charleston AFB, South Carolina, to Dhahran and Riyadh, Saudi Arabia. The aircraft departed from Charleston at 1230 Eastern Standard Time. Cargo destined for the AOR had to arrive at Charleston no later than 1030 to make that day's express mission. The 1030 cutoff time dovetailed with the overnight mail and air express parcel delivery schedules in the United States and the flight schedules of CONUS airlift contracted by MAC for Air Force Logistics Command (LOGAIR) and the Navy (QUICKTRANS). Including a stop for fuel and a crew change in Torrejon, Spain, it took a Desert Express mission about 17 hr to reach the AOR. When the C-141 landed, ground crews unloaded the Desert Express cargo, sorted it by destination, and loaded it on C-130 shuttles. Overall, Desert Express reduced response time for the highest-priority shipments from as much as 2 wk to as little as 72 hr. Its success spawned a similar arrangement in Germany between Rhein Main AB and the Persian Gulf. Called European Desert Express, it began operation on 8 December 1990. To help move a backlog of 9AU cargo, USTRANSCOM on 13 February 1991 began flying a second C-141 mission per day from Charleston. It departed at 1400 Eastern Standard Time, an hour and a half after the first, staged through Torrejon, and stopped at King Khalid Military City and Dhahran, Saudi Arabia.

By the end of the war, Desert Express had moved nearly 2040 tons of 9AU cargo and about 27 tons of 9BU cargo on 135 missions. At the end of its operation on 14 March 1991, European Desert Express had airlifted 680 tons of 9AU cargo and 761 tons of 9BU cargo on 92 missions.

Airlift Assessment

Military Airlift Command Fleet

USTRANSCOM learned much about airlift from its Desert Shield/Storm experiences. When operating in the desert, C-130 crews should wipe down wheel struts after every flight to keep sand and other grit from working into hydraulic seals. Cleaning cockpits daily to prevent sand and dust from sifting into the electronics, and regularly flushing water through engines to prevent corrosion, were also essential in the desert. Air Force Brig. Gen. Edwin Tenoso, the commander of airlift forces in the Saudi Arabia during Desert Shield/Storm, felt it would have been better to deploy whole C-130 wings rather than form provisional wings out of squadrons from several stateside units.

Brigadier General Tenoso recommended changes to the C-130 training program based on his Desert Shield/Storm experiences. Units should do more "integration training." Crews needed more experience operating with fighters, airlifters from other units, and command, control, and communications aircraft. He would like MAC to put more emphasis on flying without the use of communications and navigation equipment. Crews needed to practice high-altitude airdrops. Finally, he recommended that, for wartime-tempo operations like those he had experienced in Saudi Arabia, MAC needed to raise the C-130 crew ratio from 1:5 to 2:0. In general, he felt C-130 crew training and aircraft equipment needed to be more oriented toward war.

The command pushed its strategic airlift force to the limit during Desert Shield/Storm, which shortened the aircrafts' service life. From December 1990 through January 1991, C-5s flew nearly $3\frac{1}{2}$ times their usual peacetime rate. The normal peacetime C-141 mission rate was about 500 missions/mo. In August, C-141s completed 1041 missions, and by December they were flying over 1400 missions/mo, a pace that continued through February. Although C-141s maintained a high mission-capable rate, MAC estimated that at such a tempo of operations seven months equaled one year of programmed service life.

The C-17 Aircraft

The war emphasized the need for the C-17 to replace the aging C-141 and to increase airlift flexibility. The C-17's modern design would give it the capability to move larger quantities of equipment, munitions, fuel, and outsized cargo directly to forward areas. In his testimony to the U.S. Senate Committee on Armed Services in March of 1991, General Johnson stated:

> Because of its superior fuel efficiency, the C-17 can carry its maximum payload over a greater distance than either the C-5 or C-141. The C-17 can also airdrop outsize cargo. Its lower manpower requirements and reduced operation and support costs make it more efficient, while its exceptional ground maneuverability increases cargo throughput, adding to its effectiveness. . . . If we would have had the C-17 in place of the C-141 during Desert Shield, we could have met our airlift deployment requirements from 20 to 35 percent faster, depending on the capacity of the airfields made available in the area of operations. The C-17's impact in the first 12 days alone would have allowed us to carry enough cargo to deploy an additional three F-15, three F-16, three F-4, and three A-10 squadrons, plus two light infantry brigades. In addition to its strategic contribution, the C-17 could also have provided the equivalent in-theater airlift of a 16-aircraft C-130 squadron.

Furthermore, MAC's analysis of Desert Shield/Storm showed that by replacing 117 C-141s with 80 C-17s during the first 45 days of the operations, the command could have increased strategic lift capability by 28 percent and outsized capability by 25 percent. In summary, the C-17 would mean fewer intertheater missions, fewer crew members, less maintenance as well as additional intratheater capability, and a faster rate of cargo delivery.

En Route Basing for Strategic Airlift Aircraft

For General Johnson, Desert Shield/Storm underscored the importance of en route bases for strategic deployment. In-theater airfields, although well developed by most standards, lacked sufficient ramp space and support facilities such as fueling, billeting, and cargo handling. Consequently, MAC relied heavily on bases in Europe for such services. The percentage of airlift missions transiting European bases in support of the operation follow: Torrejon AB, Spain, 31 percent; Rhein Main AB, Germany, 27 percent; Zaragoza AB, Spain, 18 percent; Ramstein AB, Germany, 14 percent; RAF Mildenhall, England, 6 percent; and Rota, Spain, 4 percent.

The only major structural repair facility for C-5s and C-141s, Rhein Main had as many as 40 such aircraft on the ground at a time. Together, Torrejon and Rhein Main serviced up to 100 strategic airlift aircraft with 2 million gal of fuel per day. During December 1990, MAC averaged 50 missions/day from Torrejon (compared to 50/wk in peacetime) and 25 missions/day from Zaragoza. Missions at those two Spanish bases peaked at 90 and 35, respectively. The record number of strategic airlift aircraft on the ground at Torrejon during Desert Shield/Storm was 68. Consequently, General Johnson, in a letter to Secretary of Defense Cheney, stated emphatically that the United States "must retain both a Central European and an Iberian Peninsula base" and requested that USTRANSCOM be consulted on base closure issues "affecting the global strategic mobility mission."

463L Pallets

Airlift 463L pallets—along with their nets, chains, and straps—were in chronic short supply throughout the deployment. Pallets allowed MAC to carry cargo in neat packages for quick and easy transport. Although it was the responsibility of deploying units to furnish pallets for their cargo, they often turned to MAC for these items. When asked why they did not have pallets to support their deployments, units commonly replied that they "never expected to actually deploy." Pallets, once out of the airlift system, were often misused. Some became storage platforms or construction material. Others were broken or lost.

Many served as intermodal devices. Transporters and logisticians in-theater discovered that cargo "containerized" on 463L pallets fit nicely on 2½-ton and 40-ft flatbed trucks. Similarly, they used aircraft tie-down straps, chains, and nets to secure bulk cargo on trucks. At logistical bases inland, Army and Marine Corps units stockpiled their cargo on the pallets in anticipation of orders to move forward quickly by air or land.

USTRANSCOM and MAC attacked the pallet shortage problem from several angles. To meet the wartime requirement, MAC representatives in-theater, with the Army's assistance, retrieved pallets from inland staging areas for consolidation at airfields. There they cleaned and repaired them for transport via air back to the United States. USTRANSCOM and MAC arranged with Air Force Logistics Command to increase and expedite construction of new pallets and put into the airlift system 6000 pallets from the Department of Defense War Reserve Storage. They also reemphasized to users their duty to supply and protect such critical strategic deployment assets. The measures worked, but barely. Right up to the end of the war the Joint Chiefs of Staff, the supported commander in chief, and the supporting commanders in chief, feared that the shortage of 463L pallets would break or seriously degrade the strategic airlift to the Persian Gulf.

At war's end, USTRANSCOM and MAC were considering several ways to avoid pallet shortages in the future. Early in future contingencies, they would form recovery teams for deployment to the area of operations. They also contemplated adopting a "one-time-use" disposable pallet. Designing a "pallet within a pallet" system was another possible option. As envisioned, a 463L-like pallet would enclose a tactical-type pallet that could move forward by surface. The outer pallet could then return to the airlift system for additional loads. Perhaps the best solution was to consider 463L pallets and their accouterments as intermodal assets, and simply procure enough of them to satisfy both airlift and theater pipeline needs.

Safety and the C-5 Crash

MAC's safety record during Desert Shield/Storm, one of the largest and most intense airlift operations in history, should be considered excellent. On 29 August 1990, the command experienced its one and only Desert Shield/Storm catastrophic accident, when a C-5 crashed departing Ramstein AB, Germany, for the Persian Gulf with a load of medical supplies, food, and aircraft maintenance equipment. Thirteen of the 17 personnel on board were killed. Nine of those were with the 433d Military Airlift Wing, Kelly AFB, near San Antonio, Texas. One 433d Reservist survived. All the Reservists were volunteers. The other four killed and three injured were active-duty Air Force from Ramstein and nearby Hahn AB. Air Force investigators later determined, according to *Aviation Week and Space Technology*, that the "uncommanded and inadvertent" deployment of an engine thrust reverser during takeoff probably caused the crash.

Civil Reserve Air Fleet

USTRANSCOM and MAC learned much about Civil Reserve Air Fleet (CRAF) during Desert Shield/Storm. CRAF aircraft were less flexible than MAC aircraft. MAC estimated that about 85 percent of the cargo carried by air during Desert Shield/Storm could not fit on or was extremely difficult to load on civil aircraft. Of that amount, about 60 percent was oversize. The other 15 percent was "outsize," meaning it could fit only on C-5s.

Although CRAF program functioned superbly during Desert Shield/Storm, USTRANSCOM and MAC believed it could be refined. A new CRAF structure would give USTRANSCOM and MAC increased cargo lift in Stage II. It would also give the commands, for the first time, an aeromedical option in Stage II.

U.S. airline companies and their employees had a long list of lessons learned from Desert Shield/Storm. William D. Slattery, Executive Vice President for Operations, Northwest Airlines, requested that MAC give the airlines more notice of impending activation. "A 24-hour or 48-hour notice is not long enough . . . to set up an adequate support structure," he emphasized. In that vein, he recommended that in future contingencies CRAF operate from hubs, such as Frankfurt, Germany, or JFK in New York, which would increase lift capability by incorporating into CRAF the airlines' regularly scheduled flights.

Captain John Saux, Executive Vice President, Airline Pilots Association, offered several other suggestions for CRAF improvement. He noted that at the beginning of Desert Shield the airlines had difficulty assessing their capability to crew CRAF over and above reserve crew commitments, as required under the CRAF program. His organization would work with the airlines to rectify the problem. He recommended that instead of issuing blanket waivers and letting the mission fit the waiver, MAC should look at each mission and waive requirements only as needed. For example, waiving the length of the duty day for MAC crew members, whose average age was 30, worked fine, but it was tough on CRAF crew members, whose average

age was closer to 55. On the one hand, Saux recommended that MAC and the Department of Transportation restrict hazardous materials to military aircraft because CRAF crews were not trained to handle them. On the other hand, he wanted the military to train CRAF crews in Tactical Aide to Navigation and other precision radar equipment and methods. Lack of such expertise had caused some CRAF pilots to "refuse to make precision radar approaches" during Desert Shield/Storm. Lack of proper charts and ultra-high-frequency-equipped aircraft had also greatly complicated their job. Finally, he wanted the military to issue CRAF crews special-purpose gear, such as chemical warfare protective clothing, prior to or immediately upon activation.

Concerns foremost on the minds of airline executives were monetary. Airlines that volunteered their service prior to CRAF activation felt that it was unfair for MAC to exclude them from military business after activation. Several complained that during the operation the military coopted their aircraft only to let them sit idle for several days before deployment. In some cases, planes were pulled out for CRAF but never used. Days would pass before the carriers were informed their planes were not needed. A familiar complaint was lack of logistical support en route and in the AOR. Airline representatives argued that their companies lost the goodwill of their paying customers due to canceled flights. This in turn strengthened the competitors' edge. Overall, they felt that their participation in Desert Shield/Storm would result in long term losses in both the passenger and cargo business. Now that the airlines understood the real cost of the CRAF program, they were questioning their future participation in it.

MAC considered several ways to strengthen incentives for participation in the CRAF program. New contracts would institutionalize volunteers, so that volunteers remained in the system following an activation. Contracts would guarantee utilization if called up, and a reasonable release if not called up. They would make the peacetime uniform rate the basis for war rates; guarantee an eight-hour day if called up; and recognize additional costs of activation and lack of backhaul in war.

Despite CRAF's tremendous showing during Desert Shield/Storm, General Johnson considered the program's future "very uncertain" owing to the economic precariousness of many U.S. airlines. Several filed for bankruptcy during the war, and several others might soon follow. He cited as an example Pan American World Airways, which accounted for 10 percent of CRAF's wartime passenger airlift capability and 11 percent of its wartime cargo capability. He feared that "this potential loss may not be absorbed by other carriers." More importantly, the health of the U.S. airlines industry was an issue of national security. The Department of Defense did not want the U.S. airline industry to go the way of the U.S. maritime industry. More to the point, it did not want to depend on foreign-flag airlines for deploying and sustaining American troops in emergencies.

Sealift Operations

Overview

USTRANSCOM's Desert Shield/Storm sealift accomplishments were as impressive as those of airlift. At the height of the sealift on 31 December 1990, 217 ships—132 en route, 57 returning, and 28 loading or unloading—formed a virtual "steel bridge" across the Atlantic Ocean. This equated to approximately one ship every 50 mi from Savannah, Georgia, to the Persian Gulf. By the end of the war, 459 ship-loads had moved 945,000 pieces of unit equipment totaling nearly 32.7 million sq ft, enough tanks, trucks, ammunition, and food stuffs to cover every square foot of 681 football fields. Unit equipment sealifted to the United States Central Command (USCENTCOM) area of responsibility (AOR) totaled nearly 2.45 million tons. Another 701,500 tons of sustainment dry cargo traveled by sea. Mostly containerized and shipped on regularly scheduled commercial liners, it equated to about 37 containerships (2000 twenty-foot size). In all, the command transported about 9.2 million tons of cargo by sea (3.1 dry and 6.1 petroleum products) to the Persian Gulf during Desert Shield/Storm, as shown in Table D-1.

At war's end, the sustainment pipeline was open. The first week of March 1991, 70 shiploads of cargo, totaling 469,608 tons, were en route to the USCENTCOM AOR. (Only a small percentage of this cargo was delivered as planned. The remaining loads, termed "U-Turns," moved instead to various ports in the United States, Europe, or Pacific.) Fifty of the 70 shiploads carried ammunition totaling 378,590 tons, 68 percent of the total ammunition loaded for transport by sea during Desert Shield/Storm. Another 1000 rail cars of ammunition and explosives were at Sunny Point Military Ocean Terminal, North Carolina, awaiting shipment to the Persian Gulf. Obviously, the United States was prepared to fight a longer war.

Afloat Prepositioning Force

Because of the huge amount of heavy combat equipment required by the Commander in Chief, United States Central Command (USCINCCENT), the Department of Defense put sealift into motion almost immediately. First it turned to the Afloat Prepositioning Force, consisting of 13 Maritime Prepositioning Ships and 12 Afloat Prepositioning Ships. The Maritime Prepositioning Ships were divided into three Maritime Prepositioning Squadrons (MPSs), one each based in the Atlantic Ocean (MPS-1), Indian Ocean (MPS-2), and Pacific Ocean (MPS-3). Each squadron was capable of equipping and supplying a Marine Expeditionary Brigade (MEB) of approximately 16,500 Marines for 30 days. Both MPS-2 and MPS-3 were alerted for possible deployment on 7 August for the first-ever wartime test of the Afloat Prepositioning Force. On 15 August, MPS-2 roll-on/roll-off (RO/RO) vessels Anderson, Bonnyman, and Hauge, the first ships to arrive in the AOR in support of Desert Shield, began unloading their cargo at Al Jubayl, Saudi Arabia. They carried equipment and supplies for the 7th MEB, whose troops were arriving in the AOR via air. All five ships of MPS-2 had arrived in-theater by 5 September. The four ships of MPS-3, supporting the 1st MEB, began arriving in the AOR on 25 August. They closed on 30 August. Supporting elements of the II Marine Expeditionary Force, the four ships of the MPS-1, arrived in the AOR on 13 December. After their initial prepositioning voyages, 7 of the 13 Maritime Prepositioning Ships were turned over to USTRANSCOM as common-user transport ships (one in MPS-1, five in MPS-2, and one in MPS-3). While in-theater and not common-user assets, Maritime Prepositioning Ships served as floating ammunition and fuel platforms and in other sea-based logistics roles.

Long-term Military Sealift Command (MSC) charters, the Afloat Prepositioning Ships of the Afloat Prepositioning Force, began arriving in Saudi Arabia from Diego Garcia on 17 August. Carrying Army and Air Force equipment and supplies, they included four tankers and eight cargo ships. After delivering their initial loads, seven of the cargo vessels began serving as common-user strategic transports. The eighth cargo ship remained in the theater as a USCENTCOM asset. All four tankers eventually served in the common-user role. Military Sealift Command withdrew two of the tankers from the prepositioning force for common-user service at the outset of Desert Shield. The other two operated in the AOR under USCENTCOM through most of Desert Shield. They completed their first common-user voyages by mid-January 1991, just prior to D-Day, 17 January 1991.

The Afloat Prepositioning Force's contribution to Desert Shield/Storm was considerable. On their first Desert Shield voyages, serving in their prepositioning role, the Afloat Prepositioning Force delivered 281,305 tons of unit cargo to the AOR (116,977 tons by Afloat Prepositioning Ships and 164,328 tons by Maritime Prepositioning Ships). Overall, in its prepositioning and common-user roles, the Afloat Prepositioning Force carried 19 percent of Desert Shield/Storm unit cargo (8.5 percent Afloat Prepositioning Ships and 10.5 percent Maritime Prepositioning Ships).

Fast Sealift Ships and the *Antares* Casualty

The eight ships from MSC's fast sealift fleet began arriving in the AOR soon after the Afloat Prepositioning Force. Military Sealift Command activated three of the Fast Sealift Ships (FSSs) on 7 August and the remaining five on 8 August. Maintained in a reduced readiness status that allowed for activation in 96 hours or less, each had a skeleton crew of about a dozen merchant mariners kept on a four-day steaming notice. A full crew numbered about 40. FSSs had both a container and a RO/RO capability. A series of ramps allowed wheeled and tracked vehicles to be driven on and off. Thus they were ideal for carrying unit equipment. Also, two sets of twin cranes amidships and aft lifted cargo on and off.

They were huge by most any standard. Measuring 946 ft long, almost as long as an aircraft carrier, each could carry about 1000 pieces of equipment. One FSS load was roughly equivalent to 200 C-5 aircraft loads. Designed for a maximum speed of 33 kn, FSSs were also fast for a cargo ship. (FSSs during Desert Shield/Storm actually averaged about 23 kn, due primarily to bad weather and navigational considerations such as speed limitations in the Suez Canal.) The *Capella*, departing Jacksonville, Florida, on 13 August, was the first FSS to arrive in the AOR, on the 27th. It was followed by the *Altair*, which departed Savannah, Georgia, on the 14th and arrived in Ad Damman, Saudi Arabia, on the 28th. (Navy VADM Francis R. Donovan, MSC's Commander, called the first *Capella* and *Altair* voyages "a horse race.") They carried equipment for the 24th Infantry Division (24th ID). Interestingly, stevedores in Ad Damman unloaded the *Capella* in record time for an FSS, 12 hr. Learning from the experience, it took them only 7½ hr to unload the *Altair* the following day.

All but one FSS, the *Antares*, had finished their first voyage by 7 September. After departing Jacksonville, Florida, on 20 August with 24th ID equipment, the *Antares* began to have boiler problems. On the 25th, she sat dead in the water at approximately 35-48N and 68-55W.

Working with its component commands, USTRANSCOM developed a plan to speed the unit's equipment to the AOR. MSC on the 26th diverted the *Antares,* under tow by MSC's ocean tug *Apache,* to Rota, Spain. MSC also diverted *Altair* to Rota to pick up the *Antares* load and take it to the Persian Gulf. Having completed its first Desert Shield voyage, the *Altair* was in the Mediterranean en route back to the United States for another load. While the two FSSs proceeded to Rota, USTRANSCOM, working with USCENTCOM, identified high-priority 24th ID equipment on the *Antares* for airlift from Rota to the AOR.

On 9 September the *Antares* arrived at Rota, followed by the *Altair* on the 10th, when the operation commenced. With the Military Traffic Management Command (MTMC) Commander Army MG John R. Piatak on the scene, and under direction of the Commander of MTMC-Europe, 98 Army supercargoes from the *Antares* and personnel from U.S. Naval Station Rota began to transfer the *Antares* cargo to the *Altair.* The ships were nested port side to, with the *Antares* inboard. Operations included RO/RO to the pier and transloading ship to ship. Transloading was a delicate job, involving proper infusion of ballast so that the two ships remained in balance with one another. The ships had to be listed away from each other to keep their deck houses from crashing together. Simultaneously, 50 XVIII Airborne Corps troops, whom MAC had airlifted from Dhahran, Saudi Arabia, to Rota on the 8th, prepared 32 pieces of equipment, including communications vans and generators, for airlift aboard MAC C-5s and C-141s, two of each. All four MAC aircraft had departed Rota by the 11th. Transloading FSS to FSS continued through the 13th with the additional help of 135 troops from Naval Reserve Cargo Handling Battalion Four, who had arrived at Rota from Charleston AFB, South Carolina, on the 11th aboard two C-141s. The *Altair* departed Rota on the 14th and arrived in Saudi Arabia on the 23d, thus closing the 24th ID three weeks later than planned. For Desert Shield/Storm, the *Antares'* boiler failures proved fatal. Lacking the resources to fix her at Rota, MSC towed her to Royal Naval Station Gibraltar, where she remained under repair throughout the operation.

Several points in regard to the *Antares'* failure and the recovery of its cargo need highlighting. Having just completed six months of service in exercise Team Spirit, the *Antares* in August 1990 had been scheduled for major overhaul. Thus USTRANSCOM and MSC accepted a degree of risk in deciding to use her to speed the deployment. Even with a catastrophic failure, the FSS fleets' carrying capacity and speed allowed the remaining seven ships to deliver just over 13 percent of Desert Shield/Storm unit equipment on 32 voyages. Transloading ship-to-ship saved time. The entire operation took only 4½ days. Using the normal method of unloading from the first ship onto the dock and then loading the second ship would have taken 10 days. Overall, and perhaps most importantly, the *Antares* episode serves as an example of USTRANSCOM's value added. In support of USCENTCOM requirements, USTRANSCOM devised a plan to recover the 24th ID cargo and expedite its delivery to the AOR. To do so, the command integrated the transportation modes and directed the expertise of all three of its component commands: MAC airlift, MSC sealift, and MTMC port operations.

Ready Reserve Force

While readying FSSs for deployment, USTRANSCOM and MSC turned to the Maritime Administration (MARAD) to activate U.S. ships in reserve. The National Defense Reserve Fleet (NDRF) was comprised of two groups of ships. The Ready

Reserve Force (RRF) numbered 96 vessels: 83 dry cargo, 11 tankers, and 2 troop-ships, which were laid up in various states of preparedness allowing them to be ready for sea in 5 days (65 ships assigned), 10 days (28 ships assigned), or 20 days (3 ships assigned). The vessels were administrated by MARAD Reserve Fleets: James River, Virginia (38 ships); Beaumont, Texas (35 ships); and Suisun Bay, California (23 ships). (Many of the RRF ships were actually located or "outported" at various U.S. ports.) There were 116 additional vessels in the NDRF, including 71 World War II Victory ships and 45 others ranging in age from 20 to 45 yr. Their breakout times ranged from 30 to 90 days. None of the latter group was activated during the operation because of their smaller size, larger crew requirements, older propulsion systems, and slower loading and transit times.

For Desert Shield/Storm, MARAD undertook the first large-scale activation of the RRF. On 10 August, at MSC's request, MARAD activated all 17 of the RRF's RO/RO vessels. Two of those, the Cape Henry and the Cape Inscription—carrying the 1st Corps Support Command and the 197th Infantry Brigade—were the first RRF ships to reach the AOR (9 September). In all, MARAD activated 76 ships during the Desert Shield/Storm time period, 7 August 1990–10 March 1991. Of those, 72 were activated for use in Desert Shield/Storm. Seventy of the 72 were dry cargo ships. In all, 62 RRF ships used in support of Desert Shield/Storm were common-user dry cargo under USTRANSCOM. MSC estimated the average cost per ship activation to be $2.4 million. By war's end, the RRF had carried 28 percent of the unit cargo for U.S. forces.

Activation of the RRF was slower than anticipated. Only 20 of the 62 RRF common-user dry cargo ships used in Desert Shield/Storm were activated within their specified time period. Ships scheduled for 5-day breakout took, on the average, 11 days to breakout. It took an average of 16 days to break out 10-day ships. In nearly every case, MARAD attributed lateness to problems with propulsion or auxiliary machinery. Both the Department of Transportation and the Department of Defense believed the primary cause for such mechanical failures was lack of funds for maintenance and activation exercises. Congress had repeatedly cut RRF funding. In fact, only one-third of the RRF ships serving in Desert Shield/Storm had even been test-activated, and as a consequence some ships could not meet their advertised readiness levels. MARAD also discovered that some RRF ship contract managers did not have the technical expertise and resources to break out ships in a crisis. As a result, "in the best interests of the government," MARAD in November canceled reserve ship maintenance, activation, and operating contracts with two RRF ship management companies. Both companies had activated ships late. One of those ships, the *Gulf Banker,* had a catastrophic breakdown.

A few late activations were at least partly due to manning problems. Two skill groups were in particularly short supply: radio officers, and senior engineers who knew how to operate and maintain steam propulsion plants. The task of locating approximately 2400 licensed and unlicensed seafarers for RRF ships fell to MARAD, Ship Managers, and General Agents. They had a hard time locating mariners, because the activations began on a weekend and continued through the August vacation season.

Other ships could not be activated on time because they were laid up far from activation facilities. Maritime Administrator Captain Warren G. Leback noted that five-day RRF ships in Beaumont, Texas, had to be towed to New Orleans, Houston, Galveston, or Mobile, because Beaumont did not have the facilities required to activate them. Towing took up to two days. They also had to undergo a 24-hour sea trial, leaving as little as one day to ready a vessel that might not have been to sea for years. Once activated and brought to operating condition, however, RRF ships performed well. All 17 RO/RO ships activated on 10 August completed their first voyage. Overall, the RRF maintained a respectable 93.5 reliability rate.

Commercial Charters: U.S.-Flag and Foreign-Flag

Along with the prepositioning ships, FSSs, and the RRF, chartered commercial ships played a vital role in the deployment. MSC chartered sealift through the release of a worldwide Request for Proposal (RFP). In this way, MSC chartered 32 U.S. flag vessels. The first charter vessel to arrive (9 September) in the AOR (Ad Damman) was the *American Eagle*. It carried 2864 tons of 101st Airborne Division equipment from Jacksonville. Overall, the U.S. chartered commercial fleet carried approximately 13 percent of Desert Shield/Storm unit equipment.

When MSC had exhausted the U.S. merchant ships offered through RFP, it turned to allied and friendly sources of shipping. On 18 September, the first foreign charter ship, the Canadian flagged ASL *Cygnus*, arrived in the AOR (Ad Damman). It had left Savannah, Georgia, on 25 August carrying 7363 tons of 24th Infantry Division equipment. In all, MSC chartered 208 foreign vessels, including 41 RO/ROs, from 33 nations. Cyprus (28), Norway (21), Panama (21), Greece (17), and Bahamas (13) together contributed 100 vessels. The former Eastern Bloc nations of Poland and Rumania contributed five and three ships, respectively. Yugoslavia chartered two vessels to the United States. Twice, in August and December 1990, US-TRANSCOM requested, through the Department of State, use of Soviet Union dry cargo ships, and both times the Soviet Union declined, considering it "inappropriate to engage in such activities." Germany chartered only four ships. Japan, with a fleet of 2500 ships including 426 RO/RO and 439 general cargo, chartered no ships to the United States during the operation. Finally, as shown in Table D-10, U.S. allies donated sealift to the war effort, 1511 sea days' worth.

A statistical summary of commercial shipping contributions during Desert Shield/Storm follows. In all, foreign-flag vessels carried 27 percent of unit equipment. Of all dry cargo (unit equipment plus containerized and breakbulk sustainment cargo), the U.S. flag fleet (military and commercial) carried 80 percent. Foreign-flag vessels carried the remainder.

Sealift Readiness Program

During Desert Shield/Storm, USTRANSCOM could also have called on commercial ships from the Sealift Readiness Program (SRP). Administered by MSC, SRP required shipping companies that bid on MSC contracts or received government subsidies to commit 50 percent of their cargo capacity to MSC for possible use during less-than-full mobilization, contingencies, and emergencies. Of the 122 militarily useful vessels in the program, 23 were tankers and 99 were dry cargo. To activate the program, MSC had to show that (1) the NDRF ships were not available in sufficient time or numbers to meet requirements, and (2) there was insufficient shipping capability at fair and reasonable price to meet requirements, or available

Table D-10 Desert Shield/Storm Donated Sealift,
by Country (Foreign Government Value—As of
31 March 1991)

Country	Total
S. Korea	
Sea days	370
$ Value	10,596,964
Japan	
Sea days	420
$ Value	34,900,000
Kuwait	
Sea days	721
$ Value	20,629,000
Denmark	
Sea days	*
$ Value	5,945,131
Total	
Sea days	1,511
$ Value	72,071,095

*Space available on ships.

SOURCE: U.S. Transportation Command, Comptroller-Donated Lift
Reports. Prepared by: U.S. Transportation Command, Offices of History
and Comptroller (TCHO and TCAC).

shipping could not meet requirements. In addition, MARAD had to prepare a re-
port on what impact the activation would have on the commercial charter industry.
Approval authority rested with the Secretary of Defense and the Secretary of
Transportation.

For several reasons USTRANSCOM did not use SRP during Desert Shield/
Storm. Much of the U.S. maritime industry responded to the contingency voluntarily. By the end of the war USTRANSCOM had employed 62 SRP-enrolled vessels (8
tankers and 54 dry cargo, including 30 containerships under the Special Middle
East Sealift Agreement) without even activating the program. USTRANSCOM
needed RO/ROs primarily, and nearly all of them in the SRP were already supporting Desert Shield/Storm. Furthermore, USTRANSCOM considered the approval
process unresponsive to time-sensitive military operations. Finally, activating the remaining RO/ROs and container ships in the SRP could have caused the SRP companies severe and perhaps permanent financial damage by eliminating them from
the commercial liner trade.

U.S. Merchant Mariners

Nearly every crew member aboard every type of cargo ship—Afloat Prepositioning
Force, Fast Sealift Ships, Ready Reserve Force, and commercial charter—was a civilian merchant mariner. American merchant mariners fell into one of two major
categories. First, in general, civil service mariners worked on MSC-owned cargo vessels. Second, U.S.-flag charter and RRF ships were crewed for the most part by com-

mercial mariners. Merchant mariners also served aboard MSC hospital ships and auxiliaries such as oilers, combat stores ships, oceangoing tugs, and aviation logistic-support ships.

For operation Desert Storm, MARAD needed nearly 2400 additional commercial mariners to crew the RRF. Who were they? Many who heeded the unions' call for help were former merchant mariners who came out of retirement. Some of them were veterans of World War II, the Korean War, and the war in Southeast Asia. Nearly 200 were cadets at the U.S. Merchant Marine Academy, Kings Point, New York, and other U.S. maritime academies. Some were raw recruits. The Seafarers International Union expanded its entry-level training program from 60 to 200 students per month to help put bodies on ships fast. The union also increased the frequency of skill-upgrading courses for firemen and steam engineers from once a quarter to once a month. The Marine Engineers Beneficial Association/National Maritime Union, the Sailors Union of the Pacific, and other maritime unions developed similar programs to expand the pool. Enduring long working hours on multiple voyages with little or no leave, nearly 9800 American merchant mariners served during Desert Shield/Storm.

Like their counterparts in wars past, many American merchant mariners in Desert Shield/Storm voluntarily sailed into harm's way. Along with their comrades in uniform, they faced floating mines, chemical warfare, and attacks by Iraqi fighter aircraft and SCUD, Exocet, and Silkworm missiles. Why? Although motivations varied, two topped the list: patriotism and money. In praise of merchant mariners' patriotic response, General Johnson quipped, "They showed up in such numbers that we had them draw straws to see who would have the privilege of serving in the Gulf." Special wartime compensation included $130/mo, a 10 percent bonus for crews on ammunition ships, and double pay for time spent in the most dangerous parts of the Persian Gulf from D-Day to cessation of hostilities. Wages ranged from about $4800/mo for an able-bodied seaman recruit to as high as $150,000/yr for a commercial cargo ship captain. Wartime incentives also included special life insurance coverage and additional bonuses if actually attacked. Fortunately, no merchant mariners were killed due to enemy action, although at least one died (from a heart attack) while serving during the operation.

After Desert Shield/Storm, American merchant mariners did not go unrecognized for their service as they had in past wars. They were the only civilians invited to join in the National Victory Parade in Washington, D.C. The Department of Transportation minted for them a "U.S. Merchant Marine Expeditionary Medal." MARAD estimated that about 5000 U.S. merchant mariners who served in the war zone aboard U.S.-flag commercial or government-owned vessels were eligible to receive it. Congress was also considering granting American merchant mariners who served in Desert Shield/Storm tax breaks and reemployment rights.

Sealift Assessment

Decline of U.S. Maritime Industry, Impact on Strategic Deployment

The war in the Persian Gulf heightened USTRANSCOM's concerns for the health of the nation's maritime industry. At the end of World War II there were thousands of U.S.-flagged Merchant Marine ships carrying over 50 percent of U.S. foreign oceangoing trade. By 1970 the number of ships in the U.S. Merchant Marine had dropped to 894, with a corresponding decrease in the amount of U.S. trade they carried. The United States, the largest trading nation in the world, carried in 1990 less than 4 percent of its trade on U.S.-flagged ships. Due to the high cost of ship-building and crewing in the United States compared to other nations, the U.S. ship-building and commercial shipping industries were finding it increasingly difficult to compete on the world market. The importance of the issue was recognized at the highest levels. In his Maritime Day proclamation, President Bush said the victory in the Persian Gulf "demonstrated, once again, the importance of the American merchant marine to maintaining an adequate and reliable sealift capacity for the United States."

The U.S. Merchant Marine's severe decline had serious ramifications for national security. According to General Johnson, during Desert Shield/Storm "availability and timeliness of unit equipment capable ships from both U.S. and worldwide commercial fleets were not adequate to meet the supported CINC's [Commander in Chief's] surge requirements." To meet the requirement, the command used virtually every roll-on/roll-off (RO/RO) it could find: all 17 in the Ready Reserve Force (RRF), 47 U.S.-flag charter, and 41 foreign-flag charter. Competition among the allies exacerbated the problem. For example in late November, as USTRANSCOM prepared for surge deployment, the United Kingdom was contracting for 22 RO/ROs to move its 4th Mechanized Brigade to the Persian Gulf. It was during this period that the danger in the situation became most apparent. From late December 1990 to the end of the war, foreign flags carried nearly 40 percent of U.S. unit cargo. In General Johnson's words, "It worked okay this time but what if foreign governments don't go along with the operation [next time]? After all, only the United Kingdom supported our raid on Qadhafi in 1986. France would not let us fly overhead."

In fact, there were balkers during Desert Shield/Storm. For a variety of reasons—political, religious, pay disputes, and fear of entering a combat zone—foreign crews on one dozen commercial ships chartered for the operation refused to complete their voyages. Switching crews, transloading ships, and unloading ships at alternative ports minimized deployment delays.

The situation would only get worse. The Maritime Administration (MARAD) predicted that the U.S. Merchant Marine fleet would continue to decline, from 168 militarily useful dry cargo ships in 1990 to 35 by the year 2005. Additionally, commercial trends away from RO/RO and breakbulk vessels in favor of non-self-sustaining container ships (approximately 70 percent of the commercial fleet was containerized) would reduce further the military utility of the commercial fleet worldwide. For reasons of national security, General Johnson and the regional Commanders in Chief (CINCs) simply could not let the nation continue to increase its reliance on foreign countries for strategic deployment.

Ready Reserve Force Modernization

Since the Department of Defense (DOD) could do little, if anything, to improve the U.S. maritime industry's competitive edge and thus deepen the commercial pool of ships it has to draw upon in an emergency, General Johnson sought to strengthen the nation's military sealift force through a balanced program of new ship construction and purchase of existing ships for the RRF. While the maritime industry had converted to diesel-powered ships, most RRF ships still had less efficient and less reliable steam propulsion plants: 83 percent steam, 16 percent diesel, and 1 percent gas turbine. Averaging 24 years old, RRF ships were predominately breakbulk freighters and tankers, types that USTRANSCOM passed over during the war for ones more militarily useful. Consequently, General Johnson proposed adding 21 diesel-powered RO/ROs to the RRF between fiscal year 1992 and fiscal year 1995. Purchased on the world market with MARAD-appropriated funds, they should have a minimum carrying capacity of 100,000 sq ft and be able to sustain a speed of between 19 and 23 kn. They should also be placed in reduced operating status in clusters of three or four, and located at ports as near as possible to where they would be needed. MARAD wanted to assign each cluster a skeleton crew that would maintain the ships and take them out on regular sea trials. Furthermore, Deputy Maritime Administrator Robert E. Martinez planned to stiffen contracting requirements for RRF ships maintenance, activations, and operations.

As part of RRF modernization, General Johnson recommended scrapping the National Defense Reserve Fleet's World War II-vintage ships. Their military worth was extremely doubtful, and their very existence provided a false sense of security. Besides, based on USTRANSCOM's Desert Shield/Storm experiences, it was unlikely crews could be found to man them. Finally, funds used to maintain them would be much better spent on upgrading the RRF. The General Accounting Office estimated that scrapping the obsolete ships in the National Defense Reserve Fleet would save about $10 million in direct maintenance costs over the next decade and generate between $38 to $42 million to improve the RRF if ships were sold to the highest foreign or domestic bidders. Most importantly, MARAD needed Congress to guarantee adequate funding to modernize the RRF. "You cannot maintain a Ready Reserve Fleet on a year-to-year basis without knowing how much money you're going to have over time" emphasized Maritime Administrator Captain Warren G. Leback.

New Strategic Sealift Ships

In addition to modernizing the RRF, General Johnson wanted to increase the number of RO/RO ships in the MSC fleet. Specifically, he recommended building 10 strategic sealift ships in U.S. shipyards with U.S. Navy funds. With diesel power and a sustained cruising speed of 25 kn, they should have a carrying capacity of 200,000 sq ft. Although USCINCTRANS sought a balance between buying and building ships, he emphasized the necessity of buying ships immediately to fill the sealift surge shortfall. The *Saudi Abha* should serve as the example. A Saudi-flagged RO/RO with clean lines, easy access, and 202,000-sq-ft carrying capacity, the *Saudi Abha* performed superbly for transporting unit equipment during Desert Shield/Storm.

Merchant Mariner Shortages and Merchant Marine Reserve

There was another maritime issue of great concern to USTRANSCOM. Fewer ships meant fewer jobs for young sailors, and as a consequence manpower had dwindled almost 60 percent since 1970 to a current level of 10,000. MARAD projected that it would be less than half that amount by the turn of the century. In 1990 the average age of a U.S. merchant seaman was 49 years old, which meant many of the mariners who manned the RRF ships during Desert Shield/Storm were in their sixties and seventies. At least two were in their eighties. (There were teenagers as well.)

Although no RRF ship activated for Desert Shield/Storm failed to sail because of crew shortage, demographics portended big problems in the next war. MARAD predicted that by the year 2000 the nation would be short 1600 seamen to man the Ready Reserve Force, Fast Sealift Ships, and commercial vessels during initial surge deployment. The shortage would increase, MARAD estimated, to more than 7200 during sustainment operations. Additionally, according to MARAD, the DOD's "phased activation of ready reserve force vessels mitigated difficulties in repairing vessels and obtaining crews." In other words, a full mobilization with total RRF activation (including the tankers, of which only 2 of 11 were used for operations in the oil-rich Persian Gulf) likely would have depleted the mariner pool. MARAD also believed that, based on its conversations with military reservists, "many former mariners who wanted to assist in crewing RRF ships were deterred from leaving their shoreside jobs because of their lack of reemployment rights."

One possible solution would be establishment of a Merchant Marine Reserve. At war's end MARAD was considering several options, which included annual training, annual salary, prevailing wages while on duty, government health benefits, and guaranteed reemployment after active service. General Johnson applauded MARAD's efforts, but emphasized that any such program should provide incentives for long-term commitment and ensure fully manned RRF crews for initial surge operations. A Merchant Marine Reserve should not, he added, compete with the active mariner labor pool.

Commercial Industry's View

Based on their Desert Shield/Storm experiences, commercial shipping companies offered several suggestions to improve strategic deployment. All called for increased use of intermodalism in general, and containerization in particular. Most wanted to play a bigger role in military exercises and planning. For instance, Crowley Maritime's President and Chief Executive Officer, Leo L. Collar, suggested that USTRANSCOM arrange for midlevel executives from the domestic and international liner, tanker, and dry bulk operators to meet with military planners for a one- or two-week exercise each year.

Commercial transporters and USTRANSCOM recommended that the military increase its use of seasheds and flatracks to improve the nation's ability to move unit cargo. Through the Sealift Enhancement Program, the DOD constructed these large, metal cagelike pieces of equipment to adapt containerships or container sections of combination carriers (breakbulk/container, roll-on/roll-off container) for carrying a variety of vehicles and other heavy military cargo. During Desert Shield/Storm, Military Traffic Management Command (MTMC) used about 1230 of its 2010 flatracks. At Military Ocean Terminal, Bayonne, New Jersey, they allowed MTMC to load a container ship with wheeled cargo and helicopters "that otherwise would have had to wait for a breakbulk or roll-on/roll-off vessel."

MSC adapted two vessels, the RRF crane ship *Flickertail State* and the U.S.-flag charter breakbulk ship *Mallory Lykes*, with seasheds for the operation. Together they used only 19 of the Navy's 890 seasheds. (Each Fast Sealift Ship held 13 seasheds. Part of the ships, they were not purchased under the enhancement program.) US-TRANSCOM did not use more seasheds during the initial Desert Shield surge because RO/ROs were available to carry unit cargo and it did not want to take the time to make the adaptations. As the deployment developed later on, the command chose not to expand seashed use for a combination of reasons—rapidly changing requirements, type of ships available, and the location of ships and seasheds. US-TRANSCOM agreed with industry that it should increase its emphasis on sealift enhancements, and said it would do so beginning with redeployment from the Persian Gulf.

Some commercial shippers wanted greater compensation for their sacrifices in future emergencies. For example, Crowley Maritime Corporation's Leo Collar concluded that "compensation for carriers whose vessels were taken out of the commercial market was inadequate to make up for the inconvenience, loss of credibility in commercial markets, and the jobs that were lost in the private sector."

Overland Transportation and Port Operations

Overview

An integral part of the Desert Shield/Storm transportation effort was the marshaling of combat forces with their heavy equipment. USTRANSCOM's Army component command, Military Traffic Management Command (MTMC), coordinated the movement of Army, Air Force, and Marine Corps units to seaports, prepared those ports for ships and cargo, and supervised the loading operations at ports worldwide. As outlined in Table D-11, MTMC and Military Sealift Command (MSC), US-TRANSCOM's Navy component command, recorded the loading of about 2.73 million tons of equipment and dry cargo onto 538 ships at 50 commercial and military ports worldwide in support of Desert Shield/Storm.

Military and U.S. Commercial Sector Cooperation

MTMC worked behind the scenes with industry and government agencies to keep the combat units moving. On 8 August 1990, for the first time ever, MTMC initiated the Contingency Response (CORE) Program. With representatives from MTMC, Department of Transportation, and industry, CORE coordinated exemptions and waivers, and handled safety, security, facility, and transportation resource issues. Designed to facilitate volunteer cooperation between government and industry, CORE could also be directive. However, it soon became apparent that there would be adequate landlift for the operation. Therefore, MTMC deactivated the formal CORE organization on 16 October 1990, although the program continued throughout the operation to serve informally as the command's conduit to industry. For example, when the United States Central Command (USCENTCOM) identified a shortfall of

Table D-11 Summary of Desert Shield/Storm Shipments by U.S. and Foreign Ports (7 August 1990–10 March 1991)

Port	Number of ships	Total tons (dry cargo)	Major units loaded
		U.S. Ports	
Bayonne, New Jersey	33	183,933	1st Corps Support Command
Beaumont, Texas	18	87,101	3d ACR, 1st BDE, 2d ARMD DIV
Charleston, South Carolina	14	46,957	XVII ABN CORPS, 1st COSCOM
Cheatham Annex, Virginia	2	7,789	II Marine Expeditionary Force
Concord, California	9	68,361	Ammunition
Earle, New Jersey	2	11,701	Ammunition
Gulfport, Mississippi	1	3,398	Navy Construction Battalion 4
Houston, Texas	40	213,648	1st INF DIV, 13th COSCOM, 1st CAV DIV, III CORPS
Jacksonville, Florida	59	220,652	101st ABN DIV, 1st COSCOM, II MEF
Long Beach, California	17	39,538	I MEF, II MEF/5th MEB
Morehead City, North Carolina	7	13,054	II Marine Expeditionary Force
Newport News, Virginia	11	56,243	85th EVAC, 1st COSCOM/7th GRP
Norfolk, Virginia	1	5,700	Landing Craft Utility/Lash Barges
Oakland MOTBA, California	19	42,380	1st COSCOM
Port Heuneme, California	12	31,741	11th SIG BDE, Navy UE, 5th MEB
Roosevelt Roads, Puerto Rico	1	1,880	Navy Unit Equipment
South Atlantic Outport, South Carolina	2	3,534	XVIII Airborne Corps
Savannah, Georgia	12	124,987	24 INF DIV, 197 INF BDE
Sunny Point MOT, North Carolina	38	375,892	4th MEB, Ammunition
Tacoma, Washington	5	11,884	9th INF DIV, 864 ENG BN
Wilmington, North Carolina	22	132,501	II MEF, XVIII ABN CORPS, 1st COSCOM
Total	325	1,682,874	
Total number of U.S. ports:	21		

	Foreign Ports		
Amsterdam, Netherlands	5	30,341	Ammunition
Antwerp, Belgium	32	103,463	2d COSCOM, 3d ARMD DIV
Benelux (Near Rotterdam)	1	1,102	12th CMBT AVN BDE
Bogen, Denmark	1	3,708	Flight Hosp 15
Bremerhaven, Germany	48	268,883	2d ACR, VII CORPS, 1st ARMD DIV
Cartagena, Spain	1	5,455	Ammunition
Chinae, Korea	2	11,754	Ammunition
Eemshave, Netherlands	5	29,990	Ammunition
Emden, Netherlands	2	15,062	Ammunition
Gibraltar, Spain	1	5,040	Follow-On
Glen Douglas, Scotland	1	6,204	Ammunition
Guam	4	26,938	Ammunition
Lisbon, Portugal	2	14,226	Ammunition
Livorno, Italy	13	35,333	12th Aviation Brigade
Lualualei, Hawaii	1	4,852	Ammunition
Naha, Okinawa	2	8,185	Navy Unit Equipment
Newport, Wales	2	23,205	Ammunition
Nordenham, Germany	24	154,142	Ammunition
Pusan, Korea	1	3,205	US Air Force Matting
Rota, Spain	4	15,102	1st COSCOM, 24th INF DIV, 75 FA BDE
Ridham, United Kingdom	2	17,043	Ammunition
Rotterdam, Netherlands	41	151,121	2d COSCOM, 3d ARMD DIV
Sasebo, Japan	1	14,399	Ammunition
Southampton, United Kingdom	1	647	Fuel Barges
Subic Bay, Philippines	3	15,615	Ammunition
Suda Bay, Crete	1	1,210	Ammunition
Tengan, Okinawa	3	8,985	Ammunition
Tombolo, Italy	4	47,220	Ammunition
Unknown	4	11,822	Unknown
Total	213	1,034,252	
Total Foreign Ports:	29		
Conus Total:	325	1,682,874	**Ports: 21**
Foreign Total:	213	1,034,252	**Ports: 29**
Grand Total:	538	2,717,126	**50**

SOURCES: Military Sealift Command, Lift Summary Reports; Military Traffic Management Command, Port Operations Recap Report; U.S. Transportation Command, Ship Voyage Report. Prepared by: U.S. Transportation Command, Office of History (TCHO).

Heavy Equipment Transporters, MTMC coordinated the effort to locate the vehicles in the civilian sector and get them to the ports for shipment to the USCENTCOM area of responsibility (AOR).

U.S. Ports

Ports in the United States loaded 1.7 million tons of equipment and dry cargo on 325 ships, as shown in Table D-11. In the United States, the Port of Jacksonville, Florida, loaded the most ships (59) and the second most cargo (220,652 tons). Those figures represented 18.2 and 13.1 percent of the total ships and unit cargo that embarked U.S. ports in support of Desert Shield/Storm. The second leading U.S. port for number of ships loaded was Houston, Texas. Forty ships carrying 213,648 tons departed from Houston for the Persian Gulf, which represented 12.3 and 12.7 percent of the total ships and total cargo loaded at U.S. ports. MTMC's terminal at Sunny Point, North Carolina, loaded the most cargo (375,893 tons), nearly all of it ammunition, on 38 ships. Those figures represented 22.3 percent of the cargo and 11.7 percent of the ships loaded in the United States.

To help maintain unit integrity, MTMC moved, when at all possible, each major combat unit through a single port. For instance, Jacksonville loaded the 101st Airborne Division, and Savannah, Georgia, loaded the 24th Infantry Division and the 197th Infantry Brigade. The 4th Marine Expeditionary Brigade moved through Sunny Point, North Carolina, while the XVIII Airborne Corps Artillery departed from Charleston, South Carolina, and Wilmington, North Carolina. On the Gulf Coast, Beaumont, Texas, loaded the 3d Armored Division and Houston, Texas, loaded the 1st Infantry Division, 13th Corps Support Command, and 1st Cavalry Division. On the west coast, for example, the I Marine Expeditionary Force embarked from Long Beach, California.

The International Longshoremens' Association (whose members say ILA stands for "I Love America") responded immediately to the crisis. On 10 August, with the arrivals of MSC's Fast Sealift Ships at U.S. east coast and Gulf ports, they initiated Desert Shield loading operations. Many of the ILA's stevedores traveled at their own expense to where they were most needed. Work went on nonstop: 12-hour shifts, 24-hours-a-day, 7-days-a-week. During surge operations, it was not uncommon for stevedores to work 24 or more hours straight, with only 4 or 5 hours off before starting up again. They loaded ships in 100-plus degree heat on Labor Day, and in snow and ice on Christmas. To guarantee that its members were able to meet the military's demands. ILA leadership set up and conducted training courses in forklift operation, steam winchmanship, and ammunition handling and loading.

U.S. Overland Transportation

As with port operations, MTMC relied heavily on the commercial sector for overland transportation. For instance, Landstar Systems, one of MTMC's largest truck charter companies, shipped 400 truckloads of 101st Airborne Division gear from Fort Campbell, Kentucky, to the port of Jacksonville, Florida, 780 miles away, in $3\frac{1}{2}$ days. In all, MTMC used 27 commercial trucking firms in 1174 truckloads to move the 101st to Jacksonville. For Desert Shield/Storm, MTMC routed 1.2 million tons of unit cargo and equipment to U.S. seaports on nearly 16,000 commercial railcars and 54,000 commercial trucks. (MTMC estimated that it loaded 945,000 vehicles and other pieces of unit equipment on ships departing from U.S. ports.) In addition, MTMC estimated that commercial truck companies carried 70 percent of all Desert Shield/Storm ammunition. Overall, the commercial sector accounted for nearly 90 percent of the tonnage transported by truck and rail to U.S. ports. MTMC's Defense Freight Railway Interchange Fleet of 1421 heavy-duty flatcars carried the remainder, mostly heavy fighting vehicles such as M1 and M60 tanks. Because the command did not own or operate passenger transport vehicles, nearly all of the troops arrived at their CONUS embarkation points via commercial aircraft or commercial bus (about 105,000 troops by the former and 30,000 troops by the latter) under contract to MTMC.

The U.S. rail, truck, and bus industries responded patriotically to the Desert Shield/Storm mobilization and deployment. Burlington Northern Railroad created a train service dedicated to military cargo. The company moved 1500 carloads of food, ammunition, jet fuel, and other military impedimenta. Conrail moved 474 carloads of M1 tanks from manufacturing facilities to the port at Bayonne, New Jersey. It also transported 276 carloads of new "Hummer" utility vehicles, and 1209 carloads of new 5-ton trucks from the production line to air and seaports of embarkation. Sante Fe and Union Pacific moved 3851 and 2000 carloads respectively, in support of Desert Shield/Storm.

The Association of American Railroads recorded that, in descending order, CSX Transportation, Union Pacific, Southern Pacific Transportation Co., and Atchison, Topeka and Santa Fe Railway were the major haulers of military equipment during the deployment to the Persian Gulf. By war's end, CSXT estimated it had moved 13,000 carloads of unit equipment and general cargo. It also estimated that it operated 1500 trains dedicated to the military between August 1990 and the end of February 1991. Conrail, Santa Fe, Union Pacific, and Norfolk Southern willingly supplemented CSXT's fleet with cars of their own. The industry moved empty cars with the same urgency as loads. Additionally, railroad companies accepted thousands of interchanged cars during the deployment. A key CSXT rail corridor for interchange traffic ran from East Saint Louis, Illinois, through Evansville, Indiana, and Memphis and Nashville, Tennessee, to the CSXT Hamlet Railyard near Lumberton, North Carolina.

With the nation's largest bus company on strike and virtually out of the military charter business, MTMC turned to the National Motorcoach Network (NMN) to move troops over land. A consortium of 30 companies with 1500 motor coaches nationwide, NMN, participating in its first-ever large mobilization and deployment, positioned relief drivers on interstate highways around the country. Motor coach carriers were responsible for arranging meal stops for the troops. (The association noted that it intended to reward, with postwar business, eating establishments that accepted military meal vouchers.) In addition to cross-country transport of troops, NMN buses provided the military with short hauls. For example, they shuttled thousands of troops to the National Training Center, Fort Irwin, California, from local airports.

Deployment from Europe

Only a handful of ships left European ports for the Persian Gulf during the first Desert Shield surge. The largest single unit deployment was the Army's 12th Combat Aviation Brigade. Between 8 and 14 September, its cargo and equipment deployed on four ships—three from Livorno, Italy, carrying 9065 tons, and one from Rotterdam, Netherlands, carrying 1102 tons.

European ports were especially active during the Desert Shield surge deployment from mid-November 1990 through early March 1991. Throughout the operation, ports in Europe loaded 213 ships with 1,034,252 tons, most of it in support of the Army's VII Corps. Overseas, Bremerhaven, Germany, ranked number one, with 272,710 tons on 48 ships. That represented 22.5 and 26.1 percent, respectively, of the total ships and tonnage embarking from foreign ports to the AOR. Rotterdam ranked number two overseas, with 42 ships carrying 157,675 tons. Ranking third was Antwerp, Belgium, loading 32 ships with 103,463 tons.

Transporting the VII Corps' nearly 40,000 pieces of equipment and 24,000 tons of ammunition to four embarkation ports in only 42 days was a herculean task. For the deployment, U.S. Army Europe, along with the 1st Theater Army Movement Control Agency and Military Traffic Management Command–Europe, decided to maximize the use of rail and barge transport. Truck convoying would be a last resort because of dangerous winter driving conditions. They also decided to use "train equivalents" as the measurement standard for movement of the Corps. Their formula equated the Corps' unit equipment, cargo, and ammunition into a number of trains. Similar formulas converted barge and convoy loads into "train equivalents." They estimated it would take 585 "train equivalents" to move the Corps to the ports. Finally they estimated, based on a 20-day sailing time, that the force would have to be at the ports by 20 December 1990 in order for it to close in the Persian Gulf by 15 January 1991 as required.

Except for a greater reliance on convoys than originally envisioned, the Corps deployed as planned. Units moved by truck and rail from their stations to MTMC–Europe's Rhine River Terminal at Mannheim, Germany, located 250 mi inland where the Neckar River joins the Rhine. There MTMC offloaded the vehicles and equipment and then loaded them onto barges. The barges then proceeded down the Rhine on a three-day trip to Antwerp or Rotterdam for another offloading and loading, this time on ships embarking for the Persian Gulf. MTMC moved 15,000 pieces of equipment on 520 barge loads to Rotterdam and Antwerp. Overall, MTMC estimated that barges moved between 35 and 40 percent of all cargo transported to European ports in support of Desert Shield/Storm. Most of the heavy tracked equipment traveled by rail to Bremerhaven. The commander of MTMC's Bremerhaven Terminal estimated that it took about 10,000 rail cars and 9000 trucks to move 3600 tracked vehicles and 14,000 wheeled vehicles to Bremerhaven. To meet the deployment schedule, Army transporters in Europe relied on trucks to convoy about 20 percent of the Corps' equipment. They also contracted 50 commercial buses to move Corps' troops to aerial ports for deployment to the AOR. From the second week in December through mid-January, between 2000 and 3500 soldiers flew out of Germany daily. The VII Corps marked its port closure at 5:45 p.m., 20 December, when the last military truck in the final convoy of the 2d Armored Division (Forward) arrived at Bremerhaven. The final "train equivalent" count was 590.

Host government support was the key to the success of the deployment from Europe. Foreign nationals—military, civil servants, and contractors—worked side-by-side with U.S. transporters. The Dutch, for example, loaned the U.S. Army trucks and drivers. Government officials in Germany, the Netherlands, and Italy made available to U.S. forces berths and marshaling areas at their ports. Their assistance was invaluable in complying with international agreements and local and national regulations. The deployment of the 12th Combat Aviation Brigade from Wiesbaden, Germany, through France to Livorno, Italy, for example, required, on short notice, rail and customs clearances as well as overflight rights from the three countries. Host nations also granted waivers to U.S. forces for the transport of ammunition and other hazardous cargo over land and by barge. Additionally, host nations provided most of the security for ports, convoys, and rail yards.

Overland Transportation and Port Operations—An Assessment

Peacetime Operations, Exercises, and Planning

As with Desert Shield/Storm airlift and sealift, study of overland and port operations prompts some observations. For instance, peacetime operations and exercises paid dividends during the deployment. Since 1987, Military Traffic Management Command (MTMC) had used commercial ports in its annual Reforger exercises. Port authorities and civilian and military stevedores in the United States termed Reforgers "dress rehearsals." In Europe, transporters dubbed the Desert Shield/Storm deployment "Deforger," a Reforger in reverse. In early 1990 they also gained considerable experience moving some 2200 tanks, armored personnel carriers, and howitzers out of Europe under the Conventional Forces Europe Treaty. CSXT valued its regular, long-term relationship with the military: repeated and exhaustive drills "52 weeks a year" had prepared it for the deployment, according to the company's Assistant Vice President for Sales, Joe DiCarlo. He added that CSXT especially valued as "realistic rehearsals" its periodic ammunition movements from Charleston, South Carolina, to Blount Island, Florida. The commercial industry's leadership—in truck, rail, and ports—was unanimous in calling for the military to increase their participation in exercises, both live and simulated.

Leaders in the commercial transport business also wanted to be included in mobilization and deployment planning. According to Lilian G. Liburdi, Director, Port Department, Port Authority of New York and New Jersey, only then could they "intelligently address [the military's] facilities, space, and labor requirements." Benny Holland, President, South Atlantic and Gulf Coast District-International Longshoremen, agreed. "Early identification of highly active ports will help us put the manpower where it is needed," he emphasized. CSXT complained about "short lead times" and "inflated requirements," which greatly complicated their ability to allocate scarce resources. Similarly, James A. Hagan, Chairman, President, and Chief Executive Officer, Consolidated Rail Corporation, believed that the railroads' lack of information on military intentions early in the deployment hindered their ability to respond. He especially wanted the military to more clearly identify installations where rail would be required for mobilization and deployment, so industry and government could more wisely invest funds in trackage and loading dock maintenance. Trucking industry spokesman Jeff Crowe (President, Chairman, and Chief Executive Officer, Landstar Systems, Incorporated) helped to increase his trucking company's responsiveness by creating a 24-hour hotline for the military.

Commercial Assets

Truck and rail companies in the United States coped with shortages and met deployment requirements through cooperation with their competitors and the military but, in the words of Dick Davidson, President and CEO, Union Pacific Railroad, for the rail industry "it was a close fit." For example, during Desert Shield/Storm, CSXT, with the largest inventory of cars in the railroad industry, pressed into service for the military boxcars usually reserved for paper customers. CSXT reported that military-type cars, such as 50-ft boxcars and 60-ft and 89-ft flatcars, were especially hard to find. At war's end the situation sent CSXT's Bill Braman (Manager, Distribution–Car Management, Baltimore) "begging for cars" in preparation for troops scheduled to return through Blount Island.

Union Pacific's Davidson predicted greater problems in the future. With the drawdown of military forces in the post-Cold War era, there would be fewer exercises to test mobilization. As a consequence, he argued, there would be less incentive for commercial rail companies to maintain in their inventories low revenue-producing cars and other equipment specially constructed for the military. "If we don't need to provide rail equipment for training exercises," Davidson stated, "there's a good chance shortages will develop if and when the next conflict begins." He added that, had the economy been stronger, the rail industry might not have been able to meet the military's requirements during Desert Shield/Storm. Davidson's points were not lost on the military establishment. To help assure that US-TRANSCOM would be able to move unit equipment to the ports in the future, General Johnson would seek funding to expand MTMC's Defense Freight Rail Interchange Fleet.

Reliability and Safety

Although rail traffic was embargoed at several locations because of unsafe track conditions, no ships were delayed due to railcar or track reliability. In fact, of the approximately 16,000 rail cars used in the United States to deliver Desert Shield/ Storm unit equipment and cargo, less than two dozen required en route repairs. In its movement of about 54,000 truckloads of unit equipment and cargo, the commercial trucking industry suffered only one serious accident (a truck caught fire in Nevada). Landstar System's Crowe believes that luck was on the trucking industry's side. In many instances trucks had to take detours, particularly with oversize cargo, because bridges were out or unsafe. "Our national transportation infrastructure, particularly our roads and bridges, are in a deplorable state," Crowe noted in his post-Desert Shield/Storm analysis. Thomas J. Donahue, President and CEO, American Trucking Association, noted that truck shipments were delayed early in the deployment "by states enforcing strict limits on trucks with dromedary boxes used to keep fuses separate from munitions." In future contingencies, stressed Donahue, the Department of Defense (DOD) and the trucking industry should immediately petition the Department of Transportation (DOT) "to lift pertinent truck size and weight restrictions."

Military port operators registered several safety concerns. On occasion, pallets of ammunition arriving at Military Ocean Terminal Sunny Point, North Carolina, were not blocked and braced. Longshoremen found ammunition containers that had not been strapped to pallets, and compressed gas cylinders unrestrained in vehicles. Consequently they had to reload and reconfigure cargo, which slowed deployment. Such carelessness also posed unnecessary safety risks to the crowded ports. To avoid accidents and speed operations, MTMC emphasized the need for deploying units to complete packaging of unit equipment at home station.

Army MG John R. Piatak, the MTMC Commanding General, brought his area commanders to task over the issue. He told them that on visits to MTMC ports and terminals he had "observed blatant disregard of basic safety requirements such as inadequate lifting gear, absence of tag lines, and improperly dressed [contract] labor." He wanted them to increase their "on-site vigilance" making spot safety inspections and ensuring that contract laborers "meet the same safety standards that apply to our soldiers and DA [Department of the Army] civilians."

Ports Issues

For the most part, U.S. commercial ports accommodated military ships without delay during the deployment, but port authorities foresaw problems in the future. Port authority spokesperson Liburdi was especially concerned that the government and industry find ways to dispose of materials dredged from the nation's waterways. Without an active, innovative, and cooperative effort in this matter, dredging operations might be curtailed. Channels would begin to fill, thus obstructing access to the nation's ports. In fact, Military Sealift command reported that ship draft limitations at Sunny Point prevented MTMC from fully loading ammunition ships embarking for the Persian Gulf. Port authorities also solicited DOD and DOT backing in their negotiations with local communities over land use. Balancing community needs with those of the military—such as marshaling areas and road and rail access to ports—was, port authorities believed, an issue of increasing importance to national security. Perhaps of most importance, port authorities and military commanders alike theorized that, had the economy been stronger and imports up during Desert Shield/Storm, military ships would have had to compete with commercial ships for labor and berths, which in turn would have delayed the deployment. As a result, Air Force Gen. Hansford T. Johnson, Commander in Chief, United States Transportation Command, told Congress that the nation's ports need additional berthing "to accommodate an increase in surge sealift assets and ensure a smooth flow for rapidly deploying heavy units."

General Johnson was also concerned over the lack of a modern ammunition-loading facility on the west coast of the United States. Current ammunition outloading capability failed to meet wartime requirements, and as a result USTRANSCOM and MTMC, in coordination with the Army and Navy, would seek funding to build a common-user ammunition container facility at Naval Weapons Station Concord, California. Under the proposal, MTMC would operate the terminal. It should have at least the same loading capability as Sunny Point—600 20-ft-equivalent containers/day.

Labor Issues

Initially, there were labor shortages. Prior to Desert Shield/Storm, the International Longshoremen's Association (ILA) had been decreasing its membership in the Atlantic, South Atlantic, and Gulf ports, due to a weak economy and a general decline in military business. Because of their proximity to Camp Lejeune and Fort Bragg, their ammunition-loading capability, and their reliance on the same stevedore pool, the South Carolina Port of Charleston and the North Carolina Ports of Morehead City, Wilmington, and Military Ocean Terminal at Sunny Point, were particularly vulnerable during an emergency. On 7 August 1990, the area had about 300 laborers. To meet the military's requirement, ILA needed nearly 600 stevedores. For the initial August surge, the Association helped make up the difference by recruiting 175 laborers from Galveston, Philadelphia, and other ports to load ships along the North Carolina and South Carolina coasts. The ILA stevedores worked side-by-side with port operators from MTMC's Transportation Terminal Units. During surge operations in early February 1991, ships began to back up at Wilmington and Sunny Point, in part due to shortages of stevedores skilled in fork-lift operations. Again ILA volunteers from around the country, about 80 of them, broke the logjam. Based on his Desert Shield/Storm experiences, ILA's Hagan considered organizing and training a "mobile longshoremen's force" for future contingencies.

There might have been severe labor shortages in the rail industry. On 15 February the nation's major rail companies and unions, representing nearly a quarter of a million workers, faced a contract deadline. At issue was a three-year-old dispute over wages, health care costs, and work rules. To avoid a strike or lockout while the United States was at war (even if the President acted quickly to seize the rail systems, there would have been a disruption in service), they agreed on 13 February to a 60-day extension of contract talks. Fred Hardin's position on the issue reflected that held by most of the rail industry's workers and management. President of the United Transportation Union, he stated that he and his 100,000 followers were "Americans first and workers second." The new deadline would be 17 April. Similarly, ILA workers, "in the nation's best interests," continued to work throughout Desert Shield/Storm even though their contract had expired in October. (In January ILA workers, as an exception to the norm, went on strike at Baltimore, but with minimal impact on the deployment.)

Military Traffic Management Command in Europe

In Europe, moving forces overland and loading them on ships differed greatly from such operations in the United States. While it operated military port terminals in Europe much as it did in the United States, MTMC did not control inland truck and rail traffic functions in Europe. Instead, the 1st Theater Army Movement Control Agency, which reported to U.S. Army Europe, managed those transportation assets. Lack of a traffic single-manager in Europe complicated the Desert Shield/ Storm deployment, as did the need to comply with the laws and regulations of foreign nations. For example, a convoy carrying large amounts of explosives and other hazardous materials over crowded roads often required a wide variety of permits from more than one country. More importantly, as discussed earlier, host nations worked hard to facilitate the deployment.

Requiring multiple loading and unloading, barge operations in Europe appeared cumbersome, but in reality they greatly facilitated and expedited inland transport. Barge traffic decreased rail and road congestion and permitted simultaneous movement by different modes. More importantly from MTMC's perspective, barges increased the command's ability to expedite the deployment, because MTMC managed that portion of the inland traffic system. Overall, barges speeded deployment by increasing the availability of truck and rail assets to move cargo and equipment to Bremerhaven and other ports not serviced by inland waterways. Even so, MTMC estimated that in December 1990, the German rail industry was short 5000 cars. A shortfall in ammunition-certified rail cars forced the 1st Theater Army Movement Control Agency to delay transport of Air Force ammunition in favor of the VII Corps deployment. Without barges, the delays likely would have been worse.

USCINCTRANS' Conclusion

In a letter to Ronald W. Drucker, Senior Vice President and Chief Executive Officer, CSX Corporation, General Johnson summarized his thoughts on Desert Shield/Storm surface transportation activity in the United States. He believed that the nation's ability to rapidly deploy forces was "absolutely dependent upon" MTMC's relationships with commercial industry. "We must all continue to work to keep that relationship strong," he emphasized. He underscored the importance of a healthy surface transportation industry for surge capacity. He added that as the United States reduced its overseas military presence, the nation's dependence on commercial industry for surge operations would increase. He also stressed that military and commercial transporters needed to "press for improved maintenance and expansion of the nation's transportation infrastructure, particularly in the areas of highways, intermodal connections, and bridges of all types." General Johnson concluded that, over all, surface transportation support to Desert Shield/Storm was "an unqualified success for both military and commercial industry participants." He was "continually impressed by the seemingly effortless talent and professionalism displayed across the entire spectrum of the DOD–Commercial Surface Transportation Industry team as they overcame every obstacle in the path of deploying our nation's forces."

Containerization and Intermodalism

Special Middle East Sealift Agreement

During Desert Shield/Storm, Military Sealift Command (MSC) contracted with U.S. shipping companies to transport Department of Defense cargo aboard regularly scheduled United States–Middle East liner services. Through this contracting arrangement, the Special Middle East Sealift Agreement (SMESA), USTRANSCOM capitalized on the containership strength of the U.S. maritime industry to deliver almost all of the Desert Shield/Storm sustainment cargo. Several U.S. liner services participated: American President Lines, Central Gulf Lines, Farrell, Lykes, Sea-Land Services, and Waterman, among others. Military Traffic Management Command estimated that it booked, and MSC shipped, about 37,000 40-ft SMESA containers to the Persian Gulf during the operation. Under SMESA, the liners also carried some breakbulk and a small number of 20-ft and refrigerated containers. The two largest SMESA carriers, American President Lines and Sea-Land, transported about 80 percent of the SMESA cargo, just over 40 and just under 40 percent respectively.

The first large-scale military use of commercial intermodal systems, SMESA was both flexible and reliable. Awarded on 23 August 1990, the contract called for a 10-wk-long service, beginning on the 27th, with a government option for extensions. (SMESA was still in effect when redeployment began on 10 March, 1991.) A capability of 2700 40-ft containers/wk was planned, although the weekly deliveries varied from as low as 250 early in the deployment to over 3300 in mid-February 1991. Rates ranged from $7000 to $8000 per 40-ft container, based on the number hauled per week. U.S.-flag SMESA carriers sailed almost daily on their established routes to transshipment points, where they transferred their SMESA cargo to smaller, foreign-flag feeder vessels under charter to them. The foreign-flag ships then shuttled the SMESA cargo to the United States Central Command (USCENTCOM) area of responsibility (AOR). Departures from New York, Norfolk, and Charleston, transshipped at Algeciras, Spain, or Alexandria, Egypt, for shuttle to Jeddah and Ad Damman, Saudi Arabia. Likewise, sailings from Oakland/San Francisco, Seattle/Tacoma, Long Beach/San Pedro, transloaded at Singapore or Al Fujairah, United Arab Emirates, for transfer to Ad Damman. U.S.-flag SMESA ships departing Bremerhaven, Germany, and Rotterdam, Netherlands, transferred their cargo to foreign-flag companies at Alexandria for transport to Jeddah and Ad Damman. East coast, west coast, and European sailings accounted for about 56, 36, and 8 percent respectively of SMESA containers shipped. Average sailing times were 35, 30, and 15 days respectively, including feeder voyages. The SMESA contract also required carriers to arrange line-haul service in Saudi Arabia. The most important legs were between the ports of Jeddah, Ad Damman, and Al Jubayl. Containers traveled inland using the commercial companies' established infrastructure.

Military Traffic Management Command and the Jeddah Land Test

To act as an interface between the commercial companies and the in-theater military supply and transportation infrastructure, Military Traffic Management Command (MTMC) dispatched teams of transporters to Ad Damman and Jeddah. Serving as the Ocean Cargo Clearance Authority (OCCA), they administered the provisions of SMESA, enforced performance, verified carrier invoices for payment, provided technical assistance, kept track of containers, and in general attempted to expedite the deployment. For example, at USTRANSCOM request, the MTMC OCCA arranged with Sea-Land to truck 92 containers from Jeddah on the Red Sea eastward across the Saudi Arabian peninsula to Ad Damman. USTRANSCOM wanted to determine if the land route between the two ports could serve as an alternative means of distribution, should either Ad Damman or Al Jubayl come under attack or become overburdened. It also wanted to verify if the overland method was economically feasible.

MTMC completed the test on 23 September. The command determined that the land route worked and could even save time, as much as seven days compared to the one by sea. However, it also found the cost to be greater per unit, about $400 per 40-ft container and $500 per 20-ft container. The extra cost, plus problems clearing customs at Jeddah and along the way, convinced USTRANSCOM to rely exclusively on the sea link, unless circumstances at Saudi Arabia's east coast dictated differently. They did not.

Sealift Express

Early in Desert Shield, USTRANSCOM worked with MTMC and MSC to speed delivery of high-priority cargo to the AOR via sea. As a result, for a short time, Sea-Land carried military cargo direct to Saudi Arabia on its regularly scheduled Sea-Land Express. However, the small amount of Desert Shield cargo earmarked for express service prompted the company to discontinue such sailings for the military.

Expanding upon the SMESA contract, USTRANSCOM for the second surge deployment established an express sealift service to expedite delivery of air-eligible cargo that the command had diverted to sealift for lack of space on aircraft. For this new express service, dubbed "Sealift Express," Sea-Land scheduled space for about 1000 40-ft containers on each of four voyages between 23 December and 13 January. A fifth voyage was later added for February 1991. The ships departed Charleston for Algeciras with the high-priority Desert Shield/Storm cargo, for transloading to foreign-flag feeder vessels and onward movement directly to Ad Damman. Originally planned as a 23-day voyage, Sealift Express shipping times actually averaged 25 to 27 days due to "forward delivery problems" primarily related to increasing port congestion and the outbreak of war. The contract ran through 14 March.

Containerization of Ammunition and Unit Equipment

The services containerized surprisingly little ammunition and unit equipment during Desert Shield/Storm. Approximately 2100 20-ft containers of ammunition and 7000 40-ft containers of unit equipment moved to the Persian Gulf, most of the former from the United States and the latter from Europe. An additional 2000 containers were used for Deployable Medical Units.

Early in Desert Shield and throughout the operation, USTRANSCOM promoted containerization of ammunition and unit equipment. USTRANSCOM argued that containerization would free up space on Fast Sealift Ship and other roll-on/roll-off vessels for transport of vehicles, and also free up military terminals for unit deployments, since most container shipments embarked from commercial port facilities operated by commercial ocean carriers. Consequently more units could be deployed simultaneously. Containerships were much more efficient that breakbulk vessels. USTRANSCOM estimated that 6 containerships could haul the equivalent of 18 breakbulk ships. Containerization would also speed deployment, because containerships could be loaded and unloaded faster than breakbulk ships. In addition USTRANSCOM stressed that containerization of unit cargo and ammunition would speed deployment, by capitalizing on the commercial industry's intermodal expertise and capabilities. Furthermore the command argued it could save money, increase security, and improve in-transit visibility through containerization.

USTRANSCOM's success at containerizing ammunition and unit cargo was limited, for several reasons. Early in the operation the supported commander and the Army concluded that in-theater infrastructure lacked the equipment necessary to handle containerized ammunition. In particular, USCENTCOM had a limited field-ammunition supply-point material handling capability. The Army also feared that containerization would slow the deployment. "Container movement normally requires longer leadtimes for positioning of assets at shipper locations and rail transit to the port," Army Materiel Command noted. Throughout the operation, "changing priorities" and "lack of firm requirements" were in part behind the Army's hesitancy to containerize ammunition. Consequently USTRANSCOM shipped most ammunition breakbulk—the same way the Phoenicians did it, Navy VADM Francis Donovan, MSC's Commander, later was to remark.

Containerizing unit equipment was an even bigger challenge for USTRANSCOM. Unit commanders believed that containerization meant their equipment would be split up into hundreds of boxes and then transported on a multitude of ships. As a result they favored roll-on/roll-off over container vessels, so they could consolidate their cargo and equipment on as few ships as possible and thus maintain unit integrity.

They also feared that containerization would slow unit deployment. In mid-September, in response to a USTRANSCOM request (one of many during Phase I) to test the feasibility of containerizing a unit for deployment from the United States to the Persian Gulf, Forces Command (FORSCOM) replied " . . . given the sensitivities associated with closure of the currently deploying force, we recommend that the test be conducted during the deployment of rotation forces." Consequently, USTRANSCOM and FORSCOM agreed to test containerizing a unit deploying in mid-November. USTRANSCOM developed a force module consisting of units suitable for the test, then forwarded it to FORSCOM for consideration and selection. In its urgency to meet Phase II surge deployment, FORSCOM abandoned the plan.

Early in the deployment the Army, FORSCOM, USCENTCOM, and MTMC concluded that there were not enough government containers, military vans, and other intermodal devices available to support ammunition and unit equipment moves and still meet other worldwide commitments. In late January 1991, the Army's Office of the Deputy Chief for Logistics noted that up to that point most of the ammunition—for the Air Force, Navy, and Marine Corps as well as the Army—had been shipped breakbulk "due in part to lack of containers." From the beginning, many commercial containers remained in the AOR as storage boxes, so that by the time Desert Storm commenced even the SMESA contractors considered the container shortage critical. On 9 February, MTMC reported to USTRANSCOM that there was "a worldwide shortage of boxes. . . . Within the past four weeks the number of containers backlogged in theater, currently 8800 FEUs [40-ft equivalents], has more than doubled. . . . At the present return rate for empties, the number of containers in theater will double within five weeks." At war's end, USTRANSCOM was coordinating a Department of Defense (DOD) effort to buy containers, some with Japanese money.

In conclusion, the services were reluctant to containerize more of their ammunition and unit equipment because they were skeptical of, and unfamiliar with, the method. Had they really wanted to do it, they could have purchased containers early in the deployment for use later on, when the theater commander was ready to receive them. USTRANSCOM could also have done more to promote containerization. "After the war, in meeting with all the joint logistics commanders," General Johnson reminisced, "I realized that no one said no to containerization of ammunition. We simply did not push hard enough for it." In hindsight, several of USTRANSCOM's logisticians concluded that the command should have forced the issue by simply telling customers they would get containerships instead of RO/ROs for their unit equipment, and "then let them sort it out."

USTRANSCOM's Role in Post-Desert Shield/Storm Containerization; Intermodalism in DOD

As a member of the Joint Staff-sponsored General/Flag Officer Steering Group on Containerization, USTRANSCOM would continue its support and advocacy of containerization in the Department of Defense following the war. It would participate in development of the DOD Containerization Master Action Plan, and emphasize containerization during deliberate planning and Time Phased Force Deployment Data refinement conferences. It would also champion a west coast port capable of handling containerized ammunition. To make better use of containers on hand, it would improve container staging, stuffing, and stripping methods. It would also seek funds to increase the number of containers in the DOD inventory. Additionally, the command would work to make the Defense Transportation System compatible with the commercial sector's intermodal systems. Realizing that containerization was "hampered by a steep learning curve," the command would push for the Services to use containers and intermodal systems in peacetime so that they would feel comfortable using them during war. Immediately, the command would plan for containerization of units redeploying from the Persian Gulf. However, General Johnson knew that unless USTRANSCOM became a peacetime as well as wartime operational command, his power to influence service operations, short of war, would remain limited.

Special Topics

Prepositioning

Although prepositioning was ultimately a service responsibility, USTRANSCOM obviously had a stake in it. In general, prepositioning reduced the sealift requirement but, as Air Force Gen. Hansford T. Johnson, Commander in Chief, United States Transportation Command, emphasized, there was more to the equation. Prepositioning placed a large demand on airlift. Plans for deployment of a Marine Corps Expeditionary Brigade required 250 sorties, 30 of which had to be C-5, 35 of which could be Civil Reserve Air Fleet (CRAF), and the remainder should be military (C-141, C-5, or C-17). The number of missions could of course change, depending on the types of aircraft actually used. For example during Desert Shield/Storm, Military Airlift Command (MAC) required 264 C-141-equivalent airlift missions to deploy the 7th Marine Expeditionary Brigade to Saudi Arabia to unite with Maritime Prepositioning Squadron 2. Only a small portion of those flights carried troops. Even Army divisions scheduled to deploy to the European theater, with its huge prepositioned stocks, planned on substantial use of military airlift. A typical mechanized infantry division deploying to Europe would need a minimum of 69 C-5 and 221 C-141 cargo missions to supplement its very sizable commercial lift requirement. Simply put, military aircraft were required to carry equipment and armament—such as helicopters, aircraft engines, test equipment, and communications vans—that could not fit on commercial aircraft and, because of cost, security threats, or sensitivity to the elements, could not be prepositioned. Most importantly, Desert Shield/Storm had validated the Afloat Prepositioning Force concept. As a result, General Johnson intended to back service plans to expand the program.

Reserve Forces

It is readily apparent that USTRANSCOM and its component commands could not have performed their wartime missions without Reserve augmentation. At war's end the commands' augmentees—from the Air National Guard (ANG) and U.S. Air Force (USAFR), U.S. Army (USAR), and U.S. Naval (USNR) Reserves—peaked at 22,681. MAC augmentation reached 21,283 (4192 ANG and 17,091 USAFR). The remainder were distributed as follows: 43 at USTRANSCOM (37 USNR and 6 USAR); 923 at Military Traffic Management Command (MTMC—915 USAR and 8 USNR); and 432 USNR at Military Sealift Command.

The commands had a dependence on Reserve volunteers especially early in the deployment. In August, 7378 (82 percent) of their 9034 Reservists on duty were volunteers. Volunteers made up 88 percent of MAC and 100 percent of USTRANSCOM Reserve augmentation in August. At USTRANSCOM, volunteers served primarily with the Crisis Action Team (CAT), allowing a fully manned CAT to operate around the clock during the critical first weeks of the deployment. In August, volunteers made up 42 percent of MTMC's Reserve force. Most of them were in Transportation Terminal Units, loading the first Fast Sealift and Ready Reserve Force ships activated for the deployment. Volunteers also helped to load and fly the first airlift aircraft to deploy in support of Desert Shield.

General Johnson considered such heavy reliance on volunteers to be risky. He wanted to rely instead on "rapid-access" mobility reserve modules and call-up procedures for them" which USTRANSCOM and its component commands could use prior to the Presidential 200,000 Reserve activation. In essence, he wanted a guaranteed and quantifiable pool of reservists to "prime the strategic transportation system" for war.

USTRANSCOM also found invaluable the expertise it eventually gained from having a mix of services in its Reserve augmentation during Desert Shield/Storm. Consequently, it proposed to the Joint Staff the formation of a USTRANSCOM Joint Transportation Reserve Unit. Built around Naval Reserve USTRANSCOM Detachment 118, the new unit would include all the authorized USTRANSCOM reserve augmentation of 65 selected reserve billets and 31 Joint Mobilization

Augmentees. Under the proposal, the billets would be redistributed to achieve service balance, 32 each Army, Navy, and Air Force, plus 3 new Marine Corps billets. In the command's view, mobilization readiness could best be achieved if all reservists, regardless of service affiliation, trained as one unit. It was especially important to the command that it train the way it would fight. If approved, the USTRANSCOM reserve unit would be the first joint reserve unit ever.

Accounting

USTRANSCOM served as the U.S. government's focal point for tracking Desert Shield/Storm transportation costs. Based on the component commands' inputs, the USTRANSCOM Office of the Comptroller computed those costs at the end of March to be $4.577 billion, as shown in Table D-12. This included ship breakouts, ship activations, labor, travel, contracts, supplies, equipment, fuel, and in-theater transport.

The command also kept track of donated foreign airlift and sealift for the U.S. government. As seen in Table D-13, South Korea, Japan, Kuwait, and Italy had contributed by the end of March a total of 200 airlift missions worth an estimated $73.9 million. Japan was by far the largest donor with 124 airlift missions bought from other nations at an estimated worth of $46.9 million. As outlined in Table D-10, South Korea, Japan, Kuwait, and Denmark contributed 1511 sea days of sealift worth an estimated $72.1 million. Japan again led the group with donations of nearly $35 million worth of sealift. Kuwait's contribution was especially noteworthy during the surge deployment for war between January and March. During that period, Kuwait donated 505 sea days, worth an estimated $15.3 million.

Of all the Desert Shield/Storm accounting issues, those involving free fuel were probably the most challenging for USTRANSCOM. Under the Implementation Plan for Logistics Support of United States Forces in Defense of the Kingdom of Saudi Arabia, referred to as the Logistics Support Agreement (LSA), signed by the U.S. government and the Saudi Arabian government on 10 November 1990, the

Table D-12 Desert Shield/Storm Transportation Costs
(As of 31 March 1991—$000)

	USTRANSCOM	MAC	MTMC	MSC	Total
Aug. 90	21	162,674	13,401	110,576	268,672
Sep. 90	21	224,081	21,603	175,779	421,484
Oct. 90	40	229,778	10,928	176,084	416,830
Nov. 90	23	171,505	15,351	173,311	360,190
Dec. 90	37	341,508	37,752	270,321	649,618
Jan. 91	496	443,248	40,241	419,290	903,275
Feb. 91	47	430,403	47,277	297,922	775,649
Mar. 91	370	370,820	7,414	383,937	762,541
Total	1,055	2,374,017	193,967	2,007,220	4,576,259

SOURCE: U.S. Transportation Command, Comptroller Desert Shield/Storm, Transportation Cost Reports. Prepared by: U.S. Transportation Command, Offices of History and Comptroller (TCHO/TCAC).

Table D-13 Desert Shield/Storm Donated Airlift by Country (Foreign Government Value, As of 31 March 1991)

Country	Total
S. Korea	
Missions	54
$ Value	25,200,000
Japan	
Missions	124*
$ Value	46,893,333
Kuwait	
Missions	1
$ Value	260,646
Italy	
Missions	21
$ Value	1,492,176
Total	
Missions	200
$ Value	73,846,155

*Includes five missions performed by Government of Japan outside Military Airlift Command arena. Government of Japan flew their own cargo into the Area of Operations.

SOURCE: U.S. Transportation Command, Comptroller-Donated Lift Reports. Prepared by: U.S. Transportation Command, Offices of History and Comptroller (TCHO and TCAC).

Saudis agreed to provide free fuel to U.S. Desert Shield forces operating in Saudi Arabia and its surrounding waters. The agreement covered transient aircraft, such as those in the CRAF, as well as those stationed in country. It included all types of fuel and additives and provided for delivery of petroleum, oil, and lubricants to the airfields and aircraft. Under LSA, the Saudi Arabian Marketing and Refining Company (SAMAREC) agreed to provide the fuel either directly or through subcontractors.

Receiving free fuel via the LSA created a series of administrative complications. For example SAMAREC continued to bill CRAF aircraft for fuel, even though under the agreement it should have been free. In response United States Central Command (USCENTCOM) asked USTRANSCOM to collect paid invoices, then forward them to USCENTCOM for presentation to the Saudi Arabian government for reimbursement. Additionally, in an effort to alleviate the billing problem, the Joint Chiefs of Staff tasked USTRANSCOM to provide CRAF crews with forms that would identify and authorize them to receive free fuel. The Principal Deputy, Office of the Secretary of Defense (OSD) Comptroller, enacted a follow-on measure that reclaimed the value of the free fuel and allocated it back to USTRANSCOM customers by identifying it as specific dollars returned to OSD accounts. The accounts were then returned to the services in a supplemented Desert Storm appropriation. By war's end CRAF aircraft were usually receiving free fuel, but many of the improperly billed invoices were still outstanding.

Desert Shield/Storm and USTRANSCOM's Future

Joint Operation Planning and Execution System; Time Phased Force Deployment Data

Typically, strategic deployments are based on Operations Plans and their accompanying Time Phased Force Deployment Data (TPFDD, or "Tip-Fid"), which are developed and executed using the Joint Operation Planning and Execution System (JOPES). The TPFDD identifies the scheme of deployment, including the sequence in which specific units deploy, their ports of embarkation, and estimates of transportation requirements. At the outset of Desert Shield, however, the Commander in Chief, United States Central Command (USCINCCENT) did not have a TPFDD. (In fact, since 1989 there had been only one TPFDD refinement conference, and that was for the Commander in Chief, U.S. Pacific Command.) All that was available for USCINCCENT's area of responsibility (AOR) was a Concept Outline Plan and draft Operation Plan for United States Central Command's (USCENTCOM's) AOR, prepared by USCENTCOM with the assistance of USTRANSCOM and other supporting commands in the spring and summer of 1990. Essentially, USCENTCOM, USTRANSCOM, the Services, and the Joint Staff planned the initial phases of the deployment manually through direct conversations, while constructing an execution TPFDD.

Shortages of JOPES Operators and USTRANSCOM Action

One of Department of Defense's biggest deployment handicaps in the early days of Desert Shield was a shortage of JOPES-capable operators. Air Force Maj. Gen. Malcolm B. Armstrong, Special Assistant to the Director of the Joint Staff, in his report, "Implications for TRANSCOM Based on Desert Shield Observations," described the problem succinctly and authoritatively to Army Gen. Colin L. Powell, Chairman, Joint Chiefs of Staff (CJCS):

> One reason JOPES was inadequate [during Desert Shield] is that TRANSCOM components do not use this system for day-to-day peacetime activities. In peacetime, each component manages [its] portion of the nation's mobility capability using processes that are Service-oriented and predate both TRANSCOM and the notion of jointness. Thus, JOPES procedures and shortfalls were not well understood due to a lack of experience in working with JOPES. As problems arose, there was a tendency for JOPES users to abandon the process and revert to that which they were familiar with—their day-to-day systems. However, the day-to-day, peacetime management systems do not provide crucial information needed to manage a wartime deployment.

To help solve the problem, USTRANSCOM in August sent its JOPES experts to USCENTCOM at MacDill AFB, Florida, and other key commands, to assist them in refining the TPFDD data base. Once refined, it provided a foundation for system discipline, enhanced deployment procedures, enabled JOPES to begin functioning as designed, and gave USTRANSCOM the necessary perspective on total deployment requirements.

Other USTRANSCOM Deployment Planning Initiatives

USTRANSCOM's initiative helped solve other deployment management problems. The operational considerations in the AOR required USCENTCOM to repeatedly change the priority and scheduling of units. Given its current level of development, JOPES was not capable of reacting to changes of such frequency and magnitude in a timely manner. Consequently, USTRANSCOM accelerated development and brought on-line the Flow and Analysis System for TRANSCOM, which rapidly (within two to four hours) and accurately provided the Commander in Chief, US-TRANSCOM (USCINCTRANS) with transportation requirements and USCINC-CENT with closure estimates.

The command also accelerated development of the Dynamic Analysis Replanning Tool (DART). A suite of hardware and software for rapidly editing transportation scheduling data and developing and analyzing courses of action, DART included elements of JOPES Version 4, JOPES' most advanced and yet-to-be released software. USTRANSCOM deployed a DART prototype to U.S. European Command, which used it to modify and manipulate the Desert Shield/Storm TPFDD during the latter phase of the operation. DART proved such a success that USTRANSCOM intended to use it for redeployment and, in the near future, make it available to the other unified commands.

USTRANSCOM provided the transportation user with in-transit visibility, the up-to-the minute status of cargo en route, in a variety of ways. For example, USTRANSCOM and Military Airlift Command (MAC) developed interfaces between JOPES and MAC's Global Decision Support System (GDSS). JOPES, for the first time ever, presented "actual" carrier movement schedules with "real" manifests attached for movement tracking. Another USTRANSCOM initiative sent MAC teams to airlift onload locations. Primarily via GDSS and the Automatic Digital Network, they reported to USTRANSCOM what was loaded on departing aircraft. According to General Johnson, the success of these "never before attempted interfaces underscores the potential gains achievable by networking existing systems." That was why US-TRANSCOM led the Department of Defense (DOD) effort "to establish a Global Transportation Network, which would allow any user to access selected transportation information from any other user's database."

Importance of Deliberate Planning

The deployment reinforced the importance of the deliberate planning phase of the war plan preparation. General Johnson emphasized that the deployment community must maintain current, refined deployment data to avoid the confusion it experienced early in the Desert Shield deployment. Most importantly, JOPES, once loaded with a refined TPFDD, proved crucial to Desert Shield/Storm deployment order and discipline. Consequently, General Johnson recommended that the DOD maintain funding for incremental JOPES software revisions, to strengthen interfaces, enhance user friendliness, and make those who would use the system in war use it in peace as well. "Train, train, train, use, use, use" was the "real key to success with JOPES" according to General Johnson. However, under USTRANSCOM's charter, USCINCTRANS did not have authority to direct the Joint Deployment Community to use JOPES and JOPES-compatible processes in peacetime.

Centralized Traffic Management in Desert Shield/Storm

Desert Shield/Storm revealed that USTRANSCOM's centralized traffic management was the most effective and flexible method to coordinate airlift, sealift, and ground movements. The Goldwater-Nichols Department of Defense Reorganization Act of 1986 helped to strengthen joint command relationships as well as the role of unified commanders. Partly as a result of this act, USTRANSCOM was created in 1987 to provide the unified commanders with the global air, land, and sea transportation required to meet national security objectives. Acting on this authority during Desert Shield/Storm, USTRANSCOM had the ability to react quickly to changing priorities and efficiently schedule and employ transportation resources. In this case the supported Commander in Chief, Army Gen. H. Norman Schwarzkopf, needed to call only one person to satisfy his transportation requirements: Air Force Gen. Hansford T. Johnson, USCINCTRANS. Despite the success of this arrangement, Desert Shield/Storm reinforced General Johnson's belief that US-TRANSCOM was not yet the fully operational, peacetime as well as wartime, common-user transportation manager it needed to be. For example, he believed that if he had had such peacetime authorities prior to Desert Shield/Storm, he would have used them to better prepare the Services for containerization of ammunition and unit cargo.

USTRANSCOM in Peacetime Operations

Major General Armstrong, in his report dealing with USTRANSCOM in Desert Shield, outlined the problem and solution for General Powell, CJCS. The peacetime responsibilities of USCINCTRANS, especially in a crisis short of war, exceeded his authority. The USTRANSCOM Implementation Plan defined the command as "wartime-oriented." Thus, authorities not granted to USCINCTRANS in peacetime but necessary to manage a wartime strategic deployment such as Desert Shield included: (1) operational control of the three component headquarters; (2) charter to act as the single manager of all lift assets; and (3) charter to be the single traffic manager. To deny USCINCTRANS such authority, Major General Armstrong insisted,

> risks establishment of deployment priorities and allocation of deployment assets [during war] that neither match the priorities of the supported CINC, nor reflect the optimum use of mobility assets envisioned by TRANSCOM. . . . The observation that we should organize in peacetime as we will fight in wartime—avoiding separate command arrangements for peace and war—strongly applies here.

"This fact," he concluded, "appears to be strong testimony for changing the existing charter and authorities of CINCTRANS." At war's end, the command had a reorganization charter before the Secretary of Defense that would make USCINC-TRANS single manager for common-user transportation in peace and war, and affirm his position by assigning to him all common user Transportation Component Commands and all common-user transportation forces in the Forces for Unified and Specified Commands document.

Security

Throughout Desert Shield/Storm, USTRANSCOM and its component commands sought ways to improve security for overland and port operations. As in past contingencies MTMC, at the beginning of Desert Shield/Storm, contracted for port security forces and augmented them with its reserve Port Security Detachments. MTMC worked with port authorities to upgrade pass systems, and it coordinated its efforts on shore with those of the Coast Guard, which was responsible for water security at ports in the United States.

One of the most likely terrorist targets was MTMC's Military Ocean Terminal Sunny Point (MOTSU). The largest ammunition port in the United States—11,000 acres, 100 mi of railroad track, and 3 wharves with 6 berths—MOTSU was the only U.S. terminal capable of loading containerized ammunition. With local authorities, MTMC formed night vision-capable security units to patrol rail lines leading to the critical installation. As extra security for ammunition-loading operations during surge deployment, MTMC, at USTRANSCOM's direction, arranged with the Civil Air Patrol (CAP) for air surveillance of Sunny Point, North Carolina. Between 11 February and 15 March 1991, a single-propeller CAP plane patrolled above the terminal and adjacent areas for four hours daily. Onboard was an MTMC Physical Security Non-Commissioned Officer. The patrol found nothing to report.

There was a serious security breach in the United States. In early September, security guards working for Union Pacific at the Port of Houston discovered that someone had broken into a container shipped by rail from Fort Sill, Oklahoma. Missing were 7 M-60 machine guns, 33 M-16A1 rifles, and 14 50-cal machine guns. Those weapons and other items stolen in the heist were later recovered.

Such security problems led USTRANSCOM and MTMC to conclude that they relied too heavily on contract guards to police rail yards and ports, in particular Sunny Point. Contract guards were expensive, especially considering their lack of training and poor reliability in comparison to their military counterparts. The commands would in the future use military security forces whenever possible.

Overseas, where MTMC for the most part had to depend on the host government for security, the threat was even greater. On 21 January, a bomb exploded after work at the MTMC Outport Headquarters building in Istanbul, Turkey, as the Turkish police guards changed shifts. A government vehicle was damaged, three portable buildings were destroyed, and all the glass in the main building was broken. No one was injured and no one claimed responsibility.

Conclusion

One of the largest deployments in history, Desert Shield/Storm had much to teach transporters and those who rely on the Defense Transportation System. Prepositioning, overland transportation, port operations, strategic airlift (organic and commercial), strategic sealift (especially fast sealift and the Ready Reserve Force [RRF] once activated) worked extremely well. Operations like Desert Express, Sealift Express, and Special Middle East Shipping Agreement should be considered for future contingencies. The war highlighted the tremendous capability of roll-on/roll-off vessels. Staging bases in Europe were critical to strategic airlift. The Department of Defense needed to renew its deliberate planning efforts, support Joint Operation Planning and Execution System (JOPES) improvements, and enforce JOPES training in peacetime, so users would be prepared to operate the system in war. USTRANSCOM and its component command needed to push for containerization and intermodalism in the DOD. Furthermore, Desert Shield/Storm convinced USTRANSCOM that with the C-17 aircraft and mix of well-maintained, militarily useful ships in the RRF and U.S.-flag fleet—supplemented with a Merchant Marine reserve, increased afloat prepositioning, and procedures for activating reserve transportation units to prime the Defense Transportation System prior to the 200,000 presidential call-up—the nation would have the strategic deployment force it required in the twenty-first century.

Furthermore, USTRANSCOM during Desert Shield/Storm proved a value added. For the first time in U.S. military history, a single command directed all three modes of strategic lift: air, land, and sea. Relying on the Commander in Chief, USTRANSCOM (USCINCTRANS), to satisfy U.S. Central Command (USCENTCOM) transportation requirements, USCENTCOM's Commander in Chief (CINC) could concentrate on his war-fighting mission. Moreover, as a unified CINC, US-CINCTRANS worked directly with the other supporting CINCs, the Joint Chiefs of Staff, and a wide variety of government agencies to facilitate the deployment. Finally, with oversight of the entire transportation operation and authority to manage it, USTRANSCOM quickly and efficiently employed personnel, aircraft, ships, trains, trucks, and port assets to meet the customer's requirements. Finally, Desert Shield/Storm supported USCINCTRANS' position that to smooth the transition from peacetime operations to a wartime footing, USTRANSCOM needed to have the same organization and authority in peace as it had in war.

Index

ABC analysis, 3.12–3.14
Accessibility of highway trans., 10.12
Accidents:
  prevention of, 17.25, 17.26
  in shipping and receiving, 17.24, 17.25
Accumulation, 22.5, 22.7
  conveyor, 19.26
Act to Regulate Commerce of 1887, 10.6,
  10.8, 12.8
Activity-based costing (ABC), 9.2, 9.7–9.12
Activity-based object costing, 9.8
Activity-based process costing, 9.8
Activity-based product costing, 9.8
Activity cost pools, 9.8
Adaptable distribution, 1.10
Administration within logistics, 2.3
Air Cargo Deregulation Act of 1977,
  10.40
Air freight, 13.4
  (*See also* Air transportation)
Air gate, 20.9
Air Passenger Deregulation Act of 1978,
  10.40, 10.41
Air-sea, 10.27
Air transportation, 10.32
  accessibility of, 10.36
  carriers:
    charter, 10.34
    international, 10.34
    local, 10.34
    major, 10.33
    national, 10.33
    regional, 10.34
    small package and overnight,
     10.34
  commissions, 10.37
  communication, 10.38
  congestion of, 10.36, 10.44
  cost, 10.36, 10.37
  deregulation of, 10.40
    international, 10.41
  equipment:
    short-haul, 10.34
    widebody, 10.34

Air transportation (*Cont.*):
  flight frequency, 10.36
  ground-handling equipment, 10.35
  labor, 10.43
  maintenance, 10.37
  megacarriers, 10.44
    vs. niche carriers, 10.42
  rates, 12.24
    international, 12.25
  safety, 10.43
  service characteristics, 10.35
  service vs. price, 10.41
  speed, 10.35
Air waybill, 14.8
Airbill, 14.8
Airframe manufacturers, 10.35
Airline Deregulation Act, 14.15
Airport, 10.38
  congestion, 10.40
  expansion and the environment,
    10.40
  hub-and-spoke, 10.39
  services, 10.39
  user fees, 10.39
Aisles:
  cross, 16.21, 16.23
  main, 16.21
  requirements, 16.23
American Warehouseman's Association
  (AWA), 1.4
Any quantity rate, 12.37
Application engineering, 20.3
Aspect ratio, 27.3
Auto carriers, in shipping industry,
  10.22
Automated Guided Vehicle Systems
  (AGVS), A.11
  communications with, 19.20
  figure, 19.18
  pickup/delivery stations, 19.18
  routing, 19.21
  system control, 19.19
  tractors, 19.18
  traffic control, 19.21

About the Editors

JAMES A. TOMPKINS, Ph.D., is founder and president of Tompkins Associates, Inc., an internationally known consulting firm specializing in facilities planning, material handling, warehousing, distribution, and integrated manufacturing. He is a veteran of more than 800 consulting projects worldwide, and has been president of the Institute of Industrial Engineers, the International Materials Management Society, and the College-Industry Council on Material Handling Industry. His previous books include *The Warehouse Management Handbook* and *Winning Manufacturing.*

DALE HARMELINK is the distribution systems engineering manager at Tompkins Associates, Inc. He has led more than 50 major consulting projects in areas ranging from planning distribution networks to implementing systems, and has presented seminars and authored numerous articles on warehousing and distribution. Harmelink is an expert in both the science of distribution modeling as well as the art of achieving distribution excellence.